The **Rough Guide** to

Scotland

written and researched by

Rob Humphreys and Donald Reid

with additional contributions from

Helena Smith

www.roughguides.com

Contents

Scottish food and drink colour section following p.240

The great outdoors colour section following p.432

◀◀ Eilean Donan Castle ◀ Forth Rail Bridge

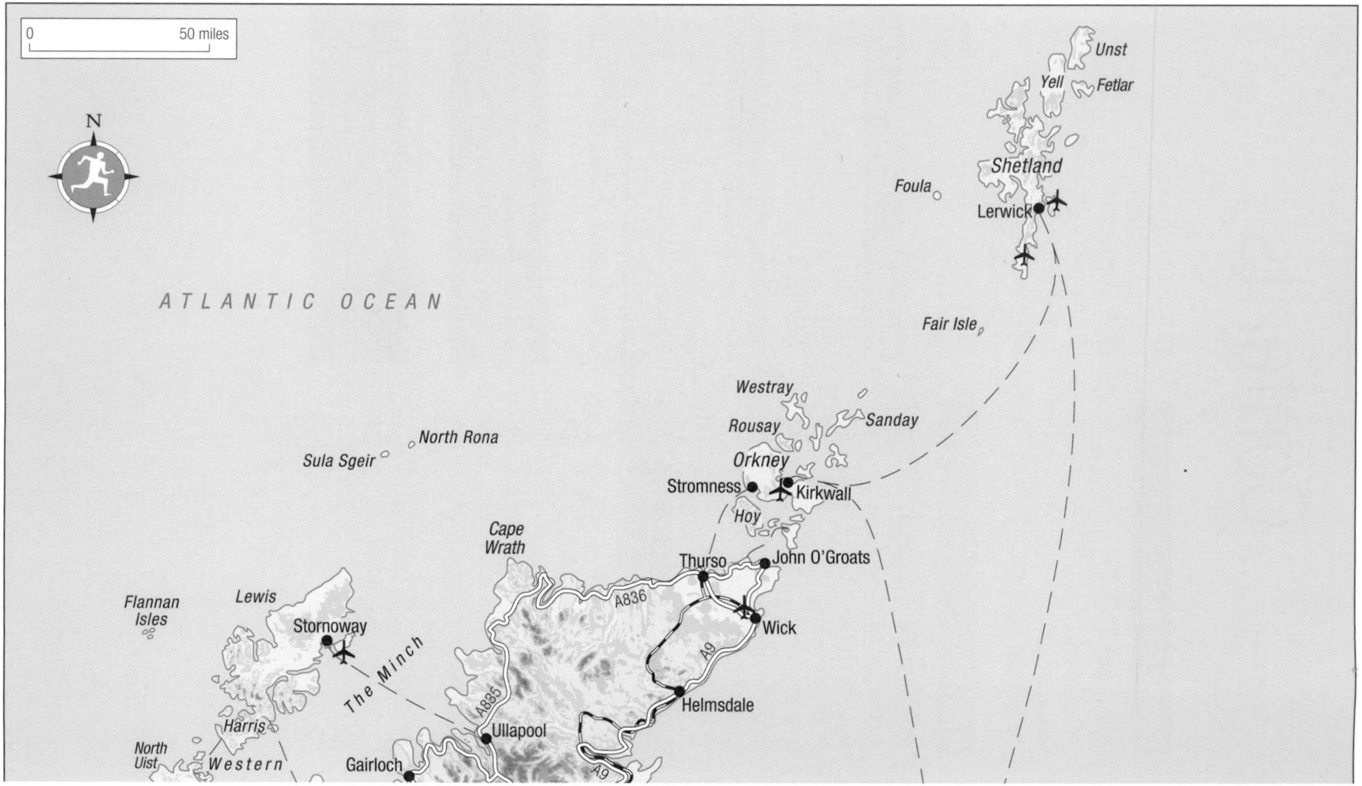

0
50 miles
N
ATLANTIC OCEAN
Unst
Yell
Fetlar
Shetland
Foula
Lerwick
Fair Isle
Westray
Rousay
Sanday
Orkney
Stromness
Kirkwall
Hoy
North Rona
Sula Sgeir
Cape Wrath
Thurso
John O'Groats
A836
Wick
A9
Helmsdale
Flannan Isles
Lewis
Stornoway
The Minch
A835
Ullapool
Harris
North Uist
Western
Gairloch

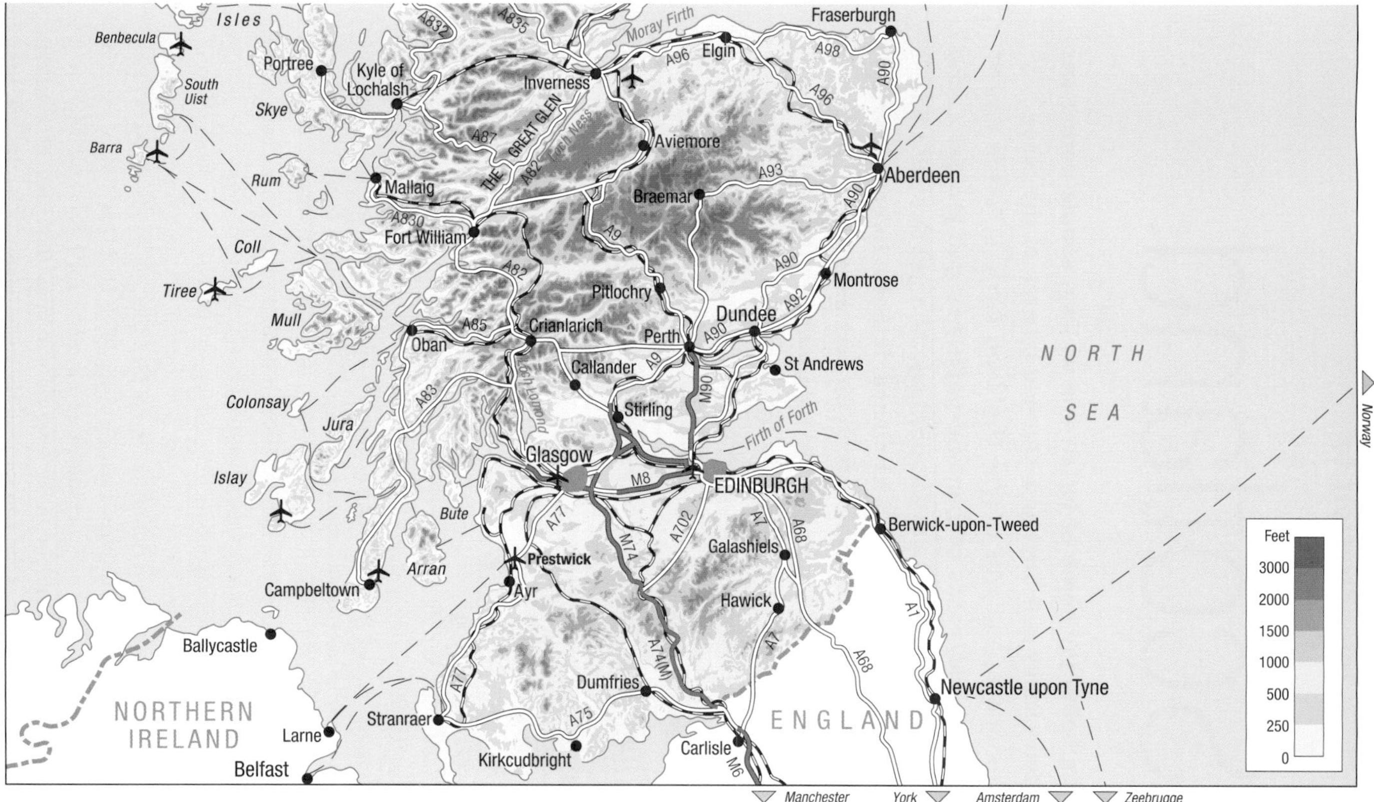
Isles
Benbecula
South Uist
Barra
Portree
Skye
Kyle of Lochalsh
Rum
Mallaig
Coll
Tiree
Mull
Colonsay
Jura
Islay
Campbeltown
Arran
Bute
A832
A835
Moray Firth
Inverness
THE GREAT GLEN
A87
A82
Loch Ness
A830
Fort William
A85
Oban
A83
Crianlarich
Loch Lomond
Callander
Pitlochry
A9
Aviemore
Braemar
A96
Elgin
Fraserburgh
A98
A90
Aberdeen
A93
Montrose
A92
Dundee
Perth
St Andrews
M90
Stirling
Firth of Forth
Glasgow
M8
EDINBURGH
A77
Prestwick
Ayr
M74
A702
A7
A68
Galashiels
Hawick
A74(M)
Dumfries
A75
Kirkcudbright
Stranraer
Carlisle
M6
Berwick-upon-Tweed
A1
Newcastle upon Tyne
ENGLAND
NORTH SEA
Norway
Ballycastle
NORTHERN IRELAND
Larne
Belfast
Manchester
York
Amsterdam
Zeebrugge
Feet
3000
2000
1500
1000
500
250
0

Introduction to Scotland

As befits the home of tartan and whisky, simple definitions don't really suit Scotland. Clichéd images of the place abound – postcards of wee Highland terriers, tartan tins of shortbread, ranks of diamond-patterned golf jerseys ... and they drive many Scots to apoplexy. And yet Scotland has a habit of delivering on its classic images: in some parts ruined castles really do perch on just about every hilltop, in summer the glens inevitably turn purple with heather and if you end up in a village on gala day you just might bump into a formation of bagpipers marching down the street.

The complexity of Scotland can be hard to unravel: somewhere deep in the country's genes a generous dose of romantic Celtic hedonism blends, somehow, with stern Calvinist prudence. There's little more splendid here than the scenery, yet half the time it's hidden under a pall of drizzly mist. The country's major contribution to medieval warfare was the chaotic, blood-curdling charge of the half-naked Highlander, yet it's civilized enough to have given the world steam power, the television and penicillin. Chefs from Paris to Pisa rhapsodize over Scottish langoustine and Aberdeen Angus steaks, while the locals are happily tucking into another deep-fried supper of haggis and chips. It's a country where the losers of battles (and football games) are more romanticized than the winners.

Naturally, the tourist industry tends to play up the heritage, but beyond the nostalgia lies a modern, dynamic nation. Oil and nanotechnology now matter more to the Scottish economy than fishing or Harris Tweed. Edinburgh still has its medieval Royal Mile, but just as many folk are drawn by its nightclubs and modern restaurants, while out in the Hebrides, the locals are more likely to be building websites than shearing sheep. The Highland huntin' shootin' fishin' set are these days outnumbered by mountain bikers and wide-eyed whale-watchers. Outdoor music festivals will draw thousands of revellers, but just as popular as the pop stars on the main stage will be the folk band

▶ Hiking in the Cairngorms

rocking the ceilidh tent with accordions and an electric fiddle.

Stuck in the far northwest corner of Europe, Scotland is remote, but it's not isolated. The inspiring emptiness of the wild northwest coast lies barely a couple of hours from Edinburgh and Glasgow, two of Britain's most dense and intriguing urban centres. Ancient ties to Ireland, Scandinavia, France and the Netherlands mean that – compared with the English at least – Scots are generally enthusiastic about the European Union, which has poured money into infrastructure and cultural projects, particularly in the Highlands and Islands. By contrast, Scotland's relationship with the "auld enemy", England, remains as problematic as ever. The Scottish Parliament in Edinburgh has helped to focus Scottish minds on Scottish affairs, but many Scots still tend to view matters south of the border with a mixture of exaggerated disdain and well-hidden envy. Ask for a "full English breakfast" and you'll quickly find yourself put right. Old prejudices die hard.

Fact file

- Scotland covers an **area** of just over 30,000 square miles, has a 2300-mile-long coastline and contains over 31,460 **lochs**. Of its 790 **islands**, 130 are inhabited. The highest point is the summit of Ben Nevis (4406ft), while the bottom of Loch Morar is 1017 feet below sea level.
- The **capital** is Edinburgh (population nearly 480,000), and the largest city is Glasgow (population 580,000). While the number of people worldwide who claim Scottish descent is estimated at more than 25 million, the **population** of the country is just over 5 million – 1.2 percent of whom (roughly 60,000 people) speak **Gaelic**.
- Scotland is a constituent territory of the **United Kingdom** of Great Britain and Northern Ireland. The head of state is Queen Elizabeth II. It is a **parliamentary democracy** whose sovereign parliament sits at Westminster in London, with elements of government business devolved to the separately elected Scottish Parliament which sits in Edinburgh.
- **Whisky** accounts for 13 percent of Scotland's exports and is worth over £3 billion annually.

Where to go

Even if you're planning a short visit, it's still perfectly possible, and quite common, to combine a stay in either Edinburgh or Glasgow with a brief foray into the Highlands. With more time at your disposal, the opportunity to experience the variety of landscapes in Scotland increases, but there's no escaping the fact that travel in the more remote regions of Scotland takes time, and – in the case of the islands – money. If you're planning to spend most of your time in the countryside, it's most rewarding to concentrate on just one or two small areas.

The initial focus for many visitors to Scotland is the capital, **Edinburgh**, a dramatically handsome and engaging city famous for its magnificent castle and historic Old Town. Come here in August and you'll find the city transformed by the Edinburgh Festival, the largest arts festival in the world. An hour's travel to the west is the country's biggest city, **Glasgow**, a place quite different in character from Edinburgh. Once a sprawling industrial metropolis, Glasgow nevertheless has an impressive architectural heritage and a lively social and cultural life. Other urban centres are inevitably overshadowed by the big two, although the transformation from industrial grey to cultural colour is injecting life into **Dundee**, while there's a defiant separateness to **Aberdeen** with its silvery granite architecture and prominent port. Other centres are less of a draw in their own right, acting as useful transport or service hubs to emptier landscapes beyond, though some do contain compelling attractions such as the wonderful castle in **Stirling** or the Burns' monuments in Ayr.

▲ Calton Hill, Edinburgh

The weather

"There's no such thing as bad weather, only inadequate clothing", the poet laureate Ted Hughes is alleged to have said when asked why he liked holidaying on Scotland's west coast, given that it always rains there. For those who don't share Hughes' cavalier attitude to the elements, the weather is probably the single biggest factor to put you off visiting Scotland. It's not so much that the weather's always bad, it's just that it is unpredictable: you could enjoy the most fabulous week of sunshine in early April and suffer a week of low-lying fog and drizzle in August. Out in the islands, they say you can get all four seasons in a day. The saving grace is that even if the weather's not necessarily good, it's generally interesting, exhilarating, dramatic and certainly photogenic. Then, the sun finally coming out is truly worth the wait. A week spent in a landscape swathed in thick mist can be transformed when the clouds lift to reveal a majestic mountain range or a hidden group of islands far offshore.

You don't have to travel far north of the Glasgow–Edinburgh axis to find the first hints of **Highland** landscape, a divide marked by the Highland Boundary Fault which cuts across central Scotland. The lochs, hills and wooded glens of the **Trossachs** and **Loch Lomond** are the most easily reached and as a consequence busier than other parts. Further north, **Perthshire** and the Grampian hills of **Angus** and **Deeside** show the Scottish countryside at its richest, with colourful woodlands and long glens rising up to distinctive mountain peaks. South of Inverness the mighty **Cairngorm** massif offers hints of the raw wilderness Scotland can still

Wildlife

From wintering wildfowl to cliff-breeding summer sea birds, Scotland is a year-round wildlife destination – all you need is a bit of patience and a pair of binoculars. While the region's vast tracts of moorland and forest support a relatively small human population, they harbour a surprisingly healthy quota of mammals and birds. Herds of red deer roam the hillsides, while buzzards and eagles patrol the skies. Out at sea, the west coast, in particular, is one of the best places in the world to spot marine mammals, from the humble porpoise to the humongous humpback whale.

provide, an aspect of the country which is at its finest in the lonely north and western Highlands. To get to the far north you'll have to cross the **Great Glen**, an ancient geological fissure which cuts right across the country from Ben Nevis to **Loch Ness**, a moody stretch of water rather choked with tourists hoping for a glimpse of its monster. Scotland's most memorable scenery is to be found on the jagged west coast, stretching from **Argyll** all the way north to **Wester Ross** and the looming hills of Assynt. Not all of central and northern Scotland is rugged Highlands, however, with the east coast in particular mixing fertile farmland with pretty stone-built fishing villages and golf courses, most notably at the prosperous university town of **St Andrews**, the spiritual home of the game. Elsewhere the whisky trail of **Speyside** and the castles and Pictish stones of the **northeast** provide plenty of scope for exploration off the beaten track, while in the southern part of the country, the rolling hills and ruined abbeys of the **Borders** offer a refreshingly unaffected vision of rural Scotland.

The grand splendour of the Highlands would be bare without the **islands** off the west and north coasts. Assorted in size, flavour and accessibility, the long chain of rocky Hebrides which necklace Scotland's Atlantic shoreline includes **Mull** and its nearby pilgrimage centre of **Iona**; **Islay** and **Jura**, famous for their wildlife and whisky; **Skye**, the most visited of the Hebrides, where the snow-tipped peaks of the Cuillin rise up from deep sea lochs; and the **Western Isles**, an elongated archipelago that is the country's last bastion of Gaelic language and culture. Off the north coast, **Orkney** and **Shetland**, both with a rich Norse heritage, differ not only from each other, but also quite distinctly from mainland Scotland in dialect and culture – far-flung islands buffeted by wind and sea that offer some of the country's wildest scenery, finest birdwatching and best archeological sites.

When to go

The **summer** months of June, July and August are regarded as high season, with local school holidays making July and early August the busiest period. While the locals celebrate a single day of bright sunshine as "glorious", the weather at this time is, at best, unpredictable; however, days are generally mild or warm and, most importantly, long, with daylight lingering until 9pm or later. August in Edinburgh is Festival time, which dominates everything in the city and means accommodation is hard to come by. Elsewhere, events such as Highland Games, folk festivals or sporting events – most of which take place in the summer months – can tie up accommodation, though normally only in a fairly concentrated local area. If you're out and about in the countryside throughout the summer, you won't be able to avoid the clouds of small biting insects called **midges**, which can be a real annoyance on still days, particularly around dusk.

Commonly, **May** and **September** throw up weather every bit as good as, if not better than, the months of high summer. You're less likely to encounter crowds or struggle to find somewhere to stay, and the mild temperatures

▲ Mountain biking, Lairig Ghru, Highlands

Munro-bagging

Just as the Inuit have hundreds of words for snow, so in Scotland a hill is rarely just a hill. Depending on where you are in the country, what it's shaped like and how high it is, a hill might be a ben, a mount, a law, a pen, a brae or even a pap (or in Gaelic, beinn, cnoc, creag, meall, sgurr or stob). Even more confusing, if you're keen on doing a bit of hillwalking, are "Munros". These are the hills in Scotland over 3000 feet in height, defined by a list first drawn up by one Sir Hugh Munro in 1891. You "bag" a Munro by walking to the top of it, and once you've bagged all 284 you can call yourself a Munroist and let your chiropodist retire in peace. Of course, there's no need to do them all: at heart, Munro-bagging is simply about appreciating the great Scottish outdoors. It's advisable, however, not to get too obsessed by Sir Hugh's challenge: after the Munros you might hear the call of the "Corbetts" (hills between 2500 and 2999 feet) or even the "Donalds" (lowland hills above 2000 feet).

combined with the changing colours of nature mean both are great for outdoor activities, particularly hiking. Note, however, that September is prime stalking season for deer, which can disrupt access over parts of the Highlands if you're hiking, fishing or riding a mountain bike.

The **spring** and **autumn** months of April and October bracket the season for many parts of rural Scotland. A large number of attractions, tourist offices and guesthouses often open for business on Easter weekend and shut up shop after the school half-term in mid-October. If places do stay open through the winter it's normally with reduced opening hours; this is the best time to pick up special offers at hotels and guesthouses. Note too that in more remote spots public transport will often operate on a reduced winter timetable.

▲ Glasgow Museum of Modern Art

▶ Loch Shiel

Winter days, from November through to March, occasionally crisp and bright, are more often cold, gloomy and all too brief, although Hogmanay and New Year has traditionally been a time to visit Scotland for partying and warm hospitality – something which improves as the weather worsens. While even tourist hotspots such as Edinburgh are notably quieter during winter, a fall of snow in the Highlands will prompt plenty of activity around the ski resorts.

Average daily temperatures and monthly rainfall

	Jan	Feb	Mar	Apr	May	Jun	Jul	Aug	Sep	Oct	Nov	Dec
Edinburgh												
°C/°F	6/43	6/44	9/47	11/52	14/58	17/63	18/65	18/65	16/61	13/56	9/48	7/45
mm	47	39	39	38	49	45	69	73	57	56	58	56
inches	1.8	1.5	1.5	1.5	1.9	1.8	2.7	2.8	2.2	2.2	2.2	2.2
Fort William												
°C/°F	6/43	7/44	9/47	11/52	15/58	17/62	17/63	17/63	15/60	13/55	9/48	7/45
mm	200	132	152	111	103	124	137	150	199	215	220	238
inches	7.8	5.1	5.9	4.3	4	4.8	5.3	5.9	7.8	8.4	8.6	9.3
Lerwick												
°C/°F	5/41	5/41	6/43	8/46	10/50	13/55	14/57	14/57	13/55	10/51	7/45	6/43
mm	127	93	93	72	64	64	67	78	113	119	140	147
inches	5	3.6	3.6	2.8	2.5	2.5	2.6	3	4.4	4.6	5.5	5.7
Tiree												
°C/°F	7/45	7/45	8/47	10/51	13/55	15/59	16/60	16/61	15/58	13/55	10/49	8/47
mm	120	71	77	60	56	66	79	83	123	125	123	123
inches	4.7	2.8	3	2.3	2.2	2.6	3.1	3.2	4.8	4.9	4.8	4.8
Wick												
°C/°F	6/42	6/42	7/45	9/49	11/52	14/58	15/60	15/60	14/57	12/53	8/47	7/44
mm	81	58	55	45	47	49	61	74	68	73	90	81
inches	3.2	2.3	2.1	1.8	1.8	1.9	2.4	2.9	2.7	2.8	3.5	3.2

things not to miss

It's not possible to see everything that Scotland has to offer on a short trip – and we don't suggest you try. What follows, in no particular order, is a selective taste of the country's highlights: absorbing sights, vibrant festivals and some of the most spectacular scenic wonders in Europe. They're arranged in five colour-coded categories, which you can browse through to find the very best things to see and experience. All highlights have a page reference to take you straight into the Guide, where you can find out more.

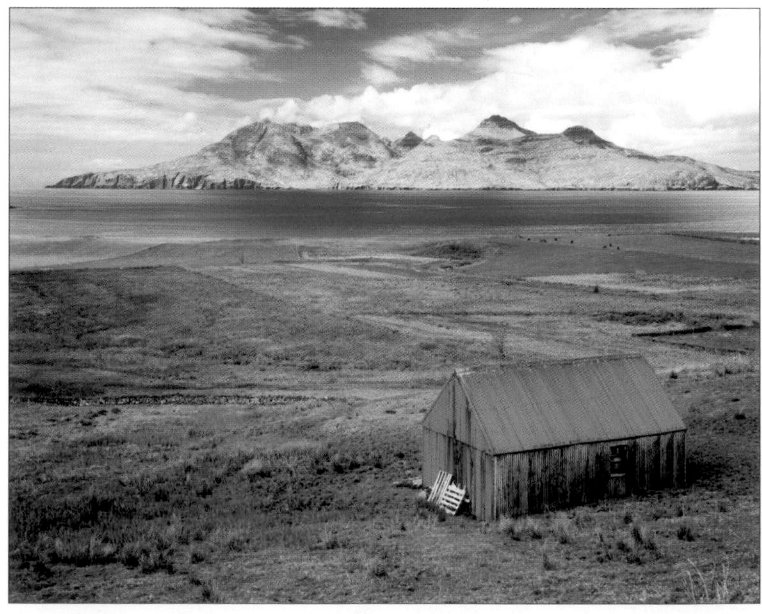

01 Eigg Page **536** • Perfect example of a tiny, friendly Hebridean island with a golden beach to lie on, a hill to climb and stunning views across the sea to its neighbour, Rùm.

02 The Cairngorm mountains Page **425** • Natural splendour and terrific outdoor activities.

03 Hogmanay Page **43** • New Year celebrations, with whisky, dancing and fireworks staving off the midwinter chill.

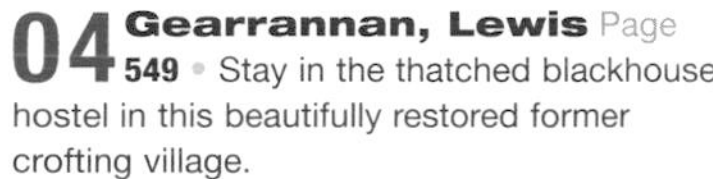

04 Gearrannan, Lewis Page **549** • Stay in the thatched blackhouse hostel in this beautifully restored former crofting village.

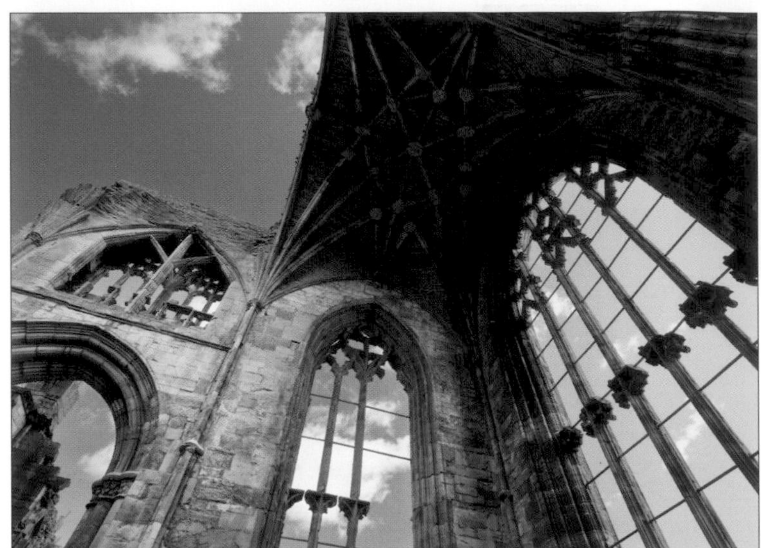

05 Melrose Abbey Page **148** • Ruined Cistercian abbey situated in the most beguiling of Border towns.

06 Tobermory Page **272** • The main town on the beautiful island of Mull, and Scotland's most picturesque fishing port.

07 Scottish Parliament

Page **89** • Enric Miralles' startling, contemporary design has transformed the old Holyrood area of Edinburgh.

08 Glen Coe Page **366** • Moody, poignant and spectacular glen within easy reach of Fort William.

09 Staffa and the Treshnish Isles Page **276** • View the basalt columns of Staffa's Fingal's Cave from the sea, and then picnic beside the puffins on the Isle of Lunga.

10 Skye Cuillin Page **527** • The most spectacular mountain range on the west coast, for viewing or climbing.

11 Edinburgh Festival Page **118** • The world's biggest festival of theatre and the arts transforms Edinburgh every August.

12 Whale-watching, Mull Page **274** • Close encounters with a very different type of Highland wildlife.

13 West Highland Railway Page **479** • One of the great railway journeys of the world.

14 Islay Page **294** • Hebridean island with no fewer than seven whisky distilleries, and wonderfully varied birdlife that includes thousands of wintering geese.

15 Jarlshof, Shetland Page **606** • An exceptional archeological site taking in Bronze Age, Iron Age, Pictish, Viking and medieval remains.

16 Shetland Folk Festival Page **602** • Shetland is the place to experience traditional folk music, and the annual Folk Festival is the best time to do it.

17 Pubs Page **39** • Forget the great outdoors and install yourself in one of Scotland's cosy and convivial hostelries.

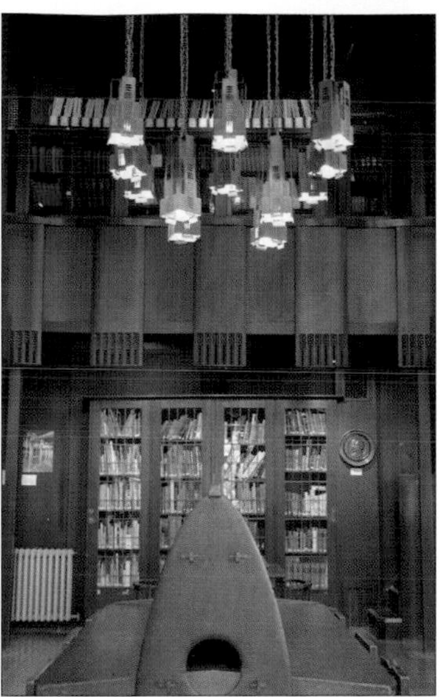

18 Glasgow School of Art Page **224** • Finest example of the unique style of Glasgow architect and designer Charles Rennie Mackintosh.

19 Burrell Collection, Glasgow Page **233** • An unconventional but impressive museum at the heart of Glasgow's cultural renaissance.

20 Mousa, Shetland Page **604** • The mother of all Iron Age brochs, on an island off the coast of Shetland.

21 Edinburgh Old Town Page **76** • Lose yourself in the capital's medieval cobbled streets and closes.

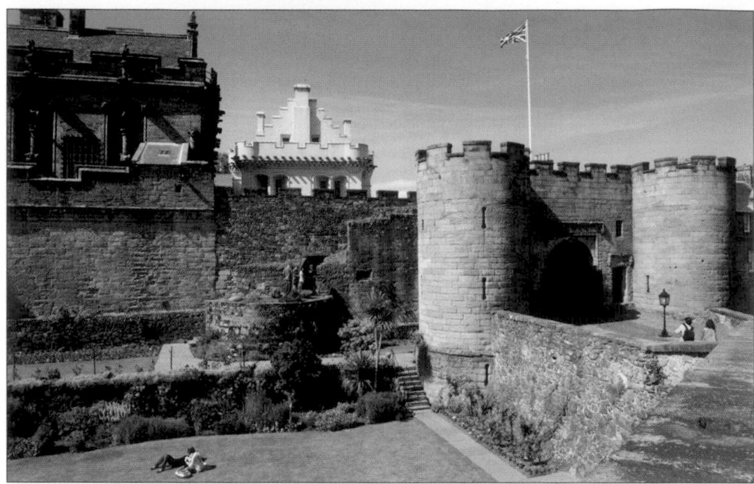

22 Stirling Castle Page **309** • The grandest castle in Scotland, with a commanding outlook over Highlands and Lowlands.

23 Loch Fyne Oyster Bar Page **259** • Pick up a picnic or enjoy fine dining at Scotland's top smokehouse and seafood outlet, located just outside Inveraray.

24 Museum of Scotland, Edinburgh Page **93** • Treasures including the ivory Lewis chessmen are housed in this striking modern museum.

25 **South Harris beaches** Page **553** • Take your pick of deserted golden beaches in South Harris, or further south in the Uists.

26 **Kinloch Castle, Rùm** Page **534** • Stay in the servants' quarters of this Edwardian hideaway or in one of its few remaining four-poster beds.

27 Iona Page **278** • The home of Celtic Christian spirituality, an island of pilgrimage today as in antiquity.

28 Caledonian forest Page **425** • Among the gnarled survivors of the great ancient forests you'll find one of Scotland's largest populations of the elusive red squirrel.

29 Dunnottar Castle Page **404** • Memorably dramatic ruined fortress, surrounded by giddy sea cliffs.

30 Calanais, Lewis Page **549** • Prehistoric standing stones that occupy a serene setting in the Western Isles.

Basics

Basics

Getting there

The quickest, easiest and cheapest way to get to Scotland is by plane. Scotland has three main international airports: Glasgow, Edinburgh and Aberdeen. Glasgow handles most nonstop scheduled flights from North America; all three have a reasonable spread of European flights.

With most airlines nowadays, how much you pay depends on how far in advance you book and how much demand there is during that period – the earlier you book, the cheaper the prices.

If you're coming from elsewhere in Britain, from Ireland or even northwest Europe, you can reach Scotland easily enough by **train**, **bus** or **ferry** – it probably won't work out cheaper or faster than flying, but it's undoubtedly better for the environment.

From England and Wales

If you're heading out to the Highlands and Islands, **flying** is the quickest way to travel. Airfares are only really competitive, however, on popular routes such as London or Birmingham to Edinburgh and Glasgow, which can cost as little as £50 return (journey time around 1hr). Once you add on the cost of taxes and getting to and from the airport, the savings on the same journey overland are often minimal – and then, of course, there's the environmental impact to consider.

Flying may be quick, but the **coach and train** fares can be pretty competitive. If you book far enough in advance, **train** fares can cost as little as £40 for a London or Manchester to Glasgow return (journey time from 4hr 45min or 3hr 30min). A more flexible or last-minute fare will obviously cost two or three times that amount. Another option is the overnight **Caledonian Sleeper** run by ScotRail from London Euston (daily except Sat; journey time around 7hr); again, if you book in advance, single overnight fares cost around £20, though most return fares are more like £100 return. The **coach** takes longer than the train (journey time around 9hr), but costs less, with a London or Birmingham to Glasgow return starting for as little as £30.

From Ireland

Travel from Ireland is quickest by plane, with **airfares** from either Belfast or Dublin to Glasgow Prestwick from as little as €40 return. There are also good **ferry** links with Northern Ireland and the train and ferry fares are very competitive: Belfast to Glasgow (via Stranraer) is just £50 return (journey time 5hr). P&O Irish Sea runs several sea crossings daily from Larne to Cairnryan (1hr) and Troon (2hr) and Stena Line operates services daily from Belfast to Stranraer (2hr 10min).

From mainland Europe

Ferries run by DFDS Seaways go overnight from IJmuiden, near Amsterdam, to Newcastle (daily; 16–17hr), less than an hour's drive south of the Scottish border. High-season return fares start at around €300, for a passenger with a car and an overnight berth. Direct Ferries (ⓦwww.directferries.co.uk) has a very useful website that gives you the latest information on crossings and allows you to compare all the options.

From the US and Canada

If you fly **nonstop to Scotland** from North America, you'll arrive in either Glasgow or Edinburgh. The majority of cheap fares, however, route through London, Manchester, Dublin or Paris. To reach any other Scottish airport, you'll definitely need to go via London, Glasgow or Edinburgh.

Figure on six to seven hours' flight time nonstop from the east coast to Glasgow, or seven hours to London plus an extra hour and a quarter from London to Glasgow or Edinburgh (not including stopover time). Add three or four hours more for travel from the west coast.

Return fares (including taxes) for nonstop flights to Glasgow from New York are $700–800; for nonstop flights from Toronto return fares are Can$700–800.

From Australia and New Zealand

Flight time from Australia and New Zealand to Scotland is at least 22 hours. There's a wide variety of routes, with those touching down in Southeast Asia the quickest and cheapest on average. To reach Scotland, you usually have to change planes either in London – the most popular choice – or in another European gateway such as Paris or Amsterdam. Given the length of the journey involved, you might be better off including a night's stopover in your itinerary, and indeed some airlines include one in the price of the flight.

The cheapest direct scheduled flights to London are usually to be found on one of the Asian airlines. Average **return fares** (including taxes) from eastern gateways to London are Aus$1500–2000 in low season, Aus$2000–2500 in high season. Fares from Perth or Darwin cost around Aus$200 less. Return fares from Auckland to London range between NZ$2000 and NZ$3000 depending on the season, route and carrier.

From South Africa

There are **no direct flights** from South Africa to Scotland, so you must change planes en route. The quickest and cheapest route to take is via London, with flight time around eleven hours, usually overnight. **Return fares** from Cape Town to London are ZAR7500–10,000; you'll save money if you buy the next leg of your journey to Scotland online – see below for details.

Airlines

Aer Arann ⓦ www.aerarann.com
Aer Lingus ⓦ www.aerlingus.com
Air Canada ⓦ www.aircanada.com
Air New Zealand ⓦ www.airnewzealand.com
Air Transat ⓦ www.airtransat.com
American Airlines ⓦ www.aa.com
Asiana Airlines ⓦ www.flyasiana.com
bmi ⓦ www.flybmi.com
bmibaby ⓦ www.bmibaby.com
British Airways ⓦ www.ba.com
Cathay Pacific ⓦ www.cathaypacific.com
Continental Airlines ⓦ www.continental.com
Delta ⓦ www.delta.com
Eastern Airways ⓦ www.easternairways.com
easyJet ⓦ www.easyjet.com
Flybe ⓦ www.flybe.com
Gulf Air ⓦ www.gulfair.com
KLM ⓦ www.klm.com
Lufthansa ⓦ www.lufthansa.com
Malaysia Airlines ⓦ www.malaysiaairlines.com
Qantas ⓦ www.qantas.com
Royal Brunei ⓦ www.bruneiair.com
Ryanair ⓦ www.ryanair.com
Scandinavian Airlines ⓦ www.flysas.com
ScotAirways ⓦ www.scotairways.com
Singapore Airlines ⓦ www.singaporeair.com
Thai Airways ⓦ www.thaiair.com
United Airlines ⓦ www.united.com
US Airlines ⓦ www.usairways.com

Virgin Atlantic Ⓦ www.virgin-atlantic.com
Widerøe Ⓦ www.wideroe.no

Agents and operators

ebookers Ⓦ www.ebookers.com. Low fares on an extensive selection of scheduled flights and package deals.
North South Travel Ⓦ www.northsouthtravel.co.uk. Friendly, competitive travel agency, offering discounted fares worldwide. Profits are used to support projects in the developing world, especially the promotion of sustainable tourism.
STA Travel Ⓦ www.statravel.com. Worldwide specialists in independent travel; also student IDs, travel insurance, car rental, rail passes, and more. Good discounts for students and under-26s.
Trailfinders Ⓦ www.trailfinders.com. One of the best-informed and most efficient agents for independent travellers.
Travel CUTS Ⓦ www.travelcuts.com. Canadian youth and student travel firm.
USIT Ⓦ www.usit.ie. Ireland's main student and youth travel specialists.

Train and coach information

East Coast Ⓦ www.eastcoast.co.uk. Trains to Edinburgh, Glasgow, Aberdeen and Inverness.
Man in Seat 61 Ⓦ www.seat61.com. The best train information website on the internet.
National Express Ⓦ www.nationalexpress.com. Coaches to Scotland.
National Rail enquiries Ⓦ www.nationalrail.co.uk. Information and fares for all train services and companies.
ScotRail Ⓦ www.scotrail.co.uk. Caledonian Sleeper train to Glasgow, Edinburgh, Aberdeen, Inverness and Fort William.
Virgin Ⓦ www.virgintrains.co.uk. Trains to Edinburgh and Glasgow.

Ferry companies

DFDS Seaways Ⓦ www.dfdsseaways.com. Ferries from Europe.
P&O Irish Sea Ⓦ www.poirishsea.com. Ferries from Ireland.
Stena Line Ⓦ www.stenaline.co.uk. Ferries from Ireland.

Getting around

The majority of Scots live in the central belt, with Glasgow in the west and Edinburgh in the east. Public transport in this region is efficient and most places are easily accessible by train and bus. Further south and north it can be a different story: off the main routes, public transport services are few and far between, particularly in more remote parts of the Highlands and Islands. With careful planning, however, practically everywhere is accessible, and the scenery is usually adequate compensation for a long journey.

By train

Scotland has a modest **rail network**, at its densest in the central belt, skeletal in the Highlands, and nonexistent in the Islands. ScotRail runs the majority of train services, reaching all the major towns, sometimes on lines rated among the great scenic routes of the world.

You can buy train **tickets** at most stations, but if the ticket office at the station is closed, or the automatic machine isn't working, you may buy your ticket on board from the inspector using cash or a credit card. Those eligible for a **national rail pass** (£26) can obtain discounted tickets, with up to a third off most fares. These include the **16–25 Railcard**, for full-time students and those aged between 16 and 25, and the **Senior Railcard** for people over 60. Alternatively, a **Family & Friends Railcard** entitles up to four adults and up to four children a reduction.

In addition, ScotRail offers several regional passes. The most flexible is the **Freedom of Scotland Travelpass**, which gives unlimited train travel within Scotland. It's also valid on all CalMac ferries, Glasgow Underground and on various buses in the remoter regions. The pass costs £114 for four days' travel in an eight-day period, or £153 for eight days' travel in a fifteen-day period. The **Highland Rover** allows unlimited train travel within the Highlands; it costs £74 for four out of eight consecutive days. Lastly, there's a **Central Scotland Rover**, which gives unlimited train travel on lines between Glasgow and Edinburgh; it costs £33 for three out of seven consecutive days.

BritRail passes (ⓦwww.britrail.com) are only available to visitors not resident in the UK and must be purchased before you leave your home country. The pass is available in a wide variety of types; for example the Adult pass allows unlimited train travel for eight days and costs US$359. If you've been resident in a European country other than the UK for at least six months, an **InterRail** pass, allowing unlimited train travel within Britain, might be worth it if Scotland is part of a longer European trip. For more details, visit ⓦwww.interrailnet.com. Note that **Eurail** passes are not valid in the UK.

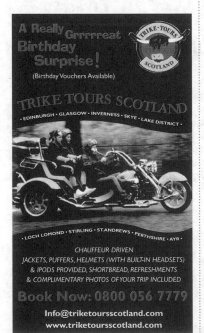

On most ScotRail routes **bicycles** are carried free, but since there are only between two and six bike spaces available, it's a good idea to reserve ahead and a requirement on longer journeys.

Useful rail contacts

ScotRail ⓦwww.scotrail.co.uk. For booking tickets and seats on all trains within Scotland, and sleeper trains from London to Scotland.

National Rail Enquiries ⓣ0845/748 4950, ⓦwww.nationalrail.co.uk. Gives details of timetables, fares and other information on rail travel throughout the UK.

By coach and bus

All of Scotland's major towns and cities are served by a few long-distance bus services, known across Britain as **coaches**.

Minibus tours

Minibus tours that operate out of Edinburgh (and Glasgow) and head off into the Highlands are popular with backpackers who want a quick taste of Scotland. Aimed at the youth market, they adopt an upbeat and irreverent approach to sightseeing, as well as offering a good opportunity to get to know fellow travellers.

The current leading operator, **Haggis** (Ⓣ0131/557 9393, Ⓦwww.haggisadventures.com), has bright yellow minibuses setting off daily on whistle-stop tours lasting between one and six days, in the company of a live-wire guide. A three-day trip round Skye starts from £99 (food and accommodation not included).

Several other companies offer similar packages, including **Macbackpackers** (Ⓣ0131/558 9900, Ⓦwww.macbackpackers.com), which runs tours linking up their own hostels round the country, and **Wild in Scotland** (Ⓣ0131/478 6500, Ⓦwww.wild-in-scotland.com), which takes in the Outer Hebrides or Orkney. The popular **Rabbie's Trail Burners** tours (Ⓣ0131/226 3133, Ⓦwww.rabbies.com) don't aim squarely at the backpacker market and have a rather more mellow outlook.

Scotland's national operator is **Scottish Citylink** (Ⓣ0871/266 3333, Ⓦwww.citylink.co.uk). On the whole, coaches are cheaper than trains and, as a result, are very popular, so for longer journeys it's advisable to book ahead.

There are various **discounts** on offer for those with children, those under 26 or over 60 and full-time students (contact Scottish Citylink for more details), as well as an **Explorer Pass**, which gives unlimited travel throughout Scotland; the £79 pass gives you eight days' travel over a sixteen-day period. Overseas passport holders can buy a **Brit Xplorer pass** (in 7-, 14- or 28-day versions) in the UK, from National Express (Ⓦwww.nationalexpress.com), or at major ports and airports; the seven-day pass costs £79, though you'd have to do a lot of bus travelling to make it worthwhile.

Local bus services are run by a bewildering array of companies, many of which change routes and timetables frequently. Local tourist offices can provide free timetables or you can contact **Traveline Scotland** (Ⓣ0871/200 2233, Ⓦwww.travelinescotland.com), which provides a reliable service both online and by phone. Some areas in the Highlands and Islands are only served by a **postbus**, vehicles carrying mail and a handful of fare-paying passengers. They set off early in the morning, usually around 8am and, though sociable, can be excruciatingly slow. You can view routes and timetables on the **Royal Mail website** (Ⓣ0845/774 0740, Ⓦwww.royalmail.com/postbus).

By car

In order to **drive** in Scotland you need a current full driving licence. If you're bringing your own vehicle into the country you should also carry your vehicle registration, ownership and insurance documents at all times.

In Scotland, as in the rest of the UK, you **drive on the left**. Speed limits are 20–40mph in built-up areas, 70mph on motorways and dual carriageways (freeways) and 60mph on most other roads. As a rule, assume that in any area with street lighting the limit is 30mph.

In the Highlands and Islands, there are still plenty of **single-track roads** with passing places; in addition to allowing oncoming traffic to pass at these points, you should also let cars behind you overtake. In remoter regions, the roads are dotted with sheep which are entirely oblivious to cars, so slow down and edge your way past; should you kill or injure one, it is your duty to inform the local farmer.

The AA (Ⓣ0800/ 887766, Ⓦwww.theaa.com), RAC (Ⓣ0844/891 3111, Ⓦwww.rac.co.uk) and Green Flag (Ⓣ0845/246 2766, Ⓦwww.greenflag.co.uk) all operate 24-hour **emergency breakdown** services. You may be entitled to free assistance through a reciprocal arrangement with a motoring organization in your home country. If not, you can make use of these emergency services by joining at the roadside, but you will incur a hefty surcharge. In remote areas, you may have a long wait for assistance.

Renting a car

Car rental in Scotland is expensive. Most firms charge £25–50 per day, or around £130–200 a week. The major chains are confined mostly to the big cities, so it may be cheaper to use small **local agencies** – we've highlighted some in the account. Remember, too that **fuel** in Scotland is expensive – petrol (gasoline) and diesel cost well over £1.20 per litre. **Automatics** are rare at the lower end of the price scale – if you want one, you should book well ahead. **Camper vans** are another option; rates start at £400 a week in the high season, but you'll save on accommodation – visit Ⓦwww.walkhighlands.co.uk to view a range of options. Few companies will rent to drivers with less than one year's experience and most will only rent to people over 21 or 25 and under 70 or 75 years of age.

UK car rental companies

Arnold Clark Ⓣ0141/237 4374, Ⓦwww.arnoldclarkrental.co.uk
Avis Ⓣ0844/581 0147, Ⓦwww.avis.co.uk
Budget Ⓣ01344/484100, Ⓦwww.budget.co.uk
easyCar Ⓣ0871/0500 444, Ⓦwww.easycar.com
Europcar Ⓣ0871/384 9847, Ⓦwww.europcar.co.uk
Hertz Ⓣ0870/844 8844, Ⓦwww.hertz.co.uk
Holiday Autos Ⓣ0871/472 5229, Ⓦwww.holidayautos.co.uk
National Ⓣ0871/384 3504, Ⓦwww.nationalcar.co.uk
Thrifty Ⓣ01494/751500, Ⓦwww.thrifty.co.uk

By ferry

Scotland has more than sixty inhabited islands, and nearly fifty of them have scheduled **ferry** links. Most ferries carry cars and vans, and the vast majority can – and should – be booked as far in advance as possible.

CalMac has a virtual monopoly on services on the River Clyde and to the Hebrides, sailing to 22 islands and 4 peninsulas. They aren't quick – no catamarans or fast ferries – or cheap, but they do have two types of reduced-fare pass. If you're taking more than one ferry, ask for one of the discounted **Island Hopscotch** tickets. If you're going to be taking a lot of ferries, you might be better off with an **Island Rover**, which entitles you to eight or fifteen consecutive days' unlimited ferry travel. It does not, however, guarantee you a place on any ferry, so you still need to book ahead. Prices for the eight-day/fifteen-day pass are around £50/£70 for passengers and around £230/£350 for cars.

Car ferries to **Orkney and Shetland** are run by Northlink Ferries. Pentland Ferries also run a car ferry to Orkney, and John O'Groats Ferries run a summer-only passenger service to Orkney. The various Orkney islands are linked to each other by Orkney Ferries; Shetland's inter-island ferries are mostly council-run so the local tourist board is your best bet for information. There are also numerous **small operators** round the Scottish coast that run fast RIB taxi services, day-excursion trips and even the odd scheduled service; their contact details are given in the relevant chapters of this guide.

Ferry companies

CalMac Ⓣ0800/066 5000, Ⓦwww.calmac.co.uk
John O'Groats Ferries Ⓣ01955/611353, Ⓦwww.jogferry.co.uk
NorthLink Ferries Ⓣ0845/600 0449, Ⓦwww.northlinkferries.co.uk
Orkney Ferries Ⓣ01856/872044, Ⓦwww.orkneyferries.co.uk
Pentland Ferries Ⓣ01856/831226, Ⓦwww.pentlandferries.co.uk

By plane

Apart from the three major **airports** of Glasgow, Edinburgh and Aberdeen, Scotland has numerous minor airports around the Scottish Highlands and Islands, some of which are little more than gravel airstrips. Airfares fluctuate enormously depending on demand – if you book early enough you can fly from Glasgow to Islay for £50 one-way, but leave it to the last minute and it could cost you more than twice that. Most flights within Scotland are operated by **flybe** (Ⓦwww.flybe.com), or its franchise partner **Loganair** (Ⓦwww.loganair.co.uk). For inter-island flights in Shetland, you need to book direct through **Directflight** (Ⓣ01595/840246). Competition emerges from time to time, with **Eastern Airways** (Ⓦwww.easternairways.com) currently offering flights from Aberdeen to Stornoway and Wick.

Accommodation

In common with the rest of Britain, accommodation in Scotland is expensive. Budget travellers are well catered for with numerous hostels and those with money to spend will relish the more expensive country-house hotels. In the middle ground, however, the standard of many B&Bs, guesthouses and hotels can be disappointing. Welcoming, comfortable, well-run places do, of course, exist in all parts of the country – and you'll find the best ones listed in the guide.

Booking hotels, guesthouses and B&Bs

VisitScotland, the country's tourist board, operates a system for grading accommodation, which is updated annually. However, not every establishment participates, and you shouldn't assume that a particular B&B is no good simply because it's not on VisitScotland's lists. The tourist board uses star awards, from one to five, which are supposed to reflect the quality of welcome, service and hospitality – though it's pretty clear that places without en-suite toilets, a TV in every room, matching fabrics or packets of shortbread on the sideboard are likely to be marked down.

Most **tourist offices** will help you find accommodation and **book a room** directly, for which they normally charge a flat fee of £4. If you take advantage of this service, it's worth being clear as to what kind of place you'd prefer, as the tourist office quite often selects something quite randomly across the whole range of their membership. Bear in mind, too, that outside the main towns and cities many places are only open for the **tourist season** (Easter to Oct): you'll always find somewhere to stay outside this period, but the choice may be limited.

Hotels

Hotels come in all shapes and sizes. At the upper end of the market, they can be huge country houses and converted castles offering a very exclusive and opulent experience. Most will have a licensed bar and offer both breakfast and dinner, and often lunch as well. In the cities the increasing prevalence of modern budget hotels and travel lodges run by national (and international) chains may not win any prizes for aesthetics or variety, but they are competitively priced and for the most part meet criteria for clean, smart, serviceable accommodation. Also making a bit of a comeback are inns (in other words, pubs), or their modern equivalent, "restaurants with rooms". These will often have only a handful of rooms, but their emphasis on creating an all-round convivial atmosphere as

Accommodation price codes

Throughout this book, accommodation prices have been graded with the **codes** below, corresponding to the cost of the least expensive double room in high season. The bulk of our recommendations fall in categories ❷ to ❺; those in the highest categories are limited to places that are especially attractive. Bear in mind that many of the chain hotels slash their tariffs at the weekend, and that a cheaper establishment may also have a selection of more expensive rooms. Price codes are not given for **campsites**, most of which charge less than £10 per person. Almost all **hostels** and **bunkhouses** charge between £10 and £15 per person per night; the few exceptions to this rule have their prices quoted in the review.

❶ £50 and under
❷ £51–60
❸ £61–70
❹ £71–80
❺ £81–100
❻ £101–120
❼ £121–150
❽ £151–200
❾ £201 and over

well as serving top-quality food often make them worth seeking out.

Guesthouses and B&Bs

Guesthouses and B&Bs offer the widest and most diverse range of accommodation. VisitScotland uses the term "guesthouse" for a commercial venture that has four or more rooms, at least some of which are en suite, reserving "B&B" for a predominantly private family home that has only a few rooms to let. In reality, however, most place offer en-suite facilities, and the different names often reflect the pretensions of the owners and the cost of the rooms more than differences in service: in general, guesthouses cost more than B&Bs.

Some guesthouses and B&Bs have decor that consists of heavy chintz and floral designs, but the location, and the chance to get an insight into the local way of life, can be some compensation. Many B&Bs, even the pricier ones, have only a few rooms, so **advance booking** is recommended, especially in the Islands.

Hostels

There's an ever-increasing number of **hostels** in Scotland to cater for travellers – youthful or otherwise – who are unable or unwilling to pay the rates charged by hotels, guest-houses and B&Bs. Most hostels are clean and comfortable, sometimes offering doubles and even singles as well as dormitory accommodation. Others concentrate more on keeping the price as low as possible, simply providing a roof over your head and a few basic facilities. Whatever type of hostel you stay in, expect to pay £10–20 per night.

The **Scottish Youth Hostels Association** (Ⓦwww.syha.org.uk), referred to throughout the Guide as "SYHA hostels", run the longest-established hostels in the Highlands and Islands. While these places sometimes occupy handsome buildings, many retain an institutionalized air. Bunk-bed accommodation in single-sex dormitories, lights out before midnight and no smoking/no alcohol policies are the norm outside the big cities. Breakfast is not normally included in the price, though most hostels have self-catering facilities.

If you're not a **member** of one of the hostelling organizations affiliated to **Hostelling International** (HI), you can pay your £10 joining fee at most hostels. **Advance booking** is recommended, and essential at Easter, Christmas and from May to August. You can book online, by phone, post and sometimes fax, and your bed will be held until 6pm on the day of arrival.

There are also loads of **independent hostels** (sometimes known as "bunkhouses") across Scotland. These are usually laidback places with no membership, fewer rules, mixed dorms and no curfew. You can find most of them in the annually updated *Independent Hostel Guide* (Ⓦ www.independenthostelguide.co.uk). Many of them are also affiliated to the Independent Backpackers Hostels of Scotland (Ⓦ www.hostel-scotland.co.uk), which has a programme of inspection and lists members in their *Blue Hostel Guide*, available for free online.

Camping and self-catering

There are hundreds of **caravan and camping parks** around Scotland, most of which are open from April to October. The most expensive sites charge about £10–15 for two people to pitch a tent, and are usually well equipped, with shops, a restaurant, a bar and, occasionally, sports facilities. Most of these, however, are aimed principally at caravans, trailers and motorhomes, and generally don't offer the tranquil atmosphere and independence that those travelling with just a tent are seeking.

That said, **informal sites** of the kind tent campers relish do exist, and are described throughout this guide, though they are few and far between. Many **hostels** allow camping, and farmers will usually let folk camp on their land for free or for a nominal sum. Scotland's relaxed land access laws allow **wild camping** in open country. The basic rule is "leave no trace", but for a guide to good practice, visit Ⓦ www.outdooraccess-scotland.com.

The great majority of **caravans** are permanently moored nose to tail in the vicinity of some of Scotland's finest scenery; others are positioned singly in back gardens or amidst farmland. Some can be booked for self-catering, and with prices starting at around £100 a week, this can work out as one of the cheapest options if you're travelling with kids in tow.

If you're planning to do a lot of camping at official camping and caravanning sites, it might be worthwhile joining the **Camping and Caravanning Club** (Ⓦ www.campingandcaravanningclub.co.uk). Membership costs around £37 and entitles you to pay only a per-person fee, not a pitch fee, at CCC sites. Those coming from abroad can get the same benefits by buying an international camping carnet, available from home motoring organizations or a CCC equivalent.

Self-catering

A huge proportion of visitors to Scotland opt for **self-catering**, booking a cottage or apartment for a week and often saving themselves a considerable amount of money by doing so. In most cases, the minimum period of let is a week, and therefore isn't a valid option if you're aiming to tour round the country. The least you can expect to pay in the high season is around £250 per week for a place sleeping four, but something special, or somewhere in a popular tourist area, might cost £500 or more. Such is the number and variety of self-catering places on offer that we've mentioned very few in the Guide. A good source of information is VisitScotland's self-catering guide, updated annually and listing more than 1200 properties, or try one of the websites listed below.

Cottages and Castles Ⓦ www.cottages-and-castles.co.uk. A range of self-catering properties, mostly in mainland Scotland.

Cottages4you Ⓦ www.cottages4you.co.uk. Hundreds of reasonably priced properties all over Scotland.

Ecosse Unique Ⓦ www.uniquescotland.com. Carefully selected cottages across mainland Scotland, plus a few in the Hebrides and Orkney.

Landmark Trust Ⓦ www.landmarktrust.org.uk. A very select number of unforgettable, upmarket historical properties; first, however, you must buy the brochure (£13, refundable on first booking).

Mackay's Agency Ⓦ www.mackays-self-catering.co.uk. A whole range of properties in every corner of mainland Scotland (plus Skye and Orkney), from chalets and town apartments to remote stone-built cottages.

National Trust for Scotland www.nts.org.uk. The NTS lets around forty of its converted historic cottages and houses.

Scottish Country Cottages www.scottish-country-cottages.co.uk. Superior cottages with lots of character scattered across the Scottish mainland, plus some of the Inner Hebrides.

Campus accommodation

A different and generally cheaper self-catering option, especially if you're staying a week or more in one of the cities, is **campus accommodation**. The universities of Glasgow, Strathclyde, Edinburgh, Stirling, St Andrews and Dundee all open their halls of residence to overseas visitors during the summer break, and some also offer rooms during the Easter and Christmas vacations. Accommodation varies from tiny single rooms in long, lonely corridors to relatively comfortable places in small shared apartments. Prices start at around £20 per night, not always including breakfast. All the useful university details are given in the Guide.

Food and drink

While Scotland isn't exactly known for its culinary heritage, the country's eating habits are changing, and from the cities to some of the furthest islands, you can often eat extremely well with a strong emphasis on fresh, local and organic produce. For more on ingredients, classic dishes including haggis, top restaurants and drinks, see the "Scottish food and drink" colour section.

Breakfast

In most hotels and B&Bs you'll be offered a **Scottish breakfast**, similar to its English counterpart of sausage, bacon and egg, but typically with the addition of black pudding (blood sausage) and potato scones. Porridge is another likely option, as is fish in the form of kippers, smoked haddock or even kedgeree. Scotland's staple drink, like England's, is **tea**, drunk strong and with milk, though **coffee** is just as readily available everywhere. However, while designer coffee shops are now a familiar feature in the cities, execrable versions of espresso and cappuccino, as well as instant coffee, are still all too familiar.

Lunches and snacks

The most common lunchtime fare in Scotland remains the **sandwich**. A bowl or cup of hearty **soup** is a typical accompaniment, particularly in winter. A **pub lunch** is often an attractive alternative. Bar menus generally have standard filling but unambitious options including soup, sandwiches, scampi and chips or steak pie and chips, with vegetarians suffering from a paucity of choice. That said, some bar food is freshly prepared and filling, equalling the à la carte dishes served in the adjacent hotel restaurant. Pubs or hotel bars are among the cheapest options when it comes to eating out – in the smallest villages, these might be your only option.

Restaurants are often, though not always, open at lunchtimes. When they tend to be less busy and generally offer a shorter menu compared with their evening service, and this can make for a more pleasant and less expensive experience. For morning or afternoon snacks, as well as light lunches, **tearooms** are a common feature; you will often find decent home baking.

As for **fast food**, chip shops, or **chippies**, abound, the best often found in coastal towns within sight of the fishing boats. Deep-fried battered fish is the standard choice – when served with chips it's known as a "fish supper", even if eaten at lunchtime – though everything from

Meal times

In many parts of Scotland outside the cities, inflexible **meal times** mean that you'll have to keep an eye on your watch if you don't want to miss out on eating. B&Bs and hotels frequently serve breakfast only until 9am, lunch is usually over by 2pm, and, despite the long summer evenings, pub and hotel kitchens often stop serving dinner as early as 8pm.

hamburgers to haggis suppers is normally on offer, all deep-fried, of course. Scotland is even credited with inventing the **deep-fried Mars bar**, the definitive badge of a nation with the worst heart disease statistics in Europe. For alternative fast food, major towns feature all the usual pizza, burger and baked potato outlets, as well as Chinese, Mexican and Indian takeaways.

Evening meals

There's no doubt that, as with the rest of the UK, eating out in Scotland is expensive. Our restaurant listings include a mix of high-quality and budget establishments. Wine in restaurants is marked up strongly, so you'll often pay £15 for a bottle selling for £5 in the shops; house wines generally start around the £10 mark.

If you're travelling in remoter parts of Scotland, or staying at a B&B or guesthouse in the countryside, ask advice about nearby options for your **evening meal**. Many B&Bs and guesthouses will cook you dinner, but you must book ahead and indicate any dietary requirements.

As for **restaurants**, standards vary enormously, but independent restaurants using good-quality local produce are now found all over Scotland. Less predictable are hotel restaurants, many of which serve non-residents. Some can be very ordinary despite the highfalutin descriptions on the à la carte menu. You could easily end up paying £30–40 a head for a meal with wine.

In central Scotland, particularly in Edinburgh and Glasgow, there's a range of **international** cuisines including Japanese, Thai, Caribbean and Turkish, as well as the more common Indian, Chinese and Italian establishments. Glasgow is one of Britain's curry capitals, while Edinburgh's restaurant scene is very lively, its seafood and vegetarian restaurants a particular strength.

Among traditional **desserts**, "clootie dumpling" is a sweet, stodgy fruit pudding bound in a cloth and cooked for hours, while Cranachan, made with toasted oatmeal steeped in whisky and folded into whipped cream flavoured with fresh raspberries, or the similar Atholl Brose, are considered more refined.

Food shopping

Most Scots get their supplies from supermarkets, but you're increasingly likely to come across good delis, farm shops and specialist **food shops**. Many stock local produce alongside imported delicacies, as well as organic fruit and veg, specialist drinks such as locally brewed beer, freshly baked bread, and sandwiches and other snacks for takeaway. Look out too for **farmers' markets** (Ⓦwww.scottishfarmersmarkets.co.uk), which take place on Saturday and Sunday mornings; local farmers and small producers from pig farmers to cheese-makers and small smokeries set up stalls to sell their specialist lines.

Scotland is notorious for its sweet tooth, and **cakes and puddings** are taken very seriously. Bakers with extensive displays of iced buns, cakes and cream-filled pastries are a typical feature of any Scottish high street, while home-made shortbread, scones or tablet (a hard, crystalline form of fudge) are considered great treats. In the summer, Scottish berries, in particular raspberries and strawberries, are particularly tasty.

You'll also find a number of specialist cheese shops, while many restaurants serve only **Scottish cheeses** after dinner. Look out for Isle of Mull, a tangy farmhouse cheddar; Dunsyre Blue, a Scottish Dolcelatte; or farmhouse Dunlop, the local version of cheddar.

Drinking

As in the rest of Britain, Scottish **pubs**, which originated as travellers' hostelries and

Making malt whisky

Malt whisky is made by soaking barley in **steeps** (water cisterns) for two or three days until it swells, after which it is left to germinate for around seven days, during which the starch in the barley seed is converted into soluble sugars – this process is known as **malting**. The malted barley or "green malt" is then dried in a **kiln** over a furnace, which can be oil-fired, peat-fired or, more often than not, a combination of the two. Only a few distilleries still do their own malting and kilning in the traditional pagoda-style kilns; the rest simply have their malted barley delivered from an industrial maltings. The first process in most distilleries is therefore **milling**, which grinds the malted barley into "grist". Next comes the **mashing**, during which the grist is infused in hot water in mashtuns, producing a sugary concoction called "wort". After cooling, the wort passes into the washbacks, traditionally made of wood, where it is fermented with yeast for two to three days. During **fermentation**, the sugar is converted into alcohol, producing a brown foaming liquid known as "wash". **Distillation** now takes place, not once but twice: the wash is steam-heated, and the vapours siphoned off and condensed as a spirit. This is the point at which the whisky is poured into oak casks – usually ones which have already been used to store bourbon or sherry – and left to age for a minimum of three years. The average **maturation** period for a single malt whisky, however, is ten years; and the longer it matures, the more expensive it is, because two percent evaporates each year. Unlike wine, as soon as the whisky is bottled, maturation ceases.

coaching inns, are the main social focal points of any community. Pubs in Scotland vary hugely, from old-fashioned inns with open fires and a convivial atmosphere, to raucous theme pubs with loud music and satellite TV. Out in the islands, pubs are few and far between, with most drinking taking place in the local hotel bar. In Edinburgh and Glasgow you'll find traditional pubs supplemented by upbeat, trendy café-bars.

The national drink is **whisky** (see *Scottish food and drink* colour section), though you might not guess it from the "alcopops" (bottles of sweet fruit drinks laced with vodka or gin) and ready-made mixers consumed on a Friday and Saturday night. Scotland also produces some exceptionally good cask-conditioned **real ales** (see also *Scottish food and drink* colour section), yet lager is much more popular. Pub **opening hours** are generally 11am to 11pm, but in the cities and towns, or anywhere where there is demand, places stay open much later. Whatever time the pub closes, "last orders" will be called by the bar staff about fifteen minutes before closing time to allow a bit of "drinking-up time". In general, you have to be 16 to enter a pub unaccompanied, though some places are relaxed about people bringing children in, or have special family rooms and beer gardens where the kids can run free. The legal drinking age is 18. As with the rest of the UK, smoking is not allowed in any pubs, bars or restaurants.

Scotland produces a prodigious amount of **mineral water**, much of which is exported – tap water is chill, clean and perfectly palatable in most parts of the country, including the areas of the Highlands and Islands where it's tinged the colour of weak tea by peat in the ground. Locally produced **Irn-Bru**, a fizzy orange, sickly sweet concoction, has been known to outsell Coke and Pepsi in Scotland.

The media

Many Scots see the UK's "national media" as London-based and London-biased, and prefer to listen to Scottish radio programmes, read Scottish newspapers, and – albeit to a much lesser extent – watch Scottish TV. Local papers are also avidly consumed, with the weekly papers in places like Orkney and Shetland read by virtually the entire adult population.

The press

The Scottish press centres on two serious **dailies** – *The Scotsman*, now published in tabloid format and based in Edinburgh, and *The Herald*, a broadsheet published in Glasgow. Both offer good coverage of the current issues affecting Scotland, along with British and foreign news, sport, arts and lifestyle pages. Scotland's biggest-selling dailies are the downmarket *Daily Record*, a tabloid from the same stable as the *Daily Mirror*, and the local edition of *The Sun*. Most of the main UK newspapers do produce specific Scottish editions, although the "quality" press, ranging between the right-wing *Daily Telegraph* and the left-of-centre *Guardian*, are justifiably seen in Scotland as being London papers.

The provincial daily press in Scotland is more widely read than its English counterpart, with the two biggest-selling regional titles being Aberdeen's famously parochial *Press and Journal*, read in the northeast, Orkney and Shetland, and the right-wing *Dundee Courier*, mostly sold in Perth, Angus, Tayside and Fife. The weekly *Oban Times* gives an insight into life in the Highlands and Islands, but is staid compared with the radical, campaigning weekly *West Highland Free Press*, printed on Skye; both carry articles in Gaelic as well as English. Further north, the lively *Shetland Times* and sedate *Orcadian* are essential weekly reads.

Many national Sunday newspapers have a Scottish edition, although Scotland has its own offerings – *Scotland on Sunday*, from the *Scotsman* stable, and the *Sunday Herald*, complementing its eponymous daily. Far more fun and widely read is the anachronistic *Sunday Post*, published by Dundee's D.C. Thomson publishing group. It's a wholesome paper, uniquely Scottish, and has changed little since the 1950s, since which time its two long-running cartoon strips, *Oor Wullie* and *The Broons*, have acquired cult status.

Scottish **monthlies** include the glossy *Scottish Field*, a parochial version of England's *Tatler*, covering countryside interests along with local travel and fashion, and the widely read *Scots Magazine*, an old-fashioned middle-of-the-road publication which promotes family values and lots of good fresh air.

TV and radio

In Scotland there are five main (sometimes called "terrestrial") **TV channels**: state-owned BBC1 and BBC2, and independent commercial channels, ITV1, Channel 4 and Five. **BBC Scotland** produces news programmes and a regular crop of local-interest lifestyle, current affairs, drama and comedy shows which slot into the schedules of both BBC channels. The commercial channel ITV1 is divided between three regional companies in Scotland: populist Scottish Television (STV), which is received in most of south-central Scotland and parts of the West Highlands; Grampian, based in Aberdeen; and Border, which transmits from Carlisle. There's also the quirkier though often trashy Channel 4, and downmarket Five, which still can't be received in some parts of Scotland.

The **BBC radio** network broadcasts six main channels in Scotland, five of which are national stations originating largely from London: Radio 1 (pop and dance music), Radio 2 (mainstream pop, rock and light music), Radio 3 (classical music), Radio 4 (current affairs, arts and drama) and Radio 5 Live (sports, news and live discussions and phone-ins). Only the award-winning BBC Radio Scotland offers a Scottish perspective on news, politics, arts, music, travel and sport, as well as providing a Gaelic network in the Highlands with local programmes in Shetland, Orkney and the Borders.

A web of local **commercial radio** stations covers the country, mostly mixing rock and pop music with news bulletins, but a few tiny community-based stations such as Lochbroom FM in Ullapool – a place famed for its daily midge count – transmit documentaries and discussions on local issues. The most populated areas of Scotland also receive UK-wide commercial stations such as Classic FM, Virgin Radio and TalkSport. With a DAB **digital radio**, you can get all the main stations crackle-free along with special interest and smaller-scale stations.

Some Scottish radio stations

BBC Radio Scotland 92–95FM, 810MW Ⓦ **www.bbc.co.uk/radioscotland.** Nationwide news, sport, music, current affairs and arts.

Clyde 1 102.5FM Ⓦ **www.radioclyde.com.** Glasgow's main contemporary rock and pop station. The slightly mellower Clyde 2 is at 1152MW.

Lochbroom FM 102.2 & 96.8FM Ⓦ **www.lochbroomfm.co.uk.** One of Britain's smallest radio stations, broadcasting to the northwest coast from Ullapool.

Moray Firth 97.4FM, 1107MW Ⓦ **www.mfr.co.uk.** Mainstream rock and pop for the youth of the Inverness area.

Nevis Radio 96.6 & 102.3FM Ⓦ **www.nevisradio.co.uk.** All that's happening in Fort William and surrounds, from the slopes of Ben Nevis.

North Sound 96.9FM, 1035MW Ⓦ **www.northsound.co.uk.** Pumps out the latest tunes for Aberdeen.

Radio Forth 97.3FM Ⓦ **www.radioforth.com.** Rock and pop for Edinburgh and around. Forth 2 at 1548MW is their easier-listening stablemate.

Radio Tay 96.4 & 102.8FM, 1161 & 1584MW Ⓦ **www.radiotay.co.uk.** Dundee's local radio.

Real Radio 100–101FM Ⓦ **www.realradiofm.com.** Mainstream pop and shock jocks for the central belt.

SIBC 96.2FM Ⓦ **www.sibc.co.uk.** Shetland's own independent station.

Events and spectator sports

Scotland offers a huge range of cultural and heritage-themed events as well as a packed sporting calendar. Many tourists will home straight in on the Highland Games and other tartan-draped theatricals, but there's more to Scotland than this: numerous regional celebrations perpetuate ancient customs, and the Edinburgh Festival is an arts celebration unrivalled in size and variety in the world. A few of the smaller, more obscure events, particularly those with a pagan bent, do not always welcome the casual visitor. The tourist board publishes a weighty list of all Scottish events twice a year: it's free and you can get it from area tourist offices or direct from their headquarters. Full details are at Ⓦwww.visitscotland.com.

Events calendar

Dec–Jan

Dec 31 and Jan 1 Hogmanay and Ne'er Day. Traditionally more important to the Scots than Christmas, the occasion is known for the custom of "first-footing" (see box opposite). More popular these days are huge and highly organized street parties, most notably in Edinburgh (Ⓦwww.edinburghshogmanay.org), but also in Aberdeen, Glasgow and other centres.

Jan 1 Stonehaven fireball ceremony. Locals swing fireballs on long sticks to welcome New Year and ward off evil spirits. Also **Kirkwall Boys' and Men's Ba' Games, Orkney**: mass, drunken football game through the streets of the town, with the castle and the harbour the respective goals. As a grand finale the players jump into the harbour.

Jan 11 Burning of the Clavie, Burghead, Moray Ⓦwww.hogmanay.net/events/burghhead. A burning tar barrel is carried through the town and then rolled down Doorie Hill. Charred fragments of the Clavie offer protection against the evil eye.

Mid- to late Jan Celtic Connections, Glasgow Ⓦwww.celticconnections.com. A major celebration of Celtic and folk music held in venues across the city.

Last Tues in Jan Up-Helly-Aa, Lerwick, Shetland Ⓦwww.visitshetland.com. Norse fire festival culminating in the burning of a specially built Viking longship. Visitors will need an invite from one of the locals, or you can buy a ticket for the Town Hall celebrations.

Jan 25 Burns Night. Scots worldwide get stuck into haggis, whisky and vowel-grinding poetry to commemorate Scotland's greatest poet, Robert Burns (see box, p.44 & p.192).

Feb–March

Feb Scottish Curling Championship Ⓦwww.royalcaledoniancurlingclub.org, held in a different (indoor) venue each year.

Feb–March Six Nations Rugby tournament, between Scotland, England, Wales, Ireland, France and Italy Ⓦwww.rbs6nations.com. Scotland's home games are played at Murrayfield stadium in Edinburgh.

March 1 Whuppity Scourie, Lanark. Local children race round the church beating each other with home-made paper weapons in a representation (it's thought) of the chasing away of winter or the warding off of evil spirits.

April–May

April Scottish Grand National, Ayr Ⓦwww.ayr-racecourse.co.uk. Not quite as testing as the English equivalent steeplechase, but an important event in the Scottish racing calendar. Also **Rugby Sevens** (seven-a-side tournaments; Ⓦwww.melrose7s.com) in the Borders and the entertaining and inclusive **Edinburgh Science Festival** Ⓦwww.sciencefestival.co.uk.

April 6 Tartan Day. Over-hyped celebration of ancestry by North Americans of Scottish descent on the anniversary of the Declaration of Arbroath in 1320. Ignored by most Scots in Scotland, other than journalists.

Early May Spirit of Speyside Scotch Whisky Festival (Ⓦwww.spiritofspeyside.com). Four-day binge with pipe bands, gigs and dancing as well as distillery crawls. **Shetland Folk Festival** (Ⓦwww.shetlandfolkfestival.com). One of the liveliest and most entertaining of Scotland's round of folk festivals.

May Scottish FA Cup Final. Scotland's premier football event, played in Glasgow.

Hogmanay

When hardline Scottish Protestant clerics in the sixteenth century abolished Christmas for being a Catholic mass, the Scots, not wanting to miss out on a mid-winter knees-up, instead put their energy into greeting the New Year, or **Hogmanay**. Houses were cleaned from top to bottom, debts were paid and quarrels made up, and, after the bells of midnight were rung, great store was laid by welcoming good luck into your house. This still takes the form of the tradition of **"first-footing"** – visiting your neighbours and bearing gifts. The ideal first-foot is a tall dark-haired male carrying a bottle of whisky; women or redheads, on the other hand, bring bad luck – though, to be honest, no one carrying a bottle of whisky tends to be turned away these days, whatever the colour of their hair. All this neighbourly greeting means a fair bit of partying, and no one is expected to go to work the next day, or, indeed, the day after that. Even today, January 1 is a public holiday in the rest of the UK, but only in Scotland does the holiday extend to the next day too.

Late May **Atholl Highlanders Parade at Blair Castle, Perthshire** ⓦ www.blair-castle.co.uk. The annual parade and inspection of Britain's last private army by their colonel-in-chief, the Duke of Atholl, on the eve of their Highland Games. Also **Burns an' a' That** (ⓦ www.burnsfestival.com), a modern celebration of poet Robert Burns, including gigs by contemporary pop acts.

June–July

June–Aug **Riding of the Marches** in border towns such as Hawick, Selkirk, Jedburgh, Langholm and Lauder. The Ridings originated to check the boundaries of common land owned by the town and also to commemorate warfare between the Scots and the English.

June **Beginning of the Highland Games season** across the Highlands, northeast and Argyll. **St Magnus Festival**, Orkney, is a classical and folk music, drama, dance and literature festival celebrating the islands ⓦ www.stmagnusfestival.com. The **Edinburgh International Film Festival** (ⓦ www.edfilmfest.org.uk) runs from mid-June for 10 days.

Late June **Royal Highland Agricultural Show**, at Ingliston near Edinburgh ⓦ www.royalhighlandshow.org. Old wooden boats and fishing craft gather for the **Traditional Boat Festival** at Portsoy on the Moray Firth coast (ⓦ www.scottishtraditionalboatfestival.co.uk). **Glasgow International Jazz Festival** (ⓦ www.jazzfest.co.uk).

Early July **T in the Park** (ⓦ www.tinthepark.com). Scotland's biggest outdoor music event, held at Balado near Kinross with a star-studded line-up of contemporary bands.

July **Scottish Open Golf Championship**. Held each year at Loch Lomond golf course, just before the **British Open** tournament, which is played in Scotland at least every alternate year.

Late July **The Wickerman Festival** of alternative music is held near Kirkcudbright (ⓦ www.thewickermanfestival.co.uk).

Aug–Sept

Aug **Edinburgh Festival** ⓦ www.edinburghfestivals.com. One of the world's great arts jamborees (see p.118). **The Edinburgh Military Tattoo** (ⓦ www.edinburgh-tattoo.co.uk) features floodlit massed pipe bands and drums on the castle esplanade. There's also the **World Pipe Band Championship** at Glasgow (ⓦ www.seeglasgow.com/piping), and plenty more Highland Games.

Early Sept **Shinty's Camanachd Cup Final** ⓦ www.shinty.com. The climax of the season for Scotland's own stick-and-ball game, normally held in one of the main Highland towns. Also various food festivals and events under the banner of **Scottish Food Fortnight** (ⓦ www.scottishfoodfortnight.co.uk).

Late Sept **Doors Open Day** (ⓦ www.doorsopendays.org.uk). The one weekend a year when many public and private buildings are open to the public; actual dates vary. Also another **Spirit of Speyside Whisky Festival** (ⓦ www.spiritofspeyside.com), and **the Scottish Book Town Festival** in Wigtown (ⓦ www.wigtown-booktown.co.uk).

Oct–Nov

Oct **Tiree Wave Classic** (ⓦ www.tireewaveclassic.com). Annual event attracting windsurfers from around the world to the breezy Hebridean island.

The National Mod (ⓦ www.the-mod.co.uk). Held over nine days at a different venue each year, the Mod is a competitive festival and features all aspects of Gaelic performing arts.

Nov 30 **St Andrew's Day**. Celebrating Scotland's patron saint. The town of St Andrews hosts a week of events leading up to it (ⓦ www.standrewsweek.co.uk).

Highland Games

Despite their name, **Highland Games** are held all over Scotland between May and mid-September, varying in size and in the range of events they offer. The Games probably originated in the fourteenth century as a means of recruiting the best fighting men for the clan chiefs, and were popularized by Queen Victoria to encourage the traditional dress, music, games and dance of the Highlands; indeed, various royals still attend the Games at Braemar.

Apart from Braemar, the most famous games take place at Oban and Cowal, but the smaller events are often more fun – like a sort of Highland version of a school sports day. There's money to be won, too, so the Games are usually pretty competitive. The most distinctive events are known as the "heavies" – tossing the caber (pronounced "kabber"), putting the stone, and tossing the weight over the bar – all of which require prodigious strength and skill and the wearing of a kilt. Tossing the caber is the most spectacular, when the athlete must lift an entire tree trunk up, cupping it in his hands, before running with it and attempting to heave it end over end. Just as important as the sporting events are the **piping** competitions – for individuals and bands – and **dancing** competitions, where you'll see girls as young as 3 tripping the quick, intricate steps of dances such as the Highland Fling.

Football

Football (soccer) is far and away Scotland's most popular spectator sport. The national team (accompanied by its distinctive and vocal supporters, known as the "Tartan Army") is a source of pride and frustation for Scots everywhere. Once a regular at World Cups where they were involved in some memorable matches against the likes of Holland and Brazil, Scotland have failed to qualify for an international tournament since 1998.

The national domestic league established in 1874 is one of the oldest in the world, but today most of the teams that play in it are little known beyond the boundaries of Scotland. The exceptions are the two massive Glasgow teams that dominate the Scottish scene – **Rangers** and **Celtic** (known collectively as the "Old Firm"; see box, p.233). The sectarian, and occasionally violent, rivalry between these two is one of the least attractive aspects of Scottish life, and their stranglehold over the **Scottish Premier League** or SPL (Ⓦwww.scotprem.com)

Burns night

To celebrate the birthday of the country's best-known poet, Rabbie Burns (1759–96), Scots all over the world gather together for a **Burns Supper** on January 25. Strictly speaking, a piper should greet the guests until everyone is seated ready to hear the first bit of Burns' poetry, *The Selkirk Grace*:

Some hae meat and canna eat,
and some wad eat that want it,
but we hae meat and we can eat,
and sae the Lord be thankit.

At this point the star attraction of the evening, the **haggis**, is piped in on a silver platter, after which someone reads out Burns's *Ode to a Haggis*, beginning with the immortal line, "*Fair fa' your honest, sonsie face/Great chieftain o' the pudding-race!*". During the **recitation**, the reader raises a knife ("*His knife see Rustic-labour dight*"), pierces the haggis, allowing the tasty gore to spill out ("*trenching its gushing entrails*"), and then toasts the haggis with the final line ("*Gie her a Haggis!*"). After everyone has tucked into their **haggis, tatties and neaps**, someone gives a paean to the life of Burns along with more of his poetry. A male guest then has to give a speech in which women are praised (often ironically) through selective quotations from Burns, ending in a Toast to the Lassies. This is followed by a (usually scathing) reply from one of the Lassies, again through judicious use of Burns's quotes. Finally, there's a stirring rendition of Burns's poem, *Auld Lang Syne*, to the familiar tune.

makes the national championship a fairly predictable affair.

As in England, foreign players have flooded the league, to the extent that home-grown players can be in the minority in the Rangers and Celtic teams. However, talented local players still have a stage on which to perform, and the new blend of continental sophistication mixed with Scottish passion and ruggedness makes for a distinctive spectacle.

The season begins in early August and ends in mid-May, with matches on Saturday afternoons at 3pm, and also often on Sunday afternoons and Wednesday evenings. Tickets range from £15 to £25 for big games; the major clubs operate telephone credit-card booking services (see the relevant city's listings section for details). For a quick overview, see Ⓦwww.scotprem.com which features details of every Scottish club, with news and match-report archives.

Rugby

Although rugby has always lived under the shadow of football in Scotland, it ranks as one of the country's major sports. Weekends when the national team is playing a home international at Murrayfield stadium in Edinburgh are colourful occasions, with kilted masses filling the capital's pubs and lining the streets leading to the ground. Internationals take place in the spring, when Scotland take on the other "home nations", along with France and Italy, in the annual **Six Nations** tournament (see p.42), although there are always fixtures in the autumn against international touring teams such as New Zealand, Australia and South Africa. Tickets for big games are hard to come by; contact the **Scottish Rugby Union** (Ⓣ0131/346 5000, Ⓦwww.sru.org.uk).

The area where the **domestic rugby** tradition runs deepest is in the Borders, where towns such as Hawick, Kelso and Galashiels can be gripped by the fortunes of their local team on a Saturday afternoon. The Borders are also the home of **seven-a-side rugby**, an abridged version of the game that was invented in Melrose in the 1890s and is now played around the world, most notably at the glamorous annual event in Hong Kong. The Melrose Sevens is still the biggest tournament of the year in Scotland (see p.42), although you'll find events at one or other of the Border towns through the spring, most going on right through an afternoon and invoking a festival atmosphere in the large crowd.

Shinty

Played throughout Scotland but with particular strongholds in the West Highlands and Strathspey, the game of **shinty** (the Gaelic *sinteag* means "leap") arrived from Ireland around 1500 years ago. Until the latter part of the nineteenth century, it was played on an informal basis and teams from neighbouring villages had to come to an agreement about rules before matches could begin. However, in 1893, the **Camanachd Association** – the Gaelic word for shinty is *camanachd* – was set up to formalize the rules, and the first Camanachd Cup Final was held in Inverness in 1896. Today, shinty is still fairly close to its Gaelic roots, like the Irish game of hurling, with each team having twelve players including a goalkeeper, and each goal counting for a point. The game, which bears similarities to an undisciplined version of hockey, isn't for the faint-hearted; it's played at a furious pace, with sticks – called camans or cammocks – flying alarmingly in all directions. Support is enthusiastic and vocal, and if you're in the Highlands during the season, which runs from March to October, it's well worth trying to catch a match: check with tourist offices or the local paper, or go to ⓦwww.shinty.com.

Curling

The one winter sport which enjoys a strong Scottish identity is **curling** (ⓦwww.royalcaledoniancurlingclub.org), occasionally still played on a frozen outdoor rink, or "pond", though most commonly these days seen at indoor ice rinks. The game, which involves gently sliding smooth-bottomed 18kg discs of granite called "stones" across the ice towards a target circle, is said to have been invented in Scotland, although its earliest representation is in a sixteenth-century Flemish painting. Played by two teams of four, it's a highly tactical and skilful sport, enlivened by team members using brushes to sweep the ice furiously in front of a moving stone to help it travel further and straighter. If you're interested in seeing curling being played, go along to the ice rink in places such as Perth, Pitlochry or Inverness on a winter evening.

Outdoor activities

Scotland boasts a landscape that, weather conditions apart, is extremely attractive for outdoor pursuits at all levels of fitness and ambition, and legislation enacted by the Scottish Parliament has ensured a right of access to hills, mountains, lochs and rivers. Within striking distance of its cities are two national parks, remote wilderness areas and vast stretches of glens and moorland, while sea-kayakers, sailors and surfers can enjoy excellent conditions along the rugged but beautiful coastline. For more on outdoor activities see our special colour section.

Walking and climbing

The whole of Scotland offers superb opportunities for **walking**, with some of the finest areas in the ownership of bodies such as the National Trust for Scotland and the John Muir Trust (ⓦwww.jmt.org); both permit year-round access. Bear in mind, though, that restrictions may be in place during lambing and deerstalking seasons. See ⓦwww.snh.org.uk/hillphones for information about **hiking safely** during the stalking season. In addition, the green signposts of the Scottish Rights of Way Society point to established paths and routes all over the country.

There are several **long-distance footpaths**, such as the well-known West Highland Way, which take between three and seven days to walk, though you can, of course, just do a section of them. Paths are generally well signposted and well supported, with a range of services from bunkhouses to baggage-carrying services. For more on long-distance footpaths see *The great outdoors* colour section.

Numerous short walks (from accessible towns and villages) and several major walks are touched on in this guide. However, you should only use our notes as general outlines, and always in conjunction with a good map. Where possible, we have given details of the best maps to use – in most cases one of the excellent and reliable **Ordnance Survey** (OS) series (see p.55), usually available from local tourist offices, which can also supply other local maps, safety advice and guidebooks/leaflets. We've These, as well as a wide range of maps, are available from most of the good outdoor stores scattered around the country.

For relatively gentle walking in the company of knowledgeable locals, look out for guided walks offered by rangers at many National Trust for Scotland, Forest Enterprise and Scottish Natural Heritage sites. These often focus on local **wildlife**, and the best can lead to some special sightings, such as a badger's sett or a golden eagle's eyrie.

Useful contacts for walkers

General information

ⓦ **www.hillphones.info** Daily information for hill walkers about deerstalking activities (July–Oct).

ⓦ **www.outdooraccess-scotland.com** All you need to know about the Scottish Outdoor Access Code.

ⓦ **www.walking.visitscotland.com** Official site from VisitScotland, with good lists of operators, information on long-distance footpaths and details of deerstalking restrictions and contact phone numbers.

ⓦ **www.wildlife.visitscotland.com** Highlights the fauna and flora you may spot on a walk.

Clubs and associations

Mountain Bothies Association ⓦwww.mountainbothies.org.uk. Charity dedicated to maintaining huts and shelters in the Scottish Highlands.

Mountaineering Council of Scotland ⓣ01738/493942, ⓦwww.mountaineering-scotland.org.uk. The representative body for all mountain activities, with detailed information on access and conservation issues.

Ramblers Association Scotland ⓦwww.ramblers.org.uk/scotland. Campaigning organization

Midges and ticks

Despite being only just over a millimetre long, and enjoying a life span on the wing of just a few weeks, the **midge** (genus: *culicoides*) – a tiny biting fly prevalent in the Highlands (mainly the west coast) and Islands – is considered to be second only to the weather as the major deterrent to tourism in Scotland. There are more than thirty varieties of midge, though only half of these bite humans. Ninety percent of all midge bites are down to the female *Culicoides impunctatus* or **Highland midge** (the male does not bite), which has two sets of jaws sporting twenty teeth each; she needs a good meal of blood in order to produce eggs.

These persistent creatures can be a nuisance, but some people also have a violent allergic reaction to midge bites. The easiest way to avoid midges is to visit in the winter, since they only appear between April and October. Midges also favour still, damp, overcast or shady conditions and are at their meanest around sunrise and sunset, when clouds of them can descend on an otherwise idyllic spot. Direct sunlight, heavy rain, noise and smoke discourage them to some degree, though wind is the most effective means of dispersing them. If they appear, cover up exposed skin and get your hands on some kind of repellent. Recommendations include Autan, Eureka, Jungle Formula (widely available from pharmacists) and the herbal remedy citronella. An alternative to repellents for protecting your face, especially if you're walking or camping, is a **midge net**, a little like a beekeeper's hat; though they appear ridiculous at first, you're unlikely to care as long as they work. The latest deployment in the battle against the midge is a gas-powered machine called a "midge magnet" which sucks up the wee beasties and is supposed to be able to clear up to an acre; each unit costs £400 and upwards, but there's been a healthy take-up by pubs with beer gardens and by campsite owners.

If you're walking through long grass or bracken, there's a possibility that you may receive attention from **ticks**, tiny parasites no bigger than a pin head, which bury themselves into your skin. Removing ticks by dabbing them with alcohol, butter or oil is now discouraged; the medically favoured way of extracting them is to pull them out carefully with small tweezers. There is a very slight risk of catching some nasty diseases, such as encephalitis, from ticks. If flu-like symptoms persist after a tick bite, you should see a doctor immediately.

with network of local groups and news on events and issues.

Scottish Mountaineering Club ⓦwww.smc.org.uk. The largest mountaineering club in the country. A well-respected organization which publishes a popular series of mountain guidebooks.

Tour operators

Adventure Scotland ⓣ08702/402676, ⓦwww.adventure-scotland.com. Highly experienced operator providing a wide range of courses and one-day adventures, from telemark skiing to climbing, kayaking and biking.

Bespoke Highland Tours ⓣ01854/612628, ⓦwww.scotland-inverness.co.uk/bht-main.htm. Offers five-to twelve-day self-led treks with a detailed itinerary along routes such as the Great Glen Way and West Highland Way, organizing baggage transfer and accommodation en route.

Cape Adventure International ⓣ01971/521006, ⓦwww.capeventure.co.uk. From a wonderfully remote northwest location near Kinlochbervie, Cape offers day, weekend and week-long individual and family adventure experiences including wilderness trips, climbing, sea-kayaking and walking.

C-N-Do Scotland ⓣ01786/445703, ⓦwww.cndoscotland.com. Prides itself on offering the "best walking holidays in Scotland". Munro-bagging for novices and experts with qualified leaders.

G2 Outdoor ⓣ07946/285612, ⓦwww.g2outdoor.co.uk. Personable, highly qualified adventure specialists offering gorge, hillwalking, rock climbing, canoeing and telemark skiing in the Cairngorms.

Glenmore Lodge ⓣ01479/861256, ⓦwww.glenmorelodge.org.uk. Based within the Cairngorm National Park, and internationally recognized as a leader in outdoor skills and leadership training.

Hebridean Pursuits ⓣ01631/563594, ⓦwww.hebrideanpursuits.com. Offers hillwalking and rock climbing in the Hebrides and West Highlands, as well as surf-kayaking and sailing trips.

Nae Limits ⓣ08450/178177, ⓦwww.naelimits.co.uk. This excellent Perthshire-based operator offers everything from wet 'n' wild rafting to bug canyoning and cliff jumping.

North-West Frontiers ⓣ01854/612628, ⓦwww.nwfrontiers.com. Based in Ullapool, offering guided mountain trips with small groups in the northwest Highlands, Hebrides and even the Shetland Islands. April–Oct.

Rua Reidh Lighthouse Holidays ⓣ01445/771263, ⓦwww.ruareidh.co.uk. From its spectacular northwest location, this company offers guided walks highlighting wildlife, rock climbing courses and week-long treks into the Torridon hills.

Vertical Descents ⓣ01855/821593, ⓦwww.verticaldescents.com. Ideally located for the Glencoe and Fort William area, activities and courses include canyoning, funyakking (a type of rafting) and climbing.

Walkabout Scotland ⓣ0131/661 7168, ⓦwww.walkaboutscotland.com. A great way to get a taste of hiking in Scotland, from exploring Ben Lomond to the Isle of Arran. Guided day and weekend walking from Edinburgh with all transport included.

Wilderness Scotland ⓣ0131/625 6635, ⓦwww.wildernessscotland.com. Guided, self-guided and customized adventure holidays and trips that focus on exploring the remote and unspoiled parts of Scotland by foot, bike, sea-kayak, yacht and even on skis.

Winter sports

Skiing and **snowboarding** take place at five different locations in Scotland – Glen Coe, the Nevis Range beside Fort William, Glen Shee, the Lecht and the Cairngorms near Aviemore. The resorts can go for months on end through the winter with insufficient snow, then see the approach roads suddenly made impassable by a glut of the stuff. When the conditions are good, Scotland's ski resorts have piste and off-piste areas that will challenge even the most accomplished alpine or cross-country skier.

Expect to pay up to £28 for a standard day-pass at one of the resorts, or around £110 for a five-day pass; rental of skis or snowboard comes in at around £25 per day, with reductions for multi-day rents. At weekends, in good weather with decent snow, expect the slopes to be packed with trippers from the central belt, although midweek usually sees queues dissolving. For a comprehensive rundown of all the resorts, including ticket prices and conditions, visit ⓦski.visitscotland.com.

Cross-country skiing (along with the related telemark or Nordic skiing) is becoming increasingly popular in the hills around Braemar near Glenshee and the Cairngorms. The best way to get started or to find out about good routes is to contact an outdoor pursuits company that offers telemark or Nordic rental and instruction; in the Aviemore area try Adventure Scotland or G2 Outdoor (see p.424). Also check out the Huntly Nordic and Outdoor Centre in Huntly, Aberdeenshire (ⓣ01466/794428, ⓦwww.nordicski.co.uk/hnoc). For equipment hire, sales or advice for Nordic and ski mountaineering equipment, contact Mountain Spirit (Ⓣ01479/811788, Ⓦwww.mountainspirit.co.uk) located at the southern entrance to Aviemore village.

Pony trekking and horse-riding

There are approximately sixty pony trekking or riding centres across the country, most approved by either the Trekking and Riding Society of Scotland (TRSS; Ⓦwww.ridinginscotland.com) or the British Horse Society (BHS; Ⓦwww.bhs.org.uk). As a rule, any centre will offer the option of **pony trekking**, **hacking** and **trail riding**. In addition, a network of special horse-and-rider B&Bs means you can ride independently on your own horse. The **Buccleuch Country Ride**, a three to four day, 57-mile long route using private tracks, open country and quiet bridleways was the first route of its kind to be opened in Scotland. For more information about this, and the B&B network for riders, contact the Scottish Borders Tourist Board, or visit Ⓦwww.buccleuch.com.

Cycling and mountain biking

Cycle touring is a great way to see some of the remoter parts of Scotland and navigate city streets (especially in Edinburgh). You'll find cycle shops in towns but few dedicated cycle lanes. In the countryside it can be tricky finding spare parts unless you are near one of Scotland's purpose-built mountain-bike trail centres.

Scotland is now regarded as one of the world's top destinations for **off-road mountain biking**. The Forestry Commission has established more than 1150 miles of excellent off-road routes. These are detailed in numerous "Cycling in the Forest" leaflets (available from Forest Enterprise offices, see p.50). Alternatively, get hold of the *Scottish Mountain Biking Guide* from tourist information centres. Some of the tougher routes are best attempted on full suspension mountain bikes although the easier (blue/green) trails can be ridden on a standard mountain or road bike. Pocket Mountain publish a series of compact cycling guides to the country (Ⓦwww.pocketmountains.com).

For up-to-date information on long-distance routes, including **The Great Glen Cycle Way**, along with a list of publications detailing specific routes, contact the cyclists campaigning group Sustrans (Ⓦwww.sustrans.co.uk), as well as the organizations listed on p.50.

Another option is to shell out on a cycling holiday package. Britain's biggest cycling organization, the **Cycle Touring Club**, or CTC (Ⓦwww.ctc.org.uk), provides lists of tour operators and rental outlets in Scotland, and supplies members with touring and technical advice, as well as insurance. Visit Scotland's "Cycling in Scotland" brochure is worth getting hold of, with practical advice and suggestions for itineraries around the

Staying safe in the hills

Due to rapid weather changes, the mountains are potentially extremely dangerous and should be treated with respect. Every year, in every season, climbers and walkers lose their lives in the Scottish hills.

- Wear sturdy, ankle-supporting footwear and wear or carry with you warm, brightly coloured and waterproof layered clothing, even for what appears to be an easy expedition in apparently settled weather.
- Always carry adequate maps, a compass (which you should know how to use), food, water and a whistle. If it's sunny, make sure you use sun protection.
- Check the weather forecast before you go. If the weather looks as if it's closing in, get down from the mountain fast.
- Always leave word with someone of your route and what time you expect to return, and remember to contact the person again to let them know that you are back.
- In an emergency, call mountain rescue on Ⓣ999.

country. The tourist board's "Cyclists Welcome" scheme gives guesthouses and B&Bs around the country a chance to advertise that they're cyclist-friendly, and able to provide an overnight laundry service, a late meal or a packed lunch.

Transporting your bike **by train** is a good way of getting to the interesting parts of Scotland without a lot of hard pedalling. Bikes are allowed free on mainline GNER and Virgin Intercity trains, as well as ScotRail trains, but you need to book the space as far in advance as possible. Bus and coach companies, including National Express and Scottish Citylink, rarely accept cycles unless they are dismantled and boxed; one notable exception is the excellent service operated by Dearman coaches (ⓣ01349/883585, ⓦwww.timdearmancoaches.co.uk) between Inverness and Durness via Ullapool (May–Sept Mon–Sat, 1 daily). Large towns and tourist centres offer **bike rental**. Expect to pay £10–20 per day; most outlets also give good discounts for multi-day rents.

Useful contacts for cyclists

Cyclists' Touring Club ⓣ01483/417217, ⓦwww.ctc.org.uk. Britain's largest cycling organization, and a good source of general advice; their handbook has lists of cyclist-friendly B&Bs and cafés in Scotland. Annual membership £34.

Forest Enterprise ⓣ0845/367 3787, ⓦwww.forestry.gov.uk/mtbscotland. The best source of information on Scotland's extensive network of forest trails – ideal for mountain-biking at all levels of ability.

Full On Adventure ⓣ07885/835838, ⓦwww.fullonadventure.co.uk. Among its many offerings, provides fully guided mountain-bike tours of Highland trails.

Highland Wildcat Trails ⓦwww.highlandwildcat.com. Scotland's most northerly dedicated mountain-bike centre complete with one of the country's longest downhill tracks.

The Hub in the Forest ⓣ01721/721736, ⓦwww.thehubintheforest.co.uk. One of Scotland's most established mountain-bike centres with a huge network of trails for all abilities in Glentress Forest near Peebles.

MBHI Bikes ⓣ07780/940342, ⓦwww.mbhi.co.uk. Whether for bike hire or a guided trip, this Cromarty-based operator is ideal if touring the east coast above Inverness.

Nevis Range ⓦwww.ridefortwilliam.co.uk. For information on all the trails around Fort William, including the home of Scotland's World Cup downhill and cross-country tracks (May–Oct) at Nevis Range.

North Sea Cycle Route ⓦwww.northsea-cycle.com. Signposted 3725-mile (6000-km) route round seven countries fringing the North Sea, including 772 miles (1242km) in Scotland along the east coast and in Orkney and Shetland.

Scottish Cycle Safaris ⓣ0131/556 5560, ⓦwww.cyclescotland.co.uk. Fully organized cycle tours at all levels, from camping to country-house hotels, with a good range of bikes available for rent, from tandems to children's bikes.

Scottish Cycling ⓣ0131/652 0187, ⓦwww.scottishcycling.com. Produces an annual handbook and calendar of cycling events (£8) – mainly road, mountain-bike and track races.

Spokes ⓣ0131/313 2114, ⓦwww.spokes.org.uk. Active Edinburgh cycle campaign group with plenty of good links and news on events and cycle-friendly developments.

Wild Adventures ⓣ01479/851374, ⓦwww.wild-adventures.co.uk. A Speyside operator offering skills courses and biking holidays.

WolfTrax Mountain Bike Centre ⓣ01528/544786, ⓦwww.forestry.gov.uk/wolftrax. This Central Highland bike centre near Newtonmore has over ten miles of routes for every standard of rider, bike hire and an excellent café.

Air sports

Scotland has its fair share of fine sunny days, when it's hard to beat scanning majestic mountain peaks, lochs and endless forests from the air. Whether you're a willing novice or an expert **paraglider** or **skydiver**, there are centres just outside Glasgow, Edinburgh and Perth which will cater to your needs. There are also opportunities to try ballooning and gliding.

British Gliding Association ⓣ0116/253 1051, ⓦwww.gliding.co.uk. Governing body for gliding enthusiasts and schools across the UK with information on where to find many clubs in Scotland.

Cloudbusters ⓣ07899/878509, ⓦwww.cloudbusters.co.uk. Highly reputable paragliding school which runs taster and fully accredited paragliding courses in the Lanarkshire hills outside Glasgow each weekend of the year. Around £120.

Flying Fever ⓣ01770/303899, ⓦwww.flyingfever.net. Based on the stunning Isle of Arran, forty miles southwest of Glasgow. From March–Oct, fully accredited paragliding courses and tandem flights can be enjoyed for around £100.

Skydive St Andrews ⓣ01334/880678, ⓦwww.skydivestandrews.co.uk. Year-round, highly professional, fully accredited parachute school that offers tandem, solo "static" line and "accelerated free-fall courses" over the Fife countryside. Tandem jump from £250.

Skydive Strathallan ⓣ01764/662572, ⓦwww.skydivestrathallan.co.uk. Located just outside Auchterarder, this non-commercial school operates year-round. Tandem jump from £250.

Golf

There are more than four hundred golf courses in Scotland, where the game is less elitist and more accessible than anywhere else in the world. **Golf** in its present form took shape in the fifteenth century on the dunes of Scotland's east coast, and today you'll find some of the oldest courses in the world on these coastal sites, known as "links". It's often possible to turn up and play, though it's sensible to phone ahead; booking is essential for the championship courses.

Public courses are owned by the local council, while **private courses** belong to a club. You can play on both – occasionally the private courses require that you are a **member** of another club, and the odd one asks for introductions from a member, but these rules are often waived for overseas visitors and all you need to do is pay a one-off fee. The cost of a round will set you back around £10 on a small nine-hole course, and more than £50 on many good-quality eighteen-hole courses.

St Andrews is the top destination for golfers: it's the home of the Royal and Ancient Golf Club, the body that regulates the rules of the game. Go to ⓦwww.scotlands-golf-courses.com for contacts, scorecards and maps of signature holes for most main courses. If you're coming to Scotland primarily to play golf, it's worth shelling out for one of the various multi-course passes or packages available that gives you access to a number of courses in any one region. There's more information at ⓦwww.scottishgolf.com and ⓦwww.visitscotland.com/golf.

Fishing

Scotland's serrated coastline – with the deep sea lochs of the west, the firths of the east and the myriad offshore islands – ranks among the cleanest coasts in Europe. Combine this with an abundance of salmon, sea trout, brown trout and pike, acres of open space and easy access, and you have a wonderful location for game-, coarse- or sea-fishing.

No licence is needed to fish in Scotland, although nearly all land is privately owned and its fishing therefore controlled by a landlord/lady or his/her agent. Permission, however, is usually easy to obtain: permits can be bought at local tackle shops, rural post offices or through fishing clubs in the area – if in doubt, ask at the nearest tourist office. Salmon and sea trout have strict **seasons**, which usually stretch from late August to late February. Individual tourist offices will know the precise dates, or see Visit Scotland's excellent "Fish Scotland" brochure (ⓦwww.fishpal.com/VisitScotland). For more information and contacts see ⓦwww.fishscotland.co.uk.

Watersports

Opportunities for **sailing** are outstanding. However, even in summer the full force of the North Atlantic can be felt, and changeable conditions combined with tricky tides and rocky shores demand good sailing and navigational skills. Yacht charters are available from various ports, either bareboat or in yachts run by a skipper and crew; contact Sail Scotland (ⓦwww.sailscotland.co.uk) or the Associated Scottish Yacht Charters (ⓦwww.asyc.co.uk).

An alternative way to enjoy Scotland under sail is to spend a week at a sailing school. Many schools, as well as small boat rental operations dotted along the coast, will rent sailing dinghies by the hour or day, as well as **windsurfers**, though you'll always need a wet suit. Scotland's top spots for windsurfing and **kitesurfing** are Troon on the Ayrshire coast, St Andrews and Tiree. The last named is internationally renowned for its beaches and waves and has an excellent surf, windsurfing and kitesurfing school, Wild Diamond Watersports (ⓦwww.surfschoolscotland.co.uk).

In recent years **sea-kayaking** has witnessed an explosion in popularity, with a host of operators offering sea-kayaking lessons and expeditions across the country. Canoe Scotland (ⓦwww.canoescotland.org) offer useful advice,

The best Scottish surf breaks

***Brimm's Ness** Five miles west of Thurso. A selection of reef breaks that pick up the smallest of swells.

Fraserburgh Thirty-nine miles north of Aberdeen. A number of beach and reef breaks – beginners should stick to the beach.

Machrihanish Bay Mull of Kintyre. Four miles of beach breaks on one of Scotland's loneliest peninsulas.

Pease Bay Near Dunbar, 26 miles east of Edinburgh. A popular break suited to all abilities; can get very crowded.

***Thurso East** Just below the castle. One of the best right-hand reef breaks in Europe.

***Torrisdale Bay** Bettyhill, 32 miles west of Thurso. An excellent right-hand river-mouth break.

***Valtos** On the Uig peninsula, Lewis. A break on one of the Outer Hebrides' most exquisite shell-sand beaches.

* Experienced surfers only

while Glenmore Lodge (ⓦwww.glenmorelodge.org.uk), Canoe Hebrides (ⓦwww.canoehebrides.com), Uist Outdoor Centre (ⓦwww.seakayakouterhebrides.co.uk) and Skyak Adventures (ⓦwww.skyakadventures.com) are highly reputable for either training or tours.

Surfing

In addition to sea-kayaking, Scotland is fast gaining a reputation as a **surfing** destination. However, the northern coastline lies on the same latitude as Alaska and Iceland, so the water temperature is very low: even in midsummer it rarely exceeds 15°C, and in winter can drop to as low as 7°C. The one vital accessory, therefore, is a good wet suit (ideally a 5/3mm steamer), wet-suit boots and, outside summer, gloves and a hood, too.

Many of the best spots are surrounded by stunning scenery, and you'd be unlucky to encounter another surfer for miles. However, this isolation – combined with the cold water and big, powerful waves – means that many of the best locations can only be enjoyed by experienced surfers. If you're a beginner, consider a lesson with a BSA-qualified coach such as Craig "Suds" Sutherland at Wild Diamond Watersports in Tiree (ⓣ07793/063849, ⓦwww.surfschoolscotland.co.uk).

Surf shops rent or sell equipment and provide good information about local breaks and events on the surfing scene. Two further sources of information are *Surf UK* by Wayne "Alf" Alderson (Fernhurst Books; £14.95), with details on more than four hundred breaks around Britain, and the British Surfing Association (ⓦwww.britsurf.co.uk).

Surf information, shops and schools

Adventure Sports 13 High St, Dunbar ⓣ01368/869734, ⓦwww.c2cadventure.com. Year-round surfing lessons and surf safaris across Scotland.

Boardwise 1146 Argyle St, Glasgow ⓣ0870/750 4423, ⓦwww.boardwise.com; 4 Lady Lawson St, Edinburgh ⓣ0870/750 4420. Surf gear, clothes and short-term rental.

Clan Surf 45 Hyndland St, Partick, Glasgow ⓣ0141/339 6523, ⓦwww.clanskates.co.uk. Combined surf, skate and snowboard shop. Lessons available.

ESP 5–7 Moss St, Elgin ⓣ01343/550129. Sales and rental only.

Granite Reef 45 The Green, Aberdeen ⓣ01224/252752, ⓦwww.granitereef.com. Sales, hire and lessons.

Tempest Surf Riverside Road, Thurso ⓣ01847/892500. At the harbourside, you'll find lessons, a shop and a café that may tempt you to remain snug indoors.

Wild Diamond Watersports Isle of Tiree, ⓣ07793/063849, ⓦwww.surfschoolscotland.co.uk. Professional instruction and hire for surfing, windsurfing, kitesurfing and kayaking.

Travel essentials

Costs

Scotland is a relatively **expensive** place to visit, with travel, food and accommodation costs higher than the EU average. The minimum expenditure for a couple travelling on public transport, self-catering and camping, is in the region of £30 each a day, rising to around £50 a day if you're staying at hostels and eating the odd meal out. Staying at budget B&Bs, eating at unpretentious restaurants and visiting the odd tourist attraction, means that you're looking at at least £75 each per day; if you're renting a car, staying in comfortable B&Bs or hotels and eating well, you should reckon on at least £100 a day per person.

Crime and personal safety

For the most part the Scottish **police** are approachable and helpful to visitors. If you're lost in a major town, asking a police officer is generally the quickest way to get help. As with any country, Scotland's major towns and cities have their danger spots, but these tend to be inner-city housing estates where no tourist has any reason to roam. The chief urban risk is pickpocketing, so carry only as much money as you need, and keep all bags and pockets fastened. Out in the Highlands and Islands, crime levels are very low. Should you have anything stolen or be involved in some incident that requires reporting, contact the local police station (listed in the Guide for the major cities); the ⓣ999 (or ⓣ112) number should only be used in emergencies – in other words if someone is in immediate danger or a crime is taking place.

Discounts

Most attractions in Scotland offer **concessions** for senior citizens, the unemployed, full-time students and children under 16, with under-5s being admitted free almost everywhere – proof of eligibility will be required in most cases. Family tickets are often available for those travelling with kids.

Once obtained, **youth/student ID cards** soon pay for themselves in savings. Full-time students are eligible for the International Student Identity Card or **ISIC** (ⓦwww.isiccard.com), which costs around £10 and entitles the bearer to special air, rail and bus fares, and discounts at museums, theatres and other attractions. If you're not a student, but you're 25 or younger, you can get an International Youth Travel Card or **IYTC**,

Historic Scotland and National Trust for Scotland

Many of Scotland's most treasured sights – from castles and country houses to islands, gardens and tracts of protected landscape – come under the control of the privately run **National Trust for Scotland** (ⓦwww.nts.org.uk) or the state-run **Historic Scotland** (ⓦwww.historic-scotland.gov.uk); we've quoted **"NTS"** or **"HS"** respectively for each site reviewed in this guide. Both organizations charge an admission fee for most places, and these can be quite high, especially for the more grandiose NTS estates. If you think you'll be visiting more than half a dozen NTS properties, or more than a dozen HS ones, it's worth taking annual membership, which costs around £40 (HS) or £46 (NTS), and allows free admission to their properties. In addition, both the NTS and HS offer short-term passes: the NTS has the **Discovery Ticket**, which costs between £20 for an adult ticket lasting three days to £60 for a family ticket lasting fourteen days; and the HS's **Explorer Pass**, ranging from £22 for three days (out of five) to £63 for seven days (out of fourteen) for a family.

which costs the same as the ISIC and carries the same benefits.

Electricity

The current is the **EU standard** of approximately 230v AC. All sockets are designed for British three-pin plugs, which are totally different from the rest of the EU. North American appliances need a transformer and **adapter**; Australasian appliances need only an adapter.

Emergencies

For **police**, **fire** and **ambulance** services phone ⓣ999.

Entry requirements

Citizens of all European countries – except Albania, Bosnia, Macedonia, Montenegro, Serbia and all the former Soviet republics (other than the Baltic states) – can enter Britain with just a **passport**, for up to three months (and indefinitely if you're from the EU). US, Canadian, Australian and New Zealand citizens can stay for up to six months, providing they have a return ticket and adequate funds to cover their stay. Citizens of most other countries require a **visa**, obtainable from the British consulate or mission office in the country of application.

Note that visa regulations are subject to frequent changes, so it's always wise to contact the nearest British embassy or high commission before you travel. If you visit ⓦwww.ukvisas.gov.uk, you can download the full range of **application forms** and information leaflets and find out the contact details of your nearest embassy or consulate. In addition, an independent charity, the Immigration Advisory Service or IAS (ⓦwww.iasuk.org), offers free and confidential advice to anyone applying for entry clearance into the UK.

If you want to **extend your visa**, you should contact the UK Border Agency (ⓦwww.ukba.homeoffice.gov.uk), a month before the expiry date given in your passport.

Gay and lesbian travellers

Both Glasgow and Edinburgh have reasonably prominent **gay and lesbian** communities, with a well-established network of bars, cafés, nightclubs, support groups and events. In **Edinburgh**, the area around Broughton Street is the heart of the city's "pink triangle", while in **Glasgow** the scene is mostly found in the Merchant City area; our entertainment listings for both cities include a number of gay bars and clubs. Elsewhere in Scotland, there are one or two gay bars in both Aberdeen and Dundee, and support and advice groups dotted around the country. Details for these, and many other aspects of the gay scene in Scotland, can be found on the website for the monthly *Scotsgay* newspaper (ⓦwww.scotsgay.co.uk).

Health

Pharmacists (known as chemists in Scotland) can dispense only a limited range of drugs without a doctor's prescription. Most pharmacies are open standard shop hours; local newspapers carry lists of late-opening pharmacies, or you can contact the local police for current details.

If your condition is serious enough, you can turn up at the Accident and Emergency (A&E) department of local **hospitals** for complaints that require immediate attention. Obviously, if it's an absolute emergency, ring for an ambulance (ⓣ999). These services are free to all. You can also get free medical advice from NHS Direct, the health service's 24-hour helpline (ⓣ0845/4647, ⓦwww.nhsdirect.nhs.uk).

Insurance

Even though EU health-care privileges apply in the UK, it's as well to take out **travel insurance** before travelling to cover against theft, loss and illness or injury. For non-EU citizens, it's worth checking whether you are already covered before you buy a new policy. If you need to take out insurance, you might want to consider the travel insurance deal we offer. For details, see the box opposite.

Internet

Internet cafés are most common in the big cities and towns, though you'll usually find somewhere you can get online even in the Highlands and Islands. The tourist office

Rough Guides travel insurance

Rough Guides has teamed up with WorldNomads.com to offer great **travel insurance** deals. Policies are available to residents of more than 150 countries, with cover for a wide range of **adventure sports**, 24hour emergency assistance, high levels of medical and evacuation cover and a **stream of travel safety information.** Roughguides.com users can take advantage of their policies online 24/7, from anywhere in the world – even if you're already travelling. And since plans often change when you're on the road, you can extend your policy and even claim online. Roughguides.com users who buy travel insurance with WorldNomads.com can also leave a positive footprint and donate to a community development project. For more information go to Ⓦ**www.roughguides.com/shop.**

should be able to help – sometimes they will have an access point – and public libraries often provide cheap or free access. If you have your own laptop or smart phone, it's relatively easy to find a café, bar, restaurant, B&B or hotel that offers **wi-fi,** either for a fee or for free. The site Ⓦwww.kropla.com gives useful details of how to plug in your laptop when abroad, phone country codes around the world and information about electrical systems in different countries.

Laundry

Coin-operated laundries can be found in Scottish cities and towns, but are becoming less and less common. A wash followed by a spin or tumble dry costs about £3; a "service wash" (having your laundry done for you in a few hours) costs about £2 extra. In the remoter regions of Scotland, you'll have to rely on hostel and campsite laundry facilities.

Mail

A **stamp** for a first-class **letter** to anywhere in the British Isles currently costs 41p and should arrive the next day; second-class letters cost 32p, taking three days. Note that there are now size restrictions: letters over 240 x 165 x 5mm are designated as "Large letters" and are correspondingly more expensive to send. Postcards and airmail letters of less than 10g cost 60p to the rest of Europe and should get there within three days; to the rest of the world they cost 67p and should get there within five days. Note, however, that in many parts of the Highlands and Islands there will only be one or two mail collections each day, often at lunchtime or even earlier. Stamps can be bought at post office counters or from newsagents and local shops, although they usually only sell books of four or ten stamps.

For general postal enquiries phone Ⓣ0845/774 0740 (Mon–Fri 8am–6pm, Sat 8am–1pm), or visit the website Ⓦwww.royalmail.com. Main **post offices** are open Monday to Friday 9am–5.30pm, Saturday 9am–noon. However, in small communities you'll find post office counters operating out of a shop, shed or even a private house and these will often keep extremely restricted hours.

Maps

The most comprehensive maps of Scotland are produced by the **Ordnance Survey** or OS (Ⓦwww.ordnancesurvey.co.uk), renowned for their accuracy and clarity. Scotland is covered by 85 maps in the 1:50,000 (pink) **Landranger** series which shows enough detail to be useful for most walkers and cyclists. There's more detail still in the full-colour 1:25,000 (orange) **Explorer** series, which covers Scotland in around 170 maps. The full Ordnance Survey range is only available at a few big-city stores or online, although in any walking district of Scotland you'll find the relevant maps in local shops or tourist offices. If you're planning a walk of more than a couple of hours in duration, or intend to walk in the Scottish hills at all, it is strongly recommended that you carry the relevant OS map and familiarize yourself with how to navigate using it.

Virtually every service station in Scotland stocks at least one large-format **road atlas**, covering all of Britain at around three miles to one inch, and generally including larger-scale plans of major towns. For an overview of the

Public holidays

Official **bank holidays** in Scotland operate on: January 1 and 2; Good Friday; the first and last Monday in May; last Monday in August; St Andrew's Day (Nov 30), Christmas Day (Dec 25); and Boxing Day (Dec 26). In addition, all Scottish towns have one-day holidays in spring, summer and autumn – dates vary from place to place but normally fall on a Monday. While many local shops and business close on these days, few tourist-related businesses observe the holidays, particularly in the summer months.

whole of Scotland on one map, Estate Publications' *Scotland* (1:500,000) is produced in cooperation with various local tourist boards and is designed to highlight places of interest. They also produce regional maps that mark all the major tourist sights as well as youth hostels and campsites, perfect if you're driving or cycling round one particular region. These are available from just about every tourist office in Scotland.

Money

The basic unit of **currency** in the UK is the pound sterling (£), divided into 100 pence (p). Coins come in denominations of 1p, 2p, 5p, 10p, 20p, 50p, £1 and £2. Bank of England £5, £10, £20 and £50 banknotes are legal tender in Scotland; in addition the Bank of Scotland (HBOS), the Royal Bank of Scotland (RBS) and the Clydesdale Bank issue their own banknotes in all the same denominations, plus a £100 note. All Scottish notes are legal tender throughout the UK, no matter what shopkeepers south of the border might say. In general, few people use £50 or £100 notes, and shopkeepers are likely to treat them with suspicion, since forgeries are widespread. At the time of going to press, £1 was worth around $1.60, €1.20, Can$1.60, Aus$1.60 and NZ$2.15. For the most up-to-date exchange rates, check the useful website ⓦwww.xe.com.

Credit/debit cards are by far the most convenient way to carry your money, and most hotels, shops and restaurants in Scotland accept the major brand cards. In every sizeable town in Scotland, and in some surprisingly small places too, you'll find a branch of at least one of the big Scottish high-street **banks**, usually with an **ATM** attached. However, on some islands, and in remoter parts, you may find there is only a **mobile bank** that runs to a timetable (usually available from the local post office). General **banking hours** are Monday to Friday from 9 or 9.30am to 4 or 5pm, though some branches are open until slightly later on Thursdays. Post offices charge **no commission**, have longer opening hours, and are therefore often a good place to change money and cheques. Lost or stolen credit/debit cards should be reported to the police and the following numbers: Mastercard ⓣ0800/964767; Visa ⓣ0800/891725.

Opening hours and public holidays

Traditional **shop hours** in Scotland are Monday to Saturday 9am to 5.30 or 6pm. In the bigger towns and cities, many places now stay open on Sundays and late at night on Thursdays or Fridays. Large supermarkets typically stay open till 8pm or 10pm and a few manage 24-hour opening (excluding Sunday). However, there are also plenty of towns and villages where you'll find precious little open on a Sunday, with many small towns also retaining an **"early closing day"** – often Wednesday – when shops close at 1pm. In the Highlands and Islands you'll find precious few attractions open outside the tourist season (Easter to Oct), though ruins, parks and gardens are normally accessible year-round. Note that last entrance can be an hour (or more) before the published closing time.

Phones

Public **payphones** are found in the Highlands and Islands, though with the ubiquity of mobile phones they're now less common and less assiduously maintained. Payphones take all coins from 10p upwards, some take only phonecards and credit cards, and others take all three – the minimum charge is usually 60p. Phonecards are available from post offices and newsagents,

Operator services

Domestic operator ⓣ100
International operator ⓣ155
Domestic directory assistance ⓣ118 500
International directory assistance ⓣ118 505

but discount call-cards with a PIN are generally cheaper for international calls.

If you're taking your **mobile/cellphone** with you to Scotland, check with your service provider whether your phone will work abroad and what the call charges will be. Unless you have a tri-band phone, it's unlikely that a mobile bought for use in the US will work outside the States and vice versa. Mobiles in Australia and New Zealand generally use the same system as the UK so should work fine. All the main UK networks cover the Highlands and Islands, though you'll still find many places in among the hills or out on the islands where there's no signal at all. If you're in a rural area and having trouble with reception, simply ask a local where the strongest signals are found nearby.

Throughout this guide, every phone number is prefixed by the **area code**, which is separated from the number by an oblique slash. You don't have to dial the code if you're calling from within the same area, unless you're using a mobile phone. Any number with the prefix ⓣ0800, ⓣ0808 and ⓣ0500 prefixes are free of charge from land lines (but not necessarily mobiles). Beware of premium-rate numbers, which are common for pre-recorded information services – and usually have the prefix ⓣ09.

Time

Greenwich Mean Time (GMT) – equivalent to Co-ordinated Universal Time (UTC) – is used from the end of October to the end of March; for the rest of the year the country switches to **British Summer Time** (BST), one hour ahead of GMT.

Tipping

There are no fixed rules for **tipping**. If you think you've received good service, particularly in restaurants or cafés, you may want to leave a tip of ten percent of the total bill (unless service has already been included). It's not normal, however, to leave tips in pubs, although bar staff are sometimes offered drinks, which they may accept in the form of money. The only other occasions when you'll be expected to tip are in hairdressers, taxis, and upmarket hotels where porters, bellboys and table waiters rely on being tipped to bump up their often dismal wages.

Tourist information

The official tourist board is known as **VisitScotland** (ⓦwww.visitscotland.com) and they run **tourist offices** (often called Visitor or Tourist Information Centres, or even "TICs") in virtually every Scottish town. Opening hours are often fiendishly complex and often change at short notice; consequently, we've simply put the days and months in which the offices are open in the relevant sections throughout the book. Beware that phone enquiries are often directed to a central call centre in Livingstone, where the staff have no knowledge of local information other than what appears on their computer screen. Consequently, we've only given telephone numbers for tourist offices where you've got a good chance of getting through to that specific office.

As well as being stacked full of souvenirs and other gifts, most TICs have a decent selection of leaflets, displays, maps and books relating to the local area. The staff are usually helpful and will do their best to help

Phoning home

To Australia ⓣ0061 + area code without the zero + number
To Ireland ⓣ00353 + area code without the zero + number
To New Zealand ⓣ0064 + area code without the zero + number
To South Africa ⓣ0027 + area code without the zero + number
To US and Canada ⓣ001 + area code + number

with enquiries about accommodation, local transport, attractions and restaurants, although it's worth being aware that they're sometimes reluctant to divulge information about local attractions or accommodation which are not paid-up members of the Tourist Board – and a number of perfectly decent guesthouses and the like choose not to pay the fees.

Travellers with disabilities

Scottish attitudes towards travellers with **disabilities** still lag behind advances towards independence made in North America and Australia. Access to many public buildings has improved, with legislation ensuring that all new buildings have appropriate facilities. It's worth keeping in mind, however, that installing ramps, lifts, wide doorways and disabled toilets is impossible or inappropriate in many of Scotland's older and historic buildings. Most **trains** in Scotland have wheelchair lifts and assistance is, in theory, available at all manned stations – for more, go to Ⓦwww.scotrail.co.uk and click on "Facilities". Wheelchair-users and blind or partially sighted people are automatically given thirty to forty percent reductions on train fares, and people with other disabilities are eligible for the Disabled Persons Railcard (£18 per year; Ⓦwww.disabledpersons-railcard.co.uk), which gives a third off most tickets. There are no bus discounts for the disabled. **Car rental** firm Avis will fit their cars with Lynx Hand Controls for free as long as you give them a few days' notice. As for accommodation, modified suites for people with disabilities do exist, but are often available only at higher-priced establishments and perhaps the odd B&B.

Websites

Throughout the Guide, we've included **websites** for specific accommodation, museums, galleries, transport, entertainment venues and other attractions. If you're looking for more general information about Scotland, or just a different take on things, then the list below is a useful starting point.

Ⓦ**adventure.visitscotland.com** Tourist-board site cataloguing various Scottish adventure-holiday options, everything from pony trekking to mountain biking.

Ⓦ**www.ceolas.org/ceolas.html** A very informative Celtic music site, both historical and contemporary, with lots of music to listen to.

Ⓦ**www.geo.ed.ac.uk/home/scotland/scotland.html** Edinburgh University's Geography Department gives you an introduction to Scottish history, geography and politics, with a myriad of links.

Ⓦ**www.met-office.gov.uk** The nation's favourite topic, the weather, discussed in detail with full regional (and shipping) forecasts.

Ⓦ**sco.wikipedia.org** Wikipedia in the Scots vernacular.

Ⓦ**www.scottish-islands-federation.co.uk** Lots of information and useful links for the Scottish islands from Arran to Shetland.

Ⓦ**shetlopedia.com** Shetland's very own version of Wikipedia.

Ⓦ**www.stonepages.com/scotland** Strangely compelling website for those hooked on cairns and stone circles.

Working in Scotland

All Swiss nationals and EEA citizens (except those from Bulgaria and Romania) can work in Scotland without a permit, although citizens of the Czech Republic, Estonia, Hungary, Latvia, Lithuania, Poland, Slovakia or Slovenia must register under the Worker Registration Scheme. Other nationals need a **work permit** in order to work legally in the UK, with eligibility worked out on a points-based system. There are exceptions to the above rules, although these are constantly changing, so for the latest regulations visit Ⓦwww.ukvisas.gov.uk

Guide

Guide

1

Edinburgh and the Lothians

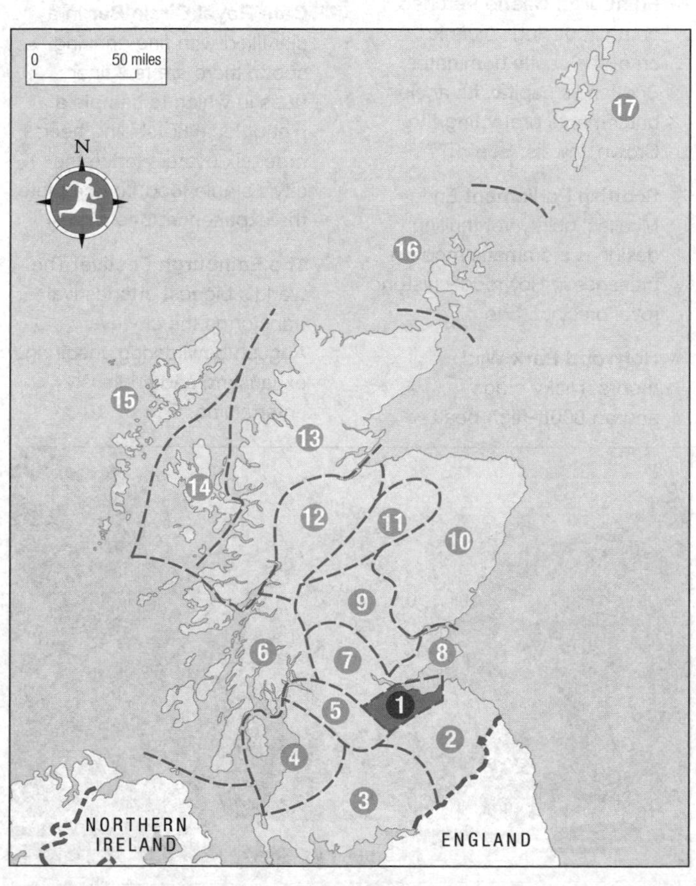

CHAPTER 1 Highlights

* **The Old Town** The evocative heart of the historic city, with its tenements, closes, courtyards, ghosts and catacombs cheek-by-jowl with many of Scotland's most important buildings. See p.76

* **Edinburgh Castle** Perched on an imposing volcanic crag, the castle dominates Scotland's capital, its ancient battlements protecting the Crown Jewels. See p.77

* **Scottish Parliament** Enric Miralles' quirky yet thrilling design is a dramatic modern presence in Holyrood's historic royal precinct. See p.89

* **Holyrood Park** Wild moors, rocky crags and an 800ft-high peak (Arthur's Seat), all slap in the middle of the city. See p.90

* **Museum of Scotland** The treasures of Scotland's past housed in a dynamic and superbly conceived building. See p.93

* **Café Royal Circle Bar** In a city filled with fine drinking spots, there are few finer pubs in which to sample a pint of local 80-shilling beer; order six oysters (once the city's staple food) to complete the experience. See p.114

* **The Edinburgh Festival** The world's biggest arts festival transforms the city every August: bewildering, inspiring, exhausting and endlessly entertaining. See p.118

▲ Edinburgh Castle

1

Edinburgh and the Lothians

Venerable, dramatic **EDINBURGH**, the showcase capital of Scotland, is a historic, cosmopolitan and cultured city. The setting is wonderfully striking: perched on a series of extinct volcanoes and rocky crags which rise from the generally flat landscape of the Lothians, with the sheltered shoreline of the Firth of Forth to the north. "My own Romantic town", Sir Walter Scott called it, although it was another native author, Robert Louis Stevenson, who perhaps best captured the feel of his "precipitous city", declaring that "No situation could be more commanding for the head of a kingdom; none better chosen for noble prospects."

The centre has two distinct parts, divided by **Princes Street Gardens**, which runs roughly east–west under the shadow of **Edinburgh Castle**, in the very heart of the city. To the north, the dignified, Grecian-style **New Town** was immaculately laid out in the eighteenth century during the Age of Reason, after the announcement of a plan to improve conditions in the city. The **Old Town**, on the other hand, with its tortuous alleys and tightly packed closes, is unrelentingly medieval, associated in popular imagination with the city's underworld lore of murderers Burke and Hare and of schizophrenic Deacon Brodie, inspiration for Stevenson's *Strange Case of Dr Jekyll and Mr Hyde*. Indeed, Edinburgh's ability to capture the literary imagination has seen it dubbed a "**World City of Literature**" by UNESCO, the same organization that previously conferred World Heritage Site status on a large section of the centre covering both Old and New towns.

Set on the hill that rolls down from the fairy-tale Castle to the royal **Palace of Holyroodhouse**, the Old Town preserves all the key landmarks from its role as a historic capital, augmented by the dramatic and unusual new **Scottish Parliament building**, opposite the palace. A few hundred yards away, a tantalizing glimpse of the wild beauty of Scotland's scenery can be had in **Holyrood Park**, an extensive area of open countryside dominated by **Arthur's Seat**, the largest and most impressive of the city's volcanoes.

In August, around a million visitors flock to the city for the **Edinburgh Festival**, in fact a series of separate festivals that make up the largest arts extravaganza in the world. Among Edinburgh's many museums, the exciting **National Museum of Scotland** houses 10,000 of Scotland's most precious artefacts, while the **National Gallery of Scotland** and its offshoot, the **Scottish National Gallery of Modern Art**, house two of Britain's finest collections of paintings.

EDINBURGH AND THE LOTHIANS

On a less elevated theme, the city's distinctive pubs, allied to its brewing and distilling traditions, make it a great **drinking** city. Its four **universities**, plus several colleges, mean that there is a youthful presence for most of the year – a welcome corrective to the stuffiness that is often regarded as Edinburgh's Achilles heel. Beyond the city centre, the most lively area is **Leith**, the city's medieval port, whose seedy edge is softened by a series of great bars and upmarket seafood restaurants, along with the presence of the former royal yacht **Britannia**, now open to visitors. The wider rural hinterland of Edinburgh, known as the **Lothians**, mixes rolling countryside and attractive country towns with some impressive historic ruins. In East Lothian, blustery cliff-top paths lead to the romantic battlements of **Tantallon Castle**, while nearby North Berwick, home of the **Scottish Seabird Centre**, looks out to the gannet-covered Bass Rock. The most famous sight in Midlothian is the mysterious fifteenth-century **Rosslyn Chapel**, while West Lothian boasts the towering, roofless **Linlithgow Palace**, thirty minutes from Edinburgh by train. To the northwest of the city, the dramatic steel geometry of the Forth Rail Bridge is best seen by walking across the parallel road bridge, starting at **South Queensferry**.

Some history

It was during the **Dark Ages** that the name Edinburgh – at least in its early forms of Dunedin or Din Eidyn ("fort of Eidyn") – first appeared. The strategic fort atop the Castle Rock volcano served as Scotland's **southernmost border post** until 1018, when King Malcolm I established the River Tweed as the permanent frontier. In the reign of Malcolm Canmore in the late eleventh century the Castle became one of the main seats of the court, and the town, which was given privileged status as a **royal burgh**, began to grow. In 1128 King David established Holyrood Abbey at the foot of the slope, later allowing its monks to found a separate burgh, known as **Canongate**.

Robert the Bruce granted Edinburgh a **new charter** in 1329, giving it jurisdiction over the nearby port of Leith, and during the following century the prosperity brought by foreign trade enabled the newly fortified city to establish itself as the permanent **capital of Scotland**. Under King James IV, the city enjoyed a short but brilliant **Renaissance era**, which saw not only the construction of a new palace alongside Holyrood Abbey, but also the granting of a **royal charter** to the College of Surgeons, the earliest in the city's long line of academic and professional bodies.

This period came to an abrupt end in 1513 with the calamitous defeat by the English at the Battle of Flodden, which led to several decades of political instability. In the 1540s King Henry VIII's attempt to force a royal union with Scotland led to the sack of Edinburgh, prompting the Scots to turn to France: French troops arrived to defend the city, while the young queen Mary was dispatched to Paris as the promised bride of the Dauphin, later (briefly) François II of France. While the French occupiers succeeded in removing the English threat, they themselves antagonized the locals, who had become increasingly sympathetic to the ideals of the **Reformation**. When the radical preacher **John Knox** returned from exile in 1555, he quickly won over the city to his Calvinist message.

James VI's rule saw the foundation of the University of Edinburgh in 1582, but following the **Union of the Crowns** in 1603 the city was totally upstaged by London: although James promised to visit every three years, it was not until 1617 that he made his only return trip. In 1633 Charles I visited Edinburgh for his coronation, but soon afterwards precipitated a crisis by introducing episcopacy to the Church of Scotland, in the process making Edinburgh a bishopric for the first time. Fifty years of religious turmoil followed, culminating in the triumph of

Presbyterianism. Despite these vicissitudes, Edinburgh grew throughout the seventeenth century – although, constrained by its city walls, it was forced to build both upwards and inwards.

The **Union of the Parliaments** of 1707 dealt a further blow to Edinburgh's political prestige, though by guaranteeing the preservation of the Church of Scotland and the legal and educational systems the act ensured that the city was never relegated to a purely provincial role. Indeed, the second half of the eighteenth century saw Edinburgh achieve the height of its intellectual influence, led by natives such as David Hume and Adam Smith. Around the same time, the city began to expand beyond its medieval boundaries, laying out the **New Town**, a masterpiece of the Neoclassical style.

Industrialization affected Edinburgh less than any other major city in the nation, and it never lost its white-collar character. Through the Victorian era Edinburgh cemented its role as a conservative bastion of the establishment, controlling Scotland's legal, ecclesiastical and education systems. Indeed, the city underwent an enormous **urban expansion** in the course of the nineteenth century, annexing, among many other small burghs, the large port of Leith.

In 1947 Edinburgh was chosen to host the great **International Festival** which served as a symbol of the new peaceful European order; despite some hiccups, it has flourished ever since, in the process helping to make tourism a mainstay of the local economy. During the 1980s Glasgow, previously the poor relation but always a tenacious rival, began to challenge the city's status as a cultural centre, and it took the re-establishment of a devolved Scottish **Parliament** in 1999 for Edinburgh to reassert its status in a meaningful way. With debates, decisions and demonstrations about crucial aspects of the government of Scotland taking place in Edinburgh, there was a marked upturn in the perceived importance of the city, augmented by notable achievements in scientific research and the arts. The city's financial sector burgeoned, with the Royal Bank of Scotland becoming the second largest banking group in the UK in the early years of the new century. Its near collapse and subsequent bail-out by the government during the 2009 economic crisis dented not just the city's self-confidence, but also the arguments made by **nationalist politicians** that Scotland has the stability and economic prowess to prosper as an independent country.

Arrival, information and transport

Edinburgh International Airport (Ⓣ0844/481 8989, Ⓦwww.edinburghairport.com) is at Turnhouse, six miles west of the city centre, close to the start of the M8 motorway to Glasgow. Airlink shuttle buses (#100; journey time 30min; £3.50; Ⓦwww.flybybus.com) connect to Waverley Rail Station in the centre of town; they run 24 hours a day, with services departing every ten or fifteen minutes between 4am and midnight, then half-hourly through the night. There are plans to reintroduce a tram service by 2012, which would link the airport to the city centre. Metered **taxis** charge around £15–20 for the same journey, while Onward Travel (Ⓣ0131/272 8222, Ⓦwww.onwardtravel.com) offers fixed-price fares in the same range, and you can pre-book larger vehicles if required. The least expensive door-to-door option is Edinburgh Shuttle (Ⓣ0845/500 5000, Ⓦwww.edinburghshuttle.com), which operates a frequent shared-taxi service using seven-seater minibuses and runs between the airport and any address in a large chunk of central Edinburgh for £8 for a single journey.

Conveniently situated at the eastern end of Princes Street, right in the heart of the city, **Waverley Station** (timetable and fare enquiries Ⓣ0845/748 4950,

Ⓦwww.nationalrail.co.uk) is the arrival point for all mainline trains. The **bus and coach** terminal for local and intercity services is located on the east side of St Andrew Square, two minutes' walk from Waverley Station.

There's a second mainline train stop, **Haymarket Station**, just under two miles west on the lines from Waverley to Glasgow, Fife and the Highlands, although this is only really of use if you're staying nearby.

Information and city tours

Edinburgh's main **tourist office** is found on top of Princes Mall near the northern entrance to the train station (April & Oct Mon–Sat 9am–6pm, Sun 10am–6pm; May, June & Sept Mon–Sat 9am–7pm, Sun 10am–7pm; July & Aug Mon–Sat 9am–8pm, Sun 10am–8pm; Nov–March Mon–Wed 9am–5pm, Thurs–Sat 9am–6pm, Sun 10am–5pm; Ⓣ0845/225 5121, Ⓦwww.edinburgh.org). Although inevitably hectic at the height of the season, it's reasonably efficient, with scores of free leaflets and a bank of computers available if you want to search for information online (£1/20min). The much smaller **airport branch** is in the main concourse, directly opposite Gate 5 (daily: April–Oct 6.30am–10.30pm; Nov–March 7am–9pm).

Despite the compactness of the city centre, open-top **bus tours** are big business, with several companies taking slightly varying routes around the main sights. All cost much the same, depart from Waverley Bridge and allow you to get on and off at leisure. The most engaging are MacTours (£12; Ⓣ0131/220 0770, Ⓦwww.edinburghtour.com), using a fleet of vintage buses. Several companies offer **walking tours**, many of which depart from the central section of the Royal Mile near the High Kirk of St Giles, including Auld Reekie Tours (Ⓣ0131/557 4700, Ⓦwww.auldreekietours.com) and Mercat Tours (Ⓣ0131/225 5445, Ⓦwww.mercat-tours.com). These two companies also offer night-time ghost tours around the Old Town, as do the entertaining Cadies and Witchery Tours (Ⓣ0131/225 6745, Ⓦwww.witcherytours.com) and the spine-tingling City of the Dead graveyard tour (Ⓣ0131/225 9044, Ⓦwww.blackhart.uk.com). Other specialist outings include the **Edinburgh Literary Pub Tour** (Ⓣ0131/226 6665, Ⓦwww.edinburghliterarypubtour.co.uk), which mixes a pub crawl with extracts from local authors acted out along the way; **Geowalks** (Ⓣ0131/555 5488, Ⓦwww.geowalks.demon.co.uk), which offers guided walks up Arthur's Seat in the company of a qualified geologist; **Rebustours** (Ⓣ0131/553 7473, Ⓦwww.rebustours.com), which traces the footsteps of Inspector Rebus, hero of Ian Rankin's bestselling detective novels (see p.637); and a **Trainspotting** tour (Ⓣ0131/555 2500, Ⓦwww.leithwalks.co.uk) which takes you round some of the scenes famous from Irvine Welsh's novels. One of the coolest ways to see the city has to be a chauffeur-driven tour on a 1600cc trike by **Trike Tours Scotland** (Ⓣ0800/056 7779, Ⓦwww.triketoursscotland.com). **Adrian's Edinburgh City Cycle Tour** (Ⓣ07966/477206, Ⓦwww.edinburghcycletour.com) uses peddle-power for an enjoyable and good value three-hour Edinburgh tour, with all equipment provided. **Advance booking** is recommended for all the above, and for the specialist tours in particular.

City transport

Although Edinburgh occupies a large area relative to its population – fewer than half a million people – most places worth visiting lie within the compact city centre, which is easily explored on foot. The reintroduction of **trams** by 2012 looks set to redefine Edinburgh's travel map, but for the meantime it's most useful

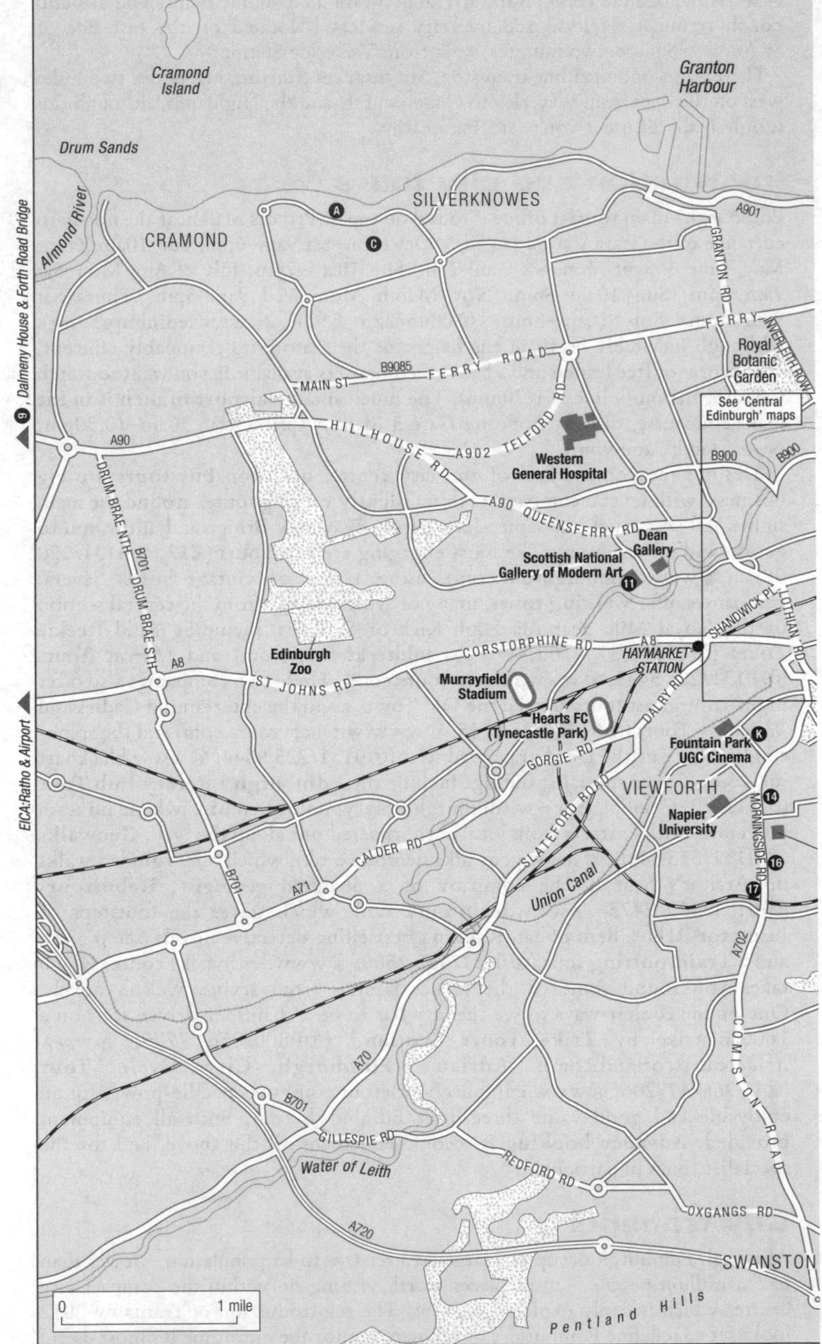
Cramond Island
Granton Harbour
Drum Sands
Almond River
SILVERKNOWES
CRAMOND
A
C
A901
GRANTON RD
FERRY
INVERLEITH ROW
Royal Botanic Garden
B9085
FERRY ROAD
MAIN ST
TELFORD RD
See 'Central Edinburgh' maps
9, Dalmeny House & Forth Road Bridge
A90
HILLHOUSE RD
A902
Western General Hospital
B900
B900
DRUM BRAE NTH
B701
DRUM BRAE STH
A90 QUEENSFERRY RD
Dean Gallery
Scottish National Gallery of Modern Art
11
SHANDWICK PL
LOTHIAN RD
Edinburgh Zoo
CORSTORPHINE RD
A8
HAYMARKET STATION
A8
ST JOHNS RD
Murrayfield Stadium
DALRY RD
EICA:Ratho & Airport
Hearts FC (Tynecastle Park)
K
Fountain Park UGC Cinema
GORGIE RD
VIEWFORTH
14
Napier University
MORNINGSIDE RD
SLATEFORD ROAD
CALDER RD
16
B701
Union Canal
A71
17
A702
A70
COMISTON ROAD
B701
GILLESPIE RD
Water of Leith
REDFORD RD
OXGANGS RD
A720
SWANSTON
0
1 mile
Pentland Hills

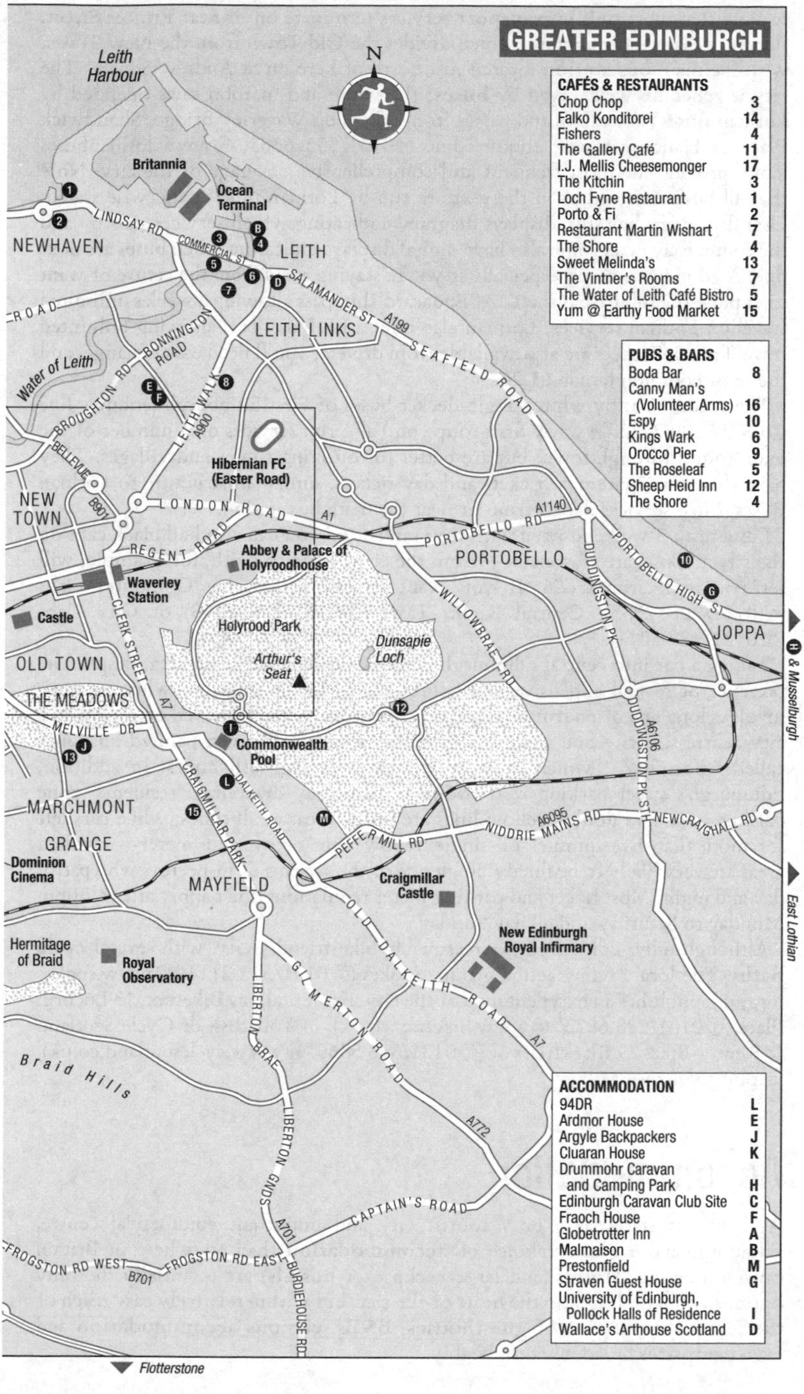

GREATER EDINBURGH

CAFÉS & RESTAURANTS

Chop Chop	3
Falko Konditorei	14
Fishers	4
The Gallery Café	11
I.J. Mellis Cheesemonger	17
The Kitchin	3
Loch Fyne Restaurant	1
Porto & Fi	2
Restaurant Martin Wishart	7
The Shore	4
Sweet Melinda's	13
The Vintner's Rooms	7
The Water of Leith Café Bistro	5
Yum @ Earthy Food Market	15

PUBS & BARS

Boda Bar	8
Canny Man's (Volunteer Arms)	16
Espy	10
Kings Wark	6
Orocco Pier	9
The Roseleaf	5
Sheep Heid Inn	12
The Shore	4

ACCOMMODATION

94DR	L
Ardmor House	E
Argyle Backpackers	J
Cluaran House	K
Drummohr Caravan and Camping Park	H
Edinburgh Caravan Club Site	C
Fraoch House	F
Globetrotter Inn	A
Malmaison	B
Prestonfield	M
Straven Guest House	G
University of Edinburgh, Pollock Halls of Residence	I
Wallace's Arthouse Scotland	D

to note that most **public transport** services terminate on or near Princes Street, the city's main thoroughfare, which divides the Old Town from the New Town, with the main **bus station** located just north of here on St Andrew Square. The city is generally well served by **buses**; the white and maroon ones operated by Lothian Buses (timetables and passes from offices on Waverley Bridge, Shandwick Place or Hanover Street; enquiry line Ⓣ0131/555 6363, Ⓦwww.lothianbuses.com) provide the most frequent and comprehensive coverage of the city. Note that all buses referred to in the text are run by Lothian unless otherwise stated. Usefully, every bus stop displays diagrams indicating which services pass by and the routes they take; some also have digital displays indicating when buses are next due. A good investment, especially if you're staying away from the centre or want to explore the suburbs, is the £13 "Ridacard" bus pass allowing a week's unlimited travel on Lothian services; Lothian also offer a LRT day pass allowing unlimited travel for £3. Tickets are also available from drivers; you'll need exact change, and the most common fare is £1.20.

The predominantly white, single-decker buses of First Edinburgh (enquiry line Ⓣ0871/ 200 2233, Ⓦwww.firstgroup.com) also run services on a number of the main routes through town, but are better for outlying towns and villages. They have their own system of tickets and day-tickets, similar in structure to Lothian Buses. Most services depart from or near the main bus station.

Edinburgh is well endowed with **taxi** ranks, and you can also hail black cabs on the street. Costs are reasonable – from the city centre to Leith, for example, will set you back around £6. If you want to call a taxi, try Computer Cabs (Ⓣ0131/228 2555), Central Radio Taxis (Ⓣ0131/229 2468) or City Cabs (Ⓣ0131/228 1211).

Taking a **car** into central Edinburgh is emphatically not a good idea: despite the presence of several expensive multistorey car parks, finding somewhere to park involves long and often fruitless searches. Private cars aren't allowed on certain key city-centre streets – and there is a growing network of green-painted bus lanes called "greenways", which must be left clear during rush hours. In addition, Edinburgh's street parking restrictions are famously draconian: residents' zone parking areas and double yellow lines are no-go areas at all times, while cars left for more than five minutes on single yellow lines or overdue meter-controlled areas are very likely to be fined £30 by one of the swarms of inspectors who patrol day and night. Most ticket and parking meter regulations don't apply after 6.30pm Monday to Saturday and all day Sunday.

Although hilly, Edinburgh is a reasonably bike-friendly city, with several **cycle paths**. The local cycling action group, Spokes (Ⓣ0131/313 2114, Ⓦwww.spokes.org.uk), publishes an excellent map of the city. For rental, try Biketrax, 13 Lochrin Place (Ⓣ0131/228 6633, Ⓦwww.biketrax.co.uk), in Tollcross, or Cycle Scotland & Rent-a-Bike, 29 Blackfriars St (Ⓣ0131/556 5560, Ⓦwww.cyclescotland.co.uk), just off the Royal Mile.

Accommodation

As befits its status as a busy tourist city and important commercial centre, Edinburgh has a greater choice of **accommodation** than anywhere in Britain outside London. **Hotels** (and large backpacker **hostels**) are essentially the only options you'll find right in the heart of the city, but within relatively easy reach of the centre the selection of **guesthouses**, **B&Bs**, **campus accommodation** and even **campsites** broadens considerably.

Prices here are significantly higher than elsewhere in Scotland, with double rooms starting at £60 per night. Budget hotel chains offer the best value if you want basic accommodation right in the centre, with rooms available for £60–80; £80–100 per night will get you something more stylish. Bear in mind that many of the guesthouses and small hotels are located in Georgian and Victorian townhouses, over three or more floors, and usually have no lift, so are not ideal for those with restricted mobility. Making **reservations** is worthwhile at any time of year, and is strongly recommended for stays during the Festival and around Hogmanay, when places can get booked out months in advance. VisitScotland operates a booking centre for accommodation all over the country, including Edinburgh; call ⓣ0845/225 5121 or go to ⓦwww.visitscotland.com. There's a £3 fee, waived if you book online. Accommodation options are shown on the maps on pp.68–69 & pp.72–73.

Hotels

There aren't many **independent hotels** left in the centre of Edinburgh: almost all, whether grand and traditional, budget or stylishly contemporary, are either part of a recognizable chain or an international marketing group. Anywhere with historic grandeur or the latest in high design is at the upper end of the market, but you will find a few places that balance style and reasonable prices. In addition, the abundance of establishments in the city centre means that you can often find good deals in **quieter periods** or through online booking sites, and it's always worth looking out for the special offers advertised by all the chains. Below we've selected a range of the more interesting, characterful and well placed across all categories. Note that smaller hotels have generally been included in the guesthouse section below.

Old Town

Apex International 31–35 Grassmarket ⓣ0131/300 3456, ⓦwww.apexhotels.co.uk. This ex-university building turned 175-bed business-oriented hotel has comfortable rooms, some with views to the Castle. Faces the happening Grassmarket. The linked *Apex City Hotel* is on the same road (at no. 61), and *Apex Waterloo Place* is also central on the side of Calton Hill. 6

Ibis Edinburgh Centre 6 Hunter Square ⓣ0131/240 7000, ⓦwww.accorhotels.com. Probably the best-located chain hotel cheapie in the Old Town, within sight of the Royal Mile; rooms are modern and inexpensive, but there are few facilities other than a rather plain bar. 2

Hotel Missoni 1 George IV Bridge ⓣ0131/220 6666, ⓦwww.hotelmissoni.com. Quite what this funky, sexy new tie-up between the Italian fashion house and Rezidor Hotels is doing in the heart of prim Edinburgh is unclear, but the zigzag fabrics, wacky lighting and mosaic-like tiling are enticing, if a little headache-inducing. 8

The Scotsman 20 North Bridge ⓣ0131/556 5565, ⓦwww.thescotsmanhotel.co.uk. The plush but unstuffy new occupant of the grand old offices of the *Scotsman* newspaper is one of Edinburgh's headline hotels. It's five-star stuff, with modern gadgets and fittings, but the marble staircase and walnut panelled lobby have been retained, and you can sleep in the editor's old office; rooms from £300. 9

Ten Hill Place 10 Hill Place ⓣ0131/662 2080, ⓦwww.tenhillplace.com. A contemporary hotel linked to the historic Royal College of Surgeons, with 78 sleek and smartly styled bedrooms, all run according to an environmentally conscious policy. Not part of a chain, but efficiently operated. 6

Travelodge Edinburgh Central 33 St Mary's St ⓣ0871/984 6137, ⓦwww.travelodge.co.uk. There's more than a hint of concrete brutalism about the look of this chain hotel, but it's well priced and centrally located, 100yd from the Royal Mile near some decent restaurants. 4

New Town

Express by Holiday Inn Edinburgh City Centre Picardy Place, Broughton ⓣ0131/558 2300, ⓣwww.hieedinburgh.co.uk. It's by a busy roundabout but otherwise a good location in an elegant old Georgian tenement near the top of Broughton St, with 161 rooms featuring neat but predictable chain-hotel decor and facilities. 6

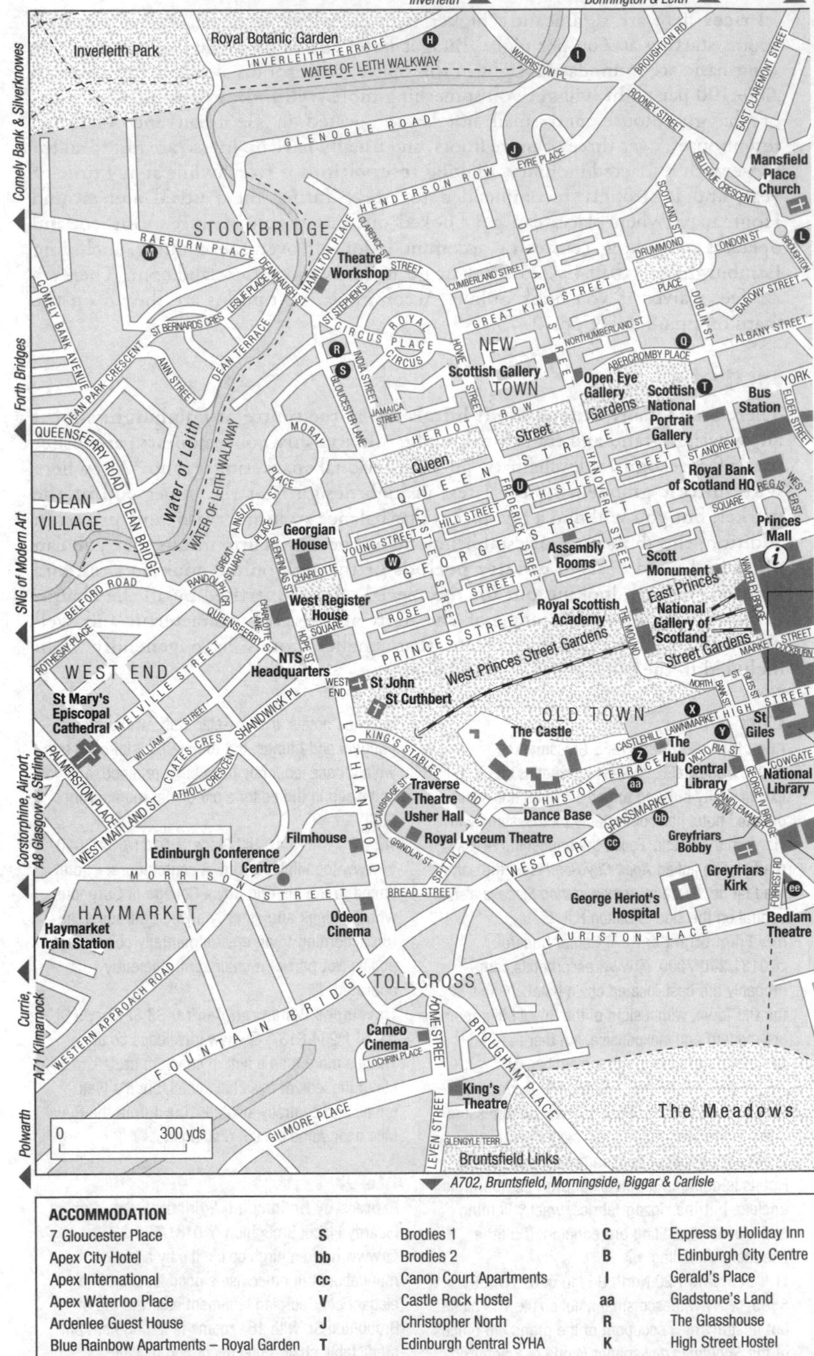

ACCOMMODATION

7 Gloucester Place	S	Brodies 1	C	Express by Holiday Inn Edinburgh City Centre
Apex City Hotel	bb	Brodies 2	B	
Apex International	cc	Canon Court Apartments	I	Gerald's Place
Apex Waterloo Place	V	Castle Rock Hostel	aa	Gladstone's Land
Ardenlee Guest House	J	Christopher North	R	The Glasshouse
Blue Rainbow Apartments – Royal Garden	T	Edinburgh Central SYHA	K	High Street Hostel

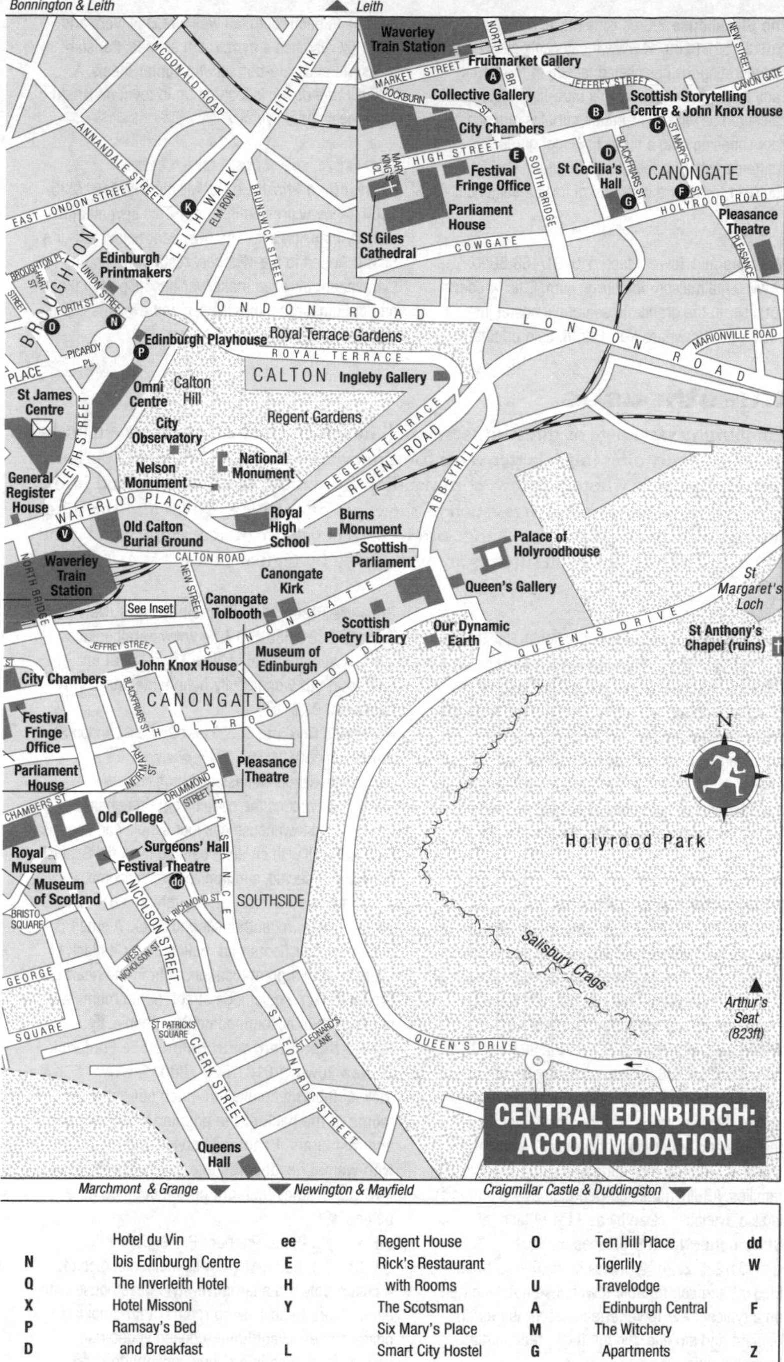

	Hotel du Vin	ee	Regent House	O	Ten Hill Place	dd
N	Ibis Edinburgh Centre	E	Rick's Restaurant		Tigerlily	W
Q	The Inverleith Hotel	H	with Rooms	U	Travelodge	
X	Hotel Missoni	Y	The Scotsman	A	Edinburgh Central	F
P	Ramsay's Bed		Six Mary's Place	M	The Witchery	
D	and Breakfast	L	Smart City Hostel	G	Apartments	Z

The Glasshouse 2 Greenside Place, Broughton ⓣ0131/525 8200, ⓦwww.theetoncollection.com. Incorporating the castellated facade of the former Lady Glenorchy's Church, this ultra-hip hotel has 65 chichi rooms with push-button curtains and sliding doors opening onto a huge, lush roof garden scattered with Philippe Starck furniture. Perfect if you're in town for a weekend of flash indulgence. ❾

Leith

Malmaison 1 Tower Place ⓣ0131/468 5000, ⓦwww.malmaison-edinburgh.com. Chic, modern hotel set in the grand old seamen's hostel just back from the wharf-side. Bright, bold original designs in each room, as well as CD players and cable TV. Also has a gym, room service, Parisian brasserie and café-bar serving lighter meals. A linked *Hotel du Vin* is located up in town on Bristo place near the university. ❻

South of the centre

Prestonfield Priestfield Rd, Mayfield ⓣ0131/225 7800, ⓦwww.prestonfield.com. This seventeenth-century mansion set in its own park below Arthur's Seat is linked to the *Witchery* restaurant, and its extravagant baroque makeover has helped make it one of Edinburgh's most lavish and over-the-top places to stay. ❾

Guesthouses

Edinburgh's vast range of **guesthouses, small hotels** and **bed & breakfast** establishments generally offer much better value for money and a far more homely experience than the larger city hotels. A few, commanding a premium rate, can be found in the very centre of the city, but areas such as the edges of the New Town and the inner suburbs of Bruntsfield and the Grange offer a perfect balance of accessibility and good value. Elsewhere, almost all suburbs are well served by regular buses.

Old Town

The Witchery Apartments Castlehill, Royal Mile ⓣ0131/225 5613, ⓦwww.thewitchery.com. Seven riotously indulgent suites grouped around this famously spooky restaurant just downhill from the Castle; expect antique furniture, big leather armchairs, tapestry-draped beds, oak panelling and huge roll-top baths, as well as ultra-modern sound systems and complementary bottles of champagne. Top of the range, unique and memorable. ❾

New Town

7 Gloucester Place 7 Gloucester Place ⓣ0131/225 2974, ⓦwww.stayinginscotland.com. Elegant, well-cared-for B&B, with three bedrooms on the upper floor of a Georgian terrace house. The best of the double rooms has graceful garden views and a classic 1930s bathroom. ❻

Ardenlee Guest House 9 Eyre Place, New Town ⓣ0131/556 2838, ⓦwww.ardenleeguesthouse.com. Welcoming non-smoking guesthouse at the foot of the New Town, with original Victorian features and nine reasonably spacious rooms, seven of which are en suite and some suitable for families. A fully furnished Georgian apartment (❻) is also available, close by at 3 Eyre Place. ❸

Christopher North 6 Gloucester Place ⓣ0131/225 2720, ⓦwww.christophernorth.co.uk. Elegant and comfortable townhouse hotel located on a typical New Town terrace. Decor is modern, opulent and striking, though it can feel a little overwhelming. ❽

Gerald's Place 21b Abercromby Place, New Town ⓣ0131/558 7017, ⓦwww.geraldsplace.com. A homely taste of New Town life at an upmarket but wonderfully hospitable and comfy basement B&B. ❼

Ramsay's Bed and Breakfast 25 East London St, Broughton ⓣ0131/557 5917, ⓦwww.ramsaysbedandbreakfastedinburgh.com. Well located just around the corner from Broughton St, this terraced townhouse has four simple and neat bedrooms, all with en-suite bathrooms. A full Scottish breakfast is served, and families are welcome. ❺

Regent House 3 Forth St, Broughton ⓣ0131/556 1616, ⓦwww.regenthousehotel.co.uk. A small hotel over four floors that makes up for its lack of glamour with a great location, right in the heart of Broughton on a quiet side street. Some rooms are big enough to accommodate 3–5 people. ❹

Rick's Restaurant with Rooms 55a Frederick St, New Town ⓣ0131/622 7800, ⓦwww.ricksedinburgh.co.uk. Ten much sought-after rooms at the back of the popular New Town bar and restaurant. Beautifully styled with beds fitted with walnut headboards and plush fabrics, plus DVD player, they look out onto a cobbled lane behind. ❼

Six Mary's Place Raeburn Place, Stockbridge ⓣ0131/332 8965, ⓦwww.sixmarysplace.co.uk. A collectively run alternative-style guesthouse with eight smart, fresh-looking rooms, a no-smoking policy and excellent home-cooked vegetarian breakfasts served in a sunny conservatory. ❻

Tigerlily 125 George St ⓣ0131/225 5005, ⓦwww.tigerlilyedinburgh.co.uk. A glitzy boutique hotel, bar and restaurant that epitomizes the new "gorgeous" George St. A classic Georgian townhouse transformed into a flamboyant design extravaganza; indulgent pink or black bedroom suites are kitted out with hi-tech gadgets and decadent fabrics. ❾

South of the centre

94DR 94 Dalkeith Rd, Newington ⓣ0131/662 9265, ⓦwww.94dr.com. A boutique guesthouse offering three different styles with its couture, bespoke and tailored rooms. Front-facing rooms have a view of Arthur's Seat. ❺

Cluaran House 47 Leamington Terrace, Viewforth ⓣ0131/221 0047, ⓦwww.cluaran-house-edinburgh.co.uk. Tasteful and welcoming B&B with lots of original features and paintings. Serves good wholefood breakfasts. Close to the Meadows with bus links (including #11 & #23) from nearby Bruntsfield Place. ❺

North Edinburgh

Ardmor House 74 Pilrig St, Pilrig ⓣ0131/554 4944, ⓦwww.ardmorhouse.com. Victorian townhouse with some lovely original features combined with smart contemporary decor. Gay-owned, straight-friendly and located halfway between the centre and Leith. ❺

Fraoch House 66 Pilrig St, Pilrig ⓣ0131/554 1353, ⓦwww.fraochhouse.com. A relaxing nine-bedroom guesthouse with a slick, modern look created by its young owners. It's a 10–15min walk from both Broughton St and the heart of Leith. ❺

The Inverleith Hotel 5 Inverleith Terrace, Inverleith ⓣ0131/556 2745, ⓦwww.inverleithhotel.co.uk. Pleasant option near the Botanic Gardens, with ten rooms of various sizes in a Victorian terraced house; all are en suite and tastefully decorated with wooden floors, antiques and tapestries. The owners also run the self-contained Brandon Apartment at 5 Brandon St. ❺

Wallace's Arthouse Scotland 41/4 Constitution St ⓣ07941/343714, ⓦwww.wallacesarthousescotland.com. Fantastic boutique B&B in Leith owned and run by a fashion designer. With its kitsch surroundings and friendly service it's one of the city's finest recent additions. ❺

East of the centre

Straven Guest House 3 Brunstane Rd North, Joppa ⓣ0131/669 5580, ⓦwww.stravenguesthouse.com. Neat, friendly place near the beach with a no-smoking policy and environmentally friendly approach; vegetarian and vegan breakfast available. No children under 12. ❹

Self-catering apartments and campus accommodation

Custom-built **self-catering serviced apartments** are popular with business travellers but, with no minimum let, are a viable alternative to guesthouses. They're also well worth considering for longer stays such as during the Festival. For a brochure of self-catering options contact the Tourist Board: we've listed some of the best below. **Campus accommodation** is available in the city during the summer months, though it's neither as useful or cheap as might be expected.

Blue Rainbow Apartments – Royal Garden York Buildings, Queen St ⓣ0845/045 2222, ⓦwww.bluerainbowapartments.com. Superbly equipped, comfortable modern one- and two-bedroom serviced apartments very centrally located opposite the Scottish National Portrait Gallery. Studio apartment from £129.

Canon Court Apartments 20 Canonmills ⓣ0131/554 2721, ⓦwww.canoncourt.co.uk. A block of smart, comfortable self-catering one- and two-bedroom apartments not far from Canonmills Bridge over the Water of Leith, at the northern edge of the New Town. One-bedroom apartments from £112.

Gladstone's Land 477b Lawnmarket, c/o National Trust for Scotland, 5 Charlotte Square ⓣ0131/243 9331, ⓦwww.nts.org.uk. Two classic Old Town apartments on the fourth floor of the historic Gladstone's Land. Set up for self-catering, both sleep two (twin beds), and there's a minimum stay of three nights (short breaks from £250).

University of Edinburgh, Pollock Halls of Residence 18 Holyrood Park Rd, Newington ⓣ0131/651 2007, ⓦwww.edinburghfirst.com. Unquestionably the best setting of any of the city's university accommodation, right beside Holyrood Park, and with a range of accommodation from single rooms (£32) and en-suite double (£79) to self-catering flats (from £425 per week). Mostly available Easter & June to mid-Sept, though some rooms available year-round.

Hostels

Edinburgh is one of the UK's most popular **backpacker** destinations, and there are a large number of hostels in and around the city centre, ranging in size, atmosphere and quality. Competition is fierce, so be prepared for a bit of enthusiastic marketing when you make an enquiry.

Argyle Backpackers 14 Argyle Place, Marchmont ⓣ0131/667 9991, ⓦwww.argyle-backpackers.com. Quiet, less intense version of the typical backpackers' hostel, pleasantly located in three adjoining townhouses near the Meadows in studenty Marchmont. It's walking distance to town, but you can get bus #41 from the door. The small dorms have single beds, and there are a dozen or so double/twin rooms (❶), as well as a pleasant communal conservatory and garden at the back.

Brodies 1 12 High St, Old Town ⓣ0131/556 6770, ⓦwww.brodieshostels.co.uk. Tucked down a typical Old Town close, with four fairly straightforward dorms sleeping up to a dozen, and limited communal areas. It's smaller than many hostels, and a little bit more homely as a result.

Brodies 2 93 High St, Old Town ⓣ0131/556 2223, ⓦwww.brodieshostels.co.uk. The mellow atmosphere at this smart hostel is even more marked than in the sister property across the road. Smaller dorms (mostly six- or eight-bed) as well as doubles (❷).

Castle Rock Hostel 15 Johnston Terrace, Old Town ⓣ0131/225 9666, ⓦwww.castlerockedinburgh.com. Tucked below the Castle ramparts, with 200 or so beds arranged in large, bright dorms, as well as triple and quad rooms and some doubles (❷). The communal areas include a games room with pool and table tennis.

Edinburgh Central SYHA 9 Haddington Place, Leith ⓣ0845/293 7373, ⓦwww.edinburghcentral.org. In a handy location at the top of Leith Walk, this five-star hostel has single, double and eight-bed rooms with en-suite facilities. There is a reasonably priced bistro or self-catering kitchen facilities. Dorms (from £16), twins (❸) and family rooms (❹) all available.

Globetrotter Inn 46 Marine Drive, Cramond ⓣ0131/336 1030, ⓦwww.globetrotterinns.com. A big departure from the buzzy city-centre hostels, in a sylvan parkland setting four miles from the centre with lovely views of the Firth of Forth. The 350-plus beds are mostly bunks with privacy curtains and individual reading lights, but there are also doubles (❷). There's access to a gym, pool table, live music and cheap bar food.

High Street Hostel 8 Blackfriars St, Old Town ⓣ0131/557 3984, ⓦwww.highstreethostel.com. Lively and popular hostel in an attractive sixteenth-century building just off the Royal Mile. Dorms only, but good communal facilities.

Smart City Hostel 50 Blackfriars St, Old Town ⓣ0131/524 1989, ⓦwww.smartcityhostels.com. A five-star hostel just off the Royal Mile, with 622 beds in twin rooms or dorms. Women-only rooms are available. A reasonable café serves good-value food and breakfasts, and there is a late-night bar for residents.

Campsites

There are only a couple of established **campsites** within half an hour's travel of central Edinburgh.

Drummohr Caravan and Camping Park Levenhall, Musselburgh ⓣ0131/665 6867, ⓦwww.drummohr.org. A large, pleasant site in Musselburgh, a coastal satellite town to the east of Edinburgh, with excellent transport connections to the city, including buses #15, #26, #30 and #44. Camping site and wooden huts available.

Edinburgh Caravan Club Site Marine Drive, Silverknowes ⓣ0131/312 6874. Caravan-dominated site in a pleasant location close to the shore in the northwestern suburbs, with a handy bus service (#42) into town. Camping May–Sept only.

The Old Town

The **OLD TOWN**, although only about a mile long and 400yd wide, represented the total extent of the twin burghs of Edinburgh and Canongate for the first 650 years of their existence, and its general appearance and character remain indubitably medieval. Containing the majority of the city's most famous tourist sights, it makes by far the best starting point for your explorations.

In addition to the obvious goals of the **Castle** and the **Palace of Holyroodhouse** at either end of the famous **Royal Mile**, you'll find scores of historic buildings along the length of the street. Inevitably, much of the Old Town is sacrificed to hard-sell tourism, and can be uncomfortably crowded throughout the summer, especially during the Festival. Yet the area remains at the heart of Edinburgh, with important daily business being conducted in the law courts, city chambers and, of course, the new **Scottish Parliament**, housed in a radical and controversial collection of buildings at the foot of the Royal Mile. It's well worth extending your explorations to the area immediately to the south of the Royal Mile, and in particular to the engaging **National Museum of Scotland**.

The Old Town is compact enough to allow a brief glance at the highlights in the course of a single day, but a thorough visit requires several days. No matter how pressed you are, make sure that you spare time for the wonderfully varied scenery and breathtaking vantage points of **Holyrood Park**, an extensive tract of open countryside on the eastern edge of the Old Town that includes Arthur's Seat, the peak of which rises so distinctively in the midst of the city.

The Castle

The history of Edinburgh, and indeed of Scotland, is tightly wrapped up with its **Castle** (daily: April–Oct 9.30am–6pm; Nov–March 9.30am–5pm, last entry 45min before closing; HS; £12–14; Ⓦ www.edinburghcastle.gov.uk), which dominates the city from a lofty seat atop an extinct volcanic rock. It requires no great imaginative feat to comprehend the strategic importance that underpinned the Castle's, and hence Edinburgh's, importance in Scotland. From Princes Street, the north side rears high above an almost sheer rock face; the southern side is equally formidable and the western, where the rock rises in terraces, only marginally less so. Would-be attackers, like modern tourists, were forced to approach the Castle from the narrow ridge to the east on which the Royal Mile runs down to Holyrood.

The disparate styles of the fortifications reflect the change in its role from defensive citadel to national monument, and today, as well as attracting more visitors than anywhere else in the country, the Castle is still a **military barracks** and home to Scotland's **Crown Jewels**. The oldest surviving part of the complex is from the twelfth century, while the most recent additions date back to the 1920s. Nothing remains from its period as a seat of the Scottish court in the reign of Malcolm Canmore; indeed, having been lost to (and subsequently recaptured from) the English on several occasions, the defences were dismantled by the Scots themselves in 1313, because of the problems that ensued when they were in the wrong hands, and weren't rebuilt until 1356, when the return of King David II from captivity introduced a modicum of political stability. Thereafter, it gradually developed into Scotland's premier castle, with the dual function of fortress and royal palace. It last saw action in 1745, when Bonnie Prince Charlie's forces, fresh from their victory at Prestonpans, made a half-hearted attempt to storm it. Subsequent advances in weapon technology diminished the Castle's importance, but under the influence of the Romantic movement it came to be seen as a great national monument.

Though you can easily take in the views and wander round the Castle by yourself, you might like to join a **guided tour** (every 15min–1hr; 20min; free), which offers a brief introduction to the key aspects of the garrison. For more in-depth information, multi-language **audio guides** (£3 if bought as part of the entrance fee) can be picked up from a booth just beyond the Portcullis Gate.

The Esplanade

The Castle is entered via the **Esplanade**, a parade ground laid out in the eighteenth century and enclosed a hundred years later by ornamental walls. For most of the year it acts as a coach park, though in the summer months huge grandstands are erected for the Edinburgh Military Tattoo (see p.122), which takes place every night during August, coinciding with the Edinburgh Festival. A shameless and spectacular pageant of swinging kilts and massed pipe bands, the tattoo makes full use of its dramatic setting.

Entry to the Esplanade is free, and if you don't have time to do the Castle justice, or don't want to pay the pricey entry fee, it does at least offer a taste of the precipitous location as well as eye-stretching views. Various memorials are dotted around the Esplanade, including an equestrian **statue of Field Marshal Earl Haig**, the controversial Edinburgh-born commander of the British forces in World War I, and the pretty Art Nouveau **Witches' Fountain** commemorating the three hundred or more women burnt at this spot on charges of sorcery, the last of whom died in 1722. Rising up to one side of the Esplanade are the higgledy-piggedly pink-and-white turrets and high gables of **Ramsay Gardens**, surely some of the most picturesque city-centre apartment buildings in the world. Most date from the 1890s, the vision of Patrick Geddes, a pioneer of the modern town-planning movement.

The lower defences

Edinburgh Castle has a single entrance, a 10ft-wide opening in the **gatehouse**, one of many Romantic-style additions made in the 1880s. Rearing up behind is the most distinctive and impressive feature of the Castle's silhouette, the sixteenth-century **Half Moon Battery**, which marks the outer limit of the actual defences. Once through the gatehouse, the main ticket office is on your right, with an information centre alongside. Continue uphill along Lower Ward, showing your ticket at the **Portcullis Gate**, a handsome Renaissance gateway of the same period as the battery above, marred by the addition of a nineteenth-century upper storey equipped with anachronistic arrow slits. Beyond this the wide main path is known as Middle Ward, with the six-gun **Argyle Battery** to the right. Further west on **Mill's Mount Battery**, a well-known Edinburgh ritual takes place – the daily firing of the **one o'clock gun**. Originally designed for the benefit of ships in the Firth of Forth, these days it's an enjoyable ceremony for visitors to watch and a useful time signal for city-centre office workers. There's an interesting little exhibition about the history of the firing of the gun in a room immediately below Mill's Mount Battery.

National War Museum of Scotland

Located in the old hospital buildings, down a ramp between the café/restaurant immediately behind the one o'clock gun and the Governor's House, the **National War Museum of Scotland** (free) covers the last four hundred years of Scottish military history. Scots have been fighting for much longer than that, of course, but the slant of the museum is very definitely towards the soldiers who fought *for* the Union, rather than against it (or against themselves). While the various rooms are packed with uniforms, medals, paintings of heroic actions and plenty of interesting memorabilia, the museum manages to convey a reflective, human tone. Just as delicate is the job of showing no favouritism to any of the Scottish regiments, each of which has strong traditions more forcefully paraded in the various regimental museums found in regions of Scotland – the Royal Scots and the Scots Dragoon Guards, for instance, both have displays in other parts of Edinburgh Castle.

St Margaret's Chapel

Near the highest point of the citadel is tiny **St Margaret's Chapel**, the oldest surviving building in the Castle, and probably in Edinburgh. Although once believed to have been built by the saint herself, and mooted as the site of her death in 1093, its architectural style suggests that it actually dates from about thirty years later, and was probably built by King David I as a memorial to his mother. Used as a powder magazine for three hundred years, it was eventually rededicated in 1934 after sympathetic restoration. Externally, its Norman style is plain and severe, but the dignified interior preserves an elaborate zigzag archway dividing the nave from the sanctuary.

The battlements in front of the chapel offer the best of all the Castle's panoramic views. Here you'll see the famous fifteenth-century siege gun, **Mons Meg**, which could fire a 500lb stone nearly two miles. It last saw active service in the 1540s, and was thereafter used occasionally as a ceremonial saluting gun before being moved to the Tower of London in 1754. Such was Meg's emblematic value that Sir Walter Scott persuaded George IV to return it for his 1822 state visit to Scotland. Just below Mons Meg there's a small **cemetery**, the last resting place of the **soldiers' pets**: it is kept in immaculate condition, particularly when contrasted with the dilapidated state of some of the city's public cemeteries. Continuing eastwards, you skirt the top of the Forewall and Half Moon Batteries, passing the 110ft-high **Castle Well** en route to **Crown Square**, the most important and secure section of the entire complex.

Crown Square

The eastern side of **Crown Square**, the historic heart of the Castle, is occupied by the **Palace**, a surprisingly unassuming edifice begun in the 1430s. It owes its Renaissance appearance to King James IV, though it was remodelled for Mary, Queen of Scots and her consort Henry, Lord Darnley, whose entwined initials (MAH), together with the date 1566, can be seen above one of the doorways. This gives access to a few historic rooms, the most interesting of which is the tiny panelled bedchamber at the extreme southeastern corner, where Mary gave birth to James VI.

A section of the Palace houses a detailed audiovisual presentation on the nation's **Crown Jewels**, properly known as the **Honours of Scotland**; the originals are housed in the Crown Room at the very end of the display. You might be put off by the slow-moving, claustrophobic queues that shuffle past the various tableaux, but the Honours still serve as one of the most potent images of Scotland's nationhood. Last used for the Scottish-only coronation of Charles II in 1651, the oldest of the three pieces comprising the Honours is the **sceptre**, which bears statuettes of the Virgin and Child, St James and St Andrew, rounded off by a polished globe of rock crystal: it was given to James IV in 1494 by Pope Alexander VI, and refashioned by Scottish craftsmen for James V. Even finer is the **sword**, a swaggering Italian High Renaissance masterpiece by the silversmith Domenico da Sutri, presented to James IV by Pope Julius II. The jewel-encrusted **crown**, made for James V by the Scottish goldsmith James Mosman, incorporates the gold circlet worn by Robert the Bruce and is topped by an enamelled orb and cross. The glass case containing the Honours has recently been rearranged to create space for the incongruously plain **Stone of Destiny** (see box, p.80).

On the south side of Crown Square is James IV's hammer-beam-ceilinged **Great Hall**, used for meetings of the Scottish Parliament until 1639, while opposite this on the north side of the square is the serene Hall of Honour housing the **Scottish National War Memorial**, created in 1927 by the architect Sir Robert Lorimer and 200 Scottish artists and craftsmen.

The Stone of Destiny

Legend has it that the **Stone of Destiny** (also called the Stone of Scone) was "Jacob's Pillow", on which he dreamed of the ladder of angels from earth to heaven. Its real history is obscure, but it is known to have been moved from Ireland to Dunadd by missionaries, and thence to Dunstaffnage, from where Kenneth MacAlpine, king of the Dalriada Scots, brought it to the abbey at Scone, near Perth, in 838. There it remained for almost five hundred years, used as a coronation throne on which all kings of Scotland were crowned.

In 1296 Edward I stole what he believed to be the Stone and installed it at Westminster Abbey, where, apart from a brief interlude in 1950 when it was removed by Scottish nationalists and hidden in Arbroath for several months, it remained for seven hundred years. All this changed in December 1996 when, after a ceremony-laden journey from London, the Stone returned to Scotland, in one of the doomed attempts by the Conservative government to convince the Scottish people that the Union was a good thing. Much to the annoyance of the people of Perth and the curators of Scone Palace (see p.355), and the general indifference of the people of Scotland, the Stone was placed in Edinburgh Castle.

However, speculation surrounds the authenticity of the Stone, for the original is said to have been intricately carved, while the one seen today is a plain block of sandstone. Many believe that the canny monks at Scone palmed this off onto the English king (some say that it's nothing more sacred than the cover for a medieval septic tank), and that the real Stone of Destiny lies hidden in an underground chamber, its whereabouts a mystery to all but the chosen few.

The rest of the complex

From Crown Square, you can descend to the **Vaults**, a series of cavernous chambers erected by James IV to provide level surface for the buildings above. They were later used as a prison for captured foreign nationals, who bequeathed a rich legacy of graffiti. Directly opposite the entrance to the Vaults is the **Military Prison**, built in 1842, when the design and function of jails was a major topic of public debate. The cells, designed for solitary confinement, are less forbidding than might be expected.

The Royal Mile

The **Royal Mile**, the name given to the ridge linking the Castle with Holyrood, was described by Daniel Defoe in 1724, as "the largest, longest and finest street for Buildings and Number of Inhabitants, not in Bretain only, but in the World". Almost exactly a mile in length, it is divided into four separate streets – Castlehill, Lawnmarket, High Street and Canongate. From these, branching out in a herringbone pattern, are a series of tightly packed closes and steep lanes entered via archways known as "pends". After the construction of the New Town much of the housing along the Royal Mile degenerated into a notorious slum, but has since shaken off that reputation, with bijou flats, holiday apartments, student residences and offices now populating the tightly packed buildings. Although marred by rather too many tacky tourist shops and the odd misjudged new development, the Royal Mile is still right at the heart of Edinburgh's appeal as a world-class tourist destination, and a thoroughfare that rewards detailed exploration.

Castlehill

Immediately east (downhill) from the Castle, the first building on the northern side of **Castlehill**, the Royal Mile's uppermost stretch, is the former reservoir for the Old Town, which has been converted into the **Edinburgh Old Town Weaving Centre**

(May–Oct Mon–Sat 9am–6.30pm, Sun 10am–6.30pm; Nov–April Mon–Sat 9am–5.30pm, Sun 10am–5.30pm). Very much a commercial enterprise, the centre contains various shops selling garish knick-knacks, kilts, rugs and other tartan adornments, while noisy looms rhythmically churn the stuff out on the floors below.

Opposite the Weaving Centre, the **Scotch Whisky Experience** (daily: June–Aug 10am–5.30pm; Sept–May 10am–5pm; £11.50; Ⓦwww.scotch-whisky-experience.co.uk) mimics the kind of tours offered at distilleries in the Highlands, and while it can't match the authenticity of the real thing, the centre does offer a thorough introduction to the "water of life" (*uisge beatha* in Gaelic), with tours featuring an entertaining tutorial on the specialized art of whisky "nosing", a gimmicky ride in a moving "barrel" car, a peek at the world's largest whisky collection and a tasting. On the ground floor, a well-stocked shop gives an idea of the sheer range and diversity of the drink, while downstairs there's a pleasant whisky bar and restaurant, *Amber* (see p.107).

Across the street, housed in the domed black-and-white turret atop the **Outlook Tower** (daily: April–Oct 9.30am–6pm, July & Aug open till 7.30pm; Nov–March 10am–5pm; £9.25; Ⓦwww.camera-obscura.co.uk), Edinburgh's camera obscura has been a tourist attraction since 1853, providing an intriguing bird's-eye view of a city going about its business. The "camera" consists of a small darkened room with a white wooden table onto which a periscope reflects live images of prominent buildings and folk walking on the streets below.

The imposing black church at the foot of Castlehill is **The Hub** (Ⓣ0131/473 2015, Ⓦwww.thehub-edinburgh.com), also known as "Edinburgh's Festival Centre". It's open year-round, providing performance, rehearsal and exhibition space, a ticket centre and a café. The building itself was constructed in 1845 to designs by James Gillespie Graham and Augustus Pugin, one of the architects of the Houses of Parliament in London – a connection obvious from the superb neo-Gothic detailing and the sheer presence of the building, whose spire is the highest in Edinburgh. If it's not in use for a function, try to check out the main hall upstairs, where the original neo-Gothic woodwork and high-vaulted ceiling is enlivened with a fabulous fabric design in Rastafarian colours. Permanent works of art have been incorporated into the centre, including more than two hundred delightful foot-high sculptures depicting Festival performers and audiences.

Lawnmarket

Below the Hub, the Royal Mile opens out into the broader expanse of **Lawnmarket**, which, as its name suggests, was once a marketplace. Doing its best to maintain its dignity among a sea of cheap tartan gifts and discounted woolly jumpers, **Gladstone's Land** (daily: April–Oct 10am–5pm, July–Aug 10am–6.30pm; NTS; £5.50) is the Royal Mile's best surviving example of a typical seventeenth-century tenement. The tall, narrow building – not unlike a canalside house in Amsterdam – would have been home to various families living in cramped conditions: the well-to-do Gledstanes, who built it in 1620, are thought to have occupied the third floor. The National Trust for Scotland has carefully restored the rooms, filling them with period furnishings and fittings; in each a well-spoken guide is on hand to answer questions and pass out a sheet detailing what's on show. The arcaded and wooden-fronted ground floor is home to a reconstructed cloth shop; pass through this and you encounter a warren of tight little staircases, tiny rooms, creaking floorboards and peek-hole windows. The finest room, on the first floor immediately above the arcade, has a marvellous painted ceiling and some fine old dark furniture. The upper floors contain apartments which are rented to visitors (see p.75).

A few paces further on, look out for the arched entranceway to Lady Stair's Close, one of a number of attractive courtyards just off the Royal Mile. Within the

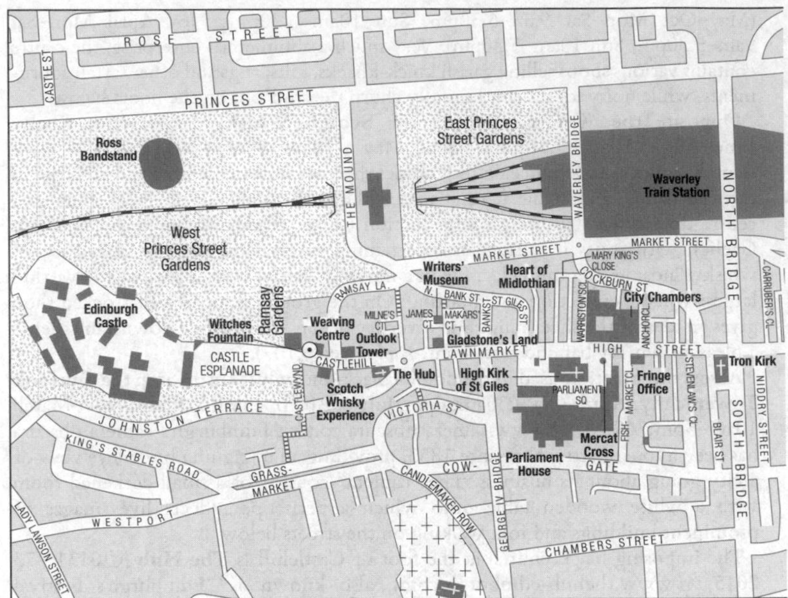

seventeenth-century Lady Stair's House is the **Writers' Museum** (Mon–Sat 10am–5pm; also Sun noon–5pm in Aug; free; Ⓦwww.edinburghmuseums.org.uk), dedicated to Scotland's three greatest literary lions: Sir Walter Scott, Robert Louis Stevenson and Robert Burns. The house itself holds as much interest as the slightly lacklustre collection of portraits, manuscripts and knick-knacks that make up the museum, its tight, winding stairs and poky, wood-panelled rooms offering a flavour of the medieval Old Town. More inspiring from a literary angle is the open courtyard outside, known as the Makars' Court after the Scots word for the "maker" of poetry or prose, which features a series of paving stones inscribed with quotations from Scotland's most famous writers and poets.

High Kirk of St Giles

Across the junction with George IV Bridge is the third and most central section of the Royal Mile, known as the **High Street**. The dominant building of the southern side of the street, the **High Kirk of St Giles** (May–Sept Mon–Fri 9am–7pm, Sat 9am–5pm, Sun 1–5pm; Oct–April Mon–Sat 9am–5pm, Sun 1–5pm; free; Ⓦwww.stgilescathedral.org.uk) is the original parish church of medieval Edinburgh, from where John Knox (see box, p.86) launched and directed the Scottish Reformation. St Giles is often referred to as a cathedral, although it has only been the seat of a bishop on two brief and unhappy occasions in the seventeenth century. According to one of the city's best-known legends, the attempt in 1637 to introduce the English Prayer Book, and thus episcopal government, so incensed a humble stallholder named Jenny Geddes that she hurled her stool at the preacher, prompting the rest of the congregation to chase the offending clergy out of the building. A tablet in the north aisle marks the spot from where she let rip.

The location and historical significance of St Giles mean that it is often used for high-profile religious services, such as when the Queen is in town or at the

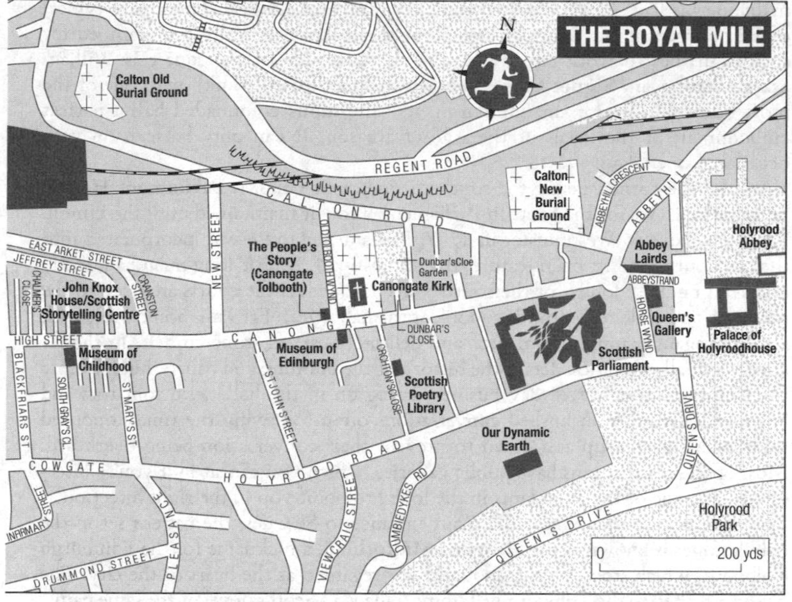

opening of Parliament, despite the fact that it is, strictly, still an ordinary parish church with a regular congregation. The resplendent **crown spire** of the kirk is formed from eight flying buttresses and dates back to 1485, while **inside**, the four massive piers supporting the tower were part of a Norman church built here around 1120. In the nineteenth century, St Giles was adorned with a whole series of funerary monuments on the model of London's Westminster Abbey; around the same time it acquired several attractive Pre-Raphaelite stained-glass windows designed by Edward Burne-Jones and William Morris. A more recent addition was the great **west window**, whose dedication to Robbie Burns in 1985 caused enormous controversy – as a hardened drinker and womanizer, the national bard was far from being an upholder of accepted Presbyterian values. Look out, too, for an elegant bronze relief of Robert Louis Stevenson on the south side of the church.

At the southeastern corner of St Giles, the **Thistle Chapel** was built by Sir Robert Lorimer in 1911 as the private chapel of the sixteen knights of the Most Noble Order of the Thistle, the highest chivalric order in Scotland. Based on St George's Chapel in Windsor, it's an exquisite piece of craftsmanship, with an elaborate ribbed vault, huge drooping bosses and extravagantly ornate stalls showing off Lorimer's bold Arts and Crafts styling.

Parliament Square

St Giles is surrounded on three sides by **Parliament Square**, which itself is dominated by the continuous Neoclassical facades of the **Law Courts**, originally planned by Robert Adam (1728–92), one of four brothers in a family of architects whose work helped imbue the New Town with much of its grace and elegance. Because of a shortage of funds and consequent delays, the present exteriors were built to designs by Robert Reid (1776–1856), the designer of the northern part of New Town, who faithfully quoted Adam's architectural vocabulary without matching his flair. Reid's elevated Ionic columns and classical statuary are typical of Edinburgh's grand Georgian style, but the location is really too cramped for such flourishes to work effectively. On the west side of the square is William Stark's flamboyant **Signet Library** (Ⓦwww.signetlibrary.co.uk), with one of the most beautiful interiors in Edinburgh, its sumptuous colonnaded hall a perfect embodiment of the ideals of the Age of Reason. It can only be seen on very occasional open days.

Around the corner, facing the southern side of St Giles, is **Parliament House**, built in the 1630s for the Scottish Parliament, a role it maintained until the Union. After the move to Westminster in 1707, Parliament House was incorporated into the law courts, and its main feature, the impressive 122-foot-long main hall, today acts as a grandiose lobby for the courtrooms beyond. As the courts are open to the public, it's possible to get inside to look at the hall (Mon–Fri 9am–5pm; free), with its extravagant hammer-beam roof and delicately carved stone corbels. In the far corner a small exhibition details the history of the building and courts, but it's more fun simply to watch everyday business going on in the hall, with solicitors and bewigged advocates in hushed conversations often following the time-honoured tradition of pacing up and down to prevent their conversation being overheard. Most of the court rooms have public galleries, which you can sit in if you're interested – ask one of the attendants in the lobby to point you in the right direction.

Outside on the square near the main entrance to St Giles, the pattern set in the cobblestones is known as the **Heart of Midlothian**, a nickname for the Edinburgh Tolbooth, which stood on this spot and was regarded as the heart of the city. The prison attached to the Tolbooth was immortalized in Scott's novel of the same name, and you may still see locals spitting on the cobblestone heart, a continuation of the tradition of spitting on the door of the prison to ward off the evil contained therein. At the other end of St Giles, public proclamations (such as the announcement of the dissolution of Parliament) have traditionally been read from the **Mercat Cross**. The present structure, adorned with coats of arms and topped by a sculpture of a unicorn, looks venerable enough, but most of it is little more than a hundred years old, a gift to the city from nineteenth-century prime minister William Ewart Gladstone. The Cross (or nearby) is a main departure point for myriad **tours** of the Old Town (see p.67 for details).

Mary King's Close

Opposite the Mercat Cross, the U-shaped **City Chambers** were designed by John Adam, brother of Robert, as the Royal Exchange. Local traders never warmed to the exchange, however, so the town council established its headquarters there instead. Beneath the City Chambers lies **Mary King's Close**, one of Edinburgh's most unusual attractions. When work on the chambers began in 1753, the existing tenements on the steeply sloping site were only partially demolished to make way for the new building being constructed on top of them. The process left large sections of the houses together with the old streets (or closes) that ran alongside them intact but entirely enclosed among the basement and cellars of the City Chambers. You can visit this rather spooky subterranean "lost city" on tours led by costumed actors (April–Oct daily 10am–9pm; Nov–March Sun–Thurs 10am–5pm, Fri & Sat 10am–9pm; every 20min; 1hr; £11; Ⓦwww.realmarykingsclose.com), who take you round the cold stone shells of the houses where various scenes from the Close's history have been recreated. As you'd expect, blood, plague, pestilence and ghostly apparitions are to the fore, though there is an acknowledgement of the more prosaic side of medieval life in the archeological evidence of an urban cow byre. The tour ends with a stroll up the remarkably well-preserved Mary King's Close itself. A little further down the High Street is **Anchor Close**, site of the printing works of William Smellie, who published the first-ever edition of the *Encyclopaedia Britannica* there in 1768.

Lower High Street

Beyond the intersection of North Bridge and South Bridge the noisy **Museum of Childhood** (Mon–Sat 10am–5pm, Sun noon–5pm; free; Ⓦwww.edinburghmuseums.org.uk) was founded in 1955 by a bachelor local councillor who heartily disliked children. In today's digital age the collection of dolls' houses, teddy bears, train sets and marionettes may be a little dull for some children, although their nostalgic charm often touches a chord with parents.

Across the street and just a little way downhill, jutting out into the street from the main line of buildings, is the fifteenth-century John Knox House, now part of the **Scottish Storytelling Centre** (Mon–Sat 10am–6pm, also Sun noon–6pm in July & Aug; £4 entry to John Knox House; Ⓦwww.scottishstorytellingcentre.co.uk). There are two distinct parts to this cultural centre: one half is a stylish contemporary development containing an excellent café, the Netherbow Theatre and an airy Storytelling Court with a small permanent exhibition about Scottish stories from ancient folk tales to Harry Potter. By contrast, John Knox House is a fifteenth-century stone-and-timber building which, with its distinctive external staircase, overhanging upper storeys and busy pantile roof, is a classic example of the Royal Mile in its medieval heyday. Inside, the house is all low doorways, uneven floors and ornate wooden panelling; it contains a series of displays about Knox (see box, p.86), the minister who led the Reformation in Scotland and established Calvinist Presbyterianism as the dominant religious force in the country. Regular performances and events, often aimed at a younger audience, take place in the centre, particularly during the Festival. To get to the lovely quiet garden behind the centre, head down Trunk's Close, a few doors uphill from John Knox House.

Canongate

For over seven hundred years, the district through which the final and most easterly section of the Royal Mile, the **Canongate**, runs, was a burgh in its own right, officially separate from the capital, which was entered through the Netherbow Port.

A notorious slum area even into the 1960s, it has been the subject of some of the most ambitious **restoration** programmes in the Old Town, though the lack of harmony between the buildings renovated in different decades can be seen fairly clearly. For such a central district, it's interesting to note that most of the buildings here are residential, and by no means are they all bijou apartments. The most dramatic slice of the redevelopment, however, is in the Holyrood area at its lower end, where the new Parliament building has brought a radical contemporary slant to the look and feel of the whole area. As you wander down the Canongate, you might be diverted by one or two of an eclectic range of shops, which include a gallery of historic maps and sea charts, an old-fashioned whisky bottler and a genuine bagpipe maker.

Dominated by a turreted steeple and an odd external box clock, the late sixteenth-century **Canongate Tolbooth** on the north side of the street has served both as the headquarters of the burgh administration and as a prison. It now houses **The People's Story** (Mon–Sat 10am–5pm, also Sun noon–5pm in Aug; free; Ⓦwww.edinburghmuseums.org.uk), which contains a series of display cases, dense information boards and rather old-fashioned tableaux dedicated to the everyday life and work of Edinburgh's population down the centuries. This isn't one of Edinburgh's essential museums, but it does have a down-to-earth reality

John Knox

Protestant reformer John Knox has been credited with, or blamed for, the distinctive national characteristic of rather gloomy reserve that emerged from the Calvinist Reformation and which has cast its shadow right up to the present. Little is known about Knox's early years: he was born between 1505 and 1514 in East Lothian, and trained for the priesthood at St Andrews University. Ordained in 1540, Knox then served as a private tutor, in league with Scotland's first significant Protestant leader, **George Wishart**. After Wishart was burnt at the stake for heresy in 1546, Knox became involved with the group who had carried out the revenge murder of the Scottish primate, Cardinal David Beaton, subsequently taking over his castle in St Andrews. The following year this was captured by the French, and Knox was carted off to work as a galley slave.

He was freed in 1548, as a result of the intervention of the English, who invited him to play an evangelizing role in the spread of their own Reformation. Following successful ministries in Berwick-upon-Tweed and Newcastle upon Tyne, Knox turned down the bishopric of Rochester, less from an intrinsic opposition to episcopacy than from a wish to avoid becoming embroiled in the turmoil he guessed would ensue if the Catholic Mary Tudor acceded to the English throne. When this duly happened in 1553, Knox fled to the Continent, ending up as minister to the English-speaking community in Geneva, which was then in the grip of the theocratic government of the Frenchman **Jean Calvin**.

In exile, Knox was preoccupied with the influence wielded by political rulers, believing that the future of the Reformation in Europe was at risk because of the opposition of a few powerful sovereigns. This prompted him to write his infamous treatise, *The First Blast of the Trumpet Against the Monstrous Regiment of Women*, a specific attack on the three Catholic women then ruling Scotland, England and France, which has made his name synonymous with misogyny ever since.

When Knox was allowed to return to Scotland in 1555, he took over as spiritual leader of the Reformation, becoming minister of St Giles in Edinburgh, where he gained a reputation as a charismatic preacher. The establishment of Protestantism as the official religion of Scotland in 1560 was dependent on the forging of an alliance with Elizabeth I, which Knox himself rigorously championed: the swift deployment of English troops against the French garrison in Edinburgh dealt a fatal blow to Franco-Spanish hopes of re-establishing Catholicism in both Scotland and England. Although the return of Mary, Queen of Scots the following year placed a Catholic monarch on the Scottish throne, Knox was reputedly always able to retain the upper hand in his famous disputes with her.

Before his death in 1572, Knox began mapping out the organization of the **Scots Kirk**, sweeping away all vestiges of episcopal control and giving lay people a role of unprecedented importance. He also proposed a nationwide education system, to be compulsory for the very young and free for the poor, though lack of funds meant this could not be implemented in full. His final legacy was the posthumously published *History of the Reformation of Religion in the Realm of Scotland*, a justification of his life's work.

For all his considerable influence, Knox was not responsible for many of the features which have created the popular image of Scottish Presbyterianism – and of Knox himself – as austere and joyless. A man of refined cultural tastes, he did not encourage the iconoclasm that destroyed so many of Scotland's churches and works of art: indeed, much of this was carried out by English hands. Nor did he promote unbending Sabbatarianism, an obsessive work ethic, or even the inflexible view of the doctrine of predestination favoured by his far more fanatical successors. Ironically, though, by fostering an irrevocable rift in the "Auld Alliance" with France, he did more than anyone else to ensure that Scotland's future was to be linked with that of England.

often missing from places dedicated to high culture or famous historical characters. Next door, **Canongate Kirk** (May–Sept Mon–Sat 10.30am–4.30pm, Sun 12.30–4.30pm depending on volunteer staff and church services; free) was built in the 1680s to house the congregation expelled from Holyrood Abbey when the latter was commandeered by James VII (James II in England) to serve as the chapel for the **Order of the Thistle**. The kirk, which has excellent acoustics and is often used for concerts, has a modesty rarely seen in churches built in later centuries, with a graceful curved facade and a bow-shaped gable to the rear. The surrounding churchyard (free access) provides an attractive and tranquil stretch of green in the heart of the Old Town and affords fine views of Calton Hill; it also happens to be one of the city's most exclusive cemeteries – well-known internees include the political economist **Adam Smith**, Mrs Agnes McLehose (better known as Robert Burns's "Clarinda") and **Robert Fergusson**, regarded by some as Edinburgh's greatest poet, despite his death at the age of 24. Fergusson's headstone was donated by Burns, a fervent admirer, and a statue of the young poet can be seen just outside the gates of the kirk.

Opposite the church, the **Museum of Edinburgh** in Huntly House (Mon–Sat 10am–5pm, also Sun noon–5pm in Aug; free; Ⓦwww.edinburghmuseums.org.uk) is the city's principal collection devoted to local history, though the museum is as interesting for the labyrinthine network of wood-panelled rooms within as for its rather quirky array of artefacts. These do, however, include a number of items of real historical significance, in particular the National Convention, the petition for religious freedom drawn up on a deerskin parchment in 1638, and the original plans for the layout of the New Town drawn by James Craig (see p.96), chosen by the city council after a competition in 1767.

Among the various closes and arched entries on this stretch of Canongate, look out for **Dunbar's Close**, on the north side of the street, which has a beautiful seventeenth-century walled garden tucked in behind its tenements. Opposite this is the entry to Crichton's Close, through which you'll find the **Scottish Poetry Library** (Tues, Wed & Fri 10am–5pm, Thurs 10am–8pm, Sat 10am–4pm; free; Ⓦwww.spl.org.uk), a small island of modern architectural eloquence amid a cacophony of large-scale developments. The building incorporates a section of an old city wall, and the attractive, thoroughly contemporary design harmoniously combines brick, oak, glass, Caithness stone and blue ceramic tiles. The library contains Scotland's most comprehensive collection of native poetry, and visitors are free to read the books, periodicals and leaflets found on the shelves, or listen to recordings of poetry in English, Scots and Gaelic. Readings and events are organized throughout the year.

Holyrood

At the foot of Canongate lies **Holyrood**, for centuries known as Edinburgh's royal quarter, with its ruined thirteenth-century **abbey** and the **Palace of Holyroodhouse**. In recent years, however, the area has been transformed by the addition of Enric Miralles' dazzling but highly controversial new Scottish Parliament, which was deliberately landscaped to mimic the cliffs and ridges of Edinburgh's most dramatic natural feature, the nearby **Holyrood Park** and its slumbering peak, Arthur's Seat.

The **legend** of Holyrood goes back to 1128, when King David I, son of Malcolm Canmore and St Margaret, went out hunting and was suddenly confronted by a stag who threw him from his horse and seemed ready to gore him. In desperation, the king tried to protect himself by grasping its antlers, but instead found himself holding a crucifix, whereupon the animal ran off. In a dream that

Admission to Holyroodhouse

Compared with most royal palaces, visitor access to Holyroodhouse is extensive. However, the Queen still makes fairly regular visits, and for this reason the palace is normally closed in mid-May, late June and mid-November, and occasionally at other times if a state function is taking place.

night, he heard a voice commanding him to "make a house for Canons devoted to the Cross"; he duly obeyed, naming the abbey Holyrood ("rood" being an alternative name for a cross). Another explanation is that David, the most pious of all Scotland's monarchs, acquired a relic of Christ's Cross and decided to build a suitable home for it.

Holyrood soon became a favoured **royal residence**, its situation in a secluded valley making it far more agreeable than the draughty Castle. At first, monarchs lodged in the abbey's monastic guesthouse, to which a wing for the exclusive use of the court was added during the reign of James II. This was transformed into a full-blown palace for James IV, which in turn was replaced by a much larger building for Charles II, although he never actually lived there. Indeed, it was something of a white elephant until Queen Victoria started travelling to Scotland frequently enough to establish an official residence.

The Palace of Holyroodhouse

In its present form, the **Palace of Holyroodhouse** (daily: April–Oct 9.30am–6pm; Nov–March 9.30am–4.30pm; last admission 1hr before closing; £10.25; Ⓦ www.royalcollection.org.uk) is largely a seventeenth-century creation, planned for Charles II. However, the tower house of the old palace was skillfully incorporated to form the northwestern block, with a virtual mirror image of it erected as a counterbalance at the other end.

Tours of the palace move through a series of royal **reception rooms** featuring some outstanding encrusted plasterwork, each more impressive than the last – an idea Charles II had picked up from his cousin Louis XIV's Versailles – while on the northern side of the internal quadrangle, the **Great Gallery** extends almost the full length of the palace and is dominated by portraits of 96 Scottish kings, painted by Jacob de Wet in 1684 to illustrate the lineage of Stewart royalty. The result is unintentionally hilarious, as it is clear that the artist's imagination was taxed to bursting point by the need to paint so many different facial types without having an inkling as to what the subjects actually looked like. Leading from this into the oldest part of the palace, known as James V's tower, the formal, ceremonial tone gives way to dark medieval history, with a tight spiral staircase leading to the chambers used by **Mary, Queen of Scots**. These contain various relics, including jewellery, associated with the queen, though the most compelling viewing is a tiny supper room, from where in 1566 Mary's Italian secretary, **David Rizzio**, was dragged by conspirators, who included her jealous husband, Lord Darnley, to the outer chamber and stabbed 56 times; a brass plaque on the wall points out what are rather optimistically identified as the bloodstains on the wooden floor.

Holyrood Abbey

Immediately adjacent to the palace are the evocative ruins of **Holyrood Abbey** (free access as part of Holyroodhouse tour), some of which date to the thirteenth century. Various invading armies paid little respect to the building over the years, and although it was patched up for Charles I's coronation in 1633 it was gutted in 1688 by an anti-Catholic mob. The roof finally tumbled down in 1768, but the melancholy scene has inspired artists down the years, among them Felix Mendelssohn, who in 1829 wrote: "Everything is in ruins and mouldering … I believe I have found the beginning of my Scottish Symphony there today." Adjacent to the abbey are the formal palace gardens, open to visitors during the summer months and offering some pleasant strolls.

The Queen's Gallery

Essentially an adjunct to Holyrood Palace, the **Queen's Gallery** (same times; £5.50 or £14.30 joint ticket with Holyroodhouse; ⓦwww.royalcollection.org.uk) is located in the shell of a former church directly between the palace and the Parliament. With just two principal viewing rooms, it's a compact space, but has an appealing contemporary style which manages to remain sympathetic to the older elements of the building. It's used to display changing exhibitions from the Royal Collection, a vast array of art treasures held by the Queen on behalf of the British nation. Because the pieces are otherwise exhibited only during the limited openings of Buckingham Palace and Windsor Castle, the exhibitions here tend to draw quite a lot of interest. Recent displays have included a priceless collection of drawings by Leonardo da Vinci and a glittering array of jewellery by Russian goldsmith Carl Fabergé.

The Scottish Parliament

For all its grandeur, Holyrood Palace is in danger of being upstaged by the striking buildings that make up the new **Scottish Parliament** (for visiting details see box below). The most controversial public building to be erected in Scotland since World War II, it houses the country's directly elected assembly, which was reintroduced into the British political scene in 1999 – Scotland's parliament was abolished in 1707, when it joined the English assembly at Westminster as part of the Union of the two nations.

Made up of various linked elements rather than one single building, the unique design of the complex was the vision of Catalan architect **Enric Miralles**, whose death in 2000, halfway through the building process, caused more than a few ripples of uncertainty as to whether the famously whimsical designer had in fact set down his final draft. Initial estimates for the cost of the building were tentatively put at £40 million; by the time the Queen cut the ribbon in October 2004, the final bill was over £400 million. A major public inquiry into the overspend blamed costing

Visiting the Scottish Parliament

There's free access into the entrance lobby of the Parliament, entered from Horse Wynd, opposite the palace, where you'll find a small exhibition providing some historical, political and architectural background. If Parliament is in session, it's normally possible to watch proceedings in the debating chamber from the public gallery, though you have to get a pass from the front desk in the lobby. To see the rest of the interior properly you'll need to join one of the regular **guided tours** (1hr; free; bookings recommended; ⓣ0131/348 5200, ⓦwww.scottish.parliament.uk), highly recommended to better appreciate the quality, detailed features and unique vision of the building's design. Special tours dedicated to the architecture of the building and its collection of contemporary Scottish art also take place, but much less frequently – check the website for details.

There's action in the debating chamber only on "Business days" (Tues–Thurs 9am–6.30pm when Parliament is sitting), but there are no guided tours on these days. On "Non-business days" (Mon & Fri when Parliament is sitting, or Mon–Fri if Parliament is in recess), the doors are open April–Sept 10am–5.30pm, Nov–March 10am–4pm, as well as Sat 11am–5.30pm throughout the year.

failures early in the project and criticized the spendthrift attitude of politicians and civil servants alike, yet the building is still an impressive – if imperfect – testament to the ambition of Miralles and the man who championed him, Scotland's First Minister, Donald Dewar, who also died before the project was completed. While locals still mutter over the cost and the oddness of the design, the building has won over the majority of the general architectural community, scooping numerous prizes including, in 2005, the most prestigious in Britain, the Royal Institute of British Architects (RIBA) Stirling Prize.

From the outside the Parliament building can appear cluttered, hemmed in by Holyrood Palace and haphazard tenements, and there's much to be said for taking a walk up the path under Salisbury Crags to get an overview of the site. Miralles had a conviction that "the Parliament sits in the land", which helps explain the leaf or petal-shaped design of the central buildings, as well as the landscaping which ties together the long grass banks of the Parliament's gardens and the wildness of the parkland beyond.

One of the most memorable features of the building is the fanciful motifs and odd architectural signatures running through the design, including the anvil-shaped panels which clad the exterior and the extraordinary windows of the offices for MSPs (Members of the Scottish Parliament), shaped like the profile of a mountain or a section of the Forth Rail Bridge and said to have been inspired by a monk's contemplative cell.

The stark concrete of the new building's interior may not be to all tastes, and while some parts of the design are undoubtedly experimental and over-elaborate, there are moments where grace and boldness convene. One example is the **Garden Lobby**, an airy, bright meeting place in the heart of the campus with a fascinating roof of glass panels forming the shape of an upturned boat. The main **debating chamber**, meanwhile, is grand yet intimate and undoubtedly modern, with light flooding in through high windows and a complex network of thick oak beams, lights and microphone wires.

Our Dynamic Earth

Next to the Scottish Parliament on Holyrood Road, beneath a pincushion of white metal struts which make it look like a miniature version of London's Millennium Dome, **Our Dynamic Earth** (April–June & Sept–Oct daily 10am–5.30pm; July–Aug daily 10am–6pm; Nov–March Wed–Sun 10am–5.30pm; last entry 1hr 30min before closing; £10.50; Ⓦ www.dynamicearth.co.uk), is a hi-tech attraction based on the wonders of the natural world and aimed at families with kids between 5 and 15. Although James Hutton, the Edinburgh-born "Father of Geology", lived nearby in the eighteenth century, there are few specific links to Edinburgh or Scotland. Galleries cover the formation of the earth and continents with crashing sound effects and a shaking floor, while the calmer grandeur of glaciers and oceans are explored through magnificent large-screen landscape footage; further on, the polar regions – complete with a real iceberg – and tropical jungles are imaginatively recreated, with interactive computer screens and special effects at every turn. Outside, the dramatic **amphitheatre**, which incorporates the steps leading up to the main entrance, serves as a great venue for outdoor theatre and music performances, most notably during the Festival.

Holyrood Park, Arthur's Seat and Duddingston

Holyrood Park, a natural wilderness in the very heart of the modern city, is one of Edinburgh's greatest assets. Packed into an area no more than five miles in diameter is an amazing variety of landscapes – hills, crags, moorland, marshes, glens, lochs and fields – representing something of a microcosm of

Scotland's scenery. While old photographs of the park show crops growing and sheep grazing, it's now most used by walkers, joggers, cyclists and other outdoor enthusiasts. A single tarred road, **Queen's Drive**, loops through the park, enabling many of its features to be seen by car, although you need to get out and stroll around to appreciate it fully. You can pick up a map of suggested walks, as well as information on the geology and flora of the park, from the Holyrood Park Information Centre (unstaffed; daily 8/9am–5/6pm; closes 3/4pm in winter) in Holyrood Lodge on Horse Wynd. For further specific information, a uniformed Historic Scotland staff member is normally on duty in the nearby car park.

Two of the most rewarding walks begin from near this point: one, along a pathway nicknamed the "Radical Road", traverses the ridge immediately below the **Salisbury Crags**, one of the main features of the Edinburgh skyline. This is arguably a finer walk than the sharper climb to the top of Arthur's Seat: note that climbing is not allowed on the crags themselves, and that there's no continuous path along the top. A better looped walk of about an hour's duration from Holyrood is to follow the "Volunteer's Walk" up the glen behind the Crags, then back along the Radical Road.

The usual starting point for the ascent of **Arthur's Seat**, which at 823ft above sea level towers over Edinburgh's numerous high points, is Dunsapie Loch, reached by following the tarred Queen's Drive in a clockwise direction from the palace gates (30–40min walk). Part of a volcano which last saw action 350 million years ago, its connections to the legendary king are fairly sketchy: the name is likely to be a corruption of the Gaelic *Ard-na-said*, or "height of arrows". From Dunsapie Loch it's a twenty-minute climb up grassy slopes to the rocky summit. On a clear day, the views might just stretch to the English border and the Atlantic Ocean; more realistically, the landmarks which dominate are Fife, a few Highland peaks and, of course, Edinburgh laid out on all sides.

Queen's Drive continues round beneath the summit to meet itself again at a roundabout near the southern point of the Salisbury Crags. At a second roundabout the first exit leads out of the park past **Duddingston Loch**, a bird sanctuary (free access) with swans, herons and grebes often seen around its reedy fringes. Perched above the loch, just outside the park boundary, Duddingston Kirk dates back in part to the twelfth century and lies at the heart of **Duddingston Village**, an unspoilt corner of the city with cobbled lanes, cute cottages and, inevitably, high price tags. The *Sheep Heid Inn* here (see p.115) is one of Edinburgh's oldest pubs and a great waypoint if you're exploring the park; out at the back of the pub there's a traditional skittle alley, still very much in working order.

Cowgate and the Grassmarket

At the bottom of the valley immediately south of the Royal Mile, and following a roughly parallel course from the Lawnmarket to St Mary's Street, the **Cowgate** is one of Edinburgh's oldest surviving streets. It was also once one of the city's most prestigious addresses, but the construction of the great **viaducts** of George IV Bridge and South Bridge entombed it below street level, condemning it to decay and neglect and leading the nineteenth-century writer, Alexander Smith, to declare: "the condition of the inhabitants is as little known to respectable Edinburgh as are the habits of moles, earthworms, and the mining population." Various nightclubs and Festival venues have established themselves – on Friday and Saturday nights the street heaves with revellers – but it remains a slightly unsalubrious spot and the contrast with the nearby Royal Mile remains stark.

The Grassmarket

At the western end of the Cowgate is an open, partly cobbled area girdled by tall tenements known as the **Grassmarket**, which was used as the city's cattle market from 1477 to 1911. Despite the height of many of the surrounding buildings, it offers an unexpected view up to the precipitous walls of the Castle and, come springtime, it's sunny enough for cafés to put tables and chairs along the pavement. Such Continental aspirations are a bit of a diversion, however, as the Grassmarket is best remembered as the location of Edinburgh's public gallows – the spot is marked by a tiny garden. The notorious serial killers William Burke and William Hare had their lair in a now-vanished close just off the western end of the Grassmarket, and for a long time before its relatively recent gentrification there was a seamy edge to the place, with brothels, drinking dens and shelters for down-and-outs. Tucked away in the northwest corner is the award-winning modern architecture of **Dance Base** (Ⓣ0131/225 5525, Ⓦwww.dancebase.co.uk), Scotland's National Centre for Dance, which holds classes, workshops and shows.

The Grassmarket's two-sided character is still on view with stag and hen parties carousing between the area's pubs, while by day you can admire the architectural quirks and a series of interesting shops, in particular the string of offbeat, independent boutiques on curving **Victoria Street**, an unusual two-tier thoroughfare, with arcaded shops below and a pedestrian terrace above. It sweeps up to George IV Bridge and the **National Library of Scotland**, a looming, windowless facade adorned with allegorical figures by Scottish sculptor Hew Lorimer. This is Scotland's largest library and one of the UK's copyright libraries (it holds a copy of every book published in the country), and you have to apply for a reader's ticket to gain access to the collection. However, there is an interesting and well-researched small exhibition on the subject of books, printing and the written word mounted in a side gallery on the ground floor (usually Mon–Fri 10am–8pm, Sat 10am–5pm, Sun 2–5pm; free; Ⓦwww.nls.uk).

Greyfriars and around

The small statue of **Greyfriars Bobby** at the junction of George IV Bridge and Candlemaker Row must rank as one of Edinburgh's more mawkish tourist attractions. Bobby was a Skye terrier acquired as a working dog by a police constable named John Gray. When Gray died in 1858, Bobby was found a few days later sitting on his grave, a vigil he maintained until his death fourteen years later. In the process, he became an Edinburgh celebrity, fed and cared for by locals who gave him a special collar to prevent him being impounded as a stray. The statue was modelled from life and erected soon after his death. Bobby's legendary dedication easily lent itself to children's books and was eventually picked up by Disney, whose 1960 feature film hammed up the story and ensured that streams of tourists have paid their respects ever since.

The grave Bobby mourned over is in the **Greyfriars Kirkyard**, which has a fine collection of seventeenth-century gravestones and mausoleums, including one to the Adam family of architects. The kirkyard is visited regularly by ghost tours (see p.67) and was known for grave-robbing as freshly interred bodies were exhumed and sold to the nearby medical school (a crime taken to a higher level by the notorious Burke and Hare, who bypassed the graveyards by simply murdering the victims they'd then sell on for dissection). More significantly, the kirkyard was the setting, in 1638, for the signing of the **National Covenant**, a dramatic act of defiance by the Presbyterian Scots against the attempts of Charles I to impose an episcopal form of worship on the country. In an undemocratic age, thousands of townsfolk as well as important nobles signed the original at Greyfriars; copies were then made and sent around the country with some 300,000 names being added.

Greyfriars Kirk itself was built in 1620 on land that had belonged to a Franciscan convent, though little of the original late Gothic-style building remains. A fire in the mid-nineteenth century led to significant rebuilding and the installation of the first organ in a Presbyterian church in Scotland; today's magnificent instrument, by Peter Collins, arrived in 1990.

At the western end of Greyfriars Kirkyard is one of the most significant surviving portions of the **Flodden Wall**, the city fortifications erected in the wake of Scotland's disastrous military defeat of 1513. When open, the gateway beyond offers a short cut to **George Heriot's Hospital**, otherwise approached from Lauriston Place to the south. The impressive four-turreted building, often mistaken for Holyrood Palace, is now one of Edinburgh's most prestigious fee-paying schools. While you can't go inside, it's possible to enter the grounds during school holidays and take a stroll around the outside of the building and the interior quadrangle to admire the architectural finery from up close.

National Museum of Scotland

Immediately opposite Greyfriars Bobby, on the south side of Chambers Street, stands the striking honey-coloured sandstone **Museum of Scotland** (Mon–Sun 10am–5pm; free; Ⓦwww.nms.ac.uk). Custom-built in the 1990s, its modern lines and imaginatively designed interior offer a fresh – but still respectful – perspective on the nation's story and its most important historic artefacts. It stands alongside the older **Royal Museum of Scotland** (for more on which, see p.95), although the two are interlinked. The cylindrical entrance tower of the National Museum, with its echoes of Edinburgh Castle, has a doorway at its base which leads to the soaring central lobby, **Hawthornden Court**; from here, you can join one of the free guided tours on different themes that depart throughout the day, or pick up an audio headset (also free) which provides detailed information on the displays. The collection tells the nation's history from earliest man to the present day and is laid out in broadly chronological order over seven different levels. The labyrinthine feel of the rooms and stairways is a little disorienting at first – the unexpected views of different parts of the museum above and below are a deliberate effect by the architect to emphasize the interconnectedness of the layers of Scotland's history.

Early Scotland

To get to the first section, **Beginnings**, take the lift or stairs from Hawthornden Court down to Level 0. Here, Scotland's story before the arrival of man is presented with audiovisual displays, artistic recreations and a selection of rocks and fossils, including some Lewisian gneiss, the oldest rock in Europe, and "Lizzie" (*Westlothiana lizziae*), the oldest known fossil reptile in the world.

The second section, **Early People**, also on Level 0, covers the period from the arrival of the first people to the end of the first millennium AD. This is the most engrossing section of the entire museum, an eloquent testament to the remarkable craftsmanship, artistry and practicality of Scotland's early people. The best way to approach this section is from the doors of the main lift, where you are confronted by eight giant bronze figures in the distinctive post-industrial style of Edinburgh-born sculptor **Sir Eduardo Paolozzi**. His trademark incorporation of geometric shapes into the human form allows the figures to "wear" different artefacts such as prehistoric bracelets and necklaces in small display compartments. The innovative use of contemporary art is continued with installations by the environmental artist **Andy Goldsworthy**, who shapes natural materials into sinuously beautiful geometrical patterns. Look out for *Hearth*, created from pieces of wood found on the construction site of the new museum, and *Enclosure*, four curved walls of slate roof tiles and four panels of cracked clay. Among the artefacts on display, highlights are the **Trappain treasure** hoard, 20kg of silver plates, cutlery and goblets found buried in East Lothian; the **Cramond Lioness**, a sculpture from a Roman tombstone found recently in the Firth of Forth; and the beautifully detailed gold, silver and amber **Hunterston brooch**, dating from around 700 AD.

Medieval Scotland

The **Kingdom of the Scots** on Levels 1 and 2 covers the period between Scotland's development as a single independent nation and the Union with England in 1707. Among the figures represented here are Robert the Bruce, Mary, Queen of Scots and her son James VI, under whom the crowns of Scotland and England became united in 1603. Star exhibits include the **Monymusk reliquary**, an intricately decorated box said to have carried the remains of St Columba, the **Lewis chessmen**, exquisitely idiosyncratic twelfth-century pieces carved from walrus ivory, and the "**Maiden**", an early form of the guillotine.

Level 3 shows exhibits under the theme **Scotland Transformed**, covering the century or so following the Union of Parliaments in 1707. This was the period that saw the last of the Highland uprisings under Bonnie Prince Charlie (whose silver travelling canteen is on display), yet also witnessed the expansion of trade links with the Americas and developments in industries such as weaving and iron and steel production. Dominating the floor is a reconstructed steam-driven **Newcomen engine**, which was still being used to pump water from a coal mine in Ayrshire in 1901. Alongside it, in contrast, is part of a thatched, cruck-frame 1720s house, of a type in which many Scots still lived during this time.

Scotland in modern times

Following the early innovations of steam and mechanical engineering, Scotland went on to pioneer many aspects of heavy engineering, with ship and locomotive production to the fore. The largest of the exhibits in **Industry and Empire** on Level 4 is the steam locomotive *Ellesmere*, which highlights the fact that in the nineteenth century Scotland was building more railway engines than anywhere else in the world. As well as industrial progress, other fields are covered too, including domestic life, leisure activities and the influence of Scots around the world, both as a result of emigration and through such luminaries as James Watt, Charles Rennie Mackintosh and Robert Louis Stevenson.

Up on Level 6, **Scotland: A Changing Nation** traces the different experiences of people living and working in twentieth- and twenty-first-century Scotland, through the five themes of war, industry, daily life, emigration and politics. Film, objects and personal stories combine to offer a picture of Scotland's recent social history, with poetry, literature, film, music and interactive activities all featured. See memorabilia too from Scotland's sporting heroes, as well as iconic objects from everyone from J.K. Rowling and Ewan McGregor to Franz Ferdinand. Visitors can also watch a short preview of the gallery's feature film *One Nation, Five Million Voices*, which takes a look at Scottish life and national identity.

Above this is a small **roof garden**, accessed by a lift. Up here, sweeping views open out to the Firth of Forth, the Pentland hills and across to the Castle and Royal Mile skyline. Other fine views can be enjoyed from the museum's stylish *Tower* restaurant.

Royal Museum of Scotland

Next door to the National Museum is the much older **Royal Museum of Scotland** (daily 10am–5pm; free; ⓦwww.nms.ac.uk), a dignified Venetian-style palace with a cast-iron interior modelled on that of the former Crystal Palace in London. A wonderful example of Victorian Britain's fascination with antiquities and natural history, it has been undergoing a comprehensive refurbishment, due to be unveiled sometime in 2011. Whereas the National Museum focuses on Scottish history, the Royal Museum offers a more global perspective. Stuffed animals and dinosaur reconstructions from the natural history collections tend to be the big draw for families, while artefacts from Samurai armour to an ancient Egyptian coffin are part of an eclectic educational treasure trove of cultural objects.

The University of Edinburgh and around

Immediately alongside the Royal Museum is the earliest surviving part of the **University of Edinburgh**, variously referred to as Old College or Old Quad, although nowadays it houses only a few university departments; the main campus colonizes the streets and squares to the south. Founded as the "Tounis College" in 1583 by James VI (later James I of England), the university is now the largest in Scotland, with nearly 20,000 students.

The **Old College** was designed by Robert Adam, but was built after his death in a considerably modified form by William Playfair (1789–1857), one of Edinburgh's greatest architects. Playfair built just one of Adam's two quadrangles (the dome, topped by a golden "Youth", was not added until 1879) and his magnificent Neoclassical Upper Library is now mostly used for ceremonial occasions. The small **Talbot Rice Art Gallery** (Tues–Sat 10am–5pm, also Sun 2pm–5pm in Aug; free; ⓦwww.trg.ed.ac.uk), housed in the southwest corner of the Old College, displays in rather lacklustre fashion part of the University's large art and bronze collection, including a number of twentieth-century works by Scots Joan Eardley and William McTaggart. The best part of the gallery, worth navigating the complex entrance route to find, is the set of rooms given to touring and temporary avant-garde exhibitions which are mounted here on a regular basis – the show held during the Festival is normally of a high standard.

A little further up Nicolson Street, the southern extension of South Bridge, is the glass-fronted **Festival Theatre** (see p.117), a refurbished music hall that opened in 1994, giving the city a long-awaited venue for presenting opera and dance on a large scale. Opposite this stands the stately facade of the **Surgeons' Hall**, a handsome Ionic temple built by Playfair as the headquarters of the Royal College of Surgeons. Inside is one of the city's most unusual and morbidly compelling museums, Surgeons' Hall Museum (Mon–Fri 10am–4pm, also Sat & Sun noon–4pm in Aug; £5; ⓦwww.rcsed.ac.uk). In the eighteenth and nineteenth century Edinburgh developed as a leading centre for medical and anatomical research, nurturing world-famous pioneers such as James Young Simpson, founder of anaesthesia, and Joseph Lister, the father of modern surgery. The history of surgery takes up one part of the museum, with intriguing exhibits ranging from early surgical tools to a pocketbook covered with the leathered skin of serial killer William Burke (see p.92). Another room has an array of gruesome instruments illustrating the history of dentistry, while nearby is a small display dedicated to a past president of the college, Joseph Bell, whose diagnostic prowess was infamously immortalized by one of his students, Arthur Conan Doyle. The third and most remarkable part of the museum, the elegant **Playfair Hall**, contains an array of specimens and jars from the college's anatomical and pathological collections dating back to the eighteenth century.

The New Town

The **NEW TOWN**, itself well over two hundred years old, stands in total contrast to the Old Town: the layout is symmetrical, the streets are broad and straight, and most of the buildings are Neoclassical. Originally intended to be residential, the entire area, right down to the names of its streets, is something of a celebration of the Union, which was then generally regarded as a proud development in Scotland's history. Today, the New Town's main streets form the bustling hub of the city's commercial, retail and business life, dominated by shops, banks and offices.

The existence of the New Town is chiefly due to the vision of **George Drummond**, who made schemes for the expansion of the city soon after becoming Lord Provost in 1725. Work began on the draining of the Nor' Loch below the Castle in 1759, a task that was to last some sixty years. The North Bridge, linking the Old Town with the main road leading to the port of Leith, was built between 1763 and 1772 and, in 1766, following a public competition, a plan for the New Town by 22-year-old architect **James Craig** was chosen. Its gridiron pattern was perfectly matched to the site: central **George Street**, flanked by showpiece squares, was laid out along the main ridge, with parallel **Princes Street** and **Queen Street** on either side below, and two smaller streets, Thistle Street and Rose Street, in between the three major thoroughfares providing coach houses, artisans' dwellings and shops. Princes and Queen streets were built up on one side only, so as not to block the spectacular views of the Old Town and Fife respectively. Architects were accordingly afforded a wonderful opportunity to play with vistas and spatial relationships, particularly well exploited by Robert Adam, who contributed extensively to the later phases of the work. The First New Town, as the area covered by Craig's plan came to be known, received a whole series of extensions in the early decades of the nineteenth century, all carefully in harmony with the Neoclassical idiom.

In many ways, the layout of the greater New Town is its own most remarkable sight, an extraordinary grouping of squares, circuses, terraces, crescents and parks with a few set pieces such as **Register House**, the north frontage of **Charlotte Square** and the assemblage of curiosities on and around **Calton Hill**. However, it also contains assorted Victorian additions, notably the **Scott Monument** on Princes Street, the **Royal Botanic Garden** on its northern fringe, as well as two of the city's most important public collections – the **National Gallery of Scotland** and, further afield, the **Scottish National Gallery of Modern Art**.

Princes Street

Although only allocated a subsidiary role in the original plan of the New Town, **Princes Street** had developed into Edinburgh's principal thoroughfare by the middle of the nineteenth century, a role it has retained ever since. Its unobstructed views across to the Castle and the Old Town are undeniably magnificent. Indeed, without the views, Princes Street would lose much of its appeal; its northern side, dominated by large outlets of the familiar national chains, is almost always crowded with shoppers, and few of the original eighteenth-century buildings remain.

The East End

With its dignified Corinthian pillars and dome, **General Register House** (Mon–Fri 9am–4.30pm; free; Ⓦwww.nas.gov.uk) is the most distinguished building on Princes Street. It's best seen on the approach from North Bridge – the same perspective is hard to achieve close up, which is why it's routinely ignored by the streams of shoppers squeezing past. Unfortunately, the majesty of the setting is marred by the **St James Centre** to the rear, a covered shopping arcade now regarded as the city's worst-ever planning blunder. Register House was designed in 1774 by Robert Adam as a custom-built home for Scotland's national archives, a function it has maintained ever since. Today it's home to the **ScotlandsPeople Centre**, a dedicated family history unit which acts as a single point of access for those researching genealogical records. Free two-hour taster sessions on how to access the digitized records are available at 10am and 2pm each weekday; if you want to delve deeper into family history, there's a search fee of £10 for a full or part-day's access. Apart from the fascinating history that can be uncovered, part of the appeal of embarking on some research is the opportunity to spend time in the elegant interior of Register House, centred on a glorious Roman rotunda, lavishly decorated with plasterwork and antique-style medallions. The adjacent **New Register House** is home to the General Register Office for Scotland (Ⓦwww.gro-scotland.gov.uk) and contains records of births, deaths and marriages.

Princes Street Gardens

It's hard to imagine that the **gardens** (dawn to dusk; free) which flank nearly the entire length of Princes Street were once the stagnant, foul-smelling Nor' Loch, into which the effluent of the Old Town flowed for centuries. The railway has since replaced the water and today a sunken cutting carries the main lines out of Waverley Station to the west and north. The gardens, split into East and West sections, were originally the private domain of Princes Street residents and their well-placed acquaintances, only becoming a public park in 1876. These days, the swathes of green lawn, colourful flower beds and mature trees are a green lung for the city centre: on sunny days local office workers appear in their droves at lunchtime, while in the run-up to Christmas the gardens' eastern section is home to an ice rink (late Nov to early Jan Mon–Wed & Sun 10am–8pm, Thurs–Sat 10am–10pm; £8–9.50) and a towering ferris wheel (same period, daily 10am–10pm; £4–5). The larger and more verdant western section has a floral clock and the Ross Bandstand, a popular Festival venue.

The Scott Monument

Facing the Victorian shopping emporium Jenners, and set within East Princes Street Gardens, the 200ft-high **Scott Monument** (April–Sept daily 10am–7pm; Oct–March Mon–Sat 9am–4pm, Sun 10am–4pm; £3) was erected in memory of prolific author and patriot Sir Walter Scott within a few years of his death. The largest monument in the world to a man of letters, the elaborate Gothic spire was created by George Meikle Kemp, a carpenter and joiner whose only building this is; while it was still under construction, he stumbled into a canal one foggy evening and drowned. The architecture is closely modelled on Scott's beloved Melrose Abbey (see p.148), and the rich sculptural decoration shows sixteen Scottish writers and sixty-four characters from Scott's famous *Waverley* novels. On the central plinth at the base of the monument is a **statue** of Scott with his deerhound Maida, carved from a thirty-ton block of Carrara marble.

Inside the recently restored memorial, a tightly winding spiral staircase climbs 287 steps to a narrow platform near the top: from here, you can enjoy some inspiring – if vertiginous – vistas of the city below and hills and firths beyond.

The National Gallery of Scotland

Princes Street Gardens are bisected by the **Mound**, one of only two direct road links between the Old and New Towns (the other is North Bridge). Its name is an accurate description: it was formed in the 1780s by dumping piles of earth and

> The National Gallery of Scotland is just one part of the national art collection housed around Edinburgh. Other works of the **National Galleries' collection** are on display at the Scottish National Portrait Gallery (closed at time of going to press but due to re-open in autumn 2011; see p.101), the Scottish National Gallery of Modern Art (p.104) and its neighbour, the Dean Gallery (p.105). A free bus service (daily: 10.45am–5pm; every 45min) connects all four buildings.

other waste brought from the New Town's building plots. At the foot of the mound on the Princes Street level are two grand Neoclassical buildings, the **National Gallery of Scotland** (daily: 10am–5pm, until 7pm Thurs; free, entrance charge for some temporary exhibitions; Ⓦ www.natgalscot.ac.uk) and the **Royal Scottish Academy** (same hours). Both were designed by William Henry Playfair (1790–1857), though the exterior of the National Gallery is considerably more austere than its bold Athenian counterpart.

Both buildings have their own entrance facing Princes Street, but the main entry point to the complex as a whole is through the much newer **Weston Link**, located beneath the galleries looking out into East Princes Street Gardens. Built in tandem with a multi-million pound refurbishment of the Royal Scottish Academy (which mostly holds temporary exhibitions), the entry point from Princes Street Gardens East is perhaps not as discreet as originally intended (its facade is couched in pompously large Clasach stone slabs), but the basement extension offers improved access to both institutions as well as a lecture theatre, shop and café-restaurant (*The Scottish Restaurant and Café*, see p.107).

Built as a "temple to the fine arts" in 1850, the National Gallery houses Scotland's premier collection of pre-twentieth-century European art, including a clutch of exquisite Old Masters and some superb Impressionist works. Though by no means as vast as national collections found elsewhere in Europe, the gallery benefits greatly from being a manageable size, its series of elegant octagonal rooms enlivened by imaginative displays and a pleasantly unrushed atmosphere.

On the ground floor the rooms have been restored to their 1850s appearance with pictures hung closely together on claret-coloured walls, often on two levels, and intermingled with sculptures and objets d'art to produce a deliberately cluttered effect. As a result some lesser works, which would otherwise languish in the vaults, are on display, a good 15ft up. Though individual works are frequently moved, the layout is broadly chronological, starting in the upper rooms above the gallery's entrance on the Mound and continuing clockwise around the ground floor.

The gallery's programme of small temporary exhibitions means that not all of the paintings mentioned are always on display. In addition, some of the art pieces tour, or are on loan, while others may be put on rotation to make room for other works.

Early works

Among the Gallery's most valuable treasures are **Hugo van der Goes**' *Trinity Panels*, on a long-term loan from the Queen. Painted in the mid-fifteenth century, they were commissioned by Provost Edward Bonkil for the Holy Trinity Collegiate Church, which was later demolished to make way for Edinburgh's Waverley Station. Bonkil can be seen amidst the company of organ-playing angels in the finest and best preserved of the four panels, while on the reverse sides are portraits of James III, his son (the future James IV) and Queen Margaret of Denmark. The panels are turned by the gallery every half-hour. One of the gallery's more recent additions is a superb painting by **Botticelli**, *The Virgin*

Adoring the Sleeping Christ Child which, along with **Raphael**'s graceful tondo *The Holy Family with a Palm Tree*, has undergone careful restoration to reveal a striking luminosity and depth of colour.

Of the four mythological scenes by **Titian**, the sensuous *Three Ages of Man* is one of his most accomplished early compositions, while *Diana and Acteon* and its pendant *Diana and Calisto*, painted for Philip II of Spain, illustrate the highly impressionistic freedom of his late style. Alongside the Titians, **Bassano**'s truly regal *Adoration of the Kings* and a dramatic altarpiece, *The Deposition of Christ*, by **Tintoretto,** as well as several other works by **Veronese**, complete the fine Venetian section.

European highlights

Poussin's *Seven Sacraments* are proudly displayed in their own room, the floor and central octagonal bench of which repeat some of the works' motifs. The series marks the first attempt to portray scenes from the life of Jesus realistically, rather than through images dictated by artistic conventions. The result is profoundly touching, with numerous imaginative and subtle details. **Rubens**' *The Feast of Herod*, recently enlivened by meticulous restoration, is an archetypal example of his sumptuously grand manner, its gory subject matter overshadowed by the gaudy depiction of the delights of the table. It was executed with extensive studio assistance, like all his large works, whereas the three small *modellos* are all from his own hand. Among the four canvases by **Rembrandt** are a poignant *Self-Portrait Aged 51* and the ripely suggestive *Woman in Bed*, which is thought to represent the biblical figure of Sarah on her wedding night, waiting for her husband Tobias to put the devil to flight. *Christ in the House of Martha and Mary* is the largest and probably the earliest of the thirty or so surviving paintings by **Vermeer**.

Contemporary art in Edinburgh

In addition to the contemporary art collections in the city's National Galleries there are a number of smaller independent galleries around the city.

The Collective Gallery 22–28 Cockburn St ⓣ0131/220 1260, ⓦwww.collectivegallery.net. Tends to focus on young local artists, and doesn't flinch from showing experimental modern work.

Edinburgh Printmakers 23 Union St ⓣ0131/557 2479, ⓦwww.edinburgh-printmakers.co.uk. A highly respected studio and gallery dedicated to contemporary printmaking.

Fruitmarket Gallery 45 Market St ⓣ0131/225 2383, ⓦwww.fruitmarket.co.uk. The stylish modern design of this dynamic and much-admired art space is the capital's first port of call for top-grade international artists – recent years have seen shows by the likes of Jeff Koons and Bill Viola.

Ingleby Gallery 15 Carlton Rd ⓣ0131/556 4441, ⓦwww.inglebygallery.com. Ingleby's reputation for ambitious projects and innovative artists makes it one of Scotland's foremost small private art galleries. Features changing exhibitions by international contemporary artists including many of Scotland's premier stars such as Alison Watt, Kenny Hunter and Callum Innes.

Open Eye Gallery 34 Abercromby Place ⓣ0131/557 1020, ⓦwww.openeyegallery.co.uk. One of the city's best commercial galleries, regularly featuring shows by Scotland's top contemporary artists.

Scottish Gallery 16 Dundas St ⓣ0131/558 1200, ⓦwww.scottish-gallery.co.uk. The longest established of a number of small galleries on this New Town street; often some of the most striking works here are in the basement area dedicated to applied art.

One of the gallery's most recent major purchases is **Canova**'s 1817 statue *The Three Graces* – saved at the last minute from the hands of the J. Paul Getty Museum in California. There's also a superb group of early Impressionist works including **Camille Pissarro**'s *Kitchen Garden L'Hermitage*. Other Impressionist masters have a strong showing, including a collection of **Degas**' sketches, paintings and bronzes, **Monet**'s *Haystacks (Snow)* and **Renoir**'s *Woman Nursing Child*. Representing the Post-Impressionists are three exceptional examples of **Gauguin**'s work, including *Vision After the Sermon*, set in Brittany; **Van Gogh**'s *Olive Trees*, and **Cézanne**'s *The Big Trees* – a clear forerunner of modern abstraction.

Scottish and English works

On the face of it, the gallery's Scottish collection, ambitiously covering the entire gamut from seventeenth-century portraiture to the Arts and Crafts movement, is a bit of an anticlimax. Most works are hung in the rather drab basement, where space and access are cramped. There are, however, a few significant works displayed within a broad European context. Both **Gavin Hamilton**'s *Achilles Mourning the Death of Patroclus*, painted in Rome, and Arts and Crafts painter **Robert Burns**' *Diana and her Nymphs* are finer examples of arresting Scottish art.

Of Sir **Henry Raeburn**'s large portraits, the swaggering masculinity of *Sir John Sinclair in Highland Dress* shows the artist's technical mastery, though he was equally confident when working on a smaller scale, as evidenced by one of the gallery's most popular pictures, *The Rev Robert Walker Skating on Duddingston Loch*. The gallery also owns a brilliant array of watercolours by **Turner**, faithfully displayed each January when damaging sunlight is at its weakest, though visitors at other times of the year can enjoy two of his fine Roman views displayed in one of the darker galleries.

George Street

To the north, running parallel to Princes Street, **George Street** is rapidly changing its role from a thoroughfare of august financial institutions to a highbrow version of Princes Street, where the big deals are done in designer-label shops. George Street was designed to be the centrepiece of the First New Town, joining two grand squares. At its eastern end lies the smartly landscaped **St Andrew Square**, centring around the Melville Monument, a towering column topped by a statue of Lord Melville, Pitt the Younger's Navy Treasurer. Around the edge of the square you'll find Edinburgh's bus station, the city's swankiest shopping arcade, Multrees Walk, and a handsome eighteenth-century town mansion, designed by Sir William Chambers. Still the ceremonial headquarters of the Royal Bank of Scotland, the palatial mid-nineteenth-century banking hall is a symbol of the success of the New Town.

Charlotte Square

At the western end of George Street is **Charlotte Square**, designed by Robert Adam in 1791, a year before his death. For the most part, his plans were faithfully implemented, an exception being the domed and porticoed church of St George, simplified on grounds of expense. Its interior was gutted in the 1960s and refurbished as **West Register House**; like its counterpart at the far end of Princes Street, it holds various historic records and features changing documentary exhibitions (Mon–Fri 9am–4.30pm; free; Ⓦ www.nas.gov.uk). Generally regarded as the epitome of the New Town's elegant simplicity, the square was once the most exclusive residential address in Edinburgh, and though much of it is now occupied by offices, the imperious dignity of the architecture is still clear to see. Indeed, the north side, the finest of Adam's drawings, is once again the city's premier address, with the official residence of the First Minister of the Scottish Government at number 6 (Bute House), the Edinburgh equivalent of 10 Downing Street. In August each year the gardens in the centre of the square are colonized by the temporary tents of the Edinburgh Book Festival (see p.121).

Restored by the National Trust for Scotland, the lower floors of neighbouring no. 7 are open to the public under the name of the **Georgian House** (daily: March 11am–4pm; April–June; Sept & Oct 10am–5pm; July & Aug 10am–6pm; Nov 11am–3pm; NTS; £5.50), the interior of which provides a revealing sense of well-to-do New Town living in the early nineteenth century. Though a little stuffy and lifeless, the rooms are impressively decked out in period furniture – look for the working barrel organ which plays a selection of Scottish airs – and hung with fine paintings, including portraits by Ramsay and Raeburn, seventeenth-century Dutch cabinet pictures and the beautiful *Marriage of the Virgin* by El Greco's teacher, the Italian miniaturist Giulio Clovio. In the basement are the original wine cellar, lined with roughly made bins, and a kitchen complete with an open fire for roasting and a separate oven for baking; video reconstructions of life below and above stairs are shown in a nearby room.

Queen Street

Queen Street, the last of the three main streets of the First New Town, is bordered to the north by gardens, and commands sweeping views across to Fife. The best preserved of the area's three main streets, it's occupied mostly by offices and has few individual attractions, with the exception of the **Scottish National Portrait Gallery** at its eastern end, just to the north of St Andrew Square. A fantastic medieval Gothic palace in red sandstone that makes an extravagant contrast to the New Town's prevailing Neoclassicism, the exterior of the building is encrusted with statues of national heroes, a theme reiterated in the stunning two-storey entrance hall by William Hole's tapestry-like frieze. The gallery was undergoing a major internal redevelopment at time of going to press, but is due to reopen in autumn 2011 with expanded exhibition space and brand-new facilities. Details on opening times and planned exhibitions are available at Ⓦ www.nationalgalleries.org.

Calton Hill

Edinburgh's longstanding tag as the "Athens of the North" is nowhere better earned than on **Calton Hill**, the volcanic crag which rises up above the eastern end of Princes Street. Numerous architects homed in on it as a showcase for their most ambitious and grandiose buildings and monuments, the presence of which emphasizes Calton's aloof air and sense of detachment. But the hill and its odd collection of edifices aren't just for looking *at*: this is also one of the best viewpoints from which to appreciate the city as a whole, with its tightly knitted suburbs, landmark Old and New Town buildings and the sea beyond – much closer to Edinburgh than many visitors expect.

Waterloo Place forms a ceremonial way from Princes Street to Calton Hill. On its southern side is **Old Calton Burial Ground**, tucked in behind a line of high, dark, forbidding walls. The picturesque assembly of mausoleums and gravestones within, some at a jaunty angle and others weathered with age, make for an absorbing wander. Notable among the monuments are the cylindrical memorial by Robert Adam to the philosopher David Hume, one of Edinburgh's greatest sons, and a piercing obelisk commemorating various political martyrs. Many visitors arriving at Waverley Station below imagine the picturesque castellated building hard up against the cemetery's eastern wall to be Edinburgh

Castle itself. In fact, it's the only surviving part of the **Calton Gaol**, once Edinburgh's main prison, most of which was demolished in the 1930s to make way for the looming Art Deco **St Andrew's House**, which is today occupied by civil servants.

Further on, set majestically on the slopes of Calton Hill looking towards Arthur's Seat, sits one of Edinburgh's greatest buildings, the **Old Royal High School**. With its bold central portico of Doric columns and graceful symmetrical colonnaded wings, Thomas Hamilton's elegant building of 1829 is regarded by many as the epitome of Edinburgh's Athenian aspirations. The capital's high school was based here between 1829 and 1968, at which point the building was converted to house a debating chamber and became Scotland's parliament-in-waiting. However, soon after the re-establishment of a Scottish parliament had been confirmed in 1997 the building was controversially rejected as too small for the intended assembly, with a brand-new building at Holyrood favoured instead. Currently used as offices by the city council, the latest plan is to convert it into a hotel. Across the road, Hamilton also built the **Burns Monument**, a circular Corinthian temple modelled on the Monument to Lysicrates in Athens, as a memorial to the national bard.

Robert Louis Stevenson reckoned that Calton Hill was the best place to view Edinburgh, "since you can see the Castle, which you lose from the Castle, and Arthur's Seat, which you cannot see from Arthur's Seat". Though the panoramas from ground level are spectacular enough, those from the top of the **Nelson Monument** (April–Sept Mon 1–6pm, Tues–Sat 10am–6pm; Oct–March Mon–Sat 10am–3pm; £3), perched near the summit of Calton Hill, are even better. Each day at 1pm, a white ball drops down a mast at the top of the monument; this, together with the one o'clock gun fired from the Castle battlements (see p.78), once provided a daily check for the mariners of Leith, who needed accurate chronometers to ensure reliable navigation at sea.

Alongside, the **National Monument** is often referred to as "Edinburgh's Disgrace", yet many locals admire this unfinished and somewhat ungainly attempt to replicate the Parthenon atop Calton Hill. Begun as a memorial to the dead of the Napoleonic Wars, the project's shortage of funds led architect William Playfair to ensure that even with just twelve of the massive columns completed, the folly would still serve as a striking landmark. It's one of those constructions which is purposeless yet still magnetic; with a bit of effort and care you can climb up and around the monument, sit and contemplate from one of the huge steps or meander around the base of the mighty pillars. New schemes for the development of the National Monument and its Calton Hill neighbours, either grandiose, foolish or both, are regularly proposed.

Designed by Playfair in 1818, the **City Observatory** is the largest of the buildings at the summit of Calton Hill. Because of pollution and the advent of street lighting, which impaired views of the stars, the observatory proper had to be relocated to Blackford Hill before the end of the nineteenth century, but the equipment here continues to be used by students. At the corner of the curtain walls is the castellated Observatory House, one of the few surviving buildings by James Craig, designer of the New Town. There are plans to turn the complex into an art gallery, but for now a stroll around its perimeter offers a broad perspective over the city, with views out to the Forth bridges and Fife.

The Northern New Town

The **Northern New Town** was the earliest extension to the First New Town, begun in 1801, and today covers roughly the area north of Queen Street between

India Street to the west and Broughton Street to the east, and as far as Fettes Row to the north. This has survived in far better shape than its predecessor: with the exception of one street, almost all of it is intact, and it has managed to preserve a predominantly residential character.

One of the area's most intriguing buildings is the neo-Norman **Mansfield Place Church**, on the corner of Broughton and East London streets, designed in the late nineteenth century for the strange, now defunct Catholic Apostolic sect. The church contains a cycle of **murals** by the Dublin-born **Phoebe Anna Traquair**, a leading light in the Scottish Arts and Crafts movement. Covering vast areas of the walls and ceilings of the main nave and side chapels, the wonderfully luminous paintings depict biblical parables and texts, with rows of angels, cherubs flecked with gold and worshipping figures painted in delicate pastel colours. The dilapidation of the church in the early 1990s prompted a campaign to save and protect the murals, which are now recognized as the city's finest *in situ* art treasure. The building now houses offices for Scottish voluntary groups and viewing of the murals is restricted to one Sunday afternoon each month, although more regular opening is normally arranged during the Festival. For more details see Ⓦwww.mansfieldtraquair.org.uk.

The Royal Botanic Garden

Just beyond the northern boundaries of the New Town is the seventy-acre site of the **Royal Botanic Garden** (daily: March & Oct 10am–6pm; April–Sept 10am–7pm; Nov–Feb 10am–4pm; free; Ⓦwww.rbge.org.uk). Filled with mature trees and a huge variety of native and exotic plants and flowers, the "botanics" (as they're commonly called) are most popular simply as a place to stroll and lounge around on the grass. The main entrance is the West Gate on Arboretum Place, through the contemporary, eco-designed John Hope Gateway, where you'll find interpretation areas, information, exhibitions, a shop and restaurant. Towards the eastern side of the gardens, a series of ten glasshouses (entry £4), including a soaring 1850s Palm House, shows off a steamy array of palms, ferns, orchids, cycads and aquatic plants, including some huge circular water lilies. Elsewhere, different themes are highlighted: the large Chinese-style garden, for example, has a bubbling waterfall and the world's biggest collection of Asian wild plants outside China, while in the northwest corner there's a Scottish native woodland which very effectively evokes the wild unkemptness of parts of the Scottish Highlands and west coast. Art is also a strong theme within the botanics, with a gallery showing changing contemporary exhibitions in the attractive eighteenth-century Inverleith House at the centre of the gardens. Scattered all around are a number of outdoor sculptures, including a giant pine cone by landscape artist Andy Goldsworthy and the striking stainless-steel east gate, designed in the form of stylized rhododendrons. Parts of the garden are also notable for their great vistas: the lawns near Inverleith House offer one of the city's best views of the Castle and Old Town's steeples and monuments. **Guided tours** (£3) leave from the John Hope Gateway at 11am and 2pm (April–Sept).

Stockbridge and Dean Village

Between the New Town and the Botanic Gardens, the busy suburb of **Stockbridge** grew up around the Water of Leith ford (and its seventeenth-century bridge) over which cattle were driven to market in Edinburgh. The hamlet was essentially gobbled up in the expansion of the New Town, but a few charming buildings and an independent character prevail in the district today. The area is a popular quarter for young professionals who can't afford the soaring property prices in the New Town proper, and as a result there's a good crop of bars, boutiques and places to eat along both Raeburn Place, the main road, and St Stephen's Street, long one of Edinburgh's more offbeat side streets.

Less than half a mile from Stockbridge, linked by a riverside path which forms part of the **Water of Leith Walkway** (Ⓦ www.waterofleith.org.uk), is the old milling community of **Dean Village**, one of central Edinburgh's most picturesque yet unexpected corners, its atmosphere of decay arrested by the conversion of numerous granaries and tall mill buildings into designer flats. Nestling close to the river, with steep banks rising up on both sides, the Victorian community has a self-contained air, its surviving features including a school, clock tower and communal drying green. High above Dean Village, **Dean Bridge**, a bravura feat of 1830s engineering by Thomas Telford, carries the main road over 100ft above the river.

The West End

The western extension to the New Town was the last part to be built, deviating from the area's overriding Neoclassicism with a number of Victorian additions, including the city's principal Episcopal church, the huge Early English Gothic-style **St Mary's Cathedral**. With its proximity to the city centre, the West End is now mostly used for offices, with a decent clutch of bars and restaurants, though there is some elegant terraced housing towards its outer edges. Here, enjoying some green space and a dignified setting are two compelling collections of contemporary art, the well-established **Scottish National Gallery of Modern Art** and its neighbour, the **Dean Gallery**, both of which regularly host worthwhile seasonal and touring exhibitions.

The Scottish National Gallery of Modern Art

Set in spacious wooded grounds at the far northwestern fringe of the New Town, about ten minutes' walk from either the cathedral or Dean Village, the **Scottish National Gallery of Modern Art** on Belford Road (daily 10am–5pm, open till 6pm in August; free, entrance charge for some temporary exhibitions; Ⓦ www.natgalscot.ac.uk), was the first collection in Britain devoted solely to twentieth-century painting and sculpture. It operates in tandem with the Dean Gallery, across the road (see opposite); both are located in impressive Neoclassical buildings which have been superbly converted into pleasant, relaxing viewing spaces, and they also have excellent cafés – if it's a sunny day head for the one at the Gallery of Modern Art, which has a pleasant outdoor terrace.

The extensive wooded grounds of the galleries serve as a **sculpture park**, featuring works by Jacob Epstein, Henry Moore, Barbara Hepworth and, most strikingly, Charles Jencks, whose prize-winning *Landform*, a swirling mix of ponds and grassy mounds, dominates the area in front of the Gallery of Modern Art. In contrast, there are few permanent works inside – one exception is Douglas Gordon's *List of Names (Random)*, an examination of "how our heads function", which lists in plain type on a white wall everyone the artist can remember meeting. Otherwise, the display space is divided between temporary exhibitions and selections from the gallery's own holdings; the latter are arranged thematically, but are almost constantly moved around. The collection starts with early twentieth-century Post-Impressionists, then moves through the Fauvists, German Expressionism, Cubism and Pop Art, with works by Lichtenstein and Warhol establishing a connection with the extensive holdings of Eduardo Paolozzi's work in the Dean Gallery. There's a strong section on living **British artists**, from Francis Bacon and Gilbert & George to Britart exponents such as Damien Hirst and Rachel Whiteread, while modern **Scottish** art ranges

Approaches to the Modern Art and Dean galleries

The most pleasant way of getting to the neighbouring Modern Art and Dean galleries is on foot along the **Water of Leith Walkway**, which can be joined at Stockbridge or Dean Village. Alternatively, a **free bus** runs every 45min (Mon–Sun 10.45am–5pm) from outside the National Gallery on the Mound, stopping at the National Portrait Gallery on the way. The only regular **public transport** running along Belford Road is bus #13, which leaves from the western end of George Street. Along the Water of Leith Walkway, look out for *6 Times*, a series of half a dozen life-size, cast-iron figures by sculptor Anthony Gormley, a number of which have been placed in the river itself between the Scottish National Gallery of Modern Art and Leith docks.

from the Colourists – whose works are attracting ever-growing posthumous critical acclaim – to the distinctive styles of contemporary Scots including John Bellany, a portraitist of striking originality, and the poet-artist-gardener Ian Hamilton Finlay. You're also likely to encounter at least one of the fifty different rooms that form part of Anthony D'Offay's permanent gift of *The Artist Rooms* to the National Galleries of Scotland and Tate, with the work of 25 international contemporary artists including Diane Arbus, Andy Warhol and Ron Mueck touring galleries large and small around the country.

The Dean Gallery

Opposite the Modern Art Gallery on the other side of Belford Road, the **Dean Gallery** (same hours; free; ⓦwww.natgalscot.ac.uk) is housed in an equally impressive Neoclassical building completed in 1833. The interior, built as an orphanage and later used as an education centre, has been dramatically refurbished specifically to make room for the work of Edinburgh-born sculptor **Sir Eduardo Paolozzi**, described by some as the father of Pop Art. The collection was partly assembled from a bequest by Gabrielle Keiller, and partly from a gift from the artist himself, who died in 2005, which included some three thousand sculptures, two thousand prints and drawings and three thousand books.

There's an awesome introduction to Paolozzi's work in the form of the huge *Vulcan*, a half-man, half-machine which squeezes into the Great Hall immediately opposite the main entrance – view it both from ground level and the head-height balcony to appreciate the sheer scale of the piece. No less persuasive of Paolozzi's dynamic creative talents are the rooms to the right of the main entrance, where his London studio has been expertly re-created, right down to the clutter of half-finished casts, toys and empty pots of glue. Hidden amongst this chaos is a large part of his bequest, with incomplete models piled four or five deep on the floor and designs stacked randomly on shelves. Elsewhere in the gallery, a selection of his sculptures and drawings are exhibited in a more traditional manner.

The ground floor also holds the Roland Penrose Gallery's world-renowned collection of **Dada** and **Surrealist** art; Penrose was a close friend and patron of many of the movements' leading figures, and Marcel Duchamp, Max Ernst and Man Ray are all represented. Look out also for Dali's *The Signal of Anguish* and Magritte's *Magic Mirror* along with work by Miró and Giacometti – all hung on crowded walls with an assortment of artefacts and ethnic souvenirs gathered by Penrose and his artist companions while travelling. Elsewhere, you'll see 2009 Turner Prize winner Richard Wright's major wall painting *The Stairwell Project*. The rooms upstairs are normally given over to special and touring exhibitions, which usually carry an entrance charge.

Eating

The last decade has seen a marked upsurge in style, sophistication and good taste in Edinburgh's cafés and restaurants. **Café culture** has hit the centre of the city, with tables spilling onto the pavements in the summer, and this has been matched by the rise of a clutch of original, upmarket and stylish **restaurants**, many identifying their cuisine as **contemporary** or **modern Scottish** and championing top-quality local meat, game and fish. With five restaurants holding Michelin stars, Edinburgh can justifiably claim second place behind London in the UK's fine-dining pecking order. Alongside, there's a well-padded mid-market populated by familiar chains and long-established Chinese, Indian and Mexican restaurants, as well as more interesting outposts of Thai, North African and Spanish cuisine.

Generally, small **diners** and **bistros** predominate, many adopting a casual French style and offering good-value set menus. Edinburgh has a number of first-rate **vegetarian** restaurants, including a couple of great Indian vegetarian places, and it's an excellent place if you like **fish and shellfish**, which have long been a speciality of the **Leith** waterfront. If you're looking for **Scottish cooking**, plenty of tourist-oriented places offer up haggis and other classic clichés, mostly with little culinary merit; a better idea is to seek out places taking care over local sourcing and embracing the good quality ingredients available from small and artisan producers around Scotland.

Most of Edinburgh's restaurants serve from noon to 2.30pm and 6pm to 10pm, and many are closed at least one day a week – it's worth checking especially before heading out on a Sunday or Monday. During the **Festival** the majority of restaurants keep longer hours, but they are also much busier. Many **pubs** (see p.113) also serve food, either in the bar itself or an attached restaurant.

Cafés and restaurants are shown on the maps on pp.68–69 and pp.108–109.

Royal Mile and around

Generally, the cafés and restaurants of the **Royal Mile** are less obviously tourist traps than the shops of the ancient thoroughfare, and it doesn't take too much investigative work to track down places of character and imagination tucked away down the lanes and closes of the Old Town, or located in unusual and interesting buildings. In summer, this is the busiest part of town, so it's advisable to book a table for an evening meal.

Cafés

Always Sunday 170 High St ⓣ0131/622 0667. Proof that there's room for a bit of real food even on the tourist-thronged Royal Mile, this pleasantly upbeat independent café serves healthy lunches, home-made cakes, fresh smoothies and Fairtrade coffee. Open daily till 6pm.

The Edinburgh Larder 15 Blackfriars St ⓣ0131/556 6922. Just 20yd off the Royal Mile, but acts like a neighbourhood café, with friendly staff, food that dares to depart from the norm, and almost all ingredients sourced from smaller producers around Edinburgh.

Foodies at Holyrood 67 Holyrood Rd ⓣ0131/557 6836. There's a dearth of decent eating places in the Holyrood quarter, and while cafés within the Parliament and Palace offer convenience, the food here is a step or two above, with freshly made sandwiches, decent veggie options, hand-baked cakes and a pleasant if undistinguished setting.

Fruitmarket Gallery Café 45 Market St ⓣ0131/226 1843. This attractive café feels like an extension of the gallery space, its airy, reflective ambience enhanced by the wall of glass onto the street. Stop in for soups, coffees or a Caesar salad. Mon–Sat 11.30am–4pm, Sun noon–4pm.

Bistros & casual dining

David Bann's Vegetarian Restaurant 56–58 St Mary's St ⓣ0131/556 5888, ⓦwww.davidbann.com. Thoroughly modern vegetarian restaurant, open long hours and offering a wide choice of interesting, unconventional dishes such as artichoke and celeriac tart or chickpea koftas with home-made curd cheese. The prices are very reasonable and the overall design is stylish and classy.

Mother India's Cafe 3–5 Infirmary St ⓣ0131/524 9801, ⓦwww.motherindiascafeedinburgh.co.uk. This Glasgow-based operation has a refreshing approach to Indian food, serving freshly prepared tapas-style dishes that allow you to eat well but also lightly, with fish dishes in particular standing out. Old stone walls and original photos on the walls help maintain an informal but buzzy atmsophere.

Spoon Café Bistro 6a Nicholson St ⓣ0131/557 4567. A lovely, large first-floor room opposite the Festival Theatre, with quirky retro fittings and a reliable menu of well-made rustic dishes with punchy flavours and good ingredients. They also make the best soup in town. Under a different name, this was the café where J.K. Rowling first penned *Harry Potter*.

Fine dining

Amber Scotch Whisky Heritage Centre, 354 Castlehill ⓣ0131/477 8477, ⓦwww.amber-restaurant.co.uk. Neat, contemporary-styled place serving a good choice of light food such as potted shrimp at lunchtime and more substantial and expensive dishes in the evenings, when there's a "whisky sommelier" on hand to suggest the best drams to accompany your honey-roast rack of Highland lamb or wild hare.

The Grain Store 30 Victoria St ⓣ0131/225 7635, ⓦwww.grainstore-restaurant.co.uk. Often missed by passers-by, this unpretentious restaurant is a relaxing haven amongst the bustle of the Old Town, serving fairly uncomplicated but top-quality modern Scottish food such as saddle of venison with beetroot fondant or toasted goat's cheese with caramelized walnuts. Reasonable lunchtime and set-price options.

La Garrigue 31 Jeffrey St ⓣ0131/557 3032, ⓦwww.lagarrigue.co.uk. A place of genuine charm and quality, with a menu and wine list dedicated to the produce and traditions of the Languedoc region of France. The care and honesty of the cooking shine through in dishes such as cassoulet or bream with chard.

Ondine 2 George IV Bridge ⓣ0131/226 1888, ⓦwww.ondinerestaurant.co.uk. Tucked in beside (but a separate venture from) the *Hotel Missoni*, this dedicated seafood restaurant from Edinburgh chef Roy Brett, once Rick Stein's main chef in Padstow, turns out some sublime dishes using native shellfish and fish from sustainable sources.

Wedgwood the Restaurant 267 Canongate ⓣ0131/558 8737, ⓦwww.wedgwoodtherestaurant.co.uk. A small but accomplished and ambitious fine-dining restaurant on the Royal Mile using local (and sometimes foraged) ingredients and introducing flavours from North Africa and the Pacific Rim. Offers an excellent £10 lunch deal.

The Witchery by the Castle 352 Castlehill ⓣ0131/225 5613, ⓦwww.thewitchery.com. An upmarket restaurant that only Edinburgh could create, set in magnificently over-the-top medieval surroundings full of Gothic panelling, tapestries and heavy stonework, all a mere broomstick-hop from the Castle. The rich fish and game dishes are pricey, but you can steal a sense of it all with a lunch or pre- or post-theatre set menu for under £15.

New Town and the West End

For the flashier end of the restaurant, club and bar scene, the **New Town** and the **West End** are the happening part of town. Many nationwide chains have restaurants on and around Princes and George streets, but it's worth exploring a little further afield to areas such as Broughton Street to find more authentic, home-grown places.

Cafés

Artisan Roast 57 Broughton St ⓦwww.artisanroast.co.uk. If you're into the black stuff, this is the must-visit coffee shop in Edinburgh. A narrow, grungy shop lined with hessian, they roast on site, make coffee with skill and care, and delight in taking pops at mainstream coffee culture. Perch on a stool in the main shop or shuffle through to cushioned benches in "The Mooch".

Eteaket 41a Frederick St ⓣ0131/226 2982, ⓦwww.eteaket.co.uk. The best of the tea boutiques in the city centre, with a restrained but contemporary decor scheme, good quality loose-leaf teas and some decent nibbles alongside.

The Scottish Café and Restaurant National Gallery of Scotland, The Mound ⓣ0131/226 6524, ⓦwww.thescottishcafeandrestaurant.com. An admirable (and mostly successful) attempt to bring the best of Scottish food to a busy venue that celebrates the best of Scottish art. Choose luxury porridge or a buttery (the local equivalent of a croissant) for morning snack, or a platter of smoked salmon or Scottish artisan cheeses for lunch.

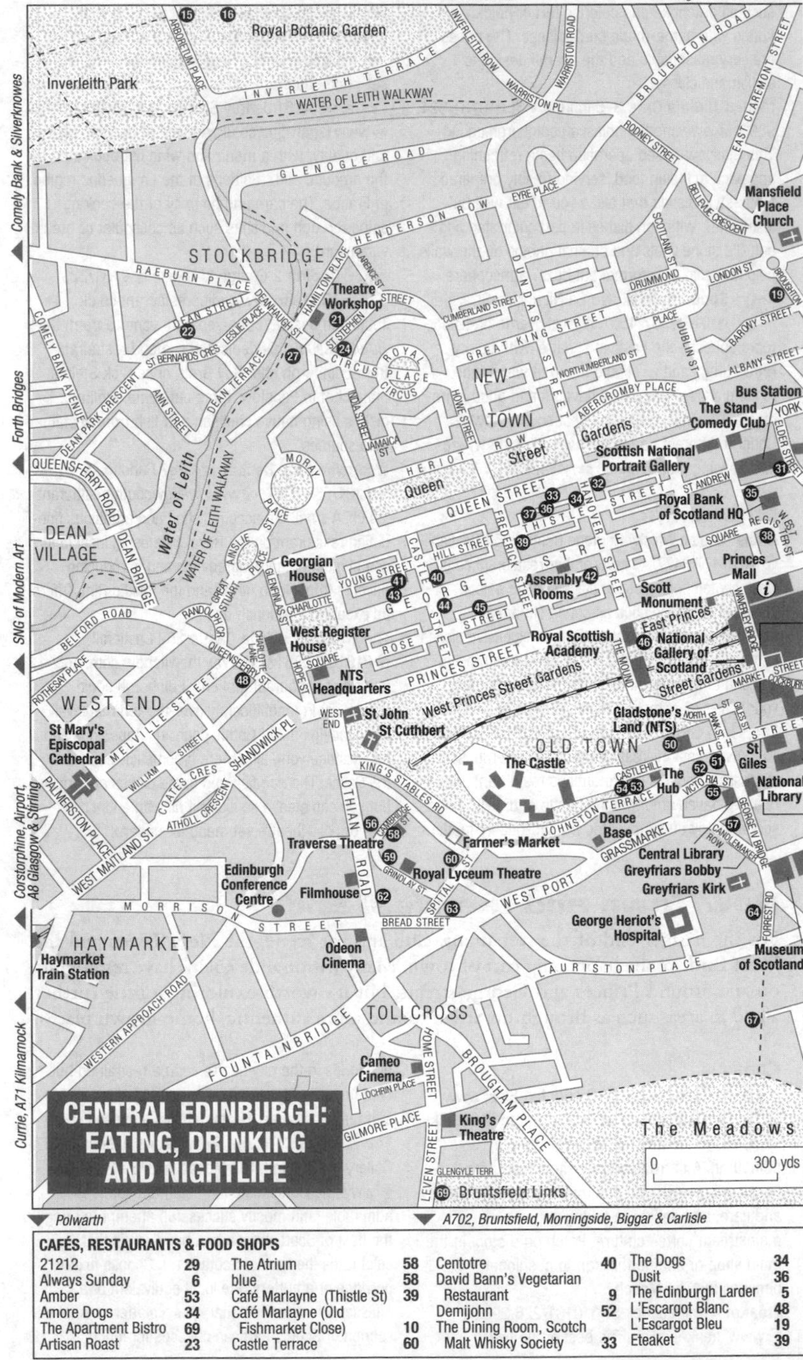

CAFÉS, RESTAURANTS & FOOD SHOPS

21212	29	The Atrium	58	Centotre	40	The Dogs	34
Always Sunday	6	blue	58	David Bann's Vegetarian Restaurant	9	Dusit	36
Amber	53	Café Marlayne (Thistle St)	39	Demijohn	52	The Edinburgh Larder	5
Amore Dogs	34	Café Marlayne (Old Fishmarket Close)	10	The Dining Room, Scotch Malt Whisky Society	33	L'Escargot Blanc	48
The Apartment Bistro	69	Castle Terrace	60			L'Escargot Bleu	19
Artisan Roast	23					Eteaket	39

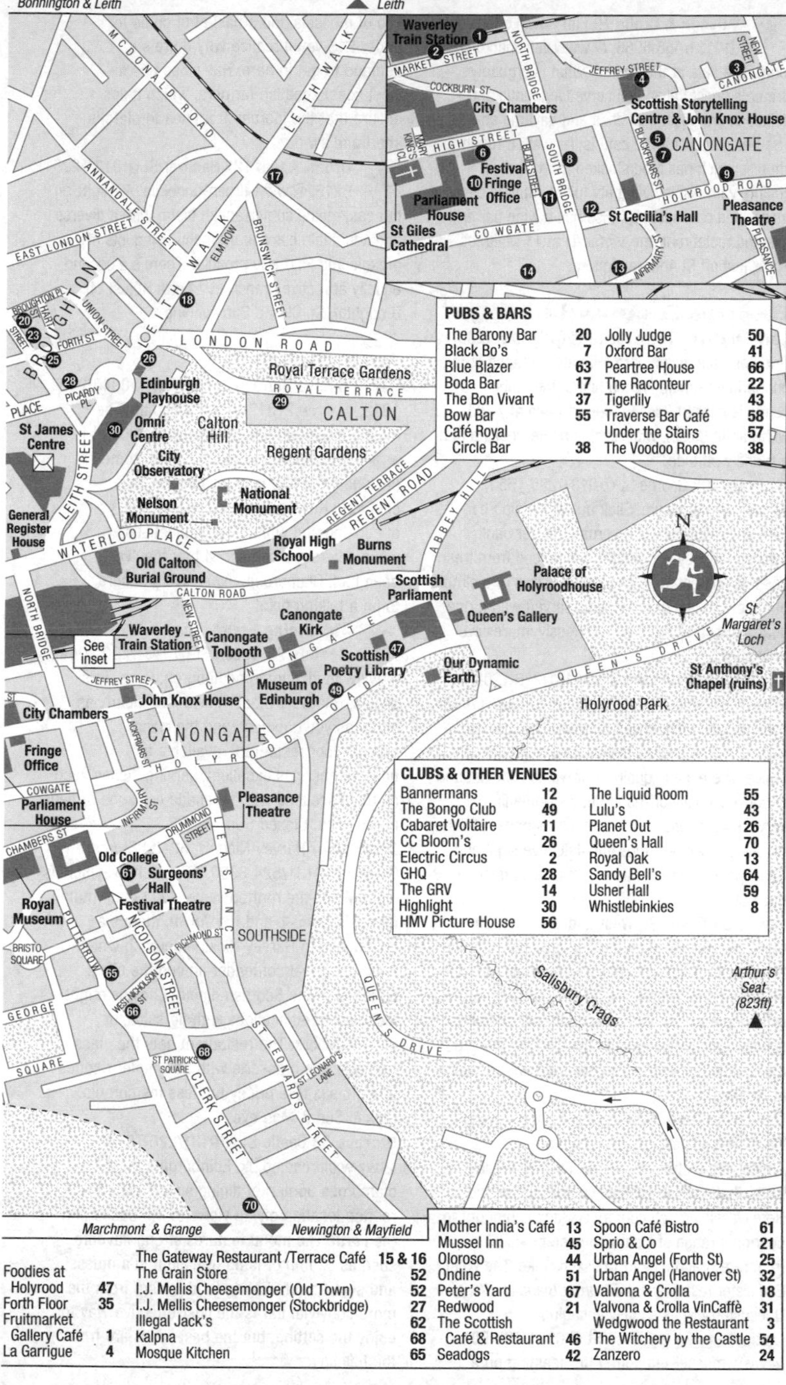

PUBS & BARS

The Barony Bar	20	Jolly Judge	50
Black Bo's	7	Oxford Bar	41
Blue Blazer	63	Peartree House	66
Boda Bar	17	The Raconteur	22
The Bon Vivant	37	Tigerlily	43
Bow Bar	55	Traverse Bar Café	58
Café Royal Circle Bar	38	Under the Stairs	57
		The Voodoo Rooms	38

CLUBS & OTHER VENUES

Bannermans	12	The Liquid Room	55
The Bongo Club	49	Lulu's	43
Cabaret Voltaire	11	Planet Out	26
CC Bloom's	26	Queen's Hall	70
Electric Circus	2	Royal Oak	13
GHQ	28	Sandy Bell's	64
The GRV	14	Usher Hall	59
Highlight	30	Whistlebinkies	8
HMV Picture House	56		

Foodies at Holyrood	47
Forth Floor	35
Fruitmarket Gallery Café	1
La Garrigue	4
The Gateway Restaurant /Terrace Café	15 & 16
The Grain Store	52
I.J. Mellis Cheesemonger (Old Town)	52
I.J. Mellis Cheesemonger (Stockbridge)	27
Illegal Jack's	62
Kalpna	68
Mosque Kitchen	65
Mother India's Café	13
Mussel Inn	45
Oloroso	44
Ondine	51
Peter's Yard	67
Redwood	21
The Scottish Café & Restaurant	46
Seadogs	42
Spoon Café Bistro	61
Sprio & Co	21
Urban Angel (Forth St)	25
Urban Angel (Hanover St)	32
Valvona & Crolla	18
Valvona & Crolla VinCaffè	31
Wedgwood the Restaurant	3
The Witchery by the Castle	54
Zanzero	24

Valvona & Crolla 19 Elm Row, Leith Walk ⓣ0131/556 6066, ⓦwww.valvonacrolla.com. The café at the back of what is arguably Britain's finest Italian deli serves authentic and delicious breakfasts, lunches and daytime snacks. The best advert for the café is the walk through the shop – which has food stacked from floor to ceiling, with display cabinets full of sublime olives, meats and cheeses. *V&C* also has a wine bar and evening restaurant (the *VinCaffè*) at 11 Multrees Walk, just off St Andrew Square.

Bistros & casual dining

Café Marlayne 76 Thistle St ⓣ0131/226 2230. Original – and even more intimate – branch of this endearingly simple French bistro (the other venue is near St Giles in the Old Town at 7 Old Fishmarket Close), with reliable home-cooking and a friendly attitude.

Centotre 103 George St ⓣ0131/225 1550, ⓦwww.centotre.com. Slick but welcoming bar, café and restaurant in an ornate former bank, offering unfussy, top-quality Italian food from fresh pastries and coffee to interesting pizzas or a simple but blissful plate of gorgonzola served with a ripe pear. All accompanied by a seriously impressive drinks list.

The Dogs 110 Hanover St ⓣ0131/220 1208, ⓦwww.thedogsonline.co.uk. Back-to-basics British cooking with offal, cheap cuts and cheaper fish served in well-cooked dishes for properly decent prices. There's an equally good-value wine list and unconventionally off-hand but well-meaning service. Variations on the formula reappear at sister restaurants *Amore Dogs* (the Italian version) and *Seadogs* (the fishy version), almost next door, at 43 Rose St.

Dusit 49a Thistle St, West End ⓣ0131/220 6846, ⓦwww.dusit.co.uk. The bold but effective blend of Thai flavours and well-sourced Scottish ingredients here brings a bit of originality and refinement to the often predictable Thai dining scene. Specialities include guinea fowl with red curry sauce or vegetables stir-fried with a dash of whisky.

L'Escargot Bleu 56 Broughton St ⓣ0131/557 1600, ⓦwww.lescargotbleu.co.uk.
A nice step on from the rustic, no-frills French bistro that's still in evidence across Edinburgh. Here classic French country cooking is brought to bear on a range of locally sourced produce, from rare-breed pigs to Trossachs pike. The West End sister restaurant, *L'Escargot Blanc* at 17 Queensferry St, is equally engaging.

Mussel Inn 61–65 Rose St ⓣ0131/225 5979, ⓦwww.mussel-inn.com. After feasting on a kilo of mussels and a basket of chips for under £15 you'll realize why there's a demand to get in here. Has close ties to west coast shellfish farmers, which helps ensure that the journey from sea to plate is short and swift.

Urban Angel 121 Hanover St ⓣ0131/225 6215, ⓦwww.urban-angel.co.uk. Right-on but easy-going subterranean bistro with a diverse and adaptable blackboard menu using lots of organic and Fairtrade produce. There's a second, equally attractive branch at 1 Forth St just off Broughton St. Closed Sun evening.

Fine dining

21212 3 Royal Terrace, Calton Hill ⓣ0845/222 1212, ⓦwww.21212restaurant.co.uk. The most challenging and polarizing restaurant to arrive in Edinburgh in recent years; some (including the Michelin inspectors) love chef Paul Kitching's shopping-list style of cooking and whimsical concoctions, while others are convinced that they've been had. Glamorous, expensive and sure to be a talking point.

The Dining Room, Scotch Malt Whisky Society 28 Queen St ⓣ0131/220 2044, ⓦwww.thediningroomedinburgh.co.uk. This stylish, relatively modern club isn't nearly as stuffy as you'd expect, and the classy ground-floor restaurant, available to non-members, is excellent, serving dishes such as roast scallops with tapenade or daube of beef in red wine. Closed Sun.

Forth Floor Harvey Nichols, 30–34 St Andrew Square ⓣ0131/524 8350, ⓦwww.harveynichols.com. While the rooftop views don't quite match its rivals *Oloroso* and the *Tower*, there's a confidence to Harvey Nicks' approach which makes it a real contender among the city's options for fine Scottish dining. Choices might include seared scallops with fig salsa, or pot-roast pork. The restaurant gets the glass frontage; the brasserie with its simpler risottos and grills is less pricey but less memorable. Closed Sun & Mon eve.

Oloroso 33 Castle St ⓣ0131/226 7614, ⓦwww.oloroso.co.uk. Edinburgh's most glamorous upmarket dining space, with a rooftop location giving views to the Castle and the Forth. The menu features strong flavours such as chump of lamb or halibut in a mussel and sorrel broth. Eating (or drinking) from the more convivial bar is the cost-effective way to enjoy the setting, but the best views are from the balcony.

Stockbridge and around

The northern fringe of the New Town, **Stockbridge** is the home of many of the city's young professionals, and the eating scene here is straightforward and pleasant.

Cafés

The Gallery Café Scottish National Gallery of Modern Art, Belford Rd, Dean Village ⓣ0131/332 8600. Far more than a standard refreshment stop for gallery visitors, the cultured setting (which includes a lovely outside eating area) and appealing, mid-priced menu of hearty soups, healthy salads and filled croissants pulls in reassuring numbers of locals. Open daily 10am–4.30pm.

The Gateway Restaurant/Terrace Café Royal Botanic Garden, Inverleith ⓣ0131/552 2674. At the West Gate of the Botanics, the new John Hope Gateway Centre has a nice-looking eating space on its upper floor, serving full breakfasts, lunches and formal afternoon tea. A few hundred yards beyond, the busy *Terrace Café* serves coffees, snacks and less formal lunches, with lots of outdoor tables and kid-friendly options.

Sprio & Co 39 St Stephen St ⓣ0131/226 7533. Halfway along one of Edinburgh's most Bohemian streets, this little coffee and piadina (flatbread) bar offers a very Milanese blend of good taste, attitude and sharp style.

Bistros & casual dining

Redwood 33a St Stephen St ⓣ0131/225 8342, ⓦwww.redwood-restaurant.co.uk. This one-chef-one-waiter show in a tiny Stockbridge basement restaurant has some of the most interesting, genuine fusion food in town. Essentially inspired by Californian cuisine, the food's still often local and well sourced. Closed Sun–Tues.

Zanzero 15 North West Circus Place ⓣ0131/220 0333, ⓦwww.zanzero.com. Upbeat, brightly coloured Italian café-bistro from the same stable as *Centotre* (see opposite), serving lighter, healthier food including pizzas, salads and fish at reasonable if not rock-bottom prices.

Lothian Road

While **Lothian Road**, just west of the Old Town, has a shabbier side, particularly around its various late-night bars and clubs, this is Edinburgh's theatre district, with a decent selection of sophisticated, lively places to eat and drink, and good value pre- and post-theatre deals.

Bistros and casual dining

blue 10 Cambridge St ⓣ0131/221 1222, ⓦwww.bluescotland.co.uk. With minimalist modern decor, this impressive café-bistro is handy for a quality pre- or post-theatre bite, with tasty, well-sourced dishes such as local fish pie or Stornoway black pudding with poached egg, and is one of the city's more sophisticated child-friendly options. Closed Sun.

Illegal Jack's 113–117 Lothian Rd ⓣ0131/622 7499, ⓦwww.illegaljacks.co.uk. Freshly made Tex-Mex in a large, sleek venue on busy Lothian Rd. The line-up on the menu is as you'd expect, but good ingredients and good attitudes prevail.

Fine dining

The Atrium 10 Cambridge St ⓣ0131/228 8882, ⓦwww.atriumrestaurant.co.uk. One of the most consistently impressive of Edinburgh's top-end restaurants. The quirky, arty design includes features such as railway-sleeper tables, while the food focuses on high-quality Scottish produce, some of it sourced from the nearby farmers' market. Closed Sun.

Castle Terrace 33–35 Castle Terrace ⓣ0131/229 1222, ⓦwww.castleterracerestaurant.com. City-centre sister restaurant to the highly successful *Kitchin* (see p.112), with chef-patron Dominic Jack bringing high-level French cooking to bear on excellent Scottish produce. Refined and stylish within, but not too formal or glitzy; set lunches available for under £20.

Southside

As the student quarter of the city, the **Southside** boasts plenty of good-value eating, but it's also an area where more progressive and interesting restaurants can establish themselves on the fringe of the more expensive city centre.

Cafés

Falko Konditorei 185 Bruntsfield Place ⓣ0131/656 0763. German master-baker Falko Burkert has brought a new level of Continental sophistication to Edinburgh's cake scene with his superb Sachertorte, Linzer tarts and cheesecakes. Chewy, tasty bread accompanies the meat platters, or you can just stop in for a coffee or tea. Closed Mon & Tues.

Peter's Yard 27 Simpson Loan (Quartermile) ⓣ0131/228 5876. Another side to the Continental baking scene, this time a Swedish outfit with the bread ovens on view and baskets of delicious loaves out front. Set on the edge of The Meadows, it's popular with flush-feeling students and professionals drawn down from the Old Town by the excellent soup, coffee and baking treats.

Yum @ Earthy Food Market 33–41 Ratcliffe Terrace, Marchmont ⓣ0131/667 2967. A daytime café has been a natural extension for Edinburgh's best fresh food shop, where you'll find fruit and veg from East Lothian alongside excellent bread, cheeses and organic dry goods. Lovely home-made tarts and smart salads top the bill.

Bistros and casual dining

The Apartment Bistro 7–13 Barclay Place, Bruntsfield ⓣ0131/228 6456. The hippest place for miles when it opened in 1999, a recent makeover under the same ownership has seen it revitalized as a sultry, Parisian-style brasserie with hearty cooking, good wines and plenty of stylish sophistication.

Kalpna 2–3 St Patrick's Square, Newington ⓣ0131/667 9890. Outstanding vegetarian restaurant serving authentic Gujarati dishes. Four set meals, including a vegan option, stand alongside the main menu for those keen to sample a range of dishes.

Mosque Kitchen Edinburgh Central Mosque, 50 Potterrow, Newington. Basic but filling and very cheap curries served from a tiny kitchen behind the mosque; the only seating is outside under a large awning. Popular with students and on sunny days.

Sweet Melinda's 11 Roseneath St, Marchmont ⓣ0131/229 7953, ⓦwwwsweetmelindas.co.uk. A pleasant seafood restaurant in a timber-panelled room with a friendly neighbourhood feel. It's worth shelling out for dishes such as mackerel served with chorizo, or exquisitely fried squid. Closed Sun & lunchtime Mon.

Leith and Newhaven

The area around the cobbled Shore of **Leith**, along the edge of the Water of Leith just as it reaches the sea, is the best-known dining quarter in Edinburgh, and lives up to its billing with good-quality, laidback seafood bistros and a concentration of Michelin stars.

Cafés

Porto & Fi 47 Newhaven Main St ⓣ0131/551 1900, ⓦwww.portofi.com. A bright daytime café not far from Newhaven's old stone harbour, with tempting cakes alongside serious daily specials including stews and fish pie from an accomplished kitchen.

The Water of Leith Café Bistro 52 Coburg St ⓣ0131/555 2613. A wee bit out on its own, but this welcoming, family-friendly spot is right beside the Water of Leith walkway. The French chef has plenty of restaurant experience which shows in the quality of food from casseroles to quiches.

Bistros & casual dining

Chop Chop 76 Commercial Quay ⓣ0131/553 1818, ⓦwww.chop-chop.co.uk. Second branch of a Chinese restaurant that specializes in northern Chinese cooking, with its dumplings a particular draw. Success on one of Gordon Ramsay's TV shows has seen it blossom.

Fishers 1 The Shore ⓣ0131/554 5666, ⓦwww.fishersbistros.co.uk. One of the first wave of seafood bistros to put Leith's dining scene on the map. The menu here has an appealing range of expensive and fancy fish, but there are also impressive bar-style snacks such as fishcakes and chowder.

Loch Fyne Restaurant 25 Pier Place, Newhaven Harbour ⓣ0131/559 3900, ⓦwww.lochfyne.com. Fantastic location by the fish market and old stone harbour at Newhaven for this English-based chain with strong connections to Scotland's west coast. Best for simple oysters and fish with a glass of wine.

The Shore 3–4 The Shore ⓣ0131/553 5080. A well-lived-in bar/restaurant with huge mirrors, wood panelling and aproned waiters who serve up good fish dishes and decent wines. Live jazz, folk and hubbub float through from the adjoining bar.

Fine dining

The Kitchin 78 Commercial Quay ⓣ0131/555 1755, ⓦwww.thekitchin.com. Opened in 2006 by young Scottish chef Tom Kitchin and the winner – less than six months later – of a Michelin star, this upwardly mobile operation puts itself at the more relaxed end of the fine-dining bracket and offers some tantalizing dishes including rolled pig's head with crispy ear salad, or razor clams with chorizo. Closed Sun & Mon.

Restaurant Martin Wishart 52 The Shore ⓣ0131/553 3557, ⓦwww.martin-wishart.co.uk. The eponymous chef is one of the leading lights of the Scottish culinary scene, and was the first Michelin-star holder in Edinburgh. Though relatively modest in size and demure in atmosphere, this place wows the gourmets with highly accomplished and exquisitely presented dishes featuring Scottish-sourced fish and meat. A two-course lunch is £24.50, a six-course evening tasting menu £65. Closed Sun & Mon.

The Vintner's Rooms 87 Giles St ⓣ0131/554 6767 ⓦwww.thevintnersrooms.com. Splendid restaurant with accompanying whisky bar in a seventeenth-century warehouse; the small but ornate Rococo dining room is a marvel and the food – from seafood to game – goes a long way to matching it. Closed Sun evening & Mon.

Specialist food shops

As in any other city in Britain, supermarkets dominate day-to-day food shopping in Edinburgh, but there are plenty of good delis and specialist food retailers if you're prepared to seek them out. Most venerated of all is **Valvona & Crolla**, 19 Elm Row, Leith Walk, where you encounter a mouthwatering array of top-notch Italian delicacies, much of it delivered directly by a weekly truck from Milan's markets. If you want to discover some locally grown produce, there's a **Farmers' Market** on Castle Terrace near the Usher Hall every Saturday morning (9am–1pm). **I.J. Mellis Cheesemonger** has three shops around town (30a Victoria St, 330 Morningside Rd and 6 Baker's Place, Stockbridge), all of which focus on expertly conditioned farmhouse and artisan cheeses from Britain and Ireland. Right next door to Mellis' Victoria Street shop is **Demijohn**, a "liquid deli" where you can fill variously sized bottles from large, bulbous demijohns filled with oils, vinegars and some wonderfully colourful liqueurs and fruit spirits, many sourced from small operations around the UK. The best food shop in the very centre of town is on the fourth floor of Harvey Nichols on St Andrew Square, but for more leisured food shopping head down Broughton Street or through the main parts of Stockbridge or Bruntsfield, where you're most likely to find small artisan shops, good delis and traditional butchers and fishmongers.

Pubs and bars

Many of Edinburgh's **pubs**, especially in the Old Town, have histories that stretch back centuries, while others, particularly in the New Town, are unaltered Victorian or Edwardian period pieces. Add a plentiful supply of trendy modern **bars**, and there's enough to cater for all tastes. The standard licensing hours are 11am–11pm (noon–11pm on Sun), but many places stay open later and, during the Festival especially, you won't have a problem finding a bar open till at least 1am.

Edinburgh has a long history of beer-making, though only one working brewery remains in the city itself, the small **Caledonian Brewery** in the western reaches of town. Owned by multinational Scottish & Newcastle, it still uses old techniques and equipment to produce some of the best specialist beers in Britain, including its popular Deuchar's IPA. For more on Scottish beer, see the *Scottish food and drink* colour section.

A fun way to explore Edinburgh's pubs is to take a **Literary Pub Tour**, a pub crawl with culture around Old and New Town watering holes. The various tours introduce you to the scenes, characters and words of the major figures of Scottish literature, including Burns, Scott and MacDiarmid, and are run by The

Scottish Literary Tour Trust (departing from the *Beehive* pub on the Grassmarket; Ⓣ0800/169 7410, Ⓦwww.edinburghliterarypubtour.co.uk) and Edinburgh Literary Tours (from the *Mitre* pub, 131 High St; Ⓦwww.edinburghbookloverstour.com).

The Royal Mile and around

Black Bo's 55 Blackfriars St. No decent ales (although there's a good selection of bottled beers), but a fine example of how to stay trendy without going minimalist, with church pews and candles alongside original art and DJ decks. Just 50yd from the Royal Mile, but well off the tourist trail.

Bow Bar 80 West Bow. Wonderful old wood-panelled bar and one of the nicest, most convivial drinking spots in the city centre. Choose from among nearly 150 whiskies or a changing selection of first-rate Scottish and English cask beers.

Jolly Judge 7a James Court. Atmospheric, low-ceilinged bar in a close just down from the Castle. Cosy in winter and pleasant outside in summer.

Under the Stairs 3a Merchant St. Comfy, shabby-chic bar with great cocktails, popular with the pre-clubbing crowd. Food served late, with sharing plates available right up till the 1am closing time.

New Town and West End

The Bon Vivant 55 Thistle St. Classy city-centre bar, with an excellent wine list and good choice of champagne by the glass, as well as interesting food available in tapas-sized portions. Open till 1am.

Café Royal Circle Bar 17 West Register St. Worth a visit just for its Victorian decor, notably the huge elliptical island bar and tiled portraits of renowned inventors. The beer and food are good, too. The *Café* is a better bet than its equally venerable, but much more staid neighbouring *Oyster Bar* restaurant.

Oxford Bar 8 Young St. An unpretentious, unspoilt, no-nonsense city bar – which is why local crime writer Ian Rankin and his Inspector Rebus like it so much. Fans duly make the pilgrimage, but fortunately not all the regulars have been scared off. Open until 1am.

Tigerlily 125 George St. The daddy of all George Street's decadent destination bars, where the locals come to see and be seen. Can be tons of fun – but only if you're wearing the right clothes. Bar open till 1am.

The Voodoo Rooms 19a West Register St. Glamorous gilt and plush booths attract a dressed-up crowd, especially at the weekend. Frequent live music, performance and club nights, including Edinburgh's legendary Vegas! Open till 1am.

Broughton and Leith Walk

The Barony Bar 81–85 Broughton St. A fine old-fashioned bar which manages to be big and lively without being spoilt. Chainification has blunted a bit of its appeal, but there's still real ale and a blazing fire.

Boda Bar 229 Leith Walk. A laidback local which has been smartened up and given a Scandinavian twist by its Swedish owners. Offers a small but interesting wine list, friendly staff and lovely locals. Open till 1am.

Stockbridge

The Raconteur 50 Dean St. Relaxed and cosy neighbourhood pub, quietly tucked away in the cobbled streets of Stockbridge, which shakes up a mean cocktail or two.

Lothian Road and Tollcross

Blue Blazer 2 Spittal St. This traditional Edinburgh howff with an oak-clad bar and church pews serves as good a selection of real ales as you'll find anywhere in the city. Open till 1am.

Traverse Bar Café Traverse Theatre, 10 Cambridge St. Much more than just a theatre bar, attracting a lively, sophisticated crowd who dispel any notion of a quiet interval drink. Good food available. One of *the* places to be during the Festival.

The Southside

Peartree House 36 West Nicolson St, Newington. Fine bar in an eighteenth-century house with old sofas and a large courtyard – one of central Edinburgh's very few beer gardens. Open Mon–Wed & Sun until 11.45pm, Thurs–Sat until 12.45am.

Leith

Kings Wark 36 The Shore. Real ale in a restored eighteenth-century pub right in the heart of Leith. There's an attached restaurant, and great bar meals – check in at the bar for a table.

The Roseleaf 23/24 Sandport Place. Chintzy-cool local that's a little off the beaten track but worth the trip for the pot-tails alone – funky cocktails served in vintage teapots. Open till 1am.

The Shore 3–4 The Shore. Atmospheric traditional bar with an adjacent restaurant (see p.112). There's regular live jazz or folk music as well as real ales and good bar snacks.

Elsewhere in the city

Canny Man's (Volunteer Arms) 237 Morningside Rd, Morningside. Atmospheric and idiosyncratic pub-cum-museum adorned with anything that can be hung on the walls or from the ceiling. Local ales and more than two hundred whiskies on offer, as well as snacks.

Espy 62–64 Bath St, Portobello. Great wee boozer slap bang in the middle of Portobello Promenade, ideal for beer on the beach on those occasions when the sun shines.

Orocco Pier 17 High St, South Queensferry. A stylish contemporary drinking spot on South Queensferry's medieval high street, with unbeatable views over the water to the Forth Bridges (see also p.135).

Sheep Heid Inn 43 The Causeway, Duddingston. One of Edinburgh's best-known historic pubs, the building has barely survived various predictable makeovers, but despite this remains an attractive spot. Decent meals are available at the bar, and there's an old-fashioned skittle alley out the back.

Nightlife and entertainment

Inevitably, Edinburgh's **nightlife** is at its best during the Festival (see p.118), which can make the other 48 weeks of the year seem like an anticlimax. However, at any time the city has plenty to offer, especially in the realm of **theatre** and **music**.

While it lacks Glasgow's clout, Edinburgh's **club scene** can be enormously enjoyable, with a mix of mainstream discos offering pop and dance music and left-field clubs with a dressed-down vibe and a wide range of nights, usually rotating on a monthly or fortnightly basis. Most of the city-centre clubs stay open till around 3am. While you can normally hear **live jazz**, **folk** and **rock** every evening in one or other of the city's pubs, for the really big rock events, ad hoc places – such as the Castle Esplanade or Murrayfield Stadium – are pressed into service. The city has permanent venues large enough to host large touring **orchestras** and **ballet** companies; elsewhere you can uncover a lively **comedy** club and a couple of excellent art-house **cinemas**.Edinburgh has a dynamic **gay** culture, for years centred round the top of Leith Walk and Broughton Street, where the first gay and lesbian centre appeared in the 1970s. Since the early 1990s, more and more gay enterprises, especially cafés and nightclubs, have moved into this area, now dubbed the "Pink Triangle".

Hogmanay

One way of celebrating **Hogmanay** is to join one of the street parties that are held in the middle of towns and cities, often centred around a prominent clockface which rings out "the bells" at midnight. These days, the largest New Year's Eve street party in Europe takes place in Edinburgh, with around 80,000 people on the streets of the city enjoying the culmination of a week-long series of events. On the night itself, stages are set up in different parts of the city centre, with big-name rock groups and local ceilidh bands playing to the increasingly inebriated masses. The high point of the evening is, of course, midnight, when hundreds of tons of fireworks are let off into the night sky above the Castle, and Edinburgh joins the rest of the world singing "**Auld Lang Syne**", an old Scottish tune with lyrics by Robert Burns, Scotland's national poet.

For information about celebrations in Edinburgh, and how to get hold of tickets for the street party, go to Ⓦwww.edinburghshogmanay.com.

The best way to find out **what's on** is to pick up a copy of *The List*, a fortnightly magazine covering both Edinburgh and Glasgow (£2.20). Alternatively, get hold of the *Edinburgh Evening News*, which appears daily except Sunday: its listings column gives details of performances in the city that day, hotels and bars included. Information on nightclubs can be found on posters and the flyers distributed to most of the pre-club bars around town. Box offices of individual halls and theatres are likewise liberally supplied with promotional leaflets about forthcoming music and theatre, and some are able to sell tickets for more than one venue – Ⓦ www.tickets-scotland.com is another useful resource.

Nightclubs

The Bongo Club Moray House, 37 Holyrood Rd Ⓣ0131/558 7604, Ⓦwww.thebongoclub.co.uk. Legendary Edinburgh club and arts venue; its line-up is eclectic but always worth checking out. Look out for the monthly dub and reggae Messenger Sound System.

Cabaret Voltaire 36–38 Blair St Ⓣ0131/220 6176, Ⓦwww.thecabaretvoltaire.com. Atmospheric nightclub in the Old Town's underground vaults, playing host to some of the city's best clubs, including deep house favourite Ultragroove.

Electric Circus 36–39 Market St Ⓣ0131/226 4224, Ⓦwww.theelectriccircus.biz. Private karaoke rooms, burlesque and live music with an indie slant. Clubs include indie/alternative night His and Hers.

The GRV 7 Guthrie St Ⓣ0131/220 2987. Intimate and innovative venue that's the home of Taste, an evening of full-on house that has long been a favourite with the city's gay community.

The Liquid Room 9c Victoria St Ⓣ0131/225 2564, Ⓦwww.liquidroom.com. Recently refurbished, with new cutting-edge sound and light system. One of the best of the larger venues, with nights such as the indie Evol, and Luvely, a popular gay-friendly house night.

Lulu's 125b George St Ⓣ0131/225 5005, Ⓦwww.luluedinburgh.co.uk. Sultry subterranean nightspot beneath OTT bar and restaurant *Tigerlily*. A place to see and be seen, with its fair share of Travolta-wannabes striding to the sound-responsive disco light floor.

Gay clubs and bars

CC Bloom's 23–24 Greenside Place Ⓣ0131/556 9331. Edinburgh's most enduring gay club, with a big dance floor, stonking rhythms and a young, friendly crowd.

Planet Out 6 Baxter's Place Ⓣ0131/556 5551. Loud and outrageous bar beside the Playhouse Theatre, a popular meeting point.

GHQ 4 Picardy Place Ⓣ0845/166 6024, Ⓦwww.socialanimal.co.uk. Stylish bar and club catering to a dressed-up crowd. Highlights on the nightly club menu include pop and dance every Friday at Kinky Disco; and the female-focused Furburger, monthly.

Live music venues

Bannermans 212 Cowgate Ⓣ0131/556 3254, Ⓦwww.bannermansgigs.co.uk. The best place in Edinburgh to discover local indie bands hoping for a big break.

HMV Picture House 31 Lothian Rd Ⓣ0131/221 2280, Ⓦwww.edinburgh-picturehouse.co.uk. A 1500-capacity city-centre venue which still manages to feel intimate. The reasonably eclectic gig list includes local bands, breakthrough chart-toppers and the occasional tribute band.

The Liquid Room 9c Victoria St Ⓣ0131/225 2564, Ⓦwww.liquidroom.com. Good-sized venue frequented by local acts and touring indie bands.

Queen's Hall 85–89 Clerk St Ⓣ0131/668 2019, Ⓦwww.thequeenshall.net. Converted Georgian church which now operates as a concert hall; it's used principally by the Scottish Chamber Orchestra and Scottish Ensemble, and much favoured by jazz, blues and folk groups.

Royal Oak 1 Infirmary St Ⓣ0131/557 2976, Ⓦwww.royal-oak-folk.com. Traditional pub hosting regular informal folk sessions and the "Wee Folk Club" on Sun.

Sandy Bell's 25 Forrest Rd Ⓣ0131/225 2751. A friendly bar and a good bet for folk music most nights of the week.

Usher Hall Corner Lothian Rd & Grindlay St Ⓣ0131/228 1155, Ⓦwww.usherhall.co.uk. Now reopened after a major refurbishment and strikingly contemporary extension, Edinburgh's main civic concert hall is excellent for choral and symphony concerts, but less suitable for solo vocalists. The upper circle seats are cheapest and have the best acoustics.

Whistlebinkies 4–6 South Bridge Ⓣ0131/557 5114, Ⓦwww.whistlebinkies.com. One of the most reliable places to find live music every night of the week – often it's rock and pop covers, though there are some folk evenings. Daily till 3am.

Theatre and dance

Assembly Rooms 54 George St ⓣ0131/220 4348, ⓦwww.assemblyrooms.co.uk. Varied complex of small and large halls. Used all year, but really comes into its own during the Fringe, featuring large-scale drama productions and mainstream comedy.
Dance Base 14–16 Grassmarket ⓣ0131/225 5255, ⓦwww.dancebase.co.uk. Scotland's sparkling new National Centre for Dance is used mostly for modern dance workshops and classes, but also hosts occasional performances.
Edinburgh Playhouse 18–22 Greenside Place ⓣ0844/847 1660, ⓦwww.edinburgh-playhouse.co.uk. The largest theatre in Britain, formerly a cinema. Used largely for extended runs of popular musicals and occasional rock concerts.
Festival Theatre Nicolson St ⓣ0131/529 6000, ⓦwww.eft.co.uk. The largest stage in Britain, principally used for Scottish Opera and Scottish Ballet's appearances in the capital, but also for everything from the children's show *Singing Kettle* to Engelbert Humperdinck.
King's Theatre 2 Leven St ⓣ0131/529 6000, ⓦwww.eft.co.uk. Stately Edwardian civic theatre that majors in pantomime, touring West End plays and the occasional major drama or opera performance.
Royal Lyceum Theatre 30 Grindlay St ⓣ0131/248 4848, ⓦwww.lyceum.org.uk. Fine Victorian civic theatre with a compact auditorium. The leading year-round venue for mainstream drama.
Traverse Theatre 10 Cambridge St ⓣ0131/228 1404, ⓦwww.traverse.co.uk. One of Britain's premier venues for new plays and avant-garde drama from around the world. Going from strength to strength in its custom-built home beside the Usher Hall, with a great bar downstairs and the popular *blue* café-bar upstairs (see p.111).

Comedy

Highlight Omni Centre, Greenside Place ⓣ0131/524 9300, ⓦwww.thehighlight.co.uk.com. An Edinburgh link in a national chain located in the huge glass-fronted Omni cinema complex at the foot of Calton Hill. Fairly reliable for a year-round chance to encounter big-name stand-up acts, with an after-party thrown in.
The Stand Comedy Club 5 York Place ⓣ0131/558 7272, ⓦwww.thestand.co.uk. The city's top comedy spot, with a different act on every night and some of the UK's top comics headlining at the weekends.

Cinemas

Cameo 38 Home St, Tollcross ⓣ0131/228 2800, ⓦwww.picturehouses.co.uk; bookings ⓣ0871/902 5723. A treasure of an art-house cinema; screens more challenging mainstream releases and cult late-nighters. Tarantino's been here and thinks it's great.
Dominion 18 Newbattle Terrace, Morningside ⓣ0131/447 4771, ⓦwww.dominioncinemas.net. A reminder of how cinemas were before multiplexes, the Dominion is still family-owned, and battling on with its screenings of popular new releases.
Filmhouse 88 Lothian Rd ⓣ0131/228 2688, ⓦwww.filmhousecinema.com. Three screens showing an eclectic programme of independent, art-house and classic films. The café is a hangout for the city's film buffs.
Odeon 118 Lothian Rd ⓣ0870/224 4007 (info and bookings), ⓦwww.odeon.co.uk. Central four-screen cinema showing the latest releases.
Vue Omni Centre, Greenside Place ⓣ0871/224 0240, ⓦwww.myvue.com. Most central of the big multiscreen venues, tucked under Calton Hill at the top of Leith Walk.

Shopping

Despite the relentless advance of the big chains, it's still possible to track down some appealing and unusual shops in central Edinburgh. **Princes Street**, one of Britain's most famous shopping streets, is all but dominated by standard chain outlets, though no serious shopper should miss out on a visit to Edinburgh's venerable department store Jenners, at 48 Princes St, opposite the Scott Monument. More fashionable upmarket shops and boutiques are to be found on and around parallel **George Street**, including an upscale shopping area on the east side of St Andrew Square. There's nothing compelling about central Edinburgh's two big shopping malls, **Princes Mall** and the **St James Centre**, which are dominated by the big names.

For more original outlets, head for **Cockburn Street**, south of Waverley Station, a hub for trendy clothes and record shops, while on **Victoria Street** and in and around the **Grassmarket** you'll find an eclectic range of antique, crafts, food and book shops. Along and around the **Royal Mile**, meanwhile, several distinctly offbeat places sit among the tacky souvenir sellers.

Books Waterstone's is the major bookselling presence in Edinburgh, with large stores at 128 Princes St (Ⓣ0843/290 8313), 13–14 Princes St (Ⓣ0843/290 8307) and 83 George St (Ⓣ0843/290 8309). A Blackwell's store at 53–62 South Bridge (Ⓣ0131/662 8222) provides a strong general/academic presence near the university. There's a good selection of antiquarian and secondhand bookshops in the city: Peter Bell, 68 West Port Ⓣ0131/229 0562; McNaughtan's Bookshop, 3a–4a Haddington Place, Leith Walk Ⓣ0131/556 5897; and Edinburgh Books, 147 West Port Ⓣ0131/229 4431.

Clothes (new) Some of the more interesting clothes shops in town include: Corniche, 2–4 Jeffrey St Ⓣ0131/556 3707 (women's and men's designer labels); Cruise, 80 George St Ⓣ0131/226 0840 (women's and men's fashion); Fabhatrix, 13 Cowgatehead Ⓣ0131/225 9222 (contemporary hats); Harvey Nichols, 32–34 St Andrew Square Ⓣ0131/524 8388 (expensive designer labels); Helen Bateman Shoes, 16 William St Ⓣ0131/220 4495 (women's designer shoes); Ness, 367 High St Ⓣ0131/226 5227 (contemporary Scottish knitwear and accessories).

Clothes (secondhand) Wm Armstrong, 83 Grassmarket Ⓣ0131/220 5557, also at 64 Clerk St Ⓣ0131/667 3056; Herman Brown, 151 West Port Ⓣ0131/228 2589; Godiva, 9 West Port Ⓣ0131/221 9212.

Crafts Anta, 91–93 West Bow, Victoria St Ⓣ0131/225 4616; Flux, 55 Bernard St, Leith Ⓣ0131/554 4075; National Museum of Scotland Shop, Chambers St Ⓣ0131/225 7534.

Maps Carson Clark, 181–183 Canongate (Ⓣ0131/556 4710), sells antique maps, charts and globes. Street maps can be found in all the main bookshops (see above) and the tourist information centre. Ordnance Survey maps for hillwalking are available from good outdoor stores.

Music Check out Avalanche, 63 Cockburn St (Ⓣ0131/225 3939) for indie music; Coda, 12 Bank St (Ⓣ0131/622 7246) for contemporary Scottish folk and roots music; McAlister Matheson Music, 1 Grindlay St (Ⓣ0131/629 9274) for classical and jazz; Underground Solu'shun, 9 Cockburn St (Ⓣ0131/226 2242) for house, garage, techno and drum'n'bass vinyl; and Vinyl Villains, 5 Elm Row (Ⓣ0131/558 1170) for secondhand records, tapes and ephemera.

Outdoors There is a concentration of useful stores on Rose St; try Tiso, 123–125 Rose St (Ⓣ0131/225 9486).

Tartan Kinloch Anderson, corner Commercial and Dock streets, Leith (Ⓣ0131/555 1390), has a large showroom; Geoffrey Tailor, 57–59 High St (Ⓣ0131/557 0256) is one of the largest and most respected retailers on the Royal Mile – as well as traditional tartan they sell a line of "21st-century kilts" in materials including leather, plain tweed and camouflage pattern.

Whisky Royal Mile Whiskies, 379–381 High St Ⓣ0131/225 3383; William Cadenhead, 172 Canongate Ⓣ0131/556 5864.

Woollen goods Bill Baber Knitwear, 66 Grassmarket (Ⓣ0131/225 3249), has garments designed and made on the premises; Ragamuffin, 278 Canongate (Ⓣ0131/557 6007), features Skye knitwear.

The Edinburgh Festival

The **Edinburgh Festival** is actually an umbrella term encompassing several different festivals taking place at around the same time in the city. The principal events are the **Edinburgh International Festival** and the much larger **Edinburgh Festival Fringe**, but there are also **Book, Jazz and Blues, Art** and **Television** festivals, as well as the **Military Tattoo** on the Castle Esplanade.

The Edinburgh International Festival

The **Edinburgh International Festival** (Ⓦwww.eif.co.uk), sometimes called the "Official Festival", was the original Edinburgh Festival, conceived in 1947 as a celebration of pan-European culture in the postwar era. Initially dominated by opera, other elements such as top-grade theatre, ballet, dance and classical music

Edinburgh's other festivals

Quite apart from August's Edinburgh Festival, the city is now promoting itself as a year-round venue, with a number of different events well established. The **Science Festival** in April (ⓣ0131/558 7666, ⓦwww.sciencefestival.co.uk) incorporates hands-on children's events as well as numerous lectures on a vast array of subjects. There's also a **Children's Festival** in late May (ⓣ0131/225 8050, ⓦwww.imaginate.org.uk), with readings, magicians and specialist children's drama. The city's annual **International Film Festival** (ⓦwww.edfilmfest.org.uk) is held in the second half of June.

During December, **Edinburgh's Christmas** (ⓦwww.edinburghschristmas.com) draws together various seasonal events, most prominently the installation of a huge ferris wheel beside the Scott Monument and an outdoor skating rink nearby. At the turn of the year, **Edinburgh's Hogmanay** (see box, p.115) is one of the world's largest New Year street parties, involving torchlight processions, folk and rock concerts and fireworks galore. There's more revelry on the night of April 30 at **Beltane** (ⓦwww.beltane.org), an ancient Celtic fire festival celebrating the arrival of spring, which has a New Age feel to it, with lots of painted flesh, beating drums and huge bonfires.

were gradually introduced, and it's still very much a highbrow event, its high production values and serious approach offering an antidote to the Fringe's slapdash vigour.

The festival generally runs over the second two weeks of August and the first week of September, culminating in a **Fireworks Concert** based in Princes Street Gardens but visible from all over the city. Performances take place at the city's larger venues such as the Usher Hall and the Festival Theatre and, while ticket prices run to over £60, it is possible to see shows for £10 or less if you're prepared to queue for the handful of tickets kept back until the day. The International Festival's year-round headquarters are located at **The Hub** (see p.81), where there's a booking office for tickets.

The Edinburgh Festival Fringe

Even standing alone, the **Edinburgh Festival Fringe** is easily the world's largest arts gathering. Each year sees over 30,000 performances from some 700 companies, with more than 12,000 participants from all over the world. There are something in the region of 1500 shows every day, round the clock, in 200 venues around the city. While the headlining names at the International Festival reinforce the Festival's cultural credibility, it is the dynamism, spontaneity and sheer exuberance of the Fringe which dominate Edinburgh every August, giving the city its unique atmosphere. Crucially, because no artistic control is imposed on those who want to produce a show as part of the Fringe, the productions range from the inspired to the diabolical; there's also a highly competitive atmosphere in which one bad review in a prominent publication means box-office disaster. Many unknowns rely on self-publicity, taking to the streets to perform highlights from their show, or pressing leaflets into the hands of every passer-by.

These days, the most prominent and ubiquitous aspect of the Fringe is **comedy**, having overtaken theatre as the largest genre in 2008. As well as sell-out audiences and quotable reviews, most of the comedy acts are chasing the Foster's Edinburgh Comedy Award (formerly the Perrier Award), given to the outstanding stand-up or comedy cabaret, and there's no doubt that the Edinburgh Festival is the place to

Doing the Festival

For the visitor, the sheer volume of the Festival's output can be bewildering: virtually every branch of **arts** and **entertainment** is represented somewhere, and world-famous stars mix with pub singers in the daily line-up. It can be a struggle to find accommodation, get hold of the tickets you want, book a table in a restaurant or simply get from one side of town to another; you can end up seeing something truly dire, or something mind-blowing; you'll inevitably try to do too much, stay out too late or spend too much money – but then again, most Festival veterans will tell you that if you don't experience these things then you haven't really done the Festival.

Dates, venues, names, star acts, happening bars and burning issues change from one year to the next. This unpredictability is one of the Festival's greatest charms, however, so while the following information will help you get to grips with it, be prepared for – indeed, enjoy – the unexpected. For up-to-the-minute **information** at any time of year, visit Ⓦwww.edinburghfestivals.co.uk, which has links to the homepages of most of the main festivals. Each festival produces its own programme well in advance, while during the Festival various publications give information about what's on day by day, among them *The Guide*, published daily by the Fringe Office, and local what's-on guide *The List*, which comes out weekly during the Festival and manages to combine comprehensive coverage with a reliably on-the-pulse sense of what's hot and what's not. Of the local newspapers, *The Scotsman* carries a dedicated daily Festival supplement with an events diary and reviews which carry a lot of weight, while *The Herald*, published in Glasgow, and the London-based papers offer more selective but generally authoritative reviews. Various freebie newspapers are also available around town – the best of these is *Fest*, which mixes news with pithy reviews and yet more listings.

catch new talent before it becomes famous, with debuts made by everyone from Monty Python to Graham Norton over the years.

Despite the growth and profile of comedy, however, the Fringe's **theatre** programme shows no signs of dying out, with hundreds of brand new works airing alongside offbeat classics and familiar Shakespearean tragedies. The venues are often as imaginative as the shows themselves – play-parks, restaurants and even parked cars have all been used to stage plays. The Fringe also offers fine musicals, dance, children's shows, exhibitions, lectures and music – after years of neglect this last, in particular, has now expanded significantly, with sub-festivals and venues dedicated to youth orchestras, folk and roots music and pop and rock, including The Edge, which is committed to programming popular music at the Edinburgh Festivals. And for those on a very tight budget the **Laughing Horse Edinburgh Free Fringe Festival** brings around 300 free comedy, music, cabaret and children's shows to fourteen venues in the city.

The full Fringe programme is usually available in June from the Festival Fringe Office (Ⓣ0131/226 0000, Ⓦwww.edfringe.com). Postal and telephone bookings for shows can be made immediately after its release, while during the Festival, tickets are sold at the Fringe Office, on the Royal Mile at no. 180 (daily 10am–9pm), as well as online or at venues. Ticket prices for most Fringe shows start at £5, and average from £8 to £12 at the main venues, with the best-known acts going for even more. Although some theatre and music shows can be longer, most performances are scheduled to run for an hour. Performances go on round the clock: if so inclined, you could sit through twenty shows in a day. The Fringe starts and finishes before the International Festival, kicking off in early August – there are often cheap deals on the opening weekend – and ending on the last weekend of the month.

Edinburgh International Book Festival

The **Edinburgh International Book Festival**, which takes place in the last two weeks of August, is the world's largest celebration of the written word. It's held in a tented village in the sedate setting of Charlotte Square and offers talks, readings and signings by a star-studded line-up of visiting authors, as well as panel discussions and workshops. Well-known Scottish authors such as Iain Banks, Ian Rankin and Alexander McCall-Smith are good for an appearance most years, while visitors from further afield have included Doris Lessing, Louis de Bernières, Vikram Seth, Joyce Carol Oates and Salman Rushdie. In addition, there's a dedicated programme of children's activities, debates, writing workshops and book-related events, an on-site café and, of course, a bookshop.

Tickets (generally £8–10) often sell out quickly, particularly for the big-name events. For tickets and info during the Festival, contact the ticket office at Charlotte Square (ⓣ0845/373 5888, ⓦwww.edbookfest.co.uk).

Edinburgh Jazz and Blues Festival

The **Edinburgh Jazz and Blues Festival** runs immediately prior to the Fringe in the first week in August, easing the city into the festival spirit with a full programme of gigs in many different locations. Scotland's own varied and vibrant jazz scene is always fully represented, and atmospheric late-night clubs complement major

Fringe venues

While the Fringe is famous for its tiny and unexpected auditoriums, the five dominant **Fringe venues** are the Assembly Rooms, the Pleasance, the Gilded Balloon, the Underbelly and "C" venues. Venue complexes rather than single spaces, these giants colonize clusters of different-sized spaces for the duration of the Festival. If you're new to the Fringe, these are all safe bets for decent shows and a bit of star-spotting.

The atmosphere at the **Pleasance Courtyard** (60 The Pleasance ⓣ0131/556 6550, ⓦwww.pleasance.co.uk) has a slighty raucous feel thanks to its busy courtyard bar, with offbeat comedy mixing with whimsical appearances by panellists on Radio 4 game shows, while the **Pleasance Dome,** located in Edinburgh University's student union at Potterrow, is a substantial supplementary venue with a busy central café/bar area. The comedy-focused **Gilded Balloon** (Teviot Row House, Bristo Square ⓣ0131/622 6555, ⓦwww.gildedballoon.co.uk) bases its operations close by in another student union, the Gothic Teviot Row. Located between this and the Pleasance Dome in Bristo Square is the unmistakeable sight of a giant, inflatable upside-down cow, "the Udderbelly", one of the fifteen comedy and cabaret venues operated by **Underbelly** (58 Cowgate ⓣ0844/545 8252, ⓦwww.underbelly.co.uk). Over in the New Town, the **Assembly Rooms** (50 George St ⓣ0131/623 3000, ⓦwww.assemblyrooms.com) provide a slick, grand setting for top-of-the-range drama and big-name music and comedy acts. They have expanded in recent years to take in the Church of Scotland's Gothic, majestic **Assembly Hall** on the Mound as well as commandeering the Ross Bandstand in **Princes Street Gardens** for its new tented venue and outdoor garden bar. The disparate locations of **C** (ⓣ0870/701 5105, ⓦwww.cthefestival.com) have the most varied programme of the big five, and in recent years have been known to stage controversial productions that other venues might be too wary to promote.

While it's nothing like as large as the venues above, you shouldn't ignore the programme put on at the **Traverse Theatre** (see p.117). Long a champion of new drama, the "Trav" combines the avant-garde with professional presentation and its plays are generally among the Fringe's most acclaimed.

concerts given by international stars. Past visitors have included B.B. King, Bill Wyman, Dizzy Gillespie, Dave Brubeck, Van Morrison, Carol Kidd, and The Blues Band. Highlights include the nightly **Jam Sessions** and a colourful New Orleans-style **Mardi Gras and street parade**.

Tickets range in price from £5 for small pub gigs to £20 for a seat in a big venue, and are available from The Hub (Ⓣ0131/473 2000, Ⓦwww.edinburghjazzfestival.com).

Edinburgh Art Festival

A relative newcomer on the scene, the **Edinburgh Art Festival** (Ⓦwww.edinburghartfestival.com) has quickly established itself as an important addition to the festivals portfolio. This is due, in large part, to the ambition and diversity of its programme, which has included high-profile exhibitions by internationally renowned contemporary artists such as Tracey Emin, Douglas Gordon and Ron Mueck as well as retrospectives of work by pioneering twentieth-century artists including sculptor Eva Hesse, photographer Robert Mapplethorpe, pop artists Gilbert & George and elder statesmen of Scottish painting Alan Davie and John Bellany. Virtually every art gallery in the city participates in the festival, from small private concerns to blockbuster shows at the National Galleries of Scotland's five venues.

Most exhibitions are free, though entry to the National Galleries' exhibitions costs £7–10 (Ⓦwww.nationalgalleries.org/tickets).

The Military Tattoo

Staged in the spectacular stadium of the Edinburgh Castle Esplanade, the **Military Tattoo** is an unashamed display of pomp and military pride. The programme of choreographed drills, massed pipe bands, historical tableaux, energetic battle re-enactments, national dancing and pyrotechnics has been a feature of the Festival for over half a century, its emotional climax provided by a lone piper on the Castle battlements. Followed by a quick fireworks display, it's a successful formula barely tampered with over the years.

Tickets (£16–50 depending on seat location) need to be booked well in advance, and it's advisable to take a cushion and rainwear. Tickets and information are available from the Tattoo Office, 32 Market St (Ⓣ0131/225 1188, Ⓦwww.edintattoo.co.uk).

Listings

Banks and exchange All the major UK banks have branches in central Edinburgh, with ATMs and currency exchange; the main concentrations are in the area between Hanover St and St Andrew Square in the east end of the central New Town. Post offices will exchange currency commission-free; you can also try Thomas Cook, 52 Hanover St (Mon–Sat 9am–5.30pm, Sun noon–5pm; Ⓣ0845/308 9277) and the currency exchange bureaus in the main tourist office (see p.67). To change money after hours, try one of the upmarket hotels – but expect a hefty commission charge.

Bike rental Biketrax, 11 Lochrin Place Ⓣ0131/228 6633, Ⓦwww.biketrax.co.uk; Edinburgh Cycle Hire, 29 Blackfriars St Ⓣ0131/556 5560, Ⓦwww.cyclescotland.co.uk.

Car rental Arnold Clark, 20B–20D Seafield Rd East Ⓣ0131/657 9120; Avis, 5 West Park Place Ⓣ0844/544 3463; Budget, Edinburgh Airport Ⓣ0844/581 2253; Europcar, 24 East London St Ⓣ0131/603 2827; Hertz, 10 Picardy Place Ⓣ0131/202 8571; Thrifty, 42 Haymarket Terrace Ⓣ0131/337 1319.

Dentist Call the NHS Helpline (Ⓣ0800/224488) for details of your nearest dental surgery. Chalmers

Dental Centre, 3 Chalmers St (Mon–Fri 9am–4.45pm; ⓣ0131/536 4800) has a walk-in centre for emergency dental work if you're not registered locally, as well as an out-of-hours service.

Flight information Edinburgh International Airport (ⓣ0844/481 8989, ⓦwww.edinburghairport.com).

Football Edinburgh has two Scottish Premier Division teams, which are normally at home on alternate weekends: Heart of Midlothian (known as Hearts) play at Tynecastle Stadium, Gorgie Rd (ⓣ0871/663 1874, ⓦwww.heartsfc.co.uk), a couple of miles west of the centre; Hibernian (or Hibs) play at Easter Rd Stadium (ⓣ0131/652 6329, ⓦwww.hibernianfc.co.uk), a similar distance northeast of the centre. Between them, the two clubs dominated Scottish football in the 1950s, but neither has won more than the odd trophy since, though one or the other periodically threatens to make a major breakthrough. Tickets start around £20.

Gay and lesbian contacts Lothian LGBT Helpline (Wed 12.30pm–7pm; ⓣ0131/556 4049); Edinburgh LGBT Centre for Health and Wellbeing, 9 Howe St (ⓣ0131/523 1100, ⓦwww.lgbthealth.org.uk).

Golf Edinburgh is awash with fine golf courses, but most are private. The best public courses are the two on the Braid Hills (ⓣ0131/447 6666); others are Carrick Knowe (ⓣ0131/337 1096), Craigentinny (ⓣ0131/554 7501) and Silverknowes (ⓣ0131/336 3843).

Hospital Royal Infirmary, Little France (ⓣ0131/536 1000), has a 24hr casualty department. There's also a minor injuries clinic at the Western General, Crewe Rd North (8am–9pm; ⓣ0131/537 1330), and a casualty department for children at Royal Hospital for Sick Children, Sciennes Rd (ⓣ0131/536 0000). NHS24 (ⓣ0845/424 2424) offers health advice and clinical assessment over the phone; it essentially covers periods when doctors' surgeries aren't open, but is available 24hr.

Internet Many hotels, guesthouses and hostels have facilities, with free wi-fi access quickly becoming the norm; in the centre of town try New Wings, 71 Nicholson St (ⓣ0131/668 4777), or Coffee Home Internet, 28 Crighton Place (ⓣ0131/477 8336), about halfway down Leith Walk.

Laundry Bendix Self-Service Laundrette, 342 Leith Walk ⓣ0131/554 2180; Canonmills Laundrette, 7–8 Huntly St ⓣ0131/556 3199; Ace Cleaning Centre, 13 South Clerk St ⓣ0131/603 3408.

Left luggage Counter by platform 2 at Waverley Station; £5 per item (daily 7am–11pm; ⓣ0131/558 3829).

Libraries Central Library, George IV Bridge (Mon–Thurs 10am–8pm, Fri 10am–5pm, Sat 9am–1pm; ⓣ0131/242 8000). In addition to the usual departments, there's a separate Scottish section, plus an Edinburgh Room which is a mine of information on the city. The National Library of Scotland, George IV Bridge (Mon–Fri 9.30am–8.30pm, Sat 9.30am–1pm; ⓣ0131/623 3700), a magnificent copyright library, is for research purposes only and accreditation is necessary to use the facilities. There is freer access to an annexe which contains the Map Room, 33 Salisbury Place (Mon–Fri 9.30am–5pm, Sat 9.30am–1pm).

Lost property Edinburgh Airport ⓣ0131/344 3486; Edinburgh Police HQ ⓣ0131/311 3141 (lost property found in taxis is sent here); Lothian Buses ⓣ0131/558 8858; Scotrail ⓣ0141/335 3276.

Pharmacy Boots, 48 Shandwick Place (Mon–Fri 8am–8pm, Sat 8am–6pm, Sun 10.30am–5pm; ⓣ0131/225 6757) has the longest opening hours.

Police In an emergency call 999. Otherwise contact Lothian and Borders Police HQ, Fettes Ave (ⓣ0131/311 3131).

Post office 8–10 St James Centre (Mon–Sat 9am–5.30pm; ⓣ0845/722 3344).

Rape crisis centre ⓣ0131/556 9437, ⓦwww.rapecrisisscotland.org.uk.

Rugby Scotland's international fixtures are played at Murrayfield Stadium, a couple of miles west of the city centre. Visit ⓦwww.scottishrugby.org or phone ⓣ0131/346 5000 for information on ticket sales, but tickets can be very hard to come by for the big games.

Swimming pools The city has one Olympic-standard modern pool, the Royal Commonwealth Pool, 21 Dalkeith Rd, which is closed for refurbishment until summer 2011. There are a number of considerably older pools at Caledonian Crescent, Dalry (ⓣ0131/313 3964); Glenogle Rd, Stockbridge (ⓣ0131/343 6376); 57 The Promenade, Portobello (ⓣ0131/669 6888) and 6 Thirlestane Rd, Marchmont (ⓣ0131/447 0052). Go to ⓦwww.edinburghleisure.co.uk for opening hours and details of facilities.

Taxis Central Radio Taxis ⓣ0131/229 2468; City Cabs ⓣ0131/228 1211.

Travel agents Flight Centre, 40 North Bridge ⓣ0131/226 7066; STA, 27 Forest Rd ⓣ0871/702 9817.

Out from the centre

There's a great deal to be discovered beyond the compact centre of Edinburgh, especially along the Firth of Forth coastline to the north and towards the Pentland Hills to the south. Just over a mile northeast of the city centre is **Leith**, the historic port of Edinburgh, a fascinating mix of cobbled streets, new developments and run-down housing, alongside some of the city's top restaurants. Nearby you can find a flavour of the city's maritime and fishing heritage at the atmospheric harbour of **Newhaven**, while the long beach at **Portobello** is still a popular spot on a sunny day. To the north and west of the city are Edinburgh's long-established **zoo** and the placid charms of the old Roman village of **Cramond**, also on the shore of the Forth.

In the southeast suburbs of the city, the imposing fifteenth-century **Craigmillar Castle** is incongruously set amid a rather grim housing estate, but there is also a rural aspect to the area, with various hills, parks and, on the southern edge of the city, the **Pentland Hills,** which offer wild walking country and terrific views.

Leith and around

Although **LEITH** is generally known as the port of Edinburgh, it developed independently of the city up the hill, its history bound up in the hard graft of fishing, shipbuilding and trade. The presence of sailors, merchants and continental traders also gave the place a cosmopolitan – if slightly rough – edge, which is still obvious today. While specific attractions are few, Leith is an intriguing place to explore, worth visiting not just for the contrasts to central Edinburgh, but also for its nautical air and the excellent eating and drinking scene, which majors on seafood but includes haute cuisine and well-worn, friendly pubs.

Leith's initial revival from down-and-out port to des-res waterfront began in the 1980s around the area known as the **Shore**, the old harbour at the mouth of the Water of Leith. More recently, the massive dock areas beyond are being transformed at a rate of knots, with landmark developments including a vast building housing civil servants from the Scottish Executive and Ocean Terminal, a shopping and entertainment complex, beside which the former royal yacht **Britannia** has settled into her retirement.

To reach Leith from the city centre, take one of the many buses going down Leith Walk, which connects with the eastern end of Princes Street and Queen Street; the roadworks you're likely to see along the way are for the tram system which will ply this route from 2012 – or possibly later.

Around the port

The best way to absorb Leith's history and seafaring connections is to take a stroll along **The Shore**, a tenement-lined road running alongside the Water of Leith. Until the mid-nineteenth century this was a bustling and cosmopolitan harbour, visited by ships from all over the world, but as vessels became increasingly large, they moored up at custom-built docks built beyond the original quays; these days, only a handful of boats are permanently moored here. Instead, the focus is on the numerous **pubs and restaurants** that line the street, many of which spill tables and chairs out onto the cobbled pavement on sunny days. Within a few hundred yards of each other, Leith now has three Michelin-starred restaurants, a concentration unmatched in any other British city outside London. The historic buildings along this stretch include the imposing Neoclassical Custom House, still used as offices by the harbour authority (and not open to the public); the round signal tower above *Fishers* restaurant (see p.112), which was originally constructed as a windmill; and the turrets and towers of the Sailors' Home, built in Scots Baronial style in the 1880s as a dosshouse for seafarers, and now home to the rather swankier digs of the *Malmaison* hotel (see p.74).

A little further south on Kirkgate, **Trinity House** (ⓣ0131/554 3289; HS; free) is the only one of the port's grand buildings open to the public. Even here access is limited – all visits must be pre-booked – but if you're interested in maritime history, it's well worth the effort. Home of the Incorporation of Masters and Mariners of Leith, the present Neoclassical villa dates from 1816 and has some impressive original interiors and plasterwork, as well as a significant collection of maritime memorabilia including paintings and ships' models.

Leith Links is an area of predominantly flat parkland on the eastern side of Leith; documentary evidence from 1505 suggests that James IV used to "play at gowf at Leithe", giving rise to Leith's claim as the birthplace of the sport. In 1744 the first written rules of golf were drawn up here by the Honourable Company of Edinburgh Golfers, ten years before they were formalized in St Andrews. However, fans keen to pay homage to the spot may be a little disappointed: other than informal practice sessions by locals, there's no golf played on the Links these days.

Britannia

A little to the west of The Shore, moored alongside **Ocean Terminal**, a huge shopping and entertainment centre designed by Terence Conran, is one of the world's most famous ships, **Britannia** (daily: April–June & Oct 10am–4pm; July–Sept 9.30am–4.30pm; Nov–March 10am–3.30pm; £11.50; ⓦwww.royalyachtbritannia.co.uk). Launched in 1953 at John Brown's shipyard on Clydeside, *Britannia* was used by the royal family for 44 years for state visits, diplomatic functions and royal holidays. Leith acquired her following decommission in 1997, against the wishes of many of the royal family, who felt that scuttling would have been a more dignified end. Alongside *Britannia*, the sleek former royal sailing yacht, *Bloodhound*, is also on view (Sept–June).

Visits to *Britannia* begin in the **visitor centre**, on the second floor of Ocean Terminal, where royal holiday snaps and video clips of the ship's most famous moments, which included the 1983 evacuation of Aden and the British handover of Hong Kong in 1997, are shown. An audio handset is then handed out and you are allowed to roam around the yacht: the **bridge**, the **engine room**, the **officers' mess** and a large part of the **state apartments**, including the cabins used by the Queen and the Duke of Edinburgh. The ship has been kept largely as she was when in service, with a well-preserved 1950s dowdiness which the audio guide loyally attributes to the Queen's good taste and astute frugality in the lean postwar years. Certainly, the atmosphere is a far cry from the opulent splendour which many expect.

The guide's commentary also reveals quirkier aspects of *Britannia*'s history: a full Marine Band was always part of the 300-strong crew; hand signals were used by the sailors to communicate orders as shouting was forbidden; and a special solid mahogany rail was built onto the royal bridge to allow the Queen to stand on deck as the ship came into port, without fear of a gust of wind lifting the royal skirt.

To get to Ocean Terminal from the city, jump on one of the tour buses that leave from Waverley Bridge; otherwise, make use of buses #11, #22 or #34 from Princes Street, or #35 from the Royal Mile.

Newhaven

To the west of Leith lies the old village (now suburb) of **NEWHAVEN**, established by James IV at the start of the sixteenth century as an alternative shipbuilding centre to Leith: his massive warship, the *Great Michael*, capable of carrying 120 gunners, 300 mariners and 1000 troops, and said to have used up all the trees in Fife, was built here. Newhaven has also been a ferry station and an important fishing centre, landing some six million oysters a year at the height of its success in the 1860s. Today, the chief pleasure is a stroll around the stone harbour, which still has a pleasantly salty feel, with a handful of boats tied up alongside or resting gently on the tidal mud – though you might want to combine your visit with a plate of oysters (admittedly, grown on the other side of Scotland) at the *Loch Fyne Restaurant* (see p.112) which overlooks the harbour. Trips out to Inchcolm Island (see p.136) on the Firth of Forth on board a high-speed RIB run from the harbour (daily April–Oct, £22; ⓣ0131/331 4857, ⓦwww.seafari.co.uk).

Portobello

Among Edinburgh's least expected assets is its **beach**, most of which falls within **PORTOBELLO**, the suburb to the southeast of Leith. Once a lively **seaside resort,** it's now a forlorn kind of place, its funfairs and amusement arcades decidedly down at heel. Nonetheless, it retains a certain faded charm, and – on hot summer weekends at least – the beach can be a mass of swimmers, sunbathers, surfers and pleasure boats. A walk along the promenade is a pleasure at any time of the year. Portobello is about three miles east of the centre of town, and can be reached by a direct route on buses #15 or #26.

Edinburgh Zoo

A couple of miles due west of the city centre, **Edinburgh Zoo** (daily: April–Sept 9am–6pm; March & Oct 9am–5pm; Nov–Feb 9am–4.30pm; £15.50; ⓦwww.edinburghzoo.org.uk) is set on an eighty-acre site on the slopes of Corstorphine Hill (buses #12, #26 & #31 from town). Established in 1913, the zoo has a reputation for preserving rare and endangered species, with the general emphasis moving away from bored animals in cages to imaginatively designed habitats and viewing areas. The latter are best seen by taking a **hilltop safari** (daily 10am–3.30pm/4.30pm; 30min), a regular, free shuttle trip to the top of Corstorphine Hill in a Land Rover-pulled trailer, passing large enclosures of camels and llamas. Once at the top, you can admire the city views, then get out and wander back down past zebra and antelope grazing in fields and a row of glass-walled pens containing tigers and lions. The place is permanently packed with kids, and the zoo's most famous attraction is its **penguin parade** (daily 2.15pm April–Sept, and sunny days March & Oct), when rangers encourage a bunch of the flightless birds to leave their pen and waddle around a short circuit of pathways lined with admiring spectators.

Cramond

Two and a half miles further northwest, roughly five miles from the city centre, **CRAMOND** is one of the city's most atmospheric – and poshest – old villages. The enduring image of Cramond is of step-gabled whitewashed houses rising uphill from the waterfront, though it also has the foundations of a Roman fort, and a tower house, church, inn and mansion, all from the seventeenth century. The best reason to come here is to enjoy a stroll around and a bit of fresh air. The **walk** along the wide promenade that follows the shoreline offers great views of the Forth; or head out across the causeway to the uninhabited bird sanctuary of Cramond Island – though be aware that the causeway disappears as high tide approaches and can leave you stranded if you get your timings wrong. For tide times, either check the noticeboard on shore, call the Coastguard (ⓣ01333/450666) or look for tide times for Leith on the BBC weather website. Aim to get to and from the island in the two hours either side of low tide. Inland of Cramond, there's another pleasant walk along a tree-lined path leading upstream along the River

Almond, past former mills and their adjoining cottages towards the sixteenth-century Old Cramond Bridge. These walks should take around an hour each.

Craigmillar Castle

Situated around five miles southeast of Edinburgh's centre, amidst green belt, **Craigmillar Castle** (April–Sept daily 9.30am–5.30pm; Oct daily 9.30am–4.30pm; Nov–March 9.30am–4.30pm, closed Thurs & Fri; HS; £4.20), is uninhabited these days, and offers an atmospheric, untrammelled contrast to packed Edinburgh Castle in the city centre. Before Queen Victoria set her heart on Balmoral, Craigmillar was considered her royal castle north of the border, a possibility which seems somewhat odd now, given its proximity to the ugly council housing scheme of Craigmillar, one of Edinburgh's most deprived districts. That said, the immediate setting feels very rural and Craigmillar Castle enjoys splendid views back to Arthur's Seat and Edinburgh Castle. The oldest part of the complex is the L-shaped tower house, which dates back to the early 1400s – this remains substantially intact, and the great hall, with its resplendent late Gothic chimneypiece, is in good enough shape to be rented out for functions. The tower house was surrounded in the 1500s by a quadrangular wall with cylindrical corner towers and was used on occasion by Mary, Queen of Scots. It was abandoned to its picturesque decay in the mid-eighteenth century, and today the peaceful ruins and their adjoining grassy lawns make a great place to explore, with kids in particular loving the run of their very own castle.

Take **bus** #8, #33 or #49, from North Bridge to Edinburgh Royal Infirmary, from where the castle is a ten-minute walk along a footpath.

The southern hills

The **hills** of Edinburgh's southern suburbs offer good, not overly demanding walking opportunities, with plenty of sweeping panoramic views. The **Royal Observatory** (only open to the public for occasional evening talks and weekly stargazing sessions; ⓣ0131/668 8404, ⓦwww.roe.ac.uk) stands at the top of Blackford Hill, just a short walk south of Morningside or Newington. Immediately to the south are the **Braid Hills**, largely occupied by two golf courses, which are closed on alternate Sundays to allow access for walkers.

Further south, the **Pentland Hills**, a chain some eighteen miles long and five wide, dominate most views south of Edinburgh and offer walkers and mountain bikers a thrilling taste of wild Scottish countryside just a few miles beyond the suburbs. Numerous bike trails and walks, from gentle strolls along well-marked paths to a ten-mile traverse of the hills and moors, are outlined in a free pamphlet available from the Regional Park Information Centre at **FLOTTERSTONE**, ten miles south of the city centre on the A702.

The simplest way to get a taste of the scenery of the Pentlands is to set off from the car park by the ski centre at **Hillend**, at the northeast end of the range; take the path up the right-hand side of the dry ski slopes, turning left shortly after crossing a stile to reach a prominent point with outstanding views over Edinburgh and Fife. If you're feeling energetic, go higher up where the vistas get even better. An alternative entry point to the Pentland Hills is **SWANSTON**, a short distance northwest of Hillend. It's an unspoiled, highly exclusive hamlet of whitewashed thatched-roof dwellings separated from the rest of the city by almost a mile of farmland; **Robert Louis Stevenson** (see box, p.128) spent his boyhood summers in Swanston Cottage, the largest of the houses, immortalizing it in the novel *St Ives*. Buses #16 and #27 will take you to Oxgangs Road, from where you can walk to Swanston along Swanston Road. Hillend, meanwhile, is connected with the city centre by buses #4 and #15, but only the less frequent McEwans coaches #100, #101 and #102 passes Flotterstone.

Robert Louis Stevenson

Though **Robert Louis Stevenson** (1850–94) is sometimes dismissed for his straight-up writing style, he was one of the best-loved writers of his generation, and one whose novels, short stories, travelogues and essays remain enormously popular over a century after his death.

Born in Edinburgh into a distinguished family of lighthouse engineers, Stevenson was a sickly child, with a solitary childhood dominated by his governess, Alison "Cummie" Cunningham, who regaled him with tales drawn from Calvinist folklore. Sent to the university to study engineering, Stevenson rebelled against his upbringing by spending much of his time in the low-life howffs and brothels of the city. He later switched his studies to law, and although called to the bar in 1875, by then he had decided to channel his energies into literature: while still a student, he had already made his mark as an **essayist**, and eventually had more than a hundred essays published, ranging from light-hearted whimsy to trenchant political analysis. A set of topographical pieces about his native city was later collected together as *Edinburgh: Picturesque Notes*, which conjure up nicely its atmosphere, character and appearance – warts and all.

Stevenson's other early successes were two **travelogues**, *An Inland Voyage* and *Travels with a Donkey in the Cevennes*, kaleidoscopic jottings based on his journeys in France, where he went to escape Scotland's weather, which was damaging his health. It was there that he met Fanny Osbourne, an American ten years his senior, who was estranged from her husband and had two children in tow. His voyage to join her in San Francisco formed the basis for his most important factual work, *The Amateur Emigrant*, a vivid first-hand account of the great nineteenth-century European migration to the United States.

Having married the now-divorced Fanny, Stevenson began an elusive search for an agreeable climate that led to Switzerland, the French Riviera and the Scottish Highlands. He belatedly turned to the novel, achieving immediate acclaim in 1881 for **Treasure Island**, a moralistic adventure yarn that began as an entertainment for his stepson and future collaborator, Lloyd Osbourne. In 1886 his most famous short story, **Strange Case of Dr Jekyll and Mr Hyde**, (despite its nominal London setting), offered a vivid evocation of Edinburgh's Old Town: an allegory of its dual personality of prosperity and squalor, and an analysis of its Calvinistic preoccupations with guilt and damnation. The same year saw the publication of the historical romance **Kidnapped**, an adventure novel which exemplified Stevenson's view that literature should seek above all to entertain.

In 1887 Stevenson left Britain for good, travelling first to the United States where he began one of his most ambitious novels, *The Master of Ballantrae*. A year later, he set sail for the South Seas, and eventually settled in **Samoa**; his last works include a number of stories with a local setting, such as the grimly realistic *The Ebb Tide* and *The Beach of Falesà*. However, Scotland continued to be his main inspiration: he wrote *Catriona* as a sequel to *Kidnapped*, and was at work on two more novels with Scottish settings, *St Ives* and *Weir of Hermiston*, a dark story of father and son confrontation, at the time of his sudden death from a brain haemorrhage in 1894. He was buried on the top of Mount Vaea overlooking the Pacific Ocean.

East Lothian

East Lothian consists of the coastal strip and hinterland immediately east of Edinburgh, bounded by the Firth of Forth to the north and the Lammermuir Hills to the south. All of it is within easy day-trip range from the capital, though there are places you can stay overnight if you're keen to explore it properly. Often mocked as the "home counties" of Edinburgh, there's no denying its well-ordered feel, with prosperous farms and large estate houses dominating the scenery. The most immediately attractive part of the area is the coastline, extending from the town of **Musselburgh**, all but joined onto Edinburgh, round to **Dunbar**. There's something for most tastes here, including the wide sandy beaches by **Aberlady**, the famous golf courses of **Gullane**, the enjoyable Seabird Centre at **North Berwick**, dramatic cliff-top ruins at **Tantallon** and the supersonic draw of **Concorde** at the Museum of Flight. Inland, at the foot of the Lammermuirs is the county town of **Haddington**, a pleasant enough place, though the attractions nearby of Gifford, a neat village deeper into the hills, or Edinburgh's "local" whisky distillery by Pencaitland, are likely to be a stronger draw.

Musselburgh to Dirleton

Though the largest town in East Lothian, with a long history connected to the development of mussel beds at the mouth of the River Esk, **MUSSELBURGH** is a place in which you're unlikely to linger long, if only for the feeling that you've hardly shaken off the dust of Edinburgh. There is, however, a **race course** here, one of the busiest in Scotland, with a regular programme of decent quality National Hunt and Flat meetings. For details of what's on, contact the course on Ⓣ0131/665 2859, Ⓦwww.musselburgh-racecourse.co.uk.

Bypassing the chimneys of the Cockenzie power station, the East Lothian coastline takes a turn for the better by **ABERLADY**, an elongated conservation village of Gothic-style cottages and mansions just sixteen miles east of Edinburgh. The salt marshes and sand dunes of the adjacent **Aberlady Bay Nature Reserve**, a birdwatchers' haven, mark the site of the old harbour.

From the nature reserve, it's a couple of miles to **GULLANE** (pronounced "Gillin"), the location of the famous shoreline links of **Muirfield Golf Course**, home of the grandly named Honourable Company of Edinburgh Golfers and occasional venue for the Open Championship. There are three other courses around Gullane, not to mention dozens more around East Lothian, but if golf isn't your thing, you might prefer the fine sandy **beaches** of Gullane Bay or the chance to explore the genteel hamlet of **DIRLETON**, two miles east of Gullane, which huddles around **Dirleton Castle** (daily: April–Sept 9.30am–5.30pm; Oct–March 9.30am–4.30pm; HS; £4.70), a romantic thirteenth-century ruin with gardens.

There are some grand places to **stay** nearby, among them the splendid *Open Arms*, opposite the castle (Ⓣ01620/850241, Ⓦwww.openarmshotel.com; ❼). Eating options are even better, with the excellent if modest-looking *La Potinière* restaurant (Ⓣ01620/843214, Ⓦwww.la-potiniere.co.uk; closed Mon & Tues, also Sun eve in winter) on the main street in Gullane and *Chez Roux* (Ⓣ01620/842144, Ⓦwww.greywalls.co.uk), one of a number of hotel restaurants run by chef Albert Roux's company, offering excellent, well-priced dining in the stunning Edwardian country-house hotel of *Greywalls*, right beside Muirfield links. For snacks or **picnic fare** head to Gullane Delicatessen at 40c High St and Falko Konditormeister, an excellent German baker a little further along the main street.

National Museum of Flight

A few miles south of Dirleton, located on an old military airfield by East Fortune, the **National Museum of Flight** (April–Oct daily 10am–5pm; Nov–March Sat & Sun 10am–4pm; £9; Ⓣ0131/247 4238, Ⓦwww.nms.ac.uk/flight) is home to *Alpha Alpha*, the first **Concorde** to fly in British Airways colours. One of the icons of the twentieth century, Concorde was the world's first supersonic passenger jet, able to zip over the Atlantic in just under three hours. Now installed in a custom-built hangar, *Alpha Alpha*, one of only twenty planes built, has been reassembled to show how she looked when decommissioned in 2003. Despite its exclusive tag, space wasn't one of the luxuries available aboard the plane known to its crew as "the toothpick", and a visit on board is restricted to a slightly stooped wander through the forward half of the aircraft, with the chance to look at the cockpit through a perspex partition. Elsewhere in the hangar, a short film tells the story of *Alpha Alpha*, including footage of its unusual journey by barge and road trailer to East Fortune, while information boards and display cabinets allow you to follow the Concorde project as a whole, from its early days of Anglo-French bickering to the tragic Paris crash of 2000. Alongside Concorde you can look inside the front section of a Boeing 707, the style of plane that ushered in the "jet age" in the 1960s, while elsewhere on the site are more than fifty vintage aircraft including a Vulcan bomber, a Spitfire and a Tigermoth. To get to the museum by public transport, catch **First Bus** #121 from North Berwick or Haddington, both of which have connections from Edinburgh.

North Berwick

NORTH BERWICK has a great deal of charm and a somewhat faded, old-fashioned air, its guesthouses and hotels extending along the shore in all their Victorian and Edwardian sobriety. The town's small harbour is set on a headland which cleaves two crescents of sand, providing the town with an attractive coastal setting, though it is the two nearby volcanic heaps, the offshore **Bass Rock** and 613ft-high **North Berwick Law**, which are the town's defining physical features.

Resembling a giant molar, the Bass Rock rises 350ft above the sea some three miles east of North Berwick and is home to some 100,000 nesting gannets in summer, as well as razorbills, terns, puffins, guillemots and fulmars. The best place to observe the rock and its inhabitants is the **Scottish Seabird Centre** (April–Sept daily 10am–6pm; Nov–Jan Mon–Fri 10am–4pm, Sat & Sun 10am–5pm; Feb, March & Oct Mon–Fri 10am–5pm, Sat & Sun 10am–5.30pm; £7.15; Ⓦwww.seabird.org), housed in an attractively designed new building by the harbour. Among the interactive exhibits and child-oriented displays there's a live link from the centre to cameras mounted on the volcanic island, which show close-up pictures of the birds in their nesting grounds. The cameras are mounted in different locations, depending on the movement of birds – in winter, for example, the gannets aren't around so it's more interesting to watch the shore birds or some peregrine falcons which have nested on Fidra Island. Weather permitting, various **boat trips** are available, including high-speed RIB trips around the Bass Rock, a longer scoot as far as the Isle of May near the Fife coast (see p.339) and a five-and-a-half-hour trip with time on the Bass Rock itself. Contact the Seabird Centre to find out what's available on any given day (Ⓣ01620/890202).

Practicalities

North Berwick is served by a regular half-hourly **train** from Edinburgh Waverley, with special travel and entry deals available for those heading for the Seabird Centre (ask at Waverley ticket office or go to Ⓦwww.scotrail.co.uk). From the station it's a ten-minute walk east to the town centre. **Buses** from Edinburgh (every 30min) run along the coast via Aberlady, Gullane and Dirleton and stop on High Street, while the hourly services from Haddington and Dunbar terminate outside the **tourist office** (April, May & Oct Mon–Sat; June–Sept daily; Nov–March Thurs–Sat; Ⓣ01620/892197), on Quality Street.

As befits a well-to-do holiday resort, there are several decent **B&Bs**, including *Beach Lodge*, 5 Beach Rd (Ⓣ01620/892257, Ⓦwww.beachlodge.co.uk; ❺), near the main street and harbour and boasting some great balcony views out to sea, and *Glebe House*, Law Rd (Ⓣ01620/892608, Ⓦwww.glebehouse-nb.co.uk; ❻), a grander eighteenth-century manse in secluded grounds further inland but still overlooking the sea.

One of the best-located **cafés** in town is at the Seabird Centre, which has panoramic views over the beach as well as outdoor decking. *Osteria* at 71 High St (Ⓣ01620/890589, Ⓦwww.osteria-no1.co.uk; closed Sun) is run by a father and daughter team, with a pricey but classy menu of classical Italian cooking – booking recommended.

Tantallon Castle

The melodramatic ruins of **Tantallon Castle** (April–Sept daily 9.30am–5.30pm; Oct daily 9.30am–4.30pm; Nov–March Mon–Wed, Sat & Sun 9.30am–4.30pm; HS; £4.70), three miles east of North Berwick on the A198, stand on the precipitous cliffs facing the Bass Rock. With a sheer drop down to the sea on three sides and a sequence of moats and ditches on the fourth, the castle's desolate invincibility is daunting, especially when the wind howls over the remaining battlements and the surf crashes on the rocks far below. Built at the end of the fourteenth century, the castle was a stronghold of the Douglases, the earls of Angus, one of the most powerful noble families in Scotland. You can reach Tantallon Castle from North Berwick by the Dunbar **bus** (Eves Coaches #120; Mon–Sat 6 daily, 2 on Sun), which takes fifteen minutes, or you can walk there from town along the cliffs in around an hour.

Dunbar

Twelve miles further along the coast lies **DUNBAR**, with its delightfully intricate double harbour set beside the shattered remains of a castle, and a wide, recently spruced-up High Street graced by several grand old stone buildings. One of these is the three-storey **John Muir Birthplace**, 126 High St (April–Oct Mon–Sat 10am–5pm, Sun 1–5pm; Nov–March Wed–Sat 10am–5pm, Sun 1–5pm; free; Ⓦwww.jmbt.org.uk), the first home of the explorer and naturalist who created the United States national park system. The house is an engaging interpretative and education centre about the pioneer's life and legacy, although a more appropriate tribute, in some respects, is the **country park** neighbouring the town, also named in Muir's honour. You can experience it on an easy three-mile walk west of the harbour, along a rugged stretch of coast to the sands of Belhaven Bay.

The **tourist office**, 143a High St (April–Oct Mon–Sat; July & Aug daily; Ⓣ01368/863353), will help with **accommodation**; try the non-smoking *Woodside* B&B, 13 North St (Ⓣ01368/862384, Ⓦwww.dunbarwoodside.co.uk; April–Sept; ❹) close to John Muir Country Park. For somewhere to **eat** in town, head to the *Creel*, near the old harbour (Ⓣ01368/863279, Ⓦwww.creelrestaurant.co.uk; closed Mon–Wed), which serves well-judged meals based on local produce.

Inland from the coast

One of Scotland's most respectable county towns, **HADDINGTON** sits on the banks of the Tyne river with the hulking mass of **St Mary's Church** (Easter–Sept Mon–Sat 11am–4pm, Sun 2–4.30pm; free), Scotland's largest parish church, rising tall near its centre. Other than a stroll along the river bank or the seventeenth-century medicinal gardens of **St Mary's Pleasance** (open during daylight hours; free) on Sidegate, there's not much to detain you in the town. Four miles south along the B6369 on the edge of the Lammermuir Hills, the pretty hamlet of **GIFFORD**, whose eighteenth-century estate cottages flank a trim white-washed church, was the birthplace (in 1723) of the Reverend John Witherspoon, a signatory of the American Declaration of Independence. The hamlet makes a good base for walkers, with several footpaths setting out across the surrounding red-soiled farmland for the Lammermuir Hills, while longer trails connect with the Southern Upland Way.

Six miles west of Gifford, meanwhile, and about the same distance from Haddington along the A6093, the **Glenkinchie Distillery** (Easter–Oct Mon–Sat 10am–5pm, Sun noon–5pm; Nov daily noon–4pm; Dec–Easter Mon–Fri noon–4pm; last tour 1hr before closing; £6) is the closest place to Edinburgh where malt whisky is made. Here, of course, they emphasize the qualities that set Glenkinchie, a lighter, drier malt, apart from the peaty, smoky whiskies of the north and west. If you want **to stay** in the area, try *Eaglescairnie Mains* (Ⓣ01620/810491, Ⓦwww.eaglescairnie.com; ❹), a substantial farmhouse a mile from Gifford with open fires and a tennis court.

Midlothian

Immediately south of Edinburgh lies the old county of **MIDLOTHIAN**, once called Edinburghshire. It's one of the hilliest parts of the Central Lowlands, with the Pentland chain running down its western side and the Moorfoots defining its boundary with the Borders to the south. Though predominantly rural, it contains a belt of former mining communities that are struggling to come to terms with the recent decline of the industry. Such charms as it has are mostly low-key, with the exception of the riotously ornate chapel at **ROSLIN**. This tranquil village lies seven miles south of the centre of Edinburgh, from where it can be reached by bus #15 from St Andrew Square. An otherwise nondescript place, the village has two unusual claims to fame: it was near here, at the Roslin Institute, that the **world's first cloned sheep**, Dolly, was created in 1997; and it's home to the mysterious, richly decorated late Gothic **Rosslyn Chapel** (April–Sept Mon–Sat 9.30am–5.30pm, Sun noon–4.15pm; Oct–March Mon–Sat 9.30am–4.30pm, Sun noon–4.15pm; £7.50; Ⓦwww.rosslynchapel.org.uk). The chapel was intended to be a huge collegiate church dedicated to St Matthew, but construction halted soon after the founder's death in 1484, and the vestry built onto the facade nearly four hundred years later is the sole subsequent addition. After a long period of neglect, a massive restoration project is underway.

Visitors are free to look around both inside and out: Rosslyn's exterior bristles with pinnacles, gargoyles, flying buttresses and canopies, while inside the **stonework** is, if anything, even more intricate. The foliage carving is particularly outstanding, with botanically accurate depictions of over a dozen different leaves and plants. Among them are cacti and Indian corn, compounding the legend that the founder's grandfather, the daring sea adventurer Prince Henry of Orkney, did indeed set foot in the New World a century before Columbus. The rich and subtle figurative sculptures have given Rosslyn the nickname of "a Bible in stone", though they're more allegorical than literal, with portrayals of the Dance of Death, the Seven Acts of Mercy and the Seven Deadly Sins.

The greatest and most original carving of all is the extraordinary knotted **Apprentice Pillar** at the southeastern corner of the Lady Chapel. According to local legend, the pillar was made by an apprentice during the absence of the master mason, who killed him in a fit of jealousy on seeing the finished work. A tiny head of a man with a slashed forehead, set at the apex of the ceiling at the far northwestern corner of the building, is popularly supposed to represent the apprentice, his murderer the corresponding head at the opposite side.

The imagery of carvings such as the floriated cross and five-pointed star, together with the history of the family, the St Clairs of Rosslyn, which owns the chapel, leave little doubt about its links to the **Knights Templar** and Freemasonry. Two members of the St Clair family, for example, were allegedly grand masters of the Prieuré de Sion, the shadowy order linked to the Templars, while the Masonic connection was said to have saved the chapel from the armies of Oliver Cromwell, himself a Freemason, which destroyed the surrounding area but spared Rosslyn. More intriguing still are claims that, because of such connections, Rosslyn Chapel has been the repository for items such as the lost Scrolls of Solomon's Temple in Jerusalem, the true Stone of Scone and, most famously, the **Holy Grail**. The chapel is regularly drawn into conspiracy theories on these themes, most famously in recent years through Dan Brown's bestseller *The Da Vinci Code*; the chapel's appearance in the film of the same name precipitated a huge surge in visitor numbers which detracts a little from the mysterious air of the place.

West Lothian

To many, West Lothian is a poor relative to the rich, rolling farmland of East and Midlothian, with a landscape dominated by motorways, industrial estates and giant hillocks of ochre-coloured mine waste called "bings". However, in the ruined royal palace at **Linlithgow**, the area boasts one of Scotland's more magnificent ruins. Not too far away, the village of **South Queensferry** lies under the considerable shadow of the Forth rail and road bridges, though it's an interesting enough place in its own right, with a historic High Street and the notable stately homes **Dalmeny** and **Hopetoun** nearby.

Linlithgow

Roughly equidistant between Falkirk, to the west, and the outskirts of Edinburgh, to the east, is the ancient royal burgh of **LINLITHGOW**. The town itself has largely kept its medieval layout, but development since the 1960s has sadly stripped it of some fine buildings, notably close to the **Town Hall** and **Cross** – the former marketplace – on the long High Street.

Though hidden from the main road, **Linlithgow Palace** (daily: April–Sept 9.30am–5.30pm; Oct–March 9.30am–4.30pm; HS; £5.20), is a splendid fifteenth-century ruin romantically set on the edge of Linlithgow Loch and associated with some of Scotland's best-known historical figures, including Mary, Queen of Scots, who was born here on December 8, 1542 and became queen six days later. A royal manor house is believed to have existed on this site since the time of David I, though James I began construction of the present palace, a process that continued through two centuries and the reign of no fewer than eight monarchs. From the top of the northwest tower, Queen Margaret looked out in vain for the return of James IV from the field of Flodden in 1513 – indeed, the views from her bower, six giddy storeys up from the ground, are exceptional. The ornate octagonal **fountain** in the inner courtyard, with its wonderfully intricate figures and medallion heads, flowed with wine for the wedding of James V and Mary of Guise.

This is a great place to take children: the elegant, bare rooms echo with footsteps and there's a labyrinthine network of spiral staircases and endless nooks and crannies. The galleried **Great Hall** is magnificent, as is the adjoining kitchen, which has a truly cavernous fireplace.

St Michael's Church, adjacent to the palace, is one of Scotland's largest pre-Reformation churches, consecrated in the thirteenth century. The present building was completed three hundred years later, with the exception of the hugely incongruous aluminium spire, tacked on in 1946.

Running through Linlithgow is part of the **Union Canal**, the 31-mile artery opened in 1822, which together with the Forth & Clyde Canal linked Edinburgh with Glasgow. At Falkirk, six miles west of here, the unusual Falkirk Wheel (see p.316) transfers boats from one canal to the other. The Linlithgow Union Canal Society runs short boat trips on the canal in the summer months (weekends Easter–Sept, daily July & Aug; Ⓦwww.lucs.org.uk).

Practicalities

Linlithgow is on the main **train** routes from Edinburgh to both Glasgow Queen Street and Stirling; the **train station** lies at the southern end of town. The **tourist office** is in the Town Hall building at the Cross (Sat & Sun; Ⓣ01506/844600), between the Palace and the High Street.

For **accommodation**, on the outskirts of town at Belsyde there's smart *Arden House* (Ⓣ01506/670172, Ⓦwww.ardenhouse-scotland.co.uk; ❺) and friendly *Belsyde Farm* (Ⓣ01506/842098, Ⓦwww.belsydehouse.co.uk; ❸), a late eighteenth-century house on a sheep and cattle farm beside the Union Canal.

Linlithgow has some decent places to **eat** including *Epulum* (Ⓣ01506/844411, Ⓦwww.epulum.net) at 121 High St, a bright, upbeat daytime café-bistro, and the grand *Champany Inn*, just outside Linlithgow on the way to Blackness (Ⓣ01506/834532, Ⓦwww.champany.com), which serves seriously expensive steaks and seafood in an upmarket restaurant, though there's also a less formal chop and ale house as well as smart rooms (❺).

EICA:Ratho

One of the hidden modern wonders of Scottish sport, **EICA:Ratho**, or Edinburgh International Climbing Arena (Mon–Fri 10am–10pm, Sat & Sun 10am–7pm; times and charges for activities vary; Ⓣ0131/333 6333, Ⓦwww.eica-ratho.com), is the world's largest indoor climbing facility, incorporating a remarkable 2870 square yards of artificial climbing wall. Having cost £24 million, the centre struggled financially until its 2005 rescue by Edinburgh Council. The spectacular vision of its architect founders was to enclose (and roof) a disused quarry, creating a giant arena that's now used for international climbing competitions as well as classes (from £20 for an hour-long taster session) for climbers of all levels, including beginners and kids. Above the arena, just under the glass roof, Aerial Assault (£9.50) is a stomach-churning obstacle course suspended 100ft off the ground, which you take on while secured into a sliding harness. Elsewhere in this multi-faceted facility are a state-of-the-art gym, spa, a climbing-themed kids' soft play area and a café which peers out over the climbing arena.

There's no direct public transport to the centre: the best you can do is take #X48 to the village of Ratho then walk for fifteen minutes along the canal towpath; if you're driving, follow the signs from the Newbridge roundabout on the A8, not far from the airport.

South Queensferry and around

Eight miles northwest of Edinburgh city centre, the small town of **SOUTH QUEENSFERRY** is best known today for its location at the southern end of the two mighty **Forth bridges** – for more on these, see p.346. Named after the saintly wife of King Malcolm Canmore, Margaret, who would often use the ferry here to travel between the royal palaces in Dunfermline and Edinburgh, it's an attractive old settlement, its narrow, cobbled High Street lined with tightly packed old buildings, most of which date from the seventeenth and eighteenth centuries. Only one row of houses separates the High Street from the water; through the gaps between these there's a great perspective of the two Forth bridges, an old stone harbour and a curved, pebbly beach, the scene each New Year's Day of the teeth-chattering "Loony Dook", when a gaggle of hungover locals (along with some foolhardy tourists) charge into the sea for the quickest of dips. The small **museum**, 53 High St (Mon & Thurs–Sat 10am–1pm & 2.15–5pm, Sun noon–5pm; free), contains relics of the town's history and information on the building of the two bridges that loom over the village. One of the best ways to get a good view of the magnificent Rail Bridge is to walk (or cycle) across the Road Bridge.

South Queensferry has a couple of excellent spots to **eat**. *The Boathouse* (Ⓣ0131/331 5429, Ⓦwww.theboathouse-sq.co.uk) at 19b High St has a moderately expensive restaurant serving classy local seafood as well as a cheaper bistro with big plate-glass windows; a few doors away at no. 17, *Orocco Pier* (Ⓣ0870/118 1664, Ⓦwww.oroccopier.co.uk) is more ostentatiously slick and contemporary, but is a good place for a drink, some pleasant bistro food or a comfy bed for the night (❻). Both have great views over the water to the bridges. You can walk from South Queensferry to both Dalmeny and Hopetoun houses (see below), although given the distances involved you're probably better off with a taxi, unless you have your own transport.

Dalmeny House

Set on a two-thousand-acre estate between South Queensferry and Cramond, **Dalmeny House** (late May to late July Mon, Tues & Sun tours at 2.15pm & 3.30pm only; £6; Ⓦwww.dalmeny.co.uk), is not the prettiest country seat you'll encounter in Scotland, and visiting opportunities are very restricted, but the quality of the items on show combined with the intriguing history of the resident Rosebery family make it a fascinating place to visit. The fifth earl (1847–1929), a nineteenth-century British prime minister, married the heiress Hannah de Rothschild, and their union is the principal reason why Dalmeny has some of the finest baroque and Neoclassical furniture produced for Louis XIV, Louis XV and Louis XVI in the hundred years before the French Revolution. Also in the collection are a very rare set of tapestries made from cartoons by Goya, and portraits by Raeburn, Reynolds, Gainsborough and Lawrence as well as a valuable collection of memorabilia relating to Napoleon Bonaparte, who clearly fascinated the fifth earl – the collection includes the desk Napoleon used on St Helena, and his ornate shaving stand.

Hopetoun House

Sitting in its own extensive estate on the south shore of the Forth, just to the west of South Queensferry, **Hopetoun House** (Easter–Sept daily 10.30am–5pm; £8 house and grounds, £3.70 grounds only; Ⓦwww.hopetounhouse.com) is one of the most impressive stately homes in Scotland. The original house was built at the turn of the eighteenth century for the first earl of Hopetoun by Sir William Bruce, the architect of Holyroodhouse. A couple of decades later, William Adam carried out an enormous extension, engulfing the structure with a curvaceous main facade and two projecting wings – superb examples of Roman Baroque pomp and swagger. Hopetoun's architecture is undoubtedly its most compelling feature, but the furnishings aren't completely overwhelmed, with some impressive seventeenth-century tapestries, Meissen porcelain and a distinguished collection of paintings, including portraits by Gainsborough, Ramsay and Raeburn. There's a free guided tour at 2pm each day. The house's grounds include a long, regal driveway and lovely walks along woodland trails and the banks of the Forth, as well as plenty of places for a picnic. If the weather's not favourable, the *Stables Tearoom* makes a classy alternative indoor venue for lunch or afternoon tea.

Inchcolm

From South Queensferry's Hawes Pier, just west of the rail bridge, a couple of ferry servies head out to the island of **Inchcolm**, located about five miles northeast of South Queensferry near the Fife shore. The island is home to the best-preserved medieval **abbey** in Scotland, founded in 1235 after King Alexander I was stormbound on the island and took refuge in a hermit's cell. Although the structure as a whole is half-ruined today, the tower, octagonal chapterhouse and echoing cloisters are intact and well worth exploring. The hour and a half you're given ashore by the boat timetables also allows time for a picnic on the abbey's lawns or the chance to explore Inchcolm's old military fortifications and extensive bird-nesting grounds. Dolphins and porpoises are sometimes sighted from the boat crossings to the island, which are run by *Maid of the Forth* (ⓣ0131/331 4857, ⓦwww.maidoftheforth.co.uk; £14.70 including landing fee) and *Forth Belle* (ⓣ0870/118 1866, ⓦwww.forthtours.com; £22.70 including bus from Edinburgh and landing fee). Both run from April to October only, with sailing varying from weekends only in spring and autumn to multiple trips in high summer. Check websites for timetables.

Travel details

Trains

Edinburgh to: Aberdeen (hourly; 2hr 20min); Birmingham (hourly; 5hr); Dunbar (8 daily; 30min); Dundee (hourly; 1hr 45min); Falkirk (every 15min; 25min); Fort William (change at Glasgow, 3 daily; 4hr 55min); Glasgow (every 15–30min; 50min); Inverness (6 daily direct; 3hr 50min); London (hourly; 4hr 30min); Manchester (3 daily; 4hr); Newcastle upon Tyne (hourly; 1hr 30min); North Berwick (hourly; 30min); Oban (2–3 daily, change at Glasgow; 4hr 10min); Perth (6 daily; 1hr 15min); Stirling (every 30min; 45min); York (hourly; 2hr 30min).

Buses

Edinburgh (St Andrew Square) to: Aberdeen (hourly; 3hr 50min); Birmingham (2–3 daily; 6hr 50min); Dundee (hourly; 1hr 45min–2hr); Glasgow (every 15min; 1hr 10min); Inverness (hourly; 3hr 30min–4hr 30min); London (10 daily; 7hr 50min); Newcastle upon Tyne (5 daily; 2hr 45min); Perth (hourly; 1hr 20min).

Flights

Edinburgh to: Belfast (Mon–Fri 8 daily; Sat & Sun 4 daily; 55min); Cardiff (1–2 daily; 1hr 10min); Dublin (4 daily; 1hr); Kirkwall (Mon–Fri 2 daily, Sat & Sun 1 daily; 1hr 55min); London City (Mon–Fri 8 daily, Sat 1, 3 on Sun; 1hr 15min); London Gatwick (Mon–Fri 12 daily, Sat & Sun 5 daily; 1hr 15min); London Heathrow (Mon–Fri 15 daily, Sat & Sun 11–15 daily; 1hr); London Luton (Mon–Fri 7 daily, Sat & Sun 4 daily; 1hr 20min); London Stansted (Mon–Fri 6 daily, Sat & Sun 4–6 daily; 1hr 10min); Stornoway (Mon–Fri 3 daily, Sat 2, Sun 1; 1hr 10 min); Sumburgh (Shetland) (2 daily; 1hr 30min); Wick (Mon–Fri 1 daily; 1hr 10min).

2

The Borders

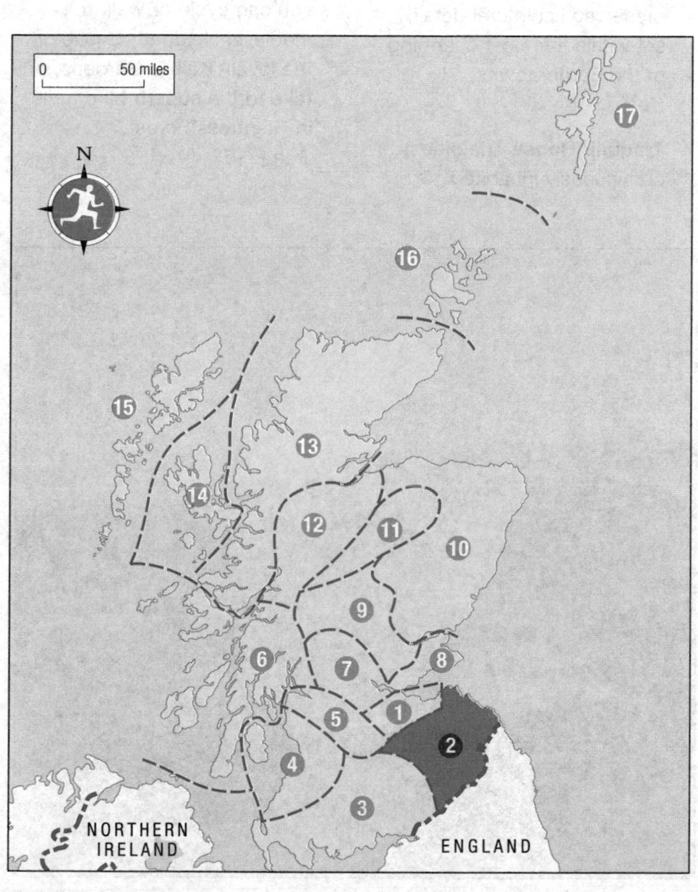

CHAPTER 2

Highlights

* **St Abb's Head** Easily accessible, spectacular coastal scenery with sea stacks and nesting seabirds galore. See p.142
* **Melrose Abbey** The Border abbey with the best-preserved sculptural detail, set within the most charming of the Border towns. See p.148
* **Traquair House** The oldest continuously inhabited house in Scotland, virtually unchanged since the fifteenth century. See p.151
* **Walking and cycling around Peebles** The banks of the Tweed are at their most scenic around Peebles, and you can cycle or walk to medieval Neidpath Castle or the lovely Kailzie Gardens, or take to the superb bike trails in Glentress Forest. See p.152

▲ St Abb's Head

2

The Borders

Sandwiched between the Cheviot Hills on the English border and the Pentland, Moorfoot and Lammermuir hills south of Edinburgh, the **Borders** (Ⓦwww.scot-borders.co.uk) is a region made up of the old shire counties of Berwick, Roxburgh, Selkirk and Peebles. Travelling from the bleak moorland of neighbouring Northumberland, you'll be struck by the green lushness of Tweeddale, whose river is the pivotal feature of the region's geography. Yet the Borders also incorporate some of the wildest stretches of the Southern Uplands, with their bare, rounded peaks and weather-beaten heathery hills.

The Borders' most famous sights are its **ruined abbeys**, founded under King David I (1124–53), whose policy of encouraging the monastic orders had little to do with spirituality. The monks of Kelso, Melrose, Jedburgh and Dryburgh were the frontiersmen of David's kingdom, helping advance his authority in areas of doubtful allegiance. This period of relative stability was interrupted in 1296 by the Wars of Independence with England.

From the first half of the sixteenth century until the Act of Union, the Borders again experienced turbulent times, bloodily fought over by the English and the Scots, and plagued by endless clan warfare and Reivers' raids (see p.146). Consequently, the countryside is strewn with ruined castles and keeps, while each major town celebrates its agitated past in the **Common Ridings**, when locals – especially the "callants" (young men) – dressed in period costume ride out to check the burgh boundaries. It's a boisterous, macho business, performed with pride and matched only by the local love of **rugby union**, which reaches a crescendo with the **Melrose Sevens** tournament in April.

Tweeddale is the Borders at its best, with the finest section between **Melrose** and **Peebles**, where you'll find a string of attractions, from the eccentricities of Sir Walter Scott's mansion at **Abbotsford** to the intriguing Jacobite past of **Traquair House**, plus the aforementioned ruined abbeys. The valley widens to the east to form the **Merse** basin, an area of rich arable land that features a series of grand stately homes, principally **Floors Castle**, **Manderston**, **Paxton** and **Mellerstain House**, all featuring the Neoclassical work of the Adam family.

To the west, the Borders have a wilder aspect, where a series of narrow valleys lead up to the border with Dumfriesshire: remote **Liddesdale**, southwest of Jedburgh; **Teviotdale**, to the north, which passes through Hawick and carries the A7 down to Carlisle; Ettrick Water, which takes you over into Eskdale; and **Yarrow Water** which connects Selkirk with Moffat in Dumfriesshire. Choose any of these four routes for the scenery. North of the Tweed, the **Lammermuir Hills** form the southern edge of Lothian and the central belt. Further east in **Berwickshire**, especially around **St Abb's Head**, the coastline becomes more rugged, its cliffs and rocky outcrops harbouring a series of desolate ruined castles, while inland, the flatness of the terrain is interrupted by the occasional extinct volcano.

The only **train** line in the Borders runs along the east coast, and travelling by **bus** takes some planning, as it's often difficult to cross between valleys – pick up timetables from the local tourist offices.

Berwickshire

Berwickshire, Scotland's easternmost county, lost its natural focus and centre when the English finally captured the town of Berwick-upon-Tweed in 1482 – in its place, unassuming **Duns** had to fill in as the old county town. The coastline is bracing rather than beguiling, with its main attractions the fishing port of **Eyemouth**, and the dramatic cliff scenery around **St Abbs**.

The Lammermuir Hills and Lauder

The gentle River Tweed marks the border between Scotland and England, but it is the **Lammermuir Hills** that form a more substantial physical barrier, and

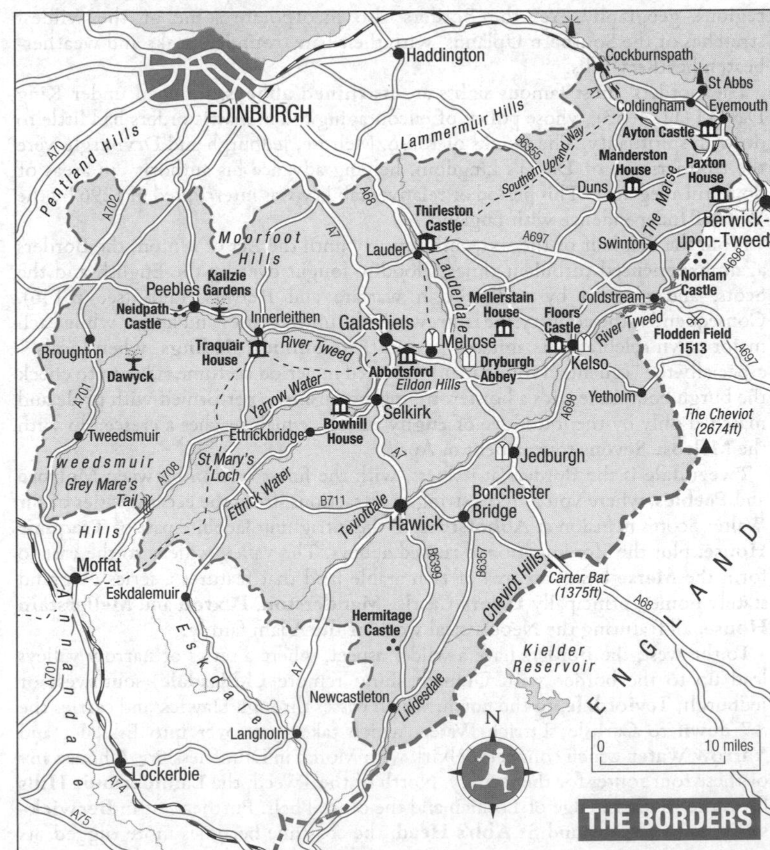

provide the setting for Walter Scott's *Bride of Lammermoor* (itself the inspiration for Donizetti's opera *Lucia di Lammermoor*). The hills are a favourite haunt of Edinburgh-based ramblers, as well as those completing the **Southern Upland Way**, which ends at Cockburnspath on the coast.

At the southwestern edge of the Lammermuir Hills sits **LAUDER** (pronounced "lorder"), a grey market town 25 miles or so southeast of Edinburgh on the A68. The reason to come here is to visit nearby **Thirlestane Castle** (Easter, May, June & Sept Wed, Thurs & Sun 10am–3.30pm; July & Aug daily except Fri & Sat; £10; guided tours until 2.30pm; grounds only £3; Ⓦwww.thirlestanecastle.co.uk), an imposing Scots Baronial pile with reddish turrets and castellated towers – to get there take the signposted footpath from the main square. Begun by John Maitland in the late sixteenth century, when he became Lord Chancellor of Scotland, and still owned by the family, the castle's somewhat undistinguished interior is redeemed by the extravagant plasterwork of the Restoration ceilings and a wealth of domestic detail from the Victorian period, including a wonderland of children's toys. There's also an adventure playground for those with children, and a woodland walk for those who wish to avoid them. In Lauder itself, the *Flat Cat Gallery & Coffee Shop* on the market square is a stylish **café**, and the *Black Bull Hotel* serves very decent bar meals.

Eyemouth and around

The history of **EYEMOUTH** (Ⓦwww.eyemouth.com), the only settlement of any size on the Borders' coastline, is forever tied up with the sea. Its long, slender harbour remains very much the focus of activity, its waters packed with deep-sea and inshore fleets and its quay strewn with tatters of old net, discarded fish and fish crates. The 1834 dredger *Bertha*, built by Isambard Kingdom Brunel, sitting in the harbour, is part of the **Eyemouth Maritime Centre** (daily 10am–5pm; £3.75; Ⓦwww.worldofboats.org), which puts on nautical exhibitions and displays an outstanding array of restored sailing craft in the old fish market building. Eyemouth also boasts three annual fishy events: the weekend **Seafood Festival** on the second weekend in June, the week-long **Herring Queen Festival** in July and the **Lifeboat Gala** in August.

The **Eyemouth Museum**, in the Auld Kirk on the Market Place (April–Sept Mon–Sat 10am–5pm, Sun noon–3pm; Oct Mon–Sat 10am–4pm; £2.50; Ⓦwww.eyemouthmuseum.org.uk) is worth a visit for the vast, modern **Eyemouth Tapestry**, commemorating the 1881 disaster when a freak storm took the lives of 129 local men, a tragedy of extraordinary proportions for a place of this size. The elegant **Gunsgreen House**, on the far side of the harbour, was designed in the 1750s by James Adam. Despite its respectable appearance – it's currently used by the local golf club – the house was once used by smugglers, with secret passages and underground tunnels leading back into town.

For something to eat, head for *Oblò Bar & Bistro*, a pleasant café-restaurant at 20 Harbour Rd; for fish and chips and home-made ice cream, try the celebrated *Giacopazzi's*, 18 Harbour Rd. The **tourist office** (April–Sept daily; Oct Mon–Sat; Ⓣ01890/750678) is down by the harbour, in the Auld Kirk on the Market Place.

St Abbs

Flanked by jagged cliffs, the remote fishing village of **ST ABBS** (Ⓦwww.stabbs.com), a couple of miles north of Eyemouth, has a rugged setting, with old cottages tumbling down to the tiny, surf-battered harbour. From the harbour, you can take sea-angling, sub-aqua-diving, birdwatching and regular sightseeing **boat trips** with a local guide (Ⓣ01890/771681). Alternatively, you can walk a mile or so up the coast to **St Abb's Head**, where the sheer, seabird-nesting cliffs rise 300ft out of the water. En route to the headland, there's a small **visitor centre** (April–Oct daily 10am–5pm) and the Kittiwake Gallery, with an adjacent coffee shop that does packed lunches. An easy-to-follow, mile-long walking trail ends at the Stevensons' lighthouse, but you only need to follow it for half a mile before being rewarded with a spectacular view of the Berwickshire coast.

Paxton House

Overlooking the River Tweed, eight miles south of Eyemouth and just four miles west of Berwick-upon-Tweed, is the perfectly proportioned Palladian mansion of **Paxton House** (April–Oct daily 11am–5pm; grounds daily 10am–sunset; £7.50, gardens and grounds only £4; Ⓦ www.paxtonhouse.co.uk), designed by the Adam brothers in 1758. It was built for Patrick Home of Billie, in a desperate and unsuccessful attempt to woo his Prussian lover, Sophie de Brandt, lady-in-waiting to Queen Elizabeth Christine, wife of Frederick the Great. Forced to return home on the murder of his mother – apparently, the butler did it – he built Paxton for his intended bride, but, sadly, they were never to meet again.

The interior features a stunning collection of Chippendale furniture, commissioned by the cousin to whom Patrick sold the house on the death of Sophie. The other highlight is the **Picture Gallery**, completed in the 1810s, with its rich Neoclassical plasterwork and changing display of works from the National Gallery of Scotland. The **grounds**, laid out by an assistant of Capability Brown, include gentle footpaths, a croquet lawn, an army-built adventure playground, a tearoom, Highland cattle, Shetland ponies, a Victorian boathouse housing a salmon-netting museum and a hide, from where you can spy on red squirrels and woodpeckers. To reach the house, take the #32 bus (Mon–Sat 2–4 daily) from Berwick.

Manderston House

Manderston House (mid-May to mid-Sept Thurs & Sun 1.30–5pm; £9; gardens Thurs & Sun 11.30am–dusk; £5; Ⓦ www.manderston.co.uk), ten miles west of Paxton on the A6105, is the very embodiment of Edwardian Britain. Between 1871 and 1905, the Miller family spent most of their herring and hemp fortune on turning their Georgian home into a prestigious country house. It's certainly a staggering sight, from the intricate plasterwork ceilings to the inlaid marble floor in the hall and the extravagant silver staircase. The whole lot is sumptuously furnished with trappings worthy of a man who'd just married into the aristocracy: James Miller married Eveline Curzon, the daughter of Lord Scarsdale, in 1893. The house is currently the home of Lord and Lady Palmer, of Huntley & Palmers biscuits fame – there's a Biscuit Tin Museum in the house to prove it. The extensive **gardens** are noted for their courtyard stables (where you can have an Edwardian-style cream tea), cloistered marble dairy, mock tower house and, of course, rhododendrons and azaleas. Manderston is a twenty-minute walk east of Duns, and on the route of bus #60 between Berwick and Melrose.

The Tweed valley

Rising in the hills far to the west, the **River Tweed** snakes its way across the Borders until it reaches the North Sea at Berwick-upon-Tweed, most of its final stretch forming the boundary between Scotland and England. This is the area known as the **Merse** (from the Old English for marsh), a flat landscape of rich farmland and wooded riverbanks where the occasional military ruin serves as a

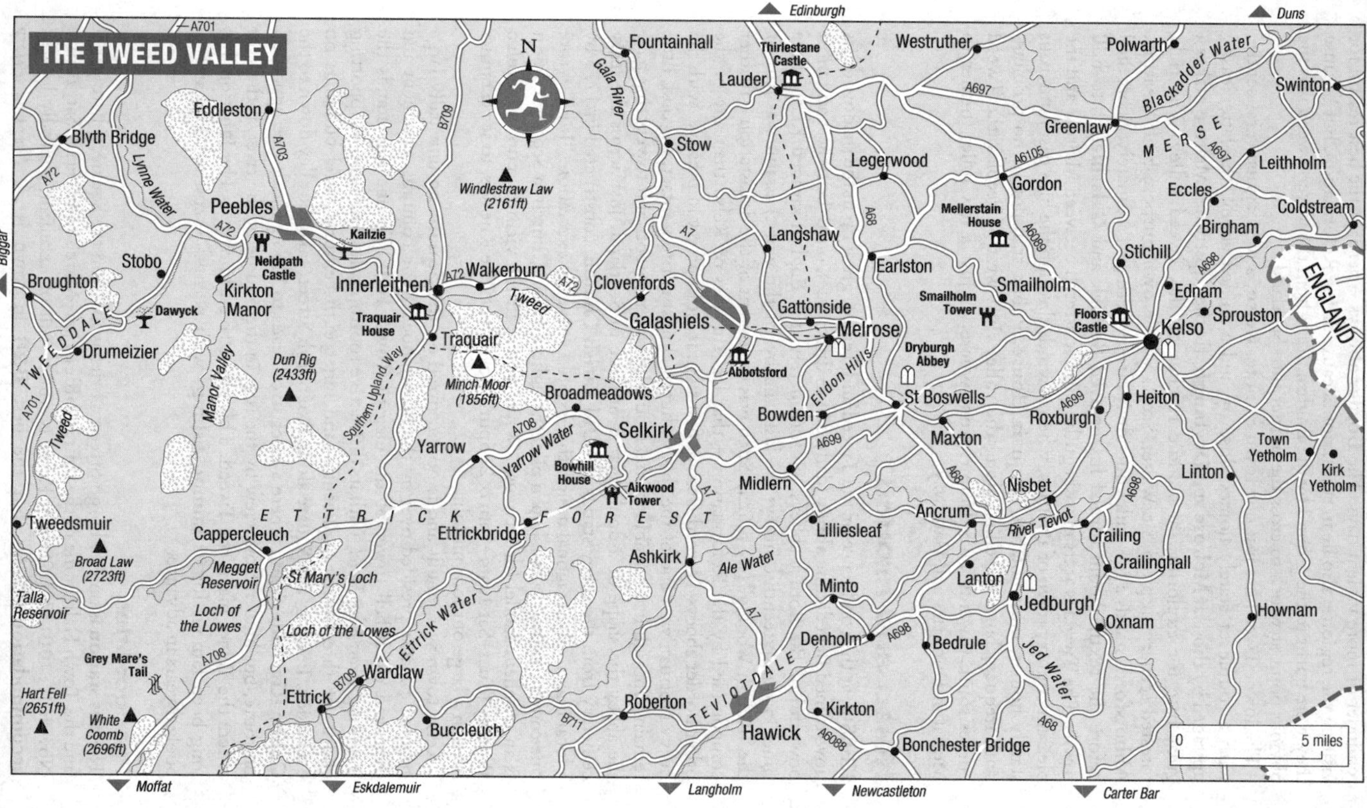
THE TWEED VALLEY
N
Edinburgh
Duns
Biggar
Moffat
Eskdalemuir
Langholm
Newcastleton
Carter Bar
ENGLAND
0 5 miles
Fountainhall
Gala River
Thirlestane Castle
Lauder
Westruther
Polwarth
Blackadder Water
Swinton
Greenlaw
MERSE
Leithholm
Eccles
Coldstream
Birgham
Stichill
Ednam
Sprouston
Kelso
Floors Castle
Eddleston
Blyth Bridge
Lynne Water
Stow
Legerwood
Gordon
Mellerstain House
Windlestraw Law (2161ft)
Peebles
Kailzie
Neidpath Castle
Stobo
Broughton
Kirkton Manor
Dawyck
Drumeizier
TWEEDDALE
Manor Valley
Dun Rig (2433ft)
Innerleithen
Walkerburn
Tweed
Traquair House
Traquair
Minch Moor (1856ft)
Southern Upland Way
Clovenfords
Galashiels
Langshaw
Earlston
Smailholm
Smailholm Tower
Gattonside
Melrose
Eildon Hills
Dryburgh Abbey
Abbotsford
Broadmeadows
St Boswells
Bowden
Heiton
Roxburgh
Town Yetholm
Kirk Yetholm
Linton
Selkirk
Yarrow
Yarrow Water
Bowhill House
Aikwood Tower
Midlern
Maxton
Nisbet
Tweedsmuir
ETTRICK FOREST
Ettrickbridge
Cappercleuch
Ancrum
River Teviot
Crailing
Lilliesleaf
Broad Law (2723ft)
Megget Reservoir
St Mary's Loch
Ashkirk
Ale Water
Crailinghall
Lanton
Talla Reservoir
Loch of the Lowes
Loch of the Lowes
Minto
Jedburgh
Hownam
Oxnam
Ettrick Water
Denholm
Bedrule
Jed Water
Grey Mare's Tail
Wardlaw
TEVIOTDALE
Hart Fell (2651ft)
Ettrick
Roberton
Kirkton
White Coomb (2696ft)
Buccleuch
Hawick
Bonchester Bridge
A701
A72
A703
B709
A7
A68
A697
A6105
A6089
A698
A699
A708
B711
A6088

reminder of more violent days. The **Border abbeys** – perhaps the best reason for visiting the region – also lie in ruins, not because of the Reformation, but because they were burnt to the ground by the English, for whom the lower Tweed was the obvious point at which to cross the border into Scotland.

The lower Tweed has just one town of note, **Kelso**, a busy agricultural centre, with a couple of stately homes close by and a ruined abbey, the latter easily upstaged by those at **Melrose** and **Dryburgh**, further upstream. Melrose makes a great base for exploring the middle reaches of the Tweed valley. The rich, forested scenery inspired Sir Walter Scott, whose own purpose-built creation, **Abbotsford**, stands a few miles outside Melrose. Perhaps fortunately, Scott died before the textile boom turned his beloved **Selkirk** and **Galashiels** into mill towns. The Tweed is at its most beguiling in the stretch between Melrose and the pleasant country town of **Peebles**, when it winds through the hills past numerous stately homes, most notably **Traquair House**. Public transport is no problem, with frequent buses travelling along the valley. Just west of Peebles, the Tweed curves south towards Tweedsmuir, from where it's just a few miles further to Moffat in Dumfries and Galloway.

Kelso and around

KELSO, at the confluence of the Tweed and Teviot, grew up in the shadow of its now-ruined Benedictine **abbey** (daily dawn–dusk; free), once the richest and most powerful of the Border abbeys. Unfortunately, the English savaged Kelso three times in the sixteenth century: the last (and by far the worst) assault was part of the "Rough Wooing" (see p.625). Such was the extent of the devastation – further compounded by the Reformation – that less survives of Kelso than any of the other Border abbeys. Nevertheless, at first sight it looks pretty impressive, with the heavy Norman west end of the abbey church almost entirely intact. Beyond, little remains, though it is possible to make out the two transepts and towers that gave the abbey the shape of a double cross, unique in Scotland. Just across the leafy cemetery from the abbey stands the **Old Parish Church**, constructed in 1773 by a local man to an octagonal design that excited universal execration. "It is," wrote one contemporary, "a misshapen pile, the ugliest Parish Church in Scotland, but it is an excellent model for a circus." While you're in the vicinity, pop into **Kelso Pottery** (Tues–Sat 10am–1pm & 2–5pm), close by at The Knowes, to see ceramics fired in a large outdoor pit kiln.

Kelso town was rebuilt and is now centred on **the Square**, an unusually large cobbled expanse presided over by the honey-hued Ionic columns, pediment and oversized clock bell tower of the elegant **Town Hall**. To one side stands the imposing *Cross Keys Hotel*, with its distinctive rooftop balustrade, and a supporting chorus of three-storey eighteenth- and nineteenth-century pastel buildings on every side. Leaving The Square along Roxburgh Street, take the alley down to the **Cobby Riverside Walk**, where a brief stroll leads to Floors Castle (see opposite). En route, but hidden from view by the islet in the middle of the river, is the spot where the Teviot meets the Tweed. This bit of river, known as The Junction, has long been famous for its **salmon fishing**, with permits – costing thousands – booked years in advance.

Practicalities

The **bus station** is on Roxburgh Street, a brief walk from the Square, where you'll find the Town Hall, home to the **tourist office** (Jan–March Mon, Fri & Sat; April–Nov daily; ⓣ01573/228055). Kelso is stuffed full of excellent, centrally located **accommodation** choices, but the best **B&B** in town is *The Old Priory*

(Ⓣ01573/223030, Ⓦwww.theoldpriorykelso.com; ④), a beautifully furnished Georgian townhouse on Woodmarket, just off the Square. Alternatively, there's *Duncan House* (Ⓣ01573/225682, Ⓦwww.duncanhouse.co.uk; ④), another very tastefully decorated Georgian house north of the Square off Roxburgh Street, with views across the river to Floors Castle. For more modest accommodation, try *Ivy Neuk* (Ⓣ01573/226270, Ⓦwww.ivyneuk.com; ③), a pleasant Victorian B&B, east of The Square at 62 Horsemarket.

Most **eating** places are just off the Square: the *Cobbles Inn* restaurant is housed in a former pub just up Bowmont Street – check the specials menu for the best dishes – and the *Cross Keys* in the Square specializes in local produce. For a snack, there's *Le Jardin* (closed Mon), next to Kelso Pottery. For picnic food, head for the *Teviot Smokery*, on the A698 five miles south of Kelso, where you can also enjoy a river walk, a stroll through the water gardens or a snack in the café.

Kelso has a very popular **racecourse** (Ⓦwww.kelso-races.co.uk) to the north of town, and an impressive annual rota of events and **festivals**: the Jim Clark Rally (May); the Border Union Dog Show (June); Civic Week (July); the Kelso Rugby Sevens (Sept); as well as St James Fair (Sept), re-enacting the death of James II and the burning of Roxburghe Castle, and the Ram Sales a week or so later.

Floors Castle

If you stand on Kelso's handsome bridge over the Tweed, you can easily make out the pepperpot turrets and castellations of **Floors Castle** (Easter & May–Oct daily 11am–5pm; £7.50, grounds & garden only £3; Ⓦwww.floorscastle.com), one mile northwest of town. The bulk of the building was designed by William Adam in the 1720s for the first Duke of Roxburghe and, despite the Victorian modifications, the interior still demonstrates his uncluttered style, while the superb views from the windows give the place an airy feel. Floors remains the home of the Duke of Roxburghe – his imperious features can be seen in a variety of portraits and photos around the house – so the public get to see only ten rooms and the basement. In 1903, the eighth duke married Mary Goelet, the wealthiest heiress in America at the time, and the **paintings**, by Matisse, Augustus John and Odilon Redon, and the Brussels and Gobelin tapestries she carried off from her family home are now the castle's highlights. There's an above-average **café** and you can wander down to the Tweed and see the holly tree that marks the spot where James II was killed by an exploding cannon during the siege of Roxburgh Castle. His son, also James, was crowned James III at the age of nine at Kelso Abbey.

Mellerstain House

Six miles northwest of Kelso off the A6089, **Mellerstain House** (guided tours: Easter–June & Sept Wed & Sun 12.30–5pm; July & Aug Mon, Wed, Thurs & Sun; Oct Sun 12.30–5pm; £7, gardens only £4; Ⓦwww.mellerstain.com) represents the very best of the Adam family's work: William designed the wings in 1725, and his son Robert the main mansion house fifty years later. Inside, it has an elegant, domestic air, lacking in pomposity. Robert Adam's love of columns, delicate roundels and friezes culminates in a stunning sequence of plaster-moulded, pastel-shaded ceilings, which still preserve the original colours; the **library** is the architectural highlight, with four unusual long panels in plaster relief of classical scenes relegating the books to second place. Perhaps the most intriguing Adam creation is the charming, but freezing, bathroom in the basement, the only one known to have been designed by him. There are also some interesting paintings by Constable, Gainsborough, Ramsay and Veronese. The house remains the home of the Earl of Haddington, descendant of the Baillie family who acquired the estate in 1642. After the tour you can wander the formal Edwardian gardens, which slope down to the lake, or venture further afield to the Fairy Glen. There's also an excellent tearoom.

Smailholm Tower

In marked contrast to Mellerstain is the craggy **Smailholm Tower** (April–Sept daily 9.30am–5.30pm; Oct–March Sat & Sun 9.30am–4.30pm; HS; £3.70), perched on a rocky outcrop a few miles to the south. It's a remote and evocative fastness that inspired Walter Scott (see p.150) and conjures up Reivers' raids (see below) and border skirmishes. The fifteenth-century tower was designed to withstand sudden attack, with the rough rubble walls 6ft thick and both the entrance – once guarded by a heavy door plus an iron yett (gate) – and the windows made disproportionately small. Inside, head for the roof, where two narrow **wall-walks**, jammed against the barrel-vaulted roof and the crow-stepped gables, provide panoramic views. On the north side the watchman's seat has also survived, stuck against the chimney stack for warmth and with a recess for a lantern.

Dryburgh Abbey

Hidden away in a U-bend in the Tweed, ten miles upstream from Kelso, the remains of **Dryburgh Abbey** (daily: Easter–Sept 9.30am–5.30pm; Oct–Easter 9.30am–4.30pm; HS; £4.70) occupy an idyllic position against a hilly backdrop, with ancient cedars, redwoods, beech and lime trees and wide lawns flattering the pinkish-red hues of the stonework. The Premonstratensians, or White Canons, founded the abbey in the twelfth century, but they were never as successful – or apparently as devout – as their Cistercian neighbours in Melrose. Their chronicles

The Border Reivers

From the thirteenth to the early seventeenth centuries, the wild, inhospitable border country stretching from the Solway Firth in the west to the Tweed valley in the east, well away from the power bases of both the Scottish and English monarchs, was overrun by outlaws known as the **Border Reivers**, *reive* being a Scots word for plunder. As George MacDonald Fraser put it in his book *The Steel Bonnets*, "The great border tribes of both Scotland and England feuded continuously among themselves. Robbery and blackmail were everyday professions; raiding, arson, kidnapping, murder and extortion were an accepted part of the social system." This, then, was no cross-border dispute, but an open struggle for power among Borders folk. Those who "shook loose the Border" included people from all walks of life – agricultural labourers, gentleman farmers, smallholders, even peers of the realm – for whom theft, raiding, tracking and ambush became second nature.

The source of this behaviour was the destruction and devastation wrought upon the region by virtually continual warfare between England and Scotland, and the "slash and burn" policy of the era. With many residents no longer able to find sustenance from the land, crime became the only way to survive. Cattle-rustling, blackmail and kidnapping led to an anarchical mindset, where feuding families would habitually wreak havoc and devastation on each other.

The legacy of the Border Reivers can still be seen today in the region's fortified farms and churches; in the **Common Riding** traditions of many border towns; in the great family names such as Armstrong, Graham, Kerr and Nixon, which once filled the hearts of Borderers with dread; and in the language – the words "blackmail" (first used to described the protection money paid by farmers to the local clan chiefs) and "bereaved" (originally referred to being robbed) have their roots in the mayhem of this period.

detail interminable disputes about land and money: one story relates how a fourteenth-century canon called Marcus flattened the abbot with his fist.

The romantic setting is second to none, but the ruins of the **Abbey Church** are much less substantial than, say, at Melrose or Jedburgh. Virtually nothing survives of the nave, but the transepts have fared better, their chapels now serving as private burial grounds for, among others, **Sir Walter Scott** and Field Marshal Haig, the World War I commander whose ineptitude cost thousands of soldiers' lives. The night stairs, down which the monks stumbled in the early hours of the morning, survive in the south transept, and lead even today to the monks' dormitory. Leaving the church via the east processional door in the south aisle, with its dog tooth decoration, you enter the cloisters, the highlight of which is the barrel-vaulted **Chapter House**, complete with low stone benches and blind interlaced arcading.

Next door to the abbey is the *Dryburgh Abbey Hotel*, a sprawling red-sandstone **hotel** that's a hunting, shooting, fishing kind of place. You don't need to stay here to have a cup of tea or a drink in the bar, or even to have a swim in the indoor pool. Dryburgh is a mile's walk north from St Boswell's on the A68 and the main bus route from Kelso to Melrose (Mon–Sat 2–4 daily), and a very pleasant three- or four-mile walk along the river from Melrose. Drivers and cyclists should approach the abbey via the much-visited **Scott's View**, to the north on the B6356, overlooking the Tweed valley, where the writer and his friends often picnicked and where Scott's horse stopped out of habit during the writer's own funeral procession. The scene inspired J.M.W. Turner's *Melrose 1831*, now on display in the National Gallery of Scotland (see p.97).

Melrose

Tucked in between the Tweed and the gorse-backed Eildon Hills, minuscule **MELROSE** is the most beguiling of towns, its narrow streets trimmed by a harmonious ensemble of styles, from pretty little cottages and tweedy shops to high-standing Georgian and Victorian facades. Its chief draw is its ruined **abbey**, by far the best of the Border abbeys, but it's also perfectly positioned for exploring the Tweed valley. Most of the year it's a sleepy little place, but as the birthplace in 1883 of the **Rugby Sevens** (seven-a-side games), it swarms during Sevens Week (second week in April), during the **Borders Book Festival** in June, and again in early September when it hosts the **Melrose Music Festival**, a popular weekend of traditional music attracting folkies from afar.

Arrival, information and accommodation

Buses to Melrose stop in Market Square, from where it's a brief walk north to the abbey ruins and the **tourist office** opposite (April–Oct daily; Nov–March Fri & Sat only; ⓣ01896/822283).

Melrose has a clutch of **hotels**, with prices generally higher than you might expect; it's in the town's simple B&Bs, however, that you'll get the real flavour of the place.

Braidwood Buccleuch St ⓣ01896/822488, ⓦwww.braidwoodmelrose.co.uk. An easy-going and comfortable cottage guesthouse, a stone's throw from the abbey. ❸

Dunfermline House 3 Buccleuch St ⓣ01896/822411, ⓦwww.dunfermlinehouse.co.uk. Solid townhouse B&B, opposite *Braidwood*; rooms have views over the garden or over to the abbey. ❸

Gibson Caravan Park ⓣ01896/822969. Lovely little campsite right in the town centre, just off the High Street, opposite the rugby ground. Open all year.

Old Bank House 27 Buccleuch St ⓣ01896/823712, ⓦwww.oldbankhousemelrose.co.uk. Solid Victorian townhouse with charming hosts and three pristinely maintained en-suite rooms. ❸

SYHA hostel ⓣ01896/822521, ⓦwww.syha.org.uk. Situated in a sprawling Georgian mansion overlooking the abbey. Open mid-March to mid-Oct.

Townhouse Market Square ⓣ01896/822645, ⓦwww.thetownhousemelrose.co.uk. Small hotel on the main square, with eleven stylishly renovated en-suite rooms, with contemporary furnishings. ❼

The abbey

The pink- and red-tinted stone ruins of **Melrose Abbey** (daily: April–Sept 9.30am–6.30pm; Oct–March 9.30am–4.30pm; HS; £5), north of the town square, soar above their riverside surroundings. Founded in 1136 by King David I, Melrose was the first Cistercian settlement in Scotland and grew rich selling wool and hides to Flanders, but its prosperity was fragile: the English repeatedly razed Melrose, most viciously under Richard II in 1385 and the Earl of Hertford in 1545. Most of the present remains date from the intervening period, when extensive rebuilding abandoned the original Cistercian austerity for an elaborate, Gothic style inspired by the abbeys of northern England. The sculptural detailing at Melrose is of the highest quality, but it's easy to miss if you don't know where to look, so taking advantage of the free audio-guide, or buying yourself a guidebook, is a good idea.

The site is dominated by the **Abbey Church**, which has lost its west front, and whose nave is reduced to the elegant window arches and chapels of the south aisle. Amazingly, however, the stone **pulpitum** (screen), separating the choir monks from their lay brothers, is preserved. Beyond, the **presbytery** has its magnificent perpendicular window, lierne vaulting and ceiling bosses intact, with the capitals of the surrounding columns sporting the most intricate of curly kale carving. In the **south transept**, another fine fifteenth-century window sprouts yet more delicate, foliate tracery and the adjacent cornice is enlivened by angels playing musical instruments, though these figures are badly weathered. This kind of finely carved detail is repeated everywhere you look in Melrose. Outside, the exterior sculpture on the south transept is even more impressive: lower niche-corbels are decorated with crouching figures holding scrolls bearing inscriptions such as "He suffered because he willed it". Elsewhere, look for the statue of the Virgin and Child, high on the south side of the westernmost surviving buttress, the Coronation of the Virgin on the east-end gable and the numerous mischievous **gargoyles**, from peculiar crouching beasts to the pig playing the bagpipes on the roof on the south side of the nave.

Legend has it that the heart of **Robert the Bruce** is buried here (his body having been buried at Dunfermline Abbey), and in 1997, when a heart cask was publicly exhumed, this theory received an unexpected boost. However, the burial location was not in accordance with Bruce's own wishes. In 1329, the dying king told his friend, Sir James Douglas, to carry his heart on a Crusade to the Holy Land in fulfilment of an old vow: "Seeing therefore, that my body cannot go to achieve what my heart desires, I will send my heart instead of my body, to accomplish my vow." Douglas tried his best, but was killed fighting the Moors in Spain – and Bruce's heart ended up in Melrose. A new commemorative stone marks its current resting place in the chapter house, north of the sacristy.

The paltry ruins of the old monastic buildings edge the church to the north and lead over the road to the **Commendator's House** (same hours as the abbey), a lovely red-sandstone building converted into a private house in 1590 by the abbey's last commendator, and now housing a modest collection of ecclesiastical bric-a-brac. Beyond the house is the mill-lade, where water used to flow in order to power the abbey's mills, and was also diverted to flush the monks' latrines.

The town

Melrose is a tiny place, centred on its busy little market square. The main event is the abbey, but there are one or two minor sights worth visiting. To the west of the abbey, on St Mary's Road, it's worth popping into the tiny, delightful **Priorwood Garden** (April–Oct Mon–Sat 10am–5pm, Sun 1–5pm; Nov & Dec Mon–Sat 10am–4pm; NTS; £6 joint ticket with Harmony Garden), whose compact walled precincts are given over to an orchard and flowers that are suitable for drying; there's a dried-flower shop, too. Peace and quiet can also be found in the three-acre **Harmony Garden** (April–Oct Mon–Sat 10am–5pm, Sun 1pm–5pm; NTS; £6 joint ticket with Priorwood Garden), a lovely Regency townhouse garden just past the tourist office, which itself has a charming walled garden where you can picnic.

Melrose's other museum, the **Three Hills Roman Heritage Centre**, just off Market Square (April–Oct daily 1.30–4.30pm; £1.50; Ⓦwww.trimontium.net), is a quirky little centre that merits a browse. Its displays include Celtic bronze axe-heads excavated from the Eildon Hills, dioramas, models and the odd archeological find outlining the three Roman occupations of the region. For further Roman adventures, the five-mile circular **Trimontium Walk** (April–Oct Thurs 1.30–5.15pm; July & Aug also Tues 1.30–5.15pm; £3) takes you past various Roman sites in the area (although there's not much left on the ground), including the Leaderfoot viaduct and the most northerly amphitheatre in the Roman Empire, and even throws in a free cuppa.

Eating and drinking

Melrose offers a good choice of **eating** options. *Marmion's Brasserie* (Ⓣ01896/822245; closed Sun), housed in a spacious Victorian house on Buccleuch Street, serves great breakfasts, lunches, afternoon teas and dinners, while *Burt's Hotel* does excellent bar meals or, if you're feeling energetic, walk 500yd past the abbey and across the old suspension bridge to Gattonside, where the *Hoebridge Inn* (Ⓣ01896/823082; closed Mon), once a bobbin mill and now one of the Borders' best restaurants, serves home-made Scottish food in relaxed, low-key surroundings. If you want a light lunch or snack, head to *Russell's* (closed Thurs), a popular, very traditional tearoom on Market Square; or *Haldane's Fish & Chip Shop* (closed Wed), next door.

Walking in the Eildon Hills

Ordnance Survey Explorer Map no. 338.

From the centre of Melrose, it's a vigorous three-mile walk to the top of the **Eildon Hills**, whose triple volcanic peaks are the Central Borders' most distinctive landmark. The tourist office sells a leaflet detailing the hike, which begins about 90yd south of – and up the hill from – Market Square, along the B6359 to Lilliesleaf.

The hills have been associated with all sorts of legends, beginning with tales of their creation by the wizard-cum-alchemist Michael Scott (1175–1230) who, in the words of Sir Walter Scott, "cleft the Eildon Hills in three". It was here that the mystic **Thomas the Rhymer** received the gift of prophecy from the Faerie Queen, and Arthur and his knights are reckoned to lie asleep deep within the hills, victims of a powerful spell. The ancient Celts, who revered the number three, also considered the site a holy place and maintained their settlements on the slopes long after the Romans' departure.

Melrose is also the starting point for the popular **St Cuthbert's Way**, a sixty-mile walk which finishes at Lindisfarne (Holy Island) on the Northumbrian coast. The tourist office can give details of the walk, though the trail is well marked by yellow arrows from the abbey up over the Eildons to the pretty village of **Bowden**, where you can make a detour to see a twelfth-century kirk, half a mile down the hill from the square, and browse secondhand books and get a really good, home-made tea at *The Old School*.

For **pubs**, try the popular *King's Arms* on the High Street, or the *Ship Inn*, on East Port at the top of the square, the liveliest in town, especially during the Folk Festival and on Saturday afternoons when the Melrose rugby team have played at home. Be sure to check out what's on at *The Wynd* (T 01896/820028, W www.thewynd.com), Melrose's very own pint-sized **theatre**, tucked away down an alleyway, north off the main square, which shows films and puts on gigs as well as live drama.

Abbotsford

Abbotsford (mid-March to May & Oct Mon–Sat 9.30am–5pm, Sun 11am–4pm; June–Sept Mon–Sat 9.30am–5pm, Sun 9.30am–5pm; £7; W www.scottsabbotsford.co.uk), a stately home a couple of miles up the Tweed from Melrose, was designed to satisfy the Romantic inclinations of **Sir Walter Scott**, who lived here from 1812 until his death twenty years later. Built on the site of a farmhouse Scott bought and subsequently demolished, Abbotsford (as Scott chose to call it) took twelve years to evolve, with the fanciful turrets and castellations of the Scots Baronial exterior incorporating copies of medieval originals: the entrance porch imitates that of Linlithgow Palace and the screen wall in the garden echoes Melrose Abbey's cloister.

Sir Walter Scott

Walter Scott (1771–1832) was born to a solidly bourgeois family in Edinburgh. Crippled by polio, he was sent by his parents to recuperate at his grandfather's farm in Smailholm, where the boy's imagination was fired by his relatives' tales of derring-do, the violent history of the Borders retold amidst the rugged landscape that he spent long summer days exploring. Throughout the 1790s he transcribed hundreds of old **Border ballads**, publishing a three-volume collection entitled *Minstrelsy of the Scottish Borders* in 1802. An instant success, *Minstrelsy* was followed by Scott's own *Lay of the Last Minstrel*, a narrative poem whose strong story and rose-tinted regionalism proved very popular.

More **poetry** was to come, most successfully *Marmion* (1808) and *The Lady of the Lake* (1810), not to mention an eighteen-volume edition of the works of John Dryden and nineteen volumes of Jonathan Swift. However, despite having two paid jobs, one as **Sheriff-Depute** of Selkirkshire, the other as clerk to the Court of Session in Edinburgh, his finances remained shaky. From 1813, Scott was writing to pay the bills and poured out a veritable flood of **historical novels** using his extensive knowledge of Scottish history and folklore. He produced his best work within the space of ten years: *Waverley* (1814), *The Antiquary* (1816), *Rob Roy* and *The Heart of Midlothian* (both 1818), as well as two notable novels set in England, *Ivanhoe* (1819) and *Kenilworth* (1821). In 1824 he returned to Scottish tales with *Redgauntlet*, the last of his quality work. As Scott's financial problems increased, the quality of his writing deteriorated, and the effort broke his health. His last years were plagued by illness, and in 1832 he died at Abbotsford and was buried at Dryburgh Abbey (see p.146).

Although Scott's interests were diverse, his historical novels focused mostly on the Jacobites, whose loyalty to the Stewarts had riven Scotland since the "Glorious Revolution" of 1688. That the nation was prepared to be entertained by such tales was essentially a matter of timing: by the 1760s it was clear that the Jacobite cause was lost for good and Scotland, emerging from its isolated medievalism, had been firmly welded into the United Kingdom. Thus its turbulent history and independent spirit was safely in the past, and ripe for romancing – as shown by the arrival of King George IV in Edinburgh during 1822 decked out in Highland dress. Yet for Sir Walter the romance was tinged with a genuine sense of loss. Loyal to the Hanoverians, he still grieved for Bonnie Prince Charlie; he welcomed a commercial Scotland but lamented the passing of feudal ties, and so his heroes are transitional, fighting men of action superseded by bourgeois figures searching for a clear identity.

Scott was proud of his *folie de grandeur*, writing to a friend, "It is a kind of conundrum castle to be sure [which] pleases a fantastic person in style and manner." That said, it was undoubtedly one of the chief causes of Scott's subsequent bankruptcy.

Despite all the exterior pomp, the interior is surprisingly small and poky, with just six rooms open for viewing on the upper floor. Visitors start in the wood-panelled **study**, with its small writing desk made of salvage from the Spanish Armada at which Scott churned out the Waverley novels at a furious rate. The heavy wood-panelled **library** contains Scott's collection of more than nine thousand rare books and an extraordinary assortment of memorabilia, the centrepiece of which is Napoleon's pen case and blotting book, Also here are Rob Roy's purse and *skene dhu* (knife), a lock of Nelson's hair – and of Bonnie Prince Charlie's – plus the latter's *quaich* (drinking cup), Flora Macdonald's pocketbook, the inlaid pearl crucifix that accompanied Mary, Queen of Scots, to the scaffold and even a piece of oatcake found in the pocket of a dead Highlander at Culloden. You can also see Henry Raeburn's famous portrait of Scott in the **drawing room**, and all sorts of weapons – notably Rob Roy's sword, dagger and gun – in the **armoury**. In the barbaric-looking **entrance hall**, hung with elk and wild cattle skulls, and spoils gathered from the battlefield of Waterloo by Scott himself, is a model of the skull of Robert the Bruce and some of Scott's dandyish clothes.

The fast and frequent Melrose–Galashiels **bus** provides easy access to Abbotsford: ask for the Tweedbank island on the A6091, from where the house is a ten-minute walk up the road. Alternatively, it's a pleasant two-mile riverside hike from Melrose.

Galashiels

It's hard to avoid **GALASHIELS**, or "Gala" as it's known locally, a hard-working textile town four miles west of Melrose whose grey-green workers' terraces spread along the valley of the Gala Water near its junction with the Tweed. It occupies a pivotal position in the Borders, and has the region's principal **bus station**, situated close to (and north of the river from) the town centre. The main street runs parallel with the river, its eastern end cheered by a melodramatic equestrian statue of a Border Reiver above the town's war memorial. The long-demolished New Gala House, a mansion that stood at the top of the town, was taken over during World War II by Edinburgh girls' school, **St Trinnean's**; the artist Ronald Searle met two of the pupils in 1941, inspiration for the unruly schoolgirls in his St Trinian's novels. If you've time to kill, drop by the **Old Gala House** (April–Oct Tues–Sat 10am–4pm, June–Aug also Mon 10am–4pm & Sun 11am–4pm; free), dating from 1583, which houses the local history museum and has a café. There's no tourist office in town, but there are plenty of leaflets at the library on Lawyers Brae, south of the river.

Traquair House

Peeping out from the trees a mile or so south of Innerleithen, eleven miles west of Galashiels, on the B709, **Traquair House** (daily: April, May & Sept noon–5pm; June–Aug 10.30am–5pm; Oct 11am–4pm; Nov Sat & Sun 11am–3pm; £7.50, grounds only £4; Ⓦwww.traquair.co.uk) is the oldest continuously inhabited house in Scotland, with the present owners – the Maxwell Stuarts – having lived here since 1491. The first laird of Traquair (pronounced "tra-quare"), inherited an elementary fortified tower, which his powerful descendants gradually converted into a mansion that was visited, it is said, by 27 monarchs, including Mary, Queen of Scots. Persistently Catholic, the family paid for its principles: the Jacobite fifth earl spent two years in the Tower of London; Protestant mill-workers repeatedly attacked their property; and by 1800 little remained of the family's once enormous estates – certainly not enough to fund any major rebuilding.

Consequently, Traquair's main appeal is in its ancient shape and structure. The whitewashed facade is strikingly handsome, with narrow windows and trim turrets surrounding the tiniest of front doors – an organic, homogeneous edifice that's a welcome change from other grandiose stately homes. Inside, you can see the original vaulted cellars, where locals once hid their cattle from raiders; the twisting main staircase as well as the earlier medieval version, later a secret escape route for persecuted Catholics; a carefully camouflaged priest's hole; and even a **priest's room** where a string of resident chaplains lived in hiding until the Catholic Emancipation Act freed things up in 1829. Of the furniture and fittings, it's not any particular piece that impresses, but rather the accumulation of family possessions and revealing letters that give a real insight into the Maxwell Stuarts' revolving-door fortunes and eccentricities. In the **museum room** there is a wealth of treasures, including a fine example of a Jacobite Amen glass, a rosary and crucifix owned by Mary, Queen of Scots and the cloak worn by the earl of Nithsdale during his dramatic escape from the Tower of London, where he was under sentence of death for his part in the Jacobite Rising of 1715. (The earl was saved by his wife who got his jailers drunk and smuggled him out disguised as a maid in spite of his red beard.)

It's worth sparing time for the surrounding **gardens** where you'll find a **hedge maze**, several craft workshops and the **Traquair House Brewery** dating back to 1566, which was revived in 1965 and claims to be the only British brewery that still ferments totally in oak. You can learn about the brewery and taste the ales in the Brewery Shop. There's also an attractive café serving above-average snacks in an estate cottage on the redundant avenue which leads to the locked **Bear Gates**; Bonnie Prince Charlie departed the house through the gates, and the then-owner promised to keep them locked till a Stuart should ascend the throne.

Most visitors come to Traquair as a day-trip from Peebles, but if you're really taken by the place, you can stay in one of its three double guest **rooms** (Ⓣ01896/830323; ❽), decked out with antiques and four-posters, on a bed-and-breakfast basis only. Campers should head for the *Tweedside Caravan Park* **campsite** (Ⓣ01896/831271, Ⓦwww.tweedsidecaravanparkinnerleithen.co.uk; April–Oct), with lovely views by the river, down Montgomery Street in Innerleithen.

Peebles

Fast, wide, tree-lined and fringed with grassy banks, the Tweed looks at its best at **PEEBLES**, a handsome royal burgh that sits on the north bank, seven miles

Walks around Peebles

A series of footpaths snake through the hills surrounding Peebles with their rough-edged burns, bare peaks and deep woods. The five-mile **Sware Trail** is one of the easiest and most scenic, weaving west along the north bank of the river and looping back to the south. On the way, it passes **Neidpath Castle,** a gaunt medieval tower house perched high above the river on a rocky bluff. The walk also goes by the splendid skew rail bridge, part of the Glasgow line, which was finished in 1850 and closed in 1969. Other, longer footpaths follow the old drove roads, like the thirteen-mile haul to **St Mary's Loch** or the fourteen-mile route to Selkirk via Traquair House (see p.151). For either of these, you'll need an Ordnance Survey map, a compass and proper hiking gear (see p.49). A more gentle stroll is the 2.5-mile amble to the privately owned **Kailzie Gardens** (daily: April–Oct 10am–5.30pm; Nov–March dawn–dusk; £3), whose fifteen acres include a walled garden, trout pond (fly-fishing tackle is available for rent) and a pleasant wood-panelled tearoom; it's also one of the places (the other being Glentress Forest) where you can see live CCTV pictures of the ospreys that have been successfully introduced into the nearby forest.

upstream from Innerleithen. The town itself has a genteel, relaxed air, its wide, handsome High Street bordered by houses in a medley of architectural styles, mostly dating from Victorian times. The soaring crown spire of the **Old Parish Church** (daily 10am–4pm) rises up at the western end of the High Street and, inside, the church has some unusual features such as the elegant oak, bronze and engraved-glass entrance screen and 22 modern oil paintings illustrating the Scriptures. Suspended from the ceiling are tattered Napoleonic flags, emblems of 1816, the year the Peebleshire Militia disbanded.

Further down the High Street is the **Tweeddale Museum & Gallery** (Mon–Fri 10.30am–12.30pm & 1–4pm, April–Oct also Sat 9.30am–12.30pm; free), housed in the Chambers Institute, which is heralded by two wonderfully ornate wrought-iron street lamps painted magenta and silver. William Chambers, a local worthy, presented the building to the town in 1859, complete with an art gallery dedicated to the enlightenment of his neighbours. He stuffed the place with casts of the world's most famous sculptures and, although most were lost long ago, today's "Secret Room", once the Museum Room, contains two handsome friezes: one a copy of the Elgin Marbles taken from the Parthenon; the other of the Triumph of Alexander, originally cast in 1812 to honour Napoleon.

Practicalities

Buses stop outside the post office, a few doors down from the well-stocked **tourist office** on the High Street (Jan–March Mon–Sat; April–Dec daily).

Peebles has a vast number of **B&Bs**: try *Rowanbrae*, a flower-infested Victorian place on a quiet cul-de-sac on Northgate, off the east end of the High Street (ⓣ01721/721630, ⓔjohn@rowanbrae.freeserve.co.uk; ❹); or *Viewfield*, 1 Rosetta Rd (ⓣ01721/721232, ⓔmmitchell38@yahoo.com; ❹), an attractive detached Victorian house, ten-minutes' walk west of the bridge, with rooms overlooking a lovely garden – take the Old Town road (the A72) and follow it round, turning right up Young Street. There are also two excellent options a couple of miles up the Edinburgh Road: *Winkston Farmhouse* (ⓣ01721/721264, ⓦwww.winkstonholidays.co.uk; ❹), a grand Georgian country house with spacious rooms, and *Cringletie House Hotel* (ⓣ01721/725750, ⓦwww.cringletie.com; ❻), a splendid Scots Baronial pile just beyond it. Of the two **campsites** on the edge of town, the *Rosetta Caravan Park* (ⓣ01721/720770, ⓦwww.rosettacaravanpark.co.uk; mid-March to Oct) is the quieter, and although the facilities could do with an upgrade, the setting, surrounded by mature woods, is lovely (directions as for *Viewfield* B&B).

The best place to **eat** is *The Sunflower* (ⓣ017221/722420; closed Sun), a tiny, brightly coloured restaurant at 4 Bridgegate, just off Northgate, which does open sandwiches at lunchtime and more adventurous evening meals (Thurs–Sat). You can munch on a baguette and get a good coffee at the café in the Eastgate Theatre (ⓦwww.eastgatearts.com; closed Sun), a state-of-the-art church conversion on Eastgate. It's also worth trying out *Osso* (ⓣ01721/724477), just east of the theatre on Innerleithen Road, which does sandwiches, tapas and comfort food for lunch, and an imaginative contemporary menu with dishes such as braised hare leg or coley risotto in the evening (Wed–Sat only). As for **pubs**, the *Crown Hotel* on the High Street is a cosy place to hunker down, while the *Tontine Hotel*, opposite, is grander, with views south over the Tweed, and a standard hotel menu. For good pub grub, try a bar meal at the *Castle Venlaw Hotel*, on the edge of town up the Edinburgh Road.

Upper Tweeddale

Upstream from Peebles, the Tweed valley is more commonly known as **Upper Tweeddale**. The valley sides gradually narrow as the road follows the river

Mountain biking in Glentress and Innerleithen

Glentress Forest, two miles east of Peebles on the A72, has some of the best opportunities for mountain biking in Scotland. Not only are there five superb, carefully crafted, purpose-built trails, colour-coded for difficulty, there's a fantastic bike centre at the entrance to the forest called **The Hub** (ⓣ01721/721736, ⓦwww.thehubintheforest.co.uk). This is a great place for mountain bikers, with changing rooms and showers, a café and a shop filled with spares that stays open late. You can choose from a whole range of excellent MTBs for all ages and there are even occasional training weekends so you can improve your technique. If you fancy staying several days it's worth checking out the timber wigwams (ⓣ01721/721007, ⓦwww.glentressforestlodges.co.uk; ❷), near The Hub. Glentress is, in fact, just one of seven forest biking centres in southern Scotland, known collectively as the **7 Stanes** (ⓦwww.7stanes.gov.uk). There's another one just a few miles southeast of Glentress near **Innerleithen**, with bike rental available a short distance away from Alpine Bikes (ⓣ01896/830880), in an old church on the Peebles Road in Innerleithen.

upstream and south to the source of the Tweed, at the border with Dumfries and Galloway. Eight miles southwest of Peebles, near Strobo, the Tweed passes **Dawyck Botanic Garden** (daily: Feb & Nov 10am–4pm; March & Oct 10am–5pm; April–Sept 10am–6pm; £5; ⓦwww.rbge.org.uk), an arboretum outstation of the Royal Botanic Garden in Edinburgh, which specializes in rare trees and shrubs, but also has an impressive display of rhododendrons and azaleas.

Two miles west of Dawyck stands the village of **BROUGHTON**, home of the excellent Broughton Ales. Inside the old Free Church, the **John Buchan Centre** (Easter & May to mid-Oct daily 2–5pm; £1.50) commemorates John Buchan, first Baron Tweedsmuir (1875–1940), author and diplomat, who spent his childhood holidays in the district. Five miles south of Broughton, off the A701, in pretty, secluded **Holmswater Glen**, is the *Glenholm Centre* (ⓣ01899/830408, ⓦwww.glenholm.co.uk; closed Jan; ❺) a working farm that is both a cosy four-room guesthouse and a wildlife centre, the perfect base for exploring the surrounding hills.

Ten miles or so further south on the A701, the Tweed eventually reaches tiny **TWEEDSMUIR**, a good base for climbing **Broad Law** (2723ft), the Southern Uplands' second highest hill. Behind the hotel there's a small workshop and craft centre, where you can watch glass-blowing displays. At Tweedsmuir, you can either head south into Dumfries and Galloway, or head east over the Tweedsmuir Hills to St Mary's Loch (see p.156). The eleven-mile single-track road, inaccessible in winter, climbs at a twenty-percent gradient past Talla Reservoir, where many men lost their lives constructing a water supply for Edinburgh in 1905.

Selkirk and around

Just south of the River Tweed, five miles southwest of Melrose, lies the royal burgh of **SELKIRK**. The old town sits high up above Ettrick Water; down in the valley by the riverside, the town's imposing grey-stone woollen mills are mostly boarded up now, an eerie reminder of a once prosperous era. Situated on the edge of some lovely countryside, the town is a good base for exploring the picturesque, sparsely populated valleys of Yarrow Water and Ettrick Water, to the west.

At the centre of Selkirk, at one end of the High Street, you'll find the tiny **Market Square**, where you should pop into *Grieves Snack Attack* and purchase the local "Selkirk Bannock", a sort of fruitcake. While munching it, you can admire Selkirk's statues, the most prominent being that of Sir Walter Scott, which stands outside the former Town House, now dubbed **Sir Walter Scott's Courtroom** (April–Sept Mon–Fri 10am–4pm, Sat 10am–2pm, May–Aug also Sun 10am–2pm; free), where he served as sheriff for 33 years. Just off Market Square to the south is **Halliwell's House Museum** (April–Sept Mon–Sat 10am–5pm, Sun 11am–3pm; Oct Mon–Sat 10am–4pm, Sun 11am–3pm; free), a reconstruction of an old-style hardware shop and an informative exhibit on the industrialization of the Tweed valley.

At the other end of the High Street is a statue of **Mungo Park**, the explorer and anti-slavery advocate, born in the county in 1771, and drowned in the River Niger in 1805. The base displays two finely cast bas-reliefs depicting his exploits; his son, who died searching for his father's body in 1827, is also commemorated. The bronze life-size African mourners, *Peace*, *War*, *Slavery*, and *Home Life in the Niger*, were added in 1913, after several petitions and newspaper editorials demanded that Park be further commemorated.

Practicalities

The **tourist office** (same hours as Halliwell's House) is in Halliwell's House, and can help with **accommodation**. First choice is the *Glen Hotel* (Ⓣ01750/20259, Ⓦwww.glenhotel.co.uk; ❺), an imposing Victorian pile near the bridge, with clean rooms and laidback staff. Another place full of character is the *Heatherlie House Hotel* (Ⓣ01750/721200, Ⓦwww.heatherliehouse.co.uk; ❹), a Victorian mansion set in its own grounds a sharp left turn up from the road to Ettrick at Heatherlie Park. **Camping** is possible beside the river, next to the swimming pool at *Victoria Park* (Ⓣ01750/720897; April–Oct), though a campsite like *Honey Cottage* (Ⓣ01750/62246, Ⓦwww.honeycottagecaravanpark.co.uk), some seventeen miles away near Wardlaw by Ettrick Water, is a far more scenic choice.

Bowhill House

Three miles west of Selkirk off the A708, **Bowhill House** (guided tours July daily 11am–5pm; Aug daily 2pm–3.30pm; £8; Ⓦwww.bowhill.org) is the property of the Duke of Buccleuch, a seriously wealthy man. Beyond the grandiose mid-nineteenth-century mansion's facade of dark whinstone is an outstanding collection of French antiques and European **paintings**: in the dining room, for example, there are portraits by Reynolds and Gainsborough, and a Canaletto cityscape, while the drawing room boasts Boulle furniture, Meissen tableware, paintings by Ruysdael, Leandro Bassano and Claude Lorraine, as well as two more family portraits by Reynolds. Look out also for the Scott Room, which features another splendid portrait of Sir Walter by Henry Raeburn, and the Duke of Monmouth's execution shirt.

The wooded hills of **Bowhill Country Park** adjoining the house (10am–5pm: April–June Sat & Sun; July & Aug daily; £3.50) are crisscrossed by scenic footpaths and cycle trails. The park also shelters a 72-seat "theatre in the forest", *Bowhill Theatre* (Ⓣ01750/22204), in the house's former game larder, which hosts the occasional production. Getting to Bowhill by **public transport** is difficult – the Selkirk to Peebles bus will drop you at General's Bridge (10min), from where it's a mile or so's walk through the grounds to the house, or you can get a taxi from Selkirk.

West along Yarrow Water

The A708, which passes by Bowhill, follows **Yarrow Water** upstream towards Dumfriesshire. A couple of miles northwest of Bowhill there's the Broadmeadows SYHA **hostel** near Yarrowford (Ⓣ01750/76372, Ⓦwww.syha.org.uk; mid-June to Aug) – the SYHA's first hostel, opened in 1931 – which serves as a convenient starting point for some good hill walks. From here, you can reach the hilltop cairns of **The Three Brethren** (1530ft), whose summit offers excellent views over the Borders. You can also link up with stretches of the Southern Upland Way by heading east down through Yair Forest, or by following an old drove road west to the Cheese Well at Minchmoor (so called because of offerings left by travellers for the faerie folk), and ending up at Traquair House near Innerleithen (see p.151).

Eight miles west of the hostel, the A708 is crossed by the B709 going north through the hills to Innerleithen and southeast to Hawick. The junction is marked by the **Gordon Arms Hotel** (Ⓣ01750/82222, Ⓦwww.thegordonarmsyarrow.com; ❷), reputedly the last meeting place of Walter Scott and James Hogg, the "Shepherd Poet of Ettrick", where framed fragments of letters from Scott are on display in an otherwise basic bar serving meals and real ale. From the hotel, which offers a transport service and a **bunkhouse** for walkers (£18.50 B&B), you can follow the course of the lovely Yarrow Water further east for about seventeen miles to Selkirk (see p.154). Buses along the Yarrow valley take you as far as the *Gordon Arms* before turning north to Peebles.

A couple of miles further up the A708 at the top of Yarrow Water lies a pair of icy lakes: **St Mary's Loch**, and its diminutive neighbour, **Loch of the Lowes**, separated by a slender isthmus and magnificently set beneath the surrounding hills. This spot was popular with the nineteenth-century Scottish literati, especially Scott and Hogg, who eulogized "the bosom of the lonely Lowes". The pair met to chew the fat at **Tibbie Shiels Inn** on the isthmus, which takes its name from Isabella Shiel, a formidable and, by all accounts, amusing woman who ruled the place till her death in 1878 at the age of 96. Today, the inn is a famous watering-hole on the Southern Upland Way, providing decent bar meals and a riverside **campsite** (with tepee). The place is popular so book ahead and phone ahead for opening times in winter (Ⓣ01750/42231, Ⓦwww.tibbieshiels.com). On the last Sunday in July the **Blanket Preaching** takes place here – an open-air service recalling a time when preachers were barred from the church.

For a short and enjoyable walk, follow a section of the Southern Upland Way from the inn along the east side of St Mary's Loch into **Bowerhope Forest**. Alternatively, the Southern Upland Way heads across the moors north to Traquair House and south to the valley of the **Ettrick Water**, both strenuous hikes that require an Ordnance Survey map, a compass and proper clothing (see p.49). If you're continuing west along the A708 into Dumfries and Galloway, don't miss the 200ft **Grey Mare's Tail Waterfall** (NTS), four miles southwest of Loch of the Lowes, which tumbles down a rocky crevasse as you descend into Dumfriesshire. The base of the falls is approached by a precipitous footpath along the left side of the stream, a ten-minute clamber each way from the road.

Teviotdale and Liddesdale

To the south of the Tweed, **Teviotdale** is an altogether gentler valley, stretched between Teviothead, in the western hills, and Kelso, where the river joins the Tweed. The chief draw here is the best preserved of all the Border abbeys, at **Jedburgh**, which lies on a tributary of the Teviot called Jed Water. The main town on the Teviot itself is **Hawick**, famous for its knitwear factories, but not an essential stop. From Hawick the busy A7 tracks up the most dramatic section of Teviotdale towards Langholm in Dumfriesshire. The alternative is to head down **Liddesdale** from Hawick along the B6399, or – if you're coming straight from Jedburgh – the B6357, both slower but even more picturesque and remote roads flanked by dense forests, barren moors and secluded heaths. If you do come this way, stop off at solitary **Hermitage Castle**.

The Galashiels to Carlisle **bus** travels along much of Teviotdale via Hawick, where buses connect with Jedburgh.

Jedburgh

Just ten miles north of the English border, **JEDBURGH** (Ⓦwww.jedburgh.org.uk) nestles in the lush valley of Jed Water near its confluence with the Teviot out on the edge of the wild Cheviot Hills. During the interminable wars between England and Scotland, Jedburgh was the quintessential frontier town, a heavily garrisoned royal burgh incorporating a mighty castle and abbey. Though the castle was destroyed by the Scots in 1409 to keep it out of the hands of the English, its memory has been kept alive by stories: in 1285, for example, King Alexander III was celebrating his wedding feast in the great hall when a ghostly apparition predicted his untimely death and a bloody civil war; sure enough, he died in a hunting accident shortly afterwards and chaos ensued. Today, Jedburgh is the first place of any size that you come to on the A68, having crossed over Carter Bar from England, and as such gets quite a bit of passing tourist trade. The ruined **abbey** is the main event, though a stroll round the old town centre is a pleasant way to while away an hour or so.

Arrival and information

Buses pick up and drop off at Canongate near the town centre; yards away on Murray's Green is the **tourist office** (April–Oct daily; Nov–March Mon–Sat only; Ⓣ01835/863170). You can rent bikes and tandems from Tandem & Bike Hire (Ⓣ01835/830326), 8 Timpendean Cottages.

Accommodation

Hundalee House Ⓣ01835/863011, Ⓔsheila.whittaker@btinternet.com. A warm welcome is guaranteed at this seventeenth-century manor house in open grounds, a mile south of town, off the A68. March–Oct. ❷

Jedwater Caravan Park Camptown, (5 miles south down the A68 Ⓣ01835/840219, Ⓦwww.jedwater.co.uk. The cheaper and more secluded choice of two campsites nearby, with a pleasant riverside site. March–Oct.

Meadhon House 48 Castlegate Ⓣ01835/862504, Ⓦwww.meadhon.com. Pronounced "mawn", this is the finest of several B&Bs among Castlegate's pleasant and antique row of houses, with a conservatory round the back overlooking a lovely sloping garden. ❷

Willow Court The Friars Ⓣ01835/863702, Ⓦwww.willowcourtjedburgh.co.uk. The attention to detail here – Egyptian cotton bed linen, flat-screen TVs – puts this a cut above most of Jedburgh's B&Bs. ❹

The Town

Despite its ruinous state, **Jedburgh Abbey** (May–Sept daily 9.30am–5.30pm; Oct–April daily 9.30am–4.30pm; HS; £5.20) still dominates the town, particularly when approached from the south. Founded in the twelfth century as an Augustinian priory by King David I, it's the best preserved of all the Border abbeys, its vast church towering over a sloping site right in the centre of town, beside Jed Water. Built in red, yellow and grey sandstone, the abbey church can appear by turns gloomy, calm or richly warm, depending on the weather and the light. The abbey was burnt and badly damaged on a number of occasions, but by far the worst destruction was inflicted by the English in the 1540s. By this time, the contemplative way of life had already fallen prey to corruption and only a few canons remained living in the ruins of the abbey, until it was finally closed in 1560. The abbey church remained the parish kirk for another three centuries and as a result has survived particularly well preserved.

Jedburgh festivals

Jedburgh is at its busiest during the town's two main festivals. The **Common Riding**, or Callants' Festival, takes place in late June or early July, when the young people of the town – especially the lads – mount up and ride out to check the burgh boundaries, a reminder of more troubled days when Jedburgh was subject to English raids. In similar spirit, early February sees the day-long **Jedburgh Hand Ba'** game, an all-male affair between the "uppies" (those born above Market Place) and the "doonies" (those born below). The aim of the game is to get a hay-stuffed leather ball – originally representing the head of an Englishman – from one end of town to the other.

Entry is through the bright **visitor centre** at the bottom of the hill, which has an optional fifteen-minute audiovisual show on the ground floor and a viewing room overlooking the site upstairs (a useful retreat if it's raining). Here, too, you'll see Jedburgh's most treasured archeological find, the **Jedburgh Comb**, carved around 1100 from walrus ivory and decorated with a griffin and a dragon. All that remains of the conventual buildings where the canons lived are the foundations and basic ground plan, but then Jedburgh's chief glory is really its **Abbey Church**, which remains splendidly preserved. As you enter via the west door, the three-storey nave's perfectly proportioned parade of columns and arches lies before you, a fine example of the transition from Romanesque to Gothic design, with pointed window arches surmounted by the round-headed arches of the triforium, which, in turn, support the lancet windows of the clerestory. Be sure you climb up the narrow staircase in the west front to the balcony overlooking the nave, where you can contemplate how the place must have looked all decked out for the marriage of Alexander III to Yolande de Dreux in 1285.

It's a couple of minutes' walk from the abbey to the small square **Market Place**, surrounded by soft oatmeal-coloured houses and centred on the 1889 Jubilee Fountain, a red-sandstone column topped by a unicorn. At the top of Castlegate stands **Jedburgh Castle Jail** (Easter–Oct Mon–Sat 10am–4.30pm, Sun 1–4pm; free), an impressive castellated nineteenth-century pile built on the site of the old royal castle, which is well worth a visit. As well as detailed information about Jedburgh's history, there's a fascinating insight into conditions in jail, deportations, crime and punishment (discover what happened to 9-year-olds who threw stones at ducks). The cells themselves are, for the period, remarkably comfortable, reflecting the influence of reformer John Howard.

Back down near the Market Place, signs will guide you to **Mary, Queen of Scots' House** (March–Nov Mon–Sat 10am–4.30pm, Sun 11am–4.30pm; free). Despite the name, it's unlikely that Mary actually stayed in this particular sixteenth-century house, though she did visit the town in 1566 for the Assizes. The attempt to unravel her complex life is cursory, the redeeming features being a copy of Mary's death mask and one of the few surviving portraits of the Earl of Bothwell, Mary's third husband. Just north of the town is **Monteviot** (Ⓦwww.monteviot.com), the early eighteenth-century home of the Marquess of Lothian and headquarters of the Clan Kerr: the garden (April–Oct daily noon–5pm; £3.50), slopes down to the Teviot and has lovely water features, herbaceous borders and roses in season; the house's interior is also open in July (daily 1–5pm; £3.50). Five miles to the south of town is **Jedforest Deer and Farm Park** (daily: April–Aug 10am–5.30pm; Sept & Oct 11am–4.30pm; £5) which provides a good family day out; there's a red deer herd and rare breeds of cattle, pigs and chickens, with falconry demonstrations thrown in.

Eating

There's a shortage of good **eating** places in Jedburgh itself, the most reliable being *Simply Scottish*, 6–8 High St (Ⓣ01835/864696), a smart but relaxed bistro-style café/restaurant serving inexpensive Scottish meals, as well as pasta dishes and the usual snacks. Try the local speciality **Jethart Snails**, sticky boiled sweets invented by a French POW in the 1700s and on sale everywhere. Further out of town, south on the A68, the comfortable *Jedforest Hotel* (Ⓣ01835/840222, Ⓦwww.jedforesthotel.com; ❻) has a restaurant with an excellent reputation. Three miles east of Jedburgh on the A698 is *Caddy Mann*, (daily in daytime, plus Fri & Sat eves) an award-winning restaurant and teashop crammed with bric-a-brac and antiques.

Hawick

Fourteen miles southwest of Jedburgh, **HAWICK** (pronounced "hoyk") is the largest town in the Borders. Despite being a busy, working mill town, Hawick has a surprising number of visitors, the majority of whom come in search of bargains from its woollen knitwear factory outlets. The town's heyday as the centre of the region's knitwear and hosiery industry was in the late nineteenth century, yet companies like Pringle, Lyle & Scott and Peter Scott continue to produce quality cashmere knitwear here. Followers of the yarn can satiate themselves at the **Hawick Cashmere Visitor Centre** (Mon–Sat 9.30am–5pm; free), on Arthur Street, east of the town centre off the A698, which has a viewing gallery overlooking the frames at work.

The Victorian architecture of Hawick's handsome, wide **High Street** reflects the confident prosperity of the late nineteenth century, particularly the Scots Baronial town hall halfway down the street. At the southwestern end of the street stands the **Borders Textile Tower House** (April–Oct Mon–Sat 10am–4.30pm, Sun noon–3pm; Nov–March Mon–Sat 10am–4pm; free) which tells the history of the textile industry with exhibits ranging from ladies' combinations from the early 1900s to Vivienne Westwood; there's lots of hands-on stuff for kids too. The **tourist office** (April–Sept daily; Oct Mon–Sat; Ⓣ01450/373993) is alongside in the **Tower Mill**, a newly transformed old water mill housing a cinema and a good café bar.

Hawick's other formal attraction is the **Hawick Museum & Gallery** (April–Sept Mon–Fri 10am–noon & 1–5pm, Sat & Sun 2–5pm; Oct–March Mon–Fri noon–3pm, Sun 1–3pm; free), a mile or so west of the town centre in Wilton Lodge Park. The museum has displays reflecting the manufacturing life of the area and a special section on Jimmie Guthrie, a local motorcycle ace who died during the German Grand Prix in 1937. There's also a gallery housing nineteenth- and twentieth-century Scottish art; more exciting, though, are the regular travelling exhibitions that the town manages to attract.

The most surprising **accommodation** is *The Bank* (Ⓣ01450/363760, Ⓦwww.thebankno12highst.com; ❸), house, as the name suggests, in a former bank right on the High Street at no. 12, with spacious rooms and contemporary, almost rock-star, decor. Another option is *Hizzy's* (Ⓣ01450/372101, Ⓦwww.hizzys.co.uk; ❹), a great, family-run guesthouse on North Bridge Street that's been comprehensively renovated. Hawick's most celebrated annual event is its **Common Riding**, which is held in early June, and commemorates a skirmish in 1514 when the local Hawick callants defeated a small English force and captured their banner.

Liddesdale

Either forming the border with England, or sticking close to it, **Liddesdale** is the only valley in the Borders whose river flows westwards. It's best approached via the hamlet of Bonchester Bridge, which sits on the A6088 from Hawick to Carter

Bar. From here, the B6357 cuts south through Wauchope Forest before reaching Liddesdale.

The valley's wild beauty is at its most striking between Saughtree and Newcastleton, where there's a turning to **Hermitage Castle** (April–Sept daily 9.30am–5.30pm; HS; £3.70), a bleak and forbidding fastness bedevilled by all sorts of horrifying legends: one owner, William Douglas, starved his prisoners to death, whilst Lord de Soulis, another occupant, engaged the help of demons to fortify the castle in defiance of the king, Robert the Bruce, who had him boiled to death. From the outside, the castle remains an imposing structure, its heavy walls topped by stepped gables and a tidy corbelled parapet. However, the apparent homogeneity is deceptive: certain features were invented during a Victorian restoration, a confusing supplement to the ad hoc alterations that had already transformed the fourteenth-century original. The ruinous interior is a bit of a letdown, but look out for the tight Gothic doorways and gruesome dungeon.

It's a short journey on to **NEWCASTLETON**, a classic estate village built for the handloom weavers of the third duke of Buccleuch in 1793. The gridiron streets fall either side of a long main road that connects three geometrically arranged squares, with the largest, Douglas Square, as the centrepiece. You can have a **drink**, sample some local trout or pheasant or even **stay** the night at the *Liddesdale Hotel* (ⓣ01387/375255, ⓦwww.liddesdalehotel.co.uk; ④), a family-run inn on Douglas Square itself. Book ahead if you plan to stay during the hugely popular **Newcastleton Traditional Music Festival** in July. There are regular **buses** along Liddesdale, from Newcastleton to Carlisle (Mon–Sat only).

Travel details

Trains

Edinburgh to: Berwick-upon-Tweed (every 1–2hr; 40–45min).

Buses

Berwick-upon-Tweed to: Duns (5–9 daily; 25min); Eyemouth (hourly; 15min); Galashiels (5–9 daily; 1hr 45min); Melrose (5–7 daily; 1hr 20min).

Duns to: Eyemouth (Mon–Sat 4 daily; 40min); Kelso (Mon–Fri 2 daily; 50min).

Edinburgh to: Coldingham (Mon–Sat every 2hr, 3 on Sun; 1hr 30min); Eyemouth (Mon–Sat 6 daily, 3 on Sun; 1hr 40min); Galashiels (Mon–Sat hourly; 2hr); Hawick (hourly; 2hr); Jedburgh (Mon–Fri hourly, 9 on Sat, 5 on Sun; 1hr 40min); Kelso (4–6 daily; 2hr); Lauder (Mon–Sat 7 hourly, 6 on Sun; 1hr 10min); Melrose (hourly; 2hr 15min); Peebles (hourly; 1hr); Selkirk (hourly; 1hr 40min).

Galashiels to: Hawick (Mon–Sat hourly, 4 on Sun; 45min); Jedburgh (Mon–Sat hourly; 5 on Sun; 50min); Kelso (Mon–Sat 7–9 daily, 5 on Sun; 1hr); Langholm (Mon–Sat 8–9 daily, 4 on Sun; 1hr 15min); Melrose (Mon–Sat hourly, 7 on Sun; 15min); Peebles (Mon–Sat hourly, 9 on Sun; 45min); Selkirk (Mon–Sat every 30min, Sun hourly; 15min).

Hawick to: Jedburgh (Mon–Sat every 30min–1hr; 25min); Kelso (hourly; 1hr); Langholm (Mon–Sat hourly, 4 on Sun; 30min); Newcastleton (Mon–Fri 3–4 daily, 2 on Sat; 45min); Selkirk (Mon–Sat hourly, 4 on Sun; 25min).

Jedburgh to: Kelso (Mon–Sat 5–7 daily; 25min); Lauder (3–4 daily; 45min); Melrose (Mon–Sat 1–2 hourly, 7 on Sun; 30min).

Kelso to: Coldstream (Mon–Sat every 1–2hr; 20min); Kirk Yetholm (Mon–Sat 6 daily; 20min); Lauder (4–6 daily; 45min); Melrose (Mon–Sat 7–9 daily, 5 on Sun; 30–40min).

Melrose to: Duns (Mon–Sat 5–7 daily, 3 on Sun; 50min); Galashiels (Mon–Sat hourly, 7 on Sun; 15min); Hawick (Wed, Fri & Sat 2 daily; 40min); Jedburgh (Mon–Sat 1–2 hourly, 7 on Sun; 30min); Kelso (Mon–Sat 8–12 daily, 4 on Sun; 30min); Peebles (Mon–Sat hourly, 6 on Sun; 1hr 10min); Selkirk (Mon–Sat hourly, 2 on Sun; 20min).

Newcastleton to: Carlisle (Mon–Fri 3–4 daily, 1 on Sat; 50min); Hawick (Mon–Fri 3–4 daily, 2 on Sat; 45min); Langholm (Mon–Sat 3–4 daily; 40min).

Selkirk to: Ettrick (Mon–Fri 2 daily; 50min); Hawick (Mon–Sat hourly, Sun every 2hr; 20min); Langholm (Mon–Sat 6–7 daily, 3 on Sun; 1hr).

3

Dumfries and Galloway

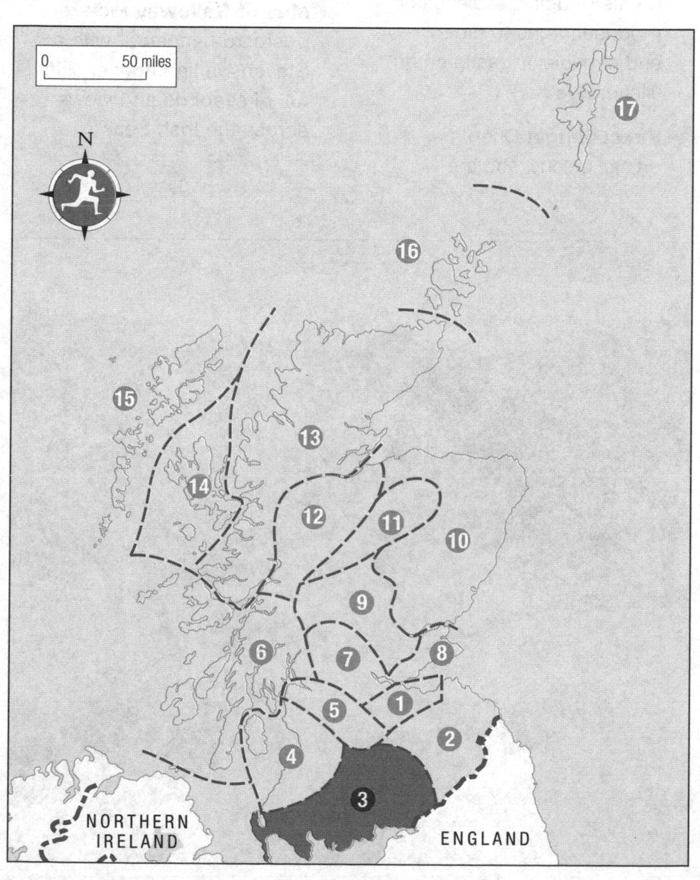

CHAPTER 3 Highlights

✱ **Caerlaverock** One of Scotland's most photogenic moated castles, beside a superb site for waterfowl and waders. See p.169

✱ **Threave Garden and Castle** The perfect day-trip from Castle Douglas: azaleas and rhododendrons to die for and a medieval castle on an island. See p.173

✱ **Kirkcudbright** One-time artists' colony, and the best-looking town in the "Scottish Riviera". See p.174

✱ **Galloway Forest Park** Go mountain biking along remote forest tracks, or hiking on the Southern Upland Way. See p.178

✱ **Mull of Galloway** Picture-postcard headland, with a Stevenson lighthouse, cliffs full of seabirds and views across the Irish Sea. See p.184

▲ Galloway Forest Park

3

Dumfries and Galloway

The southwest corner of Scotland, now known as **Dumfries and Galloway** (Ⓦwww.visitdumfriesandgalloway.co.uk), is a region set apart, with few people bothering to exit the main Carlisle–Glasgow motorway that runs through the county. Yet Dumfries and Galloway have stately homes, deserted hills and ruined abbeys to compete with the best of the Borders. They also have something the Borders don't have, and that's the Solway coast, a long, indented coastline of sheltered sandy coves that's been dubbed the "Scottish Riviera" – an exaggeration perhaps, but it's certainly Scotland's warmest, southernmost stretch of coastline.

The region has a fascinatingly diverse heritage. Originally inhabited by southern Picts, it has at various times been overrun by Romans, Anglo-Saxons from Northumberland and Celts from Ireland: the name Galloway means the "land of the stranger Gaels". It was an unruly land, where independent chieftains maintained close contacts with the Vikings rather than the Scots, right up until medieval times. Gradually, this autonomy was whittled away, and the area was swallowed up by the Scottish Crown, though Galloway continued to be a fiercely independent region, typified by local hero Robert the Bruce. Later, it became a stronghold of the Covenanters, and suffered terribly during the "Killing Times" following the Restoration, when the government forces came to impose Episcopalianism. From around the seventeenth century, the ports of the Solway coast prospered with the expansion of local shipping routes over to Ireland. The region subsequently experienced economic decline as trade routes changed, turning busy ports into sleepy backwaters.

Unless you're running away to **Gretna Green** to get married, **Dumfries** is the obvious gateway to the region, a run-down town that's only a must for those on the trail of **Robert Burns**, who spent the last part of his life here. More compelling is the nearby coast, overlooking the Solway Firth, the shallow estuary wedged between Scotland and England, famed for its wildlife and for the nearby red-sandstone ruins of **Caerlaverock Castle** and **Sweetheart Abbey**. Edged by tidal marsh and mudbank, much of the Solway shoreline is flat and eerily remote, but there are also some fine rocky bays sheltering beneath wooded hills, most notably along the **Colvend coast**. Further along the coast is **Kirkcudbright**, once a bustling port thronged with sailing ships, later an artists' retreat and now a tranquil, well-preserved little eighteenth- and early nineteenth-century town.

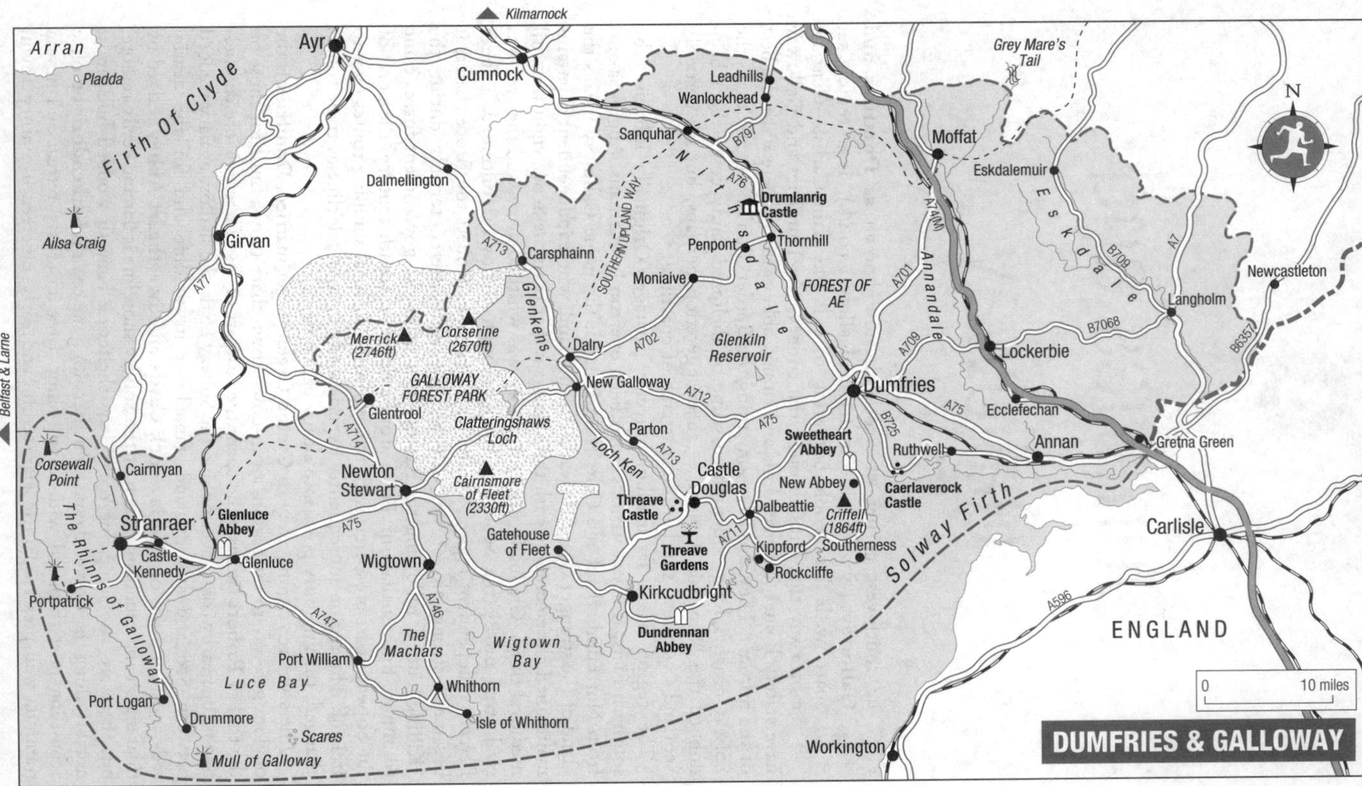
DUMFRIES & GALLOWAY
Kilmarnock
Belfast & Larne
Arran
Pladda
Firth Of Clyde
Ailsa Craig
Ayr
Cumnock
Dalmellington
Girvan
A77
Carsphainn
A713
Glenkens
Merrick (2746ft)
Corserine (2670ft)
GALLOWAY FOREST PARK
Glentrool
A714
Clatteringshaws Loch
Cairnsmore of Fleet (2330ft)
Newton Stewart
Corsewall Point
Cairnryan
Stranraer
Castle Kennedy
Glenluce Abbey
Glenluce
A75
The Rhinns of Galloway
Portpatrick
Port Logan
Drummore
Mull of Galloway
Scares
Luce Bay
A747
Port William
The Machars
A746
Wigtown
Whithorn
Isle of Whithorn
Wigtown Bay
Gatehouse of Fleet
Kirkcudbright
Dundrennan Abbey
Threave Castle
Threave Gardens
Castle Douglas
Loch Ken
Parton
A713
New Galloway
A712
Dalry
A702
Moniaive
SOUTHERN UPLAND WAY
Sanquhar
B797
Wanlockhead
Leadhills
A76
Nithsdale
Drumlanrig Castle
Penpont
Thornhill
FOREST OF AE
Glenkiln Reservoir
A701
A709
Dumfries
A75
B725
Sweetheart Abbey
New Abbey
Criffell (1864ft)
Dalbeattie
A711
Kippford
Rockcliffe
Southerness
Caerlaverock Castle
Ruthwell
Solway Firth
Annan
Ecclefechan
Lockerbie
Annandale
A74(M)
Moffat
Grey Mare's Tail
Eskdalemuir
Eskdale
B709
B7068
A7
Langholm
Newcastleton
B6357
Gretna Green
Carlisle
A596
ENGLAND
Workington
N
0
10 miles

Gretna Green marriages

Up until 1754 English couples could buy a quick and secret wedding at London's Fleet Prison, bribing imprisoned clerics with small amounts of money. The **Hardwicke Marriage Act** brought an end to this seedy wheeze, enforcing the requirement of a licence and a church ceremony. However, in Scotland, a marriage declaration made before two witnesses remained legal. The consequences of this difference in the law verged on farce: hundreds of runaway couples dashed north to Scotland, their weddings witnessed by just about anyone who came to hand – ferrymen, farmers, tollgate keepers and even self-styled "priests" who set up their own "marriage houses".

Gretna Green, due to its position beside the border on the main turnpike road to Edinburgh, became the most popular destination for the fugitives. In their rush, many people tied the knot at the first place to hand after dismounting from the stagecoach, which happened to be a **blacksmith's shop** situated at the crossroads, though the better-off maintained class distinctions, heading for the staging post at Gretna Hall. The association with blacksmiths was strengthened by one of the first "priests", the redoubtable Joseph Paisley, a 25-stone Goliath who – in business from 1754 to 1812 – gave a certain style to the ceremony by straightening a horseshoe, a show of strength rather than a symbolic act. His melodramatic feat led to stories of Gretna Green weddings being performed over the blacksmith's **anvil**, and later "priests" were more than happy to act out the rumour. Gretna Green boomed until the marriage laws were further amended in 1856, but some businesses continued right up to 1940, when marriage by declaration was made illegal.

The only marriages that take place in Gretna Green nowadays, however, are for couples taken in by the "romance" of the name – more than 4000 annually – and English couples under 18, who want to get married without the permission of their parents (Ⓦ www.gretnaweddings.com).

Like Kirkcudbright, **Threave Garden and Castle**, just outside Castle Douglas, are popular with – but not crowded by – tourists.

Contrasting with the essentially gentle landscape of the Solway coast is the brooding presence of the **Galloway Hills** to the north, their beautiful moors, mountains, lakes and rivers centred on the 150,000-acre **Galloway Forest Park**, an underused hillwalking and mountain-biking paradise. Continuing west into what used to be Wigtownshire, the landscape becomes flatter and more relentlessly agricultural. The three main points of interest here are **Whithorn**, where St Ninian introduced Christianity to Scotland; the attractive seaport of **Portpatrick** on the hammer-headed Rhinns of Galloway; and the **Mull of Galloway**, Scotland's southernmost point, and a nesting site for thousands of seabirds.

Travelling the region by **bus** presents few problems; in addition, there's a **train** line up Annandale from Carlisle to Glasgow and one up Nithsdale via Dumfries. It's also easy to travel on from southwest Scotland by **ferry** to Northern Ireland, from Stranraer to Belfast and from Cairnryan to Larne. The combination of rolling landscape and quiet back roads makes the region good for **cyclists**: five of the **7stanes** (Ⓦ www.7stanes.gov.uk) purpose-built mountain-bike routes are in the forested hills of Dumfries and Galloway. This is also excellent **walking** country, featuring the **Southern Upland Way** (Ⓦ www.southernuplandway.com), a 212-mile coast-to-coast hike from Portpatrick in the west to Cockburnspath in the east.

Dumfries and around

Situated on the wide banks of the River Nith, a short distance inland from the Solway Firth, **DUMFRIES** is by far the largest town in southwest Scotland, with a population of more than thirty thousand. Long known as the "Queen of the South" (as is its football club), it flourished as a medieval seaport and trading centre, its success attracting the attention of many English armies. Despite this, it went on to prosper with its light industries and port supplying the agricultural hinterland. The town planners of the 1960s badly damaged its appearance, but many of the warm red-sandstone buildings that distinguish Dumfries from other places in the southwest survive. The town is second only to Ayr for its associations with **Robbie Burns** (see p.192), who spent the last five years of his life here employed as an exciseman.

Arrival and information

Dumfries **train** station is five minutes' walk east of the town centre, while **buses** drop you off at Whitesands beside the River Nith. The **tourist office** (June–Sept daily; Oct–May closed Sun; ⓣ01387/253862) is also on Whitesands. Grierson and Graham, 10 Academy St (ⓣ01387/259483), offers **bike rental**, useful for reaching the nearby Solway coast.

Accommodation

Dumfries abounds in handsome sandstone villas, several of which have been turned into **guesthouses** and **B&Bs**.

Burnett House 4 Lovers Walk ⓣ01387/263164, ⓦwww.burnetthouse.co.uk. For value and convenience, you can't beat this very smartly maintained Victorian B&B near the station; cyclists are welcome. ❷

Comlongon Castle Ten miles east of Dumfries, off the A75 ⓣ01387/870283, ⓦwww.comlongon.com. A classic Scottish castle retreat (and favourite wedding venue) set in a 120-acre estate – most rooms feature four-poster beds and plush traditional furnishings, plus there's a resident ghost. ❽

Glenaldor House 5 Victoria Terrace ⓣ01387/264248, ⓦwww.glenaldorhouse.co.uk. A light and bright Victorian house near the station with four en-suite bedrooms and bountiful breakfasts. ❷

The Merlin 2 Kenmure Terrace ⓣ01387/261002. Terrace B&B in a distinctive setting, overlooking the suspension bridge over the Nith near the RBC. ❷

The Town

Orientation around Dumfries is easy, with the railway to the east, and the river to the north and west. The pedestrianized **High Street** runs roughly parallel to the Nith; at its northern end, presiding over a floral roundabout, is the **Burns Statue**, a sentimental piece of Victorian frippery in white Carrara marble, featuring the great man holding a posy in one hand while the other clutches at his heart. Further down the High Street, Burns's body lay in state at the town's most singular building, the **Midsteeple**, an appealingly wonky hotchpotch, built in 1707 to fulfil the multiple functions of town prison, clock tower, courthouse and arsenal.

If you're on Burns's trail, make sure you duck down the alleyway to the **Globe Inn** (ⓦwww.globeinndumfries.co.uk), just past the ornate red and gold Victorian fountain, a little further down the High Street. This whitewashed inn, with its own suntrap courtyard, is Burns's most famous "howff" (pub) and one of the town's few surviving seventeenth-century buildings. Burns had a fling with Annie Park, a barmaid at the *Globe Inn*, and the resultant child was taken into the Burns household by his long-suffering wife, Jean Armour.

Southeast of the High Street, in what was once Mill Vennel and is now, inevitably, Burns Street, stands **Burns House** (April–Sept Mon–Sat 10am–5pm,

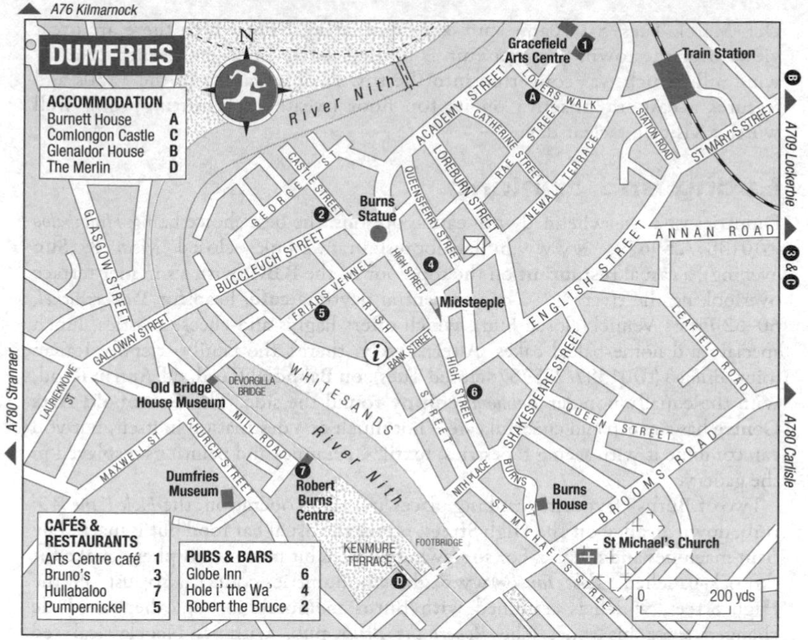

Sun 2–5pm; Oct–March Tues–Sat 10am–1pm & 2–5pm; free), a simple sandstone building where the poet died of rheumatic heart disease in 1796 aged 37, a few days before the birth of his last son, Maxwell. Burns lived here just three years before he died, though Jean Armour stayed on until her own death, some 38 years later. Inside, there's the usual collection of Burns memorabilia – manuscripts, letters, his copper kettle, nutmeg grater and the like – while one of the bedroom windows bears his signature, scratched with his diamond ring. As a member of the Dumfries Volunteers, Burns was given a military funeral, before being buried nearby in a simple grave by **St Michael's Church** (Mon–Fri 10am–4pm; free), a large red-sandstone church, built in 1745. In 1815 Burns was dug up and moved across the graveyard to a purpose-built **Mausoleum**, a bright white Neoclassical eyesore that houses a statue of him being accosted by the poetic Muse. The rest of the graveyard is packed full of large red-sandstone tombstones, including many of the poet's friends, a number of them inscribed with the most wonderfully verbose epitaphs.

The Nith is spanned by two pedestrian-only bridges, a delicate suspension bridge from 1875 and, a little further upstream, **Devorgilla Bridge**, built in 1431 and one of the oldest in Scotland. Attached to its southwestern end is the town's oldest house, built in 1660 and now housing the tiny and slightly bizarre **Old Bridge House Museum** (times as for Burns House; free), stuffed full of Victorian domestic bric-a-brac, including a teeth-chattering range of Victorian dental gear; the house was once an inn, which Burns would have undoubtedly visited.

Downstream from the Old Bridge House, an old watermill has been converted into the **Robert Burns Centre**, or RBC (times as for Burns House; £2; Ⓦ www.rbcft.co.uk), with a simple exhibition on the poet's years in Dumfries; films are also regularly shown here. On the hill above the RBC stands the **Dumfries Museum** (April–Sept Mon–Sat 10am–5pm, Sun 2–5pm;

Oct–March Tues–Sat 10am–1pm & 2–5pm; free), from which there are great views over the town. The museum is housed partly in an eighteenth-century windmill, which was converted into the town's observatory in the 1830s and features a **camera obscura** on its top floor (weather permitting; £2), well worth a visit on a clear day.

Eating and drinking

Dumfries isn't overwhelmed with eating options, the best choice being *Hullabaloo* (Ⓣ01387/259679; Ⓦwww.hullabaloorestaurant.co.uk; closed Mon & Sun evening), a casual **restaurant** on the top floor of the RBC, with a summer terrace overlooking the river. For a decent central daytime **café**, head for *Pumpernickel*, 60–62 Friars Vennel (closed Sun), which offers haggis and cheese toasties, lunch specials and home-baked cakes. Alternatively, there's the family-friendly Italian joint, *Bruno's* (Ⓣ01387/255757; closed Tues), on Balmoral Road, off Annan Road, with the equally popular *Balmoral* **chippy** round the side. The **Gracefield Arts Centre** has a cheap and cheerful café – not much of a destination in itself, but you can combine it with seeing tapestries, textiles, ceramics and paintings displayed in the gallery.

Two of Burns's favourite drinking places are still in operation: the *Hole i' the Wa'* **pub**, down an alley off the High Street, serves the usual bar food but is marred by fruit machines and muzak. For somewhere with a bit more atmosphere, make for the oak-panelled *Globe Inn* (Ⓦwww.globeinndumfries.co.uk), also just off the High Street, which is crammed with Burns memorabilia but otherwise little changed since his time. The *Robert the Bruce* pub, with its Neoclassical red sandstone portico at the top of Buccleuch Street, is a typical and very popular church conversion by the J.D. Wetherspoon chain. **Films** are shown regularly at the RBC (Tues–Sat; Ⓣ01387/264808, Ⓦwww.rbcft.co.uk).

Around Dumfries

Southeast of Dumfries, the medieval ruins of **Caerlaverock Castle** are simply magnificent, as is the adjacent nature reserve and the early Christian cross at nearby **Ruthwell**. On the west bank of the Nith estuary, the star attraction is **Sweetheart Abbey**, the best preserved of the trio of Cistercian abbeys in Dumfries and Galloway. Regular **buses** run to all these sights, with timetables available from the Dumfries tourist office.

Anyone interested in sculpture should check out the private collection that is dotted about the landscape around the remote **Glenkiln Reservoir**, some eight miles west of Dumfries (ask at the tourist office for directions and an information sheet). A naked *John the Baptist* by Jacob Epstein welcomes visitors to the car park – this is one of five startling sculptures set in the landscape, including a Rodin and two Henry Moores.

Ellisland Farm

North of Dumfries, the A76 passes **Ellisland Farm** (April–Sept Mon–Fri 10am–1pm & 2–5pm, Sun 2–5pm; Oct–March Tues–Sat 10am–5pm; £2.50; Ⓦwww.ellislandfarm.co.uk), built by Robert Burns in 1788 as a family home and working farmhouse. His three years at Ellisland were very productive: he wrote more than 130 poems and songs during his time here, including *Tam o' Shanter* and *Auld Lang Syne*. The farm – "a ruinous affair", Burns called it – didn't prosper due to the boggy soil, and eventually Burns got a salaried post as an exciseman. Ellisland remains a working farm, though it also houses a museum, where you can see Burns's fishing rod and flute, the original range installed by the poet for his wife, and his pistol and sword – essential possessions when carrying out the unpopular job of levying taxes.

Caerlaverock Castle

Caerlaverock Castle, eight miles southeast of Dumfries (daily: April–Sept 9.30am–5.30pm; Oct–March 9.30am–4.30pm; HS; £5.20), is a picture-perfect ruined castle. Not only is it moated, it's built from the rich local red sandstone and has preserved its mighty double-towered gatehouse. Built in the late thirteenth century, it clearly impressed medieval chroniclers. During the siege of 1300 by Edward I, a contemporary bard commented: "In shape it was like a shield, for it had but three sides round it, with a tower at each corner." Caerlaverock sustained further damage in 1312, this time from the Scots, and again in 1356–57 from the English, forcing numerous rebuilding programmes. The most surprising addition, however, lies inside, where you're confronted by the ornate Renaissance facade of the **Nithsdale Lodging**, erected in the 1630s by the first earl of Nithsdale. Just six years later the earl and his garrison were forced to surrender after a thirteen-week siege and bombardment by the Covenanters, who proceeded to wreck the place. It was never inhabited again.

Caerlaverock Castle is a popular family day out; it has a siege-engine playground, a tearoom and an exhibition and video on the siege of 1300, where kids can do their own heraldry – a useful wet-weather retreat. There are also **walks** marked out along the edge of the neighbouring national nature reserve, including one leading to the earthworks of the castle that preceded Caerlaverock; en route, look out for the rare natterjack toad.

Caerlaverock Wetland Centre

Three miles further east, at Eastpark, is the **Caerlaverock Wetland Centre** (daily 10am–5pm; £5.50; ⓣ01387/770200, ⓦwww.wwt.org.uk), 1400 acres of protected salt marsh and mud flat edging the Solway Firth. It's famous for the 25,000 or so Svalbard barnacle geese that winter here between September and April, but the rest of the year there's plenty of other flora and fauna to look out for, as well as the aforementioned natterjack toad. The main observatory here is linked to a score of well-situated birdwatchers' hides. Throughout the year there are daily feeding times for the wild whooper swans and the wardens run free wildlife safaris; call for up-to-date details. You can **camp** or stay in one of the **rooms** in the centre's converted farmhouse (ⓔinfo.caerlaverock@wwt.org.uk; ❸), which has its own observation tower, plus a kitchen and washing machine for guests' use. Both the castle and the centre are reached along the B725; this is the route the #371 bus takes from Dumfries, mostly terminating at the castle but sometimes continuing to the start of the two-mile lane leading off the B725 to the centre.

The Ruthwell Cross

A modest country church, seven miles east of Caerlaverock, houses the remarkable eighteen-foot **Ruthwell Cross**, an extraordinary early Christian monument from the early or mid-eighth century when Galloway was ruled by the Northumbrians. The cross was considered idolatrous during the Reformation, smashed and buried, and only finally reassembled in the nineteenth century. The decoration reveals a strikingly sophisticated style and iconography, probably derived from the eastern Mediterranean. The main inscriptions are in Latin, but running round the edge is a poem written in the Northumbrian dialect in runic figures. However, it's the biblical carvings on the main face that really catch the eye, notably Mary Magdalene washing the feet of Jesus.

New Abbey and around

NEW ABBEY is a tidy little one-street village, eight miles south of Dumfries, that originally evolved in order to service its giant neighbour, **Sweetheart Abbey** (April–Sept daily 9.30am–5.30pm; Oct daily 9.30am–4.30pm; Nov–March Mon–Wed, Sat & Sun 9.30am–4.30pm; HS; £3), which now lies romantically ruined to the east. The abbey takes its unusual name from its founder, Devorgilla de Balliol, Lady of Galloway, who carried the embalmed heart of her husband, John Balliol (of Oxford college fame) around with her for the remaining 22 years of her life – she is buried, with the casket, in the presbytery. The last of the Cistercian abbeys to be founded in Scotland, in 1273, Sweetheart is dominated by the red sandstone ruins of the abbey church, which remains intact, albeit minus its roof. Standing in the grassy nave, flanked by giant compound piers supporting early Gothic arches, and above them a triforium, it's easy to imagine what the completed church must have looked like. The central square tower is a massive, brutal structure, but the elaborate tracery in some of the windows and flamboyant corbelling below the central tower clearly mark a change from the austere simplicity of earlier Cistercian foundations. The massive precinct wall is made from rough granite boulders, and is the most complete of its kind in the country.

Award-winning *Abbey Cottage* **tearoom** is renowned for its good coffee, teas and home-made cakes, and enjoys an unrivalled view over the abbey. At the centre of the village, two **pubs** face one another across a cobbled square: the *Abbey Arms* (Ⓣ01387/850489, Ⓦwww.abbeyarmshotel.com; ❷), and the *Criffel Inn* (Ⓣ01387/850244, Ⓦwww.criffel-inn.co.uk; ❷); both have seats outside, serve pub food and do B&B. Just beyond the pubs, but before the bridge, is the eighteenth-century water-powered **New Abbey Corn Mill** (times as for abbey; HS; £4.20); at noon and 3pm the custodian puts the mill machinery through its paces. The mill pond is a lovely spot for a picnic.

Around New Abbey

Just outside New Abbey on the Dumfries road lies **Shambellie House** (April–Oct daily 10am–5pm; £4; Ⓦwww.nms.ac.uk/costume), a Scots Baronial pile designed by David Bryce in 1856. The house isn't all that grand inside, so it's only worth visiting if you want to see the dummies who now inhabit the rooms, dressed to the nines in a variety of **costumes** from the Victorian era to the 1920s. There's also a tearoom, with tables outside overlooking the house's lawn, garden and wooded grounds.

One and a half miles south of New Abbey, Ardwell Mains Farm marks the start of the walk up **Criffel** (1864ft), a hump-backed whale of a hill with great views of the Borders and the Lake District. A couple of miles further on, at Kirkbean, a small turning on the left leads to **John Paul Jones Museum** (April–June & Sept Tues–Sun 10am–5pm; July & Aug daily 10am–5pm; £2.50; Ⓦwww.jpj.demon.co.uk), where the "father of the US Navy" was born into extreme poverty in 1747. Here, you can learn about his eventful and adventurous naval career, which began when he went to sea at the age of 13, and which included a spell in the Russian navy.

Nithsdale

North of Dumfries, the A76 and the railway line to Kilmarnock travel the length of **Nithsdale**, whose gentle slopes and old forests hide one major attraction: the many-turreted seventeenth-century mansion of **Drumlanrig Castle** near

Thornhill, just one of three substantial country seats owned by the duke of Buccleuch. At the opposite end of the class system were the miners who worked the lead mines in the neighbouring Lowther Hills, to the east, now commemorated in the intriguing **Museum of Lead Mining** in Wanlockhead.

Drumlanrig Castle and around

Seventeen miles north of Dumfries, just off the A76, **Drumlanrig Castle** (mid-March to Aug daily 11am–5pm; £9, gardens and country park only £5; Ⓦwww.drumlanrig.co.uk) is, in fact, not a castle at all, but the grandiose stately home of the Duke of Buccleuch and Queensberry, one of the country's wealthiest men. Visitors approach via an impressive driveway that sweeps along an avenue of lime trees to the "Pink Palace", a seventeenth-century pink-sandstone structure with a forest of cupolas, turrets and towers. Since the theft of the castle's Leonardo da Vinci in 2003 (it has since been recovered), visits have been by guided tour only.

The highlights of the richly furnished interior are the paintings in the oak-panelled staircase hall, most notably **Rembrandt**'s *Old Woman Reading*, and **Hans Holbein**'s formal portrait of Sir Nicholas Carew, Master of the Horse to Henry VIII. Other artists to look out for include Joost van Cleef, Murillo, Jan Gossaert and van Dyck. Also be sure to check out the striking 1950s portrait by John Merton of the present duchess, all debutante coiffure and high-society décolletage, in the morning room, and, in the serving room, John Ainslie's *Joseph Florence, Chef*, a sharply observed and dynamic portrait much liked by Walter Scott.

As well as the house, Drumlanrig offers a host of other attractions, including formal **gardens** and a forested **country park** (April–Sept daily 11am–5pm). The old stableyard beside the castle contains a visitor centre, a few shops, the inevitable tearoom and also a useful **bike rental** outlet, as the park is crisscrossed by footpaths and cycle routes. There's also a **cycle museum** with a replica of the first-ever pedal bike, invented in 1839 by local boy Kirkpatrick MacMillan. Before you go for a stroll round the gardens, pick up the tree trail leaflet, which will point out significant trees, such as the red oak planted by Neil Armstrong – and don't miss out on the Victorian **Heather Hut**, either. If you're heading here by bus from Dumfries or Ayr, note that it's a one-and-a-half-mile walk from the road to the house.

Practicalities

You can **stay** the night comfortably at Thornhill, three miles south on the A76, either at the *Buccleuch and Queensberry Hotel* (Ⓣ01848/330215, Ⓦwww.buccleuchhotel.co.uk; ④), a hunting, shooting and fishing **inn** built in pink sandstone at the main crossroads, whose bar serves a range of superb real ales and good pub food, or close by at *Gillbank House* (Ⓣ01848/330597, Ⓦwww.gillbank.co.uk; ④), a smart Victorian house at 8 East Morton St, with the *Thornhill Inn* just down the road. More stylish again is *Trigony House Hotel* (Ⓣ01848/331211, Ⓦwww.trigonyhotel.co.uk; ⑥), a couple of miles further down the A76, an ivy-clad, pink-sandstone former shooting lodge, with a very warm atmosphere and a good, moderately expensive Scottish **restaurant**.

Sanquhar and Wanlockhead

Leaving Drumlanrig, the A76 slips through the wooded hills of Nithsdale, passing the turning to Wanlockhead (see below) en route to **SANQUHAR** (pronounced "Sank-er"), a trim market town and the first stop on the railway line north from Dumfries. Jutting out into the main street is Sanquhar's most notable building, the **Tolbooth** (April–Sept Tues–Sat 10am–1pm & 2–5pm, Sun 2–5pm; free), a handsome Georgian townhouse with a pedimented facade, a double-side forestair, a square clock tower and finished off with an octagonal cupola. Elsewhere, the bow-windowed shop at 39–41 High St claims to be the oldest working **post office** in Britain, dating from 1712.

From Sanquhar, it's six miles up the striking Mennock Pass to **WANLOCKHEAD**, a remote and windswept spot in the **Lowther Hills**. Sitting at 1500ft, Wanlockhead is the highest village in Scotland and now home to the fascinating open-air **Museum of Lead Mining** (daily: April–June, Sept & Oct 11am–4.30pm; July & Aug 10am–5pm; £7.25; Ⓦ www.leadminingmuseum.co.uk). After a brief foray into the main exhibition you don a hard hat and go on a guided tour of the underground **Lochnell Mine**. Afterwards there's a tour of a **miner's cottage** from the 1740s and then one from a hundred years or so later. You should also visit the remarkable eighteenth-century **Miners' Library**, its 3000-plus volumes purchased from the voluntary subscriptions of its members, and try your hand at gold panning.

Most weekends, you can travel from the Glengonnar Halt, just above Wanlockhead, to the neighbouring mining village of **LEADHILLS** on the mile-long narrow gauge **Leadhills & Wanlockhead Railway** (Easter–Sept Sat & Sun 11am–5pm; £3.50; Ⓦ www.leadhillsrailway.co.uk), Britain's highest adhesion railway. The terraced cottages of this classic "company town" were built by the mine owners for their employees, but the boom years ended in the 1830s, since when the village has been left pretty much to itself.

The Colvend coast and beyond

The **Colvend coast**, twenty miles or so southwest of Dumfries, is probably one of the finest stretches of coastline along the so-called "Scottish Riviera". The best approach is via the A710, which heads south through New Abbey (see p.170), before cutting across a handsome landscape of rolling farmland to the aptly named **SANDYHILLS**, little more than a scattering of houses dotted around a sandy bay overlooking the tidal mud flats of the Solway Firth. There's a very well-equipped **campsite**, the *Sandyhills Leisure Park* (Ⓣ 01387/780257; April–Oct), down by the beach, plus a couple of lovely **guesthouses** with stunning views over the bay: *Craigbittern* (Ⓣ 01387/780247, Ⓦ www.craigbitterncottage.co.uk; ❹), an imposing turreted greystone pile; and the nearby Edwardian villa of *Cairngill House* (Ⓣ 01387/780681, Ⓦ www.cairngill.co.uk; March to mid-Nov; ❷). A mile or so beyond is *Barcloy Farm* (Easter–Sept; closed Wed), which has an excellent farm shop and **café**.

Half a mile or so further west, a side road leads down to **ROCKCLIFFE**, a beguiling little place of comfortable villas sheltered beneath wooded hills and nestled around a beautiful rocky, sand and shell bay. Excellent B&B **accommodation** and self-catering is available at *Millbrae House* (Ⓣ 01556/630217, Ⓦ www.millbraehouse.co.uk; March–Oct; ❸), a whitewashed cottage a short stroll from the bay. For **camping**, the *Castle Point Caravan Site* (Ⓣ 01556/630248; March–Oct) is in a secluded spot, just south of the village, a stone's throw from the seashore. The *Garden House* tearoom (closed Mon & Tues), at the entrance to the village, serves sandwiches and cakes in an attractive garden.

For vehicles, Rockcliffe is a dead end, but it's the start of a pleasant half-hour walk along the Jubilee Path to neighbouring **KIPPFORD**, a tiny, lively yachting centre strung out along the east bank of the Urr estuary. En route, the path passes the Celtic hill fort of the **Mote of Mark**, a useful craggy viewpoint. At low tide you can walk over the Rough Firth causeway from the shore below across the mud flats to **Rough Island**, a humpy twenty-acre bird sanctuary owned by the National Trust for Scotland – it's out of bounds in May and June when terns and oystercatchers are nesting. The reward for your stroll is a drink and a bite to eat at the *Anchor Hotel* (Ⓣ01556/620205), right on Kippford's waterfront, which serves tasty **bar meals**. If you want to stay the night, head for *Rosemount* (Ⓣ01556/620214; Ⓦwww.rosemountguesthouse.com; Feb–Nov; ❷), a friendly **guesthouse** on the seafront, or the stylish *Roughfirth House* B&B (Ⓣ01556/620330; Ⓦwww.roughfirth.com; ❺), a whitewashed villa in the woods along the road towards Rough Firth, with wonderful views over the estuary.

Castle Douglas and around

The man responsible for the late eighteenth-century grid-plan streets of **CASTLE DOUGLAS** (Ⓦwww.castledouglas.net), eighteen miles southwest of Dumfries, was William Douglas, a local lad who made a fortune trading in the West Indies. The town has a distinctive, dead-straight main street, **King Street**, which slopes down past the landmark clock tower, built in a mixture of red sandstone and grey granite that's typical of the town. Most folk come here simply to visit the nearby attractions of **Threave Garden and Castle** (see below and p.174), and there's no real need to linger in town, though it's pleasant enough.

The **tourist office** (April–Sept daily; Ⓣ01556/502611) is at the top end of King Street. All the old coaching inns on King Street offer **accommodation**, but you're better off trying one of the Victorian guesthouses out on Ernespie Road, such as *Albion House* (Ⓣ01556/502360, Ⓦwww.albionhousecastledouglas.co.uk; March–Nov; ❸), at no. 49; just to the south of Castle Douglas. Campers should make for the town's *Lochside* **campsite** (Ⓣ01556/502949; Easter–Oct), beside Loch Carlingwark, a short walk from the bottom of King Street down Marle Street.

The best place to grab a bite **to eat** is *Designs*, 179 King St (Ⓦwww.designsgallery.co.uk; closed Sun), a daytime café at the back of an arts and crafts and book shop, with a lovely conservatory and garden. *Carlo's* at 211 King St (Ⓣ01556 503977, Ⓦwww.carlosrestaurant.co.uk; closed Mon) is a cheery, family-run Italian trattoria, while for a pint of the local Sulwath beer on draught, head for the *Douglas Arms Hotel*, on the corner of St Andrew and King streets. **Bike rental** – useful for getting out to Threave – is available from the Castle Douglas Cycle Centre on Church Street (Ⓣ01556/504542, Ⓦwww.cdbikes.co.uk; closed Sun). For weekend **entertainment**, go to the Lochside Theatre (Ⓣ01556/504506, Ⓦwww.lochsidetheatre.co.uk), housed in the former Church of St Andrew, two blocks east of King Street down Marle Street; it hosts gigs and shows films.

Threave Garden

Threave Garden (daily 9.30am–5.30pm; NTS; £6), the premier horticultural sight in Dumfries and Galloway, is a pleasant mile or so's walk or cycle south of Castle Douglas, along the shores of Loch Carlingwark. The garden features a magnificent spread of flowers and woodland across sixty acres, subdivided into more than a dozen areas, from the old-fashioned herbaceous borders of the Walled Garden to the brilliant banks of rhododendrons in the Woodland Garden and the ranks of primula, astilbe and gentian in the Peat Garden. In springtime, thousands of visitors turn up for the flowering of more than two hundred types of daffodil.

The **visitor centre** (daily: April–Oct 9.30am–5.30pm; Feb, March, Nov & Dec 10am–4pm) has maps of and an exhibition about the garden and the surrounding estate (also NTS property), though the restaurant's fruit pies and outdoor terrace are more immediately appealing. Threave is also home to the School of Practical Gardening, whose postgraduate students occupy one floor of **Threave House**, a hulking Scots Baronial mansion built by the Gordon family in 1872, and now restored to its 1938 condition; it can be visited on a guided tour (daily 11am–3.30pm; house & garden ticket £10).

Threave Castle

The nicest way of reaching **Threave Castle** (April–Sept daily 9.30am–5pm; HS; £4.20), a mile or so north of the gardens, is to walk through the estate. However you decide to get there, you should follow the signs to the Open Farm (which has the *Bothy* tearoom serving soup and sandwiches), from where it's a lovely fifteen-minute walk down to the River Dee, where you ring a brass bell for the boat to take you over to the flat and grassy island on which the stern-looking tower house stands.

Built in around 1370 for one of the Black Douglases, Archibald the Grim, first Lord of Galloway and third Earl of Douglas, the fortress was among the first of its kind, a sturdy, rectangular structure completed shortly after the War of Independence. The rickety curtain wall to the south and east is all that remains of the **artillery fortifications**, hurriedly constructed in the 1450s by the ninth earl in a desperate – and unsuccessful – attempt to defend the castle against James II's new-fangled cannon. The castle was partially dismantled in the 1640s, but enough remains of the interior to make out its general plan.

Kirkcudbright and around

KIRKCUDBRIGHT – pronounced "kir-coo-bree" (Ⓦwww.kirkcudbright.co.uk) – hugging the muddy banks of the River Dee ten miles southwest of Castle Douglas, is the only major town along the Solway coast to have retained a working harbour. In addition, it has a ruined castle and the most attractive of town centres, a charming medley of simple two-storey cottages with medieval pends, Georgian villas and Victorian townhouses, all built in a mixture of sandstone, granite and brick, and attractively painted. Not surprisingly, Kirkcudbright became something of a magnet for Scottish artists from the late nineteenth century onwards. It was also the location of much of the cult 1970s film, *The Wicker Man*, and is the nearest town for **The Wickerman Festival** (Ⓦwww.thewickermanfestival.co.uk), southwest Scotland's biggest music festival, which takes place on the third weekend in July, during which a giant Wicker Man is torched. Kirkcudbright itself also has a much smaller **jazz festival** in mid-June and a host of **summer festivities** in the middle of August.

Arrival, information and accommodation

Buses to Kirkcudbright stop by the harbour car park, next to the **tourist office** (mid-Feb to Nov daily; Ⓣ01557/330494), where you can get help finding a place to stay. There are daily **boat trips** from the slipway near Broughton House.

The town offers some excellent **accommodation** in its brightly painted villas, worth booking in advance: one of the best is *Gladstone House* (Ⓣ01557/331734, Ⓦwww.kirkcudbrightgladstone.com; ❸), an elegant, comfortable Georgian B&B set back slightly from the street, or *The Greengate* (Ⓣ01557/331895, Ⓦwww.thegreengate.co.uk; ❹), an attractive terraced cottage with just one double bedroom, which was Glasgow Girl Jessie King's former home. *Baytree House* (Ⓣ01557 330824, Ⓦwww.baytreekirkcudbright.co.uk; ❹) is an imposing Georgian

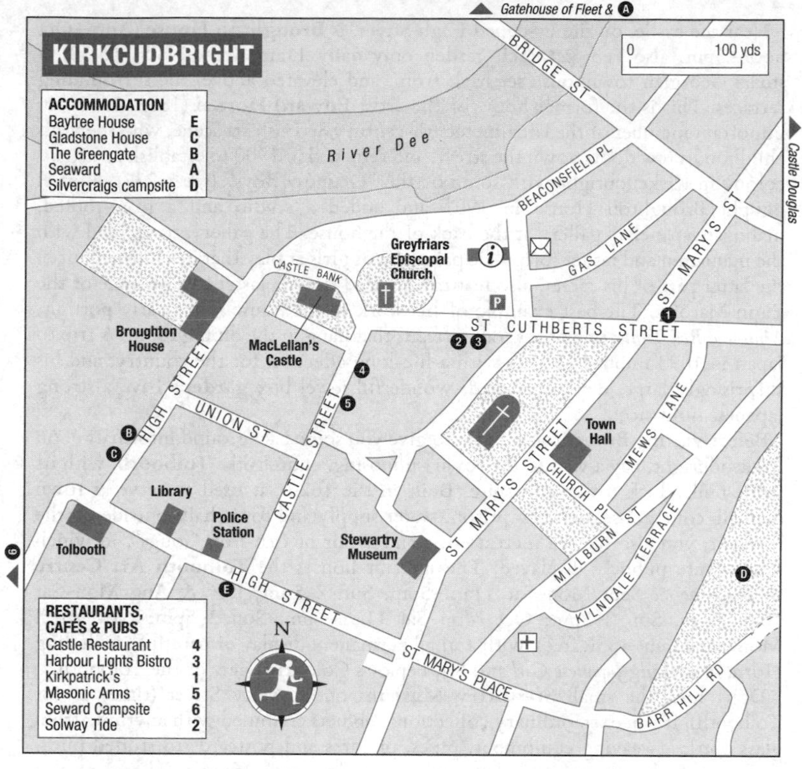

townhouse in the centre of things at 110 High St; there's a friendly welcome and a fine breakfast. The *Silvercraigs* caravan and **campsite** (ⓣ01557/330123; Easter to late Oct) is centrally located on a bluff overlooking town. Alternatively, head to *Seaward* campsite at Dhoon Bay (ⓣ01557/870267, ⓦwww.gillespie-leisure.co.uk; March–Oct), three miles southwest of town along the B727, close to the beach, which has its own outdoor swimming pool.

The Town

The most surprising sight in Kirkcudbright is **MacLellan's Castle** (April–Sept daily 9.30am–5.30pm; HS; £3.70), a pink-flecked sixteenth-century tower house that sits at one end of the High Street, by the harbourside. Part fortified keep and part spacious mansion, the castle was built in the 1570s for the Provost of Kirkcudbright, Sir Thomas MacLellan of Bombie, when a degree of law and order permitted the aristocracy to relax its defensive preoccupations and satisfy its desire for comfort and domestic convenience. As a consequence, chimneys replaced battlements and windows begin at the ground floor. Nevertheless, the walls remain impressively thick and there are a handful of wide-mouthed gun loops. The interior is well preserved, from the kitchen and vaulted storerooms in the basement, to the rabbit warren of well-appointed domestic apartments above. Keep an eye out for the spyhole known as the **"laird's lug"**, behind the fireplace of the Great Hall. MacLellan's son, Robert, amassed so many debts that on his death in 1639, the house had to be sold off, and from then on it was more or less abandoned.

Near the castle, on the L-shaped High Street, is **Broughton House** (April–Oct noon–5pm; also Feb & March garden only daily 11am–4pm; NTS; £5.50), a smart Georgian townhouse set back from, and elevated above, the surrounding terraces. This is the former home of the artist **Edward Hornel** (1863–1933), an important member of the late nineteenth-century Scottish art scene, who spent his childhood a few doors down the street, and returned in 1900 to establish an artists' colony in Kirkcudbright with some of the "Glasgow Boys" (see p.227). Hornel bought Broughton House in 1901 and added a studio and a glass-roofed, mahogany-panelled gallery at the back of the house. The gallery, now filled with the mannered and rather formulaic paintings of girls at play that he churned out in the latter part of his career, also features a scaled-down plaster cast of some of the Elgin Marbles. The best example of his work in the house is the early portrait, *Man in a Red Tunic*, one of several portraits that hang in the dining room. A trip to Japan in 1893 imbued Hornel with a life-long affection for the country, and his surprisingly large, densely packed, wonderful jewel box **gardens** have a strong Japanese influence.

Before visiting Broughton House, to give you some background information on Kirkcudbright, pay a visit to the town's imposing, church-like **Tolbooth**, with its stone-built clock tower and spire. Built in the 1620s, it used to serve as town council, courthouse, debtors' prison, water supply and town hall: outside on the forestair, you also see the mercat cross and a pair of cast-iron "jougs", in which felons were publicly displayed. The interior houses the **Tolbooth Art Centre** (May, June & Sept Mon–Sat 11am–5pm, Sun 2–5pm; July & Aug Mon–Sat 10am–5pm, Sun 2–5pm; Oct Mon–Sat 11am–4pm, Sun 2–5pm; Nov–April Mon–Sat 11am–4pm; free), with a small permanent display of paintings including Hornel's striking *Japanese Girl* and S.J. Peploe's Colourist view of the Tolbooth.

Don't miss the small **Stewartry Museum** on St Mary Street (times as for Tolbooth). It's an extraordinary collection: cabinets crammed with anything from glass bottles, weaving equipment, pipes, pictures and postcards to stuffed birds, pickled fish and the tricorne hats once worn by town officials. There are also examples of book jackets designed by Jessie King and E.A. Taylor. Incidentally, the "Stewartry" is the old name for the former county of Kirkcudbrightshire, as for centuries it was ruled by a royal steward appointed by the Balliol family.

Eating and drinking

The top choices as far as upmarket **restaurants** go are the *Castle Restaurant*, 5 Castle St (Ⓣ01557/330569, Ⓦwww.thecastlerestaurant.net; eves only & Sun lunch), a smart little place offering Scottish and French cuisine, and *Kirkpatrick's* at 29 St Cuthbert Place (Ⓣ01557/330888), which has a less appealing location but serves excellent Scottish dishes with an imaginative twist. Alternatively, there's *Solway Tide*, an attractive tearoom on Castle Street (closed Sun), which serves good coffee, smoothies, paninis, bagels and home-made scones. A few doors away, the jaunty lunch-only *Harbour Lights Bistro* has a simple menu of rolls, platters and hot specials. For a **drink**, the busy *Masonic Arms*, on Castle Street, pulls a reasonable pint of real ale.

Around Kirkcudbright

The **Galloway Wildlife Conservation Park** (Feb–Nov daily 10am–dusk; £6; Ⓦwww.gallowaywildlife.co.uk) sits a mile or so up the B727 east of Kirkcudbright. Lesser pandas, collared peccaries and Scottish wildcats are just some of the animals you can expect to see, and you can feed the goats, deer and llama. Equally popular with kids is the local ice-cream makers **Cream o' Galloway** (daily: Easter–Oct

10am–5pm, till 6pm July & Aug; £4; Ⓦwww.creamogalloway.co.uk), whose organic farm at Rainton, six miles west of Kirkcudbright, has nature trails and a large adventure playground.

More edifying than any of the above are the greystone ruins of **Dundrennan Abbey** (April–Sept daily 9.30am–5.30pm; Oct–March Sat & Sun 9.30am–4.30pm; Nov–March Sat & Sun 9.30am–4.30pm; HS; £2), hidden in the village of the same name, some six miles southeast of Kirkcudbright. Founded in 1142, Dundrennan was the mother house of the local Cistercian abbeys of Sweetheart and Glenluce, and was clearly the grandest of the lot, even though it's now reduced to just its transepts. The chief treasures of the abbey are the chapter house's finely carved cusped portal, and the medieval effigy of a tonsured abbot in the northwest corner of the nave; he was murdered – hence the faded dagger in his chest – and the figure being trampled at his feet is thought to be his assassin, in the process of being disembowelled. **Bus** #501 connects Dundrennan with Kirkcudbright (Mon–Sat).

Gatehouse of Fleet

Like Castle Douglas, **GATEHOUSE OF FLEET** (Ⓦwww.gatehouse-of-fleet.co.uk), ten miles west of Kirkcudbright, has a distinctive long, straight main street. However, the quiet streets of Gatehouse have none of the life and bustle of Castle Douglas. By contrast, in the late eighteenth and early nineteenth century, the town was a thriving industrial centre with cotton mills, shipbuilding and a brewery. By 1850 the boom was over, the town was bypassed by the railway and the mills slipped into disrepair.

As in Castle Douglas, the sloping whitewashed High Street has a landmark clock tower, in this case an incongruous freestanding one, built in grey granite and topped by strange mitre-shaped crenellations. The *Murray Arms Hotel*, the old coaching inn next to the clock tower, is where Robbie Burns wrote *Scots wha hae*. From here picturesque Ann Street gives access to the wooded grounds of **Cally House Gardens** (Easter–Sept Tues–Fri 2–5.30pm, Sat & Sun 10am–5.30pm; £2; Ⓦwww.callygardens.co.uk). A palatial Neoclassical country mansion (now the *Cally Palace Hotel*), Cally House was built in the 1760s. Back in town, the **Mill on the Fleet** (April–Oct daily 10.30am–5pm; free), opposite the car park by the river at the bottom of the High Street, traces the economic and social history of Gatehouse and Galloway from inside a restored grey granite bobbin mill; it also has a decent **café** on the ground floor and a large secondhand bookshop on the top floor.

Perched on a hill a mile southwest of Gatehouse stands **Cardoness Castle** (April–Sept daily 9.30am–5.30pm; Oct–March Sat & Sun 9.30am–4.30pm; HS; £3.70), a classic late fifteenth-century fortified tower house that once edged the Water of Fleet river. Ancient seat of the McCullochs, it has some fashionably decorated fireplaces and plenty of en-suite latrines.

Practicalities

The **tourist office** (Easter–Sept daily; Oct closed Sun; Ⓣ01557/814212) is situated by the car park by the river. The place to **stay** is the sumptuous *Cally Palace Hotel* (Ⓣ01557/814341, Ⓦwww.callypalace.co.uk; closed Jan; ❽), though make sure you're placed in the old house rather than the ugly modern extension, and dress up if you're going to eat there. **B&B** in Gatehouse itself is available at the *Bobbin Guest House*, 36 High St (Ⓣ01557/814229; ❷), or at the very comfortable *Ship Inn* (Ⓣ01557/814217, Ⓦwww.theshipinngatehouse.co.uk; ❺), formerly the

Anwoth Hotel, where Dorothy L. Sayers wrote *Five Red Herrings*. For good straightforward **pub food**, head for the bar or the conservatory of the welcoming *Masonic Arms*, just up Ann Street.

Galloway Forest Park and around

The strange thing about Galloway is that while the area around the coast is all rolling farmland, stately homes, sandy coves and estuarine mud flats, you only have to head north ten or twenty miles and you're transported to the entirely different landscape of the Galloway Hills, an environment of glassy lochs, wooded hills and bare, rounded peaks. Much of this landscape is now incorporated into the **Galloway Forest Park**, Britain's largest forest park, which stretches all the way from the southern part of Ayrshire right down to Gatehouse of Fleet, laid out on land owned by the Forestry Commission. Few people actually live here, but the park is a major draw for hikers and mountain bikers. Accommodation is sparse in the park itself: use **Newton Stewart**, to the southwest, as a base. Galloway is an official "dark sky park", with designated spots for astronomy; for more, see Ⓦ www.forestry.gov.uk.

Hiking, biking and stargazing: Galloway Forest Park

Galloway Forest Park (Ⓦ www.forestry.gov.uk/gallowayforestpark) has three **visitor centres** (times vary but are generally April–Oct daily 10.30am–4.30pm): by Clatteringshaws Loch, at Glentrool and at Kirroughtree. Each has a tearoom, several waymarked walks and lots of information on activities and events. In addition, both Glentrool and Kirroughtree have **mountain-bike trails**, which form part of southern Scotland's outstanding mountain-biking facilities, known as the 7stanes (Ⓦ www.7stanes.co.uk). Of the two, **Kirroughtree**, three miles east of Newton Stewart, is by far the most varied and fun, with lots of exciting singletrack trails for all abilities and good bike-rental facilities.

Hikers are better off heading for **Glentrool**, at the western edge of the park, about ten miles north of Newton Stewart, where a narrow lane twists the five miles over to **Loch Trool**. On the north side of the loch the **Bruce Stone**, near the lovely Buchan Waterfall, marks the spot where Robert the Bruce ambushed an English force in 1307 after routing the main body of the army at Solway Moss. From here, you can follow the Gariland Burn to Loch Neldricken and Loch Enoch, with their silver granite sands, and then on to the Devil's Bowling Green, strewn with hundreds of erratic boulders left by the retreating glaciers. Alternatively, you can head for the Range of the Awful Hand, whose five peaks include the **Merrick** (2746ft), the highest hill in southern Scotland.

The only surfaced road to cross the park is the desolate twenty-mile stretch of the A712 between Newton Stewart and New Galloway, known as the **Queen's Way**. About seven miles east of Newton Stewart, at the **Grey Mare's Tail Bridge**, there are various forest trails, all delving into the pine forests beside the road, crossing gorges, waterfalls and burns. There's also a **Wild Goat Park** and, a mile or so further up the road, a **Red Deer Range**. A few more miles on, you'll come to **Clatteringshaws Loch**, a reservoir surrounded by pine forest, and connected with the Southern Upland Way on its north side. Heading southeast from Clatteringshaws is the **Raiders Road**, a ten-mile-long toll road that shadows the River Dee, with some great waterfalls and pools for swimming in.

The park has been formally designated a "**dark sky park**"; call Ⓣ 01671/402420 or check the park website for locations of forest roads where you can best view the night skies.

Newton Stewart

NEWTON STEWART (Ⓦwww.newtonstewart.org), famous for its salmon and trout fishing, is an unassuming market town on the west bank of the River Cree. As the largest town within easy reach of the Galloway Forest Park it's a popular choice as a base for hikers and cyclists as well as anglers.

On the main square, by the bus station, you'll find the local **tourist office** (April–June & Oct Mon–Sat; July–Sept daily; Ⓣ01671/402431), which has plenty of helpful literature. The finest **hotel** is the *Creebridge House Hotel* (Ⓣ01671/402121, Ⓦwww.creebridge.co.uk; ❻), in an appealing eighteenth-century granite hunting lodge over the main bridge, just past the petrol station. It can arrange fishing permits, personal gillies (guides), and even tackle. A cheaper option is to go for one of the substantial red-sandstone Victorian villa **B&Bs**, such as *Rowallan House* (Ⓣ01671/402520, Ⓦwww.rowallan.co.uk; ❹), on Corsbie Road, west of the main street up Church Lane, or *Flowerbank* (Ⓣ01671/402629, Ⓦwww.flowerbankgh.com; ❸), a lovely stone house by the river: take a left over the bridge up Millcroft Road from the bridge. There's also a spruce SYHA **hostel** (Ⓣ0870/004 1142, Ⓦwww.syha.org.uk; April–Sept) in the old school, quarter of a mile further up the road. For something nearer to the heart of the park, there are a couple of rooms at *House O'Hill* (Ⓣ01671/840243, Ⓦwww.houseohill.co.uk; ❹), a pub eight miles up the A714 in Bargrennan. There's also a very well-equipped **campsite** (Ⓣ01671/840280, Ⓦwww.glentroolholidaypark.co.uk; March–Oct) a little distance further up the road to Glentrool, and full-on country-house glamour just outside Glentrool at *Kirroughtree House Hotel* (Ⓣ01671/402 141, Ⓦwww.mcmillanhotels.co.uk; ❻).

If you need a bite **to eat**, the daytime *Café Cree* (closed Sun) is just the place, with wooden tables, art on the walls and imaginative dishes on the menu. In the evening, the *Creebridge* has a good but pricey restaurant as well as serving decent pub food and real ales. The cinema (Ⓣ01671/403333, Ⓦwww.nscinema.co.uk) on the main street shows **films** five or six nights of the week, and stages the occasional live event.

The Glenkens

At the eastern edge of the forest park is the river valley of the **Glenkens**, which extends south as far as Castle Douglas along Loch Ken, and north along the Water of Ken as far as Carsphairn, a desolate hamlet surrounded by wild moors near the border with Ayrshire. The wooded banks of **Loch Ken** are particularly stunning in autumn, and the area is a haven for **watersports** fans. Head for the Galloway Activity Centre (Ⓣ01644/420626, Ⓦwww.lochken.co.uk), which can organize half-day, full-day and week-long watersports packages; for waterskiing, contact the Loch Ken Waterski School (Ⓣ01644/70333, Ⓦwww.skilochken.co.uk) further down the loch. To the south of Loch Ken, off the B795 near Laurieston, Bellymack Hill Farm has a **Kite Feeding Station** (daily 10am–4pm; £2.50; Ⓦwww.gallowaykitetrail.com), where you're guaranteed a spectacular view of at least a dozen red kites tucking in at around 2pm.

NEW GALLOWAY, nineteen miles east of Newton Stewart, is a smart little one-street town of stone-built whitewashed cottages at the northern tip of Loch Ken. The *Smithy* **tearoom** at the bottom of the High Street is a good source of local information, *Kitty's Tearoom* has excellent home-cooking, and the award-winning *Cross Keys Hotel* in the High Street serves real ale. New Galloway is the venue for the annual **Scottish Alternative Games** (Ⓦwww.scottish-alternative-games.com), which usually take place on the first Sunday in August and feature lots of frivolous and obscure games such as "hurlin' the curlin' stane" and snail racing.

The Southern Upland Way passes a few miles north of New Galloway through picturesque St John's Town of Dalry, better known simply as **DALRY**. Five miles north along the B7000 stands the SYHA **Kendoon hostel** (Ⓣ0845/293 7373, Ⓦwww.syha.org.uk; mid-May to mid-Sept), a simple shed-like structure. Note that it's a Rent-a-Hostel, meaning you can't book an individual bunk. It's a very pleasant twenty-minute walk through the woods from the A713 to the west; if you're travelling there on the Castle Douglas–Ayr bus, ask the driver to tell you when to get off.

The Machars

The Machars is the name given to the triangular peninsula of rolling farmland and open landscapes south of Newton Stewart. Its title comes from the Gaelic *machair*, the name for the low-lying sandy coastal grasslands. It's a neglected part of the coastline, a bit out on a limb, and with a somewhat disconsolate air. However, you could easily while away an hour or two in **Wigtown**'s numerous bookshops and, as the birthplace of Scottish Christianity, **Whithorn** is well worth a visit.

Wigtown

Seven miles south of Newton Stewart, **WIGTOWN** (Ⓦwww.wigtown-booktown.co.uk) is a tiny place, considering it was once the county town of Wigtownshire. Despite its modest size, it has a remarkable main square, a vast, triangular-shaped affair, its layout unchanged since medieval times. Dominating the square and its central bowling green are the gargantuan, exotic-looking **County Buildings**, built in French Gothic style, and now home to the town's library and, on the top floor, a camera room (May–Sept: Mon, Thurs & Sat 10am–5pm, Tues, Wed & Fri 10am–7.30pm, Sun 2–5pm; free), with a CCTV link to a local osprey nest and great views over Wigtown Bay.

Over the last decade Wigtown has reinvented itself as "Scotland's National Book Town", with more than twenty **bookshops** occupying some of the modest houses that line the square, and more elsewhere in the vicinity. *The Book Shop*, on the north side of the square, is the largest secondhand bookshop in Scotland, a wonderful rambling affair, while *Readinglasses*, on the opposite side of the square, includes a small **café**. The town also hosts a **literary festival** of some note in late September.

If you're looking for somewhere to eat or sleep, the best thing to do is to head to **BLADNOCH**, a little village with a whisky distillery, by the river a mile or so southwest. The *Fordbank Country House Hotel* (Ⓣ01988/402346, Ⓦwww.fordbankhotel.co.uk; ❹) is the former home of the local distillery owners and now a comfortable hotel.

Whithorn and around

Fifteen miles south of Wigtown is **WHITHORN** (Ⓦwww.whithorn.com), a one-street town that nevertheless occupies an important place in Scottish history, for it is thought that here in 397 **St Ninian** founded the first Christian church north of Hadrian's Wall. No one can be sure where the original church stood and very little is known about Ninian's life, but his tomb at Whithorn soon became a popular place of pilgrimage and, in the twelfth century, a Premonstratensian priory was established to service the shrine. For generations the rich and the royal made the trek here, the last being Mary, Queen of Scots in 1563, after which came the Reformation and the prohibition of pilgrimages in 1581.

These days, it takes a serious leap of the imagination to envisage Whithorn as a medieval pilgrimage centre. For this reason, it's a good idea to start by watching the audiovisual show at the **Whithorn Story** (Easter–Oct daily 10.30am–5pm; £3.50), to the right of the pend on the main street, which leads to the remains of the priory. In the excellent adjacent exhibition, there's a handful of archeological finds including a lead Viking cat-skinning trough, a carved oak statue of St Ninian, a gold pontifical ring and a copper-gilt crozier. Heading outside, the dig site is pretty uninspiring, as are the nearby ruins of the nave of **Whithorn Priory**. More compelling are the series of early Christian standing crosses and headstones housed in the on-site **Whithorn Museum**. The best preserved is the tenth-century Monteith Cross, decorated with interlaced patterns; the oldest is the Latinus stone from the mid-fifth century, the earliest Christian stone in Scotland; while the Petrus stone, with its chi-rho symbol, dates from the mid-seventh century. Grab a snack at the Whithorn Dig's *Pilgrims' Tearoom*.

The pilgrims who crossed the Solway to visit St Ninian's shrine landed at the **ISLE OF WHITHORN**, four miles south of Whithorn, no longer an island, but an antique and picturesque little seaport. If you continue to the end of the harbour, you'll pick up signs to the minuscule remains of the thirteenth-century **St Ninian's Chapel**, which some believe was the site of the original church. If you want to **stay**, try the unassuming but popular *Steam Packet Inn* (Ⓣ01988/500334, Ⓦwww.steampacketinn.biz; ❸), right on the quay in the Isle of Whithorn; it does pub food that's above average in quality and price, and has a moderately expensive **restaurant**.

The Rhinns of Galloway

West of the Machars, the hilly, hammer-shaped peninsula at the end of the Solway coast, known as the **Rhinns of Galloway**, encompasses two contrasting towns: the grimy port of **Stranraer**, from where there are regular ferries to Northern Ireland, and the old seafaring port of **Portpatrick**. At either end of the peninsula are two lighthouses: one stands above Corsewall Point, and now houses a luxury hotel, the other stands on the **Mull of Galloway**, a windswept headland at the southwest tip of Scotland, which is home to a vast array of nesting seabirds.

Stranraer and around

No one can say that **STRANRAER** (Ⓦwww.stranraer.org) is beautiful, and if you're heading to (or coming from) Ireland, there's really no reason to linger longer than you have to. If you find yourself with time to kill, head for the town's one specific attraction, the **Castle of St John** (Easter to mid-Sept Mon–Sat 10am–1pm & 2–5pm; free), a ruined four-storey tower house built around 1500, which now stands on its own little green halfway down the main street, one block inland from the harbour front. Inside, several videos trace the history of the castle, which was notorious in the 1680s as the headquarters of Graham of Claverhouse, sheriff of Wigtown and known as "bloody Clavers" for his brutal campaigns against the local Covenanters.

Practicalities

The **train station** is right at the end of the east pier by the Stena Line **ferry** terminal for Belfast (Ⓣ0870/570 7070, Ⓦwww.stenaline.co.uk). A couple of minutes' walk away, on Port Rodie, is the **bus station**. Stena Line's fast HSS catamarans depart for Belfast from the West Pier on the other side of the harbour. P&O Irish Sea ferries (Ⓣ0870/242 4777, Ⓦwww.poirishsea.com) to and from Larne, arrive not in Stranraer, but at the port of **CAIRNRYAN**, some five miles north; note, though, that bus services to Cairnryan are infrequent and aren't integrated with the ferry times.

Stranraer's **tourist office** is at 28 Harbour St (mid-June to mid-Sept daily; mid-Sept to Easter Mon–Sat; Ⓣ01776/702595) between the two piers. Should you need **accommodation**, head for the very reasonable *Harbour Guest House* (Ⓣ01776/704626, Ⓦwww.harbourguesthousestranraer.co.uk; ❷), a decent **B&B** on the seafront on Market Street, just a short stroll from either pier. You'll have few problems **eating out** if you're after fish and chips, pizzas or pub grub.

At **Corsewall Point**, eleven miles north of Stranraer, at the northern tip of the Rhinns of Galloway, the (still functioning) 1815 lighthouse has been incorporated into the luxury *Corsewall Lighthouse Hotel* (Ⓣ01776/853220, Ⓦwww.lighthousehotel.co.uk; including champagne breakfast ❺). If you don't have your own transport, the owners will collect you from Stranraer, as long as you book in advance.

Castle Kennedy Gardens

The approach to **Castle Kennedy Gardens** (April–Sept daily 10am–5pm; £4; Ⓦwww.castlekennedygardens.co.uk), three miles east of Stranraer, is splendid, passing along a tree-lined avenue that frames the ruined medieval fortress of Castle Kennedy beyond, and then across a palm-fringed canal. The castle forms the centrepiece of the gardens, on a hill squeezed between two lochs, though its ruins can no longer be visited. The 75-acre landscaped gardens, which include a lovely walled garden, stretch west as far as nearby Lochinch Castle, seat of the earl of Stair (and also inaccessible), via a giant lily pond and a stupendous avenue of monkey puzzle trees.

Glenluce Abbey

Seven miles east of Castle Kennedy, along the A75, you'll pick up signs for **Glenluce Abbey** (April–Sept daily 9.30am–6.30pm; HS; £3.20), whose ruins lie in a gentle valley by the railway, a couple of miles north of the main road. Founded in 1192 as a daughter-house of Dundrennan (see p.177), Glenluce is the most ruinous of the trio of Cistercian monasteries in the southwest. However, it does have one surviving gem: the fifteenth-century **chapter house**, which has survived pretty much intact, its ribbed-vault ceiling generating the clearest of acoustics. Notice the green man motif carved into the corbels and ceiling bosses. The one other remarkable relic at Glenluce is the monks' water-supply system, whose clay pipes (and even a lidded junction box) can be seen in and around the cloisters.

If you wish **to stay** the night or grab a bite **to eat**, head for the *Kelvin House Hotel* (Ⓣ01581/300528, Ⓦwww.kelvin-house.co.uk; ❸), a small hotel in the centre of the village, with a convivial bar. There's also a lovely **campsite** (Ⓣ01581/300412, Ⓦwww.glenlucecaravan.co.uk; March–Oct) right in the village. Note that there are no direct **buses** to the abbey, but the Glenluce–Newton Stewart bus will drop you off along the main road and you can walk the mile or so from there.

Portpatrick and around

Situated roughly halfway along the west shore of the Rhinns, **PORTPATRICK** has an attractive pastel-painted seafront that wraps itself round a small rocky bay, sheltered by equally rocky cliffs. Until the mid-nineteenth century Portpatrick was a thriving seaport, serving as the main embarkation point for Northern

Ireland, with coal, cotton and British troops heading in one direction, Ulster cattle and linen in the other. Nowadays, minus its railway, it's a quiet, comely resort enjoyed for its rugged scenery, sea-angling and gentle hikes, such as the twenty-minute stroll south along the sea cliffs to the shattered ruins of **Dunskey Castle**, a sixteenth-century L-shaped tower house, or the longer circular walk north to **Dunskey Gardens** (March–Oct daily 10am–5pm; £3.50), with its glasshouses, walled gardens, maze and tearoom, and then west down the Dunskey Glen to link up with the **Southern Upland Way** which takes you back to the quayside.

Practicalities

Portpatrick has several good **hotels** and **guesthouses**, the best of which is the lilac-painted *Waterfront Hotel* (Ⓣ01776/810800, Ⓦwww.waterfronthotel.co.uk; ❺), which has a nice terrace bar. For something a bit cheaper, *Rickwood House Hotel* (Ⓣ01776/810270, Ⓦwww.portpatrick.me.uk; ❷), with its simple bright decor, is an excellent option, set back from the harbour on Heugh Road near the golf club. Another option, if you're on an unlimited budget, is *Knockinaam Lodge* (Ⓣ01776/810471, Ⓦwww.knockinaamlodge.com; ❾), an exclusive little country-house hotel with a Michelin-starred restaurant, hidden away in its own private cove a couple of miles south of Portpatrick.

There are several caravan and **campsites** in a row on the hill overlooking Portpatrick and Dunskey Castle, quite a distance from town (and the sea), but accessed by a pleasant walk along the disused railway and cliff-top trail; *Sunnymeade* (Ⓣ01776/810293; March–Oct) has the better facilities, but *Castle Bay* (Ⓣ01776/810462; March–Oct) has the more informal atmosphere.

Portpatrick's **pubs** can get pretty lively on the weekend, and all of them offer fairly standard bar meals. The *Crown* on the seafront is the cosiest and best for food, including local seafood, though the adjacent *Harbour House Hotel* has real ale. The modern *Campbell's Restaurant* (Ⓣ01776/810314, Ⓦwww.campbellsrestaurant.co.uk) at 1 South Crescent serves great local seafood; you'll often see the owner nipping out in his boat to augment the menu. Portpatrick has an annual **Folk Festival** in the first weekend of September (call Ⓣ01776/810717 or visit Ⓦwww.stranraer.org for more details).

Port Logan

Ten miles south of Portpatrick, over gorse-covered hills and pastureland crossed by narrow country lanes and dotted with farming hamlets, you'll find the village of **PORT LOGAN**, sitting on the south side of a sandy bay. A mile or so north of the village is a peaceful little outpost of Edinburgh's Royal Botanic Garden, known as **Logan Botanic Garden** (Feb Sun only 10am–4pm; mid-March to Oct daily 10am–5pm; £5; Ⓦwww.rbge.org.uk). The Gulf Stream keeps the Rhinns almost completely free of frost, allowing subtropical species to grow. Check out the primeval giant Brazilian rhubarb in the Gunnera Bog, take a wander in the woods to the south, and head for the enormous walled gardens, where you'll find a water garden, a peat garden (the first ever), and a massive 20ft-high beech hedge. The Discovery Centre, near the entrance, is an excellent wet-weather retreat, and the garden's **salad bar** is a good place to grab a snack.

Back down at the bay, a rough track leads north along the coast to a castellated fishkeeper's house, where you'll find the **Logan Fish Pond** (daily: Feb–Sept 10am–5pm; Oct to early Nov 10am–4pm; £3.50), created as a fish larder in 1800 by the local laird (from Logan House) by adapting a natural tidal pool created by a blowhole formed during the Ice Age. The water level is now carefully controlled to enable visitors to take a look at the trout, turbot, plaice, eels and rays and feed the coleys; you can also handle starfish and admire the plants.

Mull of Galloway

It's another twelve miles from Port Logan to the **Mull of Galloway** (Ⓦwww.mull-of-galloway.co.uk) but it's well worth the ride. This precipitous headland, crowned by a classic whitewashed Stevenson lighthouse, from which on a clear day you can see the Isle of Man and the coasts of Ireland and England, really feels like the end of the road. It is, in fact, the southernmost point in Scotland, further south even than Hadrian's Wall in England. It's also a favourite nesting spot for guillemots, razorbills, kittiwakes, shag, fulmar and even a few puffin; skeins of gannets fish here, too, from their gannetry on the Scares, clearly visible to the east. The headland is also an RSPB reserve – good for linnets and twite – with a **visitor centre** (Easter–Sept daily 10.30am–5pm) in a building near the **lighthouse**, which can be climbed on summer weekends (April–Sept Sat & Sun 10am–3.30pm; £2). Just below the car park, perched on the cliff-edge and roofed with turf, is an excellent **café**, the *Gallie Craig*, serving hot meals and snacks (Ⓦwww.galliecraig.co.uk; Nov–March closed Wed & Thurs); the terrace here provides armchair birdwatching.

Travel details

Trains

Dumfries to: Carlisle (Mon–Sat every 1–2hr, 5 on Sun; 40min); Glasgow Central (Mon–Sat every 1–2hr, 2 on Sun; 1hr 45min); Kilmarnock (Mon–Sat every 1–2hr, 2 on Sun; 1hr 5min); Sanquhar (Mon–Sat every 1–2hr, 2 on Sun; 25min); Stranraer (Mon–Sat 2 daily; 2hr 55min).
Stranraer to: Ayr (Mon–Sat 7 daily, 3 on Sun; 1hr 20min); Girvan (Mon–Sat 7 daily, 3 on Sun; 55min); Glasgow (Mon–Sat 7 daily, 3 on Sun; 2hr 10min).

Buses

Castle Douglas to: Dalry (Mon–Sat 6 daily, 1 on Sun; 40min); Dumfries (Mon–Sat hourly, Sun every 2hr; 45min); Dundrennan (Mon, Wed & Fri 1 daily; 35min); Kirkcudbright (Mon–Sat hourly, Sun every 2hr; 20min); New Galloway (Mon–Sat 5 daily; 35min).
Dumfries to: Ayr (Mon–Sat every 2hr; 2hr 10min); Caerlaverock (Mon–Sat 8–11 daily, 2 on Sun; 25min); Carlisle (Mon–Sat hourly, Sun every 2hr; 1hr 35min); Castle Douglas (Mon–Sat hourly, Sun every 2hr; 45min); Dalry (Mon–Sat 1–2 daily; 50min); Edinburgh (Mon–Sat 4 daily, 2 on Sun; 2hr 40min); Gatehouse of Fleet (Mon–Sat 8 daily, 3 on Sun; 55min–1hr 25min); Gretna (Mon–Sat hourly, Sun every 2hr; 1hr); Kippford (Mon–Sat 4 daily, 2 on Sun; 1hr 10min); Kirkcudbright (Mon–Sat hourly, Sun every 2hr; 1hr); New Abbey (Mon–Sat hourly, 4–5 on Sun; 15min); New Galloway (Mon–Sat 1–2 daily; 55min); Newton Stewart (Mon–Sat every 2hr, 2 on Sun; 1hr 30min); Rockcliffe (3–4 daily; 1hr); Stranraer (Mon–Sat every 2hr, 2 on Sun; 2hr 15min); Thornhill (Mon–Sat hourly, 8 on Sun; 25min).
Gatehouse of Fleet to: Kirkcudbright (Mon–Sat every 2hr, 5 on Sun; 15min); Newton Stewart (Mon–Sat 9–11 daily, 3 on Sun; 35min); Stranraer (Mon–Sat every 2hr, 3 on Sun; 1hr 15min).
Kirkcudbright to: Dundrennan (Mon–Sat 6 daily; 10min).
Newton Stewart to: Castle Kennedy (Mon–Sat hourly, 4 on Sun; 35min); Girvan (Mon–Sat 5 daily, 2 on Sun; 1hr 10min); Glenluce (Mon–Sat hourly, 4 on Sun; 25min); Glentrool (Mon–Sat 7–8 daily, 4 on Sun; 25min); Stranraer (Mon–Sat 15 daily, 5 on Sun; 45min); Whithorn (Mon–Sat hourly, 4 on Sun; 50min); Isle of Whithorn (Mon–Sat hourly, 4 on Sun; 1hr); Wigtown (Mon–Sat hourly, 6 on Sun; 15min).
Sanquhar to: Leadhills (Mon–Sat 6 daily; 30min); Wanlockhead (Mon–Sat 6 daily; 25min).
Stranraer to: Port Logan (Mon–Sat 6–8 daily, 3 on Sun; 45min); Portpatrick (Mon–Sat 7 daily, 3 on Sun; 25min).

Ferries

(summer timetable)
Cairnryan to: Larne (7–9 daily; 1hr–1hr 45min).
Stranraer to: Belfast (6–7 daily; 1hr 45min–3hr 15min).

4

Ayrshire and Arran

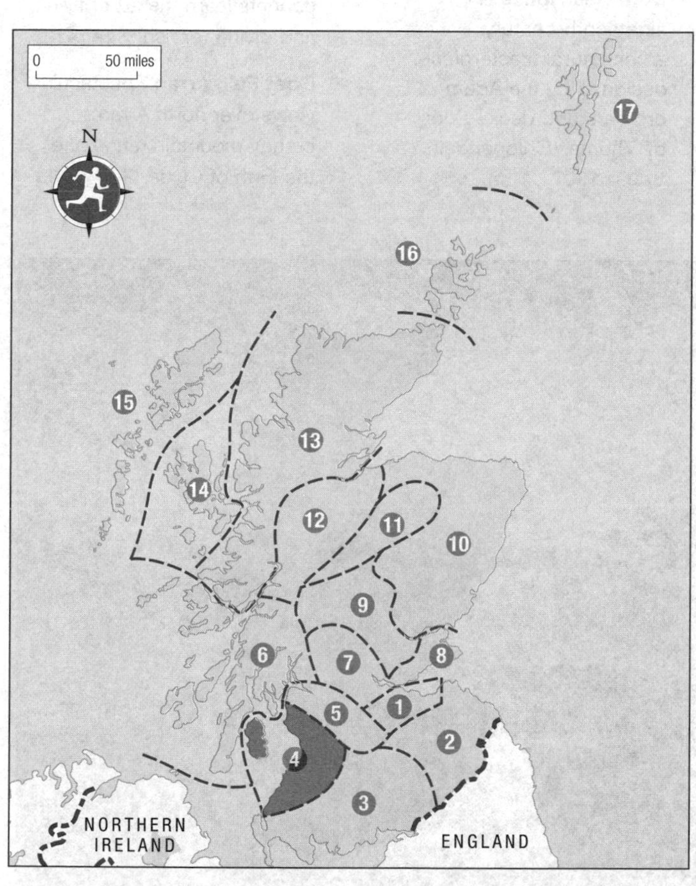

CHAPTER 4 Highlights

* **Alloway** The village where poet Robert Burns was born, and the best of many Burns pilgrimage spots in the region. See p.191
* **Dumfries House** An eighteenth-century architectural masterpiece, designed by the Adam brothers and decked out by Thomas Chippendale. See p.193
* **Culzean Castle** Stately home with a fabulous cliff-edge setting, surrounded by acres of gardens and woods reaching down to the shore. See p.194
* **Ailsa Craig** Watch baby gannets learn the art of flying and diving for fish. See p.195
* **Goat Fell, Arran** Spectacular views over north Arran's craggy mountain range and the Firth of Clyde. See p.203

▲ Culzean Castle

4

Ayrshire and Arran

The rolling hills and rich soil of **Ayrshire** make for prime farming country and, as such, are not really top of most visitors' Scottish itinerary. **Ayr**, the county town and birthplace of Robert Burns, won't keep you long, and workaday **Kilmarnock**, the largest place in the region, sees virtually no tourists. However, with Ireland only a short ferry ride away, and Glasgow a short train ride away, Ayrshire still gets plenty of visitors. Most wisely stick to the coastline, attracted by the wide, flat, sandy **beaches** and the region's vast number of **golf** courses. **Dumfries House**, in the undistinguished countryside east of Ayr, is one of the finest eighteenth-century stately homes in Britain and well worth a detour. South of the town, the most obvious points of interest are **Culzean Castle**, with its Robert Adam interior and extensive wooded grounds, and the offshore islands of **Ailsa Craig**, home to the world's second-largest gannetry. North of Ayr, where the towns benefited from the industrialization of Glasgow, there are even fewer places to detain you, with the exception of **Irvine**, home to the fascinating Scottish Maritime Museum.

The **Isle of Arran** is without doubt the most alluring destination in Ayrshire, its jagged outline visible across the Firth of Clyde from the entire length of the Ayrshire coast. Arran is often described as "Scotland in miniature", and the barren north of the island is certainly a great place to get a quick taste of the Highlands.

Ayrshire is home to the misleadingly named Glasgow Prestwick **Airport**, which lies, in fact, just outside Ayr. Both Prestwick and Ayr are served by frequent **trains** from Glasgow Central, and there's a useful train line from Ayr down the coast to Stranraer, and north to Largs. From Troon, just north of Ayr, fast **ferries** depart to Larne, and from the port of Ardrossan, further north still, you can cross to the Isle of Arran, from where you can hopscotch on to Kintyre and the Hebrides in summer.

Ayr and around

With a population of around fifty thousand, **AYR** is by far the largest town on the Firth of Clyde coast. It was an important seaport and trading centre for many centuries, rivalling Glasgow in size and significance right up until the late seventeenth century. In recognition, Cromwell made it a centre of his administration and built an enormous fortress here, long since destroyed. With the relative decline of its seaborne trade, Ayr reinvented itself in the nineteenth century as an administrative centre and a popular resort for middle-class Victorians. Nowadays,

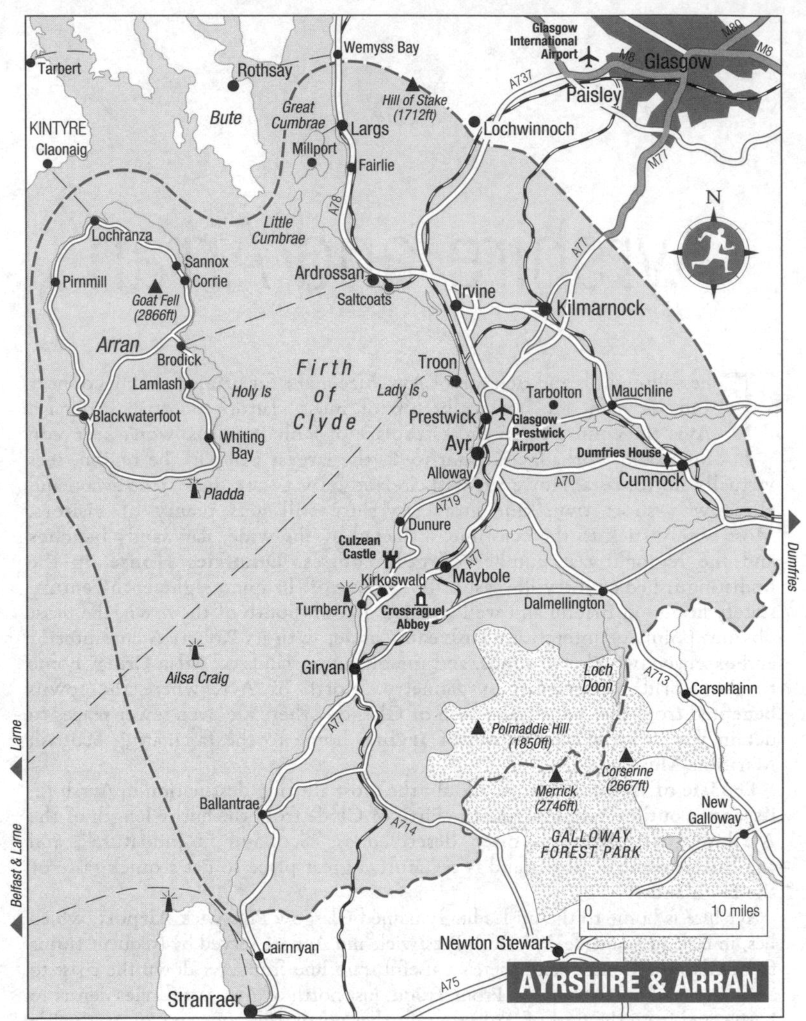

the town won't detain you long, though its prestigious **racecourse** (Ⓦwww.ayr-racecourse.co.uk) pulls in huge crowds, and the local tourist industry continues to do steady business out of the fact that Robbie Burns was born in the neighbouring village of **Alloway** (see p.191).

Arrival and information

Ayr **train** station is ten minutes' walk southeast of the town centre, while the **bus** station is in the centre at the foot of Sandgate; the **tourist office** is nearby, at 22 Sandgate (July–Sept daily; Oct–June closed Sun; Ⓣ01292/290300), and can help with accommodation, a particularly useful service during big race meetings. For details of transport options from nearby Glasgow Prestwick Airport, see p.196.

On the Burns trail

The number of memorials, museums, pubs and places across the region associated with **Robert Burns** is quite staggering. If you've only a passing interest in the poet, then you're best off visiting either his birthplace in **Alloway** (see p.191), or the town where he died and is buried, **Dumfries** (see p.167). However, the dedicated fan might also fancy checking out the following spots:

The **Bachelors' Club** (Easter–Sept Mon, Tues & Fri–Sun 1–5pm; NTS; £5.50) is a wee thatched house in the tiny village of Tarbolton, some six miles northeast of Ayr. It was here in the upstairs room that the 20-year-old Burns attended dancing classes, set up a debating society and became a Freemason.

In Kirkoswald, fourteen miles southwest of Ayr, is **Souter Johnnie's Cottage** (April–Sept Mon, Tues & Fri–Sun 11.30am–5pm; NTS; £5.50), once the home of John Davidson, Burns's boon companion and the original inspiration for Souter (cobbler) Johnnie in *Tam o' Shanter*. The restored alehouse here has life-size stone figures of Johnnie, Tam himself and other Burnsian characters, all of whom are buried in the nearby graveyard.

Scotland's largest monument to Burns is in Kilmarnock (see p.196), where his first poems were published, but there's an equally imposing Scots Baronial one in Mauchline, eleven miles east of Ayr. The **National Burns Memorial Tower**, erected in 1897 (along with half a dozen houses for the poor) on the centenary of the poet's death, stands just by the A76 northwest of the town centre (ask about access at the museum). You can also visit the **Burns House Museum** (Tues–Sat 11am–5pm; free), on Castle Street, where Burns lived at the time of his marriage to Jean Armour, and Burns's favourite drinking hole, *Poosie Nansie's*, on Loudoun Street, which retains much of its original eighteenth-century character.

Accommodation

Ayr has a vast choice of **accommodation**, the cheapest of which is generally clustered in the streets between the town centre and the Esplanade; however, the nicest places can be found in the leafy streets to the south of the town centre. Those wishing to camp should head for the *Heads of Ayr* caravan and **campsite** (ⓣ01292/442269; March–Oct), three miles south of town along the coastal A719, beside the popular Heads of Ayr Farm Park (Easter–Oct daily 10am–5pm; free; ⓦwww.headsofayrfarmpark.co.uk).

Craggallan 8 Queen's Terrace ⓣ01292/264998, ⓦwww.cragallan.com. A friendly little guesthouse – the best on the street – with quite attractive plain decor. ❷

The Crescent 26 Bellevue Crescent ⓣ01292/287329, ⓦwww.26crescent.freeserve.co.uk. A spacious and cosily furnished Victorian house with a four-poster suite available. ❹

The Dunn Thing 13 Park Circus ⓣ01292/284531, ⓦwww.thedunnthing.co.uk. Brightly decorated B&B that lets out rooms, with or without breakfast. ❷

Savoy Park Hotel 16 Racecourse Rd ⓣ01292/266112, ⓦwww.savoypark.com. A splendid red sandstone Scots Baronial building, with a lovely garden complete with gazebo and swings; it's a little lacking in atmosphere, but the public rooms are suitably grand and the bedrooms have all mod cons. ❹

The Town

Ayr's cobbled, four-arched **Auld Brig** survived the threat of demolition in the early twentieth century, thanks largely to Burns's poem *The Brigs of Ayr*, and is one of the oldest stone bridges in Scotland, having been built during the reign of James IV (1488–1513). A short stroll upstream from the bridge stands the much restored **Auld Kirk** (ⓦwww.auldkirk.org). At the lych gate, look out for the coffin-shaped

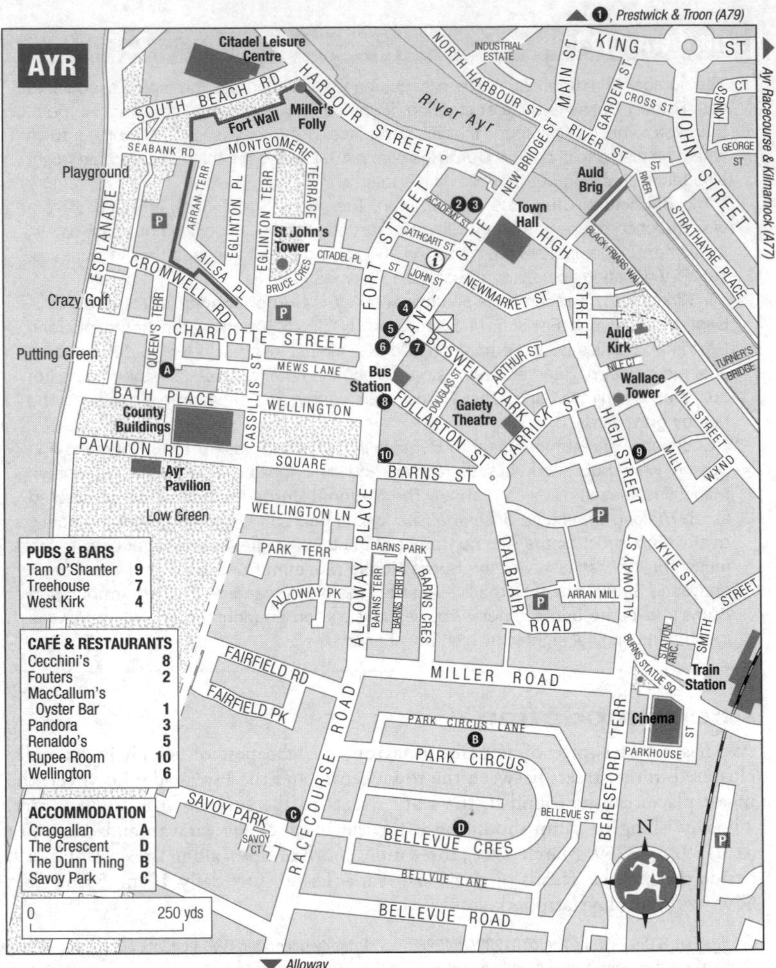

mort-safe (heavy grating) on the walls; placed over newly dug graves, these mort-safes were an early nineteenth-century security system, meant to deter bodysnatchers at a time when bodies were swiftly bought up by medical schools with no questions asked.

The rest of Ayr's busy town centre, wedged between Sandgate and the south bank of the treacly River Ayr, was rebuilt by the Victorians, and is now busy most days with shoppers from all over the county. The most conspicuous landmark is the big, grey, rather ugly, castellated **Wallace Tower**, erected in 1828 at the southern end of the High Street. It stands on what is thought to have been the site of Edward I's barracks, which were set alight by Wallace in 1297. At the junction of the High Street and Sandgate sits the more impressive Neoclassical **Town Hall**, completed in 1832, whose spectacular 226ft-high spire is guarded by griffins brandishing flaming torches, eagles and a Triton.

All you can see of Cromwell's zigzag **Citadel**, built to the west of the town centre in the 1650s, is a small section of the old walls – the area was built over, for the most part, in Victorian times, but is still known locally as "the Fort". The best-preserved section of the fortifications lies on South Harbour Street, though the one surviving corbelled corner turret is, in fact, a Victorian addition known as **Miller's Folly** after its eccentric former owner. Another survivor from the distant past is **St John's Tower** (call ⓣ01292/286385 to arrange access), which stands on its own in a walled garden at the heart of the old citadel, and is all that remains of the medieval church where the Scottish parliament met after the Battle of Bannockburn in 1315 to decide the royal succession.

To the south of the citadel are the wide, gridiron streets of Ayr's main Georgian and Regency residential development. **Wellington Square**, whose first occupants were "Gentlemen of Rich Fortune and Retired Army Officers", is the area's showpiece, its trim gardens and terraces overlooked by the **County Buildings**, a vast, imposing Palladian pile from 1820. The opening of the Glasgow-to-Ayr train line in 1840 brought the first major influx of holiday-makers to the town, but today – unless the weather's fantastic – only a few hardy types take a stroll along Ayr's bleak, long **Esplanade** and beach, which look out to the Isle of Arran. The one building of note is the distinctive whitewashed **Ayr Pavilion**, built in 1911, with its four tall corner towers and known locally as "the Piv" – it now houses the suitably tacky Pirate Pete's adventure playground.

Eating, drinking and nightlife

Ayr has some decent **eating** options. Arguably the town's best restaurant is *Fouters*, 2a Academy St (ⓣ01292/261391, ⓦwww.fouters.co.uk; closed Mon & Sun), a cellar bistro off Sandgate – its short but imaginative menu features fresh local seafood, beef and lamb. There are several good moderately priced Italian outfits, like *Cecchini's* (ⓣ01292/263607, ⓦwww.cecchinisayr.com), a fairly chic modern bistro at 72 Fort St. On the eastern side of Wellington Square, the *Rupee Room* (ⓣ01292/283002) is a popular, welcoming and inexpensive Indian restaurant, decked out with modern furnishings. Ayr's most stylish café is *Pandora*, a dark wood-panelled coffee house on Sandgate, offering standard inexpensive bistro food. You can eat-in or take away fish and chips from *Wellington*, a long-established chippy at the corner of Sandgate and Fort Street, next door to which is cheery *Renaldo's*, renowned for its authentic Italian ice cream and Ayr rock. For terrific **seafood**, head north to the harbour at Troon to the acclaimed *MacCallum's Oyster Bar* (ⓣ01292/319339).

Ayr's **pubs** are heaving most weekends. The most historic pub in town is the thatched *Tam o' Shanter*, on the High Street, which advertises its "traditional atmosphere" but also its "Sky Sports". For a quiet pint of real ale, head for the *West Kirk*, a music-free J.D. Wetherspoon church-to-pub conversion on Sandgate, with wooden balconies held up by pistachio-coloured fluted pillars. Younger folk head for the *Treehouse*, also on Sandgate, which also offers Sky Sports.

Alloway

ALLOWAY, formerly a small village but now on the southern outskirts of Ayr, is the birthplace of Robert Burns (1759–96), Scotland's national poet. There are several places in Alloway associated with Burns, all gathered under the grandly titled Burns National Heritage Park (ⓦwww.burnsheritagepark.com), and you can get a joint "passport" for the lot lasting three days (£5). Your first port of call, however, should be the **Burns Cottage and Museum** (daily: April–Sept 10am–5.30pm; Oct–March 10am–5pm; £4), opposite the village post office and shop. The poet's birthplace, a low, whitewashed, thatched cottage where animals and people lived under the same roof, with a separate section for grain storage, was quite modern in its day. Much altered over the years, you can nevertheless gain an

Robert Burns

The first of seven children, **Robert Burns**, the national poet of Scotland, was born in Alloway on January 25, 1759. His father, William, was employed as a gardener until 1766, when he became a tenant farmer at Mount Oliphant, near Alloway, moving to Lochlie Farm, Tarbolton, eleven years later. A series of bad harvests and the demands of the landlord's estate manager bankrupted the family, and William died almost penniless in 1784. These events had a profound effect on Robert, leaving him with an antipathy towards political authority and a hatred of the land-owning classes.

With the death of his father, Robert became head of the family and they moved again, this time to a farm at Mossgiel, near Mauchline. Burns had already begun writing **poetry** and **prose** at Lochlie, recording incidental thoughts in his *First Commonplace Book*, but it was here at Mossgiel that he began to write in earnest, and his first volume, *Poems Chiefly in the Scottish Dialect*, was published in Kilmarnock in 1786. The book proved immensely popular, celebrated by ordinary Scots and Edinburgh literati alike, with the satirical trilogy *Holy Willie's Prayer*, *The Holy Fair* and *Address to the Devil* attracting particular attention. The object of Burns's poetic scorn was the kirk, whose ministers had obliged him to appear in church to be publicly condemned for fornication – a commonplace punishment in those days.

Burns spent the winter of 1786–87 in the capital, lionized by the literary establishment. Despite his success, however, he felt trapped, unable to make enough money from writing to leave farming. He was also in a political snare, fraternizing with the elite, but with radical views and pseudo-Jacobite nationalist sympathies that constantly landed him in trouble. His frequent recourse was to play the part of the unlettered ploughman-poet, the noble savage who might be excused his impetuous outbursts and hectic womanizing.

He had, however, made useful contacts in Edinburgh and as a consequence was recruited to collect, write and rearrange two volumes of songs set to traditional Scottish tunes. These volumes, James Johnson's *Scots Musical Museum* and George Thomson's *Select Scottish Airs*, contain the bulk of his **songwriting**, and it's on them that Burns's international reputation rests, with works like *Auld Lang Syne*, *Scots, Wha Hae*, *Coming Through the Rye* and *Green Grow the Rushes, O*. At this time, too, though poetry now took second place, he produced two excellent poems: *Tam o' Shanter* and a republican tract, *A Man's a Man for a' That*.

Burns often boasted of his sexual conquests, and he fathered several illegitimate children, but in 1788, he eventually married **Jean Armour**, a stonemason's daughter from Mauchline, with whom he already had two children, and moved to Ellisland Farm, near Dumfries (see p.168). The following year he was appointed excise officer and could at last leave farming, moving to Dumfries in 1791. Burns's years of comfort were short-lived, however. His years of labour on the farm, allied to a rheumatic fever, damaged his heart, and he died in Dumfries on July 21, 1796, aged 37.

Burns's work, inspired by a romantic nationalism and tinged with a wry wit, has made him a potent symbol of "Scottishness". Ignoring the anglophile preferences of the Edinburgh elite, he wrote in Scots vernacular about the country he loved, an exuberant celebration that filled a need in a nation culturally colonized by England. Today, Burns Clubs all over the world mark every anniversary of the poet's birthday with the Burns Supper, complete with Scottish totems – haggis, piper and whisky bottle – and a ritual recital of Burns's *Ode to a Haggis*.

impression of what the place must have been like when Burns, the first of seven children, was born in the box bed in the only room in the house. The nearby two-room museum boasts all sorts of memorabilia: the giant family Bible, letters and manuscripts, the pistol he carried while an exciseman, a lock of his hair, plus lots of kitsch Burnsiana from through the centuries.

Ten minutes' walk down the road from the cottage is the plain, roofless ruin of **Alloway Kirk**, where Robert's father William is buried. Burns set much of *Tam o' Shanter* here. Tam, having got drunk in Ayr, passes "by Alloway's auld haunted kirk" and stumbles across a riotous witches' dance. Down the road from the church, the **Brig o' Doon**, the picturesque thirteenth-century hump-backed bridge over which Tam is forced to flee for his life, still stands, curving gracefully over the river. High above the river and bridge, in a small carefully manicured garden, towers the **Burns Monument** (daily: April–Sept 9am–5pm; Oct–March 10am–4pm; free), a striking, slightly ludicrous Neoclassical rotunda, topped by a scalloped cornice and a miniature copper-gilt baldachin. You can climb to the top for views over to the Brig, and, in the nearby **Statue House**, admire some eighteenth-century stone statues of Tam, Soutar and Nanse, which are, in fact, portraits of Burns's friends. To enter the garden, you need to approach from the nearby **Tam o' Shanter Experience** (daily: April–Sept 10am–5.30pm; Oct–March 10am–5pm; £1.50), on the opposite side of the road from Alloway Kirk. Don't bother with the "Experience" itself, however, as its low-budget audiovisual presentation of *Tam o' Shanter* fails to do justice to Burns's poem.

To reach Alloway from Ayr town centre, **buses #1** and **#57** set off from Sandgate (Mon–Sat hourly) and go right to the Tam o' Shanter Experience; otherwise, you can catch bus #58 or #60 from the bus station to Alloway.

Dumfries House

Located fourteen miles east of Ayr off the A70, just outside cumnock, **Dumfries House** (Easter–Oct 11am–4pm, pre-booked guided tour only; £10; ⓣ01290/425959, ⓦwww.dumfries-house.org.uk) is a handsome Palladian villa, an essential stop for anyone with an interest in domestic architecture.

Lively tours illuminate both the uniqueness and beauty of the furnishings, and the story of how they remain miraculously intact. The house was commissioned by the fifth earl of Dumfries, a widower who wanted to remarry and ensure he had an heir for the family estate. The house, the major early commission for the Adam brothers, was conceived as a honey trap to lure a potential wife, and, judging by the portrait of the ageing, gouty earl in the Pink Drawing Room, he needed all the help he could get. Such was the earl's urgency the house was built and decked out relatively swiftly – between 1756 and 1760 – meaning its Rococo decorative scheme is in perfect harmony with the graceful sandstone exterior. Chief amongst the treasures is a huge collection of **Chippendale furniture**, some ordered direct from Thomas himself, and some created from his "Director" (book of designs) and augmented by local craftsmen with Scottish saltires. Throughout the house, the family symbols of the wyvern (small dragon) and the thistle recur in inventive and playful touches, and exotic Oriental motifs crop up in the fanciful Adam plasterwork ceilings, tapestry fire screens and gilded pier glasses.

The earl secured a wife but died without producing an heir; the family subsequently turned their attention to creating Mount Stuart (see p.261), leaving Dumfries House to be looked after by a series of housekeepers. The recent story of the house is as remarkable as its past: the building and its contents were all up for sale in 2007, and some of the furniture had begun its journey south to Christie's when Prince Charles and a hastily assembled trust intervened to make a heritage "save". You can still see Christie's labels on some of the ceramics and furnishings.

From Glasgow take the #X77 or X76 bus from Buchanan Street Bus station; from Ayr take the #46 bus. The house has an excellent **café/tearoom**, serving sandwich platters, soup and cakes.

South of Ayr

Fifty miles from top to bottom, the **South Ayrshire coastline** between Ayr and Stranraer is largely unblemished by modern industry or major seaside developments. Glasgow is that much further away, which deters day-trippers, and the sandy beaches are frequently interspersed with coastal cliffs. The two main reasons why visitors venture here, apart from to play golf, are to visit **Culzean Castle**, Robert Adam's Neoclassical mansion on the cliffs between Ayr and Girvan, and to take a boat trip to see the gannets on **Ailsa Craig**, the giant muffin-shaped island in the Firth of Clyde. The A77 stays away from the coast until just before **Girvan**, a low-key seaside resort where boats depart for Ailsa Craig. If you keep to the main road, however, you'll pass by the area's most overlooked sight, the medieval ruins of **Crossraguel Abbey**. As for public transport, there's a good **bus** service along the coast, particularly between Ayr and Culzean, plus a **train** line from Ayr to Girvan and on to Stranraer.

Culzean Castle

Sitting on the edge of a sheer cliff, looking out over the Firth of Clyde to Arran, **Culzean Castle** (Easter–Oct daily 10.30am–5pm; Ⓦwww.culzeanexperience.org; NTS; £13) couldn't have a more impressive situation. Given its strategic position, it's hardly surprising that the Kennedy family maintained a castle at Culzean (pronounced "cullane") from the twelfth century onwards. The current castle is actually a grand, late eighteenth-century stately home, designed by the Scottish Neoclassical architect **Robert Adam** for the tenth earl of Cassillis (pronounced "cassles"), as the Kennedys had by then become. The best place to start is at the **visitor centre** in the modernized Home Farm buildings. Here you can watch an audiovisual show on the house, and pick up **free maps** – as well as wildlife leaflets – that help you to get your bearings. The visitor centre's self-service **restaurant** is good, though you might prefer to head over to the *Old Stables* **coffee house** beside the castle, a quieter spot with table service.

From the visitor centre, it's a few minutes' walk through Adam's mock-ruined arch to the **Castle** itself, which overlooks the pristine lawn and herbaceous borders of the Fountain Court on one side, with the high sea cliffs on the other. Begun in 1777, Culzean's exterior preserves a medieval aspect, with its arrow slits and battlements; the interior, however, exemplifies the delicate, harmonious Neoclassical designs that Adam loved – look out for the dolphins and swans (emblems of the Kennedy family) and the rams' heads (Adam's own favourite motif). The most brilliantly conceived work by Adam is the **Oval Staircase**, where tiers of classical columns lead up to a huge glazed cupola allowing light to stream down. After admiring the portrait of Napoleon by Lefèvre, you pass through to the impressive circular **Saloon**, whose symmetrical flourishes deliberately contrast with the natural land and seascapes on view through the windows.

It's worth leaving enough time for an exploration of the 500-acre **country park** (daily 9.30am to dusk; £8.50). You can also **stay** at Culzean (Ⓣ01655/884455; April–Oct; ⑨), on the top floor, where six double bedrooms have been done out in a comfortably genteel style. Guests eat together in the shared dining room and the chef comes in to do breakfast as well. There's also the well-maintained and very popular *Culzean Castle* **campsite** (Ⓣ01655/760627; March–Oct), located in the woods by the castle entrance, with great views across to Arran.

Crossraguel Abbey

Three miles inland from Culzean, right by the A77, lie the substantial remains of **Crossraguel Abbey** (Easter–Sept daily 9.30am–5.30pm; HS; £3.70), a Cluniac monastery – one of only two in Scotland – founded in 1250. The best place to start is in the choir of the **abbey church**, which has ornate carving over the piscina and sedilia. Better still is the fifteenth-century **sacristy**, which has kept its vaulted ceiling and its decorative capitals, corbels and bosses, embellished with squirrels, lions, a triple-faced head and a green man. Next door, off the cloisters, the vaulted **chapter house** is also intact. The **tower house**, tacked onto the eastern end of the complex, was built around 1480 to provide luxury accommodation in keeping with the abbot's high status in the outside world, and clearly illustrates the corruption of the monastic ideal that spurred the Reformation. On the opposite side of the abbey, the **gatehouse** is equally grand and has been restored, so that you can climb right up to the cap house and walk out onto the battlements. Clearly visible nearby is a beehive-shaped dovecote, a crucial part of the abbey's economy; the monks not only ate the doves but also relied on them for eggs.

South to Girvan

Beyond Crossraguel, the A77 eventually reaches the coast at the village of **TURNBERRY**, a vast purpose-built Edwardian golfing resort. Visible out on the rocks on the point to the north of the village are a lighthouse and the ruined **castle** where Robert the Bruce was born in 1274, and which was in all likelihood left to fall into rack and ruin in 1307, after Bruce himself attacked and routed the English troops garrisoned within.

Set beneath a ridge of grassy hills, **GIRVAN** (Ⓦwww.girvan-online.net), five miles south of Turnberry, is at its best round the busy harbour, a narrow slit beside the mouth of the Girvan Water. The chief reason for visiting the town is to take the boat excursion to Ailsa Craig (see below). There's a permanent exhibition about the island (and Girvan) at the **McKechnie Institute** (Tues, Thurs & Fri 1–4pm, Wed 1.30–4.30pm, Sat 10.30am–4pm; free), on Dalrymple Street, just up from **Auld Stumpy**, the great name given to the town's clock tower. Orientation is easy, with the **train station** just a short walk northeast of the harbour. If you're looking for an eco-conscious rural retreat, then head for *Drumskeoch Farm* (Ⓣ01465/841172, Ⓦwww.drumskeoch.co.uk; ❷), a lovely vegetarian B&B on an organic farm some ten miles south of Girvan, off the A714.

Ailsa Craig

As you travel along the South Ayrshire coast, the giant muffin-shaped island of **Ailsa Craig** is an intriguing presence on the horizon, stranded as it is in the middle of the Firth of Clyde. The island's name means "Fairy Rock" in Gaelic, though it was a less than enchanting place for the persecuted Catholics who escaped here during the Reformation. The island's granite has long been used for making what many consider to be the finest curling stones – a company in nearby Mauchline still has exclusive rights and sporadically collects a few boulders. In the late nineteenth century 29 people lived on the island, either working in the quarry or at the Stevenson lighthouse. With its volcanic, columnar cliffs and 1114ft summit, Ailsa Craig is now a **bird sanctuary** that's home to some 40,000 gannets, plus thousands of other seabirds. The best time to make the trip is at the end of May and in June when the fledglings are trying to fly. Several companies in Girvan offer **cruises** round the island, but only Mark McCrindle, who also organizes sea-angling trips, is licensed to land (May to late Sept 1–2 daily; Ⓣ01465/713219, Ⓦwww.ailsacraig.org.uk). It takes about an hour to reach the island, after which you get enough time to walk up to the summit of the rock and watch the birds, weather permitting. The exact timings and prices depend on the length of trip, tides and weather; booking ahead is essential.

North of Ayr

The Ayrshire coast extends some thirty miles or so north of Ayr. A train line and the busy coastal road, the A78, cut across this disparate shoreline, where rolling farmland is interrupted by the pockmarks of industrialization, interspersed with moribund seaside resorts and internationally famous links golf courses. One place that is worth a visit is **Irvine**, home to the excellent Scottish Maritime Museum. The northernmost town on the Ayrshire coast, and also easily the area's most agreeable seaside resort, is **Largs**, from where you can catch a ferry across to the nearby island of **Great Cumbrae**, a low-key but justifiably popular holiday spot.

Transport connections are excellent, with frequent **buses** and a **train** line reaching as far as Largs. **Glasgow Prestwick Airport** (Ⓣ0871/223 0700, Ⓦwww.gpia.co.uk), lies just to the northeast of Ayr and Prestwick, and has its own **train station** (alight at Prestwick Airport not Prestwick Town station), with trains (every 30min) to Glasgow (45min) and Ayr (20min); there's also an express **bus** (#X77) to Glasgow's Buchanan Street station (hourly; 50min). In addition, P&O fast ferries to Larne (Ⓦwww.poirishsea.com) depart from **Troon**, where the Open Championship was first played in 1860, some three miles north of Prestwick. Further up the coast still, dour **Ardrossan** is the departure point for CalMac ferries to the Isle of Arran (see p.199).

Kilmarnock

Twelve miles northeast from Ayr, **KILMARNOCK** is a shabby and depressed manufacturing town, known principally for being the home of Johnnie Walker whisky. The town planners of the 1960s and 1970s didn't do the place any favours, saddling it with some terrible shopping centres and a grim one-way road system. Yet "Killie" as the locals call it, isn't a bad-looking town in parts, thanks to the local red sandstone, and it does have a couple of sights.

One of the town's most handsome buildings is the **Dick Institute** (Tues–Sat 11am–5pm; free), a splendid edifice with a Corinthian portico flanked by monkey-puzzle trees, just off the B7073 (London Road). On the ground floor is the town library, and a space for temporary exhibitions; upstairs is the endearingly old-fashioned local museum. The institute's artworks include a couple of top-notch Pre-Raphaelite paintings by Alma-Tadema and Millais, and several works by Edward Hornel.

To the north of the Dick Institute, beyond Kilmarnock College and the railway, is Kay Park, site of the largest **Burns Monument** in Scotland, a Scots Baronial monstrosity erected at the highest point in the town in 1879. More uplifting is **Dean Castle** (April–Oct Wed–Sun 11am–5pm; Nov–March Sat & Sun noon–4pm; free; Ⓦwww.deancastle.com), set in beautiful wooded grounds a mile or so to the north up Kilmarnock Water, with a mini-farm, aviaries and adventure playground. Parts of the castle date back to 1360, and the highlights of the interior include several fifteenth- and sixteenth-century Brussels tapestries, plus a collection of musical instruments and a large armoury from the same period.

Practicalities

Kilmarnock's **train station** lies at the north end of John Finnie Street, which is lined with impressive red-sandstone Victorian buildings and runs parallel with the much less attractive main shopping drag, King Street, to the east. It's unlikely you'll want to **stay**, but if you do try *Dean Park Guest House* (Ⓣ01563/572794; ❷), a little sandstone villa at 27 Wellington St, just behind the train station. Head for the entirely modern, *Wheatsheaf* pub, just up from The Cross, at the northern end of King Street, if you're after something to **eat**.

Irvine

IRVINE, twelve miles north of Ayr, was once the principal port for trade between Glasgow and Ireland, and later for coal from Kilmarnock; its halcyon days are recalled by a branch of the **Scottish Maritime Museum** (April–Oct daily 10am–5pm; £3.50; Ⓦwww.scottishmaritimemuseum.org), which is spread across several locations down at the town's carefully restored old harbour.

The best place to start is in the **Linthouse Engine Shop**, on Harbour Road, a late nineteenth-century hangar-like building held up with massive iron girders, moved here brick by brick from Govan in Glasgow in 1990. Inside, the ad hoc displays include everything from old sailing dinghies, yachts and canoes to a giant ship's turbines. Free guided tours set off roughly four times a day round the nearby **Shipyard Worker's Tenement Flat**, which has been restored to something like its appearance in 1910, when a family of six to eight would have occupied its two rooms and scullery (and rented one of them out to a lodger). Moored at the **pontoons** on Harbour Street is an assortment of craft, which you can board, including a tug, a trawler, a "puffer" boat, a yacht driven by a wind turbine and the SY *Carola*, the oldest seagoing steam yacht in the country. At the nearby **Boatshop** kids can learn morse code and semaphore.

The **old town** of Irvine lies a mile or so to the east of the harbour, separated by railway lines and the gargantuan **Riverfront Shopping Mall**, an abomination through which you must walk to reach the High Street. Here and there a couple of narrow streets hint at the town's antiquity, amid the prevailing architectural gloom. The cobbled street of Glasgow Vennel, south of the High Street, features the **Vennel Gallery** (Fri–Sun 10am–1pm & 2–5pm; free), which exhibits contemporary art and crafts and shows a video on Burns, who stayed in the eighteenth-century cottage for six months at the age of 22, while learning the trade of flax-combing. He didn't enjoy it much, falling ill with pleurisy, though he did manage to taste his first whisky there, and lose his virginity. The most atmospheric street is **Seagate**, another cobbled affair, this time off the north end of the High Street, which has ancient cottages and the remains of **Seagate Castle**, a sixteenth-century fortified house.

Practicalities

Arriving at Irvine's adjacent **train** or **bus stations**, you'll find yourself exactly halfway between the harbour to the west, and the Riverfront carbuncle and old town to the east. Kilwinning Road, heading north out of Irvine, has several inexpensive **B&Bs**: *Laurelbank Guest House*, a comfortable whitewashed Victorian villa, is set back from the road at no.3 (Ⓣ01294/277153, Ⓦwww.laurelbankguesthouse.co.uk; ❷); for something a bit posher, head for *Annfield House*, 6 Castle St (Ⓣ01294/278903, Ⓦwww.annfieldhousehotel.com; ❹), a spacious Victorian mansion overlooking the river at the end of Sandgate.

Irvine has a lovely sandy beach at the far end of the harbour which is good for swimming. If the weather's not great, head for the nearby **Magnum** (Ⓦwww.kaleisure.co.uk), Scotland's largest leisure centre and swimming pool. You could also check to see if the **Irvine Folk Club** (Ⓦwww.irvinefolkclub.co.uk) is meeting up at the Vineburgh Community Centre in Quarry Road: it puts on some excellent gigs. Irvine's busiest time of the year is August, when the **Marymass Festival** (Ⓦwww.marymass.org) takes place: ten days of dog shows, flower shows and folk music, culminating in a horse-drawn procession through the town.

Largs and around

Nineteen miles north of Irvine, tucked in between the hills and the sea, **LARGS** remains the most traditional of Ayrshire's family resorts, its guesthouses and B&Bs spreading out behind an elongated seaside promenade. Largs also conceals one real gem: **Skelmorlie Aisle** (June–Aug Mon–Sat 2–5pm; keys from the museum next door; free), a slice of the Renaissance hidden away beside the old graveyard off Main Street – to get there, enter the yard opposite the WHSmith newsagent. Once the north transept of a larger church (long since gone), and now standing alone in the graveyard, the aisle was converted in 1636 into a mausoleum by Sir Robert Montgomerie, a local bigwig, in memory of his wife who died in a horseriding accident. Carved by Scottish masons following Italian patterns, the tomb is decorated with Montgomerie's coat of arms as well as symbols of mortality such as the skull, winged hourglass and inverted torch. Up above, the intricate paintwork of the barrel-vaulted ceiling includes the signs of the zodiac, biblical figures and texts.

Largs' chief historical claim to fame is the **Battle of Largs**, which took place in 1263. The battle was forced on King Haakon's Vikings when their longships were blown ashore by a gale. The invaders were attacked by the Scots and, although both sides claimed victory, the Norwegians retreated north and abandoned their territorial claims to the Hebrides three years later. The battle provides a historical link for **Vikingar!** (daily: April–Sept 10.30am–4.30pm; Oct & March 10.30am–3.30pm; £4.50; Ⓦwww.kaleisure.co.uk), a light-hearted Viking-themed extravaganza housed in a purpose-built leisure complex, swimming pool and cinema, five minutes' walk north of the pier. Largs also holds a week-long **Viking Festival** (Ⓦwww.largsvikingfestival.com) in August/September, which includes a costumed re-enactment of the famous skirmish.

The Battle of Largs is also commemorated by the distinctive **Pencil Monument**, a modern obelisk a mile south of the town centre, close to the marina, and opposite the **Kelburn Castle and Country Centre** (Easter–Oct daily 10am–6pm; £7.50; Ⓦwww.kelburncountrycentre.com), seat of the earls of Glasgow (aka the Boyle family) since the twelfth century, and now a very popular tourist attraction. The castle itself is no great shakes inside and can only be seen by guided tour. Much more enticing are the grounds, which feature a steep gorge and waterfall, 1000-year-old yew trees, an Adam monument and some lovely, relatively informal, gardens. There's also plenty for kids to do, including an adventure course, a secret forest playground (open from noon), a pets' corner, and pony riding.

Practicalities

Largs' **bus** and **train station** are both just south of Main Street, a short stroll east of the pier, and there's a tiny **tourist office** (April Mon–Sat; May–Aug daily; Sept Tues–Sat; Ⓣ01475/689962) inside the train station. Caledonian MacBrayne operates a regular **ferry service** to Great Cumbrae (every 15min in summer; Ⓣ01475/674134, Ⓦwww.calmac.co.uk) from Largs' pier. The old **paddle steamer**, the *Waverley*, also visits regularly during the summer (Ⓣ0845/130 4647, Ⓦwww.waverleyexcursions.co.uk).

Being a holiday town, Largs has no shortage of **guesthouses** and **B&Bs**. There's a cluster along Aubery Crescent, a quiet street overlooking the curving bay, ten minutes' walk north of the pier – head for the *Old Rectory* at no. 2 (Ⓣ01475/674405, Ⓦwww.oldrectorylargs.co.uk; Feb–Nov; ❸), with excellent views over to Cumbrae and Arran. Another option is *Biscayne House* (Ⓣ01475/672851, Ⓦwww.biscayneguesthouse.co.uk; ❷), up the hill by the main road, which offers B&B as well as self-catering accommodation for backpackers. *South Whittlieburn Farm* **campsite** (Ⓣ01475/675881; ❸) lies on a working sheep farm in a peaceful glen about three miles northeast of town; they also do really excellent **B&B** in the farmhouse.

As for **food**, fish and chips is the staple diet of most visitors, and there are plenty of places to choose from. Largs is famous for *Nardini's*, an Italian ice-cream parlour housed in a wonderful L-shaped Art Deco building on the Promenade, just north of the pier. Just south of town, *Fins* in Fairlie (Ⓣ01475/568989, Ⓦwww.fencebay.co.uk) is a cheerful wood-panelled **seafood restaurant** dishing up cullen skink, lobster, Cumbrae oysters, crabs and langoustines.

Great Cumbrae

Immediately offshore from Largs lies **Great Cumbrae**, a plump, hilly and wonderfully peaceful little island roughly four miles long and half as wide. The only settlement of any size is **MILLPORT** (Ⓦwww.millport.org.uk), which curves around a lovely wide bay on the south coast, overlooking the privately owned neighbouring island of Wee Cumbrae. The seafront is one long parade of Victorian seaside villas and terraces, interrupted only by **The Garrison**, a distinctive old barracks building with castellated gables. Adjacent to the house is the little **Museum of the Cumbraes** (April–Sept Thurs–Mon 10am–1pm & 2–5pm; free) with displays on local history and industries.

Hidden from view in the woods above the town is the Episcopal **Cathedral of Argyll & the Isles** (Mon–Sat 11am–4pm; July–Sept concert Sun 3pm), completed in 1851 to a design by William Butterfield, one of the leading High Victorian Gothic architects. It's pretty modest by Butterfield standards, with only the polychromatic tiling in the chancel giving any hint of his usual exuberance. However, it does have the distinction of being Britain's smallest cathedral, with seating for just a hundred worshippers. Just out of Millport, to the east, overlooking the Hunterston nuclear power station and iron-ore terminal back on the mainland, is the University Marine Biological Station. Its west wing contains the **Robertson Museum & Aquarium** (Mon–Fri 8.45am–12.15pm & 1.45–4.15pm; £1.50), which has a laudably ecological exhibition on the local marine environment, and an old-fashioned aquarium displaying giant whelks, starfish, dogfish, conger eels and cod.

The CalMac **ferry** over from Largs is very frequent (every 15min in summer), and takes just ten minutes to reach the island's northeast tip, with a connecting **bus** to Millport. Close by is the Scottish National Centre for watersports (Ⓣ01475/530757, Ⓦwww.nationalcentrecumbrae.org.uk), which offers courses in everything from kayaking to powerboating. The most popular activity on Great Cumbrae, however, is **cycling**: a circuit of the island takes no more than two hours even at a very leisurely pace, the road is very quiet, and there are a couple of good red-sandstone beaches on the west coast overlooking Bute. Several **bike rental** outfits in Millport offer very reasonable rates: try Bremner's, 17 Cardiff St (Ⓣ01475/530707).

If you don't fancy fish and chips, head for the fabulous *Ritz* **café**, in business since 1906 – they provide home-made ice cream, marshmallow ices, toasties and Millport Rock. The island is very peaceful once the day-trippers have gone home, and the most atmospheric and tranquil place **to stay** is the *College of the Holy Spirit* (Ⓣ01475/530353, Ⓦwww.island-retreats.org; ④), an Anglican retreat house adjacent to the cathedral. For B&B head for *Millerston*, 29 West Bay Rd (Ⓣ01475/530480, Ⓔthemillerston@fsmail.net; ④), a double bay-fronted villa with modern furnishings.

Isle of Arran

Shaped like a kidney bean and occupying centre stage in the Firth of Clyde, **Arran** (Ⓦwww.visitarran.net) is the most southerly (and therefore the most accessible) of all the Scottish islands. The Highland–Lowland dividing line passes right through its centre – hence the cliché about it being like "Scotland in miniature" – leaving

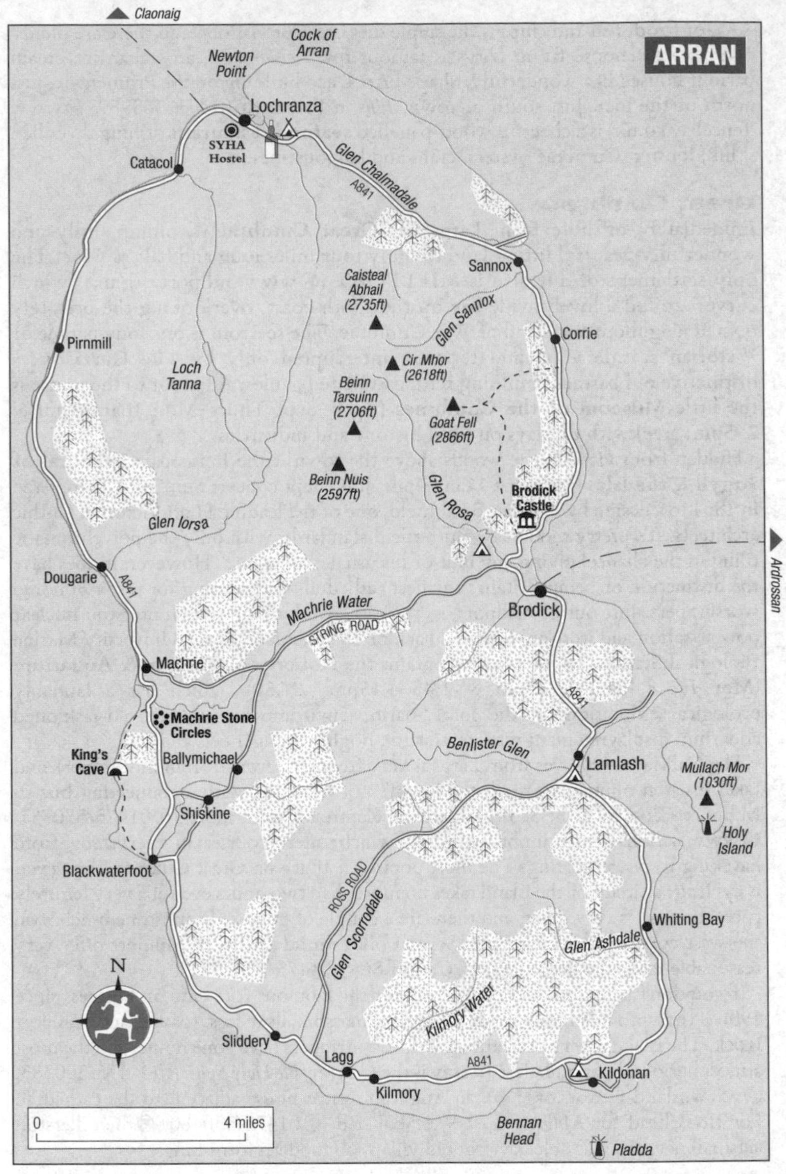

the northern half sparsely populated, mountainous and bleak, while the lush southern half enjoys a much milder climate. The population of around five thousand – many of whom are incomers – tends to stick to the southeastern quarter of the island, leaving the west and the north relatively undisturbed.

There are two big crowd-pullers on Arran: **geology** and **golf**. The former has fascinated rock-obsessed students since Sir James Hutton came here in the late eighteenth century to confirm his theories of uniformitarianism. A hundred years later, Sir Archibald Geikie's investigations were a landmark in the study of Arran's geology, and the island remains a popular destination for university and school field trips. As for golf, Arran boasts seven courses, including three of the eighteen-hole variety at Brodick, Lamlash and Whiting Bay, and a unique twelve-hole course at Shiskine, near Blackwaterfoot; an Arran Golf Pass is available for £105, giving you a round on each course.

Although **tourism** is now by far its most important industry – forty percent of the island's housing is holiday accommodation – Arran, at twenty miles in length, is large enough to have a life of its own. While the island's post-1745 history including the Clearances (set in motion by the local lairds, the Hamiltons) is as depressing as elsewhere in the Highlands, in recent years Arran's population has actually increased, in contrast with more remote islands. **Transport** on Arran itself is pretty good: daily buses circle the island (Brodick tourist office has timetables and an Arran Rural Rover day-ticket costs just under £5) and link in with the two **ferry services**: a year-round one from Ardrossan in Ayrshire to Brodick, and a smaller ferry from Claonaig on the Kintyre peninsula to Lochranza in the north (April–Oct).

Brodick

The resort of **BRODICK** (from the Norse *breidr vik*, "broad bay") is a place of only moderate charm, but it does have a grand setting in a wide, sandy bay set against a backdrop of granite mountains. Its development as a tourist resort was held back for a long time by its elitist owners, the dukes of Hamilton, though nowadays, as the island's capital and main communication hub, Brodick is by far the busiest town on Arran.

The town's shops and guesthouses are spread out along the south side of the bay, along with the tourist office and the CalMac pier. However, Brodick's tourist sights, such as they are, are clustered on the west and north side of the bay, a couple of miles from the ferry terminal. First off, on the road to the castle, there's the **Arran Heritage Museum** (April–Oct daily 10.30am–4.30pm; £3; Ⓦwww.arranmuseum.co.uk), housed in a whitewashed eighteenth-century crofter's farm, and containing an old smiddy and a Victorian cottage with box bed and range. In the old stables there are lots of agricultural bits and bobs, plus material on Arran's wartime role, its intriguing geology and a Neolithic skull found on the island.

Even if you're not based in Brodick, it's worth coming here in order to visit **Brodick Castle** (daily: April–Sept 11am–4.30pm; Oct 11am–3.30pm; NTS; £10.50), former seat of the duke of Hamilton, set on a steep bank on the north side of the bay. The bulk of the castle was built in the nineteenth century, giving it a domestic rather than a military look, and the **interior** – once you've fought your way past the 87 stags' heads on the stairs – is comfortable but undistinguished. Don't miss the portrait of the eleventh duke's faithful piper, who injured his throat on a grouse bone, was warned never to pipe again, but did so and died. Probably the most atmospheric room is the copper-filled Victorian kitchen, which conjures up a vision of the sweated and sweating labour required to feed the folk upstairs.

Much more attractive, however, are the walled **gardens** (daily 9.30am–dusk; £5.50) and extensive grounds, a treasury of exotic plants, trees and rhododendrons, which command a superb view across the bay. There's an adventure playground for kids, but the whole area is a natural playground with waterfalls, a giant pitcher plant that swallows thousands of midges daily and a maze of paths. Buried in the grounds is a bizarre Bavarian-style **summerhouse** lined entirely with pine cones, one of three built by the eleventh duke to make his wife, Princess Marie of Baden, feel at home. The castle **tearoom** serves light snacks and home-made cakes and scones.

Practicalities

Brodick's **tourist office** (March–May & Oct Mon–Sat; June–Sept daily; ⓣ01770/303776) is by the CalMac pier. Unless you've got to catch an early-morning ferry, there's little reason to stay in Brodick, though there's a decent choice should you need to. The best **rooms** close to the ferry terminal are at the excellent *Dunvegan Guest House* on Shore Road (ⓣ01770/302811, ⓦwww.dunveganhouse.co.uk; ❺); for somewhere cheaper and more peaceful, head out to *The Barn* (ⓣ01770/303615, ⓦwww.arranbarn.co.uk; ❸), a charming B&B with real style and character on the southwest edge of Brodick in Glencloy. Finally, the luxury option is the elegant and secluded *Kilmichael Country House Hotel* (ⓣ01770/302219, ⓦwww.kilmichael.com; ❽), originally built in the seventeenth century and still retaining lots of period features; a four-course dinner here is around £40 a head, but it's one of the best you'll get on the island. The nearest **campsite** is *Glen Rosa* (ⓣ01770/302380, ⓦwww.glenrosa.com), a lovely, but very basic, farm site (cold water only and no showers), two miles from town off the B880 to Blackwaterfoot.

For **food**, apart from dinner at the aforementioned *Kilmichael*, the only place that really stands out is the seafood restaurant *Creelers* (ⓣ01770/302797, ⓦwww.creelers.co.uk; Easter–Oct), which also has its own smokehouse, by the museum on the road to the castle. Nearer to the ferry terminal, the bar snacks (lunch only) at *Mac's Bar* in the *McLaren Hotel* are a cheaper option and there's real ale too. If you want to find out about any other events taking place on Arran, pick up a copy of the island's **weekly newspaper**, the *Arran Banner*.

The south

The **southern half of Arran** is less spectacular and less forbidding than the north; it's more heavily forested and the land is more fertile, and for that reason the vast majority of the population lives here. The tourist industry has followed them, though with considerably less justification.

Lamlash, Holy Island and Whiting Bay

With its distinctive Edwardian architecture and mild climate, **LAMLASH**, four miles south of Brodick, epitomizes the sedate charm of southeast Arran. The best reason for coming to Lamlash is to visit the slug-shaped hump of **Holy Island**, where a group of **Tibetan Buddhists** have established a retreat. Providing you don't dawdle, it's possible to scramble up to the top of Mullach Mór (1030ft), the island's highest point, and still catch the last ferry back. En route, you might well bump into the island's most numerous residents: feral goats, Eriskay ponies, Soay sheep and rabbits. The Holy Island ferry runs more or less hourly (ⓣ01770/600998; £8 return), and you can stay at the island's Peace Centre (ⓣ01387/373232, ⓦwww.holyisland.org; vegetarian full board ❸), where they put on a range of courses on yoga, meditation and relaxation throughout the season.

If you want to **stay** in Lamlash itself, head for the comfortable *Lilybank* (ⓣ01770/600230, ⓦwww.lilybank-arran.co.uk; Easter–Oct; ❸), overlooking the bay and offering good home-made food, or try out the stylishly refurbished rooms of the *Glenisle Hotel* (ⓣ01770/600559, ⓦwww.glenislehotel.com; ❼). The best food option is the **bar meals** at the friendly *Drift Inn*, which has tables by the shore. For something more upmarket, head for the stylish modern restaurant in the *Glenisle Hotel*.

An established Clydeside resort for over a century, **WHITING BAY**, four miles south of Lamlash, is spread out along a very pleasant bay, though it doesn't have quite the distinctive architecture of Lamlash. It does, however, have a good choice of simple **B&Bs**, such as *Mingulay* (ⓣ01770/700346; ❷), and its neighbour *Ellangowan* (ⓣ01770/700784; ❷) on Middle Road. The **food** is very good, though expensive, at the *Burlington Hotel* on Shore Road, but for home-made cakes and fresh-cooked snacks with scrumptious chips head for *The Coffee Pot* up the road.

Kildonan and around

Access to the sea is tricky along the south coast, but worth the effort, as the sandy beaches here are among the island's finest. One place where you can get down to the sea is at **KILDONAN**, an attractive small village south of Lamlash. It's set slightly off the main road, with a good sandy beach that is shared with the local wildlife. There are views from here out to the tiny flat island of **Pladda**, with its distinctive lighthouse and, in the distance, the great hump of Ailsa Craig (see p.195). Kildonan has a pleasant, laidback **campsite** (ⓣ01770/820320) right by the sea next to the nicely refurbished *Kildonan Hotel* (ⓣ01770/820207, ⓦwww.kildonanhotel.co.uk; ❺). A short stroll west along the shore road is *Mare* (ⓣ01770/820375, ⓦwww.mare-arran.co.uk; ❺), a tastefully furnished modern B&B offering superb breakfasts and stunning sea views.

The north

The **north half of Arran** – effectively the Highland part – features wonderful bare granite peaks, the occasional golden eagle and miles of unspoilt scenery, within reach only of those prepared to do some hiking. Arran's most accessible peak is also the island's highest, **Goat Fell** (2866ft) – take your pick from the Gaelic, *goath*, meaning "windy", or the Norse, *geit-fjall*, "goat mountain" – which can be ascended in just three hours from Brodick or from Corrie (return journey 5hr), though it's a strenuous hike (for the usual safety precautions, see p.49).

Corrie and Sannox

Arran's prettiest little seaside village is **CORRIE**, six miles north of Brodick, where a procession of pristine cottages lines the road to Lochranza and wraps itself around an exquisite little harbour and pier. If you want to use Corrie as a base for hiking, book ahead at the *North High Corrie Croft*, a **bunkhouse** (ⓣ01770/810218), ten minutes' steep climb above the village on a raised beach; it has one large room for group bookings, and an annexe with eight beds. The red-sandstone *Corrie Hotel*, at the centre of the village, does bar meals, and the tearoom in the *Corrie Golf Club*, confusingly in Sannox, offers good-value food all day in summer.

At **SANNOX**, two miles north, the road leaves the shoreline and climbs steeply, giving breathtaking views of the scree-strewn slopes around Caisteal Abhail (2735ft). If you make this journey around dusk, be sure to pause in **Glen Chalmadale**, on the other, northern side of the pass, to catch a glimpse of the red deer that come down to pasture by the water. Another possibility is to turn off to North Sannox, where you can park and walk along the shore to the **Fallen Rocks**, a major rock-fall of Devonian sandstone.

Lochranza

The ruined castle that occupies the mud flats of the bay and the brooding north-facing slopes of the mountains that frame it make for one of the most spectacular ensembles on the island, yet **LOCHRANZA**, despite being the only place of any size in this sparsely populated area, attracts far fewer visitors than Arran's southern resorts. The castle is worth a brief look inside, but Lochranza's main tourist attraction now is the island's modern **distillery** (mid-March to Oct Mon–Sat 10am–6pm, Sun 11am–6pm; Nov & Dec phone ⓣ01770/830264, ⓦwww.arranwhisky.com;

£3.50), distinguished by its pagoda-style roofs at the south end of the village. The tours are entertaining and slick and end with a free sample of the island's single malt.

The finest **accommodation** is to be had at the superb *Apple Lodge* (☎01770/830229; ❺), the old village manse where you'll get excellent home-cooking, or at the unusual *Castlekirk* (☎01770/830202, Ⓦwww.castlekirk.co.uk; ❷), a converted church that retains lots of original features including a rose window in the breakfast room. Lochranza also has a friendly and well-equipped SYHA **hostel** (☎01700/830631; mid-Feb to Oct), situated halfway between the distillery and the castle, with views over the bay, and a **campsite** (☎01770/830273, Ⓦwww.arran.net/lochranza; April–Oct), beautifully placed by the golf course on the Brodick road, where red deer come to graze in the early evening. The campsite has a friendly **tearoom** serving all-day breakfasts and light snacks; the bar of the *Lochranza* is the centre of the local social scene and its **bar meals** are very popular with hungry walkers. If you're just passing through, or need a **packed lunch**, go to the takeaway *Sandwich Station*, close to the CalMac slipway.

Travel details

Trains

Ayr to: Girvan (Mon–Sat 12 daily, 2 on Sun; 30min); Glasgow Central (every 30min; 50min); Irvine (every 30min; 15–20min); Kilmarnock (Mon–Sat 7 daily; 30min); Prestwick Airport (every 30min; 7min); Stranraer (Mon–Sat 7 daily, 2 on Sun; 1hr 20min).

Glasgow Central to: Ardrossan Harbour (4–5 daily; 50min); Ayr (every 30min; 55min); Irvine (every 30min; 35min); Kilmarnock (every 30min–1hr; 40min); Largs (hourly; 1hr); Prestwick Airport (every 30min; 45min); Stranraer (2 daily; 2hr 10min).

Buses

Ayr to: Ardrossan (Mon–Sat every 30min, Sun every 2hr; 55min); Cairnryan (4–7 daily; 1hr 50min); Culzean Castle (Mon–Sat hourly, Sun every 2hr; 30min); Girvan (Mon–Sat every 30min, Sun hourly; 1hr 10min); Glasgow (hourly; 55min); Kilmarnock (Mon–Sat every 30min, Sun hourly; 1hr 10min); Largs (Mon–Sat every 30min, Sun every 2hr; 1hr 20min); New Galloway (Mon–Sat 2 daily; 1hr 20min); Portpatrick (Mon–Sat 6 daily; 2hr 25min); Stranraer (4–6 daily; 2hr); Wemyss Bay (Mon–Sat every 30min, Sun every 2hr; 1hr 30min).

Brodick (Arran) to: Blackwaterfoot (Mon–Sat 8–10 daily, 4 on Sun; 30min); Corrie (3–5 daily; 20min); Kildonan (4–6 daily; 40min); Lagg (3–5 daily; 50min); Lamlash (Mon–Sat hourly, 4 on Sun; 10–15min); Lochranza (3–5 daily; 45min); Whiting Bay (Mon–Sat hourly, 4 on Sun; 25min).

Ferries

(summer timetable)

Ardrossan to: Brodick, Arran (5–6 daily; 55min).
Cairnryan to: Larne (7–9 daily; 1hr–1hr 45min).
Largs to: Great Cumbrae (every 15min; 10min).
Lochranza to: Claonaig (8–9 daily; 30min).
Stranraer to: Belfast (7–8 daily; 1hr 45min–3hr 15min).
Troon to: Larne (2 daily; 1hr 50min).

5

Glasgow and the Clyde

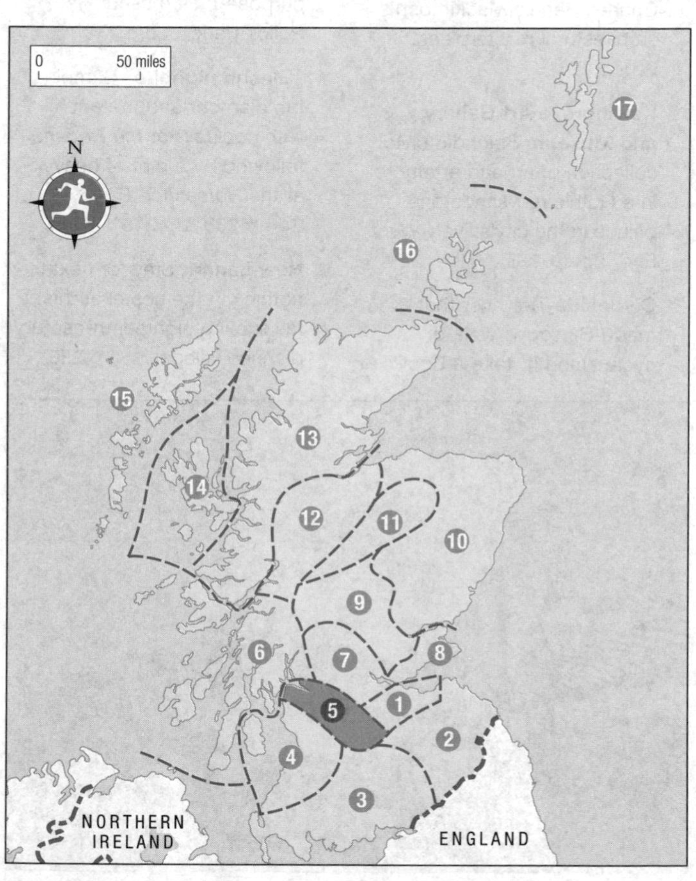

CHAPTER 5

Highlights

* **Necropolis** Elegantly crumbling graveyard on a city-centre hill behind the ancient cathedral, with great views. See p.223

* **Glasgow School of Art** Take a student-led tour of Charles Rennie Mackintosh's architectural masterpiece. See p.224

* **Kelvingrove Art Gallery and Museum** Splendid civic collection of art and artefacts in a Gothic red-sandstone palace in the city's lively West End. See p.228

* **Clydeside** The river that made Glasgow: walk or cycle along it, take a boat on it, cross a bridge over it, or get a view of it from the futuristic Science Centre. See p.230

* **Burrell Collection** An inspired and eclectic art collection displayed in a harmonious purpose-built museum in Pollok Park. See p.233

* **"Glesga nightlife"** Sample the glamour and the grit with *cocktails at the Rogano* followed by a pint of heavy at the *Horseshoe Bar*. See p.238 & p.240

* **New Lanark** Stay for next to nothing in the hostel at this fascinating eighteenth-century planned village. See p.250

▲ The "Armadillo", clydeside

5

Glasgow and the Clyde

Rejuvenated, upbeat **Glasgow**, Scotland's largest city, has not traditionally enjoyed the best of reputations. Set on the banks of the mighty River Clyde, this former industrial giant can still initially seem a grey and depressing place, with the M8 motorway screeching through the centre and dilapidated housing estates on its outskirts. However, Glasgow's image of itself changed irrevocably in 1990 when it energetically embraced its status as European City of Culture. Few visitors will be left in any doubt that the city is, in its own idiosyncratic way, a cultured and dynamic place well worth getting to know.

The city has much to offer, including some of the most imaginative museums and galleries in Britain – among them the showcase **Burrell Collection** and popular **Kelvingrove Art Gallery and Museum** – nearly all of which are free. Glasgow's **architecture** is some of the most striking in the UK, from the restored eighteenth-century warehouses of the **Merchant City** to the hulking Victorian prosperity of George Square. Most distinctive of all is the work of local luminary Charles Rennie Mackintosh, whose elegantly streamlined Art Nouveau designs appear all over the city, reaching their apotheosis in the stunning **School of Art**. Development of the old shipyards of the Clyde, notably in the space-age shapes of the new **Glasgow Science Centre**, hint at yet another string to the city's bow: combining design with innovation. The metropolis also boasts thriving live-music venues, distinctive places to eat and drink, busy theatres, concert halls and an opera house. Above all, the feature that best defines the individualism and peculiar attraction of the city is its **people**, whether rough-edged comedians on the football terraces or style-obsessed youth hitting the designer bars.

Despite all the upbeat hype, Glasgow's gentrification has passed by deprived inner-city areas such as the **East End**, home of the **Barras market** and some staunchly change-resistant pubs. Indeed, even in the more fashionable quarters of Glasgow, there's a gritty edge that's never far away, reinforcing a peculiar mix of grime and glitz that the city seems to have patented.

Glasgow is the obvious base from which to explore the **Clyde Valley and coast**, made easily accessible by a reliable train service. Chief among the draws is the remarkable eighteenth-century **New Lanark** mills and workers' village, a World Heritage Site, while other day-trips might take you to Charles Rennie Mackintosh's **Hill House** in Helensburgh or on a boat heading "doon the watter" towards the scenic Argyll sea lochs, past the old shipbuilding centres on the Clyde estuary.

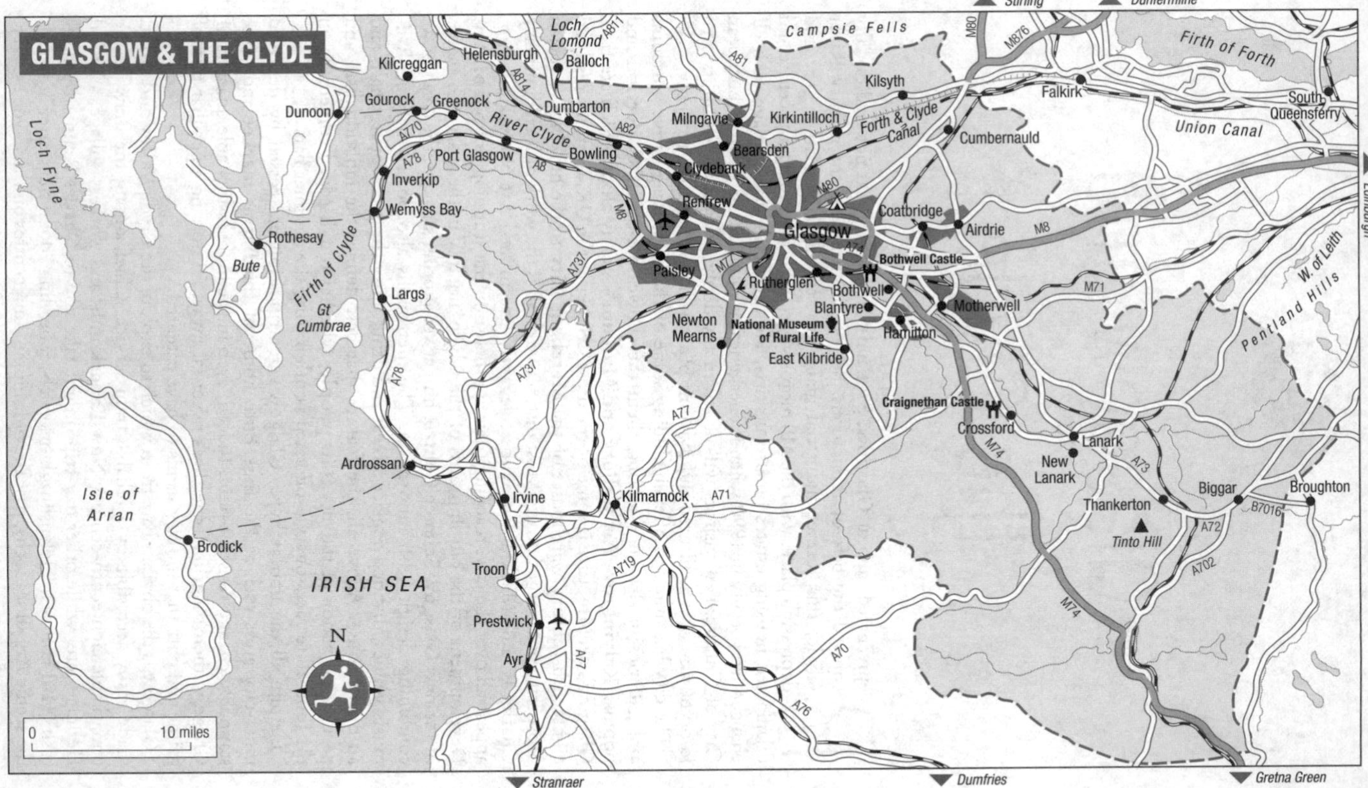
GLASGOW & THE CLYDE
Stirling
Dunfermline
Edinburgh
Stranraer
Dumfries
Gretna Green
Campsie Fells
Firth of Forth
Union Canal
Forth & Clyde Canal
Loch Lomond
Loch Fyne
River Clyde
Firth of Clyde
Pentland Hills
W. of Leith
Kilcreggan
Helensburgh
Balloch
Dunoon
Gourock
Greenock
Dumbarton
Milngavie
Kirkintilloch
Kilsyth
Falkirk
South Queensferry
Cumbernauld
Port Glasgow
Bowling
Bearsden
Clydebank
Inverkip
Wemyss Bay
Renfrew
Glasgow
Coatbridge
Airdrie
Rothesay
Bute
Paisley
Rutherglen
Bothwell Castle
Bothwell
Blantyre
Motherwell
Hamilton
Largs
Gt Cumbrae
Newton Mearns
National Museum of Rural Life
East Kilbride
Craignethan Castle
Crossford
Lanark
New Lanark
Ardrossan
Isle of Arran
Irvine
Kilmarnock
Thankerton
Biggar
Broughton
Tinto Hill
Brodick
IRISH SEA
Troon
Prestwick
Ayr
N
0
10 miles
M80
M876
M8
M71
M77
M74
A74
A81
A811
A814
A82
A770
A78
A8
A737
A77
A71
A719
A70
A76
A73
A72
A702
B7016

Glasgow

GLASGOW's earliest history, like so much else in this surprisingly romantic city, is obscured in a swirl of myth. The city's name is said to derive from the Celtic *Glas-cu*, which loosely translates as "the dear, green place" – a tag that the tourist board is keen to exploit as an antidote to the sooty images of popular imagination. It is generally agreed that the first settlers arrived in the sixth century to join. Christian missionary **Kentigern** – later to become St Mungo – in his newly founded monastery on the banks of the tiny Molendinar Burn.

William the Lionheart gave the town an official charter in 1175, after which it continued to grow in importance, peaking in the mid-fifteenth century when the **university** – the second in Scotland after St Andrews – was founded on Kentigern's site. This led to the establishment of an archbishopric, and hence city status, in 1492, and, due to its situation on a large, navigable river, Glasgow soon expanded into a major industrial **port**. The first cargo of tobacco from Virginia offloaded in Glasgow in 1674, and the 1707 Act of Union between Scotland and England – despite demonstrations against it in Glasgow – led to a boom in trade with the colonies until American independence. Following the **Industrial Revolution** and James Watt's innovations in steam power, coal from the abundant seams of Lanarkshire fuelled the ironworks all around the Clyde, worked by the cheap hands of the Highlanders and, later, those fleeing the Irish potato famine of the 1840s.

The **Victorian** age transformed Glasgow beyond recognition. The population mushroomed from 77,000 in 1801 to nearly 800,000 at the end of the century, and new tenement blocks swept into the suburbs in an attempt to cope with the choking influxes of people. Two vast and stately **International Exhibitions** were held in 1888 and 1901 to showcase the city and its industries to the outside world, necessitating the construction of huge civic monoliths such as the Kelvingrove Art Gallery and the Council Chambers in George Square. At this time Glasgow revelled in the title of the "Second City of the Empire", an unexpected epithet for a place that rarely acknowledges second place in anything.

By the turn of the twentieth century, Glasgow's industries had been honed into one massive **shipbuilding** culture. Everything from tugboats to transatlantic liners was fashioned out of sheet metal in the yards that straddled the Clyde from Gourock to Rutherglen. In the harsh economic climate of the 1930s, however, unemployment spiralled, and Glasgow could do little to counter its popular image as a city dominated by inebriate violence and (having absorbed vast numbers of Irish emigrants) sectarian tensions. The **Gorbals** area in particular became notorious as one of the worst slums in Europe.

Shipbuilding, and many associated industries, died away almost completely in the 1960s and 1970s, leaving the city depressed, jobless and directionless. Then, in the 1980s, the self-promotion began, starting with the upbeat "Glasgow's Miles Better" campaign in 1983, and snowballing towards the 1988 Garden Festival and the year-long party as European City of Culture in 1990. Glasgow then beat off competition from Edinburgh and Liverpool to become UK City of Architecture and Design in 1999, and in 2007 won the right to host the **Commonwealth Games** of 2014. These various titles have helped to reinforce the impression that Glasgow, despite its many problems, has successfully broken the industrial shackles of the past and evolved into a city of stature and confidence.

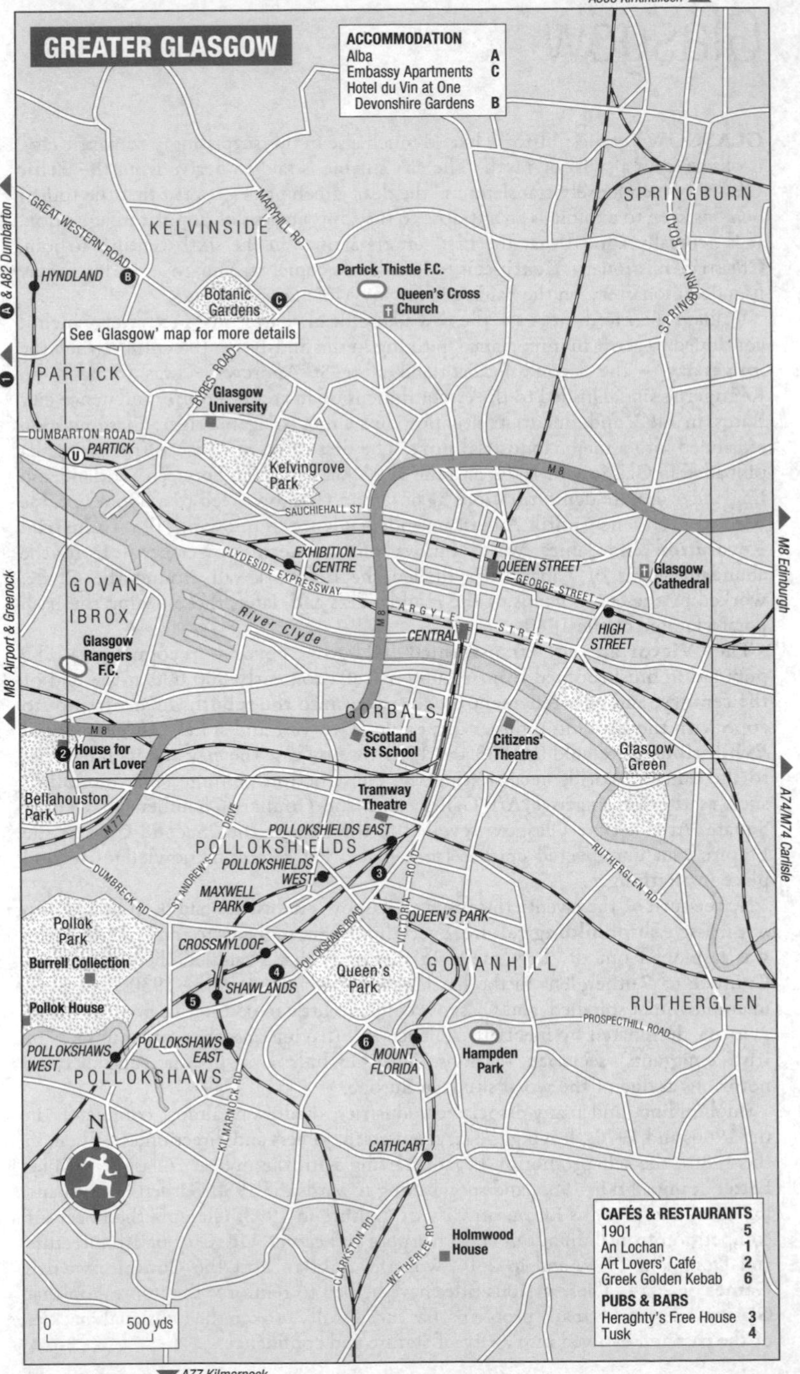
GREATER GLASGOW
ACCOMMODATION
Alba A
Embassy Apartments C
Hotel du Vin at One Devonshire Gardens B
A803 Kirkintilloch
SPRINGBURN
SPRINGBURN ROAD
KELVINSIDE
GREAT WESTERN ROAD
MARYHILL RD
A82 Dumbarton
HYNDLAND
Botanic Gardens
Partick Thistle F.C.
Queen's Cross Church
See 'Glasgow' map for more details
PARTICK
BYRES ROAD
Glasgow University
DUMBARTON ROAD
PARTICK
Kelvingrove Park
M8
SAUCHIEHALL ST
EXHIBITION CENTRE
CLYDESIDE EXPRESSWAY
QUEEN STREET
GEORGE STREET
Glasgow Cathedral
M8 Edinburgh
GOVAN
IBROX
River Clyde
ARGYLE STREET
CENTRAL
HIGH STREET
M8 Airport & Greenock
Glasgow Rangers F.C.
GORBALS
House for an Art Lover
Scotland St School
Citizens' Theatre
Glasgow Green
Bellahouston Park
M77
Tramway Theatre
POLLOKSHIELDS EAST
POLLOKSHIELDS
POLLOKSHIELDS WEST
ST ANDREW'S DRIVE
A74/M74 Carlisle
RUTHERGLEN RD
DUMBRECK RD
MAXWELL PARK
VICTORIA ROAD
QUEEN'S PARK
Pollok Park
Burrell Collection
CROSSMYLOOF
POLLOKSHAWS ROAD
Queen's Park
GOVANHILL
SHAWLANDS
Pollok House
RUTHERGLEN
PROSPECTHILL ROAD
POLLOKSHAWS WEST
POLLOKSHAWS EAST
MOUNT FLORIDA
Hampden Park
POLLOKSHAWS
KILMARNOCK RD
N
CATHCART
CLARKSTON RD
WETHERLEE RD
Holmwood House
0 500 yds
CAFÉS & RESTAURANTS
1901 5
An Lochan 1
Art Lovers' Café 2
Greek Golden Kebab 6
PUBS & BARS
Heraghty's Free House 3
Tusk 4
A77 Kilmarnock

Arrival

Glasgow International Airport (Ⓣ0844/481 5555, Ⓦwww.glasgowairport.com) is at Abbotsinch, eight miles southwest of the city – not to be confused with Glasgow Prestwick Airport, which is thirty miles south near Ayr. From the international airport, the 24-hour Glasgow Flyer bus (20min; £4.50) runs from bus stop 1 into the central Buchanan Street bus station every ten minutes during the day. Airport taxis charge around £18–20. **Glasgow Prestwick** is 45 minutes away from the city by train; for more details see p.196.

Nearly all **trains** from England come into **Central station**, which sits over Argyle Street, one of the city's main shopping thoroughfares. Bus #398 from the front entrance on Gordon Street shuttles every ten minutes to **Queen Street station**, at the corner of George Square, terminus for trains serving Edinburgh and the north. The walk between the two takes less than ten minutes. Bus #398 also stops at **Buchanan Street bus station**, arrival point for regional and intercity **coaches**.

Orientation

Glasgow is a sprawling place, built on some punishingly steep hills, and with no really obvious focus, although, as most transport services converge on the area around **Argyle Street** and, 200yd to the north, **George Square**, this pocket is the most obvious candidate for city-centre status. However, with the renovated, upmarket **Merchant City** immediately to the east and the main business and commercial areas to the west, the centre, when the term is used, actually refers to a large swathe from **Charing Cross** and the M8 in the west through to **Glasgow Green** in the run down **East End**.

The **West End** begins just over a mile west of Central station, and covers most of the area beyond the M8 motorway. In the nineteenth century, as the East End tumbled into poverty, the West End ascended the social scale with great speed, a process crowned by the arrival of the **university**. Today, this is still very much the student quarter of Glasgow, though one with a distinctly decorous air, with graceful avenues and parks, and inexpensive, interesting shops and cafés.

While the Clyde figures large in Glaswegian identity, it has generally had a divisive effect, relegating the "**Southside**" to secondary status. The redevelopment of **Clydeside** is going some way to adjust that perspective. Parts of the Southside have always been very pleasant: the leafy enclaves of **Queen's Park** are home to the national football stadium, Hampden Park, with **Pollok Park** and the **Burrell Collection** undisputed highlights of the city. The Southside attractions can be easily reached by bus.

Information

The city's efficient **tourist office** is located at 11 George Square (April & May Mon–Sat 9am–6pm, Sun 10am–6pm; June & Sept Mon–Sat 10am–7pm, Sun 10am–6pm; July & Aug Mon–Sat 9am–8pm, Sun 10am–6pm; Sept–March Mon–Sat 9am–6pm; Ⓣ0141/204 4400, Ⓦwww.seeglasgow.com). From outside the tourist office on George Square a couple of hop-on-hop-off **tour buses** with commentary set off at regular intervals around a loop that incorporates the cathedral, Clydeside, the university and West End as well as the main sights in the city centre. There's also an **airport** branch of VisitScotland in the international arrivals hall (daily 7.30am–5pm, except Oct–April Sun 8am–5pm; Ⓣ0141/848 4440).

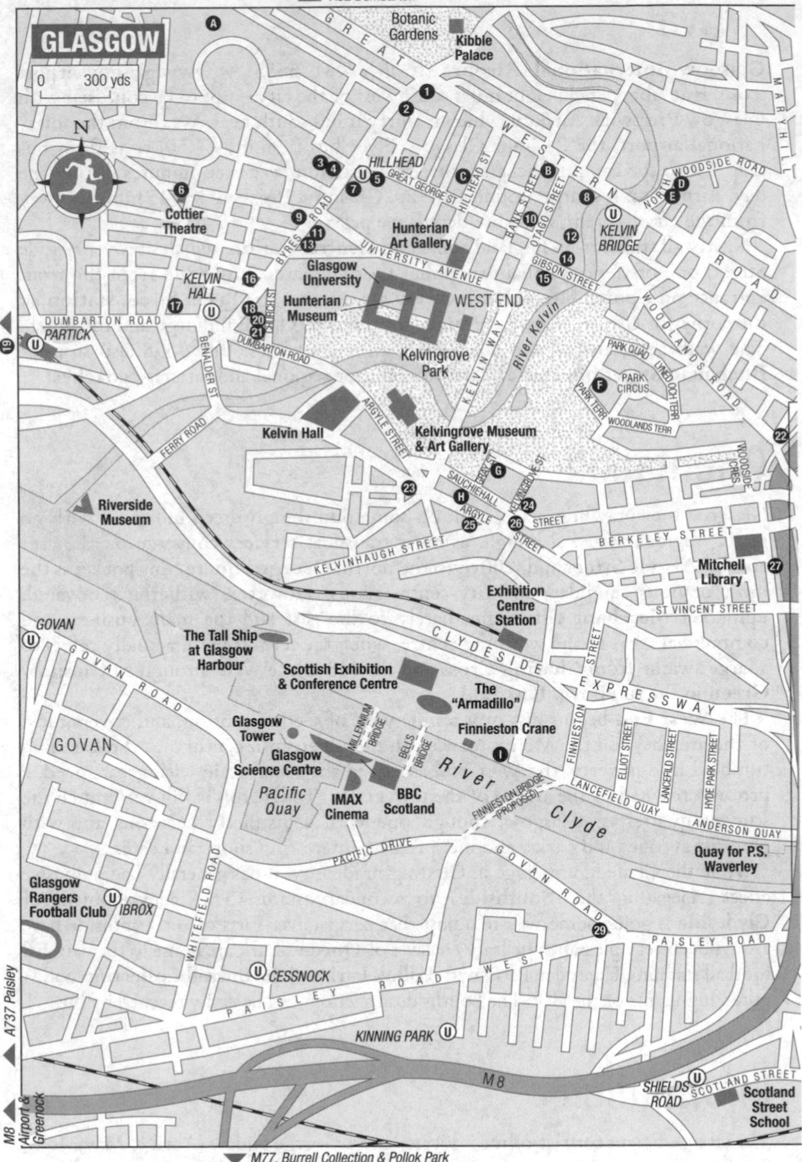

City transport

Walking is the best way of exploring any one part of the city. However, as the main sights are scattered – the West End, for example, is a good thirty-minute walk from the centre – you'll probably need to use the comprehensive **public transport** system.

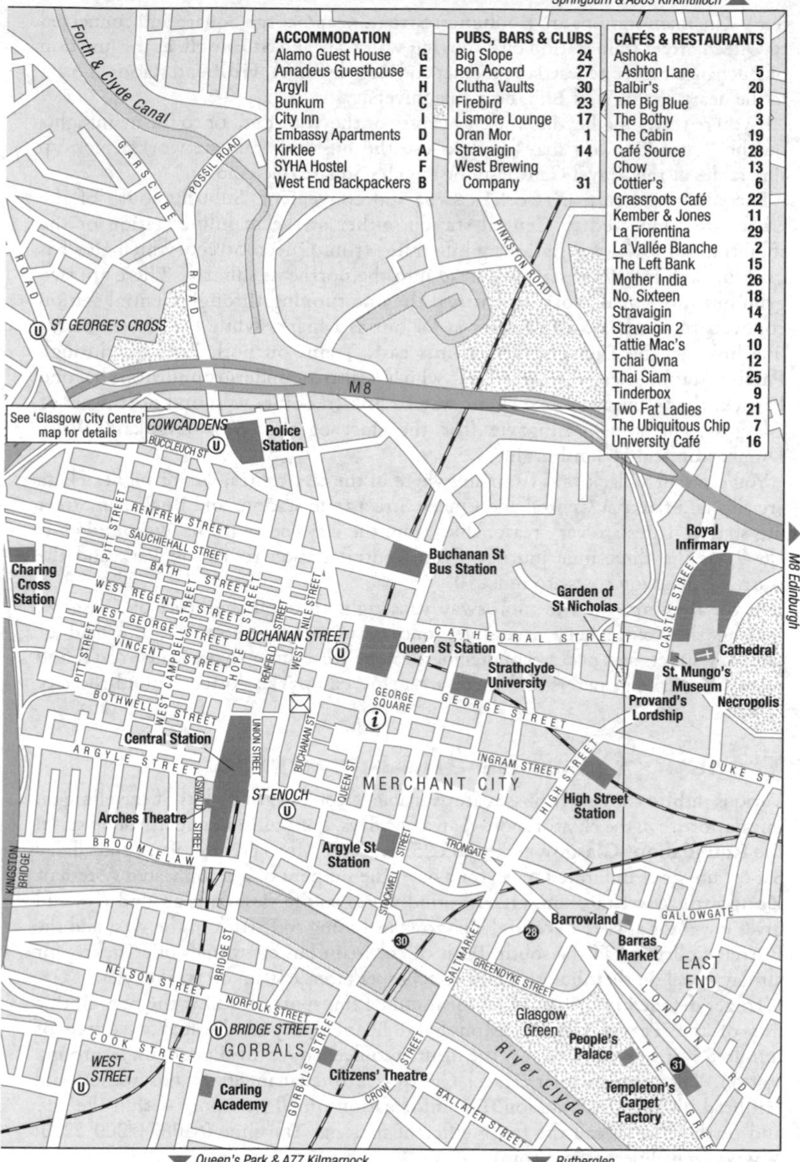

The best way to get between the city centre and the West End is to use the **Underground** (Mon–Sat 6.30am–11pm, Sun 10am–6.30pm), whose stations are marked with a large orange U. Affectionately known as the "Clockwork Orange" (there's only one, circular route and the trains are a garish bright orange), the service is extremely easy to use. There's a flat fare of £1.20, or you can buy a **day ticket** (called a Discovery Ticket) for £3.50 (Mon–Sat after 9.30am and all day

Sun). The main stations are **Buchanan Street**, near George Square and connected to Queen Street train station by a moving walkway, and **St Enoch**, at the junction of Buchanan Street pedestrian precinct and Argyle Street. **Hillhead** station is bang in the heart of the West End, near the university.

If you're travelling beyond the city centre or the West End, or to the main sights on the Southside, you may need to use the bus and train networks; pick up timetables at the Travel Centre on St Enoch's Square (see below).

The suburban **train** network is swift and convenient. Suburbs south of the Clyde are connected to Central station, either at the mainline station or the subterranean low-level station, while trains from Queen Street (which also has mainline and low-level stations) head into the northeast suburbs. There are two grim but functional **cross-city lines**: the one running through Central station connects to southeastern districts as far out as Lanark, while the Queen Street line links to the East End and points east. Trains on both lines go through **Partick** station, near the West End, which is also an underground stop; beyond Partick, the trains are an excellent way to link to points west and northwest of Glasgow, including Milngavie (for the start of the West Highland Way), Dumbarton and Helensburgh.

You can hail a black **taxi** from anywhere in the city centre, day or night. There are also taxi ranks at Central and Queen Street train stations and Buchanan Street bus station. Fares are very reasonable; from the city centre to the West End costs £6–7, or the three-mile journey from Central station to Pollok Park and the Burrell Collection costs around £10.

As for **driving**, the M8 motorway runs right through the heart of Glasgow, making the centre very accessible; once you're there, however, the grid of one-way streets and pedestrian precincts can be frustrating to navigate. You'll find plenty of parking meters and there are many **car parks** dotted around the city centre.

Transport passes and information

Various **public transport passes** are available if you plan to do lots of travelling on one day or are in the city for more than a few days. For train and underground travel the **Roundabout Glasgow** ticket (£5.25; available Mon–Fri after 9am, and all day Sat & Sun) gives unlimited travel for a day. The simplest of a complicated system of **Zonecards**, covering train, underground, buses and ferries, costs around £14 and gives travel for a week in central Glasgow, including to Partick in the west and the Burrell Collection in the south. Both of the main bus companies offer tickets for all-day travel on their buses, which are cheaper after 9.30am on weekdays.

To get detailed information on local public transport, head for the neo-Gothic hut of the **Travel Centre** (Mon–Sat 8.30am–5.30pm), located a couple of hundred yards southwest of the tourist office above St Enoch underground station. There are smaller Travel Centres at Buchanan Street bus station and Hillhead underground station. For information on all transport within the city and further afield, call the fairly efficient national Traveline (Ⓣ0871/200 2233, Ⓦwww.travelinescotland.com).

City tours

City Sightseeing (April–Oct daily 9.30am–4.30pm; £10) run tours of Glasgow's sights by **open-top bus**, which leave every half-hour from George Square on a continuous circuit of all the major attractions in the city centre and West End, allowing you to get on and off as you please. Tickets are valid for two days.

Accommodation

There's a good range of **accommodation** in Glasgow, from a large, well-run youth hostel through to some highly fashionable (and not over-priced) designer hotels in the centre. The majority of the best guesthouses and B&Bs can be found in the West End. Given that many hotels are business-oriented, you can often negotiate good deals at weekends. For locations, see the maps on p.210, pp.212–213 & pp.218–219.

Hotels and guesthouses

It's worth booking ahead at **hotels and guesthouses** to ensure a good room, especially in summer. If you're prepared to sacrifice character, ambience and home comforts, you'll often find the cheapest decent rooms in the city at the **budget chain hotels** found throughout the city centre. Big players include Ibis (Ⓣ0141/225 6000, Ⓦwww.ibishotel.com), Travelodge (Ⓣ0871/984 6141, Ⓦwww.travelodge.co.uk), Premier Inn (Ⓣ0871/527 8440, Ⓦwww.premierinn.co.uk) and Express by Holiday Inn (Ⓣ0141/331 6800, Ⓦwww.hiexpressglasgow.co.uk) – these last two also have hotels in a handy position near Glasgow International Airport.

City centre

ABode Glasgow 129 Bath St Ⓣ0141/221 6789, Ⓦwww.abodehotels.co.uk. Part of the upmarket mini-chain linked to chef Michael Caines, with sixty stylish rooms right in the city centre and excellent dining on site. ❻

Adelaide's 209 Bath St Ⓣ0141/248 4970, Ⓦwww.adelaides.co.uk. Eight simple, functional rooms (some good for families) in a beautifully restored church building, run by pleasant staff as part of a broad-thinking, approachable Baptist church community. ❸

Babbity Bowster 16–18 Blackfriars St, off High St Ⓣ0141/552 5055. Best known as a pub (see p.240), *Babbity Bowster* also features six plain but serviceable rooms that provide visitors with a great Merchant City location. The rate doesn't include breakfast. ❸

Blythswood Square 11 Blythswood Square Ⓣ0141/248 5888, Ⓦwww.townhousecompany.com. A swish but respectful conversion of the landmark Georgian Royal Scottish Automobile Club, on one of the city's loveliest squares. Features a luxury spa. ❼

The Brunswick 106 Brunswick St Ⓣ0141/552 0001, Ⓦwww.brunswickhotel.co.uk. A small, independent and individual designer hotel in the heart of the Merchant City; fashionable but good value with minimalist furniture and a smart bar and restaurant. Ask for a room on one of the higher levels to avoid traffic noise. ❸

Malmaison 278 West George St Ⓣ0141/572 1000, Ⓦwww.malmaison.com. Glasgow's version of the sleek, chic mini-chain, an austere Grecian-temple frontage masking a superbly comfortable designer hotel. ❼

Mark's Hotel 110 Bath St Ⓣ0141/353 0800, Ⓦwww.markshotels.com. Angular, glass-fronted central hotel, with rooftop views from the upper floors and 103 smartly appointed rooms. Double, triple and family rooms available at a year-round flat rate. ❺

Millennium George Square Ⓣ0141/332 6711, Ⓦwww.millenniumhotels.co.uk. The location on George Square couldn't be more central, and this new conversion of a row of tall Victorian townhouses is a cut above the usual bland chain hotels. Check the website for discount deals. ❹

Park Inn Glasgow City Centre 2 Port Dundas Place Ⓣ0141/333 1500, Ⓦwww.glasgowparkinn.co.uk. Big, sassy and classy modern hotel with a spa, trendy restaurants and lots of mod cons. ❻

Pipers' Tryst 30–34 McPhater St Ⓣ0141/353 0220, Ⓦwww.thepipingcentre.co.uk. Eight sound-proofed, (fortunately), hotel-grade rooms attached to the bagpiping centre; a café on the ground floor (Mon–Sat) serves breakfasts and evening meals. ❸

Saint Judes 190 Bath St Ⓣ0141/352 8800, Ⓦwww.saintjudes.com. Elegant contemporary boutique hotel with six rooms and some flash designer touches. ❻

West End and Clydeside

Alamo Guest House 46 Gray St Ⓣ0141/339 2395, Ⓦwww.alamoguesthouse.com. Good-value, family-run boarding house next to Kelvingrove Park. Small but comfortable rooms, including two singles. ❶

Amadeus Guesthouse 441 North Woodside Rd Ⓣ0141/339 8257, Ⓦwww.amadeusguesthouse.co.uk. Stylish en-suite rooms in a welcoming Victorian townhouse. It's handily located near Great Western Road but on a surprisingly quiet street, opposite the deep green gully of the River Kelvin. ❶

Argyll 973 Sauchiehall St Ⓣ0141/337 3313, Ⓦwww.argyllhotelglasgow.co.uk. Lots of tartan trimmings, but this well-run hotel near Kelvingrove Museum and Art Gallery has neat rooms and friendly staff. ❺

City Inn Finnieston Quay ⓣ0141/240 1002, ⓦwww.cityinn.com. One of the better of the chain hotels, made interesting by its riverside location right under the Finnieston Crane, with stylish rooms and competitive rates. ❺

Hotel du Vin at One Devonshire Gardens 1 Devonshire Gardens, Great Western Rd ⓣ0141/339 2001, ⓦwww.hotelduvin.com. Glasgow's most exclusive and exquisite small hotel, set in a handsome row of converted townhouses a 10min walk up the Great Western Road from the Botanic Gardens. ❼

Kirklee 11 Kensington Gate ⓣ0141/334 5555, ⓦwww.kirkleehotel.co.uk. Characterful West End B&B in a red-brick Edwardian townhouse, with antique furniture and walls crammed with paintings and etchings. ❹

Hostels and self-catering

Glasgow isn't short of **hostel** bed space, thanks to the seven-storey *Euro Hostel* smack in the centre of the city at 318 Clyde St (ⓣ0141/222 2828, ⓦwww.euro-hostels.co.uk). Its 360 beds are all bunks but they're in smart en-suite rooms sleeping two, four, six or more – some of which have great views. The popular and well-equipped *SYHA Hostel*, 7–8 Park Terrace (ⓣ0870/004 1119, ⓦwww.syha.org.uk), is located in a wonderful townhouse in one of the West End's grandest terraces. All the dorms are en suite, and there's a large apartment with park views for families. It's a ten-minute walk south of Kelvinbridge underground station; bus #44 from the city centre leaves you with a short stroll west up Woodlands Road.

The West End is home to two decent **independent hostels**: *Bunkum*, 26 Hillhead St (ⓣ0141 581 4481, ⓦwww.bunkumglasgow.co.uk); and *West End Backpackers* at 3 Bank St (ⓣ0141/337 7000, ⓦwww.glasgowwestendbackpackers.co.uk). A little further out in Anniesland, *Alba* at 6 Fifth Ave is a spruce and popular townhouse hostel (ⓣ0141 334 2952, ⓦwww.albahostelglasgow.co.uk).

Self-catering

Low-priced if rather bland **self-catering** rooms and flats are available at the University of Glasgow (ⓣ0141/330 4116, ⓦwww.cvso.co.uk) from June to mid-September, mostly located in the West End, with prices starting at around £19 per person per night. The University of Strathclyde (ⓣ0141/553 4148, ⓦwww.rescat.strath.ac.uk) has various sites available during the same period, most of which are gathered around the cathedral: B&B in single rooms is available near the main campus in Cathedral Street starting at £22.50 per person per night, though you can get four-bed rooms for under £60 if you're staying a minimum of four nights.

Queensgate Apartments (ⓣ0141/339 1615, ⓦwww.queensgateapartments.com) feature a choice of characterful and cosy flats in traditional West End tenement buildings, while *Embassy Apartments*, 8 Kelvin Drive (ⓣ0141/946 6698, ⓦwww.glasgowhotelsandapartments.co.uk; ❹), have useful one- to six-person self-catering apartments in locations near Byres Road and at Kelvinbridge, available on a nightly basis. Slicker serviced apartments in a magnificent Scots Baronial building in the Merchant City are available from *Fraser Suites* at 1 Albion St (ⓣ0141 553 4288, ⓦglasgow.frasershospitality.com; ❺).

The City Centre

Glasgow's large **city centre** is ranged across the north bank of the River Clyde. At its geographical heart is **George Square**, a nineteenth-century municipal showpiece crowned by the enormous **City Chambers** at its eastern end. Behind this lies one of the greatest marketing successes of the 1980s, the **Merchant City**, an area that blends magnificent Victorian architecture with yuppie conversions. The grand buildings and trendy cafés cling to the borders of the run-down **East End**, a strongly working-class district that chooses to ignore its rather showy neighbour. The oldest part of Glasgow, around the **cathedral**, lies immediately north of the East End.

Called by poet John Betjeman "the greatest Victorian city in the world", Glasgow's commercial core spreads west of George Square, and was built mostly on a large grid system with ruler-straight roads rising up severe hills to grand, sandblasted buildings. The same style was copied by many North American cities, and indeed parts of Glasgow have been pressed into service as nineteenth-century New York in films such as *House of Mirth*. The main shopping areas here are **Argyle Street**, running parallel to the river, and **Buchanan Street**, which links Argyle Street to the pedestrianized shopping thoroughfare, **Sauchiehall Street**. Just to the northwest of here is Charles Rennie Mackintosh's famous **Glasgow School of Art**. Lying between the commercial bustle of Argyle and Sauchiehall streets, and to the immediate west of Buchanan Street, are the contours of an ice age drumlin, now known as **Blythswood Hill**. In comparison with the bustling shopping parades surrounding it on three sides, this area is remarkably quiet and reserved, with streets of Georgian buildings crowned by neat Blythswood Square.

George Square and around

Now hemmed in by the city's grinding traffic, the imposing architecture of **George Square** reflects the confidence of Glasgow's Victorian age. The wide-open plaza almost has a continental airiness about it, although there isn't much subtlety about the eighty-foot column rising up at its centre, which is topped by a statue of Sir Walter Scott. Haphazardly dotted around the great writer's plinth are a number of dignified statues of assorted luminaries, ranging from Queen Victoria to Scots heroes such as James Watt and Robbie Burns. The florid splendour of the **City Chambers**, opened by Queen Victoria in 1888, occupies the entire eastern end of the square. Built from wealth gained by colonial trade and heavy industry, it epitomizes the aspirations and optimism of late Victorian city elders. Its intricately detailed facade includes high-minded friezes typical of the era: the four nations which then comprised the United Kingdom at the feet of the throned queen, the British colonies and allegorical figures representing Religion, Virtue and Knowledge. You can head inside and wander around the ground floor, where you'll see domed mosaic ceilings and two mighty Italian marble stairwells, but to get any further you'll need to join one of the **guided tours** of the labyrinthine interior (Mon–Fri 10.30am & 2.30pm; free).

The Gallery of Modern Art

Queen Street leads south from George Square to **Royal Exchange Square**, where the focal point is the graceful mansion built in 1775 for tobacco lord William Cunninghame. This was the most ostentatious of the Glasgow merchants' homes and, having served as the city's Royal Exchange and central library, now houses the **Gallery of Modern Art** (Mon–Wed & Sat 10am–5pm, Thurs 10am–8pm, Fri & Sun 11am–5pm; free). Surrounded by controversy from the day it opened in 1996, GOMA has not lived up to the potential of the marvellous building and location, though as it's free it does merit a quick visit. The mirrored reception area leads you straight into the spacious ground-floor gallery, a striking room with rows of Corinthian pillars and huge windows. It's principally used for temporary exhibitions of conceptual art. Down in the basement there's a library and an unenticing café, while the smaller galleries on the two upper floors are either linked together for larger exhibitions or used to show smaller themed shows.

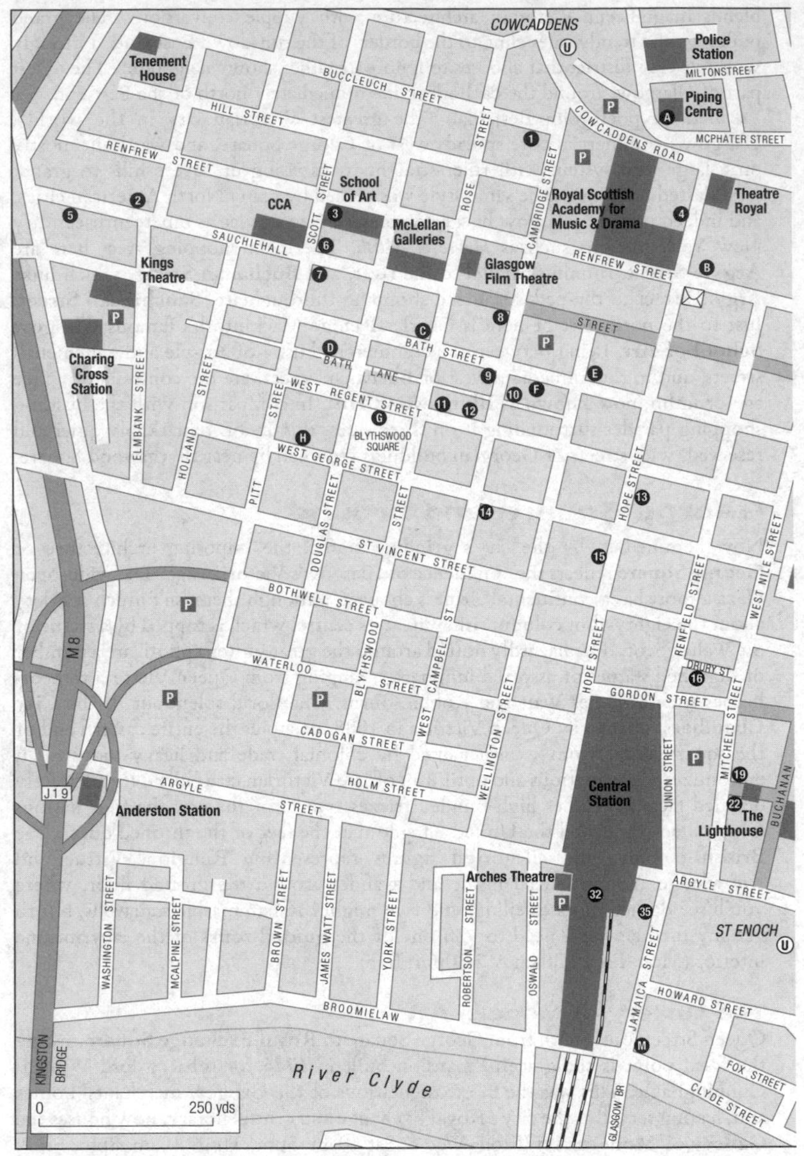

Along Buchanan Street

Buchanan Street runs north–south one block west of George Square, defining Glasgow's main shopping district. At the southern end of the street is **Princes Square**, one of the most stylish and imaginative shopping centres in the country, hollowed out of the innards of a soft sandstone building. The interior, all recherché Art Deco and ornate ironwork, has lots of pricey fashionable shops, set to a soothing background of classical music.

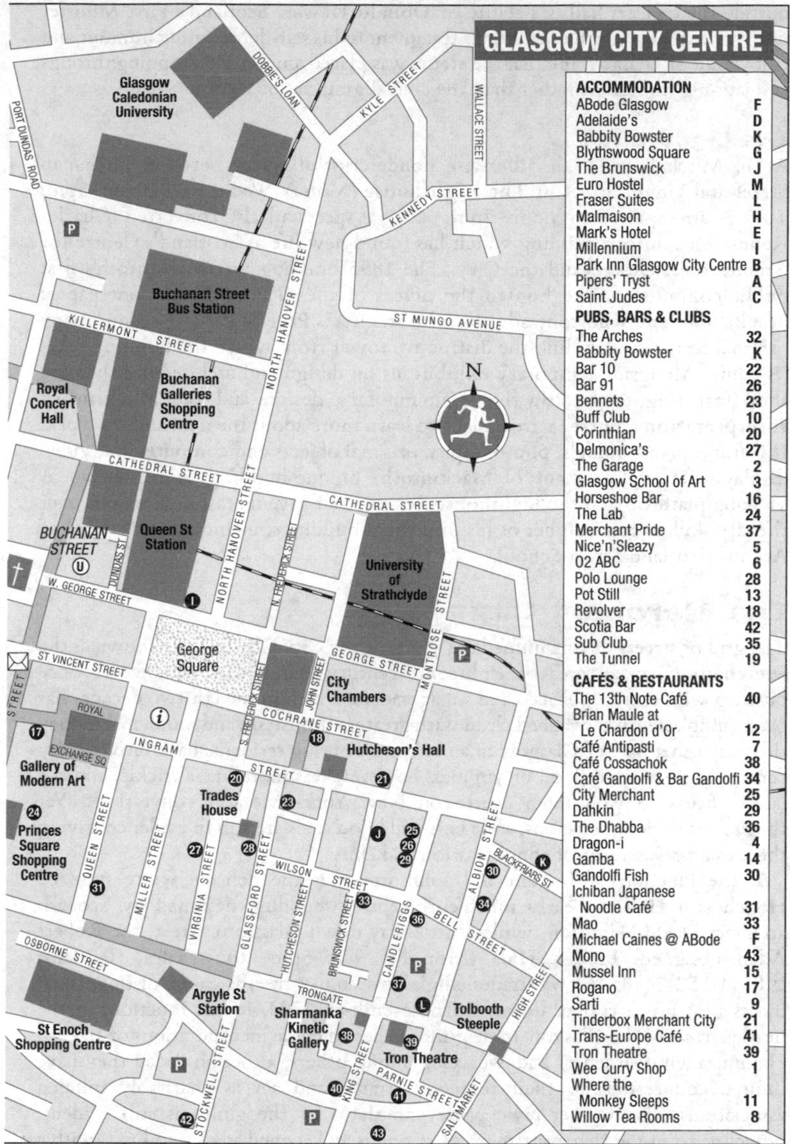

Glaswegians' voracious appetite for shopping is fed further at the northern end of Buchanan Street, just beyond the underground station, in the **Buchanan Galleries**, a bewilderingly vast shopping mall of some 600,000 square feet stuffed with most of the predictable chain stores. Next door is the anonymous £30-million **Royal Concert Hall**, with only three huge flagpoles protruding to proclaim that this is, in fact, a building of note. The showpiece hall does, however, have an excellent auditorium that plays host to world-class musical events. Standing outside the concert hall is a statue of **Donald Dewar**, Scotland's First Minister until his untimely death in 2000; it's testament to his self-depreciating humour and enjoyment of Glasgow life that the statue was placed among the shopping throngs and late-night revellers rather than the civic dignitaries of George Square.

The Lighthouse

At 11 Mitchell Lane, an otherwise nondescript alleyway between Buchanan Street and Union Street, is **The Lighthouse** (Mon & Wed–Sat 10.30am–5pm, Tues 11am–5pm, Sun noon–5pm; £3), a spectacularly converted Charles Rennie Mackintosh building which has found new life as Scotland's Centre for Architecture, Design and the City. The 1895 building was Mackintosh's first public commission, and housed the offices of the *Glasgow Herald* newspaper; despite glass and sandstone additions by architects Page & Park, it retains many original features, including the distinctive tower from which the building takes its name. Alongside temporary exhibitions on design and architecture there's a shop featuring some attractive contemporary design and the **Mackintosh Interpretation Centre**, a great place to learn more about the man and his work. It features plans, models, photographs, original objects and computer and video displays that explore many of Mackintosh's unique buildings and interiors. A viewing platform and the Lighthouse Tower itself give fantastic views out over the city skyline to a number of his important buildings, including the School of Art and Scotland Street School.

The Merchant City

The grid of streets that lie immediately east of the City Chambers is known as the **Merchant City**, an area of eighteenth-century warehouses and homes once bustling with cotton, tobacco and sugar traders, which in the last two decades has been sandblasted and swabbed clean with greater enthusiasm and municipal money than any other part of Glasgow in an attempt to bring residents back into the city centre. The expected flood of yuppies, however, was more like a trickle, and the latest efforts to woo them centre on New York-style loft conversions. Yet the expensive designer shops, style bars and bijou cafés are still in evidence, giving the area a pervasive air of sophistication and chic.

At the junction of Ingram and John streets is the delicate white spire of **Hutcheson Hall**, an early nineteenth-century building designed by Scottish architect David Hamilton, while a little way down Glassford Street, the Robert Adam-designed **Trades Hall** (Mon–Fri 9am–5pm, tour Tues 10.30am; Ⓣ0141/552 2418, Ⓦwww.tradeshallglasgow.co.uk; free) is easily distinguished by its neat green copper dome. Purpose-built in 1794, it still functions as the headquarters of the Glasgow trade guilds. These include incorporations of Bakers, Hammermen, Gardeners and Weavers, among others, although today they have limited connections to their respective trades and act as charitably minded associations. The former civic pride and status of the guilds is still evident, however, from the rich assortment of carvings and stained-glass windows, with a lively pictorial representation of the different trades in the silk frieze around the walls of the first-floor grand hall. Visitors are free to look around the building, restricted only if there is a function taking place.

Trongate 103 and Sharmanka Kinetic Gallery

Behind a sleek glass frontage amongst otherwise nondescript and downmarket shops on Trongate you'll find **Trongate 103** (Tues–Sat 10am–5pm, Sun noon–5pm; open Thurs till 9pm Feb–Dec; Ⓦwww.trongate103.com), a sparkling new arts centre that incorporates a number of organizations including the Glasgow Print Studio, Street Level Photoworks and Transmission Gallery. The six-storey converted building is used to show printmaking, contemporary photography, video work and ceramics in airy light-filled spaces.

Trongate 103 is also home to Glasgow's most unusual attraction. Founded by Russian émigrés Eduard Bersudsky and Tatyana Jakovskaya, the **Sharmanka Kinetic Gallery** (Ⓣ0141/552 7080, Ⓦwww.sharmanka.com) is like a mad inventor's magical workshop, with dozens of allegorical contraptions made from old wheels, levers, lights, carved wooden figures and scrap metal which spark into life during performances. A unique art form, Sharmanka (Russian for barrel organ or hurdy-gurdy) is at once hypnotic, playful and deeply poignant, with its mechanical sculptures, or "kinemats" imprisoned in their relentless routine, while choreographed lighting draws you from one part of the show to the next and rather sinister fairground-style music plays in the background. It takes half an hour for the sculptures to "perform", so the full programmes are only run a few times during the week (Wed–Sun 3pm, Sat & Sun also 1pm; Thurs & Sun 7pm; 70min show; £5/8).

The East End

East of Glasgow Cross, down Gallowgate beyond the train lines, lies the **East End**, the district that perhaps most closely corresponds to the old perception of Glasgow. Hemmed in by Glasgow Green to the south and the old university to the west, this densely packed industrial area essentially created the city's wealth. The Depression caused the closure of many factories, leaving communities stranded in an industrial wasteland. Today, isolated pubs, tatty shops and cafés sit amid this dereliction, in sharp contrast to the gloss of the Merchant City only a few blocks to the west. You're definitely off the tourist trail, but unless you're here after dark it's not as threatening as it may feel, and there's no doubt that the area offers a rich flavour of working-class Glasgow.

Three hundred yards from Glasgow Cross down either London Road or Gallowgate is **The Barras**, Glasgow's largest and most popular weekend market (Sat & Sun 10am–5pm; Ⓦwww.glasgow-barrowland.com). Red iron gates announce its official entrance, but boundaries are breached as the stalls – selling household goods, bric-a-brac, secondhand clothes and records, none of it of particularly high quality – spill out into the surrounding cobbled streets. The fast-talking traders, lively atmosphere and entertaining vignettes of Glasgow life make it an offbeat diversion from shopping-mall banality.

Between London Road and the River Clyde are the wide and tree-lined spaces of **Glasgow Green**. Reputedly the oldest public park in Britain, the Green has been common land since at least 1178, when it was first mentioned in records. Glaswegians hold it very dear, considering it to be an immortal link between themselves and their ancestors, for whom a stroll on the Green was a favourite Sunday afternoon jaunt. Various memorials are dotted around the lawns: the 146ft-high **Nelson Monument**; the ornate terracotta **Doulton Fountain**, rising like a wedding cake to a pinnacle where Queen Victoria oversees her Empire; and the stern monument extolling the evils of drink and the glory of God that was erected by the nineteenth-century **Temperance movement** – now a meeting place for local drunks. On the northeast side of the Green, just beyond the People's Palace, it's worth taking a look at the extraordinary **Templeton's Carpet Factory**, a massive brick edifice of turrets, arched windows, mosaic-style patterns and castellated grandeur designed in the style of the Doge's Palace in Venice and built in 1892. It has been converted into apartments, but also houses the West wing Company's excellent bier halle and microbrewery (see p.240).

The People's Palace

Opposite Templeton's Carpet Factory on Glasgow Green you can still see some poles erected to hang out washing, recalling the days when the Green was very much a public space in daily use. Beside these, the **People's Palace** (Tues–Thurs & Sat 10am–5pm, Fri & Sun 11am–5pm; free) houses a wonderfully haphazard evocation of the city's history. This squat, red-sandstone Victorian building, with a vast semicircular glasshouse tacked on the back, was purpose-built as a museum back in 1898 – almost a century before the rest of the country caught onto the fashion for social history collections. Many of the displays are designed to instill a warm glow in the memories of older locals: the museum is refreshingly unpretentious and Glaswegian families almost always outnumber visitors.

The **west wing** looks at famous Glasgow products through history, with displays of everything from cast-iron railings and biscuit wrappers to a giant portrait of Billy Connolly. In the **East Gallery**, an entertaining sound-and-light show reconstructs a "single-end" or one-roomed house, a typical setting for the daily life of hundreds of thousands of Glasgow people through the years. Downstairs, various themes with a particular resonance in Glasgow are explored, including alcohol, and some guidance to understanding "the Patter" – Glaswegians' idiosyncratic version of the Queen's English. The glasshouse at the back of the palace contains the **Winter Gardens**, with a café, water garden, twittering birds and assorted tropical plants and shrubs.

The cathedral area

Rising north up the hill from the Tolbooth Steeple at Glasgow Cross is Glasgow's **High Street**. In British cities, the name is commonly associated with the busiest central thoroughfare, and it's a surprise to see how forlorn and dilapidated Glasgow's version is, long superseded by the grander thoroughfares further west. The High Street leads up to the **cathedral**, on the site of Glasgow's original settlement.

Glasgow Cathedral

Built in 1136, destroyed in 1192 and rebuilt soon after, stumpy-spired **Glasgow Cathedral** (April–Sept Mon–Sat 9.30am–5.30pm, Sun 1–5.30pm; Oct–March Mon–Sat 9.30am–4pm, Sun 1–4pm; free; Ⓦwww.glasgowcathedral.org.uk) was not completed until the late fifteenth century, with the final reconstruction of the chapter house and the aisle designed by Robert Blacader, the city's first archbishop. Thanks to the intervention of the city guilds, it is the only Scottish mainland cathedral to have escaped the hands of religious reformers in the sixteenth century. The cathedral is dedicated to the city's patron saint and reputed founder, St Mungo.

Because of the sloping ground on which it is built, at its east end the cathedral is effectively on two levels, the crypt being part of the lower church. Either side of the nave, the narrow **aisles** are illuminated by vivid stained-glass windows, most of which date from the last century. Threadbare Union flags and military pennants hang listlessly beneath them, serving as a reminder that the cathedral is very much a part of the Unionist Protestant tradition. Beyond the nave, the **choir** is hidden from view by the curtained stone pulpit, making the interior feel a great deal smaller than might be expected from the outside. In the choir's northeastern corner, a small door leads into the gloomy **sacristy**, in which Glasgow University was founded over five hundred years ago. Wooden boards mounted on the walls detail the alternating Roman Catholic and Protestant clergy of the cathedral, testimony to the turbulence and fluctuations of the Church in Scotland.

Two sets of steps from the nave lead down into the **lower church**, where you'll see the dark and musty **chapel** surrounding the tomb of St Mungo. The saint's relics were removed in the late Middle Ages, although the tomb still forms the centrepiece. The chapel itself is one of the most glorious examples of medieval architecture in Scotland, best seen in the delicate fan vaulting rising up from the thicket of cool stone columns.

The Necropolis

Rising up behind the cathedral, the atmospheric **Necropolis** is a grassy mound covered in a fantastic assortment of crumbling and tumbling gravestones, ornate urns, gloomy catacombs and Neoclassical temples. Inspired by the Père Lachaise cemetery in Paris, developer John Strong created a garden of death in 1833, and it quickly became a fitting spot for the great and the good of wealthy nineteenth-century Glasgow to indulge their vanity. Various paths lead through the rows of eroding, neglected graves, and from the summit, next to the column topped with an indignant John Knox, there are superb **views** of the steaming chimneys of the Tennants brewery, the traffic on the M8 motorway, the crowded city-centre offices, the serene cathedral itself and a wide cityscape of spires and high-rise blocks to the south and east.

Cathedral Square

Back in Cathedral Square, the **St Mungo Museum of Religious Life and Art** (Mon–Thurs & Sat 10am–5pm, Fri & Sun 11am–5pm; free), housed in a rather bland late twentieth-century pastiche of a Scots medieval townhouse, focuses on objects, beliefs and art from Christianity, Buddhism, Judaism, Islam, Hinduism and Sikhism. In addition to the main exhibition there is a small collection of photographs, papers and archive material looking at religion in Glasgow, the zealotry of the nineteenth-century Temperance movement and Christian missionaries (local boy David Livingstone in particular). Outside is Britain's only permanent "dry stone" Zen Buddhist garden.

Across the square, the oldest house in the city, the **Provand's Lordship** (same times; free) dates from 1471, and has been used as an ecclesiastical residence and an inn, amongst other things. Inside, the re-creations of life in the fifteenth century aren't particularly arresting unless you've an interest in period furniture. As a reminder of the manse's earthier history, the upper floor contains pictures of assorted low-life characters, such as the notorious drunkards and prostitutes of eighteenth- and nineteenth-century Glasgow.

Behind the Provand's Lordship lies the small **Garden of St Nicholas**, a herb garden contrasting medieval and Renaissance aesthetics and approaches to medicine, with muddled clusters of herbs amid stone carvings of the heart and other organs, and a controlled arrangement of plants around a small ornate fountain.

Sauchiehall Street and around

Glasgow's most famous street, **Sauchiehall Street**, runs in a straight line west from the northern end of Buchanan Street, past some unexciting shopping malls to a few of the city's most interesting sights. Charles Rennie Mackintosh fans should head for the **Willow Tea Rooms** (Ⓦ www.willowtearooms.co.uk), not all that easy to spot at first, above Henderson the Jeweller at 217 Sauchiehall St. Impressive if lacking in atmosphere, this is a faithful reconstruction (opened in 1980 after more than 50 years of closure) on the site of the 1904 original, which was created for Kate Cranston, one of Rennie Mackintosh's few contemporary supporters in the city. Ask for a table in the Salon de Lux, where everything, from the fixtures and fittings right down to the teaspoons and menu cards, was designed by Mackintosh. Taking inspiration from the word *Sauchiehall*, which means "avenue of willow", he chose the willow leaf as a theme to unify the whole structure from the tables to the mirrors and the ironwork. The motif is most apparent in the stylized linear panels of the bow window which continues into the intimate dining room as if to surround the sitter, like a willow grove, and is echoed in the high-backed silver and purple chairs. These elongated forms were used to enhance the small space and demonstrate Mackintosh's superb ability to fuse function with decoration. Tea is served here from 9am until 5pm Mondays to Saturdays, and 11am–4.15pm on Sundays in summer (see p.236).

A few blocks further west at no. 350, it's usually worth wandering into the **CCA** (Centre for Contemporary Arts; ⓣ0141/352 4900, ⓦwww.cca-glasgow.com), where eclectic exhibitions of international and home-grown conceptual art, combined with a stunning atrium bar and café, consistently make this one of the city's trendier cultural hotspots.

The Glasgow School of Art

Rising above Sauchiehall Street to the north is one of the city centre's steepest hills, with Dalhousie and Scott streets veering up to Renfrew Street, where you'll find Charles Rennie Mackintosh's **Glasgow School of Art** at no. 167 (guided tours April–Sept daily on the hour 10am–4pm; Oct–March Mon–Sat 11am, 2pm & 3pm; booking advised; £8.75; ⓣ0141/353 4530, ⓦwww.gsa.ac.uk), one of the most prestigious art schools in the UK. Widely considered to be the pinnacle of Mackintosh's work, the school is a characteristically angular building of warm sandstone that, due to financial constraints, had to be constructed in two sections (1897–99 and 1907–09). There's a clear change in the architect's style from the mock-Baronial east wing to the softer lines of the western half.

The only way to see the school is to take one of the student-led **guided tours**, or during the degree show in June. All over the school, from the roof to the stairwells, Mackintosh's unique touches recur – Japanese lantern shapes, images of seeds and roses and stylized Celtric illuminations. Even before entering the building up the gently curving stairway, you cannot fail to be struck by the soaring height of the north-facing windows, which light the art studios and were designed, characteristically, to combine aesthetics with practicality.

In the side entrance hall, the school shop sells tour tickets and a good selection of Mackintosh books, posters and cards. Hanging in the hall stairwell is the artist's highly personal wrought-iron version of the legend of St Mungo represented on the city's coat of arms. Above this, the **Gallery**, the largest space in the school, is a classic example of the architect's use of contrasts, with light flooding in from a skylight yet dark beams lowering the perceived space to create a degree of intimacy. Forbidding wrought-iron work gives the sense of a Highland castle, while half-hidden alcoves with unexpected windows look out over the city. Below this is the school's most spectacular room, the glorious two-storey **Library**. Designed to give the sense of a clearing in a forest, sombre oak panelling is set against angular lights, hanging in seemingly random clusters. The dark bookcases sit precisely in their fitted alcoves, and the most unusual piece of furniture is the central periodical desk, whose oval central strut displays perfect and quite beautiful symmetry. The **Furniture Gallery**, reached at the end of your tour, shelters an Aladdin's cave of designs – numerous tall-backed chairs, a semicircular settle designed for the Willow Tea Rooms, domino tables and a chest of drawers with highlighted silver panels.

Charles Rennie Mackintosh

The work of the architect **Charles Rennie Mackintosh** (1868–1928) has come to be synonymous with the image of Glasgow. Historians may disagree over whether his work was a forerunner of the Modernist movement or merely the sunset of Victorianism, but he undoubtedly created buildings of great beauty, idiosyncratically fusing Scots Baronial with Gothic, Art Nouveau and modern design. Though the bulk of his work was conceived at the turn of the twentieth century, since the 1970s Mackintosh's ideas have become particularly fashionable, giving rise to a certain amount of ersatz "**Mockintosh**" in his home city, with his distinctive lettering and small design features used time and again by shops, pubs and businesses. Fortunately, there are also plenty of examples of the genuine article, making the city something of a pilgrimage centre for art and design students from all over the world. A one-day **Mackintosh Trail Ticket** (£16), which includes entry to twelve principal Mackintosh buildings as well as unlimited Underground and bus travel, is available from the tourist office, the attractions on the trail and the **Charles Rennie Mackintosh Society**, which is based in the Mackintosh-designed Queens Cross Church in the northwest of the city (Mon–Fri 10am–5pm, also Sun 2–5pm from March–Oct; £4; ⓣ0141/946 6600, ⓦwww.crmsociety.com).

Mackintosh's big break came in 1896, when he won the competition to design a new home for the **Glasgow School of Art** (see opposite). This is his most famous work, but a number of smaller buildings created during his tenure with the architects Honeyman and Keppie, which began in 1889, document the development of his style. One of his earliest commissions was for a new building to house the *Glasgow Herald* on Mitchell Lane, off Argyle Street. A massive tower rises up from the corner, giving the building its popular name of **The Lighthouse**; it now houses the Mackintosh Interpretation Centre (see p.220).

In the 1890s Glasgow went wild for tearooms, where the middle classes could play billiards and chess, read in the library or merely chat. The imposing Miss Cranston, who dominated the Glasgow teashop scene, commissioned Mackintosh to plan the interiors for her growing business. Over the next twenty years he designed articles from teaspoons to furniture and, finally, as in the case of the **Willow Tea Rooms** (see p.223 & p.236), the structure itself.

The spectre of limited budgets was to haunt Mackintosh throughout his career, and he never had the chance to design and construct with complete freedom. However, these constraints didn't manage to dull his creativity, as demonstrated by the **Scotland Street School** of 1904, just south of the river (see p.232). It is his most symmetrical work, with a whimsical nod to history in the Scots Baronial conical tower roofs and sandstone building material. Mackintosh's forceful personality and originality did not endear him to construction workers: he would frequently change his mind or add details at the last minute, often overstretching a budget. This lost him the support of local builders and architects and prompted him to move to Suffolk in 1914 to escape the "philistines" of Glasgow and to re-evaluate his achievements. Indeed, the building that arguably displays Mackintosh at his most flamboyant was one he never saw built, **the House for an Art Lover** (see p.232), constructed in Bellahouston Park in 1996, 95 years after plans for it were submitted to a German architectural competition.

The Tenement House

Just a few hundred yards northwest of the School of Art – on the other side of a sheer hill – is the **Tenement House**, 145 Buccleuch St (March–Oct daily 1–5pm; NTS; £5.50). Glasgow's tenements were originally conceived as a convenient way to house the influx of workers in the late 1800s, though it didn't take long for the wealthy middle classes to realize their potential. Rising three to five storeys, they have two or three apartments per floor; important rooms are picked out with bay windows, middle storeys are emphasized by architraves or decorated panels below sill or above lintel, and street junctions are given importance by swelling bay windows, turrets and domes.

This is a typical tenement block still lived in on most floors, except for the ground and first floors, where you can see the respectable if cramped home of Agnes Toward, who moved here with her mother in 1911, changing nothing and throwing very little out until she was hospitalized in 1965. On the ground floor, the National Trust for Scotland has constructed a fascinating display on the development of the humble tenement block as the bedrock of urban Scottish housing, with a poignant display of relics – ration books, letters, bills, holiday snaps and so forth – from Miss Toward's life. Upstairs, you have to ring the doorbell to enter the flat, which gives every impression of still being inhabited, with a cluttered hearth and range, kitchen utensils, recess beds, framed religious tracts and sewing machine all untouched. The only major change since Miss Toward left has been the reinstallation of the flickering gas lamps she would have used in the early days. Tenement flats were home for the vast majority of Glaswegians for much of the twentieth century, and as such developed a culture and vocabulary all of their own: the "hurley", for example, was the bed on castors which was kept below the box bed in an alcove off the kitchen.

The Piping Centre

Behind the hulking Royal Scottish Academy for Music and Drama, a short way east of the Tenement House, the **National Piping Centre**, at 30–34 McPhater St, prides itself on being an international centre for the promotion of the bagpipe. Equipped with rehearsal rooms, performance halls, conference centre, accommodation (see p.215), museum and a café, it is a meeting place for fans and performers from all over the world. For the casual visitor, the single-room **museum** (May–Sept Mon–Fri 9.30am–4.30pm, Sat 9am–1pm, also Sun 10am–4pm May–Sept; £3; Ⓦwww.thepipingcentre.co.uk) is of most interest, with a collection of instruments and related artefacts from the fourteenth century to the present day. Headsets provide a taped commentary with musical examples at relevant stages and the museum shop contains a stack of related material, from tapes and videos to manuscripts and piping accessories.

The West End

The urbane **West End** seems a world away from Glasgow's industrial image and the hustle and bustle of the city centre. In the 1800s the city's wealthy merchants established huge estates away from the soot and grime of city life, and in 1870 the ancient university was moved from its cramped home near the cathedral to a spacious new site overlooking the River Kelvin. Elegant housing swiftly followed, the Kelvingrove Art Gallery and Museum was built to house the 1888 International Exhibition, and, in 1896, the Glasgow District Subway – today's Underground – started its circuitous shuffle from here to the city centre.

The hub of life in this part of Glasgow is **Byres Road**, running between Great Western Road and Dumbarton Road past Hillhead underground station. Shops, restaurants, cafés, some enticing pubs and hordes of roving young people, including thousands of students, give the area a sense of style and vitality. Glowing red-sandstone tenements and graceful terraces provide a suitably upmarket backdrop to this cosmopolitan district.

The Glasgow Boys and the Colourists

In the 1870s a group of Glasgow-based painters formed a loose association that was to imbue Scottish art with a contemporary European flavour far ahead of the rest of Britain. Dominated by five men – Guthrie, Lavery, Henry, Hornel and Crawhall – **"The Glasgow Boys"** came from very different backgrounds, but all violently rejected the eighteenth-century conservatism which spawned little other than sentimental, anecdotal renditions of Scottish history peopled by "poor but happy" families. They dubbed these paintings **"gluepots"** for their use of megilp, an oily substance that gave the work the brown patina of age, and instead began to experiment with colour, liberally splashing paint across the canvas. The content and concerns of the paintings, often showing peasant life and work, were as offensive to the art establishment as their style: until then most of Glasgow's public art collections had been accrued by wealthy tobacco lords and merchants, who had a taste for Classical style and noble subjects.

Sir James Guthrie, taking inspiration from the *plein air* painting of the Impressionists, spent his summers in the countryside, painting everyday life. Instead of happy peasants, his work shows individuals staring out of the canvas, detached and unrepentant, painted with rich tones but without undue attention to detail or the play of light. Typical of his finest work during the 1880s, *A Highland Funeral* (in the Kelvingrove collection, see p.228) was hugely influential for the rest of the group, who found inspiration in its restrained emotional content, colour and unaffected realism. It persuaded **Sir John Lavery**, then studying in France, to return to Glasgow. Lavery was eventually to become an internationally popular society portraitist, his subtle use of paint revealing his debt to Whistler, but his earlier work, depicting the middle class at play, is filled with fresh colour and figures in motion.

Rather than a realistic aesthetic, an interest in colour and decoration united the work of friends **George Henry** and **E.A. Hornel**. The predominance of colour, pattern and design in Henry's *Galloway Landscape*, for example, is remarkable, while their joint work *The Druids*, in thickly applied impasto, is full of Celtic symbolism; both are part of the Kelvingrove collection. In 1893 the two artists set off for Japan, funded by Alexander Reid and later William Burrell, where their vibrant tone and texture took Scottish painting to the forefront of European trends.

Newcastle-born **Joseph Crawhall** was a reserved and quiet individual who combined superb draughtsmanship and simplicity of line with a photographic memory to create watercolours of an outstanding naturalism and freshness. Again, William Burrell was an important patron.

The Glasgow Boys school had reached its height by 1900 and did not outlast World War I, but the influence of their work cannot be underestimated, shaking the foundations of the artistic elite and inspiring the next generation of Edinburgh painters, who became known as the **"Colourists"**. Samuel John Peploe, John Duncan Fergusson, George Leslie Hunter and Francis Cadell shared an understanding that the manipulation of colour was the heart and soul of a good painting. All experienced and took inspiration from the avant-garde of late nineteenth-century Paris as well as the landscapes of southern France. **J.D. Fergusson**, in particular, immersed himself in the bohemian, progressive Parisian scene, rubbing shoulders with writers and artists including Picasso. Some of his most dynamic work, which can be seen in the Fergusson Gallery in Perth (see p.353), displays elements of Cubism, yet is still clearly in touch with the Celtic imagery of Henry, Hornel and, indeed, Charles Rennie Mackintosh. The influence of post-Impressionists such as Matisse and Cézanne is obvious in the work of all four, with their seascapes, society portraits and still lifes bursting with fluidity, unconventionality and, above all, manipulation of colour and shape. The work of the Scottish Colourists has become highly fashionable and valuable over the last couple of decades, with galleries and civic collections throughout the country featuring their work prominently.

The main sights straddle the banks of the cleaned-up River Kelvin, which meanders through the gracious acres of the **Botanic Gardens** and the slopes, trees and statues of **Kelvingrove Park**. Overlooked by the Gothic towers and turrets of **Glasgow University**, Kelvingrove Park is home to the pride of Glasgow's civic collection of art and artefacts, **Kelvingrove Museum and Art Gallery**, off Argyle Street. Note that the much-loved Transport Museum has closed, and its collection moved to the new Riverside Museum (see p.230).

Kelvingrove Art Gallery and Museum

Founded on donations from the city's Victorian industrialists and opened at an international fair held in 1901, the huge, red sandstone fantasy castle of **Kelvingrove Art Gallery and Museum** (Mon–Thurs & Sat 10am–5pm, Fri & Sun 11am–5pm; free; Ⓦwww.glasgowmuseums.com) is a brash statement of Glasgow's nineteenth-century self-confidence. Intricate and ambitious both in its riotous outside detailing and within, where a superb galleried main hall running the length of the building gives way to attractive upper balconies and small, interlinked display galleries, Kelvingrove (as it's popularly known) offers an impressive and inviting setting for the engaging display of art and artefacts within. There are recitals on a giant ornate organ daily at 1pm.

The displays are organized under two principal headings: **Life**, in the western half of the building, encompassing archeology, local history and stuffed animals, and **Expression**, in the eastern half, which houses much of the superb art collection. The wide and sometimes bizarre range of the exhibits, from a World War II Spitfire suspended from the roof of the West Court to suits of armour, ancient Egyptian relics and priceless paintings by Rembrandt, Burne Jones, Whistler and Raeburn, has led to accusations that the museum is somewhat ill-defined. Countering this is the argument that this is a rich and deliberately varied civic collection, gathered from legacies, astute purchases and serendipitous good fortune, which principally aims to educate, enlighten and entertain the people of Glasgow.

Most visitors will be drawn to the **paintings**, most famous of which is Salvador Dali's radically foreshortened *St John of the Cross*, located on the West Balcony. The focus of huge controversy when it was purchased by the city in 1952 for what was regarded as the vast sum of £8200, it has become an icon of the collection and essential viewing on any visit here. Other favourites include Rembrandt's calm *A Man in Armour*, Van Gogh's portrait of Glasgow art dealer Alexander Reid, Whistler's muted study of Thomas Carlyle, Titian's *Adulteress brought before Christ* and some notable paintings by Pissarro, Monet and Renoir. You can also acquaint yourself with significant **Scottish art** including works by the Glasgow Boys and the Scottish Colourists (see box, p.227), as well as more contemporary work such as Joan Eardley's gritty *Two Children* and Stephen Conroy's arresting *Self Portrait*. There's a special section of paintings, furniture and murals devoted to Charles Rennie Mackintosh and the "**Glasgow Style**" that he and his contemporaries inspired. Various busts and pieces of **sculpture** are sprinkled around the galleries, most of them Classical in form, while Sophie Cave's 95 hanging face masks fill the East Court with all sorts of facial expressions and emotions.

Glasgow University and the Hunterian bequests

Dominating the West End skyline, the gloomy turreted tower of **Glasgow University** (Ⓦwww.gla.ac.uk), designed by Sir George Gilbert Scott in the mid-nineteenth century, overlooks the glades edging the River Kelvin. Access to the main buildings and museums is from University Avenue, running east from

Byres Road. In the dark neo-Gothic pile under the tower you'll find the **University Visitor Centre & Shop** (Mon–Sat 9.30am–5pm) which, as well as giving information for potential students, has a small café and distributes leaflets about the various university buildings and the statues around the campus. From April to September **guided tours** of the campus are run from here (Wed–Sat 11am; bookings advised on ⓣ0141/330 5511; £3.50).

Beside the visitor centre is the **Hunterian Museum** (Mon–Sat 9.30am–5pm; free), Scotland's oldest public museum, dating back to 1807. The collection was donated to the university by ex-student William Hunter, a pathologist and anatomist whose eclectic tastes form the basis of a diverting zoological and archeological jaunt. Exhibits include Scotland's only dinosaur, Lord Kelvin's scientific instruments, some gruesome medical specimens and a vast numismatic collection (coins, in other words).

The Hunterian Art Gallery

Opposite the university, across University Avenue, is Hunter's more frequently visited bequest, the **Hunterian Art Gallery** (Mon–Sat 9.30am–5pm; free), best known for its wonderful works by James Abbott McNeill Whistler: only Washington DC has a larger collection. Whistler's portraits of women give his subjects a resolute strength in addition to their occasionally winsome qualities: look out especially for the trio of full-length portraits, *Harmony of Flesh Colour* and *Black, Pink and Gold: The Tulip* and *Red and Black: The Fan*, as well as his dreamy night-time visions of the Thames.

The gallery's other major collection is of nineteenth- and twentieth-century Scottish art, including the quasi-Impressionist Scottish landscapes of William McTaggart, a forerunner of the Glasgow Boys movement, itself represented here by Guthrie and Hornel. Taking the aims of this group one step further were the Scottish Colourist and, the monumental dancing figures of J.D. Fergusson's *Les Eus* preside over a small collection of work by this group, including Peploe, Hunter and Cadell, who left a vibrant legacy of thickly textured, colourful landscapes and portraits. A small selection of French Impressionism includes works by Boudin and Pissarro, with Corot's soothing *Distant View of Corbeil* being a highlight from the Barbizon school.

A side gallery leads to the **Mackintosh House** (£3, free after 2pm Wed), a re-creation of the interior of the now-demolished Glasgow home of Margaret MacDonald and Charles Rennie Mackintosh. An introductory display contains photographs of the original house sliding irrevocably into terminal decay, from where you are led into an exquisitely cool interior that contains more than sixty pieces of Mackintosh furniture on three floors. In addition, a permanent Mackintosh exhibition gallery shows a selection of his two-dimensional work, from watercolours to architectural drawings.

The Botanic Gardens

At the northern, top end of Byres Road, where it meets the Great Western Road, is the main entrance to the **Botanic Gardens** (daily 7am–dusk; free). The best-known glasshouse here, the hulking, domed **Kibble Palace** (10am–4.45pm or 4.15pm in winter; free), was built in 1863 for wealthy landowner John Kibble's estate on the shores of Loch Long, where it stood for ten years before he decided to transport it into Glasgow, drawing it up the Clyde on a vast raft pulled by a steamer. For over two decades it was used not as a greenhouse but as a Victorian pleasure palace, before the gardens' owners put a stop to the drunken revels that wreaked havoc with the lawns and plant beds. Today the palace is more sedate, housing lush ferns, exotic blooms and swaying palms from around the world. Nearby, the **Main Range Glasshouse** (same times) is home to lurid flowers and plants luxuriating in the humidity, including stunning orchids, cacti, ferns and tropical fruit. Between the two in the old curator's house is a small **visitor centre** (daily 11am–4pm; free) with art exhibitions and computer games aimed at younger visitors.

In addition to the area around the main glasshouses, there are some beautifully remote paths in the gardens that weave along the closely wooded banks of the deep-set River Kelvin, linking up with the walkway that runs alongside the river all the way down to Dumbarton Road, near its confluence with the Clyde.

Clydeside

"The **Clyde** made Glasgow and Glasgow made the Clyde" runs an old saw, full of sentimentality for the days when the river was the world's premier shipbuilding centre, and when its industry lent an innovation and confidence which made Glasgow the second city of the British Empire. Despite the hardships that heavy industry brought, every Glaswegian would follow the progress of the skeleton ships under construction in the riverside yards, cheering them on their way down the Clyde as they were launched. The last of the great liners to be built on **Clydeside** was the *QE2* in 1967, yet such events are hard to visualize today, with the banks of the river all but devoid of any industry: shipbuilding is now restricted to a couple of barely viable yards, as derelict warehouses, crumbling docks and overgrown wastelands crowd the river's flanks.

Glasgow is often accused of failing to capitalize on its river, and it's only in the last few years, with a flurry of construction, that it's once again becoming a focus of attention. Striking constructions such as the titanium-clad "**Armadillo**" concert hall, the creatively lit **Clyde Arc** (known as "the squinty bridge"), the curvaceous **Glasgow Science Centre** and the box-like new home of **BBC Scotland** have become icons of the city's forward-thinking image, though the shipbuilding heritage is not forgotten, with attractions such as the **Tall Ship at Glasgow Harbour** and **Clydebuilt** striving to recreate the river's heyday. The culmination of this activity is the **Riverside Museum**, due to open in 2011.

The easiest way to reach the cluster of Clydeside attractions is to **walk** the mile or so west along the riverside footpath from the city centre. Otherwise, jump on a **train** from Glasgow Central low-level station to the Exhibition Centre station and use the footbridge to cross the river to the Science Centre on the south bank, also served by Arriva buses #23 or #24 from Renfield Street.

The Riverside Museum

At the time of writing, work was underway on a major new **Riverside Museum** on the Clyde, due to open in 2011. The museum building, designed by Zaha Hadid, will incorporate exhibits from the much-loved and now closed Glasgow Transport Museum, as well as providing a dock for an attraction known

The Waverley

One of Glasgow's best-loved treasures is the **Waverley**, the last seagoing paddle steamer in the world, which spends the summer cruising to various ports on the Firth of Clyde and the Ayrshire coast from its base at the new Riverside Museum (see above). Built on Clydeside as recently as 1947, she's an elegant vessel to look at, not least when she's thrashing away at full steam with the hills of Argyll or Arran in the background. The booking office (Ⓣ0845/130 4647, Ⓦwww.waverleyexcursions.co.uk) has information on sailing times and her itinerary.

as **The Tall Ship at Glasgow Harbour**, the square-rigger *Glenlee*, a 245ft-long, three-masted barque launched on the river in 1896 and now one of only five large sailing vessels built on Clydeside that are still afloat. See Ⓦwww.glasgowlife.org.uk/museums for opening hours and details.

The north bank

Immediately south of the West End and just over a mile west of the city centre is the harshly re-landscaped Scottish Exhibition and Conference Centre, or **SECC**. It was built on a reclaimed dock in 1985 to kick-start the revival of the riverbank: two vast adjoining red and grey sheds that make a dutifully utilitarian venue for travelling fairs, mega-concerts and anonymous bars and cafés. Although the huge **Finnieston Crane**, retained as an icon of shipbuilding days, stands alongside the SECC, the site was rescued from bland obscurity by the arrival in 1997 of a supplementary concert hall officially entitled the Clyde Auditorium but universally nicknamed "**the Armadillo**" for its rounded exterior of armour-plating. It's like a poor man's Sydney Opera House but has quickly established itself as one of the city's architectural landmarks.

The Glasgow Science Centre

On the south bank of the river, linked to the SECC by a pedestrian bridge, are the three space-age, titanium-clad constructions which make up the **Glasgow Science Centre** (daily 10am–5pm; £9.95; IMAX features £8.95; Ⓦwww.gsc.org.uk). Of the three buildings, the largest is the curvaceous, wedge-shaped **Science Mall**. Behind the vast glass wall that faces the river are four floors of interactive exhibits ranging from lift-your-own-weight pulleys to high-tech thermograms. Described as "hands-on info-tainment for the genome generation", it's like all your most enjoyable school science experiments packed into one building, with in-house boffins demonstrating chemical reactions and pensioners and toddlers alike captivated by cockroach colonies and jigsaw puzzles of human organs. The centre covers almost every aspect of science, from simple optical illusions to cutting-edge computer technology, including a section on moral and environmental issues – lots of good fun, although weekends and school holidays are busy and noisy. Within the mall, an impressive planetarium and 3D virtual science theatre put on regular shows through the day.

Alongside the Science Mall is the bubble-like **IMAX theatre**, which shows a range of science- and nature-based documentaries as well as 3D spectaculars on its giant screen, with programmes changing regularly. Also on the site is the 417ft-high **Glasgow Tower**, the tallest freestanding structure in Scotland, built with an aerofoil-like construction to allow it to rotate to face into the prevailing wind. Glass lifts ascend to the viewing cabin at the top, offering terrific panoramic views of central Glasgow. In the dock behind the Science Centre is the base for Scotland's only regular passenger **seaplane** service, which plies routes to places such as Loch Lomond and Oban (Ⓣ01436/675030, Ⓦwww.lochlomondseaplanes.com).

The Southside

The section of Glasgow south of the Clyde is generally described as the **Southside**, though within this area there are a number of districts with recognizable names, including the notoriously deprived Gorbals and Govan, which are sprinkled with new developments but still obviously derelict and tatty in many parts. There's little reason to venture here unless you're making your way to the Science Centre (see above), the famously innovative Citizens' Theatre (see p.242) or one of the revived architectural gems of Charles Rennie Mackintosh – the **Scotland Street School** and the **House for an Art Lover**.

Moving further south, inner-city decay fades into altogether gentler and more salubrious suburbs, including Queen's Park, home to Scotland's national football stadium, **Hampden Park**; Pollokshaws and the rural landscape of Pollok Park, which contains two of Glasgow's major museums, the **Burrell Collection** and **Pollok House**; and Cathcart, location of Alexander "Greek" Thomson's **Holmwood House**.

Southside attractions are fairly widely spread. The **Underground** will get you to Scotland Street School and the House for an Art Lover, while taking the **train** from Central station is best for Hampden Park (Mount Florida station) and Holmwood House (Cathcart station). For Pollok Park either take the train to Pollokshaws West station (not to be confused with Pollokshields West) or **bus** #45, #47, #48 or #57 to Pollokshaws Road. From the park gates a **free minibus** runs every half-hour between 10am and 4.30pm to both the Burrell Collection and Pollok House.

Scotland Street School Museum

Opposite Shields Road underground station is the **Scotland Street School Museum** (Tues–Thurs & Sat 10am–5pm, Fri & Sun 11am–5pm; free), another of the city's Charles Rennie Mackintosh treasures. Mackintosh's distinctively designed school opened in 1906, and since its closure in 1979 has been entertainingly refurbished to house a fascinating collection of memorabilia related to classroom life. There are reconstructed classrooms from the Victorian and Edwardian eras, World War II and the 1960s, as well as changing rooms, a primitive domestic science room and re-creations of the school matron's sanatorium and a janitor's lair. If you visit on a weekday during term time, you may stumble on a period lesson, local schoolkids struggling with their ink blotters, gas masks and archly unsympathetic teachers, the faint smell of antiseptic conjuring up memories of scuffed knees and playground tantrums.

House for an Art Lover

A mile and a half west of Scotland Street School, tucked just inside Bellahouston Park, is Charles Rennie Mackintosh's **House for an Art Lover** (call for opening hours as the building may be closed to the public due to functions; £4.50; Ⓣ0141/353 4770, Ⓦwww.houseforanartlover.co.uk). Designed in 1901 for a German competition, it was not until 1996, after years of detailed research, that the building was actually constructed and opened as a centre for Glasgow School of Art postgraduate students, with a limited number of rooms open to the public.

It's all quintessential Mackintosh, the exquisitely stylish and original nature of the design making it hard to imagine it suffering the wear and tear of day-to-day life. On the upper floor, you can watch a video giving a detailed account of the building's history, then pass into the delicate **Oval Room**, intended for women to retire to after dinner. From here, a small corridor leads into the main **hallway**, where massive windows cast a cool light upon an area designed for large parties. In direct contrast, the dazzling white **Music Room** has bow windows opening out to a large balcony, though the garden view is marred by an artificial ski slope. The **Dining Room** is decorated with darkened stained wood and enhanced by some beautiful gesso tiles.

On the ground floor, the **café** (daily 10am–5pm) is particularly popular with locals on Sunday mornings; there's an attractive menu, and it's open every day (even if the rest of the house is closed to the public) and sometimes also in the evenings.

Hampden Park and the Scottish Football Museum

Two and a half miles south of the city centre, just west of leafy Queen's Park, the floodlights and giant stands of Scotland's national football stadium, **Hampden Park**, loom over the surrounding suburban tenements and terraces. Home of Queen's Park Football Club, the fact that it's the venue for Scotland's international fixtures and major cup finals makes it a place of pilgrimage for the country's football fans. Regular **guided tours** (daily 11am–3.30pm; £6, or £9 including entry to the museum; Ⓦwww.hampdenpark.co.uk) offer the chance to see the changing rooms, warm-up areas and inside the stadium itself, complete with anecdotes of players past and the story of the ground. Also here is the engaging **Scottish Football Museum** (Mon–Sat 10am–5pm, Sun 11am–5pm; £6), with extensive collections of memorabilia, video clips and displays covering almost every aspect of the game.

The Burrell Collection

Located in the expansive and attractive Pollok Park some six miles southwest of the city centre is the outstanding **Burrell Collection** (daily except Fri 10am–5pm; free; Ⓦwww.glasgowlife.org.uk), the lifetime collection of shipping magnate Sir William Burrell (1861–1958) and, for some, the principal reason for visiting Glasgow. Unlike many other art collectors, Sir William's only real criterion for buying a piece was whether he liked it or not, enabling him to buy many "unfashionable" works, which cost comparatively little but subsequently proved their worth. He wanted to leave his 9000-piece collection of art, sculpture and antiquities for public display, but stipulated in 1944 that they should be housed "in a rural setting far removed from the atmospheric pollution of urban conurbations, not less than sixteen miles from the Royal Exchange".

Football in Glasgow

Football is one of Glasgow's great passions – and one of its great blights. While the city can claim to be one of Europe's premier footballing centres, it's known above all for one of the most bitter rivalries in any sport, that between **Celtic** and **Rangers**. Two of the largest clubs in Britain, with weekly crowds regularly topping 60,000, the Old Firm, as they're collectively known, have dominated Scottish football for a century, lavishing vast sums of money on foreign talent in an often frantic effort both to outdo each other and to keep up with the top English and European teams.

The roots of Celtic, who play at Celtic Park in the eastern district of Parkhead (Ⓣ0141/551 8653, Ⓦwww.celticfc.co.uk), lie in the city's immigrant Irish and **Catholic** population, while Rangers, based at Ibrox Park in Govan on the Southside (Ⓣ0870/600 1993, Ⓦwww.rangers.co.uk), have traditionally drawn support from local **Protestants**. As a result, sporting rivalries have been enmeshed in a sectarian divide which many argue would not have remained so long, nor so deep, had it been divorced from the footballing scene. While large-scale violence on the terraces and streets has not been seen for some time – thanks in large measure to canny policing – Old Firm matches often seethe with bitter passions, and sectarian-related assaults do still occur in parts of the city.

However, there is a less intense side to the game in Glasgow. The city's smaller clubs actively distance themselves from the Old Firm and plod along in the lower reaches of the Scottish league. **Queen's Park**, residents of Hampden (Ⓣ0141/632 1275, Ⓦwww.queensparkfc.co.uk), **St Mirren**, the Paisley team (Ⓣ0141/840 4100, Ⓦwww.stmirrenfc.co.uk), and the much-maligned **Partick Thistle**, who play at Firhill Stadium in the West End (Ⓣ0141/579 1971, Ⓦwww.ptfc.co.uk), offer the best chances of experiencing the more down-to-earth side of Glaswegian football.

For decades, these conditions proved too difficult to meet, with few open spaces available and a pall of industrial smoke ruling out any city site. However, by the late 1960s, after the nationwide Clean Air Act had reduced pollution, and vast **Pollok Park** had been donated to the city, plans began for a new, purpose-built gallery, which finally opened in 1983. Today the simplicity and clean lines of the Burrell building are its greatest assets, with large picture windows giving sweeping views over woodland and serving as a tranquil backdrop to the objects inside. The major part of the collection, including the sculpture and antiques, are arranged in a fairly fluid style on the **ground floor**, while a **mezzanine** above displays most of the paintings.

The courtyard

On entering the building, head past the information desk and shop to an airy covered **courtyard** where the most striking piece, by virtue of sheer size, is the **Warwick Vase**, a huge bowl containing fragments of a second-century AD vase from Emperor Hadrian's villa in Tivoli. Next to it is a series of sinewy and naturalistic bronze casts of **Rodin sculptures**, among them *The Age of Bronze*, *A Call to Arms* and the famous *Thinker*. On three sides of the courtyard, a trio of dark and sombre panelled rooms have been re-erected in faithful detail from the Burrells' Hutton Castle home, their heavy tapestries, antique furniture and fireplaces displaying the same eclectic taste as the rest of the museum.

The ground floor

From the courtyard, go through the massive sandstone portal and door from Hornby Castle, incorporated into the building, to the start of the **Ancient Civilizations** collection – a catch-all title for Greek, Roman and earlier artefacts – which includes an exquisite mosaic Roman cockerel from the first century BC and a 4000-year-old Mesopotamian lion's head. The bulk of it is Egyptian, however, with rows of inscrutable gods and kings. Nearby, also illuminated by enormous windows, the **Oriental Art** collection forms nearly a quarter of the whole display, ranging from Neolithic jades through bronze vessels and Tang funerary horses to cloisonné. One of the earliest pieces, from around the second century BC, is a loveable earthenware watchdog from the Han Dynasty, but most dominant is the serene fifteenth-century *Lohan* (disciple of Buddha), who sits cross-legged and contemplative against the background of a glass wall and the trees of Pollok Park.

Burrell considered his **Medieval and Post-Medieval European Art**, which encompasses silverware, glass, textiles and sculpture, to be the most valuable part of his collection. Ranged across a maze of small galleries, the most impressive sections are the sympathetically lit stained glass and the numerous tapestries, including the riotous fifteenth-century *Peasants Hunting Rabbits with Ferrets*. Among these are a selection from Burrell's vast fine art collection, the highlight of which is one of Rembrandt's evocative early self-portraits.

The mezzanine

Upstairs, the cramped and comparatively gloomy **mezzanine** is probably the least satisfactory section of the gallery, not the best setting for its sparkling array of paintings. The range of works on show does change, but it can make incongruous leaps from a small gathering of fifteenth-century religious works to Géricault's darkly dynamic *Prancing Grey Horse* and Degas's thoughtful and perceptive *Portrait of Edmond Duranty*. Manet, Cézanne and Boudin are also represented.

Pollok House

Also within Pollok Park, a quarter of a mile down rutted tracks west of the Burrell Collection, lies the lovely eighteenth-century **Pollok House** (daily 10am–5pm;

NTS; April–Oct £8.50, Nov–March free; café and gardens free year-round), the manor of the Pollok Park estate and once home of the Maxwell family, local lords and owners of most of southern Glasgow until well into the last century. Designed by William Adam in the mid-1700s, the house is typical of its age: graciously light and sturdily built, it looks out onto the pristine raked and parterre gardens, whose stylized daintiness contrasts with the heavy Spanish paintings inside, among them two El Greco portraits and works by Murillo and Goya.

The house recently came under the management of the National Trust for Scotland – a happy reunion, as it was in the upstairs smoking room in 1931 that the then-owner, Sir John Stirling Maxwell, held the first meetings with the Eighth Duke of Atholl and Lord Colquhoun of Luss that led to the formation of the NTS. The Trust has made a deliberate effort to return the house to the layout and style it enjoyed when the Stirling Maxwells were living here in the 1920s and 1930s. As a result, the **paintings** range from the Spanish masterpieces in the morning room and some splendid Dutch hunting scenes in the dining room to Sir John's own worthy but noticeably amateur efforts which line the upstairs corridors. Generally, the rooms have the flavour of a well-to-do but unstuffy country house, with the odd piece of attractive furniture and some pleasant rooms, but little that can be described as outstanding. The servants' quarters downstairs, however, do capture the imagination – the virtually untouched labyrinth of tiled Victorian parlours and corridors includes a good **tearoom** in the old kitchen. Free tours of the house are available from the front desk, or you can wander around at your own pace.

Holmwood House

Four miles south of the city centre in the suburb of Cathcart, **Holmwood House** (April–Oct Mon & Thurs–Sun noon–5pm; NTS; £5.50), the finest domestic design by rediscovered Glasgow architect Alexander "Greek" Thomson, has recently been restored and opened to the public. A commission by James Couper, co-owner of a paper mill on the nearby River Carth, the house shows off Thomson's bold classical concepts, with exterior pillars on two levels and a raised main door, as well as his detailed and highly imaginative interiors. The restoration is ongoing, as you'll see from the patches of exquisite stencilling revealed beneath the wallpaper, and the fact that the rooms are unfurnished.

A free audio-guide provides some background information and explanation in each of the rooms. One room upstairs is given over to a series of displays about Thomson and the history of the house. Also on the upper floor is the **drawing room** – look for the white marble fireplace and the night-time star decorations on the ceiling, which contrast with a black marble fireplace and sunburst decorations in the room immediately underneath on the downstairs level, the **parlour**, which also features a delightful round bay window. Across the corridor, the **dining room** has a frieze of scenes from the *Iliad*, along with a skylight at the back of the room designed to allow the Greek gods to peer down on the feasts being consumed inside. One unusual feature not designed by Thomson is the small hatch cut in the interconnecting door between the dining room and the butler's pantry; the house was last occupied by a sisterhood of nuns, who used the dining room as a chapel and created the small hatch for use as a confessional.

Eating

Glaswegians have long enjoyed going out, and while this traditionally meant an evening of drinking and dancing, or going to a show, dining out now fits comfortably into the social agenda. Glasgow's **restaurant** scene is reasonably dynamic, with new places replacing old (and sometimes not very old) every year, but the city also has some venerable landmarks alongside its ambitious new ventures.

The city's more casual bar/diners and bistros are typically **open** from 11am right through the day and evening. Most of the more formal restaurants usually serve lunch between noon and 2.30pm and dinner from 5–6pm to about 10.30pm. Some places (especially in the **city centre**) are not open on Sundays, and Monday is another common day off. Most places to eat are concentrated in the commercial hub and **Merchant City** district of the **city centre**, as well as in the trendy **West End**. For locations, see the maps on p.210, pp.212–213 & pp.218–219.

For comprehensive listings and reviews of bars, cafés and restaurants, buy the *List Eating & Drinking Guide* at newsagents and larger bookshops. If you're travelling on a budget, note that many restaurants have excellent pre-theatre or early dining deals – it's worth logging onto the restaurant-booking website Ⓦwww.5pm.co.uk, which lists Glasgow restaurants offering special lunch and early evening deals.

Cafés, diners and café-bars

For inexpensive to moderately priced food, **cafés** and **café-bars** – in addition, of course, to local **diners**, pubs, fast-food outlets and that perennial fall-back, the fish and chip shop – are the best bets, serving filling snacks all day and often into the evening. The best of these are concentrated in districts where younger folk and students congregate: the West End, particularly on Byres Road, and the Merchant City.

City centre and the Merchant City

Café Gandolfi and Bar Gandolfi 64 Albion St Ⓣ0141/552 6813, Ⓦwww.cafegandolfi.com. *Gandolfi* was one of the first to test the waters in the revived Merchant City in the 1980s and today it's a landmark. Designed with distinctive wooden furniture from the Tim Stead workshop, *Gandolfi* serves up Scottish staples (including great black pudding), soups, salads, fish dishes and Continental cuisine, with mains around £15. The bar upstairs is more contemporary in feel but the food's equally good. New to the scene, just up the street, is *Gandolfi Fish* (Ⓣ0141/552 9475).

Café Source 1 St Andrew's Square Ⓣ0141/548 6020, Ⓦwww.cafesource.co.uk. In the basement of St Andrew's, an eighteenth-century church that is now a folk music and Scottish dance centre, this café serves up inexpensive Scottish favourites featuring local produce. Frequent live jam sessions and a monthly jazz supper club.

Tinderbox Merchant City 14 Ingram St Ⓣ0141/552 6907. Following on after the success of its West End outlet (see opposite), this branch features the same cutting-edge design and strong espresso coffees, as well as offering food put together by one of the city's leading delis.

Trans-Europe Café 25 Parnie St Ⓣ0141/552 7999, Ⓦwww.transeuropecafe.co.uk. A fun railway-style diner which takes culinary inspiration from various European capitals and dishes up excellent soup and gourmet sandwiches; handy for a visit to 103 Trongate (see p.220).

Tron Theatre Chisholm St, off Trongate Ⓣ0141/552 8587, Ⓦwww.tron.co.uk. A rather arty hangout (see p.243), particularly with writers and theatrical types, who adore both the contemporary street-side café-bar and the Victorian pub/dining room further inside. Mains start at £9.

Where the Monkey Sleeps 182 West Regent St Ⓣ0141/226 3406, Ⓦwww.monkeysleeps.com. Owned by graduates of the nearby Glasgow School of Art who acquired their barista skills between classes, this hip home-grown café features freshly prepared sandwiches and salads, and the espresso is superb. Usually closes at 5pm.

Willow Tea Rooms 217 Sauchiehall St Ⓣ0141/332 0521, Ⓦwww.willowtearooms.co.uk. A semi-authentic bit of architectural heritage on the Charles Rennie Mackintosh trail, the first-floor dining room here offers tea with scones and midday meals. Closes before 5pm.

West End

Kember & Jones 134 Byres Rd Ⓣ0141/337 3851, Ⓦwww.kemberandjones.co.uk. This stylish café and deli has become a popular spot in the competitive Byres Road market, serving freshly made salads, sandwiches and irresistible cakes and pastries.

The Left Bank 33–35 Gibson St Ⓣ0141/339 5969, Ⓦwww.theleftbank.co.uk. Part bar and part bistro, this relatively new addition to the

Hillhead neighbourhood adjacent to the university dishes up wholesome and rustic food in a chic modern setting.
Stravaigin 2 8 Ruthven Lane ⓣ0141/334 7165, ⓦwww.stravaigin.com. A popular diner/bistro just off busy Byres Road that serves excellent burgers (from £8.95) alongside excellent Moroccan, Italian and fish dishes; it's similar to the award-wining modern Scottish *Stravaigin* restaurant (see p.239).
Tchai Ovna 42 Otago Lane ⓣ0141/357 4524, ⓦwww.tchaiovna.com. A low-key and inexpensive bohemian hangout that overlooks the Kelvin River, serving savoury vegetarian options, cakes, snacks and a selection of teas from around the world.
Tinderbox 189 Byres Rd ⓣ0141/339 3108. A modern espresso café-bar offering an array of lattes, cappuccinos and the like. Even in trendy Glasgow, it remains amazingly successful.
University Café 87 Byres Rd ⓣ0141/339 5217. This institution dates from the 1910s and has been adored by at least three generations of students and West End residents, with its formica tables in snug booths, glass counters and original architectural features. The favourites here are fish'n'chips or mince'n'tatties rounded off with an ice-cream cone.

Southside

1901 1534 Pollokshaws Rd ⓣ0141/632 0161. This French-influenced bistro/pub near Pollok Country Park is a lesser-known gem serving hearty and moderately priced Mediterranean food. Open for lunch and dinner.

Restaurants

Despite some ubiquitous chain restaurants and bars, not to mention multinational fast-food outlets, Glasgow still has a high percentage of independent and locally owned establishments. If you're on a budget, set-price lunch menus are affordable options at the more expensive restaurants in town. Near the heart of things, the Merchant City combines hip bars and good restaurants – practically wall-to-wall on **Candleriggs** – amid the warehouse conversions. Two other city-centre hotbeds of dining and drinking activity are **Bath Street** and more famous **Sauchiehall Street**, especially in the Charing Cross neighbourhood of the latter. The West End has an attractive selection of bars, cafés and restaurants, thanks to the local university population and the area's perennially young, affluent and creative vibe. The focus of activity is around the Hillhead underground station on **Byres Road**: the chock-a-block restaurants and pubs of nearby cobbled **Ashton Lane** make up a particularly lively and attractive strip. The Southside is quieter, more residential and less intense, featuring some family-run restaurants with a welcoming ambience, particularly on Pollokshaws and Kilmarnock roads.

City centre and Merchant City

The 13th Note Café 50–60 King St ⓣ0141/553 1638, ⓦwww.13thnote.co.uk. Vegetarian and vegan food with Greek and other Mediterranean influences in one of Glasgow's hipper drinking and indie/experimental music haunts on arty King St. All mains are under a tenner.
Brian Maule at Le Chardon d'Or 176 West Regent St ⓣ0141/248 3801, ⓦwww.brianmaule.com. Owner/chef Maule once worked with the Roux brothers at *Le Gavroche* restaurant in London. Fancy but not pretentious French-influenced food; mains start at £20. Closed Sun & bank holidays & two weeks July/Aug.
Café Antipasti 305 Sauchiehall St ⓣ0141/332 9002. A busy and bright Italian bistro with a handsome wood interior, serving tasty and well-priced pastas and salads.
Café Cossachok 10 King St, or access it via Trongate 103 (see p.220) ⓣ0141/553 0733, ⓦwww.cossachok.com. Hearty Slavic-style dishes accompanied by Russian musicians on occasion and plenty of chilled vodka. Closed Mon.
City Merchant 97 Candleriggs ⓣ0141/553 1577, ⓦwww.citymerchant.co.uk. Popular brasserie that blazed the Merchant City trail that plenty of others have followed. Fresh Scottish produce, from Ayrshire lamb to the house speciality: west-coast seafood (£24). Closed Sun.
Dakhin 89 Candleriggs ⓣ0141/553 2585, ⓦwww.dakhin.com. Owned by the same people as *The Dhabba* (see below), this first-floor restaurant (above *Bar 91*) specializes in South Indian cuisine. Be sure and try a rice dosa (around £10).
The Dhabba 44 Candleriggs ⓣ0141/553 1249, ⓦwww.thedhabba.com. This is not your typical Glasgow curry house. Prices are higher, portions are

smaller but the menu has some truly interesting options and fresh ingredients that place it steps above most others.

Dragon-i 311–313 Hope St ⓣ0141/332 7728, ⓦwww.dragon-i.co.uk. The dishes at this stylish, modern restaurant across from the Theatre Royal offer an intriguing mix of Chinese and Far East influences; good pre-theatre menu (3 courses for £16.95).

Gamba 225a West George St ⓣ0141/572 0899, ⓦwww.gamba.co.uk. This modern basement restaurant offers one of the best meals in Glasgow. Continental contemporary sophistication prevails, with dishes such as roasted line-caught sea bass (£18.50) or Isle of Gigha halibut (£23). If you love fish, come here. Closed Sun.

Ichiban Japanese Noodle Café 50 Queen St ⓣ0141/204 4200, ⓦwww.ichiban.co.uk. Japanese-style informal and cheap eating, with long benches and tables shared by diners. Bowls (or plates) of noodles are specialities here and service is efficient.

Mao 84 Brunswick St ⓣ0141/564 5162, ⓦwww.cafemao.com. Bright café-bar in the Merchant City with a range of Asian-influenced cuisine, including spicy Korean and Indonesian dishes.

Michael Caines @ ABode 129 Bath St ⓣ0141/572 6011, ⓦwww.michaelcaines.com. Located in the *ABode* hotel and a little low on atmosphere, *Michael Caines* is nonetheless an essential stop for Glasgow foodies. Ambitious staff serve up modern French-inspired recipes using local produce, with mains starting at £19.

Mono 12 King's Court ⓣ0141/553 2400, ⓦwww.monocafebar.com. This place combines a fully vegan restaurant, Fairtrade food shop, bar and indie CD shop. Lots of space and organic beer and wine.

Mussel Inn 157 Hope St ⓣ0141/572 1405, ⓦwww.mussel-inn.com. Like the Edinburgh flagship, this branch concentrates on simply prepared pots of fresh mussels (from £5), grilled scallops (from £7.40) and other delights from the sea in relaxed, buzzy environs.

Rogano 11 Exchange Place ⓣ0141/248 4055, ⓦwww.rogano.co.uk. An Art Deco fish restaurant and Glasgow institution since 1935, decked out in the style of the *Queen Mary* ocean liner. *Café Rogano*, in the basement, is cheaper with mains around £10, or you can just have cocktails or oysters at the bar.

Sarti 133 Wellington St, 121 Bath St & 42 Renfield St ⓣ0141/204 0440, ⓦwww.sarti.co.uk. The Sarti brothers' flagship Italian café and restaurant: authentic and popular. The slightly more formal dining space is accessed from the Bath St entrance; the atmospheric café round the corner opens in the mornings.

Wee Curry Shop 7 Buccleuch St ⓣ0141/353 0777. Tiny but welcoming place near the Glasgow Film Theatre and Sauchiehall St shops (there's also a branch in the West End on Ashton Lane), serving home-made bargain meals to compete with the best in town. BYOB.

West End

An Lochan 340 Crow Rd ⓣ0141/338 6606 ⓦwww.anlochan.co.uk. If you want the best in fresh, unadulterated west-coast Scottish fish (mains starting at £10), there's no better place in Glasgow, although it is off the beaten track, in the Jordanhill district. Closed Mon.

Ashoka Ashton Lane 19 Ashton Lane ⓣ0141/337 1115, ⓦwww.ashokarestaurants.com. Lively and moderately priced curry house which has franchises across the west of Scotland; all offer consistent quality. Other *Ashoka* restaurants are at 1284 Argyle St (ⓣ0141/339 3371), and on the Southside at 268 Clarkston Rd (ⓣ0141/637 0711).

Balbir's 7 Church St ⓣ0141/339 7711. Owner Balbir Singh Sumal is one of the city's long-standing curry kings, and this modern restaurant with plenty of space reflects his wholesome approach to affordable Indian cuisine.

The Big Blue 445 Great Western Rd ⓣ0141/357 1038. A casual Italian restaurant and bar with outdoor tables overlooking the River Kelvin; particularly good for pizza.

The Bothy 11 Ruthven Lane ⓣ0141/334 4040, ⓦwww.bothyrestaurant.co.uk. Set in a lovely 1870s stone mansion, cosy inside and with bench seating in the yard outside. The menu is a bit of a laugh with its broad Scots vernacular, but the traditional food is largely accomplished – especially given the reasonable prices of most dishes.

The Cabin 996 Dumbarton Rd ⓣ0141/569 1036, ⓦwww.cabinglasgow.com. One sitting per night for three courses of upmarket Scottish food (£30) with a hint of Irish influence in a cosy, rather old-fashioned restaurant, but it's best known for the "Celtic soul" singalong on Wed. Best for parties of four or more, and you'll need to book in advance. Closed Mon.

Chow 98 Byres Rd ⓣ0141/334 9818. Proof that Chinese restaurants can be modern and non-kitsch. This bijou diner offers excellent value-for-money meals.

Cottier's 93–95 Hyndland St ⓣ0141/357 5825. Not pure Mexican, as it takes in Latin American and Caribbean, this place has a welcoming West End vibe and is located on the top floor of a church annexe adjacent to Cottier's Theatre.

Grassroots Café 93 St George's Rd ⓣ0141/333 0534. Although the competition is not especially stiff, this vegetarian outlet (just across the M8 motorway from the city centre) has the best reputation for meat-free food in Glasgow. Fresh, creative cooking and a relaxed atmosphere.

La Vallée Blanche 360 Byres Rd ⓣ0141/334 3333, ⓦwww.lavalleeblanche.com. The elegant wooden-panelled upstairs dining room is a snug winter or wet-weather retreat, serving French classics with a nod towards Alpine cuisine and Scottish ingredients (mains £12.50–22.50).

Mother India 28 Westminster Terrace, off Sauchiehall St ⓣ0141/221 1663, ⓦwww.motherindiaglasgow.co.uk. One of the best Indian restaurants in Glasgow, offering home cooking with some original specials as well as the old favourites at affordable prices in laid-back but elegant surroundings. Try the nearby spin-off *Mother India's Café*, 1355 Argyle St (ⓣ0141/339 9145), if you're on a budget; they serve Indian food in tapas-style portions.

No. Sixteen 16 Byres Rd ⓣ0141/339 2544, ⓦwww.number16.co.uk. A local favourite, with daily menus of Scottish produce, from venison (£17.50) to black bream (£15.95).

Stravaigin 28–30 Gibson St ⓣ0141/334 2665, ⓦwww.stravaigin.com. Adventurous fine dining in this basement restaurant, where Scottish meats and fish are given an international makeover using a host of exotic ingredients, offering unusual flavour combinations. Mains are £9–22. Look out for the occasional "wild food" nights.

Tattie Mac's 61 Otago St ⓣ0141/337 2282, ⓦwww.tattiemacs.co.uk. A stylish and moderately priced bistro on quiet Otago St, with a modern European menu and a nicely pared down interior.

Thai Siam 1191 Argyle St ⓣ0141/229 1191, ⓦwww.thaisiamglasgow.com. A friendly neighbourhood ambience with excellent Thai-born chefs. Decor and menu are fairly traditional but it's a reliable spot.

Two Fat Ladies 88 Dumbarton Rd ⓣ0141/339 1944, ⓦwww.twofatladiesrestaurant.com. A long-time West End favourite for well-cooked fish and shellfish dishes (around £20) with an intimate 25-seat dining room. A second outlet trades at 118a Blythswood St (ⓣ0141/847 0088) in the city centre, as well as at the traditional *Buttery*, 625–654 Argyle St (ⓣ0141/221 8188).

The Ubiquitous Chip 12 Ashton Lane ⓣ0141/334 5007, ⓦwww.ubiquitouschip.co.uk. Opened in 1971, *The Chip* led the way in headlining Scotland's quality fresh produce at the heart of a stylish upmarket dining experience. Some say it trades on its reputation, but it's still up there. The set three-course dinner is £39.95.

Southside

Art Lovers' Café House for an Art Lover (see p.232), Bellahouston Park ⓣ0141/353 4779. The dining room in this showcase house looks onto a charming garden and offers sublime lunches; there's a Little Art Lovers' menu for kids. Closed evenings.

Greek Golden Kebab 34 Sinclair Drive ⓣ0141/649 7581, ⓦwww.greekgoldenkebab.com. The longest-running Greek restaurant in Glasgow probably hasn't changed its rustic and affordable cooking in forty years. Worth seeking out. Near the south corner of Queens Park; closed Mon–Wed.

La Fiorentina 2 Paisley Rd West ⓣ0141/420 1585, ⓦwww.la-fiorentina.com. A critical favourite that also tops popular surveys, this Tuscan-oriented restaurant has become an institution. The three-course inclusive Tuscan meal (daily except Sat) is a bargain £15. Not far from the Glasgow Science Centre in Govan.

Specialist food shops

There are a host of specialist outlets around Glasgow where you can stock up on good food, the best of them being in the West End. Heart Buchanan Fine Food & Wine, 380 Byres Rd, sets the highest standards with excellent pre-prepared meals, as well as **deli**, dry goods and wine. I.J. Mellis, 492 Great Western Rd, is a wonderful, old-fashioned **cheesemonger** specializing in farmhouse cheeses from the British Isles, though they also keep a selection of the best from the Continent. Mansfield Park, just off Dumbarton Road, hosts Glasgow's **farmers' market** on the second and fourth Saturday of every month from 10am till 2pm. Grassroots, 93 Woodlands Rd, is the best **vegetarian** and Fairtrade food shop in the city, while Roots'n'Fruits, 351 Byres Rd, is piled high with organic fruit and veg. Those looking for Mexican, American and Asian treats should visit Lupe Pintos at 313 Great Western Rd, while there's a quirky foodie attraction at the **Liquid Deli**, 382 Byres Rd, lined with demijohns of olive oil, vinegar, whisky and wine.

Drinking

Many drinking dens in Glasgow's **city centre**, the adjoining **Merchant City** and buzzy **West End** are places to experience real local bonhomie. The city's mythical tough-guy image was once linked to its **pubs**, mistakenly believed by a few to be no-go areas for visitors. Today, however, the city is much changed, and windowless, nicotine-stained working men's taverns are much harder to find than airy modern bars (except in neighbourhoods that you're unlikely to visit).

If you tire of trendier **bars**, set out for the slightly edgier **Saltmarket** district near the Clyde and Glasgow Green, where the local spit-and-sawdust establishments offer a welcome change. The liveliest area for nightlife remains the West End, with students mixing with locals around Byres Road, as well as in the nearby Woodlands and Kelvingrove districts. A pub crawl through either the West End or city centre is easily done on foot. Decent pubs are more widely scattered across the **Southside**, but you'll find a handful of pleasant spots, ranging from stylish hangouts to historic locals.

As for **opening hours**, Glasgow's licensing regulations give bars and pubs more freedom than they have had historically. From Sunday to Thursday, many pubs and bars often keep serving until midnight, although some outside the centre close at 11pm during the week. On Friday and Saturday, you'll often find bars open until 1am – and occasionally later. After closing time, your option is to head to a nightclub (see opposite), some of which don't close until 5am.

City centre and Merchant City

The Arches 253 Argyle St. This basement bar is in a centre for drama and contemporary performance (see opposite), under the railway lines leaving Central station. Decent pub grub and an arty clientele.

Babbity Bowster 16–18 Blackfriars St, off High St. Lively place with a kitsch-free Scottish feel that features spontaneous folk sessions at the weekend. Good beer and wine, tasty food and outdoor seating.

Bar 10 10 Mitchell St. Across from the Lighthouse architecture centre, this is considered the grand-daddy of Glasgow style bars, and suitably chic and popular.

Bar 91 91 Candleriggs. This Merchant City style bar tends to be friendlier, less pretentious and draws a more diverse crowd than most.

Corinthian 191 Ingram St. A remarkable renovation of a florid early Victorian Italianate bank, with three distinct bars and a restaurant: dress smartly if you're arriving in a large pub-crawling group.

Horseshoe Bar 17 Drury St. An original "Gin Palace" with the longest continuous bar in the UK, this is among Glasgow's busiest drinking holes; karaoke (if you dare) upstairs. A must for pub aficionados.

The Lab 26 Springfield Court ⓣ0141/222 2116. Shots served in test tubes give *The Lab* its name; on sunny days you can sit in the secluded beer garden that's a stone's throw from hectic Buchanan St.

Nice'n'Sleazy 421 Sauchiehall St. Better known for its indie rock performance space (see p.242), the ground-floor bar has the feel of New York's East Village, with the best jukebox in the city.

Pot Still 154 Hope St. Whisky galore! At least five hundred different single malts are found in this traditional pub, which offers a decent real ale selection as well.

West Brewing Company Templeton's Carpet Factory, Glasgow Green. Near the People's Palace museum, this place is fashioned after Bavarian beer halls and brews its own excellent Munich-style lager, free of additives and preservatives.

Saltmarket

Clutha Vaults 167 Stockwell St. Slightly more scrubbed and less atmospheric than the nearby *Scotia* (see below) but host to a similar line-up of free live music.

Scotia Bar 112 Stockwell St, ⓦwww.scotiabar.net. Billy Connolly began his career here, telling jokes between singing folk songs; today it's a place for semi-pro live blues, folk and skiffle sessions.

West End

Big Slope 36a Kelvingrove St. Near Kelvingrove Park and nearby guesthouses, this is a hip bar where Alpine hunting lodge meets Manhattan's Lower East Side.

Bon Accord 153 North St ⓦwww.bonaccordweb.co.uk. This pub began the real-ale revival in Glasgow, and often hosts UK beer festivals. At the eastern edge of the West End, adjacent to the M8.

Firebird 1321 Argyle St. Airy modern drinking spot near the Kelvingrove Art Gallery, with a wood-stoked

Scottish food and drink

Scottish produce – particularly its beef, fish, shellfish and game – can be outstanding, and in whisky the country lays almost complete claim to one of the world's most popular alcoholic drinks. In modern Scottish cooking, this produce is combined with foreign influences from classic French cooking to Asian fusion to create a cuisine that can far exceed visitors' expectations.

Venison, a favourite on Scottish menus ▲

Haggis: dee-licious ▼

Scotland's natural larder

Scottish **fish and shellfish** is the envy of Europe, with a vast array of different types of fish, prawns, lobster, mussels, oysters, crab and scallops found round the extensive coastline. The prevalence of fish-farming, now a significant industry in the Highlands and Islands, means that the once-treasured **salmon** is widespread and relatively inexpensive. Both salmon and **trout**, another commonly farmed fish, are frequently smoked and served cold with bread and butter.

Scottish-reared **beef** is often delicious, especially the Aberdeen Angus breed, though Highland cattle is also rated for its depth of flavour. **Venison**, the meat of the red deer, also features large – low in cholesterol and very tasty, it's served roasted or in casseroles, often cooked with juniper and red wine. Other forms of **game** include grouse, which when cooked properly is strong, dark and succulent;

Classic dishes

Arbroath smokies Powerful smoked haddock.

Cullen skink Rich soup made from smoked haddock, potatoes and cream.

Haggis Rich sausage meat (spiced liver, offal, oatmeal and onion) cooked inside a bag made from a sheep's stomach. Tasty and satisfying, particularly when eaten with its traditional accompaniments "bashed neeps" (mashed turnips) and "chappit tatties" (mashed potatoes).

Porridge A breakfast staple, this is properly made simply with oatmeal and water cooked with a pinch of salt. Some folk prefer to add milk and honey, fruit or sugar to sweeten.

Scots broth Hearty soup made with stock (usually mutton), vegetables and barley.

pheasant, a lighter meat; and the less commonly served, but still tasty, pigeon and rabbit.

Beer

Traditional Scottish beer is a thick, dark ale known as **heavy**, served at room temperature in pints or half-pints, with a full head. Quite different in taste from English "bitter", heavy is a more robust, sweeter beer with less of an edge. All of the big-name breweries – McEwan's, Tennents, Belhaven and Caledonian – produce a reasonable selection of heavies. However, if you really want to discover Scottish beer, look out for the products of small **local breweries** such as Aviemore, the Black Isle, Arran, Fyne Ales, Skye, Orkney or Shetland. Look out, too, for Fraoch, available mostly in bottles, a very refreshing, lighter-coloured ale made from heather according to an ancient recipe.

Top five restaurants

The Kitchin, Edinburgh The youthful, unstuffy side of Michelin-starred dining, and seasonal Scottish produce at every turn. See p.112

Loch Fyne Oyster Bar, Argyll A lochside oyster shack done good, and now a standard-bearer for sustainable seafood from the west coast. See p.259.

Mhor Fish, Callander Fish and chips from a family of chefs who like to do things properly, and locally. See p.327.

Three Chimneys, Skye Anywhere offering a menu entitled "Seven Courses of Skye" is on decent terms with its neighbouring suppliers. See p.530.

The Ubiquitous Chip, Glasgow Proper Scottish produce and traditional recipes have been practised in this most urbane of settings for 40 years. See p.239.

▲ Arbroath smokies

▼ Mhor Fish

Speyside-based Macallan ▲

Checking the still at Laphroaig ▼

Ardbeg whisky aged in oak barrels ▼

Whisky

Whisky – *uisge beatha*, or the "water of life" in Gaelic – has been produced in Scotland since the fifteenth century, but only really took off in popularity after the 1780 tax on claret made wine too expensive for most people. The taxman soon caught up with whisky distilling, however, and drove the stills underground. Today, many distilleries operate on the site of simple cottages that once distilled the stuff illegally. In 1823, Parliament revised its Excise Laws, in the process legalizing whisky production, and today the drink is Scotland's chief export.

Despite the dominance of the blended whiskies such as Johnnie Walker, Bell's, Teacher's and The Famous Grouse, **single malt whisky** is infinitely superior, and, as a result, a great deal more expensive. Single malts vary in character enormously depending on the amount of peat used for drying the barley, the water used for mashing, and the type of oak cask used in the maturing process. Malt whisky is best drunk with a splash of water to release its distinctive flavours.

The two most important whisky regions are **Speyside** (see p.434), home of famous varieties such as Glenlivet, Glenfiddich and Macallan, and **Islay** (see p.298), which produces distinctively peaty whiskies such as Laphroaig, Lagavulin and Ardbeg. Many distilleries offer guided tours that range from slick and streamlined to small and friendly. All of them offer visitors a "wee dram" as a finale, and those distilleries that charge an entrance fee often give a discount if you buy a bottle at the end, though prices are no lower at source than in the shops – between £20 and £30 for the average 70cl bottle.

pizza oven producing some tasty snacks, plus DJs to keep the pre-clubbing crowd entertained. It's also a nice daytime haunt, with free wi-fi.

Lismore Lounge 206 Dumbarton Rd. Decorated with specially commissioned stained-glass panels depicting the Highland Clearances, this bar is a meeting point for the local Gaels, who come here to chat, relax and listen to impromptu music sessions.

Oran Mor Byres Rd, at Great Western Rd ⓣ0141/357 6200. Arguably the most impressive addition in many years to the nightlife scene, with a big bar, club venue (see p.242) and performance space/auditorium (plus two different dining rooms) all within the tastefully – and expensively – restored Kelvinside parish church.

Stravaigin 28 Gibson St. Above the expensive restaurant of the same name (see p.239) is this lively and amiable local pub, with an excellent wine selection and excellent food.

Southside

Heraghty's Free House 708 Pollokshaws Rd. Authentic Irish pub that prides itself on pouring the perfect pint of Guinness. Still living down its history of not having a women's loo: one's been installed for several years now.

Tusk 18 Moss Side Rd. Operated by the same company behind the *Corinthian* (see opposite), *Tusk* is almost as flamboyant, with a giant golden Buddha as the focal point. Serves decent Asian food to match.

Nightlife and entertainment

Glasgow has a thriving **contemporary music** community and hot new bands emerge practically every year. There is a clutch of venues, from the famous Barrowland ballroom to King Tut's Wah Wah Hut, where you've a good chance of catching a live act. Additionally, the city's **clubbing scene** is rated among the best in the UK, with the city attracting top DJs from around the world and also breeding a good deal of local talent. Establishments are pretty mixed and an underground scene thrives, while some mega-clubs in this designer-label-conscious city insist on dress codes. Opening hours hover between 11pm to 3am, though some stay open until 5am. Cover charges are variable: expect to pay around £5 during the week and up to £25 at the weekend. Drinks are usually about thirty percent more expensive than in the pubs.

On the **performing arts** scene, Glasgow is no slouch either: it's home to Scottish Opera, Scottish Ballet, the Royal Scottish National Orchestra, and the BBC Scottish Symphony Orchestra. All told, the city's cultural programme offers a range of **music**, from contemporary to heavyweight classical, plus **dance**, **theatre** (both mainstream and experimental/performance art), as well as **cinema**. Most of the larger theatres, cinema multiplexes and concert halls are in the city centre; the West End is home to one or two venues while the Southside has the Citizens, much-loved theatre noted for cutting-edge drama.

For detailed **listings** on what's on, pick up the comprehensive fortnightly magazine *The List* (£2.20), which also covers Edinburgh, or consult Glasgow's *Herald* or *Evening Times* newspapers. To book **tickets** for theatre productions or big concerts, try Tickets Scotland, 239 Argyle St, under Central station's platforms (Mon–Wed, Fri & Sat 9am–6pm, Thurs 9am–7pm, Sun noon–5pm; ⓣ0141/204 5151, ⓦwww.tickets-scotland.com).

Clubs

The Arches 30 Midland St, off Jamaica St ⓣ0870/240 7528, ⓦwww.thearches.co.uk. In converted arches under Central station, the renowned club portion of this arts venue offers house and techno.

Buff Club 142 Bath Lane ⓣ0141/248 1777, ⓦwww.thebuffclub.com. The playlist of vintage disco, funk and northern soul draws an eclectic crowd of clubbers.

The Garage 490 Sauchiehall St ⓣ0141/332 1120 ⓦwww.garageglassow.co.uk Medium-sized, indie-oriented student club that also hosts gigs across the rock'n'roll spectrum.

Glasgow School of Art 167 Renfrew St ⓣ0141/332 0691. Blissfully unadorned space for hipsters, with music that includes some of the best hip-hop in town.

02 ABC 300 Sauchiehall St ⓣ0141/553 1638, ⓦwww.02glasgow.co.uk. Also a live music venue (see below), *ABC* has become one of the hippest and hottest clubs in the city centre with a focus on indie, classic soul and even punk.

Oran Mor Byres Rd, at Great Western Rd ⓣ0141/357 6200. This converted church offers the West End's classiest and most enjoyable clubbing experience. see also p.241

Sub Club 22 Jamaica St ⓣ0141/248 4600, ⓦwww.subclub.co.uk. Near-legendary venue and base for the noteworthy Optimo club as well as Saturday night's Subculture, this is the home for house and techno lovers in the west of Scotland.

The Tunnel 84 Mitchell St ⓣ0141/204 1000. Contemporary and progressive house music club with arty decor (dig the gents' cascading waterfall walls) and fairly strict dress codes.

Gay clubs and bars

Bennets 90 Glassford St, Merchant City ⓣ0141/552 5761, ⓦwww.bennetsnightclub.co.uk. Glasgow's longest-running gay club: predominantly male and fairly traditional with commercially oriented music. Closed Tues.

Delmonica's 68 Virginia St ⓣ0141/552 4803. One of Glasgow's liveliest and largest gay bars, in a popular area with a mixed, hedonistic crowd and nightly entertainment or events.

Merchant Pride 20 Candleriggs ⓣ0141/564 1285. Formerly the *Candle Bar*. Relaxed and Unpretentious if a little dated, with DJs, karaoke and quiz nights.

Polo Lounge 84 Wilson St, off Glassford St ⓣ0141/553 1221. Original Victorian decor – marble tiles and open fires – and a gentleman's club atmosphere upstairs, with a dark, pounding nightclub underneath which attracts a gay and gay-friendly crowd.

Revolver 6a John St ⓣ0141/553 2456, ⓦwww.revolverglasgow.co.uk. This bar is geared more towards the art of conversation than dance, although the jukebox (free) is tops; welcomes men and women.

Live music venues

02 ABC 300–330 Sauchiehall St ⓣ0141/332 2232, ⓦwww.02glasgow.co.uk. Opened in 2005 and more proof that Glasgow's a gig-hungry town, this small- to medium-sized hall offers an intimate setting to see bands.

Barrowland 244 Gallowgate ⓣ0141/552 4601, ⓦwww.glasgow-barrowland.com. Legendary East End ballroom that hosts some of the sweatiest and best gigs you may ever encounter. With room for a couple of thousand, it mostly books bands securely on the rise but still hosts some big-time acts who return to it as their favourite venue in Scotland.

Carling Academy 121 Eglington St ⓣ0141/418 3000, ⓦwww.glasgow-academy.co.uk. With a capacity for 2500, this is the city's principal mid-sized venue.

The Garage 490 Sauchiehall St ⓣ0141/332 1120, ⓦwww.garageglasgow.co.uk. Nightclub which converts to a medium-sized venue for bands that are just about to make it big.

King Tut's Wah Wah Hut 272a St Vincent St ⓣ0141/221 5279, ⓦwww.kingtuts.co.uk. Famous as the place where Oasis were discovered, and still with one of the city's best live music programmes. Also has a good bar, with an excellent jukebox.

Nice'n'Sleazy 421 Sauchiehall St ⓣ0141/333 0900, ⓦwww.nicensleazy.com. Alternative and indie-oriented acts play most nights in the performance space below this city-centre bar (see p.240); don't be put off by the name – this is a great small venue.

Queen Margaret Union 22 University Gardens ⓣ0141/339 9784, ⓦwww.qmu.org.uk. Indie and dance-oriented acts, plus the Revolution club night on a Tues.

Theatres and comedy venues

Arches Theatre 253 Argyle St ⓣ0141/565 1000, ⓦwww.thearches.co.uk. Home to its own avant-garde theatre company, reviving old classics and introducing new talent in this hip subterranean venue.

Citizens' Theatre 119 Gorbals St ⓣ0141/429 0022, ⓦwww.citz.co.uk. The "Citz" has evolved from its 1960s working-class roots into one of the most respected and innovative contemporary theatres in Britain. Three stages, concession rates for students and free preview nights.

Cottier Theatre 93–95 Hyndland St ⓣ0141/357 3868, ⓦwww.thecottier.com. This performance space in the old Dowanhill church hosts touring shows, dance and music gigs. An adjoining bar with beer garden is a favourite on warm summer evenings.

King's Theatre 297 Bath St ⓣ0844/871 7648, ⓦwww.ambassadortickets.com, ⓦwww.kings-glasgow.co.uk. Gorgeous interiors within an imposing red-sandstone Victorian building; the programme is good quality, if safely mainstream.

Ramshorn Theatre 98 Ingram St ⓣ0141/552 3489, ⓦwww.strath.ac.uk/culture/ramshorn. Another church conversion, this Merchant City venue features student and other productions at bargain prices.

The Stand 333 Woodlands Rd ⓣ0870/600 6055, ⓦwww.thestand.co.uk. Sister to the first-rate comedy club in Edinburgh, booking local, national and international acts.
Theatre Royal 282 Hope St ⓣ0844/871 7648, ⓦwww.ambassadortickets.com. This late nineteenth-century playhouse was revived in the mid-1970s as the opulent home of Scottish Opera. It also plays regular host to visiting theatre groups, including the Royal Shakespeare Company, as well as orchestras.
Tramway 25 Albert Drive, off Pollokshaws Rd ⓣ0845/330 3501, ⓦwww.tramway.org. Based in a converted tram terminus, whose lofty proportions qualified it as the only suitable UK venue for Peter Brook's famous production of the *Mahabharata* in 1998.
Tron Theatre 63 Trongate ⓣ0141/552 4267, ⓦwww.tron.co.uk. Varied repertoire of some mainstream and, more importantly, challenging productions from leading local companies, such as Glasgow's Vanishing Point. Folk music performances in theatre bar.

Concert halls

City Halls Candleriggs ⓣ0141/353 8000, ⓦwww.glasgowconcerthalls.com. Completely renovated Victorian halls and old fruit market, this Merchant City performance space is home to the BBC Scottish Symphony Orchestra and hosts many of the annual Celtic Connections concerts.
Glasgow Royal Concert Hall 2 Sauchiehall St ⓣ0141/353 8000, ⓦwww.glasgowconcerthalls.com. One of Glasgow's less memorable modern buildings, though with great acoustics, this is the venue for big-name touring orchestras and the home of the Royal Scottish National Orchestra. Also features major rock and r'n'b stars.
Scottish Exhibition and Conference Centre, and Clyde Auditorium Finnieston Quay ⓣ0870/040 4000, ⓦwww.secc.co.uk. The SECC is a gigantic airplane hangar-like space with dreadful acoustics that, unfortunately, is the only indoor venue in Scotland for world-touring megastars from Bob Dylan to McFly. The adjacent Clyde Auditorium – better known as the Armadillo – is smaller but more melodic.

Cinemas

Cineworld 7 Renfrew St ⓣ0871/200 2000. A gigantic multistorey cinema with first-run Hollywood mainstream movies, plus a few art and independent films as well.
Glasgow Film Theatre 12 Rose St ⓣ0141/332 6353, ⓦwww.gft.org.uk. Dedicated art, independent and repertory cinema house in an Art Deco building; it's home to the Glasgow Film Festival in February. The in-house *Café Cosmo* is an excellent place for pre-show drinks.
Grosvenor 24 Ashton Lane ⓣ0845/166 6002, ⓦwww.socialanimal.co.uk. Renovated two-screen neighbourhood film house with bar – and sofas you can reserve for screenings of mostly mainstream films.
IMAX Theatre Glasgow Science Centre, 50 Pacific Quay ⓣ0141/420 5000, ⓦwww.glasgowsciencecentre.org. 3D and super-screen documentaries and features.

Shopping

Glasgow's **shopping** is amongst the best in the UK, after London. While the city's gritty industrial reputation doesn't appear to fit with its status as an oasis of retail therapy, Glaswegians have long enjoyed dressing up to go out. The main area for spending in the city centre is formed by the Z-shaped and mostly pedestrianized route of **Argyle, Buchanan and Sauchiehall streets**. Along the way you'll find Princes Square, the city's poshest mall (see p.218), plus major department stores and branches of upmarket chains. The Buchanan Galleries, a bland complex built around John Lewis, features some high-fashion budget stores; more interesting is the Parisian-style Victorian Argyle Arcade, specializing in antique and contemporary jewellery.

Otherwise, make for the **Merchant City** or the **West End** which have more individual offerings – the latter has quirky vintage and one-off fashion boutiques, and is the only district in the city with secondhand and antiquarian **bookshops**.

For more on delis and specialist **food** shopping see p.239.

Arts and crafts Shops in the Glasgow School of Art and The Lighthouse (see p.224 & p.220) are well stocked with tasteful gifts and original design items.
Books Waterstone's has a large outlet at 153 Sauchiehall St (Ⓣ0141/332 9105). For secondhand books head to the West End and try Caledonian Bookshop, 483 Great Western Rd (Ⓣ0141/334 9663) or tatty, overflowing Voltaire & Rousseau Books, 18 Otago Lane (Ⓣ0141/339 1811).
Camping and outdoors gear Tiso, 129 Buchanan St (Ⓣ0141/248 4877) and 50 Couper St, northeast of Buchanan bus terminal (Ⓣ0141/559 5450), features an ice-climbing wall, a waterfall (to test cagoules) and a 300ft walking-boot test track.
Fashion Fashionistas with money to burn should head for the chichi and pricey Italian Centre in the Merchant City for some imported glamour, or home-grown Cruise at180 Ingram St for designer wear. By far the best option for more affordable and stylish gear is the West End, specifically Byres Rd and the cluster of vintage stores on Ruthven Lane. Starry Starry Night, 19 Dowanside Lane, near Byres Rd (Ⓣ0141/337 1837), has vintage clothes including some antique pieces such as top hats, and incorporates Bethsy Gray's handmade silver jewellery store; Glorious, 41 Ruthven Lane (Ⓣ0141/357 5582), sells good-quality secondhand women's clothes arrayed by colour, with plenty of decent high-street brands; De Courcy's Arcade, 5 Cresswell Lane, features an appealing collection of cute boutiques and vintage stores, as well as a retro teashop serving tea and cupcakes; while Vintage Circus, 100 Byres Rd (Ⓣ0141/339 2577) combines outré vintage gear with a handy alteration service and a wi-fi café. Otherwise, the Barras market, 244 Gallowgate (Sat & Sun 10am–5pm), has clothes and a whole lot more at its raft of stalls.
Music One of the better shops for local, indie and secondhand music is tiny Avalanche, 34 Dundas St, near Queen St station (Ⓣ0141/332 2099). Also good for non-mainstream music are Monorail inside Mono café/bar, Kings Court, 10 King St (Ⓣ0141/552 9458); 23rd Precinct on 23 Bath St, staffed by local DJs; and Missing Records at 247 Argyle St.
Tartan/woollen Places to select your tweeds and tartans are James Pringle Weavers of Inverness, 130 Buchanan St; Hector Russell Kiltmakers, 110 Buchanan St; and Geoffrey (Tailor) Kiltmakers and Weavers, 309 Sauchiehall St.

Listings

American Express 66 Gordon St (Mon–Fri 8.30am–5.30pm, except Wed 9.30am–5.30pm, Sat 9am–noon; Ⓣ0141/225 2908).
Banks and exchange Bank of Scotland/Halifax, 54–62 Sauchiehall St; Clydesdale Bank, 30 St Vincent Place. Post offices in Hope and St Vincent streets operate bureaux de change as does Glasgow Tourist Information Centre (see p.211).
Bike rental and routes A good selection can be found at West End Cycles, 16 Chancellor St (Ⓣ0141/357 1344), which is located close to the start of the Glasgow to Loch Lomond route, one of a number of cycle routes which radiate out from the city. For further details, check Ⓦwww.sustrans.co.uk.
Bus and coach information Traveline (Ⓣ0871/200 2233, Ⓦwww.travelinescotland.com) has comprehensive information. Operators include Buchanan Street bus station (Ⓣ0141/332 6811); Citylink coaches Ⓣ0871/266 3333, Ⓦwww.citylink.co.uk; First Glasgow (local services; Ⓣ0141/423 6600, Ⓦwww.firstgroup.com).
Car rental Arnold Clark, multiple branches (Ⓣ0844/815 2129); Avis, 70 Lancefield St (Ⓣ0844/544 6064); Budget, West St Trading Estate (0844/544 4606). Car rental at the airport includes Budget (Ⓣ0844/544 4606) and Hertz (Ⓣ0870/850 2677).
Dentist For emergency dental care call Ⓣ0845/602 6417; after 6pm and at weekends dial Ⓣ0845/424 2424. Glasgow Dental Hospital is at 378 Sauchiehall St (Ⓣ0141/211 9600).
Flight information Glasgow International Airport (Ⓣ0141/887 1111, Ⓦwww.glasgowairport.com). Glasgow Prestwick International Airport (Ⓣ0871/223 0700, Ⓦwww.gpia.co.uk).
Gay and lesbian contacts Strathclyde Lesbian and Gay Switchboard (Ⓣ0141/847 0447).
Golf The city operates several inexpensive municipal courses. One of the best maintained and longest is Littlehill, Auchinairn Rd (Ⓣ0141/276 0704).
Hospital 24hr Accident & Emergency at the Royal Infirmary, 84 Castle St near Glasgow Cathedral (Ⓣ0141/211 5608).
Internet Many cafés, bars and hotels offer free wi-fi, along with public libraries. You'll also find terminals at Sip'n'Surf, 521 Great Western Rd (Ⓣ0141/339 4449).
Laundry Garnethill Cleaners, 39 Dalhousie St; Majestic Laundrette, 1110 Argyle St.

Left luggage Buchanan St bus station and lockers at Central or Queen St train stations (depending on current security restrictions).
Libraries Mitchell Library, 533 North St (☎0141/287 2999), is the largest public reference library in Europe.
Pharmacies Boots, Buchanan Galleries (Mon–Sat 9am–6pm, Sun 11am–5pm; ☎0141/333 9306), and branches throughout the city.
Police Strathclyde Police HQ, 173 Pitt St (☎0141/532 2000). For emergencies, dial 999.
Post office General information (☎0845/722 3344). Main office at 47 St Vincent St (Mon–Fri 8.30am–5.45pm, Sat 9am–5.30pm); city centre branch at 87–91 Bothwell St.
Swimming pools At city-run leisure centres in the Gorbals (☎0141/276 1490); Scotstoun (☎0141/959 4000); Tollcross (Olympic size; ☎0141/276 0801).
Taxis Glasgow Taxi Ltd (☎0141/429 7070).
Train information National Rail enquiries (☎0845/748 4950, www.nationalrail.co.uk); Strathclyde Passenger Transport (☎0141/332 6811, www.spt.co.uk); Transcentre ticket office, St Enoch underground station.
Travel agents STA Travel Ltd, 184 Byres Rd (☎0871/702 9821).

The Clyde

The **River Clyde** is the dominant physical feature of Glasgow and its environs, an area that comprises the largest urban concentration in Scotland, with almost two million people living in the city and satellite towns. Little of this immediate hinterland can be described as beautiful, with crisscrossing motorways and relentlessly grim housing estates dominating much of the landscape. However, there are pockets of interest, many related to the river itself or the industries that grew up from it. Beyond the urban sprawl, rolling green hills, open expanses of water and attractive countryside hold the promise of wilder country beyond.

West of the city, regular trains and the M8 motorway dip down from the southern bank of the Clyde to **Paisley**, where the distinctive cloth pattern gained its name, before heading back up to the edge of the river again as it broadens into the **Firth of Clyde**. Here the former shipbuilding towns of **Port Glasgow**, **Greenock** and **Gourock** look out over the water to the lochs and hills of Argyll, a prospect which also serves as a backdrop to two towns on the north bank of the firth – the ancient Strathclyde capital of **Dumbarton**, and **Helensburgh**, birthplace of architect Charles Rennie Mackintosh and the site of one of his greatest buildings, the Hill House.

North of Glasgow lies some wonderful upland countryside. Trains terminate at tiny Milngavie (pronounced "Mill-guy"), which makes great play of its status as the start of Scotland's best-known long-distance footpath, the **West Highland Way** (see box, p.321). Nearby, the rolling beauty of the Campsie Fells provides excellent walking and stunning views down onto Glasgow and the glinting river that runs through it.

Heading southeast out of Glasgow, the industrial landscape of the **Clyde Valley** eventually gives way to a far more attractive scenery of gorges and towering castles. Here lie the stoic town of **Lanark**, where eighteenth-century philanthropists built their model workers' community around the mills of **New Lanark**, and the spectacular **Falls of Clyde**, a mile upstream. Even further beyond, deep into the rolling countryside of South Lanarkshire where the Clyde is little more than a widening stream, the market town of **Biggar** with its unusual clutch of museums serves as a useful orientation point for the hill-farming country of the Scottish Borders beyond.

The Firth of Clyde – south bank

The swift journey from Glasgow along the M8, coupled with the proximity of the international airport, can belie the fact that **Paisley** is not a suburb of Glasgow but a town in its own right, with a long and distinctive history, particularly in the textile trade. Further west, the motorway and train line rejoin the Clyde by the **Erskine Bridge**, a huge concrete parabola that carries cars between the two banks of the river. As the estuary widens, the former shipbuilding centres of Port Glasgow and **Greenock** crowd the riverbank, followed by the old-fashioned seaside resort of **Gourock**, and eventually **Wemyss Bay**, jumping-off point for the ferry to Rothesay on Bute. Of the four, Greenock is by far the most interesting, with an excellent town museum that examines the life and achievements of local boy James Watt.

Paisley

Founded in the twelfth century as a monastic settlement around an abbey, **PAISLEY** expanded rapidly after the eighteenth century as a linen-manufacturing town, specializing in the production of highly fashionable imitation Kashmiri shawls. The town quickly eclipsed other British centres producing the cloth, eventually lending its name to the swirling pine-cone design.

South of the train station, down Gilmour or Smithills streets, lie the bridge over the White Cart Water and the burgh's ponderous **town hall**. Opposite, the **abbey** (Mon–Sat 10am–3.30pm; free) was built on the site of the town's original settlement and was massively overhauled in the Victorian age. Inside the squat grey building, the elongated choir, rebuilt extensively throughout the last two centuries, is illuminated by jewel-coloured stained glass from a variety of ages and styles. The abbey's oldest monument is the tenth-century Celtic cross of St Barochan, at the eastern end of the north aisle.

Paisley's bland pedestrianized **High Street** leads westwards from the town hall to the **Museum and Art Gallery** (Tues–Sat 10am–5pm, Sun 2–5pm; free), sheltering behind Ionic columns that face the grim buildings of Paisley University. Inside, it's a reasonably attractive civic building, but the main reason for coming here is to see the Shawl Gallery, which deals with the growth and development of the Paisley pattern and shawls, showing the familiar pine-cone (or teardrop) pattern from its simple beginnings to elaborate later incarnations. The Upper Gallery houses a small art collection including works by Glasgow Boys Hornel, Guthrie and Lavery (see p.227), as well as paintings by local boy John Byrne, artist and playwright best known for his plays *The Slab Boys* and *Tutti Frutti*.

On Oakshaw Street, which runs along the crest of the hill above the Art Gallery, the **Coats Observatory** (Tues–Sat 10am–5pm, Sun 2–5pm; free) has recorded astronomical and meteorological information since 1884. The telescopes are used for public viewing from October till March (6.30–9.30pm, weather permitting).

Practicalities

Regular **trains** from Glasgow Central run to Paisley's Gilmour Street station in the centre of town, and they're a faster, more convenient option than **buses** #9 (First), #36, #38 or #39 (all Arriva) from Glasgow city centre. Buses leave Paisley's Gilmour Street forecourt every ten to fifteen minutes for Glasgow International Airport, two miles north of the town. The **tourist office** is right in the centre at 9a Gilmour St (Mon–Sat; ⓣ0141/889 0711).

Few people **stay** in Paisley, but if you do, try neat and elegant Georgian *Ashtree House*, 9 Orr Square (ⓣ0141 848 6411, ⓦwww.ashtreehousehotel.com; ❺). For **food** the Paisley Arts Centre has a small bar, daytime café and outside seating; not far away, *Cardosi's* on Storie Street has decent evening menus.

Greenock and around

GREENOCK, west of Glasgow, was the site of the first dock on the Clyde, founded in 1711, and the community has grown on the back of shipping ever since. Despite its ranks of anonymous tower blocks and sterile shopping centres, the town still retains a few features of interest. To get there, you'll pass through **Port Glasgow**, a small fishing village until 1688, when the burghers of Glasgow bought it and developed it as their main harbour. As you come into the town, look out for sturdy fifteenth-century **Newark Castle** right on the banks of the river (April–Sept daily 9.30am–5.30pm; HS; £3.70).

From the Central train station in Greenock (also served by hourly Citylink buses from Glasgow's Buchanan Street station), it's a short walk down the hill to **Cathcart Square**, where an exuberant 245ft-high Victorian tower looms high over the elegant Council House. On the dockside, reached by crossing the dual carriageway behind the square, the Neoclassical **Custom House** is Greenock's finest building, splendidly located looking out over the river. From the dock in front, tens of thousands of nineteenth-century emigrants departed for the New World. These days, **Clyde Marine Cruises** (Ⓣ01475/721281, Ⓦwww.clyde-marine.co.uk) operates from Victoria Harbour, a few minutes from Central Station; it runs a ferry link and cruise to Loch Long and Loch Goil (May–Sept Mon–Fri 10.30am & 12.45pm, July & Aug also on Sat; £11).

A hundred yards from the well-proportioned **George Square**, close to Greenock West station, the **McLean Museum and Art Gallery** in Union Street (Mon–Sat 10am–5pm; free) contains pictures and contemporary records of the life and achievements of Greenock-born **James Watt**, prominent eighteenth-century industrialist and pioneer of steam power, as well as featuring exhibits on the shipbuilding industry and other local trades. The small art gallery on the ground floor contains work by Glasgow Boys Hornel and Guthrie plus Colourists Fergusson, Cadell and Peploe.

Accommodation is particularly scarce in Greenock, so it's advisable to book ahead. *The Tontine Hotel* is in Ardgowan Square, a few minutes' walk west of the Art Gallery (Ⓣ01475/723316, Ⓦwww.tontine-hotel.co.uk; ❹); the budget option in town is at the *James Watt Halls of Residence* (Ⓣ01475/731360, Ⓦwww.jameswatt.ac.uk; ❷) on Customhouse Quay, overlooking the river, where you can find clean and tidy en-suite twin rooms all year round. Greenock's eating options are restricted to predictable high-street cafés and takeaways, though neighbouring Gourock has a slightly better selection, including *Café Continental* on Kempock Street, which serves bar/bistro food and has views across the Clyde.

Gourock

On the train line west of Greenock, Fort Matilda station perches below **Lyle Hill**, an invigorating 450ft climb that is well worth the effort for the astounding views over the mountains of Argyll. West of here lies the dowdy old resort of **GOUROCK**, once a holiday destination for generations of Glaswegians, but today only of significance as a **ferry** terminal: both CalMac (Ⓣ0800/066 5000, Ⓦwww.calmac.co.uk) and the more frequent Western Ferries (Ⓣ01369/704452, Ⓦwww.western-ferries.co.uk) ply the twenty-minute route across the Firth of Clyde to Dunoon on the Cowal peninsula (see p.259), while a passenger-only ferry runs year-round to Kilcreggan and Helensburgh on the north bank of the Clyde (Mon–Sat 13 daily, also 5 on Sun in summer; £2.25 single; Ⓦwww.spt.co.uk/ferry). By the seafront there's a heated outdoor **swimming pool** (May–Sept Mon, Wed & Fri 9.30am–8.30pm, Tues & Thurs 8.30am–8.30pm, Sat & Sun 10am–4.30pm; £2.40) with a spectacular backdrop of the Argyll mountains.

Wemyss Bay

There's not much south of Gourock apart from a gruesome power-station chimney and large yacht marina at **Inverkip**, until you reach **WEMYSS** (pronounced "Weems") **BAY**, the terminus of the southern branch of the train line from Port Glasgow, which clips the edge of Greenock before curling around the mountains and moors. The most memorable part of the journey is the arrival at the grand and historic Wemyss Bay station, an impressive wrought-iron and glass palace which serves as a reminder of the great glory days when thousands of Glaswegians would alight for their steamer trip "doon the watter". It's now the departure point for the CalMac **ferry** over to Rothesay, capital of the Isle of Bute (see p.261).

The Firth of Clyde – north bank

Heading west out of Glasgow, the A82 road and the train tracks both follow the north bank of the river, passing through Clydebank, another ex-shipbuilding centre, and Bowling, the western entry point of the newly reopened Forth & Clyde Canal (see p.316). At **Dumbarton**, an ancient regional capital, the main road swings north towards Loch Lomond (see p.319), while the railway and A814 carry on along the shores of the Firth of Clyde to wealthy **Helensburgh**, before turning north along the shores of Gare Loch and Loch Long to Arrochar, which marks the beginning of Argyll (see p.258).

Dumbarton

Founded in the fifth century, the town of **DUMBARTON** today is for the most part a brutal concrete sprawl, fulfilling every cliché about postwar planning and architecture. It's best to avoid the town itself – though Talking Heads fans might be interested to know that David Byrne was born here – and head a mile southeast to **Dumbarton Castle** (April–Sept daily 9.30am–5.30pm; Oct daily 9.30am–4.30pm, Nov–March Sat–Wed 9.30am–4.30pm; £4.20), which sits atop a twin outcrop of volcanic rock surrounded by water on three sides. First founded as a Roman fort, the castle became a royal seat, from which Mary, Queen of Scots, sailed for France to marry Henri II's son in 1548. From the 1600s, the castle has been used on and off as a garrison and artillery fortress to guard the approaches to Glasgow; most of the current buildings date from this period.

Dumbarton is also home to a quirky but fascinating piece of industrial heritage relating to the glory days of Clyde shipbuilding, housed on Castle Street, between the castle and the town centre. The **Denny Tank** (Mon–Sat 10am–4pm; £2), houses the world's oldest working ship-model experiment tank, at around 110yd long. It's still used to test scale models of ships prior to the expensive business of construction.

For the most part, however, Dumbarton is just a waypoint for those heading into the Loch Lomond and the Trossachs National Park, either via Helensburgh and the coast or more directly through Balloch (see p.319). There's a **tourist office** (daily April–Oct) a couple of miles east of town by the side of the main A82 road.

Helensburgh

HELENSBURGH, twenty miles or so northwest of Glasgow, is a smart, Georgian grid-plan settlement overlooking the Clyde estuary. In the eighteenth century it was a well-to-do commuter town for Glasgow and also a seaside resort, whose bathing-master, **Henry Bell**, invented one of the first steamboats, the *Comet*. Today, Helensburgh is a stop on the route of the paddle steamer **Waverley** (see box, p.230), and there's also a passenger-only **ferry** service across the Clyde to Kilcreggan and

Gourock (see p.247); pick up timetables for both services from the **tourist office**, on the ground floor of the old Italianate church tower by the Clyde (daily Easter–Oct).

The inventor of TV, John Logie Baird, was born here, as was Charles Rennie Mackintosh, who in 1902 was commissioned by the Glaswegian publisher Walter Blackie to design **Hill House** on Upper Colquhoun Street (April–Oct daily 1.30–5.30pm; NTS; £8.50). Without doubt the best surviving example of Mackintosh's domestic architecture, the house is stamped with his very personal, elegant interpretation of Art Nouveau – right down to the light fittings and fire irons. Various upstairs rooms are given over to interpretative displays on the architect's use of light, colour, form and texture, while changing exhibitions on contemporary domestic design from around Britain are a testament to Mackintosh's ongoing influence and inspiration. After exploring the house, head for the **tearoom** in the kitchen quarters, or wander round the beautifully laid-out **gardens**.

Practicalities

Hill House is a good twenty-minute walk up Sinclair Street from Helensburgh Central **train** station, or just five minutes from Helensburgh Upper train station (where trains to and from Oban and Fort William stop). The town's **B&Bs** include antique-filled, non-smoking *Lethamhill*, 20 West Dhuhill Drive (Ⓣ01436/676016, Ⓦwww.lethamhill.co.uk; ⑤), set in the attractive, leafy villa district near Helensburgh Upper; and *Ravenswood*, 32 Suffolk St (Ⓣ01436/672112; ⑤), a family home in the western part of town. Helensburgh isn't short of **tearooms** and coffee shops; try tartanified *Craigard*, at 51 Sinclair St (Ⓣ01436/677787, Ⓦwww.craigard-tearoom.co.uk), which serves Scottish bistro food.

The Clyde Valley

The journey southeast of Glasgow into Lanarkshire, while mostly following the course of the Clyde upstream, is dominated by endless suburbs, industrial parks and wide strips of concrete highway. The principal road here is the M74, though you'll have to get off the motorway to find the main points of interest. Less than ten miles from central Glasgow, **Bothwell Castle** lies about a mile northeast of the **Blantyre** millworkers' tenement in which the explorer David Livingstone was born. Five miles west of Blantyre, on the outskirts of the new town of East Kilbride, the **National Museum of Scottish Country Life** offers an in-depth look at the history of agriculture in Scotland.

From here, the Clyde winds through lush market gardens and orchards before passing beneath the sturdy little town of **Lanark**, the best base from which to explore the valley. **New Lanark**, on the riverbank, is a remarkable eighteenth-century planned village. Ten miles further upstream, the attractive country town of **Biggar** has a surprising number of rather quirky museums, and marks the transition from the industrial central belt to rolling Border country.

Blantyre and around

BLANTYRE, now a colourless suburb of Hamilton, was a remote hamlet based around a mill on the banks of the Clyde when explorer and missionary David Livingstone was born there in 1813. First Bus's **bus** #267 from Glasgow (Buchanan St) to Hamilton runs via Blantyre, or there are frequent **trains** from Glasgow Central's lower level.

A separate tenement block set in a quiet country park near the river houses the **David Livingstone Centre** (April–Dec Mon–Sat 10am–5pm, Sun 12.30–5pm; NTS; £5). In 1813, the block consisted of 24 one-room tenements, each occupied by an entire family of mill-workers. Today, one room shows the claustrophobic conditions under which Livingstone was brought up; all the others feature slightly defensive exhibitions on the missionary movement, with tableaux of scenes from his life in Africa, including his "discovery" of the Victoria Falls and the famous meeting with Henry Stanley ("Dr Livingstone, I presume?").

A mile or so north of Blantyre, **Bothwell Castle** (April–Sept daily 9.30am–5.30pm; Oct daily 9.30am–4.30pm; Nov–March Sun–Wed 9.30am–4.30pm; HS; £3.70) is one of Scotland's most dramatic citadels, its great red-sandstone bulk looming high above a loop in the river. The oldest section is the solid donjon built by the Moray family in the late thirteenth century to protect themselves against the English king Edward I during the Scottish wars of independence. Edward only succeeded in capturing it after ordering the construction and deployment of a massive siege engine, wheeled in from Glasgow in order to lob huge stones at the castle walls. First Bus operates **bus** #255 from Glasgow (Buchanan St) to Hamilton and Motherwell, which will drop you off on the Bothwell Road near the castle entrance. By car, it is best approached from the B7071 Bothwell–Uddingston road.

National Museum of Rural Life

On the edge of **EAST KILBRIDE** new town, five miles west of Blantyre and seven miles southeast of Glasgow centre, the **National Museum of Rural Life** (daily 10am–6pm; NTS; £5) is an unexpected union of historic farm and modern museum. The site of the museum, **Kittochside**, is a 170-acre farm which avoided the intensive farming that came to dominate agriculture in Britain after World War II, and it has been retained as a working model farm showcasing traditional methods of farming. A tractor and trailer shuttle visitors the half-mile from the museum up to the eighteenth-century **farmhouse**, which is furnished much as it would have been in the 1950s. Transport isn't straightforward if you don't have your own vehicle. **Bus** #31 from Glasgow's St Enoch Centre to East Kilbride takes you past the museum (Stewartfield Way), or you can get the **train** from Glasgow Central to East Kilbride, and then take a taxi for the final three miles to the museum.

Lanark and New Lanark

The neat little market town of **LANARK** is an old and distinguished burgh, sitting in the hills high above the River Clyde, its rooftops and spires visible for miles around. Beyond the **world's oldest bell**, cast in 1130 and on show in the Georgian church of St Nicholas, there's little to see in town unless you're around during the lively **Lanimer** celebrations in early June, one of Scotland's oldest ceremonies of riding the marches or boundaries, which goes back to 1140. Most people head straight on for the village of **NEW LANARK** (Ⓦwww.newlanark.org), a mile below the main town on Braxfield Road.

Although New Lanark is served by an hourly **bus** from Lanark train station, it's well worth the steep downhill walk to get there. The first sight of the village, hidden away down in the gorge, is unforgettable: large broken curving walls of honeyed warehouses and tenements, built in Palladian style, are lined up along the turbulent river's edge. The community was founded by David Dale and Richard Arkwright in 1785 to harness the power of the Clyde waterfalls in their cotton-spinning industry, but it was Dale's son-in-law, Robert Owen, who revolutionized the social side of the experiment in 1798, creating a "village of unity". Believing the welfare of the workers to be crucial to industrial success, Owen built adult educational facilities, the world's first day nursery and playground, and schools in which dancing and music were obligatory and there was no punishment or reward.

While you're free to wander around the village, which is still partially residential, to get into any of the **exhibitions** (daily: April–Sept 10am–5pm; Oct–March

11am–5pm) you need to buy a passport ticket (£5.95; various discount tickets are available from the train station, including an all-in ticket covering admission and the return train and bus trip from Glasgow). The Neoclassical building that now houses the visitor reception was opened by Owen in 1816 under the utopian title of **The Institute for the Formation of Character**. These days, it contains the **New Millennium Experience**, which whisks visitors on a chairlift through a social history of the village.

Other parts of New Lanark village prove just as fascinating: you can wander through the 1820s shop, and find out how the workers lived in the **New Buildings**, then poke around the domestic kitchen, study and living areas of **Robert Owen's House**. In the **School for Children** there's a clever cinematic show giving an unsentimental picture of village life through the imaginary perspective of a young mill girl. Situated in the Old Dyeworks, the **Scottish Wildlife Trust Visitor Centre** (daily Jan & Feb daily noon–4pm; March–Dec 11am–5pm; £2) provides information about the history and wildlife of the area, with evening trips organized to view bats or a local badger sett. Beyond the visitor centre, a riverside path leads you the mile or so to the major **Falls of the Clyde**, where, at the stunning tree-fringed Cora Linn, the river plunges 90ft in three tumultuous stages.

Practicalities

Lanark is the terminus of **trains** from Glasgow Central. The town's **tourist office** (May–Sept daily; Oct–April closed Sun; ⓣ01555/661661) is housed in the Horsemarket, next to Somerfield supermarket, 100yd west of the station.

By far the most original **accommodation** options in the area, at both ends of the market, make use of reconstructed mill buildings in New Lanark: the SYHA **hostel** (ⓣ0870/004 1143, ⓦwww.syha.org.uk) has two-, four- and five-bed rooms in the cutely named Wee Row on Rosedale Street, and the *New Lanark Mill* (ⓣ01555/667200, ⓦwww.newlanarkhotel.co.uk; ❷) is a four-star **hotel** with good views and lots of character. The best of the **B&Bs** are a little out of town: try Mrs Findlater at attractive whitewashed Jerviswood Mains Farm (ⓣ01555/663987, ⓦwww.jerviswoodmains.com; ❷). There are plenty of cheap **cafés** and takeaways on the High Street in Lanark, as well as some more pricey Indian and Italian **restaurants** along Wellgate, while the unpretentious *Crown Tavern*, a quiet drinking haunt in Hope Street, does reasonable food until 9.30pm.

Biggar and around

Travelling further south, you leave industrial Lanarkshire behind and come instead to the gentle undulations of the Border hills. **BIGGAR**, twelve miles from Lanark, is an old market town, its wide main street lined with rather dated shops. For a town of its size, Biggar has an inordinate number of museums; none could be described as essential, though each has its own quirky appeal. The most general is the **Moat Park Heritage Centre** (June–Sept Mon–Sat 11am–4.30pm, Sun 2–4.30pm; £2) on Kirkstyle, which traces the geological and archeological history of Upper Clydesdale, while tucked away on North Back Road the **Gladstone Court Museum** (May–Sept Mon–Sat 2–5pm, Sun 2–4.30pm; £2) has a re-created street of Victorian shops, including a telephone exchange, bank and cobbler. The **Biggar Gasworks Museum** (June–Sept daily 2–5pm; £1) on Gas Works Road has the appearance of a Lilliputian power station. Built in 1839, it is the only coal-based gasworks still standing; most were demolished in the 1970s when the North Sea gas grid was developed. Finally, on Broughton Road near the country park, the **Biggar Puppet Theatre** (daily 10am–4.30pm; call ⓣ01899/220631 or go to ⓦwww.purvespuppets.com for details of shows), stages regular shows and workshops for children in its Victorian building.

Regular **bus** services to Biggar arrive from a wide range of towns; from Lanark, take bus #191, but there are also services from Edinburgh, Peebles, Moffat, Dumfries and more. They stop on High Street, near the **tourist office** (May–Aug daily; April & Sept Mon–Sat; ⓣ01899/221066). There's an attractive and reasonably priced **hotel**, *Cornhill House*, just to the south of the town (ⓣ01899/220001, ⓦwww.cornhillhousehotel.com; ❺), and **camping** at *Biggar Caravan Park* on Broughton Road (ⓣ01899/220319; April–Oct). For **food**, *Restaurant 55* at 55 High St (ⓣ01899/231555) serves modern Scottish cuisine in relaxed, contemporary surroundings, while the *Elphinstone Hotel* and the *Crown*, both also on High Street, serve up hearty pub grub. For a friendly cup of tea and good home-baking make for the *Gillespie Centre* in Biggar Kirk, facing the two hotels.

Around Biggar

Six miles west of Biggar along the A72/73, near the village of Thankerton, the solitary peak of **Tinto Hill**, or "hill of fire" was the site of Druidic festivals in honour of the sun-god Baal, or Bel. It's a relatively easy walk up the footpath to the 2320ft summit, from where the views are splendid – you'll also see a druidic circle and a Bronze Age burial cairn on the summit. Regular **buses** between Biggar and Lanark stop at Thankerton.

Travel details

Trains

Glasgow Central to: Ardrossan for Arran ferry (every 30min; 50min); Ayr (every 30min; 50min); Birmingham (9 daily; 4hr); Blantyre (every 30min; 20min); Carlisle (hourly; 1hr 10min); East Kilbride (every 30min; 30min); Gourock (every 30min; 45min); Greenock (every 30min; 40min); Lanark (every 30min; 50min); Largs (hourly; 1hr); London (hourly; 4hr 30min); Paisley (every 10min; 10min); Queens Park (every 15min; 6min); Stranraer (4 direct daily; 2hr 30min); Wemyss Bay (hourly; 50min).
Glasgow Queen St to: Aberdeen (hourly; 2hr 30min); Aviemore (3 daily; 2hr 40min); Balloch (every 30min; 45min); Dumbarton (every 20min; 35min); Dundee (hourly; 1hr 20min); Edinburgh (every 15min; 50min); Fort William (Mon–Sat 3 daily, Sun 1–2 daily; 3hr 40min); Helensburgh (every 30min; 45min); Inverness (3 daily direct; 3hr 25min); Mallaig via Fort William (Mon–Sat 3 daily, Sun 1–2 daily; 5hr 15min); Milngavie (every 30min; 25min); Oban (Mon–Sat 3 daily, Sun 1–3 daily; 3hr); Perth (hourly; 1hr); Stirling (every 20min; 25–40min).

Buses

Glasgow Buchanan St to: Aberdeen (hourly; 2hr 40min); Campbeltown (3 daily; 4–5hr); Dundee (twice hourly; 1hr 50min); Edinburgh (every 15min; 1hr 10min); Fort William (4 daily; 3hr); Glen Coe (4 daily; 2hr 30min); Inverness (1 direct daily; 3hr 20min); Kyle of Lochalsh (3 daily; 5–6hr); Loch Lomond (hourly; 45min); London (5 daily; 8–9hr); Oban (3 daily; 2hr 50min); Perth (hourly; 1hr–1hr 35min); Portree (3 daily; 6–7hr); Stirling (hourly; 45min).

Flights

Glasgow International to: Barra (2 daily; 1hr 10min); Belfast (Mon–Fri 7 daily; Sat & Sun 3 daily; 45min); Benbecula (Mon–Sat 2 daily; 1 on Sun; 1hr); Campbeltown (Mon–Fri 2 daily; 40min); Dublin (3 daily; 1hr); Islay (Mon–Fri 2 daily,1 on Sat; 45min); Kirkwall (1 daily; 2hr); London City (Mon–Fri 4 daily, 1 on Sun; 1hr 30min); London Gatwick (Mon–Fri 11 daily, Sat & Sun 4 daily; 1hr 30min); London Heathrow (Mon–Fri 18 daily, Sat & Sun 10 daily; 1hr 30min); London Luton (Mon–Fri 5 daily,3 on Sat, 4 on Sun; 1hr 15min); London Stansted (Mon–Fri 5 daily,3 on Sat, 4 on Sun; 1hr 30min); Shetland (Mon–Fri 2 daily, Sat & Sun 1 daily; 1hr 30min); Stornoway (Mon–Fri 4 daily, Sat & Sun 2 daily; 1hr 10min); Tiree (Mon–Sat 1 daily; 50min).
Glasgow Prestwick to: Dublin (Mon–Fri 3 daily, Sat & Sun 2 daily; 45min); London Stansted (4 daily; 1hr 10min).

Argyll and Bute

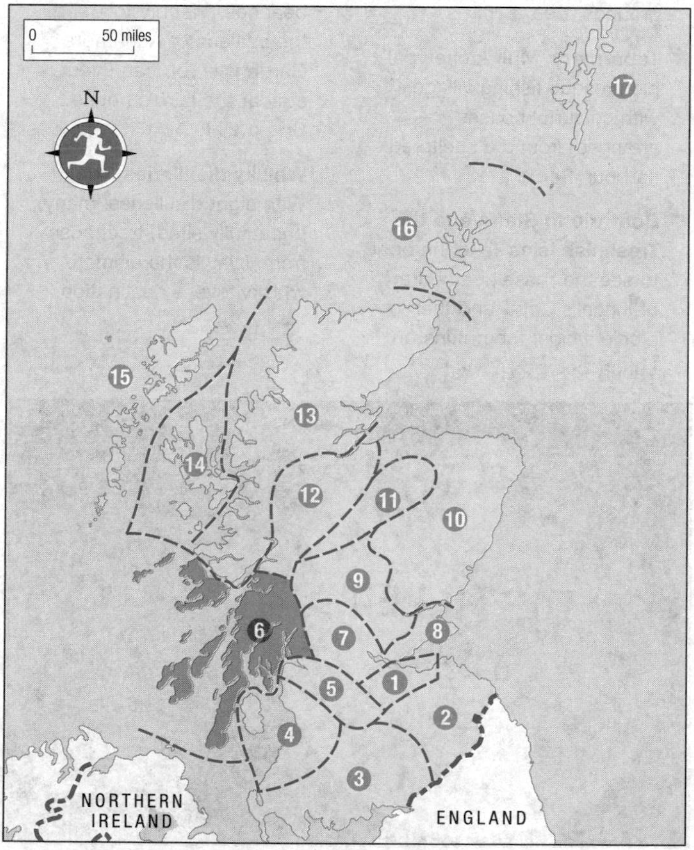

CHAPTER 6

Highlights

* **Loch Fyne Oyster Bar, Cairndow** Dine in or take away at Scotland's finest smokehouse and seafood outlet. See p.259
* **Mount Stuart, Bute** Explore this architecturally overblown mansion set in magnificent grounds. See p.261
* **Tobermory, Mull** Archetypal picturesque fishing village, with colourful houses arranged around a sheltered harbour. See p.272
* **Boat trip to Staffa and the Treshnish Isles** Take the boat to see the "basalt cathedral" of Fingal's Cave, and then picnic amidst the puffins on Lunga See p.276
* **Golden beaches** Kiloran Bay on Colonsay is one of the most perfect sandy beaches in Argyll, but there are plenty more on Islay, Coll and Tiree. See p.284
* **Isle of Gigha** The perfect island escape: sandy beaches, friendly folk and the azaleas of Achamore Gardens – you can even stay at the laird's house. See p.291
* **Whisky distilleries, Islay** With eight distilleries, many beautifully sited, to choose from, Islay is the ultimate whisky lover's destination. See p.298

▲ Laphroaig whisky, Islay

6

Argyll and Bute

Cut off for centuries from the rest of Scotland by the mountains and sea lochs that characterize the region, **Argyll** remains remote, its scatter of offshore islands forming part of the Inner Hebridean archipelago (the remaining Hebrides are dealt with in Chapters 14 & 15). Geographically as well as culturally, this is a transitional area between Highland and Lowland, boasting a rich variety of scenery, from lush, subtropical gardens warmed by the Gulf Stream to flat and treeless islands on the edge of the Atlantic. It's in the folds and twists of the countryside, the interplay of land and water and the views out to the islands that the strengths and beauties of mainland Argyll lie. The one area of man-made sights you shouldn't miss, however, is the cluster of **Celtic** and **prehistoric sites** in mid-Argyll near Kilmartin.

Overall, the population is tiny (just 90,000); even **Oban**, Argyll's chief ferry port, has just 8000 inhabitants, while the prettiest settlement, **Inveraray**, has only 500. Much of mainland Argyll is comprised of remote peninsulas separated by a series of long sea lochs. The first peninsula you come to from Glasgow is **Cowal**, cut off from the rest of Argyll by a set of mountains including the Arrochar Alps. Nestling in one of Cowal's sea lochs is the **Isle of Bute**, whose capital, Rothesay, is probably the most appealing of the old Clyde steamer resorts. **Kintyre**, the long finger of land that stretches south towards Ireland, is less visually dramatic than Cowal, though it does provide a stepping stone for several Hebridean islands, as well as Arran (see p.199).

Of the islands covered in this chapter, mountainous **Mull** is the most visited, though it is large enough to absorb the crowds, many of whom are only passing through en route to the tiny isle of **Iona**, a centre of Christian culture since the sixth century, or to **Tobermory**, the island's impossibly picturesque port (aka "Balamory"). **Islay**, best known for its distinctive malt whiskies, is fairly quiet even in the height of summer, as is neighbouring **Jura**, which offers excellent walking opportunities. And, for those seeking further solitude, there's the island of **Colonsay**, with its beautiful golden sands, and the windswept islands of **Tiree** and **Coll**, which also have great beaches and enjoy more sunny days than anywhere else in Scotland.

Public transport throughout Argyll is minimal, though buses do serve most major settlements, and the train line reaches all the way to Oban. In the remoter parts of the region and on the islands, without your own car, you'll have to rely on a combination of walking, hitching, bike rental, shared taxis and the postbus. If you're planning to take a car across to one of the islands, it's essential that you book both your outward and return journeys as early as possible, as the ferries can get very booked up.

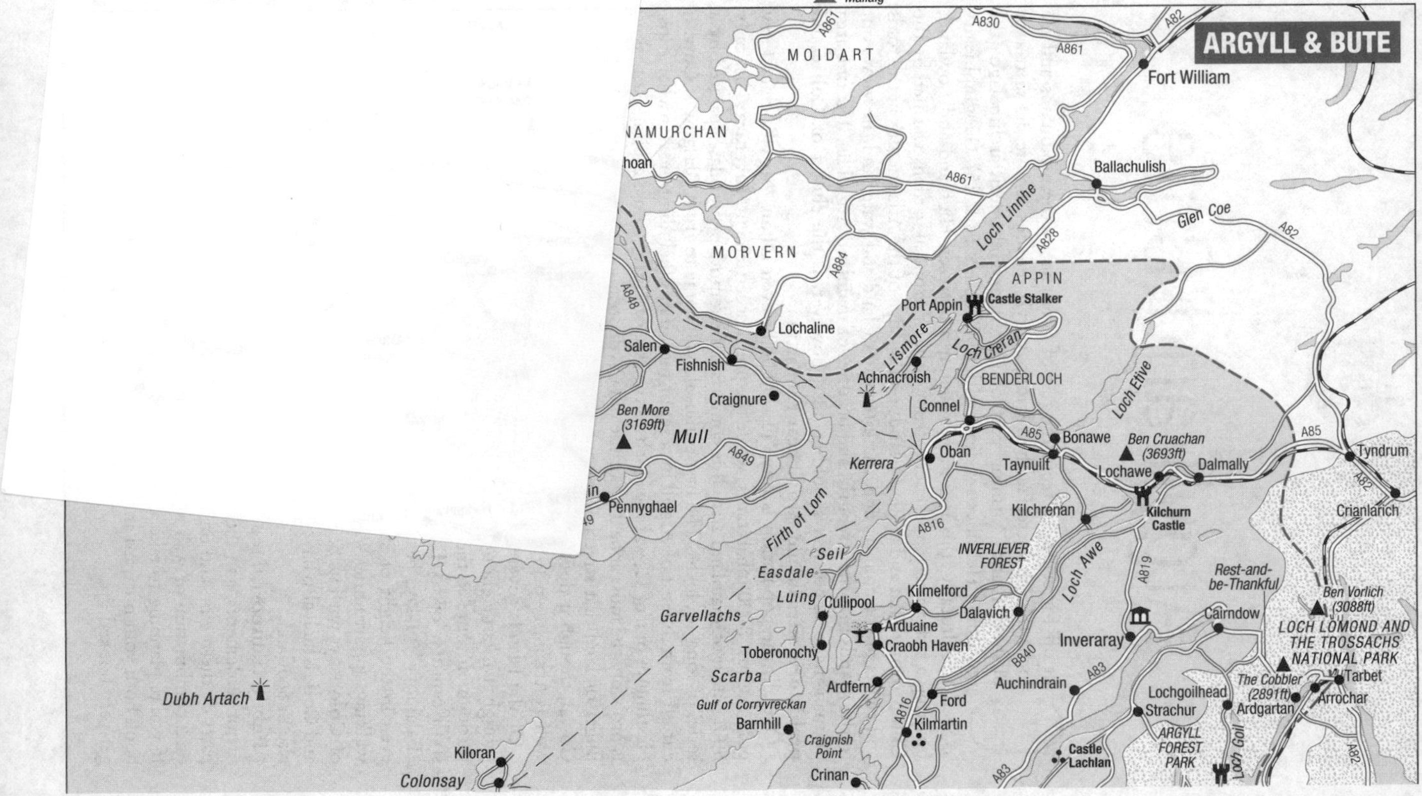

ARGYLL & BUTE

Mallaig
A861
A830
A82
A861
MOIDART
Fort William
NAMURCHAN
hoan
Ballachulish
A861
Glen Coe
A82
Loch Linnhe
A828
MORVERN
A884
APPIN
A848
Port Appin
Castle Stalker
Lochaline
Lismore
Loch Creran
Salen
Fishnish
Achnacroish
BENDERLOCH
Loch Etive
Craignure
Connel
Ben More
(3169ft)
Mull
A85
Bonawe
Ben Cruachan
(3693ft)
A85
Tyndrum
A849
Kerrera
Oban
Taynuilt
Lochawe
Dalmally
A82
Pennyghael
Kilchrenan
Kilchurn
Castle
Crianlarich
Firth of Lorn
A816
INVERLIEVER
FOREST
Seil
Loch Awe
A819
Easdale
Rest-and-
be-Thankful
Ben Vorlich
(3088ft)
Luing
Cullipool
Kilmelford
Dalavich
Garvellachs
Arduaine
Cairndow
LOCH LOMOND AND
THE TROSSACHS
NATIONAL PARK
Inveraray
Toberonochy
Craobh Haven
B840
Scarba
A83
The Cobbler
(2891ft)
Tarbet
Dubh Artach
Ardfern
Auchindrain
Lochgoilhead
Arrochar
Gulf of Corryvreckan
Ford
Strachur
Ardgartan
A816
Barnhill
Kilmartin
A82
Craignish
Point
Castle
Lachlan
ARGYLL
FOREST
PARK
Loch Goil
Kiloran
Colonsay
Crinan
A83

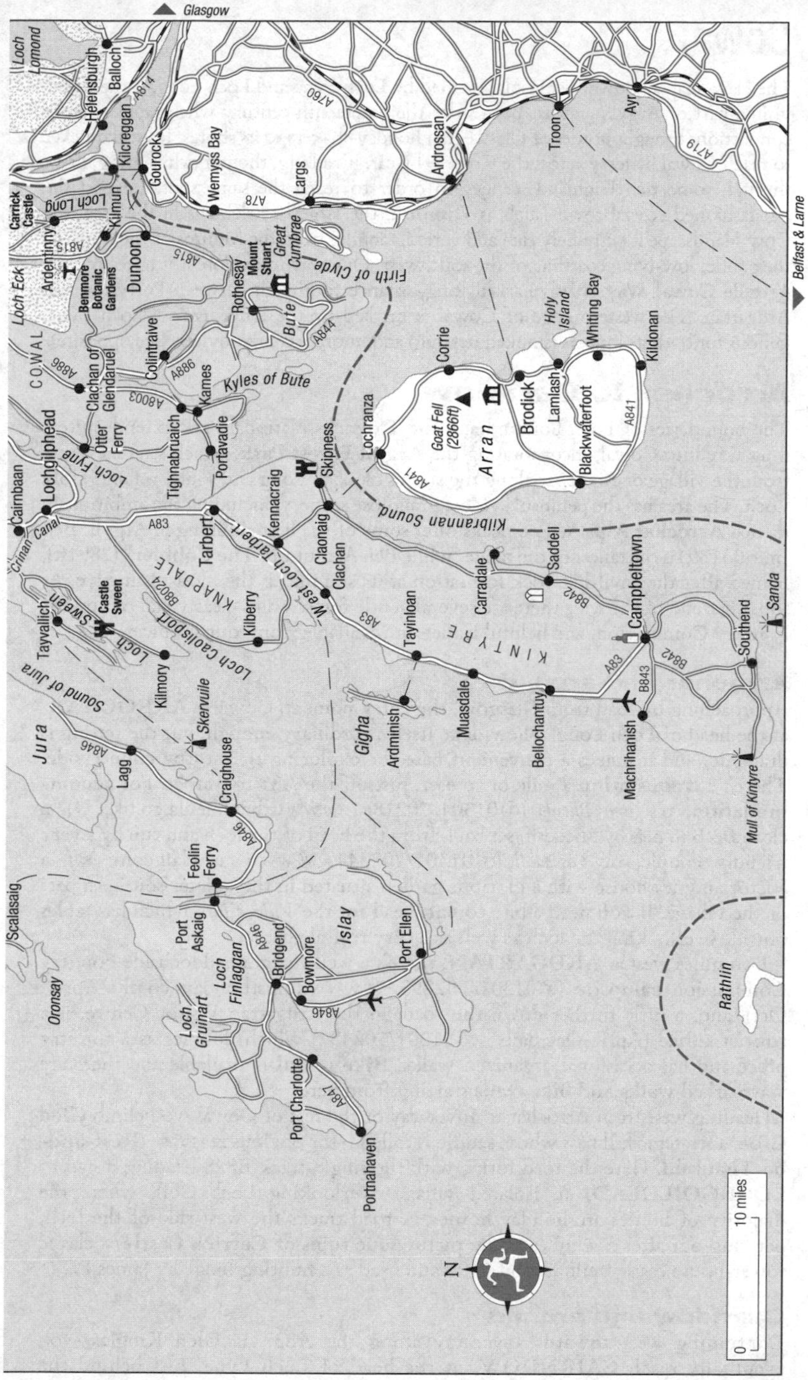

Glasgow
Belfast & Larne
Loch Lomond
Balloch
Helensburgh
Kilcreggan
A814
Gourock
Wemyss Bay
Largs
A78
A760
Ardrossan
Troon
Ayr
A719
Carrick Castle
Loch Long
Kilmun
Ardentinny
A815
Loch Eck
Benmore Botanic Gardens
Dunoon
Rothesay
Mount Stuart
Great Cumbrae
Bute
A844
Firth of Clyde
COWAL
A886
Clachan of Glendaruel
Colintraive
Kyles of Bute
A8003
Tighnabruaich
Kames
Portavadie
Otter Ferry
Loch Fyne
Lochgilphead
Cairnbaan
Crinan Canal
A83
Tarbert
KNAPDALE
B8024
Kilberry
West Loch Tarbert
Kennacraig
Claonaig
Clachan
Skipness
Lochranza
A841
Arran
Goat Fell (2866ft)
Corrie
Brodick
Lamlash
Holy Island
Whiting Bay
Blackwaterfoot
Kildonan
Kilbrannan Sound
Carradale
Saddell
B842
KINTYRE
Tayinloan
Muasdale
Bellochantuy
Campbeltown
A83
B843
Machrihanish
Southend
Sanda
Mull of Kintyre
Rathlin
Gigha
Ardminish
Castle Sween
Loch Sween
Tayvallich
Loch Caolisport
Kilmory
Skervuile
Sound of Jura
Jura
A846
Lagg
Craighouse
Feolin Ferry
Port Askaig
Islay
Loch Finlaggan
Bridgend
Bowmore
Port Ellen
Loch Gruinart
Port Charlotte
A847
Portnahaven
Oronsay
Scalasaig
N
0
10 miles

Cowal

The claw-shaped **Cowal** peninsula, formed by Loch Fyne and Loch Long, is the most-visited part of Argyll, and has been since the nineteenth century when rapid steamer connections brought hordes of Glaswegian holiday-makers to its shores. It's still quicker to reach Cowal by ferry across the Clyde – by car, it's a long, though exhilarating, drive through some rich Highland scenery in order to reach the same spot. Beyond the old-fashioned coastal towns such as **Dunoon**, the largest settlement in the area, the Cowal landscape is extremely rich and varied, ranging from the Munros of the north to the gentle, low-lying coastline of the southwest. One way to explore it is to follow the 47-mile **Cowal Way**, a waymarked long-distance foothpath between Portvadie and Ardgartan. The western edge of Cowal is marked by the long, narrow Loch Fyne, famous for both its kippers (smoked herring) and, more recently, oysters (see opposite).

Arrochar to Carndow

The boundaries of Loch Lomond and the Trossachs National Park extend quite a long way into Cowal, incorporating the **Argyll Forest Park**, which stretches west from the village of Arrochar along the shores of Loch Long and south as far as Holy Loch. The area has the peninsula's most grandiose scenery, including the ambitiously named **Arrochar Alps**, whose peaks offer some of the best climbing in Argyll: Ben Ime (3318ft) is the tallest of the range, while Ben Arthur or **"The Cobbler"** (2891ft), named after the anvil-like rock formation at its summit, is the most distinctive. At the other end of the scale there are several gentle forest walks clearly laid out by the Forestry Commission, and helpful leaflets are available from tourist offices.

Arrochar and around

Approaching by road from Glasgow, the entry point to Cowal is **ARROCHAR**, at the head of Loch Long. The village itself is ordinary enough, but the setting is dramatic, and it makes a convenient base for exploring the nearby countryside. There's a **train station** a mile or so east, just off the A83 to Tarbet. For **accommodation**, try *Ben Bheula* (ⓣ01301/702184, ⓦwww.benbheula.co.uk; ❷), a clean B&B in nearby Succoth, set back from the head of the loch and run by a very friendly couple, or *Fascadail* (ⓣ01301/702344, ⓦwww.fascadail.com; ❸), a Victorian guesthouse with a glorious garden situated in the quieter southern part of the village. If you need a bite **to eat**, head for the *Village Inn*, which has tables outside overlooking the loch as well as a cosy real-ale bar.

Two miles west at **ARDGARTAN**, there's a well-maintained lochside Forestry Commission **campsite** (ⓣ01301/702293, ⓦwww.forestholidays.co.uk; April–Oct), and, a little further down the road, in the Ardgartan Visitor Centre, is a **tourist office** (April–Oct daily; ⓣ01301/702432) which doubles as a forestry office and has occasional organized walks. **Bike rental** is available and there are waymarked **walks and bike trails** starting from here.

Heading west from Arrochar to Inveraray or the rest of Cowal, you climb **Glen Croe**, a strategic hill pass whose saddle is called – for obvious reasons – **Rest-and-be-Thankful**. Here the road forks, with the single-track B828 heading down to **LOCHGOILHEAD**, an isolated village overlooking Loch Goil, where the majority of houses are holiday homes. A road tracks the west side of the loch, petering out after five miles at the picturesque ruins of **Carrick Castle**, a classic tower-house castle built around 1400 and used as a hunting lodge by James IV.

Cairndow and around

Continuing west towards Inveraray along the A83 via Glen Kinglas, you eventually reach **CAIRNDOW**, at the head of Loch Fyne. Just behind the village, off the main road, you'll find the **Ardkinglas Woodland Garden** (daily dawn–dusk; £3.50; Ⓦwww.ardkinglas.com), which contains exotic rhododendrons, azaleas and a superb collection of conifers, one of which is, at 210ft, the tallest tree in Britain. In the southern part of the gardens stands **Ardkinglas House** (April–Oct guided tour last Fri of month 2pm; £6), a particularly handsome Scottish Baronial mansion, built in 1907 by Robert Lorimer for the Noble family. In Cairndow itself, the *Stagecoach Inn* is good for a pint and inexpensive pub food, but for something a bit special continue a mile or so further along on the A83 to the famous **Loch Fyne Oyster Bar and Shop** (Ⓣ01499/600236, Ⓦwww.loch-fyne.com), which sells more oysters than anywhere else in the country, plus lots of other fish and seafood treats. You can assemble a gourmet picnic in the shop or stock up on provisions, and the moderately expensive **restaurant** is excellent, though booking is advisable at busy times.

Dunoon

The principal entry point into Cowal by sea is **DUNOON**. In the nineteenth century it grew from a village to a major Clyde seaside resort and favourite holiday spot for Glaswegians, but nowadays there's really little to tempt you to stay, particularly with attractive countryside beckoning just beyond.

The centre of town is dominated by a grassy lump of rock known as **Castle Hill**, in the town centre, where you'll find the **Castle House Museum** (Easter–Oct Mon–Sat 10.30am–4.30pm, Sun 2–4.30pm; £2; Ⓦwww castlehousemuseum .org.uk). There's some good hands-on nature stuff for kids and an excellent section on the Clyde steamers as well as more about "Highland Mary", betrothed to Robbie Burns (despite the fact that he already had a pregnant wife), who died of typhus before the pair could see through their plan to elope to the West Indies.

Dunoon's **tourist office**, on Alexandra Parade, is the principal one in Cowal (open daily all year round). There are two **ferry** crossings across the Clyde from Gourock to Dunoon; the shorter, more frequent service is on Western Ferries to Hunter's Quay, a mile north of the town centre; CalMac's boats, though, arrive at the main pier, and have better transport connections if you're on foot.

Dunoon has some good mid-range **accommodation**, like the welcoming *Abbot's Brae*, a beautiful family-run Victorian villa, set in woods above West Bay with lovely views over the Clyde (Ⓣ01369/705021, Ⓦwww.abbotsbrae.co.uk; ❺), or the smart *Dhailling Lodge* (Ⓣ01369/701253, Ⓦwww.dhaillinglodge .com; ❹), another attractive villa closer to town on Alexandra Parade, run by a very welcoming Glaswegian couple. *Chatters*, 58 John St (Ⓣ01369/706402, Ⓦwww.chattersdunoon.co.uk; Wed–Sat only), is Dunoon's best restaurant by far, offering delicious Scottish cuisine, while the nicest café is the bright, modern *Perk Up* (closed Sun), up Ferry Brae from the main street. Dunoon has a two-screen **cinema** (a rarity in Argyll) on John Street, but the town's most famous entertainment is the **Cowal Highland Gathering**, the largest of its kind in the world, held here on the last weekend in August, and culminating in the awesome spectacle of the massed pipes and drums of more than 150 bands marching through the streets.

Benmore Botanic Garden

Six miles north of Dunoon, along the A815, is **Benmore Botanic Garden** (daily: March & Oct 10am–5pm; April–Sept 10am–6pm; £5), at the foot of **Loch Eck**. An offshoot of Edinburgh's Royal Botanic Garden, the beautifully laid-out garden occupies 120 acres of lush hillside; the mild, moist climate allows a vast range of unusual plants to grow here, with different sections devoted to rainforest species native to places as exotic as China, Chile and Bhutan. The garden boasts 300 species of rhododendron and a memorably striking avenue of great redwoods, planted in 1863 and now over 150ft high. There's a pleasant, inexpensive **café** (April–Oct daily; Nov–March Wed–Sun) by the entrance. Alternatively, there are two **pubs** on the eastern shores of Loch Eck itself: the *Coylet Inn* and, further north, the *Whistlefield Inn* (Ⓣ01369/860440, Ⓦwww.whistlefield.com; ❷). Both are good for a pint, but the *Whistlefield* is the place to go for food and **accommodation**, with both comfortable en-suite rooms and a **bunkhouse** to choose from.

Southwest Cowal

The mellower landscape of **southwest Cowal** stands in complete contrast to the bustle of Dunoon or the Highland grandeur of the Argyll Forest Park. There are few more beautiful sights in Argyll than the **Kyles of Bute**, the slivers of water that separate Cowal from the bleak bulk of the Isle of Bute and constitute some of the best sailing territory in Scotland. **COLINTRAIVE**, on the eastern Kyle, marks the narrowest point in the area – barely more than a couple of hundred yards across – and is where the CalMac ferry departs to Bute. The *Colintraive Hotel* (Ⓣ01700/841207, Ⓦwww.colintraivehotel.com; ❺), south of the ferry slipway, is worth seeking out; a favourite with yachties, it serves up delicious fresh dishes and has some lovely rooms, too.

The most popular spot from which to appreciate the Kyles is along the A8003 as it rises dramatically above the sea lochs before descending to the peaceful, lochside village of **TIGHNABRUAICH**, best known for its excellent **sailing school** (Ⓣ01700/811717, Ⓦwww.tssargyll.co.uk). You can stay at the impressive *An Lochan* by the waterside (Ⓣ01700/811239, Ⓦwww.anlochan.co.uk; ❻), which serves exceptionally good seafood bar meals and has wonderful views over the Kyles; not quite so grand, but justifiably popular with sailors and walkers, is the *Kames Hotel* (Ⓣ01700/811489, Ⓦkames-hotel.com; ❺) in neighbouring **KAMES**. You can also get B&B at *Ardeneden Guest House* (Ⓣ01700/811354; ❸), run by the same people who look after the excellent *Burnside Restaurant* in the village.

Isle of Bute

The island of **Bute** (Ⓦwww.isle-of-bute.com) is in many ways simply an extension of the Cowal peninsula, from which it is separated by the narrow Kyles of Bute. Thanks to its mild climate and its ferry link with Wemyss Bay, Bute has been a popular holiday and convalescence spot for Clydesiders for over a century. In its heyday in the 1880s, thirty steamers a day would call in at the island's capital, **Rothesay**, which easily eclipses Dunoon as the most attractive seaside resort on the Clyde, thanks to some splendid Victorian architecture, decent accommodation and eating options and the chance to visit **Mount Stuart**, one of Scotland's most singular aristocratic piles. Bute's inhabitants live around the two wide bays on the island's east coast, which resembles one long seaside promenade. To escape the crowds head for the sparsely populated west coast, which, in any case, has the sandiest beaches. Bute holds its own **Highland Games** on the third weekend in August, an international **folk festival** on the third weekend in July, and a (mainly trad) **jazz festival** over May Bank Holiday.

Rothesay

Bute's only town, **ROTHESAY** is a handsome Victorian resort, set in a wide, sweeping bay, backed by green hills, with a classic palm-tree promenade and 1920s pagoda-style pavilion originally built to house the Winter Gardens. Its **Victorian toilets** (daily: Easter–Sept 8am–7.45pm; Oct–Easter 9am–4.45pm; 20p), built in 1899 by Twyfords, are a feast of marble, ceramics and brass so ornate that they're now one of the town's most celebrated sights. The Victorians didn't make provision for ladies' conveniences, so the women's half is a modern add-on, but if the coast is clear the attendant – attired in a neat burgundy waistcoat – will allow ladies a tour of the gents.

Rothesay also boasts the militarily useless, but architecturally impressive, moated ruins of **Rothesay Castle** (April–Sept daily 9.30am–5.30pm; Oct–March Mon–Wed, Sat & Sun 9.30am–4.30pm; HS; £4.20), hidden amid the town's backstreets. Built around the twelfth century, it was twice captured by the Vikings; such vulnerability was the reasoning behind the unusual, almost circular, curtain wall, with its four big drum towers, only one of which remains fully intact.

A mile or so east of Rothesay along the coastal road is the **Ascog Hall Gardens** (Easter–Oct Wed–Sun 10am–5pm; £4), which features a really unusual **Victorian fernery**, a beautiful, dank place, sunk into the ground, and featuring ferns from all over the world.

Practicalities

Rothesay's **tourist office** (open daily all year round) is in the **Winter Gardens**, whose "Discovery Centre" has some well-presented displays on the life and times of Bute. There's no shortage of **accommodation** in and around Rothesay: try *Cannon House* (Ⓣ01700/502819, Ⓦwww.cannonhousehotel.co.uk; ④), a really elegant Georgian hotel close to the pier on Battery Place; alternatively, the *Boat House* (Ⓣ01700/502696, Ⓦwww.theboathouse-bute.co.uk; ③) at no. 15 is a stylish "boutique B&B" with classy contemporary furnishings and decor; for a truly memorable stay, there's *Balmory Hall* (Ⓣ01700/500669, Ⓦwww.balmoryhall.com; ⑦), a luxurious Victorian mansion, superbly run, and set in its own grounds in Ascog. Bute has just one **hostel**, *Bute Backpackers* (Ⓣ01700/501876), conveniently located at 36 Argyle St, five minutes' walk along the seafront towards Port Bannatyne.

The best **food** option in Rothesay is the *Squat Lobster* (Ⓣ01700/503603; closed Mon & Sun), 29 Gallowgate, which specializes in seafood – bring your own alcohol. During the day, the small but stylish veggie café, *Musicker* (closed Mon & Sun), just across from the castle has decent snacks and even better music. Outside Rothesay, in Port Bannatyne, there's the highly original and engaging *Port Royal Hotel*, a "Russian Tavern" that serves fresh smoked sprats and razorfish with blini, washed down with real ales, or *The Pier at Craigmore*, a good café on the road to Ardencraig Gardens. It's worth knowing that Rothesay has a **cinema** – confusingly known as the Discovery Theatre – at the back of the Winter Gardens.

Mount Stuart

Bute's most compelling sight is **Mount Stuart** (May–Sept; phone Ⓣ01700/503877 for times; £8, gardens only £4; Ⓦwww.mountstuart.com), a huge, fantasy Gothic mansion set amidst acres of lush woodland gardens overlooking the Firth of Clyde four miles south of Rothesay, and ancestral home of the seventh marquess of Bute, also known as Johnny Bute (or, in his Formula One racing days, as Johnny Dumfries). The building was created by the marvellously eccentric third marquess and architect Robert Rowand Anderson after a fire in 1877 destroyed the family seat. With little regard for expense, the marquess shipped in tons of Italian marble, built a railway line to transport it down the coast and employed craftsmen who had worked with William Burges on the marquess's other medieval concoction, Cardiff Castle.

Mount Stuart's sleek modern **visitor centre** contains an excellent **café/restaurant** serving light lunches and giving great views into the trees. The house itself is a fifteen-minute walk through the grounds (daily 10am–6pm). The *pièce de resistance* is the columned **Marble Hall**, its vaulted ceiling and stained-glass windows decorated with the signs of the zodiac, reflecting the marquess's taste for mysticism. He was equally fond of animal and plant imagery; hence you'll find birds feeding on berries in the dining-room frieze and monkeys reading (and tearing up) books and scrolls in the library. Look out also for the unusual heraldic ceiling in the drawing room. After all the heavy furnishings, seek aesthetic relief in the vast **Marble Chapel**, built entirely out of dazzling white Carrara marble, with a magnificent Cosmati floor pattern. Upstairs, along with three impressive bathrooms, check out the **Horoscope Room**, where you can see a fine astrological ceiling and adjacent observatory/conservatory.

Around Bute

The Highland–Lowland dividing line passes through the middle of Bute, which is all but sliced in two by the freshwater Loch Fad. As a result, the northern half of the island is hilly, uninhabited and little visited, while the southern half is made up of Lowland-style farmland.

Six miles south of Rothesay, east-facing **Kilchattan Bay** has a lovely arc of sand overlooked by a row of grand Victorian houses, including *Kingarth Hotel*, which has a very convivial bar.

Over on the west coast, **St Blane's Chapel** is a twelfth-century ruin beautifully situated in open countryside amid the foundations of an earlier Christian settlement established in the sixth century by St Catan, uncle to the local-born St Blane. Bute's finest sandy beach is further up the west coast, at **Ettrick Bay**, which has a tearoom (April–Oct) and basic campsite (open all year) at its north end.

Inveraray

The traditional county town of Argyll, and a classic example of an eighteenth-century planned town, **INVERARAY** was built in the 1770s by the Duke of Argyll in order to distance his newly rebuilt castle from the hoi polloi in the town, and to establish a commercial and legal centre for the region. Inveraray has changed very little since and remains an absolute set piece of Scottish Georgian architecture, with a truly memorable setting, the brilliant white arches of Front Street reflected in the still waters of Loch Fyne.

The Town

Despite its picture-book location, there's not much more to Inveraray than its distinctive **Main Street** (perpendicular to Front Street), flanked by whitewashed terraces, characterized by black window casements. At the top of the street, the road divides to circumnavigate the town's Neoclassical church: originally the southern half served the Gaelic-speaking community, while the northern half served those who spoke English.

East of the church is **Inveraray Jail** (daily: April–Oct 9.30am–6pm; Nov–March 10am–5pm; £8.25; Ⓦwww.inverarayjail.co.uk), whose attractive Georgian courthouse and grim prison blocks ceased to function in the 1930s. The jail is now a thoroughly enjoyable museum, which graphically recounts prison conditions from medieval times to the twentieth century. You can try out the minute "Airing Yards" where the prisoners got to exercise for an hour a day, and also sit in the semicircular courthouse, with its great views over the loch, and listen to a re-enactment of a trial of the period.

A ten-minute walk north of Main Street, **Inveraray Castle** (April–Oct Mon–Sat 10am–5.45pm, Sun noon–5.45pm; £6.30; Ⓦwww.inveraray-castle.com) remains the family home of the Duke of Argyll. Built in 1745, it was given a touch of the Loire in the nineteenth century with the addition of dormer windows and conical corner spires. Inside, the most startling feature is the armoury hall, whose displays of weaponry – supplied to the Campbells by the British government to put down the Jacobites – rise through several storeys; otherwise, the interior's pretty unremarkable, with the exception of Rob Roy's rather sad-looking sporran and dirk handle.

Practicalities

Inveraray's **tourist office** is on Front Street (open daily all year round; Ⓣ01499/302063), as is the town's chief **hotel**, the *Argyll*, formerly the *Great Inn*, where Dr Johnson and Boswell once stayed. A better **place to stay**, however, is *Rudha-Na-Craige* (Ⓣ01499/302668, Ⓦwww.rudha-na-craige.f2s.com; ❺), a beautifully restored Scottish Baronial house on the southern edge of town, or *Newton Hall* (Ⓣ01499/302484, Ⓦwww.newtonhallinveraray.com; ❹), a nearby former church, now a B&B with views over the loch.

The SYHA **hostel** (Ⓣ0870/004 1125, Ⓦwww.syha.org.uk; mid-March to Oct) is in a modern building a short walk up the A819, while the old Royal Navy base, two miles down the A83 to Lochgilphead, has been converted into the excellent, fully equipped *Argyll Caravan Park* (Ⓣ01499/302285, Ⓦwww.argyllcaravanpark.com; April–Oct). *Brambles*, on Main Street, does classic café food, plus home-made cakes, and the **bar** of the *George Hotel*, opposite, is the town's liveliest spot, and also serves decent bar **meals**. To sample Loch Fyne's delicious fresh fish and seafood, though, you should head for the restaurant of the nearby *Loch Fyne Oyster Bar* (see p.259).

Oban and around

The solidly Victorian resort of **OBAN** (Ⓦwww.oban.org.uk) enjoys a superb setting – the island of Kerrera to the southwest providing its bay with a natural shelter – distinguished by a bizarre granite amphitheatre, dramatically lit at night, on the hilltop above the town. Despite a population of just 8000, it's by far the largest port in northwest Scotland, the second-largest town in Argyll, and the main departure point for ferries to the Hebrides. If you arrive late, or are catching an early boat, you may have to spend the night here if so, never mind: it's a great place to eat fresh seafood.

Arrival and information

Arriving in Oban **by car** can be a bit of a nightmare in the summer, when traffic chokes the main drag. If you're heading straight for the ferry, make sure you leave an extra hour to allow for sitting in the tailbacks. The CalMac **ferry terminal** (Ⓣ01631/566688, Ⓦwww.calmac.co.uk) for the islands is on Railway Pier, a stone's throw from the **train station**, which is itself adjacent to the bus stops on

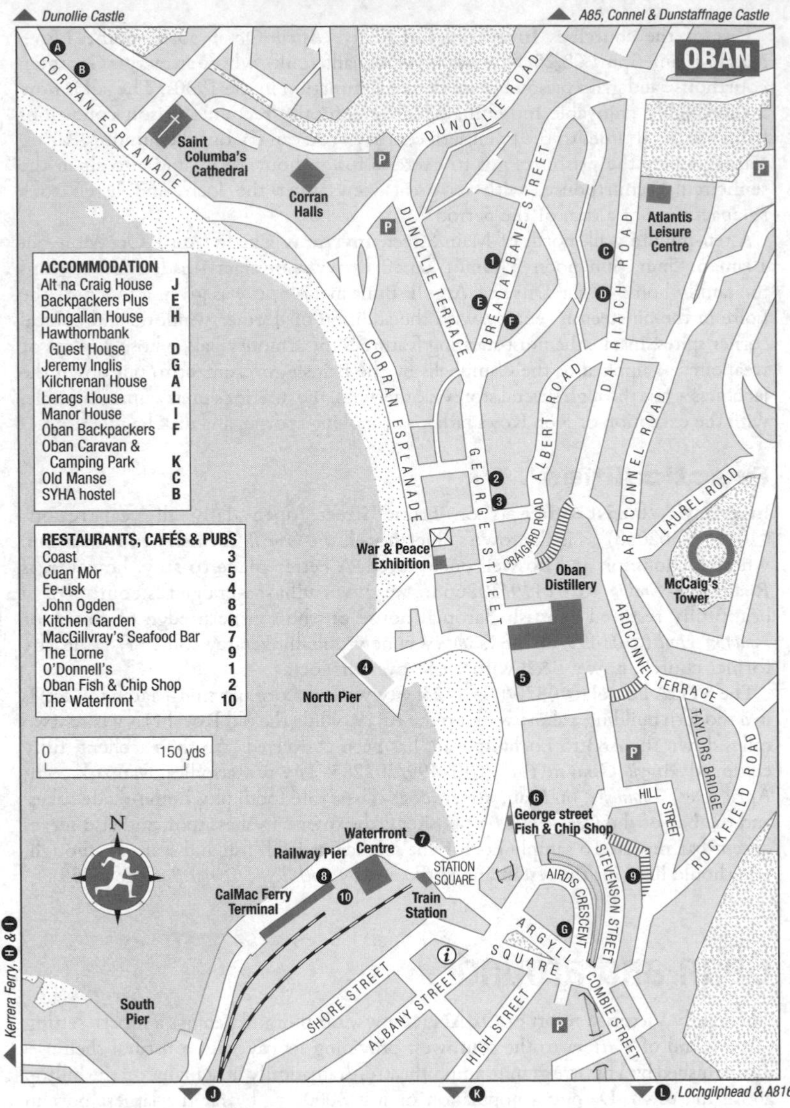

Station Square. Six miles north of town, tiny **Oban Airport** (Ⓣ0845/805 7465, Ⓦwww.hebrideanair.co.uk) in North Connel has flights to Coll, Tiree, Islay and Colonsay; the nearest train station to the airport is Connel Ferry, or take bus #405 from Oban to Barcaldine.

The **tourist office** (open daily year round; Ⓣ01631/563122) is housed in a converted church on Argyll Square, and has heaps of leaflets and books as well as internet access. For **car and bike rental** go to Flit on Glencruitten Road (Ⓣ01631/566553, Ⓦwww.flitselfdrive.co.uk). If you fancy taking the plunge and trying your hand at some **diving**, contact the Puffin Dive Centre, based a mile south of Oban at Port Gallanach (Ⓣ01631/566088, Ⓦwww.puffin.org.uk).

Accommodation

Oban is positively heaving with **hotels** and **B&Bs**, most of them very reasonably priced and many on or near the quayside.

Hotels and B&Bs

Alt na Craig House Glenmore Road ⓣ01631/564524, ⓦwww.guesthouseinoban.com. A handsome Victorian house just south of town, with a woodland garden, beautifully furnished rooms and views of the bay. ❻

Dungallan House Hotel Gallanach Road ⓣ01631/563799, ⓦwww.dungallanhotel-oban.co.uk. Solid Victorian villa hotel with a dozen rooms set in its own woodland grounds, hidden away on the Gallanach Road, with great views across the Sound of Kerrera. No under-12s. ❽

Hawthornbank Guest House Dalriach Road ⓣ01631/562041. Decent, traditional guesthouse in the lower backstreets of Oban, just across the road from the swimming pool. ❸

Kilchrenan House Corran Esplanade ⓣ01631/562663, ⓦwww.kilchrenanhouse.co.uk. A bright and hospitable home located near the Cathedral, with ten rooms, most of which have sea views. ❸

Lerags House Lerags ⓣ01631/563381, ⓦwww.leragshouse.com. A super special option located four miles south of Oban – *Lerags House* is a Georgian mansion somewhere between a B&B and a country-house hotel with chic decor and excellent food – the tariff includes dinner. ❽

Manor House Hotel Gallanach Road ⓣ01631/562087, ⓦwww.manorhouseoban.com. Beautiful eighteenth-century manor house, peacefully located on the fringes of town by the shores of the Sound of Kerrera, with a top-notch restaurant attached. ❾

Old Manse Dalriach Road ⓣ01631/564886, ⓦwww.obanguesthouse.co.uk. Spotlessly clean guesthouse run by a very welcoming couple, with a beautiful garden and lovely views over the sea. ❸

Hostels and campsites

Jeremy Inglis 21 Airds Crescent ⓣ01631/565065. Halfway between a hostel and a B&B, with an eccentric proprietor who also runs *McTavish's Kitchens*. Located near the train station, with shared rooms, doubles or family rooms available, plus kitchen facilities; it's the cheapest bed in town, with breakfast included. ❶

Oban Backpackers Breadalbane St ⓣ01631/562107, ⓦwww.obanbackpackers.com. Friendly and central Oban hostel, with a pool table, real fire, internet access and breakfast included. March–Oct & Christmas–New Year. Round the corner, *Backpackers Plus* is slightly more expensive and is good for couples on a budget as it has doubles, as well as rooms for small groups. ❷

Oban Caravan & Camping Park Gallanach Rd ⓣ01631/562425, ⓦwww.obancaravanpark.com. Huge site with lots of camping space and great views, with a good chance of a breeze to blow the midges away. A mile and a half from Oban up a pretty glen. Open April–Oct.

SYHA hostel Corran Esplanade ⓣ01631/562025, ⓦwww.syha.org.uk. Converted Victorian house, with a quieter, modern annexe behind, both a fair trek with a backpack from the ferry terminal along the Corran Esplanade. Two-, three- and four-bed en-suite rooms available. ❶

The Town

Apart from the setting and views, the only truly remarkable sight in Oban is the town's landmark, **McCaig's Tower**, a stiff ten-minute climb from the quayside. Built in imitation of Rome's Colosseum, it was the brainchild of a local businessman a century ago, who had the twin aims of alleviating off-season unemployment among the local stonemasons and creating a museum, art gallery and chapel. Originally, the plan was to add a 95-foot central tower, but work never progressed further than the exterior granite walls before McCaig died. In his will, McCaig gave instructions for the lancet windows to be filled with bronze statues of the family, though no such work was ever undertaken. Instead, the folly has been turned into a sort of walled garden which is a popular rendezvous for Oban's youth after dark, but for the rest of the time simply provides a wonderful seaward panorama, particularly at sunset.

Down in the centre of town, you can pass a few hours admiring the boats in the harbour and looking out for scavenging seals in the bay. If the weather's bad, the best option is to sign up for one of the excellent guided tours around **Oban Distillery** (Feb Mon–Fri 12.30–4pm; March–Dec Mon–Fri 9.30am–5pm; June–Oct also Sat 9.30am–4.30pm; July & Aug also Sun 12.30–4.30pm; £7), slap in the centre of town off George Street. The tour ends with a generous dram of Oban's lightly peaty malt. Another refuge is the **War and Peace Exhibition** (May–Oct daily 10am–4pm; May–Sept Mon–Sat 10am–6pm, Sun 10am–4pm; free; Ⓦwww.obanmuseum.org.uk) in the old *Oban Times* building beside the Art Deco *Regent Hotel* on the Esplanade; stuffed full of memorabilia and staffed by enthusiasts, it tells the story of the intriguing wartime role of the area around Oban as a flying-boat base, mustering point for Atlantic convoys and as a training centre for the D-Day landings.

Eating, drinking and nightlife

Oban has become a terrific place to get good fresh seafood. If you're only here to catch a ferry, grab a quick langoustine sandwich or dressed fresh crab from John Ogden's excellent **takeaway** seafood shack near the CalMac terminal, or head to nearby *MacGillivray's Seafood Bar*, another alfresco harbour place which serves pan-fried scallops and lobster tails. Of course, there's always fish and chips, from *Oban Fish & Chip Shop & Restaurant* at 116 George St, or the *George Street Fish & Chip Shop* by the seafront.

You should be able to catch some **live music** at the weekend at *O'Donnell's* Irish pub, underneath an incongruously flash bar called *Paparazzi* on Breadalbane Street, or in *The Lorne*, a more attractive and popular pub on Stevenson Street which also serves real ales, forty malts and local seafood.

Cafés and restaurants

Coast 104 George St Ⓣ01631/569900, Ⓦwww.coastoban.com. A slick place with a metropolitan atmosphere, serving acclaimed and original fish, game and meat dishes. Mains start at £15.

Cuan Mòr 60 George St Ⓣ01631/565078, Ⓦwww.cuanmor.co.uk. Contemporary bistro-pub with lots of fish and seafood dishes, plus bangers and mash, baguettes and salads, all for under £12.

Ee-usk North Pier Ⓣ01631/565666, Ⓦwww.eeusk.com. A lively restaurant with plenty of glass that makes the most of the harbour views. They serve glistening seafood platters, fresh fish dishes and lighter snacks such as Thai fish cakes (£12.95) or mussels (£6.95). Moderate–expensive.

Kitchen Garden 14 George St Ⓣ01631/566332, Ⓦwww.kitchengardenoban.co.uk. Impressive, central deli and licensed café offering all day breakfast and delicious snacks on the mezzanine, open in the evenings in peak season.

The Waterfront 1 Railway Pier Ⓣ01631/563110, Ⓦwww.waterfrontoban.co.uk. Despite the unprepossessing exterior, this is a great place with an open kitchen rustling up impressive dishes using scallops, langoustine and the best of the daily catch. Mains average £15, or you can get fish and chips for under a tenner.

Isle of Kerrera

One of the best places to escape from the crowds that plague Oban is the low-lying island of **Kerrera**, which shelters Oban Bay from the worst of the westerly winds. Measuring just five miles by two, the island is easily explored on foot. The island's most prominent landmark is the **Hutcheson's Monument**, commemorating David Hutcheson, one of the Victorian founders of what is now Caledonian MacBrayne. The most appealing vistas, however, are from Kerrera's highest point, **Càrn Breugach** (620ft), over to Mull, the Slate Islands, Lismore, Jura and beyond.

The ferry lands roughly halfway down the east coast, at the north end of **Horseshoe Bay**, where King Alexander II died in 1249. If the weather's good and you feel like lazing by the sea, head for the island's finest sandy beach, **Slatrach**

Bay, on the west coast, one mile northwest of the ferry jetty. Otherwise, there's a very rewarding trail down to the cliff-top ruin of **Gylen Castle** and back to the ferry via the Drove Road.

The passenger and bicycle **ferry** crosses regularly (summer every 30min; winter every 1–2hr; ⓣ01631/563665; £5) through the day from the mainland two miles down the Gallanach road from Oban. In summer, **bus** #431 from Oban train station connects with the ferry once a day. Kerrera has a population of around thirty – and no shop, so if you're planning to self-cater then bring food. However, you can eat home-made veggie **snacks** at the *Kerrera Teagarden* (Easter–Sept Wed–Sun only), located in a nice spot at Lower Gylen, a 45-minute walk from the ferry. Right beside this is the seven-bed *Kerrera Bunkhouse* (ⓣ01631/570223, ⓦwww.kerrerabunkhouse.co.uk), a converted eighteenth-century stable building, with a byre living space for hire by the evening. They also rent a room in the farmhouse for B&B (❶). For more **B&B** or self-catering accommodation enquire at *Ardentrive Farm* (ⓣ01631/567180, ⓔdavid@ardentrive.fsnet.co.uk; ❶), at the north of the island.

Connel and Benderloch

Five miles up the A85 from Oban, at **CONNEL**, you can't fail to admire the majestic, steel cantilever **Connel Bridge**, built in 1903 to take the old branch railway line across the sea cataract at the mouth of Loch Etive, north to Fort William. The name "Connel" comes from the Gaelic *conghail* ("tumultuous flood"), created by tidal streams rushing over a ledge of rock. Known as the Falls of Lora, this is one of the few tidal waterfalls in the country and looks as menacing as it does spectacular. If you want to stay out here in Connel as a mellower alternative to Oban, *Ards House* (ⓣ01631/710255, ⓦwww.ardshouse.com; ❺), a whitewashed Victorian villa by the main road overlooking the water, is a pleasant option, while a good place to admire the kayakers tackling the tidal falls is modern *Strumhor* guesthouse (ⓣ01631/710167, ⓦwww.strumhor.co.uk; ❸), whose proprietors run sea-kayaking courses from beginners upwards (ⓦwww.seafreedomkayak.co.uk).

On the north side of the Connel Bridge lies the hammerhead peninsula of **Benderloch** (from *beinn eadar da loch*, "hill between two lochs"), which harbours three of Argyll's more interesting **places to stay**. Standing on its own, right above the beach just west of the village of Benderloch, A *Dun Na Mara* (ⓣ01631/720233, ⓦwww.dunnamara.com; ❺) is a fine Arts and Crafts-style holiday home where highly stylish contemporary decor is complemented by the warm hospitality (and lavish breakfasts) of its two young architect owners. Further up the A828 you can stay at *Barcaldine House* (ⓣ01631/720219, ⓦwww.barcaldinehouse.co.uk; ❼), elegant, early Georgian house built for the Campbells of Barcaldine. If you have an unlimited budget you might like to stay at the area's most exclusive hotel, the *Isle of Eriska*, a luxury, turreted, Scottish Baronial place with a spa, pool and upmarket dining room. It's run by the Buchanan-Smiths on their own three-hundred-acre island off the northern point of Benderloch (ⓣ01631/720371, ⓦwww.eriska-hotel.co.uk; ❾).

Since the weather in this part of Scotland can be bad at almost any time of the year, it's as well to know about the **Scottish Sea Life Sanctuary** (daily 10am–5pm, with earlier closing time in winter; £12.50 though cheaper if bought online; ⓦwww.sealsanctuary.co.uk), which is to be found on the A828, along the southern shores of Loch Creran. Here you can see loads of sea creatures at close quarters, touch the (non-)stingrays, do a bit of rock-pool dipping, keep a look out for the resident otters and learn about how common seal orphan pups are rescued and returned to the wild.

Appin

The next peninsula after Benderloch is **Appin**, best known as the setting for Robert Louis Stevenson's *Kidnapped*, a fictionalized account of the "Appin Murder" of 1752, when Colin Campbell was shot in the back, allegedly by one of the disenfranchised Stewart clan.

The name Appin derives from the Gaelic *abthaine*, meaning "lands belonging to the abbey", in this case the one on the island of Lismore (see below), which is linked to the peninsula by passenger ferry from **PORT APPIN**, a pretty little fishing village at the peninsula's westernmost tip. Overlooking a host of tiny little islands dotted around Loch Linnhe, with Lismore and the mountains of Morvern and Mull in the background, this is, without doubt, one of Argyll's most picturesque spots. The *Pierhouse Hotel* (Ⓣ01631/730302, Ⓦwww.pierhousehotel.co.uk; ❻), nicely situated right by the ferry, has a popular bar and an expensive seafood restaurant.

Framed magnificently as you wind along the single-track road to Port Appin is one of Argyll's most romantic ruined castles, the much-photographed sixteenth-century ruins of **Castle Stalker** (open irregular hours; Ⓣ01631/740315/730354, Ⓦwww.castlestalker.com). Offering one of the best outlooks over the castle, the pleasant, modern *Castle Stalker View* **café** and shop (Nov–Dec Thurs–Sun, closed Jan) is a short distance up the road to Ballachullish. **Bike rental** is available from Port Appin Bikes (Ⓣ01631/730391) and it's worth noting that bicycles travel for free on the passenger ferry to Lismore (see below). For other **outdoor pursuits**, head for the Linnhe Marine Water Sports Centre (Ⓣ07721/503981; May–Sept) in Lettershuna (just north of Castle Stalker), which rents out boats of all shapes and sizes, offers sailing and windsurfing lessons, not to mention waterskiing, clay-pigeon shooting and even pony trekking.

Isle of Lismore

Lying in the middle of Loch Linnhe, to the north of Oban, and barely rising above a hillock, the narrow island of **Lismore** (Ⓦwww.isleoflismore.com) offers wonderful gentle walking and cycling opportunities, with unrivalled views, in fine weather, across to the mountains of Morvern, Lochaber and Mull. Legend has it that St **Columba** and **Moluag** both fancied the skinny island as a missionary base, but as they raced towards it Moluag cut off his finger and threw it ashore ahead of Columba, claiming the land for himself. Of Moluag's sixth-century foundation nothing remains, but from 1236 until 1507 the island served as the seat of the bishop of Argyll. Lismore is one of the most fertile of the Inner Hebrides – its name derives from the Gaelic *lios mór*, meaning "great garden" – and before the Clearances (see p.631) it supported nearly 1400 inhabitants; the population today is only 180, half of them over 60.

Lismore is about ten miles long and a mile wide, and the ferry from Oban lands at **ACHNACROISH**, roughly halfway along the eastern coastline. To get to grips with the history of the island and its Gaelic culture, follow the signs to the Heritage Centre, **Ionad Naomh Moluag** (May–Sept daily 11am–5pm; March, April & Oct to mid Nov daily noon–3pm; £3.50), a turf-roofed, timber-clad building with a permanent exhibition on Lismore, a reference library, a gift shop and a **café** with an outdoor terrace. Your ticket also covers entry to the nearby restored nineteenth-century cottar's (landless tenant's) cottage, **Tigh Iseabal Dhaibh**, with its traditionally built stone walls, birch roof timbers and thatched roof. In **CLACHAN** you'll find the diminutive, whitewashed fourteenth-century **Cathedral of St Moluag**, whose choir was reduced in height and converted into the parish church in 1749. Due east of the church – head north up the road and take the turning signposted on the right – the circular **Tirefour Broch**, over two thousand years old, occupies a commanding position and has walls almost 10ft thick in places.

Practicalities

Two **ferries** serve Lismore: a small CalMac car ferry from Oban to Achnacroish (Mon–Sat 4–5 daily, 2 on Sun; 50min), and a shorter passenger- and bicycle-only crossing from Port Appin to Point, the island's north point (daily hourly; 10min). **Accommodation** on the island is extremely limited: try the budget B&B at the *Schoolhouse* (ⓣ01631/760262; ❶), north of Clachan, which also serves evening meals; or Elizabeth Kilmurray's popular B&B in Achnacroish (ⓣ01631/760260 or 07760/260008). **Bike rental** is available from Lismore Bike Hire (ⓣ01631/760213) – they'll deliver to the ferry if asked.

Loch Awe

Legend has it that **Loch Awe**, twenty miles east of Oban, was created by a witch and inhabited by a monster even more gruesome than the one at Loch Ness. At more than 25 miles in length, Loch Awe is actually the longest stretch of fresh water in the country, but most travellers only encounter the loch's north end as they speed along its shores by car or train on the way to or from Oban. Several tiny islands on the loch sport picturesque ruins, including the fifteenth-century ruins of **Kilchurn Castle**, strategically situated on a rocky spit (once an island) at the head of the loch; to visit the castle, you can approach by foot from the A85 to the east. The castle is essentially a shell, but its watery setting and imposing outlines make it well worth a detour.

The main attraction on the shores of Loch Awe is, however, rather less picturesque. **Cruachan Power Station** (Easter–Oct daily 9.30am–5pm; Nov–March 10am–3.45pm; £6; ⓦwww.visitcruachan.co.uk) is actually constructed inside mighty Ben Cruachan (3693ft), which looms over the head of Loch Awe; it was built in 1965 as part of the hydroelectric network which generates around ten percent of Scotland's electricity. Half-hour guided tours set off every half-hour from the **visitor centre** by the loch, taking you to a viewing platform above the generating room deep inside the "hollow mountain", a cavern big enough to contain the Tower of London. The whole experience of visiting an industrial complex hidden within a mountain is very James Bond, and it certainly pulls in the tour coaches. They have a basic **café** with loch views.

There are some terrific though pricey **places to stay** on the peaceful north-western shores of Loch Awe around the hamlet of **KILCHRENAN**, reached by a back road from Taynuilt. The *Taychreggan Hotel* (ⓣ01866/833211, ⓦwww.taychregganhotel.co.uk; ❻) is an old drovers' inn by the loch now plumped up into an upmarket retreat, while the *Ardanaiseig Hotel* (ⓣ01866/833333, ⓦwww.ardanaiseig.com; ❼; closed Jan) is a wonderfully secluded, romantic escape set in a palatial Scottish Baronial pile four miles to the northeast down a dead-end track. Both these hotels have superb, though expensive, restaurants, and the *Ardanaiseig* also has its own glorious **gardens** (daily 9.30am–dusk), home of rare species of azalea and rhododendron, worth visiting even if you're not staying here. *Roineabhal Country House* is a superior B&B (ⓣ01866/83320, ⓦwww.roineabhal.com, minimum 2-night booking; ❻), very stylish and comfortable and serving fine dinners as well as breakfast.

Isle of Mull

The second largest of the Inner Hebrides, **Mull** (Ⓦ www.holidaymull.co.uk) is by far the most accessible: just forty minutes from Oban by ferry. As so often, first impressions largely depend on the weather – it is the wettest of the Hebrides (and that's saying something) – for without the sun the large tracts of moorland, particularly around the island's highest peak, Ben More (3169ft), can appear bleak and unwelcoming. There are, however, areas of more gentle pastoral scenery around **Dervaig** in the north and **Salen** on the east coast, and the indented west coast varies from the sandy beaches around **Calgary** to the cliffs of Loch na Keal. The most common mistake is to try and "do" the island in a day or two: flogging up the main road to the picturesque capital of **Tobermory**, then covering the fifty-odd miles between there and Fionnphort, in order to visit **Iona**. Mull is a place that will grow on you only if you have the time and patience to explore.

Historically, crofting, whisky distilling and fishing supported the islanders (*Muileachs*), but the population – which peaked at 10,000 – decreased dramatically in the late nineteenth century due to the Clearances and the 1846 potato famine. On Mull, it is a trend that has been reversed, mostly owing to the large influx of settlers from elsewhere in the country, which has brought the current population up to more than 2500. One of the main reasons for this resurgence is, of course, tourism – more than half a million visitors come here each year. Mull makes particular efforts to draw visitors to **special events** through the year: these annual events include a wildlife week in May, the Mendelssohn on Mull Festival in July, which commemorates the composer's visit here in 1829, and a rally car event around the island's winding roads in October.

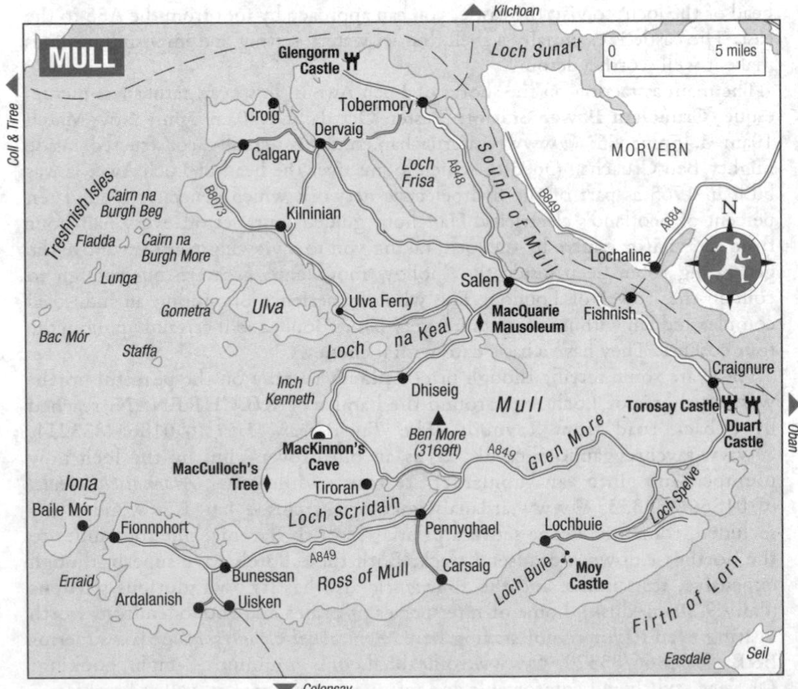

Craignure is the main ferry terminal, with a frequent daily **car ferry** link to Oban (booking ahead advisable). A smaller and less expensive car ferry crosses daily from Lochaline on the Morvern peninsula (see p.475) to Fishnish, six miles northwest of Craignure. Another even smaller car ferry connects Kilchoan on the Ardnamurchan peninsula (see p.477) with Tobermory, the island capital. **Public transport** on Mull is not too bad on the main A849, but there's more or less no service along the west coast. If **driving**, note that the roads are still predominantly single-track, with passing places, which can slow journeys down considerably. To rent a cottage on Mull, try Ⓦwww.isleofmullcottages.com and Ⓦwww.islandholidaycottages.com, which feature some good rustic options.

Craignure and around

CRAIGNURE is little more than a scattering of cottages, though there is a small shop, a bar, some toilets and a CalMac ticket and **tourist office** – the only one on the island open daily all year round – situated opposite the pier. The eighteenth-century whitewashed *Craignure Inn* (Ⓣ01680/812305, Ⓦwww.craignure-inn.co.uk; ❹), just a minute's stroll up the road towards Fionnphort, is a snug **pub** to hole up in, with decent rooms and food. Along the side road leading to Mull Rail, there's also a well-equipped **campsite** run by Shieling Holidays (Ⓣ01680/812496, Ⓦwww.shielingholidays.co.uk; April–Oct) set above a shingle beach with good views over to the Morvern shore. The campsite also offers accommodation in "shielings" (large, furnished, hard-top tents), and has boats, canoes and bikes for rent. Another pleasant place to camp is the well-equipped *Balmeanach Park* site (Ⓣ01680/300342; April–Oct), five miles up the A849 at Fishnish, which has a small tearoom attached. There are several B&Bs in the area, but the best **guest-house** is the *Old Mill Cottage* (Ⓣ01680/812442, Ⓦwww.oldmillmull.com; ❹), a sensitively converted mill, three miles south on the A849 in Lochdon; they also provide attractive self-catering accommodation.

The most memorable mode of transport available at Craignure is the diminutive, narrow-gauge Mull & West Highland Railway, commonly known as **Mull Rail** (Easter–Oct; £5 return; Ⓣ01680/812494, Ⓦwww.mullrail.co.uk), built in the 1980s and the only working railway in the Scottish islands. The Craignure station is situated beyond the Shieling Holidays campsite, and the line stretches southeast for about a mile and a half to Torosay Castle (see below). You may prefer to take the train one way only as it's a lovely thirty-minute walk along the coast (with the possibility of spotting an otter). The company uses diesel and steam locomotives, so ring ahead if you want to be sure of a steam-driven train.

Torosay and Duart castles

Two castles lie immediately southeast of Craignure. The first, a mile-long walk or short train-ride from Craignure, is **Torosay Castle,** a full-blown Scottish Baronial creation whose magnificent **gardens** feature an avenue of eighteenth-century Venetian statues, a Japanese section and views up Loch Linnhe. At the time of writing the castle was for sale; to check whether it is open to the public, contact the tourist office in Craignure.

Very different in style is **Duart Castle** (April Mon–Thurs 10.30am–4pm; May to mid-Oct daily 10.30am–5.30pm; £5.30; Ⓦwww.duartcastle.com), a couple of miles east of Torosay, which is perched on a rocky promontory sticking out into the Sound of Mull, making it a striking landmark from the Oban–Craignure ferry. Duart was headquarters of the once-powerful MacLean clan from the thirteenth century, but was burnt down by the Campbells and confiscated after the 1745 rebellion. In 1911 the 26th clan chief, Fitzroy MacLean (1835–1936) – not to be confused with the

Scottish writer of the same name – managed to buy it back and restore it. Buffeted by winds and weather, the castle is by no means a luxurious country seat: you can peek at the dungeons, climb up to the ramparts, study the family photos and learn about the world scout movement (the 27th clan chief became Chief Scout in 1959). After your visit, head to the castle's pretty, barnlike tearoom (May to mid-Oct), where there's an impressive array of home-made cakes on offer.

A short way past Torosay Castle, a turn-off leads to **Wings over Mull** (Easter–Oct 10.30am–5.30pm; £4.50; Ⓦwww.wingsovermull.com), a conservation centre and sanctuary devoted to birds of prey. The visitors' centre here, based in a converted steading, has lots of background information about all kinds of owls, hawks, falcons and eagles, as well as details about the work done at the centre to rescue and preserve these species. Flying displays take place at noon, 2pm and 4pm each day.

Tobermory

Mull's chief town, **TOBERMORY,** at the northern tip of the island, is easily the most attractive fishing port on the west coast of Scotland, its clusters of brightly coloured houses and boats sheltering in a bay backed by a steep bluff. Founded in 1788 by the British Society for Encouraging Fisheries, it never really took off as a fishing port and only survived due to the steady influx of crofters evicted from other parts of the island during the Clearances. With a population of more than 800, it is the most important settlement on Mull, and if you're staying any length of time on the island you're bound to want to visit, not least because it has a Womble named after it (or, if you're under 10, because it's the setting for the children's TV show *Balamory*).

Information and accommodation

The **tourist office** (April–Oct daily) is in the same building as the CalMac ticket office on the pier at the far end of Main Street. If you want to **rent a bike**, head to Archibald Brown, the endearingly old-fashioned ironmongers on Main Street (Ⓣ01688/302020, Ⓦwww.browns-tobermory.co.uk). At the large whitewashed Harbour Visitor Centre you can book a variety of **boat outings**, from a half-hour seal trip (£6) to an all-day Whalewatch Explorer Cruise (£59) with an island landing for lunch.

The small, friendly SYHA **hostel** is on Main Street (Ⓣ0870/004 1151, Ⓦwww.syha.org.uk; March–Oct) and has internet and laundry facilities. The nearest **campsite** is spruce *Newdale* (Ⓣ01688/302624, Ⓦwww.tobermory-campsite.co.uk; April–Oct), nicely situated one and a half miles uphill from Tobermory on the B8073 to Dervaig.

Baliscate Guest House Salen Road Ⓣ01688/302251, Ⓦwww.baliscate.co.uk. Good-quality self-catering apartments in an imposing whitewashed Victorian guesthouse with a large garden, set back from the road to Salen on the edge of Tobermory. ❺

Glengorm Castle Near Tobermory Ⓣ01688/302321, Ⓦwww.glengormcastle.co.uk. Fairy-tale, rambling Baronial mansion in a superb, secluded setting, five miles northwest of Tobermory, with incredible coastal views, lovely gardens and local walks. Guests get use of the castle's wood-panelled library and lounge; the bedrooms are large and full of splendid features and there are self-catering cottages available too. ❼

Highland Cottage Breadalbane St Ⓣ01688/302030, Ⓦwww.highlandcottage.co.uk. Super-luxury B&B run by a very welcoming couple in a quiet street high above the harbour; the four-course Scottish menu in the restaurant costs around £40 a head, but is outstanding. ❽

Sonas House Upper town, by the golf course Ⓣ01688/302304, Ⓦwww.sonashouse.co.uk. Fairly plain but comfortable rooms with terrific views over the Sound of Mull; they have a small swimming pool. ❼

Strongarbh House Upper Tobermory Ⓣ01688/302319, Ⓦwww.strongarbh.com. A super-stylish but friendly B&B in a large Victorian villa, with a library, boardgames and wi-fi. Two rooms have four-posters. ❺

Tobermory Hotel Main St ⓣ01688/302091, ⓦwww.thetobermoryhotel.com. Smallish, fairly smart and comfortable hotel converted from fishermens' cottages, with fifteen rooms situated right on the harbour front. ❺

Western Isles Hotel Above the harbour ⓣ01688/302012, ⓦwww.westernisleshotel.com. The decor – moth-eaten stag heads and floral drapes – isn't for everyone, but the *Western Isles* is undergoing gradual renovation. The setting above town is impressive, and the hotel has a glamorous pedigree as a location for the Powell and Pressburger classic *I Know Where I'm Going.* ❺

The Town

The harbour – known as **Main Street** – is one long parade of multicoloured hotels, guesthouses, restaurants and shops, and you could happily spend an hour or so meandering around. A good wet-weather retreat is the **Mull Museum** (Easter to mid-Oct Mon–Fri 10am–4pm, Sat 10am–1pm; free), further along Main Street, a tiny room with a great deal of information and artefacts – including a few objects salvaged from the *San Juan de Sicilia*, a ship from the Spanish Armada which lies at the bottom of Tobermory harbour.

A stiff climb up Back Brae will bring you to the island's main arts centre, **An Tobar** (March–Dec Mon–Sat 10am–5pm; May–Sept also Sun 1–4pm; free; ⓦwww.antobar.co.uk), housed in a converted Victorian schoolhouse. The small but attractive centre hosts exhibitions and a variety of live events, and contains a café with comfy sofas set before a real fire. The rest of the upper town, laid out on a classic grid-plan, merits a stroll, if only for the great views over the bay.

Alternatively, there's the minuscule **Tobermory Distillery** (Easter–Oct Mon–Fri 10am–4/5pm; £3.50) at the south end of the bay, founded in 1795 but closed down three times since then. Today, it's back in business and offers a fairly desultory guided tour, rounded off with a dram. Meanwhile, five miles northwest of town, along a dead-end single-track road, lies **Glengorm Castle**, a Scots Baronial pile overlooking the sea which offers accommodation (see opposite) and also has an attractively converted steading, housing a café, well-stocked farm shop, craft shop and art gallery (Easter to mid-Oct). You can walk around their attractive walled garden or make for the longer forest, archeological and coastal trails.

Eating

Main Street heaves with **places to eat**, including a highly rated *Fish & Chip Van* (Mon–Sat) on the old pier which serves up scallops and chips alongside more traditional fish suppers. Fine **picnic** fodder, fresh bread and goodies can be found at the excellent Tobermory Bakery, also on the harbour front.

Café Fish The Pier ⓣ01688/301253, ⓦwww.thecafefish.com. Great little place above the tourist office, which cooks up the best of the catch from their own boat.

The Glassbarn Tearooms Glengorm Road ⓣ01688/302235. The prettiest eating option on Mull – a spacious glasshouse with sofas and wooden furniture serving good coffee, snacks and cakes. Walk through the cottage garden to visit the farm shop of the Isle of Mull dairy.

Highland Cottage Breadalbane St ⓣ01688/302030, ⓦwww.highlandcottage.co.uk. B&B restaurant that serves dishes such as Tobermory scallops with parsnip mash and roast saddle of Ardnamurchan venison for around £37 for four courses.

Mull Pottery Salen Rd ⓣ01688/302347. This pleasant café/bistro above Mull Pottery is a good option for imaginatively prepared meals using Mull produce including beef, venison and seafood.

Water's Edge Main St ⓣ01688/302091, ⓦwww.thetobermoryhotel.com. Restaurant in the *Tobermory Hotel* which serves up elegant seafood dishes.

Pubs, live music and entertainment

The lively bar of the *Mishnish Hotel on Main Street* has been the most popular local **drinking** hole for many years, and features live music at the weekend. On the

Wildlife boat trips around Mull

Boat trips leave from several different places around Mull, with prices ranging from around £6 for a half-hour seal cruise to £59 for a full day **whale-watching**. **Sea Life Surveys** (Easter–Oct; ⓣ01688/302916, ⓦwww.sealifesurveys.com), linked to the Hebridean Whale and Dolphin Trust, focuses on seeking out the whales (minke and even killer whales are the most common), porpoises, dolphins and basking sharks that spend time in the waters around the Hebrides. Based in the Harbour Visitor Centre in Tobermory, the same outfit also operates friendly Ecocruz, which sticks to coastal waters, and is particularly good for families. Rather more sedate are the wildlife cruises with **Hebridean Adventure** (mid-May to Sept Mon–Sat ⓣ01688/302044, ⓦwww.hebrideanadventure.co.uk; half-day £35, full day £70), which head out of Tobermory harbour; they also do a dinner cruise.

opposite side of the bay, near the distillery, is *MacGochan's*, a purpose-built, though pleasant enough, pub, which also offers occasional live music. For the latest **events** in Tobermory (or anywhere else on Mull), pick up the free monthly newsletter *Round & About*, and/or buy a copy of *Am Muileach*, the monthly island newspaper. An Tobar is an excellent venue for concerts and ceilidhs; and the Mull Theatre (ⓣ01688/302828, ⓦwww.mulltheatre.com) performs around the island and has a box office at the far end of Main Street.

Dervaig and Calgary

The gently undulating countryside west of Tobermory, beyond the freshwater Mishnish lochs, provides some of the most beguiling scenery on the island. Added to this, the road out west, the B8073, is exceptionally dramatic, with fiendish switchbacks much appreciated during the annual Mull Rally, which takes place each October. Loch Frisa, a long slash in the landscape south of the road, is an established nesting place for **white-tailed (or sea) eagles**. There's a well-placed hide which has close-up, live CCTV pictures of the nest; between April and July, when the birds are nesting, guided access to the hide is available through the RSPB (£3; bookings on ⓣ01688/302038).

The only village of any size on this side of the island is **DERVAIG**, which nestles beside narrow Loch Chumhainn, just eight miles southwest of Tobermory, distinguished by its unusual pencil-shaped church spire and single street of dinky whitewashed cottages and old corrugated-iron shacks. Dervaig has a shop, a bookshop/café and a wide choice of **places to stay**. At the upper end of the scale, Victorian *Druimard Country House* (ⓣ01688/400345, ⓦwww.druimard.co.uk; ❹), located on the fringe of Dervaig, is a pleasant, comfy place serving good dinners. Local food is also served at the *Druimnacroish Hotel* (ⓣ01688/400274, ⓦwww.druimnacroish.co.uk; March–Nov; ❸), a lovely country house in a rural setting two miles out on the Salen road, though you need to book in advance. There are several pleasant B&Bs, including the excellent *Cuin Lodge* (ⓣ01688/400346, ⓦwww.cuinlodgemull.co.uk; ❹), an old shooting lodge overlooking the loch, to the northwest of the village. There's also a modern **bunkhouse** (ⓣ01688/400491 or ⓣ07919/870664) in the village hall, with bedding provided and disabled facilities, while the *Bellachroy*, a rugged early seventeenth-century **inn** with an attractive whitewashed interior, serves good seafood and real ales and offers six plain but cosy rooms (ⓣ01688/400314, ⓦwww.bellachroyhotel.co.uk; ❺).

The cross-country road takes you on to *Am Birlinn* (Ⓣ01688/400619, Ⓦwww.ambirlinnw5.com), a contemporary chalet-like **restaurant** serving up elegant food: lobster, scallops, venison and mussels feature. Beyond here is **CALGARY**, once a thriving crofting community, now a quiet glen which opens out onto Mull's finest sandy bay, backed by low-lying dunes and machair, with wonderful views over to Coll and Tiree. A few hundred yards back from the beach is the delightful *Calgary Farmhouse* (Ⓣ01688/400256, Ⓦwww.calgary.co.uk), providing glamorous self-catering accommodation and an art-filled daytime **café**. A sculpture trail winds through the wooded hills behind the farm; you can buy a map (£1) at the entrance gate to help identify the artworks amongst the trees. Down by the beach itself, there's a spectacular and very popular spot for **camping** rough; the only facilities are the basic public toilets.

Salen and around

SALEN, on the east coast halfway between Craignure and Tobermory, lies at the narrowest point on Mull, and is not a bad place to base yourself. **Accommodation** choices range from the hostel-style *Arle Lodge* (Ⓣ01680/300299, Ⓦwww.arlelodge.co.uk; ❸), four miles north of Salen on the road to Tobermory, with twin and family rooms to the pretty Victorian *Gruline Home Farm* **B&B** (Ⓣ01680/300581, Ⓦwww.gruline.com; ❻), a former farmhouse four miles southwest near the shores of Loch Na Keal, which serves up excellent and elaborate dinners (non-residents must reserve). Simpler, less expensive B&B is available next door at *Barn Cottage* (Ⓣ01680/300451, Ⓦwww.barncottagemull.co.uk; ❷). Salen itself has a great place to **eat**: *Mediterranea* (Ⓣ01680/300200, Ⓦwww.mull-cuisine.co.uk; lunch Thurs–Sun, dinner nightly), which mixes engaging Scottish hospitality with Sicilian cooking. You can **rent bikes** from On Yer Bike (Ⓣ01680/300501), which has mountain bikes, hybrids and child trailers to rent.

Isle of Ulva

Ulva's (Ⓦwww.ulva.mull.com) population peaked in the nineteenth century at a staggering 850, sustained by the huge quantities of kelp which were exported for glass and soap production. That was before the market for kelp collapsed and the 1846 potato famine hit, after which the remaining population was brutally evicted. Nowadays around fifteen people live here, and the island is littered with ruined crofts. It's great walking country, however, with several clearly marked paths crisscrossing the native woodland and the rocky heather moorland interior – and you're almost guaranteed to spot some of the abundant wildlife.

To **get to Ulva**, which lies just a hundred yards or so off the west coast of Mull, follow the signs for "Ulva Ferry" west from Salen or south from Calgary – if you've no transport, a postbus can get you there, but you'll have to make your own way back. From **Ulva Ferry**, a small bicycle/passenger-only ferry (£5 return) is available on demand (Mon–Fri 9am–5pm; June–Aug also Sun; at other times by arrangement on Ⓣ01688/500226). *The Boathouse*, near the ferry slip on the Ulva side, serves as a licensed **tearoom** selling soup, cakes, snacks, Guinness and Ulva oysters. You can learn more about the history of the island from the exhibition upstairs, and pop into the newly restored thatched smiddy nearby, housing **Sheila's Cottage**, which has been restored to the period when islander Sheila MacFadyen lived there in the first half of the last century. There's no accommodation, but with permission from the present owners (Ⓣ01688/500264, Ⓔulva@mull.com) you can **camp** rough overnight.

Isle of Staffa and the Treshnish Isles

Five miles southwest of Ulva, **Staffa** is one of the most romantic and dramatic of Scotland's many uninhabited islands. On its south side, the perpendicular rockface features an imposing series of black basalt columns, known as the Colonnade, which have been cut by the sea into cathedralesque caverns, most notably **Fingal's Cave**. The Vikings knew about the island – the name derives from their word for "Island of Pillars" – but it wasn't until 1772 that it was "discovered" by the world. Turner painted it, Wordsworth explored it, but Mendelssohn's *Die Fingalshöhle* (the lovely "*Hebrides Overture*"), inspired by the sounds of the sea-wracked caves he heard on a visit here in 1829, did most to popularize the place – after which Queen Victoria gave her blessing, too. The polygonal basalt organ-pipes were created some sixty million years ago when a huge mass of molten basalt burst forth onto land and, as it cooled, solidified into hexaganol crystals. The same phenomenon produced the Giant's Causeway in Northern Ireland and Celtic folk tales often link the two with rival giants Fionn mac Cumhail (Irish) and Fingal (Scottish) throwing rocks at each other across the Irish Sea.

Northwest of Staffa lie the **Treshnish Isles**, an archipelago of uninhabited volcanic islets, none more than a mile or two across. The most distinctive is **Bac Mór**, shaped like a Puritan's hat and popularly dubbed the Dutchman's Cap. **Lunga**, the largest island, is a summer nesting-place for hundreds of seabirds, in particular guillemots, razorbills and puffins, as well as a breeding ground for seals. The two most northerly islands, **Cairn na Burgh More** and **Cairn na Burgh Beag**, have the remains of ruined castles, the first of which served as a lookout post for the Lords of the Isles and was last garrisoned in the Civil War; Cairn na Burgh Beag hasn't been occupied since the 1715 Jacobite uprising.

From April to October several operators offer **boat trips** to Staffa and the Treshnish Isles. Long-established Turus Mara (Ⓣ0800/085 8786, Ⓦwww.turusmara.com) sets out from Ulva Ferry and is a classy outfit, charging around £50 return, as does Gordon Grant Marine (Ⓣ01681/700338, Ⓦwww.staffatours.com), who depart from Fionnphort. If you just want to go to Staffa, try Iolaire (Ⓣ01681/700358, Ⓦwww.staffatrips.co.uk), who charge around £20 for passage from Fionnphort.

Ben More and the Ardmeanach peninsula

From the southern shores of Loch na Keal, which almost splits Mull in two, rise the terraced slopes of **Ben More** (3169ft) – literally "big mountain" – a mighty extinct volcano, and the only Munro in the Hebrides outside of Skye. It's most easily climbed from Dhiseig, halfway along the loch's southern shores, though an alternative route is to climb up to the col between Beinn Fhada and A'Chioch, and approach via the mountain's eastern ridge. Further west along the shore the road carves through spectacular overhanging cliffs before heading south past the Gribun rocks which face the tiny island of **Inch Kenneth**, where Unity Mitford lived until her death in 1948. There are great views out to Staffa and the Treshnish Isles as the road leaves the coast behind, climbing over the pass to Loch Scribain, where it eventually joins the equally dramatic Glen More road (A849) from Craignure.

If you're properly equipped for walking, however, you can explore the **Ardmeanach peninsula**, to the west of the road. The area, which features a large sea cave and a fossilized tree, is NTS-owned and there is a car park just before *Tiroran House* (Ⓣ01681/705232, Ⓦwww.tiroran.com; ❻ including afternoon tea), a beautiful secluded **hotel** with six rooms, cosy lounges, good home-cooking and a lovely, lush, south-facing garden.

The Ross of Mull

Stretching for twenty miles west as far as Iona is Mull's rocky southernmost peninsula, the **Ross of Mull**, which, like much of Scotland, appears blissfully tranquil in good weather, and desolate and bleak in bad climes. Most visitors simply drive through the Ross en route to Iona, but if you have the time it's definitely worth considering exploring, or even staying, in this little-visited part of Mull.

The most scenic spots on the Ross are hidden away on the south coast, starting with **LOCHBUIE**, which lies on a fertile plain beside the sea. The bay here is rugged and wide, and overlooked by the handsome peak of Ben Buie (2352ft), to the northwest. Hidden behind a patch of Scots pine are the ivy-strewn ruins of **Moy Castle**, an old MacLean stronghold; in the fields to the north is one of the few **stone circles** in the west of Scotland, dating from the second century BC, the tallest of its stones about 6ft high. The best **accommodation** in the vicinity is at *Barrachandroman* (Ⓣ01680/814220, Ⓦwww.barrachandroman.co.uk; ❹), a converted stone barn in Kinlochspelve, overlooking the sea loch. A popular and fairly easy walk is the five-mile hike west from Lochbuie along the coastal path to Carsaig (see below).

The main A849 road, single-track (for the most part), hugs the northern coastline of the Ross, passing, first off, the tiny settlement of **PENNYGHAEL**, home to the *Pennyghael Hotel* (Ⓣ01681/704288, Ⓦwww.pennyghaelhotel.com; ❺), which has a good restaurant serving island produce including crab, mussels, pork and Tobermory cheeses. A cheaper option is the rustic *Smithy* B&B (Ⓣ01681/704034, Ⓦwww.mull-bedandbreakfast.com; ❷), which also has a pretty waterside location and a view of Ben More. A rickety single-track road heads south four miles to **CARSAIG**, which enjoys an idyllic setting, looking south out to Colonsay, Islay and Jura. Most folk come here either to walk east to Lochbuie, or west under the cliffs, to the **Nuns' Cave**, where nuns from Iona are alleged to have hidden during the Reformation, and then, after four miles or so, at Malcolm's Point, the spectacular **Carsaig Arches**, formed by eroded sea caves, which are linked to basalt cliffs.

Meanwhile, the main road continues for another eleven miles to **BUNESSAN**, the largest village on the peninsula, roughly two-thirds of the way along the Ross. Bunessan has a few useful shops and a reasonable pub, *The Argyll Arms Hotel*. A road connects Bunessan with the sandy bays of the south coast. A couple of miles out of the village, modern *Ardachy House Hotel* (Ⓣ01681/700505, Ⓦwww.ardachy.co.uk; March–Oct; ❻) overlooks the wide expanse of **Ardalanish Bay**. Just beyond the hotel, drop in at Ardalanish Weavers (daily tour 1pm; Ⓣ01681/700265, Ⓦwww.ardalanishfarm.co.uk), where beautiful durable organic tweed is produced on Victorian looms originally from Torosay Castle. The tweed is snapped up by upmarket high-street stores, and is used for the elegant couture collection displayed in the small shop; you can also buy smaller items such as scarves, and balls of wool. The road continues to the more sheltered bay of sand and granite outcrops at neighbouring **UISKEN**, a mile to the east. The beach is a wonderful spot for wild **camping**, but ask permission first at *Uisken Croft* (Ⓣ01681/700307), just up the hill. From Uisken, the Lorn Ferry Service (April–Oct; Ⓣ01951/200320) runs an occasional **passenger-only ferry** to Colonsay.

Fionnphort

The road ends at **FIONNPHORT**, facing Iona, probably the least attractive place to stay on the Ross. Partly to ease congestion on Iona, and to give their neighbours a slice of the tourist pound, Fionnphort was chosen as the site for the little-visited **Columba Centre** (Easter–Sept daily 10am–1pm & 2–5.30pm;

free), whose small but well-presented exhibition outlines Iona's history, tells a little of Columba's life, and has a few facsimiles of the illuminated manuscripts produced by the island's monks.

For **B&B** in Fionnphort, try the sandstone Victorian villa of *Seaview* (ⓣ01681/700235, ⓦwww.seaview-mull.co.uk; ❸) or whitewashed *Staffa House* (ⓣ01681/700677, ⓦwww.staffahouse.co.uk; ❸), both of which are close to the ferry and the local pub, the *Keel Row*, which serves reasonable meals. For a treat, head to stylish and upmarket *Ninth Wave* (ⓣ01681/700757, ⓦwww.ninthwaverestaurant.co.uk) just outside the village, where the owner catches and then serves up crab and lobster; veg is supplied from their kitchen garden. The simple *Fidden Farm* **campsite** (ⓣ01681/700427; April–Sept), a mile or so south of Fionnphort, is a lovely place to camp, with direct access to the golden sands of Fidden beach. Fidden beach looks out to the **Isle of Erraid**, where Robert Louis Stevenson is believed to have written *Kidnapped* while staying in one of the island's cottages. **Bikes** can be rented from *Seaview* B&B.

Isle of Iona

Less than a mile off the southwest tip of Mull, **IONA** (ⓦwww.isle-of-iona.com) – just three miles long and not much more than a mile wide – has been a place of pilgrimage for several centuries, and a place of Christian worship for more than 1400 years. For it was to this flat Hebridean island that St Columba fled from Ireland in 563 and established a monastery which was responsible for the conversion of more or less all of pagan Scotland as well as much of northern England. This history and the island's splendid isolation have lent it a peculiar religiosity; in the much-quoted words of Dr Johnson, who visited in 1773, "That man is little to be envied … whose piety would not grow warmer among the ruins of Iona." Today, however, the island can barely cope with the constant flood of day-trippers, so to appreciate the special atmosphere and to have time to see the whole island, including the often overlooked west coast, you should plan on staying at least one night.

Baile Mór

The passenger ferry from Fionnphort drops you off at the island's main village, **BAILE MÓR** (literally "Large Village"), which is in fact little more than a single terrace of cottages facing the sea. Just inland lie the extensive pink-granite ruins of the **Augustinian nunnery**, disused since the Reformation. A beautifully maintained garden now occupies the cloisters, and if nothing else the complex gives you an idea of the state of the present-day abbey before it was restored. Across the road to the north, in the former manse, is the **Iona Heritage Centre** (Easter–Oct Mon–Sat 10.30am–4.30pm; £3), with displays on the social history of the island over the last 200 years, including the Clearances, which nearly halved the island's population of 500 in the mid-nineteenth century. At a bend in the road, just south of the manse and church, stands the fifteenth-century **MacLean's Cross**, a fine, late medieval example of the distinctive, flowing, three-leaved foliage of the Iona school.

Iona Abbey

No buildings remain from Columba's time: the present **abbey** (daily: April–Sept 9.30am–5.30pm; Oct–March 9.30am–4.30pm; HS; £4.70) dates from the arrival of the Benedictines in around 1200; it was extensively rebuilt in the

St Columba and Iona

There is very little that is known for certain about **St Columba** (Colum Cille), but legend has it that he was born in Donegal in northwestern Ireland some time around 521. A scholar and soldier priest who founded numerous monasteries in Ireland, he is thought to have become involved in a bloody dispute with the king which culminated in the Battle of Cúl Drebene (Cooldrumman), at which Columba's forces won, though with the loss of more than 3000 lives. Repenting the bloodshed, Columba went into exile with twelve other monks, in 563, settling on Iona and eventually becoming something of a cult figure by the time of his death in 597.

In the sixth and seventh centuries Iona enjoyed a great deal of autonomy from Rome, establishing a specifically **Celtic Christian** tradition. Missionaries were sent out to the rest of Scotland and parts of England, and Iona quickly became a respected seat of learning and artistry; the monks compiled a vast library of intricately **illuminated manuscripts** – most famously the *Book of Kells* (now on display in Trinity College, Dublin) – while the masons excelled in carving peculiarly intricate crosses. Two factors were instrumental in the demise of the Celtic tradition: a series of Viking raids, the worst of which was the massacre of 68 monks on the sands of Martyrs' Bay in 806; and relentless pressure from the established Church, beginning with the Synod of Whitby in 664 which chose Rome over the Celtic Church, and culminated in its suppression by King David I in 1144.

In 1203, Iona became part of the mainstream Church with the establishment of an **Augustinian nunnery** and a **Benedictine monastery** by Reginald, son of Somerled, Lord of the Isles. During the Reformation, the entire complex was ransacked, the contents of the library burnt and all but three of the island's 360 crosses destroyed. Although plans were drawn up at various times to turn the abbey into a Cathedral of the Isles, nothing came of them until 1899, when the then-owner, the eighth Duke of Argyll, donated the abbey buildings to the **Church of Scotland**, who restored the abbey church for worship over the course of the next decade. Iona's modern resurgence began in 1938, when **George MacLeod**, a minister from Glasgow, established a group of ministers, students and artisans to begin rebuilding the remainder of the monastic buildings. What began as a mostly male, Gaelic-speaking, strictly Presbyterian community is today a lay, mixed and ecumenical retreat. The entire abbey complex has been successfully restored, and is now looked after by Historic Scotland, while the island, apart from the church land and a few crofts, is in the care of the NTS.

fifteenth and sixteenth centuries, and restored virtually wholesale last century. Iona's oldest building, the plain-looking eleventh-century **St Oran's Chapel**, lies south of the abbey, to your right. Legend has it that the original chapel could only be completed through human sacrifice. Oran apparently volunteered to be buried alive, and was found to have survived the ordeal when the grave was opened a few days later. Declaring that he had seen hell and it wasn't all bad, he was promptly reinterred for blasphemy. Oran's Chapel stands at the centre of Iona's sacred burial ground, **Reilig Odhráin** (Oran's Cemetery), which is said to contain the graves of sixty kings of Norway, Ireland, France and Scotland, including Duncan and Macbeth. The best of the early Christian gravestones and medieval effigies that once lay in the Reilig Odhráin have been removed to the Infirmary Museum, behind the abbey, and to various other locations within the complex.

Approaching the abbey itself, from the ticket office, you cross an exposed section of the evocative medieval **Street of the Dead**, whose giant pink-granite cobbles once stretched from the abbey, past St Oran's Chapel, to the village. Beside the road stands the most impressive of Iona's Celtic high crosses, the

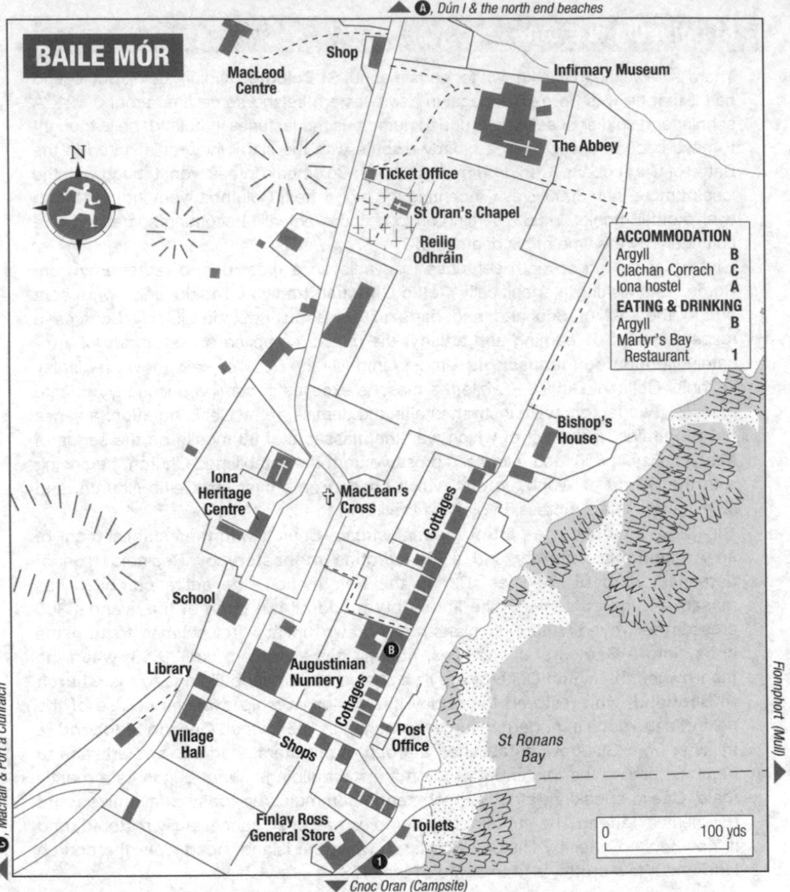

eighth-century **St Martin's Cross**, smothered with figural scenes – the Virgin and Child at the centre, Daniel in the lion's den, Abraham sacrificing Isaac, and David with musicians in the shaft below. The reverse side features Pictish serpent-and-boss decoration. Standing directly in front of the abbey are the base of St Matthew's Cross (the rest of which is in the Infirmary Museum) and, to the left, a concrete cast of the eighth-century **St John's Cross**, decorated with serpent-and-boss and Celtic spiral ornamental panels. Before you enter the abbey, take a look inside **St Columba's Shrine**, a small steep-roofed chamber to the left of the main entrance. Columba is believed to have been buried either here or under the rocky mound to the west of the abbey, known as Tórr an Aba.

The **Abbey** itself has been simply and sensitively restored to incorporate the original elements. You can spot many of the medieval capitals in the south aisle of the choir and in the south transept, where the white marble effigies of the eighth Duke of Argyll and his wife, Ina, lie in a side chapel – an incongruous piece of Victorian pomp in an otherwise modest and tranquil place. The finest pre-Reformation effigy is that of John MacKinnon, the last abbot of Iona, who died around 1500, and now lies on the south side of the choir steps. For reasons of sanitation, the **cloisters** were placed, contrary to the norm, on the north side of the church (where running water was available); entirely reconstructed in the late 1950s, they now shelter lots of medieval grave slabs. There are free daily guided tours of the abbey (the times are posted up at the ticket office).

The rest of the island

Not many day visitors get further than the village and abbey, but it's perfectly possible to walk to the stunning sandy beaches and turquoise seas at the **north end** of the island, or up to the highest point, **Dún I**, a mere 328ft above sea level but with views on a clear day to Skye, Tiree and Jura. Alternatively, it takes about half an hour to walk over to the **machair**, or common grazing land, on the west side of Iona, which lies adjacent to the evocatively named Bay at the Back of the Ocean, a crescent of pebble and shell-strewn sand with a spouting cave to the south. Those with more time (2–3hr) might hike over to the **south** of the island, where Port a'Churaich ("Bay of the Coracle", also known as St Columba's Bay), the saint's traditional landing place on Iona, is filled with smooth round rocks and multicoloured pebbles and stones.

Practicalities

There's no **tourist office** on Iona, and as demand far exceeds supply you should organize **accommodation** well in advance; and for those who are stuck, there's an information board just up from the jetty that lists all the options. Of the island's two **hotels**, the stone-built *Argyll* (Ⓣ01681/700334, Ⓦwww.argyllhoteliona.co.uk; Feb–Nov; ❻), in the village's terrace of cottages overlooking the Sound of Iona, is by far the nicer. As for **B&Bs**, try *Clachan Corrach* (May–Oct; Ⓣ01681/700323; ❷), a croft in the middle of the island. For **camping** head to the *Cnoc-Oran* site (Ⓣ01681/700112) a fifteen-minute walk beyond *Martyr's Bay Restaurant*. There's a terrific **hostel** (Ⓣ01681/700781, Ⓦwww.ionahostel.co.uk) at the north of the island, where the main room is filled with lovely wooden furniture and there are views out to the Treshnish Isles; to reach it, follow the road past the abbey for half a mile. If you want to stay with the **Iona Community** (Ⓣ01681/700404, Ⓦwww.iona.org.uk), either in the abbey itself or the *MacLeod Centre* (popularly known as "The Mac"), you must be prepared to participate fully in the daily activities, prayers and religious services.

Eating options aren't bad: the restaurant at the *Argyll* uses home-grown vegetables and organic produce, whenever possible, and they have a pretty tea garden by the water. The pub grub at the bar adjoining the *Martyr's Bay Restaurant* by the jetty is reasonable too, often serving the freshest possible seafood. For something lighter during the day, head for the **tearoom** beside the Heritage Centre, which serves home-made soup and tasty cakes and has an idyllic garden setting.

Visitors are not allowed to bring cars onto the island, but **bikes** can be rented in Fionnphort (see p.277) or from the Finlay Ross general store in the village (Ⓣ01681/700357, Ⓦwww.finlayrossiona.co.uk; ❷); they also do basic B&B. There's also a taxi on the island (Ⓣ01681/700776). Mark Jardine's Alternative Boat Hire (Ⓣ01681/700537, Ⓦwww.boattripsiona.com), based on Iona, takes the lovely wooden gaff-rigged sailing boat *Freya* on short trips to some of the less-visited spots around the Sound of Iona and Erraid. There are also trips to Staffa (Ⓣ01681/700358) and whale-watching and wildlife outings (Ⓣ01681/700362, Ⓦwww.volanteiona.com)

Coll and Tiree

Coll and **Tiree** are among the most isolated of the Inner Hebrides, and if anything have more in common with the outlying Western Isles than with their closest neighbour, Mull. Each is roughly twelve miles long and three miles wide, both are low-lying, treeless and exceptionally windy, with white sandy beaches and the highest sunshine records in Scotland. Like most of the Hebrides, they were once ruled by Vikings, and didn't pass into Scottish hands until the thirteenth century. In the 1830s Coll's population peaked at 1440, Tiree's at a staggering 4450, but both were badly affected by the Clearances, which virtually halved their populations in a generation.

Throughout the summer, the CalMac **ferry** from Oban calls daily at Coll (2hr 40min) and Tiree (3hr 40min). On Thursdays – though the day may change – the ferry continues to Barra in the Western Isles, and calls in at Tiree on the way back, making a **day-trip from Oban** possible; a minibus tour of the island is thrown in as part of the package. Tiree also has an **airport** with daily flights (Mon–Sat) to and from Glasgow. The majority of visitors on both islands stay for at least a week in self-catering accommodation (see p.36), though there are B&Bs and hotels on the islands – advance booking is essential (and that goes for the ferry crossing, too).

Isle of Coll

The fish-shaped rocky island of **Coll**, with a population of around a hundred, lies less than seven miles off the coast of Mull. The ferry docks at Coll's only real village, **ARINAGOUR**, whose whitewashed cottages line the western shore of Loch Eatharna, a popular safe anchorage for boats. Half the island's population lives in the village, and it's here you'll find the island's hotel and pub, post office, churches and a couple of shops. The island's petrol pump is also in Arinagour, and is run on a volunteer basis – effectively it's open when the ferry arrives.

On the southwest coast there are two edifices, both confusingly known as **Breachacha Castle**, and both built by the MacLeans. The older, at the head of Loch Breachacha, is a fifteenth-century tower house with an additional curtain wall, now used by Project Trust overseas aid volunteers as a training centre (Ⓦwww.projecttrust.org.uk). The less attractive "new castle", to the northwest, is made up of a central block built around 1750 and two side pavilions added a century later, now converted into holiday cottages. It was here that Dr Johnson and Boswell stayed in 1773 after a storm forced them to take refuge en route to Mull. Much of the surrounding area is now owned by the RSPB, in the hope of protecting the island's corncrakes. To the west are some **giant sand dunes**, with two glorious golden sandy bays stretching for over a mile on either side. At the far western end is *Caolas*, where you can get a cup of tea and home-baked goodies.

Practicalities

Aside from self-catering cottages, **accommodation** options are very limited. In Arinagour, the small, family-run *Coll Hotel* (Ⓣ01879/230334, Ⓦwww.collhotel.com; ❺) provides decent **accommodation**, or else there's *Tigh-na-Mara* (Ⓣ01879/230354, Ⓦwww.sturgeon.dircon.co.uk; ❷), a modern guesthouse near the pier. *Garden House* (Ⓣ01879/230374), down a track on the left before the turn-off for the castles, runs a **campsite** in the shelter of what was formerly a walled garden; wild camping is also possible behind the *Coll Hotel* – contact them for permission. The *Coll Hotel* doubles as the island's social centre, does excellent **meals** and has a dining-room overflow. Another good eating option is the *First Port of Coll* café (Ⓣ01879/230488, Ⓦwww.firstportofcoll.com), in the old harbour stores overlooking the bay, which offers hot meals all day. The three-bedroom flat above the shop is available to rent.

Isle of Tiree

Tiree, as its Gaelic name *tir-iodh* (land of corn) suggests, was once known as the breadbasket of the Inner Hebrides, thanks to its acres of rich machair. Nowadays crofting and tourism are the main sources of income for the resident population of around 750. One of the most distinctive features of Tiree is its architecture, in particular the large numbers of "pudding" or "spotty" houses, where only the mortar is painted white. In addition, there are numerous "white houses" (*tigh geal*) and traditional "blackhouses" (*tigh dubh*). With no shortage of wind, Tiree's sandy beaches attract large numbers of windsurfers for the Tiree Wave Classic (Ⓦwww.tireewaveclassic.com) every October.

The ferry calls at Gott Bay Pier, now best known for **An Turas** (The Journey), Tiree's award-winning "shelter", a structure that consists of two parallel white walls connected via a black felt section to a glass box which punctures a stone dyke and frames a seaview. Just up the road from the pier is the village of **SCARINISH**, home to a post office, some public toilets, a supermarket, the butcher's and the bank, with a petrol pump back at the pier. Also in Scarinish you'll find **An Iodhlann** (June–Sept Mon–Fri 9am–5pm; Oct–May Tues–Fri 11am–5pm; £3; Ⓦwww.aniodhlann.org.uk) – "haystack" in Gaelic – the island's two-roomed archive, which puts on exhibitions in the summer.

The island's most intriguing sights lie in the bulging western half of the island, where Tiree's two landmark hills rise up. Below the higher of the two is **HYNISH** whose **harbour** was designed by Alan Stevenson in the 1830s to transport building materials for the magnificent 140-foot-tall **Skerryvore Lighthouse**, which lies on a sea-swept reef some twelve miles southwest of Tiree. Up on the hill behind the harbour, beside the row of lighthouse keepers' houses, stands a stumpy granite signal tower, whose signals used to be the only contact the lighthouse keepers had with civilization. The tower now houses a **museum** telling the history of the herculean effort required to erect the lighthouse; weather permitting, you can see the lighthouse from the tower's viewing platform.

On the other side of Ben Hynish, a mile or so across the golden sands of Balephuil Bay, is the spectacular headland of **Ceann a'Mhara** (pronounced "kenavara"), home to thousands of seabirds, including fulmars, kittiwakes, guillemots, razorbills, shags and cormorants, with gannets and terns feeding offshore. In the scattered west coast settlement of **SANDAIG**, to the north of Ceann a'Mhara, three thatched white houses in a row have been turned into the **Taigh Iain Mhoir** (June–Sept Mon–Fri 2–4pm; free), which gives an insight into how the majority of islanders lived in the nineteenth century.

Practicalities

If you're arriving at the **airport**, about three miles west of Scarinish, you should arrange for your hosts to collect you (most will). Tiree has a Ring'n'Ride **minibus** service (Mon–Sat 7am–6pm, Tues until 10pm; Ⓣ01879/220419) which will take you anywhere on the island; **bike rental** (Ⓣ01879/220428) or MacLennans **car rental** (Ⓣ01879/220555) are the other options.

The island has two **hotels**, with the *Scarinish* (Ⓣ01879/220308, Ⓦwww.tireescarinishhotel.com; ❹), overlooking the old harbour, the better of the two. Other options include *Kirkapol House* (Ⓣ01879/220729, Ⓦwww.kirkapoltiree.co.uk; ❹), a friendly **B&B** in a tastefully converted kirk, a mile or so east of

Scarinish along Gott Bay; *Glebe House* (Ⓣ01879/220758, Ⓦwww.glebehousetiree.co.uk; ❸), the renovated former manse overlooking the pier in Scarinish; and the very welcoming *Cèabhar* (Ⓣ01879/220684, Ⓦwww.ceabhar.com; ❹), a guesthouse and **restaurant** in Sandaig. Great **hostel** accommodation is available at *Millhouse* (Ⓣ01879/220435, Ⓦwww.tireemillhouse.co.uk), a converted barn near Loch Bhasapol, in the northwest of the island. For **camping**, contact Wild Diamond Watersports (Ⓣ01879/220399, Ⓦwww.wilddiamond.co.uk) who operate a site in the southwest of the island; their watersports activities centre around Loch Bhasapol.

As for **eating**, the bar meals at both hotels are good, and local goodies such as crab, lobster and langoustine are served at the homely *Elephant's End* (Ⓣ01879/220694, Ⓦwww.elephantsend.com) in Kirkapol. For a **map** of the island and the daily papers, you need to go to the supermarket at Crossapol.

Isle of Colonsay

Isolated between Mull and Islay, **Colonsay** (Ⓦwww.colonsay.org.uk) – measuring just eight miles by three – is nothing like as bleak and windswept as Coll or Tiree. Its craggy, heather-backed hills even support the occasional patch of woodland, plus a bewildering array of plant and birdlife, wild goats and rabbits, and a very fine quasi-tropical garden. The population of around a hundred is down from a pre-Clearance peak of nearly a thousand. With only one hotel and infrequent ferry links with the mainland, there's no fear of mass tourism taking over.

The ferry terminal is at **SCALASAIG**, on the east coast, where there's a post office/shop, a petrol pump, a brewery, a café and the island's hotel. Two miles north is **Colonsay House**, built in 1722 by Malcolm MacNeil. In 1904, the island and house were bought by Lord Strathcona, who made his fortune building the Canadian Pacific Railway (and whose descendants still own the island). He was also responsible for the house's romantically dilapidated woodland **gardens** (April–Sept Wed & Fri noon–5pm; £2.50), which shelter the strange eighth-century **Riasg Buidhe Cross**, decorated with an unusually lifelike mug shot (possibly of a monk) – ask for directions from the tearoom.

To the north of Colonsay House is the island's finest sandy beach, the breathtaking **Kiloran Bay**, where the breakers roll in from the Atlantic. There's another unspoilt sandy beach backed by dunes at Balnahard, two miles northeast along a rough track; en route, you might spot wild goats, choughs and even a golden eagle.

Isle of Oronsay

Whilst on Colonsay, it's worth taking a day out to visit the **Isle of Oronsay**, half a mile to the south, with its ruined Augustinian priory. The two islands are separated by "The Strand", a stretch of tidal mud flats, which act as a causeway for two hours either side of low tide (check locally for timings); you can drive over to the island at low tide, though most people park their cars and walk across. Legends (and etymology) link saints Columba and Oran with Colonsay and Oronsay, although the ruins only date back to the fourteenth century. You can, nevertheless, still make out the original church and tiny cloisters, abandoned since the Reformation and now roofless. The highlight, though, is the **Oronsay Cross**, a superb example of late medieval artistry from Iona which, along with thirty or so beautifully carved grave slabs, can be found in the restored side chapel. It takes about an hour to walk from the tip of Colonsay across The Strand to the priory (Wellington boots are a good idea).

Practicalities

CalMac **ferries** run from Oban (daily except Tues & Sat; 2hr 20min) and once a week from Kennacraig via Islay (Wed; 3hr 35min), when a day-trip is possible, giving you around six hours on the island. There are also scheduled **flights** from Oban (Tues & Thurs, plus Fri & Sun during school terms) run by Hebridean Air (Ⓣ01631/524568). There's no public transport, but a **minibus** meets the Wednesday ferry and takes folk on a tour of the island, and Archie McConnel (Ⓣ01951/200355) will rent out **bikes**.

A cosy eighteenth-century inn at heart, and a short stroll from the pier in Scalasaig, the island's only **hotel** is *The Colonsay* (Ⓣ01951/200316, Ⓦwww.thecolonsay.com; ❺) which has transformed itself into a really stylish, comfortable place to stay; it has a good restaurant, serves very decent bar snacks and acts as the island's social centre. There are also a couple of modern **B&Bs** to choose from, though most visitors rent **self-catering** accommodation, the majority of which is run by the estate. Note that self-catering cottages tend to be booked from Friday to Friday, because of the ferries. Wild **camping** is, of course, an option, or you can sleep at the Colonsay Estate's *Backpackers' Lodge* (Ⓣ01951/200312, Ⓦwww.colonsayestate.co.uk), a very comfortable **hostel** with a real fire, overlooking Loch Fada. An alternative to **eating out** at the hotel bar is *The Pantry*, above the pier in Scalasaig, which offers simple home-cooking as well as tea and cakes (phone ahead for evening meals; Ⓣ01951/200325).

Mid-Argyll

Mid-Argyll loosely describes the central wedge of land south of Oban and north of Kintyre. **Lochgilphead**, on Loch Fyne is the chief town in the area, though it has little to offer beyond its practical uses. The highlights of this gently undulating scenery lie along the sharply indented and remote western coastline. Closest to Oban are the melancholy former slate mining settlements of Seil, Easdale and Luing, known collectively as the **Slate Islands**. Further south, the rich Bronze Age and Neolithic remains in the **Kilmartin** valley comprise one of the most important prehistoric sites in Scotland. Separating Kilmartin Glen from the **Knapdale** peninsula is the **Crinan Canal**, a short cut for boats disinclined to round the Mull of Kintyre, which ends in the pint-sized, picturesque port of **Crinan**.

The Slate Islands

Eight miles south of Oban, a road heads off the A816 west to the miniscule **Slate Islands**, which at their peak in the mid-nineteenth century quarried over nine million slates annually. Today the old slate villages are sparsely populated, and an inevitable air of melancholy hangs over them, but their dramatic setting amid crashing waves makes for a rewarding day-trip.

Isle of Seil

The most northerly of the Slate Islands is **Seil**, a lush island, now something of an exclusive enclave. It's separated from the mainland only by the thinnest of sea channels that is spanned by an elegant humpback **Clachan Bridge**, built in 1793 and popularly known as the "Bridge over the Atlantic".

The main village on Seil is **ELLENABEICH**, its neat white terraces of workers' cottages crouching below black cliffs on the westernmost tip of the island. This was once the tiny island of Eilean a'Beithich (hence Ellenabeich) separated from the mainland by a slim sea channel until the intensive slate quarrying succeeded in silting it up. Confusingly, the village is often referred to by the same name as the nearby island of Easdale, since they formed an interdependent community based exclusively around the slate industry. The **Slate Islands Heritage Centre** (April–Oct daily 10.30am–1pm & 2–5pm; free; Ⓦwww.slateislands.org.uk), in one of the little white cottages, has a model of the slate quarry as it would have been in its heyday.

For home-made pasties, seafood and real ale, pop inside the snug wood-panelled bar of the *Oyster Brewery* (Ⓣ01852/300121, Ⓦwww.seilislandpub.co.uk), on the way to the ferry. High-adrenaline **boat trips** are offered by Sea.fari (Ⓣ01852/300003, Ⓦwww.seafari.co.uk), who are based at the Ellenabeich jetty; the boats are rigid inflatables (RIBs) and travel at some speed round the offshore islands and through the Corryvrechan Whirlpool (see box below).

Isle of Easdale

Easdale (Ⓦwww.easdale.org) remains an island, though the few hundred yards that separate it from Ellenabeich have to be dredged to keep the channel open. Up to the eve of a great storm in 1881, Easdale supported an incredible 452 inhabitants, despite being less than a mile across at any one point. That night, waves engulfed the island and flooded the quarries and the island never really recovered. Many of the old workers' cottages now serve as holiday homes, and one is home to the interesting **Easdale Folk Museum** (daily: April–June, Sept & Oct 11am–4.30pm; July & Aug 11am–5pm; £2.50; Ⓦwww.easdalemuseum.org), near the main square, which sells a useful historical map of the island.

The **ferry** from Ellenabeich runs more or less on demand (press the buttons in the ferry shed or phone Ⓣ01852/300559), and you have recourse to *The Puffer* **bar/tearoom** (Ⓣ01852/300022, Ⓦwww.pufferbar.com) if you've failed to put together a picnic. With lots of wonderfully flat stones freely available, Easdale makes the perfect venue for the annual **World Stone Skimming Championships** (Ⓦwww.stoneskimming.com), held on the last Sunday of September.

Arduaine Garden

A great spot at which to stop and have a picnic on the A816 from Oban to Lochgilphead is **Arduaine Garden** (daily 9.30am–dusk; NTS; £5.50; Ⓦwww.arduaine-garden.org.uk), overlooking Asknish Bay and the islands of Shuna, Luing, Scarba and Jura. The gardens are stupendous, particularly in May and

Whirlpools and witches

Between the islands of Scarba and Jura is the raging **Corryvreckan Whirlpool** (Ⓦwww.whirlpool-scotland.co.uk; see also box, p.300), one of the world's most spectacular whirlpools, thought to be caused by a rocky pinnacle some 100ft below the sea. Exactly how the whirlpool appears depends on the tide and wind, but there's a potential tidal flow of over eight knots, which, when accompanied by gale force winds, can create standing waves up to 15ft high. Inevitably there are numerous legends about the place – known as *coire bhreacain* (speckled cauldron) in Gaelic – concerning *Cailleach* (Hag), the Celtic storm goddess.

From the land, the best place from which to view it is the northern tip of Jura (see p.300). If you're interested in taking a **boat trip** to Scarba, Corryvreckan or the nearby Garvellach islands, contact Sea.fari (Ⓣ01852/300003, Ⓦwww.seafari.co.uk), based at Easdale, or Craignish Cruises (Ⓣ07747/023038, Ⓦwww.craignishcruises.co.uk), in Ardfern.

June, and have the feel of an intimate private garden, with immaculately mown lawns, lily-strewn ponds, mature woods and spectacular rhododendrons and azaleas. For good bar meals, a great view, or pristine **accommodation** for the night, look no further than the *Loch Melfort Hotel* (Ⓣ01852/200233, Ⓦwww.lochmelfort.co.uk; ❼), adjacent to the garden.

Kilmartin Glen

The chief sight on the road from Oban to Lochgilphead is **Kilmartin Glen**, the most important prehistoric site on the Scottish mainland. The most remarkable relic is the **linear cemetery**, where several cairns are aligned for more than two miles, to the south of the village of Kilmartin. These are thought to represent the successive burials of a ruling family or chieftains, but nobody can be sure. The best view of the cemetery's configuration is from the Bronze Age **Mid-Cairn**, but the Neolithic **South Cairn**, dating from around 3000 BC, is by far the oldest and the most impressive, with its large chambered tomb roofed by giant slabs.

Close to the Mid-Cairn, the two **Temple Wood stone circles** appear to have been the architectural focus of burials in the area from Neolithic times to the Bronze Age. Visible to the south are the impressively cup-marked **Nether Largie standing stones** (no public access), the largest of which looms over 10ft high. **Cup- and ring-marked rocks** are a recurrent feature of prehistoric sites in Kilmartin Glen and elsewhere in Argyll. There are many theories as to their origin: some see them as Pictish symbols, others as primitive solar calendars. The

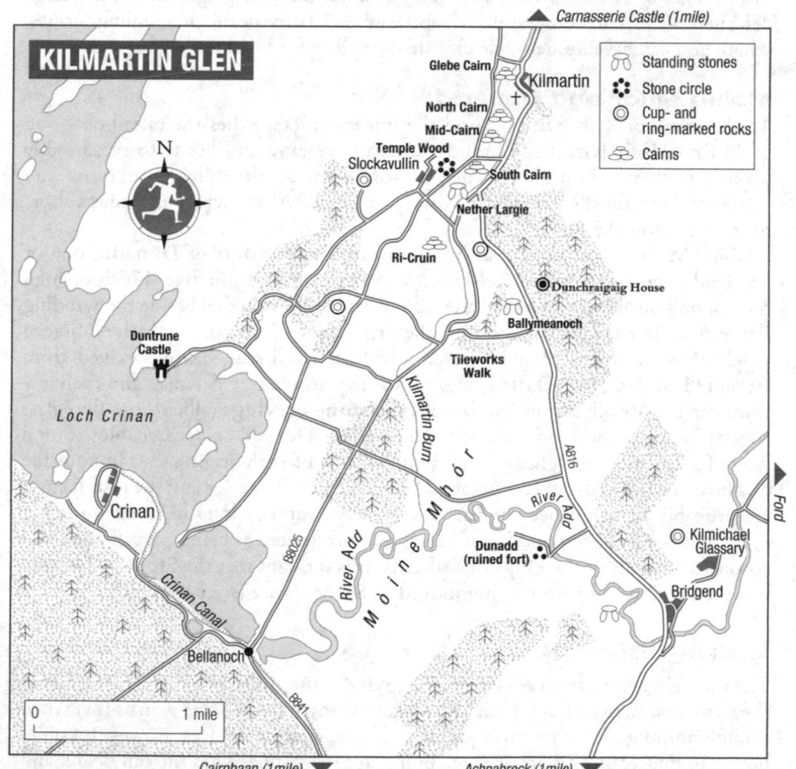

most extensive markings in the entire country are at **Achnabreck**, off the A816 towards Lochgilphead.

Kilmartin

Situated on high ground to the north of the cairns is the tiny village of **KILMARTIN**, where the old manse adjacent to the village church now houses a **Museum of Ancient Culture** (March–Oct daily 10am–5.30pm; £4.60; Ⓦwww.kilmartin.org), which is both enlightening and entertaining. Not only can you learn about the various theories concerning prehistoric crannogs, henges and cairns, but you can practise polishing an axe, examine different types of wood, and listen to a variety of weird and wonderful sounds (check out the Gaelic bird imitations).

Nearby **Kilmartin church** shelters several richly sculptured graves and crosses, while a separate enclosure in the graveyard houses a large collection of medieval grave slabs of the Malcolms of Poltalloch. Kilmartin's own castle is ruined beyond recognition; head instead for the much less ruined **Carnasserie Castle**, on a high ridge a mile up the road towards Oban. Built in the 1560s, the castle is a good example of the transition between fully fortified castles and later mansion houses, and has several original finely carved stone fireplaces and doorways, as well as numerous gun-loops and shot holes.

For something to eat, try the museum's *Glebe Cairn* **café**, with home-baked produce on offer – it's open in the evening too (Thurs–Sat). The nearest **B&B** is at *Dunchraigaig House* (Ⓣ01546/605209, Ⓦwww.dunchraigaig.co.uk; ④), a large detached Victorian house situated opposite the Ballymeanoch standing stones, where you can have home-made clootie dumpling for breakfast.

Mòine Mhór and Dunadd

To the south of Kilmartin, beyond the linear cemetery, lies the raised peat bog of **Mòine Mhór** (Great Moss), now a nature reserve and home to remarkable plant, insect and birdlife. To get a close look at the sphagnum moss and wetlands, head for the Tileworks Walk, just off the A816, which includes a short boardwalk over the bog.

Mòine Mhór is best known as home to the Iron Age fort of **Dunadd**, one of Scotland's most important Celtic sites, occupying a distinctive 176-foot-high rocky knoll once surrounded by the sea but currently stranded beside the winding River Add. It was here that Fergus, the first king of Dalriada – which embraced much of what is now Argyll – established his royal seat, having arrived from Ireland in around 500 AD. Its strategic position, the craggy defences and the view from the top are all impressive, but it's the **stone carvings** (albeit now fibreglass copies) between the twin summits which make Dunadd so remarkable: several lines of inscription in Ogham (an ancient alphabet of Irish origin), the faint outline of a boar, a hollowed-out footprint and a small basin. The boar and the inscriptions are probably Pictish, since the fort was clearly occupied long before Fergus got there, but the footprint and basin have been interpreted as being part of the royal coronation rituals of the kings of Dalriada. It is thought that the Stone of Destiny was used at Dunadd before being moved to Scone Palace (see box, p.80).

Lochgilphead

The unlikely administrative centre of Argyll & Bute, **LOCHGILPHEAD**, lies at the head of an arm of Loch Fyne. It's a planned town in the same vein as Inveraray, though nothing like as picturesque. If you're staying in the area, however, you're bound to find yourself here at some point, as Lochgilphead has the only bank and supermarket for miles. The **tourist office**, 27 Lochnell St (April–Oct daily), can help find you **accommodation** in the area. If you need a place in Lochgilphead itself, try *The Corran* (ⓣ01546/603866, ⓦwww.lamonthoy.co.uk; ❸), an attractive Victorian villa with spacious rooms on Poltalloch Street by the lochside; otherwise, try *Allt-na-Craig* (ⓣ01546/603245, ⓦwww.allt-na-craig.co.uk; ❺), a very handsome, stylish, detached Victorian guesthouse set back from the road to Ardrishaig. Those on a tight budget should head for the attractive **bunkhouse** at Brenfield (ⓣ01546/603274, ⓦwww.brenfield.co.uk), a horse-loving farm three miles south. The nicest **café** in town is *The Smiddy*, on Smithy Lane (closed Sun), which does simple café food. For high-class picnic provisions, call in at *Cockles*, a smart deli on the main street that also sells fresh and smoked fish and delicious home-made bread. **Bike rental** is available from Crinan Cycles, 34 Argyll St (ⓣ01546/603511, ⓦwww.crinancycles.co.uk; closed Sun).

Knapdale

Forested **Knapdale** – from the Gaelic *cnap* (hill) and *dall* (field) – forms a buffer zone between the Kintyre peninsula and the rest of Argyll, bounded to the north by the Crinan Canal and to the south by West Loch Tarbert and consisting of three progressively fatter fingers of land, separated by Loch Sween and Loch Caolisport.

Crinan Canal

The nine-mile-long **Crinan Canal** opened in 1801, linking Loch Fyne, at Ardrishaig south of Lochgilphead, with the Sound of Jura, thus cutting out the long and treacherous journey around the Mull of Kintyre. John Rennie's original design, although an impressive engineering feat, had numerous faults, and by 1816 Thomas Telford was called in to take charge of the renovations. The canal runs parallel to the sea for quite some way before cutting across the bottom of Mòine Mhór and hitting a flight of locks either side of **CAIRNBAAN** (there are fifteen in total); a walk along the towpath is both picturesque and pleasantly unstrenuous. A useful pit stop is the *Cairnbaan Hotel* (ⓣ01546/603668), an eighteenth-century coaching inn overlooking the canal with a decent restaurant and bar meals featuring local seafood.

The most relaxing place from which to view the canal in action is **CRINAN**, the pretty little fishing port at the canal's western end. Crinan's tiny harbour is, for the moment at least, still home to a small fishing fleet; a quick burst up through Crinan Wood to the hill above the village will give you a bird's-eye view of the sea-lock and its setting. It's worth having a pint or one of the excellent **bar meals** at the *Crinan Hotel* as it enjoys one of the most beautiful views in Scotland, especially at sunset, when the myriad islets and the distinctive Paps of Jura are reflected in the waters of the loch. Down on the lockside there's a cheap and cheerful **café** called the *Coffee Shop* (Easter–Oct), serving mouth-watering cakes and wonderful clootie dumplings.

For **accommodation**, it's best to head out of Crinan: try *The Stables* (ⓣ01546/850276, ⓦwww.thestablesbandb.co.uk; ❸), part of an old hunting lodge in Achnamara, five miles south, or the superb *Bellanoch House* (ⓣ01546/830149, ⓦwww.bellanochhouse.co.uk; ❺), a grand old schoolhouse with stripped pine floors and lots of character, right on the canal, a mile or so before Crinan.

Tayvallich, Loch Sween and Kilberry

Continuing down the western finger of Knapdale you come to the village of **TAYVALLICH** (ⓦwww.tayvallich.com), with its attractive, sheltered horseshoe bay, after which the peninsula splits again. The western arm leads eventually to the medieval **Chapel of Keills**, housing a display of late medieval carved stones. If you want to eat or drink round here, then head for the *Tayvallich Inn* (Ⓣ01546/870282), in the eponymous village.

Six miles south of Achanamara, on the eastern shores of **Loch Sween**, is the eleventh-century **Castle Sween** or "Key of Knapdale", the earliest stone castle in Scotland, but in ruins since 1647. The tranquillity and beauty of the setting are spoilt by the nearby caravan park, an eyesore that makes a visit pretty depressing. You're better off continuing south to the thirteenth-century **Kilmory Chapel**, also in ruins but with a new roof protecting the medieval grave slabs and the well-preserved MacMillan's Cross, an eight-foot fifteenth-century Celtic cross showing the Crucifixion on one side and a hunting scene on the other.

The bulk of Knapdale is isolated and fairly impenetrable, but it's worth persevering the fourteen miles of single-track road in order to reach **KILBERRY**, where you can **camp** at *Port Bàn* (Ⓣ01880/770224, Ⓦwww .portban.com; April–Oct), and enjoy the fantastic sunsets and views over Jura, or **stay the night** in comfort and style at the *Kilberry Inn* (Ⓣ01880/770223, Ⓦwww.kilberryinn .com; April–Oct Tues–Sun; ❽); the inn's **food** is superb, from the home-smoked mackerel to the Loch Fyne queenies. There's also a church worth viewing in Kilberry and a small collection of carved medieval grave slabs. Look out, too, for the **concerts** put on at *Crear* (Ⓣ01880/770369, Ⓦwww.crear.co.uk), a barn a mile from the village, which attracts top classical musicians.

Kintyre

But for the mile-long isthmus between West Loch Tarbert and the much smaller East Loch Tarbert, the little-visited, sparsely populated peninsula of **KINTYRE** (Ⓦwww.kintyre.org) – from the Gaelic *ceann tire*, "land's end" – would be an island. Indeed, in the eleventh century, when the Scottish king, Malcolm Canmore, allowed Magnus Barefoot, King of Norway, to lay claim to any island he could circumnavigate by boat, Magnus dragged his boat across the Tarbert isthmus and added the peninsula to his Hebridean kingdom. Despite its relative proximity to Scotland's Central Belt, Kintyre remains quiet and unfashionable; its main towns of **Tarbert** and **Campbeltown** have few obvious attractions, but that's part of their appeal. In many ways, it's a peninsula in a kind of time warp, where you can hole up for a week in perfect solitude.

There are regular daily **buses** from Glasgow to Campbeltown, via Tarbert and the west coast, and even a skeleton service down the single-track east coast road. There's a **ferry** to Tarbert from Portavadie on the Cowal peninsula, and a summer-only one from Lochranza on Arran. Campbeltown has an airport, with daily flights from Glasgow, which is only 40 miles away by air, compared to over 120 miles by road.

Tarbert

A distinctive rocket-like church steeple heralds the fishing port of **TARBERT** (in Gaelic *An Tairbeart*, meaning "isthmus"), sheltering an attractive little bay backed by rugged hills. Tarbert's herring industry was mentioned in the Annals of Ulster as far back as 836 AD, though right now the local fishing industry is down to its lowest level ever. Ironically, it was local Tarbert fishermen, who, in the 1830s, pioneered the method of herring fishing known as trawling, seining or ring-netting, which eventually wiped out the Loch Fyne herring stocks. Tourism is now an increasingly important source of income, though there's nothing much to see in Tarbert itself. Most people simply pass through or visit in late May, when the Scottish Series yacht races take place, and in early July when traditional boats and a seafood festival hit town. Tarbert is also the starting point of the newly marked-out **Kintyre Way** (ⓦwww.kintyreway.com), an 89-mile walk that zigzags its way down the peninsula to Southend.

Tarbert's **tourist office** (April–Oct daily; ⓣ01880/820429) is on the harbour. There's no shortage of **accommodation**: try *The Knap* (ⓣ01880/820015, ⓦwww.knapguesthouse.co.uk; ❸), a pristinely refurbished Victorian townhouse right in the centre of Tarbert, or *Struan House* (ⓣ01880/820190, ⓦwww.struan-house-lochfyne.co.uk; ❸), built in 1846 as a small hotel, overlooking the harbour a short distance along Harbour Street. The *Ca'Dora* is the caff to head for on the seafront, while *The Anchor* pub, also overlooking the harbour, is a good option for a seafood lunch. The best **food** is to be had courtesy of the French chef at the *Corner House Bistro* (ⓣ01880/820263), just by the side of the *Corner House* pub.

Isle of Gigha

Gigha (ⓦwww.gigha.org.uk) – pronounced "Geeya", with a hard "g" – is a low-lying, fertile island, with a population of around 150, just three miles off the west coast of Kintyre. The island's Ayrshire cattle produce over a quarter of a million gallons of milk a year to produce the island's distinctive (occasionally fruit-shaped) cheese. Like many of the smaller Hebrides, Gigha was bought and sold numerous times after its original lairds, the MacNeils, sold up, and was finally bought by the islanders themselves in 2002.

The ferry from Tayinloan, 23 miles south of Tarbert, deposits you at the island's only village, **ARDMINISH**, where you'll find the post office and shop. The main attraction on the island is the **Achamore Gardens** (daily 9am–dusk; £4), a mile and a half south of Ardminish. Established by the first postwar owner, Sir James Horlick of hot-drink fame, their spectacularly colourful display of azaleas are best seen in early summer. To the southwest of the gardens, the ruins of the thirteenth-century **St Catan's Chapel** are floored with weathered medieval gravestones. The real draw of Gigha, however, apart from the peace and quiet, are the white sandy beaches – including one at Ardminish itself – that dot the coastline.

Gigha is small – six miles by one mile – and most visitors come here just for the day; CalMac **ferries** depart more or less hourly from Tayinloan for the twenty-minute crossing. However, it's a great place to **stay** too: contact *Tighnavinish* (ⓣ01583/505378, ⓦwww.gigha.net; ❷), a modern crofthouse B&B half a mile north of the post office, or the *Gigha Hotel* (ⓣ01583/505254, ⓦwww.gigha.org.uk; ❺), the social centre of the island and a very welcoming place to stay, just to the south of the post office. And if you want to stay in the style of a laird, book into one of the grand rooms at *Achamore House* (ⓣ01583/505400, ⓦwww.achamorehouse.com; ❺), the beautiful house in the midst of Achamore Gardens. For advice about **camping**, you should contact the *Gigha Hotel*. The licensed *Boathouse* (April–Oct; ⓦwww.boathouse-bar.com), by the pier, is the place to go for delicious **food** and, occasionally, live music and quiz nights. **Bike rental** is available from the post office.

The west coast

Kintyre's bleak **west coast** ranks among the most exposed stretches of coastline in Argyll. Atlantic breakers pound the rocky shoreline, while the persistent westerly wind forces the trees against the hillside. However, when the weather's fine and the wind not too fierce, there are numerous deserted sandy beaches to enjoy, with great views over to Gigha, Islay, Jura and even Ireland.

There are several **campsites** to choose from along the stretch of coast around **TAYINLOAN**, ranging from the big *Point Sands Caravan Park* (ⓣ01583/441263, ⓦwww.pointsands.co.uk; April–Oct), two miles north, set back a long way from the main road near a long stretch of sandy beach, to the smaller, more informal *Muasdale Holiday Park*, three miles south (Ⓣ01583/421207, Ⓦwww.muasdaleholidays.com; Easter–Oct), squeezed between the main road and beach.

The only major development along the entire west coast is **MACHRIHANISH**, at the southern end of Machrihanish Bay, the longest continuous stretch of sand in Argyll. There are two approaches to the **beach**: from Machrihanish itself, or from Westport, at the north end of the bay, where the A83 swings east towards Campbeltown; either way, the sea here is too dangerous for swimming. Machrihanish itself was once a thriving salt-producing and coal-mining centre – you can still see the miners' cottages at neighbouring Drumlemble – but now survives solely on tourism. The main draw, apart from the beach, is the exposed championship **golf links** between the beach and Campbeltown Airport on the nearby flat and fertile swath of land known as the Laggan.

Several of the imposing, detached Victorian townhouses overlooking the bay in Machrihanish, such as *Ardell House* (Ⓣ01586/810235; March–Oct; ❸), offer **accommodation**; there's also a large, fully equipped and very exposed family-run **campsite** (Ⓣ01586/810366, Ⓦwww.campkintyre.co.uk; Feb–Oct & Dec) overlooking the golf links, which even has an array of heated wooden "wigwams" (❶). In the evening, *The Beachcomber* bar is the liveliest place in Machrihanish.

Campbeltown

CAMPBELTOWN's best feature is its setting, in a deep bay sheltered by Davaar Island and the surrounding hills. With a population of around 5000, it's Kintyre's largest town, and its shops are by far the best place to stock up on supplies. Originally known as Kinlochkilkerran (*Ceann Loch Cill Chiaran*), the town was renamed in the seventeenth century by the Earl of Argyll – a Campbell – when it became one of the main points for immigration from the Lowlands. As is evident from the architecture, Campbeltown's heyday was the Victorian era, when shipbuilding was going strong, coal was shipped by canal from Drumlemble, the fishing fleet was vast and Campbeltown Loch was said to be made of whisky.

The Town

Nineteenth-century visitors to Campbeltown frequently found the place engulfed in a thick fog of pungent peat smoke from the town's 34 **whisky distilleries**. Today, only three distilleries are left to maintain this regional subgroup of single malt whiskies (see also *Scottish food and drink* colour section). If you're interested in whisky, pop into **Cadenhead's** whisky shop at 7 Bolgam St (Ⓣ01586/551710), which runs parallel with Longrow, where you can sign up for a guided tour of the nearby **Springbank** distillery, (Ⓦwww.springbankwhisky.com; Mon–Fri 10am & 2pm, Sat & Sun by appointment; £6–20 depending on the tour), a deeply traditional, family-owned business that does absolutely everything from malting to bottling, on its own premises, and produces three different single malts

The **Campbeltown Cross**, a fourteenth-century blue-green cross with figural scenes and spirals of Celtic knotting, presides over the main roundabout on the quayside. Further along the palm-tree-dotted waterfront is the **Wee Pictures**, a dinky Art Deco cinema on Hall Street, built in 1913, community-owned and run, and still going strong (daily except Fri; Ⓣ01586/553899, Ⓦwww.weepictures.co.uk). Next door is the **Burnett Building** (Mon–Fri 9am–5pm; free), built as the town library in 1897, crowned by a distinctive lantern and decorated with four relief panels depicting the town's main industries at the time. The building harbours a very old-fashioned one-room local museum, and also includes the **Linda McCartney Memorial Garden**, which you should approach from Shore Street. Here, you'll find a slightly ludicrous bronze statue of Linda holding a lamb, a piece commissioned by the ex-Beatle, who spent many happy times with Linda and the kids on the farm he owns near Campbeltown.

The former Lorne Street Church, with its stripy bell-cote and pinnacles, is now the **Campbeltown Heritage Centre** (April–Sept Mon–Sat 11.30am–4.30pm, Sun 2–4.30pm; £2). A beautiful wooden skiff from 1906 stands where the main altar once was, and there's plenty on the local whisky and fishing industries, plus a model of the Victorian harbour front with the light railway running along Hall Street.

Campbeltown's most popular attraction is the **Scottish Owl Centre** (April–June & Sept Wed–Sat 1.30–4.30pm; July & Aug Mon–Sat 1.30–4.30pm; £6; Ⓦwww.scottishowlcentre.tk), signposted off the B842 to Machrihanish, five minutes' walk out of town. As well as being actively involved in conservation work, the centre has a huge collection of owls spread out in terraced aviaries, ranging from the tiny Scops Owl to the world's largest, the Eurasian Eagle Owl. Try to time your visit with the daily flight display at 2.30pm.

Practicalities

Campbeltown's **tourist office** is on the Old Quay (April Mon–Sat; May–Oct daily; Nov–March Mon–Fri; Ⓣ01586/552056), and will happily hand out a free map of the town. The **airport** (Ⓣ01586/553797) lies three miles west, towards Machrihanish; there's a bus connection, but you need to phone ahead to book it (Ⓣ01586/552319) – it's part of Campbeltown's **Ring'n'Ride** service, which also operates around the town and to Southend.

There's a good choice of **accommodation** in Campbeltown, from *Redknowe* (Ⓣ01586/550374, Ⓦwww.redknowe.co.uk; ❶), a very welcoming sandstone B&B on the edge of town up the B842, to the very well-run *Ardshiel Hotel* (Ⓣ01586/552133, Ⓦwww.ardshiel.co.uk; ❼), a former whisky distiller's Victorian mansion situated on a lovely leafy square, just a block or so back from the harbour front. Another place worth considering is *Oatfield House* (Ⓣ01586/551551, Ⓦwww.oatfield.org; ❺), a beautifully renovated whitewashed laird's house set in its own grounds, three miles down the B842 to Southend.

As for **places to eat**, the *Gallery 10*, on Longrow South (closed Mon & Sun), serves up the best coffee and tea in town, plus an excellent "smoked platter". The best bar meals are to be found at the *Ardshiel Hotel*, while the *Commercial Inn* on Cross Street is a good drinking hole. There are a couple of good **mountain-bike trails** in Beinn Ghuilean Forest, to the south of town; **bike rental** is available from the Cycle Shop, Longrow (Ⓣ01586/554443). If you're here in the middle of August, be prepared for the **Mull of Kintyre Music & Arts Festival** (Ⓦwww.mokfest.com), which pulls in a few old rock bands, plus some good traditional Irish and Scottish bands.

Southend and the Mull of Kintyre

The bulbous, hilly end of Kintyre, south of Campbeltown, features some of the peninsula's most spectacular scenery, interspersed with large swathes of Lowland-style farmland. **SOUTHEND** itself, a bleak, blustery spot, comes as something of a disappointment, though it does have a golden sandy beach. Below the cliffs to the west of the beach, a ruined thirteenth-century chapel marks the alleged arrival point of St Columba prior to his trip to Iona, and on a rocky knoll nearby a pair of footprints carved into the rock are known as **Columba's footprints**, though only one is actually of ancient origin. A couple of miles out to sea from Southend lies **Sanda Island**, which contains the remains of an ancient Celtic chapel, two crosses, a holy well, an unusual lighthouse comprised of three sandstone towers and lots of seabirds, including Manx shearwaters, storm petrels and puffins.

Most people venture south of Campbeltown to make a pilgrimage to the **Mull of Kintyre**, made famous by the mawkish number-one hit by sometime local resident Paul McCartney, with the help of the Campbeltown Pipe Band. It's also infamous as the site of the RAF's worst peacetime accident when, on June 2, 1994, a Chinook helicopter on its way from Belfast to Inverness crashed, killing all 29 on board. A small memorial can be found on the hillside, not far from the **Gap** (1150ft) – after which no vehicles are allowed. The Mull is the nearest Britain gets to Ireland, just twelve miles away, and the Irish coastline appears remarkably close on fine days. There's nothing specifically to see, but the trek down to the lighthouse, itself 300ft above the ocean waves, is challengingly tortuous.

Southend's derelict Art Deco *Keil Hotel* cuts a forlorn figure, set back from the bay, but you can stay in the simple, but clean rooms above the *Argyll Arms* (Ⓣ01586/830622, Ⓦwww.argyllarmshotel; ❷), the local **pub**, unremarkable except for the fact that it has a post office inside it. Alternatively, you can stay at *Ormsary Farm* (Ⓣ01586/830665, Ⓦwww.holidaymullofkintyre.co.uk; April–Sept; ❷), a small working dairy farm up Glen Breakerie, northwest of Southend. **Camping** is possible in the field right by Southend beach, run by *Machribeg Farm* (Ⓣ01586/830249; Easter–Sept).

The east coast

The **east coast** of Kintyre is gentler than the west, sheltered from the Atlantic winds and in parts strikingly beautiful, with stunning views across to Arran. However, be warned that the bus service only reaches as far as the fishing village of **CARRADALE**, some thirteen miles up the coast. The village itself is rather drab, but the tiny, very pretty harbour with its small fishing fleet, and the wide, sandy beach to the south, make up for it. On the road into town, there's the small, but informative **Network Carradale Heritage Centre** (April–Sept daily except Thurs 10am–5.30pm; Oct–March daily except Wed & Thurs 11am–4pm; free), with good home baking to be had in the tearoom.

The bar of the *Carradale Hotel* is the hub of village social life, but if you want **accommodation**, head for *Ashbank Hotel* (Ⓣ01583/431650, Ⓦwww.ashbankhotel.com; ❹), a dinky little place in the heart of the village run by two very welcoming sisters. Another option is to head out to *Dunvalanree* (Ⓣ01583/431226, Ⓦwww.dunvalanree.com; ❻), the big Victorian house overlooking the sheltered little bay of Port Righ, towards Carradale Point, which also serves up great food. The nearest **campsite** is the superbly equipped *Carradale Bay Caravan Park* (Ⓣ01583/431665, Ⓦwww.carradalebay.com; March–Oct), right by the sandy beach.

The B842 ends twelve miles north of Carradale at **CLAONAIG**, little more than a slipway for the small summer car ferry to Arran. Beyond here, a dead-end road winds its way along the shore a few miles further north to the tiny village of **SKIPNESS**, where the considerable ruins of the enormous thirteenth-century **Skipness Castle** and a chapel look out across the Kilbrannan Sound to Arran. You can sit outside and admire both, whilst enjoying fresh oysters, delicious queenies (queen scallops), mussels and home-baked cakes from the excellent **seafood cabin** (late May to Sept daily except Sat). There are also several gentle **walks** laid out in the nearby mixed woodland, up the glen.

Isle of Islay

The fertile, largely treeless island of **ISLAY** (pronounced "eye-la") is famous for one thing – single malt **whisky**. The smoky, peaty, pungent quality of Islay whisky is unique, recognizable even to the untutored palate, and all eight of the island's distilleries will happily take visitors on a guided tour, ending with the customary complimentary tipple. Yet, despite the fame of its whiskies, Islay still remains relatively undiscovered, especially when compared with Arran, Mull or Skye. Part of the reason may be the expense of the two-hour ferry journey from Kennacraig on Kintyre. If you do make the effort, however, you'll be rewarded with a genuinely friendly welcome from islanders proud of their history, landscape and Gaelic culture.

In medieval times, Islay (Ⓦwww.isle-of-islay.com) was the political centre of the Hebrides, with **Finlaggan**, near Port Askaig, the seat of the MacDonalds, Lords of the Isles. The picturesque, whitewashed villages you see on Islay today, however, date from the planned settlements founded by the Campbells in the late eighteenth and early nineteenth centuries. Apart from whisky and solitude, the other great draw is the **birdlife** – there's a real possibility of spotting a golden eagle, or the rare crow-like chough, and no chance of missing the white-fronted and barnacle geese that winter here in their thousands. In late May, the **Feis Ile**, or Islay Festival of Malt and Music (Ⓦwww .feisile.org), takes place, with whisky tasting, piping recitals, folk dancing and other events celebrating the island's Gaelic roots.

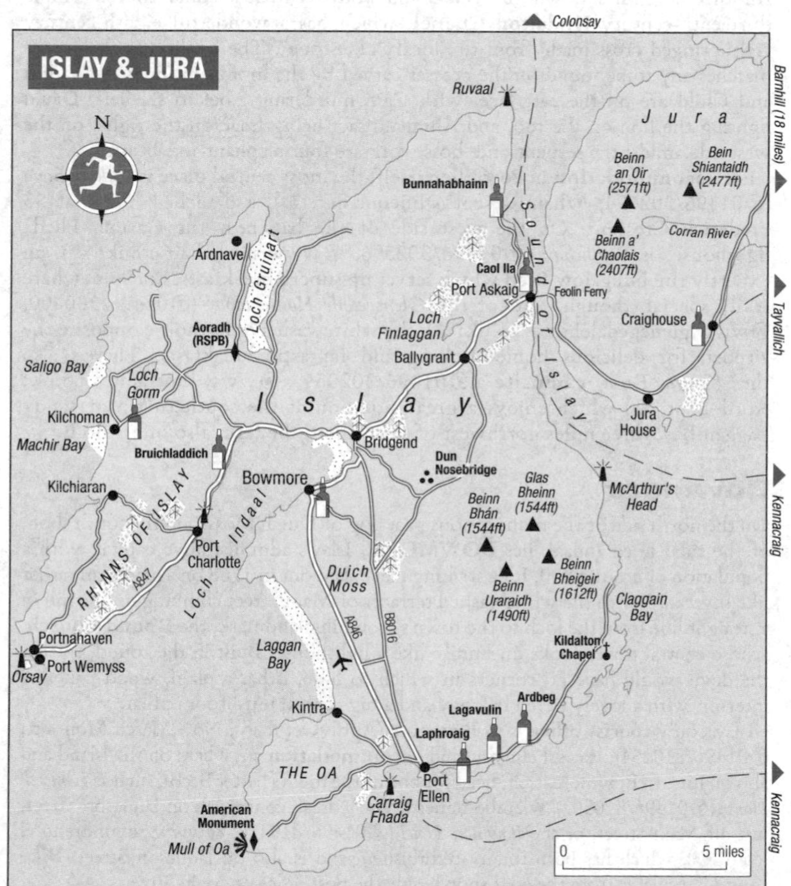

CalMac **ferries** from Kennacraig on Kintyre connect with both Port Ellen and Port Askaig and the island's airport has regular **flights** to and from Glasgow. Public transport will get you from one end of the island to the other, but if you're thinking of bringing your own vehicle, it's worth considering **car hire** on the island itself and saving on ferry fares – Islay Car Hire (Ⓣ01496/810544, Ⓦwww.islaycarhire.co.uk) will deliver to both ferry terminals. For a local point of view and news of upcoming events, pick up a copy of the fortnightly *Ileach* (Ⓦwww.ileach.co.uk); the island also has its own website (Ⓦwww.islayinfo.com).

Port Ellen and around

Laid out as a planned village in 1821 by Walter Frederick Campbell, and named after his wife, **PORT ELLEN** is the chief port on Islay, with the island's largest fishing fleet, and main CalMac ferry terminal. The neat whitewashed terraces that overlook the town's bay of golden sand are pretty enough, but the view is dominated by the village's modern maltings, whose powerful odours waft across the town.

The only reason to pause in this part of the island is to head off east along a dead-end road that passes three **distilleries** in as many miles (see box, p.298). Another six miles down the track and you eventually come to the simple thirteenth-century **Kildalton Chapel**, which has a wonderful eighth-century Celtic ringed cross made from the local "bluestone". The quality of the scenes matches any to be found on the crosses carved by the monks in Iona: the Virgin and Child are on the east face, with Cain murdering Abel to the left, David fighting the lion on the top, and Abraham sacrificing Isaac on the right; on the west side amidst the serpent-and–boss work are four elephant-like beasts.

For **accommodation** in Port Ellen itself, the most central place is *Caladh Sona* (Ⓣ01496/302694, Ⓔhamish.scott@lineone.net; ❸), a detached house at 53 Frederick Crescent. On the west side of the bay near the Carraig Fhada lighthouse, is *Samhchair* (Ⓣ01496/302596, Ⓦwww.samhchair.co.uk; ❺), an expertly run bungalow B&B which serves up superb breakfasts. For somewhere really special, though, opt for the *Glenegedale House Hotel* (Ⓣ01496/300400, Ⓦwww.glenegedalehouse.co.uk; ❻), the whitewashed guesthouse opposite the airport, for delicious home-cooking and fantastic breakfasts. There's also the *Kintra Farm* **campsite** (Ⓣ01496/302051, Ⓦwww.kintrafarm.co.uk; April–Sept; ❸) which enjoys a great situation at the southern tip of sandy Laggan Bay, three miles northwest of Port Ellen; the farm also offers B&B.

Bowmore

On the north side of the monotonous peat bog of Duich Moss, and the south shore of the tidal Loch Indaal, lies **BOWMORE**, Islay's administrative capital, with a population of around 800. It's a striking place, laid out in 1768 on a grid plan rather like Inveraray, with the whitewashed terraces of Main Street climbing up the hill in a straight line from the loch to the town's crowning landmark, the **Round Church**, whose central tower looks uncannily like a lighthouse. Built in the round, so that the devil would have no corners in which to hide, it has a plain, wood-panelled interior, with a lovely tiered balcony and a big central mushroom pillar.

Islay's only **tourist office** is in Bowmore (April–Oct daily; Nov–March Mon–Fri; Ⓣ01496/810254); it can help you find **accommodation** anywhere on the island and also on Jura. In Bowmore itself, head for one of the town's better B&Bs, such as *Lambeth House* (Ⓣ01496/810597, Ⓔlambethguesthouse@tiscali.co.uk; ❸), on Jamieson Street, just off Main Street, or the *Bowmore Hotel* (Ⓣ01496/810416, Ⓦwww.bowmorehotel.com; ❺), which has been totally refurbished, and is also on Jamieson Street. **Bike rental** is available from the craft shop beside the post office on Main Street.

At the *Harbour Inn* on Main Street, you can warm yourself by a peat fire in the **pub**, where they also do lunchtime bar snacks. At the other end of the scale, there's a decent **bakery** on Main Street, and, further up on the same side of the street, *The Cottage* (closed Sun), a cheap and friendly greasy spoon.

Loch Gruinart to Kilchoman

Between mid-September and the third week of April, it's impossible to miss the island's staggeringly large wintering population of **Greenland barnacle** and **Greater White-fronted geese**. You can see the geese just about anywhere on the island – there are an estimated 15,000 white-fronted and 40,000 barnacles here (and rising) – though they are usually at their most concentrated in the fields between Bridgend and Ballygrant. In the evening, they tend to congregate in the tidal mud flats and fields around **Loch Gruinart**. The nearby farm of Aoradh (pronounced "oorig") is run by the RSPB, and contains a **visitor centre** (daily 10am–5pm; free), with an observation point with telescopes and a CCTV link with the mud flats; there's also a hide across the road looking north over the salt flats at the head of the loch, though you're more likely to see ducks than geese.

Without doubt the best sandy beaches on Islay are to be found on the isolated northwest coast near the village of **KILCHOMAN**, in particular, the lovely golden beach of **Machir Bay**, which is backed by great white-sand dunes. The sea here has dangerous undercurrents, however, and is not safe to swim in (the same goes for the much smaller Saligo Bay, to the north), but the beaches are still lovely to walk across.

Port Charlotte and around

PORT CHARLOTTE, founded in 1828 by Walter Frederick Campbell and named after his mother, is generally agreed to be Islay's prettiest village, its immaculate whitewashed cottages clustered round a sandy cove overlooking Loch Indaal. On the northern fringe of the village, in a whitewashed former chapel, the imaginative **Museum of Islay Life** (April–Oct Mon–Sat 10.30am–4.30pm; Nov–March Mon–Sat 10am–4pm; £3; Ⓦwww.islaymuseum.org) has a children's corner, quizzes, a good library of books about the island, and tantalizing snippets about eighteenth-century illegal whisky distillers. The **Wildlife Information Centre** (Easter–Oct daily except Sat 10am–4pm; June–Aug daily 10am–4pm; £2.50), housed in the former distillery warehouse, is also worth a visit for anyone interested in the island's fauna and flora. As well as an extensive library to browse, there's lots of hands-on stuff for kids: microscopes, a touch table full of natural goodies, a sea-water aquarium, a bug world, and owl pellets to examine. Tickets are valid for a week, allowing you to go back and identify things you've seen on your travels.

Port Charlotte is the perfect place to base yourself. The welcoming *Port Charlotte Hotel* (Ⓣ01496/850360, Ⓦwww.portcharlottehotel.co.uk; ❽) has the finest **accommodation** – the seafood lunches served in the bar are very popular, and there's a good, more expensive restaurant. For B&B, you're actually better off heading out along the road to Portnahaven as far as Nerabus. There, you'll find *The Monachs* (Ⓣ01496/850049, Ⓦwww.islayguesthouse.co.uk; ❻), a spacious new luxury villa B&B with stupendous sea views, and the excellent *Octofad Farm* (Ⓣ01496/850594, Ⓦwww.octofadfarm.com; April–Oct; ❸). Port Charlotte itself is also home to Islay's SYHA **hostel** (Ⓣ0870/004 1128, Ⓦwww.syha.org.uk; April–Sept), housed in an old bonded warehouse, by the sea, next door to the Wildlife Information Centre. In addition, there's now a community-run **campsite** at the Port Mòr Centre (Ⓣ01496/850441, Ⓦislandofislay.co.uk), with sea views and tip-top facilities, just outside the village on the road to Portnahaven. For inexpensive food, there's a choice between the *Croft Kitchen* (Ⓣ01496/850230; April–Oct), opposite the museum, and the café in the Port

Islay whisky

Islay has woken up to the fact that its **whisky distilleries** are a major tourist attraction. Nowadays, every distillery offers guided tours, traditionally ending with a generous dram, and a refund (or discount) for your entrance fee if you buy a bottle in the shop. Phone ahead to make sure there's a tour running, as times do change frequently.

Ardbeg Ⓣ01496/302244, Ⓦwww.ardbeg.com. Ardbeg is traditionally considered the saltiest, peatiest malt on Islay (and that's saying something). Bought by Glenmorangie in 1997, the distillery has been thoroughly overhauled and restored, yet it still has bags of character inside. The *Old Kiln Café* is excellent (June–Aug daily 10am–5pm; Sept–May Mon–Fri 10am–5pm). Guided tours regularly 10.30am, noon & 3pm; £4.

Bowmore Ⓣ01496/810671, Ⓦwww.bowmore.co.uk. Bowmore is the most touristy of the Islay distilleries, too much so for some. However, it is by far the most central (with unrivalled disabled access), and also one of the few still doing its own malting and kilning. Daily guided tours Easter–June Mon–Sat 9am–5pm; July to mid-Sept daily 9am–5pm, Sun noon–4pm; mid-Sept to Easter Mon–Fri 9am–5pm, Sat 9am–noon; £4.

Bruichladdich Ⓣ01496/850190, Ⓦwww.bruichladdich.com. Rescued in 2001 by a group of whisky fanatics, this independent distillery offers regular guided tours and is currently planning to build a new distillery in Port Charlotte. Guided tours: Easter–Oct Mon–Fri 10.30, 11.30am & 2.30pm, Sat 11.30am & 2.30pm; Nov–Easter Mon–Fri 11.30am & 2.30pm, Sat 11.30am; £4.

Bunnahabhainn Ⓣ01496/840646, Ⓦwww.bunnahabhain.com. A visit to Bunnahabhain (pronounced "Bunna-have-in") is really only for whisky obsessives. The road from Port Askaig is windy, the whisky the least characteristically Islay and the distillery itself only in production for a few months each year. Guided tours April–Oct Mon–Fri 10.30am, 2 & 3.15pm; Nov–March by appointment; £4.

Caol Ila Ⓣ01496/302760, Ⓦwww.discovering-distilleries.com. Caol Ila (pronounced "Cull-eela"), just north of Port Askaig, is a modern distillery, the majority of whose lightly peaty malt goes into blended whiskies. Guided tours April–Oct Mon–Fri 9.30 & 10.45am, 1.45 & 3.15pm, Sat 1.45 & 3.15pm; at other times by appointment; £6 (joint ticket with Lagavulin).

Kilchoman Ⓣ01496/850011, Ⓦwww.kilchomandistillery.com. Established in 2005 as the first new distillery on Islay for over a century, Kilchoman is a very welcoming, tiny, farm-based enterprise that grows its own barley, as well as distilling, maturing and bottling its whisky on site. The first single malt has appeared (and sold out) and it's peaty. The café serves good coffee, plus home-made soup and baked items (Mon–Sat 10am–5pm). Guided tours April–Oct Mon–Sat 11am & 3pm; Nov–March Mon–Fri 11am & 3pm; £4.50.

Lagavulin Ⓣ01496/302730, Ⓦwww.discovering-distilleries.com. Lagavulin probably is the classic, all-round Islay malt, with lots of smoke and peat. The distillery enjoys a fabulous setting and is extremely busy all year round. Guided tours April–Oct Mon–Fri 9.30 & 11.15am, 2.30 & 3.45pm, Sat 9.30 & 11.15am; Nov–March Mon–Fri 9.30am & 11.15am; £6 (joint ticket with Caol Ila).

Laphroaig Ⓣ01496/302418, Ⓦwww.laphroaig.com. Another classic smoky, peaty Islay malt, and another great setting. One bonus at Laphroaig is that you get to see the malting and see and smell the peat kilns. Guided tours March–Oct Mon–Fri 10 & 11.30am; 2 & 3.30pm; free.

Mòr Centre. The **bar** of the *Port Charlotte* is very-easygoing, while the crack (and occasional live music) goes on at the *Lochindaal Inn*, down the road, where you can also tuck into a very good local-bred steak. **Bike rental** is available from 33 Main Street (Ⓣ01496/850488), opposite the hotel.

The main coastal road culminates seven miles south of Port Charlotte at **PORTNAHAVEN**, a fishing and crofting community since the early nineteenth century. The familiar whitewashed cottages wrap themselves prettily around the steep banks of a deep bay, where seals bask on the rocks in considerable numbers; in the distance, you can see Portnahaven's twin settlement, **PORT WEMYSS**, a mile south. The communities share a little whitewashed church, located above the bay in Portnahaven, with separate doors for each village. For a drink, head for *an tígh seínnse* in Portnahaven, a tiny **pub** where you can sit outside and enjoy the view in fine weather.

Finlaggan and Port Askaig

Just beyond Ballygrant, on the road to Port Askaig, a narrow road leads off north to **Loch Finlaggan**, site of a number of **prehistoric crannogs** (artificial islands) and, for four hundred years from the twelfth century, headquarters of the Lords of the Isles, semi-autonomous rulers of the Hebrides and Kintyre. The site is evocative enough, but there are, in truth, very few remains beyond the foundations. Remarkably, the palace that stood here appears to have been unfortified, a testament perhaps to the prosperity and stability of the islands in those days. Unless you need shelter from the rain, or are desperate to see the head of the commemorative medieval cross found here, you can happily skip the **information centre** (Easter & Oct Tues, Thurs & Sun 2–4pm; May–Sept daily except Sat 2.30–5pm; £2), to the northeast of the loch, and simply head on down to the site itself (access at any time), which is dotted with interpretive panels. Duckboards allow you to walk out across the reed beds of the loch and explore the main crannog, **Eilean Mor**, where several carved gravestones are displayed under cover in the chapel, all of which seem to support the theory that the Lords of the Isles buried their wives and children there, while having themselves interred on Iona. Further out into the loch is another smaller crannog, **Eilean na Comhairle**, originally connected to Eilean Mor by a causeway, where the Lords of the Isles are thought to have held meetings of the Council of the Isles.

Islay's other ferry connection with the mainland, and its sole link with Colonsay and Jura, is from **PORT ASKAIG**, a scattering of buildings which tumbles down a little cove by the narrowest section of the Sound of Islay or Caol Ila. This part of Islay has several superb places to stay. First, there's *Skerrols House* (Ⓣ01496/810520, Ⓦwww.skerrolshouse.com; ❻), a lovely whitewashed house a mile or so out of Bridgend off the A846 to Port Askaig. Further along the road, just southwest of Ballygrant is another fine whitewashed farmhouse *Kilmeny Farmhouse* (Ⓣ01496/840668, Ⓦkilmeny.co.uk; ❻), a place which richly deserves all the superlatives it regularly receives, its rooms furnished with antiques and its dinners (Tues & Thurs only) worth the extra £35 a head. The *Ballygrant Inn* is a good pub in which to grab a pint (and a bar meal), while the *Port Askaig Hotel* enjoys a wonderful position by Port Askaig pier, with views over to the Paps of Jura. For high-adrenalin **boat trips**, contact Islay Sea Safari (Ⓣ01496/840510, Ⓦwww.islayseasafari.co.uk), which is based in Port Askaig and best known for whizzing round the distilleries in a rigid inflatable. It's also possible to take a day-trip to Colonsay (see p.284) on a CalMac ferry on Wednesday.

Isle of Jura

Twenty-eight miles long and eight miles wide, the long whale-shaped island of **Jura** is one of the wildest and most mountainous of the Inner Hebrides, its entire west coast uninhabited and inaccessible except to the dedicated walker. The distinctive **Paps of Jura**, so called because of their smooth breast-like shape, seem to dominate every view off the west coast of Argyll, their glacial rounded tops covered in a light dusting of quartzite scree. The island's name is commonly thought to derive from the Norse *dyr-oe* (deer island) and, appropriately enough, the current deer population of 6000 outnumbers the 180 humans 33 to 1; other wildlife to look out for include mountain hares and eagles. With just one road, which sticks to the more sheltered eastern coast of the island, and only one hotel, a couple of B&Bs and some self-catering cottages, Jura is an ideal place to go for peace and quiet and some great walking.

If you're just coming over for the day from Islay, pop into the **Feolin Research Centre** (daily; free), near the ferry slipway, which has information and displays on the island, and then head off, five miles up the road, to the lovely wooded grounds of **Jura House** (daily 9am–5pm; Ⓦwww .jurahouseandgardens.co.uk; £2.50), originally built by the Campbells in the early nineteenth century. Pick up a booklet about the house at the entrance to the grounds, and follow the path that takes you down to the sandy shore, a perfect picnic spot in fine weather. Closer to the house itself, there's an idyllic **walled garden**, divided in two by a natural rushing burn that tumbles down in steps. The garden specializes in antipodean plants, which flourish in the frost-free climate; in season, you can buy some of the garden's organic produce or take tea in the **tea tent** (June–Aug Mon–Fri).

Anything that happens on Jura happens in the island's only real village, **CRAIGHOUSE**, eight miles up the road from Feolin Ferry. The village enjoys a sheltered setting, overlooking Knapdale on the mainland – so sheltered, in fact, that there are even a few palm trees thriving on the seafront. There's a shop/post office, the island hotel and a tearoom, plus the tiny **Isle of Jura distillery** (Ⓣ01496/820240, Ⓦwww.isleofjura.com), which is very welcoming to visitors and offers free guided tours. It's also worth popping inside **The Antlers**, opposite the shop, which is a tiny ad hoc interpretive centre, with lots of old photos and a children's corner.

George Orwell on Jura

In April 1946, Eric Blair (better known by his pen name of **George Orwell**), intending to give himself "six months' quiet" in which to complete his latest novel, moved to a remote farmhouse called **Barnhill**, at the northern end of Jura, which he had visited for the first time the previous year. He appears to have relished the challenge of a spartan existence here with his adopted 3-year-old son Richard, and later his sister Avril; fishing almost every night, shooting rabbits, laying lobster pots and even attempting a little farming. The book Orwell was writing, under the working title *The Last Man in Europe*, was to become *1984* (the title was arrived at by simply reversing the last two digits of the year in which it was finished – 1948). During his time on Jura, however, Orwell was suffering badly from tuberculosis, and eventually he was forced to return to London, where he died in January 1950.

Barnhill, 23 miles north of Craighouse, is as remote today as it was in Orwell's day. The road deteriorates rapidly beyond Lealt, where vehicles must be left, leaving pilgrims a four-mile walk to the house itself. Alternatively, the Richardsons of Kinauachdrachd (Ⓣ07899/912116) can organize a taxi and guided walk, and also run a bunkhouse. Orwell wrote most of the book in the bedroom (top left window as you look at the house); the place is now a self-catering cottage (Ⓣ01786/850274). If you're keen on making the journey out to Barnhill, you might as well combine it with a trip to the nearby **Corryvreckan Whirlpool** (see box, p.286), which lies between Jura and Scarba, to the north. Orwell nearly drowned in the whirlpool during a fishing trip in August 1947, along with his three companions (including Richard): the outboard motor was washed away, and they had to row to a nearby island and wait for several hours before being rescued by a passing fisherman. The best place to view the whirlpool from Jura is Carraig Mhor, seven miles from Lealt.

The family-run *Jura Hotel* in Craighouse is the island's one and only **hotel** (ⓣ01496/820243, ⓦwww.jurahotel.co.uk; ❹), not much to look at from the outside, but warm and friendly within, and centre of the island's social scene. The hotel does the usual bar meals, and has a shower block and laundry facilities round the back for those who wish to **camp** in the hotel gardens. For **B&B**, try *Sealladh na Mara* (ⓣ01496/820349, ⓦwww.isleofjura.net; ❷), a modern croft house four miles north of Craighouse. If you're planning to explore the north end of the island, it's worth knowing about the **bunkhouse** at Kinauachdrachd (ⓣ07899/912116). Jura has its own (unlicensed) bistro **restaurant**, *The Antlers* (ⓣ01496/820123; closed Mon eve), which serves up burgers, sandwiches and salads for lunch, and beautifully presented Jura lamb, pork and salmon in the evening.

Very occasionally a **minibus** (ⓣ01496/820314) meets the **car ferry** (ⓣ01496/840681) from Port Askaig – phone ahead to check times. The ferry itself will not run if there's a strong northerly or southerly wind, so bring your toothbrush if you're coming for a day-trip. There's also a **passenger ferry** service (ⓣ07768/450000, ⓦwww.jurapassengerferry.com) from Tayvallich, on the Argyll mainland, to Craighouse.

Travel details

Trains

Glasgow (Queen St) to: Arrochar and Tarbert (Mon–Sat 3–4 daily, Sun 1–3 daily; 1hr 15min); Dalmally (Mon–Sat 3–4 daily, Sun 1–3 daily; 2hr 15min); Oban (Mon–Sat 3–4 daily, Sun 1–3 daily; 3hr).

Mainland buses (not postbuses)

Arrochar to: Carrick Castle (Mon–Sat 1–2 daily; 50min); Inveraray (3 daily, 2 on Sun; 35min); Lochgilphead (3 daily; 1hr 30min).
Campbeltown to: Carradale (Mon–Sat 4–5 daily, 2 on Sun; 45min); Machrihanish (Mon–Sat 9 daily, 3 on Sun; 20–30min); Saddell (Mon–Sat 4–5 daily, 2 on Sun; 25min); Southend (Mon–Sat 4–5 daily, 2 on Sun; 25min).
Colintraive to: Dunoon (2 daily; 1hr); Tighnabruaich (Mon–Thurs 1–2 daily; 35min).
Dunoon to: Colintraive (2 daily; 1hr); Inveraray (Mon–Sat 3 daily, Sun 0–3 daily; 1hr 10min).
Glasgow to: Arrochar (3–5 daily; 1hr 10min); Campbeltown (3 daily; 4hr 5min); Dalmally (Mon–Sat 4 daily, 2 on Sun; 2hr 20min); Inveraray (4–6 daily; 2hr); Kennacraig (Mon–Sat 2 daily, 1 on Sun; 3hr 30min); Lochgilphead (3 daily; 2hr 40min); Oban (Mon–Sat 4 daily, Sun 2 daily; 3hr); Tarbert (3 daily; 3hr 15min); Taynuilt (Mon–Sat 4 daily, 2 on Sun; 2hr 45min).
Inveraray to: Dalmally (Mon–Sat 3 daily, 2 on Sun; 25min); Dunoon (3 daily; 1hr 10min); Lochgilphead (2–3 daily; 40min); Oban (Mon–Sat 3 daily, Sun 2 daily; 1hr 5min); Tarbert (2–3 daily; 1hr 30min).
Kennacraig to: Claonaig (Mon–Sat 3 daily; 15min); Skipness (Mon–Sat 3 daily; 20min).
Lochgilphead to: Campbeltown (4–7 daily; 1hr 45min); Crinan (Mon–Sat 3–4 daily; 20min); Kilmartin (Mon–Sat 2–5 daily; 15min); Tarbert (Mon–Fri 7–10 daily, Sat & Sun 3 daily; 30min); Tayvallich (3–4 daily; 25min).
Oban to: Appin (Mon–Sat 2–3 daily; 30min); Benderloch (Mon–Sat hourly; 20min); Connel (Mon–Sat hourly; 10–15min); Ellenabeich (Mon–Sat 4–5 daily; 50min); Fort William (Mon–Sat 4 daily; 1hr 30min); Kilmartin (Mon–Sat 2–4 daily; 1hr 20min); Lochgilphead (Mon–Sat 2–4 daily; 1hr 20min); Mallaig (April–Oct daily; 2hr 30min).
Tarbert to: Campbeltown (Mon–Sat 4 daily, 2 on Sun; 1hr 15min); Claonaig (Mon–Sat 3 daily; 30min); Kennacraig (3–6 daily; 15min); Skipness (Mon–Sat 3 daily; 35min); Tayinloan (3–6 daily; 30min).
Tighnabruaich to: Portavadie (Mon–Sat 3–4 daily; 25min); Rothesay (Mon–Thurs 1–2 daily; 1hr).

Island buses

Bute

Rothesay to: Kilchattan Bay (Mon–Sat 4 daily, 3 on Sun; 30min); Mount Stuart (every 45min; 15min); Rhubodach (Mon–Fri 1–2 daily; 20min).

Colonsay

Scalasaig to: Kilchattan Bay (Mon–Sat 4 daily, 3 on Sun; 30min); Mount Stuart (every 45min; 15min); Rhubodach (Mon–Fri 1–2 daily; 20min).

Islay

Bowmore to: Port Askaig (Mon–Sat 6–8 daily, 4 on Sun; 25min); Port Charlotte (Mon–Sat 5–6 daily, 3 on Sun; 25min); Port Ellen (Mon–Sat 10 daily, 4 on Sun; 20–30min); Portnahaven (Mon–Sat 6 daily, 3 on Sun; 50min).

Mull

Craignure to: Fionnphort (Mon–Sat 3–4 daily, 1 on Sun; 1hr 10min); Fishnish (1–4 daily; 10min); Salen (3–6 daily; 20min); Tobermory (3–6 daily; 45min).
Tobermory to: Calgary (Mon–Sat 2–3 daily; 45min); Dervaig (Mon–Sat 2–4 daily; 25min); Fishnish (2–4 daily; 40min).

Ferries

Car ferries

Summer timetable indicated.
To Arran: Ardrossan–Brodick (5–6 daily; 55min); Claonaig–Lochranza (8–9 daily; 30min).
To Bute: Colintraive–Rhubodach (frequently; 5min); Wemyss Bay–Rothesay (every 45min; 30min).
To Coll: Barra–Coll (Thurs 1 daily; 4hr); Oban–Coll (daily except Wed & Fri; 2hr 40min).
To Colonsay: Kennacraig–Colonsay (Wed 1 daily; 3hr 40min); Oban–Colonsay (daily except Tues & Sat; 2hr 15min); Port Askaig–Colonsay (Wed 1 daily; 1hr 10min).
To Dunoon: Gourock–Dunoon (hourly; 20min); McInroy's Point–Hunter's Quay (every 30min; 20min).
To Gigha: Tayinloan–Gigha (hourly; 20min).
To Islay: Colonsay–Port Askaig (Wed 1 daily; 1hr 10min); Kennacraig–Port Askaig/Port Ellen (3–4 daily; 2hr 5min–2hr 20min).
To Jura: Port Askaig–Feolin Ferry (Mon–Sat hourly, Sun 7–8 daily; 10min).
To Kintyre: Portavadie–Tarbert (hourly; 25min).
To Lismore: Oban–Achnacroish (Mon–Sat 4–5 daily, 2 on Sun; 50min).
To Luing: Cuan Ferry (Seil)–Luing (every 30min; 5min).
To Mull: Kilchoan–Tobermory (Mon–Sat every 2hr; May–Aug daily; 35min); Lochaline–Fishnish (daily hourly; 15min); Oban–Craignure (daily every 2hr; 45min).
To Tiree: Barra–Tiree (Thurs 1 daily; 2hr 45min); Oban–Tiree (1 daily; 3hr 40min).

Passenger-only ferries

Summer timetable indicated
To Iona: Fionnphort–Iona (daily frequently; 5min).
To Kerrera: Gallanach–Kerrera (every 30min; 10min).
To Lismore: Port Appin–Lismore (hourly; 5min).

Flights

Glasgow to: Campbeltown (Mon–Fri 2 daily; 35min); Islay (Mon–Fri 2 daily, 1 on Sat; 40min); Tiree (Mon–Sat 1 daily; 45min).
Oban to: Coll (Mon & Wed 2–3 daily; 30min); Colonsay (Tues & Thurs 2 daily, Fri & Sun 1 daily; 30min); Islay (Tues & Thurs 2 daily; 40min); Tiree (Mon & Wed 2 daily; 1hr).

7

Stirling, Loch Lomond and the Trossachs

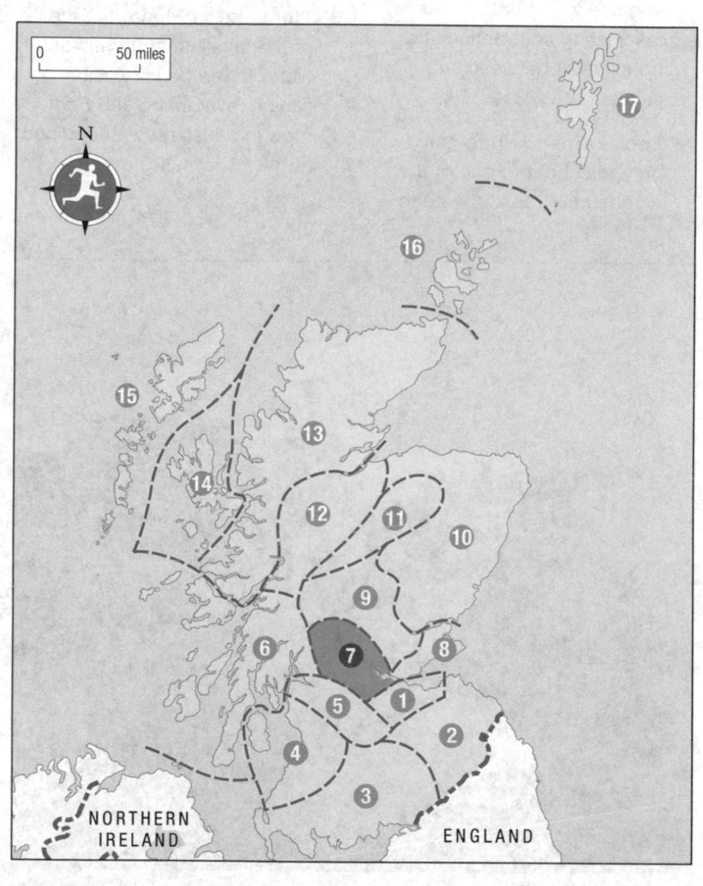

CHAPTER 7

Highlights

* **Stirling Castle** Impregnable, impressive and resonant with history. If you see only one castle in Scotland, make it this one. **See p.309**
* **Falkirk Wheel** The most remarkable piece of modern engineering in Britain, this fascinating contraption lifts boats 100ft between two canals. **See p.316**
* **Loch Lomond** Putter out on a mail boat to one of the wooded islands at the heart of Scotland's first national park. **See p.320**
* **The Trossachs** Pocket Highlands with shining lochs, wooded glens and noble peaks. Great for hiking and mountain biking. **See p.323**
* **The Lake of Menteith** One of the loveliest stretches of water in the country, with fishing, swimming and boat trips to an island with a ruined abbey. **See p.325**

▲ Stirling Castle

7

Stirling, Loch Lomond and the Trossachs

The central lowlands of Scotland were, for several centuries, the most strategically important area in the country. In 1250, a map of Britain was compiled by a monk of St Albans, which depicted Scotland as two separate land masses connected only by the thin band of Stirling Bridge; although this was obviously a figurative interpretation, Stirling was once the only **gateway** from the fertile central belt to the rugged, mountainous north. For long periods of Scotland's history kings, queens, nobles, clan chiefs and soldiers wrestled for control of the area, and it's no surprise that today the landscape is littered with remnants of the past – well-preserved medieval towns and castles, royal residences and battle sites.

Lying at the heart of Scotland, **Stirling** and its fine castle, from where you can see both snowcapped Highland peaks and Edinburgh, are unmissable for anyone wanting to grasp the complexities of Scottish history. To the south of the city, on the road to Edinburgh, lies **Falkirk**, its industrial heritage now enlivened by the intriguing Falkirk Wheel; to the east, the gentle **Ochil Hills** run towards Fife, while the flat plain extending west, the **Carse of Stirling**, has the little-visited **Campsie Fells** on its southern edge and the fabled mountains, glens, lochs and forests of the **Trossachs**, stretching west from **Callander** to Loch Lomond, to the north.

On the western side of the region, **Loch Lomond** is the largest – and most romanticized – stretch of fresh water in Scotland. Now at the heart of the Loch Lomond and the Trossachs National Park, the peerless scenery of the loch and its famously "bonnie banks" can be tainted by the sheer numbers of tourists and day-trippers who stream towards it in summer. It can get similarly clogged in parts of the neighbouring Trossachs, although there's much to appreciate once you break away from the main routes. The area is particularly good for **outdoor activities**: it's traversed by the **Glasgow–Loch Lomond–Killin cycleway**; well-managed forest tracks are ideal for mountain biking; the hills of the Trossachs provide great walking country; and the **West Highland Way**, Scotland's premier long-distance footpath, winds along the length of Loch Lomond up to Fort William in the Highlands.

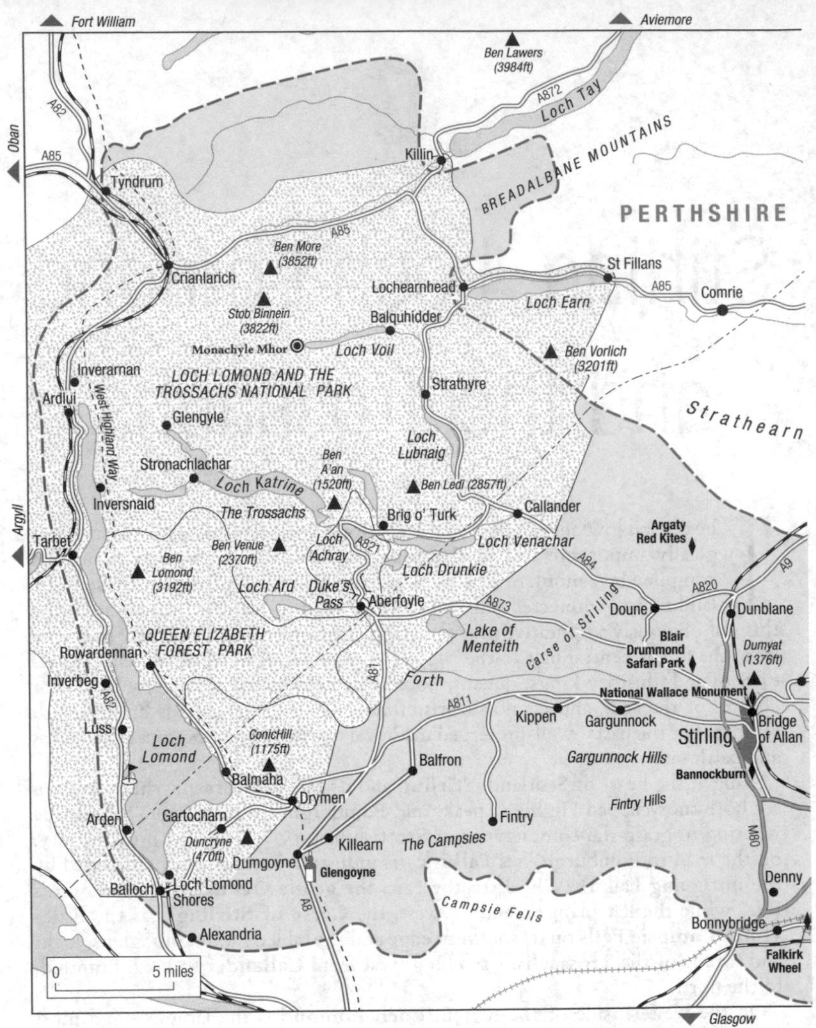

Stirling

Straddling the River Forth a few miles upstream from the estuary at Kincardine, **STIRLING** (Ⓦ www.visitstirling.org) appears at first glance like a smaller version of Edinburgh. With its crag-top castle, steep, cobbled streets and mixed community of locals, students and tourists, it's an appealing place, though it lacks the cosmopolitan edge of its near neighbours Edinburgh and Glasgow.

Stirling was the scene of some of the most significant developments in the evolution of the Scottish nation. It was here in 1297 that the Scots, under William Wallace, defeated the English at the **Battle of Stirling Bridge**, only to fight – and win again – under Robert the Bruce just a couple of miles away at the **Battle of Bannockburn** in 1314. Stirling enjoyed its golden age in the fifteenth to seventeenth centuries, most notably when its castle was the favoured residence

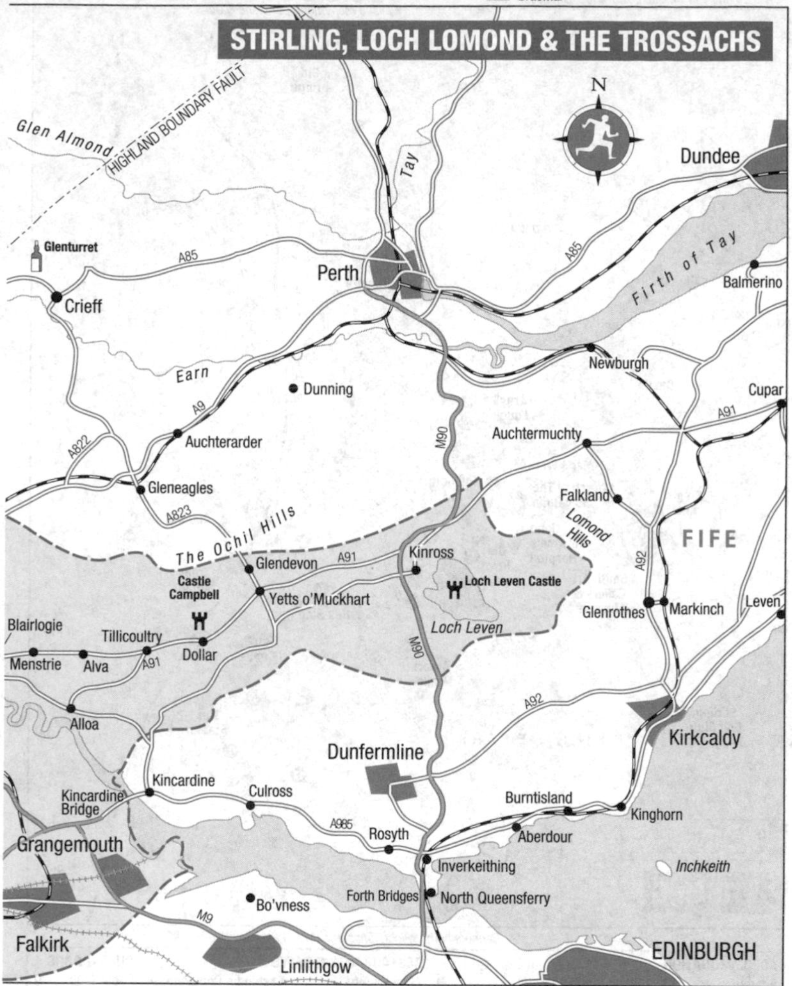

of the Stuart monarchy and the setting for the coronation in 1543 of the young Mary, future Queen of Scots.

Today Stirling is best known for its **castle** – arguably the best in Scotland, and certainly as atmospheric as Edinburgh's – and the lofty **Wallace Monument**, a mammoth Victorian monolith high on Abbey Craig to the northeast.

Arrival, information and orientation

The **train station** is near the centre of town on Station Road, just two minutes' walk from the **bus station** on Goosecroft Road. The main **tourist office** (daily; ⓣ01786/475019) is a ten-minute walk away at 41 Dumbarton Rd; as well as the usual range of books, maps and leaflets it offers an accommodation booking service (£4) and internet access. Because Stirling is a compact town, sightseeing in the Old

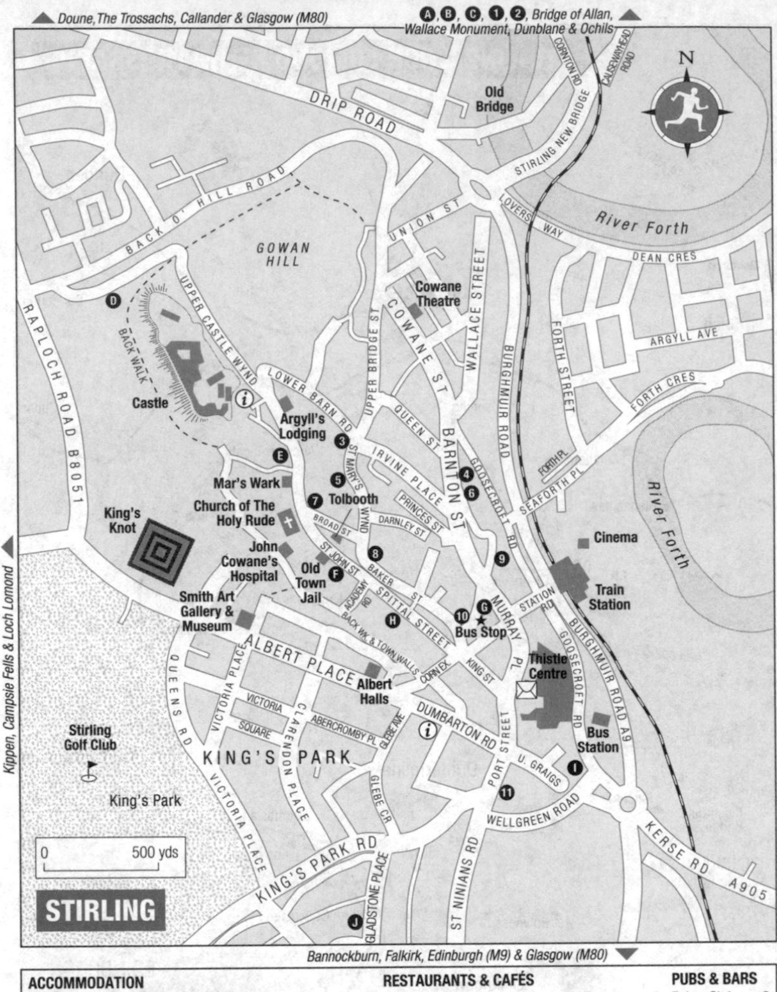

ACCOMMODATION				RESTAURANTS & CAFÉS				PUBS & BARS	
Adamo	I	Stirling Highland Hotel	H	Allan Water Café	2	East India Company	4	Fubar Club	9
Castlecroft	D	Stirling University	C	Clive Ramsay	1	Greengrocer Down the Pend	11	No 2 Baker Street	10
Kilronan House	B	SYHA hostel	F	Darnley Coffee House	8	Hermann's	7	Settle Inn	3
No. 10	J	Willy Wallace Independent Hostel	G			Mediterranea	6	Whistlebinkies	5
The Portcullis	E	Witches Craig campsite	A						

Town is best done **on foot**, though you'll need to take local buses to reach the attractive satellite town of **Bridge of Allan**, the university, Wallace Monument and Bannockburn; you can also access Bridge of Allan by train from Stirling.

Accommodation

It's worth **booking accommodation** as far in advance as possible, especially from May to October. Stirling has reasonable options in most accommodation categories and is understandably popular both as a lower-key alternative to Glasgow or Edinburgh, and as a base for exploring central Scotland.

Hotels and B&Bs

Adamo 78 Upper Craigs ⓣ01786/430890, ⓦwww.adamohotels.com. Stirling's attempt at a boutique hotel, in a sturdy stone mansion close to the city centre. Lots of purple and black contemporary styling, mod cons in the rooms and an all-day menu in the restaurant. There's a sister hotel in central Bridge of Allan in a similarly handsome building. ❼

Castlecroft Ballengeich Rd ⓣ01786/474933, ⓦwww.castlecroft-uk.com. Modern guesthouse with six en-suite rooms on the site of the King's Stables just beneath the castle rock, with terrific views north and west and a very friendly welcome. ❷

Kilronan House 15 Kenilworth Rd, Bridge of Allan ⓣ01786/831054, ⓦwww.kilronan.co.uk. A grand Victorian family house built in 1853 with spacious en-suite B&B rooms, in Bridge of Allan, just a couple of miles north of Stirling and easily reached by regular buses (First #54 & #58) and trains. ❷

No. 10 10 Gladstone Place ⓣ01786/472681, ⓦwww.cameron-10.co.uk. Modernized Victorian home with neat, uncluttered decor providing friendly and pleasant B&B accommodation. It's close to the city centre, but on a quiet and elegant King's Park street. ❷

The Portcullis Castle Wynd ⓣ01786/472290, ⓦwww.theportcullishotel.com. Traditional hotel with four en-suite rooms in an imposing building built in 1787 and a dramatic Old Town location adjacent to the castle. Cosy bar, open log fire and beer garden. ❺

Stirling Highland Hotel Spittal St ⓣ01786/272727, ⓦwww.barcelo-hotels.co.uk. Upmarket if rather pretentiously genteel hotel in a handsome Victorian Gothic building that once housed Stirling High School and still maintains an observatory on the top floor. It features comfortable rooms and has good leisure facilities, including a 15m pool and a gym. The location, in the Old Town just 500yd from the castle, is excellent. ❼

Hostel, campsite and campus accommodation

Stirling University ⓣ01786/467141, ⓦwww.holidays.stir.ac.uk. Campus accommodation in halls of residence and self-catering flats a couple of miles north of the town centre. The campus is served by regular buses from Murray Place in the town centre. ❶ room only or ❷ B&B; June to early Sept.

SYHA hostel St John St ⓣ01786/473442, ⓦwww.syha.org.uk. Situated at the top of the town, a strenuous trek with a backpack, in a converted church with an impressive 1824 Palladian facade. Dorms are small and all have showers and toilets en suite, and facilities include a games room and internet access.

Willy Wallace Independent Hostel 77 Murray Place ⓣ01786/446773, ⓦwww.willywallacehostel.com. Located 100yd from the station in a Victorian building on a busy street, this is the liveliest (and noisiest) budget option in town, with a big common room, five dorms, a family room and a couple of double and twin rooms (both ❶).

Witches Craig Campsite Blairlogie ⓣ01786/474947, ⓦwww.witchescraig.co.uk. A very attractive sylvan spot tucked under the Ochil Hills, three miles east off the A91 road to St Andrews. Take #62 bus from Stirling. April–Oct.

The Town

Stirling evolved from the top down, starting with its castle and gradually spreading south and east onto the low-lying flood plain. At the centre of the original **Old Town**, Broad Street was the main thoroughfare, with St John Street running more or less parallel, and St Mary's Wynd forming part of the original route to Stirling Bridge below. In the eighteenth and nineteenth centuries, as the threat of attack decreased, the centre of commercial life crept down towards the River Forth, with the modern town growing on the edge of the plain over which the castle stands guard.

Stirling Castle

Stirling Castle (daily: April–Sept 9.30am–6pm; Oct–March 9.30am–5pm; £9, includes entry to Argyll's Lodging – see p.310; ⓦwww.stirlingcastle.gov.uk) presented would-be invaders with a formidable challenge. Its impregnability is most daunting when you approach the town from the west, from where the sheer 250ft drop down the side of the crag is most obvious. The rock was first fortified during the Iron Age, though what you see now dates largely from the fifteenth and sixteenth centuries. Built on many levels, the main buildings are interspersed with delightful gardens and patches of lawn, while endless battlements, cannon ports, hidden staircases and other nooks and crannies make it thoroughly explorable and inspiring.

The souvenir-choked **visitor centre** is in a whitewashed cottage on one side of the esplanade car park (£2); bypass this and head straight for the main castle entrance, where you can get tickets and pick up a comprehensive audio-guide in six languages (£2). Alternatively, excellent free **guided tours** begin a little further into the castle at the well in the Outer Close. The castle's efficiently run **café** is a better-than-average spot for a simple soup and sandwich or coffee and cake.

Shortly after the castle entrance, a passageway to the left leads to a former bowling lawn and the entrance to the **Castle Exhibition**, a comprehensive run-through of the castle's history. Moving through to the central part of the castle, the **Outer Close** is the first of two main courtyard areas. Looming over it is the magnificently restored **Great Hall**, dating from 1501–03 and used as a barracks by the British army until 1964. The building stands out across Stirling for its controversially bright, creamy yellow cladding, added after the discovery during renovations of a stretch of the original sixteenth-century limewash behind a bricked-up doorway. Inside, the hall has been restored to its original state as the finest medieval secular building in Scotland, complete with five gaping fireplaces and an impressive hammer beam ceiling of rough-hewn wood.

The exterior of the **Palace**, the largest building in the castle, dates from 1540–42 and is richly decorated with grotesque carved figures and Renaissance sculpture, including, in the left-hand corner, the glaring bearded figure of James V in the dress of a commoner. Inside in the royal apartments are the **Stirling Heads**, 56 elegantly carved oak medallions that once comprised the ceiling of the Presence Chamber, where visitors were presented to royalty. A major restoration of the Palace will be completed in 2011, with specially commissioned tapestries and furniture returning the rooms to their appearance in the mid sixteenth century.

On one side of the Inner Close, the steeply sloping upper courtyard of the castle, is the **Chapel Royal**, built in 1594 by James VI for the baptism of his son. Alongside, the **King's Old Building**, at the highest point in the castle, now houses the museum of the Argyll and Sutherland Highlanders regiment, with its collection of well-polished silver and memorabilia, including a seemingly endless display of Victoria Crosses. Go through a narrow passageway between the King's Old Building and the Chapel Royal to get to the **Douglas Gardens**, reputedly the place where the eighth earl of Douglas, suspected of treachery, was thrown to his death by James II in 1452. It's a lovely, quiet corner of the castle, with mature trees and battlements over which there are splendid views of the rising Highlands beyond, as well as a bird's-eye view down to the **King's Knot**, a series of grassed octagonal mounds which in the seventeenth century were planted with box trees and ornamental hedges.

The Old Town

As you leave the castle, head downhill into the old centre of Stirling, which is fortified behind the massive, whinstone boulders of the **town walls**, built in the mid-sixteenth century and intended to ward off the advances of Henry VIII, who had set his sights on the young Mary, Queen of Scots as a wife for his son, Edward. The walls now constitute some of the best-preserved town defences in Scotland, and can be traced by following the path known as **Back Walk**. This walkway was built in the eighteenth century and in the upper reaches leads right under the castle, taut along the edge of the crag. Though a little overgrown in places, it's a great way to take in the castle's setting, and gives panoramic views of the countryside.

At the top of Castle Wynd, **Argyll's Lodging** (guided tour only, book on ⓣ01786/450000; HS; free with ticket to Stirling Castle) is a romantic Renaissance townhouse built by Sir William Alexander of Menstrie in the seventeenth century.

Once the home of Alexander, the first earl of Stirling, it was later used as a military hospital and youth hostel. The oldest part of the building, with its low ceilings and tiny windows, is the Great Kitchen, whose enormous fireplace comes complete with a special recess for salt, while the Drawing Room, hung with lavishly decorated purple tapestries, contains the ninth earl's imposing chair of state.

Further down Castle Wynd at the top of Broad Street, a richly decorated facade hides ruined **Mar's Wark**, a would-be palace that the first earl of Mar, regent of Scotland and hereditary Keeper of Stirling Castle, started in 1570. His dream house was never to be realized, however, for he died two years later and what had been built was left to ruin, its degeneration speeded up by extensive damage during the 1745 Jacobite rebellion. Behind here is the **Church of the Holy Rude** (Easter–Sept daily 11am–4pm), a fine medieval structure, the oldest parts of which, including the impressive oak hammer-beam ceiling, date from the early fifteenth century. Just south of the church on the edge of the crag, the rugged, whitewashed **John Cowane's Hospital** was built in 1649 as an almshouse for, at its founder John Cowane's request, "decayed [unsuccessful] members of the Guild of Merchants". Above the entrance, Cowane, a wealthy merchant himself, is commemorated in a painted statue that, it is said, comes alive at Hogmanay.

A short walk down St John Street, a sweeping driveway leads up to the impressive **Old Town Jail** (end May to Oct daily 10am–5pm; £6.50; Ⓦwww.oldtownjail.com), built by Victorian prison reformers as an alternative to the depravity of the medieval Tolbooth (see below). Subsequently used as a military jail, it was rescued from dereliction in 1994, with part of the building turned into offices and a substantial section used to create an entertaining visitor attraction. Telling the history of the building and prisons in general, tours are taken by actors, who enthusiastically change costumes and character a number of times; among the features of the jail they'll introduce you to is a working example of the dreaded crank, a lever that prisoners had to turn 14,400 times a day. Take the glass lift up to the prison roof to admire spectacular views across Stirling and the Forth Valley. Opposite and just uphill from the entrance to the Old Town Jail on St John Street, look out for the **Boy's Club**, a 1929 conversion of the town's old butter market, with its encouraging little mottoes engraved above the door such as "Keep smiling" and "Quarrelling is taboo".

Directly opposite the Old Town Jail, between St John Street and Broad Street, is the original medieval prison, the **Tolbooth** (daily from 9am; Ⓦwww.stirling.gov.uk/tolbooth), now an innovative music and arts centre. Originally built in 1705, the striking modern redevelopment received an architectural award as the UK's best public building. During the renovations a secret staircase was discovered, as was a complete skeleton, thought to have been that of the last man publicly hanged in Stirling. Inside there's a top-floor viewing platform looking out over the Old Town rooftops and a box office where you can find out about the centre's programme, which focuses on folk, experimental and jazz music. There are music workshops for adults and kids year-round, and summer ceilidhs. The Tolbooth is also home to the **Changing Room** (Tues–Sat 10am–6pm; free; Ⓦwww.stirling.gov.uk/changingroom), a contemporary art space.

Back on Broad Street, the town's former marketplace, there are various historical buildings and monuments including the stone **Mercat Cross** (the unicorn on top is known, inexplicably, as "the puggy") and **Darnley's House**, where Mary, Queen of Scots' husband is believed to have lodged while she lorded it up in the castle; it now houses a good little coffee shop (see p.313).

The Lower Town and around

The further downhill you go in Stirling's Lower Town, as the area on the lower eastern flanks of the castle hill is known, the more recent the buildings become.

By the time the two main streets of the Old Town merge into King Street, austere Victorian facades block the sun from the cobbled road. The only sight of note in the centre is the **Smith Art Gallery and Museum** (Tues–Sat 10.30am–5pm, Sun 2–5pm; free; Ⓦwww.smithartgallery.demon.co.uk), a short walk west near the King's Knot. Founded in 1874 with a legacy from local painter and collector Thomas Stuart Smith, it houses "The Stirling Story", a reasonably entertaining whirl through the history of the town, balancing the stories of kings and queens with more social and domestic history. Among the exhibits is the world's oldest known football, made out of a pig's bladder; it was found in the rafters of the Queen's Chamber in the castle and is thought to date from the 1540s. The small art gallery includes changing displays of mostly local arts and crafts, contemporary art and photography, and there's a pleasant café.

The fifteenth-century **Old Bridge** over the Forth lies to the north on the edge of the town centre (a 20min walk from Murray Place). Although once the most important river crossing in Scotland – the lowest bridging point on the Forth until the new bridge was built in 1831 – it now stands virtually forgotten, an incidental reminder of Stirling's former importance. An earlier wooden **bridge** nearby, no trace of which survives, was the focus of the Battle of Stirling Bridge in 1297, where William Wallace defeated the English.

The National Wallace Monument

A mile and a half north of the Old Town, the prominent **National Wallace Monument** (daily: April–June & Sept–Oct 10am–5pm; July & Aug 10am–6pm; Nov–March 10.30am–4pm; £7.50; Ⓦwww.nationalwallacemonument.com) is a freestanding, five-storey tower built in the 1860s as a tribute to Sir William Wallace, the freedom fighter who led Scottish resistance to Edward I, the "Hammer of the Scots", in the late thirteenth century. The crag on which the monument is set was the scene of Wallace's greatest victory, when he sent his troops charging down the hillside onto the plain to defeat the English at the Battle of Stirling Bridge in 1297. An audio-tour handset (free) leads you round inside the tower, where you can find Wallace's long steel sword and the Hall of (Scottish) Heroes, a row of stern white marble busts featuring John Knox and Adam Smith, as well as a life-size "talking" model of Wallace, who tells visitors about his preparations for the battle. If you can manage the climb – up 246 spiral steps – to the top of the 220ft tower, you'll be rewarded with superb views across to Fife and Ben Lomond. Various local buses including First's #63 will get you here.

Bannockburn

A couple of miles south of Stirling centre, on the A872, all but surrounded by drab suburban housing, the **Bannockburn Heritage Centre** (daily: April–Oct 10am–5.30pm; Nov–March 10am–5pm; NTS; £5.50) commemorates the most famous battle in Scottish history, when King Robert the Bruce won his mighty victory over the English at the **Battle of Bannockburn** on June 24, 1314. It was this battle, the climax of the Wars of Independence, which united the Scots under Bruce and led to independence from England, sealed by the Declaration of Arbroath (1320) and the Treaty of Northampton (1328).

Within the centre there is an audiovisual presentation on the battle and the background to it, highlighting the brilliantly innovative tactics Bruce employed in mustering his army to defeat a much larger English force. Outside, there's free access across the surrounding grounds to a concrete rotunda that encloses a flagpole and cairn, said to mark Bruce's command post for an early phase of the fighting. Pondering the scene is a stirring equestrian **statue** of Bruce, set against the skyline of Stirling Castle, the English army's approach to which he was intentionally blocking. The actual site of the main battle is still a matter of debate. Most agree that it didn't take place near the present visitor centre; a cogent theory argues that it took place on a boggy carse a mile or so to the west. Get to Bannockburn on local services #24, #52 or #57 from Stirling bus station or Murray Place.

Eating

Stirling doesn't have a strong reputation for its **restaurants**, with venues struggling to hang around long enough to earn a good name. However, there are places serving quality contemporary Scottish cuisine and **bistro**-style food.

Allan Water Café 15 Henderson St, Bridge of Allan. Established in 1902, this trad Italian café serves inexpensive fish suppers with mushy peas and its very own ice cream, made to a secret family recipe.

Clive Ramsay Café and Restaurant 28 Henderson St, Bridge of Allan ⓣ01786/831616. This is not a deluxe dining experience, but a relaxed, friendly and reasonably stylish lunch or pre-cinema option. The menu is varied and makes use of good Scottish ingredients, with haggis a popular choice.

Darnley Coffee House Bow St (the continuation of Broad St). A bit old-fashioned but with plenty of Old Town atmosphere and serving reasonably priced lunches, teas and home-made cakes in an impressive barrel-vaulted interior.

East India Company 7 Viewfield Place ⓣ01786/471330. Good Indian food, Raj-style decor and the friendliest service in town.

Greengrocer Down the Pend 81 Port St ⓣ01786/479159. A handy coffee or lunch stop, this lively deli/café tucked down a pend (passageway) in the centre of town serves delicious home-made soups, hearty sandwiches, scones and cakes.

Hermann's 58 Broad St ⓣ01786/450632, ⓦwww.hermanns.co.uk. The classiest option in Stirling, *Hermann's* is set in the historic Mar Place House towards the top of the Old Town. It operates brasserie-style at lunchtime and offers upmarket Austrian-Scottish dining such as *jager schnitzel* (veal) or Scottish lamb with cheese potatoes in the evening.

Mediterranea 4 Viewfield Place ⓣ01786/478534. Spanish tapas and moderately priced pan-Mediterranean dishes in an upbeat atmosphere.

Drinking, nightlife and entertainment

The nightlife scene in Stirling is nothing to write home about, with the cluster of mainstream bars and pubs changing hands frequently. By far the best option for a night out is the ★ *Tolbooth* (see p.311), with its eclectic **live music** programme, top-of-the-town location and glamorous high-ceilinged bar (open only when there's an event on). Look out for its boisterous summer ceilidhs in July and August.

The *Settle Inn*, 91 St Mary's Wynd, is Stirling's oldest alehouse (est.1733) and serves Scottish real ales, though it has recently undergone an unsympathetic makeover. Nearby *Whistlebinkies* features regular live music, as does *N. 2 Baker Street*, which is a good, if somewhat characterless, option for real ales. If you want to carry on after the pubs close, try *Fubar Club* in Maxwell Place, off Murray Place, a student-oriented **nightclub**. The main venue for **film** is the Vue cinema behind the train station, while the MacRobert Arts Centre (ⓣ01786/466666, ⓦwww.macrobert.org) on the university campus shows mainstream and art-house films, as well as occasional jazz and dance performances.

Around Stirling

If Stirling's strategic position between the Highlands and Lowlands made it important in medieval times, it was the town's proximity to the Forth that gave it renewed significance as the Industrial Revolution grew across Scotland's central belt. To the north and west of Stirling, the historic aspect of the region is reflected in the cathedral at **Dunblane**, the imposing castle at **Doune** and the attractive settlements of the **Carse of Stirling**, while to the east and south, on either side of the Forth, the county of **Clackmannanshire** at the foot of the **Ochil Hills**, and the less enticing area around **Falkirk** tell of a rich industrial heritage. An undoubted highlight of this hinterland is the massive **Falkirk Wheel**, a spectacular feat of modern engineering that transfers canal boats up and down a 100ft drop at the interchange of the newly restored Forth and Clyde and Union canals.

Dunblane

Small, attractive **DUNBLANE** has been an important ecclesiastical centre since the seventh century, when the Celts founded the church of St Blane here. **Dunblane Cathedral** (April–Sept Mon–Sat 9.30am–12.30pm & 1.30–5pm, Sun 2pm–5pm; Oct–March Mon–Sat 9.30am–4pm, Sun 2–4pm; HS; free) dates mainly from the thirteenth century, and restoration work carried out a century ago returned it to its Gothic splendour. Inside, note the delicate blue-purple stained glass, and the exquisitely carved pews, screen and choir stalls, all crafted in the early twentieth century. There are various memorials, including a tenth-century Celtic cross-slab standing stone and a modern, four-sided standing stone by Richard Kindersley commemorating the tragic shooting in 1996 of sixteen Dunblane schoolchildren and their teacher by local man, Thomas Hamilton. The cathedral, praised in the highest terms by John Ruskin, stands serenely amid a clutch of old buildings, among them the seventeenth-century Dean's House, which houses the small **Dunblane Museum** (May to early Oct Mon–Sat 10.30am–4.30pm; free) with exhibits on local history. Close by stands the **Leighton Library** (April–Sept Mon–Tues & Thurs–Fri 11am–2pm; donation Ⓣ01786/822296). Established in 1684, it's the oldest private lending library in Scotland and houses 4500 books in ninety languages, printed between 1500 and 1840. Visitors can browse through some of the country's rarest books, including a first edition of Sir Walter Scott's *Lady of the Lake*.

Frequent trains and occasional **buses** (#47 and #C48 from Stirling bus station) make the journey five miles north of Stirling to Dunblane. If you want to **stay**, try *Chimes House B&B* (Ⓣ01786/822481, Ⓦwww.bedandbreakfast-scotland.co.uk; ❷), which overlooks the cathedral in Cathedral Square and offers pleasant en-suite doubles and a good Scottish breakfast. The trad *Tappit Hen* on Kirk Street is a good place for a **pint**, and has regular folk music nights.

Doune and around

DOUNE, eight miles northwest of Stirling and three miles due west of Dunblane, is a sleepy village surrounding a fourteenth-century **castle** (April–Sept daily 9.30am–5.30pm; Oct daily 9.30am–4.30pm; Nov–March Mon–Wed & Sat–Sun 9.30am–4.30pm; HS; £4.20), a marvellous semi-ruin standing on a small hill in a bend of the River Teith. Today the most prominent features of the castle are its mighty 95ft-high gatehouse, with spacious vaulted rooms, and the kitchens, complete with medieval rubbish chute. Built by Robert, Duke of Albany, it ended up in the hands of the second earl of Moray, James Stewart – son of James V and half-brother of Mary, Queen of Scots – who was murdered in 1592 and immortalized in the ballad *The Bonnie Earl of Moray*; it was also used as a prison by Bonnie Prince Charlie's army after the battle of Falkirk. The castle's greatest claim to fame today, however, is as the setting for the 1970s movie *Monty Python and the Holy Grail*. With legions of Python fans arriving here on pilgrimage, Historic Scotland sells a selection of film souvenirs including bottles of the local Holy Grail Ale and even hosts an annual Monty Python Day in early September. Close to the castle,

accommodation is available at the excellent *Glenardoch House*, Castle Road (ⓣ01786/841489; ⓦwww.glenardochhouse.moonfruit.com; May–Sept; ❹), an eighteenth-century country-house B&B with two comfortable en-suite rooms and a beautiful riverside garden.

Three miles south of Doune, families may be tempted by the **Blair Drummond Safari Park** (mid-March to Sept daily 10am–5.30pm; £11.50; ⓦwww.blairdrummond.com), a bizarre attempt to re-create the African bush in the Scottish countryside. The regular #59 bus between Stirling bus station and Callander stops here. A better experience of real Scottish wildlife can be had at the **Argaty Red Kite Centre** (March–Oct arrive for 2.30pm; Nov–Feb arrive for 1.30pm; £4; ⓦwww.argatyredkites.co.uk) where you can observe these magnificent reintroduced birds at their specified feeding time; follow the signs north out of Doune on the minor road towards Bridge of Allan.

The Carse of Stirling

West of Stirling, the wide flood plain of the Forth River is known as the Carse of Forth or **Carse of Stirling**. This is fertile farmland bounded on the south by the Gargunnock and Fintry hills, which gradually blend into the **Campsie Fells**. To the north are the Trossachs, which inevitably draw away many visitors, with the main road west of Stirling, the A811, connecting to Loch Lomond through the carse. The hourly bus #12 from Stirling to Balfron goes through Gargunnock and Kippen.

You can find out about the rich ecology and history of the carse's reclaimed marshland at the **Flanders Moss** nature reserve; to reach it take a right off the A811 towards Callander, and follow the signs. You walk through the bog on raised boardwalks, spotting dragonflies, damselflies, pond skaters and green tiger beetles amongst the spaghnum moss and heather. Nearby **KIPPEN**, a scenic village with strong Rob Roy associations, has good accommodation options in the form of its two excellent pubs, the *Inn at Kippen* (ⓣ01786/870500, ⓦwww.theinnatkippen.co.uk; ❺), which has a fine restaurant, and the *Cross Keys* (ⓣ01786/870293, ⓦwww.kippencrosskeys.com; ❹). The village deli/café, *Berits & Brown*, is also a cut above. If you're in a group, consider a stay at *Gargunnock House*, a wonderful country house with a Georgian facade and plush interiors operated by the Landmark Trust (ⓣ01628/825925, ⓦwww.landmarktrust.org.uk).

At the western end of the Campsie Fells, all roads (including the West Highland Way – see box, p.312) meet at the small village of **DRYMEN**, an ancient ecclesiastical centre and stopover point for Highland drovers, which sits peacefully in the hills overlooking the winding Endrick Water as it nears Loch Lomond. In the village square, the flower-bedecked *Winnock Hotel* (ⓣ01360/660245, ⓦwww.winnockhotel.com; ❻) has comfortable en-suite **rooms**. Avoid its restaurant though, and head across the green, either to the 1734 *Clachan Inn*, an atmospheric spot for great simple **pub grub** and a pint, or to the nearby *Pottery*, which has a lively upstairs pub (with pool table) serving plain but tasty fish and chips, burgers and pizzas, and a downstairs coffee shop, with a nice timbered roof and a pretty garden, serving delicious locally baked cakes. South of Drymen, not far from Killearn, popular **Glengoyne Distillery** (tours on the hour daily: March–Nov 10am–4pm; Dec–Feb 11am–3pm; £6.50; ⓣ01360/550254, ⓦwww.glengoyne.com) is the closest whisky distillery to Glasgow that offers tours.

Falkirk and around

Southeast of Stirling, along the south bank of the widening Forth Estuary, farmland gives way to industry, notably BP's gargantuan petrochemical plant at

Grangemouth. The lights and fires of the refineries are spectacular at night, and inspired Bertrand Tavernier to make his dour 1979 sci-fi film *Death Watch* in Scotland. Despite its nondescript industrial surroundings, **FALKIRK** – located about halfway between Stirling and Edinburgh on the M9 motorway – has a good deal of visible history, going right back to the remains of the Roman Antonine Wall. It was also the site of two major battles, one in 1298 when William Wallace's army fell victim to the English under Edward I, and the other in 1746, when Bonnie Prince Charlie's disintegrating force, retreating northwards, sent the Hanoverians packing in one of its last victories. Traditionally a livestock centre, Falkirk became better known for its industry, with the founding in 1759 of the now-redundant Carron Ironworks which manufactured carronades (small cannons) for Nelson's fleet. The town was further transformed later in the eighteenth century by the construction of first the Forth and Clyde Canal, allowing easy access to Glasgow and the west coast, and then the Union Canal, which continued the route through to Edinburgh. Just twenty years later, the trains arrived, and the canals gradually fell into disuse, but have been regenerated in recent years for leisure boating and cycling.

The town is a busy local shopping hub, whose only formal attraction, set in Callendar Park, is **Callendar House** (Mon–Sat 10am–5pm; April–Sept also Sun 2–5pm; free), which was owned by the staunchly Jacobite Livingston family. It's now an entertaining local history museum, housing heritage displays and a contemporary art and craft gallery, alongside its centerpiece working Georgian kitchen, with its gleaming utensils and a huge mechanized spit. In the park, a small section of the Antonine Wall (see opposite) can be made out. The oak-panelled Victorian library of the house contains the Falkirk Council Archives (Mon–Fri 10am–12.30pm & 1.30–5pm; free), where staff will gladly help you delve into local family history.

The Falkirk Wheel

The leisure potential of Falkirk's two long-neglected canals has only recently been realized, thanks to British Waterways' £84.5 million **Millennium Link** project to restore the canals and re-establish a navigable link between east and west coasts. The icon of this project is the remarkable **Falkirk Wheel** (Ⓦwww.thefalkirkwheel.co.uk), two miles west of Falkirk town centre, which was opened in 2002.

The wheel, which looks more like a giant metal claw, was designed to solve the problem of the 115ft gap between the Union and Forth and Clyde canals. Back in the 1930s, before the canals went to rack and ruin, barges had to spend a day passing though eleven locks. To solve the problem, engineers designed the giant lift, which scoops a boat in one claw and an equal weight of water in the other. The simple process of rotating the perfectly weighted claws and depositing the boat in the other canal is said to use only the same energy that it takes to boil eight kettles.

Located right underneath the wheel, the **visitor centre** (daily 9.30am–6pm) is a good place to head for background information and to buy tickets for a **boat trip** (daily: April–Oct every 30min 9.30am–4.30pm; Nov–March hourly 10am–3pm; £7.95) – basically, a one-hour journey from the lower basin into the wheel, along the Union Canal for a short distance, then back down to the basin again via the wheel. However, the boat trip certainly isn't essential if you just want to see the wheel in action, which can be done by **walking** around the basin and adjoining towpaths. From lock 16 on the Forth and Clyde Canal, about halfway between the wheel and the centre of Falkirk, the *Bonny Barge* offers cruises (from £14; Ⓣ07859/336136, Ⓦwww.scottishcanalcruising.com) along the canal, including a four-hour trip up to and through the wheel. The frequent bus #3 from Falkirk town centre will take you to the wheel; alternatively, it's a pleasant twenty-minute walk along the Union Canal from Falkirk High train station.

Practicalities

Falkirk's centrally located **bus** station is at Callendar Riggs. Regular **trains** run from Edinburgh to Stirling via Falkirk **Grahamston Station**, while Falkirk **High Station**, which is further from the centre, is a stop on the Edinburgh–Glasgow line. In the town centre you can get **information** at the office run by the local council at the Steeple on the High Street. For B&B **accommodation** try elegant Edwardian villa *Oaklands* (ⓣ01324/610671, ⓦwww.oaklandsbedandbreakfast.co.uk; ❸) at 32 Polmont Rd.

The spacious modern *Wheelhouse* **restaurant** and bar (ⓣ01324/673490, ⓦwww.wheelhousefalkirk.com) on Millennium Wheel Drive, just ten minutes' walk from the Falkirk Wheel, is the best bet for food with its wide-ranging contemporary menu. In town, *Comma Bar Café*, 14 Lint Riggs, is a brasserie-style café and trendy bar. If you're strolling by the canal, call in at the three-storey *Union Inn* by lock 16, which dates from the days when bargemen would stop for a drink after a hard day's toil working the locks.

Around Falkirk

Unlikely as it might seem, **BONNYBRIDGE**, a largely nondescript settlement five miles west of Falkirk, claims more UFO sightings than anywhere else in Britain. Quite what attracts aliens to the area is a puzzle, as the only sight hereabouts is **Rough Castle**, one of the forts set up, at two-mile intervals, to defend the entire length of the Roman **Antonine Wall**. The most northerly frontier of the Roman Empire, the wall was built in 142 AD, of turf rather than stone, and streched for 37 miles right across the country from the Forth to the Clyde. Assailed by skirmishing Picts and the grim Scottish weather, it didn't take long for the Romans to abandon the wall and retreat to Hadrian's Wall, just south of Scotland's present border with England. The signposted site lies along a potholed back road, and though little more than a large grassy mound interpreted by a couple of information boards, the remains at Rough Castle are the best-preserved part of the wall, which has UNESCO World Heritage Site status.

The Hillfoots and Loch Leven

The rugged **Ochil Hills** stretch for roughly forty miles northeast of Stirling, forming a steep-faced range that drops down to the flood plain of the Forth Valley and is sliced by a series of deep-cut, richly wooded glens. Tucked up against the southern slopes of the Ochils is a string of settlements known as the **Hillfoot villages,** which were at the centre of Scotland's wool production for centuries. The only essential stop here is **Dollar**, for the walk up the glen to the moody castle; at **Alva**, the tourist office and visitor centre has displays recalling the weaving industry; and **Alloa** is famous as a centre for brewing beer. The Stagecoach **bus** service #23 between Stirling and St Andrews travels along the A91 through the Hillfoot villages.

Dollar

Nestling in a fold of the Ochils on the northern bank of the small River Devon, where mountain waters rush off the hills, affluent **DOLLAR** is known for its Academy, founded in 1820 with a substantial bequest from local lad John MacNabb; its pupils and staff account for around a third of the town's population. Above the town, the steep ravine of **Dollar Glen** is commanded by **Castle Campbell** (April–Sept daily 9.30am–5.30pm; Oct daily 9.30am–4.30pm; Nov–March Mon–Wed, Sat & Sun 9.30am–4.30pm; HS; £4.70), formerly, and unofficially, known as Castle Gloom – a fine and evocative tag but, prosaically, a derivation of "Gloume", an old Gaelic name. A one-and-a-half-mile-long road leads up from Dollar's main street, but becomes very narrow and steep and stops short of the castle, with only limited parking at the top. A series of marked **walks** leads up the glen, taking in mossy crags, rushing streams and, if you strike out on the three-hour hike to the top of Dollar Hill, great views. There's a map showing the walks on a board on the way up to the castle, though it's advisable to buy the relevant OS map (Explorer 366) if you're setting off for the longer hike.

The *Strathallan Hotel* on Chapel Road is a good spot for a pub **lunch** with real ale and outside seating, while there's great **B&B** in a pretty former gamekeeper's cottage at Dollarbeg, just south of town (ⓣ01259/742186, ⓦwww.guesthousescotland.co.uk; ❸)

Kinross and Loch Leven

Although by no means a large place, **KINROSS**, ten miles east of Dollar, has been transformed in the last couple of decades by the construction of the nearby M90 Edinburgh–Perth motorway. Not far from here is Balado Farm, location of the annual **T in the Park** (ⓦwww.tinthepark.com), one of the largest outdoor weekend music events in Britain.

Without doubt the most attractive part of Kinross is by the shores of trout-filled **Loch Leven**, signposted from the main street. The whole of the loch is a National Nature Reserve; it's a good place to see visiting geese and various types of duck. From the shore a small ferry chugs over to an island on which stands the ruined fourteenth-century **Loch Leven Castle** (daily: April–Sept 9.30am–5.30pm; Oct 9.30am–4.30pm; HS; £4.70 including ferry trip – buy tickets on the island; ⓣ07778/040483), where Mary, Queen of Scots was imprisoned for eleven months in 1567–68. This isn't the only island fortress Mary spent time in and it's easy to imagine the isolation of the tragic queen, who is believed to have miscarried twins while here. She managed to charm the 18-year-old brother of the castle's owner, Sir William Douglas, into helping her escape: he stole the castle keys, secured a boat in which to row ashore, locked the castle gates behind them and threw the keys into the loch – from where they were retrieved three centuries later.

Loch Lomond

The largest stretch of fresh water in Britain (23 miles long and up to five miles wide), **Loch Lomond** is the epitome of Scottish scenic splendour, thanks in large part to the ballad that fondly recalls its "bonnie, bonnie banks". The song was said to have been written by a Jacobite prisoner captured by the English, who, sure of his fate, wrote that his spirit would return to Scotland on the low road much faster than his living compatriots on the high road.

The **Loch Lomond and the Trossachs National Park** (ⓦwww.lochlomond-trossachs.org) covers over seven hundred square miles of scenic territory from the shores of Loch Long in Cowal to Loch Earn and Loch Tay, on the southwest fringes of Perthshire. Running along the south and western edges of the park is the Highland Boundary Fault, the geological fault that marks Highland from Lowland and is seen most clearly in the line of islands that cut across the widest part of Loch Lomond.

Though scenically splendid, the park is no untouched wilderness, with many parts of it close to being over-run with tourists and some large (and by no means beautiful) towns and villages situated within it. Balancing the needs of the park's 15,000 residents with those of its visitors and its wildlife is one of the principal challenges facing its guardians. The centrepiece is undoubtedly Loch Lomond, and

High roads and low roads around Loch Lomond

Ordnance Survey Explorer Map nos. 347 & 364.

The popularity of hiking and biking within Loch Lomond and the Trossachs National Park has been recognized in an initiative entitled "4Bs" which aims to co-ordinate and enhance the links between boats, boots (ie walking), bikes and buses around the park. Good signposting and information is an increasing facet of the park, with new cycle paths and trails being set out all the time, in addition to enhanced provision for walking and nature trails. Indeed, with a seaplane and wooden mail boats operating on Loch Lomond as well as a 100-year old steamship on Loch Katrine, getting around the park is as much part of the experience as getting to it.

For those keen to take to the high road in the vicinity of Loch Lomond there are three obvious targets offering different levels of challenge. Most prominent of all, **Ben Lomond** (3192ft) is the most southerly of the "Munros" (see p.12) and one of the most popular hills in Scotland, its commanding position above Loch Lomond affording amazing views of both the Highlands and Lowlands. The well-signposted route to the summit and back from Rowardennan takes five to six hours. If you're looking for an easier climb, but an equally impressive view over Loch Lomond, start at Balmaha for the ascent of **Conic Hill** (1175ft), a two- to three-hour walk through forest and open hillside.

Finally, you need less than an hour to complete the ascent of **Duncryne** (470ft), a small conical hill beside Gartocharn to the east of Balloch on the south side of the loch. The route up is undemanding and the view wonderfully rewarding.

the most popular gateway is **Balloch**, the town at the loch's southern tip; with Glasgow city centre just nineteen miles away, both Balloch and the southwest side of the loch around **Luss** are often packed with day-trippers and tour coaches. Many of these continue up the western side of the loch, though the fast A82 road isn't ideal for tourists who wish to enjoy a leisurely drive.

Very different in tone, the verdant eastern side of the loch, abutting the Trossachs, operates at a different pace, with wooden ferryboats puttering out to a scattering of tree-covered islands off the village of **Balmaha**. Much of the eastern shore can only be reached by boat or on foot, although the West Highland Way long-distance footpath (see box, p.321) and the distinctive peak of **Ben Lomond** ensure that even these parts are well traversed.

Balloch

The main settlement by Loch Lomond is **BALLOCH** at the southwestern corner of the loch, where the water channels into the River Leven for its short journey south to the sea in the Firth of Clyde. Surrounded by housing estates and overstuffed with undistinguished guesthouses, Balloch has few redeeming features and is little more than a suburb of the factory town of Alexandria. Accessible from Glasgow by both car and train, it's the site of a large development, **Loch Lomond Shores** (Ⓦwww.lochlomondshores.com), which has a "retail crescent" of shops including branches of Edinburgh's venerable department store, Jenners, and of the city's best deli, Valvona & Crolla. The centre can be accessed from town on a miniature train, or by the lakeside path. Alongside, **Drumkinnon Tower** is a striking, stone-built, cylindrical building that houses an aquarium (daily 10am–5pm; £12; Ⓣ01389/721000).

There are a number of **activities** available, including nature walks, canoe, bike and even pedalo rental with Can You Experience (Ⓣ01389/602576, Ⓦwww.canyouexperience.com), based right beside Drumkinnon Tower; they also organize "aquasphering" in summer, allowing kids to literally walk on water, in large plastic balls. A short stroll away, restored 1950s **paddle steamer** *The Maid of the Loch* is permanently moored at the pier (May–Sept daily 11am–4pm, Oct–April Sat & Sun 11am–4pm; free); aboard you can find out about her glory days sailing the loch and have a cup of tea in the on-board café.

In the centre of town near the bridge, Sweeney's Cruises (Ⓣ01389/752376, Ⓦwww.sweeney.uk.com) make **loch trips**, including a two-hour sailing to Luss. Otherwise, head across the river to the extensive mature grounds of **Balloch Castle Country Park**, where you can enjoy various shore-side and sylvan walks.

Practicalities

Balloch has a direct **train** connection with Glasgow Queen Street. Opposite the train station is a small **tourist office** (daily). There's really little point in basing yourself in Balloch, although you could make an exception for one of Scotland's most impressive SYHA **hostels** (Ⓣ0870/004 1136, Ⓦwww.syha.org.uk; April–Oct); this grand country house with turrets, stained-glass windows and walled gardens lies two miles northwest of Balloch train station, just off the A82. If you're travelling by Citylink's coach services from Glasgow to Oban, Fort William or Cambeltown, ask the driver to drop you off.

The exclusive DeVere *Cameron House* resort (Ⓣ01389/755565, Ⓦwww.cameronhouse.co.uk; ⑨), just north of Balloch, has its own spa and championship golf course as well as the area's best **restaurant**, an offshoot of Edinburgh's *Martin Wishart*. At Loch Lomond Shores, *Café Zest* is useful for a daytime snack, while *Cucina* and *Sarti's*, near the tourist office on Balloch Road, are both lively family-run Italian places though unprepossessing from the outside.

The eastern shore of Loch Lomond and the islands

The tranquil **eastern shore** is far better for walking and appreciating the loch's natural beauty than the overcrowded western side. The dead-end B837 from Drymen (see p.315) will take you halfway up the east bank to Rowardennan, as far as you can get by car or bus (#309 from Balloch and Drymen runs to Balmaha every 2hr), while the West Highland Way sticks close to the shores for the entire length of the loch, beginning at the tiny lochside settlement of **BALMAHA**, which stands on the Highland Boundary Fault. If you stand on the viewpoint above the pier, you can see the fault line clearly marked by the series of woody islands that form giant stepping stones across the loch. Many of the loch's 37 **islands** are privately owned, and, rather quaintly, an old wooden mail boat still delivers post to four of them. It's possible to join the **mail boat cruise**, which is run by MacFarlane & Son, from the jetty at Balmaha (May–Oct Mon, Thurs & Sat 11.30am returns 2pm; July & Aug daily 11.30am returns 2pm; Oct–April Mon & Thurs 10.50am returns 12.50pm; £9; Ⓣ01360/870214, Ⓦwww.balmahaboatyard.co.uk). The timetable allows a one-hour stop on Inchmurrin Island, which has just ten permanent residents; it has the ruins of a monastery and castle, and food is served in the bar of the *Inchmurrin Hotel* (Ⓣ01389/850245).

If you're looking for an island to explore, however, a better bet is **Inchcailloch**, the closest to Balmaha. Owned by Scottish Natural Heritage, there's a two-mile-long nature trail signposted round the island, which was extensively planted with oaks to provide bark for the local tanning industry. Along the way you'll encounter the ruins of a fourteenth-century nunnery and associated burial ground, and there's a picnic and camping site at Port Bawn on the southwestern side of the island, near a pleasant sandy beach. Until the mid-seventeenth century parishioners on the far (western) shore of Loch Lomond used to row across to Inchcailloch for Sunday services at the church linked to the nunnery. It's possible to row here yourself using a boat rented from MacFarlane & Son (from £10/hr or £30/day), or use their on-demand ferry service (£5 return).

Balmaha gets very busy in summer, not least with day-trippers on the West Highland Way. Beside the large car park is a **National Park Centre** (daily: April–Sept 9.30am–4pm) where you can find out about local forest walks and occasional wildlife workshops. You can **stay** at the well-run *Oak Tree Inn* (ⓣ01360/870357, ⓦwww.oak-tree-inn.co.uk), set back from the boatyard, in one of its en-suite double rooms (❹) or bunk-bed quads (❸). There's also a convivial pub with all-day **food**. A cheaper, more basic option is the *Balmaha Bunkhouse Lodge* (ⓣ01360/870084) just down and across the road, or the idyllically located *Passfoot Cottage* **B&B** (ⓣ01360/870324, ⓦwww.passfoot.com; ❸), which is set in a whitewashed toll

The West Highland Way

Opened in 1980, the spectacular **West Highland Way** was Scotland's first long-distance footpath, stretching some 95 miles from Milngavie (pronounced "mill-guy"), six miles north of central Glasgow, to Fort William, where it reaches the foot of Ben Nevis, Britain's highest mountain. Today, it is by far the most popular such footpath in Scotland, and while for many the range of scenery, relative ease of walking and nearby facilities make it a classic route, others find it a little too busy in high season, particularly in comparison with the isolation of many other parts of the Highlands.

The route follows a combination of ancient **drove roads**, along which Highlanders herded their cattle and sheep to market in the lowlands, military roads, built by troops to control the Jacobite insurgency in the eighteenth century, old coaching roads and disused railway lines. In addition to the stunning scenery, which is increasingly dramatic as the path heads north, walkers may see some of Scotland's rarer **wildlife**, including red deer, feral goats – ancestors of those left behind after the Highland Clearances – and, soaring over the highest peaks, golden eagles.

Passing through the lowlands north of Glasgow, the route runs along the eastern shores of Loch Lomond, over the Highland Boundary Fault Line, then round Crianlarich, crossing open heather moorland across the **Rannoch Moor** wilderness area. It passes close to **Glen Coe** (see p.445) notorious for the massacre of the MacDonald clan, before reaching **Fort William** (see p.448). Apart from a stretch between Loch Lomond and Bridge of Orchy, when the path is within earshot of the main road, this is wild, remote country: north of Rowardennan on Loch Lomond, the landscape is increasingly exposed, and you should be well prepared for sudden and extreme weather changes.

Though this is emphatically not the most strenuous of Britain's long-distance walks – it passes between lofty mountain peaks, rather than over them – a moderate degree of fitness is required as there are some steep ascents. If you're looking for an added challenge, you could work a climb of Ben Lomond or Ben Nevis into your schedule. You might choose to walk individual sections of the Way (the eight-mile climb from Glen Coe up the Devil's Staircase is particularly spectacular), but to tackle the whole thing you need to set aside at least seven days; avoid a Saturday start from Milngavie and you'll be less likely to be walking with hordes of people, and there'll be less pressure on accommodation. Most walkers tackle the route from south to north, and manage between ten and fourteen miles a day, staying at hotels, B&Bs and bunkhouses en route. Camping is permitted at recognized sites.

Although the path is clearly waymarked, you may want to check one of the many maps or guidebooks published: the **official guide**, published by Mercat Press (£16.99), includes a foldout map as well as descriptions of the route, with detailed cultural, historical, archeological and wildlife information. Further details about the Way, including a comprehensive accommodation list, can be found at ⓦwww.west-highland-way.co.uk, which also has links to tour companies and transport providers, who can take your luggage from one stopping point to the next.

cottage with a lochside garden. **Camping** is available two miles north, on the water at Milarrochy Bay (Ⓣ01360/870236; March–Oct), or, a couple of miles or so further up the road, at Cashel, a lovely, secluded Forestry Commission campsite also on the shores (Ⓣ01360/870234; mid-March to Oct).

Public transport ends at Balmaha, but another seven miles north through the woods brings you to the end of the road at **ROWARDENNAN**, a scattered settlement that sits below Ben Lomond (see p.319). Passenger ferries (Easter–Sept 2 daily; Ⓣ01301/702356, Ⓦwww.cruiselochlomond.co.uk) cross from Tarbert, on the west shore, and **accommodation** is available at the newly refurbished *Rowardennan Hotel* (Ⓣ01360/870273, Ⓦwww.rowardennanhotel.co.uk; ④), and, half a mile beyond, at a wonderfully situated SYHA **hostel** (Ⓣ0870/004 1148, Ⓦwww.syha.org.uk; March–Oct), a classic turreted Scots Baronial lodge with lawns running down to the shore. Nightlife centres on the hotel's *Clansman Bar*, with open fires and weekend live music.

Only walkers can continue further north up the lochside, where the only other settlement is seven miles north of Rowardennan at **INVERSNAID**, made famous by a poem of the same name by Gerard Manley Hopkins about a frothing waterfall nearby ("This darksome burn, horseback brown/His rollrock highroad roaring down…"). Though remote, the *Inversnaid Hotel* (Ⓣ01877/386223; ④) by the shore is mainly used by coach tours, who arrive via the only road in, the remote B829 from Aberfoyle, though walkers can sometimes snap up any free rooms. It's also possible to get to or from Inversnaid by **ferry** (£4 one-way/£5 return), which crosses from Inveruglas, directly opposite on the western shore. You'll have to phone the *Inversnaid Hotel* to make arrangements.

The western shore of Loch Lomond

Despite the roar of traffic hurtling along the upgraded A82, the **west bank** of Loch Lomond is an undeniably beautiful stretch of water. **LUSS** is without doubt the prettiest village in the region, with its prim, identical sandstone and slate cottages garlanded in rambling roses, and its narrow sand and pebble strand. However, its charms are no secret and its streets and beach can become crowded in summer. If you want to escape the hordes, pop into the parish **church**, which is a haven of peace and has a lovely ceiling made from Scots pine rafters and some fine Victorian stained-glass windows. You can pick up local information at the neighbouring **Luss Visitor Centre**. The modern *Lodge on Loch Lomond* (Ⓣ01436/860201, Ⓦwww.loch-lomond.co.uk; ⑦), just north of town, has a string of **rooms** with balconies and views over the loch, and serves decent meals in its restaurant, *Colquhoun's*. The *Coach House* tearoom is a must, a spruce and lively little place serving a range of teas, cakes, ciabattas, Orkney ice cream and its own take on haggis.

Ten miles north of Luss is the small settlement of **TARBET**, where the West Highland **train** – the line from Glasgow to Fort William and Mallaig, with a branch line to Oban – reaches the shoreline at the point where the A83 heads off west into Argyll; the A82 continues north along the banks of the loch towards Crianlarich. Tarbet has a small **tourist office** (April–Oct daily; Ⓣ01301/702260). At the pier over the road from the prominent *Tarbet Hotel* you can hop on an hour-long **loch cruise** run by Cruise Loch Lomond (Ⓣ01301/702356, Ⓦwww.cruiselochlomond.co.uk). The same operator also offers trips to Inversnaid and Rowardennan on the eastern side.

North of Tarbet, the A82 turns back into the narrow, winding road of old, making for slower but much more interesting driving. There's one more **train station** on Loch Lomond at Ardlui, at the mountain-framed head of the loch, but most travellers continue a couple of miles further north to **INVERARNAN**, where the Drover's Inn (T 01301/704234, W www.thedroversinn.co.uk; 4) is, arguably, the most idiosyncratic **hotel** in Scotland. The bar has a roaring fire, barmen dressed in kilts, weary hillwalkers sipping pints and bearded musicians banging out folk songs. Down the creaking corridors, past moth-eaten stuffed animals, are a number of supposedly haunted and resolutely old-fashioned rooms.

Crianlarich and Tyndrum

CRIANLARICH, some eight miles north of the head of Loch Lomond, is an important staging post on various transport routes, including the West Highland Railway which divides here, one branch heading due west towards Oban, the other continuing north over Rannoch Moor to Fort William. The West Highland Way long-distance footpath (see box, p.321) also trogs past. Otherwise, there's little reason to stop here, unless you're keen on tackling some of the steep-sided hills that rise up from the glen.

Five miles further north from here on the A82/A85, the village of **TYNDRUM** owes its existence to a minor (and very short-lived) nineteenth-century gold rush, but today supports little more than a busy service station and several characterless hotels. Right beside Tyndrum Lower railway station is a good campsite and small bunkhouse at *By The Way Hostel and Campsite* (T 01838/400333, W www.tyndrumbytheway.com), and, for a refreshingly different roadside dining experience, it's well worth trying the airy *Real Food Café* (daily until 10pm) on the main road for fresh, fast food that's locally sourced and cooked to order. At Tyndrum the road divides, with the A85 heading west to Oban, and the A82 heading for Fort William via Glen Coe.

The Trossachs

Often described as the Highlands in miniature, the **Trossachs** area boasts a magnificent diversity of scenery, with distinctive peaks, silvery lochs and mysterious, forest-covered slopes. It is country ripe for stirring tales of brave kilted clansmen, a role fulfilled by Rob Roy Macgregor, the seventeenth-century outlaw whose name seems to attach to every second waterfall, cave and barely discernible path. Strictly speaking, the name "Trossachs", normally translated as either "bristly country" or "crossing place", originally referred only to the wooded glen between **Loch Katrine** and Loch Achray, but today it is usually taken as being the whole area from **Callander** right up to the eastern banks of Loch Lomond, with which it has been grouped as one of Scotland's national parks.

The Trossachs' high tourist profile was largely attributable in the early days to Sir Walter Scott, whose novels *Lady of the Lake* and *Rob Roy* were set in and around the area. According to one contemporaneous account, after Scott's *Lady of the Lake* was published in 1810, the number of carriages passing Loch Katrine rose from fifty the previous year to 270. Since then, neither the popularity nor beauty of the region has waned, and in high season the place is jam-packed with coaches full of tourists as well as walkers and mountain bikers taking advantage of the easily accessed scenery. Autumn is a better time to come, when the hills are blanketed in rich, rusty colours and the crowds are thinner. In terms of where to stay, **Aberfoyle** has a rather dowdy air while **Callander** feels somewhat overrun, and you're often better off seeking out one of the guesthouses or B&Bs tucked away in secluded corners of the region.

If you're not driving, try **Demand Responsive Transport** (DRT), which offers a taxi-type service for the price of a bus fare (T 0844/567 5670, W www.aberfoylecoaches.com); you're advised to book trips 24hr in advance.

Rob Roy

A member of the outlawed Macgregor clan, **Rob Roy** (meaning "Red Robert" in Gaelic) was born in 1671 in Glengyle, just north of Loch Katrine, and lived for some time as a respectable cattle farmer and trader, supported by the powerful duke of Montrose. In 1712, finding himself in a tight spot when a cattle deal fell through, Rob Roy absconded with £1000, some of it belonging to the duke. He took to the hills to live as a brigand, his feud with Montrose escalating after the duke repossessed Rob Roy's land and drove his wife from their house. He was present at the Battle of Sheriffmuir during the Jacobite uprising of 1715, ostensibly supporting the Jacobites but probably as an opportunist: the chaos would have made cattle-raiding easier. Eventually captured and sentenced to transportation, Rob Roy was pardoned and returned to **Balquhidder** (see p.328), northeast of Glengyle, where he remained until his death in 1734.

Rob Roy's status as a local hero in the mould of Robin Hood should be tempered with the fact that he was without doubt a bandit and blackmailer. His life has been much romanticized, from Sir Walter Scott's 1818 novel *Rob Roy* to the 1995 film starring Liam Neeson, although the tale does serve well to dramatize the clash between the doomed clan culture of the Gaelic-speaking Highlanders and the organized feudal culture of lowland Scots, which effectively ended with the defeat of the Jacobites at Culloden in 1746. His **grave** in Balquhidder, a simple affair behind the ruined church, is one of the principal sights on the unofficial Rob Roy trail, though the peaceful graveyard is mercifully underdeveloped and free of the tartan trappings that plague parts of the Trossachs, predictably dubbed "Rob Roy Country" by the tourist board.

Aberfoyle and the Lake of Menteith

Each summer the sleepy little town of **ABERFOYLE**, twenty miles west of Stirling, dusts itself down for its annual influx of tourists. Though of little appeal itself, Aberfoyle's position in the heart of the Trossachs is ideal, with **Loch Ard Forest** and **Queen Elizabeth Forest Park** stretching across to Ben Lomond and Loch Lomond to the west, the long curve of Loch Katrine and Ben Venue to the northwest, and Ben Ledi to the northeast.

Don't come here for lively nightlife or entertainment, but for a good, healthy blast of the outdoors. From Aberfoyle you might like to wander north of the village to **Doon Hill**: cross the bridge over the Forth, continue past the cemetery and then follow signs to the **Fairy Knowe** (knoll). A toadstool marker points you through oak and holly trees to the summit of the Knowe where there is a pine tree said to contain the unquiet spirit of the Reverend Robert Kirk, who studied local fairy lore and published his inquiries in *The Secret Commonwealth* (1691). Legend has it that, as punishment for disclosing supernatural secrets, he was forcibly removed to fairyland where he has languished ever since, although his mortal remains can be found in the nearby graveyard. This short walk should preferably be made at dusk, when it is at its most atmospheric.

Practicalities

Regular **buses** from Stirling pull into the car park on Aberfoyle's Main Street. The adjacent **tourist office** (April–Oct daily 10am–5pm; Nov–March Sat & Sun only; ⓣ08707/200604) has full details of local accommodation, sights and outdoor activities. The nearby **Scottish Wool Centre** (daily: May–Sept 9.30am–5.30pm; Oct–April 10am–5pm; free) – a popular stop-off point with tour buses – is a glorified country knitwear shop selling all the usual jumpers and woolly toys as well as featuring daily seasonal displays of sheep gathering and shearing.

Accommodation options in Aberfoyle itself aren't all that inspiring. Head a mile west out of the town to *Creag-Ard House* (Ⓣ01877/382297, Ⓦwww.creag-ard.co.uk; ❺; Easter–Oct), which serves lovely breakfasts in a Victorian house overlooking Loch Ard. The **Lake of Menteith** (see below) is another beautiful place to stay: the *Lake of Menteith Hotel* (Ⓣ01877/385258, Ⓦwww.lake-hotel.com; ❼) at Port of Menteith has a lovely waterfront setting next to the Victorian Gothic parish church, as well as a classy restaurant. Near the lake in a beautiful hillside setting is *Inchie Farm*, a farmstay/B&B (Ⓣ01877/385233, Ⓦinchiefarm.co.uk; ❷).

For **camping**, a couple of miles south of Aberfoyle, off the A81 and on the edge of Queen Elizabeth Forest Park, there's *Cobleland* (Ⓣ01877/382392, Ⓦwww.forestholidays.co.uk; mid-March to mid-Jan), run by the Forestry Commission, which covers five acres of woodland by the River Forth (little more than a stream here). Further south, the excellent family-run *Trossachs Holiday Park* (Ⓣ01877/382614, Ⓦwww.trossachsholidays.co.uk; March–Oct) is twice the size and has **bikes** for rent.

The Lake of Menteith

About four miles east of Aberfoyle towards Doune, the **Lake of Menteith** is a superb fly-fishing centre and Scotland's only lake (as opposed to loch), so named due to a historic mix-up with the word *laigh*, Scots for "low-lying ground", which applied to the whole area. To rent a **fishing boat** or a rod contact the Lake of Menteith Fisheries (Ⓣ01877/385664; April–Oct). There are also some nice secluded spots along the shore for picnics and swims.

From the northern shore of the lake, you can take a little ferry out to the **Island of Inchmahome** (daily: April–Sept 9.30am–4.30pm; Oct 9.30am–3.30pm; HS; £4.70 including ferry) in order to explore the lovely ruined Augustinian abbey. Founded in 1238, **Inchmahome Priory** is the most beautiful island monastery in Scotland, its remains rising tall and graceful above the trees. The masons

Hiking and biking in the Trossachs

The Trossachs are ideal for exploring on **foot** or on a **mountain bike**. This is partly because the terrain is slightly more benign than the Highlands proper, but much is due to the excellent management of the **Queen Elizabeth Forest Park**, a huge chunk of the national park that lies between Loch Lomond and Loch Lubnaig. The main visitor centre for the area, David Marshall Lodge (see p.326), is just outside Aberfoyle, and is well worth a visit.

For **hillwalkers**, the prize peak is Ben Lomond (3192ft), best accessed from Rowardennan (see p.322). Other highlights include Ben Venue (2370ft) and Ben A'an (1520ft) on the shores of Loch Katrine, as well as Ben Ledi (2857ft), just northwest of Callander, which all offer relatively straightforward but very rewarding climbs and, on clear days, stunning views. Walkers can also choose from any number of waymarked routes through the forests and along lochsides; pick up a map of these at the visitor centre.

Bikers are served by a network of forest paths and one of the more impressive stretches of the National Cycle Network cutting through the region from Loch Lomond to Killin. If you don't have your own bike, head for the best **rental** place in the area, Wheels Cycling Centre (Ⓣ01877/331100, Ⓦwww.scottish-cycling.com), next to *Trossachs Tryst Backpackers* (see p.327) a mile and a half southwest of Callander; it stocks front or full suspension models, as well as baby seats and children's cycles. Try also the *Trossachs Holiday Park* (see above) on the A81 two miles south of Aberfoyle, and Mounter Bikes (Ⓣ01877/331052, Ⓦwww.callandercyclehire.co.uk) beside the visitor centre in the centre of Callander (see p.327).

employed to build the priory are thought to be those who built Dunblane Cathedral (see p.314); certainly the western entrance there resembles that at Inchmahome. The nave of the church is roofless, but in the choir are preserved the graves of important families from the surrounding area. Most touching is a late thirteenth-century double effigy depicting Walter, the first Stewart earl of Menteith, and his countess, Mary, who, feet resting on lion-like animals, turn towards each other and embrace.

Also buried here is the adventurer and scholar Robert Bontine Cunninghame Graham, once a pal of Buffalo Bill and Joseph Conrad, and first president of the National Party of Scotland. Five-year-old Mary, Queen of Scots was hidden at Inchmahome in 1547 before being taken to France, and there's a formal garden in the west of the island, known as Queen Mary's Bower, where she played, according to legend. Traces remain of an orchard planted by the monks, but the island is thick now with oak, ash and Spanish chestnut. Visible on a nearby but inaccessible islet is the ruined castle of **Inchtalla**, the home of the earls of Menteith in the sixteenth and seventeenth centuries.

Aberfoyle to Callander

North of Aberfoyle, the A821 road to Loch Katrine winds its way into the Queen Elizabeth Forest, snaking up **Duke's Pass** (so called because it once belonged to the duke of Montrose). You can walk or drive the short distance from Aberfoyle to the park's excellent **visitor centre** at David Marshall Lodge (daily: March–June, Sept & Oct 10am–5pm; July & Aug 10am–6pm; Nov & Dec 10am–4pm; Jan Sat & Sun 10am–4pm; Feb Thurs–Sun 10am–4pm; car park £2; ⓣ01877/382258), where you can pick up maps of the walks and cycle routes in the forest, get background information on the area's flora and fauna (there's a video-relay to the nests of local peregrine falcons, pine martens and ospreys) or settle into the café with its splendid views out over the tree tops. Adjacent to the centre is the Go Ape adventure course (April–Oct daily 9am–5pm; Feb & March Sat & Sun 9am–5pm; £30; bookings ⓣ0870/428 2710, ⓦwww.goape.co.uk), which involves an extended series of 40ft-high rope bridges, tarzan swings and high-wire slides though the forest. The only road in the forest open to cars is the **Achray Forest Drive**, just under two miles further on from the centre, which leads through the park and along the western shore of **Loch Drunkie** before rejoining the main road.

Loch Katrine

Heading down the northern side of the Duke's Pass you come first to **Loch Achray**, tucked under Ben A'an. Look out across the loch for the small **Callander Kirk** in a lovely setting alone on a promontory. At the head of the loch a road follows the short distance through to the southern end of **Loch Katrine** at the foot of Ben Venue (2370ft), from where the elegant Victorian passenger **steamer**, the SS *Sir Walter Scott* (April–Oct daily; £12 return; ⓣ01877/376315, ⓦwww.lochkatrine.co.uk), has been plying the waters since 1900, chugging up to the wild country of Glengyle. It makes various cruises each day, but only the first (departing at 10.30am) stops off at Stronachlachar most days, though on Wednesdays and weekends there's a second trip to Stronachlachar departing at 2.30pm; the shorter one-hour cruises don't make any stops (£11). A popular combination is to **rent a bike** from the Katrinewheelz (ⓣ01877/376366, ⓦwww.katrinewheelz.co.uk) hut by the pier, take the steamer up to Stronachlachar, then cycle back by way of the road around the north side of the loch.

From Loch Katrine the A821 heads due east past the tiny village of **Brig o'Turk**, where it's worth looking in on the *Byre Inn*, a tiny pub and classy restaurant set in an old stone barn with wooden pews and a welcoming open fire; it's the starting point for waymarked walks to lochs Achray, Drunkie and Venachar. The cosy, wooden-clad *Brig o'Turk Tea-Room* (Easter–Sept 11am–4pm) is also a good place to refresh after a walk or cycle. From here, carry on along the shores of Loch Venachar, where you'll find a stylish new building, *Venacher Lochside* (Ⓣ01877/330011, Ⓦwww.trossachs-leisure.co.uk), which houses an attractive café serving meals on the lochside terrace and a fishing centre offering boat rental and fly-fishing tuition.

Callander and around

CALLANDER, on the eastern edge of the Trossachs, sits on the banks of the River Teith at the southern end of the **Pass of Leny**, one of the key routes into the Highlands. Significantly larger than Aberfoyle, it suffers in high season for being right on the main tourist trail from Stirling through to the west Highlands. Callander first came to fame during the "Scottish Enlightenment" of the eighteenth and nineteenth centuries, with the glowing reports of the Trossachs given by Sir Walter Scott and William Wordsworth. Development was given a further boost when Queen Victoria chose to visit, and then by the arrival of the train line – long since closed – in the 1860s. Tourists have arrived in throngs ever since, as the plethora of restaurants, tearooms, gift shops and shops selling woollens and crafts testifies.

Callander's **tourist office** is situated in a converted church at Ancaster Square on the main street (Ⓣ08707/200628; March–Oct daily); there's **bike rental** at Mounter Bikes (Ⓣ01877/331052, Ⓦwww.callandercyclehire.co.uk), also on Ancaster Square.

Accommodation

Arden House Bracklinn Rd Ⓣ01877/330235, Ⓦwww.ardenhouse.org.uk. A grand Victorian guesthouse in its own gardens with good views and woodland walks from the back door. April–Oct. ❹

Burnt Inn House Brig o'Turk Ⓣ01877/376212, Ⓦwww.burntinnhouse.co.uk. Simple, farmhouse-style B&B right in the heart of the Trossachs countryside: a good alternative to staying in Callander. ❷

Callander Meadows 24 Main St Ⓣ01877/330181, Ⓦwww.callandermeadows.co.uk. Centrally located rooms in an attractive townhouse that has three comfortable en-suite rooms and a decent restaurant. Full board available. ❹

Roman Camp Country House Hotel Main St Ⓣ01877/330003, Ⓦwww.romancamphotel.co.uk. The town's upmarket option is this romantic, turreted seventeenth-century hunting lodge in twenty-acre gardens on the River Teith. ❼

Trossachs Tryst Invertrossachs Rd Ⓣ01877/331200, Ⓦwww.scottish-hostel.com. A friendly, well-equipped and comfortable 32-bed hostel and activity centre with self-catering dorms and family rooms, located a mile southwest of town down a turn-off from the A81 to Port of Menteith. Bike rental available. ❶

Eating and drinking

Despite Callander's tourist throngs, the town itself has few **restaurants** worth recommending. *Callander Meadows* (see above; restaurant closed Mon & Tues) serves up decent, freshly cooked lunches and dinners. Also on the main drag, at no.75 is *Mhor Fish*, is one of a new breed of fish and chip shops; it has a sustainable fish policy, daily specials and everything from snacks to bistro-style seafood dishes – the takeaway section serves fish suppers, burgers, pies and haggis. For coffee, cheeses and other deli items head for cheerful *Deli Ecosse*, beside the church on Ancaster Square. There's **pub food** at the convivial *Lade Inn* in Kilmahog, a mile west of Callander, where the owners are particularly keen on real ales, and there's an on-site shop selling bottled beers from all over Scotland.

North of Callander

North of town, you can walk or ride the scenic six-mile Callander to Strathyre (Route 7) Cycleway, which forms part of the network of cycleways between the Highlands and Glasgow. The route is based on the old Caledonian train line to Oban, which closed in 1965, and runs along the western side of Loch Lubnaig.

Beyond the northern end of Loch Lubnaig is tiny **BALQUHIDDER**, most famous as the site of the **grave of Rob Roy**, which you'll find in the small yard behind the ruined church. Refreshingly, considering the Rob Roy fever that plagues the region, his grave – marked by a rough stone carved with a sword, cross and a man with a dog – is remarkably understated. The village's tiny wood-panelled library – built by the laird as a distraction to the pub across the road – is now a tearoom (Easter–Oct daily 10am–5pm) serving freshly baked scones to passing cyclists and walkers. Avoid the plethora of Rob Roy-themed **accommodation** in Balquhidder, and drive six miles beyond the village to the award-winning *Monachyle Mhor* hotel (Ⓣ01877/384622, Ⓦwww.monachylemhor.com; ❼), an eighteenth-century farmhouse with stylish modern rooms and a terrific restaurant (open to non-residents, but book ahead). They specialize in locally sourced food – much of it from the family's farm and bakery – and there's the added bonus of lovely views over Loch Voil. On the road to the hotel is the unexpected sight of the Dhanakosa Buddhist retreat centre (Ⓣ01877/384213, Ⓦwww.dhanakosa.com) – they run weekend or week-long retreats here, with courses ranging from t'ai chi to hillwalking.

North of Balquhidder the busy A84 slides past Lochearnhead, at the western end of Loch Earn, and Killin, at the western end of Loch Tay, both of which are covered in the Perthshire chapter (see p.359 & p.363), before swinging west towards Crianlarich (see p.323) and the west coast.

Travel details

Trains

Balloch to: Glasgow Queen Street (every 30min; 50min).
Crianlarich to: Fort William (3–4 daily Mon–Sat, 1–3 on Sun; 1hr 50min); Glasgow Queen Street (6–8 daily Mon–Sat, 1–3 on Sun; 1hr 50min); Oban (3–4 daily Mon–Sat, 1–3 on Sun; 1hr 15min).
Falkirk to: Edinburgh (every 15–30min; 30min); Glasgow Queen Street (every 15–30min; 25min); Stirling (every 30min; 15min).
Stirling to: Aberdeen (hourly; 2hr 5min); Dundee (hourly; 55min); Edinburgh (every 30min; 1hr); Falkirk (every 30min; 30min); Glasgow Queen Street (every 20min; 25–40min); Inverness (3–5 daily; 2hr 55min); Perth (hourly; 30min).

Buses

Aberfoyle to: Callander (late June to mid-Oct 4 Thurs–Tues; 25min); Port of Menteith (late June to mid-Oct 4 Thurs–Tues; 10min).
Balloch to: Balmaha (every 2hr; 25min); Luss (hourly; 15min).
Callander to: Loch Katrine (late June to mid-Oct 4 Thurs–Tues; 55min).
Luss to: Tarbet (hourly; 10min).
Stirling to: Aberfoyle (4 daily; 45min); Callander (1–2 hourly; 45min); Dollar (every 2hr; 35min); Doune (1–2 hourly; 25min); Dunblane (hourly; 20min); Dundee (hourly; 1hr 30min); Edinburgh (hourly; 1hr); Falkirk (hourly; 30min); Glasgow (hourly; 50min); Inverness (every 2hr; 3hr 20min); Perth (hourly; 40min); St Andrews (every 2hr; 1hr 55min).

8

Fife

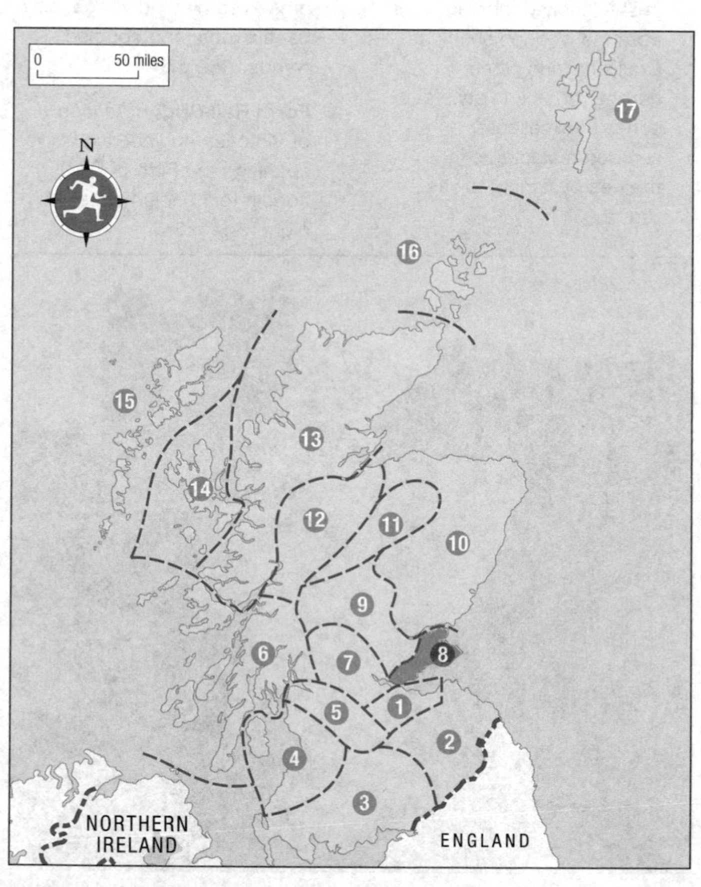
0
50 miles
N
17
16
15
13
14
12
11
10
9
6
7
8
1
5
2
4
3
NORTHERN IRELAND
ENGLAND

CHAPTER 8 # Highlights

* **Himalayas putting green, St Andrews** The world's finest putting course right beside the world's finest golf course; a snip at £1.50 a round. See p.333

* **The East Neuk** Buy freshly cooked lobster from the wooden shack at Crail's historic stone harbour or dine in style at a series of excellent seafood restaurants in the nearby fishing towns. See p.338

* **Falkland Palace** The former hunting retreat of the Stuart kings, an atmospheric semi-ruin set in lovely gardens within a charming village. See p.341

* **Culross** Scotland's best-preserved historic village, all pantile roofs and cobbled wynds. See p.344

* **Forth Rail Bridge** An icon of Victorian engineering spanning the Firth of Forth, floodlit to stunning effect at night. See p.347

▲ Golf at St Andrews

8

Fife

The ancient Kingdom of **Fife**, designated as such by the Picts in the fourth century, is a small area barely fifty miles at its widest point, but one which has a definite identity, inextricably linked with the waters that surround it on three sides – the Tay to the north, the Forth to the south, and the cold North Sea to the east. Despite its small size, Fife encompasses several different regions, with a marked difference between the rural north and the semi-industrial south. Tourism and agriculture are the economic mainstays of the **northeast** corner of Fife, where the landscape varies from gentle hills in the rural hinterland to windswept cliffs, rocky bays and sandy beaches. Fishing still has a role, but ultimately it is to **St Andrews**, Scotland's oldest university town and the home of the world-famous Royal and Ancient Golf Club, that most visitors are drawn. Development here has been cautious, and both the town itself and the surrounding area retain an appealing and old-fashioned feel. South of St Andrews, the tiny stone harbours of the fishing villages of the **East Neuk** are a deeply appealing extension to any visit to this part of Fife.

Inland from St Andrews, the central Fife settlements of Glenrothes, an unremarkable postwar new town, and Cupar, a more interesting market town, are overshadowed by the absorbing village of **Falkland** with its impressive ruined palace. In the **south**, the closure of the coal mines over the last thirty years has left local communities floundering to regain a foothold, and the squeeze on the fishing industry may well lead to further decline. In the meantime, a number of the villages have capitalized on their appeal and welcomed tourism in a way that has enhanced rather than degraded their natural assets; the perfectly preserved town of **Culross** is the most notable of these with its cobbled streets and historic buildings. Otherwise, southern Fife is dominated by the town of **Dunfermline**, a former capital of Scotland, and industrial **Kirkcaldy**, with the Forth rail and road bridges the most memorable sights of this stretch of coastline.

The main **road** into the region is the M90, which links the Forth Road Bridge northwest of Edinburgh with Perth. The A92 cuts a swathe across the county, linking Dunfermline, Glenrothes and the Tay Road Bridge in the north. However, there are innumerable back-road alternatives throughout Fife, with the coastal roads inevitably the most attractive. The **train** line follows the coast as far north as Kirkcaldy and then cuts inland towards Dundee, stopping on the way at Cupar and Leuchars (from where buses run to St Andrews). Exploration by public transport of the eastern and western fringes requires some planning as there is no train service and buses are few and far between. Fife's relatively flat terrain and network of quiet backroads have seen it marketed as great **cycle touring** country (Ⓦ www.fife-cycleways.co.uk), which holds true when the weather's fair, but it can be harder going with a cold wind whipping in off the North Sea.

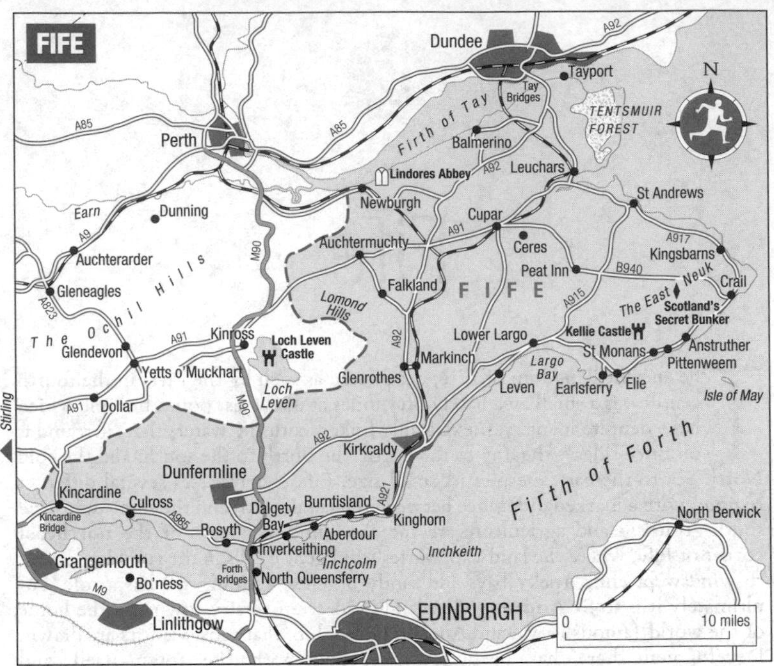

St Andrews and the East Neuk

Confident, poised and well groomed, if a little snooty, **ST ANDREWS**, Scotland's oldest **university town** and a pilgrimage centre for **golfers** from all over the world, is situated on a wide bay on the northeastern coast of Fife. Of all Scotland's universities, St Andrews is the one most often compared to Oxford or Cambridge, both for the dominance of gown over town and for the intimate, collegiate feel of the place. The university attracts a significant proportion of English students including, famously, Prince William, who spent four years studying here.

According to legend, the town was founded, pretty much by accident, in the fourth century. **St Rule** – or Regulus – a custodian of the bones of St Andrew in Patras in southwestern Greece, had a vision in which an angel ordered him to carry five of the saint's bones to the western edge of the world, where he was to build a city in his honour. The conscientious courier set off, but was shipwrecked on the rocks close to the present harbour. Struggling ashore with his precious burden, he built a shrine to the saint on what subsequently became the site of the **cathedral**; St Andrew became Scotland's patron saint and the town its ecclesiastical capital.

St Andrews isn't a large place, with only three main streets and an open, airy feel encouraged by the long stretches of sand on either side of town and the acreage of golf links all around. Almost the entire centre consists of listed buildings, while the ruined castle and cathedral have all but been rebuilt in the efforts to preserve their remains.

From St Andrews, the attractive beaches and little fishing villages of the **East Neuk** (*neuk* is Scots for "corner") are within easy reach, although the area can also be approached from the Kirkcaldy side. Though golf and coastal walks are a shared characteristic, the East Neuk villages have few of the grand buildings and bustle of

St Andrews, with old cottages and merchants' houses huddling round stone-built harbours in groupings that are fallen upon with joy by artists and photographers. A fun way to approach these settlements is on the **Fife Coastal Path** (Ⓦwww.fifecoastalpath.co.uk); it runs round the coast for 150 miles in total.

Arrival and information

St Andrews is not on the train line – the nearest **train station** is at Leuchars on the Edinburgh–Dundee line, five miles northwest across the River Eden, from where regular buses make the fifteen-minute trip into town. (When you buy your rail ticket to Leuchars, ask for a St Andrews rail-bus ticket which includes the bus fare.) Frequent **buses** from Edinburgh and Dundee terminate at the bus station on City Road at the west end of Market Street. The **tourist office** is at 70 Market St (April–Oct daily; Nov–March closed Sun; Ⓣ01334/472021).

Golf in St Andrews

St Andrews **Royal and Ancient Golf Club** (or "R&A") is the international governing body for golf, and dates back to a meeting of 22 of the local gentry in 1754, who founded the Society of St Andrews Golfers, being "admirers of the ancient and healthful exercise of golf". The game itself has been played here since the fifteenth century. Those early days were instrumental in establishing Scotland as the home of golf, for the rules were distinguished from those of the French game by the fact that participants had to manoeuvre the ball into a hole, rather than hit an above-ground target. It was not without its opponents, however – particularly James II who, in 1457, banned his subjects from playing since it was distracting them from archery practice.

The approach to St Andrews from the west runs adjacent to the famous **Old Course**, one of seven courses in the immediate vicinity of the town. The R&A's strictly private **clubhouse**, a stolid, square building dating from 1854, is at the eastern end of the Old Course overlooking both the eighteenth green and the long strand of the West Sands. The British Open Championship was first held here in 1873, having been inaugurated in 1860 at Prestwick in Ayrshire, and since then it has been held at St Andrews regularly, pulling in enormous crowds. Pictures of golfing greats from Tom Morris to Tiger Woods, along with clubs and a variety of memorabilia donated by famous players, are displayed in the admirable **British Golf Museum** on Bruce Embankment, along the waterfront below the clubhouse (April–Oct Mon–Sat 9.30am–5.30pm, Sun 10am–5pm; Nov–March Mon–Sat 10am–4pm; £6). Guided walks of the Old Course are available (see p.335), though any golf aficionado will savour a stroll around the immediate environs of the golf courses, where there are numerous golf shops, including a couple selling and repairing old-fashioned hickory-shafted clubs.

Where to play

It is possible to play any of the town's courses, ranging from the nine-hole Balgove course (from £8 per round) to the venerated **Old Course** itself – though for the latter you'll need a valid handicap certificate and must enter a daily ballot for tee times; if you're successful the green fees are £130 in summer. All this and more is explained at the clubhouse of the **St Andrews Links Trust** (Ⓦwww.standrews.org.uk), the organization that looks after all the courses in town, and is located alongside the fairway of the first hole of the Old Course. Arguably the best golfing experience in St Andrews, even if you can't tell a birdie from a bogey, is the **Himalayas** (April–Sept Mon–Sat 10.30am–6.30pm, Sun noon–6.30pm; £1.50), a fantastically lumpy eighteen-hole putting course in an ideal setting right next to the Old Course and the sea. Officially the Ladies Putting Club, founded in 1867, with its own clubhouse, the grass is as perfectly manicured as the championship course, and you can have all the thrill of sinking a six-footer in the most famous location in golf for a bargain price.

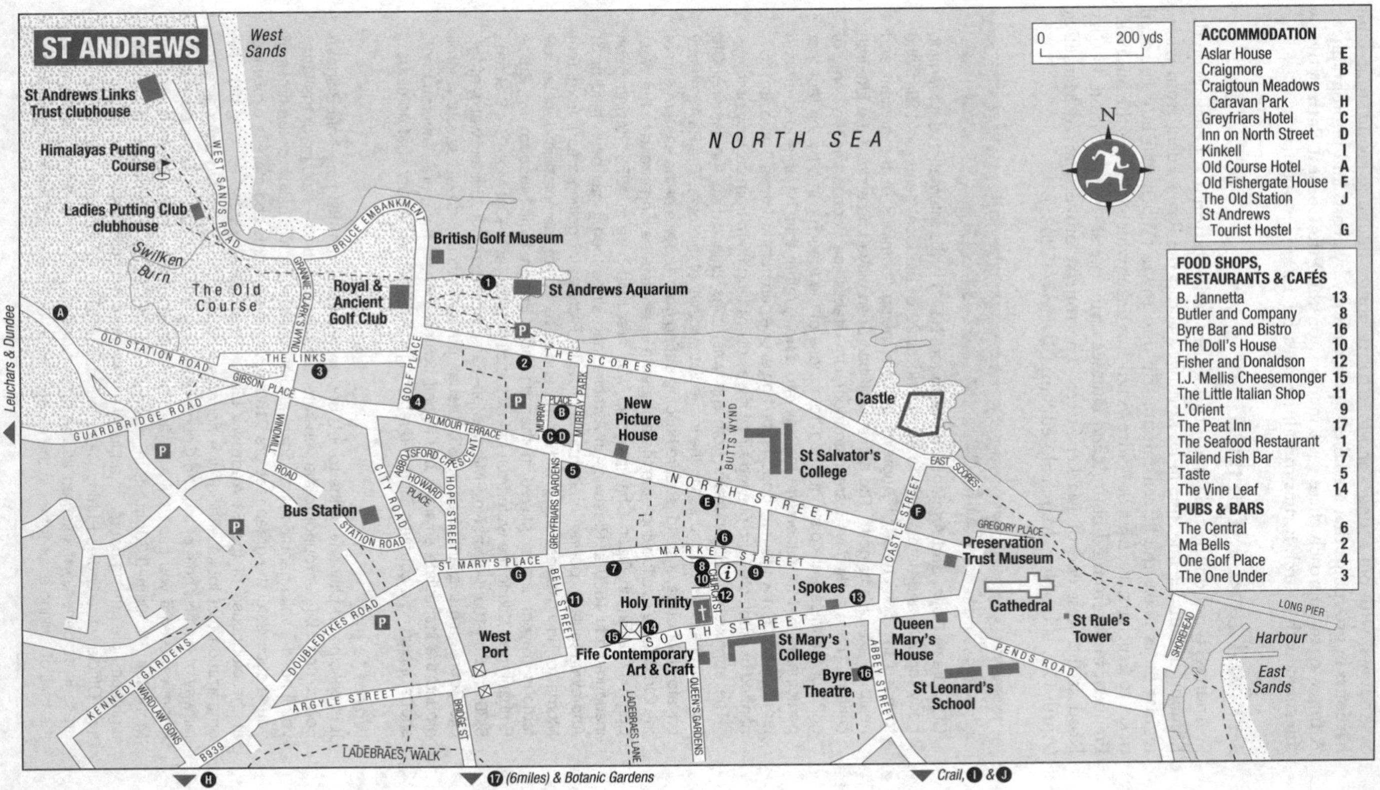
ST ANDREWS
NORTH SEA
N
0 200 yds
ACCOMMODATION
Aslar House E
Craigmore B
Craigtoun Meadows Caravan Park H
Greyfriars Hotel C
Inn on North Street D
Kinkell I
Old Course Hotel A
Old Fishergate House F
The Old Station J
St Andrews Tourist Hostel G
FOOD SHOPS, RESTAURANTS & CAFÉS
B. Jannetta 13
Butler and Company 8
Byre Bar and Bistro 16
The Doll's House 10
Fisher and Donaldson 12
I.J. Mellis Cheesemonger 15
The Little Italian Shop 11
L'Orient 9
The Peat Inn 17
The Seafood Restaurant 1
Tailend Fish Bar 7
Taste 5
The Vine Leaf 14
PUBS & BARS
The Central 6
Ma Bells 2
One Golf Place 4
The One Under 3
West Sands
St Andrews Links Trust clubhouse
Himalayas Putting Course
Ladies Putting Club clubhouse
Swilken Burn
The Old Course
Royal & Ancient Golf Club
British Golf Museum
St Andrews Aquarium
West Sands Road
Bruce Embankment
Grannie Clark's Wynd
The Links
Old Station Road
Gibson Place
Guardbridge Road
Golf Place
The Scores
Pilmour Terrace
Murray Place
Murray Park
New Picture House
Butts Wynd
St Salvator's College
Castle
East Scores
North Street
Castle Street
Gregory Place
Preservation Trust Museum
Cathedral
St Rule's Tower
Long Pier
Shorehead
Harbour
East Sands
Windmill Road
Bus Station
Station Road
City Road
Abbotsford Crescent
Howard Place
Hope Street
Greyfriars Gardens
St Mary's Place
Market Street
Church St
Bell Street
Holy Trinity
Spokes
South Street
West Port
Fife Contemporary Art & Craft
St Mary's College
Byre Theatre
Abbey Street
Queen Mary's House
Pends Road
St Leonard's School
Doubledykes Road
Kennedy Gardens
Wardlaw Gdns
Argyle Street
Bridge St
Ladebraes Walk
Ladebraes Lane
Queen's Gardens
B939
Leuchars & Dundee
H
17 (6miles) & Botanic Gardens
Crail, I & J

Tours and getting around

Most of the organized tours take place in summer only. An open-topped hop-on/hop-off **bus tour** (July & Aug daily 11am–3pm; £7) takes a one-hour spin around the main sights, although the town is compact enough to explore thoroughly on **foot**. Black Hart runs the **Twisted Tales tour** (nightly; 80min; £7.50; ⓣ0800/0842220, ⓦwww.blackhart.uk.com) seeking out the spooky spots around town. To get a bracing introduction to the importance of **golf** to the town, the St Andrews Links Trust runs guided walking tours of the Old Course, starting from the golf shop just behind the eighteenth green (July & Aug daily 11am–4pm; June Sat & Sun same times; £2.50; ⓣ01334/466694, ⓦwww.standrews.org.uk). Spokes, at 37 South St (ⓣ01334/477835), offers **bike rental**.

Accommodation

With St Andrews' wide-ranging appeal to visitors, there's no shortage of **accommodation** both in town and around, although average prices in all categories vie with Edinburgh's as the highest in Scotland. Upmarket **hotels** are thick on the ground, notably around the golf courses. There are plenty of **guesthouses**, though rooms often get booked up in the summer, when you should definitely book in advance. For **camping**, the nicest spot is *Craigtoun Meadows Caravan Park* (ⓣ01334/475959, ⓦwww.craigtounmeadows.co.uk; March–Oct), just over a mile west from the centre of town.

Hotels

Greyfriars Hotel 129 North St ⓣ01334/474906, ⓦwww.greyfriarshotel.com. Not the most inspiring place from the outside, but the interior styling is contemporary, the facilities in each room impressive and the rates decent. ❺

Inn on North Street 127 North St ⓣ01334/473387, ⓦwww.theinnonnorthstreet.com. Contemporary if slightly pricey option with a youthful feel and modern Gaelic style: tasteful rooms, wooden floors, DVD players and a lively bar and restaurant area. ❺

Old Course Hotel ⓣ01334/474371, ⓦwww.oldcoursehotel.co.uk. The best-known hotel in St Andrews, an imposing, luxurious resort located just a sliced two-iron from the seventeenth tee. Includes a spa. ❾

B&Bs, hostel and campus accommodation

Aslar House 120 North St ⓣ01334/473460, ⓦwww.aslar.com. A smart guesthouse in a three-storey townhouse with an unusual round tower at the back. ❺

Craigmore 3 Murray Park ⓣ01334/472142, ⓦwww.standrewscraigmore.com. A neat, non-smoking guesthouse with seven en-suite rooms in a very central location. ❺

Old Fishergate House North Castle St ⓣ01334/470874, ⓦwww.oldfishergatehouse.co.uk. Seventeenth-century townhouse in the oldest part of town with two spacious twin rooms full of period features. ❺

St Andrews Tourist Hostel St Mary's Place ⓣ01334/479911, ⓦwww.hostelsaccommodation.com/hostels. Handily placed backpacker hostel in a converted townhouse right above *The Grill House* restaurant with plenty of dorm beds, but no doubles. The cheapest option in town, and not the quietest.

University of St Andrews ⓣ01334/462000, ⓦwww.discoverstandrass.com. Rents out rooms in various student residences between June & Sept, all on a B&B basis. Self-catering houses also available. Single rooms from £31, twin ❹

Out-of-town accommodation

Kinkell By Brownhills ⓣ01334/472003, ⓦwww.kinkell.com. Countryside B&B in a lovely family farmhouse near the beach, about two miles south of town off the A917. ❺

The Old Station Stravithie Bridge ⓣ01334/880505, ⓦwww.theoldstation.co.uk. A couple of miles south of the town on the B9131 to Anstruther; you can stay in tasteful rooms in the main house (based around a former station waiting room) or in an imaginatively designed suite in an old railway carriage parked alongside. Main house ❺, carriage ❼

The Town

The centre of St Andrews still follows its medieval layout. On the three main thoroughfares, **North Street**, **Market Street** and **South Street**, which run west to east towards the ruined Gothic cathedral, are several of the original university buildings from the fifteenth century. Narrow alleys connect the cobbled streets; attic windows and gable ends shape the rooftops; and here and there you'll see the old wooden doors with heavy knockers and black iron hinges.

St Andrews Cathedral and around

The ruin of the great **cathedral** (visitor centre: April–Sept daily 9.30am–5.30pm; Oct–March 9.30am–4.30pm; HS; £4.20, joint ticket with castle £7.20; grounds: year-round 9am–5.30pm; free), at the east end of town, gives only an idea of the importance of what was once the largest cathedral in Scotland. Though founded in 1160, it was not finished and consecrated until 1318, in the presence of Robert the Bruce. On June 5, 1559, the Reformation took its toll, and supporters of John Knox, fresh from a rousing meeting, plundered the cathedral and left it to ruin. Stone was still being taken from the building for various local projects as late as the 1820s.

The cathedral site, above the harbour where the land drops to the sea, can be a blustery place, with the wind whistling through the great east window and down the stretch of turf that was once the central aisle. In front of the window a slab is all that remains of the high altar, where the relics of St Andrew were once enshrined. Previously, it is believed that they were kept in **St Rule's Tower**, the austere Romanesque monolith next to the cathedral, which was built as part of an abbey in 1130. From the top of the tower (a climb of 157 steps), there's a good view of the town and surroundings, and of the remains of the monastic buildings that made up the priory. Around the entire complex is a sturdy wall dating from the sixteenth century, over half a mile long and with three gateways.

Southwest of the cathedral enclosure lies **The Pends**, a huge fourteenth-century vaulted gatehouse which marked the main entrance to the priory, and from where the road leads down to the harbour, passing prim **St Leonard's**, once one of Scotland's leading private schools for girls, though now co-ed. The sixteenth-century, rubble-stonework building on the right as you go through the Pends is **Queen Mary's House**, where the queen is believed to have stayed in 1563. The house was restored in 1927 and is now used as the school library.

Down at the **harbour**, gulls screech above the fishing boats, keeping an eye on the lobster nets strewn along the quay. If you come here on a Sunday morning, you'll see students parading down the long pier, red gowns billowing in the wind, in a time-honoured after-church walk. The beach, **East Sands**, is a popular stretch, although it's cool in summer and bitterly cold in winter. A path leads south from the far end of the beach, climbing up the hill past the caravan site and cutting through the gorse; this makes a pleasant walk on a sunny day, taking in hidden coves and caves.

St Andrews Castle

Not far north of the cathedral, the rocky coastline curves inland to the ruined **castle** (same hours as cathedral; HS; £5.20, joint ticket with cathedral £7.20), with a drop to the sea on two sides and a moat on the inland side. Founded around 1200 and extended over the centuries, it was built as part of the palace of the bishops and archbishops of St Andrews and was consequently the scene of some fairly grim incidents at the time of the Reformation. There's not a great deal left of the castle, since it fell into ruin in the seventeenth century – most of what can be seen dates from the sixteenth century, apart from the fourteenth-century Fore Tower.

Around the university

A little way down North Street from the cathedral, and is housed in a picturesque sixteenth-century cottage with a low wooden door, is the **St Andrews Preservation Trust Museum and Garden** (June–Sept daily 2–5pm; Oct–May 2–5pm only when exhibitions are on; free; Ⓦ www.standrewspreservationtrust.co.uk), which presents an intimate picture of the town's history and glamorous golf connections.

Further along North Street is the enclosed quadrangle of **St Salvator's College**, the oldest part of the town's scattered **university campus**. St Andrews University is the oldest in Scotland, founded in 1410 by Bishop Henry Wardlaw, although James I, to whom the bishop was tutor, is the nominal founder (and was a great benefactor). The original building was on the site of the Old University Library and by the end of the Middle Ages three colleges had been built: St Salvator's (1450), **St Leonard's** (1512) on Pends Road and **St Mary's** (1538) on South Street. At the time of the Reformation, St Mary's became a seminary of Protestant theology, and today it houses the university's Faculty of Divinity. Its **quad** features beautiful gardens and some magnificent old trees, perfect for flopping under on a warm day. Almost all of the oldest and most attractive university buildings are found along North and South streets, with more recent parts of the campus dotted around the centre of town and further out.

The beaches, Botanic Garden and Aquarium

St Andrews has two great beaches, the **West Sands**, stretching for two miles from just below the R&A Clubhouse, and the shorter, more compact East Sands curving round from the harbour (see opposite). The West Sands are best known from the opening sequences of the Oscar-winning film *Chariots of Fire*; while they're still used by budding athletes, less energetic activities include sandcastle competitions, breath-taking dips in the North Sea, and birdwatching at the lonely north end. The blustery winds that are the scourge of golfers and walkers alike do at least make the beach a great place to fly a kite.

Another way to escape the bustle of the town is to head to the **Botanic Garden** on Canongate (daily: April–Sept 10am–7pm; Oct–March 10am–4pm; £2; Ⓦ www.st-andrews-botanic.org), a peaceful retreat just ten minutes' walk south of South Street. If you've got children in tow you may want to visit the huge **St Andrews Aquarium** (Feb–Dec daily 10am–5pm; Jan Sat & Sun 10am–5pm; £7.10; Ⓣ 01334/474786, Ⓦ www.standrewsaquarium.co.uk) on The Scores, at the west end of town close to the golf museum. Here you can see and touch marine life of all shapes and sizes, and there are observation pools and daily feeding sessions with the resident seals.

Eating and drinking

St Andrews has no shortage of **restaurants** and **cafés**. There are a number of blow-out options, but given the local student population, there's also plenty of choice at the cheaper end of the market, as well as lots of good **pubs**. For **picnic** food, you'll find tempting deli treats at Butler and Company, 10 Church St, the Little Italian Shop, 33 Bell St, or I.J. Mellis Cheesemonger, 149 South St. Fisher and Donaldson, at 13 Church St, has patisserie goodies as well as Scottish strawberry tarts and bridies. You'll also get a great **ice cream** at B. Jannetta, 31 South St – flavours include Scottish tablet and Irn Bru sorbet.

Restaurants and cafés

Byre Bar and Bistro Abbey St. Ⓦ www.byretheatre.com. One of the nicer spots in town for a leisurely coffee or light meal: risotto, burgers and steamed salmon are on the moderately priced menu.

The Doll's House 3 Church Square Ⓣ 01334/477422, Ⓦ www.dolls-house.co.uk. Stylish modern dishes based around Scottish meat and fish, with a continental feel to the outdoor tables.

L'Orient 62 Market St. ⓣ01334/470000, ⓦwww.l-orient.co.uk. Upbeat place serving reasonably priced Japanese and Thai food with a bit of European fusion thrown in for good measure.

The Peat Inn Cupar, 6 miles southwest of town ⓣ01334/840206, ⓦwww.thepeatinn.co.uk. With a reputation as one of Scotland's gourmet hot spots for the past 25 years, *The Peat Inn* offers fine dining featuring top local produce in an intimate dining room. Menus range from a three-course set lunch (£16) to a six-course tasting menu (£55). Also has eight plush if pricey suites attached (8). Closed Sun & Mon.

The Seafood Restaurant The Scores ⓣ01334/479475, ⓦwww.theseafoodrestaurant.com. Sister to its acclaimed namesake in St Monans (see p.340), this restaurant has an amazing location in a custom-built glass building on the beach between the Aquarium and the Old Course. The venue has as much wow-factor as its expensive, fish-dominated menu.

Tailend Fish Bar 130 Market St. A terrific and popular takeway – a modern twist on the trad chippy, dishing up locally sourced fresh fish. There are fish suppers with crisp batter and excellent chips, plus specials which may include sea bass, swordfish or skate.

Taste 131 North St. A small but cultured coffee shop selling good brews and a few snacks but not much else; it's one of St Andrews' bona fide hip hangouts and the best bet for breakfast.

The Vine Leaf 131 South St ⓣ01334/477497, ⓦwww.theseafoodrestaurant.com. A long-established, tucked-away place with a colourful dining room and a strong line in pricey seafood dishes, including lobster. Closed Mon.

Pubs and bars

The Central Market St. Prominent, popular old pub right in the heart of town serving real ales and pub grub.

Ma Bells 40 The Scores. In the basement of the *St Andrews Golf Hotel*, this is a lively pub serving cheap food and often thronged with students.

One Golf Place 1 Golf Place. Packed with golfers and music fans alike (there's live music at weekends) this is one of the most popular pubs in town.

The One Under 16 Pilmour Links. Hotel bar with views of the Old Course and gastro pub food.

Art and entertainment

As you'd expect of a university town, St Andrews has a healthy cultural scene. The place to start if you're interested in **visual arts** is Fife Contemporary Art and Crafts in the Town Hall, Queen's Gardens (generally Mon–Fri 10am–5pm; free), which hosts a few changing exhibits and looks after temporary shows around the town and in other parts of Fife. The other important arts venue in town is the **Byre Theatre** (ⓣ01334/475000, ⓦwww.byretheatre.com), which began life in an old cowshed in 1933 and now occupies a stylishly designed modern building on Abbey Street, complete with a pleasant café/bistro. Productions range from important Scottish drama to populist musicals. There's also a small **cinema**, the New Picture House (ⓣ01334/473509, ⓦwww.nphcinema.co.uk), on North Street.

The East Neuk

Extending south of St Andrews as far as Largo Bay, the **East Neuk** is famous for its series of quaint fishing villages, all crow-stepped gables and red pantiled roofs, the Flemish influence in the architecture indicating a history of strong trading links with the Low Countries. Inland, gently rolling hills provide some of the best farmland in Scotland, with quiet country lanes more redolent of parts of southern England than north of the border. Not surprisingly, the area is dotted with windy **golf courses**, though if you prefer your walk unspoilt there are plenty of bracing coastal paths, including one out to Fife Ness, the "nose" of Fife sticking out into the North Sea, or along the waymarked **Fife Coastal Path** (see p.347), which traces the shoreline all the way between St Andrews and the Forth Rail Bridge, and is at its most scenic in the East Neuk stretch. **Bus** #95 runs from Leven around the coast to St Andrews.

Well patronized by holiday-makers and weekenders from the central belt, the area's highlights are arts and crafts and good food; the **restaurants** are well known for serving fresh seafood, often complemented by produce from the fertile Fife farmland.

Crail

CRAIL is the archetypally charming East Neuk fishing village, its maze of rough cobbled streets leading steeply down to a tiny stone-built harbour surrounded by piles of lobster creels, with fishermen's cottages tucked into every nook and cranny in the cliff. Though often populated by artists at their easels and camera-toting tourists, it is still a working harbour, and if the boats have been out you can often buy fresh lobster and crab cooked to order from a small wooden shack right on the harbour edge. Beyond the harbour is a sand beach, and above are perched the grander merchants' houses, as well as twelfth-century **St Mary's Church**, where legend has it that the large blue stone by the gate was tossed there by the Devil, all the way from the offshore Isle of May (see below). You can trace the history of the town at the **Crail Museum and Heritage Centre**, 62 Marketgate (April Sat 10am–5pm, Sun noon–5pm; May–Sept Mon–Sat 10am–5pm, Sun noon–5pm; free; ⓣ01333/450869), which also doubles up as the town's **tourist office**. The **Crail Pottery**, 75 Nethergate (Mon–Fri 9am–5pm, Sat & Sun 10am–5pm), is an unmissable stop for its wide range of locally made pottery, while the **Jerdan Gallery**, 42 Marketgate South (daily except Tues 10.30am–5pm), displays an array of contemporary painting, sculpture and ceramics by top Scottish artists.

Accommodation choices include *The Hazelton*, 29 Marketgate North (ⓣ01333/450250, ⓦwww.thehazelton.co.uk; ❹), a pleasant B&B just across the road from the tourist office, and the *Marine Hotel*, 54 Nethergate South (ⓣ01333/450207; ❹), a traditional inn with sea views and a welcoming attitude. Also well worth considering is the upmarket B&B at *Cambo House* (ⓣ01333/450054, ⓦwww.camboestate.com; ❻), a grand house set among some stunning parkland and beautifully tended gardens near the small village of Kingsbarns, between Crail and St Andrews. The *Sauchope Links Park* (ⓣ01333/450460, ⓦwww.sauchope.co.uk; March–Oct) is a very pleasant **campsite**, a few miles north of Crail. Tucked into a wee cottage on the way down to the harbour, *Crail Harbour Gallery and Tearoom* (daily 11am–5pm) serves fresh **coffee**, nice cakes and toasted panini and has a terrace overlooking the Isle of May. Apart from that and Mrs Riley's shack selling lobster and crab down at the harbour (mid-April to early Oct Tues–Sun noon–4pm), there's nowhere notable to sit down and **eat**, particularly in comparison with what's on offer elsewhere in the East Neuk. The various hotels in the village serve bar meals, and you can get fish and chips from *Cassy's Chippy* on the High Street.

Anstruther and around

ANSTRUTHER is the largest of the East Neuk fishing harbours, but it too has an attractively old-fashioned air and no shortage of character in its houses and narrow streets. It is home to the wonderfully unpretentious **Scottish Fisheries Museum** (April–Oct Mon–Sat 10am–5.30pm, Sun 11am–5pm; Nov–March Mon–Sat 10am–4.30pm, Sun noon–4.30pm; £5). Set in an atmospheric complex of sixteenth- to nineteenth-century buildings with timber ceilings and wooden floors, it chronicles the history of the Scottish fishing and whaling industries with ingenious displays, including a whole series of exquisite model ships, built on site by a resident model-maker. Anstruther's helpful **tourist office** (April–Oct daily; ⓣ01333/311073) is next to the museum.

Located on the rugged **Isle of May**, several miles offshore from Anstruther, is a lighthouse erected in 1816 by Robert Louis Stevenson's grandfather, as well as the remains of Scotland's first lighthouse, built in 1636, which burnt coals as a beacon. The island is now a nature reserve and bird sanctuary, and can be reached by a daily boat (May & June no sailing Tues; July–Sept daily; £19; ⓣ01333/310103, ⓦwww.isleofmayferry.com) from Anstruther. Between April and July the dramatic sea cliffs are covered with breeding kittiwakes, razorbills, guillemots and shags, while inland there are thousands of puffins and eider ducks. Grey seals also make the occasional appearance. Allow between four and five hours for a round trip: an hour each way, and a couple of hours on the island. You'll also need warm, waterproof clothing.

Anstruther has a decent choice of places to stay and eat. For **B&B**, try *The Spindrift* (Ⓣ01333/310573, Ⓦwww.thespindrift.co.uk; ❺), on Pittenweem Road, or the more contemporary rooms attached to the middle-of-the-road *Waterfront* restaurant (Ⓣ01333/312200, Ⓦwww.anstruther-waterfront.co.uk; ❺) on Shore Street. Tucked in beside the museum in one of the village's oldest buildings, once a cooperage and smokehouse, is the East Neuk's most impressive fish **restaurant**, *The Cellar*, 24 East Green (Ⓣ01333/310378); booking is recommended. For decent fish and chips, head for the *Anstruther Fish Bar* at 44 The Shore, a regular award winner.

Scotland's Secret Bunker

Four miles inland from Anstruther on the B940 towards St Andrews is **Scotland's Secret Bunker** (April–Oct daily 10am–5pm; £9; Ⓦwww.secretbunker.co.uk), as idiosyncratic a tourist attraction as you are likely to find. Long a top-secret part of the military establishment, the bunker was opened to the public in 1994 following its decommissioning at the end of the Cold War. Above ground is an innocent-looking farmhouse, although the various pieces of military hardware parked outside and the rows of barbed wire fencing hint that something more sinister is afoot. From the farmhouse, you walk down a long ramp to the bunker, which comprises a vast subterranean complex of operations rooms 100ft below ground and encased in 15ft of reinforced concrete. In the event of a nuclear war this was to have become Scotland's new administrative centre with room for three hundred people; it has not been spruced up for tourists, and remains uncompromisingly spartan, with various rooms showing dormitories, radio rooms and kitsch James Bond-type control centres.

Pittenweem and around

West of Anstruther are more fishing villages, all undeniably attractive and rewarding. Two miles from Anstruther, **PITTENWEEM** has a busy harbour and fish market, as well as a number of small art galleries. The village has become something of an artists' colony and its annual arts festival (Ⓦwww.pittenweemartsfestival.co.uk) in early August is a unique event, with dozens of locals turning their houses into temporary art galleries for the week. Three miles north of Pittenweem on the B9171, **Kellie Castle** (April–Sept Thurs–Mon 1–5pm; Oct Thurs–Mon 1–4pm; £8.50; grounds year-round daily 9.30am–5.30pm; NTS; £3) has an unusual but harmonious mix of twin sixteenth-century towers linked by a seventeenth-century building. Abandoned in the early nineteenth century, it was discovered in 1878 by Professor James Lorimer, a distinguished political philosopher, who took on the castle as an "improving tenant". The wonderful **gardens**, where space is broken up by arches, alcoves and paths that weave between profuse herbaceous borders, were designed by the professor's son Robert, aged just 16. He later became a well-known architect specializing in restorations and war memorials; among his restoration works is the Hill of Tarvit in Cupar (see p.342).

Pittenweem almost merges into **ST MONANS**, the smallest of the East Neuk fishing villages – if you take the coastal footpath between the two you'll encounter a reconstructed stone windmill, a reminder of the area's link with the Low Countries, standing above some old saltpans. St Monans is worth a visit for its splendid *Seafood Restaurant* (Ⓣ01333/730327) at the far end of the harbour (there's a glamorous new namesake in St Andrews, see p.338). Beyond a dignified old bar is the smart restaurant perched right on the high tide line with panoramic views out to sea; the sophisticated cooking uses the freshest local fish and crustaceans.

Elie

Three miles on from St Monans is **ELIE**, gathered round a curve of golden-brown sand twelve miles south of St Andrews, and a popular escape for middle-class Edinburgh families who come for the bracing air and golf courses. This was once a popular bathing spot; east of Elie bay stands a tower built for Lady Janet Anstruther in the late eighteenth century as a summerhouse, with a changing room to allow her to bathe in a pool in the rocks below. The essential stop in Elie is the relaxed and convivial *Ship Inn*, overlooking the beach near the harbour, where you'll find great **bar food** and, come summer, lots of local banter in the beer garden. There's yet another excellent **restaurant** here, *Sangster's* (Ⓣ01333/331001, Ⓦwww.sangsters.co.uk; closed Mon) on the High Street. The sheltered bay is understandably popular for **watersports** – if you fancy a spin on a windsurfer or sailing dinghy, head for Elie Watersports (Ⓣ01333/330962, Ⓦwww.eliewatersports.com) at the harbour.

Central Fife

The main A92 road cuts right through **Central Fife**, ultimately connecting the Forth Road Bridge on the southern coast of Fife with the Tay Road Bridge on the northern coast. Inland from Kirkcaldy, the old mining towns of Cowdenbeath, Kelty, Lochgelly and Cardenden huddle together, routinely ignored by visitors shooting up to St Andrews on the coastal route or zooming along the M90 to Perth. Take the train, however, and you'll weave through this forlorn stretch as the line leaves the coast and heads inland. The main settlement of this region is the largely generic **Glenrothes**, ten miles inland from Kirkcaldy, a new town created after World War II in old coal-mining territory. Generally, the scenery in this part of the county is pleasant rather than startling, though it is worth making a detour to seek out **Falkland** and its magnificent ruined palace, and the sights around **Cupar**, the county town on the road to St Andrews.

Falkland

The **Howe of Fife**, north of Glenrothes, is a low-lying stretch of ground (or "howe") at the foot of the twin peaks of the heather-swathed **Lomond Hills** – West Lomond (1696ft) and East Lomond (1378ft). Nestling in the lower slopes of East Lomond is **FALKLAND**, whose narrow streets are lined with fine and well-preserved seventeenth- and eighteenth-century buildings. The village grew up around **Falkland Palace** (March–Oct Mon–Sat 10am–5pm, Sun 1–5pm; NTS; £10.50), which stands on the site of an earlier castle, home to the Macduffs, the earls of Fife. James IV began the construction of the present palace in 1500; it was completed and embellished by James V, and became a favoured country retreat for the royal court. Charles II stayed here in 1650 when he was in Scotland for his coronation, but after the Jacobite rising of 1715 and temporary occupation by Rob Roy the palace was abandoned, remaining so until the late nineteenth century when the keepership was acquired by the third marquess of Bute. He completely restored the palace, and today it is a stunning example of Early Renaissance architecture, complete with corbelled parapet, mullioned windows, round towers and massive walls. Inside there's a stately drawing room, the Chapel Royal (still used for Mass) and the Tapestry Gallery, swathed with splendid seventeenth-century Flemish hangings. Outside, the **gardens** are worth a look, their well-stocked herbaceous borders lining a pristine lawn. Don't miss the high walls of the oldest real (or royal) tennis court in Britain – built in 1539 for James V and still used.

Falkland is also a good base for **walks**, with several leading from the village; but for the more serious hikes to the summits of East and West Lomond, you have to start from Craigmead car park, about two miles west. **Accommodation** includes *Ladywell House B&B* (Ⓣ01337/858414, Ⓦwww.ladywellhousefife.co.uk; ❹), a fine Georgian country house half a mile from the village and set in walled gardens. The *Covenanter Hotel* (Ⓣ01337/857224, Ⓦwww.covenanterhotel.co.uk; ❸ in separate cottage; ❹ in hotel), is a comfortable traditional inn in the heart of the village with a great pub; attached to the hotel is *Luigino's*, a small restaurant serving wood-fired pizzas. *Kind Kyttock's Kitchen* on Cross Wynd is a little Scottish tearoom serving oatcake platters, shortbread and so on. Not far out of Falkland on the A912 you'll find a great little farm shop and **café**, *Pillars of Hercules Organic Farm* (daily 9am–6pm plus monthly restaurant night with live music; Ⓣ01337/857749, Ⓦwww.pillars.co.uk); you can **camp** here, and there's a bothy available to rent.

Cupar and around

Straddling the small River Eden and surrounded by gentle hills, **CUPAR** is the capital of Fife, despite the fact that St Andrews' star is these days a fair bit brighter. In 1276 Alexander III held an assembly in Cupar, bringing together the Church, aristocracy and local burgesses in an early form of Scottish parliament. For his troubles he subsequently became the butt of Sir David Lindsay's *Ane Pleasant Satyre of the Thrie Estaitis* (1535), one of the first great Scottish dramas.

Situated at the centre of Fife's road network, Cupar's main street is part of the main road from Edinburgh to St Andrews and is subsequently plagued with traffic jams. The **Mercat Cross**, stranded in the midst of the lorries and cars that grind through the centre, now consists of salvaged sections of the seventeenth-century original, following its destruction by an errant lorry some years ago.

One of the best reasons for stopping off at Cupar is to visit the **Hill of Tarvit** (daily: house April–Oct 1–5pm; gardens all year 9.30am–5.30pm; NTS; £8.50), an Edwardian mansion two miles south of town remodelled by Sir Robert Lorimer from a late seventeenth-century building. The house, formerly the home of the geographer and cartographer Sir John Scott, contains an impressive collection of eighteenth-century Chippendale and French furniture, Dutch paintings, Chinese porcelain and a restored Edwardian laundry. Also on the estate is a five-storey, late sixteenth-century **Scotstarvit Tower**, three-quarters of a mile west of the present house (keys available from the house April–Oct); a fine example of a Scots tower house, providing both fortification and comfort.

Practicalities

Cupar's **train station** is immediately south of the centre; **buses** from Dundee, Edinburgh, St Andrews and Stirling stop outside. If you want to **stay**, try *Westfield House* on Westfield Road (Ⓣ01334/655699, Ⓦwww.standrews4.freeserve.co.uk; ❹), an upmarket B&B set in a landscaped garden. There are some good **restaurants** in the area; follow the B940 east to the renowned *Peat Inn* (see p.338), or try the excellent *Ostler's Close*, 25 Bonnygate (Ⓣ01334/655574, Ⓦwww.ostlersclose.co.uk). During the day, you'll find simple sandwiches and home-baking at *Café Moka*, also tucked down a close at 29 Bonnygate.

Around Cupar

At **Cairnie Fruit Farm** just north of Cupar, kids may well be enthralled by a huge **maze** (April–June & Sept–Oct Tues–Sun 10am–5pm; July & Aug daily 9.30am–6pm; £4.50; Ⓦwww.cairniefruitfarm.co.uk), cut each summer in about five acres of maize; the corn grows to about 8ft, making it a serious navigational challenge. To refuel afterwards, the farm has lots of strawberries, raspberries and other soft fruit that you can pick yourself, and there's a good café and farm shop along with other activities such as go-carts.

A couple of miles southeast of Cupar, **CERES**, set around a village green, is a pleasantly slow-paced hamlet home to the **Fife Folk Museum** (April–Oct daily 10.30am–4.30pm; £3.50; Ⓣ01334/828180, Ⓦwww.fifefolkmuseum.org). Occupying several well-preserved seventeenth- to nineteenth-century buildings, it exhibits all manner of historical farming and agricultural paraphernalia. Also in the village is **Griselda Hill Pottery** (Mon–Fri 9am–5pm, Sat & Sun noon–5pm), where you can see brightly hand-painted pottery being made in a distinctive style known as Wemyss Ware – developed in Fife in the 1880s and highly prized by collectors.

The Tay coast

North of Cupar, Fife's **Tay coast** is a tranquil wedge of rural hinterland on the edge of the River Tay looking across to Dundee and Perthshire. Gentle hills fringe the shore, sheltering the villages that lie in dips and hollows along the coast.

LEUCHARS, five miles north of St Andrews, is known for its RAF base, from where low-flying jets screech over the hills, appearing out of nowhere and sending sheep, cows and horses galloping for shelter. There's a beautiful twelfth-century church in the village, with fine Norman stonework. Northeast of Leuchars, **Tentsmuir Forest**, which occupies the northeasternmost point of the Fife headland, is a nature reserve with a good beach and peaceful woodland walks. The main road, however, is busy with traffic heading for the **Tay Road Bridge**, which links Fife with Dundee. A couple of miles to the west, the current Tay **rail bridge** is the second to span the river on this spot, the first having collapsed in a terrifying disaster during a storm on December 28, 1879, which claimed the lives of around a hundred people in a train crossing the bridge at the time. The event was recorded by the poet William McGonagall, who has gone down in history as being responsible for some of the most banal verse ever written:

The storm Fiend did loudly bray,
Because ninety lives had been taken away,
On the last Sabbath day of 1879,
Which will be remember'd for a very long time.

There's a **camping** and **caravan** site (March–Oct; Ⓣ01382/552334) at **TAYPORT**, a popular resort a couple of miles east of the road bridge. Here the "silvery Tay" more than justifies its traditional description, shimmering in the light whatever the season. There are good views across the river from most points along the banks of Tay on the Fife side, though there's little of note until you get to **Lindores Abbey**, a now-ruined Benedictine settlement dating back to the twelfth century. The abbey is associated with the first records of whisky production in Scotland, exchequer rolls from 1494 indicating that James IV had placed an order for eight bols (about 400 bottles) while staying at Falkland Palace.

Southern Fife

Although the coast of **southern Fife** is predominantly industrial – with everything from cottage industries to the refitting of nuclear submarines – only a small part has been blighted by insensitive development. Thanks to its proximity to the early coal mines, the charming village of **Culross** was once a lively port which enjoyed a thriving trade with Holland, the Dutch influence obvious in its lovely gabled houses. It was from nearby **Dunfermline** that Queen Margaret ousted the

Celtic Church from Scotland in the eleventh century; her son, David I, founded an abbey here in the twelfth century. Southern Fife is linked to Edinburgh by the two **Forth bridges**, the red-painted girders of the rail bridge representing one of Britain's great engineering spectacles. East of the bridges are a string of historic coastal settlements dominated by the ancient royal burgh of **Kirkcaldy**, known as "The Lang Toun" for its four-mile-long esplanade. Largely industrial, it's unlikely to keep you for long; from here you can either head east for the picturesque villages of the East Neuk (see p.338), or turn north along the main A92 road towards Central Fife. Trains link the towns and villages of southern Fife, complemented by a good local bus service.

Culross

The A985 crosses the Forth Road Bridge, with unattractive views of the shipyard at Inverkeithing and the naval dock at Rosyth (now used as a port for ferry crossings to Zeebrugge in Belgium), before heading west along the Forth estuary to **CULROSS** (pronounced "Coorus"), one of Scotland's most picturesque settlements, all cobbled streets and squat cottages with crow-stepped gables. The town's development began in the fifth century with the arrival of St Serf on the northern side of the Forth at Cuileann Ros ("point where holly grows"), and is also said to have been the birthplace of St Mungo, founder of Glasgow Cathedral. Culross today is the best-preserved seventeenth-century town in Scotland, thanks in large part to the work of the National Trust for Scotland, which has been renovating its whitewashed, pantiled buildings since 1932. Stagecoach **bus** #78 between Dunfermline and Stirling passes through hourly.

For an excellent introduction to the burgh's history, head to the **National Trust visitor centre** (April, May & Sept Thurs–Mon noon–5pm; June–Aug daily noon–5pm; Oct Thurs–Mon noon–4pm; NTS; £8.50 joint ticket for Town House, Palace and Study), located in the **Town House** facing Sandhaven, where goods were once unloaded from ships. The upper floor of the house is where some of the four thousand witches executed in Scotland between 1560 and 1707 were tried and held while awaiting their fate in Edinburgh. Behind the ticket office is a tiny prison with built-in manacles. The most impressive building in the village is the nearby ochre-coloured **Culross Palace** (same hours), built by wealthy coal merchant George Bruce in the late sixteenth century; it's not a palace at all – its name comes from the Latin *palatium*, or "hall" – but a grand and impressive house, with lots of small rooms and connecting passageways. Inside, regular guided tours take you round the wonderful painted ceilings, pine panelling, antique furniture and curios; outside, dormer windows and crow-stepped gables dominate the walled court in which the house stands. The garden is planted with grasses, herbs and vegetables of the period, carefully grown from seed.

The charm of Culross is evident by wandering through its narrow streets or investigating crooked passageways with names such as "Wee Causeway" and "Stinking Wynd". Leading uphill from the Town House is a cobbled alleyway known as **Back Causeway**, complete with a raised central aisle formerly used by noblemen to separate them from the commoners. The alleyway leads up to the **Study** (same hours as visitor centre), a restored house that takes its name from the small room at the top of the corbelled projecting tower, reached by a turnpike stair. Built in 1610, its Dutch Renaissance-style oak panelling is further indication of the links with the Low Countries that are evident in much of Culross's architecture.

Further up the hill from the Study lie the remains of **Culross Abbey**, founded by Cistercian monks on land given to the Church in 1217 by the earl of Fife. The nave of the original building is a ruin – a lawn studded with great stumps of columns.

The choir of the abbey became the **parish church** in 1633; inside, wooden panels detail the donations given by eighteenth-century worthies to the parish poor, and a tenth-century Celtic cross in the north transept is a reminder of the abbey's origins. Many of the stones in the **graveyard** are eighteenth century, with symbols depicting the occupation of the person who is buried; the gravestone of a gardener has a crossed spade and rake as well as an hourglass with the sand run out.

There are very few **accommodation** options in Culross itself: one is *St Mungo's Cottage* (Ⓣ01383/882102, Ⓔmartinpjackson@hotmail.com; ❷), which offers B&B and has views out to the Forth.

Dunfermline

Scotland's capital until the Union of the Crowns in 1603, **DUNFERMLINE** lies inland seven miles east of Culross, north of the Forth bridges. This "auld, grey toun" is built on a hill, dominated by the **abbey** and ruined **palace** at the top. In the eleventh century, Malcolm III (Malcolm Canmore) offered refuge here to Edgar Atheling, heir to the English throne, and his family, who were shipwrecked in the Forth while fleeing the Norman Conquest. Malcolm married Edgar's Catholic sister Margaret in 1067, and in so doing started a process of reformation that ultimately supplanted the Celtic Church. Until the late nineteenth century, Dunfermline was one of Scotland's foremost linen producers as well as a major coal-mining centre, and today the town is a busy, sprawling place.

The Town

Dunfermline's **centre**, at the top of the hill around the abbey and palace, features narrow, cobbled streets, pedestrianized shopping areas and gargoyle-adorned buildings.

The abbey and palace

The oldest part of **Dunfermline Abbey** (April–Sept daily 9.30am–5.30pm; Oct–March Mon–Wed & Sat 9.30am–4.30pm, Thurs 9.30am–12.30pm, Sun 2–4.30pm; HS; £3.70; Ⓦwww.dunfermlineabbey.co.uk) is attributable to Queen Margaret, who began building a Benedictine priory in 1072, the remains of which can still be seen beneath the nave of the present church; her son, **David I**, raised the priory to the rank of abbey in the following century. In 1303, during the first of the **Wars of Independence**, the English king Edward I occupied the palace, had the church roof stripped of lead to provide ammunition for his army's catapults, and also appears to have ordered the destruction of most of the monastery buildings. **Robert the Bruce** helped rebuild the abbey and when he died of leprosy was buried here, although his body went undiscovered until building began on a new parish church in 1821. Inside, the stained glass is impressive, and the thick columns are artfully carved with chevrons, spirals and arrowheads.

The guesthouse of Margaret's Benedictine monastery, south of the abbey, became the **palace** in the sixteenth century under James VI, who gave both it and the abbey to his consort, Queen Anne of Denmark. Charles I, the last monarch to be born in Scotland, entered the world here in 1600. Today, all that is left of the palace is a long sandstone facade, especially impressive when silhouetted against the evening sky.

Near the entrance to the abbey, pink-harled **Abbot House** (daily 10am–5pm; Nov–Feb closes 4pm; £4; Ⓦwww.abbothouse.co.uk), possibly fourteenth-century, has been used as an iron foundry, an art school and a doctor's surgery. Now a museum, it houses a rather haphazard array of exhibits and "experiences" designed to bring different parts of Dunfermline's past to life, from an audiovisual ghost to a 1960s living room. It also has a good café (see p.346).

Pittencrieff Park and around

Pittencrieff Park, known to locals as "the Glen", covers a huge area in the centre of Dunfermline, and is an attractive green haven. Bordering the ruined palace, the 76-acre park used to be owned by the lairds of Pittencrieff, whose 1610 estate house, built of stone pillaged from the palace, still stands within the grounds. In 1902, however, the entire plot was purchased by rags-to-riches industrialist and philanthropist Andrew Carnegie, who donated it to his home town. This was just as much sweet revenge as beneficent public-spiritedness: the young Carnegie had been banned from the estate, according to a former laird's edict that no Morrison would pass through the gates. Since his mother had been a Morrison, Carnegie could do little more than gaze through the bars on the one day a year that the estate was open to the public. Today **Pittencrieff House** (daily: April–Sept 11am–5pm; Oct–March 11am–4pm; free) has exhibits on local history, and the glasshouses are filled with exotic blooms.

Just beyond the southeast corner of the park, the modest little cottage at the bottom of St Margaret Street is **Andrew Carnegie's Birthplace** (March–Dec Mon–Sat 11am–5pm, Sun 2–5pm; free; Ⓦwww.carnegiebirthplace.com). The son of a weaver, Carnegie (1835–1919) lived upstairs with his family as a child, while the room below housed his father's loom shop. When the family emigrated to America in 1848, Carnegie worked first on the railroads and then in the iron and steel industries; he began acquiring steel-production firms in the 1870s and was so successful that by the time he retired in 1901 he was one of the richest men in the world. For the next eighteen years he devoted himself to giving the money away, endowing educational establishments and free libraries around the world, including some six hundred in Britain.

Practicalities

Trains from Edinburgh stop at Dunfermline's **train station**, halfway down the long hill of St Margaret's Drive, southeast of the centre. It's a fifteen-minute walk up the hill from here to the **tourist office** (April–June & Sept Mon–Sat 9am–5pm, Sun 11am–4pm; July–Aug Mon–Sat 9am–5.30pm, Sun 11am–4pm; Oct–March Mon–Sat 9am–5pm; Ⓣ01383/720999) at 1 High St, immediately opposite the City Chambers. An hourly bus from Edinburgh comes in at the **bus station**, in the unprepossessing Kingsgate Centre, on the north side of town. It's not an obvious town for a stopover, but you could try traditional *Davaar House Hotel*, 126 Grieve St (Ⓣ01383/721886, Ⓦwww.davaar-house-hotel.com; ❺), or the more affordable *Hillview House* B&B, 9 Aberdour Rd (Ⓣ01383/726278, Ⓦhillviewhousebb.co.uk; ❷). For something to **eat**, the best choice is the café at Abbot House (see p.345), serving home-made soup and cakes in the barrel-vaulted interior or outside in the pretty herb garden. *The Old Inn*, just down Kirkgate, serves bar meals and has *The Creepy Wee Pub* right next door.

The Forth bridges to Kirkcaldy

Fife's **south coast** curves sharply north at the mouth of the Firth of Forth, exposing the towns and villages to an icy east wind that somewhat undermines the sunshine image of the beaches. The highlight of the coast is one of the largest man-made structures in Scotland, the impressive Forth Rail Bridge, which joins Fife at **North Queensferry**. East from here you'll find a straggle of Fife fishing communities such as **Aberdour** and **Kinghorn** which have depended on the sea for centuries, and now make popular, although not especially attractive, holiday spots as well as being part of Edinburgh's commuter belt. The fast route from the Forth Road Bridge to Kirkcaldy and the rest of Fife is along the inland A92 dual carriageway; a pleasant but more time-consuming alternative route is along the A921 which follows the northern shore of the Firth. Both the **train** line from Inverkeithing and the twice-hourly **buses** #7 and #7a from Dunfermline stop at all towns, making it quite possible to take on a section of the 81-mile-long **Fife Coastal Path**, a waymarked walking trail which begins underneath the Forth Rail Bridge at North Queensferry and links every coastal settlement including Kirkcaldy, Crail and St Andrews, finishing up at the Tay Road Bridge at Newport-on-Tay (details and leaflets available from local tourist offices).

North Queensferry

Cowering on a rocky outcrop beneath the Forth bridges, **NORTH QUEENSFERRY** is a small fishing village which was once a nineteenth-century bathing resort. Everything in North Queensferry is quite literally overshadowed by the two great bridges, each about a mile and a half in length, which traverse the **Firth of Forth** at its narrowest point. The cantilevered **Forth Rail Bridge**, built from 1883 to 1890 by Sir John Fowler and Benjamin Baker, ranks among the supreme achievements of Victorian engineering. Some fifty thousand tons of steel were used in the construction of a design that manages to express grace as well as might.

Derived from American models, the suspension format chosen for the **Forth Road Bridge** alongside makes an interesting modern complement to the older structure. Erected between 1958 and 1964, it finally killed off a 900-year-old ferry, and now attracts a heavy volume of traffic. For the best **panorama** of the rail bridge, make use of the pedestrian and cycle lane on the east side of the road bridge. For more on the bridge head to the museum in South Queensferry (see p.134).

Tucked underneath the mighty geometry of the rail bridge is **Deep Sea World** (Mon–Fri 10am–5pm, Sat & Sun 10am–6pm; £12; Ⓣ01383/411880, Ⓦwww.deepseaworld.com), a popular family attraction whose highlight is a huge aquarium with the world's largest underwater viewing tunnel, through which you glide on a moving walkway while sharks and conger eels swim past. You can see the sharks being fed by divers (Wed & Sat 1pm), or for a few more thrills, get into the tank alongside them. The two-hour session, which includes about twenty minutes in the water, costs £165. Bookings are essential, and it's for over 16-year-olds only, but you don't need a dive qualification.

One of the best places to **eat** in southern Fife is the *Wee Restaurant*, 17 Main St (Ⓣ01383/616263, Ⓦwww.theweerestaurant.co.uk; closed Mon), an unassuming venue serving pleasantly simple but tasty seasonal food at reasonable prices.

Aberdour

Four miles east of North Queensferry, **ABERDOUR** clings to the walls of its **castle** (April–Sept daily 9.30am–5.30pm; Oct–March Mon–Wed, Sat & Sun 9.30am–4.30pm; HS; £4) at the southern end of the main street. Once a Douglas stronghold, the castle is on a comparatively modest scale, with gently sloping lawns, and a large enclosed seventeenth-century garden and terraces. There's little else to see here apart from the town's popular **silver sands** beach which, along with its watersports, golf and sailing, has earned Aberdour the rather optimistic soubriquet the "Fife Riviera". Off Aberdour is **Inchcolm Island**, with a ruined abbey dating back to 1123; to get to the island you have to join a boat trip leaving from South Queensferry (see p.134).

Kinghorn

Shortly before reaching **KINGHORN**, the coastal road from Aberdour via Burntisland passes a **Celtic cross** commemorating Alexander III, the last of the Celtic kings, who plunged over the cliff near here one night in 1286 when his horse stumbled. At the southern end of town, a hill lined with Spanish-style villas leads down to the waterfront and the beach at **Pettycur Bay**, where fishing boats cluster round the small harbour and brightly coloured lobster nets dot the sands. There's an interesting diversion inland by pretty Kinghorn Loch, where Craigencalt Farm Ecology Centre is home to the UK's first **Earthship** (Mon–Thurs 9am–5pm, Fri 9am–6pm; tours £5; ⓣ01592/891884, ⓦwww.sci-scotland.org.uk), a diminutive house built into the hillside from recycled materials such as aluminium cans and old car tyres and providing its own heating, power, water and sewage treatment. Even if the Earthship isn't open, you can wander around the gardens beside it where polytunnels, a waterwheel, wind turbine, compost bins and beds of vegetables and wild flowers offer a healthy-looking vision of sustainable living.

Kirkcaldy

KIRKCALDY (pronounced "kir-coddy"), birthplace of the eighteenth-century political economist Adam Smith, doesn't hold a great deal of interest for the visitor as its charms have been largely obliterated by overdevelopment. If you're here in mid-April, you'll see the historic **Links Market** (ⓦwww.linksmarket.org.uk), a week-long funfair that dates back to 1305 and is possibly the largest street fair in Britain. The town's history is chronicled in its **Museum and Art Gallery** (Mon–Sat 10.30am–5pm, Sun 2–5pm; free) in the colourful War Memorial Gardens between the train and bus stations, a short way uphill from the front. The museum covers everything from archeological discoveries to the tradition of the local Wemyss Ware pottery. Since its inception in 1925, the gallery has built up its collection to around three hundred works by some of Scotland's finest painters from the late eighteenth century onwards, including paintings by the portraitist Sir Henry Raeburn, the historical painter Sir David Wilkie, the Scottish Colourists, the Glasgow Boys and William McTaggart. For a town known primarily for linoleum production and with a reputation firmly rooted in the prosaic, the gallery is an unexpected draw.

Travel details

Trains

Dunfermline to: Edinburgh (every 30min; 40min); Kirkcaldy (every 30min; 40min).
Kirkcaldy to: Aberdeen (hourly; 2hr 15min); Dundee (hourly; 45min); Edinburgh (every 30min; 50min); Perth (hourly; 45min).
Leuchars (for St Andrews) to: Aberdeen (1–2 hourly; 1hr 30min); Dundee (1–2 hourly; 15min); Edinburgh (1–2 hourly; 1hr).

Buses

Dumfermline to: Culross (hourly; 20min); Edinburgh (every 30min; 40min); Glasgow (twice hourly; 1hr 10min); Kirkcaldy (hourly; 30min); Stirling (every 2hr; 1hr 15min).
Glenrothes to: Edinburgh (hourly; 1hr 10min); Glasgow (hourly; 1hr 45min); Kirkcaldy (every 30min; 30min); St Andrews (hourly; 40min).
Kirkcaldy to: Anstruther (hourly; 55min); Edinburgh (hourly; 1hr 5min); Glasgow (hourly; 1hr 40min); St Andrews (twice hourly; 1hr).
St Andrews to: Dundee (every 15min; 35min); Dunfermline (hourly; 1hr 15min); Edinburgh (twice hourly; 1hr 50min); Glasgow (twice hourly; 2hr 25min); Glenrothes (hourly; 40min); Kirkcaldy (twice hourly; 1hr); Stirling (every 2hr; 2hr).

Ferries

Rosyth to: Zeebrugge (3 weekly; 18hr).

9

Perthshire

0
50 miles
N
17
16
15
13
14
12
11
10
9
6
7
8
5
1
2
4
3
NORTHERN
IRELAND
ENGLAND

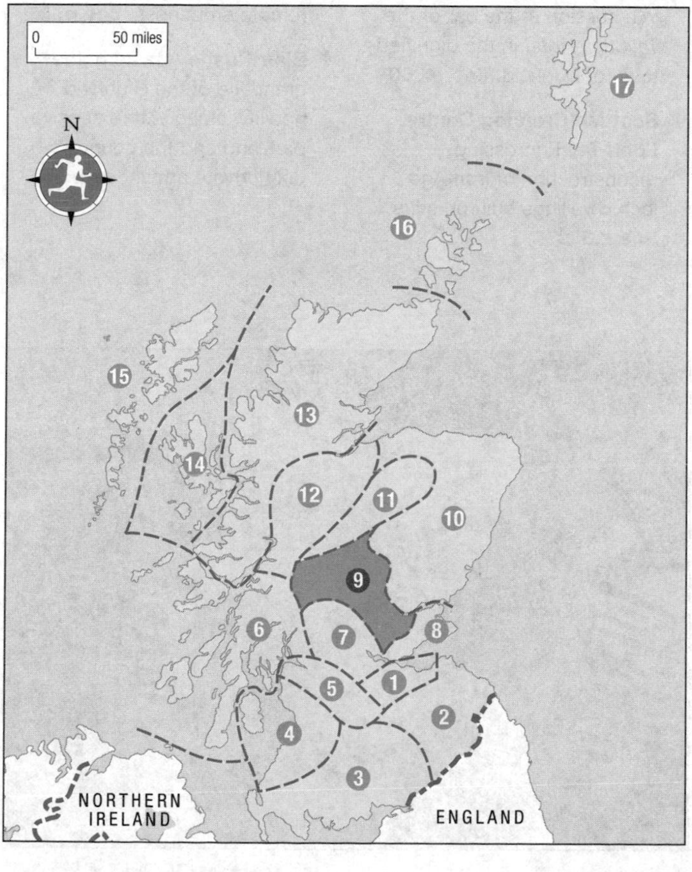

CHAPTER 9

Highlights

- **The Fergusson Gallery, Perth** A touch of Antibes in Perthshire: the gallery celebrates the vibrant work of J.D. Fergusson and his dancer wife Margaret Morris. **See p.353**
- **Folk music, Dunkeld** Join in a session at the bar of the *Taybank Hotel* in the dignified town of Dunkeld. **See p.360**
- **Scottish Crannog Centre, Loch Tay** Engrossing reconstruction of Iron Age loch dwellings built on stilts. **See p.362**
- **Schiehallion** Scale Perthshire's "fairy mountain" for the views over lochs, hills, glens and moors. **See p.366**
- **Rannoch Moor** One of the most inaccessible places in Scotland, where hikers can discover a true sense of remote emptiness. **See p.366**
- **Blair Castle** A taste of the grand life of the Highland nobility, along with extensive parkland and the country's only private army. **See p.367**

▲ Live music at the *Taybank Hotel*

Perthshire

Genteel, attractive **Perthshire** is, in many ways, the epitome of well-groomed rural Scotland. An area of gentle glens, mature woodland, rushing rivers and peaceful lochs, it's the long-established domain of Scotland's well-to-do country set. First settled over eight thousand years ago, it was ruled by the Romans and then the Picts before Celtic missionaries established themselves, enjoying the amenable climate, fertile soil and ideal defensive and trading location.

Occupying a strategic position at the mouth of the River Tay, the ancient town of **Perth** has as much claim as Stirling to be the gateway to the Highlands. Salmon, wool

Out and about in Perthshire

To many, Perthshire is a celebration of the great outdoors, with **activities** from gentle strolls through ancient oak forests to white-knuckle rides down frothing waterfalls. The variety of landscapes and their relative accessibility from the central belt has also led to a significant number of operators being based in the area. Many of these are linked to the tourist board's **Perthshire Adventure Line** (Ⓣ01887/829010 Ⓦwww.perthshire.co.uk/adventure), which gives advice and contacts. For canyoning, cliff-jumping and "sphere-ing", which involves tumbling down a hillside inside a giant plastic ball, get in touch with adrenaline junkies **Nae Limits** (Ⓣ01796/482600, Ⓦwww.naelimits.co.uk), based in Dunkeld and Ballinluig. For rafting on larger craft through the best rapids on the Tay at Grandtully, try **Splash** (Ⓣ01887/829706, Ⓦwww.rafting.co.uk) or **Freespirits** (Ⓣ01887/840400, Ⓦwww.freespirits-online.co.uk), both based in or near Aberfeldy. Also in Aberfeldy is the **National Kayak School** (Ⓦwww.nationalkayakschool.com) and the rather more sedate **Highland Safaris** (Ⓣ01887/820071, Ⓦwww.highlandsafaris.net), which offers an introduction to wild Scotland in which you're taken by four-wheel-drive vehicle to search for golden eagle eyries, stags and pine martens (see p.362).

and, by the sixteenth century, whisky – Bell's, Dewar's and the Famous Grouse brands all hail from this area – were exported from here. At nearby **Scone**, Kenneth MacAlpine established the capital of the kingdom of the Scots and the Picts in 846. When this settlement was washed away by floods in 1210, William the Lion founded Perth as a royal burgh and it stood as Scotland's capital until the mid-fifteenth century.

Rural Perthshire is dominated by the gathering mountains of the Highlands, topography that tolerates little development. There's plenty of good agricultural land, however, and the area is dotted with neat, confident towns and villages like **Crieff**, at the heart of the rolling Strathearn Valley, **Dunkeld**, with its mature trees and lovely ruined cathedral, and **Aberfeldy**, set deep amid farmland east of Loch Tay. Among the wealth of historical sites in Perthshire is splendid Baronial **Blair Castle** north of Pitlochry and the impressive Italianate gardens at **Drummond Castle** near Crieff.

North and west of Perth, **Highland Perthshire** begins to weave its charms: mighty woodlands blend with gorgeously rich scenery, particularly along the banks of the River Tay, overlooked by **Ben Lawers**, the area's tallest peak. Further north, the countryside becomes more sparsely populated and spectacular, with some wonderful walking country, especially around **Pitlochry**, **Blair Atholl** and the wild expanses of **Rannoch Moor** to the west.

Transport connections in the region are at their best if you head straight north from Perth, along the main A9 road and train line to Inverness, but buses – albeit often infrequent – also serve the more remote areas.

Perth and around

Surrounded by fertile agricultural land and beautiful scenery, the bustling market town of **PERTH** was Scotland's capital for several centuries. During the reign of James I, Parliament met here on several occasions, but its glory was short-lived: the king was murdered in the town's Dominican priory in 1437 by Sir Robert Graham, who was captured in the Highlands and tortured to death in Stirling. In May 1559, during the Reformation, John Knox preached a rousing sermon in St John's Kirk, which led to the destruction (by those Knox later condemned as "the rascal multitude") of the town's four monasteries, an event that quickened the pace of reform in Scotland. Despite decline in the seventeenth century, the community expanded in the eighteenth and has prospered ever since; today the whisky and insurance trades employ significant numbers, and Perth remains an important town. It has a long history in **livestock trading**, a tradition continued throughout the year, with regular Aberdeen Angus shows and sales from June to September, while its position at the heart of one of Scotland's richest food-producing areas encouraged a regular **farmers' market**, which takes place on King Edward Street in the centre of town on the first Saturday of every month (9am–2pm; Ⓦwww.perthfarmersmarket.co.uk).

Arrival, information and accommodation

Perth is on the main train lines north from Edinburgh and Glasgow and is well connected by bus; the **bus** and **train stations** are on opposite sides of the road at the west end of town where Kings Place runs into Leonard Street. The **tourist office** is a five-minute walk north on West Mill Street (April–Oct daily; Nov–March Tues–Sat 10am–4pm; Ⓣ01738/450600, Ⓦwww.perthshire.co.uk).

Of the numerous central **hotels**, aim for the fourteen-bedroom *Parklands Hotel*, 2 St Leonards Bank (Ⓣ01738/622451, Ⓦwww.theparklandshotel.com; ❻), close to the train station, which has a touch of contemporary styling with flatscreen TVs and broadband in all rooms; it has a good restaurant and bistro. Decent **B&Bs**

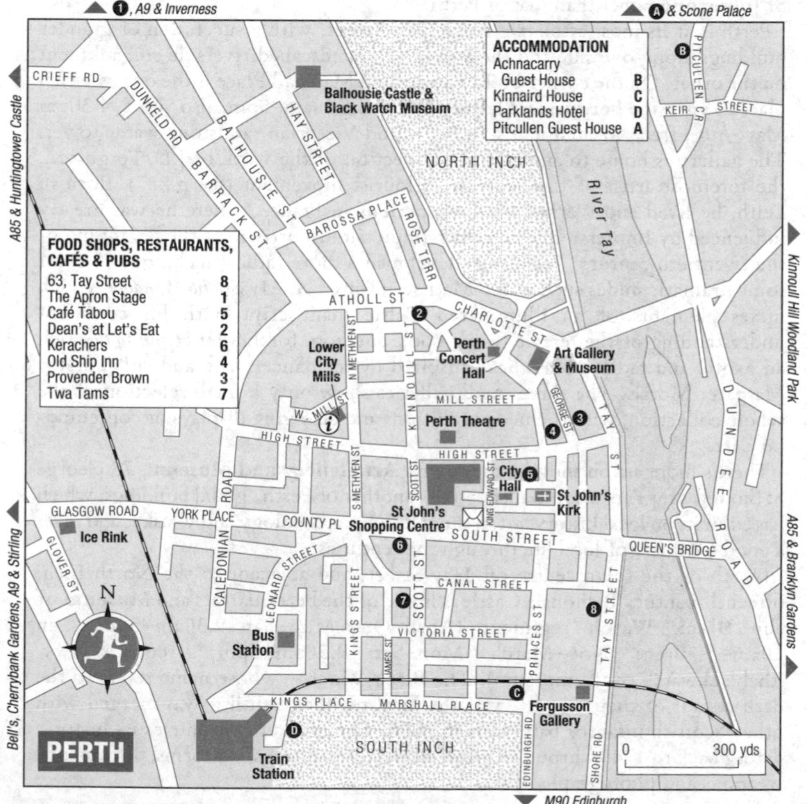

within easy reach of the centre include *Kinnaird House*, 5 Marshall Place (Ⓣ01738/628021, Ⓦwww.kinnaird-guesthouse.co.uk; ❹), overlooking South Inch Park; Victorian *Achnacarry Guest House*, at 3 Pitcullen Crescent, on the east bank of the Tay (Ⓣ01738/621421, Ⓦwww.achnacarry.co.uk; ❷); and, also on the crescent at no.17, the swish *Pitcullen Guest House* (Ⓣ01738/626506, Ⓦwww.pitcullen.co.uk; ❹). You can **camp** in pleasant surroundings by Scone Palace (Ⓣ01738/552323) on the outskirts of town, from where there are regular buses to Perth town centre.

The Town

Perth's compact **centre** occupies a small patch on the west bank of the Tay, flanked by two large areas of green parkland, known as the North and South Inch. The city's main shopping areas are **High Street** and **South Street**, as well as St John's shopping centre on King Edward Street.

Opposite the entrance to the centre is the imposing **City Hall**, used by Scotland's politicians for party conferences. Behind here lies the solid and attractive **St John's Kirk** (Mon–Sat 10am–4pm, Sun 12.30–2pm, except during services; free), surrounded by cobbled lanes and cafés. It was founded by David I in 1126, although the present building dates from the fifteenth century and was restored in 1923–28 to house a war memorial chapel designed by Robert Lorimer. Perth was once known as "St John's Town", and the local football team takes the name **St Johnstone** rather than that of Perth.

Perth is at its most attractive along **Tay Street**, with a succession of grander buildings along one side and the attractively landscaped riverside embankment on the other. On the corner of Tay Street and Marshall Place is the one essential place to visit, the **Fergusson Gallery** (Mon–Sat 10am–5pm, also Sun 1–4.30pm May–Aug; free), located in a striking round Victorian sandstone water tower. The gallery is home to an extensive collection of the work of J.D. Fergusson, the foremost artist of the Scottish Colourist movement (see p.227). Born in Leith, he lived and worked for long periods in France, where he was greatly influenced by Impressionist and post-Impressionist artists. At the beginning of the twentieth century, Fergusson developed a more radical technique to paint some dramatic nudes such as the Matisse-inspired *At My Studio Window*, which mixes elements of an illuminated Celtic manuscript with his confident understanding of the female form. Look out, too, for *Eastre: Hymn to the Sun*, an exotic and radiant brass head inspired by his dancer wife and collaborator Margaret Morris. The three small galleries show only a small selection of the whole collection, with themed exhibitions and changing displays of contemporary art.

There's more art on show at the town's **Art Gallery and Museum**, 78 George St (hours as for Fergusson Gallery; free), another of Perth's grand buildings, which has exhibits on local history, art, natural history, archeology and whisky, and gives a good overview of local life through the centuries.

North of the town centre off Hay Street, and adjacent to the North Inch, fifteenth-century Balhousie Castle is home of the headquarters and **Museum of the Black Watch** regiment (April–Oct Mon–Sat 9.30am–5pm, Sun 10am–3.30pm; Nov–March Mon–Sat 9.30am–5pm; free; Ⓦwww.theblackwatch.co.uk/museum). The Black Watch – whose name refers to the dark colour of their tartan – was the local regiment until it was merged with other Scottish infantry battalions in 2006. The museum chronicles its history, dating back to 1740, through a good display of paintings, uniforms, documents, weapons and photographs.

Eating and drinking

Perth has some excellent **restaurants**. At the top end of the market is *63, Tay Street* (Ⓣ01738/441451, Ⓦwww.63taystreet.co.uk; closed Sun & Mon), serving classy and expensive modern Scottish food; *Deans at Let's Eat*, 77 Kinnoull St (Ⓣ01738/643377, Ⓦwww.letseatperth.co.uk; closed Sun & Mon), with innovative dishes in a pleasantly homely environment; and *Kerachers*, 168 South St (Ⓣ01738/449777, Ⓦwww.kerachers-restaurant.co.uk), best known for its elegant fish dishes. For more moderately priced food try *Café Tabou* at 4 St John's Place (Ⓣ01738/446698) with its menu of French classics and outdoor seating. A homely and fun option just north of town in the village of Stanley is *The Apron Stage* (5 King St; book in advance on Ⓣ01738/828888), with bistro dishes rustled up in a tiny kitchen.

Perth's best **deli**, Provender Brown, is at 23 George St. Of the many **pubs** in the town centre, *Twa Tams* on Scott Street has a good beer garden as well as regular live music, while near the High Street on Skinnergate, the long-established *Old Ship Inn* serves real ale and pub grub.

Around Perth

Almost as well known as Perth itself is **Scone**, one-time home of the Stone of Destiny and the first capital of a united Scotland. The present palace at Scone exudes graceful Scottish country living, and there are some pleasant walks in the grounds. A starker contrast is **Huntingtower Castle**, the best of the relatively few fortified buildings on view in the Perthshire hinterland, just to the west of town.

Scone Palace and around

Just a couple of miles north of Perth on the A93 (catch the open-topped tour bus, or bus #3 or #56 from South St) is **Scone Palace** (pronounced "skoon"; April–Oct daily 9.30am–5.30pm; £9, grounds only £5.10; Ⓦwww.scone-palace.co.uk). Owned and occupied by the Earl and Countess of Mansfield, whose family has held it for almost four centuries, the two-storey building on the eastern side of the Tay is more a home than a monument: the rooms, although full of antiques and lavish furnishings, feel lived-in and used.

Scone was once the capital of Pictavia, and it was here that Kenneth MacAlpine, first king of a united Scotland, brought the famous Coronation **Stone of Destiny**, or Stone of Scone, which is now to be found in Edinburgh Castle (see p.80). A replica of the (surprisingly small) stone can be found on Moot Hill, immediately opposite the palace. Moot Hill, as its name suggests, was the place where Scottish earls came to swear loyalty to their king and discuss the affairs of state in an early form of national parliament. In a symbolic gesture, oak trees from the estate were used in the construction of Scotland's parliament at Holyrood in Edinburgh.

Inside the palace, the library houses one of the foremost collections of porcelain in the world, with items by Meissen, Sèvres, Chelsea, Derby and Worcester. Elsewhere, look out for some beautiful papier-mâché dishes, Marie Antoinette's writing desk and John Zoffany's exquisite eighteenth-century joint portrait of Lady Elizabeth Murray (daughter of the second earl) and Dido, her black companion. In the **grounds** you'll find strutting peacocks, a beech-hedge maze and avenues of venerable trees. Scone was the birthplace of botanist and plant collector **David Douglas**, and following the trail named after him you'll encounter a fragrant pinetum planted in 1848 alongside many of the exotics he discovered in California and elsewhere.

Huntingtower Castle

Nothing like as grand as Scone, but intriguing for its historical connections, is **Huntingtower Castle** (April–Sept daily 9.30am–5.30pm; Oct daily 9.30am–4.30pm; Nov–March Sun–Wed & Sat 9.30am–4.30pm; HS; £4), three miles northwest of Perth on the A85 (catch bus #13 from South Street to Perth Mart). Two three-storey towers formed the original fifteenth- and sixteenth-century tower house, linked in the seventeenth century by a range to provide more room. Formerly known as Ruthven Castle, it was here that the Raid of Ruthven took place in 1582, when the 16-year-old James VI, at the request of William, fourth Earl of Ruthven, came to the castle only to be held captive by a group of conspirators demanding the dismissal of favoured royal advisers. The plot failed, and the young James was released ten months later. Today the castle's chief attractions are its splendid sixteenth-century painted ceilings in the main hall in the east tower.

Strathearn

Strathearn – the valley of the River Earn – stretches west of Perth for some forty miles to **Loch Earn**, a popular watersports spot located just to the north of the Trossachs. Agricola was here around two thousand years ago, trying to establish a foothold in the Highlands; later the area was frequented by Bonnie Prince Charlie and Rob Roy, both bound up in the north–south struggle between Highlands and Lowlands. Today the main settlement in the valley is the well-heeled town of **Crieff**, which, despite its prosperous air, has some hints of wilder Highland countryside close by, notably around the popular **Glenturret Distillery**.

Auchterarder and around

At the southern edge of Strathearn, twelve miles southwest of Perth on the A9, the large village of **AUCHTERARDER** (known as "the Lang Toun" – long town), is recognized mainly for its proximity to Scotland's finest five-star hotel, **Gleneagles** (Ⓣ0800/389 3737, Ⓦwww.gleneagles.com; ⑨), home to three championship golf courses. If staying here is beyond your means, you might consider eating at the main restaurant, the refreshingly unstuffy *Andrew Fairlie at Gleneagles* (Ⓣ0800/704705; Mon–Sat dinner only; £65 for three courses); with two Michelin stars, it is the finest restaurant in Scotland, with highly innovative, dynamic dishes created by Fairlie.

Just to the east of the hotel, the village of **BLACKFORD** is famous for its spring water – in 1488 James IV demanded beer made from the village's water be served at his coronation, while these days it's bottled as Highland Spring mineral water. Not surprisingly, the local whisky **distillery**, Tullibardine (daily 10am–5pm; tours £5; Ⓦwww.tullibardine.com), makes much of the benefits the quality of water adds to their product. You can take a distillery tour or stop in at the café at the new visitors centre located on the edge of the village right beside the A9.

The area's other main attraction is in the quiet village of **DUNNING**, five miles east of Auchterarder on the B8062, where **St Serf's** (April–Sept daily 9.30am–5.30pm; Oct–March access by arrangement; free; Ⓣ01786/450000), a rugged church with a Norman tower and arch, houses the magnificent **Dupplin Cross**, reckoned to be the finest surviving carved Pictish stone. Dating from the early ninth century, it was made in honour of Constantine, the first king of the Picts who also reigned over the Scots of Dalriada (Argyll). The combination of Pictish and Christian imagery – intricately carved Celtic-knot patterns, depictions of animals and warriors – illustrates the developing relationship between king and the Church. On the edge of the village is a strange rough-hewn monument commemorating Maggie Wall, burnt as a witch in 1657.

Crieff

At the heart of Strathearn sits the old spa town of **CRIEFF**, in a lovely position on a south-facing slope of the Grampian foothills. Cattle drovers used to come to a market, or "tryst", here in the eighteenth century, but Crieff really came into its own with the arrival of the railway in 1856. Shortly after that, Morrison's Academy, a local private school, took in its first pupils, and in 1868 the grand *Crieff Hydro*, then known as the *Strathearn Hydropathic*, opened its doors to Victorian visitors seeking water-therapy cures. These days, Crieff values its respectability and has an array of fine Edwardian and Victorian houses, with a busy little centre that retains something of the atmosphere of the former spa town. The **Crieff Visitor Centre** at the bottom of the hill (daily 10am–4.30pm; ⓦwww.crieff.co.uk) incorporates a garden centre, an exhibition about cattle drovers and the Caithness Glass visitor centre and factory, which you can tour for free. The **tourist office** is in the town hall on High Street (Mon–Sat; ⓣ01764/652578), while **Strathearn Gallery**, 32 West High St, is worth a visit, with displays of ceramics, jewellery and landscape paintings.

The imposing *Crieff Hydro* (ⓣ01764/655555, ⓦwww.crieffhydro.com; ❼ dinner, bed & breakfast) is still the grandest place to **stay** in town, despite the institutional atmosphere, and has splendid leisure facilities including a pool and horseriding. A cheaper alternative is friendly *Galvelmore House* on Galvelmore Street (ⓣ01764/655721, ⓦwww.galvelmore.co.uk; ❷), with a lovely oak-panelled lounge; it also has a pretty two-bedroom self-catering apartment. The nearest **hostel** is *Comrie Croft Hostel* (ⓣ01764/670140, ⓦwww.comriecroft.com), a largish bunkhouse set on a working sheep farm halfway between Crieff and Comrie, with its own private fishing loch, mountain-bike rental and network of paths and walks; you can also **camp** here.

Your best bet for fine **food** is bistro-style *Yann's at Glenearn*, which serves French Alpine dishes from Yann's home province and also has attractive rooms (ⓣ01764/650111, ⓦwww.yannsatglenearnhouse.com; Wed–Fri dinner, Sat & Sun lunch & dinner; ❹). Otherwise, head downhill from the tourist office to swish Italian café *Delivino* (ⓣ01764/655665, ⓦwww.delivino.net) at 6 King St; it serves antipasti, tapas, good pizzas, coffee and cakes, and has a small but selective wine list. Crieff features an eclectic selection of old-fashioned and independent shops, including McNee's, a handy grocer/deli located near the tourist office, and the wood-lined whisky shop near Strathearn Gallery.

Around Crieff

From Crieff, it's a short drive or a twenty-minute walk north to the **Famous Grouse Experience** (daily: March–Dec 9am–6pm, tours 9.30am–4.30pm; Jan–Feb 10am–4.30pm, tours 10.30am–3pm; £8.50; ⓦwww.thefamousgrouse.com), located at the venerable **Glenturret Distillery** just off the A85 to Comrie. To get there on public transport, catch any bus going to Crieff, Comrie or St Fillans and ask the driver to drop you at the bottom of the Glenturret Distillery road, from where it's a five-minute walk. Glenturret is Scotland's **oldest distillery**, established in 1775, and still one of the more attractive, with whitewashed buildings and pagoda roofs situated beside a gurgling stream. In recent years it has become the home of the Famous Grouse blend. While the corporate edge may be hard to avoid, and the coach park often full, this is one distillery that makes a decent effort to be family-friendly and to avoid much of the romanticized pomposity which comes with other parts of the malt whisky trail.

A complete contrast, certainly in terms of visitor numbers, is the delightfully hidden **Innerpeffray Library** (March–Oct Wed–Sat 10am–12.45pm & 2–4.45pm, Sun 2–4pm; Nov–Feb phone for appointment; £5; ⓣ01764/652819, ⓦwww.innerpeffraylibrary.co.uk), four miles southeast of Crieff on the B8062 road to Auchterarder. Situated in an attractive eighteenth-century building right by the River Earn, beside an old stone chapel and schoolhouse, the serene and studious public library, founded in 1680, is the oldest in Scotland. It's a must for bibliophiles, its shelves containing some four thousand cloth and leather-bound books, mainly on theological and classical subjects, which visitors are allowed to browse.

The most impressive of the attractions around Crieff are the magnificent **Drummond Castle Gardens** (May–Oct daily 1–6pm; £5; ⓦwww.drummondcastlegardens.co.uk) near Muthill, two miles south of Crieff on the A822 (bus #47 from Crieff towards Muthill, then a mile and a half walk up the castle drive). The approach to the garden is impressive, up a splendid avenue of beech trees; crossing the courtyard of the castle to the grand terrace you can view the garden in all its symmetrical glory. It was begun as early as 1630 (the date of the tall central sundial), though the design of the French/Italianate parterre is Victorian: it depicts a St Andrew's cross and incorporates other images associated with the Drummonds, including two crowns and the wavy motif found on the family crest. Italian marble statues punctuate the long lines of the cross, and the overall effect is of exceptional harmony and grace. Beyond the formal garden, figs, grapes, veg and abundant roses and dahlias grow in the Victorian greenhouse and kitchen garden. The castle itself (no public access) is a wonderful mixture of architectural styles, a blunt medieval keep on a rocky crag adjoining a much-modified Renaissance mansion house.

If you want to stay in **MUTHILL**, a handsome eighteenth-century village with an ancient church, the obvious choice is *Barley Bree* (ⓣ01764/681451, ⓦwww.barleybree.com; ❺), with its chic bright rooms and acclaimed French/Scottish cooking.

Comrie

COMRIE, a pretty conservation village another five miles from the turn-off to Glenturret along the River Earn, has the dubious distinction of having the most seismic tremors recorded in Britain, owing to its position on the Highland Boundary Fault. Earthquake readings are still taken at the curious **Earthquake House**, a tiny building set atop a mound all on its own in the middle of a field. If you walk up to the building you can read information panels outside, or peer through the windows at a model of the world's first seismometer, set up here in 1874, as well as some rather more up-to-date equipment. To find the house, follow the signs to Dalrannoch over the hump-backed stone bridge towards the western end of Comrie, then head 600yd or so along the road. There's **accommodation** and fine dining in the village at the *Royal Hotel* (ⓣ01764/679200, ⓦwww.royalhotel.co.uk; ❼).

Loch Earn

At the western edge of Strathearn is **Loch Earn**, a gently lapping Highland loch dramatically edged by mountains. The A85 runs north along the loch shore from the village of **ST FILLANS**, at the eastern tip, to a slightly larger settlement,

LOCHEARNHEAD, at the western end of the loch, where it meets the A84 linking the Trossachs to Crianlarich (see p.323). The wide tranquil expanse of Loch Earn is popular for **watersports**, particularly engine-based pursuits like water-skiing, powerboating and jet-skiing. Lochearnhead Watersports (ⓣ07834/446 7059, ⓦwww.lochearnhead-water-sports.co.uk) offers water-skiing, wake-boarding and the like, as well as a basic licensed café with picture windows looking out to the loch. Another operator, Active Scotland (ⓣ01567/830321, ⓦwww.activescotland.com), is based a little further down the lakeshore in a little office in the *Clachan Cottage Hotel*.

For **accommodation**, try the cheerful *Lochearnhead Hotel* (ⓣ01567/830229, ⓦwww.lochearnhead-hotel.co.uk; ⑤), or the very friendly *Earnknowe* B&B (ⓣ01567/830238, ⓦwww.earnknowe.co.uk; ②), both overlooking the water at Lochearnhead. Perhaps the best choice for this locale, though, is the chalet-like *Four Seasons Hotel* (ⓣ01764/685333, ⓦwww.thefourseasonshotel.co.uk; ⑥) in St Fillans, with its wonderful waterside location. It's also the best place to **eat**; indeed, there are few other good options in the area.

Strath Tay to Loch Tay

Heading due north from Perth, both the railway and main A9 trunk road carry much of the traffic heading into the Highlands, often speeding straight through some of Perthshire's most attractive countryside in its eagerness to get to the bleaker country to the north. Perthshire has been dubbed "**Big Tree Country**" by the tourist board in recognition of some magnificent woodland in the area, including a number of individual trees that rank among Europe's oldest and tallest specimens. Many of these are found around the valley – or "strath" – of the River Tay as it heads towards the sea from attractive **Loch Tay**, set up among the high Breadalbane Mountains which include the striking peak of **Ben Lawers**, Perthshire's highest, and the hills that enclose the long, enchanting **Glen Lyon**. Studded around Loch Tay are remains of crannogs, ancient dwellings built on man-made islands, which are brought to life at the **Crannog Centre** beside the village of Kenmore. Not far downriver is the prosperous small town of **Aberfeldy**; from here the Tay drifts southeast between the unspoilt twin villages of **Dunkeld and Birnam** before meandering its way past Perth.

Dunkeld and Birnam

DUNKELD, twelve miles north of Perth on the A9, was proclaimed Scotland's ecclesiastical capital by Kenneth MacAlpine in 850. Its position at the southern boundary of the Grampian Mountains made it a favoured meeting place for Highland and Lowland cultures, and the town is one of the area's most pleasant communities, with handsome whitewashed houses, appealing arts and crafts shops and a charming cathedral. The **tourist office** is at The Cross in the town centre (April–Oct daily; ⓣ01350/727688).

Dunkeld's partly ruined **cathedral** (daily: May–Sept 9.30am–6.30pm; Oct–April 9.30am–4pm; free; ⓦwww.dunkeldcathedral.org.uk) is on the northern side of town, in an idyllic setting amid lawns and trees on the east bank of the Tay. Construction began in the early twelfth century and continued throughout the next two hundred years, but the building was more or less ruined at the time of the Reformation. The present structure consists of the fourteenth-century choir and the fifteenth-century nave; the choir, restored in 1600 (and several times since), now serves as the parish church, while the nave remains roofless apart from the clock tower. Inside, note the leper's peep near the pulpit in the north wall, through which lepers could receive the sacrament without coming into contact with the congregation. Also look out for the effigy of the **Wolf of Badenoch**, Robert II's son, born in 1343. The Wolf acquired his name and notoriety when, after being excommunicated for leaving his wife, he took his revenge by burning the towns of Forres and Elgin and sacking the latter's cathedral.

Birnam

Dunkeld is linked to its sister community, **BIRNAM**, by Thomas Telford's seven-arched bridge of 1809. This little village has a place in history thanks to Shakespeare, for it was on Dunsinane Hill, to the southeast of the village, that Macbeth declared: "I will not be afraid of death and bane/Till Birnam Forest come to Dunsinane."

The **Birnam Oak**, a gnarly old character propped up by crutches which can be seen on the waymarked riverside walk, is inevitably claimed to be a survivor of the infamous mobile forest. Several centuries after Shakespeare, another literary personality, Beatrix Potter, drew inspiration from the area, recalling her childhood holidays here when penning the Peter Rabbit stories. A Potter-themed exhibition and garden can be found in the impressive barrel-fronted **Birnam Institute** (daily 10am–4.30pm; £1; Ⓦwww.birnaminstitute.com), a lively theatre, arts and community centre.

Practicalities

Dunkeld is well served by **public transport**: by train between Perth and Inverness, and bus from Perth #23 (Stagecoach) and #957 (Scottish Citylink). There are several large **hotels** in Dunkeld and Birnam, including the central *Royal Dunkeld*, Atholl Street (Ⓣ01350/727322, Ⓦwww.royaldunkeld.co.uk; ⑤), which also has cheaper twin rooms in an annexe (②). Priciest is the rather corporate *Dunkeld House Hilton* (Ⓣ01350/727771, Ⓦwww.hilton.co.uk/dunkeld; ⑧ dinner, B&B), a vast country estate house on the banks of the Tay to the north of town that incorporates a spa, swimming pool and excellent facilities for outdoor pursuits. Local **B&Bs** include the *Waterbury Guest House* (Ⓣ01350/727324, Ⓦwww.waterbury-guesthouse.co.uk; ③) in a turreted Victorian villa on Murthly Terrace in Birnam, and *The Pend* (Ⓣ01350/727586, Ⓦwww.thepend.com; ④), an elegantly furnished option just off the main street in Dunkeld.

The central *Taybank Hotel* (Ⓣ01350/727340, Ⓦwww.thetaybank.com; ②) is a characterful beacon for music fans, who come for the regular live sessions in the convivial bar. For **food**, there are decent bar meals at the *Taybank* (the stovies are a speciality), coffee, cakes and light meals at the *Foyer Café* in the Birnam Institute, and snacks, sandwiches, Scottish beers and fresh fruit at the Robert Menzies deli in Dunkeld, where there's also a tiny café.

Around Dunkeld

Dunkeld and Birnam are surrounded by some lovely countryside, both along the banks of the Tay and in the deep surrounding forest. One of the most rewarding walks is the mile and a half from Birnam to **The Hermitage**, set in a grandly wooded gorge of the plunging River Braan. Here you'll find a pretty eighteenth-century folly, also known as Ossian's Hall, which was once mirrored to reflect the water – the mirrors were smashed by Victorian vandals and the folly was more tamely restored. The hall, appealing yet incongruous in its splendid setting, neatly frames a dramatic waterfall. Nearby you can crane your neck to look up at a Douglas fir that claims the title of tallest tree in Britain – last time the tape was out it managed 212ft.

Two miles east of Dunkeld, the **Loch of the Lowes** is a nature reserve that offers a rare chance to see breeding **ospreys** and other wildfowl; the visitor centre (April–Sept 10am–5pm; £3; ⓣ01350/727337) has video-relay screens and will point you in the direction of the best vantage points. If the surroundings seem appealing enough to warrant lingering a day or two, you could head for the mellow *Wester Caputh Independent Hostel* (ⓣ01738/710449, ⓦwww.westercaputh.co.uk), four miles downstream along the Tay from Dunkeld, which has small dorms and makes for a great base with a relaxing and welcoming atmosphere; there's also a self-catering house.

Aberfeldy and around

From Dunkeld the A9 runs north alongside the Tay for eight miles to Ballinluig, a little place marking the turn-off along the A827 to **ABERFELDY**, a prosperous settlement of large stone houses that acts as a service centre for the wider Loch Tay area. The **tourist office** (April–June, Sept & Oct Mon–Sat 9.30am–5pm, Sun 10am–4pm; July & Aug Mon–Sat 9.30am–5.30pm, Sun 10am–4pm; Nov–March Mon–Sat 10am–4pm; ⓣ01887/820276) at The Square in the town centre is good for advice on local accommodation and details of nearby walking trails. If you want to **rent a bike**, head to Girvans outdoor store (ⓣ01887/820254), behind the filling station on your way into town from the east.

Aberfeldy sits at the point where the Urlar Burn – lined by the silver birch trees celebrated by Robert Burns in his poem *The Birks of Aberfeldy* – flows into the River Tay. The Tay is spanned by the humpbacked, four-arch **Wade's Bridge**, built by General Wade in 1733 during his efforts to control the unrest in the Highlands, and one of the general's more impressive pieces of work. Overlooking the bridge from the south end is the **Black Watch Monument**, depicting a pensive, kilted soldier; it was erected in 1887 to commemorate the first muster of the Highland regiment gathered as a peace-keeping force by Wade in 1740.

The main set-piece attraction in town is **Dewar's World of Whisky** at the Aberfeldy Distillery (April–Oct Mon–Sat 10am–6pm, Sun noon–4pm; Nov–March Mon–Sat 10am–4pm; £6.50; ⓦwww.dewarswow.com), which puts on an impressive show of describing the making of whisky. A **Deluxe Tour** (£18) and **Signature Tour** (£30) are available for connoisseurs, giving a more in-depth look around the distillery and a chance to taste (or "nose") the whisky at different stages in its life. The rest of the small town centre is a busy mixture of craft and tourist shops, the most interesting by far being **The Watermill** on Mill Street (Mon–Sat 10am–5pm, Sun noon–5pm; ⓦwww.aberfeldywatermill.com), an inspiring bookshop, contemporary art gallery and café located in the town's superbly restored early nineteenth-century mill.

Practicalities

For accommodation there's *Guinach House* (ⓣ01887/820251, ⓦwww.guinachhouse.co.uk; ⑥) by The Birks, a tastefully decorated guesthouse/holiday rental in well-tended grounds; while the stylish and unpretentious *Balnearn Guest House* (ⓣ01887/820431, ⓦwww.balnearnhouse.com; ③) is on Crieff Road. The closest **bunkhouse** is *Adventurer's Escape* (ⓣ01887/820498, ⓦwww.adventurers-escape.co.uk), a brightly painted lodge right next to the

Weem Hotel on the road to Castle Menzies. As you'd expect, it's well tuned into the many adventure sports and outdoor pursuits that are available locally.

Aberfeldy isn't short on **cafés** and **tearooms**; the best bet for a good cup of coffee, a bowl of lunchtime soup or afternoon tea is the relaxed café in The Watermill (see p.361), with its pretty riverside garden. Decent bar meals can be found over the Wade Bridge in Weem at the *Ailean Chraggan Inn*.

Castle Menzies and around

One mile west of Aberfeldy, across Wade's Bridge, **Castle Menzies** (April to mid-Oct Mon–Sat 10.30am–5pm, Sun 2–5pm; £3.50; Ⓦ www.menzies.org) is an imposing, Z-shaped, sixteenth-century tower house which until the middle of the last century was the chief seat of the Clan Menzies (pronouced "Ming-iss"). With the demise of the line, the castle was taken over by the Menzies Clan Society, which since 1971 has been involved in the lengthy process of restoring it. Much of the interior is on view, most of it refreshingly free of fixtures and fittings, displaying an austerity that is much more true to medieval life than many grander, furnished castles elsewhere in the country.

A mile or so further along the road by the hamlet with the unfortunate name of **DULL** is Highland Safaris (Ⓣ01887/820071, Ⓦ www.highland adventuresafaris.net), where you can join Land Rover trips into the heather-clad hills nearby in search of wildlife such as eagles, red deer and grouse. At the lodge you can try your hand at gold and mineral panning (£4), a big hit with kids; there's also a deer park, play area and a good farm shop/café. Shortly after this point the road splits: you can strike out for the hills of Glen Lyon (see p.363), or head north past the striking mountain Schiehallion to Loch Tummel (see p.366).

Loch Tay

Aberfeldy grew up around a crossing point on the River Tay, which leaves it six miles adrift of **Loch Tay**, a fourteen-mile-long stretch of fresh water connecting the western and eastern Highlands. Guarding the northern end of the loch is **KENMORE**, where whitewashed estate houses and well-tended gardens cluster around the gate to the extensive grounds of **Taymouth Castle**, built by the Campbells of Glenorchy in the early nineteenth century. The rocket-like eighteenth-century **church** contains an ancient "poor box", and memorials to soldiers of the Black Watch Regiment. The main attraction here, though, is the **Scottish Crannog Centre** (daily: April–Oct 10am–5.30pm; Nov 10am–4pm; £6.50; Ⓦ www.crannog.co.uk). Crannogs are Iron Age loch dwellings built on stilts over the water, with a gangway to the shore which could be lifted up to defy a hostile intruder, whether animal or human. Following underwater excavations in Loch Tay, the team here has superbly reconstructed a crannog, and visitors can now walk out over the loch to the thatched wooden dwelling, complete with sheepskin rugs, wooden bowls and other evidence of the way life was lived 2500 years ago.

The nicest place to **stay** is the pleasant and well-run *Kenmore Hotel* on the village square (Ⓣ01887/830205, Ⓦ www.kenmorehotel.com; ❼); established in 1572, it's Scotland's oldest inn. Two miles to the west, *Rock House* (Ⓣ01887/830336, Ⓦ www.lochtay.co.uk; ❼) is a wonderfully swish B&B overlooking the loch, while *Culdees* (Ⓣ01887/830519, Ⓦ www.culdeesbunkhouse.co.uk; ❶), four miles along the loch's north shore at Fearnan, has family-friendly bunkhouse and B&B accommodation on a farm with an emphasis on permaculture and spiritual values. For something to **eat**, head to *The Courtyard*

(Ⓣ01887/830756, Ⓦwww.taymouthcourtyard.com) beside the Kenmore golf course, comprising a smart restaurant, large bar and deli/gift shop.

Dominating the northern side of Loch Tay is moody **Ben Lawers** (3984ft), Perthshire's highest mountain; from the top there are incredible views towards both the Atlantic and the North Sea. The ascent – which shouldn't be tackled unless you're properly equipped for Scottish hillwalking (see p.49) – takes around three hours from the NTS visitor centre (April–Sept daily 10am–5pm), located at 1300ft and reached by a winding hill road off the A827. The centre has an audiovisual show, slides of the mountain flowers – including the rare alpine flora found here – and a nature trail with accompanying descriptive booklet.

Killin

The mountains **of Breadalbane** (pronounced "bred–albin", from the Gaelic "braghaid Albin" meaning high country of Scotland) loom over the southern end of Loch Tay. Glens Lochay and Dochart curve north and south respectively from the small town of **KILLIN**, right in the centre of which the River Dochart comes rushing down over the frothy **Falls of Dochart** before disgorging into Loch Tay. A short distance west of Killin the A827 meets the A85, linking the Trossachs with Crianlarich (see p.323), an important waypoint on the roads to Oban, Fort William and the west coast.

There's little to do in Killin itself, but it makes a convenient base for some of the area's best walks. The **tourist office** (April–Oct daily; Ⓣ01567/820254) is located on the ground floor of the old watermill by the falls; upstairs is the **Breadalbane Folklore Centre** (same times; £2.95). The centre explores the history and mythology of Breadalbane and holds the 1300-year-old "healing stones" of St Fillan, an early Christian missionary who settled in Glen Dochart.

Killin is littered with **B&Bs**, including *Fairview House*, halfway along Main Street (Ⓣ01567/820667, Ⓦwww.fairview-killin.co.uk; ❷), a Victorian villa with decent rooms and breakfasts. At the eastern edge of town behind the large *Killin Hotel* you'll find the friendly but shambolic *Braveheart Backpackers*, with timber-lined en-suite dorms and family rooms (Ⓣ01567/829089; ❶). The place to grab a bite to **eat** is the *Falls of Dochart Inn*, which has an attractive stone-walled pub right above the famous rapids; a café adjoins the pub supplying coffee and cakes. If you're interested in **outdoor activities**, make for the helpful and enthusiastic Killin Outdoor Centre and Mountain Shop (Ⓣ01567/820652, Ⓦwww.killinoutdoor.co.uk) on Main Street, which rents out mountain bikes, canoes and tents.

Glen Lyon

North of Breadalbane, the mountains tumble down into **Glen Lyon** – at 34 miles long, the longest enclosed glen in Scotland – where, legend has it, the Celtic warrior Fingal built twelve castles. The narrow single-track road through the glen starts at **KELTNEYBURN**, near Kenmore at the northern end of the loch, although a road does struggle over the hills past the Ben Lawers visitor centre (see above) to **Bridge of Balgie**, halfway down the glen, where the post office does good tea and scones (April–Oct). Either way, it's a long, winding journey. A few miles on from Keltneyburn, the village of **FORTINGALL** is little more than a handful of pretty thatched cottages, though locals make much of their 5000-year-old yew tree – believed (by them at least) to be the oldest living thing in Europe. The venerable tree can be found in the churchyard, with a timeline nearby listing some of the events the yew has lived through. One of these, bizarrely, is the birth of Pontius Pilate, reputedly the son of a Roman officer stationed near Fortingall. If you're taken by the peace and remoteness of Glen Lyon, you can **stay** at the attractive, upmarket *Fortingall Hotel* (Ⓣ01887/830367, Ⓦwww.fortingallhotel.com; ❼), with its Arts and Crafts heritage, eleven bedrooms and excellent restaurant; it organizes fishing and walking packages.

Highland Perthshire

North of the Tay Valley, Perthshire doesn't discard its lush richness immediately, but there are clear indications of the more rugged, barren influences of the Highlands proper. The principal settlements of **Pitlochry** and **Blair Atholl**, both just off the A9, are separated by the narrow gorge of Killiecrankie. Though there are reasons to stop in both places, inevitably the greater rewards are to be found further from the main drag, most notably in the winding westward road along the shores of **Loch Tummel** and **Loch Rannoch** past the distinctive peak of **Schiehallion**, which eventually leads to the remote wilderness of **Rannoch Moor**.

Pitlochry

PITLOCHRY is undoubtedly a useful place to find somewhere to stay or eat en route to or from the Highlands. However, there's little charm to be found on its main street, with crawling traffic and endless shops selling cut-price woollens and knobbly walking sticks. The one attraction with some distinction is the **Edradour Distillery** (March & April, Nov & Dec Mon–Sat 10am–4pm, Sun noon–4pm; May & Oct Mon–Sat 10am–5pm, Sun noon–5pm; June–Sept Mon–Sat 9.30am–5pm, Sun noon–5pm; Jan & Feb Mon–Sat 10am–4pm; £5; Ⓦwww.edradour.co.uk), Scotland's smallest, in its idyllic position tucked into the hills a couple of miles east of Pitlochry on the A924. Although the tour of the distillery itself isn't out of the ordinary, the lack of industralization and the

Walks around Pitlochry

Ordnance Survey Explorer Map no. 368

Pitlochry is surrounded by good walking country. The biggest lure has to be **Ben Vrackie** (2733ft), which provides a stunning backdrop for the town and deserves better than a straight up-and-down walk; however, the climb should only be attempted in settled weather conditions and if you're properly prepared (see p.49).

The direct route up the hill follows the course of the Moulin burn past the inn of the same name. Alternatively, a longer but much more rewarding circular route heads north out of Pitlochry, along the edge of Loch Faskally, then up the River Garry to go through the **Pass of Killiecrankie**. This is looked after by the NTS, which has a visitor centre (April–Oct daily 10am–5.30pm) detailing the famous battle here as well as the abundant natural history of the gorge. From the NTS centre follow the route past Old Faskally to meet the main track at Loch a'Choire.

Other worthwhile walks in the area include the trip right round **Loch Faskally**, or you could follow the walk above but turn back from Killiecrankie. A lovely short hill walk from the south end of Pitlochry follows a path through oak forests along the banks of the **Black Spout** burn; when you emerge from the woods it's a few hundred yards further uphill to the lovely Edradour Distillery (see above).

fact that the whole traditional process is done on site give Edradour more personality than many of its rivals.

On the western edge of Pitlochry, just across the river, lies Scotland's renowned "Theatre in the Hills", the modern **Pitlochry Festival Theatre** (ⓣ01796/484626, ⓦwww.pitlochry.org.uk). A variety of productions – mostly mainstream theatre from the resident repertoire company, along with regular music events – are staged in the summer season (May–Oct) and on ad hoc dates the rest of the year. By day it's worth coming here to wander around **Explorers: the Scottish Plant Hunters' Garden** (April–Oct daily 10am–5pm; £4, tours £1 extra; ⓦwww.explorersgarden.com), a garden and forest area beside the theatre that pays tribute to Scottish botanists and collectors who roamed the world in the eighteenth and nineteenth centuries in search of new plant species. An open-air amphitheatre is sometimes used for outdoor performances.

A short stroll upstream from the theatre is the **Pitlochry Power Station and Dam**, a massive concrete wall that harnesses the water of the artificial Loch Faskally, just north of the town, for hydroelectric power. The **visitor centre** (April–Oct Mon–Fri 10.30am–5.30pm; £3) offers a pretty thorough rundown on how hydro schemes work, but what draws most attention is the **salmon ladder**, a staircase of murky glass boxes through which you might see some nonplussed fish making their way upstream past the dam.

Practicalities

Pitlochry is on the main **train** line to Inverness, and the regular **buses** from Perth stop near the train station on Station Road, five minutes' walk up the main street from the **tourist office**, 22 Atholl Rd (April–Oct daily; Nov–March closed Sun; ⓣ01796/472215). The office can sell you a guide to walks in the surrounding area (50p) and also offers an accommodation booking service. For **bike rental**, advice on local cycling routes, as well as general outdoor gear, try Escape Route, 3 Atholl Rd (ⓣ01796/473859, ⓦwww.escape-route.biz).

Pitlochry is packed with grand houses converted into good-quality **accommodation**. The *Moulin Hotel* (ⓣ01796/472196, ⓦwww.moulinhotel.co.uk; ❹), at Moulin on the outskirts along the A924, is a pleasant old travellers' inn with a great bar and its own brewery, while *Craigatin House and Courtyard* (ⓣ01796/472478, ⓦwww.craigatinhouse.co.uk; ❹) on the northern section of the main road through town, is an attractive, contemporary **B&B** with large beds, soothing decor and a pretty garden; *Beinn Bhracaigh*, Higher Oakfield, is similarly chic (ⓣ01796/470355, ⓦwww.beinnbhracaigh.com; ❹). Otherwise, try *Ferryman's Cottage*, Port-na-Craig (ⓣ01796/473681, ⓦwww.ferrymanscottage.co.uk; ❷), a traditional and welcoming B&B in a beautiful position next to the River Tummel and the theatre. Right in the centre is *Pitlochry Backpackers Hotel*, 134 Atholl Rd (ⓣ01796/470044, ⓦwww.pitlochrybackpackershotel.com; March–Oct), a **hostel** based in a former hotel offering dorms along with around ten twin and double rooms (❶).

Pitlochry is the domain of the tearoom and you have to hunt to find decent **places to eat**. *The Old Armoury* (ⓣ01796/474281, ⓦwww.theoldarmouryrestaurant.com) on a back road between the train station and dam is a civilized restaurant serving expensive meals in the evening, and also has a secluded tea garden. There's more moderately priced bistro food in the *Strathgarry Hotel* in the centre of town; the same owners run the *Port-na-Craig Inn* which has a beautiful riverside location near the theatre. The best bet for traditional **pub grub** is the *Moulin Inn*, handily placed at the foot of Ben Vrackie, while *Food for Thought*, 8 West Moulin Rd, is a good **deli**, serving sandwiches and coffee.

Loch Tummel and Loch Rannoch

West of Pitlochry, the B8019/B846 makes a memorably scenic, if tortuous, traverse of the shores of **Loch Tummel** and then **Loch Rannoch**. These two lochs and their adjoining rivers were much changed by the massive hydroelectric schemes built in the 1940s and 1950s, yet this is still a spectacular stretch of countryside and one that deserves leisurely exploration. **Queen's View** at the eastern end of Loch Tummel is an obvious vantage point, looking down the loch to the misty peak of **Schiehallion** (3553ft); the name comes from the Gaelic meaning "Fairy Mountain". It's a popular, fairly easy and inspiring mountain to climb (3–4hr), with views on a good day to the massed ranks of Highland peaks; the path up starts at Braes of Foss, just off the B846 that links Aberfeldy with Kinloch Rannoch. You'll get a good view of the mountain from the cosy *Loch Tummel Inn* (ⓣ01882/634272, ⓦwww.lochtummelinn.co.uk; ❺), about halfway along Loch Tummel, which serves real ale, local venison and salmon.

Beyond Loch Tummel, marking the eastern end of Loch Rannoch, the small community of **KINLOCH RANNOCH** doesn't see a lot of passing trade – fishermen and hillwalkers are the most common visitors. Otherwise, the only real destination here is Rannoch Station, a lonely outpost on the Glasgow–Fort William West Highland train line, sixteen miles further on. The road goes no further. Here you can contemplate the bleakness of **Rannoch Moor** (see box below), a wide expanse of bog, heather and wind-blown pine tree that stretches right across to the imposing entrance to Glen Coe (see p.449). A local bus service (Broons Bus #85) from Kinloch Rannoch and a postbus from Pitlochry (#223; Mon–Sat 8am) provide connections to the railway station.

In Kinloch Rannoch, *Bunrannoch House* (ⓣ01882/632407, ⓦwww.bunrannoch.co.uk; ❹), a former Victorian shooting lodge, with lovely views, is a good choice for **accommodation** (it also serves evening meals). Otherwise, there's the *Dunalastair Hotel* (ⓣ01882/632323, ⓦwww.dunalastair.co.uk; ❼), which dominates the main square of the village and has a cosy pub, bar-brasserie and

Rannoch Moor

Rannoch Moor occupies roughly 150 square miles of uninhabited and uninhabitable peat bogs, lochs, heather hillocks, strewn lumps of granite and a few gnarled Caledonian pines, all of it over one thousand feet above sea level. Perhaps the most striking thing about the moor is its inaccessibility: one road, between Crianlarich and Glen Coe, skirts its western side, while another struggles west from Pitlochry to reach its eastern edge at Rannoch Station. The only regular form of transport is the **West Highland Railway**, which stops at **Rannoch** and, a little to the north, Corrour station, which has no road access at all. There is a simple tearoom in the station building at Rannoch, as well as a pleasant small hotel, the *Moor of Rannoch* (ⓣ01882/633238, ⓦwww.moorofrannoch.co.uk; mid-Feb–Oct; ❺), but even these struggle to diminish the feeling of isolation. **Corrour**, meanwhile, stole an unlikely scene in the film *Trainspotting* when the four central characters headed here for a taste of the great outdoors; a wooden SYHA hostel is located a mile away on the shores of **Loch Ossian** (ⓣ0870/004 1139, ⓦwww.syha.org.uk; April–Oct) and is only accessible on foot, making the area a great place for hikers seeking somewhere genuinely off the beaten track. From Rannoch Station it's possible to catch the train to Corrour and walk the nine miles back; it's a longer slog west to the *Kingshouse Hotel* (see p.450) at the eastern end of Glen Coe, the dramatic peaks of which poke up above the moor's western horizon. Determined hillwalkers will find a clutch of Munros around Corrour, including remote Ben Alder (3765ft), high above the forbidding shores of Loch Ericht.

formal dining room, as well as a linked Activity Centre (Ⓦ www.activityscotland.com) that caters for most pursuits, from white-water rafting to quad biking.

North of Pitlochry

Four miles north of Pitlochry, the A9 cuts through the **Pass of Killiecrankie**, a breathtaking wooded gorge that falls away to the River Garry below. This dramatic setting was the site of the **Battle of Killiecrankie** in 1689, when the Jacobites crushed the forces of General Mackay. Legend has it that one soldier of the Crown, fleeing for his life, made a miraculous jump across the eighteen-foot **Soldier's Leap**, an impossibly wide chasm halfway up the gorge. Queen Victoria, visiting here 160 years later, contented herself with recording the beauty of the area in her diary. Exhibits at the slick NTS **visitor centre** (daily: April–Oct 10am–5.30pm; parking £2) recall the battle and examine the gorge in detail. The surroundings here are thick, mature forest, full of interesting plants and creatures – the local ranger leads **guided walks** from the visitor centre which are well worth joining.

Blair Atholl

Three miles north of Killiecrankie, the village of **BLAIR ATHOLL** makes for a much quieter and more idiosyncratic stop than Pitlochry. At the **Atholl Estates Information Centre** (April–Oct daily 9am–4.45pm; Ⓣ 01796/481646, Ⓦ www.athollestatesrangerservice.co.uk) you can get details of the extensive network of local walks and bike rides as well as information on surrounding flora and fauna. Rent **bikes** locally from Base Camp Bikes (pre-booking required; Ⓣ 01796/481256, Ⓦ www.basecamp-bikes.co.uk). Right beside the Estates Info Centre, the modest **Atholl Country Life Museum** (May–Sept daily 1.30–5pm, July & Aug from 10am Mon–Fri; £3; Ⓣ 01796/481232, Ⓦ www.athollcountrylifemuseum.org) offers a homespun and nostalgic look at the history of life in the local glens; in among the old photos and artefacts the star attraction is a stuffed, full-sized Highland cow. The grand but reasonably priced *Atholl Arms Hotel* (Ⓣ 01796/481205, Ⓦ www.athollarms.co.uk; ④) is the best place in town for a drink or a bar meal. Nearby, you can wander round the **Water Mill** on Ford Road (April–Oct daily 10.30am–5.30pm; free; Ⓦ www.blairathollwatermill.co.uk), which dates back to 1613, and witness flour being milled; better still, you can enjoy home-baked scones and light lunches in its pleasant timber-beamed tearoom.

Blair Castle

Seat of the Atholl dukedom, whitewashed, turreted **Blair Castle** (April–Oct daily 9.30am–last admission 4.30pm; Nov–March Tues & Sat only 9.30am–12.30pm; £8.75, grounds only £4.75; Ⓦ www.blair-castle.co.uk), surrounded by parkland and dating from 1269, presents an impressive sight as you approach up the drive. A piper, one of the Atholl Highlanders, may be playing in front of the castle; this select group was retained by the duke as his private army – a unique privilege afforded to him by Queen Victoria, who stayed here in 1844.

Thirty or so rooms display a selection of paintings, antique furniture and plasterwork that is sumptuous in the extreme. Highlights are the soaring **entrance hall**, with every spare inch of wood panelling covered in weapons of some description, and the vast **ballroom**, with its timber roof, antlers and mixture of portraits.

As impressive as the castle's interior are its surroundings: Highland cows graze the ancient landscaped grounds and peacocks strut in front of the castle. There is a **riding stable** from where you can take treks, and formal woodland walks take you to various parts of the castle grounds, including the walled water garden and the towering giant conifers of Diana's Grove. There is also a busy but attractive caravan and **camping** park (Ⓣ01796/481263, Ⓦwww.blaircastlecaravanpark.co.uk; April–Nov) in the grounds.

Travel details

Trains

Perth to: Aberdeen (hourly; 1hr 40min); Blair Atholl (3–7 daily; 40min); Dundee (hourly; 25min); Dunkeld (3–7 daily; 20min); Edinburgh (every 1–2hr; 1hr 20min–1hr 50min); Glasgow Queen St (hourly; 1hr); Inverness (4–9 daily; 2hr); Pitlochry (4–9 daily; 30min); Stirling (hourly; 30min).

Rannoch to: Corrour (3–4 daily; 12min); Fort William (3–4 daily; 1hr); Glasgow Queen St (3–4 daily; 2hr 45min); London Euston (sleeper service; Sun–Fri daily; 11hr).

Buses

Aberfeldy to: Perth (6 daily; 1hr 20min).

Crieff to: Stirling (8 daily; 50min).

Kinloch Rannoch to: Pitlochry (3 daily; 50min); Rannoch Station (4 daily; 40min).

Perth to: Aberfeldy (8 daily; 1hr 15min); Crieff (hourly; 45min); Dundee (hourly; 45min); Dunkeld (hourly; 30min); Edinburgh (hourly; 1hr 5min); Glasgow (hourly; 1hr 35min); Gleneagles (hourly; 25min); Inverness (hourly; 2hr 45min); Pitlochry (hourly; 45min); Stirling (hourly; 50min).

10

Northeast Scotland

0
50 miles
N
17
16
15
13
14
12
11
10
9
6
7
8
5
1
2
4
3
NORTHERN IRELAND
ENGLAND

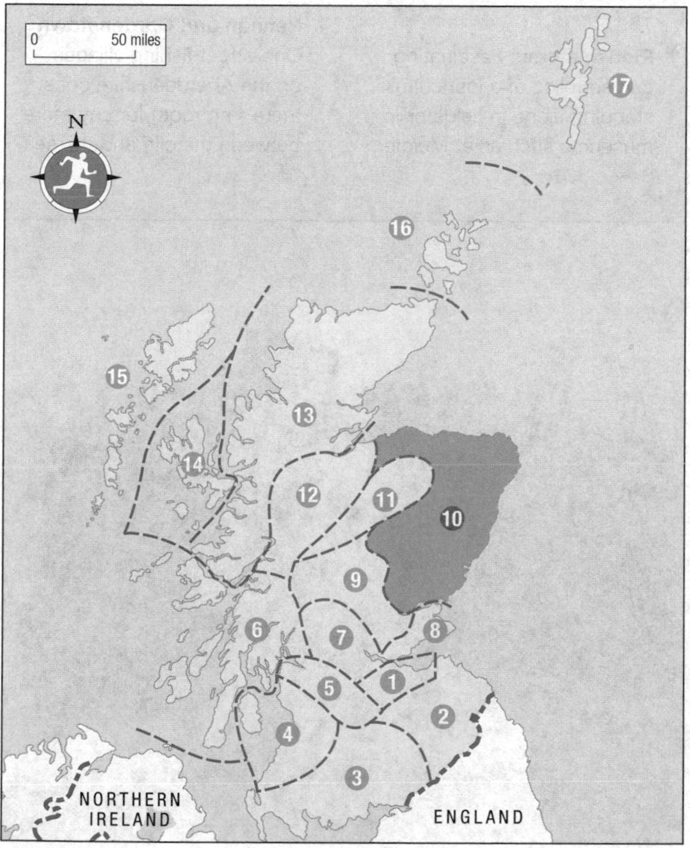

CHAPTER 10

Highlights

* **DCA** Arts centre/cinema/café at the hip heart of Dundee's up-and-coming cultural scene. See p.378

* **Arbroath smokie** A true Scottish delicacy: succulent haddock still warm from the oak smoker. See p.381

* **Pictish stones** Fascinating carved relics of a lost culture, standing alone in fields or in museums such as at Meigle. See p.386

* **Dunnottar Castle** The moodiest cliff-top ruin in the country. See p.404

* **Museum of Scottish Lighthouses** Lights, lenses and legends at one of the best small museums in the country. See p.413

* **Pennan and Gardenstown** One-street fishing villages on the Aberdeenshire coast: there's no room for any more between the cliff and the sea. See p.413

▲ Dunnottar Castle

10

Northeast Scotland

A large triangle of land thrusting into the North Sea, **northeast Scotland** comprises the area east of a line drawn roughly from Perth north to the fringe of the Moray Firth at Forres. The area takes in the county of Angus and the city of Dundee to the south and, beyond the Grampian Mountains, the counties of Aberdeenshire and Moray and the city of Aberdeen. Geographically diverse, the landscape in the south of the region is comprised predominantly of undulating farmland, but as you travel further north of the Firth of Tay, this gives way to wooded glens, mountains and increasingly harsh land fringed by a dramatic coast of cliffs and long sandy beaches.

The northeast was the southern kingdom of the **Picts**, reminders of whom are scattered throughout the region in the form of beautifully carved stones found in fields, churchyards and museums, such as the one at **Meigle**. Remote, self-contained and cut off from the centres of major power in the south, the area never grew particularly prosperous, and a handful of feuding and intermarrying families grew to wield disproportionate influence, building many of the region's **castles** and religious buildings and developing and planning its towns.

Many of the most appealing settlements are along the coast, but while the fishing industry is but a fondly held memory in many parts, a number of the northeast's ports were transformed by the discovery of **oil** in the North Sea in the 1960s – particularly **Aberdeen**, Scotland's third largest city. Aberdeen remains a sophisticated city, which, for the time being, still rides a diminishing wave of oil-based prosperity. The northeast's next largest metropolis, **Dundee**, is valiantly trying to shed its depressed post-industrial image with a reinvigorated cultural scene and **Discovery**, the ship of Captain Scott ("of the Antarctic"). A little way up the Angus coast lie the historically important towns of **Arbroath** and **Montrose** while, inland, the picturesque **Angus glens** cut into the Grampian Mountains, offering a readily accessible taste of wild Highland scenery to both hikers and skiers.

North of the glens and west of Aberdeen, **Deeside** is a fertile yet ruggedly attractive area made famous by the Royal Family, who have favoured the estate at **Balmoral** as a summer holiday retreat ever since Queen Victoria fell in love with it back in the 1840s. Beyond Deeside and the similarly endowed although less visited **Don Valley** are the eastern sections of the **Cairngorm National Park**, while the northeast coast offers yet another aspect of a diverse region, with rugged cliffs, empty beaches and historic fishing villages tucked into coves and bays.

Northeast Scotland is well served by an extensive **road** network, with fast links between Dundee and Aberdeen, while the area north and west of Aberdeen is dissected by a series of efficient routes. **Trains** from Edinburgh and Glasgow connect with Dundee, Aberdeen and other coastal towns, while an inland line

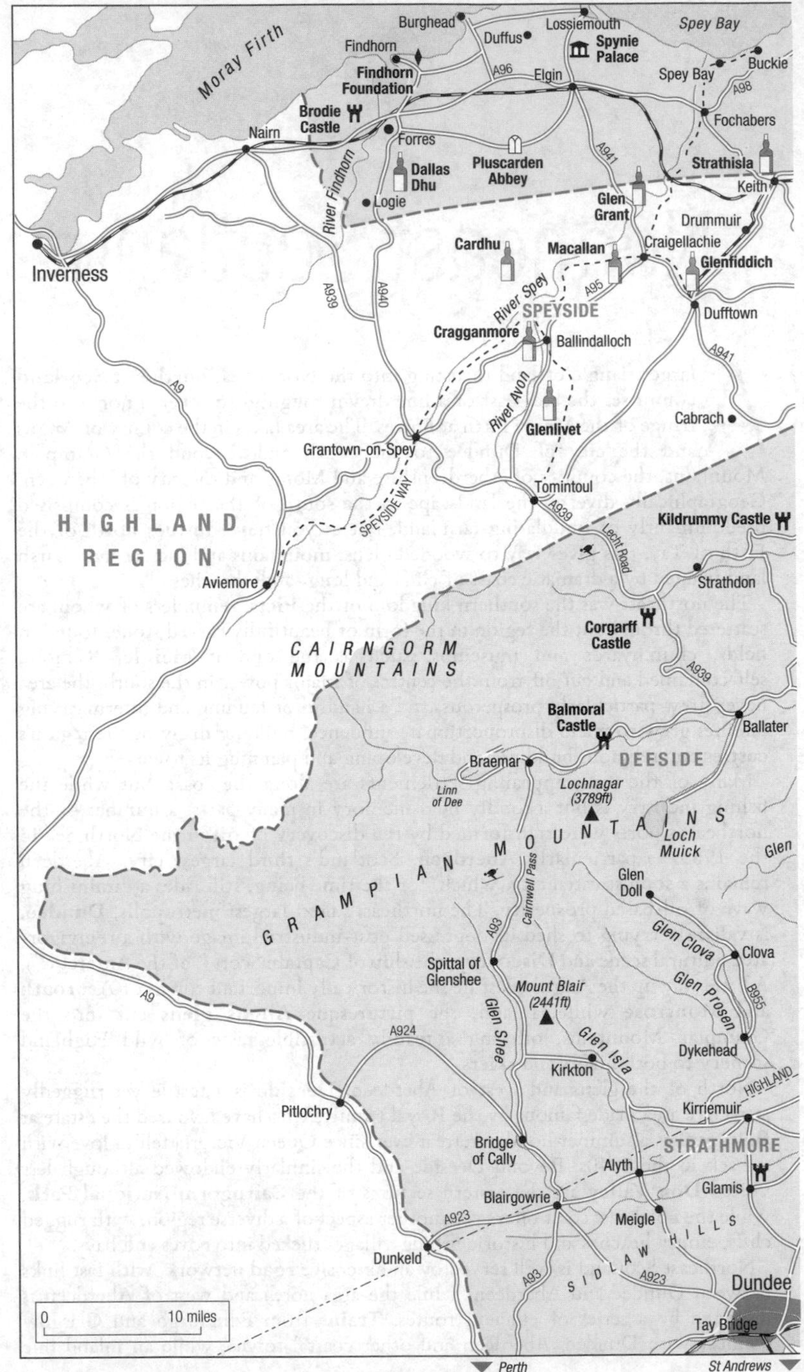
Burghead
Lossiemouth
Spey Bay
Moray Firth
Findhorn
Duffus
Spynie Palace
Buckie
Findhorn Foundation
A96
Elgin
Spey Bay
A98
Brodie Castle
Nairn
Forres
Fochabers
River Findhorn
Dallas Dhu
Pluscarden Abbey
A941
Strathisla
Keith
Logie
Glen Grant
Drummuir
Inverness
Cardhu
Macallan
Craigellachie
Glenfiddich
A939
A940
River Spey
A95
SPEYSIDE
Dufftown
Cragganmore
Ballindalloch
A941
A9
River Avon
Glenlivet
Cabrach
Grantown-on-Spey
Tomintoul
A939
HIGHLAND REGION
SPEYSIDE WAY
Lecht Road
Kildrummy Castle
Aviemore
Strathdon
Corgarff Castle
CAIRNGORM MOUNTAINS
A939
Balmoral Castle
Ballater
Braemar
DEESIDE
Linn of Dee
Lochnagar (3789ft)
Loch Muick
GRAMPIAN MOUNTAINS
Glen
Glen Doll
Cairnwell Pass
A93
Glen Clova
Clova
Spittal of Glenshee
Glen Prosen
B955
Mount Blair (2441ft)
A9
Glen Shee
Glen Isla
A924
Dykehead
Kirkton
HIGHLAND
Pitlochry
Kirriemuir
STRATHMORE
Bridge of Cally
Alyth
Glamis
Blairgowrie
A923
Meigle
SIDLAW HILLS
Dunkeld
A93
A923
Dundee
0
10 miles
Tay Bridge
Perth
St Andrews

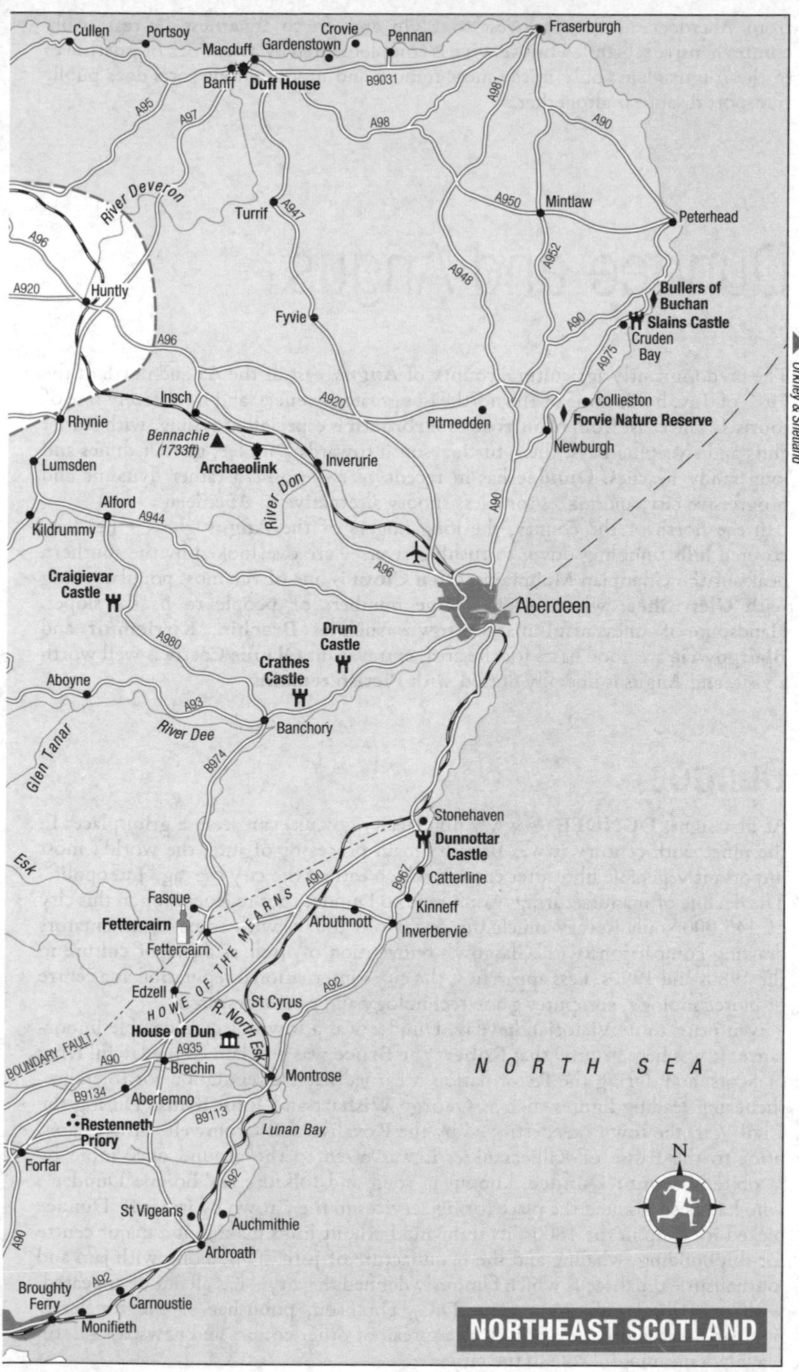

10

NORTHEAST SCOTLAND

Orkney & Shetland

from Aberdeen heads northwest to Elgin and on to Inverness. A reasonably comprehensive scheduled **bus service** is complemented by a network of **postbuses** in the Angus glens: only in the most remote and mountainous parts does public transport disappear altogether.

Dundee and Angus

The predominantly agricultural county of **Angus**, east of the A9 and north of the Firth of Tay, holds some of the northeast's greatest scenery and is relatively free of tourists. The coast from **Montrose** to **Arbroath** is especially inviting, with scarlet cliffs and sweeping bays, then, further south towards Dundee, gentler dunes and long sandy beaches. **Dundee** has in recent years become a rather dynamic and progressive city, and makes for a less snooty alternative to Aberdeen.

In the north of the county, the long fingers of the **Angus glens** – heather-covered hills tumbling down to rushing rivers – are overlooked by the southern peaks of the Grampian Mountains. **Glen Clova** is one of the most popular, along with **Glen Shee**, which attracts large numbers of people to its ski slopes. Handsome if uneventful market towns such as **Brechin**, **Kirriemuir** and **Blairgowrie** are good bases for the area, extravagant **Glamis Castle** is well worth a visit, and Angus is liberally dotted with **Pictish remains**.

Dundee

At first sight, **DUNDEE** (Ⓦwww.dundeecity.gov.uk) can seem a grim place. In the nineteenth century it was Britain's main processor of jute, the world's most important vegetable fibre after cotton, which earned the city the tag "Juteopolis". The decline of manufacturing wasn't kind to Dundee, but regeneration in this city of 145,000 souls is very much the buzzword today, with some commentators drawing comparisons with Glasgow's reinvention of itself as a city of culture in the 1980s and 1990s. Less apparent is the city's international reputation as a centre of biotechnology, computer game technology and cancer research.

Even prior to its Victorian heyday, Dundee was a town of considerable importance. It was here in 1309 that **Robert the Bruce** was proclaimed the lawful King of Scots, and during the Reformation it earned itself a reputation for tolerance, sheltering leading figures such as **George Wishart** and **John Knox**. During the Civil War, the town was destroyed by the Royalists and Cromwell's army. Later, prior to the Battle of Killiecrankie, it was razed to the ground once more by Jacobite **Viscount Dundee**, known in song and folklore as "Bonnie Dundee", who had been granted the place for his services to the Crown by James II. Dundee picked itself up in the 1800s, its train and harbour links making it a major centre for shipbuilding, whaling and the manufacture of **jute**. This, along with jam and journalism – the three Js which famously defined the city – has all but disappeared, with only local publishing giant D.C. Thomson, publisher of the timelessly popular *Beano* and *Dandy*, as well as a spread of other comics and newspapers, still playing a meaningful role in the city.

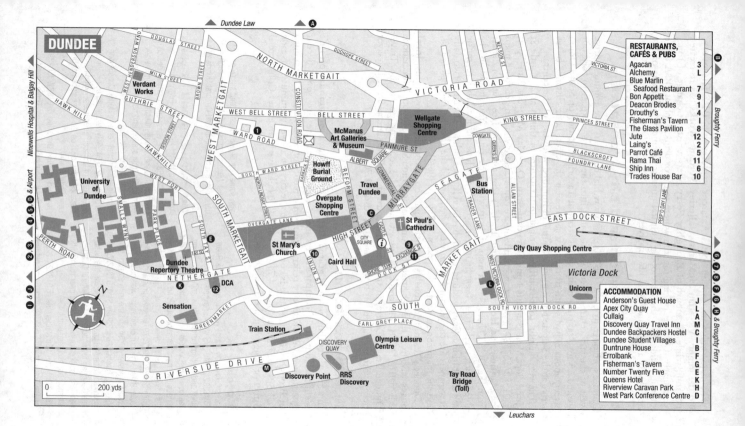

DUNDEE

RESTAURANTS, CAFÉS & PUBS

Agacan	3
Alchemy	L
Blue Marlin Seafood Restaurant	7
Bon Appetit	9
Deacon Brodies	1
Drouthy's	4
Fisherman's Tavern	I
The Glass Pavilion	8
Jute	12
Laing's	2
Parrot Café	5
Rama Thai	11
Ship Inn	6
Trades House Bar	10

ACCOMMODATION

Anderson's Guest House	J
Apex City Quay	L
Cullaig	A
Discovery Quay Travel Inn	M
Dundee Backpackers Hostel	C
Dundee Student Villages	I
Duntrune House	B
Errolbank	F
Fisherman's Tavern	G
Number Twenty Five	E
Queens Hotel	K
Riverview Caravan Park	H
West Park Conference Centre	D

Dundee Law
A
B
Broughty Ferry
6, 7, 8, F, G, H & Broughty Ferry
Leuchars
Ninewells Hospital & Balgay Hill
2, 3, 4, 5, D & Airport
I & J
Douglas Street
Dudhope Street
North Marketgait
Victoria Road
Victoria St
Nelson St
West Henderson Wynd
Verdant Works
Miln Street
Brown Street
Guthrie Street
Hawk Hill
West Bell Street
Constitution Road
Bell Street
West Marketgait
Ward Road
McManus Art Galleries & Museum
Panmure St
Wellgate Shopping Centre
King Street
Princes Street
Cowgate
Queen's St
Blackscroft
Foundry Lane
Session Street
Hawkhill
Albert Square
Commercial St
Murraygate
Seagate
Bus Station
Allan Street
Trader Lane
Peep'o Day Lane
University of Dundee
West Port
South Ward Street
Barrack St
Howff Burial Ground
Reform Street
Travel Dundee
Overgate Shopping Centre
North Lindsay Street
Smalls Wynd
Park Place
South Marketgait
Overgate Lane
High Street
St Paul's Cathedral
Castle St
City Square
East Dock Street
Perth Road
South Tay St
Tay Sq
St Mary's Church
Union St
Caird Hall
Exchange St
Shore Terr
Dock St
Market Gait
City Quay Shopping Centre
West Victoria Dock Rd
Victoria Dock
Dundee Repertory Theatre
Nethergate
DCA
Unicorn
Sensation
South
South Victoria Dock Rd
Greenmarket
Earl Grey Place
Train Station
Discovery Quay
Olympia Leisure Centre
Riverside Drive
Discovery Point
RRS Discovery
Tay Road Bridge (Toll)
0 200 yds
N

The major sights are Captain Scott's Antarctic explorer ship, **RRS Discovery**, and the mighty Victorian **McManus Galleries**. **Verdant Works** is a re-created jute mill, while the suburb of **Broughty Ferry** offers a distinct change of tone, particularly if you're looking for somewhere to eat or drink. Upbeat **DCA** is the totemic building of the developing cultural quarter around which most of the city's lively artistic and social life revolves.

Arrival, information and city transport

Dundee's **airport** (Ⓣ01382/662200, Ⓦwww.hial.co.uk) is five minutes' drive west of the city centre. There are no buses into the centre – expect to fork out around £5 for a taxi. By **train**, you'll arrive at Taybridge Station on South Union Street, about 300yd south of the city centre near the river. Long-distance **buses** arrive at the Seagate bus station, a couple of hundred yards east of the centre.

The very helpful **tourist office** is right in the centre of things at 21 Castle St (June–Sept Mon–Sat 9am–6pm, Sun noon–4pm; Oct–May Mon–Sat 9am–5pm; Ⓣ01382/527527, Ⓦwww.angusanddundee.co.uk). Here you can get route maps for Maritime and Heritage Walking Trails (1–2hr duration; free), which depart from the DCA. There's also a map of a citywide cycle route. You should also be able to pick up the free *Accent* listings magazine, which details local theatre, music and exhibitions; Ⓦwww.dundee.com has local listings online. The city's two daily newspapers are the morning *Courier & Advertiser* and the *Evening Telegraph & Post*, and the main commercial radio station is Tay FM (96.4).

Dundee's centre is reasonably compact and you can walk to most sights; **local buses** leave from the High Street or from nearby Union Street; for bus information, call Ⓣ01382/201121, check Ⓦwww.traveldundee.co.uk or go to the Travel Dundee Travel Centre, in the Forum Centre at 92 Commercial St. A Daysaver ticket, with unlimited bus travel for a day, costs £2.70.

Accommodation

In a city that's only recently geared itself up for tourists, **accommodation** isn't plentiful, but it is comparatively inexpensive and there are some decent guesthouses out of the city centre. You'll find plenty of rooms out by the suburb of Broughty Ferry, which is connected to the city by a twenty-minute bus ride (£1.50) on Strathtay buses #71, #73 and #76 (all leave from either Commercial Street or Seagate in the town centre).

Hotels

Apex City Quay Hotel West Victoria Dock Road Ⓣ01382/202404, Ⓦwww.apexhotels.co.uk. Large, sleek and modern hotel which stands out among the new developments of the dockland area, incorporating a spa, swimming pool and restaurant. ❺

Discovery Quay Premier Travel Inn Riverside Drive Ⓣ08701/977079, Ⓦwww.premiertravelinn.com. Bland, modern chain hotel well positioned beside Discovery Point and the train station. ❹

Number Twenty Five 25 Tay St Ⓣ01382/200399, Ⓦww.socialanimal.co.uk. Right beside the action in a Georgian townhouse in the Cultural Quarter, with just four colour-themed designer rooms above a trendy bar and restaurant. ❹

Queen's Hotel 160 Nethergate Ⓣ01382/322515, Ⓦwww.queenshotel-dundee.com. Grand old hotel with some fine period touches that's now part of the Best Western group. Comfortable enough and handy for the city sights and Cultural Quarter. ❺

Guesthouses and B&Bs

Andersons Guest House 285 Perth Rd Ⓣ01382/668585, Ⓦwww.andersonsdundee.co.uk. Comfortable sandstone guesthouse 15min walk west of the train station and handy for routes north and south of Dundee. ❷

Cullaig Rosemount Terrace, Upper Constitution St Ⓣ01382/322154, Ⓦwww.cullaig.co.uk. Victorian six-bedroom terraced guesthouse, within walking distance from town on the lower slopes of Dundee Law. Child-friendly. ❷

Duntrune House Duntrune Ⓣ01382/350239, Ⓦwww.duntrunehouse.co.uk. Three spacious rooms in a wing of a grand but welcoming country house built in 1826 and standing in lovely mature gardens five miles northeast of Dundee. ❺

Errolbank 9 Dalgleish Rd ⓣ01382/462118, ⓦwww.errolbank-guesthouse.com. Friendly Victorian villa with clean bright rooms and good views of the Tay. Hearty Scottish breakfast. ❸

Fisherman's Tavern 10–16 Fort St, Broughty Ferry ⓣ01382/775941, ⓦfishermanstavern.co.uk. Neat contemporary rooms, mostly en suite, above a cosy and popular traditional pub with a roaring fire. Seafood and real ales a speciality. ❸

Hostel, campus accommodation and camping

Dundee Backpackers Hostel 57 High St ⓣ01382/224646 or 0131/220 2200, ⓦwww.hoppo.com. Dundee's only backpackers' hostel, with ninety beds located in a building constructed in 1560. ❶

Dundee Student Villages ⓣ01382/573111, ⓦwww.Scotland2000.com/seabraes. En-suite single or double rooms (❶) or exclusive use of self-catered flats sleeping up to eight (from £180 for 3 nights), located at Seabraes, just west of the city centre; bland but cheap. July & Aug only.

Riverview Caravan Park Marine Drive Monifieth ⓣ01382/535471, ⓦwww.riverview.co.uk. Well-run, year-round caravan park (no tents) in a suburb beyond Broughty Ferry. On-site sauna and gym.

West Park Conference Centre Perth Road ⓣ01382/647177, ⓦwww.westparkcentre.com. Comfortable, en-suite B&B-style accommodation within a grand, attractive Victorian mansion used mostly for conferences. June–Aug. ❷

The City and around

The best approach to Dundee is across the modern mile-and-a-half-long **Tay Road Bridge** from Fife. While the Tay bridges aren't nearly as spectacular as the bridges over the Forth near Edinburgh, they do offer a magnificent panorama of the city on the northern bank of the firth. Running parallel half a mile upstream is the **Tay Rail Bridge**, opened in 1887 to replace the spindly structure which collapsed in a storm in December 1879 only eighteen months after it was built, killing the crew and 75 passengers on a train passing over the bridge at the time.

Dundee's city centre, dominated by large shopping malls filled with mundane chain stores, is focused on attractive **City Square**, a couple of hundred yards north of the Tay. The main street, which is pedestrianized as it passes City Square, starts as Nethergate in the west, becomes High Street in the centre, and then divides into Murraygate (which is also pedestrianized) and Seagate. Opposite this junction is the mottled spire of **St Paul's Episcopal Cathedral** (hours vary; free), a rather gaudy Gothic Revival structure by George Gilbert Scott, notable for its vivid if sentimental stained glass and floridly gilded high altar. Immediately in front of the cathedral is a statue to one of the city's heroes, **Admiral Duncan of Camperdown**, who defeated a Dutch fleet not far offshore from Dundee during the Napoleonic Wars. Back where Reform Street meets City Square, look out for a couple of other statues to Dundee heroes: **Desperate Dan** and **Minnie the Minx**, both from the *Dandy* comic, which is produced a few hundred yards away in the D.C. Thomson building on Albert Square.

The **McManus Art Galleries and Museum** (Mon–Sat 10.30am–5pm, Sun 12.30–4.30pm; last entry 15min before closing; free; ⓦwww.mcmanus.co.uk), Dundee's most impressive Victorian structure, is located in Albert Square in the heart of the city. Recently reopened after a major restoration, this is an unmissable stop for art lovers. The ground-floor rooms explore the nature of museums, the surrounding natural landscape and the making of modern Dundee, while upstairs there's the splendid Victoria gallery, its curved red walls hung with an impressive collection of works by masters including Rossetti and Henry Raeburn. The rest of this floor is equally engrossing: Dundee and the World shows an eclectic ethnographic collection; the 20th Century Gallery showcases work by the Scottish Colourists and others; the Long Gallery is lined with historic and modern ceramics; while Here and Now displays fine art acquisitions, including contemporary photography. The museum's bright and attractive **café** is a good pit stop, especially on a sunny day when you can sit on the stone terrace outside.

There isn't much else in the way of tourist attractions in the heart of the city centre, though some visitors enjoy a snoop around the **Howff Burial Ground** (daily 9am–dusk), located across Ward Road from the museum, which has some great carved tombstones dating from the sixteenth to nineteenth centuries. Five minutes' walk west of here, on West Henderson Wynd in Blackness, an award-winning museum, **Verdant Works** (April–Oct Mon–Sat 10am–6pm, Sun 11am–6pm; Nov–March Wed–Sat 10.30am–4.30pm, Sun 11am–4.30pm; £7, joint ticket with Discovery Point £11.50; Ⓦwww.rrsdiscovery.com), tells the story of jute from its harvesting in India to its arrival in Dundee on clipper ships. The museum, set in an old jute mill, makes a lively attempt to re-create the turn-of-the-century factory floor, the highlight being the chance to watch jute being processed on fully operational quarter-size machines originally used for training workers.

The Cultural Quarter

Immediately west of the city centre, High Street becomes Nethergate and passes into what is now being dubbed, with a fair amount of justification, Dundee's "**Cultural Quarter**". As well as the university and the highly respected Rep Theatre, the area is also home to the best concentration of pubs and cafés in the city. Principal among the many arts venues is the hip and exciting **DCA**, or Dundee Contemporary Arts, at 152 Nethergate (Mon–Sat 10am–midnight, Sun noon–midnight; galleries Tues–Sat 10.30am–5.30pm, until 8.30pm Thurs, Sun noon–5.30pm; Ⓣ01382/909900, Ⓦwww.dca.org.uk), a stunning five-floor complex which incorporates galleries, a print studio, a classy design shop and an airy café-bar (see p.380). It's worth visiting for the stimulating temporary and touring exhibitions of contemporary art, as well as an eclectic programme of art-house films and cult classics.

Tucked in behind DCA is another modern building, **Sensation** (daily 10am–5pm; £7.25; Ⓣ01382/228800, Ⓦwww.sensation.org.uk), best approached from Greenmarket, off Marketgate. Aimed squarely at families and schoolchildren, it's a fun-packed exploration of science, using eighty different interactive exhibits and participatory experiments.

The waterfront

Just south of the city centre, at the water's edge alongside the Tay Road Bridge, the domed **Discovery Point** is an impressive development centring on the Royal Research Ship *Discovery* (April–Oct Mon–Sat 10am–6pm, Sun 11am–6pm; Nov–March Mon–Sat 10am–5pm, Sun 11am–5pm; £7.75, joint ticket with Verdant Works £11.50; Ⓦwww.rrsdiscovery.com). Something of an icon for Dundee's renaissance, *Discovery* is a three-mast steam-assisted vessel built in Dundee in 1901 to take Captain Robert Falcon Scott on his polar expeditions. A combination of brute strength and elegance, she has been beautifully restored, with polished wood panels and brass trimmings giving scant indication of the privations suffered by the crew. In the Antarctic, temperatures on board would plummet to -28°C and turns at having a bath came round every 47 days. Before you step aboard there are a series of interactive displays about the construction of the ship and Scott's journeys, including the chill-inducing "Polarama" about life in Antarctica.

In total contrast is the endearingly simple wooden frigate **Unicorn** (April–Oct daily 10am–5pm; Nov–March Wed–Fri noon–4pm, Sat & Sun 10am–4pm; £5; Ⓦwww.frigateunicorn.org), moored on the other side of the road bridge near the multi-million pound redevelopment of Victoria Dock (a footpath connects the two ships). Built in 1824, it's the oldest British warship still afloat and was in active service up until 1968. Although the interior is sparse, the cannons, the splendid figureheads and the wonderful model of the ship in its fully rigged glory (the real thing would have featured over 23 miles of rope) are fascinating.

Out from the centre

A mile or so north of town, **Dundee Law** is the plug of an extinct volcano and, at 571ft, the city's highest point. Once the site of a seventh-century defensive hill fort, it's now an impressive lookout, with great views across the whole city and the Tay; the climb is steep and often windy. It takes thirty minutes to walk to the foot of the Law from the city centre, or you can take bus #4 or #71 from Albert Square.

The city's other volcanic outcrop sits a mile to the west of Dundee Law. **Balgay Hill** is skirted by the wooded **Lochee Park**, while on its summit sits the **Mills Observatory** (April–Sept Tues–Fri 11am–5pm, Sat & Sun 12.30–4pm; Oct–March Mon–Fri 11am–10pm, Sat & Sun 12.30–4pm; free; ⓣ01382/435967), Britain's only full-time public observatory with a resident astronomer. The best time to go is after dark on winter nights; in summer there's little to be seen through the telescope, but well-explained, quirky exhibits and displays chart the history of space exploration and astronomy, and on sunny days you can play at being a human sundial and take in the fantastic views over the city through little telescopes. From October to March the **planetarium** runs a fortnightly show (Fri; £1), while the observatory also has special opening times to coincide with eclipses and other astronomical events. Buses #11, #9 or #17 from Nethergate drop you in Glamis Road, at the entrance to the park.

Broughty Ferry and around

Four miles east of Dundee's city centre lies the seaside settlement of **BROUGHTY FERRY** (ⓦwww.cometobroughty.co.uk) now engulfed by the city as a reluctant suburb. The ferry referred to in the name was a railway ferry, carrying carriages travelling between Edinburgh and Aberdeen, which was inevitably closed following the building of the first ill-fated Tay Rail Bridge. Comprising an eclectic mix of big villas built by jute barons up the hillside and small fishermen's cottages along the shoreline, "The Ferry", as it's known, has experienced a recent resurgence in popularity. It's now a pleasant and relaxing spot with some good restaurants and pubs, and both the beach and the castle's "green", or grounds, are popular run-around spots for kids. The striking **Broughty Castle and Museum**, right by the seashore (April–Sept Mon–Sat 10am–4pm, Sun 12.30–4pm; Oct–March Tues–Sat 10am–4pm, Sun 12.30–4pm; free), is worth a look. Built in 1496 to protect the estuary, its four floors now house local history and military exhibits and cover the story of Broughty Ferry from 400 million years ago to its development as a fishing village.

Just north of Broughty Ferry, at the junction of the A92 and B978, the chunky bricks of **Claypotts Castle** (limited opening hours – details on ⓣ01786/431324; free) constitute one of Scotland's most complete Z-shaped tower houses. Built between 1569 and 1588, its two round towers have stepped projections to support extra rooms, a sixteenth-century architectural practice that makes Claypotts look like it's about to topple.

Eating, drinking and nightlife

The west end of Dundee, around the main university campus and Perth Road, is the best area for **eating and drinking**; the city centre has a few good pubs and one or two decent restaurants tucked away. Broughty Ferry is a pleasant alternative, with a good selection of pubs and restaurants that get particularly busy on summer evenings. The best of the local **delis** is *Taste Fresh* at 11 Union St, while *Robertson's* on Brook Street is the best place to stock up in Broughty Ferry.

Restaurants and cafés

Agacan 113 Perth Rd ⓣ01382/644227. Tiny, moderately priced Turkish restaurant with an unmistakeable colourful exterior, and rough-hewn walls inside; they serve up decent kebabs and stuffed pittas, and also do takeaways. Closed lunchtimes & all day Mon.

Alchemy Apex Dundee City Quay ⓣ0845/365 0002, ⓦwww.apexhotels.co.uk. A style-led but still pleasant restaurant space on the ground floor of the dockland's sleekest hotel. Imaginative, fairly expensive Scottish cuisine with themed tasting menus. Thurs–Sat. The moderately priced *Metro Brasserie & Bar* shares the same space and is open daily.

The Blue Marlin 9 Reform St, Monifieth ⓣ01382/534001, ⓦwww.thebluemarlin.co.uk. As the name suggests, a dedicated seafood restaurant serving lunches and dinners of crab cakes, langoustines, halibut and the like. Closed Sun & Mon.

Bon Appetit 22–26 Exchange St ⓣ01382/809000, ⓦwww.bonappetit-dundee.com. Probably the most reliable (if not necessarily glamorous) spot for well-sourced, confidently cooked food in the city. Friendly service and authentic, good-value French cuisine. Closed Sun.

The Glass Pavilion The Esplanade, Broughty Ferry ⓣ01382/732738, ⓦwww.theglasspavilion.co.uk. Dramatic, glass-fronted former (1930s) bathing shelter with Art Deco styling serving delicious home-baking, healthy light meals and a sumptuous traditional high tea (5–7pm; £12.95). Closed Mon. Dinner Fri/Sat only.

Jute Café-Bar DCA, 152 Nethergate. ⓣ01382/809000. An airy café, popular with trendy students and offering well-priced pre-theatre dining.

Parrot Café 91 Perth Rd ⓣ01382/206277. Art on the walls, and home-made soups, sarnies and cakes on the tables in this traditional wee café.

Rama Thai 32–34 Dock St ⓣ01382/223366, ⓦwww.rama-thai.co.uk. Grand Thai restaurant with chunky carved furniture and a tasty, well-executed menu. Good-value three-course set lunch.

Pubs

Deacon Brodies 15 Ward Rd ⓣ01382/204137, ⓦdeaconbrodies.co.uk. Central bar with good-value meals and nightly karaoke for budding crooners.

Drouthy's 142 Perth Rd. Revamped and glamourized pub with regular live music: rock, jazz and Scottish.

Fisherman's Tavern 10–16 Fort St, Broughty Ferry. Just off the shore in a busy traditional cottage, this pub serves a variety of real ales and is a popular weekend haunt for seafood lunches including Arbroath Smokie Pie.

Laing's 8 Roseangle, off Perth Rd ⓦwww.laingsbar.co.uk. Packed on warm summer nights, thanks to its beer garden and great river views. Lively student haunt and footie screenings.

Ship Inn 121 Fisher St, Broughty Ferry ⓣ01382/779176, ⓦwww.theshipinn-broughty-ferry.co.uk. A narrow pub with a warm atmosphere and nautical feel right on the waterfront with good views over the Tay. Good seafood dishes with fine selection of beers.

Trades House Bar 40 Nethergate. A converted bank fronted with stained-glass windows that offers drinkers a convivial atmosphere in the heart of the city.

Nightlife

When it comes to post-pub **nightlife**, Dundee is muted to say the least. The main **nightclubs** are *Fat Sam's* at 31 South Ward Rd (ⓦwww.fatsams.co.uk) and *Déjà Vu* at 25–29 Cowgate, while **live music** venues include hip and studenty *The Social* on South Tay Street and *Hustlers* at 66 North Lindsay St.

Right at the heart of the Cultural Quarter on Tay Square, north of Nethergate, is the prodigious Dundee Repertory Theatre (ⓣ01382/223530, ⓦwww.dundeereptheatre.co.uk), an excellent place for indigenously produced contemporary **theatre** and the home of the only permanent repertory company in Scotland. The best venue for **classical music**, including visits by the Royal Scottish National Orchestra and other bigwigs, is Caird Hall (ⓣ01382/434940, ⓦwww.cairdhall.co.uk), whose bulky frontage dominates City Square. For **movies**, DCA (ⓣ01382/909900, ⓦwww.dca.org.uk) has two comfy auditoriums showing an appealing range of foreign and art-house movies alongside the more challenging mainstream releases; otherwise you have to head a fair way out of the centre to the Cineworld multiplex at Camperdown Leisure Park (ⓣ0871/200 2000; bus #3 or #4 from Albert Square) or the Odeon at Douglasfield, east of the city (ⓣ0871/224 4007; bus #15 or #29).

Listings

Bike rental Easy Ride Cycles, off William Fitzgerald Way, Barns of Claverhouse ⓣ01382/505683 (from £6/day).

Books Black Hole Comic Shop (secondhand comics), 5 Victoria Rd; Waterstone's, 35 Commercial St.

Bus information Scottish Citylink ⓣ0871/266 3333; Stagecoach Strathtay for regional buses ⓣ01382/228345; Traveline Scotland ⓣ0871/200 2233.

Car rental Arnold Clark, East Dock St ⓣ01382/225382; Alamo, 45–53 Gellatly St ⓣ0870/400 4562; Hertz, 18 West Marketgate ⓣ01382/223711.

Flight information ⓣ01382/662200, ⓦwww.hial.co.uk.

Gay, lesbian and bisexual Switchboard ⓣ01382/202620 (Mon 7–9pm), ⓦwww.diversitay.org.uk.

Internet At the Central Library (see below) and the tourist office.

Library The Central Library is in the Wellgate Shopping Centre (Mon–Fri 9.30am–8.30pm, Sat 9.30am–4.30pm).

Medical facilities Ninewells Hospital in the west of the city has an Accident and Emergency department (ⓣ01382/660111). Dundee Dental Hospital (ⓣ01382/425791). Boots pharmacy is at 49–53 High St (ⓣ01382/221756, Mon–Sat 8.30am–6pm, Thurs closes 7.30pm, Sun 11am–5pm).

Police Tayside Police HQ, West Bell St ⓣ01382/223200.

Post office 4 Meadowside (Mon–Fri 9am–5.30pm, Sat 9am–12.30pm).

Sport The city has two leading football clubs, Dundee (ⓣ01382/889966, ⓦwww.dundeefc.co.uk) and Dundee United (ⓣ01382/833166, ⓦwww.dundeeunitedfc.co.uk), whose stadiums face each other across Tannadice St in the north of the city. Fortunes fluctuate for the teams, but one or the other is usually playing in the Premier League. There are public golf courses at Ashludie, Golf Ave, Monifieth (ⓣ01382/535553); Caird Park (ⓣ01382/438871); and Camperdown Country Park (ⓣ01382/431820). Other courses along the Angus coast include Carnoustie (ⓣ01241/853789, ⓦwww.carnoustiegolflinks.co.uk), a British Open venue. The Olympia Leisure Centre, beside Discovery Point, has a swimming pool (during school term: Mon–Fri 10am–8.30pm, Sat & Sun 10am–5.30pm; ⓣ01382/432300 or 432331).

Taxis There are taxi ranks on Nethergate, or call Dundee Private Hire ⓣ01382/203020; Handy Taxis ⓣ01382/889176; or 505050 Taxis ⓣ01382/505050.

The Angus coast

Two roads link Dundee to Aberdeen and the northeast coast of Scotland. By far the more pleasant option is the slightly longer A92 coast road, which joins the inland A90 at Stonehaven, just south of Aberdeen. Intercity **buses** follow both roads, while the coast-hugging train line from Dundee is one of the most picturesque in Scotland, passing attractive beaches and impressive cliffs, and stopping in the old seaports of **Arbroath** and **Montrose**.

Arbroath and around

Since it was settled in the twelfth century, local fishermen have been landing their catches at **ARBROATH**, situated on the Angus coast where it starts to curve in from the North Sea towards the Firth of Tay, about fifteen miles northeast of Dundee. The name of the town stems from Aber Brothock, the burn which runs into the sea here, and although it has a great location, with long sandy beaches and stunning sandstone cliffs on either side of town as well as an attractive old working harbour, Arbroath – like Dundee – has suffered from short-sighted development.

The town's most famous product is the **Arbroath smokie** – line-caught haddock, smoke-cured over smouldering oak chips, and still made here in a number of family-run smokehouses tucked in around the harbour. One of the most approachable and atmospheric is M&M Spink's tiny whitewashed premises at 10 Marketgate (ⓣ01241/875287); chef and cookery writer Rick Stein described the fish here, warm from the smoke, as "a world-class delicacy".

Down by the harbour, the elegant Regency **Signal House Museum** (Mon–Sat 10am–5pm, July & Aug also Sun 2–5pm; free) stands sentinel as it has since 1813 when it was built as the shore station for the Bell Rock lighthouse, improbably erected on a reef eleven miles offshore by Robert Stevenson. The interior is now given over to some excellent local history displays: a schoolroom, fisherman's cottage and lighthouse kitchen have all been carefully re-created.

Arbroath Abbey

By the late eighteenth century, chiefly due to its harbour, Arbroath had become a trading and manufacturing centre, famed for boot-making and sail-making (the *Cutty Sark*'s sails were made here). The town's real glory days, however, came much earlier in the thirteenth century with the completion in 1233 of **Arbroath Abbey** (daily: April–Sept 9.30am–5.30pm; Oct–March 9.30am–4.30pm; HS; £4.70; ⓣ01241/878756, ⓦwww.historic-scotland.gov.uk), whose rose-pink sandstone ruins, described by Dr Johnson as "fragments of magnificence", stand on Abbey Street. Founded in 1178 but not granted abbey status until 1285, it was the scene of one of the most significant events in Scotland's history when, on April 6, 1320, a group of Scottish barons drew up the **Declaration of Arbroath**, asking the pope to reverse his excommunication of Robert the Bruce and recognize him as king of a Scottish nation independent from England. The wonderfully resonant language of the document still makes for stirring reading: "For so long as one hundred of us remain alive, we will never in any degree be subject to the dominion of the English, since it is not for glory, riches or honour that we do fight, but for freedom alone, which no honest man loses but with his life." It was duly dispatched to Pope John XXII in Avignon, who in 1324 agreed to Robert's claim.

The abbey was dissolved during the Reformation, and by the eighteenth century it was little more than a source of red sandstone for local houses. However, there's enough left to get a good idea of how vast the place must have been: the semicircular **west doorway** is more or less intact, complete with medieval mouldings, and the **south transept** has a beautiful round window, once lit with a beacon to guide ships. In the early 1950s, the **Stone of Destiny** had a brief sojourn here when it was stolen from London by a group of Scottish nationalists and appeared, wrapped in a Scottish flag, at the High Altar. It was duly returned to Westminster Abbey, where it stayed until its relatively recent move to Edinburgh Castle (see p.80). A **visitor centre** at the Abbey Street entrance offers background on these events and other aspects of the history of the building.

Around Arbroath: St Vigeans and Auchmithie

Although now little more than a northwestern dormitory of Arbroath, the pristine and peaceful hamlet of **ST VIGEANS** is a fine example of a Pictish site colonized by Christians: the church is set defiantly on a pre-Christian mound at the centre of the village. Many **Pictish stones** and fragments, dating back to 842 AD are housed in the wonderful little museum, including the Drosten Stone, presumed to be a memorial. One side depicts a hunt, laced with an abundance of Pictish symbolism, while the other side bears a cross.

Four miles north of Arbroath by road or coastal footpath, the cliff-top village of **AUCHMITHIE** is the true home of the Arbroath smokie. However, the village didn't have a proper harbour until the nineteenth century – local fishermen, apparently, were carried to their boats by their wives to avoid getting wet feet – so Arbroath became the more important port and laid claim to the delicacy. Now an attractive little fishing village, Auchmithie's main attraction is the busy *But'n'Ben* **restaurant** (ⓣ01241/877223; closed Tues), one of the best along this coast, which specializes in delicious, moderately priced seafood and serves a fabulous high tea.

Practicalities

Arbroath's helpful **tourist office** enjoys views over the sea from its new location at Fishmarket Quay in the revamped harbour area (July & Aug daily; Sept–June Mon–Sat; ⓣ01241/872609). The **bus** station is on Catherine Street, about a five-minute walk south of the tourist office, and **trains** arrive at the station just across the road on Keptie Street.

For somewhere **to stay**, the central and friendly *Old Vicarage* (ⓣ01241/430475, ⓦwww.theoldvicaragebandb.co.uk; ④) offers a breakfast table that includes smokies, a freshly baked loaf and home-made preserves. There's also the *Five Gables House* (ⓣ01241/871632, ⓦwww.fivegableshouse.co.uk; ③), a mile south of Arbroath on the A92, in a great position overlooking the sea. The best way to sample Arbroath smokies is while they're still warm, straight from one of the smokehouses. *The Old Brewhouse* (ⓣ01241/879945) is a convivial and moderately priced restaurant-cum-pub by the harbour wall at the end of High Street. The locals' favourite chippy is *Peppo's* by the harbour at 51 Ladybridge St.

Montrose and around

Here's the Basin, there's Montrose, shut your een and haud your nose.

As the old rhyme indicates, **MONTROSE**, a seaport and market town since the thirteenth century, can sometimes smell a little rich, mostly because of its position on the edge of a virtually landlocked two-mile-square lagoon of mud known as the Basin. But with the wind in the right direction, the ancient Royal Burgh of Montrose is a great town to visit, with a pleasant old centre and an interesting museum. The Basin too is of interest: flooded and emptied twice daily by the tides, it's a nature reserve for the host of geese, swans and wading birds who frequent the ooze. On the south side of the Basin, a mile out of Montrose along the A92, the **Montrose Basin Wildlife Centre** (March–Oct daily 10.30am–5pm; Nov–Feb Fri–Sun 10.30am–4pm; £4; ⓦwww.montrosebasin.org.uk) has binoculars, high-powered telescopes, bird hides and remote-control video cameras.

Montrose locals are known as "Gable Endies", because of the unusual way in which the town's eighteenth- and nineteenth-century merchants, influenced by architectural styles they had seen on the continent, built their houses gable-end to the street. The few remaining original gabled houses line the wide **High Street**.

Two blocks behind the soaring kirk steeple at the lower end of High Street, the **Montrose Museum and Art Gallery** (Mon–Sat 10am–5pm; free), on Panmure Place on the western side of Mid Links Park, is one of Scotland's oldest museums, dating from 1842. In the local history section, look out for the mechanical paper sculpture of the town, with a green train running along the top and yachts sailing by.

Outside the museum entrance stands a winsome study of a boy by local sculptor William Lamb (1893–1951). More of his work can be seen in the moving **William Lamb Memorial Studio** on Market Street (July to mid-Sept daily 2–5pm; at other times, ask at the museum; free), including bronze heads of the Queen, Princess Margaret and the Queen Mother. A superbly talented but largely unheralded artist, Lamb is the more impressive because he taught himself to sculpt with his left hand, having suffered a war wound in his right. You can see another Lamb sculpture, *Whisper*, outside the library on the High Street.

Finally, don't ignore the town's fabulous golden **seashore**. The beach road, Marine Avenue, across from the town museum, heads down through sand dunes and golf links to car parks fringing the fine, wide beach overlooked by a slender white lighthouse.

Practicalities

Most **buses** stop in the High Street, while the **train** station lies a block back on Western Road. For attractive B&B **accommodation**, try *36 The Mall*, in the north of town (ⓣ01674/673464, ⓦwww.36themall.co.uk; ❷). *Lunan Lodge* (ⓣ01241/830679, ⓦwww.lunanlodge.co.uk; ❹), located just south of Montrose by Inverkeilor near the sweep of Lunan Bay, is an Angus gem. The friendly owners will pick you up from Montrose or Arbroath train station and in addition to a gargantuan breakfast can rustle up a picnic lunch or hearty dinner.

For **eating**, the liveliest (though hardly cosiest) place in Montrose is unquestionably *Roo's Leap* (ⓣ01674/672157, ⓦwww.roosleap.com), a sports bar and restaurant by the golf club off the northern end of Trail Drive, with an unlikely but decent mix of moderately priced Scottish and Australian cuisine.

Around Montrose: the House of Dun

Across the Basin, four miles west of Montrose, is the Palladian **House of Dun** (April–June & Sept–Oct Wed–Sun 12.30pm–5pm; July & Aug daily 11.30am–5pm; NTS; £8.50), accessible on the hourly Montrose–Brechin Strathtay Scottish bus #30; ask the driver to let you off outside. Built in 1730 for David Erskine, Laird of Dun, to designs by William Adam, the house was opened to the public in 1989 after extensive restoration, and is crammed full of period furniture and *objets d'art*. Inside, the ornate relief plasterwork is the most impressive feature, extravagantly emblazoned with Jacobite symbolism. The buildings in the courtyard – a hen house, gamekeeper's workshop and potting shed – have been renovated, and include a tearoom and a craft shop. Bikes can be rented from the shop.

Strathmore and the Angus glens

Immediately north of Dundee, the low-lying Sidlaw Hills divide the city from the rich agricultural region of **Strathmore**, whose string of tidy market towns lies on a fertile strip along the southernmost edge of the heather-covered lower slopes of the Grampian Mountains. These towns act as gateways to the tranquil **Angus glens**, offering some of the most rugged and majestic landscapes in northeast Scotland. **Glen Clova** in particular is well and truly on the tourist circuit, with the rolling hills and dales attracting hikers, birdwatchers and botanists in the summer, grouse shooters and deer-hunters in autumn and winter skiers who pray for a bountiful snowfall. The most useful road through the glens is the A93, which cuts through **Glen Shee**, linking Blairgowrie to Braemar on Deeside (see p.408). It's pretty dramatic stuff, threading its way over Britain's highest main road, the **Cairnwell Pass** (2199ft).

Public transport in the region is limited: to get up the glens you'll have to rely on the **postbuses** from Blairgowrie (for Glen Shee and Glen Isla) and Kirriemuir (for Glen Clova).

Blairgowrie and Glen Shee

The upper reaches of **Glen Shee**, the most dramatic and best known of the Angus glens, are dominated by its **ski fields**, ranged over four mountains above the Cairnwell mountain pass. During the season (Dec–March), ski lifts and tows give access to gentle beginners' slopes, while experienced skiers can try the more intimidating Tiger run. In summer it's all a bit sad, although there are some excellent hiking and mountain-biking routes.

To get to Glen Shee from the south you'll pass through the well-heeled little town of **BLAIRGOWRIE**, set among raspberry fields on the glen's southernmost

Skiing at Glen Shee

Scotland's **ski resorts** may not amount to much more than gentle training slopes in comparison with those of the Alps or North America, but they all make for a fun day out for everyone from beginners to experienced skiers. The strongest card of all the resorts is probably their scenic surroundings, and given that **Glen Shee** is both the most extensive and the most accessible of Scotland's ski areas, just over two hours from both Glasgow and Edinburgh, it's as good an introduction as any to the sport in Scotland.

For information, contact Ski Glenshee (ⓣ013397/41320, ⓦwww.ski-glenshee.co.uk), which also offers ski rental and lessons, as does Cairnwell Mountain Sports (ⓣ01250/885255, ⓦwww.cairnwellmountainsports.co.uk), at the Spittal of Glenshee. For the latest snow and **weather conditions**, phone Ski Glenshee or check out the Ski Scotland website (ⓦski.visitscotland.com). For **cross-country** skiing, there are some good touring areas in the vicinity; contact Cairnwell Mountain Sports or Braemar Mountain Sports (ⓣ013397/41242, ⓦwww.braemarmountainsports.com) for information and equipment rental.

tip and a good place to pick up information and plan your activities. Strictly two communities – Blairgowrie and **Rattray**, set on either side of the River Ericht – the town's modest claim to fame is that St Ninian once camped at Wellmeadow, a pleasant grassy triangle in the town centre. If you've time to kill here, wander up the leafy riverbank past a series of old mill buildings. Altogether more ambitious is the 64-mile **Cateran Trail** (ⓦwww.caterantrail.org), a long-distance footpath that starts in Blairgowrie, then heads off on a long loop into the glens to the north following some of the drove roads used by caterans, or cattle thieves. It's a four- to five-day tramp, though of course it's possible to walk shorter sections of the way.

Blairgowrie's friendly **tourist office** (April–Oct daily; Nov–March Tues–Sat; ⓣ01250/872960, ⓦwww.perthshire.co.uk) on the high side of Wellmeadow can help with **accommodation**. A number of Blairgowrie's grand houses offer B&B, among them *Heathpark House* (ⓣ01250/870700, ⓦwww.heathparkhouse.com; ❹) on the Coupar Angus Road. Otherwise, try the airy and comfortable rooms at *West Freuchies* in the village of Glenisla (ⓣ01575/582716, ⓦwww.glenisla-westfreuchies.co.uk; ❸). **Camping** is available at the year-round *Blairgowrie Holiday Park* on Rattray's Hatton Road (ⓣ01250/876666), within walking distance of Wellmeadow.

Blairgowrie has plenty of places to **eat**: *Cargills* (ⓣ01250/876735, ⓦwww.cargillsbistro.com) by the river on Lower Mill Street serves inexpensive formal meals and civilized coffee and cakes; *Antiquary* (ⓣ01250/873232), along the same road, provides more upmarket dining; while the inexpensive *Dome Restaurant*, just behind the tourist office, is a cheery place serving hearty platefuls of traditional grub. On Reform Street, pop into Blairgowrie Farm Shop for jams, vegetables, organic breads and deli items, while for a good local **pub** try the convivial and historic *Ericht Alehouse* on Wellmeadow. Alternatively, head six miles north of town on the A93 to the welcoming *Bridge of Cally Hotel* (ⓣ01250/886231, ⓦwww.bridgeofcallyhotel.com; ❺), which serves food all day, plus real ale by an open fire. Back in Blairgowrie you can rent **bikes** from Scottish Cycling Holidays, 87 Perth St (ⓣ01250/876100).

Nearly twenty miles north of Blairgowrie, the small settlement of **SPITTAL OF GLENSHEE** (the name derives from the same root as "hospital", indicating a refuge), though ideally situated for skiing, has little to commend it other than the busy *Gulabin Bunkhouse* (❶) on the A93, run by Cairnwell Mountain Sports (see box above). Tucked away among the hills behind Spittal, *Dalmunzie House*

(Ⓣ01250/885224, Ⓦwww.dalmunzie.com; ❼) is a lovely Highland retreat in a magnificent turreted mansion, with first-class dining and over sixty malt whiskies. From Spittal the road climbs another five miles or so to the ski centre at the crest of the Cairnwell Pass.

Blairgowrie is well linked by hourly **bus** #57 to both Perth and Dundee and the #71 runs at least twice daily (Mon–Sat) to Pitlochry via Bridge of Cally. To travel up Glen Shee, you'll have to rely on the **postbus**, which leaves town at 7.30am (not Sun) and returns from the Spittal of Glenshee at 12.30pm.

Meigle and Glen Isla

Fifteen miles north of Dundee on the B954 lies the tiny settlement of **MEIGLE**, home to Scotland's most important collection of early Christian and Pictish **inscribed stones**. Housed in a modest former schoolhouse, the **Meigle Museum** (April–Sept daily 9.30am–5.30pm; HS; £3.20) displays some thirty pieces dating from the seventh to the tenth centuries, all found in and around the nearby churchyard. The majority are either gravestones that would have lain flat, or cross slabs inscribed with the sign of the cross, usually standing. Most impressive is the seven-foot-tall great cross slab, said to be the gravestone of Guinevere, wife of King Arthur. The exact purpose of the stones and their enigmatic symbols is obscure, as is the reason why so many of them were found at Meigle. The most likely theory suggests that Meigle was once an important ecclesiastical centre that attracted secular burials of prominent Picts.

Glen Isla

Three miles north of Meigle is **ALYTH**, near which, legend has it, Guinevere was held captive by Mordred. The sleepy village lies at the south end of **Glen Isla**, which runs parallel to Glen Shee and is linked to it by the A926. Dominated by Mount Blair (2441ft), Glen Isla suffers from an excess of angular conifers alongside great bald chunks of hillside waiting to be planted. Heading north along the B954, the River Isla narrows and then plunges some 60ft into a deep gorge to produce the classically pretty waterfall of **Reekie Linn**, or "smoking fall", so called because of the water mist produced when the fall hits a ledge and bounces a further 20ft into a deep pool known as the Black Dub. Just after this, a side road leads east to the pleasant Loch of Lintrathen while, back into the glen proper, you'll come to the tiny hamlet of **KIRKTON OF GLENISLA** ten miles or so up the glen. Here, the cosy *Glenisla Hotel* (Ⓣ01575/582223, Ⓦwww.glenisla-hotel.com; ❹) is good for classy home-made bar food and convivial drinking. There are some relatively easy **hiking** trails in the nearby Glenisla forest, while just before Kirkton, a turn-off on the right-hand side leads northeast up a long bumpy road to the *Glenmarkie Guesthouse Health Spa and Riding Centre* (Ⓣ01575/582295, Ⓦwww.glenmarkie.co.uk; ❷), where the treats include reiki, massage and the chance to fish or pony trek.

Transport connections into the glen are limited: Alyth is on the main bus routes linking Blairgowrie with Dundee and Kirriemuir, while hourly bus #57 from Dundee to Perth passes through Meigle. Transport up to Kirkton is limited to a postbus that leaves Blairgowrie at 7am (not Sun) and travels via Alyth to arrive around 10.35am.

Forfar and around

Around fifteen miles north of Dundee on the main A90 lies **FORFAR**, Angus's county town and the ancient capital of the Picts. The wide High Street is framed by some impressive Victorian architecture and small old-fashioned shops. Midway along, at 20 West High St, the **Meffan Institute Museum and Art Gallery** (Mon–Sat 10am–5pm; free) exhibits Neolithic, Pictish and Celtic remains and a thoroughly enjoyable collection of re-created historical street scenes. The most disturbing examines the town's seventeenth-century passion for witch-hunting, with a taped re-creation of locals baying for blood.

A series of glacial lochs peters out in the west of the town at **Forfar Loch**, now surrounded by a pleasant country park with a visitor centre and three-mile nature trail. Two miles east and situated in the middle of farmland are the remains of **Restenneth Priory** (free access), approached along a hard-to-spot side road off the B9113. King Nechtan of the Picts was thought to have established a place of worship here in the eighth century, although the oldest parts of the present structure are from an Augustinian priory erected on the spot around 1100. A little way south of this, off the B9128, a cairn in the village of **DUNNICHEN** commemorates a battle at nearby Nechtansmere in 685 in which the Picts unexpectedly defeated a Northumbrian army, thus preventing the Angles from extending their kingdom northwards.

While on Forfar's High Street, it's worth popping into the quaint shops and bakers that proudly stock the famous **Forfar Bridie**, a semicircular folded pastry-case of mince, onion and seasonings: MacLarens at 8 West High St is the locals' favourite. Note that many shops close on a Thursday afternoon. Try *O'Hara's* **pub** at 41 West High St for decent pub grub and real ales.

Glamis Castle

Bus #22 from Forfar runs regularly to Dundee via the pink-sandstone **Glamis Castle** (daily 10am–6pm, last tour 4.30pm; £8.75; Ⓦ www.glamis-castle.co.uk), located a mile north of the picturesque village of **GLAMIS** (pronounced "glahms"). A wondrously over-the-top, L-shaped five-storey pile set in an extensive landscaped park, this is one of Scotland's most famous castles. Shakespeare chose it as a central location in *Macbeth*, and its **royal connections** (as the childhood home of the late Queen Mother and birthplace of the late Princess Margaret) make it one of the essential stops on every coach tour of Scotland.

Approaching the castle down the long main drive, a riot of turrets, towers and conical roofs appears fantastically at the end of the sweeping avenue of trees, framed by the Grampian Mountains. The bulk of the current building dates from the fifteenth century, although many of the later additions give it its startling Disneyesque appearance. Glamis began life as a comparatively humble hunting lodge, used in the eleventh century by the kings of Scotland. In 1372 King Robert II gave the property to his son-in-law, Sir John Lyon, who built the core of the present building. His descendants, the earls of Kinghorne and Strathmore, have lived here ever since.

Obligatory guided tours take in the fifteenth-century **crypt**, where the 12ft-thick walls enclose a haunted "lost" room, reputed to have been sealed with the red-bearded lord of Glamis and Crawford inside, after he dared to play cards with the Devil one Sabbath. In the family **chapel**, completed in 1688, artist Jacob de Wet was commissioned to produce the frescoes, and his depictions of Christ wearing a hat and St Peter in a pair of glasses have raised eyebrows ever since. **Duncan's Hall**, a fifteenth-century guardroom, is the traditional – but inaccurate – setting for Duncan's murder by Macbeth (it actually took place near Elgin).

Glamis' **grounds**, including the Italian Gardens, are worth a few hours in their own right. There are lead statues of James VI and Charles I at the top of the main drive, a seventeenth-century Baroque sundial, a commemorative archway to Princess Margaret and verdant walks out to Earl John's Bridge and through the woodland. In Glamis village, on the edge of the castle's grounds, the humble

Angus Folk Museum (April–June & Sept Sat noon–5pm, Sun 1–5pm; July & Aug Mon–Sat 11am–5pm, Sun 1–5pm; NTS; £5), housed in six low-slung cottages in Kirk Wynd, has a bewildering array of local ephemera.

Aberlemno

Five miles east of Forfar, straddling the ridge-topping B9134, the hamlet of **ABERLEMNO** is home to a superb collection of open-air Pictish stones, unfortunately boxed out of sight in winter (Oct–April) in weatherproofed wood. In the churchyard, just off the main road, an eighth-century cross slab combines a swirling Christian Celtic cross with Pictish beasts on one side and an elaborate Pictish battle scene on the other, thought to commemorate victory over the Northumbrians in 685. Three other stones, bristling with Pictish and early Christian symbols, sit by the main road, overlooking huge sweeps of valley and mountain. The Forfar to Brechin **bus** #21A stops in Aberlemno.

Kirriemuir and glens Prosen, Clova and Doll

The sandstone town of **KIRRIEMUIR**, known locally as Kirrie, is set on a hill six miles northwest of Forfar on the cusp of glens Clova and Prosen. Despite the influx of hunters up for the "season", it's still a pretty special place, a haphazard confection of narrow closes, twisting wynds and steep braes. The main cluster of streets have all the appeal of an old film set, with their old-fashioned bars, tiled butcher's shop, tartan outlets and haberdasheries somehow managing to avoid being contrived and quaint.

Kirrie was the birthplace of **J.M. Barrie**. A local handloom-weaver's son, Barrie first came to notice with his series of novels about "Thrums", a village based on his home town, in particular *A Window in Thrums* and his third novel, *The Little Minister*. The story of Peter Pan, the little boy who never grew up, was penned by Barrie in 1904 – some say as a response to a strange upbringing dominated by the memory of his older brother, who died as a child. **Barrie's birthplace**, a plain little whitewashed cottage at 9 Brechin Rd (April–June & Sept–Oct Mon–Wed & Sat noon–5pm, Sun 1–5pm; July & Aug daily 11am–5pm; NTS; £5.50, includes entrance to the camera obscura), has a series of small rooms decorated as they would have been during Barrie's childhood, as well as displays about his life and works. The wash house outside was apparently the model for the house built by the Lost Boys for Wendy in Never-Never Land. Despite being offered a prestigious plot at London's Westminster Abbey, Barrie chose to be buried in Kirrie, and the unassuming family grave can be seen in the town cemetery, a short walk from the **camera obscura** (April–June Sat & Sun noon–5pm; July–Sept Mon–Sat noon–5pm, Sun 1–5pm; NTS; £3 or £5.50 combined with Barrie's birthplace), in the old cricket pavilion above town just off West Hill Road. This unexpected treasure was donated to the town in 1930 by Barrie, and offers splendid views of Strathmore and the glens. Another local son who attracts a handful of rather different pilgrims is **Bon Scott** of the rock band AC/DC, who was born and lived here before emigrating to Australia.

More on Scott can be found at Kirriemuir's **Gateway to the Glens Museum** (April–Sept Mon–Sat 10am–5pm; Oct–March Mon, Wed & Fri–Sat 10am–5pm, Thurs 1–5pm; free), in the old Town House on the main square. The oldest building in Kirrie, it has seen service as a tollbooth, court, jail, post office, police station and chemist; these days you can find two floors of interactive displays and exhibits on the town and the Angus Glens, including a scale model of Kirrie in 1604.

Reasonable **accommodation** is available at the attractive, inn-styled *Airlie Arms*, St Malcolm's Wynd (Ⓣ01575/572847, Ⓦwww.theairliearms.co.uk; ❹), while on the edge of town, and offering a taste of the rolling countryside, is *Muirhouses Farm* (Ⓣ01575/573128, Ⓦwww.muirhousesfarm.co.uk; ❸), a working cattle farm with bright plain rooms. Six miles from town towards Glen Isla, the cosy and luxurious *Falls of Holm* guesthouse (Ⓣ01575/575867, Ⓦwww.fallsofholm.com; ❷) offers an attractive alternative. Back in town by the square, *Visocchi's* is great for daytime **snacks** and ice cream, while *Hook's Hotel* on Bank Street serves good food in the evening. The hourly #20 bus runs from Kirriemuir High Street to Forfar and Dundee.

Glen Prosen

Five miles north of Kirrie, and past Memus where *The Drovers Inn* serves good-value bar lunches, the low-key hamlet of **DYKEHEAD** marks the point where **Glen Prosen** and Glen Clova divide. A mile or so up Glen Prosen, you'll find the house where Captain Scott and fellow explorer Doctor Wilson planned their ill-fated trip to Antarctica in 1910–11, with a roadside **stone cairn** commemorating the expedition. From here on, Glen Prosen remains essentially a quiet wooded backwater, with all the wild and rugged splendour of the other glens but without the crowds. To explore the area thoroughly you need to go on foot, but a good road circuit can be made by crossing the river at the tiny village of **GLENPROSEN** and returning to Kirriemuir along the western side of the glen via Pearsie. Alternatively, the reasonably easy four-mile **Minister's Path** links Prosen with Clova. It is clearly marked and leaves from near the church in the village.

Glen Clova and Glen Doll

With its stunning cliffs, heather slopes and valley meadows, **Glen Clova** – which in the north becomes **Glen Doll** – is one of the loveliest of the Angus glens. Although it can get unpleasantly congested in peak season, the area is still

Walks from Glen Doll

Ordnance Survey Explorer maps nos. 388 & 387

These **walks** are some of the main routes across the Grampians from the Angus glens to Deeside, many of which follow well-established old drovers' roads. All three either fringe or cross the royal estate of Balmoral, and Prince Charles's favourite mountain – **Lochnagar** – can be seen from all angles. The walks all begin from the car park at the end of the tarred road where Glen Clova meets Glen Doll; all routes should always be approached with care, and you should follow the usual safety precautions.

Capel Mounth to Ballater (15 miles; 7hr). Initially, the path zigzags its way up fierce slopes before levelling out to a moorland plateau, leading to the eastern end of Loch Muick. It then follows the River Muick to Ballater.

Capel Mounth round-trip (15 miles; 8hr). Follows the above route to Loch Muick, doubling back along the loch's southern shore. The dramatic Streak of Lightning path that follows Corrie Chash leads to a ruined stables below Sandy Hillock; the descent passes the waterfall by the bridge at Bachnagairn, where a gentle burn-side track leads back to Glen Doll car park.

Jock's Road to Braemar (14 miles; 7hr). A signposted path leads below Cairn Lunkhard and along a wide ridge towards the summit of Crow Craigies (3018ft). From here, the path bumps down to Loch Callater then follows the Callater Burn, eventually hitting the A93 two miles short of Braemar.

remote enough to enable you to leave the crowds with little effort. Wildlife is abundant, with deer on the mountains, wild hares and even grouse and the occasional buzzard. The meadow flowers on the valley floor and arctic plants (including great splashes of white and purple saxifrage) on the rocks make it a botanist's paradise.

The B955 from Dykehead and Kirriemuir divides at the Gella bridge over the swift-coursing River South Esk. Six miles north of Gella, the two branches of the road join up once more at the hamlet of **CLOVA**, little more than the hearty *Glen Clova Hotel* (Ⓣ01575/550350, Ⓦwww.clova.com; ❺), which also runs a bunkhouse and a private fishing loch. The restaurant serves up traditional Scottish food, such as venison casserole and haggis. An excellent, if fairly strenuous, four-hour walk from behind the old school at the back of the hotel leads up into the mountains and around the lip of **Loch Brandy**.

North from Clova village, the road turns into a rabbit-infested lane coursing along the riverside for four miles to the car park, a useful starting point for numerous superb **walks** (see box, p.389). There are no other facilities beyond the village.

Brechin

Twelve miles or so northeast of Kirriemuir, **BRECHIN** is an attractive town whose red sandstone buildings give it a warm, welcoming feel. The chief attraction is the old **cathedral** on Bishop's Close, off the High Street. There's been a religious building of sorts here since the arrival of evangelizing Irish missionaries in 900 AD, and the red-sandstone structure has become something of a hotchpotch of architectural styles. What you see today dates chiefly from an extensive rebuilding in 1900, with the oldest surviving part of the cathedral being the 106ft-high round tower, one of only two in Scotland. The cathedral's doorway, built 6ft above the ground for protection against Viking raids, has some notable carvings, while inside you can see various Pictish stones, illuminated by the jewel-coloured stained-glass windows. Also in town, just off St Ninian Square, is the train station of the **Caledonian Railway** (Ⓣ01356/622992 or 01561/377760, Ⓦwww.caledonianrailway.com), which operates steam trains every Sunday (June–Aug) and Saturday (July–Aug) along four miles of track from Brechin to the Bridge of Dun.

A mile from the town centre along the Forfar road in the Brechin Castle Park is **Pictavia** (March–Oct Mon–Sat 9am–5pm, Sun 10am–5pm; Nov–Feb, Sat 9am–5pm, Sun 10am–5pm; £3.25; Ⓦwww.pictavia.org.uk), a custom-built tourist attraction in a country park with the grandly titled Brechin Castle Centre (garden centre/restaurant) as its hub; this is also where you'll find Brechin's **tourist office** (same times as Pictavia; Ⓣ01356/623050). Based on the history and heritage of the Picts, it's a little lacking in substance.

For **accommodation**, it's worthwhile briefly retracing your steps along the B957 to Tannadice where you'll find the eco-designed *Kalulu House* (Ⓣ01307/860205, Ⓦwww.kalulu-house.co.uk; ❸), which has a swimming pool and sauna. Brechin is on main **transport** routes: bus #30 runs hourly to Montrose, nine miles east, and it's also served by regular Citylink coaches between Dundee and Aberdeen.

Edzell and Glen Esk

Travelling around Angus, you can hardly fail to notice the difference between organic settlements and planned towns that were built by landowners who forcibly rehoused local people in order to keep them under control, especially after the Jacobite uprisings. One of the better examples of the latter, **EDZELL**, five miles north of Brechin on the B966 (and linked to it by buses #21, #29 and #30), was cleared and rebuilt with Victorian rectitude a mile to the west of its original site in the 1840s. Through the Dalhousie Arch at the entrance to the village the long, wide and ruler-straight main street is lined with prim nineteenth-century buildings, which now do a roaring trade as genteel teashops and antiques emporia.

The original village (identifiable from the cemetery and surrounding grassy mounds) lay immediately to the west of the wonderfully explorable red-sandstone ruins of **Edzell Castle** (April–Sept daily 9.30am–5.30pm; Oct–March Mon–Wed, Sat & Sun 9.30am–4.30pm; HS; £4.70), itself a mile west of the planned village. The main part of the old castle is a good example of a comfortable tower house, where luxurious living rather than defence became a priority. However it's the **pleasance garden** overlooked by the castle tower that makes a visit to Edzell essential, especially in late spring and early to mid-summer. The garden was built by Sir David Lindsay in 1604, at the height of the optimistic Renaissance, and its refinement and extravagance are evident. The walls contain sculpted images of erudition: the Planetary Deities on the east side, the Liberal Arts on the south and, under floods of lobelia, the Cardinal Virtues on the west wall. In the centre of the garden, low-cut box hedges spell out the family mottoes and enclose voluminous beds of roses.

Four miles southwest of Edzell, lying either side of the lane to Bridgend which can be reached either by carrying on along the road past the castle or by taking the narrow road at the southern end of Edzell village, are the **Caterthuns**, twin Iron Age hill forts that were probably occupied at different times. The surviving ramparts on the White Caterthun (978ft) – easily reached from the small car park below – are the most impressive, and this is thought to be the later fort, occupied by the Picts in the first few centuries AD.

Just north of Edzell, a fifteen-mile road climbs alongside the River North Esk to form **Glen Esk**, the most easterly of the Angus glens and, like the others, sparsely populated. Ten miles along the Glen, the excellent **Glenesk Retreat, Folk Museum and Restaurant** (Easter–Sept daily noon–6pm; ⓣ01356/648070, ⓦwww.gleneskretreat.btik.com) brings together records, costumes, photographs, maps and tools from the Angus glens, depicting the often harsh way of life for the inhabitants. The museum (£2) is housed adjacent to a former shooting lodge known as The Retreat, and is run independently and enthusiastically by the local community. Sunday hikers who labour up the winding glen will be heartened to find tasty and inexpensive home-baking, haggis and steak pies in the restaurant. There are some excellent **hiking** routes further up the glen (see ⓦwww.visitcairngorms.com), including one to Queen Victoria's Well in Glen Mark and another up Mount Keen, Scotland's most easterly Munro.

In Edzell, *Alexandra Lodge*, Inveriscandye Road (ⓣ01356/648266, ⓦwww.alexandralodge.co.uk; April–Oct; ❸), is a friendly **B&B** located in a little **Edwardian lodge**. The best of the **hotels** in town is the *Panmure Arms* (ⓣ01356/648950, ⓦwww.panmurearmshotel.co.uk; ❹), at the far end of the main street near the turn-off to the castle, offering sizeable rooms and predictable bar meals. Further up the glen, one and a half miles north of the village, you can **camp** at the small, child-friendly *Glenesk Caravan Park* (ⓣ01356/648565; April–Oct).

Aberdeenshire and Moray

Aberdeenshire and Moray cover a large chunk of northern Scotland – some 3500 square miles, much of it open and varied country dotted with historic and archeological sights, from eerie prehistoric rings of standing stones to quiet kirkyards, and including a rash of dramatic castles. Geographically, the counties break down into two distinct areas: the **hinterland**, once barren and now a patchwork of fertile farms, rising towards high mountains, sparkling rivers and gentle valleys; and the **coast**, a classic stretch of rocky cliffs, remote fishing villages and long, sandy beaches.

For visitors, the large city of **Aberdeen** is the obvious focal point of the region, with intriguing architecture, attractive museums and a lively social scene. From here, it's a short hop west to **Deeside**, visited annually by the Royal Family, where the trim villages of **Ballater** and **Braemar** act as a gateway to the spectacular mountain scenery of the Cairngorms National Park. To the north lies the meandering **Don Valley**, a quiet area notable for **castles** such as Kildrummy and Corgarff, both appealingly remote. Further north, the dramatic **coast** is punctuated by picturesque fishing villages, and there's a handful of engaging sights including **Duff House**, an outpost of the National Galleries of Scotland, and the New Age community at **Findhorn**.

Aberdeen has an **airport**, and is connected by **trains** to Inverness and major points further south. **Buses** in the hinterland can be few and far between, often running on schooldays only, but the main centres are well served.

Aberdeen

The third-largest city in Scotland, **ABERDEEN** (Ⓦwww.aberdeen-grampian.com), commonly known as the "Granite City", lies 120 miles northeast of Edinburgh on the banks of the rivers Dee and Don, smack in the middle of the northeast coast. While some extol the many tones and colours of Aberdeen's **granite** buildings, others see only uniform grey and find the city grim and cold: it lies on a latitude north of Moscow.

Since the 1970s, **oil** has made Aberdeen a hugely wealthy and self-confident place. Despite (or perhaps because of) this, it can seem a soulless city and sometimes it seems to exist only as a departure point for the transient population of some ten to fifteen thousand who live on the 130 oil platforms out at sea. That said, Aberdeen's **architecture** is undeniably striking – a granite cityscape created in the nineteenth century by three fine architects: Archibald Simpson and John Smith in the early years of the century and, later, A. Marshall Mackenzie. Classical inspiration and Gothic Revival styles predominate, giving grace to a material once thought of as only good enough for tombs and paving stones. In addition, the urban **parks** are some of the most beautiful in Britain. This positive floral explosion – Aberdeen was once barred from "Britain in Bloom" competitions because it won too often – certainly cheers up the general greyness.

Staying in such a prosperous place has its advantages. There are some reasonable restaurants and hotels, while certain sights, including Aberdeen's splendid **Art Gallery** and the excellent **Maritime Museum**, are free. Furthermore, the fact that the city is the bright light in a wide hinterland helps it to sustain a lively **nightlife**, with some decent pubs and a colourful arts and cultural scene.

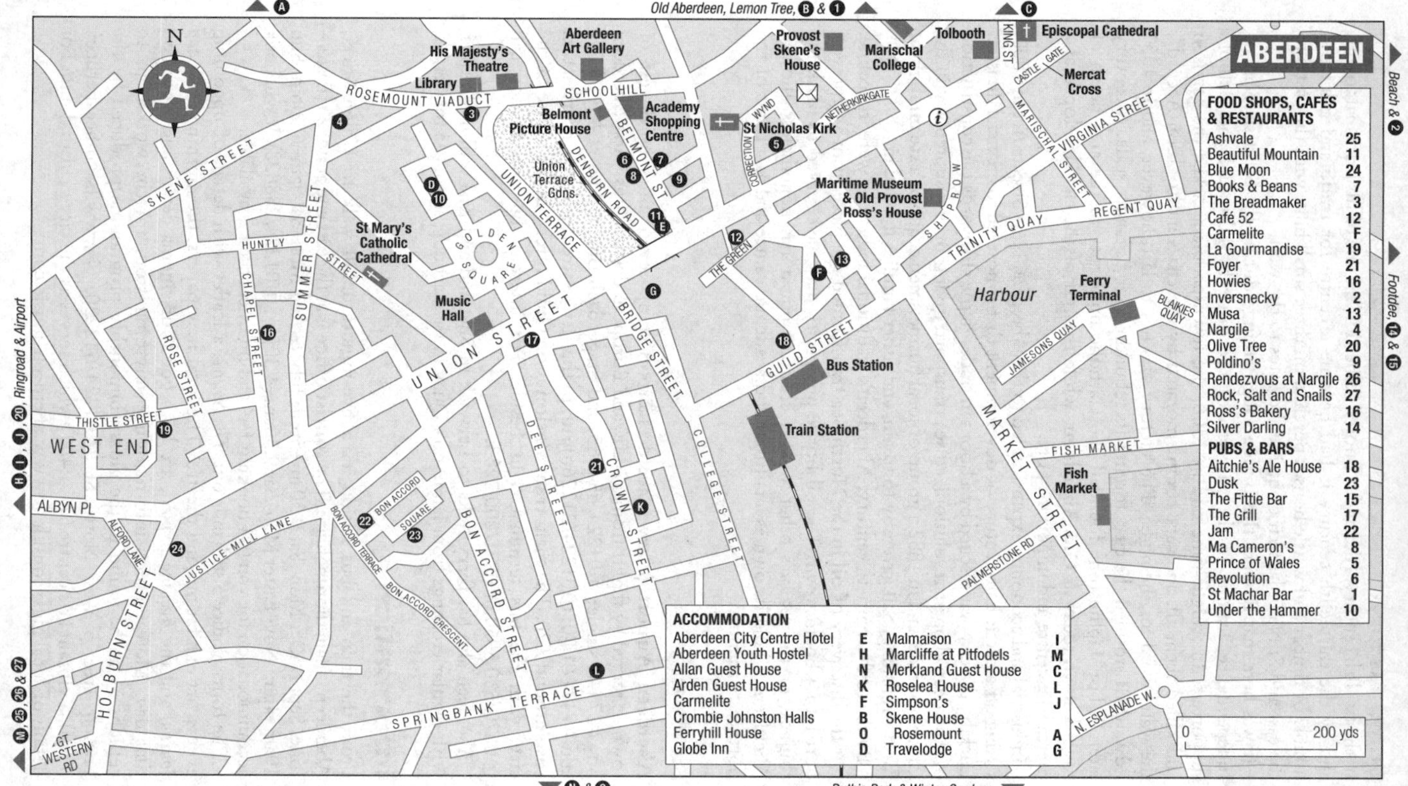
ABERDEEN
FOOD SHOPS, CAFÉS & RESTAURANTS
Ashvale 25
Beautiful Mountain 11
Blue Moon 24
Books & Beans 7
The Breadmaker 3
Café 52 12
Carmelite F
La Gourmandise 19
Foyer 21
Howies 16
Inversnecky 2
Musa 13
Nargile 4
Olive Tree 20
Poldino's 9
Rendezvous at Nargile 26
Rock, Salt and Snails 27
Ross's Bakery 16
Silver Darling 14
PUBS & BARS
Aitchie's Ale House 18
Dusk 23
The Fittie Bar 15
The Grill 17
Jam 22
Ma Cameron's 8
Prince of Wales 5
Revolution 6
St Machar Bar 1
Under the Hammer 10
ACCOMMODATION
Aberdeen City Centre Hotel E
Aberdeen Youth Hostel H
Allan Guest House N
Arden Guest House K
Carmelite F
Crombie Johnston Halls B
Ferryhill House O
Globe Inn D
Malmaison I
Marcliffe at Pitfodels M
Merkland Guest House C
Roselea House L
Simpson's J
Skene House Rosemount A
Travelodge G
0 200 yds
A
Old Aberdeen, Lemon Tree, B & 1
C
Beach & 2
Footdee, 14 & 15
Duthie Park & Winter Gardens
N & O
M, 25, 26 & 27
H, I, J, 20, Ringroad & Airport
His Majesty's Theatre
Library
Aberdeen Art Gallery
Belmont Picture House
Academy Shopping Centre
Provost Skene's House
St Nicholas Kirk
Marischal College
Tolbooth
Episcopal Cathedral
Mercat Cross
Maritime Museum & Old Provost Ross's House
St Mary's Catholic Cathedral
Music Hall
Bus Station
Train Station
Harbour
Ferry Terminal
Fish Market
Union Terrace Gdns.
WEST END
ROSEMOUNT VIADUCT
SCHOOLHILL
BELMONT ST
DENBURN ROAD
UNION TERRACE
UNION STREET
GOLDEN SQUARE
SKENE STREET
HUNTLY STREET
SUMMER STREET
CHAPEL STREET
ROSE STREET
THISTLE STREET
ALBYN PL
ALFORD LANE
JUSTICE MILL LANE
HOLBURN STREET
GT. WESTERN RD
BON ACCORD SQUARE
BON ACCORD TERRACE
BON ACCORD CRESCENT
BON ACCORD STREET
SPRINGBANK TERRACE
DEE STREET
CROWN STREET
BRIDGE STREET
COLLEGE STREET
THE GREEN
CORRECTION WYND
NETHERKIRKGATE
GUILD STREET
SHIPROW
TRINITY QUAY
REGENT QUAY
VIRGINIA STREET
MARISCHAL STREET
CASTLE GATE
KING ST
JAMESONS QUAY
BLAIKIES QUAY
FISH MARKET
MARKET STREET
PALMERSTONE RD
N. ESPLANADE W.

Some history

In the twelfth century, Alexander I noted "Aberdon" as one of his principal towns, and by the thirteenth century it had become a centre for **trade** and fishing, a jumble of timber and wattle houses perched on three small hills, with the castle to the east and St Nicholas's kirk outside the gates to the west.

It was here that **Robert the Bruce** sought refuge during the Scottish Wars of Independence, leading to the garrison of the castle by Edward I and Balliol's supporters. In a night-time raid in 1306, the townspeople attacked the garrison and killed them all, an event commemorated by the city's motto "Bon Accord", the watchword for the night. The victory was not to last, however, and in 1337 Edward III stormed the city, forcing its rebuilding on a grander scale. A century later Bishop Elphinstone founded the Catholic university in the area north of town known today as **Old Aberdeen**, while the rest of the city developed as a mercantile centre and important port.

Industrial and economic expansion led to the Aberdeen New Streets Act in 1800, setting off a hectic half-century of development that almost led to financial disaster. Luckily, the city was rescued by a boom in trade: in the **shipyards** the construction of Aberdeen clippers revolutionized sea transport, giving Britain supremacy in the China tea trade, and in 1882 a group of local businessmen acquired a **steam** tugboat for trawl fishing. Sail gave way to steam, and fisher families flooded in.

By the mid-twentieth century, Aberdeen's traditional industries were in decline, but the discovery of **oil** in the North Sea transformed the place from a depressed port into a boom town. The oil-borne prosperity may have served to mask the thinness of the region's other wealth creators, but it has nonetheless allowed Aberdeen to hold its own as a cultural and academic centre and as a focus of the northeast's identity.

Arrival

Aberdeen Airport (Ⓦwww.aberdeenairport.com), seven miles northwest of town, is served by flights from 37 UK and European destinations. First Aberdeen bus #27 (£2 single; Ⓣ01224/650065) and Stagecoach Bluebird buses #10, #727 and #747 (£1.70; Ⓣ01224/212266) run to the city centre from the airport; a taxi costs around £20. The main **train station** is on Guild Street, in the centre of the city, with the **bus** terminal right beside. For intercity bus information call Ⓣ0870/550 5050 or 0871/200 2233.

Aberdeen also has **ferry** links to Lerwick in Shetland and Kirkwall in Orkney, with regular crossings from Jamieson's Quay in the harbour; see p.403 for details.

Information

From the train and bus station it's a five-minute uphill walk to Union Street, Aberdeen's main thoroughfare. The **tourist office** is at the east end at no. 23 (Easter–June, Sept & Oct Mon–Sat 9.30am–5pm; July & Aug Mon–Sat 9am–6.30pm, Sun 10am–4pm; Nov–Easter Mon–Sat 9.30am–4.30pm; Ⓣ01224/288828). It will book accommodation for you (£4 booking fee) and internet access is available.

The tourist office also hands out *The Source*, a leaflet with details of upcoming events, art exhibitions and theatre. The local newspapers, the morning *Press and Journal* and the *Evening Express*, are both good for cinema details and what's on that day. More esoteric information – anything from t'ai chi workshops to ceilidhs – can be found in the glossy bimonthly programme produced by the Lemon Tree, 5 West North St (Ⓣ01224/642230, Ⓦwww.boxofficeaberdeen.com), a vibrant arts centre (see p.402) which serves as the city's cultural hub. For details of local gigs, consult Ⓦwww.aberdeen-music.com.

City transport and tours

Aberdeen's centre is best explored on foot, but you might need to use **buses**, most of which pass along Union Street, to reach some sights. An all-day ticket covering all city routes costs £4.20 (£3.50 after 9.30am on weekdays), and you can get a weekly pass for £15. If you plan to use the buses a lot, you can buy a **Farecard** (in £10 or £20 denominations) from the depot at 395 King St or the travel centre at 47 Union St, which also hands out transport **maps**; each time you travel the fare is deducted from the card. Late-night services on Friday and Saturday – the last leaving at 3.15am – cost flat £2, and head to six separate destinations on the city's outskirts. For information on city bus services, call the Busline (ⓣ01224/650000, ⓦwww.firstgroup.com).

Taxis operate from ranks throughout the city centre, all of which attract long queues after the pubs and clubs empty at the weekend. If you don't manage to hail one, call Rainbow Taxis (ⓣ01224/725500).

Accommodation

As befits a high-flying business city, Aberdeen has a large choice of **accommodation**. Despite some characterless and expensive chain hotels targeting the business trade, there are also now a number of boutique hotels. Predictably, the best budget options are the **B&Bs** and **guesthouses**, many of which are strung along Bon Accord and Crown streets (served by buses #6 and #17 to and from Union Street), and Great Western Road (buses #18, #19 and #24). Cheapest of all are the **hostel** and **student halls** left vacant for visitors in the summer. The emphasis on business trade means weekday rates can be considerably more expensive than weekends; the price codes below are for the lowest rates quoted.

Hotels

Aberdeen City Centre Hotel 9 Belmont St ⓣ01224/658406, ⓦwww.aberdeencitycentrehotel.co.uk. A smart little modern place tucked away on pedestrian Belmont St; the rooms feature spa baths. Bargain weekend rates, and they also have apartments to rent. ❹

Carmelite Stirling St ⓣ01224/589101, ⓦwww.carmelitehotels.com. A boutique hotel with its fusion of trad and modern style in a revamped 1820s hotel. The kitchen serves up a surprisingly modestly priced taste of Scotland. ❻

Ferryhill House 169 Bon Accord St ⓣ01224/590867, ⓦwww.ferryhillhousehotel.co.uk. A mansion set in its own grounds within walking distance of Union St. Good-value lunches and a great Malt Room for guests to sample real ales and whisky by a roaring fire. Beer garden. ❻

Malmaison 49–53 Queens Rd ⓣ0845/365 4247, ⓦwww.malmaison.com. Opened in 2008, the former Queen's Hotel has been refurbished and upgraded as part of the stylish Malmaison chain, with striking contemporary decor and all the latest in hi-tech features as well as a restaurant encircling an open grill. ❻

Marcliffe at Pitfodels North Deeside Rd, Pitfodels ⓣ01224/861000, ⓦwww.marcliffe.com. Four miles west of the city centre, this forty-room hotel in its own grounds is by far the most luxurious and tasteful option in the Aberdeen area. There's a spa, and a fine restaurant with a suitably upmarket ambience. ❼

Simpson's 59–63 Queens Rd ⓣ01224/327777, ⓦwww.simpsonshotel.co.uk. Independent hotel in a former granite terrace house, with a decent brasserie that serves good-value midweek lunches. Good weekend room rates. ❻

Travelodge 9 Bridge St ⓣ0870/191 1617, ⓦwww.travelodge.co.uk. Typically bland budget option – but you can't beat the convenient location, right next to Union St and minutes from the stations. It's worth enquiring about weekend deals. ❹

Guesthouses and B&Bs

Allan Guest House 56 Polmuir Rd ⓣ01224/584484, ⓦwww.theallan.co.uk. Recently refurbished traditional guesthouse not far from Duthie Park and 5min from the city centre by bus. Digital TV, wi-fi and good breakfasts. ❸

Arden Guest House 61 Dee St ⓣ01224/580700, ⓦwww.ardenguesthouse.co.uk. Comfortable and very central for the bus station and Union St though if you want to sleep in you'll miss breakfast (served 7–8.30am). ❸

Globe Inn 13–15 North Silver St ⓣ01224/624258, ⓦwww.the-globe-inn.co.uk. Easy-going city-centre inn with seven en-suite rooms above a bar that hosts live jazz and blues Fri & Sat. Rate includes continental breakfast. ❸

Merkland Guest House 12 Merkland Rd East ⓣ01224/634451. Standard but comfortable B&B handy for the beach. Will cater for vegan and vegetarian guests. ❷

Roselea House 12 Springbank Terrace ⓣ01224/583060, ⓦwww.roseleahouse.co.uk. Welcoming guesthouse near the bus station with accommodation suitable for people with restricted mobility. Reduced rates for children. ❷

Hostel, campus and self-catering accommodation

Aberdeen Youth Hostel 8 Queens Rd ⓣ0870/004 1100, ⓦwww.syha.org.uk. Hostel in a grand stone mansion a mile from the train station, with dorms and private rooms. Doors close at 2am but you can arrange to get in later. Bus #14 or #15 from Union St.

Crombie Johnston Halls College Bounds, Old Aberdeen ⓣ01224/273444, ⓦwww.abdn.ac.uk/summer_accommodation. Private rooms in the city's best student halls, in one of the most interesting parts of town. Available from early July to Sept, though there's also some year-round accommodation. ❶

Skene House Rosemount 96 Rosemount Viaduct ⓣ01224/645971, ⓦwww.skene-house.co.uk. There are 98 self-catering apartments here with one to three rooms, all with continental breakfast and TVs, and some with internet. Good central location. ❺

The City

Aberdeen divides neatly into five main areas. The **city centre**, roughly bounded by Broad Street, Union Street, Schoolhill and Union Terrace, features the opulent **Marischal College**, the colonnaded **Art Gallery** with its fine collection, the burgeoning nightlife of Belmont Street, and homes that pre-date Aberdeen's nineteenth-century town planning and have been preserved as **museums**. Union Street leads west to the twin diversions of gentrified shopping and raucous nightlife that defines the **West End**. To the south, the **harbour** still heaves with boats serving the fishing and oil industries, while north of the centre lies attractive **Old Aberdeen**, a village neighbourhood presided over by **King's College** and **St Machar's Cathedral** and influenced by the large student population. The long sandy **beach** marks Aberdeen's eastern border just a mile or so from the heart of the city.

The city centre

The centre of Aberdeen is dominated by mile-long **Union Street**, still the grandest and most ambitious single thoroughfare in Scotland. The challenge for the early nineteenth-century city planners who conceived the street was the building of the ambitious **Union Street bridge**, spanning two hills and the Denburn gorge. The first attempt, a triple-span design by Glasgow architect David Hamilton, bankrupted the city and collapsed during construction. The famous Thomas Telford then proposed the single-arch structure that became an engineering wonder of its age. Since completion in 1805 the bridge has been widened twice, the second time, in 1963, adding a row of shops to the southern side that obscures the dramatic impact of the structure.

Castlegate and around

Any exploration of the **city centre** should begin at the open, cobbled **Castlegate**, where Aberdeen's long-gone castle once stood. At its centre is the late seventeenth-century **Mercat Cross**, carved with a unique gallery of Stewart sovereigns alongside some fierce gargoyles. Castlegate was once the focus of city life but nowadays seems rather lifeless unless you dart along the easily missed lane to **Peacock Visual Arts**, 21 Castle St (Tues–Sat 9.30am–5.30pm; free; ⓦwww.peacockvisualarts.co.uk), a hub for the northeast's contemporary art scene which also hosts live music events.

As Union Street begins you have to crane your neck to see the towering, turreted spire of the **Town House**, though the steely grey nineteenth-century exterior is in fact a facade behind which lurks the early seventeenth-century **Tolbooth** (July–Sept Tues–Sat 10am–4pm, Sun 12.30–3.30pm; free; Ⓣ01224/621167), one of the city's oldest buildings. A jail for centuries, the Tolbooth now houses a museum of crime and imprisonment.

Nearby, on King Street, the sandstone **St Andrew's Episcopal Cathedral** (mid-May to mid-Sept Tues–Fri 11am–4pm, Sat 10.30am–1pm, Sun for worship; free), where Samuel Seabury, America's first bishop, was ordained in 1784, offers welcome relief from the uniform granite. Inside, spartan whiteness is broken by florid gold ceiling bosses representing the (then) 48 states of the USA and 48 local families who remained loyal to the Episcopal Church during the eighteenth-century Penal Laws.

Heading west, Union Street brings you to Broad Street where, tucked behind at 45 Guestrow, **Provost Skene's House** (Mon–Sat 10am–5pm; free) is Aberdeen's oldest-surviving private house, dating from 1545. The house is now a museum, with a costume gallery, archeological exhibits, period rooms and a café-bar. Don't miss the Painted Gallery, where a cycle of beautiful religious tempera paintings from the mid-seventeenth century show scenes from the life of Christ.

Marischal College and museum

On Broad Street stands Aberdeen's most imposing edifice, and the world's second-largest granite building after the Escorial in Madrid – exuberant **Marischal College**, whose tall, steel-grey pinnacled neo-Gothic facade is in absolute contrast to the hideously utilitarian concrete office blocks opposite. This spectacular building, with all its soaring, surging lines, has been painted and sketched more than any other in Aberdeen, though it's not to everyone's taste – it was once described by a minor art historian as "a wedding cake covered in indigestible grey icing". The college was founded in 1593 by the fourth Earl Marischal, and coexisted as a separate Protestant university from Catholic King's, just up the road, for over two centuries. It was long Aberdeen's boast to have as many universities as the whole of England, and it wasn't until 1860 that the two were united as the University of Aberdeen. In 1893, the central tower was more than doubled in height by A. Marshall Mackenzie and the profusion of spirelets added, though the facade, which fronts an earlier quadrangle designed by Archibald Simpson in 1837–41, was not completed until 1906.

Behind the tower, through the college entrance, the **Mitchell Hall**'s east window illustrates the history of the university in stained glass. You're unlikely to get a good view of this, however, since the university has all but moved from the college, and the building is largely closed to the public. What you can see is the **Marischal Museum** (Mon–Fri 10am–5pm, Sun 2–5pm; free) and its wealth of weird exhibits, many gathered by Victorian anthropologists and other collectors who roamed the world filling their luggage with objects. Sensitive to the cultural crassness this represents to modern tastes, the museum concentrates as much on the phenomenon of these collectors as on what they brought back.

St Nicholas Kirk

Between Upperkirkgate and Union Street stands **St Nicholas Kirk** (May–Sept Mon–Fri noon–4pm; Oct–April contact church office; free; Ⓣ01224/643494, Ⓦwww.kirk-of-st-nicholas.org.uk). It's actually two churches in one, with a solid, central bell tower, from where the 48-bell carillon, the largest in Britain, regularly chimes. There's been a church here since 1157 or thereabouts, but as the largest kirk in Scotland it was severely damaged during the Reformation and divided into the West and the East Church, separated today by the transepts and crossing; only the north transept, known as Collinson's aisle, survives from the twelfth century. The Renaissance-style **West Church**, formerly the nave of St Nicholas, was designed in the mid-eighteenth century by James Gibbs, architect of St Martin in the Fields in London. The **East Church** was rebuilt over the groin-vaulted crypt of the restored fifteenth-century St Mary's Chapel (entered from Correction Wynd), which in the 1600s was a place to imprison witches: you can still see the iron rings to which they were chained.

The Aberdeen Art Gallery and around

A little further west up Schoolhill is Aberdeen's first-rate **Art Gallery** (Tues–Sat 10am–5pm, Sun 2–5pm; free; Ⓦwww.aagm.co.uk), purpose-built in 1884 to a Neoclassical design by Mackenzie. You enter via the airy **Centre Court**, dominated by Barbara Hepworth's central fountain and thick pillars running down from the upper balcony, each hewn from a different local marble. The walls highlight the policy of acquiring contemporary art, with British work to the fore. The **Side Court** contains *Jungled*, a garish, erotic spin on stained-glass windows by Gilbert and George, and works by YBAs (Young British Artists) gifted by the Saatchi collection. The **Memorial Court**, a calming, white-walled circular room under a skylit dome, serves as the city's principal war memorial. It also houses the Lord Provost's book of condolence for the 167 people who died in the 1988 Piper Alpha oil rig disaster.

The **upstairs** rooms house the main body of the gallery's painting collection. This includes a superb collection of Victorian narrative art, some decent twentieth-century British painting and a collection of Impressionist art that includes works by Boudin, Courbet, Sisley, Monet, Pissarro and Renoir. The strong connections between the French schools and the development of modernism in Scottish painting saw the emergence of the "Glasgow Boys" in the 1880s (see p.227), exemplified here by John Lavery's *The Tennis Party*. The Scottish Colourists are also in evidence, and you'll find a good selection of modern Scottish artists, including Peter Howson and Joan Eardley, who captured the landscape around Catterline, a coastal village just south of Aberdeen, so memorably.

Opposite the gallery is Aberdeen's answer to a Bohemian quarter: cobbled Belmont and Little Belmont streets feature a number of the city's more interesting bars, shops and restaurants, and farmers' markets take place on the first and last Saturday of each month. West of Belmont Street, across the Denburn gorge, spanned by the Union Bridge and Schoolhill viaduct, the sunken **Union Terrace Gardens** are a welcome relief from the hubbub of Union Street. From here there are views across to the three domes of the Central Library, St Mark's Church and His Majesty's Theatre, traditionally referred to as "Education, Salvation and Damnation". Outside the theatre stands a hulking statue of William "Braveheart" Wallace, erected in 1888. The crumbling red-brick spire at the other end of the viaduct tops **Triple Kirks**. Built in 1843 and one of Archibald Simpson's most famous creations, it was Scotland's only example of a single building hosting three churches for three denominations.

The West End

The **West End**, the area around the westernmost part of Union Street, begins more or less at the great granite columns of the city's **Music Hall**. A block north is **Golden Square** – a misnomer as the trim houses, pubs and restaurants surrounding the statue of the Duke of Gordon are uniformly grey. The city has invested much in gentrifying the area north of Union Street, resulting in neat cobbles, old-fashioned lamps, a growing restaurant scene and a string of somewhat stuffy designer boutiques around Thistle Street. Huntly Street, west of Golden Square, heads off towards the curiously thin spire of **St Mary's Catholic Cathedral** (Mon–Fri 8am–4pm, Sat 8am–8pm, Sun 8am–8.30pm), a typical example of Victorian Gothic church architecture.

To the south of Union Street, wedged between Bon Accord Street and Bon Accord Terrace, **Bon Accord Square** is a typical, charming Aberdeen square. A grassy centre surrounds a huge solid block of granite commemorating **Archibald Simpson**, architect of much of nineteenth-century Aberdeen.

The harbour

Old, cobbled Shiprow winds down from Castlegate at the east end of Union Street to the north side of the **harbour**. Just off this steep road, peering towards the harbour through a striking glass facade, is the **Maritime Museum** (Tues–Sat 10am–5pm, Sun noon–3pm; free; Ⓦwww.aagm.co.uk), which combines a modern, airy museum with the aged labyrinthine corridors of **Provost Ross's House**. The museum is a thoroughly engrossing, imaginative tribute to Aberdeen's maritime traditions.

Just inside the front entrance you'll see a blackboard updated every day with the price of a barrel of crude oil. Suspended above the foyer and visible from five different levels is a spectacular 27ft-high model of an oil rig, which, along with terrific views over the bustling harbour, serves as a constant reminder that Aberdeen's maritime links remain very much alive. The older industries of herring fishing, whaling, shipbuilding and lighthouses also have their place, with well-designed displays and audiovisual presentations, many drawing heavily on personal reminiscences. Passages lead into Provost Ross's House, where intricate ship's models and a variety of nautical paintings and drawings are on display. At the bottom of Shiprow the cobbles meet **Market Street**, which runs the length of the harbour with its brightly painted oil-supply vessels, sleek cruise ships and peeling fishing boats. Follow your nose to the **fish market**, off Market Street, best visited early (Mon–Fri opens 7.30am) when the place is in full swing. Be warned, however, that it's not set up for visitors and entry is not guaranteed. The current market building dates from 1982, but fish have been traded here for centuries: the earliest record, from 1281, shows that an envoy of Edward I was invoiced for 1000 barrels of sturgeon and 5000 salt fish.

At the north end of Market Street, Trinity Quay runs past industrial yards and down York Street towards **Footdee**, or Fittie (an easy walk or bus #14 or #15 from Union St), a quaint nineteenth-century fishermen's village of higgledy-piggledy cottages backing onto the sea. Their windows and doors face inwards for protection from storms but also, so they say, to stop the devil sneaking in the back door. Here, in a great setting beside the lighthouse at the channel into the harbour, is *Silver Darling* (see p.402), one of the northeast's finest seafood restaurants.

From Market Street it's a twenty-minute walk or ten-minute bus ride (#6 from Market St or #16 and #17 from Union Street) to **Duthie Park** (daily 9.30am–dusk; free), on the banks of the Dee at the end of Polmuir Road. The rose garden here, known as Rose Mountain due to its profusion of blooms, can be stunning in summer, but the real treat is the **Winter Gardens** (daily: April & Nov 9.30am–5pm; May–Sept 9.30am–9pm; Oct 9.30am–8.30pm; Dec–March 9.30am–4pm; free), a steamy paradise of enormous cacti and exotic plants. By the obelisk, a parterre garden has been installed and outdoor concerts are occasionally held at the restored vintage bandstand. From the northwestern corner of Duthie Park a great cycle and walkway, the **Old Deeside Railway Line**, heads west out of the city past numerous long-gone train stations.

Old Aberdeen

An independent burgh until 1891, tranquil **Old Aberdeen**, a ten-minute ride north of the city centre on bus #20 from Marischal College on Littlejohn Street, has maintained a village-like identity. Dominated by King's College and St Machar's Cathedral, its medieval cobbled streets, wynds and little lanes are beautifully preserved. Despite the current tranquillity, the establishment of a single University of Aberdeen was a tempestuous affair. The **King's College Visitor Centre** (Mon–Sat 10am–5pm, Sun noon–5pm; free) highlights the university's turbulent history before finally, in 1860, Protestant Marischal College and sceptical King's College were merged, over two hundred years after the first attempt. Rivalry between the two, which sometimes led to well-charted brawls in the streets, has long faded.

The southern half of cobbled High Street is overlooked by **King's College Chapel** (Mon–Fri 8am–4pm; free), the first and finest of the college buildings, completed in 1495, with a chunky Renaissance spire. Named in honour of James IV, the chapel's west door is flanked by his coat of arms and that of his queen. It stands on the quadrangle, whose gracious buildings retain a medieval plan but were built much later; those immediately north were designed by Mackenzie early in the last century, with the exception of Cromwell Tower at the northeast corner, completed in 1658. The highlights of the interior, which, unusually, has no central aisle, are the ribbed arched wooden ceiling and the rare and beautiful examples of medieval Scottish woodcarving in the screen and the stalls. The remains of Bishop Elphinstone's tomb and the carved pulpit from nearby St Machar's are also here. From the college, High Street leads a short way north to **St Machar's Cathedral** on the leafy Chanonry (daily 9am–5pm; free; ⓣ01224/485988), overlooking Seaton Park and the River Don. The site was reputedly founded in 580 AD by Machar, a follower of Columba, when he was sent by the latter to find a grassy platform near the sea, overlooking a river shaped like the crook on a bishop's crozier. This setting fitted the bill perfectly, and the cathedral, a huge fifteenth-century fortified building, became one of the city's first great granite edifices. Inside, the stained-glass windows are a dazzling blaze of colour and the heraldic oak ceiling above the nave dates from 1520 and shows nearly fifty different coats of arms from Europe's royal houses and Scotland's bishops and nobles.

Also on the Chanonry, the University of Aberdeen-funded **Natural History Centre** (Mon–Fri 9am–5pm) incorporates the sunken gardens, secret paths and pretty flower beds of the **Cruickshank Botanic Gardens** (May–Sept Mon–Fri 9am–4.30pm, Sat & Sun 2–5pm; Oct–April irregular opening; free). A wander through Seaton Park, immediately to the north of St Machar's, brings you to the thirteenth-century **Brig o'Balgownie**, which gracefully spans the River Don nearly a mile north of the cathedral. The bridge is best visited at sunset; Byron, who spent much of his childhood in Aberdeen, remembered it as a favourite place.

The beach

Aberdeen can surely claim to have the best sandy **beach** of all Britain's large cities. Less than a mile east of Union Street is a great two-mile sweep of clean sand, broken by groynes and lined all along with an esplanade. To reach the beach, hop aboard bus #14 from Union Street. The massive **Beach Leisure Centre** (ⓣ01224/655401) includes flumes and a wave machine, and a ten-minute walk south will take you to sprawling **Codona's Amusement Park** (ⓦwww.codonas.com) complete with its rollercoaster, slides and restaurant areas. Just to the west in Links Road, the brand new **Transition Extreme** centre (daily 10am–10pm; various prices; ⓣ01224/626279, ⓦwww.transition-extreme.com) is where to head for street basketball, BMX biking, skateboarding or climbing. Further north (buses #6 and #11), most of the beach's hinterland is devoted to golf links.

A little way inland, the city's old tram depot at 179 Constitution St, near the *Patio Beach Boulevard* hotel, houses **Satrosphere** (daily 10am–5pm; £5.75; ⓣ01224/640340, ⓦwww.satrosphere.net), Aberdeen's entertaining and educational hands-on science exhibition aimed at kids.

Eating, drinking and nightlife

Aberdeen is not short of good **cafés** and **restaurants**, many of which are clustered around Union and Belmont streets, though you'll find them pricier than elsewhere in northeast Scotland. Although you'll find no shortage of loud, flashy **bars**, there are still a number of more traditional **pubs** that, though usually packed, are well worth a visit.

As far as **delicatessens** go, tiny La Gourmandise, 63 Thistle St, stocks gorgeous fresh patisserie fare, while Rocksalt and Snails, 40 St Swithin St (Mon–Fri 8am–6pm, Sat until 5pm), sells an array of speciality European and Scottish produce including olives, cheeses, Hebridean hot smoked salmon and northeast preserves.

Cafés

Beautiful Mountain 11 Belmont St ⓣ01224/645353. Welcoming daytime café and takeaway with a range of good-value sandwiches, including ample vegetarian and organic options.

Books and Beans 22 Belmont St ⓣ01224/646438. As the name suggests, secondhand books go hand in hand here with decent coffee and fresh soups and sandwiches.

The Breadmaker 50–52 Rosemount Viaduct ⓣ01224/641520, ⓦwww.thebreadmaker.org.uk. Enjoy a coffee and fresh baking in a cosy facility that gives people with learning difficulties training and meaningful employment. Closed Sun.

Inversnecky Beach Esplanade. Established in 1908, this beachfront café continues to serve up good-value breakfasts, lunches and teas.

Musa Exchange St ⓣ01224/571771, ⓦwww.musaaberdeen.com. Based in an old church and banana warehouse, the terrific day time vibe in the good-value art café continues into the evening with live music and mouthwatering sourced from dining; produce is sourced from small Scottish suppliers. 10am till late.

Ross's Bakery 44 Chapel St ⓣ01224/643527. Night owls (it's open till 5am) will love the home-made traditional stovies and rowies (a local pastry).

Restaurants and bistros

Ashvale 42–48 Great Western Rd ⓣ01224/596981 ⓦwww.theashvale.co.uk. Diners who finish the "Ashvale Whale", a 1lb cod fillet (£9.95) receive another for free at this renowned northeast chippy and family-oriented restaurant.

Blue Moon 11 Holburn St ⓣ01224/589977, ⓦwww.bluemoon-aberdeen.com. This continues to be the pick of Aberdeen's Indian restaurants, with sleek surroundings and dozens of inventive, moderately priced dishes.

Café 52 52 The Green ⓣ01224/590094, ⓦwww.cafe52.net. Cosy, bohemian hangout by day that turns into a hip restaurant by night with Cullen skink soup, game and vegetarian meals among the tasty, reasonably priced options. Great seating outside, screened by bamboo, on an attractive quiet street. Closed Sun evening and Mon daytime.

Carmelite Stirling St ⓣ01224/589101, ⓦwww.carmelitehotels.com. One of Aberdeen's newer dining experiences with a stylish interior and tasty Scottish-influenced cuisine served with simplicity.

Foyer 82a Crown St ⓣ01224/582277, ⓦwww.foyerrestaurant.com. A light, bright and stylish restaurant and contemporary art gallery. It's expensive, but it supports a charity which aims to prevent youth homelessness and unemployment. Closed Sun & Mon.

Howies 50 Chapel St ⓣ01224/639500, ⓦwww.howies.uk.com. Aberdeen outpost of an Edinburgh institution, serving modern Scottish cooking in a stylish environment. Well-priced set meals and house wine.

Nargile 77–79 Skene St ⓣ01224/636093. Much-loved and very friendly family-run Turkish restaurant. Good-value set-meal dinners with tasty *meze* (starters). Open 5pm until late. West end sister restaurant in Forest Ave, *Rendezvous at Nargile*, is also open at lunchtime.

Olive Tree 32 Queen's Rd ⓣ01224/208877, ⓦwww.olivetreegroup.co.uk. Seasonal specials, and stylish and fresh European cuisine with a Scottish twist. The *Black Olive Brasserie* is less formal. Closed Sun.

Poldino's 7 Little Belmont St ⓣ01224/647777, ⓦwww.poldinos.co.uk. An Aberdonian Italian institution for thirty years that combines fine flavours and quality with convivial dining.

Silver Darling Pocra Quay, North Pier ⓣ01224/576229, ⓦwww.silverdarling.co.uk. Attractively located at the harbour in Footdee. The French owner specializes in tickling your taste buds with delicious, freshly caught seafood. Pricey. Closed Sat lunchtime & Sun.

Pubs and bars

Aitchie's Ale House 10 Trinity St. Close to the railway station, this is where to meet some local worthies over real ale and stovies.

Dusk Langstane Place ⓣ01224/594430, ⓦwww.duskbegins.co.uk. Sleek and moody, with cocktails and evening sophistication.

The Fittie Bar 18 Wellington St. Close to the harbour, you'll find good-value lunches, local bearded mariners and a sense of history in this atmospheric pub.

The Grill 213 Union St. Another of the city's older pubs with a distinctive old-world charm. Real ales on tap, dozens of malts and hot stovies.

Jam 67 Langside Place. This trendy watering hole has DJs putting out a nightly beat of Indie and party anthem tunes. Noon–midnight.

Ma Camerons 6–8 Little Belmont St. A good bet if looking for haddock or haggis at lunchtime and a taste of Scottish real ales. Roof terrace and cosy snug bar where impromptu folk music takes place on Sat afternoons.

Prince of Wales 7 St Nicholas Lane. Opened in 1850, the quintessential Aberdeen pub has a 20ft-long bar and flagstone floor. With fine pub grub, renowned real ales and a Sun evening folk session, it's little wonder that it's often crowded.

St Machar Bar 97 High St, Old Aberdeen. The medieval quarter's only pub, a poky, old-fashioned bar attracting an intriguing mix of King's College students and workers.

Under the Hammer 11 North Silver St. This snug little basement wine bar has a continental vibe and is a popular refuge when icy winter winds hit the city. Relax in the knowledge there's no TV to drown out your convivial evening chat.

Nightlife, live music and entertainment

A number of **nightlife** venues feature regular jazz, folk and rock **music sessions**, while the Lemon Tree Arts Centre has as good a selection of touring theatre, bands and workshops as anywhere of its size in Scotland. From pop to underground, the city's **clubs** cater for eclectic tastes and are lively at weekends. You can buy tickets for most events at Aberdeen's **theatres** and **concert halls** from the box office beside the Music Hall on Union Street (Mon–Sat 9.30am–6pm; ⓣ01224/641122).

Clubs, live music venues and concert halls

Aberdeen Exhibition and Conference Centre Off Ellon Rd at Bridge of Don ⓣ01224/824824, ⓦwww.aecc.co.uk. Huge hall hosting the biggest rock and pop acts.

Babylon 9 Alford Place ⓣ01224/595001. Bills itself as one of Aberdeen's coolest and hippest nightspots, the Gothic-styled interior here reverberates to the beat of the latest dance tunes. Popular with an older crowd. Fri & Sat 10pm–3am.

The Blue Lamp 121 Gallowgate ⓣ01224/647472. A spacious bar featuring live jazz, usually at weekends, and a Mon folk session; there's also a much smaller snug for relative peace and quiet.

Cowdray Hall Schoolhill ⓣ01224/523700, ⓦwww.aagm.co.uk. Classical music venue, often with visiting orchestras playing; it also hosts chamber music concerts.

The Globe Inn 13–15 North Silver St ⓣ01224/624258, ⓦwww.the-globe-inn.co.uk. Pleasant city-centre inn with traditional folk music from 9pm on Tues and a variety of musical genres on weekend evenings.

Lemon Tree 5 West North St ⓣ01224/642230, ⓦwww.boxofficeaberdeen.com. The fulcrum of the city's arts scene, with live music, club nights and comedy.

Music Hall Union St ⓣ01224/632080 or 641122, ⓦwww.musichallaberdeen.com. Big-name comedy and music acts.

Revolution Bar 25 Belmont St. This trendy drinking spot with its own "Vodka bible" is where you'll also find DJs spinning decks every night of the week.

Snafu 5 Union St ⓣ01224/622660, ⓦwww.clubsnafu.com. Aberdeen's best Indie-rock-electro-rock dance club that will appeal to the true clubber.

The Tunnels Carnegies Brae ⓣ01224/211121, ⓦwww.thetunnels.co.uk. One of the city's most popular live music venues, established within old tunnels under Union St. Live bands and a different musical genre every evening including reggae, hip-hop, ska and Northern Soul.

Theatres and cinemas

Aberdeen Arts Centre 33 King St ⓣ01224/635208, ⓦwww.aberdeenartscentre.org.uk. Hosts a variety of theatrical productions, lectures and exhibitions.

Belmont Picture House 9 Belmont St ⓣ01224/343536, ⓦwww.picturehouses.co.uk. Art-house cinema showing the more cerebral new releases alongside classic, cult and foreign-language films. There's a comfortable café-bar inside and some good places nearby for a bite before or after.

Cineworld Queen's Links Leisure Park, Links Rd ⓣ0871/200 2000. Huge multiplex cinema close to the beachfront and showing all the mainstream releases.

His Majesty's Rosemount Viaduct ⓣ01224/641122, ⓦww.boxofficeaberdeen.com. The city's recently refurbished main theatre resides in a beautiful Edwardian building, and its extensive programme ranges from highbrow drama and opera to pantomime. The good-value *Matcham's* restaurant and café ensure the place has a bit of a buzz at all times of the day.

Lemon Tree (see opposite). Avant-garde events with off-the-wall comedians and plays, many coming hotfoot from the Edinburgh festivals.

Listings

Bookshops The largest is Waterstone's, 269–271 Union St and there are various WHSmith outlets including in the St Nicholas Centre. The Old Aberdeen Bookshop, 140 Spital, is best for secondhand, while Books and Beans, 22 Belmont St, offers a more populist selection.

Bus information First Aberdeen Busline ⓣ01224/650000.

Car rental Arnold Clark, Girdleness Rd ⓣ01224/249159, Lang Stracht (airport pick-ups) ⓣ01224/663723; Budget, Wellheads Drive (airport pick-ups) ⓣ01224/793333; National, 16 Broomhill Rd ⓣ01224/595366 and airport ⓣ0870/400 4502.

Ferry information ⓣ0845/600 0449, ⓦwww.northlinkferries.co.uk.

Flight information ⓣ0870/040 0006, ⓦwww.aberdeenairport.com.

Internet Free access in the Central Library (see below). Otherwise, try the tourist office, or the Family History Society at 158–164 King St.

Left luggage Small lockers at the train station.

Lesbian and gay helpline PHACE Scotland (Mon–Fri 9am–5pm; ⓣ0845/241 2151).

Library Central Library, Rosemount Viaduct (Mon–Thurs 9am–8pm, Fri & Sat 9am–5pm; ⓣ01224/652500).

Medical facilities The Royal Infirmary, on Foresterhill, northeast of the town centre, has a 24hr casualty department (ⓣ01224/681818). Boots pharmacy is in The Bon Accord Centre on George St (Mon–Wed, Fri & Sat 8.30am–6pm, Thurs 8.30am–8pm, Sun 10am–5.30pm; ⓣ01224/211592). For late-night pharmacies, Tesco's at Bridge of Don until 9pm or Morrisons supermarket on King St (ⓣ01224/624404) until 8pm.

Outdoor supplies Tiso, 26 Netherkirkgate (ⓣ01224/634934), TISO Transition Extreme, Queen's Links (ⓣ01224/646045), and Blacks, 135 George St (ⓣ01224/622272), have everything for hiking and outdoor pursuits, including maps and tips on where to go.

Police Main station is on Queen St (ⓣ0845/600 5700), including the lost property office.

Post office The central office is upstairs in the St Nicholas Centre, between Union St and Upperkirkgate (Mon–Sat 9am–5.30pm), with other branches at 371 George St (Mon–Fri 9am–5.30pm, Sat 9am–12.30pm) and 489 Union St (hours same as George St).

Sports The local football team, Aberdeen, struggles to live to up its golden era of the 1980s when then-manager Alex Ferguson brought home league titles and European trophies. Home fixtures take place at Pittodrie Stadium (ⓣ0871/983 1903, ⓦwww.afc.co.uk), between King St and the beach. There are golf courses all over the northeast; the municipal King's Links (ⓣ01224/641577, ⓦwww.craig-group.com) skirts the beach, while Murcar Golf Club (ⓣ01224/704354, ⓦwww.murcar.co.uk), a testing links five miles north of Aberdeen, is only open to visitors at certain times, but has an attractive nine-hole course, Strabathie, beside it. Bon Accord Baths and Leisure Centre, Justice Mill Lane (ⓣ01224/587920), has a 40yd (36.6m) swimming pool; Beach Leisure Centre (ⓣ01224/655401; noon–8pm) on the Esplanade has a fun pool with flumes and slides.

Taxis Rainbow City Taxis ⓣ01224/878787 or 494949.

Stonehaven and the Mearns

South of Aberdeen, the A92 and the main train line follow the coast to **Stonehaven**, a pretty harbour town and base for nearby **Dunnottar Castle**, a stunningly moody ruin perched on the cliffs. The area to the south and west is known as the **Mearns**, an agricultural district of scattered population and gathering hills famous for its links to Scots author Lewis Grassic Gibbon.

Stonehaven is easily reached by **bus** or **train** from Aberdeen or Montrose, although public transport inland into the Mearns is virtually nonexistent.

Stonehaven and around

A busy, pebble-dashed town, **STONEHAVEN** attracts hordes of holiday-makers in the summer due to the sheltered Kincardine coastline, and in early July in particular because of its respected **folk festival**. The town itself is split into two parts, the picturesque working harbour area being most likely to detain you. On one side of the harbour, Stonehaven's oldest building, the **Tolbooth** (June–Sept daily except Tues 1.30–4.30pm; free), built as a storehouse during the construction of Dunnottar Castle (see below), is now a museum of local history and fishing. On calm summer evenings, you can take **boat trips** from the harbour to fish (May–Sept; £30/hr) or to the RSPB reserve at **Fowlsheugh** (May–July; min. charge £50 or five passengers at £10pp; ⓣ01569/765064 or 07880/702831).

The old High Street, lined with some fine town houses and civic buildings, connects the harbour and its surrounding old town with the late eighteenth-century planned centre on the other side of the River Carron. On New Year's Eve, High Street is the location for the ancient ceremony of **Fireballs**, when locals parade its length swinging metal cages full of burning debris around their heads to ward off evil spirits for the coming year. The **new town** focuses on the market square, overlooked by the dusky-pink granite market hall with its impressive steeple. In the northern part of the new town is Stonehaven's wonderful open-air Art Deco **swimming pool** (June–Sept; £4.70; ⓦwww.stonehavenopenairpool.co.uk), opened in 1934 and always packed with locals on a sunny day. As well as regular daytime hours, it's open for midnight swims on Wednesdays during July and early August (10pm–midnight).

Practicalities

The helpful **tourist office** is at 66 Allardice St, the main street past the square (April–June, Sept & Oct Mon–Sat July & Aug daily; ⓣ01569/762806). For **B&B** accommodation, try attractive *Arduthie House* on Ann Street (ⓣ01569/762381, ⓦwww.arduthieguesthouse.com; ❸), or the revamped *Marine Hotel* on the harbour (ⓣ01569/762155, ⓦwww.marinehotelstonehaven.co.uk; ❻).

For **food**, try the glamorous Art Deco surroundings of the smart *Carron Restaurant* at 20 Cameron St (ⓣ01569/760460, ⓦwww.carron-restaurant.co.uk; closed Sun & Mon) or the moderately expensive and beautifully sited *Tolbooth Seafood Restaurant* (ⓣ01569/762287, ⓦwww.tolbooth-restaurant.co.uk; closed Sun & Mon), above the museum on the harbour. Here you will also find the cosy seventeenth-century *Ship Inn* **pub** and restaurant (ⓣ01569/767074), which serves tasty, moderately priced fresh seafood and real ales, whilst the *Bervie Chipper* on David Street is a good place to tuck into a hearty takeaway of fish and chips.

Dunnottar Castle, Kinneff and Arbuthnott

Two miles south of Stonehaven (the tourist office sells a walking guide for the scenic amble there), **Dunnottar Castle** (Easter to mid-Oct daily 9am–6pm;

mid-Oct to Easter Fri–Mon 10.30am–sunset; £5; Ⓦ www.dunnottarcastle.co.uk) is one of Scotland's finest ruined castles, a huge ninth-century fortress set on a three-sided sheer cliff jutting into the sea – a setting striking enough to be chosen as the backdrop for Zeffirelli's movie version of *Hamlet*. Once the principal fortress of the northeast, the ruins are worth a good root around, and there are many dramatic views out to the crashing sea. Siege and bloodstained drama splatter the castle's past: in 1297 the whole English Plantagenet garrison was burnt alive here by William Wallace, while one of the more gruesome tales from the castle's history tells of the imprisonment and torture of 122 men and 45 women Covenanters in 1685 – an event, as it says on the Covenanters' Stone in the churchyard, "whose dark shadow is for evermore flung athwart the Castled Rock".

Four miles south of Dunnottar Castle, **CATTERLINE** is a cliff-top hamlet typical of those along this stretch of coast – worth a visit for the views and the delicious, moderately priced seafood and game in the cosy *Creel Inn* (Ⓣ 01569/750254, Ⓦ www.thecreelinn.co.uk).

Some five miles inland, the straggling village of **ARBUTHNOTT** was the home of prolific local author, **Lewis Grassic Gibbon** (1901–35), whose romanticized realism perfectly encapsulates the spirit of the agricultural Mearns area. *Sunset Song*, his most famous work, is an essential read for those travelling in this area. The community-run **Grassic Gibbon Centre** and café (April–Oct daily 10am–4.30pm; £3), on the B967 through the village, is a great introduction to this fascinating and self-assured man who died so young. He is buried (under his real name of James Leslie Mitchell) in the corner of the little village graveyard, overlooking the forested banks of the Bervie Water off the main road. The parish **church** itself, one of the few surviving intact in Scotland that pre-date the Reformation, is interesting for its Norman arch, unusual fifteenth-century circular bell tower and glorious thirteenth-century chancel.

Deeside

More commonly known as **Royal Deeside**, the land stretching west from Aberdeen along the River Dee revels in its connections with the Royal Family, who have regularly holidayed here, at **Balmoral**, since Queen Victoria bought the estate. Eighty thousand Scots turned out to welcome her on her first visit in 1848. Victoria adored the place and the woods were said to remind Prince Albert of Thuringia, his homeland.

Deeside is undoubtedly handsome in a fierce, craggy, Scottish way, and the royal presence has helped keep a lid on any unattractive mass development. The villages strung along the A93, the main route through the area, are well heeled and have something of an old-fashioned air. Facilities for visitors hereabouts are first class, with a number of bunkhouses and hostels, some decent hotels and plenty of castles and grounds to snoop around. It's also an excellent area for **outdoor activities**, with hiking routes into both the Grampian and Cairngorm mountains, alongside good mountain biking, horseriding and skiing.

Stagecoach Bluebird **buses** #201, #202 and #203 from Aberdeen regularly chug along the A93, serving most of the towns on the way to Braemar.

To Drum Castle and Crathes Castle

West of Aberdeen, you'll pass through low-lying land of mixed farming, forestry and suburbs. On the B9077 six miles west of the city, children (and adults) will be diverted by a collection of more than one hundred life-sized rhyme and fairytale characters at **Storybook Glen** (daily: April–Sept 10am–6pm; Oct–March 10am–4pm; £5.40). Back on the main A93, ten miles west of Aberdeen, **Drum Castle** (April–June & Sept–Oct Mon & Thurs–Sun 11am–5pm; July & Aug daily 11am–5pm; Garden of Historic Roses April–Oct daily 10am–6pm; NTS; £8.50, grounds only £3) stands in a clearing in the ancient **woods of Drum**, made up of the splendid pines and oaks that covered this whole area before the shipbuilding industry precipitated mass forest clearance. The castle itself combines a 1619 Jacobean mansion with Victorian extensions and the original, huge thirteenth-century keep, which has been restored and reopened. Given by Robert the Bruce to his armour-bearer, William de Irvine, in 1323 for services rendered at Bannockburn, the castle remained in Irvine hands for 24 generations until the NTS took over in 1976. The main part of the house is Victorian in character, with grand, antique-filled rooms and lots of family portraits. The finest room is the library, within the ancient tower; you'll get an even better sense of the medieval atmosphere of the place by climbing up to the upper levels of the tower, with the battlements offering views out over the forest.

Further along the A93, four miles west of Drum Castle, **Crathes Castle** (April–May & Sept–Oct daily except Fri 10.30am–4.30pm; June–Aug daily 10.30am–5pm; Jan–March & Nov–Dec Sat & Sun 10.30am–3.45pm; NTS; £10.50) is a splendid sixteenth-century granite tower house adorned with flourishes such as overhanging turrets, gargoyles and conical roofs. Its thick walls, narrow windows and tiny rooms loaded with heavy old furniture make Crathes rather claustrophobic, but it is still worth visiting for some wonderful painted ceilings; the earliest dates from 1602.

By the entrance to Crathes, a cluster of restored stone cottages house various **craft shops** and **galleries** as well as the *Milton* (Ⓣ01330/844566, Ⓦwww.themilton.co.uk), an unexpectedly upmarket **restaurant** serving moderately priced à la carte meals, terrific breakfasts and summer barbecues.

Banchory

BANCHORY, meaning "fair hollow", is a one-street town that acts essentially as a gateway into rural Deeside. The small local **museum** on Bridge Street, behind High Street (Mon, Fri & Sat 11am–1pm & 2pm–4pm; extended hours July & Aug; free), may warrant half an hour or so if you're a fan of local boy James Scott Skinner, renowned fiddler and composer of such tunes as *The Bonnie Lass o' Bon Accord*.

The **tourist office** in the museum (April–June & Sept–Oct Mon–Sat; July & Aug daily; Ⓣ01330/822000) can provide information on walking and fishing in the area. Though there's an understandable temptation to push on into the attractive Deeside countryside, there are one or two places **to stay** in town, including the smart *Tor-Na-Coille Hotel* (Ⓣ01330/822242, Ⓦwww.tornacoille.com; ❼), once a retreat for Charlie Chaplin and his family. *Raemoir House* (Ⓣ01330/824884, Ⓦwww.raemoir.com; ❼), 5km to the north, is a glamorous country-house hotel set in spacious parkland. The Dee Larder on Watson Lane, off the main street, is a good deli; for memorable home-baking, drop into the *Shieling* coffee shop on Dee Street.

Aboyne and Glen Tanar

Twelve miles west of Banchory on the A93, **ABOYNE** is a typically well-mannered Deeside village at the mouth of **Glen Tanar**, which runs southwest from here for ten miles or so deep into the Grampian hills. The glen, with few steep gradients and some glorious stands of mature Caledonian pine, is ideal for walking, mountain biking or horseriding; the ranger information point two miles into the glen off the B976 has details of suitable routes, while the Glen Tanar Equestrian Centre (Ⓣ01339/886448, Ⓦwww.glentanar.co.uk) offers one- and two-hour **horse rides** (from £25). Alternative activities hereabouts include **flights** from the Deeside Gliding Club (Ⓣ01339/853339, Ⓦwww.deesideglidingclub.co.uk), while a handful of family-oriented thrills from year-round sledging to go-karts can be found at the **Deeside Activity Park** (daily 9am–5pm; Ⓣ01339/883536, Ⓦwww.deesideactivitypark.com), signposted off the A93 a couple of miles east of Aboyne, where there's also a farm shop and restaurant. Aboyne itself has some handy retreats for **food**: the excellent *Sign of the Black Faced Sheep* coffee shop just off the main road serves home-baking and light lunches, while the *Boat Inn* on Charlestown Road right beside the bridge over the Dee does good-quality pub grub.

Ballater

Ten miles west of Aboyne is the neat and ordered town of **BALLATER**, attractively hemmed in by the river and fir-covered mountains. The town was dragged from obscurity in the nineteenth century when it was discovered that waters from the local Pannanich Wells might be useful in curing scrofula. Deeside water is now back in fashion, though these days it's bottled and sold far and wide as a natural mineral water.

It was in Ballater that Queen Victoria first arrived in Deeside by train from Aberdeen back in 1848; she wouldn't allow a station to be built any closer to Balmoral, eight miles further west. Although the line has long been closed, the town's rather self-important royalism is much in evidence at the restored **train station** in the centre (daily: July & Aug 9am–6pm; rest of year 10am–5pm). The local shops that supply Balmoral with groceries and household basics also flaunt their connections, with oversized "By Appointment" crests.

If you prefer to discover the fresh air and natural beauty that Victoria came to love so much, you'll find Ballater an excellent base for local **walks and outdoor activities**. There are numerous hikes from Loch Muik (pronounced "mick"), nine miles southwest of town, including the Capel Mounth drovers' route over the mountains to Glen Doll (see p.389), and a well-worn but strenuous all-day trek up and around Lochnagar (3789ft), the mountain much painted and written about by the current Prince of Wales. Good-quality **bikes** can be rented from Cabin Fever (Ⓣ013397/54004; £15/day), beside the station on Station Square, or Cycle Highlands (Ⓣ013397/55864, Ⓦwww.cyclehighlands.com; £16/day, or £30/day for full suspension) at 16 Bridge St.

Practicalities

The **tourist office** (daily; Ⓣ013397/55306) is in the renovated train station. Good-quality **bunkhouse** accommodation with breakfast is available at the *Schoolhouse*, Anderson Road (Ⓣ013397/56333, Ⓦwww.theschool-house.eu; ❷), complete with ghost walks and storytelling, or at the excellent and well-equipped *Habitat@Ballater* on Bridge Square (Ⓣ013397/53752, Ⓦwww.habitat-at-ballater.com; ❶). There are plenty of reasonable **B&Bs** in town, including *Inverdeen House* on Bridge Square (Ⓣ013397/55759, Ⓦwww.inverdeen.com; ❷), which offers a wide choice of breakfasts, most involving local produce and home-baking. Another choice is the welcoming *Deeside Hotel* on the main road through town at 45 Braemar Rd (Ⓣ013397/55420, Ⓦwww.deesidehotel.co.uk; ❻). For **camping**, head for *Anderson Road Caravan Park* (Ⓣ013397/55727; Easter–Oct) down towards the river.

There are numerous **places to eat**, from smart hotel restaurants to bakers and coffee shops. The *Green Inn Restaurant*, 9 Victoria Rd, has comfortable en-suite rooms attached (❻). *The Auld Kirk* is, as the name suggests, based in a renovated church (ⓣ01339/755762, ⓦwww.theauldkirk.co.uk; ❻), and is pricey but excellent with locally sourced game on the menu, while *La Mangiatoia* (ⓣ013397/55999), on Bridge Square, is a cheaper and cheerful family pizza/pasta place. A couple of miles east of Ballater at Cambus O'May there's also the *Crannach Coffee Shop and Gallery* (closed Mon), a cultured spot offering good coffees, snacks and light meals, as well as superb cakes and bread from its in-house organic bakery. For a **dram** with the locals, try the back bar (entrance down Golf Street) of the Prince of Wales, which faces the main square, and the nearby *Coilacreich Inn*.

Balmoral Estate and Crathie Church

Originally a sixteenth-century tower house built for the powerful Gordon family, **Balmoral Castle** (April–July daily 10am–5pm; £8.70; ⓣ013397/42534, ⓦwww.balmoralcastle.com) has been a royal residence since 1852, when it was converted to the Scottish Baronial mansion that stands today. The Royal Family traditionally spend their summer holidays here each August, but despite its fame it can be something of a disappointment even for a dedicated royalist. For the three months when the doors are nudged open, the general riffraff are permitted to view only the ballroom, an exhibition room and the grounds. With so little of the castle on view, it's worth making the most of the grounds and larger estate by following some of the country walks, heading off on a Land Rover safari (£45 per person for 3hr) or joining a two-hour ranger-led walk of the estate (April–July Wed 2pm; included in entrance price to castle).

Opposite the castle's gates on the main road, the otherwise dull granite church of **Crathie**, built in 1895 with the proceeds of a bazaar held at Balmoral, is the royals' local church. A small **tourist office** operates in the car park by the church on the main road (daily; ⓣ013397/42414).

Braemar

Continuing westwards for another few miles, the road rises to 1100ft above sea level in the upper part of Deeside and the village of **BRAEMAR**, situated where

Deeside and Donside Highland Games

Royal Deeside is the home of the modern **Highland Games**, claiming descent from gatherings organized by eleventh-century Scottish king Malcolm Canmore to help him recruit the strongest and fittest clansmen for his army. The most famous of the local games is undoubtedly the **Braemar Gathering**, held on the first Saturday in September, which can see crowds of 15,000 and usually a royal or two as guest of honour. Vying for celebrity status in recent years has been the **Lonach** Gathering in nearby Strathdon on Donside, held the weekend before Braemar, where local laird Billy Connolly dispenses drams of whisky to marching village men and has been known to invite some Hollywood chums along – Steve Martin has appeared dressed in kilt and jacket, while Robin Williams has competed in the punishing hill race. For a true flavour of the spirit of Highland gatherings, however, try to get to one of the events that take place in other local towns and villages at weekends throughout July and August, where locals outnumber tourists and the competitions are guaranteed to be hard-fought and entertaining. Local tourist offices and the tourist board website (ⓦwww.aberdeen-grampian.com) should be able to tell you what's happening where.

three passes meet and overlooked by an unremarkable **castle**. It's an invigorating, outdoor kind of place, well patronized by committed hikers, but probably best known for its Highland Games, the annual **Braemar Gathering**, on the first Saturday of September (ⓦwww.braemargathering.org). Since Queen Victoria's day, successive generations of royals have attended and the world's most famous Highland Games have become rather an overcrowded, overblown event. You're not guaranteed to get in if you just turn up; the website has details of how to book tickets in advance.

A pleasant diversion from Braemar is to head six miles west to the end of the road and the **Linn of Dee**, where the river plummets savagely through a narrow rock gorge. From here there are countless walks into the surrounding countryside or up into the heart of the Cairngorms (see p.421), including the awesome Lairig Ghru pass which cuts all the way through to Strathspey.

Practicalities

Braemar's **tourist office** is in the modern building known as the Mews, in the middle of the village on Mar Road (daily; ⓣ013397/41600). **Accommodation** is scarce in Braemar in the lead-up to the Games, but at other times there's a wide choice. *Clunie Lodge Guest House*, Clunie Bank Road (ⓣ013397/41330, ⓦwww.clunielodge.com; ❸), on the edge of town, is a good **B&B** with lovely views up Clunie Glen, and there's a large SYHA **hostel** at Corrie Feragie, 21 Glenshee Rd (ⓣ013397/41659, ⓦwww.syha.org.uk; Jan–Oct). Cheery *Rucksacks*, an easy-going bunkhouse that's well equipped for walkers and backpackers, is just behind the Mews complex (ⓣ013397/41517) while the *Invercauld Caravan Club Park* (ⓣ013397/41373), just south of the village off Glenshee Road, has thirty **camping** pitches. A quarter of a mile south of town on Glenshee Road, you'll also find the cosy *Braemar Lodge Bunkhouse* (ⓣ013397/741627, ⓦwww.braemarlodge.co.uk).

For **food**, avoid the large hotels, which tend to be filled with coach parties, and try either *Taste*, a coffee shop and moderately priced contemporary restaurant on the road out to the Linn of Dee, or *The Gathering Place* bistro (ⓣ013397/41234, ⓦwww.the-gathering-place.co.uk) in the heart of the village (by Braemar Mountain Sports) where for lunch or dinner you'll find mouthwatering, though pricey, freshly prepared Scottish-based cuisine.

Advice on **outdoor activities**, as well as ski, mountain-bike and climbing equipment rental, is available from Braemar Mountain Sports (daily 8.30am–6pm; ⓦwww.braemarmountainsports.com).

The Don valley

The quiet countryside around the **Don valley**, once renowned for its illegal whisky distilleries and smugglers, lies at the heart of Aberdeenshire's prosperous agricultural region. From Aberdeen, the River Don winds northwest through **Inverurie**, where it takes a sharp turn west to **Alford**, then continues past ruined castles through the **Upper Don valley** and the heather moorlands of the eastern Highlands. This remote and under-visited area is positively littered with ruined castles, Pictish sites, stones and hillforts.

Inverurie is served by the regular Aberdeen to Inverness **train** and various **bus** services up the A96. Stagecoach Bluebird buses #210, #215, #217 and #220 link Aberdeen with Alford, but getting any further by public transport is all but impossible.

Inverurie and around

Some seventeen miles northwest of Aberdeen, the prosperous – if largely unexciting – farming town of **INVERURIE** lies fairly central to the numerous relics and castles in the area as well as the **Glen Garioch distillery** in Old Meldrum (Mon–Sat 10am–4pm, ⓣ01651/873450, ⓦwww.glengarioch.com; £4). The **tourist office** (April–Oct Mon–Sat; ⓣ01467/625800) shares space with a bookshop at 18 High St, not far from the station.

Bennachie and Archaeolink

The granite hill **Bennachie**, five miles west of Inverurie, is possibly the site of Mons Graupius, Scotland's first-ever recorded battle, when the Romans defeated the Picts in 84 AD. At 1733ft, this is one of the most prominent tors in the region, with tremendous views, and it makes for a stiff two-and-a-half-hour walk. The best route starts from the **Bennachie Centre** (Tues–Sun: April–Oct 10.30am–5pm; Nov–March 9.30am–4pm), a countryside ranger station and interactive interpretation centre located two miles south of **Chapel of Garioch** (pronounced "geery"). A mile immediately west of Chapel of Garioch is one of the region's most notable Pictish standing stones, the **Maiden Stone**, a 10ft-high slab inscribed with marine monsters, an elephant-like beast, and the mirror and comb for which it's named.

A further four miles northwest of Chapel of Garioch on the B9002 at Oyne, the **Archaeolink Prehistory Park** (April–Oct daily 10am–5pm; £6.10; ⓦwww.archaeolink.co.uk) gives an insight into the area's Pictish heritage. An ambitious attraction, it includes a reconstructed Iron Age farm, a hillside archeological site and an innovative grass-roofed building containing lively audiovisual displays and hands-on exhibits.

Alford and around

ALFORD (pronounced "aa-ford"), 25 miles west of Aberdeen, only exists at all because it was chosen, in 1859, as the terminus for the Great North Scotland Railway. A fairly grey little town now firmly within the Aberdeen commuter belt, it's still well worth making the trip here for the **Grampian Transport Museum** on Main Street (April–Oct daily 10am–5pm; £6; ⓦwww.gtm.org.uk). Here you'll find a large, diverse display of transport through the ages, from tramcars to sleek designs that have won endurance events for eco-friendly designs. Exhibits include the Craigevar Express, a strange, three-wheeled steam-driven vehicle developed by the local postman for his rounds, and that famous monument to British eccentricity and ingenuity, the Sinclair C5 motorized tricycle.

Practically next door is the terminus for the **Alford Valley Railway** (April, May & Sept Sat & Sun 1–4.30pm; June Mon–Fri 10.30pm–2.30pm, Sat & Sun 1–4.30pm; July & Aug daily 1–4.30pm; ⓣ07879/293934, ⓦwww.alfordvalleyrailway.org.uk), a narrow-gauge train that runs for about a mile from Alford Station through wooded vales to the wide open space of **Murray Park**; the return journey (£4) takes an hour. The station is also home to the neat **tourist office** (April–Sept daily; ⓣ019755/62052).

Craigievar Castle

Six miles south of Alford on the A980, **Craigievar Castle** (noon–5.30pm: May–June & Sept Mon, Tues & Fri–Sun; July & Aug daily; NTS; £10; ⓣ08444/932174) is a fantastic pink confection of turrets, gables, balustrades and cupolas bubbling over from its top three storeys. It was built in 1626 by a Baltic trader known as Willy the Merchant, who evidently allowed his whimsy to run riot. The **grounds** are open all year (9.30am to sunset; £1).

The Upper Don valley

Travelling west from Alford, settlements become noticeably more scattered and remote as the countryside takes on a more open, familiarly Highland appearance. Ten miles from Alford stand the impressive ruins of the thirteenth-century **Kildrummy Castle** (April–Sept daily 9.30am–5.30pm; HS; £3.70), where Robert the Bruce sent his wife and children during the Wars of Independence. The castle blacksmith, bribed with as much gold as he could carry, set fire to the place and it fell into English hands. Bruce's immediate family survived, but his brother was executed and the entire garrison hanged, drawn and quartered. Meanwhile, the duplicitous blacksmith was rewarded for his help by having molten gold poured down his throat. The sixth earl of Mar used the castle as the headquarters of the ill-fated Jacobite risings in 1715, but after that Kildrummy became redundant and it fell into disrepair. Beside the ruins, the separate **Kildrummy Castle Gardens** (April–Oct daily 10am–5pm; £3.50) are quite a draw, boasting everything from swathes of azaleas in spring to Himalayan poppies in summer.

Ten miles further west, the A944 sweeps round into the parish of **STRATHDON**, little more than scattered buildings by the roadside. Four miles north of here, up a rough track leading into Glen Nochty, lies the unexpected **Lost Gallery** (daily except Tues 11am–5pm; Ⓦwww.lostgallery.co.uk), which shows work by some of Scotland's leading modern artists in a wonderfully remote and tranquil setting. A further eight miles west, just beyond the junction of the Ballater road, lies **Corgarff Castle** (April–Sept daily 9.30am–5.30pm; Oct–March Sat & Sun 9.30am–4.30pm; HS; £4.70), an austere tower house with an unusual star-shaped curtain wall and an eventful history. Built in 1537, it was turned into a barracks in 1748, in the aftermath of Culloden, by the Hanoverian government in order to track down local Jacobite rebels; a century later, English redcoats were stationed here with the unpopular task of trying to control whisky smuggling. Today the place has been restored to resemble its days as a barracks, with stark rooms and rows of hard, uncomfortable beds – authentic touches which also extend to graffiti on the walls and peat smoke permeating the building from a fire on the upper floor.

Leading to the castle from the south is the old military road, which, unusually, hasn't been covered over by the present road and is fairly clear for about three miles. A mile or so along this from the castle, approached from the main road by the track beside Rowan Tree Cottage, is *Jenny's Bothy* at Dellachuper (Ⓣ019756/51449, Ⓦwww.jennysbothy.co.uk), a beautifully remote and simple **bunkhouse** with a cosy wood-burning stove. You'll have to bring your own supplies, but it's a great base for hiking, cycling and skiing, or just detaching yourself from the madding crowd for a day or two. Another bunkhouse, along with standard **B&B** accommodation and good-value bar meals can be found at the *Allargue Arms Hotel* (Ⓣ019756/51410, Ⓦwww.allarguearmshotel.co.uk; ❷), an old wayside inn overlooking Corgarff Castle and a cosy base for skiing, fishing or hiking trips.

The **Lecht Road**, crossing the area of bleak but wonderfully empty high country to the remote mountain village of Tomintoul (see p.432), passes the Lecht ski centre at 2090ft above sea level, but is frequently impassable in winter due to snow.

The coast

The **coast** of northeast Scotland from Aberdeen to Inverness has a rugged, sometimes bleak fringe with pleasant if undramatic farmland rolling inland. Still, if the weather is good, it's well worth spending a couple of days meandering through the various little fishing villages and along the miles of deserted, unspoilt beaches. The largest coastal towns are **Peterhead** and **Fraserburgh**, both dominated by sizeable fishing fleets; while neither has much to offer, the latter's Museum of Scottish Lighthouses is one of the most attractive small museums in Scotland. More appealing to most visitors are the quieter spots along the Moray coast, including the charming villages of **Pennan**, **Gardenstown**, **Portsoy** and nearby **Cullen**. The other main attractions are **Duff House** in Banff, a branch of the National Gallery of Scotland; the working abbey at **Pluscarden** by Elgin; and the **Findhorn Foundation**, near Forres.

The main towns and larger villages are fairly well served by **buses**, while **trains** from Aberdeen and Inverness stop at Elgin, Forres and Nairn.

The coast road towards Peterhead

Fifteen miles north of Aberdeen, a turning (signposted to Collieston) leads off the main A92 coast road to **Forvie National Nature Reserve**. This area incorporates the Sands of Forvie, one of Britain's largest and least disturbed dune systems, home to Britain's largest colony of breeding eider duck. There's a small but informative **visitor centre** (April–Sept daily 9am–5pm; call ⓣ01358/751330 for winter hours), from which a network of trails winds along the coast and through the dunes, with one leading to the site of a fifteenth-century village, buried by the shifting sands.

COLLIESTON itself is a pleasant hamlet with a harbour but little else; for somewhere to eat or stay it's worth making for **NEWBURGH**, essentially a satellite town of Aberdeen at the mouth of the Ythan River, itself a good place to spot wildfowl.

Cruden Bay

Superb sandy beaches can also be found eight miles north of Forvie at **Cruden Bay**, from where a pleasant fifteen-minute walk leads to the huge pink-granite ruin of **Slains Castle**. The ruin itself is not especially interesting – it was over-modernized in the nineteenth century – though its stark cliff-top beauty is striking and it claims notoriety as the place that inspired Bram Stoker to write *Dracula*. The best approach is to pull into the Meikle Partans car park on the A975 north of the village and follow the obvious path until you begin to see the ruins.

From a car park a little further up the A975, or a precarious three-mile walk north from Slains Castle along the cliffs, you can reach the **Bullers of Buchan**, a splendid 245ft-deep sea chasm, where the ocean gushes in through a natural archway eroded by the sea. This is some of the finest cliff scenery in the country and attracts a huge number of (smelly) nesting seabirds.

Peterhead and around

PETERHEAD, the easternmost mainland town in Scotland, stands in sharp contrast to the picturesque fishing villages on this stretch of coast. As notable for its high-security prison and ugly power station as its busy harbour, it's an unashamedly functional place. Although in recent years the oil industry has created a surge in wealth and population, Peterhead's *raison d'être* is **fishing**, and it was for many years the busiest white fish port in Europe. The boom is now over, however, and Peterhead has felt the consequences of the overfishing of the North Sea.

The oldest building in town is the four hundred-year-old **Ugie Salmon Fish House** on Golf Road at the mouth of the River Ugie, at the north end of town (Mon–Fri 9am–5pm, Sat 9am–noon; free; Ⓦ www.ugie-salmon.co.uk), where you can often watch the traditional methods of oak-smoking salmon and trout in Scotland's oldest smokehouse; the finished product is for sale at reasonable prices. On the beach just off the main road, one of the town's newer buildings houses the **Peterhead Maritime Heritage**, a combined college and museum (June–Aug Mon–Sat 10.30am–5pm, Sun 11.30am–5pm; free) that tells the story of the town's fishing industry from the old herring fleet to the modern day. Listen out for the recordings of old fishermen and women, who still speak the distinctive Doric dialect.

Peterhead has no official tourist office, but you should be able to find somewhere **to stay**; in town there's the comfortable and welcoming *Alexander's Invernettie Guest House* on South Road (Ⓣ 01779/473530, Ⓦ www.alexandersinvernettieguesthouse.co.uk; ❷), while the old lighthouse cottages at remote Rattray Head (Ⓣ 01346/532236, Ⓦ www.rattrayhead.net; ❷), halfway between Peterhead and Fraserburgh, offer B&B, a self-catering cottage (from £450pw) and a backpacker hostel. For **food**, the friendly though workaday *Dolphin* serves mince and tatties, fish pie and gargantuan fish and chips from as early as 4am until 6pm (Mon–Fri) from right next to the fish market in the harbour area. There's also the reasonable *Maritime Café* at Peterhead Maritime Heritage.

Fraserburgh

Twenty miles north of Peterhead, **FRASERBURGH** (Ⓦ www.visitfraserburgh.com) is a large and fairly severe-looking place. At the northern tip of the town, an eighteenth-century lighthouse protrudes from the top of sixteenth-century **Fraserburgh Castle**. The lighthouse was one of the first to be built in Scotland and is now part of the excellent **Museum of Scottish Lighthouses** (April–June, Sept & Oct Mon–Sat 11am–5pm, Sun noon–5pm; July & Aug Mon–Sat 10am–6pm, Sun 11am–6pm; Nov–March Mon–Sat 11am–4pm, Sun noon–4pm; £5; Ⓦ www.lighthousemuseum.org.uk), where you can see a collection of huge lenses and prisms gathered from decommissioned lighthouses, and a display on various members of the famous "Lighthouse" Stevenson family. Highlight of the museum is the tour of Kinnaird Head lighthouse itself, preserved as it was when the last keeper left in 1991, with its century-old equipment still in perfect working order.

Next door, and also well worth a visit, is the **Fraserburgh Heritage Centre** (April–Oct Mon–Sat 11am–5pm, Sun 1–5pm; £4.50; Ⓦ www.fraserburghheritage.com), a wide-ranging exhibition on the history of the town, with small boats, audiovisual presentations and details of some experiments in wireless communication performed in town by Marconi in 1904.

Fraserbugh's **tourist office**, in Saltoun Square (April–Oct Mon–Sat; Ⓣ 01346/518315), gives out information about the surrounding area. For a bite to **eat**, try *Zanres* opposite the tourist office, which does decent fish and chips, while *Lonmay Old Manse* (Ⓣ 01346/532227, Ⓦ www.lonmay.co.uk) south of the town offers excellent **B&B** in a handsome 1820 manse.

Fraserburgh to Gardenstown

The coast road between Fraserburgh and Pennan, twelve miles west, is particularly attractive: inland there are villages with pretty churches and cottages, while countless paths lead off it to ruined castles, cliff-top walks and lonely beaches. **PENNAN** itself, a tiny fishing hamlet, lies just off the road, down a steep and hazardous hill. Consisting of little more than a single row of whitewashed stone cottages tucked between a cliff and the sea, the village leapt into the limelight when the British movie *Local Hero* was filmed here in 1982. You can stay at one of the identifiable landmarks from the film, the *Pennan Inn* (ⓣ01346/561201, ⓦthepennaninn.co.uk; ❸), where you can also grab a drink or something to eat.

Locals in tiny and equally appealing **CROVIE** (pronounced "crivie"), another village in the same style on the other side of Troup Head from Pennan, frequently have their doorsteps washed by the sea. The Head itself supports over 1500 gannet nests. Wedged in against the steep cliffs, Crovie is so narrow that its residents have to park their cars at one end of the village and continue to their houses on foot. **GARDENSTOWN**, a short way west, is similar if a little larger and supports the *Garden Arms Hotel* (ⓣ01261/851260, ⓦwww.gardenarms.co.uk; ❷), as well as the Gallery 83 art space.

Macduff and Banff

Heading west along the coast from Pennan brings you, after ten miles, to **MACDUFF**, a famous spa town during the nineteenth century that now has a thriving and pleasant harbour. **Macduff Marine Aquarium**, 11 High Shore (daily 10am–5pm; £5.65; ⓦwww.macduff-aquarium.org.uk), has an intriguing display on the Moray Firth marine habitat with a huge centre-piece aquarium tank open to the air where visitors can watch divers feed the fish. From the harbour, North 58 (ⓣ01542/819900, ⓦwww.north58.co.uk) and Puffin Cruises (ⓣ01542/832560, ⓦwww.puffincruises.com) both offer a variety of wildlife-spotting and sightseeing **boat trips** along the coast.

Macduff and its neighbour **BANFF** are separated by little more than the beautiful seven-arch bridge over the River Deveron. Banff's **tourist office** (April–Oct Mon–Sat; ⓣ01261/812419) is housed in the old gatehouse of Duff House in St Mary Square.

Duff House

Banff has a mix of characterful old buildings and boarded-up shops, which give little clue to the extravagance of **Duff House** (generally April–Oct daily 11am–5pm; Nov–March Thurs–Sun 11am–4pm; HS; £6.55; ⓦwww.duffhouse.org.uk), the town's main attraction. Built to William Adam's design in 1730, this elegant four-floor Georgian Baroque house was originally intended for one of the northeast's richest men, William Braco, who became earl of Fife in 1759. It was clearly built to impress, and could have been even more splendid had Adam been allowed to build curving colonnades either side; Braco's refusal to pay for carved Corinthian columns to be shipped in from Queensferry caused such bitter argument that the laird never came to live here, and even shut his coach curtains whenever he passed by.

The house has been painstakingly restored and reopened as an outpost of the **National Gallery of Scotland**'s extensive collection, and while the emphasis is on displaying period artwork rather than any broader selection of the Gallery's paintings, temporary exhibitions of work from the collections are mounted regularly. Beyond the house there are extensive **grounds** with an adventure playground, some pleasant parkland and riverside walks, and various odd buildings including a fishing "temple" and the Duff dynasty's mausoleum.

Practicalities

One option for **accommodation** is *The Knowes* (ⓣ01261/832152, ⓦwww.knoweshotel.co.uk; ❸), a small hotel on the hill above Macduff with plain rooms and great outlooks over both towns. There are also numerous B&Bs in and around

Macduff and Banff. At *Durno House* (Ⓣ01261/821203, Ⓦwww.durnohouse-scotland.co.uk; ❶), five minutes from Banff, you'll find extensive grounds, organic produce and a warm welcome, while *St Helens Guest House* (Ⓣ01261/818241, Ⓦwww.sthelensbanff.demon.co.uk; ❷) on Bellevue Road in Banff is another friendly option. **Camping** is best near the beach to the west of Banff, at the windy *Banff Links Caravan Park* (Ⓣ01261/812228; April–Oct).

For **food** it's best to head to Macduff, where the *Cornerstone Teahouse* on Market Street hits the mark with delicious home-baking and light meals (closed Tues; Ⓣ01261/833352). Reasonably priced bar food with a view of the coastline is available from *The Knowes Hotel* (see opposite). More upmarket but still moderately priced is the French restaurant in the grand *County Hotel* in Banff (Ⓣ01261/815353, Ⓦwww.thecountyhotel.com).

Cullen and Portsoy

Twelve miles west of Banff is **CULLEN**, served by bus #305 from Aberdeen. Strikingly situated beneath a superb series of arched viaducts, which were built because the earl and countess of Seafield refused to allow the railway to pass through the grounds of Cullen House, the town is made up of two sections: Seatown, by the harbour, and the new town on the hillside. There's a lovely stretch of sheltered sand by Seatown, where the colourful houses – confusingly numbered according to the order in which they were built – huddle end-on to the sea.

You can pick up leaflets about local walks at the town's independent **tourist office** on the main square of the new town, but as it's run by volunteers the opening hours can be sporadic (generally June–Aug daily 11am–5pm). Grand *Seafield Arms* (Ⓣ01542/840791, Ⓦwww.theseafieldarms.co.uk; ❺) is a well-run nineteenth-century coaching **inn**. The local delicacy, **Cullen skink** – a soup made from milk (or cream), potato and smoked haddock – is available at the *Seafield* and elsewhere, including *Puddleduck Patch* on Seafield Street.

Six miles east is the quiet village of **PORTSOY**, renowned for its green marble once shipped to Versailles, and its annual traditional boat festival in early July. The *Shore Inn* by the atmospheric old stone harbour is a good spot for a beer or a meal on a sunny day.

Buckie and Spey Bay

West of Cullen, the scruffy working fishing town of **BUCKIE** marks one end of the **Speyside Way** long-distance footpath (see p.432). This follows the coast west for five miles to windy **Spey Bay**, at the mouth of the river of the same name, which can also be reached by a small coastal road from Buckie. It's a remote spot bounded by sea, river and sky; interpretation is offered by a small but dedicated **wildlife centre** (April–Oct daily 10.30am–5pm; Nov–March Sat & Sun 10.30am–5pm; free; Ⓦwww.wdcs.org/wildlifecentre), whose main mission is researching the Moray Firth dolphin population (for more on which, see p.464). The centre, run by the Whale and Dolphin Conservation Society, houses an exhibition and a café; alongside, the Tugnet **ice house**, a partially subterranean, thick-walled house with a turf roof used by fishermen in the days before electric refrigeration to store their ice and catches, makes for an atmospheric auditorium in which films of the underwater world are shown. The centre can advise on accredited local operators if you want to head out onto the Firth itself to look for sea life. It is sometimes possible, however, to see dolphins feeding if you wander along the long pebbly spit by the mouth of the Spey; this is also a good spot to see otters and birds, including ospreys. To **stay**, try the simple *Beach House B&B* (Ⓣ01343/829220; ❸), where the living room affords excellent views over the sea.

Elgin and around

The lively market town of **ELGIN**, just inland about fifteen miles west of Cullen, grew up around the River Lossie in the thirteenth century. The centre has mostly kept its medieval street plan, and while the busy main street is choked with chain stores, it does open out onto an old cobbled marketplace with a tangle of wynds and pends on either side.

On North College Street, a few blocks from the tourist office and clearly signposted, is the lovely ruin of **Elgin Cathedral** (April–Sept daily 9.30am–5.30pm; Oct–March Mon–Wed, Sat & Sun 9.30am–4.30pm; HS; £4.70, joint ticket with Spynie Palace (see opposite) £6). Once considered Scotland's most beautiful cathedral, rivalling St Andrews in importance, it's little more than a shell today, though it does retain its original facade. Founded in 1224, the three-towered building was extensively rebuilt after a fire in 1270, and stood as the region's highest religious house until 1390 when the inimical Wolf of Badenoch (illegitimate son of Robert II) burned the place down, along with the rest of the town, in retaliation for having been excommunicated by the bishop of Moray when he left his wife. The cathedral suffered further during the post-Reformation period, when all its valuables were stripped and the building was reduced to a common quarry for the locals. Unusual features include the Pictish cross slab in the middle of the ruins and the cracked gravestones with their *memento mori* of skulls and crossbones. Across the road from the cathedral, the three-acre **Biblical Garden** (May–Sept daily 10am–7pm; free) has been planted with all 110 plants mentioned in the Bible, interspersed with some rather stiff-looking statues depicting the parables.

At the very top of High Street is one of Britain's oldest museums, the **Elgin Museum** (April–Oct Mon–Fri 10am–5pm, Sat 11am–4pm; Nov–March open on request or if staff are in the building; £4; ⓣ01343/543675, ⓦelginmuseum.org.uk), which has been housed here since 1843. Following a major refurbishment, it has plenty of modern touches, with displays on local history and some weird anthropological artefacts including a shrunken head from Ecuador. In addition, you can see an excellent collection of fossils, some well-explained Pictish relics and a display on the important Birnie hoard of silver Roman dinarii from 197 AD found nearby.

Elgin is on the edge of whisky country, and while the attractive local **distillery**, **Glen Moray** (Mon–Fri 9am–5pm, May–Sept Sat also 10am–4.30pm; £3; ⓦwww.glenmoray.com) isn't part of the official Malt Whisky Trail (see p.434), tours are still available – the distinctive thing here is that your guide is quite likely to be the stillman, mashman or one of the other workers from the distillery floor. For those feeling a bit more energetic, the sprawling "Moray Monster Trails" nine miles south of Elgin offer some excellent **mountain biking** (ⓦwww.moraymountainbikeclub.co.uk).

Practicalities

Elgin is well served by public transport, though the **train station** served by the Aberdeen–Inverness line is slightly detached from the city centre on the south side of town.

The helpful **tourist office**, 17 High St (April–Sept daily; Oct–March Mon–Sat; ⓣ01343/542666), will book local **accommodation**. *The Lodge*, 20 Duff Ave (ⓣ01343/549981, ⓦwww.thelodge-elgin.com; ❸), provides B&B in a house built for a former tea-plantation owner, offering guests dinner and an appetizing breakfast menu, while *The Pines*, East Road (ⓣ01343/552495, ⓦwww.thepinesguesthouse.com; ❸), makes for a pleasant alternative. Five miles east of town, the *Old Church of Urquhart* (ⓣ01343/843063, ⓦwww.oldchurch.eu; ❸) is the most appealing place to stay in the area, an unusual and comfortable B&B in an imaginatively converted church on Meft Road; there's also a self-catering apartment.

For **food**, *Aspire* on Moss Street (Ⓣ01343/540932) serves memorable, moderately priced lunches and dinners with a European twist in the setting of a converted church. *Ashvale* at 11 Moss St does good sit-down fish and chips. For a great coffee (and free wi-fi access) head for *Restaurant 55* at 55 High St between the tourist office and the museum. You can pick up some great **picnic** foods at the old-fashioned high-street store Gordon & McPhail, 58–60 South St, an Aladdin's cave of delicacies; they claim to have the largest selection of whiskies in the world.

Pluscarden Abbey

Set in an attractive, verdant valley seven miles southwest of Elgin, **Pluscarden Abbey** (daily 9am–5pm; free; Ⓦwww.pluscardenabbey.org), looms impressively large in a peaceful clearing off an unmarked road. One of only two abbeys in Scotland with a permanent community of monks, it was founded in 1230 for a French order and, in 1390, became another of the properties burnt by the Wolf of Badenoch (see p.360); recovering from this, it became a priory of the Benedictine Abbey of Dunfermline in 1454 and continued as such until monastic life was suppressed in Scotland in 1560. In 1948 a small group of Benedictine monks from Gloucester established the present community. They are an active bunch, running stained-glass workshops, making honey and even recording Gregorian chants on CDs. The abbey itself is airy and tranquil, with the monks' singing often eerily floating through from the connecting chapel. It is possible to **stay** here on retreat for a few days; see the website for details.

Lossiemouth, Spynie Palace and Duffus

Five miles north of Elgin across the flat land of the Laich of Moray, Elgin's nearest seaside town, **LOSSIEMOUTH** (generally known as Lossie), is a cheery golf-oriented seaside town blessed with lovely sandy beaches; the glorious duney spit of the East Beach is reached over a footbridge across the River Lossie from the town park. In the easternmost part of the older harbour's grid of stone streets, Pitgaveny Street has the tiny **Fisheries Museum** (April–Sept Mon–Sat 10.30am–5pm; £1.50), which includes some interesting scale models of fishing boats and a re-creation of the study of local lad James Ramsay Macdonald (1866–1937), Britain's first Labour prime minister. The town's only blight is the frequent sky-tearing noise of military aircraft from the nearby RAF base.

Lossiemouth's development as a port came when the nearby waterways of **SPYNIE**, three miles inland, silted up and became useless to the traders of Elgin. Little remains of the settlement except hulking **Spynie Palace** (April–Sept daily 9.30am–5.30pm; Oct–March Sat & Sun 9.30am–4.30pm; HS; £3.70, joint ticket with Elgin Cathedral, opposite, £6.20), home of the bishops of Moray from 1107 until 1686. The enormous rectangular David's Tower – visible for miles around – offers stunning views from the top over the Moray Firth and the Spynie Canal, the much-diminished sea loch.

Straight roads and water ditches crisscross the flat land west of Spynie. Past the sinister shapes of the planes and hangars of RAF Lossiemouth is the spread-eagled settlement of **DUFFUS**, five miles west of Lossie. Old Duffus is no more than a farm or two and a motte and bailey **castle** (free access), part of which leans at a rakish angle. New Duffus, two miles northwest, is best known as the gateway to **Gordonstoun School**, the spartan (but hugely expensive) public school favoured by royalty, although Prince Charles reportedly despised its fresh-air-and-cold-showers puritanism.

Burghead

Another of this coastline's tightly packed, stone-built fishing villages, windswept **BURGHEAD** (served by hourly bus #331 from Elgin) was once the site of an important Iron Age fort and the ancient Pictish capital of Moray. In 1805–09 a fishing village was built on the promontory where the ancient fort had sat, in the course of which some unique Pictish stone carvings known as the **Burghead Bulls** were discovered. One is on display in the small **Burghead Visitor Centre** (Easter–Sept daily noon–4pm; entry by donation) built into the round white lookout tower at the tip of the promontory; others can be seen in Elgin Museum, the National Museum in Edinburgh and the British Museum in London. The tower offers great views of the Moray Firth, while inside are displays about Pictish times and the dramatic annual fire ceremony known as the **Burning of the Clavie**, one of only a few that still take place in Scotland. A burning tar barrel is carried around the town on January 11 to mark the old calendar's new year, before being rolled into the sea, sparks and embers flying.

Findhorn and the Moray Arts Centre

A wide sweep of sandy beach stretches five miles around Burghead Bay to **FINDHORN**, a tidy village with some neat fishermen's cottages, a delightful harbour dotted with moored yachts, a small **Heritage Centre** (May & Sept Sat & Sun 2–5pm; June–Aug daily 2–5pm; free) in the village's former salmon-net sheds and grass-roofed ice house, and a couple of good pubs: on a sunny day, a pint or some seafood on the terrace at the popular *Kimberley Inn* is hard to beat. Equally attractive is the centrally located *Bakehouse*, a café-restaurant run by the Findhorn Foundation (see box opposite). With all food freshly prepared on site, its moderately priced daytime and evening (Thurs–Sun only) menu includes organic local cheeses, meats and fish as well as the chance for some al fresco dining.

Like Lossiemouth, however, it's hard to escape the military presence in the area, with **RAF Kinloss**, one of the UK's most important front-line airfields, right on its doorstep. Findhorn is best known, however, for the controversial **Findhorn Foundation**, based beside the town's caravan park about a mile before you reach the village itself. Visitors are generally free to stroll around the community, but it's worth trying to take a more informed look at the different activities and projects by means of a **guided tour** (April–Sept Mon, Wed & Fri–Sun 2pm; no Sun tour in April & Sept; £5); you can also guide yourself via a booklet (£3.50) available from the shop or visitor centre. During a tour you can stop off at the community's excellent *Blue Angel* **café**, which serves healthy soups and irresistible organic cakes (daily 10am–5pm) produced by the community's Phoenix Bakery (now relocated into Findhorn village itself). Beside the café is the Universal Hall Arts Centre, an occasional venue for good touring folk and jazz bands, while the Phoenix Community Store near the entrance to the foundation is a richly stocked **delicatessen** with lots of organic produce and bread baked on site; there's also a small craft and book section.

Don't miss the **Moray Art Centre** (Ⓣ01309/692426, Ⓦwww.morayartcentre.org), on the edge of the foundation but not officially a part of it. The centre is located in a terracotta-hued eco-friendly building; it hosts eclectic and imaginative temporary exhibitions and regular art classes.

The **visitor centre** (Mon–Fri 10am–5pm, also open Sat & Sun 1–4pm in summer; Ⓣ01309/690311, Ⓦwww.findhorn.org) has information on staying within the community, either as part of an introductory "Experience Week", or simply overnighting – a number of the eco-houses offer B&B (❷–❸); try *Sunflower* (Ⓣ01309/692080, Ⓦwww.sunflower-findhorn.co.uk), where they serve a good

The Findhorn Foundation

In 1962, with little money and no employment, Eileen and Peter Caddy, their three children and friend Dorothy Maclean, settled on a caravan site at Findhorn. Dorothy believed that she had a special relationship with what she called the "devas … the archetypal formative forces of light or energy that underlie all forms in nature – plants, trees, rivers", and from the uncompromising sandy soil they built a remarkable garden filled with plants and vegetables, far larger than had ever been seen in the area.

A few of those who came to see the phenomenon stayed to help out and tune into the spiritual aspect of the daily life of the nascent community. With its emphasis on inner discovery and development, but unattached to any particular doctrine or creed, the **Findhorn Foundation** (ⓦwww.findhorn.org) has today blossomed into a permanent community of a couple of hundred people, with a well-developed series of courses and retreats on subjects ranging from astroshamanic healing to organic gardening, drawing another eight thousand or so visitors each year. The original caravan still stands, surrounded by a whole host of newer timber buildings and other caravans employing solar power, earth roofs and other green initiatives. The most intriguing of these are a group of round houses made from huge barrels reclaimed from a Speyside whisky distillery, while elsewhere you can see an ecological sewage treatment centre, a huge wind generator and various community businesses including a café, pottery and weaving studio.

The foundation is not without controversy: a community leader once declared that "behind the benign and apparently religious front lies a hard core of New Agers experimenting with hallucinatory techniques marketed as spirituality." Whatever the truth, Findhorn can be accused of being overly well heeled, as betrayed by a glance into the shop or a tally of the smart cars parked outside the well-appointed eco-houses. However, there's little doubt that the community appeals to large numbers of people: it continues to prosper and it is well known around the world. The reputation of the place is such that it attracts visitors both sympathetic and sceptical – and both find something to feed their preconceptions.

organic breakfast, or the *Strawbale House* (ⓣ01309/692188). Despite the enormous growth of the community, it is still situated on Findhorn's caravan and **camping park** (ⓣ01309/690203, ⓦwww.findhornbayholidaypark.com; April–Oct), which has tent pitches, stationary caravans (❷) and some unusual eco-chalets (£745per week in high season). The foundation is located on the B9011 about five miles northeast of Forres and served by bus #336 linking Forres High Street with Findhorn and Elgin.

Forres

FORRES (ⓦwww.forresweb.net), four miles southwest of Findhorn, is one of Scotland's oldest agricultural towns, and of little note except for its pretty flower-filled parks and the 20ft-high **Sueno's Stone** on the eastern outskirts of town, one of the most remarkable Pictish stones in Scotland. Now housed in what looks like a huge glass telephone box as protection against further erosion, the stone was found buried in 1726 and mistakenly named after Swein Forkbeard, King of Denmark, though it more probably commemorates a battle between the people of Moray and the Norse settlers in Orkney. Carvings on the east face can be read as one of the earliest examples of war reportage, with the story told from the arrival of the leader at the top to the decapitated corpses of the vanquished at the bottom.

Forres is on the main Inverness–Aberdeen **train** line; the train station sits half a mile west of the tourist office near the north end of Market Street and the **Ben Romach whisky distillery** (May–Sept Mon–Sat 9.30pm–5pm, June–Aug also

Sun noon–4pm; Oct–April Mon–Fri 9.30am–5pm; £3.50; Ⓣ01309/675968, Ⓦwww.benromach.com), established in 1898. **Bus** #10 between Aberdeen/Elgin and Inverness stops outside St Leonard's Church on High Street, a little way along from the friendly **tourist office** at no. 116 (April–Oct Mon–Sat; Ⓣ01309/672938). For **accommodation**, head three miles or so west of Forres to Dyke, where the *Old Kirk* (Ⓣ01309/641414, Ⓦwww.oldkirk.co.uk; ❸) has three rooms in a bright, modern conversion of a Victorian country church. Hearty sandwiches and home-baking are served at *Time Out Café*, 79 High St (Ⓣ01309/672425). Out of Forres, recommended places to **eat** include *The Loft Bistro* (Ⓣ01343/850111, Ⓦwww.eastgrange.co.uk; closed Mon) at East Grange farm near Kinloss – where you can also **camp** or sleep in a wigwam – or the daytime café at *Logie Steading* (Ⓦwww.logie.co.uk), a conversion of an old farm outbuilding that also houses a secondhand bookshop, art gallery and other small shops, located six miles south of Forres.

Travel details

Trains

Aberdeen to: Arbroath (every 30min; 1hr); Dundee (every 30min; 1hr 15min); Edinburgh (1–2 hourly; 2hr 35min); Elgin (Mon–Sat 10 daily, 5 on Sun; 1hr 30min); Forres (Mon–Sat 10 daily, 5 on Sun; 1hr 45min); Glasgow (hourly; 2hr 35min); Inverness (Mon–Sat 10 daily, 5 on Sun; 2hr 15min); Inverurie (Mon–Sat minimum of 10 daily, 5 on Sun; 20min); London (Sun–Fri sleeper service; 10hrs); Montrose (every 30min; 45min); Nairn (Mon–Sat 10 daily, 5 on Sun; 1hr 50min);
Stonehaven (every 30min; 15min).
Dundee to: Aberdeen (every 30min; 1hr 15min); Arbroath (every 30min; 20min); Edinburgh (1–2 hourly; 1hr 15min); Glasgow (1–2 hourly; 1hr 30min); Montrose (1–2 hourly; 30min).
Elgin to: Forres (at least once every 2hr; 20min); Nairn (hourly; 25min).

Buses

Aberdeen to: Ballater (hourly; 1hr 45min); Banchory (hourly; 55min); Banff (hourly; 1hr 55min); Braemar (at least once every 2hr; 2hr 10min); Crathie for Balmoral (at least once every 2 hours; 1hr 55min); Cruden Bay (hourly; 50min); Cullen (hourly; 2hr 30min); Dundee (hourly; 2hr); Elgin (hourly; 3hr 20min); Forres (hourly; 4hr); Fraserburgh (hourly; 1hr 30min); Inverurie (hourly; 50min); Macduff (hourly; 1hr 50min); Peterhead (every 30min; 1hr 15min); Stonehaven (every 15min; 50min).
Dundee to: Aberdeen (hourly; 1hr 20min); Arbroath (hourly; 50min); Blairgowrie (7 daily; 50min); Forfar (hourly; 30min); Glamis (5 daily; 35min); Kirriemuir (5 daily; 55min); Meigle (hourly; 40min); Montrose (hourly; 1hr 10min).
Elgin to: Aberdeen (hourly; 3hr 30min); Burghead (hourly; 25min); Duffus (hourly; 15min); Forres (hourly; 25min); Inverurie (hourly; 1hr 30min); Lossiemouth (every 30min; 20min); Nairn (hourly; 45min); Pluscarden (1 daily schooldays only; 20min).
Forres to: Elgin (hourly; 25min); Findhorn (hourly; 20min).
Fraserburgh to: Banff (2 daily; 55min); Macduff (2 daily; 45min).
Montrose to: Brechin (every 30min; 20min).

Ferries

Aberdeen to: Kirkwall, Orkney (Thurs, Sat & Sun plus Tues in summer; 6hr); Lerwick, Shetland (daily; 10–12hr overnight).

Flights

Aberdeen to: Belfast (1 daily, 1hr 15min); Birmingham (Mon–Fri 5 daily, Sat & Sun 2 daily; 1hr 30min); Dublin (1 daily; 1hr 5min); East Midlands (3 daily Mon–Fri; 1 Sun; 1hr 25min), Exeter (1 daily; 1hr 50min); Kirkwall, Orkney (1 daily; 55min); Liverpool (1 daily, 1hr); London Gatwick (min 3 daily; 1hr 35min); London Heathrow (Mon-Fri, min 7 daily, Sat & Sun min 2; 1hr 30min); London Luton (2 daily; 1hr 30min); Manchester (Mon–Fri 6 daily, Sat & Sun 2 daily; 1hr 20min); Newcastle (Mon–Fri 5 daily, Sat–Sun 1 daily; 55min); Sumburgh, Shetland (Mon–Fri 5 daily, Sat & Sun 2 daily; 1hr).
Dundee to: London City (Mon–Fri 4 daily,1 on Sat, 2 on Sun; 1hr 25min).

The Cairngorms and Speyside

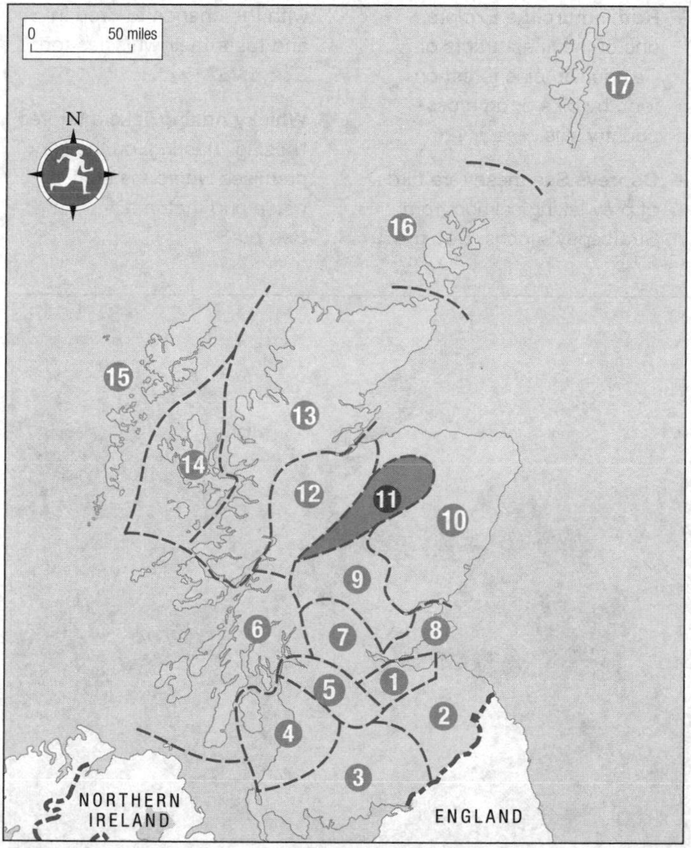

CHAPTER 11 **Highlights**

* **The Cairngorms** Scotland's grandest mountain massif, located within Britain's largest national park, where rare plants, wild animals, inspiring vistas, and challenging outdoor activities abound. See p.425

* **Rothiemurchus** Explore one of the finest tracts of Caledonian pine forest on foot, by bike or on cross-country skis. See p.426

* **Ospreys** See these rare birds of prey taking salmon from Strathspey's lochs. See p.429

* **Shinty** An ancient indigenous sport that's a wild mix of hockey and golf; watch a game at Kingussie or Newtonmore. See p.431

* **Speyside Way** Walking route taking in Glenfiddich, Glenlivet and Glen Grant, with the chance to drop in and taste their whiskies too. See p.432

* **Whisky nosing** Take a tutored "nosing" (tasting) on the very premises where the stuff is made and matured. See p.434

▲ A stag in the Cairngorms

The Cairngorms and Speyside

Rising high in the heather-clad hills above remote Loch Laggan, forty miles due south of Inverness, the **River Spey**, Scotland's second longest river, drains northeast towards the Moray Firth through one of the Highlands' most spellbinding valleys. Famous for its ancient forests, salmon fishing and ospreys, the area around the upper section of the river, known as **Strathspey**, is dominated by the sculpted **Cairngorms**, Britain's most extensive mountain massif, unique in supporting subarctic tundra on its high plateau. Though the area has been admired and treasured for many years as one of Scotland's prime natural assets, the Cairngorms National Park was only declared in 2004. Outdoor enthusiasts flock to the area to take advantage of the superb hiking, biking, watersports and winter snows, aided by the fact that the area is easily accessible by road and rail from both the Central Belt and Inverness.

A string of villages along the river provide useful bases for setting out into the wilder country, principal among them **Aviemore**, a rather ugly straggle of housing and hotel developments which nevertheless has a lively, youthful feel to it. A little way north, **Grantown-on-Spey** is more attractive, with solid Victorian mansions but much less vitality, while smaller settlements such as **Boat of Garten** and **Kincraig** are quieter, well-kept villages.

Downriver, Strathspey gives way to the area known as **Speyside**, famous as the heart of Scotland's **malt whisky** industry. In addition to the Malt Whisky Trail that leads round a number of well-known distilleries in the vicinity of villages such as **Dufftown** and **Craigellachie**, the lesser-known **Speyside Way**, another of Scotland's long-distance footpaths, offers the chance to enjoy the scenery of the region, as well as its whiskies, on foot.

Strathspey

Of Strathspey's scattered settlements, **Aviemore** absorbs the largest number of visitors, particularly in midwinter when it metamorphoses into the UK's busiest ski resort. The village struggles to reflect the charm of its surrounding area, but it's a good first stop for information, to sort out somewhere to stay or to find out about nearby outdoor activities, which are likely to seem very enticing after a

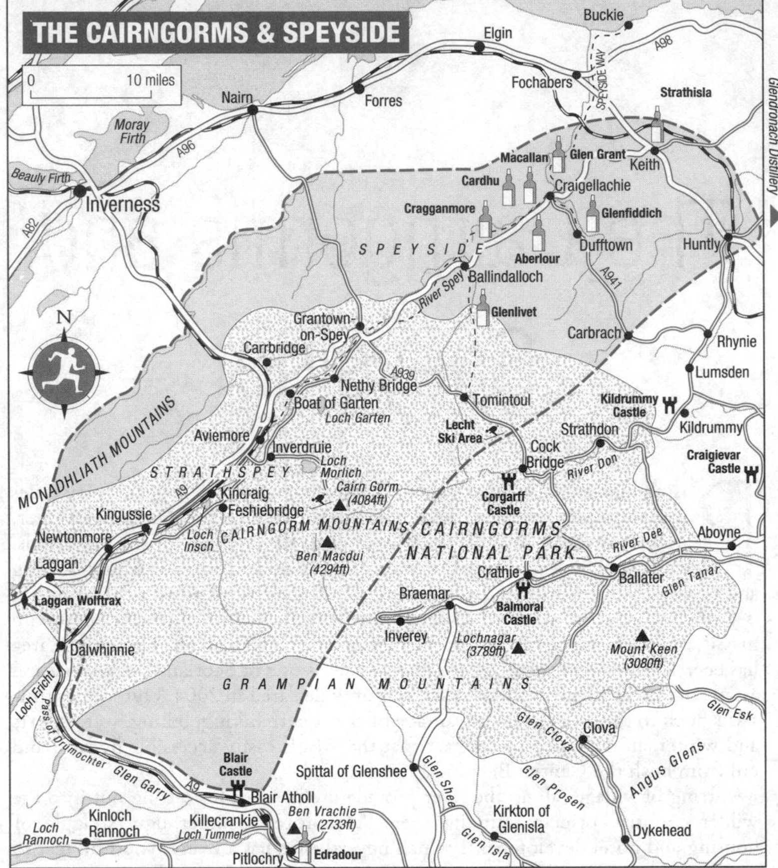

glimpse of the 4000-foot summit plateau of the Cairngorms. The planned Georgian town of **Grantown-on-Spey** makes a good alternative base for summer visitors. Further upriver, the sedate villages of **Newtonmore** and **Kingussie** are older-established holiday centres, popular more with anglers and grouse hunters than canoeists and climbers. The whole area boasts a wide choice of good-quality accommodation, particularly in the budget market, with various easy-going hostels run by and for outdoor enthusiasts.

Aviemore and around

The once-sleepy village of **AVIEMORE** was first developed as a ski and tourism resort in the mid-1960s and, over the years, fell victim to profiteering developers with scant regard for the needs of the local community. More recently, an ambitious hotel and spa development has finally replaced most of the glaring planning eyesores, but the town remains a soulless hotchpotch of retail outlets, café-bars and characterless housing developments. That said, Aviemore is undeniably well equipped with services and facilities and is the most convenient base for the Cairngorms.

The main attractions of Aviemore are its **outdoor pursuits**, though train enthusiasts are drawn to the restored **Strathspey Steam Railway**, which chugs the short distance between Aviemore and Broomhill, just beyond Boat of Garten village, four times daily through the summer (June–Sept; less regular service at other times; ⓣ01479/810725, ⓦwww.strathspeyrailway.co.uk). The more energetic can head for the fabulous **Aviemore Indoor Climbing** Wall (daily 9am–5pm; Tues & Thurs till 10pm; £5; ⓣ01479/812466, ⓦwww.extreme-dream.com). The most useful local **bus** route is the #34, which runs hourly from Aviemore to the Cairn gorm Mountain Railway (see p.428) via Rothiemurchus and Loch Morlich. The same service runs regularly (5 daily) to Grantown via the Osprey Centre at Boat of Garten.

Aviemore's businesslike **tourist office** is in the heart of things at 7 The Parade, Grampian Rd (daily; ⓣ01479/810930). It offers an accommodation booking service and reams of leaflets on local attractions.

Cairngorms National Park

The **Cairngorms National Park** (ⓦwww.cairngorms.co.uk) covers some 1500 square miles and incorporates the **Cairngorms massif**, the largest mountainscape in the UK and the only sizeable plateau in the country over 2500ft. It's the biggest national park in Britain, and while Aviemore and the surrounding area are regarded as the main point of entry, particularly for those planning outdoor activities, it's also possible to access the eastern side of the park from both Deeside and Donside in Aberdeenshire. Crossing the range is a significant challenge: by road the only connection is the A939 Tomintoul to Cock Bridge, frequently impassable in winter due to snow, while on foot the only way to avoid the high peaks is to follow the old cattle drovers' route called the **Lairig Ghru**, a very long day's walk between Inverdruie at the edge of Rothiemurchus and the Linn of Dee, near Inverey.

The name Cairngorm comes from the Gaelic *An Carm Gorm*, meaning "the blue hill" after the blueish-tinged stones found in the area, and within the park there are 52 summits over 2953ft, as well as a quarter of Scotland's native woodland and a quarter of the UK's threatened wildlife species. The conservation of the landscape's unique flora and fauna is, of course, one of the principal reasons national park status was conferred. However, an important role for the park is to consider the needs of an estimated 17,000 people living and working within its boundaries and to integrate the array of outdoor activities enjoyed by visitors.

Vegetation in the area ranges from one of the largest tracts of ancient **Caledonian pine and birch forest** remaining in Scotland at Rothiemurchus, to subarctic tundra on the high plateau, where **alpine flora** such as starry saxifrage and the star-shaped pink flowers of moss campion peek out of the pink granite in the few months of summer that the ground is free of snow. In the pine forests of the river valleys, strikingly coloured **birds** such as crested tits, redwings and goldfinches can be observed, along with rarely seen **mammals** such as the red squirrel and pine marten. On the heather slopes above the forest, red and black grouse are often encountered, though their larger relative, the capercaillie, is a much rarer sight, having been reintroduced in 1837 after dying out in the seventeenth century. Birds of prey you're most likely to see are **osprey**, best seen at the osprey observation centre (see p.429) at Loch Garten or fishing on the lochs around Aviemore, though golden eagles and peregrine falcons can occasionally be seen higher up. Venturing up to the plateau you'll have the chance of seeing the shy **ptarmigan**, another member of the grouse family, which nests on bare rock and has white plumage during winter, or even the dotterel and snow bunting, rare visitors from the Arctic, along with mountain (blue) hares, which also turn white in winter and are best seen in spring as they scurry across patches of brown hillside where the snow has melted.

Summer activities

In summer, the main activities around Aviemore are **walking** (see box, p.428) and **watersports**, and there are great opportunities for mountain biking, pony trekking and fly-fishing. Two centres offer sailing, windsurfing and canoeing: the Loch Morlich Watersports Centre (Ⓣ01479/861221, Ⓦwww.lochmorlich.com), seven miles east of Aviemore, and the Loch Insh Watersports Centre (Ⓣ01540/651272, Ⓦwww.lochinsh.com) six miles up-valley near Kincraig. The latter also rents mountain bikes, boats for fishing, runs boat-based wildlife tours (May–Sept) and gives ski instruction on a 200ft-long dry slope. If you want still more action, G2 Outdoor (Ⓣ01479/811008, Ⓦwww.g2outdoor.co.uk) will take you kayaking and canyoning whilst Full On Adventure (Ⓣ07885/835838, Ⓦwww.fullonadventure.com) runs **white-water rafting** trips on the Findhorn River.

Riding and **pony trekking** are on offer up and down the valley: try Alvie Stables near Kincraig (Ⓣ07831/495397, Ⓦwww.alvie-estate.co.uk), or Strathspey Highland Ponies (Easter–Oct Ⓣ01479/812345), where you can ride this ancient Highland breed on hacks and treks from Rothiemurchus Visitor Centre at Inverdruie. **Fishing** is very much part of the local scene; you can fish for trout and salmon on the River Spey, and the Rothiemurchus Estate (Ⓣ01479/810703, Ⓦwww.rothiemurchus.com) has a stocked rainbow trout-fishing loch (June–Aug 9am–9pm; Sept–May 9am–5pm; 1hr introductory package £13) at **Inverdruie**, where success is virtually guaranteed. The Abernethy Angling Association (Ⓦwww.river-spey.com) is a good source of information for the seasons, locations and costs of renting a rod and tackle. The Aviemore tourist office provides a brochure outlining the permits required.

For both the adventurous and novice cyclist, the entire region is great for **mountain biking**. The Rothiemurchus Estate has several excellent (and non-technical) way-marked trails running through its extensive lands. However, for the best advice, including guiding, maps and high-quality (front suspension) bike rental (£15/half day, £20/day), stop in at Bothy Bikes (Ⓣ01479/810111, Ⓦwww.bothybikes.co.uk) beside the tennis courts at Inverdruie. To buy (and, in some instances, rent) other outdoor equipment, in particular **climbing** and **hill-walking** gear, pop into the friendly and professional Mountain Spirit (Ⓣ01479/811788) shop at 62 Grampian Rd or try Cairngorm Mountain Sports in the centre of Aviemore (Ⓣ01479/810903).

Winter activities

Scottish **skiing** on a commercial level first really took off in Aviemore. By continental European and North American standards it's all on a tiny scale, but occasionally snow and sun coincide to offer beginner and expert alike a great day on the pistes. February and March are usually the best times, but there's a chance of decent snow at any time between mid-November and April. Several places sell or rent standard equipment though The Ski School (Ⓦwww.theskischool.co.uk) in the Day Lodge at Corie Cas on Cairngorm mountain is your best bet for ski/board rental and lessons. For ski mountaineering/cross-country rental, Mountain Spirit in Aviemore (see above) is the place to go, while the experts at G2 Outdoor (see above) will provide one-to-one tuition in the art of telemarking and back- country skiing. For an overview of skiing in the area check out Ⓦwww.ski.visitscotland.com.

The **Cairngorm Ski Area** (Ⓣ01479/861319, Ⓦwww.cairngormmountain.com), nine miles southeast of Aviemore, above Loch Morlich in Glenmore Forest Park, is well served during winter by buses from Aviemore. From here, the year-round **funicular railway** (see p.428) is the principal means of getting to the top of the ski slopes.

For a crash course in surviving Scottish winters, you could do worse than try a week at the National Outdoor Training Centre at *Glenmore Lodge* (see below) in the heart of the Glenmore Forest Park at the east end of Loch Morlich. This superbly equipped and organized centre (complete with cosy après-ski bar) offers winter and summer courses in hillwalking, mountaineering, alpine ski-mountaineering, avalanche awareness and much more. To add to the winter scene, there's a herd of reindeer at the **Cairngorm Reindeer Centre** by Loch Morlich (daily 10am–5pm; guided excursions 11am, & 2.30pm, July & Aug also 3.30pm; £9.50; ⓣ01479/861228, ⓦwww.reindeer-company.demon.co.uk), while between Loch Morlich and Inverdruie the **Cairngorm Sleddog Adventure Centre** (ⓣ07767/270526, ⓦwww.sled-dogs.co.uk), the UK's only sleddog centre, has a small museum (£8), as well as two- to three-hour trips on a wheeled or ski-based sled pulled by ten dogs (Oct–April only; £60 per person).

Accommodation

There's a good range of accommodation in Aviemore, and no shortage of **campsites**: two of the best are *Rothiemurchus Caravan Park*, among the tall pine trees at Coylumbridge on the way to Loch Morlich (ⓣ01479/812800, ⓦwww.rothiemurchus.net), and the Forestry Enterprise site beside the banks of Loch Morlich (ⓣ01479/861271).

Hotels and B&Bs

Corrour House Hotel Inverdruie, 2 miles southeast of Aviemore ⓣ01479/810220, ⓦwww.corrourhousehotel.co.uk. A secluded small hotel with a distinctly upmarket atmosphere. ❹

Glenmore Lodge 8 miles east of Aviemore ⓣ01479/861256, ⓦwww.glenmorelodge.org.uk. Specialist outdoor pursuits centre with excellent accommodation in twin rooms (with shared facilities) and self-catered lodges – guests can make use of the superb facilities, which include a pool, weights room, sauna and indoor climbing wall. ❷

Macdonald Aviemore Highland Resort Aviemore ⓣ0845/608 3734, ⓦwww.macdonaldhotels.co.uk/aviemore. A huge resort incorporating four separate hotels, self-catering chalets, several restaurants, a spa, luxury boutique shopping and a golf course. Modern and rather soulless. ❻

Ravenscraig Guest House Grampian Rd ⓣ01479/810 278. A handy central location and a welcoming and family-friendly B&B. ❸

Rowan Tree Country Hotel 3 miles south of Aviemore, overlooking Loch Alvie ⓣ01479/810207, ⓦwww.rowantreehotel.com. A relaxed, comfortable alternative to staying in town. ❺

Hostels

Aviemore Bunkhouse Dalfaber Rd ⓣ01479/811181, ⓦwww.aviemore-bunkhouse.com. A large modern place beside the *Old Bridge Inn* within walking distance from the station, with a family room and a double. ❶

Aviemore SYHA 25 Grampian Rd ⓣ0870/004 1104, ⓦwww.syha.org.uk. Aviemore's large and well-equipped SYHA hostel is within walking distance of the centre of the village.

Cairngorm Lodge ⓣ0870/004 1137. A SYHA hostel towards the Cairngorms at Loch Morlich, located in an old shooting lodge. Jan–Oct.

Eating

All along Aviemore's main drag are bistros, hotels and takeaways serving fairly predictable, run-of-the-mill **food**. One exception is the reasonably priced *Mountain Café* (ⓣ01479/812473), above Cairngorm Mountain Sports (see opposite), which serves an all-day menu of wholesome snacks and freshly prepared meals, often using local produce. Nearby, *RD's* (ⓣ01479/811633) is a safe bet for good-value dinners, while *The Einich* (ⓣ01479/812334), tucked away at the Rothiemurchus Visitor Centre at Inverdruie, is a delight and open for tasty home-bakes and lunches every day, and moderately priced evening meals from Wednesday to Saturday. Alternatively, there's *The Old Bridge Inn* on the east side of the railway on Dalfaber Road, which dishes up decent Scottish dinners and tasty pub grub and real

Walks around Aviemore

Ordnance Survey Explorer Maps nos. 402 & 403 or OS Outdoor Leisure Map no. 3

Walking of all grades is a highlight of the Aviemore area, though you should heed the usual safety guidelines (see p.49). These are particularly important if you want to venture into the subarctic climatic zone of the Cairngorms. However, as well as the high mountain trails, there are some lovely and well-signposted **low-level walks** in the area. It takes an hour or so to complete the gentle circular walk around pretty **Loch an Eilean** (with its ruined castle) in the **Rothiemurchus Estate**, beginning at the end of the back road that turns east off the B970 a mile south of Inverdruie. The helpful estate **visitor centres** at the lochside and by the roadside at Inverdruie provide more information on other woodland trails.

Another good, shortish (half-day) walk leads along a well-surfaced forestry track from Glenmore Lodge up towards the **Ryvoan Pass**, taking in An Lochan Uaine, known as the "Green Loch" and living up to its name, with amazing colours that range from turquoise to slate grey depending on the weather. The **Glenmore Forest Park Visitor Centre** by the roadside at the turn-off to Glenmore Lodge is the starting point for the three-hour round-trip climb of Meall a' Bhuachallie (2654ft), which offers excellent views and is usually accessible year-round. The centre has information on other trails in this section of the forest.

ales in a mellow, cosy setting, while *Café Mambo* adjacent to Aviemore Shopping Centre on Grampian Road, has a cheerful burger'n'chips-style menu.

Cairn Gorm mountain

From Aviemore, a road leads past Inverdruie and Loch Morlich and winds its way up into the Cairngorms, reaching the Coire Cas car park at a height of 2150ft. Here there's the base station for the ski area and the departure point for the **Cairn Gorm Mountain Railway** (daily 10am–5pm, last train up 4.20pm; every 20min; £9.75; Ⓦwww.cairngormmountain.com), a two-car funicular system that runs to the top of the ski area. A highly controversial £15 million scheme that was bitterly opposed by conservationists, the railway whisks skiers in winter, and tourists throughout the year, along a mile and a half of track to the top station at an altitude of 3600ft, not far from the summit of Cairn Gorm mountain. The top station incorporates an exhibition/interpretation area and a café/restaurant from which spectacular views can be had on clear days; there is no access beyond the confines of the top station and its open-air viewing terrace unless you're embarking on winter skiing, so anyone wanting to walk on the subarctic Cairngorm plateau will have to trudge up from the car park at the bottom.

At the base station there's a **ranger office** (daily: April–Oct 9am–5pm; Nov–March 8.30am–4.30pm) where you can find out about various trails and even join occasional guided walks, as well as check the latest weather report. The simplest of the walks is around a **Mountain Garden Trail**, which features shrubs and trees native to the Cairngorms. The *Ptarmigan* **restaurant** at the top station offers self-service meals through the day and, in summer (July–Sept), more formal three-course "sunset dining" on Friday and Saturday evenings, as well as a three-course meal and ceilidh on Thursday evenings (July & Aug only); pre-booking is required for both (Ⓣ01479/861341).

Carrbridge

Worth considering as an alternative to Aviemore – particularly as a skiing base – **CARRBRIDGE** is a pleasant, quiet village about seven miles north. Look out for the spindly Bridge of Carr at the northern end of the village, built in 1717 and still making a graceful stone arch over the River Dulnain. The main attraction in the village is the **Landmark Forest Heritage Park** (daily: April to mid-July 10am–6pm; mid-July to Aug 10am–7pm; Sept–March 10am–5pm; £11.55; Ⓦwww.landmark-centre.co.uk), which offers families a host of excellent outdoor and indoor activities including forest walks, nature trails, water fun rides and Britain's highest wooden tower. For local **accommodation** both *Carrmoor Guest House*, Carr Road (Ⓣ01479/841244, Ⓦwww.carrmoorguesthouse.co.uk; ❸), and the very friendly *MellonPatch* B&B (Ⓣ01479/841592, Ⓦwww.mellonpatch.com; ❷) on Station Road are good options. The cosy, basic *Carrbridge Bunkhouse* (Ⓣ01479/841250, Ⓦwww.carrbridge-bunkhouse.co.uk), a timber-lined cabin with a wood-burning stove, is a good base for walkers; it's half a mile or so north of the village on the Inverness road.

Loch Garten and around

The **Abernethy Forest RSPB Reserve** on the shore of **LOCH GARTEN**, seven miles northeast of Aviemore and eight miles south of Grantown-on-Spey, is famous as the nesting site of one of Britain's rarest birds. A little over fifty years ago, the **osprey**, known in North America as the fish hawk, had completely disappeared from the British Isles. Then, in 1954, a single pair of these exquisite white-and-brown raptors mysteriously reappeared and built a nest in a tree half a mile or so from the loch. One year's eggs fell victim to thieves, and thereafter the area became the centre of an effective high-security operation. There are now believed to be up to 150 pairs nesting across the Highlands. The best time to visit is between April and August, when the ospreys return from West Africa to nest and the RSPB opens an **observation centre** (daily 10am–6pm; £3; Ⓣ01479/831476), complete with powerful telescopes and CCTV monitoring of the nest. The reserve is also home to several other rare species, including the Scottish crossbill, capercaillie, whooper swan and red squirrel; once-weekly **guided walks** leave from the observation centre (Wed 9.30am), while during the spring lekking season (April to mid-May) when male capercaillie gather and joust with each other, the centre opens very early for "Caperwatch" (daily 5.30–8am; £3). Rent two-wheeled transport from Cairngorm Bike and Hire by the station (Ⓣ01479/831745, Ⓦwww.cairngormbikeandhike.co.uk), from where **steam trains** run to Aviemore.

Loch Garten is about a mile and a half west of **BOAT OF GARTEN** village: from the village, cross the Spey then take the Grantown road, and the reserve is signposted to the right. An attractive wee place, Boat of Garten has a number of good **accommodation** options, the most elegant being the *Boat Hotel and Restaurant* (Ⓣ01479/831258, Ⓦwww.boathotel.co.uk; ❺). *Fraoch Lodge*, 15 Deshar Rd (Ⓣ01479/831331, Ⓦwww.scotmountain.co.uk; ❶), is an excellent hostel with four twin rooms and a family room sleeping four, and provides high-quality home-cooked meals along with good facilities such as a purpose-built drying room. It's enthusiastically run by experienced mountaineers, who also offer guided walking holidays and instruction in mountain skills. Alternatively, try the *Old Ferryman's House* (Ⓣ01479/831370; ❷), just across the Spey, which is a wonderfully homely, hospitable B&B, with no TVs, lots of books and delicious evening meals and breakfasts. *Anderson's* **restaurant** on Deshar Road is a homely and attractive place serving creative dishes based on local ingredients (closed Tues).

Kincraig

At **KINCRAIG**, six miles southwest of Aviemore on the B9152 towards Kingussie, there are a couple of unusual encounters with animals which offer a memorable diversion if you're not setting off on outdoor pursuits. The **Highland**

Wildlife Park (daily: June–Aug 10am–6pm; April, May, Sept & Oct 10am–5pm; Nov–March 10am–4pm; last entry 2hr before closing; £13.50; Ⓣ01540/651270, Ⓦwww.highlandwildlifepark.org), with its captive animals, will not appeal to everyone; it is a charity run by the Royal Zoological Society of Scotland where you can see wolves and bison, as well as many rarely seen natives, including pine martens, capercaillie, wildcat and eagles. Nearby, the engrossing **Working Sheepdogs** demonstrations at Leault Farm (May–Oct Sun–Fri 4pm; £5; Ⓣ01540/651310, Ⓦwww.leaultworkingsheepdogs.co.uk) afford the rare opportunity to see a champion shepherd herd a flock of sheep with up to eight dogs, using whistles and other commands. The fascinating hour-long display also includes a chance to see traditional hand-shearing, duck-herding and collie-pup training. Meanwhile, the Loch Insh Watersports Centre (see p.426) runs a **wildlife passenger boat trip** around Loch Insh and into Inchmarsh RSPB reserve (daily May & June 11am, 2pm & 4pm; also 6pm July & Aug; £8).

There are some good low-price **accommodation** options nearby. The Loch Insh Watersports Centre (Ⓣ01540/651272, Ⓦwww.lochinsh.com) has basic but practical en-suite B&B rooms (❷) as well as a decent waterfront café/restaurant (Ⓣ01540/651394). At the remote *Glen Feshie Hostel* at Balachroick (Ⓣ01540/651323, Ⓦwww.glenfeshiehostel.co.uk), three miles from Loch Insh down beautiful Glen Feshie, the price includes as much porridge as you like for breakfast.

Grantown-on-Spey

Buses run from Aviemore and Inverness to the small town of **GRANTOWN-ON-SPEY** (Ⓦwww.grantownonspey.com), about fifteen miles northeast of Aviemore and another alternative base for exploring the Strathspey area. Life is concentrated around the central square, with its attractive Georgian architecture; the **tourist office** is on the High Street (March–Oct daily).

As with much of Speyside, there's a decent choice of **accommodation**. There's top-notch **B&B** in luxury organic *Eden House*, outside of town in the village of Cromdale (Ⓣ01479/872112, Ⓦwww.theedenhouse.co.uk). In Grantown itself, *Parkburn Guest House* (Ⓣ01479/873116, Ⓦwww.parkburnguesthouse.co.uk; ❷) on the High Street is welcoming; if you're after something more upmarket head for the large seventeenth-century *Garth Hotel*, at the north end of the square (Ⓣ01479/872836, Ⓦwww.garthhotel.com; ❺) where the restaurant serves respectable, traditional meat-based dinners. There's also the smart *Muckrach Lodge Hotel and Restaurant* (Ⓣ01479/851257, Ⓦwww.muckrach.co.uk; ❺), three miles southeast of Grantown by Dulnain Bridge.

In the budget range, you'll find a bunkhouse at Ardenbeg Outdoor Centre (Ⓣ01479/872824, Ⓦwww.ardenbeg.co.uk), on Grant Road, parallel to the High Street, a base for courses in hillwalking, climbing, canoeing and skiing, while a mile or two south of town at Nethy Bridge, between Grantown and Boat of Garten, is the tiny, eight-bed *Lazy Duck Hostel* (Ⓣ01479/821642, Ⓦwww.lazyduck.co.uk), a peaceful and comfortable retreat with woodland **camping** and great moorland walking on its doorstep. For **bike rental**, head just south of town to Craggan Outdoor Centre (Ⓣ01479/873283; £25/day) by the Craggan Golf Course.

To **eat** out in grand style, try *Muckrach Lodge*, which offers a thoughtfully prepared and moderately pricey menu whilst within Grantown itself, the *Glass House* restaurant on Grant Road (Ⓣ01479/872980, Ⓦwww.theglasshouse-grantown.co.uk) serves excellent, moderate-to-expensive contemporary Scottish food in a relaxed conservatory dining room. You can watch red squirrels at play over a coffee and tremendous cakes at the beautiful 350-acre *Revack Highland Estate and Adventure Park* (Ⓣ01479/872234), located just a mile out of town.

Newtonmore, Kingussie and Laggan

Twelve miles southwest of Aviemore, close neighbours **NEWTONMORE** and **KINGUSSIE** (pronounced "king-*yoos*-ee") are pleasant villages at the head of the Strathspey Valley separated by a couple of miles of farmland. On the **shinty** field their peaceful coexistence is forgotten and the two become bitter rivals; in recent years Kingussie has been dominant in the game, a fierce, indigenous sport from which ice hockey and golf evolved. Otherwise, the excellent **Highland Folk Museum** at Newtonmore (April–Aug daily 10.30am–5.30pm; Sept & Oct 11am–4.30pm; donation; Ⓦwww.highlandfolk.com) is the chief attraction here. The outdoor site is a living history museum, with an old vintage bus offering a jump-on/jump-off tour round reconstructions of a working croft, a water-powered sawmill and a church where recitals on traditional Highland instruments are given.

Kingussie is also notable for the ruins of **Ruthven Barracks** (free access), standing east across the river on a hillock. The best-preserved garrison built to pacify the Highlands after the 1715 rebellion, it makes for great exploring by day and is impressively floodlit at night.

Eight miles southwest of Newtonmore on the A86, just beyond the junction with the A889 from Dalwhinnie, **Laggan Wolftrax mountain-bike centre** (£20/day; Ⓣ01528/544786, Ⓦwww.basecampmtb.com) is a superb facility boasting a café and over nine miles of trails to suit all abilities.

Practicalities

In Newtonmore, the best place for local **tourist information** is the Craft Centre (Feb–Dec Mon–Sat 9am–5pm) opposite the Co-op supermarket. The Wildcat Centre (April–Sept Mon–Fri 9.30am–12.30pm & 2–5pm, Sat 9.30am–12.30pm; Oct–March Wed–Sat 9.30am–12.30pm; Ⓣ01540/673131) also offers local information and details of some well-organized walking trails in the area.

One of the most appealing places **to stay** in the whole of Speyside is the relaxed but stylish *The Cross* (Ⓣ01540/661166, Ⓦwww.thecross.co.uk; ❻) "restaurant with rooms" located in a converted tweed mill on the banks of the River Gynack in Kingussie. On the edge of Newtonmore, *Coig Na Shee* (Ⓣ01540/670109, Ⓦwww.coignashee.co.uk; ❹) is a soothingly decorated **B&B** in an Edwardian hunting lodge. Newtonmore has a number of good **hostels** including *Newtonmore Hostel* (Ⓣ01540/673360, Ⓦwww.highlandhostel.co.uk), a welcoming and well-equipped place. In Kingussie, you'll find a comfortable, cheap bed in *The Laird's Bothy* (Ⓣ01540/661334, Ⓦwww.thetipsylaird.co.uk). The most convenient accommodation for Laggan is *The Pottery Bunkhouse* and coffee shop (Ⓣ01528/544231, Ⓦwww.potterybunkhouse.co.uk), which offers convenient, comfortable rooms and even an outdoor hot tub. For camping, those with transport will find good amenities at the *Invernahavon Holiday Park* (Ⓣ01540/673534), three miles south of Newtonmore.

The most ambitious **food** in the area is served at *The Cross* (see above; restaurant closed Sun & Mon), where the meals, though expensive, make imaginative use of local ingredients, complemented by a vast wine list. Cheaper food is available at several cafés and pubs in both towns – *Gilly's Kitchen* on the main street in Kingussie is open during the day (Tues–Sat 10am–5pm; Ⓦwww.gillyskitchen.com) for simple home-made soup and light lunches. Also on High Street, the *Tipsy Laird* (Ⓣ01540/661334) is a good spot for a light lunch or an inexpensive evening meal.

Speyside

Strictly speaking, the term **Speyside** refers to the entire region surrounding the Spey river, but to most people the name is synonymous with the **whisky triangle**, stretching from just north of Craigellachie, down towards Tomintoul in the south and east to Huntly. Indeed, there are more whisky distilleries and famous brands (including Glenfiddich, Glenlivet and Macallan) concentrated in this small area than in any other part of the country. Running through the heart of the region is the River Spey, whose clean, clear, fast-running waters play a vital part in the whisky industry and are also home to thousands of salmon, making it one of Scotland's finest angling locations. Obviously fertile, the tranquil glens of the area have none of the ruggedness of other parts of the Highlands; tourism blends into a local economy kept healthy by whisky and farming, rather than dominating it.

At the centre of Speyside is the quiet market town of **Dufftown**, full of solid, stone-built workers' houses and dotted with no fewer than nine whisky distilleries. Along with the well-kept nearby villages of **Craigellachie** and **Aberlour**, it makes the best base for a tour of whisky country, whether on the official Malt Whisky Trail or more independent explorations. Fewer visitors take the chance to discover the more remote glens, such as **Glenlivet**, which push higher up towards the Cairngorm massif, nestled into which is Britain's highest village, **Tomintoul**, situated on the edge of both whisky country and a large expanse of wild uplands. Though not surrounded by distilleries, the market town of **Huntly** has an impressive ruined castle and serves as a useful point of entry if you're coming into the region from the Aberdeenshire side.

Transport connections are poor through the area, with irregular buses connecting the main villages and (from Grantown) only one bus a day crossing to Ballater via Tomintoul. The only mainline railway stops in the area are at Keith, twelve miles northeast of Dufftown, and Huntly.

Dufftown

The cheery community of **DUFFTOWN**, founded in 1817 by James Duff, fourth Earl of Fife, proudly proclaims itself "Malt Whisky Capital of the World" for the

The Speyside Way

The **Speyside Way**, with its beguiling blend of mountain, river, wildlife and whisky, is fast establishing itself as an appealing and less taxing alternative to the popular West Highland and Southern Upland long-distance footpaths. Starting at **Buckie** on the Moray Firth coast (see p.415), it follows the fast-flowing River Spey from its mouth at Spey Bay south to **Aviemore** (see p.424), with branches linking it to **Dufftown**, Scotland's malt whisky capital, and **Tomintoul** on the remote edge of the Cairngorm mountains. Some 65 miles long without taking on the branch routes, the whole thing is a five- to seven-day expedition, but its proximity to main roads and small villages means that it is excellent for shorter walks or even bicycle trips, especially in the heart of **distillery** country between Craigellachie and Glenlivet: Glenfiddich, Glenlivet, Macallan and Cardhu distilleries, as well as the Speyside Cooperage, lie directly on or a short distance off the route. Other highlights include the chance to encounter an array of **wildlife**, from dolphins at Spey Bay to ospreys at Loch Garten, as well as the restored **railway** trips on offer at Dufftown and Aviemore. The path uses disused railway lines for much of its length, and there are simple campsites and good B&Bs at strategic points along the route. For more details contact the Speyside Way Visitor Centre at Aberlour (Ⓣ01340/881266, Ⓦwww.speysideway.org).

The great outdoors

For outdoor enthusiasts, Scotland provides a wonderfully rugged and diverse landscape where you can take a bracing walk through an ancient oak forest or practise ice-climbing for the Himalayas a thousand feet up. Hillwalkers take to picking off Munros (hills over 3000ft in height), mountain bikers get muddy and, if you're into watersports, there's white water, waves and wind a plenty. And while it's always tempting to postpone your outdoor foray on account of the unreliable weather, it's worth keeping in mind that the poorer the conditions, the cosier the pub at the end of the day.

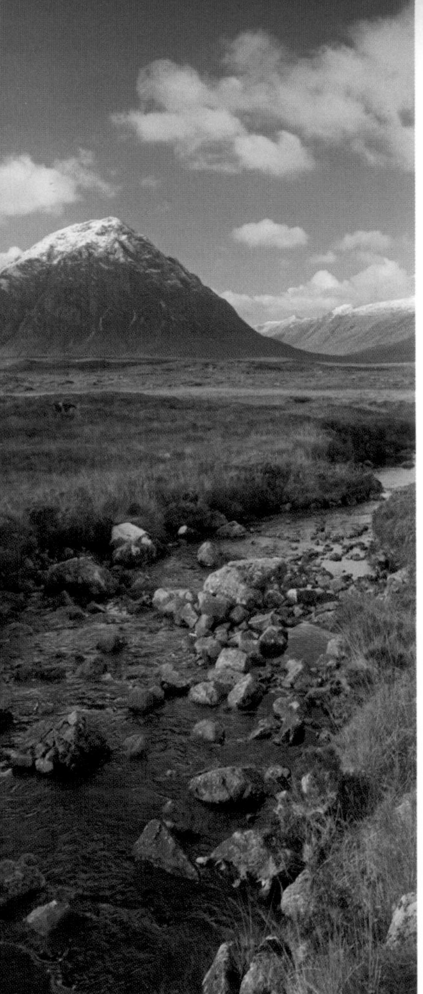

Buachaille Etive, Glen Coe ▲

Road sign, Kilmartin Valley ▼

To the hills

Walking in Scotland needn't necessarily mean uphill, though it is hard to go far without encountering a slope. The country as a whole is remarkably well suited to **hillwalking:** access is generally free, though there may be restricted access during lambing (April and May) and deerstalking seasons (July 1 to October 20); there are a range of good paths or forest tracks; and, despite the popularity of walking, the hills aren't nearly as busy as, say, the Lake District in northern England. Serious hillwalkers usually aim for the spectacular Highlands, in particular the tough ranges around **Glen Coe** or **Torridon**, though for many the ultimate challenge remains the dragon-back **Cullin** ridge on Skye.

Long-distance trails

West Highland Way This five-day, 95-mile trek along well-marked paths between north Glasgow and Fort William, via Loch Lomond and Rannoch Moor, is the doyen of Scotland's official long-distance footpaths. See p.321.

Great Glen Way You can choose to detour up a couple of Munroes, but otherwise, this is a straightforward, low-level 73-mile hike from Fort William to Inverness. See p.443.

Speyside Way A gentle, 65- to 84-mile wander (depending on the route chosen) through whisky country from the Cairngorms to the sea. See p.432.

Southern Upland Way Though the hills don't rival the Highlands, this ten-day, 212-mile, coast-to-coast walk is a pretty serious undertaking. See p.165.

Cowal Way Argyll's regional footpath is a fairly gentle, 47-mile walk from Portavadie in the southwest of the peninsula to Inveruglas on Loch Lomond. See p.258.

On your bike

Scotland is one of the world's top five **mountain-bike destinations**, with over a thousand miles of remote terrain to challenge even the most accomplished cyclist. Dedicated mountain-bike centres, such as those in the Borders or on the Black Isle, provide waymarked trails designed for every level of rider, from white-knuckle **black runs** to leisurely rides through National Parks and Forestry Commission areas. A number of long-distance routes, including The **Great Glen Cycle Way** (see p.443), have been established using a combination of specially built cycle paths and quieter back roads. The rural roads are infinitely more enjoyable, particularly in the gentler landscapes of the south and east of the country, where generally amiable gradients and a decent concentration of pubs and B&Bs make the area perfect for cycle touring.

▲ Mountain biking, Great Glen

▼ Sea-kayaking, Staffa

Worth a surf

One thing Scotland isn't short of is water, so it's no surprise that **watersports** are popular on inland lochs and around the coast. The Outer Hebrides in particular are regarded as world class for **sea-kayaking**, with their innumerable skerries, sea caves and remote white-sand beaches; yacht racing and **sailing** are excellent on the protected Firth of Clyde, while **cruising** is the main focus on the west coast. And though the climate can't quite match Bondi or Malibu, serious **surfers** will tell you that it's not the sun but the waves that count. There are world-class breaks near Thurso, in the Moray Firth and on the islands Coll, Tiree and Islay. Other remote spots include the Outer Hebrides and the Mull of Kintyre. Just pack some cocoa with the surf wax.

Ice climbing, Aonach Mhòr ▲

Windsurfers at the Tiree Wave Classic ▼

The crazy stuff

The long-standing image of Scotland as a place to play a testing but well-mannered round of golf, or to pull on your waders and tweed cap to spend a relaxing day fishing, is fast being overtaken by the lycra and neon blur of adrenaline junkies revelling in the wild conditions the country has to offer. Near Fort William there's a purpose-built downhill **mountain-bike track** that descends 1800ft in little over two miles – it's used for world championships and is definitely not one for Sunday riders. Out in Tiree there's also first-class sporting action in the annual **windsurfing Wave Classic**, while each year sailors and fell-runners team up for the exhausting **Scottish Islands Peak Race** to the top of the highest summits on the islands of Mull, Jura and Arran. In winter, there's downhill and cross-country **skiing** action in places such as Cairngorm National Park, Glen Shee and Ben Nevis, while Glencoe is popular with **ice-** and **rock-climbers** training for international high-altitude expeditions; in recent years some of the world's finest indoor facilities for both sports have been built at the likes of Kinlochleven near Fort William and Ratho near Edinburgh. Thrill-seekers in Scotland aren't put off by the weather – it merely sets the agenda. A day of gentle zephyrs is perfect for a spot of paragliding in Ayrshire, while a fresh breeze has **kite-surfers** and power-, buggy- or blo-karters heading for the gloriously empty beaches of the Outer Hebrides. A good dump of rain, on the other hand, will see white-water **rafters** and **canoeists** heading for frothing white rivers such as the Tay, Orchy and Etive. Alternatively, why not enter for the **Hebridean Challenge**, Europe's most extreme endurance race, which involves five days of running, cycling, swimming and kayaking around a 400-mile course in the Outer Hebrides?

reason that it produces more of the stuff than any other town in Britain. A more telling statistic, perhaps, is that as a result Dufftown also reportedly raises more capital for the exchequer per head of population than anywhere else in the country. There are nine distilleries around Dufftown (not all of them still working), as well as a cooperage and a coppersmith, and an extended stroll around the outskirts of the town gives a good idea of the density of whisky distilling going on, with glimpses of giant warehouses and whiffs of fermenting barley or peat smoke lingering on the breeze.

There isn't a great deal to do in the town, but it's a useful starting point for orienting yourself towards the whisky trail. The small, volunteer-run **Whisky Museum** at 24 Fife St (mid-June to Sept Mon–Fri 1–4pm; free) has a slightly disorganized collection of illicit distilling equipment, books and old photographs. On the edge of town along the A941 is the town's largest working distillery, **Glenfiddich** (see box, p.434), as well as the old Dufftown train station, which has been restored by enthusiasts in recent years and is now the departure point for the **Keith & Dufftown Railway** (April–Sept 3 trips Sat & Sun, June–Aug also Fri; 40min; £9.50 return; Ⓣ01340/821181, Ⓦwww.keith-dufftown-railway.co.uk for journey times), which uses various restored diesel locomotives to chug through whisky country to Keith, home of the Strathisla distillery (see box, p.435). Beside the platform at Dufftown a permanent buffet car serves coffee, tea, soup and home-baked cakes.

Practicalities

Dufftown's four main streets converge on its main square, scene of a lively annual party on Hogmanay when free drams are handed out to revellers. The official **tourist office** is located inside the handsome clock tower at the centre of the square (April–Oct daily; Ⓣ01340/820501), though an informal information and accommodation booking service has developed across the road, at The Whisky Shop (Ⓣ01340/821097, Ⓦwww.whiskyshopdufftown.co.uk), which boasts an array of six hundred malts and umpteen beers, produced not just on Speyside but all over Scotland. Nosings and other special events are regularly organized here, most notably the twice-yearly **Spirit of Speyside Whisky Festival** (Ⓦwww.spiritofspeyside.com), which draws whisky experts and enthusiasts to the area in late April and late September.

There's a handful of places to stay in Dufftown itself, although you may choose to look elsewhere in Speyside where you will feel a bit closer to the attractive countryside. The only **hostel** accommodation nearby is the small self-catering *Swan Bunkhouse* (Ⓣ01542/810334) located at Drummuir, which has facilities suitable for wheelchair users. Located three miles northeast of Dufftown, it's possible to camp (£5), rent kayaks (£12) and fish (£18) at the Loch Park Adventure Centre (Ⓣ01542/810334, Ⓦwww.lochpark.co.uk), one mile away; though unfortunately, there's no public transport this far. In town, *Morven*, on the main square (Ⓣ01340/820507, Ⓦwww.morvendufftown.co.uk; ❷), offers simple, inexpensive **B&B**. *Tannochbrae and Restaurant*, 22 Fife St (Ⓣ01340/820541, Ⓦwww.tannochbrae.co.uk; ❸), is a pleasant, enthusiastically run former provost's house with a lovely restaurant and bike rental (£15/day).

The smartest of Dufftown's **restaurants** are the expensive (and child-friendly) *La Faisanderie*, on the corner of The Square and Balvenie Street (Ⓣ01340/821273; closed Tues), which serves local produce such as trout and game in a French style, and *Taste of Speyside*, 10 Balverie St (Ⓣ01340/820860; closed Mon), just off The Square, where you'll pay around £20 for three courses of Scottish cuisine. Alternatively, the rustic setting of *Noah's Ark Bistro and Café* (Ⓣ01542/821428) on Balvenie Street offers good value and wholesome daytime home-bakes, lunches and dinners.

Touring malt whisky country

Speyside is the heart of Scotland's **whisky** industry, and the presence of more than fifty distilleries is testimony to a unique combination of clear, clean water, benign climate and gentle upland terrain. Yet for all the advertising-influenced visions of timeless traditions, whisky is a multimillion-pound business dominated by huge corporations, and to many working distilleries visitors are an afterthought, if not a downright nuisance. That said, plenty are located in attractive historic buildings that now go to some lengths to provide an engaging experience for visitors. Mostly this involves a tour around the essential stages in the whisky-making process, though a number of distilleries now offer pricier connoisseur tours with a tutored tasting (or **nosing**, as it's properly called) and in-depth studies of the distiller's art. Some tours have restrictions on children.

There are eight distilleries on the official **Malt Whisky Trail** (Ⓦwww.maltwhiskytrail.com), a clearly signposted seventy-mile meander around the region. Unless you're seriously interested in whisky, it's best to just pick out a couple that appeal. All offer a guided tour (some are free, others charge but then give you a voucher redeemable against a bottle of whisky from the distillery shop), with a tasting to round it off; if you're driving you'll often be offered a miniature to takeaway. You could cycle or walk parts of the route, using the Speyside Way (see box, p.432). The following is a list of selected highlights.

Cardhu, on the B9102 at Knockando (April–June Mon–Fri 10am–5pm; July–Sept Mon–Sat 10am–5pm, Sun noon–4pm; Oct–April Mon–Fri 11am–3pm; tours at 11am, 1pm & 2pm; £4 including voucher). Established over a century ago, when the founder's wife would raise a red flag to warn crofters if the authorities were on the lookout for their illegal stills. With attractive, pagoda-topped buildings, it sells rich, full-bodied whisky with distinctive peaty flavours that comes in an attractive bulbous bottle.

Glen Grant, Rothes (mid-Jan to mid-Dec Mon–Sat 9.30am–5pm, Sun noon–5pm; £3.50 including voucher). A well-known, floral whisky aggressively marketed to the younger customer. The highlight here is the attractive Victorian gardens, a mix of well-tended lawns and mixed, mature trees which include a tumbling waterfall and a hidden whisky safe.

Glenfiddich, on the A941 just north of Dufftown (Jan to mid-Dec Mon–Sat 9.30am–4.30pm, Sun noon–4.30pm; free). The biggest and slickest of all the Speyside

Whisky isn't in short supply in the local pubs and hotels, but for a choice of more than seven hundred different whiskies you have to head to the *Grouse Inn* at Cabrach, tucked among the hills six miles out along the A941 to Rhynie.

Craigellachie

Four miles north of Dufftown, the small settlement of **CRAIGELLACHIE** (pronounced "Craig-*ell*-ach-ee") sits above the confluence of the sparkling waters of the Fiddich and the Spey. From the village, you can look down on a beautiful iron bridge over the Spey built by Thomas Telford in 1815. The local distillery isn't open to the public, though Glen Grant (see box above) with its attractive gardens is only a few miles up the road at Rothes, and, for an unusual alternative to a distillery tour, the **Speyside Cooperage** (Mon–Fri 9.30am–4pm; £3.30) is well worth a visit. After a short exhibition explaining the ancient and skilled art of cooperage, you're shown onto a balcony overlooking the large workshop where the oak casks for whisky are made and repaired.

For somewhere **to stay** in the village there's an extremely welcoming and tasteful B&B attached to the *Green Hall Gallery* on Victoria Street (Ⓣ01340/871010, Ⓦwww.aboutscotland.com/greenhall; ④) while just along the road, the grand *Craigellachie Hotel* (Ⓣ01340/881204, Ⓦwww.craigellachie.com; ⑦) is the epitome of distilleries, despite the fact that it's still owned by the same Grant family who founded it in 1887. It's a light, sweet whisky packaged in triangular bottles – unusually, the bottling is still done on the premises and is part of the tours (offered in various languages).

Glenlivet, on the B9008 to Tomintoul (April–Oct Mon–Sat 9.30am–4pm, Sun noon–4pm; free). A famous name in a lonely hillside setting. This was the first licensed distillery in the Highlands, following the 1823 act that aimed to reduce illicit distilling and smuggling. The Glenlivet 12-year-old malt is a floral, fragrant, medium-bodied whisky. The Speyside Way passes through the distillery grounds.

Strathisla, Keith (April–Oct Mon–Sat 9.30am–4pm, Sun noon–4pm; £5). A small, old-fashioned distillery claiming to be Scotland's oldest (1786); it's certainly one of the most attractive, with classic pagoda-shaped buildings and the River Isla rushing by. Inside there's an old-fashioned mashtun and brass-bound spirit safes. The malt itself has a rich, almost fruity taste and is pretty rare, but is used as the heart of the better-known Chivas Regal blend. You can arrive here on one of the restored trains of the Keith & Dufftown Railway (see p.433).

The **Speyside Cooperage** at Craigellachie (see opposite) is also part of the official trail, with fascinating glimpses of a highly skilled and vital part of the industry.

Other distilleries, not on the official trail, include:

Aberlour, in Aberlour (April–Oct daily 10.30am & 2pm; Nov & Dec Mon–Fri; £7.50; booking essential ⓣ01340/881249). The twice-daily tours are quite specialized, with a tutored nosing and the chance to buy and fill your own bottle of cask-strength single malt.

Cragganmore, at Ballindalloch (tours April–Sept Mon–Fri 11.30, 2pm; £4; booking essential ⓣ01479/874700). Offers a personalized, exclusive tour by appointment.

Glendronach, 8 miles northeast of Huntly (Mon–Sat 10am–4.30pm, Sun noon–4pm; £3). An isolated distillery that makes much of the fact that, uniquely, the stills are heated in the traditional method by coal fires.

Macallan, near Craigellachie (April–Oct Mon–Sat 9.30am–4.30pm; Nov–March Mon–Fri 11am–3pm; ⓣ01340/872280). Small tours, and a classy whisky aged in sherry casks to give it a rich colour and flavour.

sumptuous "tartan-draped" Scottish hospitality, with classy cuisine and a bar lined with whisky bottles. In Archiestown, a few miles west of Craigellachie, the pleasant, traditional *Archiestown Hotel* (ⓣ01340/810218, ⓦwww.archiestownhotel.co.uk; ❼) serves good evening **meals** and has some comfy rooms upstairs. In good weather, it's also a fine spot for al fresco dining. There's moderately priced pub grub in the busy *Highlander Inn* (ⓣ01340/881446, ⓦwww.whiskyinn.com; ❺) on Victoria Street in Craigellachie, which has five smallish rooms and also hosts frequent folk **music sessions**. The tiny *Fiddichside Inn*, on the A95 just outside Craigellachie, is a wonderfully original and convivial **pub** with a garden by the river; quite unfazed by the demands of fashion, it has been in the hands of just two landladies (mother and daughter) for the last seventy years or so.

Aberlour

Two miles southwest from Craigellachie is **ABERLOUR**, officially "Charlestown of Aberlour". Founded in 1812 by Charles Grant, its long main street, neat, flower-filled central square and well-trimmed lawns running down to the Spey have all the markings of a planned village. Though you can visit the distillery here, it's another local produce – **shortbread** – that is exported in greater quantity around the world, mostly in tartan tins adorned with kilted warriors. A local baker, **Joseph Walker**, set up shop here at the turn of the twentieth century, quickly gaining a reputation for the product which seems to epitomize the Scottish sweet tooth. If you're keen, you can join the coachloads who visit the factory shop on the outskirts of the village.

Aberlour is just a few miles from the extensive **Moray Monster (Mountain-bike) Trails** at Ben Aigen (Ⓦwww.moraymountainbikeclub.co.uk). The town is also right on the Speyside Way (see box, p.432) and the **visitor centre** occupies half of the old train station, just back from the main square (May–Oct daily; Nov–April open when ranger in office; Ⓣ01340/881266, Ⓦwww.speysideway.org). The centre has detailed information boards about natural history and other aspects of the way, and there's a wee tearoom next door (June–Sept Mon–Sat 10am–noon & 2–4.30pm, Sun 2–4.30pm). Though the **campsite** here, *Aberlour Gardens Caravan Park* (Ⓣ01340/871586, Ⓦwww.aberlourgardens.co.uk; March–Dec), is the most pleasant in the area, it's a walk of a mile and a half from either Aberlour or Craigellachie. Alternatively, there's reasonable **B&B** at *Knockside* (Ⓣ01340/881561, Ⓦwww.speyside.moray.org/Aberlour/knockside.html; ❷). The best place to **eat and drink** is the *Mash Tun* (Ⓣ01340/881771, Ⓦwww.mashtun-aberlour.com), a pleasant, traditional pub at 8 Broomfield Square that serves up freshly prepared bar meals, real ales and all the local whiskies in the heart of Aberlour near the Spey; it also has cosy rooms and a luxury suite (❺). There's a range of deli produce at the Spey Larder, right by the village square.

Glenlivet

Beyond Aberlour, the Spey and the main road both head generally southwest to Ballindalloch and, a dozen miles beyond that, Grantown-on-Spey, at the head of the Strathspey region (see p.430). South from Ballindalloch are the quieter, remote glens of the Avon (pronounced "*A'an*") and Livet rivers. Allegedly, in the days of the despised tax excisemen, the Braes of Glenlivet once held over one hundred illicit whisky stills. The (legal) distillery at **GLENLIVET**, founded in 1824 by George Smith, is one of the most famous on Speyside, and certainly enjoys one of the more attractive settings. You can **stay** in George Smith's former house, right beside the distillery; *Minmore House* (Ⓣ01807/590378, Ⓦwww.minmorehousehotel.com; ❼) has a lovely country-house feel with antique furniture and a wood-panelled bar. The owner is a chef and the superb **meals**, including a cake-laden afternoon tea by the open fire, are available to non-residents if they book ahead.

Tomintoul

South of Glenlivet, deep into the foothills of the Cairngorms, **TOMINTOUL** (pronounced "*tom*-in-towel") is, at 1150ft, the highest village in the Scottish Highlands, and the northern gateway to the **Lecht** ski area (see box opposite). Its long, thin layout is reminiscent of a Wild West frontier town; Queen Victoria wrote that it was "the most tumble-down, poor looking place I ever saw". A spur of the Speyside Way connects Ballindalloch through Glenlivet to Tomintoul, and there are plenty of other terrific walking opportunities in the area, as well as some great routes for mountain biking. Many of these are on the Glenlivet Crown Estate (Ⓦwww.crownestate.co.uk/glenlivet), an extensive tract of carefully managed land abutting Tomintoul; information and useful maps about its wildlife (including reindeer) and numerous paths and bike trails are available from the tourist office or the estate **ranger's office** at the far end of the long main street (Ⓣ01807/580283). Land Rover and walking safaris are offered locally by Glenlivet Wildlife (Ⓣ01807/590241, Ⓦwww.glenlivet-wildlife.co.uk), including trips out to see black grouse, birds of prey and roe deer.

Skiing and go-karting at the Lecht

The Lecht is the most remote of Scotland's ski areas, but it works hard to make itself appealing with a range of winter and summer activities. While its twenty runs include some gentle beginners' slopes there's little really challenging for experienced skiers other than a Snowboard Fun Park, with specially built jumps and ramps. Snow-making equipment helps extend the snow season beyond January and February, while there are also various summer activities, including quad bikes (£10) and "Deval karts" (£6) – go-karts with balloon tyres imported from the Alps which you can use to speed down the slopes from the top of the chairlift. A day's ski pass is £25; ski rental costs £17 a day from the ski school at the base station. For information on skiing and road conditions, call the base station on ⓣ01975/651440 or check ⓦwww.lecht.co.uk or ⓦski.visitscotland.com. There's also a lovely café at the base station with views across the pistes.

In the central square, the helpful **tourist office** (April–June, Sept & Oct Mon–Sat; July & Aug daily; ⓣ01807/580285) also acts as the local **museum** (same times; free), with mock-ups of an old farm kitchen and a smithie. It is possible to **camp** beside the Glenlivet Estate ranger's office, though there are no facilities here. There's a good SYHA **hostel** situated in the old schoolhouse on Main Street (ⓣ0870/004 1152; mid-May to mid-Sept). Of the **B&Bs**, try *Findron Farmhouse*, a working farm half a mile south of town on the Braemar road (ⓣ01807/580734, ⓦwww.ballindalloch-guesthouse.com; ❶), while the *Glenavon* (ⓣ01807/580218, ⓦwww.glenavon-hotel.co.uk; ❸) is the most convivial of the **hotels** gathered around the main square.

Huntly

The ancient burgh of **HUNTLY**, ten miles east of Dufftown on the main train route from Aberdeen to Inverness, has one of the smallest and prettiest, albeit rather skeletal, castles in the area. **Huntly Castle** (April–Sept daily 9.30am–5.30pm; Oct–March Sun–Wed & Sat 9.30am–4.30pm; HS; £4.70), power centre of the Gordon family, sits in a peaceful clearing on the banks of the Deveron River, a ten-minute walk from the town centre down Castle Street. Built over a period of five centuries, it became the headquarters of the Counter-Reformation in Scotland in 1562. During the Civil War the earl of Huntly, who had supported Charles I, was shot against his castle's walls, after which the place was left to fall into ruin. Today you can still make out the twelfth-century **motte**, a grassy mound on the west side of the complex. In the basement, a narrow passage leads to the **prisons**, where medieval graffiti of tents, animals and people adorn the walls. Huntly is on the fringe of whisky country, with the isolated **Glendronach Distillery** (see box, p.435) the nearest to town.

Practicalities

Huntly's **tourist office** (April–June, Sept & Oct Mon–Sat; July & Aug daily; ⓣ01466/792255) is on the main square. **Accommodation** options range from the former home of the duke of Gordon, the *Castle Hotel* (ⓣ01466/792696, ⓦwww.castlehotel.uk.com; ❻), which stands at the end of a long driveway behind the castle ruins, to B&B at handsome and tasteful *Coynachie Guesthouse* in nearby Gartly (ⓣ01466/720383, ⓦwww.coynachieguesthouse.com; ❸). The *Rose and Thistle* on Duke Street is a reasonable pub with regular folk music, and serves pub meals, though your best choice for a decent **meal** is the *Castle Hotel*. For daytime snacks, the *Park Lane* café on the road to Keith is a good bet. **Bikes** can be rented from the Huntly Nordic & Outdoor Centre near the castle (Ⓣ01466/794428, Ⓦhnoc.nordicski.org.uk; Mon–Fri 10am–4pm, Sat–Sun 9am–5pm), where you can also roller-ski or brush up your cross-country skiing skills on all-weather tracks if there's no snow.

Travel details

Trains

Aviemore to: Edinburgh (Mon–Sat 9 daily, 5 on Sun; 2hr 50min); Glasgow (9 daily, 5 on Sun; 2hr 30min); Inverness (Mon–Sat 9 daily, 5 on Sun; 40min).
Huntly to: Aberdeen (1–2 hourly; 55min); Elgin (every 1–2hr; 35min); Inverness (every 1–2hr; 1hr 25min).
Kingussie to: Edinburgh (Mon–Sat 9 daily, 5 on Sun; 2hr 40min); Glasgow (Mon–Sat 9 daily, 5 on Sun; 2hr 30min); Inverness (Mon–Sat 9 daily, 5 on Sun; 55min).

Buses

Aviemore to: Cairngorm ski area (hourly; 30min); Edinburgh (5 daily; 2hr 30min–3hr 30min); Glasgow (7 daily; 3hr 30min); Grantown-on-Spey (Mon–Sat twice hourly; 35min); Inverness (Mon–Sat 6 daily, 5 on Sun; 45min).
Dufftown to: Aberlour (Mon–Sat hourly; 5 on Sun; 15min); Elgin (Mon–Sat hourly; 5 on Sun; 50min).
Huntly to: Aberdeen (Mon–Sat hourly, 2 on Sun; 1hr 30min); Elgin (Mon–Sat hourly, 6 on Sun; 1hr); Inverness (Mon–Sat hourly, 3 on Sun; 2hr 15min).
Kingussie/Newtonmore to: Edinburgh and Glasgow (Mon–Fri 5 daily, Sat & Sun 3 daily; 2hr 30min–3hr 30min); Inverness (Mon–Fri 6 daily, Sat & Sun 5 daily; 1hr).
Tomintoul to: Aviemore (May–Sept Sat & Sun only 2 daily; 45min); Ballater (May–Sept 2 daily; 1hr 30min); Elgin (May–Sept Sat & Sun only 2 daily; 1hr 45min); Grantown (May–Sept 2 daily; 20min).

The Great Glen

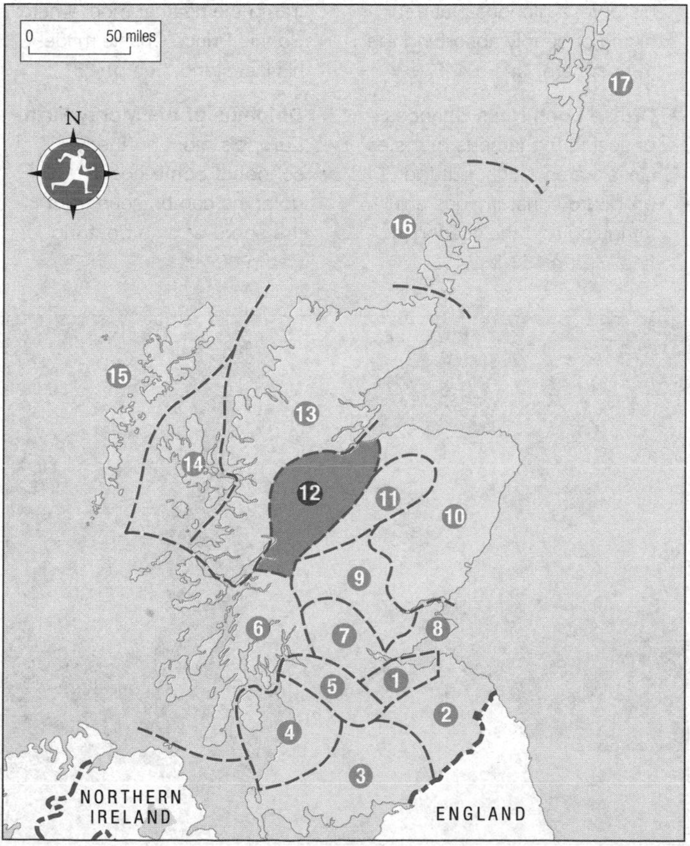

CHAPTER 12 # Highlights

* **Commando Memorial** An exposed but dramatic place to take in sweeping views over Scotland's highest ben (Nevis) and its longest glen (the Great Glen). See p.448

* **Glen Coe** Spectacular, moody, poignant and full of history – a glorious place for hiking or simply absorbing the atmosphere. See p.449

* **Cruise Loch Ness** Chances of seeing the famous monster Nessie aren't high, but the on-board sonar images are intriguing and the scenery's fine. See p.453 & p.458

* **Glen Affric** Some of Scotland's best-hidden scenery, with ancient Caledonian forests and gushing rivers. See p.456

* **Culloden battlefield** Experience the cannon-fire in a "battle immersion theatre" and tramp the heather moor where Bonnie Prince Charlie made his last stand. See p.463

* **Dolphins of the Moray Firth** Europe's most northerly school of bottle-nosed dolphins can be seen from the shore or on a boat trip. See p.464

▲ The Commando Memorial

12

The Great Glen

The **Great Glen**, a major geological faultline cutting diagonally across the Highlands from Fort William to Inverness, is the defining geographic feature of the north of Scotland. A huge rift valley was formed when the northwestern and southeastern sides of the fault slid in opposite directions for more than sixty miles, while the present landscape was shaped by glaciers that retreated only around 8000 BC. The glen is impressive more for its sheer scale than its beauty, but the imposing barrier of loch and mountain means that no one can travel into the northern Highlands without passing through it. With the two major service centres of the Highlands at either end, it makes an obvious and rewarding route between the west and east coasts.

Of the Great Glen's four elongated lochs, the most famous is **Loch Ness**, home to the mythical monster; lochs **Oich**, **Lochy** and **Linnhe** (the last of these a sea loch) are less renowned though no less attractive. All four are linked by the **Caledonian Canal**. The southwestern end of the Great Glen is dominated by the town of **Fort William**, the self-proclaimed "Outdoor Capital of the UK". Situated at the heart of the Lochaber area, it is a utilitarian base, with plenty of places to stay and excellent access to a host of adventure sports. While the town itself is charmless, the surrounding countryside is a magnificent blend of rugged mountain terrain and tranquil sea loch. Dominating the scene to the south is **Ben Nevis**, Britain's highest peak, best approached from scenic Glen Nevis. The most famous glen of all, **Glen Coe**, lies on the main A82 road half-an-hour's drive south of Fort William, the two separated by the coastal inlet of **Loch Leven**. Nowadays the whole area is unashamedly given over to tourism, with Fort William swamped by bus tours throughout the summer, but, as ever in the Highlands, within a thirty-minute drive you can be totally alone.

At the northeastern end of the Great Glen is the capital of the Highlands, **Inverness**, a sprawling city with some decent places to eat; it's most often used as a springboard to remoter areas further north. Inevitably, most transport links to the northern Highlands, including Ullapool, Thurso and the Orkney and Shetland islands, pass through Inverness.

The region has a turbulent and bloody **history**. Founded in 1655 and named in honour of William III, Fort William was successfully held by government troops during both of the Jacobite risings; the country to the southwest is inextricably associated with Bonnie Prince Charlie's flight after **Culloden**. Glen Coe is another historic site with a violent past, renowned as much for the infamous massacre of 1692 as for its magnificent scenery.

The main **A82** road runs the length of the Great Glen, although relatively high traffic levels mean that it's not a fast or particularly easy route to drive. The area is reasonably well served by **buses**, with several daily services between Inverness and

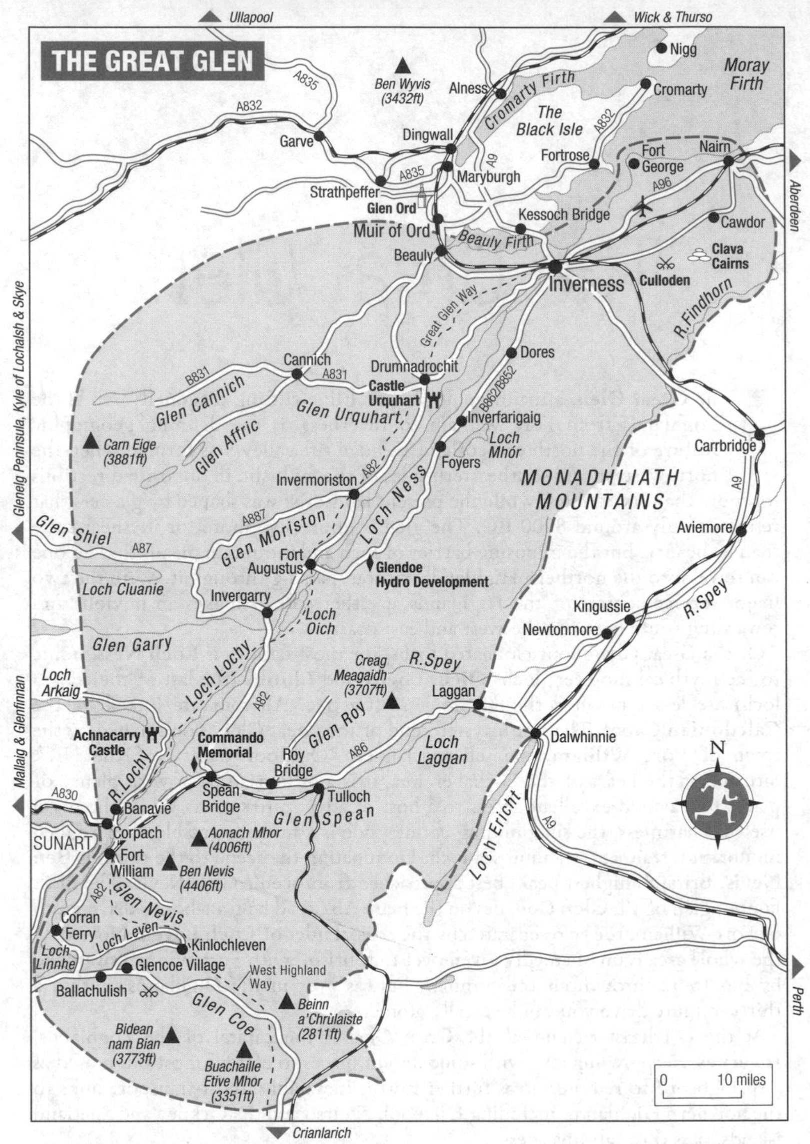

Fort William, and a couple of extra buses covering the section between Fort William and Invergarry during school terms. However, the traditional and most rewarding way to travel through the Glen itself is by **boat**: a flotilla of kayaks, small yachts and pleasure vessels take advantage of the **Caledonian canal** and its old wooden locks during the summer. Alternatively, an excellent **cycle path** traverses the Glen, as well as a long-distance footpath, the 73-mile **Great Glen Way**, which takes five to six days to walk in full (see box opposite).

Fort William

With its stunning position on Loch Linnhe, tucked in below the snow-streaked bulk of Ben Nevis, **FORT WILLIAM** (known by the many walkers and climbers that come here as "Fort Bill") should be a gem. Sadly, the same lack of taste that nearly saw the town renamed "Abernevis" in the 1950s is evident in the ribbon bungalow development and ill-advised dual carriageway – complete with grubby pedestrian underpass – which have wrecked the waterfront. The main street and the little squares off it are more appealing, though occupied by some decidedly tacky tourist gift shops.

Arrival and information

Just across the A82 dual carriageway from the north end of the High Street you'll find Fort William's **train station** (a stop on the scenic West Highland Railway direct from Glasgow). Intercity **coaches** from Glasgow and Inverness stop outside here. The busy and very helpful **tourist office** is on the High Street (April–Sept daily; Oct–March Mon–Sat; Ⓣ01397/701801, Ⓦwww.visithighlands.com).

You'll find a host of outdoor-activity specialists in town. High-spec **mountain bikes** are available for rent at Off Beat Bikes, 117 High St (Ⓣ01397/704008, Ⓦwww.offbeatbikes.co.uk); they know the best routes, issue free maps and also have a branch open at the Nevis Range gondola base station (June–Sept; Ⓣ01397/705825) – a location that boasts forest rides and a world-championship standard downhill track. Local **mountain guides** include Alan Kimber of *Calluna* (see p.444) and the **Snowgoose Mountain Centre** (Ⓣ01397/772467, Ⓦwww.highland-mountain-guides.co.uk), set beside *Smiddy Bunkhouse and Blacksmith's Hostel*, which offers instruction, rental and residential courses for activities such as mountaineering. For sea-kayak coaching, half-day and weekend trips, Rockhoppers in Corpach is a good bet (Ⓣ07739/837344, Ⓦwww.rockhopperscotland.co.uk).

The Great Glen Way and cycle path

The 73-mile cleft of the Great Glen is the most obvious – and by far the flattest – way of traversing northern Scotland from coast to coast. The **Great Glen Way** long-distance footpath (Ⓦwww.greatglenway.com) is a relatively undemanding five-to-six-day hike that uses a combination of canal towpath and forest- and hill-tracks between Fort William and Inverness. Accommodation is readily available all the way along the route in campsites, hostels, bunkhouses and B&Bs, though in high season you should book ahead and if you know you're going to arrive late somewhere it's worth checking that you can still get a meal either where you're staying or somewhere nearby. The maps you'll need to do the whole thing are *Ordnance Survey Landranger maps 41*, *34* and *26*. Alternatively, *The Great Glen Way and Cycle Route* published by Footprint (£4.95) also maps out the way. There are various other guidebooks that describe the route, including *The Great Glen Way* published by Rucksack Readers (£10.99). A **cycle path** also traverses the Glen, offering a tranquil alternative to the hazardous A82. The path, which shares some of its route with the footpath but also utilizes stretches of minor roads, is well signposted and can be managed in one long day or two easier days, though of course you can tackle shorter sections. Bikes can be rented at Fort William, Banavie, Drumnadrochit and Inverness. The Forestry Commission publishes *Cycling in the Forest, The Great Glen*, a handy booklet highlighting the various sections of the route (Ⓣ01320/366322 or 01397/702184, Ⓦwww.forestry.gov.uk). The suggested **direction** for following both routes is from west to east – to take advantage of the prevailing southwesterly wind.

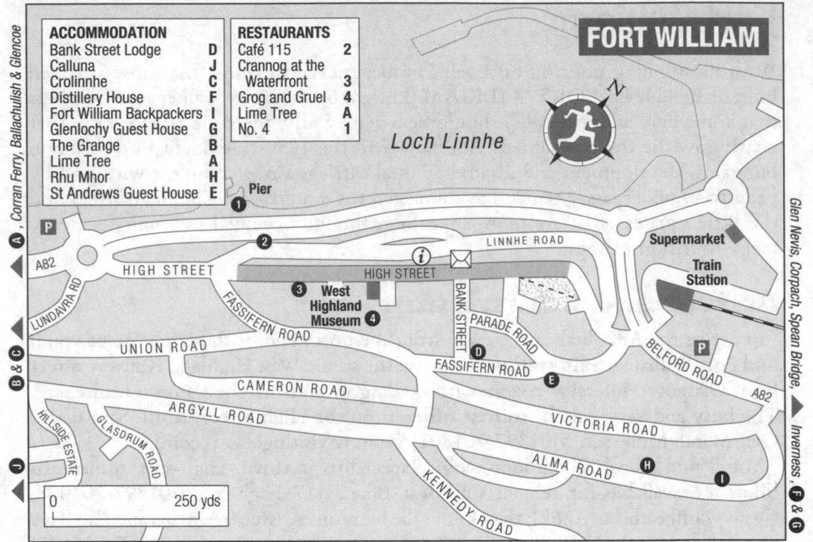

Accommodation

The town itself isn't the most characterful place to base yourself, but Fort William's plentiful **accommodation** ranges from large luxury hotels to budget hostels and bunkhouses. Numerous B&Bs are also scattered across town, many of them in the suburb of Corpach on the other side of Loch Linnhe, three miles along the Mallaig road (served by regular buses), where you'll also find a couple of good hostels.

Town hotels and B&Bs

Crolinnhe Grange Rd ⓣ01397/702709, ⓦwww.crolinnhe.co.uk. Beautifully appointed guesthouse overlooking Loch Linnhe. Quite grand and upmarket. ❻

Distillery House North Rd ⓣ01397/700103, ⓦwww.stayinfortwilliam.co.uk. Very comfortable, well-equipped upper-range guesthouse a 10min walk north of the town centre near the Glen Nevis turn-off, with singles, doubles and "superior" rooms. ❺

The Grange Grange Rd ⓣ01397/705516, ⓦwww.thegrange-scotland.co.uk. Top-grade accommodation in a striking old stone house, with log fires, views towards Loch Linnhe and luxurious en-suite doubles. Vegetarian breakfasts on request. Open April–Oct. ❻

Lime Tree Achintore Rd ⓣ01397/701806, ⓦwww.limetreefortwilliam.co.uk. A stylish and relaxing option in an old manse, with a great modern restaurant and an excellent gallery; they've also got the practicalities covered with a drying room, map room and bike storage. ❺

Rhu Mhor Alma Rd ⓣ01397/702213, ⓦwww.rhumhor.co.uk. Congenial and characterful B&B, a 10min walk from the town centre, offering good breakfasts; vegetarians and vegans catered for on request. ❸

St Andrews Guest House Fassifern Rd ⓣ01397/703038, ⓦwww.standrewsguesthouse.co.uk. Comfortable, central and very reasonable B&B in a converted granite choir school featuring various inscriptions and stained-glass windows. ❶

Town hostels and campsites

Bank Street Lodge Bank St ⓣ01397/700070, ⓦwww.bankstreetlodge.co.uk. A clean and bright 43-bed hostel handy for transport and the town centre.

Calluna Heathercroft, Connachie Rd ⓣ01397/700451, ⓦwww.fortwilliamholiday.co.uk. Well-run self-catering and hostel accommodation a 10min walk from the centre of town, configured for individual, family and group stays. Free pick-up from town available, along with on-site laundry and mountain-guiding services (see ⓦ westcoast-mountainguides.co.uk).

Fort William Backpackers Alma Rd ⓣ 01397/700711, ⓦ www.scotlands-top-hostels.com. A busy 38-bed, rambling, archetypal backpacker hostel a 5min walk up the hill from town, with great views and large communal areas.

Out of town hotels and B&Bs

Achintee Farm Guest House Glen Nevis ⓣ 01397/702240, ⓦ www.achinteefarm.com. Friendly B&B with adjoining hostel and self-catering cottage, right by the *Ben Nevis Inn* at the start of the Ben Nevis footpath. ❹

Inverlochy Castle Torlundy, 2 miles north of town on the A82 ⓣ 01397/702177, ⓦ www.inverlochycastlehotel.co.uk. Built on the site of a thirteenth-century fortress, this is one of Scotland's grandest and most luxurious country-house hotels with fantastic accommodation and Michelin-star food. ❾

Rhiw Goch Banavie ⓣ 01397/772373, ⓦ www.rhiwgoch.co.uk. Comfortable and welcoming B&B overlooking Neptune's Staircase with great views to Ben Nevis. For a super-healthy breakfast, try the great fresh-fruit platter. Bike and canoe rental also available. ❷

Out of town hostels and campsites

Ben Nevis Inn Achintee, Glen Nevis ⓣ 01397/701227, ⓦ www.ben-nevis-inn.co.uk. A basic and cosy twenty-bed bunkhouse in the basement of a lively 250-year-old pub, 500m north of *Achintee Farm Guest House* (see opposite). Terrific pub grub and atmosphere.

Chase the Wild Goose Hostel Banavie ⓣ 01397/772531, ⓦ www.great-glen-hostel.com. A small, comfortable hostel close to Neptune's Staircase and handy for the Great Glen Way.

Farr Cottage Lodge Corpach, on the main A830 ⓣ 01397/772315, ⓦ www.farrcottage.co.uk. Well-equipped, lively place with range of dorms and double/twin rooms (❶). Offers a multitude of outdoor activities including canyoning and sea-fishing; evening entertainment includes whisky tastings.

Glen Nevis Caravan and Camping Park Glen Nevis, 2 miles up the Glen Nevis road ⓣ 01397/702191, ⓦ www.glennevisholidays.co.uk. Offers a range of lodges and rentable caravans as well as camping pitches. Facilities include hot showers, a shop and restaurant, and disabled facilities.

Glen Nevis SYHA hostel Glen Nevis, 2.5 miles up the Glen Nevis road, opposite the start of the path to the summit ⓣ 01397/702 336, ⓦ www.syha.org.uk. Though far from town, this friendly hostel is an excellent base for walkers. Very busy in summer.

Smiddy Bunkhouse and Blacksmith's Hostel Snowgoose Mountain Centre, Station Rd, Corpach ⓣ 01397/772467, ⓦ www.highland-mountain-guides.co.uk. Alpine hostel and bunkhouse on the site of an old blacksmith's workshop. It's four miles from Ben Nevis at the southwestern end of the Caledonian Canal.

The Town

Fort William's aesthetic decline started in the nineteenth century when the original fort, which gave the town its name, was demolished to make way for the train line. There's little to detain you except the splendid and idiosyncratic **West Highland Museum**, on Cameron Square, just off the High Street (June–Sept Mon–Sat 10am–5pm, July & Aug also Sun 10am–4pm; Oct–May Mon–Sat 10am–4pm; £4). Its collections cover virtually every aspect of Highland life and the presentation is traditional, but very well done, making a refreshing change from state-of-the-art heritage centres. There's a secret portrait of Bonnie Prince Charlie and the long Spanish rifle used in the famous Appin Murder, and even a 550kg slab of aluminium, the stuff that's processed into silver foil just five miles north of town (you'll see the huge pipes running down the mountainside).

Excursions from town include the 84-mile round-trip to Mallaig (see p.481) on the **West Highland Railway** Line aboard the **Jacobite Steam Train** (mid-May to Oct Mon–Fri; July–Aug also Sat & Sun; depart Fort William 10.20am, return 2.10pm; £31; ⓣ 01524/737751 or 737753, ⓦ www.westcoastrailways.co.uk). Heading along the shore of Loch Eil to the west coast via historic Glenfinnan (see p.479), the train passes through some of the region's most spectacular scenery, though these days it's as popular for its role as the locomotive used in the *Harry Potter* films. Several **cruises** also leave from the town pier every day, offering the chance to spot the marine life of Loch Linnhe, which includes seals and seabirds. Try Crannog Cruises (April to mid-Sept; 90min; £10; ⓣ01397/705589, ⓦwww.crannog.net) or Seaventures, who offer exhilarating fast boat trips (March–Nov; incl 90min Loch Linnhe trip; £10; ⓣ01397/701687, ⓦwww.seaventuresscotland.com).

Eating and drinking

Fort William has a reasonable range of places to **eat** and **drink**. If your budget won't stretch to the Michelin-starred fare at *Inverlochy Castle*, the pick of the bunch is the *Lime Tree Restaurant* (ⓣ01397/701806, ⓦwww.limetreefortwilliam.co.uk) in the Old Manse on Achintore Road, which serves excellent contemporary Scottish food. At *Crannog at the Waterfront* (ⓣ01397/705589, ⓦwww.oceanandoak.co.uk), located at the pier just off the bypass on entering Fort William, you'll find lochside views and fresh seafood, including lobster, oak-smoked salmon and langoustines, alongside a reasonable wine list. Another option is *No. 4* (ⓣ01397/704222), at the top end of Cameron Square, with dishes including lamb, venison and a handful of traditional Scottish dishes. On the High Street, loud and friendly *Grog and Gruel* is a good bet for Scottish real ales, malts, entertainment and some traditional pub grub, while *Café 115* is decent for coffee.

Around Fort William

Any disappointment you harbour about the dispiriting flavour of Fort William town should be offset by the wealth of scenery and activities in its immediate vicinity. Most obvious – on a clear day, at least – is **Ben Nevis**, the most popular, though hardly the most rewarding, of Scotland's high peaks. The path up leaves from **Glen Nevis**, also a starting point for some other excellent walks of various lengths and elevations. The mountain abutting Ben Nevis is **Aonach Mhòr**, home of Scotland's most modern ski resort and an internationally renowned honey-pot for downhill mountain-bike enthusiasts. Some of the best views of these peaks can be had from **Corpach**, a small village opposite Fort William that marks the start of the **Caledonian Canal** (see p.461).

The main road travelling up the Great Glen from Fort William towards Inverness is the A82, ten miles along which is the small settlement of **Spean Bridge**, a good waypoint for getting to various remote and attractive walking areas with several backpacker hostels, notably glens **Spean** and **Roy**, found along the A86 trunk road, which links across the central highlands to the A9 and the Speyside region.

Glen Nevis

A ten-minute drive south of Fort William, **GLEN NEVIS** is indisputably among the Highlands' most impressive glens: a classic U-shaped glacial valley hemmed in by steep bracken-covered slopes and swathes of blue-grey scree. With the forbidding mass of Ben Nevis rising steeply to the north, it's not surprising that the valley has served as a location in the films *Rob Roy* and *Braveheart*. Apart from its natural beauty, Glen Nevis is also the starting point for the ascent of Ben Nevis, and you can rent **mountain equipment** at the trailhead. One of the best maps is *Harvey's Ben Nevis Walkers Map and Guide*, available from Fort William's tourist office and most local bookshops and outdoor stores. **Bus** #41 runs from the bus station in Fort William via the SYHA hostel to the Lower Falls car park almost five miles up the Glen Nevis road.

The Nevis Range

Situated seven miles northeast of Fort William by the A82, on the slopes of **Aonach Mhòr**, one of the high mountains abutting Ben Nevis, the **Nevis Range** (Ⓣ01397/705825, Ⓦwww.nevis-range.co.uk) is Scotland's highest ski area. All year round, bus #41 runs from Fort William at least five times a day (Mon–Sat; 3 on Sun) to the base station of the country's only **gondola** system (daily: 10am–5pm; July & Aug 9.30am–6pm; closed mid-Nov to mid-Dec; £10.50 return). The one-and-a-half-mile gondola trip (15min), rising 2000ft, gives an easy approach to some high-level walking as well as spectacular views from the terrace of the self-service restaurant at the top station. There's also a Discovery Centre here, providing insights into the mountain's geology and wildlife. From the top of the gondola station, you can experience a white-knuckle ride down Britain's only World-Cup standard **downhill mountain-bike course** (mid-May to mid-Sept 11am–3pm; £12 including gondola one-way; £19 multi-trip), a hair-raising 3km route that's not for the faint-hearted. There's also over 25 miles of waymarked off-road bike routes, known as the Witch's Trails, on the mountainside and in the Leanachan Forest, ranging from gentle paths to cross-country scrambles. Off Beat Bikes (Mon–Sat 9am–5.30pm, Sun 10am–5pm; £12/half-day, £17/day; Ⓣ01397/704008, Ⓦwww.offbeatbikes.co.uk) rents general mountain bikes as well as full-suspension ones for the downhill course from its shops in Fort William and at the gondola base station (mid-May to mid-Sept). The base station area also has a café and there's a play area and nature trail nearby.

A great **low-level walk** (six miles round-trip) runs from the end of the road at the top of Glen Nevis. The good but very rocky path leads through a dramatic gorge with impressive falls and rapids, then opens out into a secret hanging valley, carpeted with wild flowers, with a high waterfall at the far end. If you're really energetic (and properly equipped) you can walk the full twelve miles on over **Rannoch Moor** to **Corrour Station** (see p.366), where you can pick up one of three daily trains to take you back to Fort William.

Of all the walks in and around Glen Nevis, the **ascent of Ben Nevis** (4406ft), Britain's highest summit, inevitably attracts the most attention. In high summer the trail is teeming with hikers – around 100,000 summit each year. However, this doesn't mean that the mountain should be treated casually. It can snow at the summit any day of the year and people die on the slopes, so take the necessary precautions (see p.49); in winter, of course, the mountain should be left to the experts. The most obvious **route**, a Victorian pony-path up the whaleback south side of the mountain, built to service the observatory that once stood on the top, starts from the helpful Glen Nevis visitor centre (daily: Easter to mid-May & Oct 9am–5pm; mid-May to end Sept 9am–6pm) a mile and a half southeast of Fort William along the Glen Nevis road (bus #42 from Fort William). Ask here for the useful leaflet *Ben Nevis: Safety information for walking the mountain track*. Return via the main route or, if the weather is settled and you're confident enough, make a side-trip from the wide saddle into the **Allt a'Mhuilinn glen** for spectacular views of the great cliffs on Ben Nevis's north face. Allow a full day for the climb (8hr) and check the weather forecast at your accommodation before setting out.

Neptune's Staircase

In the suburb of **BANAVIE**, three miles north of the centre of Fort William along the A830 to Mallaig, the Caledonian Canal climbs 64ft in less than half a mile via a punishing but picturesque series of eight locks known as **Neptune's Staircase**. There are stunning views from here of Ben Nevis and its neighbours, and it's a popular point from which to walk or cycle along the canal towpath. *Moorings Hotel* near the staircase does decent pub food. Canoes (£25/day) can be rented from *Rhiw Goch* B&B (see p.445) a half-mile up the B8004 in Banavie, whilst the Snowgoose Mountain Centre in Corpach (Ⓣ01397/772467) also rents kayaks and canoes. If you do choose to cycle along the Caledonian Canal, look out for *The Eagle Inn* at Laggan Locks at the head of Loch Lochy, where fresh seafood and real ale are on offer aboard a wonderful 1920s Dutch barge (Ⓣ07789/858567 or 07811/956893; Easter–Oct).

Spean Bridge and around

Ten miles northeast of Fort William, the village of **SPEAN BRIDGE** marks the junction of the A82 with the A86 from Dalwhinnie and Kingussie (see p.431). If you're here, it's well worth heading a mile out of the village on the A82 towards Inverness to the **Commando Memorial**, a group of bronze soldiers commemorating the men who trained in the area during World War II. The statue looks out on an awesome sweep of moor and mountain that takes in the wider Lochaber area and the Ben Nevis massif. A few hundred yards from the memorial, on the minor B8004 to Gairlochy, is the welcoming and upmarket *Old Pines Hotel and Restaurant* (Ⓣ01397/712324, Ⓦwww.oldpines.co.uk; ⑧), where guests are treated to locally sourced game and shellfish as well as home-baking, pasta and ice cream.

Three miles east of Spean Bridge, a minor road turns off up **Glen Roy**. A couple of miles along the glen, you'll see the so-called "parallel roads": not roads at all, but ancient beaches at various levels along the valley sides, which mark the shorelines of a loch confined here by a glacial dam in the last Ice Age. Back on the A86 at **ROY BRIDGE**, four miles from Spean Bridge, you can enjoy some tasty home-made soup and bar food under the gaze of stag heads in the *Roy Bridge Hotel*, which runs the adjacent cosy *Grey Corrie Lodge* backpackers hostel (Ⓣ01397/712236, Ⓦwww.roybridgehotel.co.uk). Just 500m further north, the *Stronlossit Inn* (Ⓣ01397/712253, Ⓦwww.stronlossit.co.uk; ⑤) serves standard bar food and has several real ales on tap. Two miles east of Roy Bridge, *Aite Cruinnichidh* (Ⓣ01397/712315, Ⓦwww.highland-hostel.co.uk) is a comfortable wood-lined **bunkhouse** in a beautiful setting, with good facilities including family rooms and a sauna, as well as local advice for walkers and cyclists. The nearby Roy Bridge Store is handy for provisions while Jimmy Couts (Ⓣ01397/712812, Ⓦwww.fishing-scotland.co.uk) is the man to call for **fly-fishing** tuition and excursions.

Five miles further east from *Aite Cruinnichidh*, the railway line and road part company at **TULLOCH**, and trains swing south to pass Loch Treig and cross Rannoch Moor (see p.366). The station building at Tulloch is now a friendly and well-equipped **hostel**, *Station Lodge* (Ⓣ01397/732333, Ⓦwww.stationlodge.co.uk), which can provide breakfasts and dinners with advance notice. The Caledonian sleeper train from London stops right at the door. Further east, the A86 runs alongside the artificial **Loch Laggan** with the picturesque Ardverikie Castle on its southern shore and the attractive walking area of **Creag Meagaidh National Nature Reserve** to the north.

Glen Coe and around

Glen Coe, half-an-hour's drive south of Fort William on the main A82 road to Glasgow, is one of Scotland's most inspiring places. Arriving from the south across the desolate reaches of Rannoch Moor, you're likely to find the start of the glen – with **Buachaille Etive Mhòr** to the south and **Beinn a'Chrùlaiste** to the north – little short of forbidding. By the time you've reached the heart of the glen, with the three huge rock buttresses known as the **Three Sisters** on one side and the Anoach Eagach ridge on the other combining to close up the sky, you'll almost certainly want to stop. Added to the compelling emotional mix is the story of the notorious **massacre of Glen Coe** in 1692, nadir of the long-standing enmity between the clans MacDonald and Campbell. At its western end, Glen Coe meets Loch Leven: the main road goes west and over the bridge at **Ballachulish** en route to Fort William, while at the eastern end of the loch is the slowly reviving settlement of **Kinlochleven**, site of the world's largest indoor ice-climbing centre and a waypoint on the West Highland Way long-distance footpath (see box, p.321).

Glen Coe

Breathtakingly beautiful **Glen Coe** (literally "Valley of Weeping"), sixteen miles south of Fort William on the A82, is a spectacular mountain valley between velvety-green conical peaks, their tops often wreathed in cloud, their flanks streaked by cascades of rock and scree. In 1692 it was the site of a notorious massacre, in which the MacDonalds were victims of an abiding government desire to suppress the clans. Fed up with what they regarded as unacceptable lawlessness, and a groundswell of Jacobitism and Catholicism, the government offered a general pardon to all those who signed an oath of allegiance to William III by January 1, 1692. When clan chief **Alastair MacDonald** missed the deadline, a plot was hatched to make an example of "that damnable sept", and **Campbell of Glenlyon** was ordered to billet his soldiers in the homes of the MacDonalds, who for ten days entertained them with traditional Highland hospitality. In the early morning of February 13, the soldiers turned on their hosts, slaying around forty and causing more than three hundred to flee in a blizzard.

Walks around Glen Coe

Ordnance Survey Explorer map no. 384

Flanked by the sheer-sided Munros, **Glen Coe** offers some of the Highlands' most challenging **hiking** routes, with long steep ascents over rough trails and notoriously unpredictable weather conditions that claim lives every year. The walks outlined below number among the glen's less-ambitious routes, but still require a map. It's essential that you take the proper precautions (see p.49), and stick to the paths, both for your own safety and the sake of the landscape, which has become badly eroded in places. For a broader selection of walks, get hold of the Ordnance Survey *Pathfinder Guide: Fort William and Glen Coe Walks*.

A good introduction to the splendours of Glen Coe is the half-day hike over the **Devil's Staircase**, which follows part of the old military road that once ran between Fort William and Stirling. The trail, part of the West Highland Way (see p.321), starts at the village of **Kinlochleven** and is marked by thistle signs, which lead uphill to the 1804ft pass and down the other side into Glen Coe.

Set right in the heart of the glen, the half-day **Allt Coire Gabhail** hike starts at the car park opposite the distinctive Three Sisters massif on the main A82. This explores the so-called "Lost Valley" where the Clan MacDonald fled and hid their cattle when attacked. Once in the valley, there are superb views of the upper slopes of Bidean nan Bian, Gearr Aonach and Beinn Fhada, which improve as you continue on to its head, another twenty-to-thirty-minute walk.

Undoubtedly one of the finest walks in the Glen Coe area that doesn't entail the ascent of a Munro is the **Buachaille Etive Beag** circuit, which follows the textbook glacial valleys of Lairig Eilde and Lairig Gartain, ascending 1968ft in only nine miles of rough trail. Park near the waterfall at **The Study** – the gorge part of the A82 through Glen Coe – and walk up the road until you see a sign pointing south to "Loch Etiveside".

Beyond the small village of **GLENCOE** at the western end of the glen, the glen itself (a property of the NTS since the 1930s) is virtually uninhabited, and provides outstanding climbing and walking. The attractive NTS **visitor centre** (March daily 10am–4pm; April–Aug daily 9.30am–5.30pm; Sept & Oct daily 10am–5pm; Nov to mid-Dec, Jan & Feb Thurs–Sun 10am–4pm; NTS; £5.50) sits in woodland a mile south of the village. It has a good exhibition, with film, giving a balanced account of the massacre, information about the area's natural history and conservation issues, and some entertaining material on rock- and hill-climbing through the years. There's also a cabin area providing information on the local weather and wildlife, and you may be able to join a ranger-led **guided walk** (Easter & June–Sept). Unfortunately the café food doesn't live up to its nice-looking interior. Meanwhile, in Glencoe village, you can pay a visit to the delightful heather-roofed **Glencoe Folk Museum** (April–Oct Mon–Sat 10am–5.30pm; £3). Various games and activities for kids can be enjoyed within this cosy 1720 croft where items include a chair that reputedly once belonged to Bonnie Prince Charlie.

At the eastern end of Glen Coe beyond the looming massif of Buachaille Etive Mhòr, the landscape opens out onto vast Rannoch Moor. From the **Glen Coe Mountain Resort** (ⓣ01855/851226, ⓦwww.glencoemountain.com; Jan–Oct & Dec daily) a chairlift (£8) climbs 2400ft to Meall a Bhuiridh, giving spectacular views over Rannoch Moor and to Ben Nevis. At the base station, there's a simple but pleasant café.

Practicalities

To get to the heart of Glen Coe from Fort William, hop on the Glasgow-bound Scottish Citylink **coach** service (4 daily; 30min). Bus #44 from Fort William also stops at least five times a day (3 on Sun) at Glencoe village en route to Kinlochleven.

There's a good selection of **accommodation** in Glen Coe and the surrounding area. Basic options include an SYHA **hostel** (ⓣ01855/811219, ⓦwww.syha.org.uk) on a back road halfway between Glencoe village and the *Clachaig Inn* (see below); a cheaper neighbouring **independent hostel** (ⓣ01855/811906, ⓦwww.glencoehostel.co.uk) in rustic whitewashed buildings; the sylvan year-round *Red Squirrel* **campsite** nearby (ⓣ01855/811256, ⓦwww.redsquirrelcampsite.co.uk; campfires permitted); and the *Caravanning and Camping Club* site (ⓣ01855/811397; April–Oct) beside the NTS visitor centre on the main road.

Glencoe village has a few comfortable **B&Bs**, such as the secluded and friendly *Scorry Breac* (ⓣ01855/811354, ⓦwww.scorrybreac.co.uk; ❷), while the best-known **hotel** in the area is the lively *Clachaig Inn* (ⓣ01855/811252, ⓦwww.clachaig.com; ❺), a great place to reward your exertions with cask-conditioned ales and heaped platefuls of food; it's three miles south of Glencoe village on the minor road off the A82, a stroll away from the campsite and hostels. The other famous hotel in the glen is the historic though run-down *Kingshouse Hotel* (ⓣ01855/851259, ⓦwww.kingy.com; ❸), ten miles south of here on the edge of the empty wilds of Rannoch Moor. If nothing else, it's worth stopping for a pint at the atmospheric *Climber's Bar* within. Ten miles further south at Bridge of Orchy station is the cosy *West Highland Way Sleeper Hostel* (ⓣ01838/400548, ⓦwww.westhighlandwaysleeper.co.uk). You can enjoy reasonably priced pub grub in the nearby *Bridge of Orchy Hotel*.

Ballachulish and Onich

From 1693 to 1955, the village of **BALLACHULISH**, just one mile west of Glencoe village, was a major centre for the quarrying of roofing slates, shipping out 26 million of them at the height of production in the mid-nineteenth century. There's a short, well-maintained footpath leading from directly opposite

Ballachulish tourist office into the now-disused slate quarry – a few information boards tell the history of the quarry, which, like many former industrial sites, has an eerie stillness to it. Ballachulish has two parts – the main village on the south of the loch and North Ballachulish on the other side of the road bridge, which spans the mouth of Loch Leven. Beyond North Ballachulish on the road to Fort William is the roadside settlement of **ONICH**, a mile or so on from which is **CORRAN**, from where a car ferry crosses the narrowest point of Loch Linnhe, providing access to the Morvern and Ardnamurchan peninsulas.

Ballachulish's **tourist office** is on Albert Road, sharing space with a coffee and gift shop (daily; ⓣ01855/811866); you can use its freephone line to organize somewhere to stay. For a cheap bed, head to the *Corran Bunkhouse* (ⓣ01855/821000, ⓦwww.corranbunkhouse.co.uk) by the ferry jetty at Corran, or welcoming *Inchree Lodge* (ⓣ0800/3101536, ⓦwww.inchreecentre.co.uk) at Onich, where accommodation is available in a bunkhouse or chalets and there's a decent real-ale **pub** and bistro, *The Four Seasons*. The excellent activity operator Vertical Descents (ⓣ01855/821593, ⓦwww.verticaldescents.com) is also based at Onich; through them you can try a host of activities including wet-and-wild watersports and adrenaline-pumping canyoning (both around £55/half-day).

In Ballachulish village, *Fern Villa* (ⓣ01855/811393, ⓦwww.fernvilla.org.uk; ❷) is a friendly **B&B**, while *Cuildorag House* (ⓣ01855/821529, ⓦwww.cuildoraghouse.com; ❷) in Onich is a particularly pleasant vegetarian and vegan B&B, renowned for its great breakfasts. For **hotels**, the luxurious *Ballachulish Hotel* (ⓣ0844/855 9133, ⓦwww.ballachulishhotel.com; ❸), just outside the village, offers sumptuous accommodation, pricey fine dining, terrific mountain views, its own nine-hole golf course and a fine dose of Scottish history (including a role in Robert Louis Stevenson's literary classic *Kidnapped*). Another option is the family-friendly *Isles of Glencoe Hotel* (ⓣ01855/831800, ⓦwww.islesofglencoe.com; ❺), which has a swimming pool. At the adjacent Lochaber Watersports (ⓣ01855/821391, ⓦwww.lochaberwatersports.co.uk) you can rent a small sailing dinghy, rowing boat or canoe from £12 per hour.

Kinlochleven

At the easternmost end of Loch Leven, the settlement of **KINLOCHLEVEN** is steadily reviving its fortunes after many years of being a tourism backwater best known as the site of a huge, unsightly aluminium smelter built in 1904. The tale of the area's industrial past is told in **The Aluminium Story** (Mon–Fri 10am–1pm & 2–5pm, Oct–March closed Fri afternoon; free), a small series of displays in the same building as the town library and tourist office. The disused smelter is now the home of an innovative indoor mountaineering centre called **The Ice Factor** (ⓣ01855/831100, ⓦwww.ice-factor.co.uk). This impressive facility includes the world's largest artificial ice-climbing wall (13.5m) as well as a range of more traditional climbing walls plus equipment rental, and a steam room and sauna. There's a bar upstairs and food is available. Alongside, another part of the aluminium smelter has been transformed into the **Atlas Brewery**, open for tours on summer evenings (groups can arrange tours at other times; ⓣ01855/831111, ⓦwww.atlasbrewery.com). As well as being close to Glen Coe, Kinlochleven stands at the foot of the Mamore hills, popular with Munro-baggers; it's also a convenient overnight stop on the **West Highland Way**, with Fort William a day's walk away.

For hikers looking to spend the night in Kinlochleven, the *Blackwater* **hostel** (ⓣ01855/831253, ⓦwww.blackwaterhostel.co.uk) beside the river is decidedly upmarket, with TVs and en-suite facilities in dorms with two, three, four or eight beds, and a communal kitchen/dining area. For £5 per person you can also **camp** here. There's fine hospitality at the Edwardian-built *Edencoille Guest House*

(Ⓣ01855/831358, Ⓦwww.kinlochlevenbedandbreakfast.co.uk; ❷) where, with notice, you can organize packed lunches, evening meals and guided walking trips. There are also two decent **hotels** in Kinlochleven: *MacDonald Hotel* (Ⓣ01855/831539, Ⓦwww.macdonaldhotel.co.uk; ❺), whose *Bothy Bar* is popular with walkers and where you can also camp (£4), and the *Tailrace Inn* on Riverside Road (Ⓣ01855/831777, Ⓦwww.tailraceinn.com; ❹), offering reasonable rooms and food (including breakfast and packed lunches for non-residents), along with regular entertainment. The best place to eat near here is the *Lochleven Seafood Café* (Ⓣ01855/821048, Ⓦwww.lochlevenseafoodcafe.co.uk; closed Mon & Tues), a relaxed restaurant with an attractive outdoor terrace specializing in local shellfish, located a few miles along the B836 following the north side of the loch.

Loch Ness and around

Twenty-three miles long, unfathomably deep, cold and often moody, **Loch Ness** is bounded by rugged heather-clad mountains rising steeply from a wooded shoreline and attractive glens opening up on either side. Its fame, however, is based overwhelmingly on its legendary inhabitant Nessie, the "Loch Ness monster",

Nessie

The world-famous **Loch Ness monster**, affectionately known as **Nessie** (and by serious aficionados as *Nessiteras rhombopteryx*), has been a local celebrity for some time. The first mention of a mystery creature crops up in St Adamnan's seventh-century biography of **St Columba**, who allegedly calmed an aquatic animal that had attacked one of his monks. Present-day interest, however, is probably greater outside Scotland than within the country, and dates from the building of the road along the loch's western shore in the early 1930s. In 1934 the *Daily Mail* published London surgeon R.K. Wilson's sensational photograph of the head and neck of the monster peering up out of the loch, and the hype has hardly diminished since. Recent encounters range from glimpses of ripples by anglers to the famous occasion in 1961 when thirty hotel guests saw a pair of humps break the water's surface and cruise for about half a mile before submerging.

Photographic evidence is showcased in two separate exhibitions located at Drumnadrochit, but the most impressive of these exhibits – including the renowned black-and-white movie footage of Nessie's humps moving across the water, and Wilson's original head-and-shoulders shot – have now been exposed as fakes. Indeed, in few other places on earth has watching a rather lifeless and often grey expanse of water seemed so compelling, or have floating logs, otters and boat wakes been photographed so often and with such excitement. Yet while even high-tech sonar surveys carried out over the past two decades have failed to come up with conclusive evidence, it's hard to dismiss Nessie as pure myth. After all, no one yet knows where the unknown layers of silt and mud at the bottom of the loch begin and end: best estimates say the loch is over 750ft deep, deeper than much of the North Sea, while others point to the possibilities of underwater caves and undiscovered channels connected to the sea. What scientists have found in the cold, murky depths, including pure white eels and rare arctic char, offers fertile grounds for speculation, with different theories declaring Nessie to be a remnant from the dinosaur age, a giant newt or a huge visiting Baltic sturgeon. Technological advances have also expanded the scope for Nessie-watching: Ⓦwww.lochness.co.uk offers round-the-clock **webcams** for views across the loch, while Ⓦwww.lochnessinvestigation.org is packed with research information.

whose fame ensures a steady flow of hopeful visitors to the settlements dotted along the loch, in particular **Drumnadrochit**. Nearby, the impressive ruins of **Castle Urquhart** – a favourite monster-spotting location – perch atop a rock on the lochside and attract a deluge of bus parties during the summer. Almost as busy in high season is the village of **Fort Augustus**, at the more scenic southwest tip of Loch Ness, where you can watch queues of boats tackling one of the Caledonian Canal's longest flight of locks.

Away from the lochside, and seeing a fraction of Loch Ness's visitor numbers, the remote glens of **Urquhart** and **Affric** make an appealing contrast, with Affric in particular boasting narrow, winding roads, gushing streams and hillsides dotted with ancient Caledonian pine forests. The busiest of these glens to the north is the often bleak high country of **Glen Moriston**, a little to the southwest of Glen Affric, through which the main road between Inverness and Skye passes.

Although most visitors drive along the tree-lined A82 road, which runs along the western shore of Loch Ness, the sinuous single-track B862/B852 (originally a military road built to link Fort Augustus and Fort George) that skirts the eastern shore is quieter and affords far more spectacular views. However, buses from Inverness along this road only run as far south as **Foyers**, so you'll need your own transport to complete the whole loop around the loch, a journey which includes a most impressive stretch between Fort Augustus and the high, hidden **Loch Mhor**, overlooked by the imposing Monadhliath range to the south.

Fort Augustus

FORT AUGUSTUS, a tiny, busy village at the scenic southwestern tip of Loch Ness, was named after George II's son, the chubby lad who later became the "Butcher" duke of Cumberland of Culloden fame; it was built as a barracks after the 1715 Jacobite rebellion. Today, it's dominated by comings and goings along the **Caledonian Canal**, which leaves Loch Ness here, and by its large former **Benedictine abbey**, a campus of grey Victorian buildings founded on the site of the original fort in 1876. Until relatively recently this was home to a small but active community of monks, but it has now been converted into luxury flats. From its berth by the Clansman Centre, **Cruise Loch Ness** (March–Oct; 1hr; £11; ⓣ01320/366277, ⓦwww.cruiselochness.com) sails five miles up Loch Ness, using sonar technology to provide passengers with impressive live 3D imagery of the deep where underwater cave systems, salmon, cannibalistic trout (and, some would speculate, Nessie) are to be found.

Fort Augustus's very helpful **tourist office** (April–Sept daily; Oct–Dec & mid-Feb to March Sat & Sun; ⓣ01320/366779) hands out useful free walking leaflets and stocks maps of the Great Glen Way (see box, p.443). They'll also advise on fishing permits for the loch or nearby river. There's **hostel** accommodation at *Morag's Lodge* (ⓣ01320/366289, ⓦwww.moragslodge.com) at Bunoich Brae on the Loch Ness side of town, where the atmosphere livens up with the daily arrival of backpackers' minibus tours, and at the well-equipped thirty-bed *Stravaigers Lodge* (ⓣ01320/366257, ⓦwww.highlandbunkhouse.co.uk) on Glendoe Road. *Abbey Cottage* (ⓣ0845/471 8332, ⓦwww.abbeycottagelochness.co.uk; ❷) is a nicely renovated **B&B** on the main street, and there's the spacious *Cumberlands Campsite* a five-minute walk from the loch (ⓣ01320/366257, ⓦwww.cumberlands-campsite.com). Of the **hotels**, try either the small, friendly *Caledonian* (ⓣ01320/366256, ⓦwww.thecaledonianhotel.com; ❹) or the distinctly upmarket *Lovat Arms Hotel* opposite (ⓣ0845/450 1100, ⓦwww.lovatarms-hotel.com; ❹), built on the site of the 1718 Kilwhimen Barracks and refurbished along eco-friendly principles.

Both of the above hotels provide decent **food**, or try the *Lock Inn* by the canal, with its attractive wood-panelled interior and upscale pub food. There are tables outside by the lock for summer days, and regular live-music events. *The Scots Kitchen* opposite the tourist office does moderately priced, home-cooked food including steak-and-ale pie or clootie dumpling. There are some good **cycling** routes locally, notably along the Great Glen cycle route. The best place to rent bikes or watersports equipment, including boats and canoes, is at Monster Activities (Ⓣ01809/501340, Ⓦwww.monsteractivities.com), South Laggan, eight miles or so southwest at the head of Loch Lochy.

The east side of Loch Ness

The tranquil and scenic **east side** of Loch Ness is skirted by General Wade's old military highway, now the B862/B852. From Fort Augustus, the narrow single-track road swings up, away from the lochside through the near-deserted **Stratherrick** valley, dotted with tiny lochans. To the southeast of Fort Augustus you'll pass the massive earth workings of the new Glendoe Hydro Station. From here, the road drops down to rejoin the shores of Loch Ness at **FOYERS**, where there are numerous marked forest trails and an impressive waterfall. In Upper Foyers village you can find the *Red Squirrel Café*, which runs a live web-cam of red squirrels nesting (April–June) across the road, and the friendly *Foyers House* (Ⓣ01456/486405, Ⓦwww.foyershouse-lochness.com; no children; ④), located by the signposted waterfall. This secluded B&B has fabulous views of the loch from its terrace and a **restaurant** serving up game pie, venison and local salmon (daily 7–9pm Easter to Sept; Ⓣ01463/711870).

Past **Inverfarigaig** – where a road up a beautiful, steep-sided river valley leads east over to Loch Mhor – is the sleepy village of **DORES**, nestled at the northeastern end of Loch Ness, the whitewashed *Dores Inn* providing a pleasant pit stop. Only nine miles southwest of Inverness, the old **pub** is popular with Invernessians, who trickle out here on summer evenings for a stroll along the grey pebble beach and some monster-spotting. Note that a local **bus** from Inverness runs down the east side of the loch to Foyers (Mon–Fri 3 daily; 2 on Sat).

Invermoriston and west

On the other shore, heading north from Fort Augustus along the main A82, **INVERMORISTON** is a tiny, attractive village situated just above the loch. Here you can follow well-marked woodland footpaths past a series of grand waterfalls, and a good stop for lunch or a drink is provided by the *Glenmoriston Arms Hotel* (Ⓣ01320/351206, Ⓦwww.glenmoristonarms.co.uk), a whitewashed stone building with a popular bar. The A887 leads west from Invermoriston to the west coast (via the A87) on the main commercial route to the Skye Bridge. Rugged and somewhat awesome, the stretch through **Glen Moriston**, beside **Loch Cluanie**, has serious peaks on either side and little sign of human habitation. At the western end of the loch, you'll find the isolated *Cluanie Inn* (Ⓣ01320/340238, Ⓦwww.cluanieinn.com; ⑦), a popular place with outdoor types, serving good food in its real-fire pub; one of the bedrooms has a jacuzzi bath and a four-poster. West from here, the road drops gradually down **Glen Shiel** into the superb mountainscape of Kintail.

Drumnadrochit and around

Situated above a verdant, sheltered bay of Loch Ness fifteen miles southwest of Inverness, **DRUMNADROCHIT** is the southern gateway to remote Glen Affric and the epicentre of Nessie-hype, complete with a rash of tacky souvenir shops and two rival monster exhibitions whose head-to-head scramble for punters occasionally erupts into acrimonious exchanges, detailed with relish by the local press. Of the pair, the **Loch Ness Centre & Exhibition** (daily: Easter–May 9.30am–5pm; June & Sept 9am–6pm; July & Aug 9am–8pm; Oct 9.30am–5.30pm; Nov–Easter 10am–3.30pm; £6.50) is the better bet, offering an in-depth rundown of eyewitness accounts and information on various Nessie research projects. The **Nessieland Monster Centre** (daily: April–June & Sept–Nov 9am–5pm; July & Aug 9am–9pm; Dec–March 9am–4pm; £5) is a worthwhile stop if only for the in-house bakery in the adjacent hotel (❺) where guests can search for the resident ghost within the heavily wood-panelled and tartanized interior.

Cruises on the loch aboard Deep Scan Cruises run from the Loch Ness 2000 Exhibition (hourly; Easter–Sept 10am–6pm; 1hr; £10; ⓣ01456/450218), while the *Nessie Hunter* (hourly: Easter–Dec 9am–6pm; 50min; £10; ⓣ01456/450395, ⓦwww.loch-ness-cruises.com) can be booked at the Nessieland Monster Centre; there's a decent little shop here where all the crafts are made in Scotland. If you want to turn your back on all the hype, you could opt for the well-run **pony trekking** available at Borlum Farm (ⓣ01456/450220, ⓦwww.borlum.co.uk; from £23/hr) just two minutes' drive north of Urquhart Castle.

Most photographs allegedly showing the monster have been taken a couple of miles east of Drumnadrochit, around the thirteenth-century ruined lochside **Castle Urquhart** (daily: April–Sept 9.30am–6pm; Oct–March 9.30am–5pm; HS; £6.50). Built as a strategic base to guard the Great Glen, the castle was taken by Edward I of England and later held by Robert the Bruce against Edward III, only to be blown up in 1692 to prevent it from falling to the Jacobites. Today it's one of Scotland's classic picture-postcard ruins, particularly splendid at night when it's floodlit and the crowds have gone. In the small visitor centre, a short film (in six languages) highlights the turbulent history of the castle. There's a footpath alongside the A82 road between Drumnadrochit and the castle, though the constant stream of cars, caravans and tour buses doesn't make it a particularly pleasant stroll.

Practicalities

Drumnadrochit's helpful **tourist office** (April, May, Sept & Oct Mon–Sat; June–Aug daily; ⓣ01456/459086) shares space with a Highland Council service point in the middle of the main car park in the village. There's a good range of **accommodation** around Drumnadrochit and in the adjoining village of Lewiston. A very welcoming **B&B** is *Gillyflowers* (ⓣ01456/450641, ⓦwww.cali.co.uk/freeway/gillyflowers; ❷), a renovated 1780s farmhouse on a country lane in Lewiston. Otherwise, try the cluster of cottage B&Bs on the village green. **Hotels** include the friendly and simply furnished *Benleva* (ⓣ01456/450080, ⓦwww.benleva.co.uk; ❹), also in Lewiston, with several real ales on tap and locally sourced game on the menu. Two miles west of Drumnadrochit along the Cannich road is a particularly relaxed country-house hotel, *Polmaily House* (ⓣ01456/450343, ⓦwww.polmaily.co.uk; ❻), a family-oriented option with a heated indoor swimming pool and hot tub. For **hostel** beds you can also head for the immaculate and friendly *Loch Ness Backpackers Lodge* (ⓣ01456/450807, ⓦwww.lochness-backpackers.com; ❶), at Coiltie Farmhouse in Lewiston; follow the signs to the left when coming from Drumnadrochit. As well as dorms, the hostel has one double and two family rooms and facilities include bike rental and pony trekking. A special Sunday bus into Glen Affric can be arranged. There's scenic **camping** at Borlum Farm (see above).

Most of the hotels in the area – the *Benleva* in particular – serve good bar **food**; in Drumnadrochit try the *Karasia* Indian restaurant (ⓣ01456/450002) or the inexpensive *Glen Café* on the village green for reasonable lunches and snacks. Next door, the slightly more upmarket *Fiddlers' Café Bar* offers local steaks, salmon and hearty lunches.

Glen Affric

Due west of Drumnadrochit lies a vast area of high peaks, remote glens and few roads. The reason most folk head this way is to explore the picturesque native forests and grand mountains of **Glen Affric**, heaven for walkers, climbers and mountain bikers. If you're driving, note that the nearest petrol stations are in Drumnadrochit and Beauly to the north. Coming by public transport, Ross's Minibus (Ⓣ07801/988491, Ⓦwww.ross-minibuses.co.uk) runs a handy Dial-a-Bus service, as well as scheduled buses; its vehicles will also carry bikes if given advance notice. It's worth getting your hands on the excellent Glen Affric and Strathglass tourist map (Ⓦwww.glenaffric.info), usually available from local businesses and tourist offices.

The approach to the glen is through the small settlement of **CANNICH**, fourteen miles west of Drumnadrochit on the A831. Keen mountain bikers may want to stop off at the (free) **Balnain Bike Park** five miles west of Drumnadrochit where a variety of timber-based obstacles will test your riding ability. Look out for the Glen Urquhart Forestry Commission sign for access off the main road. Cannich is a quiet and uninspiring village, but it has an excellent campsite (Ⓣ01456/415364) where mountain bikes can be rented, and there's also the friendly neighbouring *Glen Affric Backpackers Hostel* (Ⓣ01456/415263), which offers inexpensive twin or four-bed rooms. For food, the best option is the chalet-like *Bog Cotton Café* (daily 9am–3pm) at the campsite. Otherwise, try the modest *Slaters Arms* or buy supplies from the village Spar shop.

Hemmed in by a string of Munros, Glen Affric is great for picnics and pottering. From the car park at the head of the single-track road along the glen, ten miles southwest of Cannich, there's a selection of **walks**: the trip around **Loch Affric** will take you a good five hours but allows you to appreciate the glen, its wildlife and Caledonian pine and birch woods in all their remote splendour. For details of **volunteer work** in Glen Affric helping with the restoration of the woodland, get in touch with Trees for Life (Ⓦwww.treesforlife.org.uk). You could also do some serious **hiking**. Munro-baggers (see p.12) are normally much in evidence, and it is possible to tramp 25 miles all the way through Glen Affric to Shiel Bridge, on the west coast near Kyle of Lochalsh. The utterly remote *Allt Beithe* SYHA hostel (Ⓣ0845/293 7373, Ⓦwww.syha.org.uk; April–Oct) near the head of Glen Affric, makes a convenient if rudimentary stopover halfway. A wind turbine and solar panels provide the hostel with electricity, but note that you'll need to bring all your own food: the nearest shop is 21 miles away.

Inverness

Straddling a nexus of major road and rail routes, **INVERNESS** is the busy hub of the Highlands, and an inevitable port of call if you're exploring the region by public transport. Over a hundred miles from any other major settlement yet with a population rapidly approaching 100,000, Inverness is the only city in the Highlands. Crowned by a pink crenellated **castle** and lavishly decorated with flowers, the city centre still has some hints of its medieval street layout, though unsightly concrete blocks do an efficient job of masking it. Within walking distance of the centre are peaceful spots along by the Ness, leafy parks and friendly B&Bs located in prosperous-looking stone houses.

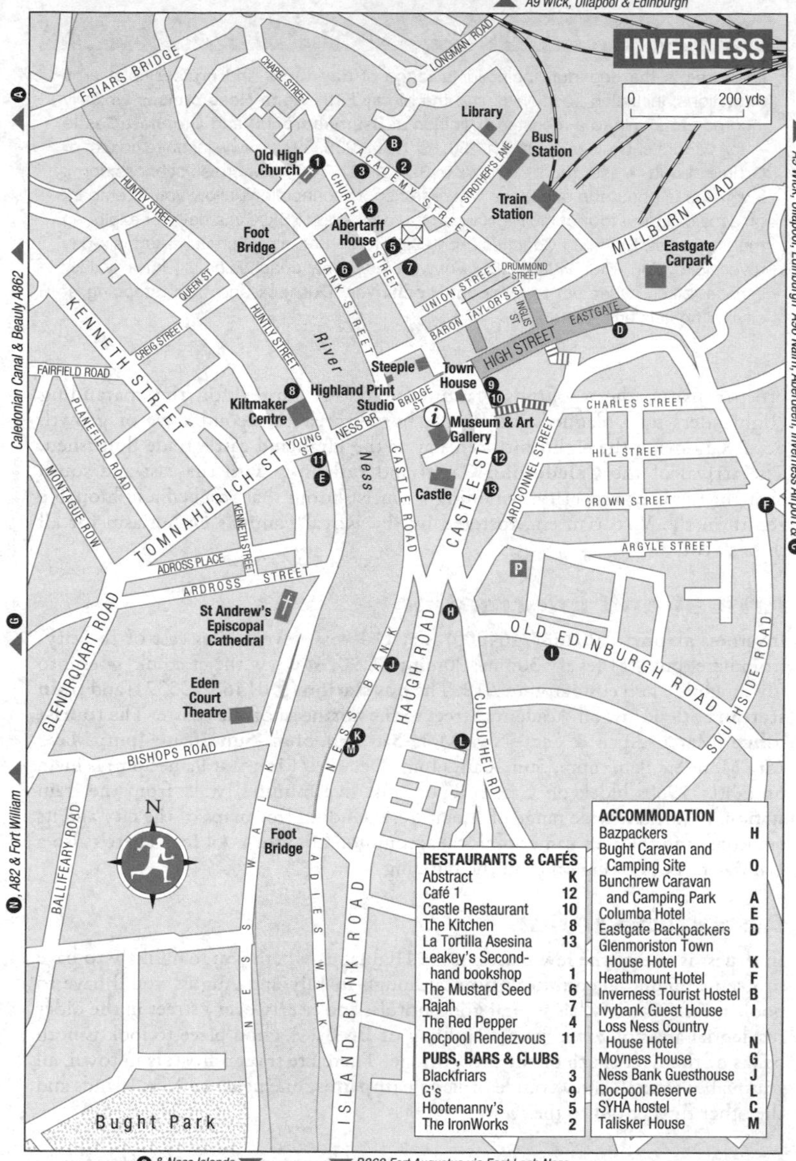

The sheltered **harbour** and proximity to the open sea made Inverness an important entrepôt and shipbuilding centre during medieval times. David I, who first imposed a feudal system on Scotland, erected a castle on the banks of the Ness to oversee maritime trade in the early twelfth century, promoting it to royal burgh status soon after. Bolstered by receipts from the lucrative export of leather, salmon and timber, the town grew to become the kingdom's most

Tours and cruises from Inverness

Inverness is the departure point for a range of **day-tours** and **cruises** to nearby attractions, including Loch Ness and the Moray Firth. **Loch Ness cruises** typically incorporate a visit to a monster exhibition at **Drumnadrochit** and **Urquhart Castle** – try Jacobite Cruises (from £11.50; ⓣ01463/233999, ⓦwww.jacobite.co.uk) or **Cruise Loch Ness** (from £11; ⓣ01320/366277, ⓦwww.cruiselochness.com). Inverness is about the one place where transport connections allow you to embark on a major **grand tour** of the Highlands or a round-trip to Skye in a day. For exploring the northwest, Dearman Coaches (April–Sept Mon–Sat, also Sun July–Aug; six-day rover ticket £36; ⓣ01349/883585, ⓦwww.timdearmancoaches.co.uk) have a daily service (bikes accepted) to **Ullapool**, **Lochinver**, **Durness** and back stopping at several hostels en route.

prosperous northern outpost, and an obvious target for the marauding Highlanders who plagued this remote border area. A second wave of growth occurred during the eighteenth century as the Highland cattle trade flourished. The arrival of the **Caledonian Canal** and **rail** links with the east and south brought further prosperity, heralding a tourist boom that reached a fashionable zenith in the Victorian era, fostered by the Royal Family's enthusiasm for all things Scottish.

Arrival and information

Inverness **airport** (ⓣ01667/464000) is at Dalcross, seven miles east of the city; from here, bus #11 (every 30min; 20min; £2.90; ⓦwww.thejet.co.uk) goes into town, while a taxi costs around £12. The **bus station** (ⓣ01463/233371) and **train station** both lie just off Academy Street to the northeast of the centre. The **tourist office** (March–April & Sept–Nov Mon–Sat 9am–5pm, Sun 10am–4pm; May–Aug Mon–Sat 9am–6pm, Sun 10am–4pm; Dec–Feb Mon–Sat 9am–5pm) is in an unsightly 1960s block on Castle Wynd, just five minutes' walk from the train station. It stocks a wide range of literature, including free maps of the city and its environs, and the staff can book local accommodation for a £4 fee. There's also a CalMac ferry booking office in the building.

Accommodation

Inverness is one of the few places in the Highlands where you're unlikely to have problems finding **accommodation**, although in July and August you'll have to book ahead. The city has several good **hotels**, and nearly every street in the older residential areas of town has a sprinkling of **B&Bs**. A good place to look is both banks of the river south of the Ness Bridge. There are several **hostels** in town, all reasonably central, and a couple of large **campsites**, one near the Ness Islands and the other further out to the west.

Hotels

Columba Hotel 7 Ness Walk ⓣ08444/146600, ⓦwww.oxfordhotelsandinns.com/ourhotels/Columba. A great location on the river and a handsome Victorian building make this a decent city-centre option. 6

Glenmoriston Town House Hotel 20 Ness Bank ⓣ01463/223777, ⓦwww.glenmoristontownhouse.com. An upmarket, contemporary hotel by the riverside just a few minutes' walk from the town centre. Muted decor and a good dining experience at *Abstract*. 7

Loch Ness Country House Hotel Off the A82 Fort William Rd ⓣ01463/230512, ⓦwww.lochnesscountryhousehotel.co.uk. Luxurious country-house hotel, three miles west of central Inverness. Attractive modern Scottish food, fine wines and more than two hundred malts, as well as very comfortable and spacious rooms. ❽

Heathmount Hotel Kingsmill Road ☎01463/235877, ⓦwww.heathmounthotel.com. Reasonably central boutique hotel with rather overstyled but comfortable rooms. ❻

Rocpool Reserve Culduthel Road ☎01463/240089, ⓦwww.rocpool.com. Only a 10min walk south from the castle, this acclaimed boutique hotel and restaurant offers hip, chic and decadent rooms and upmarket modern dining. ❽

B&Bs

Ivybank Guest House 28 Old Edinburgh Rd ☎01463/232796, ⓦwww.ivybankguesthouse.com. A grand Georgian home just up the hill from the castle, with open fires and a lovely homely interior. ❷

Moyness House 6 Bruce Gardens ☎01463/233836, ⓦwww.moyness.co.uk. Warm, welcoming, upmarket B&B on the west side of Inverness, with original Victorian features and a nice walled garden. ❺

Ness Bank Guesthouse 7 Ness Bank ☎01463/232939, ⓦwww.nessbankguesthouse.co.uk. Five lovely, tasteful rooms in Grade II listed Victorian house on the river; good for large get-togethers. ❷

Talisker House 25 Ness Bank ☎01463/236221, ⓦwww.scotland-inverness.co.uk/talisker. Pleasant 1830s B&B in a riverside location just a 5min walk from the centre. ❹

Hostels

Bazpackers Top of Castle St ☎01463/717663, ⓦwww.bazpackershostel.co.uk. The most cosy and relaxed of the city's hostels, with more than thirty beds including two doubles and a twin (❶); some dorms are mixed. Good location, great views and a garden, which is used for barbecues.

Eastgate Backpackers Hostel 38 Eastgate ☎01463/718756, ⓦwww.eastgatebackpackers.com. Well-maintained former hotel with single, twin and double rooms (❶). Bike rental, internet access and left-luggage storage.

Inverness Tourist Hostel 24 Rose St ☎01463/241962, ⓦwww.invernesshostel.com. A central, clean, well-equipped sixty-bed hostel offering top-notch amenities including wide-screen TVs and internet access.

SYHA hostel Victoria Drive, off Millburn Road, about three-quarters of a mile east of the centre ☎01463/231771, ⓦwww.syha.org.uk. Well equipped with large kitchens and communal areas, and ten four-bed family rooms among the 166-bed total. However, it's quite far from the centre, and the building is devoid of character.

Campsites

Bught Caravan and Camping Site Bught Park ☎01463/236920, ⓦwww.invernesscaravanpark.com. Inverness's main campsite, south of the centre, on the west bank of the river near the sports centre. Good facilities, but it can get very crowded at the height of the season. Easter to mid-Sept.

Bunchrew Caravan and Camping Park Bunchrew, 3 miles west of Inverness on the A862 ☎01463/237802, ⓦwww.bunchrew-caravanpark.co.uk. Well-equipped site with lots of space for tents on the shores of the Beauly Firth, plus hot water, showers, laundry and a shop. Very popular with families. March–Nov.

The Town

Looming above the city and dominating the horizon is **Inverness Castle**, a predominantly nineteenth-century red-sandstone building perched above the river. The original castle formed the core of the ancient town, which had rapidly developed as a port trading with Europe after its conversion to Christianity by St Columba in the sixth century. Robert the Bruce wrested the castle back from the English during the Wars of Independence, destroying much of the structure in the process, and while held by the Jacobites in both the 1715 and the 1745 rebellions, it was blown up by them to prevent it falling into government hands. Today's edifice houses the Sheriff Court and is not open to the general public. However, there are good views down the River Ness and various plaques and statues in the grounds including a small plinth marking the start of the 73-mile Great Glen Way.

Below the castle, the revamped **IMAG** (Inverness Museum and Art Gallery; Mon–Sat 10am–5pm, July & Aug Sun 1–5pm; free; ⓦwww.invernessmuseum.com) on Castle Wynd offers an insight into the social history of the Highlands, with treasures from the times of the Picts and Vikings, taxidermy exhibits such as

"Felicity" the puma, caught in Cannich in 1980, and interactive features including an introduction to the Gaelic language. It also has impressive temporary art exhibitions.

Leading north from the castle, medieval **Church Street** is home to the town's oldest surviving buildings. On the corner with Bridge Street stands the **Steeple** (1791), whose spire had to be straightened after an earth tremor in 1816. The **Old High Church**, founded in 1171 and rebuilt on several occasions since, stands just along the street, hemmed in by a walled graveyard. Those Jacobites who survived the massacre of Culloden were brought here and incarcerated prior to their execution in the cemetery. If you look carefully you may see the bullet holes left on gravestones by the firing squads.

The truth about tartan

To much of the world, **tartan** is synonymous with Scotland. It's the natural choice of packaging for Scottish exports from shortbread to Sean Connery, and when the Scottish football team travels abroad to play a fixture, the high-spirited "Tartan Army" of fans is never far behind. Tartan is big business for the tourist industry, yet the truth is that romantic fiction and commercial interest have enclosed this ancient Highland art form within an almost insurmountable wall of myth.

The original form of tartan, the kind that long ago was called **Helande**, was a fine, hard and almost showerproof cloth spun in Highland villages from the wool of the native sheep, dyed with preparations of local plants and with patterns woven by artist-weavers. It was worn as a huge single piece of cloth, or **plaid**, which was belted around the waist and draped over the upper body, rather like a knee-length toga. The natural colours of old tartans were clear but soft, and the broken pattern gave superb camouflage, unlike modern versions, where garish, clashing colours are often used to create impact.

The myth-makers were about four centuries ahead of themselves in dressing up the warriors of the film *Braveheart* in plaid: in fact tartan did not become popular in the Lowlands until the beginning of the eighteenth century, when it was adopted as the anti-Union badge of the **Jacobites**. After Culloden, a ban on the wearing of tartan in the Highlands lasted some 25 years; in that time it became a fondly held emblem for emigrant Highlanders in the colonies and was incorporated into the uniforms of the new Highland regiments in the British Army. Then **Sir Walter Scott** set to work glamorizing the clans, dressing George IV in a kilt (and, just as controversially, flesh-coloured tights) for his visit to Edinburgh in 1822. By the time Queen Victoria set the royal seal of approval on both the Highlands and tartan with her extended annual holidays at Balmoral, the concept of tartan as formal dress rather than rough Highland wear was assured.

Hand in hand with the gentrification of the kilt came "rules" about the correct form of attire and the idea that every clan had its own distinguishing tartan. To have the right to wear tartan, one had to belong, albeit remotely, to a clan, and so the way was paved for the "what's-my-tartan?" lists that appear in tartan picture-books and souvenir shops. Great feats of genealogical gymnastics were performed: where lists left gaps, a marketing phenomenon of themed tartans developed, with new patterns for different districts, companies and even football teams being produced.

Scotsmen today will commonly wear the **kilt** for weddings and other formal occasions; properly made kilts, however – comprising some four yards of one hundred percent wool – are likely to set you back £300 or more, with the rest of the regalia at least doubling that figure. If the contents of your sporran don't stretch that far, most places selling kilts will rent outfits on a daily basis. The best place to find better-quality material is a recognized Highland outfitter rather than a souvenir shop: in Inverness, try the Scottish Kiltmaker Visitor Centre at the Highland House of Fraser shop (see opposite).

Along the River Ness

Just across Ness Bridge from Bridge Street is the **Scottish Kiltmaker Visitor Centre** in Highland House of Fraser (daily 9am–9pm, open later summer; £2). Entered through the factory shop, this imaginative small attraction, complete with the outfits worn by actors for the *Braveheart* and *Rob Roy* films, sets out everything you ever wanted to know about tartan. There's an interesting seven-minute film and on weekdays (9am–5pm) you can watch various tartan products being made in the workshop. The finished products are, of course, on sale in the showroom downstairs, along with all manner of Highland knitwear, woven woollies and Harris tweed.

On the opposite bank, the new base of the **Highland Print Studio** (Ⓣ01463/718999, Ⓦwww.highlandprintstudio.co.uk) is well worth a visit, both to browse the collection of prints for sale, or to improve your artistic skills: they run courses in all types of printmaking, and have an impressive digital suite.

Rising from the west bank directly opposite the castle, **St Andrews Episcopal Cathedral** (built 1869) was intended by its architects to be one of the grandest buildings in Scotland. However, funds ran out before the giant twin spires of the original design could be completed. The interior is pretty ordinary, too, though it does claim an unusual octagonal chapterhouse. Alongside the cathedral, the **Eden Court Theatre and Cinema** (Ⓦwww.eden-court.co.uk) is a major multi-arts venue in Scotland and hub for theatrical performances in the Highlands.

From here, you can wander a mile or so upriver to the peaceful **Ness Islands**, an attractive, informal public park reached and linked by footbridges. Laid out with mature trees and shrubs, the islands are the favourite haunt of local anglers. Half a mile further upstream, the river runs close to the **Caledonian Canal**, designed by Thomas Telford in the early nineteenth century as a link between the east and west coasts, joining lochs Ness, Oich, Lochy and Linnhe. Today its main use is recreational, and there are cruises through part of it to Loch Ness (see box, p.452), while the towpath provides relaxing walks with good views.

Eating and drinking

Inverness has lots of places to eat, including a few excellent-quality gourmet options, while for the budget-conscious there's no shortage of **pubs**, **cafés** and **restaurants** around the town centre. **Takeaways** cluster on Young Street, just across the river, and at the ends of Eastgate and Academy Street.

The liveliest **nightlife** revolves around the pubs and, on Friday and Saturday nights, in nightclubs such as *G's* on Castle Street. The *Ironworks* on Academy Street (Ⓦwww.ironworksvenue.com) hosts touring bands. The far end of Academy Street features a cluster of good **pubs**; there's a lively atmosphere at *Blackfriars*, where you can enjoy folk and ceilidh music five nights a week. *Hootananny's*, on Church Street, continues to be a popular and lively pub with excellent ceilidhs, real ale and tasty "Thai Tananny" bar food.

Cafés

Castle Restaurant 41 Castle St. There's little finery here but this long-established family-run café does a roaring trade in hearty breakfasts, meat pies and great haggis. Open at 8am for breakfast; closed Sun.

Leakey's Second-Hand Bookshop Church St Ⓣ01463/239947. Prise yourself away from the old books and maps for delicious soup and open sandwiches.

The Red Pepper 74 Church St. Reasonable coffee-bar hangout with freshly made sandwiches. Takeaway available.

Restaurants

Abstract 20 Ness Bank Ⓣ01463/223777, Ⓦwww.abstractrestaurant.com. This award-winning French restaurant within *Glenmoriston Town House Hotel* (see p.458) serves delicious creations with panache; mains start at £14.

Closed Mon. *The Contrast Brasserie* (☎01463/227889) is more affordable and relaxed but still good quality.
Café 1 75 Castle St ☎01463/226200. Contemporary Scottish cooking including venison fillet and gateaux of haggis, served in a bistro-style setting. Its "express" pre-theatre menu (until 6.45pm) is very good value (£9.50 for two courses). Closed Sun.
The Kitchen 15 Huntly St ☎01463/259119, Ⓦwww.kitchenrestaurant.co.uk. Beneath a distinctive wavy roof, this stylish sister restaurant of *The Mustard Seed* has riverside views and thoughtfully prepared seafood and meat dishes (around £15).
La Tortilla Asesina 99 Castle St ☎01463/709809. Simple but lively tapas restaurant, serving all the old favourites as well as some "tartan tapas" concentrating on local ingredients.
The Mustard Seed 16 Fraser St ☎01463/220220, Ⓦwww.mustardseedrestaurant.co.uk. Airy, welcoming restaurant with great-value Mediterranean-style lunches and tasty, à la carte dining: a starter and a main will set you back around £25.
Rajah Post Office Ave ☎01463/237190. One of a couple of decent and affordable Indian restaurants in town, tucked away in a backstreet basement.
Rocpool Rendezvous 1 Ness Walk ☎01463/717274. Another of the city's excellent, smartish dining options, with a smart contemporary setting, attentive staff and delicious bistro food. Around £30 for a three-course meal.

Listings

Bike rental Fancy a Ride? (☎07902/242301, Ⓦwww.tickettoridehighlands.co.uk; from £20/day) will deliver bikes to you and also offer tours. For cycle kit try Bikes of Inverness, 39 Grant St ☎01463/225965.
Bookshops Leakey's, Scotland's largest used bookshop, is located in a former church on Church St and filled with almost 100,000 secondhand books. A great spot to browse, with a warming wood stove in winter and a cosy, inexpensive café (see p.461). There's also Waterstones at 50–52 High St.
Car rental Budget, Railway Terrace, behind the train station (☎01463/713333); Turner Hire Drive, Lotland St (☎01463/716058); Focus Vehicle Rental, 36 Shore St (☎01463/709517); Aberdeen 4x4 Self-Drive, 15b Harbour Rd (☎01463/871083).
Cinemas Vue, Inverness Retail Park, Eastfield Way ☎08712/240240; Eden Court Theatre and Cinema, Bishops Road ☎01463/234234.
Dentist Contact the Scotland-wide National Health Service Line (☎08454/242424) for local and emergency dentists or The Dental Clinic within Optical Express on High St (☎01463/248871; Mon–Sat 9am–5pm).
Hospital Raigmore Hospital (☎01463/704000) on the southeastern outskirts of town close to the A9.
Internet Highland libraries provide 30min free internet access.
Laundry Young Street Laundrette, 17 Young St ☎01463/242507.
Left luggage Train-station lockers cost £3–5 for 24hr (can only deposit 8am–6.30pm); the left-luggage room in the bus station costs £1 per item per day (Mon–Sat 8.30am–6pm, Sun 12.30pm–6.30pm).
Library Inverness Library (Mon–Fri 9am–6.30pm, Sat 9am–5pm; ☎01463/236463), housed in a Neoclassical building on the northeast side of the bus station, has an excellent genealogical research unit (Mon–Fri 10am–1pm & 2–5pm; ext 9).
Outdoor supplies Macpherson's "traditional mountaineering shop", 34 Church St ☎01463/711427; Tiso, 41 High St ☎01463/716617; Tiso Outdoor Experience, 2 Henderson Rd, Longman Estate ☎01463/729171.
Pharmacy Boots, 1–11 Eastgate Shopping Centre (Mon–Wed & Fri 8.45am–6pm, Thurs 8.45am–7pm, Sat 8.30am–6pm, Sun 11am–5pm; ☎01463/225167).
Post office 14–16 Queensgate (Mon–Thurs 9am–5.30pm, Fri 9.30am–5.30pm, Sat 9am–1pm ☎01463/234111); also noon–5pm at Tesco's.
Public toilets Just behind tourist information on Castle St.
Radio The local radio station is Moray Firth Radio on 97.4FM and 1107AM.
Sports centre Inverness Sports Centre & Aquadome leisure pool (Mon–Fri 10am–8pm, Sat & Sun 9am–5pm; ☎01463/667502), a mile or so south of the town centre off the A82, has a large pool with flumes and waves, also gym, health suite and climbing wall.
Taxis Tartan Taxis ☎01463/222777. Expect to pay £14 from city centre to airport.

Around Inverness

A string of worthwhile sights punctuates the approach to Inverness along the main route from Aberdeen. The low-key resort of **Nairn**, with its long white-sand beaches and championship golf course, stands within striking distance of several monuments, including whimsical **Cawdor Castle**, best known for its role in Shakespeare's *Macbeth*, and **Fort George**, one of several impressive Hanoverian bastions erected in the wake of the Jacobite rebellion. The infamous battle and ensuing massacre that ended Bonnie Prince Charlie's uprising took place on the outskirts of Inverness at **Culloden**, where a brand-new visitor centre and memorial stones beside a heather-clad moor recall the gruesome events of 1746. The area's gentle, undulating green landscape is well tended and tranquil, a fertile contrast to the windswept moorland and mountains which almost surround it.

East of Inverness

East of Inverness lies the fertile, sheltered coastal strip of the **Moray Firth** and its hinterland, the pastoral countryside contrasting with the scenic splendours you'll encounter once you head further north into the Highlands. Primary target is **Culloden**, the most poignant battlefield site in Scotland, where Bonnie Prince Charlie's Jacobites were routed in 1746. Further east are **Cawdor Castle** and **Fort George**, two of the best-preserved fortified structures in the Highlands. **Nairn**, the main town of the district, has a pretty harbour as well as appealing walks and cycle routes.

The overloaded A96 traverses this stretch and the region is well served by public transport, with all the historic sites and castles accessible on day-trips from Inverness, or en route to Aberdeen. Stagecoach buses (Ⓣ01463/239292) run from Inverness to Fort George, Cawdor Castle and Culloden.

Culloden

The windswept moorland of **CULLODEN** (site open all year; free), five miles east of Inverness, witnessed the last-ever battle on British soil when, on April 16, 1746, the Jacobite cause was finally subdued – a turning point in the history of the Scottish nation.

The second Jacobite rebellion had begun on August 19, 1745, with the raising of the Stuarts' standard at **Glenfinnan** on the west coast (see p.479). Shortly after, Edinburgh fell into Jacobite hands, and Bonnie Prince Charlie began his march on London. The English had appointed the ambitious young duke of Cumberland to command their forces, and his pursuit, together with bad weather and lack of funds, eventually forced the Jacobites to retreat north. They ended up at Culloden, where, ill fed and exhausted after a pointless night march, they were hopelessly outnumbered by the English. The open, flat ground of Culloden Moor was totally unsuitable for the Highlanders' style of courageous but undisciplined fighting, which needed steep hills and lots of cover to provide the element of surprise, and they were routed. After the battle, in which 1500 Highlanders were slaughtered (many of them as they lay wounded on the battlefield), Bonnie Prince Charlie fled west to the hills and islands, where loyal Highlanders sheltered and protected him. He eventually escaped to France, leaving his supporters to their fate – and, in effect, ushering in the end of the clan system. The clans were disarmed, the wearing of tartan and playing of bagpipes forbidden, and the chiefs became landlords greedy for higher and higher rents. The battle also unleashed an orgy of violent reprisals on Scotland, as unruly English troops raped and pillaged their way across the region; within a century, the Highland way of life had changed out of all recognition.

The dolphins of the Moray Firth

The **Moray Firth**, a great wedge-shaped bay forming the eastern coastline of the Highlands, is one of only three areas of UK waters that support a resident population of **dolphins**. More than a hundred of these beautiful, intelligent marine mammals live in the estuary, the most northerly breeding ground in Europe for this particular species – the bottle-nosed dolphin (*Tursiops truncatus*) – and you stand a good chance of spotting a few, either from the shore or a boat.

One of the best places in Scotland, if not in Europe, to look for them is **Chanonry Point**, on the Black Isle (see p.509) – a spit of sand protruding into a narrow, deep channel, where converging currents bring fish close to the surface, and thus the dolphins close to shore; a rising tide is the most likely time to see them. **Kessock Bridge**, one mile north of Inverness, is another prime dolphin-spotting location. You can go all the way down to the beach at the small village of North Kessock, underneath the road bridge or stop above the village in a car park just off the A9 at the **Dolphin and Seal Visitor Centre** and listening post (June–Sept daily 9.30am–12.30pm & 1–4.30pm; free), run by the Whale and Dolphin Conservation Society (WDCS), where hydrophones allow you to eavesdrop on the clicks and whistles of underwater conversations.

In addition, several companies run dolphin-spotting **boat trips** around the Moray Firth. However, researchers claim that the increased traffic is causing the dolphins unnecessary stress, particularly during the all-important breeding period when passing vessels are thought to force calves underwater for uncomfortably long periods. So if you decide to go on a cruise to see the dolphins, which also sometimes provides the chance of spotting minke whales, porpoises, seals and otters, make sure that the operator is a member of the Dolphin Space Programme's Accreditation Scheme (Ⓦwww.dolphinspace.org). Operators currently accredited include Phoenix, based in Nairn (Ⓣ01667/456078, Ⓦwww.phoenix-boat-trips.co.uk); Inverness Dolphin Cruises, Inverness (Ⓣ01463/717900, Ⓦwww.inverness-dolphin-cruises.co.uk); and the WDCS Wildlife Centre, Spey Bay (Ⓣ01343/820339). In addition, Dolphin Trips Avoch (Ⓣ01381/622383, Ⓦwww.dolphintripsavoch.co.uk) and the highly regarded Ecoventures, Cromarty (Ⓣ01381/600323, Ⓦwww.ecoventures.co.uk), are based on the Black Isle, on the northern side of the firth. Trips with all operators, most of which operate between April and October, cost from £10 for one hour. All these trips are very popular, so be sure to book them well in advance. To reach the dolphin sites, take bus #26 (Mon–Sat hourly, irregular Sun) from Inverness Union Street to Avoch, Rosemarkie and Cromarty. Bus #12 also stops in the village of North Kessock.

The visitor centre and battlefield

Today, this historic site annually attracts more than 200,000 visitors. Your first stop should be the superb eco-friendly **visitor centre** (daily: April–Oct 9am–6pm; Nov–March 10am–4pm; £10; NTS; Ⓦwww.nts.org.uk/culloden). The sleek building hosts costumed actors and state-of-the-art audiovisual and interactive technology, all employed to tell the tragedy of Culloden through the words, songs and poetic verse of locals and soldiers who experienced it. The *pièce de résistance* is the powerful "battle immersion theatre" where visitors are surrounded by lifelike cinematography and the sounds of the raging, bloody fight.

Go up to the rooftop platform to enjoy the elevated view across the actual battlefield before walking around the battle site, (armed with a free audioguide that makes use of global positioning software) on twenty-, forty-five- and sixty-minute routes with yet more evocative narrative. Flags mark out the positions of the two armies while simple headstones mark the **clan graves**. The **Field of the English**, for many years unmarked, is a mass grave for the fifty or so English soldiers who died. Half a mile east of the battlefield, just beyond the crossroads on the main road, is the **Cumberland Stone**, thought for many years to have been the point from where the duke watched the battle. It is more likely, however, that he was much further forward and simply used the stone for shelter. Elsewhere, the restored **Leanach cottage** marks the spot where thirty injured Jacobites were burnt alive.

Every April, on the Saturday closest to the date of the battle, there's a small commemorative service. The visitor centre has a reference library and will check for you if you think you have an ancestor who died here. The beautifully designed **café** serves good cooked meals, as well as snacks and cakes.

The Clava Cairns

If you're visiting Culloden with your own transport, it's worth making a short detour to the **Clava Cairns**, an impressive collection of prehistoric burial chambers clustered around the south bank of the River Nairn, a half-mile southeast of the battlefield. Erected some time before 2000 BC, the Bronze Age cairns, which are encircled by standing stones in a spinney of mature beech trees, are of two different kinds: one large and one very small **ring-cairn**, and two **passage graves**, which have a narrow passageway from edge to centre. Though cremated remains have been found in both types of structure, and unburnt remains in the passage graves, little is known about the nomadic herdsmen who are thought to have built them. For refreshments, pop into the refurbished *Culloden Moor Inn* near the Cairns and Culloden battlefield.

Cawdor Castle

The pretty village of **CAWDOR**, eight miles east of Culloden, is the site of **Cawdor Castle** (May–Oct daily 10am–5.30pm; £8.30, £4.50 gardens & nature trails only; Ⓦ www.cawdorcastle.com), a setting intimately linked to Shakespeare's *Macbeth*: the fulfilment of the witches' prediction that Macbeth was to become thane of Cawdor sets off his tragic desire to be king. Though visitors arrive here in their droves each summer because of the site's literary associations, the castle, which dates from the early fourteenth century, could not possibly have witnessed the grisly historical events on which the Bard's drama was based. However, the immaculately restored monument – a fairy-tale affair of towers, turrets, hidden passageways, dungeons, gargoyles and crenellations whimsically shooting off from the original keep – is still well worth a visit.

Six centuries on, the Campbells of Cawdor still spend their winters here, and the castle feels like a family home, albeit one with tapestries, pictures and opulent furniture (all catalogued with mischievous humour). As you explore, look out for the **Thorn Tree Room**, a vaulted chamber complete with the remains of an ancient holly tree that has been carbon-dated to 1372 – an ancient pagan fertility symbol believed to ward off fairies and evil spirits. The **grounds** of the castle are impressive, with an attractive walled garden, a maze, small golf course, putting green and nature trails. It's also worth visiting the village for a drink or delicious meal at the traditional *Cawdor Tavern*. To get here, take **bus** #12 from Inverness.

Fort George

Eight miles of undulating coastal farmland separate Cawdor Castle from **Fort George** (daily: April–Sept 9.30am–5.30pm; Oct–March 9.30am–4.30pm; HS; £6.70), an old Hanoverian bastion with walls a mile long, considered by military architectural historians to be one of the finest fortifications in Europe. Crowning a sandy spit that juts into the middle of the Moray Firth, it was built between 1747 and 1769 as a base for George II's army, in case the Highlanders should attempt to rekindle the Jacobite flame. By the time of its completion, however, the uprising had been firmly quashed and the fort has been used ever since as barracks; note the armed sentries at the main entrance and the periodic crack of live gunfire from the nearby firing ranges.

Apart from the sweeping panoramic views across the Firth from its ramparts, the main incentive to visit Fort George is the **Regimental Museum** of the Queen's Own Highlanders. It displays a predictable array of regimental silver, coins, moth-eaten uniforms and medals, along with some macabre war trophies, ranging from bloodstained nineteenth-century Sudanese battle robes to Iraqi gas masks gathered in the first Gulf War. The **chapel** is also worth a look – squat and solid outside, and all light and grace within.

Walking on the northern, grass-covered casemates, which look out into the estuary, you may be lucky enough to see a school of bottle-nosed **dolphins** (see box, p.464) swimming in with the tide. This is also a good spot for birdwatching: a colony of kittiwakes occupies the fort's slate rooftops. B**us** #11 from Queensgate in Inverness serves the fort.

Nairn

One of the driest and sunniest places in the whole of Scotland, **NAIRN**, sixteen miles east of Inverness, began its days as a peaceful community of fishermen and farmers. The former spoke Gaelic, the latter English, allowing James VI to boast that a town in his kingdom was so large that people at one end of the main street could not understand those at the other end. Nairn became popular in Victorian times, when the train line offered a convenient link to its revitalizing sea air and mild climate, and today the 11,000-strong population still relies on tourism, with all the ingredients for a traditional seaside holiday – sandy beach, ice-cream shops and fish-and-chip stalls. It boasts two championship golf courses, and Thomas Telford's **harbour** is filled with leisure craft rather than fishing boats. The **Nairn Museum**, Viewfield House, King Street (May–Oct Mon–Fri 10am–4.30pm, Sat 10am–1pm; £3; Ⓦwww.nairnmuseum.co.uk), provides a general insight into the history and prehistory of the area; the **Fishertown Room** illustrates the parsimonious and puritanical life of the fishing families.

Nairn no longer has a tourist office but there is a freephone accommodation booking service within the main library at 68 High St. For **places to stay**, the pick of the bunch is the luxurious *Boath House Hotel and Spa* (Ⓣ01667/454896, Ⓦwww.boath-house.com; ❽) in the village of Auldearn just outside Nairn, a fine Georgian country house set in magnificent gardens where guests are lavished with attention and mouthwatering (if pricey) cooking that draws upon organic produce and regional dairy, fish and meat suppliers. For an affordable taste of such luxury, book a lunchtime table in the Michelin-starred restaurant. Alternatively, there's *Cawdor House*, a bright and attractive **B&B** *(*Ⓣ01667/455855, Ⓦwww.cawdorhousenairn.co.uk; ❹*)*, and *Greenlawns*, 13 Seafield St (Ⓣ01667/452738, Ⓦwww.greenlawns.uk.com; ❸), a spacious friendly home where kedgeree and smoked salmon feature on the breakfast menu.

For a reasonably priced **meal** try the family-run Italian restaurant in the *Aurora Hotel*, 2 Academy St (Ⓣ01667/453551); *The Classroom*, 1 Cawdor St, continues to be Nairn's most popular coffee shop serving tasty light bites, lunches and dinners (daily 11am–11pm). **Bike rental** is available from Bike and Buggy at 2 Leopold St (Ⓣ01667/455416, Ⓦwww.bikeandbuggy.co.uk). Delnies Wood, two miles west of Nairn, has an excellent campsite (April–Oct; Ⓣ01667/455281).

West of Inverness

West of Inverness, the Moray Firth becomes the **Beauly Firth**, a sheltered sea loch bounded by the Black Isle in the north and the wooded hills of the Aird to the south. At the head of the firth is the medieval village of **Beauly**, seat of the colourful Lovat clan, with the small settlement of **Muir of Ord**, known for its whisky, close by. Most northbound traffic uses Kessock Bridge to cross the Moray Firth from Inverness, so this whole area is quieter, and the A862, which skirts the shoreline and the mud flats, offers a more scenic alternative to the faster A9.

Beauly

The self-confident stone-built village of **BEAULY** lies ten miles west of Inverness, at the point where the Beauly River – one of Scotland's most renowned salmon-fishing streams – flows into the Firth. It's arranged around a single main street that widens into a spacious marketplace, at the north end of which stand the skeletal red-sandstone remains of **Beauly Priory** (daily 9.30am–4.30pm; free). Founded in 1230 by the Bisset family for the Valliscaulian order, and later becoming Cistercian, it was destroyed during the Reformation and is now in ruins. Beside this, the refurbished **Beauly Centre** (daily 10am–6pm) provides local tourist information and a bookshop. Just outside of town, the **Kilmorack Gallery** (Ⓣ01463/783230, Ⓦwww.kilmorackgallery.co.uk) is based in a beautiful vaulted church, and shows changing exhibitions of contemporary Scottish art: a refreshing change from the more twee galleries hereabouts.

Beauly has a surprising number of **places to stay**. The most comfortable is the modern *Priory Hotel* (Ⓣ01463/782309, Ⓦwww.priory-hotel.com; ❻) on the picturesque village square. The *Lovat Arms Hotel* (Ⓣ01463/782313, Ⓦwww.lovatarms.com; ❻), at the opposite end of the main street, is more traditional and has a decent restaurant. Within the row of Victorian houses past the *Lovat Arms* visitors will find several reasonable B&Bs, including *Heathmount Guest House* (Ⓣ01463/782411; ❷). For a bolt-hole in the tranquil hamlet of Struy in Strathglass, nine miles south on the A831, the rustic *Cnoc Hotel* (Ⓣ01463/761264, Ⓦwww.thecnochotel.co.uk; ❺) is a good bet for hearty food and a comfortable bed. For daytime **eating** in Beauly, the *Corner on the Square* delicatessen on the High Street offers tasty home-baked quiches and cakes (open till 10pm on Thurs).

Around Beauly

MUIR OF ORD, a sprawling village four miles north of Beauly, is notable only for the **Glen Ord Distillery** (Jan–March & Oct–Dec Mon–Fri 11am–3pm; April–Sept Mon–Fri 10am–5pm, July–Sept also Sat & Sun noon–4pm; £5 including discount voucher; Ⓦwww.discovering-distilleries.com/glenord) on its northern outskirts. Here, as at other distilleries, the mysteries of whisky production are explained with a tour that winds up in the cellars, where you get to sample the 12-year-old Glen Ord single malt. No buses stop outside the distillery, but it's a ten-minute walk from Muir of Ord, which you can reach on **buses** #17, #18, #19 from Union Street in Inverness; these travel several times a day via Beauly (Mon–Sat) to Dingwall. More helpfully, the **train** from Inverness stops at Muir of Ord station (20min; Mon–Sat 6 daily; 2 on Sun).

You can also visit a family-run **winery** at **Moniack Castle** (April–Oct Mon–Sat 10am–5pm; Nov–March Mon–Fri 11am–4pm; £2), four miles east of Beauly, just off the A862, where you can taste and buy more than thirty different home-made products, including silver-birch or meadowsweet wine, sloe-berry liqueur, juniper chutney and rosehip jam.

Travel details

Trains

Fort William to: Crianlarich (Mon–Sat 3 daily, 2 on Sun; 1hr 50min); Glasgow (Mon–Sat 3 daily, 2 on Sun; 3hr 50min); London (1 daily, 2 nightly; 9hr 25min–12hr); Mallaig (Mon–Sat 3 daily, 2 on Sun; 1hr 25min).

Inverness to: Aberdeen (Mon–Sat 10 daily; 5 on Sun; 2hr 15min); Aviemore (Mon–Sat 9 daily, 5 on Sun; 40min); Edinburgh (Mon–Sat 5 daily, 3 on Sun; 3hr 30min); Glasgow (Mon–Sat 3 daily; 3 on Sun; 3hr 20min); Kyle of Lochalsh (Mon–Sat 2–3 daily, 1 on Sun; 2hr 25min); London (Mon–Fri & 4 on Sun, 1 nightly; 8hr 30min–11hr); Thurso (Mon–Sat 2 daily, 1 on Sun; 3hr 25min); Wick (Mon–Sat 3 daily, 1 on Sun; 4hr 20min).

Buses

Fort William to: Drumnadrochit (8 daily; 1hr 30min); Edinburgh (4 daily; 4hr); Fort Augustus (5 daily; 1hr); Glasgow (4 daily; 3hr); Inverness (6 daily; 2hr); Mallaig (Mon–Fri 1daily; 1hr 20min); Oban (Mon–Sat 4 daily; 1hr 30min); Portree, Skye (2 daily; 3hr).

Inverness to: Aberdeen (hourly; 3hr 40min); Aviemore (Mon–Sat 6, 5 Sun; 45min); Drumnadrochit (8 daily; 25min); Fort Augustus (5 daily; 1hr); Fort William (6 daily; 2hr); Glasgow (6 daily direct; 3hr 35min–4hr 25min); Kyle of Lochalsh (3 daily; 2hr); Nairn (hourly; 50min); Perth (10 daily; 2hr 35min); Portree (3 daily; 3hr); Thurso (Mon–Sat 5 daily, 2 on Sun; 3hr 30min); Ullapool (2 Mon, Tues, Thurs & Sat; 3 Wed & Fri; 2hr 25min); Wick (Mon–Sat 3 daily, 2 on Sun; 3hr).

Flights

Inverness to: Dublin (Mon–Fri 2 daily, 1 on Sun; 1hr 30min); Edinburgh (Mon–Fri 2 daily, 1 Sat; 45min); Kirkwall (Mon–Fri 2 daily, 1 Sat & Sun; 45min); London (Gatwick 4 daily Mon–Fri, 3 Sat & Sun; Heathrow 1 daily; Luton Mon–Fri 1 daily, 2 daily Sat & Sun; 1hr 30min); Manchester (Mon–Fri 2 daily, 1 Sun; 1hr 25min); Shetland (Mon–Fri 2 daily; 1 daily Sat & Sun; 1hr 40min); Stornoway (Mon–Fri 4 daily, 2 on Sat, 1 on Sun daily; 40min).

13

The north and northwest Highlands

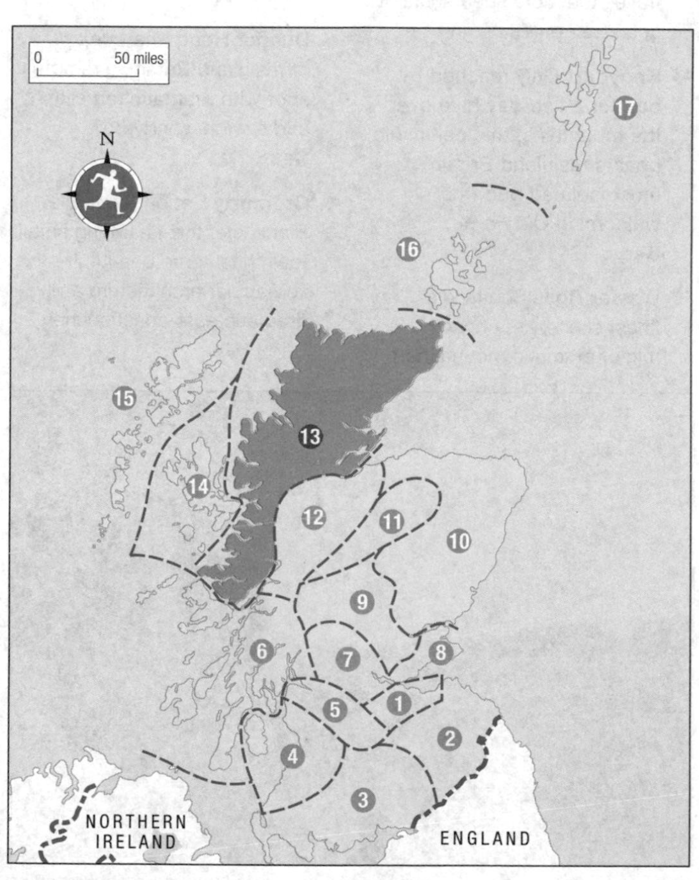

CHAPTER 13

Highlights

- **Loch Shiel** This romantic, unspoilt loch is where Bonnie Prince Charlie first raised an army. See p.475
- **West Highland Railway** From Glasgow to Mallaig via Fort William; the further north you travel, the more spectacular it gets. See p.479
- **Knoydart** Only reached by boat or a two-day hike over the mountains, this peninsula boasts mainland Britain's most isolated pub, the welcoming *Old Forge*. See p.481
- **Wester Ross** Scotland's finest scenery – a heady mix of dramatic mountains, rugged sea lochs, sweeping bays, scattered islands and idyllic Applecross. See p.488
- **Ceilidh Place, Ullapool** The best venue for modern Highland culture, with evenings of music, song and dance. See p.494
- **Dunnet Head** The true tip of mainland Britain, a remote spot with dramatic red cliffs and a wide, sandy bay. See p.506
- **Cromarty** Set on the fertile Black Isle, this charming small town has some beautiful vernacular architecture and dramatic east-coast scenery. See p.509

▲ Mountain scenery, Wester Ross

13

The north and northwest Highlands

The **north and northwest Highlands**, the area beyond the Great Glen, holds some of Scotland's most spectacular scenery: a classic combination of bare mountains, remote glens, dark lochs and tumbling rivers, surrounded on three sides by a magnificently rugged coastline. The inspiring landscape and the tranquility and space that it offers are without doubt the main attractions of the region. You may be surprised at just how remote much of it still is: the vast peat bogs in the north, for example, are among the most extensive and unspoilt wilderness areas in Europe, while a handful of the west coast's crofting villages can still be reached only by boat.

Different weather conditions and cultural influences have given each of the three coastlines its own distinct character. The beautiful **west coast**, with its indented shoreline and the dramatic mountains of **Torridon** and **Assynt**, is a place whose charm and poetic scenery just about hold their own against the intrusions of the touring hordes in summer. West of Fort William lies the remote and tranquil **Ardnamurchan peninsula** and the "Road to the Isles" to the fishing port of **Mallaig**, railhead of the famous West Highland Railway. From Mallaig, ferries cross to Skye and **Knoydart**, a magical peninsula with no road access that's home to the remotest pub in Britain. The more direct route to Skye is across the famous Skye Bridge at **Kyle of Lochalsh**, not far from which are charming coastal villages such as **Glenelg** and **Plockton**. Between Kyle of Lochalsh and **Ullapool**, the main settlement in the northwest, lies **Wester Ross**, with quintessentially west-coast scenes of sparkling sea lochs, rocky headlands and sandy beaches set against some of Scotland's most dramatic mountains, with Skye and the Western Isles on the horizon.

The little-visited **north coast**, stretching from stormy **Cape Wrath**, at the very northwest tip of the mainland, to **John O'Groats**, is even more rugged than the west, its sheer cliffs and sand-filled bays bearing the brunt of frequently fierce Atlantic storms. The main settlement is **Thurso**, jumping-off point for the main ferry service to Orkney.

On the fertile **east coast** of the Highland region, stretching north from Inverness to the old herring port of **Wick**, green fields and woodland run down to the sweeping sandy beaches of the **Black Isle** and the **Cromarty** and **Dornoch firths**. This region is rich with historical sites, including the contentious **Sutherland Monument** by Golspie, **Dornoch**'s fourteenth-century sandstone cathedral, and a number of places linked to the **Clearances**, a tragic chapter in the story of the Highlands.

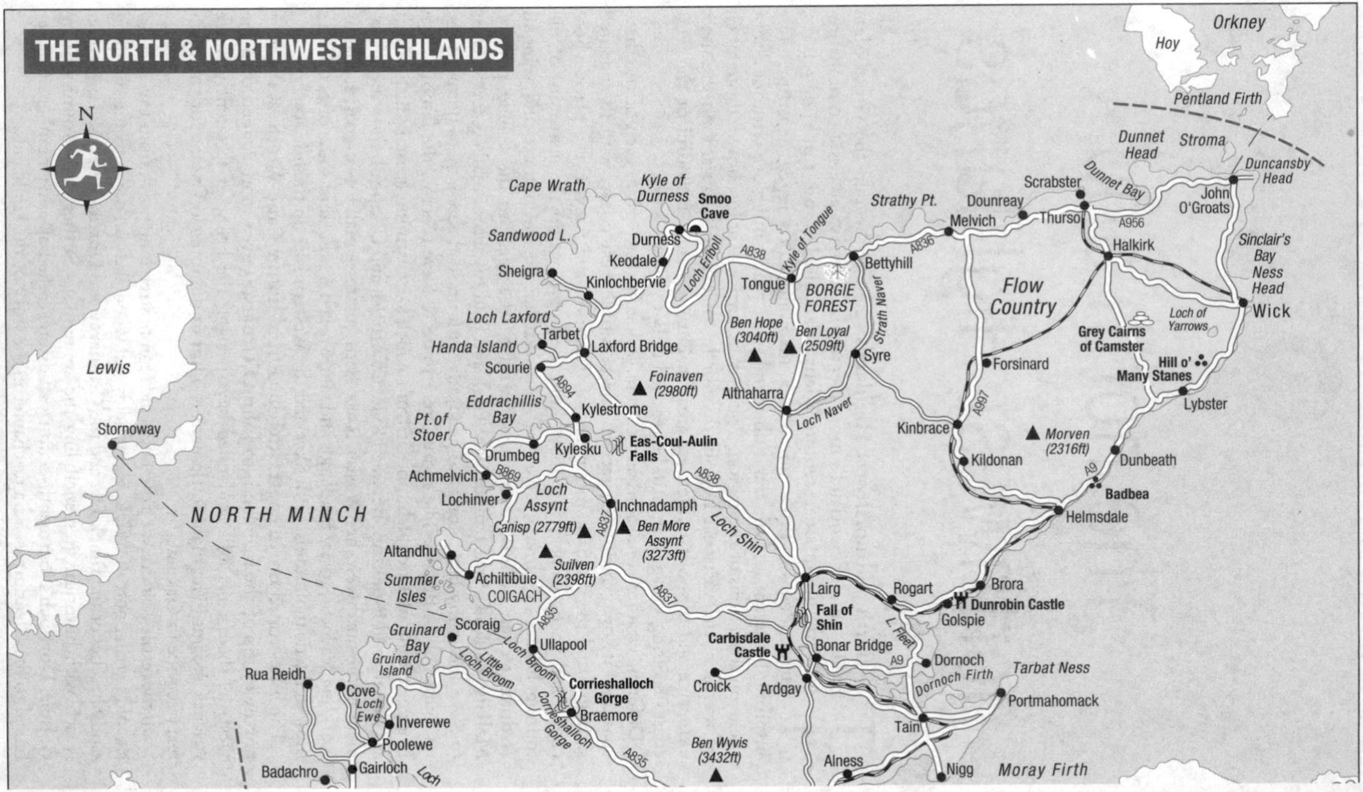

THE NORTH & NORTHWEST HIGHLANDS

N
Orkney
Hoy
Pentland Firth
Dunnet Head
Stroma
Duncansby Head
Dunnet Bay
Scrabster
John O'Groats
A956
Cape Wrath
Kyle of Durness
Smoo Cave
Strathy Pt.
Dounreay
Melvich
Thurso
Halkirk
Sinclair's Bay
Ness Head
Wick
Sandwood L.
Durness
Keodale
Loch Eriboll
A838
Kyle of Tongue
A836
Bettyhill
Sheigra
Kinlochbervie
Tongue
BORGIE FOREST
Strath Naver
Flow Country
Loch of Yarrows
Loch Laxford
Tarbet
Handa Island
Laxford Bridge
Ben Hope (3040ft)
Ben Loyal (2509ft)
Syre
Grey Cairns of Camster
Hill o' Many Stanes
Lewis
Scourie
A894
Foinaven (2980ft)
Altnaharra
Forsinard
Lybster
Eddrachillis Bay
Kylestrome
Loch Naver
Kinbrace
A997
Pt. of Stoer
Stornoway
Drumbeg
Kylesku
Eas-Coul-Aulin Falls
Morven (2316ft)
Kildonan
Dunbeath
Achmelvich
B869
A838
A9
Badbea
Lochinver
Loch Assynt
Inchnadamph
NORTH MINCH
Canisp (2779ft)
A837
Ben More Assynt (3273ft)
Loch Shin
Helmsdale
Altandhu
Suilven (2398ft)
Summer Isles
Achiltibuie
COIGACH
A837
Lairg
Rogart
Brora
Dunrobin Castle
Golspie
Fall of Shin
L. Fleet
Gruinard Bay
Scoraig
A835
Ullapool
Gruinard Island
Loch Broom
Little Loch Broom
Carbisdale Castle
Bonar Bridge
A9
Dornoch
Tarbat Ness
Rua Reidh
Cove
Loch Ewe
Corrieshalloch Gorge
Croick
Ardgay
Dornoch Firth
Portmahomack
Inverewe
Braemore
Corrieshalloch Gorge
Tain
Poolewe
A835
Ben Wyvis (3432ft)
Alness
Badachro
Gairloch
Loch
Nigg
Moray Firth

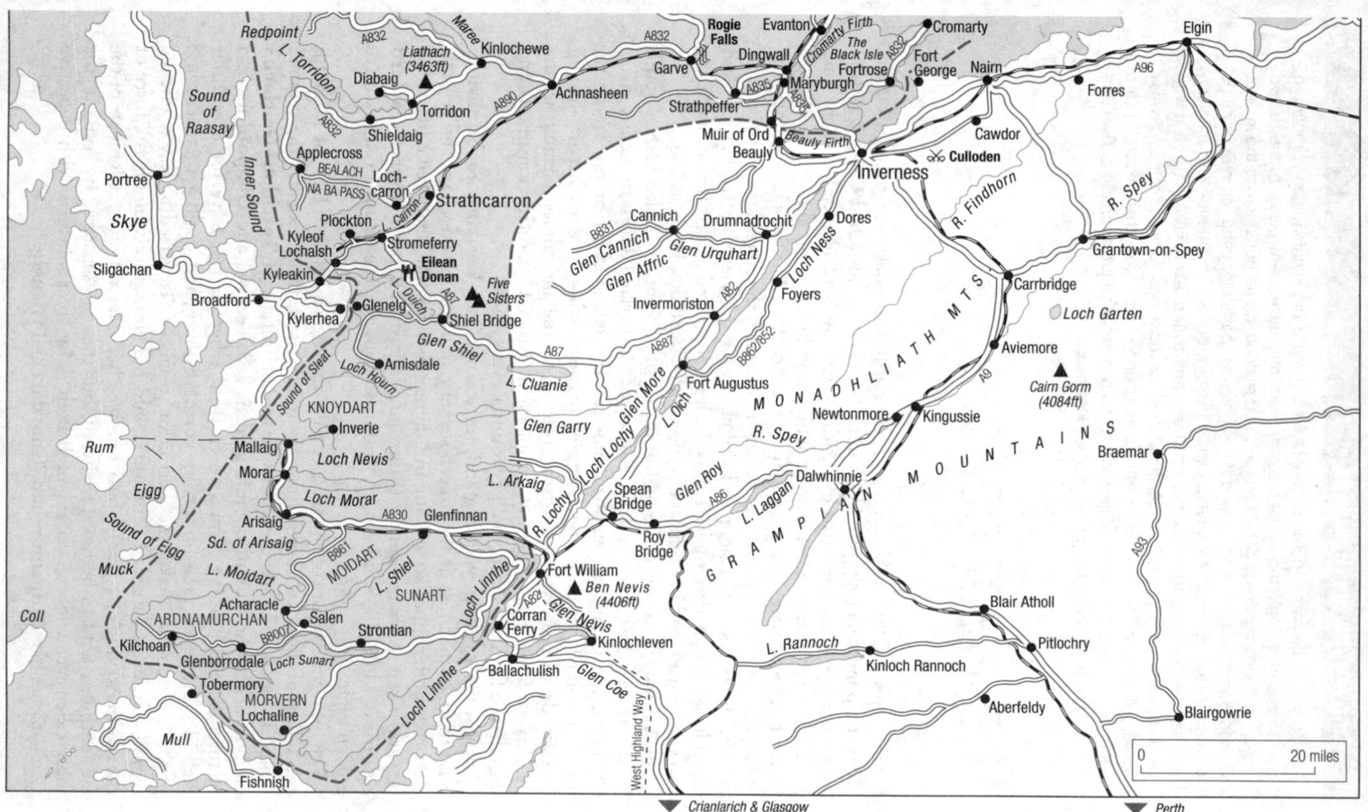
Redpoint
L. Torridon
A832
Maree
Kinlochewe
Liathach
(3463ft)
Diabaig
Torridon
Shieldaig
A890
Achnasheen
A832
Rogie
Falls
Garve
Evanton
Cromarty Firth
The
Black Isle
A832
Cromarty
Dingwall
Maryburgh
A835
Fortrose
Fort
George
Nairn
Elgin
A96
Forres
Strathpeffer
Muir of Ord
Beauly
Beauly Firth
Inverness
Cawdor
Culloden
Sound
of
Raasay
Inner Sound
Applecross
BEALACH
NA BA PASS
Loch-
carron
Strathcarron
Portree
Skye
Plockton
L. Carron
Kyleof
Lochalsh
Stromeferry
Eilean
Donan
Sligachan
Kyleakin
Broadford
Kylerhea
Glenelg
L. Duich
A87
Five
Sisters
Shiel Bridge
Glen Shiel
Arnisdale
Loch Hourn
Sound of Sleat
KNOYDART
Inverie
Rum
Mallaig
Loch Nevis
Morar
Loch Morar
Eigg
Arisaig
A830
Glenfinnan
Sound of Eigg
Sd. of Arisaig
B861
MOIDART
L. Shiel
SUNART
Muck
L. Moidart
Acharacle
Salen
ARDNAMURCHAN
B8007
Strontian
Kilchoan
Glenborrodale
Loch Sunart
Tobermory
MORVERN
Lochaline
Mull
Fishnish
Coll
Loch Linnhe
Cannich
B831
Glen Cannich
Glen Affric
Glen Urquhart
Drumnadrochit
Dores
Loch Ness
Foyers
Invermoriston
A82
A87
A887
B862/852
L. Cluanie
Glen Garry
Glen More
L. Oich
Fort Augustus
Loch Lochy
L. Arkaig
R. Lochy
Spean
Bridge
Roy
Bridge
Glen Roy
A86
L. Laggan
Fort William
Ben Nevis
(4406ft)
A82
Glen Nevis
Corran
Ferry
Kinlochleven
Ballachulish
Glen Coe
West Highland Way
R. Findhorn
R. Spey
Grantown-on-Spey
Carrbridge
Loch Garten
MONADHLIATH MTS
Aviemore
A9
Cairn Gorm
(4084ft)
Newtonmore
Kingussie
R. Spey
Dalwhinnie
GRAMPIAN MOUNTAINS
Braemar
A93
Blair Atholl
Pitlochry
L. Rannoch
Kinloch Rannoch
Aberfeldy
Blairgowrie
0
20 miles
Crianlarich & Glasgow
Perth

Getting around the Highlands

Unless you're prepared to spend weeks on the road, the Highlands are simply too vast to see in a single trip. Most visitors, therefore, base themselves in one or two areas, exploring the coast or hills on foot, and making longer hops across the interior by car, bus or train. Getting around the Highlands, particularly the remoter parts, is obviously easiest if you've got your own transport, but with a little forward planning you can see a surprising amount using **buses** and **trains**, especially if you fill in with **postbuses** (for which you can get timetables at most post offices, or see Ⓦwww.royalmail.com/postbus). It is worth remembering, however, that much of the Highlands comes to a halt on **Sundays**, when bus services are sporadic at best and you may well find most shops and restaurants closed.

The west coast

For many people, the Highlands' starkly beautiful **west coast** – stretching from the **Morvern peninsula** (opposite Mull) in the south to wind-lashed **Cape Wrath** in the far north – is the finest part of Scotland. Cut by fjord-like sea lochs, the long coastline is scattered with windswept white-sand beaches and cliff-girt headlands, with rugged mountains sweeping up from the shoreline. The fast-changing weather rolling off the North Atlantic can be harsh, but when the sun shines, the sparkle of the sea, the richness of colour and the clarity of the views out to the scattered Hebrides are simply irresistible. This is the least populated part of Britain, with just two small towns, and yawning tracts of moorland and desolate peat bog.

The **Vikings**, who ruled the region in the ninth century, called it the "South Land", from which the modern district of Sutherland takes its name. After Culloden, the Clearances emptied most of the inland glens of the far north, however, and left the population clinging to the coastline, where a herring-fishing industry developed. Today, tourism, crofting, fishing and salmon farming are the mainstays of the local economy, supplemented by EU construction grants and subsidies to farm the sheep you'll encounter everywhere.

For visitors, **cycling**, **walking** and, increasingly, sea-kayaking are the obvious ways to make the most of the superb scenery, and countless lochans and crystal-clear rivers offer superlative trout and salmon **fishing**. The shattered cliffs of the far northwest harbour some of Europe's largest and most diverse **sea-bird colonies**, while the area's craggy mountaintops are the haunt of the elusive golden eagle.

The most visited part of the west coast is the stretch between Kyle of Lochalsh and Ullapool. Lying within easy reach of Inverness, this sector has the region's more obvious highlights: the awesome mountainscape of **Torridon**, **Gairloch**'s sandy beaches, the famous botanic gardens at **Inverewe**, and **Ullapool** itself, a picturesque and bustling fishing town from where ferries leave for the Outer Hebrides. However, press on further north, or south, and you'll get a truer sense of the isolation that makes the west coast so special. Traversed by few roads, the remote northwest corner of Scotland is wild and bleak, receiving the full force of the North Atlantic's frequently ferocious weather. The scattered settlements of the far southwest tend to be more sheltered, but they are separated by some of the most extensive wilderness areas in Britain – lonely peninsulas with evocative Gaelic names like **Ardnamurchan**, **Knoydart** and **Glenelg**.

Practicalities

Tempered by the Gulf Stream, the west coast's **weather** ranges from stupendous to diabolical. Never count on a sunny morning meaning a fine day; it can rain here at any time, and go on raining for days. Beware, too, of the dreaded **midge**, which drives even the hardiest of locals to distraction on warm summer evenings.

Without your own vehicle, **transport** can be a problem. There's a reasonable **train** service from Inverness to Kyle of Lochalsh and from Fort William to Mallaig, and a useful **summer bus** service connects Inverness to Ullapool, Lochinver, Scourie and Durness. However, services peter out as you venture further afield, where you'll have to rely on **postbuses**, which go just about everywhere, albeit slowly and at odd times of day. **Driving** is a much simpler option: the roads aren't busy, though they are frequently single-track and scattered with sheep. Refuel whenever you can since pumps are few and far between, and make sure your vehicle is in good condition; in a crisis, even if you manage to reach the nearest garage, spares may well have to be sent over from Inverness.

Morvern to Knoydart: the "Rough Bounds"

The remote and sparsely populated southwest corner of the Highlands, from the empty district of **Morvern** to the isolated peninsula of **Knoydart**, is a dramatic, lonely region of mountain and moorland, its rocky, indented coast studded by stunning white beaches which enjoy wonderful views to Mull, Skye and other islands. Its Gaelic name, *Garbh-chiochan*, translates as the "**Rough Bounds**", implying a region geographically and spiritually apart. Even if you have got a car, you should spend some time here exploring on foot.

The southwest Highlands' main road is the A830, often described as "the Road to the Isles", which winds in tandem with the rail line through the glens from Fort William to the road- and railhead at **Mallaig**, a busy fishing port with ferry connections to Skye. Along the way, the road passes **Glenfinnan**, the much-photographed spot at the head of stunning **Loch Shiel** where Bonnie Prince Charlie gathered the clans to start the doomed Jacobite uprising of 1745. There are regular buses and trains along the main road; elsewhere in the region you'll usually have to rely on daily post- or schoolbuses. If you have your own transport, the five-minute ferry crossing at **Corran Ferry** (every 20–30min; Mon–Sat 6.30am–9.20pm, Sun 8.45am–9.20pm; car and passengers £6.40, foot passengers and bicycles go free), a nine-mile drive south of Fort William down Loch Linnhe, provides a more direct point of entry for Morvern and the rugged **Ardnamurchan** peninsula. *The Inn at Ardgour* (Ⓣ01855/841225, Ⓦwww.ardgour.biz; ❹), on the Morvern side, is a pleasant stop for a drink or a bite to eat.

Morvern

Bounded on three sides by sea lochs and in the north by desolate Glen Tarbet, the large, mountainous **Morvern** peninsula lies at the southwest corner of the Rough Bounds region. The landscape can seem unremittingly bleak and empty – until, that is, you reach the coast, which reveals some lovely views over to Mull. Most visitors only travel through here to get to **LOCHALINE** (pronounced "loch-*aa*lin"), a remote community on the **Sound of Mull**, from where a small car ferry chugs to **Fishnish** – the shortest crossing from the mainland (and cheaper than the main Oban–Craignure crossing if you're taking a car onto Mull). Lochaline village, little more than a scattering of houses around a small pier, has a diving centre specializing in underwater archeology (Ⓣ01967/421627, Ⓦwww.lochalinedivecentre.co.uk) and is a popular anchorage for yachts cruising the west coast.

For **accommodation**, the dive centre offers two self-catering options: a ten-bed facility in the *Old Post Office* and 24 beds in the *Dive Lodge*. You could also try the straightforward and friendly *Lochaline Hotel* (Ⓣ01967/421657; ❷). The best reason to stop here, however, is to **eat** at the superb *White House Restaurant* (Ⓣ01967/421777, Ⓦwww.thewhitehouserestaurant.co.uk; closed Mon) which specializes in delicious, freshly prepared dishes using local meat and seafood, plus coffee and home-baked scones. You can also *Catch a Snack* in the wooden hut by the pier: they do a mean venison burger.

As you'd expect, **transport** links here (other than the Fishnish ferry) are extremely limited, with a bus running to and from Fort William on a Tuesday, Thursday and Friday only, plus a Saturday service in summer (check with Shiel Buses Ⓣ01967/431272, Ⓦwww.shielbuses.co.uk). By request, the bus goes as far as the road end at **Drimnin** at the northwest corner of Morvern, from where you can cross to Tobermory on Mull with Ardnamurchan Charters (Ⓣ01972/500208, Ⓦwww.west-scotland-marine.com). Booking is essential, and trips depend on passenger numbers. The same company also runs wildlife excursions and trips to outlying islands.

Sunart and Ardgour

North of Morvern, the predominantly roadless regions of **Sunart** and **Ardgour** make up the country between Loch Shiel, Loch Sunart and Loch Linnhe. The heart of Jacobite support in the mid-eighteenth century, they're Catholic strongholds to this day. The area's only real village is sleepy **STRONTIAN**, grouped around a green on an inlet of Loch Sunart. In 1722, lead mines here yielded the first-ever traces of the element **strontium**, which was named after the village.

You can get to Strontian on the one **bus** a day (Mon–Sat; Ⓣ01967/431272), which leaves Fort William at 1.25pm and reaches Strontian at 2.15pm before continuing to Kilchoan. Strontian's **tourist office** (Easter–Oct Mon–Sat; June–Sept also Sun; Ⓣ01967/402382) is by the roadside as you pass through the village. The six-bedroom *Strontian Hotel* (Ⓣ01967/402029, Ⓦwww.thestrontianhotel.co.uk; ❺) offers reasonable bar meals on the main road looking over the water. You can also cross the bridge heading north through the village and turn right for the *Ariundle Centre* (Ⓣ01967/402279), a wood-beamed café and craft centre with a plain but decent **bunkhouse**. **B&B** is available at the delightfully secluded *Craigrowan Croft* (Ⓣ01967/402253, Ⓦwww.craigrowancroft.co.uk; ❷), a little way up the Ariundle turn-off. Six miles west of Strontian, only two miles before Salen, *Resipole Farm* (Ⓣ01967/431235, Ⓦwww.resipole.co.uk; April–Oct) has a great set-up, with a **camping** and caravan park and (year-round) self-catering accommodation. The reception stocks basic foodstuffs. For dinner, drive a few minutes to the *Salen Hotel* (see opposite).

The Ardnamurchan peninsula

The tortuous single-track B8007 road winds west from Salen to the wild **Ardnamurchan peninsula**, the most westerly point on the British mainland. The unspoilt landscape is relatively gentle and wooded at the eastern end, with much of the coastline of long Loch Sunart fringed by ancient oakwoods. The further west you travel, however, the trees disappear and are replaced by a wild, salt-sprayed moorland. The peninsula, once ruled by Norse invaders, lost most of its inhabitants during the infamous Clearances, and only a handful of tiny crofting settlements cling to its jagged coastline.

Yet Ardnamurchan, with its pristine, empty beaches and wonderful sea vistas, can be an inspiring place. The peninsula harbours a huge variety of birds, mammals and wild flowers such as thrift and wild iris, making **walking** an obvious attraction. More than forty walks are detailed in a guide to the peninsula produced annually by the local community (available from tourist offices and most shops), while **guided walks** are also available at most of the nature reserves dotted along the Loch Sunart shoreline. For wildlife-spotting, stop off at the turf-roofed Garbh Eilean hide (free access), five miles west of Strontian on the A861, from where you can see seals, seabirds and the occasional eagle.

Salen to Glenborrodale

The coastal hamlet of **SALEN** marks the turn-off for Ardnamurchan Point: from here it's a further 25 miles of slow, scenic driving along the single-track road which follows the northern shore of Loch Sunart. Salen is a sheltered anchorage, and yachties often row ashore for a drink at the *Salen Hotel* (Ⓣ01967/431 1661, Ⓦwww.salenhotel.co.uk; ❷), which has some neat rooms and serves good seafood bar meals. There's not much more until you get to the engaging **Ardnamurchan Natural History Centre** (April–Oct Mon–Sat 10.30am–5.30pm, Sun noon–5.30pm; £4; Ⓦwww.ardnamurchannaturalhistorycentre.co.uk), an inspiring introduction to the diverse flora, fauna and geology of Ardnamurchan just west of the hamlet of **GLENBORRODALE**. The centre is housed in a sensitively designed timber structure complete with turf roof, bark floor and wildlife ponds. Live-cam recordings show the comings and goings of heron, a pine marten's nest, and sea and golden eagles feeding nearby. The *Antler Tearoom* here dishes up sandwiches and good home-baked cakes, and evening meals are sometimes served in summer (Ⓣ01972/500209).

Kilchoan and Ardnamurchan Point

KILCHOAN, nine miles west of the Glenmore Centre, is Ardnamurchan's main village – a straggling but appealing crofting township overlooking the Sound of Mull. A **car ferry** runs from here to Tobermory (Mon–Sat 8am–6.40pm 3–4 daily, plus May–Aug Sun 10.15am–4.45pm 5 daily; 35min). The community centre in the village houses a **tourist office** (Easter–Oct daily; Ⓣ01972/510222, Ⓦwww.ardnamurchan.com) that also serves coffee and lunchtime soup. For **boat trips** out of Kilchoan to observe wildlife, including dolphins, seals, whales and possibly the rare sea eagle, contact Ardnamurchan Charters (Ⓣ01972/500208, Ⓦwww.west-scotland-marine.com). The only direct **bus** to Kilchoan leaves from Fort William at 3.20pm (Mon–Sat), travelling via the Corran Ferry and arriving three hours later.

The road continues beyond Kilchoan to the rocky, windy **Ardnamurchan Point** and its famous 36m-high **lighthouse**. The lighthouse buildings house a small café and an absorbing **exhibition** (daily April–Oct 10am–5pm; £5; Ⓣ01972/510210, Ⓦwww.ardnamurchanlighthouse.com). Best of all is the chance to climb up the inside of the Egyptian-style tower; at the top, a guide will show you the lighting mechanism. Minke whales sometimes surface in the waters off the point.

Also worth exploring around the peninsula are the myriad coves, beaches and headlands along the long coastline. The finest of the sandy beaches is about three miles north of the lighthouse at **Sanna Bay**, a shell-strewn strand and series of dunes which offers unforgettable vistas of the Small Isles to the north, circled by gulls, terns and guillemots.

Practicalities

Accommodation isn't plentiful in Kilchoan, and in summer you're well advised to book far ahead. You can normally camp in the gardens of the *Kilchoan House Hotel*, and there's a good campsite with lovely coastal views by the Ardnamurchan Study Centre (ⓣ07787/812084, ⓦwww.ardnamurchanstudycentre.co.uk), about half a mile past the Ferry Stores. For B&B, try friendly *Doirlinn House* (ⓣ01972/510209, ⓔdoirlinnhouse@ardnamurchan-holidays.com; ❷; March–Oct) or nearby two-bedroom *Torrsolais* (ⓣ01972/510389, ⓦwww.ardnamurchan-holidays.co.uk; ❷). Both have lovely views over the bay and Sound of Mull.

Options for lunch and evening meals in the area are limited, with the Kilchoan community centre serving good-value snacks and lunches and *Kilchoan House Hotel* (ⓣ01972/510200, ⓦwww.kilchoanhousehotel.co.uk; ❹) the best bet for an evening meal – it also has half a dozen rooms, including some family rooms. The Ferry Stores in Kilchoan makes an impressive effort to carry fresh food and local produce when it's available.

Acharacle and around

At the eastern end of Ardnamurchan, just north of Salen where the A861 heads north towards the district of Moidart, the main settlement is **ACHARACLE**, an attractive ancient crofting village set back a few hundred yards from the seaward end of freshwater **Loch Shiel**. The pleasant *Loch Shiel House Hotel* (ⓣ01967/431224, ⓦwww.lochshielhotel.co.uk; ❷) is a comfortable, friendly place to stay, stop for a drink or eat, while *Ardshealach Lodge* (ⓣ01967/431399, ⓦwww.ardshealach-lodge.co.uk; ❹) serves lunch, afternoon tea and dinner in an attractive house in its own grounds with a great outlook over the loch and hills. The *Chimneys B&B* (ⓣ01967/431528, ⓦwww.chimneysmoidart.co.uk; ❷) is another option, and you can head to the *Blue Parrot Café* for daytime snacks and home-baking.

You can get to Acharacle by **boat** from Glenfinnan at the head of Loch Shiel with Loch Shiel Cruises (Wed only; Easter to mid-Oct; £15 single, £22 return; ⓣ01687/470322, ⓦwww.highlandcruises.co.uk), or on infrequent **buses** from Mallaig or Fort William.

Castle Tioram

A mile north of Acharacle, a side road running north off the A861 winds for three miles or so past a secluded estuary lined with rhododendron thickets and fishing platforms to **Loch Moidart**, a calm and sheltered sea-loch. Perched atop a rocky promontory jutting out into the loch is **Castle Tioram** (pronounced "cheerum"), one of Scotland's most atmospheric monuments. Reached via a sandy causeway that's only just above the high tide, the thirteenth-century fortress, whose Gaelic name means "dry land", was the seat of the MacDonalds of Clanranald until it was destroyed by their chief in 1715 to prevent it from falling into Hanoverian hands.

The Road to the Isles

The "**Road to the Isles**" (ⓦwww.road-to-the-isles.org.uk) from Fort William to Mallaig, followed by the West Highland Railway and the narrow, winding A830, traverses the mountains and glens of the Rough Bounds before breaking out near **Arisaig** onto a spectacularly scenic coast of sheltered inlets, stunning white beaches and wonderful views to the islands of Rùm, Eigg, Muck and Skye. This is a country commonly associated with **Bonnie Prince Charlie**, whose adventures of 1745–46 began and ended on this stretch of coast, with his defiant gathering of the clans at **Glenfinnan**.

Glenfinnan

GLENFINNAN, nineteen miles west of Fort William at the head of lovely Loch Shiel, was where Bonnie Prince Charlie raised his standard to signal the start of the Jacobite uprising of 1745. Surrounded by no more than two hundred loyal clansmen, the young rebel prince waited here to see if the Cameron of Loch Shiel would join his army. The drone of this powerful chief's pipers drifting up the glen was eagerly awaited, for without him the Stuarts' attempt to claim the English throne would have been sheer folly. Despite strong misgivings, Cameron did decide to support the uprising, and arrived at Glenfinnan on a sunny August 19 with eight hundred men, thereby encouraging other clan leaders to follow suit. The prince raised his red-and-white silk colour, proclaimed his father as King James III of England and set off on the long march to London – from which only a handful of the soldiers gathered at Glenfinnan would return. The spot is marked by a column (now a little lopsided), crowned with a clansman in full battle dress, erected as a tribute by Alexander Macdonald of Glenaladale in 1815.

The **visitor centre** and run-of-the-mill café (daily: April, May, June, Sept & Oct 10am–5pm; July & Aug 9.30am–5.30pm; NTS; £3), opposite the monument, gives an account of the '45 uprising through to the rout at **Culloden** eight months later (see p.463). Loch Shiel Cruises (ⓣ01687/470322, ⓦwww.highlandcruises.co.uk) run a number of **boat trips** on the loch, all offering a worthwhile opportunity to view the remote, beguiling scenery and occasionally a golden eagle. Cyclists can also disembark at the Polloch Pontoon and return by the lochside track to Glenfinnan.

The West Highland Railway

Scotland's most famous railway line, and a train journey counted by many as among the world's most scenic, is the brilliantly engineered **West Highland Railway**, running from Glasgow to Mallaig via Fort William. The line is in two sections: the southern part travels from **Glasgow** Queen Street station along the Clyde estuary and up Loch Long before switching to the banks of Loch Lomond on its way to **Crianlarich**, where the train divides, with one section heading for Oban. After climbing around Beinn Odhar on a unique horseshoe-shaped loop of viaducts, the line traverses desolate **Rannoch Moor**, where the track had to be laid on a mattress of tree roots, brushwood and thousands of tons of earth and ashes. By this point the line has diverged from the road, and travels through country that can otherwise be reached only by long-distance footpaths. The train then swings into Glen Roy, passing through the dramatic **Monessie Gorge** and entering **Fort William** from the northeast.

The second leg of the journey, from Fort William to Mallaig, is arguably even more spectacular, and from mid-May to mid-October one of the scheduled services is pulled by the **Jacobite Steam Train** (Mon–Fri, also Sat & Sun July & Aug; departs Fort William 10.20am, departs Mallaig 2.10pm; day-return £28; book on ⓣ01524/737751, ⓦwww.steamtrain.info). Shortly after leaving Fort William the railway crosses the Caledonian Canal beside Neptune's Staircase by way of a swing bridge at **Benavie**, before travelling along the shores of Locheil and crossing the magnificent 21-arch viaduct at **Glenfinnan**, where the steam train, in its "Hogwarts Express" livery, was filmed for the *Harry Potter* movies. At Glenfinnan station there's a small **museum**, a restaurant and a bunkhouse (see p.480). Not long afterwards the line reaches the coast, with views of the Small Isles and Skye as it runs past the famous silver sands of **Morar** and up to **Mallaig**, where there are ferry connections to Armadale on Skye.

If you're planning on travelling the West Highland line, and in particular linking it to other train journeys (such as the similarly attractive route between Inverness and Kyle of Lochalsh), it's worth considering one of First ScotRail's multi-day **Highland Rover tickets**, details of which are given on p.29.

Glenfinnan is one of the most spectacular parts of the **West Highland Railway** line (see box p.479), not only for the glimpse it offers of the monument and graceful Loch Shiel, but also for the mighty 21-arched Loch nan Uamh **viaduct**, built in 1901 and one of the first ever large constructions made out of concrete: it is now famed as a *Harry Potter* film location. You can learn more of the history of this section of the railway at the **Glenfinnan Station Museum** (June to mid-Oct daily 9am–5pm; 50p; Ⓦwww.glenfinnanstationmuseum.co.uk) set in the old station booking office. Right beside the station, two old railway carriages have been pressed into use as a highly original **restaurant** and **bunkhouse**; the *Dining Car* (June–Sept daily 10am–5pm; Ⓣ01397/722300) is open for light lunches and home-baking (phone ahead for evening meals), while the *Sleeping Car* (Ⓣ01397/722295; year-round), a converted 1958 camping coach, sleeps ten in bunk beds and makes for a memorable, if slightly restricted, place to stay. The best of the more conventional accommodation options is the *Lochailort Inn* (Ⓣ01687/470208, Ⓦwww.lochailortinn.co.uk; ❺), about ten miles on from Glenfinnan towards Arisaig (and also on the train line, although you have to request to stop here).

Arisaig

West of Glenfinnan, the A830 runs alongside captivating Loch Eilt in the district of **Morar**, through Lochailort – where it meets the road from Acharacle – and onwards to white sands, turquoise seas and rocky islets draped with orange seaweed. **ARISAIG**, scattered round a sandy bay at the west end of the Morar peninsula, makes a good base for exploring this area. A **bypass** now whizzes cars (and, more importantly, fish lorries) to Mallaig, but the slower coast road enjoys the best of the scenery.

The only specific attraction in Arisaig village is the **Land, Sea and Islands Centre** (Easter to mid-Oct Mon–Fri 10am–3pm, Sun 1pm–4pm; £2.50), a small, volunteer-run community project whose displays give intriguing detail on local events, including secret operations during World War II and background on local characters such as the man who inspired Robert Louis Stevenson's Long John Silver. There's a small seal colony at nearby **Rhumach**, reached via the single-track lane heading west out of Arisaig village along the headland. A **boat** also leaves from here (11am) daily during the summer for the Small Isles (see p.533), operated by Arisaig Marine (Ⓣ01687/450224, Ⓦwww.arisaig.co.uk).

Accommodation in the village is plentiful: *Hilbre* (Ⓣ01687/450685, Ⓦwww.road-to-the-isles.org.uk/hilbre.html; ❷; March–Oct) is modern and comfortable with fine sea views, while the more upmarket *Old Library Lodge and Restaurant* (Ⓣ01687/450651, Ⓦwww.oldlibrary.co.uk; ❺; April–Oct) has a handful of well-appointed rooms, though only two overlook the seafront. For **food**, the restaurant at the *Old Library* serves tasty if rather pricey fare, while meals and plain rooms are available at the characterless *Arisaig Hotel* (Ⓣ01687/450210, Ⓦwww.arisaighotel.co.uk; ❻).

Morar

Stretching for eight miles or so north of Arisaig is a string of stunning white-sand **beaches** backed by flowery machair, with barren granite hills and moorland rising up behind, and wonderful seaward views of Eigg and Rùm. The next settlement of any significance is **MORAR**, where the famous beach scenes from *Local Hero* were shot. There are umpteen **campsites** along the coast road, and **B&B** at the home of adventurer Tom McClean, *Invermorar House* (Ⓣ01687/462274, Ⓦwww.road-to-the-isles.org.uk/invermorar.html; ❷; July to mid-Sept only). He runs outdoor activities at Ardintigh, a ninety-minute sail up Loch Nevis.

Much closer is **Loch Morar** – rumoured to be the home of a monster called Morag, a lesser-known rival to Nessie – which runs east of Morar village into the heart of a huge wilderness area. For boat rental or to obtain a fishing permit for Loch Morar call ⓣ01687/462388. Delicious, freshly prepared Thai takeaways can be had in Morar from *Sunset* (ⓣ01687/462259; closed Mon) on the main drag.

Mallaig

A cluttered, noisy port whose pebble-dashed houses struggle for space with great lumps of exposed granite, **MALLAIG**, 47 miles west of Fort William, is not pretty. Before the railway line reached here in 1901 it consisted of only a few cottages, but it's now bustling and, as the main ferry-stop for Skye, the Small Isles and Knoydart, always full of visitors. Once one of Europe's busiest herring ports, the continuing source of the village's wealth is its **fishing** industry.

Alongside the train station, apart from the daily hubbub of the harbour, the **Mallaig Heritage Centre** (April, May & Oct Mon–Sat 11am–4pm; June–Sept Mon–Fri 9.30am–4.30pm, Sat & Sun noon–4pm; £2; ⓣ01687/462085, ⓦwww.mallaigheritage.org.uk) is worth a browse for its displays on the area's past, and for information about lifeboats, fishing and the ancient highland galleys that once plied the waters of the Inner Hebrides. The walking trail to **Mallaigmore** (1hr), a small cove with a white-sand beach and isolated croft, begins at the top of the harbour on East Bay; follow the road north past the tourist office and turn right when you see the signpost between two houses.

Practicalities

Mallaig is concentrated around the harbour, where you'll find the **tourist office** (April–Oct Mon–Sat; ⓣ01687/462064 for winter opening hours), and the **bus** and **train stations**. The CalMac ticket office (ⓣ01687/462403), serving passengers for Skye and the Small Isles, is also nearby. You can arrange transport to Knoydart by calling Bruce Watt Cruises (ⓣ01687/462320, ⓦwww.knoydart-ferry.co.uk), which sail to Inverie, on the Knoydart peninsula, every morning and afternoon (mid-May to mid-Sept Mon–Fri; mid-Sept to mid-May Mon, Wed & Fri); the loch is quite sheltered, so crossings are rarely cancelled. To fish, spot dolphins and seals or be put ashore for a day as a "castaway", contact fluent Gaelic-speaker Ewen Nicholson (ⓣ01687/462652).

There are plenty of **places to stay**. The *West Highland Hotel* (ⓣ01687/462210, ⓦwww.westhighlandhotel.co.uk; ❺) is a typically bland but comfortable Scottish Highland hotel; some rooms have excellent sea views. For **B&B**, head around the harbour to East Bay, where you'll find the cheery *Western Isles Guest House* (ⓣ01687/462320, ⓦwww.road-to-the-isles.org.uk/western-isles.html; ❸). *Sheena's Backpackers' Lodge* (ⓣ01687/462764, ⓦwww.mallaigbackpackers.co.uk), a refreshingly laidback independent **hostel** overlooking the harbour, has mixed dorms and the (licensed) *Tea Garden Restaurant*, a great place to watch the world go by while you tuck into Cullen skink, a pint of prawns or home-made scones. Another fishy and slightly more upmarket **eating** option, though it's not much to look at, is the *Fishmarket Restaurant* across the road. Fresh fish and chips – or scallops and chips if you're feeling decadent – are served at the *Cornerstone*, across from the tourist office.

The Knoydart peninsula

Many people regard the **Knoydart peninsula** as mainland Britain's most dramatic and unspoilt wilderness area. Flanked by **Loch Nevis** ("Loch of Heaven") in the south and the fjord-like inlet of **Loch Hourn** ("Loch of Hell") to the north,

Knoydart's knobbly green peaks – three of them Munros – sweep straight out of the sea. To get to the heart of the peninsula, you must catch a **boat** from Mallaig or Glenelg, or else **hike** for a couple of days across rugged moorland and mountains and sleep rough in old stone bothies (most marked on OS maps). Unsurprisingly, the peninsula attracts walkers, lured by well-maintained trails that wind east into the wild interior, where Bonnie Prince Charlie is rumoured to have hidden out after Culloden.

At the end of the eighteenth century, around a thousand people eked out a living from this inhospitable terrain through crofting and fishing. Evictions in 1853 began a dramatic decrease in the population, which continued to dwindle through the twentieth century as a succession of landowners ran the estate as a hunting and shooting playground, prompting a famous land raid in 1948 by a group of crofters known as the "Seven Men of Knoydart", who claimed ownership of portions of the estate. Although their bid failed, their cause was invoked when the crofters of Knoydart finally achieved a community buy-out in 1998. These days the peninsula supports around seventy people, most in the hamlet of **INVERIE**. Nestled beside a sheltered bay on the south side of the peninsula, it has a pint-sized post office and shop, a ranger post (with internet access) advising on local walks and wildlife, and mainland Britain's most remote pub, the *Old Forge*.

Bruce Watt Cruises' **boat** chugs into Inverie from Mallaig (see p.481). To arrange for a (passenger) boat crossing from Arnisdale on the Glenelg peninsula to the north coast of Knoydart or Kinloch Hourn, contact Billy Mackenzie (see p.486).

There are two main **hiking routes** into Knoydart. The trailhead for the first is **KINLOCH HOURN**, a crofting hamlet at the far east end of Loch Hourn which you can get to by road (turn south off the A87 six miles west of Invergarry). From Kinloch Hourn, a well-marked path winds around the coast to Barrisdale (where there's a year-round bothy and campsite; ⓦwww.barisdale.com) before continuing ten miles to Inverie. The second path into Knoydart starts west of Loch Arkaig, approaching the peninsula via Glen Dessary. Take wet-weather gear, a decent map, plenty of food, warm clothes and a good sleeping bag, and leave your name and expected time of arrival with someone when you set off.

You can rent **mountain bikes** from *The Pier House* and there are plans to develop cycle trails in the area. Your best source of information for walking and wildlife (including guided walks) is the ranger post (ⓣ01687/462242) beside the *Old Forge*.

Accommodation

Most of Knoydart's surprisingly numerous **accommodation** options are concentrated in and around Inverie. If you want to wild camp, for a small donation to the ranger office you can pitch on "long beach" just ten minutes from the only pub.

Hotels and B&Bs

Doune Stone Lodges ⓣ01687/462667, ⓦwww.doune-knoydart.co.uk. Rebuilt from ruined crofts and offering pine-fitted en-suite doubles right on the shore, this place provides both total isolation and creature comforts, with delicious meals served in the dining room. Owner Martin gives advice about walks and provides OS maps and compasses for wild walks. It's not easy to get to Doune by land, but they'll pick you up by boat from Mallaig (£20pp). Minimum stay three nights. Full board ❼.

The Gathering Inverie ⓣ01687/460051, ⓦwww.thegatheringknoydart.co.uk. Situated in Inverie itself, this friendly B&B has some bunk-bed options and beautiful wood furnishings. ❺

Knoydart Lodge Inverie ⓣ01687/460129, ⓦwww.knoydartlodge.co.uk. Beautifully located near the pub and the beach, this wooden lodge provides a warm welcome and elegant en-suite rooms. ❺

The Pier House Inverie ⓣ01687/462347, ⓦwww.thepierhouseknoydart.co.uk. This cosy abode, with fine views over the loch, is the most convenient option for the pub and ranger post. It has its own restaurant with dinner available to non-residents. ❻

Hostels

Knoydart Foundation Bunkhouse Inverie ⓣ01687/462242, ⓦwww.knoydart-foundation.com. Simple and straightforward option, with adequate facilities in old steadings a 10min walk from the pub.

Torrie Shieling Inverie ⓣ01687/462669, ⓔtorrie@knoydart.org. Upmarket, independent hostel just east of the village on the side of the mountain, and offering top-notch self-catering facilities, comfortable wooden beds in four-person rooms and open fires in the convivial living room. It also has a Land Rover and boat for ferrying guests around the peninsula, and to neighbouring lochs and islands.

Eating

The *Old Forge* is one of Scotland's finer **pubs**, with a convivial atmosphere where visitors and locals mix. You'll find generous bar meals often featuring recently caught seafood, real ales, an open fire, terrific loch views and a good chance of live music of an evening. *The Pier House* (see p.482) is also a good option for eating.

Kyle of Lochalsh and around

As the main gateway to Skye, **Kyle of Lochalsh** used to be an important transit point, though with the construction of the Skye Bridge in 1995, it was left as merely the terminus for the train route from Inverness. Of much more interest to most visitors is nearby **Eilean Donan Castle**, perched at the end of a stone causeway on the shores of **Loch Duich**. It's not hard, however, to step off the tourist trail: remote **Glenelg** peninsula is just to the south side of Loch Duich. A few miles north of Kyle of Lochalsh, the delightful village of **Plockton** is a refreshing alternative to its utilitarian neighbour, with cottages grouped around a bay and Highland cattle wandering the streets. Plockton lies on the southern shore of **Loch Carron**, a long inlet which acts as a dividing line between Kyle of Lochalsh and the splendours of Wester Ross to the north.

Kyle of Lochalsh

KYLE OF LOCHALSH is not particularly attractive and with the building of the **Skye Bridge**, traffic has little reason to stop before rumbling over the channel a mile to the west. Just about the only reason to pause in Kyle is to take a ride on the *Atlantis* (Easter–Oct; ⓣ01471/822716 or 0800/980 4846, ⓦwww.seaprobeatlantis.com), the UK's only semi-submersible glass-bottomed **boat**, aboard which you can visit the protected seal and bird colonies on Seal Island (£12.50) or see the World War II wreck of HMS *Port Napier* (£15).

Buses run to Kyle of Lochalsh from Glasgow via Fort William and Invergarry (3 daily; 5hr) and from Inverness via Invermoriston (3 daily; 2hr 10min). You should book in advance for all of them (ⓣ0870/550 5050, ⓦwww.citylink.co.uk). All continue at least as far as Portree on Skye. Buses also shuttle across the bridge to Kyleakin on Skye every thirty minutes or so. **Trains** run to Kyle of Lochalsh from Inverness (Mon–Sat 4 daily, 2 on Sun; 2hr 30min), curving north through Achnasheen and Glen Carron; the line is a rail enthusiast's dream. Kyle's helpful **tourist office** (April–Oct daily), on top of the small hill near the old ferry jetty, can book **accommodation** – a useful service as there are surprisingly few options. The best hotel is probably the welcoming *Kyle Hotel* in Main Street, with a menu including fresh seafood and game (ⓣ01599/534204, ⓦwww.kylehotel.co.uk; ❺). Spacious and comfortable *Ardenlea* on Church Street (ⓣ01599/534630; ❷) or nearby *A'Chomraich* (ⓣ01599/534210; ❷) are both good central B&Bs. There's a simple bunkhouse in town, *Cúchulainn's* (ⓣ01599/534492), above a pub across the main street from the tourist office, and you'll find tent pitches at pleasant

Reraig Caravan Park at Balmacara, a few miles east of Kyle (Ⓣ01599/566215, Ⓦwww.reraig.com). To **eat**, sample the fresh dishes and delicious home-made puddings of the tiny *Waverley Restaurant* on the main street (5.30–9.30pm, closed Thurs; Ⓣ01599/534337), while for a snack visit *Sheila's Café* opposite the tourist office.

Loch Duich

Skirted on its northern shore by the A87, **Loch Duich**, the boot-shaped inlet just to the south of Kyle of Lochalsh, features prominently on the tourist trail, and buses from all over Europe thunder down the sixteen miles from **SHIEL BRIDGE** to Kyle of Lochalsh on their way to Skye. The main road, which connects to the Great Glen at Invermoriston (see p.454) and Invergarry, makes for a dramatic approach to the loch out of Glen Shiel, where, to the north, the **Five Sisters of Kintail** surge impressively up to heights of 3000ft. There's comfortable **accommodation** to be had in Shiel Bridge itself at the *Kintail Lodge Hotel* (Ⓣ01599/511275, Ⓦwww.kintaillodgehotel.co.uk; ❻); the hotel also offers dorm-style **hostel** accommodation in the appropriately named *Wee Bunkhouse* and in twins and singles in the *Trekkers' Lodge*. At **RATAGAN**, a mile or so up the southern shore from Shiel Bridge, the excellent SYHA **hostel** (Ⓣ01599/511243, Ⓦwww.syha.org.uk; March–Oct) is popular with walkers newly arrived off the Glen Affric trek from Cannich (see p.456). However, for fine food, views and comfort, head for *Grants at Craigellachie* (Ⓣ01599/511331, Ⓦwww.housebytheloch.co.uk; ❻) in Ratagan. There's scenic camping at the *Shielbridge Caravan Park & Campsite* (Ⓣ01599/511221, Ⓦwww.shielbridgecaravanpark.co.uk).

Eilean Donan Castle

After Edinburgh's hilltop fortress, **Eilean Donan Castle** (April–Oct daily 10am–5pm; opens 9am July–Aug; £5.50; Ⓦwww.eileandonancastle.com), ten miles north of Shiel Bridge on the A87, has to be Scotland's most photographed monument. Presiding over the once strategically important confluence of lochs Alsh, Long and Duich, the forbidding crenellated tower rises from the water's edge, joined to the shore by a narrow stone bridge and with sheer mountains as a backdrop. The castle was established in 1230 by Alexander II to protect the area from the Vikings. Later, during a Jacobite uprising in 1719, it was occupied by troops dispatched by the king of Spain to help the **"Old Pretender"**. In response, George I sent frigates to recapture the castle. The formidable walls withstood the bombardment for three days, only falling when the Hanoverian forces came ashore for an assault: having taken the castle, they lit its magazine, shattering its walls. Thereafter, it lay in ruins until John Macrae-Gilstrap had it rebuilt between 1912 and 1932. Eilean Donan has since featured in *Highlander*, *Entrapment* and the James Bond adventure *The World is Not Enough*. Three floors, including the banqueting hall, the bedrooms and the troops' quarters are open to the public, with various Jacobite and clan relics also on display.

There are a couple of places to **stay** less than a mile away from the castle, in the hamlet of **DORNIE**, though both trade on the location, so you may want to go further afield. There's whitewashed *Dornie Hotel*, Francis Street (Ⓣ01599/555205; ❺), and the *Loch Duich Hotel* (Ⓣ01599/555213; ❺), whose small **restaurant** serves bar snacks and evening meals. On Sunday nights a **folk music** session takes place in the bar. Along from the *Dornie Hotel*, reasonable bar meals and ales are offered at the *Clachan Pub*. However, to escape the hordes, head for the splendidly remote *Whitefalls Retreat* (Ⓣ01599/588205) bunkhouse in Camusluinie, eight miles north.

Hiking in Glen Shiel

Ordnance Survey Explorer map no. 414

The mountains of **Glen Shiel**, sweeping southeast from Loch Duich, offer some of the best hiking routes in Scotland. Rising dramatically from sea level to over 3000ft in less than a couple of miles, they are also exposed to the worst of the west coast's notoriously fickle weather. Don't underestimate either of these two routes. Tracing the paths on a map, they can appear short and easy to follow; nonetheless, walkers come unstuck here every year, often failing to allow enough time to get off the mountain by nightfall or suffering a sudden change in the weather. Only attempt them if you're confident in your walking experience, and have a map and a compass. A detailed trekking guide can also be very useful – *Hill Walks in Northwest Scotland* or *The Munros*, both published by SMC, are recommended. Also make sure to follow the usual safety precautions outlined on p.49.

Taking in a bumper crop of Munros, the **Five Sisters traverse** is deservedly the most popular trek in the area. Allow a full day to complete the whole route. The distinctive chain of mountains across the glen from the Five Sisters is the **Kintail Ridge**, with breathtaking views south across Knoydart and the islands of the west. It's another full-day trek, beginning from the *Cluanie Inn* (see p.454) on the A87.

The Glenelg peninsula

South of Loch Duich, the isolated and little-known **Glenelg peninsula**, jutting out into the Sound of Sleat, is the crofting area featured in Gavin Maxwell's otter novel *Ring of Bright Water*. Maxwell disguised the identity of this pristine stretch of coast by calling it "Camusfearnà", and it has remained a tranquil backwater in spite of the traffic that trickles through during the summer for the Kylerhea ferry to Skye (see p.525 for details of the museum at Eilean Bàn, once Maxwell's home).

The landward approach to the peninsula is from the east by turning off the fast A87 at Shiel Bridge on Loch Duich, from where a narrow single-track road climbs a tortuous series of switchbacks to the Mam Ratagan Pass (1115ft), affording spectacular views over the awesome **Five Sisters** massif. There's a terrific picnic stop halfway up the road. Following the route of an old drovers' trail, the road, covered by both the postbus and Skyeways bus service (both Mon–Fri) from Kyle of Lochalsh, drops down the other side through Glen More, with the magnificent Kintail Ridge visible to the southeast, towards the peninsula's main settlement, **GLENELG**, on the Sound of Sleat.

Glenelg itself is a row of picturesque whitewashed houses, surrounded by trees. The *Glenelg Inn* (ⓣ01599/522273, ⓦwww.glenelg-inn.com; ❼) is a wonderful spot, boasting seven luxurious (en-suite) **rooms** overlooking the bay and offering moderately priced fresh food all day and occasional live music.

The community-run, six-car **Glenelg–Kylerhea ferry** (daily: Easter–Oct 9am–6pm, June–Aug 10am–7pm; ⓣ01599/522313, ⓦwww.skyeferry.co.uk) shuttles to Skye every fifteen minutes across the Sound of Sleat, one of the fastest tidal races in the UK, from a jetty northwest of the village; minke whale and dolphin may be spotted. In former times, this choppy channel used to be an important drovers' crossing: eight thousand cattle each year were herded head to tail across from Skye to the mainland.

One and a half miles south of Glenelg village, a left turn up Glen Beag leads to the **Glenelg Brochs**, some of the best-preserved Iron Age monuments in the country. Standing in a sheltered stream valley, the circular towers – Dun Telve and Dun Troddan – are thought to have been erected around two thousand years ago to protect the surrounding settlements from raiders. About a third of each main structure remains, with the curving dry-stone walls and internal passages still impressively intact.

Arnisdale

A narrow backroad snakes its way southeast beyond Glenelg village through a scattering of old crofting hamlets and timber forests. The views across the Sound of Sleat to Knoydart grow more spectacular at each bend, reaching a high point at a windy pass that takes in a vast sweep of sea, loch and islands. Below the road at **Sandaig** is where Gavin Maxwell and his otters lived in the 1950s: the site of his house is now marked by a cairn.

Swinging east, the road winds down to the waterside again, following the north shore of Loch Hourn as far as **ARNISDALE**, departure point for the boat to Knoydart (see p.481). Arnisdale is made up of the two hamlets of **Camusbane** and **Corran**, the former consisting of a single row of old cottages ranged behind a long pebble beach, with a massive scree slope behind, while the latter, a mile along the road, is a minuscule whitewashed fishing hamlet at the water's edge. Aside from the arrival of electricity and a red telephone box, the only major addition to this gorgeous hamlet in the last hundred years has been Mrs Nash's friendly **B&B** and tea hut (ⓣ01599/522336; ❶), with home-baking, breathtaking views and dinner options such as tasty fish pie (order in advance).

Unless you're prepared to walk the nine miles from Glenelg, reaching Arnisdale requires forward planning. With the demise of the postbus service, your only option is to use the MacRae community bus that links Kyle of Lochalsh with *Ratagan Youth Hostel* and Glenelg (plus Arnisdale on request). Book ahead on ⓣ01599/511384.

Billy Mackenzie's year-round fast-boat **passenger ferry** from Arnisdale across Loch Hourn to Barrisdale (and to Kinlochhourn) provides an excellent means for walkers and cyclists to explore the most inaccessible parts of the Knoydart peninsula (April–Sept; ⓣ01599/522247, ⓦwww.arnisdaleferry.com; £12 single). The boat can also be chartered for wildlife trips and fishing.

Plockton

A fifteen-minute train ride north of Kyle at the seaward end of islet-studded Loch Carron lies the unbelievably picturesque village of **PLOCKTON**: a chocolate-box row of cottages ranged around the curve of a tiny harbour and backed by a craggy landscape of heather and pine. Originally known as Am Ploc, the settlement was a crofting hamlet until the end of the eighteenth century, when a local laird transformed it into a prosperous fishery, renaming it "Plocktown". In high season it's packed with tourists, yachties and second-home owners, and the unique brilliance of the light has also made it something of an artists' hangout.

The *Haven Hotel*, on Innes Street (ⓣ01599/544223; ❻), the almost adjacent family-run *Plockton Inn* (ⓣ01599/544222, ⓦwww.plocktoninn.co.uk; ❺) and the *Plockton Hotel* on Harbour Street (ⓣ01599/544274, ⓦwww.plocktonhotel.co.uk; ❻) all have comfortable accommodation within their respective, atmospheric, walls, live music in summer, and the last also offers terrific harbour and loch views. Of the fifteen or so **B&Bs**, try comfortable *Mackenzie's* on the main street (ⓣ01599/544306; ❷) or, beyond the tiny post office, *Heron's Flight* (ⓣ01599/544220, ⓦwww.heronsflight.org; March–Nov; ❸), with loch views from its two upstairs bedrooms. At the cosy main-street retreat *An Caladh*, "the resting place on the shore" (ⓣ01599/544356, ⓦwww.plockton.uk.com; ❸), guests have free use of two wooden sailing dinghies and can watch the owner sail in with his morning catch. On the outskirts of Plockton, meanwhile, opposite the railway station, the attractive *Station Bunkhouse* (ⓣ01599/544235) features four- and six-person dorms and an open-plan kitchen and living area; check in at friendly *Nessun Dorma*: the owners also do B&B (❶). On the other side of the tracks, *Off the Rails* (ⓣ01559/544306, ⓦwww.plocktonstation.co.uk) provides self-catering accommodation in the delightful wood-panelled station building. Follow the road for Stromferry to *Duncraig Castle* (ⓣ01599/544295, ⓦwww.duncraigcastle.com; ❻), which provides B&B in a Scots baronial pile romantically sited across the bay from Plockton.

For a small village, Plockton offers a number of good places to **eat**. Fresh seafood is a staple on the evening menus at *The Haven*, the *Plockton Inn* and the *Plockton Hotel*. The latter two sell local real ales, and it's hard to beat the views over the bay from the hotel. All of the above, plus the modern café/restaurant in *Plockton Stores* at the seafront, serve filling breakfasts, good-value lunches and dinner. For fish and chips, pizza and so on, try the tiny *Harbour* takeaway. Calum's Seal Trips (Easter–Oct daily; £8; free if no seals; ⓣ01599/544306 or 07761/263828) provides an interesting one-hour excursion as well as a two-hour dolphin trip; Calum also rents out canoes (£10/hr). **Bike rental** (£14/day) is available from Gordon Mackenzie at Plockton Cottages. Call ⓣ01599/544255 or 07922/934630.

Strathcarron and Kishorn

The sea lochs immediately north of Plockton are the dual inlets of **Loch Kishorn**, so deep it was once used as an oil-rig construction site, and **Loch Carron**, which cuts inland to **STRATHCARRON**, a useful link between Kyle of Lochalsh and Torridon to the north. Strathcarron has a station on the Kyle–Inverness line and provides a postbus connection to Shieldaig (for Applecross) and Torridon (Mon–Sat 10am). Right by Strathcarron station, housed in the old station building, is the helpful Strathcarron **tourist information, shop and post office** (Mon–Sat; ⓣ01520/722218). A mile south, along the road to Kyle, the *Carron Pottery, Crafts and Restaurant* (ⓣ01520/722488) serves fresh home-made meals and you can browse local crafts. Another mile or so south, **Alladale** (Mon–Sat 10am–5.30pm) is an attractive "artist's garden" with sculptures scattered throughout.

There are several more **accommodation** options two or three miles away in **LOCHCARRON**, a pretty little village of whitewashed cottages stretched out along the northern shore of the loch. One of the best is *Rockvilla Hotel* (ⓣ01520/722379, ⓦwww.rockvilla-hotel.co.uk; ❹), a small hotel in the centre of the village that serves moderately priced bar meals, real ales and good breakfasts using organic yoghurt, breads and local produce. There are numerous B&Bs to choose from, including the five-bedroom *Old Manse* (ⓣ01520/722208, ⓦwww.theoldmanselochcarron.com; ❸), just off the road to Strome Castle. **Camping** is possible at the simple *Wee Campsite* (ⓣ01520/722898; Easter to end Oct), above the village. Further down towards Strome Castle is the much-heralded **Lochcarron Weavers** (ⓦwww.lochcarronweavers.co.uk), housed in an old-fashioned timber-clad workshop, where you can watch weaving demonstrations. Another wet-weather option is the **Lochcarron Old Smiddy Heritage Centre** (April to mid-Oct Mon–Sat 8am–5.30pm, Sun noon–5.30pm; free; ⓣ01520/722108), a restored smithy and forge established in 1810 on the road between Strathcarron and Lochcarron, which houses a small exhibition and video on local history.

From here, a single-track road leads over the hillside to **KISHORN**, at the head of the loch of the same name. The wooden chalet of the *Kishorn Seafood Bar* (ⓣ01520/733240; Mon–Sat 10am–9pm, Sun & noon–5pm) is worth a stop to indulge in **fresh local shellfish** or coffee, home-baking and bacon rolls.

Wester Ross

Wester Ross, the western seaboard of the old county of Ross-shire, is widely regarded as the most glamorous stretch of this coast. Here, all the classic elements of Scotland's **coastal scenery** – dramatic mountains, sandy beaches, whitewashed crofting cottages and shimmering island views – come together in spectacular fashion. Settlements such as **Applecross** and the peninsulas north and south of **Gairloch** maintain an endearing simplicity and sense of isolation. There is some tough but wonderful **hiking** to be had in the mountains around **Torridon** and **Coigach**, while **boat trips** and the prolific sea- and birdlife are another draw. The main settlement is the attractive fishing town of **Ullapool**, the port for ferry services to Stornoway in the Western Isles, and a pleasant enough place to use as a base, not least for its active social and cultural scene.

The Applecross peninsula

The most dramatic approach to the **Applecross peninsula** (the English-sounding name is a corruption of the Gaelic *Apor Crosan*, meaning "estuary") is from the south, up a classic glacial U-shaped valley and over the infamous **Bealach na Bà** ("Pass of the Cattle"). Crossing the forbidding hills behind Kishorn and rising to 2053ft, with a gradient and switchback bends worthy of the Alps, this route – a popular cycling piste – is hair-raising in places, but the panoramic views across the Minch to Raasay and Skye more than compensate. The other way in is from the north: a beautiful coast road that meanders slowly from Shieldaig on Loch Torridon, with tantalizing glimpses of the Skye Cuillin to the south. For transport between Strathcarron and Achasheen, calling at Applecross, contact Dial-A-Bus (ⓣ01520/722205).

The sheltered, fertile coast around **APPLECROSS** village, where Irish missionary monk Maelrhuba founded a monastery in 673 AD, comes as a surprise after the bleakness of the approach: you can wander along lanes banked with wild iris and orchids, and explore beaches and rock pools. There's a small **Heritage Centre** (April–Oct Mon–Sat noon–4pm; ⓦwww.applecrossheritage.org.uk) overlooking Clachan church and graveyard, and a number of **waymarked trails** along the shore – great for walking off a pub lunch. Local experts Applecross Mountain & Sea (ⓣ01520/744394, ⓦwww.applecross.uk.com), based at the entrance of the village, organize mountain expeditions and sea-kayaking.

The family-run *Applecross Inn* (ⓣ01520/744262; ❻), right beside the sea, is the focal point of the community, with seven refurbished **rooms** upstairs, and a lively bar (with occasional ceilidh) that serves good, freshly prepared local seafood and produce (noon–9pm). A mile down the road, the excellent *Potting Shed Café and Restaurant* (ⓣ01520/744440; March to end Oct Mon–Sat 11am–8.30pm, Sun 11am–4pm) is a culinary and visual delight, where the walled Victorian garden, woods and sea provide rich pickings for the chefs, who serve delicious dishes in a laidback atmosphere. Fairly inexpensive in its daytime incarnation as a café, it's pricier in the evening; it operates a rickshaw service to take you to and from Applecross. There's an excellent **B&B** in the village: *Littlehill of My Heart* (ⓣ01520/744432, ⓦwww.applecrossaccommodation.com; ❹), with classy spacious rooms and a delicious breakfast. You'll also find several good B&Bs on the peninsula: *Tigh na Mara* (ⓣ01520/744277; ❸) at Lonbain provides views of Raasay whilst, nearer Shieldaig, *Tigh a' Chracaich* (ⓣ01520/755367, ⓦwww.lochtorridon.net; ❸) sits in a small bay with spectacular views over Loch Torridon. *Applecross Campsite* (ⓣ01520/744268, ⓦwww.applecross.uk.com/campsite) is located as you come into the village from the pass; it features the cheery *Flower Tunnel* café/bar (daily from 9am).

Loch Torridon

Loch Torridon marks the northern boundary of the Applecross peninsula, its awe-inspiring setting enhanced by the appealingly rugged mountains of **Liathach** and **Beinn Eighe**, hulks of reddish 750-million-year-old Torridonian sandstone tipped by streaks of white quartzite. Some 15,000 acres of the massif are under the protection of the National Trust for Scotland, which also looks after **Shieldaig Island**, where a heronry has been established among the tall Scots pines. The island lies in a sheltered bay off the prim but pretty village of **SHIELDAIG** ("herring bay") on the southern shore of Loch Torridon, where the popular Shieldaig Fete is held at the beginning of August every year.

There's an attractive small **hotel** and snug bar by the shore in the village, *Tigh-an-Eilean* (Ⓣ01520/755251, Ⓦwww.tighaneilean.co.uk; March–Oct; ❽), with live music every Friday in summer. The *Rivendell* B&B (Ⓣ01520/755250; ❸) is nearby and a simple **campsite** affords terrific loch views a little way up the hill. At **TORRIDON** village, at the east end of the loch, the main road heads inland through Glen Torridon, while the minor road runs through the village along the northern shore. At the road junction, past the Torridon Mountain Rescue post, a **Countryside Centre** (Easter to end Sept Mon–Sat 10am–5pm; £3) gives information on local geology, flora and fauna, plus advice on mountain walks.

On the south side of the loch stands one of the area's grandest **hotels**, the smart, rambling *Torridon* (Ⓣ01445/791242, Ⓦwww.thetorridon.com; ❾), a Victorian building set amid well-tended lochside grounds. The hotel also runs the adjacent *Torridon Inn* (March–Oct; ❺), a cyclist- and walker-friendly modern farmstead conversion with neat twins and doubles and a moderately priced bar/bistro serving real ales, boar sausage and the like. Torridon Activities, run from the hotel, offers pursuits including hillwalking, mountain biking and sea-kayaking. Close to the Countryside Centre is a rather unsightly SYHA **hostel** (Ⓣ0870/004 1154, Ⓦwww.syha.org.uk; March–Oct) and a council-run **campsite**.

Walks around Torridon

Ordnance Survey Explorer map no. 433

With the support of Scottish Natural Heritage (SNH), large tracts of Torridon's Beinn Eighe National Nature Reserve are being replanted with native trees including birch, Scots pine and rowan. Good paths lead through the woodlands, but venture higher and conditions can be difficult, and the weather can change very rapidly. If you're relatively inexperienced but want to do the magnificent ridge walk along the **Liathach** (pronounced "lee-ach") massif, or the strenuous traverse of **Beinn Eighe** (pronounced "ben ay"), you can join a National Trust Ranger Service guided hike (July & Aug; Torridon Countryside Centre; Ⓣ01445/791221).

For those confident to go it alone, one of many possible routes takes you behind Liathach and down the pass, **Coire Dubh**, to the main road in Glen Torridon. This covers thirteen miles and takes in superb landscapes: weather permitting, you can make the rewarding diversion up to the **Coire Mhic Fhearchair**, widely regarded as the most spectacular corrie in Scotland. Allow yourself the whole day.

Even in rough weather, the undulating, seven-mile hike up the coast from **Lower Diabaig**, ten miles northwest of Torridon village, to **Redpoint** is a rewarding one, and on a clear day the views across to Raasay and Applecross are wonderful. If you're staying in Shieldaig, the track that winds up the peninsula running north from the village makes a pleasant ninety-minute round walk. For any of these walks, ensure you are properly equipped with waterproofs, warm clothing and provisions.

Loch Maree

About eight miles north of Loch Torridon, **Loch Maree**, dotted with Caledonian-pine-covered islands, is one of the west's scenic highlights, best viewed from the A832 road that drops down to its southeastern tip through Glen Docherty. At the southeastern end of the loch, the A896 from Torridon meets the A832 from Achnasheen at small **KINLOCHEWE** (Ⓦ www.torridon-mountains.com), a good base if you're heading into the hills. There's a twelve-bed **bunkhouse** as well as good meals at the *Kinlochewe Hotel* (Ⓣ 01445/760253, Ⓦ www.kinlochewehotel.co.uk; ❺). The corrugated-iron *Whistle Stop Café* is handy for breakfast, hot food and cakes, while Kinlochewe Store opposite the hotel contains the post office (which opens Mon–Sat 9–11am) and the basic *Teapot Café*, and sells outdoor kit including maps and camping gas.

The A832 skirts the southern shore of Loch Maree, passing the **Beinn Eighe Nature Reserve**, the UK's oldest wildlife sanctuary. Parts of the reserve are forested with Caledonian pinewood, which once covered the whole of the country, and it is home to pine martens, wildcats, buzzards and golden eagles. A mile north of Kinlochewe, the well-run **Beinn Eighe Visitor Centre** (Easter & May–Oct daily 10am–5pm) on the A832, informs visitors about the area's rare species. Outside, the "talking trails" provide an easy walk through the vicinity, while several interesting **walks** start from the car park, a mile north of the visitor centre. There's also a basic campsite here.

Loch Maree is surrounded by some of Scotland's finest **deerstalking** country: the remote, privately owned Letterewe Lodge on the north shore, accessible only by helicopter or boat, lies at the heart of a famous deer forest. In 1877, Queen Victoria stayed at the wonderfully sited *Loch Maree Hotel*, now an exclusive self-catering lodge. Just 100m away, set back from the loch and road amidst trees, *The Old Mill and Highland Lodge* (Ⓣ 01445/760271, Ⓦ www.theoldmillhighlandlodge.co.uk; ❽) is a pleasant if pricey place **to stay**.

Gairloch and around

GAIRLOCH spreads around the northeastern corner of the wide sheltered bay of Loch Gairloch. In summer it thrives as a low-key holiday resort, with several tempting sandy beaches and some excellent coastal walks within easy reach. The township is divided into pretty, distinct areas spread over nearly two miles of shoreline: to the south, in **Flowerdale Bay**, are the old pier and harbour; past the bank, at the turn-off to Melvaig, **Achtercairn** is the centre of Gairloch; and along the north side of the bay, on the road to Melvaig, are the strung-out crofts of **Strath**. The main supermarket and helpful **tourist office** (June–Sept daily; Oct–May Mon–Sat) are in Achtercairn, right by the **Gairloch Heritage Museum** (March–Sept daily 10am–5pm; Oct Mon–Sat 10am–1.30pm; £3; Ⓦ www.gairlochheritagemuseum.org), whose eclectic, appealing displays range from a mock-up of a croft house to an early knitting machine. Probably the most interesting section is the archive made by elderly locals – an array of photographs, maps, genealogies, lists of place names and taped recollections, mostly in Gaelic. The little whitewashed **Solas Gallery** (Ⓣ 01445/712626, Ⓦ www.solasgallery.co.uk) is worth a look for its displays of local ceramics and watercolours.

Gairloch has a good choice of **accommodation**, but you might prefer to stay out along the road north to Melvaig or south to Redpoint (see p.489). There are some good **B&Bs**: in Strath, try Miss Mackenzie's child-friendly *Duisary* (Ⓣ 01445/712252, Ⓦ www.duisary.freeserve.co.uk; April–Oct; ❶). At the southern edge of the village, just before the turn-off to Badachro, the atmospheric and tastefully furnished *Kerrysdale House* (Ⓣ 01445/712292, Ⓦ www.kerrysdalehouse.co.uk; ❷) is set back in its own lovely gardens. North of town you'll find the *Sands Holiday Centre* (Ⓣ01445/712152, Ⓦwww.sandsholidaycentre.co.uk) for **camping**.

For **food**, head for the harbour, where the *Old Inn* (Ⓦwww.theoldinn.net; ❺) offers moderately priced seafood on its bar menu, a very good range of Scottish real ales and snug rooms. There's also good-value lunch and evening fare at the *Harbour Lights Café*; for **snacks**, try the bistro-style *Blueprint Café* across the road – where you'll also find the chip shop.

One leisurely way to explore the coast is on a wildlife-spotting **cruise**. There are several operators, but try the pier-based Gairloch Marine Life Centre & Cruises (Easter–Oct; from £10; Ⓣ01445/712636, Ⓦwww.porpoise-gairloch.co.uk), who run enjoyable trips across the bay in search of dolphins, seals and even the odd whale. They also deploy a mini-sub that sends underwater pictures back to the boat whilst a hydrophone picks up audio from the sea life. Take a cruise, go sea-angling or **rent a boat** for the day through the Gairloch Chandlery (Ⓣ01445/712458), at the pier, or go **pony trekking** with Gairloch Trekking Centre (Ⓣ01445/712652, Ⓦwww.gairlochtrekkingcentre.co.uk; closed Thurs). From the car park on the north side of the Flowerdale river, a sheltered glen provides a scenic woodland walk: ask at the tourist office for directions. For bike rental, call Ⓣ01445/712030.

Rubha Reidh and around

The area's real attraction is its beautiful **coastline**. To get to one of the most impressive stretches, head around the north side of the bay and follow the single-track B8021 to **BIG SAND**, which has a cleaner and quieter **beach** than the one in Gairloch, as well as an excellent **campsite** just above the beach (Ⓣ01445/712152). At Carn Dearg, just before Big Sand, a former hunting lodge is now an SYHA **hostel** (Ⓣ01445/712219, Ⓦwww.syha.org.uk; April–Sept), spectacularly set on the edge of a cliff with views to Skye. The B8021, and the postbus from Gairloch, terminate at the tiny crofting hamlet of Melvaig, where a white-stone former Free Church provides a rustic setting for simple, hearty bar meals and a pint at the *Melvaig Inn* (Tues–Sun; Ⓣ01445/771212, Ⓦwww.melvaig-inn.co.uk).

From Melvaig, it's another three miles out to **Rubha Reidh** (pronounced "roo-a-ray"). You can stay at the headland's still operational *Rua Reidh Lighthouse* (Ⓣ01445/771263, Ⓦwww.ruareidh.co.uk; ❶), which was built in 1910 and looks straight out to the Outer Hebrides. Comfortable accommodation options include a bunkhouse, double and family rooms (meals extra; book ahead in high season). Fran, the cheerful owner, can provide breakfast (£6) and a pre-booked evening meal (£15). Guided walking and climbing courses are also offered.

Around the headland from Rubha Reidh lies the secluded and beautiful **Camas Mor** beach, a spot sought out by expert surfers. For a great half-day walk, follow the marked footpath inland (southeast) from here along the base of a sheer scarp slope, and past a string of lochans, ruined crofts and a remote wood to **MIDTOWN** on the east side of the peninsula, four miles north of Poolewe on the B8057. However, unless you leave a car at the end of the trail or arrange to be picked up, you'll have to walk or hitch back to Gairloch.

Badachro and Redpoint

Three miles south of Gairloch, a narrow single-track lane (built with the Destitution Funds raised during the nineteenth-century potato famine) winds west from the main A832, past wooded coves and inlets on its way south of the loch to **BADACHRO**, a sleepy former fishing village in a very attractive setting with a wonderful pub, the *Badachro Inn* (Ⓦwww.badachroinn.com), right by the water's edge, where you can sit in the beer garden watching the boats come and go and tuck into quite pricey fresh seafood with a real ale. At the eastern edge of Badachro, secluded *Shieldaig Lodge Hotel* (Ⓣ01445/741250, Ⓦwww.shieldaiglodge.com; ❸) has reasonable accommodation in a former Victorian shooting lodge. Accessed via a floating bridge and a short drive away, *Dry Island* is a great self-catering option (Ⓣ01445/741263, Ⓦwww.dryisland.co.uk). The owner runs two-hour "creel trips" (£17.50) from his pier, giving you the chance to see octopus, prawns and lobster being hauled in. Evening fishing trips for mackerel can also be organized.

Beyond Badachro, the road winds for five more miles along the shore to **REDPOINT**, a straggling hamlet with beautiful beaches of peach-coloured sand and great views to Raasay, Skye and the Western Isles. It also marks the trailhead for the wonderful coast walk to Lower Diabaig (see box, p.489). Even if you don't fancy a full-blown hike, following the path a mile or so brings you to the exquisite **beach** hidden on the south side of the headland.

Poolewe and around

It's a fifteen-minute hop by bus over the headland from Gairloch to the trim little village of **POOLEWE**, which sits by a small bay at the sheltered southern end of Loch Ewe, where the (very short) River Ewe rushes down from Loch Maree. One of the area's best **walks** begins near here, signposted from the layby-cum-viewpoint on the main A832, a mile south of the village. It takes a couple of hours to follow the easy trail across open craggy moorland to the shores of **Loch Maree** (see p.490), and thence to the car park at Slattadale, seven miles southeast of Gairloch. If you reach the *Loch Maree Hotel* before 5pm (June–Sept Mon–Sat) you should be able to pick up the Wester bus from Inverness back to Gairloch and Poolewe.

The ten-mile drive along the small side road running along the west shore of Loch Ewe leads to **COVE**, where you'll find an atmospheric cave that was used by the severe Presbyterian "Wee Frees" as a church into the twentieth century; it's a perilous scramble up, however, and there's little here to see other than the cave.

For **accommodation** Poolewe has a popular and well-equipped **campsite** (Ⓣ01445/781249; May–Oct), whilst the family-run and refurbished *Poolewe Hotel* (Ⓣ01445/781241, Ⓦwww.poolewehotel.co.uk; ❺) on the Cove road, serves seafood and game dinners. For a taste of luxury, relax in the sumptuous interior of the *Pool House Hotel* (Ⓣ01445/781272, Ⓦwww.poolhousehotel.co.uk; ❽), which once belonged to Osgood MacKenzie (see below). At Aultbea, *Cartmel* (Ⓣ01445/731375, Ⓦwww.cartmelguesthouse.com; ❸) is a welcoming 1970s four-bedroom guest-house. In Poolewe itself, *The Bridge Cottage Café and Gallery*, in a neat white cottage opposite the post office, offers home-baking and tasty, freshly prepared snacks.

Inverewe Gardens

Half a mile across the bay from Poolewe on the A832, **Inverewe Gardens** (daily: April, May & Sept 10am–5pm; June–Aug 10am–6pm; Oct 10am–4pm; Nov–March 10am–3pm; NTS; £8.50), a verdant oasis of foliage and riotously colourful flower collections, forms a vivid contrast to the wild, heathery crags of the adjoining coast. The gardens were the brainchild of **Osgood MacKenzie**, who inherited the surrounding 12,000-acre estate from his stepfather, the laird of Gairloch, in 1862. Taking advantage of the area's famously temperate climate, Mackenzie collected plants from all over the world for his walled garden, which still forms the nucleus of the complex. Protected from Loch Ewe's corrosive salt breezes by a dense brake of Scots pine, rowan, oak, beech and birch trees, the fragile plants flourished on rich soil brought here as ballast on Irish ships to overlay the previously infertile beach gravel and sea grass. By the time MacKenzie died in 1922, his garden sprawled over the whole peninsula, surrounded by a hundred acres of woodland. Thousands of visitors pour through here annually, but the place rarely feels overcrowded. Interconnected by a labyrinthine network of twisting paths and walkways, a few accessible by wheelchair, more than a dozen gardens feature exotic plant collections from as far afield as Chile, China, Tasmania and the Himalayas. Mid-May to mid-June is the best time to see the rhododendrons and azaleas, while the herbaceous garden reaches its peak in July and August, as does the wonderful Victorian vegetable and flower garden beside the sea. You'll need at least a couple of hours, particularly if you explore the Pinewood Trail and still leave time for the **visitor centre** (April–Sept daily 9.30am–5pm), which is the starting point for **guided walks**. There's also a pleasant **restaurant**.

Gruinard Bay and Little Loch Broom

At **LAIDE**, ten miles north of Poolewe, the road skirts the shores of **Gruinard Bay**, offering fabulous views and, at the inner end of the bay, some excellent sandy beaches. During World War II, the bay's **Gruinard Island** was used as a testing ground for biological warfare. After much protest, the Ministry of Defence had the island decontaminated and it was finally declared "safe" in 1990. As befits the stunning scenery, there are some lovely **accommodation** choices all along this stretch, including the pleasant *Gruinard Bay* campsite (Ⓣ01445/731225) and the welcoming *Old Smiddy Guest House* (Ⓣ01445/731696, Ⓦwww.oldsmiddyguesthouse.co.uk; ❹) on the main road in Laide.

Corrieshalloch Gorge

The road heads inland before joining the A835, the main Inverness–Ullapool road, at **Braemore Junction**, above the head of Loch Broom. Just nearby, and easily accessible from a layby on the A835, the spectacular 50m **Falls of Measach** plunge through the mile-long Corrieshalloch Gorge, formed by glacial meltwaters. You can overlook the cascades from a precarious observation platform, or from the impressive, wobbly Victorian suspension bridge that spans the chasm, whose 60m vertical sides are draped in wych elm, goat willow and bird cherry. The A835 from the head of Loch Broom to Ullapool is one of the so-called **Destitution Roads**, built to give employment to local people during the nineteenth-century potato famines.

Ullapool

ULLAPOOL (Ⓦwww.ullapool.co.uk), the northwest's principal centre of population, was founded at the height of the herring boom in 1788 by the British Fisheries Society, on a sheltered arm of land jutting into Loch Broom. The grid-plan town is still an important fishing centre, though the **ferry** link to Stornoway on Lewis (see p.545) means that in high season it's swamped by visitors. You can make a day-long return ferry/bus visit (summer only Wed & Fri) to Lewis (departs Ullapool 9.30am and Stornoway at 7pm with Caledonian MacBrayne summer only Ⓣ01854/612358; £30.20). Though busy, Ullapool remains a hugely appealing place and a good base for exploring the northwest Highlands. Regular **buses** run from here to Inverness and Durness and there is a reasonable service north to Achiltibuie (Mon–Sat; Ⓣ01463/222444) and southwest to Poolewe and Gairloch (Mon, Wed, Thurs & Sat; Ⓣ01445/712255). Accommodation is plentiful and Ullapool is an obvious hideaway if the weather is bad, with cosy pubs and a lively **arts centre**, *The Ceilidh Place*.

Arrival, information and accommodation

Forming the backbone of its grid plan, Ullapool's two main thoroughfares run parallel, with **Shore Street** on the lochside and **Argyle Street** further inland. **Buses** stop at the pier, in the town centre near the ferry dock, from where it's

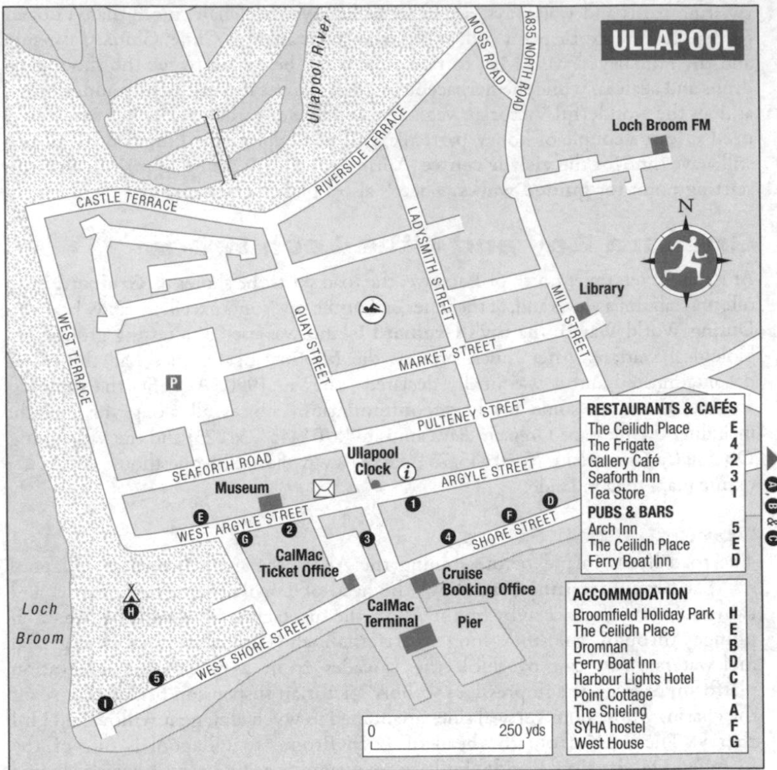

easy to get your bearings. The well-run **tourist office** (April–May Mon–Sat; June–Aug daily; Oct Mon–Fri; call ⓣ01854/612486 for winter opening hours) on Argyle Street offers an accommodation booking service. Ullapool has all kinds of **places to stay**, including a couple of welcoming hostels and some decent guesthouses and B&Bs, though it's worth booking ahead to get any of the places listed below.

Hotels, guesthouses and B&Bs

The Ceilidh Place West Argyle St ⓣ01854/612103. Renowned for its live music and ceilidhs, the tastefully furnished interior of this charismatic place includes thirteen en-suite bedrooms, an excellent café-bar and bookshop specializing in Scottish literature, history and art. You can also call to reserve a bed in its small bunkhouse (1), directly across the road. 7

Dromnan Garve Rd ⓣ01854/612333, ⓦwww.dromnan.co.uk. Excellent B&B run by welcoming hosts, who serve up a hearty breakfast. Has lovely sea views, and from the dining area you can walk onto the patio or down to the shore. 3

Ferry Boat Inn Shore St ⓣ01854/612366, ⓦwww.ferryboat-inn.com. Traditional inn right on the waterfront with a convivial atmosphere and reasonable food. 5

Harbour Lights Hotel Garve Rd ⓣ01854/612222, ⓦwww.harbour-lights.co.uk. A modern, family-run hotel with nineteen comfortable en-suite bedrooms. 3

Point Cottage 22 West Shore St ⓣ01854/612494, ⓦwww.pointcottage.co.uk. Rustic, very well-equipped B&B at the quieter end of the seafront. Guests can borrow OS maps that have been already marked up with walking routes. 3

The Shieling Garve Rd ⓣ01854/612947, ⓦwww.thesheilingullapool.co.uk. Another friendly, comfortable guesthouse overlooking the loch, with immaculate, spacious rooms (4 and 5 have the best views), superb breakfasts and a sauna. Free fishing for brown trout is also available. ❸

West House West Argyle St ⓣ01854/613126, ⓦwww.westhousebandb.co.uk. A former manse, centrally located and newly refurbished with four bright rooms. ❹

Hostel and campsite

Broomfield Holiday Park West Shore St ⓣ01854/612020. Large, good-value campsite, a 5-min walk from town. Exposed to the wind off Loch Broom but offers great views and warm showers.

SYHA Hostel Shore St ⓣ01854/612254, ⓦwww.syha.org.uk. Busy hostel on the front, with internet access, laundry and lots of good information about local walks. March–Oct.

The Town

Day or night, most of the action in Ullapool centres on the **harbour**, which has an authentic and salty air, especially when the boats are in. By day, attention focuses on the comings and goings of the ferry, fishing boats and smaller craft, while, in the evening, yachts swing on the current, the shops stay open late, and customers from the *Ferry Boat Inn* line the sea wall. During summer, both the *Summer Queen* (ⓣ01854/612472, ⓦwww.summerqueen.co.uk) and *Centaur* fast-rib boat (ⓣ01854/633708, ⓦwww.sea-scape.co.uk) run wildlife cruises and trips to the uninhabited **Summer Isles** to view sea-bird colonies, grey seals, dolphins, porpoises and the occasional whale.

The only conventional attraction in town is the award-winning **museum**, in the old parish church on West Argyle Street (Easter–Oct Mon–Sat 10am–5pm; by prior arrangement in winter; ⓣ01854/612987; £3), where photographs, audio-visual and touch-screen displays provide an insight into life in a Highland community, including crofting, fishing, local religion and emigration. During the Clearances, Ullapool was one of the ports through which evicted crofters left to start new lives abroad.

Eating, drinking and entertainment

There are several good **pubs** in Ullapool; notably the *Ferry Boat Inn* (or "FBI"), where you can enjoy a pint of real ale at the lochside – midges permitting – and the *Arch Inn* on West Shore Street. Live Scottish **folk music** is a special feature at *The Ceilidh Place* and often at the *FBI*. The atmospheric *Ceilidh Place* also periodically holds art exhibitions.

Though the interior is hardly intimate, the busy *Seaforth Inn* on Quay Street serves terrific-value mains and starters, including a scrumptious fish pie. This busy bar/restaurant also hosts regular live-music performances, and there's an adjacent chip shop. Though pricier, *The Ceilidh Place* is another popular destination, offering lunch, snacks and dinners in a pleasant bistro area. On the shorefront, the *Frigate* is a good bet for coffee and sandwiches. For a no-frills option, try the tiny locals' favourite the *Tea Store* on Argyle Street (opposite the tourist information) which serves up hearty, inexpensive breakfasts, home-baking and a refreshing cuppa. Nearby, *Gallery Café* on West Argyle Street above an outdoor shop, provides all-day breakfasts, soup and sandwiches and has changing exhibitions of local landscape photography.

Assynt

If you've come as far as Ullapool it really is worth continuing further north into the dramatic, remote and highly distinctive hills of **Assynt**, which marks the transition from Wester Ross into Sutherland. One of the least populated areas in

Ceilidhs

The **ceilidh** is essentially an informal, homespun kind of entertainment, the word being Gaelic for a "visit". In remote Highland communities, talents and resources were pooled, people gathering to play music, sing, recite poems and dance. The dances themselves are thought to be ancient in origin; the Romans wrote that the Caledonians danced with abandon round swords stuck in the ground, a practice echoed in today's formalized sword dance, where the weapons are crossed on the floor and a quick-stepping dancer skips over and around them.

Highland ceilidhs, fuelled by whisky and largely extemporized, must have been an intoxicating, riotous means of fending off winter gloom. Like much of clan culture, however, the traditions died or were forced underground after the defeat of the Highlanders at Culloden and the passing of the 1747 Act of Proscription, which forbade the wearing of the plaid and other expressions of Highland identity.

Ceilidhs were enthusiastically revived in the reign of tartan-fetishist Queen Victoria, and in the twentieth century became the preserve of the village hall and hotel ballroom, buoyed to some extent by the popularity of jaunty 1950s TV programmes such as *The White Heather Club*, which showed rather prim demonstrations of Scottish country dancing and made a star out of master accordionist Jimmy Shand. More recently, though, the ceilidh has thrown off some of these stale associations, with places such as *The Ceilidh Place* in Ullapool and the *Taybank Hotel* in Dunkeld (see p.360) restoring some of its spontaneous, infectious fun to a night of Scottish music and dancing.

Europe, this is a landscape not of mountain ranges but of extraordinary peaks, rising individually from the moorland. The area boasts some of the world's oldest rock formations, and occasional signs by the roadside highlight the whole region's considerable geological importance (Ⓦ www.northwest-highlands-geopark.org.uk). It's an area of peaceful, slow backroads, which, after twisting past idyllic crofts, invariably end up at a deserted beach or windswept headland with superb clear-day views west to the Outer Hebrides. **Lochinver**, midway along the west coast and still an important fishing port, is the main settlement, though the crofting villages along the coast, like those around **Achiltibuie**, are more appealing. If you're keen to climb the mountains, head for **Inchnadamph**, which sits below the region's two Munros.

Coigach

Coigach (Ⓦ www.coigach.com) is the peninsula immediately to the north of Loch Broom, accessible via a slow, winding, single-track road that leaves the A835 ten miles north of Ullapool, squeezing between the northern shore of Loch Lurgainn and the lower slopes of Cul Beag (2523ft) and craggy Stac Pollaidh (2012ft). To the southeast, the awesome bulk of Ben More Coigach (2439ft) presides over the district, which contains some spectacular coastal scenery. Coigach's main settlement is **ACHILTIBUIE**, an old crofting village scattered across the hillside above a series of beaches and rocks that taper into the Atlantic. A mile offshore lies Tanera Mor, the largest island of the **Summer Isles**. For **boat** trips round the isles, including some time ashore on Tanera Mor, *Hectoria* (Ⓣ 01854/622315) usually runs twice a day from the Badentarbert pier at Achiltibuie (Easter–Oct; 3hr 30min; £22). Once on the island, you can buy "Summer Isles" stamps from the post office, rent kayaks or take a stroll.

The other attraction in the area is the **Achiltibuie Smokehouse** (Ⓣ 01854/622353, Ⓦ www.summerislesfoods.co.uk; free) at **ALTANDHU**, along the coast road west of Achiltibuie. Here you can see meat, fish and game being cured in the traditional way and buy some afterwards. Next to this, the *Am Fuaran* bar serves lunches, snacks and evening meals, including fresh hand-dived scallops, and, like everywhere else along this stretch, enjoys terrific views.

For **accommodation**, the *Summer Isles Hotel* (Ⓣ01854/622282, Ⓦwww.summerisleshotel.co.uk; Easter–Oct; ❼) enjoys a perfect setting with views over the islands. It's also a memorable (if pricey) Michelin-starred spot for a seafood lunch or dinner. Of Achiltibuie's several **B&Bs**, *Dornie House* (Ⓣ01854/622271, Ⓔdorniehousebandb@aol.com; Easter–Nov; ❶), halfway to Altandhu, is welcoming and provides huge breakfasts. Four miles west of the village there's a basic campsite at *Achnahaird Farm* (Ⓣ01854/622348; Easter–Sept).

There's also a beautifully situated twenty-bed SYHA **hostel** (Ⓣ01854/622482, Ⓦwww.syha.org.uk; May–Sept), three miles southeast of Achiltibuie down the coast at **ACHININVER**, handy for accessing Coigach's mountain hikes. If you're experienced and can use a map and compass, you can walk the ten-mile path to the hostel from Ullapool.

Lochinver and around

The twisting, narrow road north from Achiltibuie through Inverkirkaig is unremittingly spectacular, threading its way through a tumultuous landscape of heaving valleys, moorland and bare rock, past the startling shapes of Cul Beag (2523ft), Cul Mor (2785ft) and the distinctive sugar-loaf **Suilven** (2398ft). You pass thick-walled, idyllic crofts and the start of several community woodland walking trails, before a sheltered bay heralds your arrival at **LOCHINVER**, sixteen miles north of Ullapool (although more than thirty by road). One of the busier fishing harbours in Scotland, it's a workaday and not very attractive place from where large trucks head off for the continent. The **tourist office** (April–Oct Mon–Sat, June–Sept also Sun; Ⓣ01571/844330) in the excellent **Assynt Visitor Centre** gives an interesting rundown on the area's geology, wildlife and history and has a CCTV link to a nearby heronry. A handy leaflet, *Walks around Assynt*, is available from the tourist office, highlighting 31 low- and high-level walks.

Lochinver has a wide choice of good **B&Bs**. On the north side of the loch, *Davar* (Ⓣ01571/844501, Ⓦwww.davar-lochinver.co.uk; March–Oct; ❷) is very welcoming, while you'll enjoy fine views and comfort in three-bedroom *Veyatie B&B* (Ⓣ01571/844424, Ⓦwww.veyatie-scotland.co.uk; ❹) in Baddidarrach. Closer to the tourist office, comfortable *Polcraig* (Ⓣ01571/844429, Ⓔcathelmac@aol.com; ❷) serves up fabulous breakfasts and can arrange fishing. Combining fine dining with a relaxed, upmarket stay, the beautifully appointed *Albannach Hotel* (Ⓣ01571/844407, Ⓦwww.thealbannach.co.uk; ❾; March–Dec; no children under 12) at Baddidarrach, an attractive nineteenth-century building set in a walled garden, offers sumptuous accommodation and memorable five-course dining based on croft-reared produce and fresh seafood; non-guests can dine for £49. Lochinver's most popular **food** halt is the *Larder Riverside Bistro* on the main street, where the moderately priced food includes excellent home-made pies such as wild boar, port and prune served with mash. Reasonably priced bar meals and a good selection of real ales are available at the *Caberfeidh* next door, which is also the most convivial place to head for a drink.

Inverkirkaig Falls

Approaching Lochinver from the south, the road bends sharply through a wooded valley where a signpost for **Falls of Kirkaig** marks the start of a long but gentle **walk** to the base of **Suilven** – the most distinctive mountain in

Scotland, its huge sandstone dome rising above the heather boglands of Assynt. Serious hikers use the path to approach the mighty peak, but you can also follow it for an easy five-mile, three-hour (return) ramble, taking in a waterfall and a secluded loch. Just by the start of the trail but tucked away among the dark pine trees, **Achins Bookshop** must rate as the Highland's best-hidden nook. You can browse the shelves of heavyweight classics and local-interest titles, then head to the **coffee shop** for soup or home-baking. Fishing permits are also available here.

North of Lochinver

Heading **north** from Lochinver, there are two possible routes: the fast A837, which runs eastwards along the shore of Loch Assynt (see p.498) to join the north-bound A894, or the narrow, more scenic B869 **coast road** that locals dub the "Breakdown Zone", because its ups and downs claim so many victims during summer. Hugging the indented shoreline, this route offers superb views as well as a number of rewarding side-trips to beaches and dramatic cliffs.

The first village worthy of a detour is **ACHMELVICH**, three miles northwest of Lochinver, where a tiny bay cradles a stunning white-sand beach lapped by startlingly turquoise water. There's a **campsite** and a basic 36-bed SYHA **hostel** (Ⓣ01571/844480, Ⓦwww.syha.org.uk; April–Sept) just behind the largest beach. However, there are plenty of equally seductive beaches up the coast, including one by the hamlet of Clachtoll, dominated by another beautiful bay with a basic campsite (Easter–Sept; Ⓣ01571/855377, Ⓦwww.clachtollbeachcampsite.co.uk); nearby you'll find the former Clachtoll Salmon Station – now preserved by the Assynt Historical Society.

The side road that branches north off the B869 between **STOER** and **CLASHNESSIE** ends abruptly by the automatic lighthouse at **Raffin**, Stevenson-built in 1870. You can continue for two miles along a boggy, slightly tricky track to the Point of Stoer, named after a colossal rock pillar, the **Old Man of Stoer**, which stands offshore, surrounded by sheer cliffs and splashed with guano from the sea-bird colonies that nest on its 200ft-high sides. Overlooking the Bay of Stoer is the wonderfully remote and snug *Stac Fada B&B* (Ⓣ0845/345 5349, Ⓦwww.stacfada.co.uk; ❷). Some five miles east of Clashnessie, the Drumbeg Stores is unexpectedly well stocked with some deli items, local food and good wine. Next door you can find rooms and a hearty salmon steak or steak and ale pie at the *Drumbeg Hotel* (Ⓣ01571/833236, Ⓦwww.drumbeghotel.co.uk; ❹), while just up the road is a small tea garden and craft shop.

Loch Assynt and around

The area east of Lochinver, traversed by the A837, centred on **Loch Assynt** and bounded by the gnarled peaks of the Ben More Assynt massif, is a wilderness of mountains, moorland, mist and scree. Dotted with lochs and lochans, it's also an angler's paradise, home to the only non-migratory fish in northern Scotland, the brown trout, and numerous other species, including the Atlantic salmon, sea trout, arctic char and ferox, a mysterious, cannibalistic strain of trout.

The displays within the grass-roofed, unstaffed **Knockan Crag** (Creag a' Chnocain; Ⓦwww.knockan-crag.co.uk) visitor centre, thirteen miles south of Loch Assynt on the A835 to Ullapool and part of the Inverpolly National Nature Reserve, outline what is one of the most important geological sites in the world. In 1859, the theory of thrust faults was developed by eminent geologist James Nicol, and two interpretive **trails** (one 15min, the other 1hr) show you how to detect the movement of rock plates in the nearby ancient cliffs.

Kylesku and around

At **KYLESKU**, 33 miles north of Ullapool on the A894, a long, curving road bridge sweeps over the mouth of lochs Glencoul and Glendhu. During World War II, these deep waters provided a secret training base for the brave crews of the x-craft mini-submarines. A small, poignant memorial stands in the car park at the northern end of the Kylesku road bridge.

The congenial *Kylesku Hotel* (ⓣ01971/502231, ⓦwww.kyleskuhotel.co.uk; March–Oct; ❺), by the water's edge above the old ferry slipway, has a welcoming bar with real ales where guests can feast on reasonably priced dishes including **fresh seafood**. Alternatively, there's *Newton Lodge* (ⓣ01971/502070, ⓦwww.newtonlodge.co.uk; ❺), a modern, friendly and comfortable small **hotel** two miles south of Kylesku offering guests fine views over Loch Glencoul and the chance to spot seals on the shoreline. Statesman Cruises runs entertaining **boat trips** (March–Oct twice daily except Sat; round trip 2hr; ⓣ01971/502345; £15) from the jetty below the *Kylesku Hotel* to the 650ft **Eas-Coul-Aulin**, Britain's highest waterfall, located at the head of Loch Glencoul; otters, seals, porpoises and minke whales can occasionally be spotted along the way. You can get dropped off in the morning and/or picked up in the afternoon if you arrange it beforehand.

The far northwest coast

The Sutherland coastline north of Kylesku is a bridge too far for some, yet for others the stark, elemental beauty of the Highlands is to be found on the **far northwest coast** as nowhere else. Here, the peaks become more widely spaced and settlements smaller and fewer, linked by twisting single-track roads and shoreside footpaths that make excellent hiking trails. Places to stay and eat can be thin on the ground, particularly out of season.

Scourie

Ten miles north of Kylesku, the widely scattered crofting community of **SCOURIE**, on a bluff above the main road, surrounds a beautiful sandy beach whose safe bathing has made it a popular holiday destination for families; there's plenty to do for walkers and trout anglers, too. The Inverness to Durness bus service (Mon–Sat, via Lairg station) stops here. Scourie itself has some good **accommodation**, including the charming *Scourie Lodge* (ⓣ01971/502248, ⓦwww.scourielodge.co.uk; March–Oct; ❺), an old three-bedroomed shooting retreat surrounded by trees on the north side of the sandy bay, with a lovely garden. There's a **campsite**, the modest *Scourie Caravan and Camping Park* (ⓣ01971/502060; April–Sept) two minutes' walk away.

Tarbet and Handa Island

Visible just offshore to the north of Scourie, **Handa Island** is a huge chunk of red Torridon sandstone surrounded by sheer cliffs, carpeted with machair and purple-tinged moorland and teeming with seabirds. A **wildlife reserve** administered by the Scottish Wildlife Trust (ⓦwww.swt.org.uk), the island supports one of the largest sea-bird colonies in northwest Europe. It's a real treat for ornithologists, with razorbills and guillemots breeding on its guano-covered cliffs during summer. From late May to mid-July, large numbers of puffins waddle comically over the turf-covered cliff-tops where they dig their burrows. Until the mid-nineteenth century, Handa supported a community of crofters, who survived on a diet of fish, potatoes and seabirds. The islanders, whose ruined cottages still cling to the slopes by the jetty, devised their own system of government, with a "queen" (Handa's oldest widow) and "parliament" (a council of men who met each morning to discuss the day's business). Uprooted by the 1847 potato famine, most of the villagers emigrated to Canada's Cape Breton.

Weather permitting, **boats** (ⓣ07780/967800) leave for Handa throughout the day (Easter–Sept Mon–Sat 9.30am–2pm outbound; £10) from the tiny cove of **TARBET**, three miles northwest of the main road and accessible by postbus from Scourie, where there's a small car park and jetty. You're encouraged to make a donation towards Handa's upkeep. You'll need about three hours to follow the **footpath** around the island – an easy and enjoyable walk taking in the north shore's Great Stack rock pillar and some fine views across the Minch: a detailed route guide is featured in the SWT's free leaflet, available from the warden's office when you arrive. Camping is not allowed, and only volunteers and scientists for the nature reserve can use the small bothy. Tarbet's unexpected and delightful *Shorehouse* **restaurant** (ⓣ01971/502251; Easter–Sept Mon–Sat), in a conservatory just above the jetty, serves delicious, moderately priced fresh seafood – some of it caught by the owner – as well as a good selection of home-made cakes and dessert.

Kinlochbervie to Sandwood Bay

North of Scourie, the road sweeps inland through the starkest part of the Highlands, in which rocks piled on rocks, bog and water create an almost alien landscape, and the bare, stony coastline looks increasingly inhospitable. The B801 side road branches off to **KINLOCHBERVIE**, near which the welcoming *Old School Restaurant and Rooms* (ⓣ01971/521383, ⓦwww.oldschoolklb.co.uk; March–Oct; ❹) offers comfortable beds – including a cute separate en-suite single (£45) – and good-value evening meals. In Kinlochbervie itself, the eponymous *Kinlochbervie Hotel* (ⓣ01971/521275, ⓦwww.kinlochberviehotel.com; ❺) overlooks an incongruously huge fish market and modern concrete harbour from where trucks from all over Europe pick up cod and shellfish. There's a mobile bank, petrol pump and nearby shop; if you're in need of sustenance, try **fish and chips** at the *Fishermen's Mission* (Mon–Fri).

A single-track road continues northwest of Kinlochbervie through isolated **OLDSHOREMORE**, a working crofters' village scattered above a stunning white-sand beach (where you can camp rough), to **BLAIRMORE**, where a four-mile walk leads across peaty moorland to **Sandwood Bay**. After an unremarkable walk-in, the shell-white sandy **beach** at the end of the rough track is a breathtaking sight and one of the most beautiful in Scotland. Flanked by rolling dunes and lashed by fierce gales for much of the year, the dramatic leaning rock-stack to the south is said to be haunted by a bearded mariner – one of many sailors to have perished on this notoriously dangerous stretch of coast since the Vikings first navigated it over a millennium ago. Around the turn of the twentieth century, the beach, whose treacherous undercurrents make it unsuitable for swimming, also witnessed Britain's most recent recorded sighting of a **mermaid**. Turning back and past Blairmore at **SHEIGRA**, you can wild camp (there are no facilities) behind the beach.

It's possible to trek overland from Sandwood Bay north to Cape Wrath (see p.502), the northwestern tip of mainland Britain, a full day's walk away. If you're planning to meet the Cape Wrath minibus to Durness, contact them first since it won't run if the weather turns bad, leaving you stranded.

The north coast

Though a constant stream of sponsored walkers, caravans and tour groups makes it to the dull town of **John O'Groats**, surprisingly few visitors travel the whole length of the Highlands' wild **north coast**. Those who do, however, rarely return disappointed. Scotland's rugged northern shore is backed by barren mountains in the west, and by lochs and open rolling grasslands in the east. Mile upon mile of crumbling cliffs and sheer rocky headlands shelter bays whose perfect white beaches are nearly always deserted – they're also home to Scotland's best surfing waves (see **The great outdoors** colour section).

Though only a wee place, **Durness** is a good jumping-off point for rugged **Cape Wrath**, the windswept promontory at Scotland's northwest tip, which has retained an end-of-the-world mystique lost long ago by John O'Groats. Continuing east, **Loch Eriboll** is probably the most spectacular of the north-coast sea lochs, while Tongue, ten miles further east, enjoys the most attractive setting of the coast's small crofting villages. **Thurso**, the largest town on the north coast, is really only visited by those en route to Orkney. More enticing are the huge sea-bird colonies clustered in clefts and on remote stacks at **Dunnet Head** and **Duncansby Head**, to the east of Thurso.

Durness and around

Scattered around a string of sheltered sandy coves and grassy cliff-tops, **DURNESS** (Ⓦwww.durness.org), the most northwesterly village on the British mainland, straddles the turning point on the main A838 road as it swings east from the peat bogs of the interior to the north coast's fertile strip of limestone machair. Durness village itself sits above its own sandy bay, Sango Sands, while half a mile to the east is **SMOO**, which used to be an RAF station. In between Durness and Smoo, the millennial village hall features a windblown and rather forlorn community garden that harbours a memorial commemorating the Beatle **John Lennon**, who came to Durness on family holidays and revisited in the 1960s with Yoko.

It's worth pausing at Smoo to see the 200ft-long **Smoo Cave**, a gaping hole in a sheer limestone cliff formed partly by the action of the sea and partly by the small burn that flows through it. Tucked away at the end of a narrow sheer-sided sea cove, the main chamber is accessible via steps from the car park by the A838. The much-hyped rock formations are less memorable than the short rubber-dinghy trip you have to make in the other two caverns, the whole experience enlivened after wet weather by a waterfall that crashes through the middle of the cavern. Twenty-minute walk/boat trips (May–Sept; £3) are run on request, weather permitting, by Colin Coventry (Ⓣ01971/511704).

A narrow road winds a mile or so northwest of Durness to **BALNAKIEL**, passing **Balnakiel Craft Village** en route. Disabuse yourself of any notion of quaint cottages, as the village is housed in a grim 1940s military base, transformed in the 1960s into a sort of industrial estate for arts and crafts. A dozen or so eclectic businesses (generally daily 10am–5.30pm) continue to function, including a printmakers and woodcarving studio and a pottery. The Loch Croispol bookshop runs a modest daytime café (Ⓣ01971/511777) whilst the nearby *Balnakeil Bistro* (March–Oct; Ⓣ01971/511232) serves reasonably priced lunches and evening meals and sells crafts and books. At *Cocoa Mountain*, you can watch chocolates and truffles being made before sitting down in the bright modern café for a coffee or hot chocolate (Ⓣ01971/511233).

Balnakiel is also known for its **golf course** (£15), whose ninth and final hole involves a well-judged drive over the Atlantic; you can rent equipment from the clubhouse. The white-sand beach on the east side of **Balnakiel Bay** is stunning in any weather, but most spectacular on sunny days when the water turns to brilliant turquoise. For the best views, walk along the path that winds north through the dunes (pockmarked from naval bombing exercises) behind it; this eventually leads to **Faraid Head** – from the Gaelic *Fear Ard* (High Fellow) – where there's a very small colony of nesting puffins (ask the tourist office for directions). The fine views east to the mouth of Loch Eriboll and west to Cape Wrath make this round walk (3–4hr) the best in the Durness area.

Practicalities

Public transport is sparse; the key service is the Dearman Coaches link (May–Sept Mon–Sat 1 daily; also Sun in July & Aug) from Inverness via Ullapool, Lochinver and Scourie. The bus has a cycle carrier. Postbuses provide a more complicated year-round alternative and meet trains at Lairg; check schedules at the post office or the helpful Durness **tourist office** (March–April & Oct Mon–Sat; May–Sept daily; Nov–Feb Mon–Fri). This incorporates a small **visitor centre and ranger post** that features excellent panels detailing the area's history, geology, flora and fauna. Information about walks and cycle tracks, including guided ranger walks, can be sourced from here. Next to *Mackays* (see below), the old telephone exchange has been converted into **Surf Wrath** (ⓣ07752/501333, ⓦwww.surfwrath.co.uk), where you can rent gear and book surfing and coasteering courses.

In terms of **accommodation**, *Mackays Rooms and Restaurant*, at the western edge of the village, stands out for its welcoming personal touches and a dinner menu (from 7pm, changes daily) featuring locally sourced seafood, lamb and beef (book in advance; ⓣ01971/511202, ⓦwww.visitmackays.com; ❺). The proprietor also runs the congenial and attractive *Lazy Crofter Bunkhouse* (ⓣ01971/511202, ⓦwww.durnesshostel.com) next door. A shed-like SYHA **hostel** (ⓣ01971/511264, ⓦwww.syha.org.uk; Easter–Sept), sits beside the Smoo Cave car park, a bleak half-mile east of the village. There are also a number of **B&Bs**, including *Glengolly B&B* in the village, which has two en-suite rooms in a working croft (ⓣ01971/511255, ⓦwww.glengolly.com; ❸). The **campsite** (ⓣ01971/511222), on an exposed spot near the tourist office, has views over Sango Sands; close by is the local village **pub**. In addition to *Mackays*, the *Seafood Platter* (May–Sept; ⓣ01971/511215) on the eastern fringe of the village opposite the SYHA hostel is simple, tasty and moderately priced; it also does takeaway snacks.

Cape Wrath

An excellent day-trip from Durness begins two miles southwest of the village at **KEOLDALE**, where (tides and Ministry of Defence permitting) a foot-passenger **ferry** (daily: May, June & Sept 11am & 1.30pm; July & Aug 4 trips between 9.30am and 6.30pm; £5.50 return; ⓣ01971/511376 for ferry) crosses the spectacular Kyle of Durness estuary to link up with a **minibus** (May–Sept; £10 return; ⓣ01971/511343) that makes the forty-minute, fourteen-mile run out to **Cape Wrath**, the British mainland's most northwesterly point. Note that Garvie Island (An Garbh-eilean) is an air bombing range, and the military regularly close the road to Cape Wrath. The headland takes its name not from the stormy seas that crash against it for most of the year, but from the Norse word *hvarf*, meaning "turning place" – a throwback to the days when Viking warships used it as a navigation point during raids on the Scottish coast. These days, a Stevenson lighthouse warns ships away from the treacherous rocks; looking east to Orkney and west to the Outer Hebrides, it stands above the famous **Clo Mor cliffs**, the highest sea cliffs in Britain and a prime breeding site for seabirds.

Loch Eriboll

The road east of Durness passes several spectacular sandy bays en route to deep and sheltered **Loch Eriboll**, the north coast's most spectacular sea loch, where, above the shoreline, high mountains accentuate the sense of wildness and isolation. Servicemen stationed here during World War II to protect passing Russian convoys nicknamed it "Loch 'Orrible", but it's wild and unspoilt; porpoises and otters are a common sight along the rocky shore, and minke whales occasionally swim in from the open sea.

Tongue to Thurso

There's great drama in the landscape between Tongue and Thurso, as the A836 – still single-track for some of the way – wends its way over bleak and often totally uninhabited rocky moorland, intercut with sandy sea lochs. Tiny little **Tongue** is pleasant enough, as is the settlement of **Bettyhill**, to the east, but the real reason to venture this far is to explore the countryside: **Ben Hope** (3040ft), the most northerly Munro, and the fascinating blanket bog of the **Flow Country** even further inland.

Tongue and around

The road takes a wonderfully slow and circuitous route around Loch Eriboll and east over the top of AMhoine moor to the pretty crofting township of **TONGUE**. Dominated by the ruins of **Castle Varrich** (Caisteal Bharraich), a medieval stronghold of the Mackays (three-mile return walk), the village is strewn above the east shore of the **Kyle of Tongue**, which you can cross either via a new causeway, or by following the longer and more scenic single-track road around its southern side. When the tide recedes, this shallow estuary becomes a mass of golden sand flats, superb on sunny days, with the sharp profiles of **Ben Hope** (3040ft) and **Ben Loyal** (2509ft) looming like twin sentinels to the south, and the Rabbit Islands a short way out to sea.

The best **accommodation** in Tongue is the nineteen-bedroom *Tongue Hotel* (ⓣ01847/611206, ⓦwww.tonguehotel.co.uk; April–Oct; ❻), the plush former hunting lodge of the Duke of Sutherland. The large and well-equipped SYHA **hostel** (ⓣ01847/611789, ⓦwww.syha.org.uk), right beside the causeway a mile north of the village centre on the Kyle's east shore, is the best budget option. Over on the western side of the Kyle, five miles away from Tongue at **TALMINE**, a converted nineteenth-century church with great views out towards the Orkney Islands is the home of the popular *Cloisters* B&B (ⓣ01847/601286, ⓦwww.cloistertal.demon.co.uk; ❷). There is also a very basic **campsite** opposite the sandy beach.

Bettyhill and around

Twelve miles east of Tongue, **BETTYHILL** is a major crofting village, set among rocky green hills. In Gaelic it was known as *Am Blàran Odhar* ("Little Dun-coloured Field"), but the origins of the English name are unknown; it was, however, definitely not named after Elizabeth, Countess of Sutherland, who presided over the Strathnaver Clearances. The story of those terrible times is told by local schoolchildren at the delightful and loyally maintained **Strathnaver Museum** (April–Oct Mon–Sat 10am–5pm; £2), housed in the old Farr church, east of the main village. Inside, you can see a reconstructed croft, some Pictish stones and a 3800-year-old early Bronze Age beaker. The 24-mile Strathnaver Trail, running south from Bettyhill along the B873 to Altnaharra, highlights numerous historical sites from the Neolithic, Bronze and Iron Age periods.

A short stroll north of the church, sheltered **Farr beach** forms a splendid unbroken arc of pure white sand between the Naver and Borgie rivers. Even more visually impressive is the River Naver's narrow tidal estuary, to the west of Bettyhill, and **Torrisdale beach** (popular with surfers; access off the road to Borgie five miles west of Bettyhill), which ends in a smooth white spit that forms part of the **Invernaver Nature Reserve**. During summer, arctic terns nest here on the riverbanks, which are dotted with clumps of rare Scottish primrose, and you stand a good chance of spotting an otter or two.

In the museum car park, the small **tourist office** houses the basic *Café at Bettyhill* (closed Sun & weekdays in winter). Nearby, the *Farr Bay Inn*, known locally as the "FBI", also serves good meals. The *Bettyhill Hotel* (Ⓣ01641/521352, Ⓦwww.bettyhill.info; ❷) offers good-value **rooms** and bar meals. Bettyhill's large campsite affords excellent bay views. Sheltered in woods four or five miles west of Bettyhill, the friendly, old-fashioned *Borgie Lodge Hotel* (Ⓣ01641/521332, Ⓦwww.borgielodgehotel.co.uk; ❺) is a popular base for salmon- and sea-fishing.

Dounreay

As you move east from Bettyhill, the north coast changes dramatically as the hills on the horizon recede to be replaced by fields fringed with flagstone walls. It provides an incongruous setting for **Dounreay Nuclear Power Station** (Ⓦwww.dounreay.com), a surreal collection of chimney stacks and box-like buildings, plus the famous golf-ball-shaped DFR (Dounreay Fast Reactor). Established in 1955, Dounreay pioneered the development of fast reactor technology and was the first in the world to provide mains electricity. The reactors themselves have long since closed, though Dounreay remains by the far the biggest employer on the north coast, with decommissioning of the 130-acre site estimated to last until 2033 and cost £2.9 billion.

The Flow Country

At a junction six miles before Dounreay, you can head forty miles or so south towards Helmsdale on the A897, through the **Flow Country**, whose name comes from *flói*, an Old Norse word meaning "marshy ground". This huge expanse of "blanket bog" is a valuable carbon sink and home to a wide variety of wildlife. At the train station at **FORSINARD**, fourteen miles south of Melvich and easily accessible from Thurso, Wick and the south by train, there is an RSPB **visitor centre** (April–Oct daily 9am–6pm; Ⓣ01641/571225), with CCTV coverage of hen harriers nesting, and a **Peatland Centre**, which explains the wonders of peat.

To get to grips with the whole concept of blanket bog, of which eight square miles is currently being restored from forestry use to its natural state, take a leaflet and follow the mile-long **Dubh Lochan Trail** that's been laid out over the flagstones, through peat banks to some nearby black lochans. En route, you get to see bog asphodel, bogbean, sphagnum moss and the insect-trapping sundew and butterwort; you've also got a good chance of spotting greenshanks, golden plovers and hen harriers. The visitor centre runs twice-weekly guided walks (May to end July Tues & Thurs; 2–5pm; 3hr walk; £5) through the area. The *Forsinard Hotel* (Ⓣ01641/571221; ❻), opposite the station, serves reasonable bar food, is popular with anglers and stalkers and runs hawking packages for guests. Right beside the RSPB centre, Sue Grimshaw's **B&B** (Ⓣ01641/571262; ❷) offers guests a comfortable stay and tasty three-course evening meals (£13) made with local produce.

Thurso

Approached from the isolation of the west, **THURSO** feels like a metropolis. In reality, it's a relatively small service centre visited mostly by people passing through to the adjoining port of **Scrabster** to catch the ferry to Orkney, or by increasing numbers of surfers attracted to the waves on the north coast.

Arrival and information

Trains from Inverness (all of which go via Wick) arrive at Thurso **train station**, adjacent to the **bus station**, both a ten-minute walk down Princes Street and Sir George's Street from the helpful riverside **tourist office** (April, May, June, Sept & Oct Mon–Sat; July & Aug daily). There's also an office at Caithness Horizons (see below). The **Scrabster ferry terminal** is a mile or so northwest of town, with regular buses from the train station in the morning, and from Olrig Street in the afternoon. For more on **ferries to Orkney** from Scrabster, Gills Bay and John O'Groats, see p.507.

If you're coming to **surf**, want a lesson, need to rent a board (£10/day) or simply want a coffee and home-baking before hitting the waves, ask at *Tempest Surf* on Riverside Road by Thurso harbour (ⓣ01847/892500).

Accommodation

The nearest **campsite** (ⓣ01847/805503) sits out towards Scrabster alongside the main road, though there are better views at Dunnet Bay (ⓣ01847/821319) a few miles east (see p.506).

Forss House Hotel 3 miles west of Thurso on the A836 ⓣ01847/861201, ⓦwww.forsshousehotel.co.uk. Built in 1810, this thirteen-bedroom family-owned hotel offers an upmarket stay in spacious grounds. ❼

Murray House 1 Campbell St ⓣ01847/895759, ⓦwww.murrayhousebb.com. Central, comfortable and friendly and will rustle up a tasty three-course dinner for £15 per person. ❸

Pentland Lodge ⓣ01847/895103. Nine-bedroom B&B on the west side of Thurso offering comfort and views over Thurso Bay. ❺

Sandra's 24/26 Princes St ⓣ01847/894575, ⓦwww.sandras-backpackers.ukf.net. A refurbished, clean and well-run place that's affiliated to the SYHA and owned by the popular chippy downstairs. All rooms are en suite and guests have free use of bikes and internet access. ❶

Tigh na Abhainn ⓣ01847/893443. B&B in an old house by the river serving kippers and such like for breakfast. ❷

The Townhouse 2 Braehead House ⓣ01955/611291, ⓦwww.thesurfdirectory.co.uk. A smart two-bedroom self-catering option right by the sea, and popular with surfers.

The Town

The town's name derives from the Norse word *Thorsa*, literally "River of the God Thor", and in Viking times this was a major gateway to the mainland. Later, ships set sail from here for the Baltic and Scandinavian ports loaded with meal, beef, hides and fish. Much of the town, however, dates from the 1790s, when Sir John Sinclair built a large new extension to the old fishing port. The nearby Dounreay Nuclear Power Station ensured continuing prosperity after World War II, tripling the population when workers from the plant settled in Thurso.

Thurso's grid-plan streets have some rather handsome Victorian architecture in the local, greyish sandstone. The main attraction is in the revamped Victorian Town Hall on the High Street, where **Caithness Horizons** (Mon–Sat 10am–6pm, Sun 11am–6pm; ⓦwww.caithnesshorizons.co.uk) comprises a museum, tourist office and café. The museum uses interactive technology and evocative old photos to explore local geology, history, farming and fishing, with treasures including a Bronze Age beaker and a Viking brooch. Downstairs there's a display on the decommissioning of Dounreay.

If you continue north up the High Street, you'll reach **Old St Peter's Church**, a substantial ruin with origins in the thirteenth century, and the old part of town, near the harbour.

Eating

Thurso has several good options for when you're feeling peckish.

Captain's Galley The Harbour, Scrabster ⓣ01847/894999, ⓦwww.captainsgalley.co.uk. A former ice-house and salmon bothy which now serves the best, most expensive seafood in the area; each day the menu details the boats the fish have come in on. Closed Sun & Mon.

Gallery Café Caithness Horizons museum. The museum's cheerful daytime café serves sandwiches, soup and home-baking, and has a kids' menu.

Le Bistro 2 Traill St ⓣ01847/893737. Popular option where the reasonably priced menu includes traditional fare such as Cullen skink. Closed Sun & Mon.

Tempest Surf Café Riverside Road. Inexpensive snacks by the harbour, and the place to warm up after a play in the waves.

The Upper Deck *The Ferry Inn*, Scrabster ⓣ01847/872814. The place to head for a huge (if pricey) steak, along with hearty seafood dishes and surf'n'turf classics.

Dunnet Head and the Castle of Mey

Thurso doesn't have much of a beach, so if you want to sink your toes into sand, head five miles east along the A836 to **Dunnet Bay**, a vast golden beach backed by huge dunes. One of the reef breaks here, known as "Thurso East", is regarded as one of Europe's finest, and the bay is popular with surfers even in the winter. At the northeast end of the bay, the new **Seadrift Visitor and Ranger Centre** (April–Sept Tues–Fri 2–5pm, Sat & Sun 2–6pm; free), near the excellent campsite, holds an exhibition about the area's seabirds, marine life and ecology amidst the sand dunes. You can also pick up information on good local history and nature walks, including a short self-guided trail into nearby **Dunnet Forest**.

To the north of the bay is the small village of **DUNNET**, where it's worth stopping in at **Mary-Ann's Cottage** (June–Sept Tues–Sun 2–4.30pm; £3), a farming croft vacated in 1990 by the then 93-year-old Mary-Ann Calder, whose grandfather had built the cottage, and maintained just as she left it, full of reminders of the three generations who lived and worked there over the last 150 years. For a welcoming **B&B**, try the *Dunnet Head B&B* at Brough, three miles south of Dunnet Head on the B855 and housed in the former post office (ⓣ01847/851774, ⓦwww.dunnethead.iberacal.com; ❷). The owners can advise on the archeology and wildlife in the area, including the chance to spot seals in the bay. The Thurso-to-John O'Groat's bus stops near the B&B but you'll need to walk to the lighthouse.

Despite the publicity that John O'Groats customarily receives, mainland Britain's most northerly point is in fact **Dunnet Head**, north of Dunnet along the B855, which runs for four miles over bleak heather and bog to the tip of the headland, crowned with a Stevenson lighthouse. In early summer, puffins may be spotted on the impressive red cliffs whilst seals bathe off rocks below the weirdly eroded rock stacks. On a clear day you can see the whole northern coastline from Cape Wrath to Duncansby Head, and across the treacherous **Pentland Firth** to Orkney.

Roughly fifteen miles east of Thurso, just off the A836, lies the late Queen Mother's former Scottish home, the **Castle of Mey** (May–July & mid-Aug to Sept daily 10.30am–4pm; £9.50; ⓦwww.castleofmey.org.uk). It's a modest little place, hidden behind high flagstone walls, with great views north to Orkney and a herd of the Queen Mum's beloved Aberdeen Angus grazing out front. The original castle was a sixteenth-century Z-plan affair, owned by the earls of Caithness until 1889, and bought in a state of disrepair in 1952, the year the queen mother's husband, George VI, died. She used to spend every August here, and it's unstuffy inside, the walls hung with works by local amateur artists (and watercolours by Prince Charles, who visits every August). There's a reasonable tearoom, or try nearby *Simply Unique* in Mey for traditional home-baking and coffee.

John O'Groats and around

Romantics expecting to find a magical meeting of land and water at **JOHN O'GROATS** (Ⓦwww.visitjohnogroats.com) are invariably disappointed – sadly, it remains an uninspiring tourist trap. The views north to Orkney are fine enough, but the village offers little more than a string of souvenir and craft shops and several refreshment stops thronged with coach parties. The village gets its name from the Dutchman, Jan de Groot, who obtained the ferry contract for the hazardous crossing to Orkney in 1496. The eight-sided house he built for his eight quarrelling sons (so that each one could enter by his own door) is echoed in the octagonal tower of the much-photographed but now vacant and dilapidated *John O'Groats Hotel*, which shares the same owners as Cornwall's *Land's End Hotel*, to and from which point walkers and cyclists make their epic journeys. Long overdue plans to redevelop the hotel seem to have stalled.

The **tourist office** (March–Oct daily) is by the car park. The working croft at *Bencorragh House* **B&B** (Ⓣ01955/611449, Ⓦwww.bencorraghhouse.com; March–Oct; ❷) provides farmhouse accommodation and spectacular views at Upper Gills near Canisbay, three miles southwest of John O'Groats. The small SYHA **hostel** (Ⓣ01955/611761, Ⓦwww.syha.org.uk; April–Oct) is in Canisbay itself. *Stroma View* **campsite** (Ⓣ01955/611313; March–Sept), one mile along the Thurso road, is less exposed than the windswept but well-equipped *John O'Groats* site (Ⓣ01955/611329). To **eat**, seek out the cosy, wood-furnished *School House Restaurant* (Ⓣ01955/611714, Ⓦwww.dinecaithness.co.uk; Wed–Sun). There are several **boat trips** to be had: John O'Groats Ferries (Ⓣ01955/611353, Ⓦwww.jogferry.co.uk) offers a leisurely afternoon cruise, which will take you round the sea-bird colonies and stacks of Duncansby Head or the seal colonies of Stroma (mid-June to Aug daily 2.30pm; 1hr 30min; £15); North Coast Marine Adventures (Easter–Oct daily; Ⓣ01955/611797, Ⓦwww.northcoast-marine-adventures.co.uk) arranges more high-adrenaline thirty-minute white-water trips in a rigid inflatable (£20; under-12s free) and a one-hour wildlife scenic tour (£25).

If you're disappointed by John O'Groats, press on a couple of miles further east to **Duncansby Head**, which, with its lighthouse, dramatic cliffs and well-worn coastal path, has a lot more to offer. The birdlife here is prolific, and south of the headland lie spectacular 200ft-high cliffs, cut by sheer-sided clefts known locally as *geos*, and several impressive sea stacks.

The east coast

The **east coast** of the Highlands, between Inverness and Wick, is nowhere near as spectacular as the west, with gently undulating moors, grassland and low cliffs where you might expect sea lochs and mountains. Washed by the cold waters of the North Sea, it's markedly cooler, too.

While many visitors speed up the main A9 road through this region in a headlong rush to the Orkneys' prehistoric sites, those who dally will find a wealth of brochs, cairns and standing stones, many in remarkable condition. The area around the Black Isle and the Tain was a Pictish heartland, and has yielded important finds. Further north, from around the ninth century AD onwards, the **Norse** influence was more keenly felt than in any other part of mainland Britain, and dozens of Scandinavian-sounding names recall the era when this was a Viking kingdom.

Culturally and scenically, much of the east coast is more lowland than highland, and Caithness in particular evolved more or less separately from the Highlands, avoiding the bloody tribal feuds that wrought such havoc further south and west. Later, however, the nineteenth-century **Clearances** hit the region hard, as countless ruined cottages and empty glens show. Hundreds of thousands of crofters were evicted and forced to emigrate, or else take up fishing in one of the numerous herring ports established on the coast. The fishing heritage is a recurring theme along this coast, though there are only a handful of working boats scattered around the harbours today, and while oil has brought a transient prosperity to one or two, the area remains one of the country's poorest, reliant on sheep farming, fishing and tourism.

The one stretch of the east coast that's always been relatively rich is the **Black Isle**, just over the Kessock Bridge heading north out of Inverness, whose main village, **Cromarty**, is the region's undisputed highlight, with a crop of elegant mansions and appealing fishermen's cottages clustered near the entrance to the Cromarty Firth. In late medieval times, pilgrims, including James IV of Scotland, poured through here en route to the red-sandstone town of **Tain** to worship at the shrine of St Duthus, where the former sacred enclave has now been converted into one of the many "heritage centres" that punctuate the route north. Beyond **Dornoch**, a renowned golfing resort recently famous as the site of Madonna's wedding, the ersatz-Loire château **Dunrobin Castle** is the main tourist attraction, a monument as much to the iniquities of the Clearances as to the eccentricity of Victorian taste. The relatively flat landscapes of this northeast corner – windswept peat bog and farmland dotted with lochans and grey-and-white crofts – are a surprising contrast to the more rugged country south and west of here.

The Black Isle and around

Sandwiched between the Cromarty Firth to the north and the Moray and Beauly firths which separate it from Inverness to the south, the **Black Isle** is not an island at all, but a fertile peninsula whose rolling hills, prosperous farms and stands of deciduous woodland make it more reminiscent of Dorset or Sussex than the Highlands. It probably gained its name because of its mild climate: there's rarely frost, which leaves the fields "black" all winter; another explanation is that the name derives from the Gaelic word for black, *dubh* – a possible corruption of St Duthus (see p.512).

The Black Isle is littered with dozens of **prehistoric sites**, but the main incentive to make the detour east from the A9 is to visit the picturesque eighteenth-century town of **Cromarty**, huddled at the northeast tip of the peninsula. A string of villages along the south coast is also worth stopping off in en route, and one of them, Rosemarkie, has an outstanding small **museum** devoted to Pictish culture. Nearby Chanonry Point is among the best **dolphin-spotting** sites in Europe.

The southern Black Isle

Just across the Kessock Bridge from Inverness is a roadside lay-by that hosts a **tourist office** (Easter–Oct daily; ⓣ01463/731701), as well as a small **dolphin and**

seal centre (June–Sept daily 9.30am–4.30pm; free), which offers the chance to observe (and listen to) the popular creatures.

Fortrose and Rosemarkie

FORTROSE, ten miles northeast of Inverness, is a quietly elegant village dominated by the beautiful ruins of an early thirteenth-century **cathedral** (daily 9.30am–5.30pm; free). Founded by King David I, it now languishes on a lovely green bordered by red-sandstone and colourwashed houses, where a horde of gold coins dating from the time of Robert III was unearthed in 1880.

There's a memorial plaque to the seer at nearby **Chanonry Point**, reached by a back road from the north end of Fortrose; the thirteenth hole of the golf course here marks the spot where he met his death. Jutting into a narrow channel in the Moray Firth (deepened to allow warships into the estuary during World War II), the point, fringed on one side by a beach of golden sand and shingle, is an excellent place to look for **dolphins** (see box, p.464).

ROSEMARKIE, a lovely one-street village a mile north of Fortrose at the opposite (northwest) end of the beach, is thought to have been evangelized by St Boniface in the early eighth century. The cosy **Groam House Museum** (May–Oct Mon–Sat 10am–5pm, Sun 2–4.30pm; Nov–April Sat & Sun 2–4pm; free; Ⓦ www.groamhouse.org.uk), at the bottom of the village, displays fifteen intricately carved Pictish standing stones (among them the famous Rosemarkie Cross Slab) dating from as early as the eighth century and shows an informative video highlighting Pictish sites in the region. Good **bar food** in this area is available at the *Plough Inn*, just down the main street from the museum in Rosemarkie, and there's a branch of the Cromarty Bakery on the main street.

Cromarty

According to legend, the twin headlands flanking the entrance to the **Cromarty Firth**, known as The Sutors (from the Gaelic word for shoemaker), were once a pair of giant cobblers who used to protect the Black Isle from pirates. Nowadays, however, the only giants in the area are the partially deconstructed oil rigs marooned in the estuary off Nigg and Invergordon like metal monsters marching out to sea. They form a surreal counterpoint to the web of tiny streets and chocolate-box workers' cottages of **CROMARTY**, the Black Isle's main settlement. The town, an ancient ferry crossing point on the pilgrimage trail to St Duthus's shrine in Tain, lost much of its trade during the nineteenth century to places served by the railway; a branch line to the town was begun but never completed. Although a royal burgh since the fourth century, Cromarty didn't become a prominent port until 1772 when the entrepreneurial local landlord, George Ross, founded a hemp mill here, fuelling a period of prosperity during which Cromarty acquired some of Scotland's finest Georgian houses; these, together with the terraced fishers' cottages of the nineteenth-century herring boom, have left the town with a wonderful concentration of Scottish domestic architecture.

To get a sense of Cromarty's past, wander through the town's pretty streets to the **museum** housed in the old **Courthouse** on Church Street (April–Oct Sun–Thurs 10am–5pm; £2), which tells the history of the courthouse and town using audiovisuals and animated figures. You are also issued with an audio handset and a map for an excellent **walking tour** around the town. **Hugh Miller**, a nineteenth-century stonemason turned author, geologist, folklorist and Free Church campaigner, was born in Cromarty, and his **birthplace** (May–Sept Sun–Wed 1–5pm; NTS; £5.50), a thatched cottage on Church Street, has been restored to give an idea of what Cromarty must have been like in his day. There's also a wild garden and reading room.

Tucked-away **Cromarty Pottery** at 49 Shore St (Ⓦwww.cromarty-pottery.com) is well worth a peek, and otherwise Cromarty is simply a fascinating place just to wander around, and there's an excellent four-mile circular **walk** out to the south Sutor stacks. Pick up the route by leaving town to the east on Miller Road, and turning right when the lane becomes "The Causeway". For a simpler shoreline walk, turn left here, following the path to the water.

Dolphin- and other wildlife-spotting trips (2hr; £22) are offered locally by EcoVentures (Ⓣ01381/600323, Ⓦwww.ecoventures.co.uk), who travel out through the Sutors to the Moray Firth in a powerful RIB. The tiny two-car **Nigg–Cromarty ferry** (June to end Sept daily 8am–6.15pm, until 7.15pm July and Aug; £2.50) is Scotland's smallest. Embark from the jetty near the lighthouse.

Practicalities

Buses run to Cromarty from Inverness Union Street, returning from Victoria Hall. During summer, **accommodation** is in short supply. The most upmarket option is the traditional *Royal Hotel* (Ⓣ01381/600217, Ⓦwww.royalcromartyhotel.co.uk; ❺), down at the harbour, which has nicely furnished rooms overlooking the Firth. For **B&B**, try the modest but friendly *Trade Winds* in the Fishertown area (Ⓣ01381/600430; ❷), *Gisborne B&B* (Ⓣ01381/600376; ❸) on Marine Terrace, once the cottage hospital, or grand red-brick *Sydney House* (Ⓣ01381/600451, Ⓦwww.sydneyhouse.co.uk; ❸).

For something **to eat**, there's the *Royal Hotel* which specializes in seafood, and the *Cromarty Arms* on Church Street which is good for a pub lunch, but there are few more down-to-earth but satisfying restaurants in the Highlands than *Sutor Creek* at 21 Bank St (Ⓣ01381/600855, Ⓦwww.sutorcreek.co.uk; Wed–Sun 11am–late). It serves organic wines, delicious seafood and fresh pizza cooked in a wood-fired oven, though the imaginative toppings are local and seasonal rather than conventionally Italian. Further up the road at the *Cromarty Bakery* (closed Sun) you'll find tasty home-bakes, fresh breads such as spinach and walnut, and whisky cake.

For **bike rental** (£12/half-day, £20/day) contact the friendly operator of MBHI (Ⓣ07780/940342, Ⓦwww.mbhi.co.uk) just along from *Cromarty Bakery* at 5 Bank St.

Dingwall and the Cromarty Firth

Most traffic nowadays takes the upgraded A9 north from Inverness, bypassing the small market town of **DINGWALL** (from the Norse *thing*, "parliament", and *vollr*, "field"), a royal burgh since 1226. Once a port, it was left high and dry when the river receded during the nineteenth century, and today it has succumbed to the curse of British provincial towns and acquired an ugly business park and characterless pedestrian shopping street. However, there are two handy late-night petrol stations. Dingwall's only real claim to fame is that it was the birthplace of Macbeth, whose family occupied the now ruined castle on Castle Street. You're unlikely to want to hang around here for long – for somewhere pleasant to stay move on to Strathpeffer or push on north.

Strathpeffer

STRATHPEFFER, a mannered and leafy Victorian spa town four miles west of Dingwall, complete with Victorian street lamps and surrounded by wooded hills, is pleasant enough but does suffer from a high density of coach parties. During its heyday, this was a renowned European **health resort** reached by the tongue-twisting Strathpeffer Spa Express train from Aviemore. A recent face-lift has seen the town's attractive grand hall transformed into a performing arts centre, the Strathpeffer Pavilion (Ⓦwww.strathpefferpavilion.org), and the nearby **Upper**

Pump Room (April–Sept Mon–Sat 10am–6pm, Sun 2–5pm; donation) converted into a visitor centre, where displays and videos tell the history of the resort. You can sample three waters drawn from five different wells, which were supposed to treat all manner of ailments – most of today's visitors, however, find the sulphurous-smelling liquid more masochistic than medicinal.

Also making the most of the Victorian theme is the **Highland Museum of Childhood** (Easter–Oct Mon–Sat 10am–5pm, until 7pm July & Aug, Sun 2–5pm; £2.50; Ⓦwww.highlandmuseumofchildhood.org.uk), located at the restored Victorian train station half a mile east of the main square. The museum looks at growing up in the Highlands, from home- and school-life to folklore and festivals, with some well-displayed photographs, display cabinets with toys and games and a colourful series of commissioned murals. In other parts of the station are a pleasant café and a woodworking craftshop.

Strathpeffer is within striking distance of the bleak **Ben Wyvis**, helping make it a popular base for walkers. One of the best hikes in the area is up the hill of Cnoc Mor, where the vitrified Iron Age hill fort of **Knock Farril** affords superb panoramic views to the Cromarty Firth and the surrounding mountains.

Buses run regularly between Dingwall and Strathpeffer, dropping passengers in the square. **Tourist information** is available in the front section of Upper Pump Room (see above for opening hours). The large **hotels** in the village are very popular with bus tours, so it's better to opt for **B&B** such as upmarket *Craigvar* (Ⓣ01997/421622, Ⓦwww.craigvar.com; ❹), which overlooks the square, or luxurious Edwardian villa *Linnmhor House* on Park Road (Ⓣ01997/420072, Ⓦwww.linnmhor-house.co.uk; ❺). Try the moderately priced *Red Poppy* in the Pavilion (Ⓣ01997/423332; Tues–Sat 11am–9pm) for reasonable **lunches** and **dinners** or *Richmond Hotel*, a pleasant dinner haunt with a cosy bar serving real ale. Anyone with a sweet tooth might enjoy paying a visit to *Maya* on Main Street, just across from the Pump Room, an attractive café and chocolate shop (Tues–Sat 10am–5pm) with a viewing window through to the production area where you can sometimes see the Belgian proprietor at work. There's also an excellent **bike** shop right on the Square, *Square Wheels* (Ⓣ01997/421000, Ⓦwww.squarewheels.biz; closed Mon), which rents out bikes and offers good advice on some great local routes.

The Dornoch Firth and around

North of the Cromarty Firth, the hammer-shaped **Fearn peninsula** can still be approached from the south by the ancient ferry crossing from Cromarty to Nigg, though to the north the link is a more recent causeway over the **Dornoch Firth**, the inlet which marks the northern boundary of the peninsula. On the southern edge of the Dornoch Firth, the A9 bypasses the quiet town of **Tain**, probably best known as the home of Glenmorangie whisky. Inland, at the head of the firth, there's not much to the village of **Bonar Bridge**, but fans of unusual hostels travel from far and wide to spend a night with the ghosts at the duchess of Sutherland's imposing former home, **Carbisdale Castle**. Further inland, the lonely village of **Lairg** is a connection point between west and east coasts, with roads spearing through the glens from northwest Sutherland and the railway making a laboured detour in from the east coast.

Back on the coast, on the north side of the Dornoch Firth, the neat town of **Dornoch** itself, long known for its impressive cathedral and well-manicured golf courses, found renewed fame in 2000 as the venue for an outbreak of Madonna-mania, when it hosted the pop star's wedding to Guy Ritchie.

Tain

The peninsula's largest settlement is **TAIN**, reputedly Scotland's oldest Royal Burgh and an attractive if old-fashioned small town of grand whisky-coloured sandstone buildings, notably the castle-like early eighteenth-century Tolbooth. It was the birthplace of **St Duthus**, an eleventh-century missionary who inspired great devotion in the Middle Ages. His miracle-working relics were enshrined in a sanctuary here in the eleventh century, and in 1360 St Duthus Collegiate Church was built. It was subsequently visited annually by James IV, who usually arrived here fresh from the arms of his mistress, Janet Kennedy, whom he had conveniently installed in nearby Moray. A good place to get to grips with the peninsula's past is the revamped **Tain Through Time** exhibition (April–Oct Mon–Sat 10am–5pm; £3.50), which makes creative use of three old buildings around the church and graveyard, leading you round using an audioguide. The ticket price also includes a walking tour of the town and the neighbouring **museum** (£1.50 museum only) on Castle Brae (just off the High Street), which houses an interesting display of the much-sought-after work of the Tain silversmiths, along with mediocre archeological finds and clan memorabilia. Also on Castle Brae, **Brown's Gallery** (Ⓣ01862/893884, Ⓦwww.brownsart.com) shows contemporary Scottish art in a light-filled gallery. Tain's other main attraction is the **Glenmorangie whisky distillery**, where the highly rated malt is produced (shop Mon–Fri 9am–5pm, June–Aug also Sat 10am–4pm & Sun noon–4pm; tours Mon–Fri 10.30am–3.30pm, Sat 10.30am–2.30pm, Sun 12.30–2.30pm; £2.50; Ⓣ01862/892477 Ⓦwww.glenmorangie.com); it lies beside the A9 on the north side of town. Booking is recommended for the tours.

For **accommodation**, there's the *Carnegie Lodge Hotel* (Ⓣ01862/894039, Ⓦwww.carnegiehotel.co.uk; ❹) on Viewfield Road, tucked away behind a housing estate on the west side of the A9 from the main part of Tain; it looks and feels a bit like a golf clubhouse but offers decent and reasonably priced rooms. The more modest *Golf View House* (Ⓣ01862/892856, Ⓦwww.golf-view.co.uk; Feb–Nov; ❸), three minutes' drive south of the town centre on Knockbreck Road, offers comfortable B&B and lovely views to the Dornoch Firth. The best option for simple but filling **food** in Tain is cheery *Sunflowers Café* on the High Street. Otherwise, there's Scottish-based fare in the bistro at the *Carnegie Lodge Hotel*, or the *Royal Hotel* (Ⓣ01862/892013; ❺), a lovely sandstone building at the western end of the main street, which does reasonably priced bar meals.

Portmahomack

Unless they're making use of the Cromarty–Nigg ferry, not many people visit the Fearn peninsula to the east of Tain. It has a couple of delightful discoveries, however, including the green, windswept village of **PORTMAHOMACK**, which huddles around a curving sandy beach. On the edge of the village, ongoing archeological digs by the **Tarbat Discovery Centre** (daily: April & Oct 2–5pm; May–Sept 10am–5pm; £3.50) have unearthed original Pictish sculpted artefacts, suggesting the area around the twelfth-century church was highly significant to the Picts. From Portmahomack, narrow roads run through fertile farmland to the gorse-covered point at **Tarbat Ness**, where there's a lighthouse – one of the highest in Britain. A good seven-mile **walk** starts here (2–3hr round-trip): head south from Tarbat Ness for three miles, following the narrow passage between the foot of the cliffs and the foreshore, until you get to the hamlet of Rockfield. A path leads past a row of fishermen's cottages from here to Portmahomack, then joins the tarmac road running northeast back to the lighthouse. Further south on the peninsula there are impressive Pictish **standing stones** at Hilton and at Shandwick, while near Fearn village the unexpectedly well-groomed Anta factory shop (April–Dec Mon–Sat 9.30am–5.30pm, Sun 11am–5pm; Ⓦ www.anta.co.uk) sells attractive though still pricey modern tweed and tartan fabrics, as well as pottery. There's a nice wee **café** inside.

In Portmahomack, the *Oystercatcher* on Main Street (Ⓣ 01862/871560, Ⓦ www.the-oystercatcher.co.uk; closed Mon & Tues; pre-booking advised) is one of the **restaurant** highlights of this stretch of the east coast, serving a big selection of sumptuous seafood dishes. For **accommodation**, there's a small double (❹) and a larger en-suite double (❹) above the restaurant. For boat trips from the harbour to fish or spot dolphins, call Ⓣ 01862/871257.

Bonar Bridge and around

Before the causeway was built across the Dornoch Firth, traffic heading along the coast used to skirt west around the estuary, crossing the Kyle of Sutherland at the uninspiring village of **BONAR BRIDGE**. In the fourteenth and fifteenth centuries, the village harboured a large iron foundry. Ore was brought across the peat moors of the central Highlands from the west coast on sledges, and fuel for smelting came from the oak forest draped over the northern shores of the nearby kyle. However, James IV, passing through here on his way to Tain, was shocked to find the forest virtually clear-felled and ordered that oak saplings be planted in the gaps. Now hemmed in by spruce plantations, the beautiful ancient woodland east of Bonar Bridge dates from this era.

West of the village on the road towards Croik is one of Scotland's most intriguing accommodation options: exclusive and remote **Alladale Lodge** (Ⓣ 01863/755338, Ⓦ www.alladale.com; ❾). The lodge itself and two equally luxurious stone bothies sit in a vast hunting estate owned by Paul Lister, an entrepreneur turned conservationist who aims to return the land to its pristine natural state. A high-profile plan to reintroduce predators such as wolves and bears has run up against stiff opposition and legal obstacles, but in the meantime a serious programme of reforestation is underway. Excellent ranger tours for guests explain the complexities of land management, and you can undertake a range of other outdoor activities, including shooting your very own stag. Book in advance to stay at the lodge; casual visits are not welcome.

CROIK itself is well worth a detour for its humble little **church**, which vividly illuminates the tragedy of the Clearances. Evicted from their homes in 1845, ninety villagers from Glencalvie took shelter in the churchyard, scratching poignant messages on the east window of the church that can still be deciphered.

Carbisdale Castle

Towering high above the River Shin, three miles northwest of Bonar Bridge, the daunting neo-Gothic profile of **Carbisdale Castle** overlooks the Kyle of Sutherland, as well as the battlefield where the gallant Marquis of Montrose was defeated in 1650, finally forcing Charles II to accede to the Scots' demand for Presbyterianism. The castle was erected between 1906 and 1917 for the dowager Duchess of Sutherland, following a protracted family feud.

Designed in three distinct styles (to give the impression that it was added to over a long period of time), Carbisdale was eventually acquired by a Norwegian shipping magnate in 1933, and finally gifted, along with its entire contents and estate, to the SYHA, which has turned it into what must be one of the most opulent **hostels** in the world, full of white Italian-marble sculptures, huge gilt-framed portraits, sweeping staircases and magnificent drawing rooms alongside standard facilities such as self-catering kitchens, games and TV rooms and thirty dorms, including some four-bed family rooms (Ⓣ 01549/421232, Ⓦ www.syha.org.uk; March–Oct). You can tuck into a hearty three-course dinner at the hostel's restaurant for £11.50 before wandering the supposedly haunted corridors in search of ghosts. Bring a bike to take advantage of the several miles of **mountain-biking trails** in the nearby Balblair and Carbisdale woods. The best way to get here by public transport is to take a **train from Inverness** to nearby Culrain station, which lies within half a mile of the castle. Citylink buses (minimum 4 daily) stop in Tain, from where Macleod's Coaches buses (Mon–Sat 3 daily; 20min; ⓣ01408/641354) run as far as **Ardgay**, three miles from Carbisdale Castle.

Lairg and around

North of Bonar Bridge, the A836 parallels the River Shin for eleven miles to **LAIRG**, a bleak and scattered settlement at the eastern end of lonely **Loch Shin**. On fine days, the vast wastes of heather and deergrass surrounding the village can be beautiful, but in the rain it becomes a deeply depressing landscape. Lairg is predominantly a transport hub, and there's nothing much to see in town. The Ferrycroft Countryside Centre and **tourist office**, on the west side of the river (daily; ⓣ01549/402160), is friendly and helpful, and has a good free display on the woodlands and history of the area; the on-site ranger (ⓣ01549/402638) can offer advice on local wildlife and walks.

Four miles south of Lairg, the **Falls of Shin** in Achany Glen are one of the best places in Scotland to see **salmon** leaping on their upstream migration; there's a viewing platform and a moderately priced restaurant (ⓦwww.fallsofshin.co.uk) by the car park catering to bus parties. The new adventure playground also enables children to let off steam. Lairg hosts an annual lamb sale every August, one of the largest such one-day markets in Europe, when more than 30,000 animals from all over the north of Scotland are bought and sold.

Lairg's train station is a mile south of town on the road to Bonar Bridge; buses stop right on the lochside. Should you want to **stay**, try *Ambleside* B&B (ⓣ01549/402130, ⓦwww.amblesidelairg.co.uk; ❷) which offers good views, as does the grander *Park House* (ⓣ01549/402208, ⓦwww.parkhousesporting.com; ❺) on Station Road, overlooking Loch Shin, which is a welcoming spot if you're planning walking, fishing or cycling in the area. Guests can also enjoy dinner here. Alternatively, you'll find six comfortable en-suite rooms and reasonable **bar food** at the *Highland Hotel* (ⓣ01549/402243; ❺) next to the post office. You can also pitch a tent at *Dunroamin Caravan and Camping Park* (ⓣ01549/402447, ⓦwww.lairgcaravanpark.co.uk) in the village.

Dornoch

DORNOCH, a genteel and appealing town eight miles north of Tain, lies on a flattish headland overlooking the **Dornoch Firth**. Surrounded by sand dunes and blessed with an exceptionally sunny climate by Scottish standards, it's a middle-class holiday resort, with solid Edwardian hotels, trees and flowers in profusion, and miles of sandy beaches giving good views across the estuary to the Fearn peninsula. The town is also renowned for its championship **golf course** (ⓣ01862/810219 ext 185), Scotland's most northerly first-class course. Dornoch was the scene for Scotland's most prestigious rock'n'roll wedding of recent times, when Madonna married Guy Ritchie at nearby **Skibo Castle** and had her son baptized in Dornoch cathedral. *Skibo*, an exclusive, private hotel used as a hideaway by the world's rich and powerful, is just to the west of Dornoch. Only members of the hugely expensive Carnegie Club (ⓦwww.carnegieclub.co.uk) or their guests, however, will get anywhere near the place.

Dating from the twelfth century, Dornoch became a royal burgh in 1628. Among its oldest buildings, which are all grouped round the spacious square, the exquisite **cathedral** was founded in 1224 and built of local sandstone. The original building was horribly damaged by marauding Mackays in 1570, and much of what you see today was restored by the Countess of Sutherland in 1835, though her worst Victorian excesses were removed in the twentieth century when the interior stonework was returned to its original state. The vaulted roof is particularly appealing; the stained-glass windows in the north wall were later additions, endowed by the expat Andrew Carnegie. Opposite, the fortified sixteenth-century **Bishop's Palace**, a fine example of vernacular architecture with stepped gables and towers, has been refurbished as a hotel (see below). Next door, the castellated **Old Town Jail** is home to a series of upmarket craft shops under the banner Jail Dornoch, while tucked in behind the *Castle Hotel* is the local **Historylinks Museum** (April, May & Oct Mon–Fri 10am–4pm; June–Sept daily 10am–4pm; Nov–March Wed & Thurs only; Ⓦwww.historylinks.org.uk; £2), which tells the story of Dornoch, from local saints and golfers to Madonna herself.

Practicalities

The council-run **tourist information** office (Easter to end-Sept Mon–Fri, June–Sept also Sat, July & Aug also Sun; Ⓣ01862/810594;) is based in the sheriff courthouse right next to the *Castle Hotel*. There's no shortage of **accommodation**: *Tordarroch B&B* (Ⓣ01862/810855; March–Oct; ❷) offers good value and has a great location opposite the cathedral, as does the friendly *Trevose* (Ⓣ01862/810269; March–Sept; ❷), which is swathed in roses. The fifteenth-century *Dornoch Castle Hotel* (Ⓣ01862/810216, Ⓦwww.dornochcastlehotel.com; ❻), in the Bishop's Palace on the Square, has a decent restaurant and a cosy, old-fashioned bar with an 11ft-wide fireplace, though the revamped interior doesn't live up to the buttressed, turreted facade. The *Caravan Park* (Ⓣ01862/810423, Ⓦwww.dornochcaravans.co.uk; April–Oct) is attractively set between the manicured golf course and the vegetation of the sand dunes that fringe the beach; it also offers **camping**.

Expensive gourmet meals are available at the *2 Quail* **restaurant** (Ⓣ01862/811811; May–Sept Tues–Sat; Oct–April Fri & Sat) on Castle Street, which also has tasteful rooms (❼); otherwise, try *Luigi's* on Castle Street, for familiar but decent Italian-style snacks and meals, and the *Dornoch Patisserie* on the High Street for delicious cakes.

North to Wick

North of Dornoch, the A9 hugs the coastline for most of the sixty or so miles to **Wick**, the principal settlement in the far north of the mainland. Perhaps the most important landmark in the whole stretch is the **Sutherland Monument** near Golspie, erected in memory of the first duke of Sutherland, the landowner who oversaw the eviction of thousands of his tenants during the Clearances. The bitter memory of those times resonates through most of the small towns and villages on this stretch, including **Brora**, **Dunbeath**, **Lybster** and the gold-prospecting village of **Helmsdale**. With sites dotted around recalling Iron Age settlers and Viking rule, many of these settlements also hark back to the days of a thriving fishing trade, none more so than the main town of Wick, once the busiest herring port in Europe.

Golspie and around

Ten miles north of Dornoch on the A9 lies the straggling red-sandstone town of **GOLSPIE**, whose status as an administrative centre does little to relieve its dullness. It does, however, boast an eighteen-hole golf course and a sandy beach, while half a mile further up the coast the **Big Burn** has several rapids and waterfalls that can be seen from an attractive **woodland trail** beginning at the *Sutherland Arms Hotel*. Notably, Golspie village is also the jumping-off point for the brilliant Highland Wildcat (mountain-bike) Trails (Ⓦ www.highlandwildcat.com) within the forested hills half a mile to the west. The (colour-coded) trails include a huge descent from the summit of Ben Bhraggie to sea level and a ride past the statue of the Duke of Sutherland.

Dunrobin Castle

Mountain-bikers aside, the main reason to stop in Golspie is to look around **Dunrobin Castle** (April, May, Sept & early Oct Mon–Sat 10.30am–4.30pm, Sun noon–4.30pm; June–Aug daily 10.30am–5.30pm; £8.50), overlooking the sea a mile north of town. Approached via a long tree-lined drive, this fairy-tale confection of turrets and pointed roofs – modelled by the architect Sir Charles Barry (designer of London's Houses of Parliament) on a Loire château – is the seat of the infamous Sutherland family, at one time Europe's biggest landowners, with a staggering 1.3 million acres, and the principal driving force behind the Clearances in this area. The castle is on a correspondingly vast scale, boasting 189 furnished rooms, of which the tour takes in only seventeen. Staring up at the pile from the midst of its elaborate **formal gardens**, it's worth remembering that such extravagance was paid for by uprooting literally thousands of crofters from the surrounding glens.

The castle's opulent **interior** is crammed full of fine furniture, paintings (including works by Landseer, Allan Ramsay and Sir Joshua Reynolds), tapestries and *objets d'art*. The attractive gardens are pleasant to wander around, and it's worth diverting through them to get to Dunrobin's unusual **museum**, housed in an eighteenth-century building at the edge of the garden. Inside, hundreds of disembodied animals' heads and horns peer down from the walls, alongside other more macabre appendages, from elephants' toes to rhinos' tails.

Conveniently – though not too surprisingly, considering the duke built the railway – the castle has its own **train** station (summer only) on the main Inverness–Wick line.

The Sutherland Monument

Approaching Golspie, you can't miss the 100ft-high **monument** to the first duke of Sutherland, which peers proprietorially down from the summit of the 1293ft-high **Beinn a'Bhragaidh** (Ben Bhraggie). An inscription cut into its base recalls that the statue was erected in 1834 by "a mourning and grateful tenantry [to] a judicious, kind and liberal landlord". Unsurprisingly, there's no reference to the fact that the duke, widely regarded as Scotland's own Josef Stalin, forcibly evicted 15,000 crofters from his million-acre estate – a fact which, in the words of one local historian, makes the monument "a grotesque representation of the many forces that destroyed the Highlands". A campaign to have the statue smashed and scattered over the hillside has largely died down.

It's worth the stiff **climb** to the top of the hill (round-trip 1hr 30min) for the wonderful views south along the coast past Dornoch to the Moray Firth and west towards Lairg and Loch Shin. The path is steep and strenuous in places, however, and there's no view until you're out of the trees, about twenty minutes from the top. Head up Fountain Road about halfway along Golspie's main street; after crossing the railway line and pass (or park) at Rhives Farm steading. From here, follow the Beinn a'Bhragaidh footpath (BBFP) signs along the path into the woods.

Loch Fleet and Rogart

Just to the south of Golspie, the A9 fringes **Loch Fleet**, a tidal estuary harbouring some delicate coastal and woodland vegetation, as well as a range of birdlife including greylag geese and arctic terns, and sealife such as seals and otters. Four miles northwest of Loch Fleet on the A839 to Lairg is one of Scotland's most unusual and imaginative **hostels**, *Sleeperzzz.com* (Ⓣ01408/641343, Ⓦwww.sleeperzzz.com), where you can stay in one of three first-class railway carriages parked in a siding beside the station on the Inverness–Thurso line in the tiny settlement of **ROGART**. Each of the comfortable compartments has a bunk bed on one side and the original seats on the other, while the two end compartments are used as a kitchen and common room. A small reduction is offered to those making their journey by train or bicycle. The owners have free **mountain bikes** available to explore the local countryside, and the place stands a hundred yards from a convivial local **pub**, the *Pittentrail Inn*, where the bar/bistro serves moderately priced evening meals.

Helmsdale and around

Eleven scenic miles north along the A9 from Golspie, **HELMSDALE** (Ⓦwww.helmsdale.org) is an old herring port, founded in the nineteenth century to house the evicted inhabitants of Strath Kildonan, which lies behind it. Today, the main draw in the sleepy, steadily rejuvenating village is the attractively designed **Timespan Heritage Centre** beside the river (Easter–Oct Mon–Sat 10am–5pm, Sun noon–5pm; £4; Ⓣ01431/821327). It's an ambitious venture for a place of this size, the refurbished museum telling the local story of Viking raids, witch-burning, Clearances and fishing through high-tech displays, sound effects and an audiovisual programme. The story of the Kildonan Gold Rush Trail uses twenty-first-century GPS technology: visitors are issued with an interactive hand-held audiovisual device for a self-guided tour (1hr 30min; £6 deposit) of the nearby **Baile an** Or gold-prospecting area. The centre also has an art gallery, café and geology garden.

There's no official tourist office in town, but you'll pick up local information at the very friendly Strath Ullie Crafts on the harbour (Ⓣ01431/821402). At the end of Dunrobin Street is the *Bridge Hotel* (Ⓣ01431/821100, Ⓦwww.bridgehotel.net; ❻), a pleasantly grand and comfortable **hotel** with wood-panelling, big open fireplaces and two large aquariums holding freshly caught live lobsters – available at the discerning *Green Stag* restaurant; the *Red Lobster* restaurant is less formal. There are several good-value **B&Bs**, including *Broomhill House* on Navidale Road (Ⓣ01431/821259, Ⓦwww.blancebroomhill.com; ❶), which has bedrooms in a turret added to the former croft by a miner who struck it lucky in the Kildonan gold rush. Evening meals are also available. Alternatively, try Mrs McDonald at *Customs House* on the harbour, which offers terrific views and a great breakfast (Ⓣ01431/821648 and 821643; ❶). There's also a small SYHA-affiliated **youth hostel** (Ⓣ08701/553255, Ⓦwww.helmsdalehostel.co.uk; April–Oct; family room ❶), beside the A9 as it climbs north up from the harbour; it's located in a sensitively converted gymnasium, with high ceilings and a wood-burning stove.

If you're looking for somewhere to **eat** in Helmsdale, the seasonal game and seafood on the menu of the *Green Stag* in the *Bridge Hotel* won't disappoint, though your eye may well be drawn to the bizarre *Mirage* restaurant (Ⓦwww.lamirage.org) on Dunrobin Street. The late former proprietor of the *Mirage* became something of a local celebrity, modelling herself on the romantic novelist Barbara Cartland. Under new owners, the furnishings remain suitably garish, including a lampshade with fishnet tights round the stand and framed photographs of visiting personalities covering the walls. There's a long menu, which includes large helpings of fish and chips. *Gilbert's* antique shop and tearoom on Dunrobin Street is terrific for cakes, while Timespan's bright daytime café looks onto its beautiful herbaceous garden and the bridge.

Dunbeath and around

Just north of Helmsdale, the A9 begins its long haul up the **Ord of Caithness**. This steep hill used to form a pretty impregnable obstacle, and the desolate road still gets blocked during winter snowstorms. Once over the pass, the landscape changes dramatically, as heather-clad moors give way to miles of treeless green grazing lands, peppered with derelict crofts and latticed by long dry-stone walls. As you come over the pass, look out for signs to the ruined village of **Badbea**, reached via a ten-minute walk from the car park at the side of the A9. Built by tenants cleared from nearby Ousdale, the settlement now lies deserted, although its ruined hovels show what hardship the crofters had to endure: the cottages stood so near the windy cliff-edge that children had to be tethered to prevent them from being blown into the sea.

DUNBEATH, hidden at the mouth of a small strath twelve miles north of Ord of Caithness, was another village founded to provide work in the wake of the Clearances. The local landlord built a harbour here in 1800, at the start of the herring boom, and the settlement briefly flourished. The novelist Neil Gunn was born here, in one of the terraced houses under the flyover that now swoops above the village; you can find out more about him at the **Dunbeath Heritage Centre** (Easter–Oct daily 10am–5pm; Nov–March Mon–Fri 11am–3pm; £2). The staff can advise you on several good walks along the Highland River of Gunn's novel; his other famous book, *The Silver Darlings*, was also set on this coastline. The best of the handful of modest **B&Bs** here is *Tormore Farm* (Ⓣ01593/731240; May–Oct; ❶), a large farmhouse with three comfortable rooms, half a mile north of the harbour on the A9.

Just north of Dunbeath is the simple but moving **Laidhay Croft Museum** (Easter–Oct daily 10am–5pm; £2), housed in a long thatched croft, which has a lovely tearoom and offers a useful perspective on the sometimes over-romanticized life of the Highlander before the Clearances. A little further up the coast, the **Clan Gunn Heritage Centre and Museum** (June–Sept Mon–Sat 11am–1pm & 2–4pm; £2.50) is mainly a place for members of the Clan Gunn and its septs (branches), although it also doles out a bit more local history and a few titbits for those on the trail of Neil Gunn.

Lybster and around

The final stretch of road before Wick gives great views out to the sea and the oil rigs on the horizon. The planned village of **LYBSTER** (pronounced "libe-ster"), established at the height of the nineteenth-century herring boom, once had two hundred-odd boats working out of its harbour: now there are just a handful. The **Water Lines** heritage centre by the harbour (May to mid-Oct daily 11am–5pm; £2.50) is an attractive place, with CCTV footage of seabirds on the nearby cliffs and modern displays about the "silver darlings" and the fishermen that pursued them; there's a snug café downstairs. There's not much else to see here apart from the harbour; the upper town is a grim collection of grey pebble-dashed bungalows centred on a broad main street.

The **Grey Cairns of Camster**, seven miles due north, are one of the most memorable sights on the northeast coast. Surrounded by bleak moorland, these two enormous reconstructed prehistoric burial chambers, originally built four or five thousand years ago, were immaculately designed, with corbelled dry-stone roofs in their hidden chambers, which you can crawl into through narrow passageways. More extraordinary ancient remains lie at **East Clyth**, two miles north of Lybster on the A99, where a path leads to the **"Hill o'Many Stanes"**. Some two hundred boulders stand in the ground here, forming 22 parallel rows that run north to south; no one has yet worked out what they were used for, although archeological studies have shown there were once six hundred stones in place. A fourteen-mile track waymarked as a cycle path leads between the two sites, entering the forest at a car park half a mile south of the Camster Cairns and emerging near the single-track road which passes the Hill o'Many Stanes and connects with the A99.

Another relatively unknown historic site in the area is the **Whaligoe staircase**, ten miles north of Lybster on the A99 at the north end of the village of **Ulbster**. The stairway, which has 365 steps constructed out of the distinctive local slab stone, leads steeply down from the side of the house beside the car park to a natural harbour surrounded by cliffs. At the bottom you'll see a few remnants of the harbour used by herring fishermen in the last century, as well as vast numbers of seabirds, including cormorant, skua and puffin; the daunting climb back up is made a little bit easier by the thought that, unlike the women of Ulbster, you don't have a creel full of herring to carry all the way to the top. The stairway is steep and uneven for much of the way down, so be particularly careful if the steps are wet. To get to the stairway, turn off towards the sea at the junction signposted on its landward side to the "Cairn o'Get".

Wick

Originally a Viking settlement named *Vik* (meaning "bay"), **WICK** has been a royal burgh since 1589. It's actually two towns: Wick proper, and **Pultneytown**, immediately south across the river, a messy, rather run-down community planned by Thomas Telford in 1806 for the British Fisheries Society to encourage evicted crofters to take up fishing. Wick's heyday was in the mid-nineteenth century, when it was the busiest herring port in Europe, with a fleet of more than 1100 boats, exporting tons of fish to Russia, Scandinavia and the West Indian slave plantations. Robert Louis Stevenson described it as "the meanest of man's towns, situated on the baldest of God's bays", and though redevelopment of the harbour is under way, including the installation of pontoons and facilities for yachts, something of that down-at-heel atmosphere remains. If you're here for a few hours, scout out the huge area around the harbour in Pultneytown where builders and redevelopers are steadily transforming the rows of fishermen's cottages, derelict net-mending sheds, stores and cooperages. It all gives an insight into the sheer scale of the former fishing trade.

The town's story is told in the loyally volunteer-maintained **Wick Heritage Centre** in Bank Row, Pultneytown (Easter–Oct Mon–Sat 10am–5pm; Ⓦwww.wickheritage.org; £3), which contains a fascinating, jumbled array of artefacts from the old fishing days, including fully rigged boats, original boat models, the old Noss Head lighthouse light and a huge photographic collection dating from the 1880s. The other visitor attraction nearby is the fairly simple **Pulteney Distillery** (Mon–Fri 10am–1pm & 2–4pm; tours at 11am & 2pm or by arrangement; £4, includes discount voucher; Ⓣ01955/602371) on Huddart Street, a few blocks back from the sea. Much is made here of the maritime character of both the distillery and the whisky – the coopers who made barrels for the distillery, for example, also made them for storing cured herrings bound for Russia and Germany.

The **train** station and **bus** stops are next to each other immediately south and west of the bridge that crosses the River Wick in the centre of town. Frequent local buses run to Thurso and up the coast to John O'Groats. Wick also has an **airport** (Ⓣ01955/602215), a couple of miles to the north, with direct flights to and from Edinburgh and Aberdeen.

In Macallans's menswear shop on the High Street (Mon–Sat 9am–5.30pm; Ⓣ01955/602547), you'll find the small **tourist office**. The best of the **hotels** is *Mackay's*, on the south side of the river in the town centre (Ⓣ01955/602323, Ⓦwww.mackayshotel.co.uk; ❻), while reasonable **B&B** options include *Quayside*, 25 Harbour Quay (Ⓣ01955/603229, Ⓦwww.quaysidewick.co.uk; ❹), and *The Clachan*, 13 Randolph Place on South Road (Ⓣ01955/605384,

Ⓦ www.theclachan.co.uk; ❸). Five miles towards Thurso is seventeenth-century *Bilbster House* (April–Oct, in winter by prior arrangement; Ⓣ01955/621212; ❷), a lovely eighteenth-century manor house with walled gardens.

Good **eating** options don't abound, though the moderately priced *Bord de l'Eau* (Ⓣ01955/604400; closed Mon) on Market Street, which runs along the north side of the river, offers a reasonable menu of classic French standards.

Travel details

Trains

Fort William to: Arisaig (Mon–Sat 3–4 daily, 1–2 on Sun; 1hr 10min); Glenfinnan (Mon–Sat 3–4 daily, 2–4 on Sun; 35min); Mallaig (Mon–Sat 3–4 daily, 2–4 on Sun; 1hr 25min).

Inverness to: Dingwall (Mon–Sat 3–4 daily, 1–2 on Sun; 25min); Helmsdale (Mon–Sat 3 daily, 2 on Sun; 2hr 20min); Kyle of Lochalsh (Mon–Sat 3–4 daily, 1–2 on Sun; 2hr 40min); Lairg (Mon–Sat 3 daily, 2 on Sun; 1hr 40min); Plockton (Mon–Sat 3–4 daily, 1–2 on Sun; 2hr 15min); Thurso (Mon–Sat 3 daily, 2 on Sun; 3hr 25min); Wick (Mon–Sat 3 daily, 2 on Sun; 3hr 45min).

Kyle of Lochalsh to: Dingwall (Mon–Sat 3–4 daily, 1–2 on Sun; 2hr); Inverness (Mon–Sat 3–4 daily, 1–2 on Sun; 2hr 40min); Plockton (Mon–Sat 3–4 daily, 1–2 on Sun; 15min).

Thurso to: Dingwall (Mon–Sat 4 daily, 2 on Sun; 3hr); Inverness (Mon–Sat 4 daily, 2 on Sun; 3hr 20min); Lairg (Mon–Sat 4 daily, 2 on Sun; 1hr 50min); Wick (Mon–Sat 3 daily, 2 on Sun; 35min).

Wick to: Dingwall (Mon–Sat 4 daily, 2 on Sun; 3hr 30min); Inverness (Mon–Sat 4 daily, 2 on Sun; 4hr); Lairg (Mon–Sat 4 daily, 2 on Sun; 2hr 20min).

Buses

Fort William to: Acharacle (Mon–Sat 1–2 daily; 1hr 30min); Inverness (5 daily; 2hr 15min); Kilchoan (1–2 daily on request only from Acharacle; 3hr 35); Mallaig (Mon–Fri 3 daily; 1hr 20min).

Gairloch to: Inverness (Mon–Sat 1 daily; also ScotBus 1 daily Mon–Sat, June–Sept only; 2hr 45min); Ullapool (Mon, Wed, Thurs & Sat 1 daily). To Redpoint and Melvaig only Dial-a-bus service Ⓣ01445/712255.

Inverness to: Durness (Mon–Sat 1 daily; 2hr 40min; also bike bus, May to end Sept Mon–Sat 1 daily, also July & Aug 1 on Sun); Thurso (4–5 daily; 3hr 35min); Wick (Mon–Fri 4 daily, Sat & Sun 3 daily; 2hr 55min).

Kyle of Lochalsh to: Fort William (3 daily; 1hr 50min); Glasgow (3 daily; 5hr); Inverness (3 daily; 2hr).

Lochinver to: Inverness (May to end Sept 1 daily; plus July & Aug 1 on Sun; 3hr 10min); Ullapool (Mon–Sat 2 daily;1hr).

Thurso to: Inverness (4–5 daily; 3hr 30min); John O' Groats (Mon–Fri 4 daily, 3 on Sat; 1hr); Wick (Mon–Sun 4 daily; 35min).

Ullapool to: Durness (May–Sept Mon–Sat 1 daily; also July & Aug 1 on Sun; 3hr); Inverness (Mon–Sat 2 daily; 1hr 30min).

Wick to: John O' Groats (4 daily Mon–Sat; 50min).

Ferries

To Lewis: Ullapool–Stornoway (Mon–Sat 2 daily; 2hr 45min).

To Mull: Kilchoan–Tobermory (Mon–Sat 7 daily; also May–Aug 5 on Sun; 35min); Lochaline–Fishnish (Mon–Sat every 50min, Sun hourly; 15min).

To Orkney: Gill's Bay–St Margaret's Hope (3 daily; 45min); John O'Groats–Burwick (passengers only; 2–4 daily; 40min); Scrabster–Stromness (2–3 daily; 90min).

To Skye: Glenelg–Kylerhea (every 15–30min; 15min); Mallaig–Armadale (Mon–Sat 8 daily; also mid-May to mid-Sept Sun at least 4 daily; 30min).

Mallaig to the Small Isles: Eigg (Mon, Thurs & Sat 1 daily; 1hr 15min; Rùm (Mon, Wed, Fri & Sat 1 daily; 1hr 20min); Muck (Tues, Thurs, Fri, Sat 1 daily; 2hr 5min); Canna (Mon, Wed, Fri & Sat 1 daily; 2hr 30min).

To Nigg from Cromarty: May–Oct, daily from 8am and every 30min until 6pm.

Flights

Wick to: Edinburgh (Mon–Fri 1 daily; 1hr 10min); Aberdeen (Mon–Fri 4 daily; 35min).

14

Skye and the Small Isles

0 50 miles
N
17
16
15
13
14
12
11
10
9
6
7
8
5
1
2
4
3
NORTHERN
IRELAND
ENGLAND

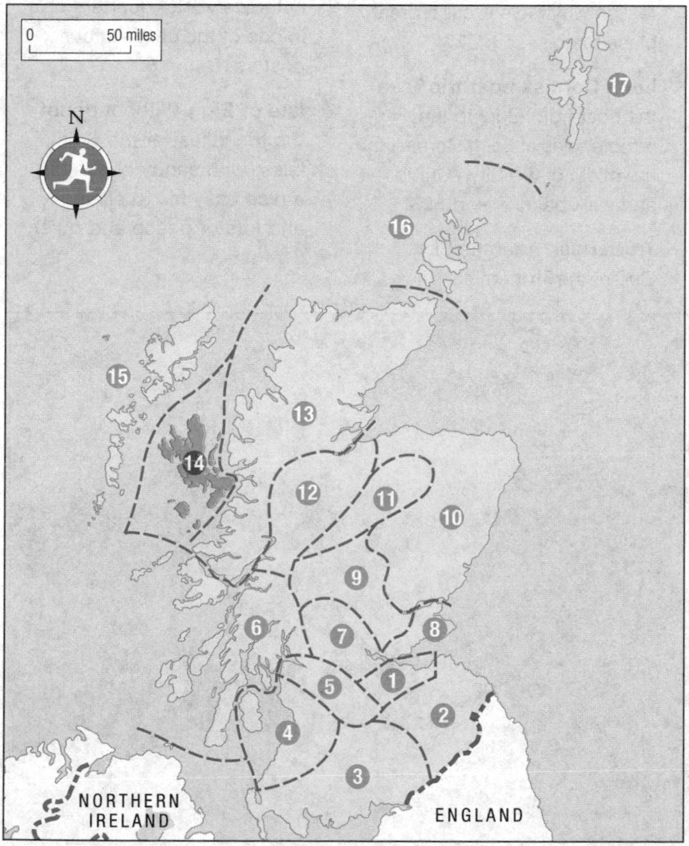

CHAPTER 14

Highlights

* **Isle of Raasay** Just off the coast of Skye, Raasay is well off the beaten track, yet offers a wide variety of outdoor pursuits from windsurfing to hillwalking. See p.526
* **Skye Cuillin** The jagged peaks of the Skye Cuillin are the real reason why Skye is still a great place to go. See p.527
* **Loch Coruisk boat trip** Take the boat from Elgol to the remote, glacial Loch Coruisk in the midst of the Skye Cuillin, and walk back. See p.528
* **Trotternish** After the Skye Cuillin, the Trotternish peninsula is the most distinctive landscape on Skye, with its basalt intrusions and massive landslides. See p.532
* **Kinloch Castle, Isle of Rùm** Visit this outrageous Edwardian pile, or better still, stay in the hostel housed in the servants' quarters or in one of the castle's four-posters. See p.534
* **Isle of Eigg** Without doubt the friendliest of the Small Isles, with sandy beaches, a nice easy hill to climb and lots of peace and quiet. See p.536

▲ Black Cuillin, Isle of Skye

14

Skye and the Small Isles

Some say the **Isle of Skye** (An t-Eilean Sgiathanach) was named after the Old Norse word for "cloud" (*skuy*), earning itself the Gaelic moniker *Eilean a' Cheò* (Island of Mist). Yet, despite the unpredictability of the weather, tourism has been an important part of the island's economy for over a century, since the railway reached Kyle of Lochalsh in 1897. From here, it was a brief boat trip across to Skye, and the Edwardian bourgeoisie was soon swarming over to walk its mountains, whose beauty had been proclaimed by the Victorians. Since the building of the Skye Bridge, the island has been busier than ever, and at the height of the summer the roads are crammed with coach tours, minibuses and caravans. Yet Skye is a deceptively large island, and you'll get the most out of it – and escape the worst of the crowds – if you take the time to explore the more remote parts of the island.

The Clearances saw an estimated 30,000 indigenous *Sgiathanachs* (pronounced "ski-anaks") emigrate in the mid-nineteenth century; today, the population is just over 9000. Tourism is now by far the island's biggest earner and has attracted hundreds of incomers from the rest of Britain over the last couple of decades. Nevertheless, Skye remains the most important centre for **Gaelic culture** and language outside the Western Isles. Over a third of the population is fluent in Gaelic, the Gaelic college on Sleat is the most important in Scotland, and the Free Church maintains a strong presence. A good way of finding out what's going on in the region is to read the weekly *West Highland Free Press*, a refreshingly vociferous campaigning newspaper published in Broadford.

One way to avoid the crowds on Skye is to head off to the so-called **Small Isles** – the improbably named **Rùm**, **Eigg**, **Muck** and **Canna** – to the south. Each with a population of fewer than a hundred, they are easily accessible by ferry from Mallaig and Arisaig, though with limited accommodation available, a visit requires forward planning.

Skye

Jutting out from the mainland like a giant butterfly, the bare and bony promontories of **Skye** (Ⓦ www.skye.co.uk) fringe a deeply indented coastline. The island's most popular destination is the **Cuillin** ridge, whose jagged peaks dominate the

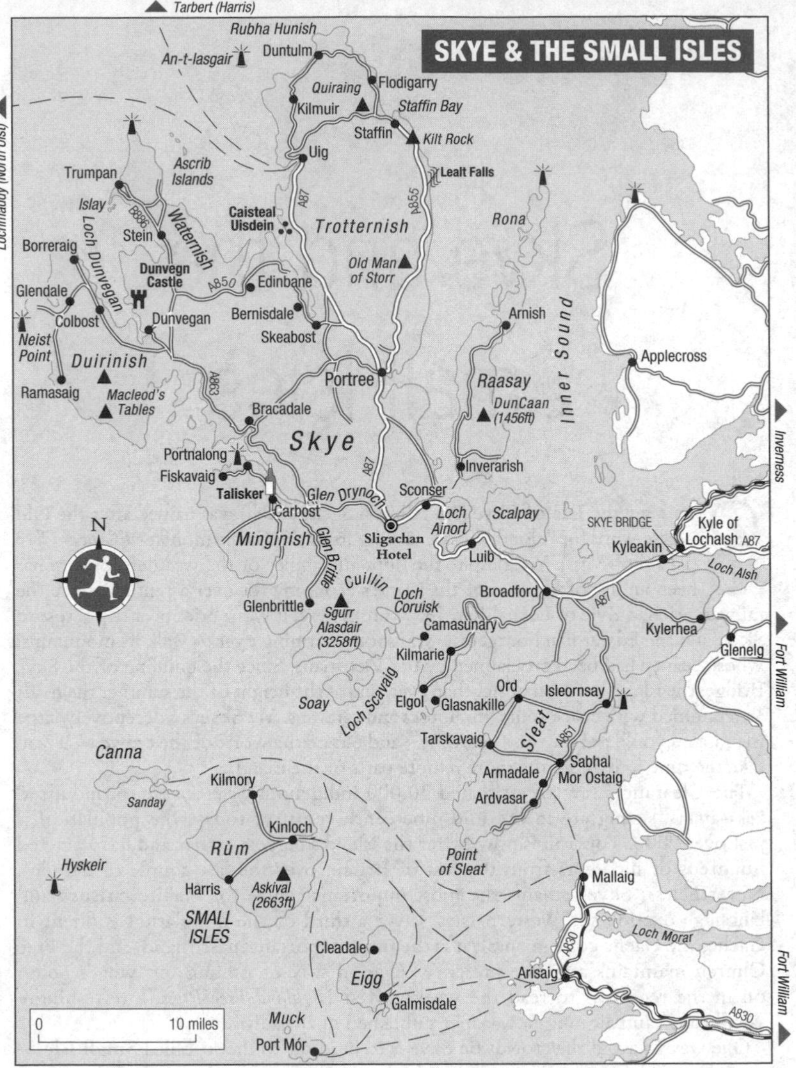

island during clear weather; to explore them at close quarters you'll need to be a fairly experienced and determined walker. More accessible and equally dramatic in their own way are the rock formations of the **Trotternish** peninsula, in the north, from which there are inspirational views across to the Western Isles. Of the two main settlements, **Portree** is the only one with any charm, and a useful base for exploring the Trotternish. If you want to escape the summer crush, head for the **Isle of Raasay**, off Skye's east coast.

Most visitors reach Skye via the **Skye Bridge**, which sweeps across the sea from Kyle of Lochalsh, itself linked to Inverness by train. The more scenic approach is via **Armadale** on the Sleat peninsula, linked by **ferry** with Mallaig, at the end of the train line from Fort William. A third option is to arrive at **Kylerhea** via the tiny **car ferry** that leaves from Glenelg, south of Kyle of Lochalsh. If you're heading for the Western Isles, it's 57 miles from Armadale and 49 miles from Kyleakin to **Uig**, from where ferries leave for Tarbert on Harris and Lochmaddy on North Uist.

Skye has several substantial **campsites**, and numerous **hostels** or bunkhouses, plenty of B&Bs and a string of pricey, but excellent **hotels**. If you're travelling by **public transport**, it's worth knowing that a Sky Roverbus ticket is available (£6 for one day; £15 for three). Services do peter out in the more remote areas, and many close down on Sundays.

Sleat

Ferries from Mallaig (see p.481) connect with the **Sleat** (pronounced "Slate") **peninsula**, Skye's southern tip, an uncharacteristically fertile area known as "The Garden of Skye". The CalMac ferry terminal is at **ARMADALE** (Armadal), an elongated hamlet stretching along the wooded shoreline. If you need a bite **to eat**, pop into the *Pasta Shed* next door, which does a great seafood pizza (eat-in or takeaway).

There are several good **accommodation options** in neighbouring Ardvasar, from the traditional, whitewashed *Ardvasar Hotel* (Ⓣ01471/844223, Ⓦwww.ardvasarhotel.com; ❼), which has a good restaurant specializing in local seafood and a lively bar, to *Morar* (Ⓣ01471/844378, Ⓦwww.accommodation-on-skye.co.uk; ❹), a modern crofthouse B&B, just beyond the hotel, with superb sea views and an indoor swimming pool. There's also the *Flora MacDonald Hostel* (Ⓣ01471/844272, Ⓦwww.skye-hostel.co.uk; ❷), two miles or so up the road to Broadford, which is a converted barn run by locals, with cheap bunks in mixed dorms, and a Lodge with a double, triple and quad. **Bike rental** is available from the local petrol station (Ⓣ01471/844249), close to the pier; **boat trips** operate from Armadale with Sea.fari (Ⓣ01471/833316, Ⓦwww.seafari.co.uk).

A little further along the A851, past the youth hostel, you'll find one of the best tourist attractions on the island, the **Armadale Castle Gardens** (April–Oct daily 9.30am–5.30pm; £6.95; Ⓦwww.clandonald.com). Within the handsome forty-acre gardens lies the shell of the MacDonalds' neo-Gothic castle, a café and a library for those who want to chase up their ancestral Donald connections. The gardens' slick, purpose-built **Museum of the Isles** has a good section on the Jacobite period and its aftermath, featuring a few Bonnie Prince Charlie keepsakes and a couple of cannonballs fired at the castle by HMS *Dartmouth*, sent by William and Mary to shell the castle, which "sent them scampering to the hills" (those who surrendered were hanged). There're also one or two top-notch works of art: a splendid portrait of a young, theatrical Glengarry (on whom Walter Scott modelled the hero of the *Waverley* novels) by Angelika Kauffman, and a portrait of his more conventional brother, MacDonell, by Raeburn.

Continuing northeast, it's another six miles to **ISLEORNSAY** (Eilean Iarmain), a secluded little village of whitewashed cottages that was once Skye's main fishing port. With the mountains of the mainland on the horizon, the views out across the bay are wonderful, overlooking a necklace of seaweed-encrusted rocks and the tidal **Isle of Ornsay**. You can stay at the *Eilean Iarmain* **hotel** (Ⓣ01471/833332, Ⓦwww.eilean-iarmain.com; ❽), a Victorian hotel in Isleornsay, whose bar and **restaurant** serves great seafood.

Kyleakin

Built in 1995, the **Skye Bridge** was once the most expensive toll bridge in Europe, and no cheaper than the ferry it replaced. Protests and non-payment eventually persuaded the Scottish government to buy the bridge in 2004 and abolish the tolls. Strictly speaking there are, in fact, two bridges, with an island in the middle, **Eilean Bàn**, whose lighthouse cottages were briefly the home of author and naturalist Gavin Maxwell. One of the houses is now a museum and can be visited, along with the lighthouse, on a guided tour (£6); numbers are limited and must be booked in advance through the **Bright Water Visitor Centre** (phone for times; Ⓣ01599/530040, Ⓦwww.eileanban.org) in nearby Kyleakin.

Most folk don't actually bother to stop in the old ferry port of **KYLEAKIN** (pronounced "ka*la*kin", with the stress on the second syllable), which has now become something of a backpackers' hangout. If you're looking for a party atmosphere, *Saucy Mary's* (Ⓣ01599/534845, Ⓦwww.saucymarys.com) is the **hostel** to head for; otherwise, snuggle down at the cosy *Dun Caan Hostel* (Ⓣ01599/534087, Ⓦwww.skyerover.co.uk). You can grab a bite to eat at *Harry's* and **bike rental** is available from the hostels.

Broadford

From the west, there's no avoiding the island's second-largest village, charmless **BROADFORD** (An t-Àth Leathann), strung out along the main road. Despite its rather unlovely appearance, Broadford makes a useful base for exploring the southern half of Skye, and has one of the island's best wet-weather retreats, the unusual **Skye Serpentarium** (Easter–Oct Mon–Sat 10am–5pm; July & Aug daily; £2.50; Ⓦwww.skyeserpentarium.org.uk), housed in an old mill by the main road heading east out of town. There are over fifty animals on display, all of them abandoned or rescued, ranging from tiny tree frogs to large iguanas and there's usually a snake you can handle.

Broadford's **tourist office** (Easter–Oct Mon–Sat only; July & Aug daily; Ⓣ08452/255121) is by the 24-hour garage on the main road, where there's a laundry, small shop and bureau de change. At the west end of the village there's a bank, a bakery, a café and a post office. The SYHA **hostel**, on the west shore of Broadford Bay (Ⓣ0870/004 1106, Ⓦwww.syha.org.uk; March–Oct), is no beauty, but it's clean and well-equipped. There's a surfeit of **B&Bs**, but a couple stand out from the crowd: *Berabhaigh* (Ⓣ01471/822372, Ⓦwww.isleofskye.net/berabhaigh; March–Oct; ❸), a spotlessly clean, whitewashed Victorian house close to the centre of the village, run by a very hospitable couple; and *Tigh an Dochais* (Ⓣ01471/820022, Ⓦwww.skyebedbreakfast.co.uk; ❺), a striking piece of contemporary architecture as well as a very comfortable guesthouse, with stunning views across Broadford Bay (binoculars provided). If you want a bite **to eat**, try the justifiably popular *Creelers Seafood Restaurant* (Ⓣ01471/822281, Ⓦwww.skye-seafood-restaurant.co.uk; closed Sun) at the south end of the bay. **Bike rental** is available from the SYHA hostel and *Fairwinds* (Ⓣ01471/822270), on the road to Elgol.

Isle of Raasay

Cha chuirear brithran air boidhche,	No words can be put on beauty,
Cha deanar dealbh no ceol no dan dhi	No picture words or poem made for it.

from *Screapadal* by Sorley MacLean

Despite lying less than a mile offshore, the long, hilly island of **Raasay** (Ratharsair) sees surprisingly few visitors. For much of its history, Raasay was the property of a branch of the staunchly Jacobite MacLeods of Lewis. When the MacLeods were finally forced to sell up in 1843, the Clearances started in earnest, a period of the island's history immortalized in verse by Raasay poet, Sorley MacLean (Somhairle MacGill-Eain). In 1921, seven ex-servicemen and their families from the neighbouring isle of **Rona**, to the north, illegally squatted crofts on Raasay, and were imprisoned, causing a public outcry. As a result, both islands were bought by the government the following year and remain in state hands. Raasay's population now stands at around two hundred, many of them members of the Free Presbyterian Church. Strict observance of the Sabbath is the most obvious manifestation for visitors, who should respect the islanders' feelings.

The ferry docks in Churchton Bay, near **INVERARISH**, the island's tiny village set within thick woods on the southwest coast. The grandest house on the island is the Georgian mansion of **Raasay House** built by the MacLeods in the late 1740s, and all but ruined a few years later by government troops. The place was run as an outdoor centre until a fire gutted it in 2009; it's currently being housed in *Borodale House* (see below). The island's interior – a rugged and rocky terrain of sandstone in the south and gneiss in the north – is well worth exploring. The most obvious spot to head for is the curiously truncated basalt cap on top of **Dun Caan** (1456ft), where Boswell "danced a Highland dance" on his visit to the island with Dr Johnson in 1773. The trail to the top of the peak is fairly easy to follow, a splendid five-mile trek up through the forest and along the burn behind Inverarish.

The CalMac **ferry** departs for Raasay from **Sconser** (Mon–Sat 8–10 daily, 2 on Sun; 25min). Many visitors go for the day, since there's plenty to do within walking distance of the pier – you could stay in Sconser at *Loch Aluinn* (Ⓣ01478/650288, Ⓦwww.isleofskye.net/loch-aluinn; March–Oct; ③), a good modern crofthouse **B&B** by the shore. If you do take a car, be warned, there's no petrol on the island. A rough track cuts up the steep hillside from the village to Raasay's isolated but beautifully placed SYHA **hostel** (Ⓣ01478/660240, Ⓦwww.syha.org.uk; mid-May to mid-Sept). Accommodation is also available at *Allt Arais* (Ⓣ01478/660237, Ⓦwww.allt-arais.co.uk; ③), a modern **B&B**, with free wi-fi and a large lounge with great views over the bay. Raasay Outdoor Centre is currently being run out of *Borodale House* (Ⓣ01478/660266, Ⓦwww.raasay-house.co.uk), the former Estate Manager's House, while Raasay House is out of action. The centre's activity programme includes everything from sailing and kayaking to climbing and hillwalking, and includes optional accommodation in one of their twelve en-suite rooms. There's a restaurant and a café serving good local food.

The Cuillin and the Red Hills

For many people, the **Cuillin**, whose sharp snow-capped peaks rise mirage-like from the flatness of the surrounding terrain, are the *raison d'être* for a visit to Skye. When the clouds finally disperse, they are the dominating feature of the island, visible from every other peninsula. There are basically three approaches to the Cuillin: from the south, by foot or by boat from Elgol; from the *Sligachan Hotel* to the north; or from Glen Brittle to the west of the mountains. Glen Sligachan is one of the most popular routes, dividing as it does the granite of the round-topped **Red Hills** (sometimes referred to as the Red Cuillin) to the east from the dark, coarse-grained jagged-edged gabbro of the real Cuillin (sometimes referred to as the Black Cuillin) to the west. With some twenty Munros between them, these are mountains to be taken seriously, and many routes through the Cuillin are for experienced climbers only (for more on safety, see p.49).

Elgol, Loch Coruisk and Glen Sligachan

The road to **ELGOL** (Ealaghol), fourteen miles southwest of Broadford at the tip of the Strathaird peninsula, is one of the most dramatic on the island, leading right into the heart of the Red Hills and then down a precipitous slope, with a stunning view from the top down to Elgol pier. The chief reason for visiting Elgol is to take a boat across **Loch Scavaig** to a jetty near the entrance of **Loch Coruisk** (*Coire Uisg* or "cauldron of waters"). An isolated, glacial loch, this needle-like shaft of water, nearly two miles long but only a couple of hundred yards wide, lies in the shadow of the highest peaks of the Black Cuillin, a wonderfully overpowering landscape.

The journey takes about an hour and passengers are dropped to spend time ashore. From Easter to October, two boats currently offer the trip: the *Bella Jane* (ⓣ0800/731 3089, ⓦwww.bellajane.co.uk), and the *Misty Isle* (ⓣ01471/866288, ⓦwww.mistyisleboattrips.co.uk; Mon–Sat only). **Walkers** use the boat simply to get to Loch Coruisk, from where you can hike amid the Red Hills, or over the pass into **Glen Sligachan**. Alternatively, you can walk round the coast to the sandy bay of **Camasunary**, over two miles to the east – a difficult walk that involves a tricky river crossing and negotiating "The Bad Step", an overhanging rock with a thirty-foot drop to the sea – and either head north to Glen Sligachan, continue south three miles along the coast to Elgol or continue east to the Am Màm shoulder, for a stunning view of mountains and the islands of Soay, Rùm and Canna. From Am Màm, the path leads down to the Elgol road, joining it at Kilmarie.

If you want a bite to eat, try the coffee shop, or the excellent seafood **restaurant** in *Coruisk House* (ⓣ01471/866330, ⓦwww.seafood-skye.co.uk; April–Oct; ❺), which also offers **B&B** in its bright and cheerful rooms. Alternatively, head for *Rowan Cottage* (ⓣ01471/866287, ⓦwww.rowancottage-skye.co.uk; March–Oct; ❸), a lovely B&B a mile or so east in Glasnakille. For walkers and climbers, by far the most popular place to stay is the roadside **campsite** and the secluded **bunkhouse** (ⓣ01478/650204, ⓦwww.sligachan.co.uk; April–Oct) **run** by the *Sligachan Hotel* on the A87, at the northern end of Glen Sligachan. The hotel's huge *Seamus Bar* serves food for weary walkers until 11pm, and quenches their thirst with its own real ales, and often has live bands.

Glen Brittle

Three miles along the A863 to Dunvegan, halfway along **Glen Drynoch**, *Bla Bheinn* B&B (ⓣ01478/640269, ⓦwww.blabheinn.co.uk; ❹) makes a good little base for attacking the Cuillin from the north. Further on, a turning signed "Carbost and Portnalong" leads to the entrance to stony **Glen Brittle**, edging the most spectacular peaks of the Cuillin. At the foot of the glen, idyllically situated by the sea, is the village of **GLENBRITTLE**. Climbers and serious walkers tend to congregate at the SYHA **hostel** (April–Sept; ⓣ01478/640278, ⓦwww.syha.org.uk) or the beautifully situated, but basic, **campsite** (April–Oct; ⓣ01478/640404), a mile or so further south behind the wide sandy beach at the foot of the glen. Both the hostel and the campsite have grocery stores, the only ones for miles.

From the valley, a score of difficult and strenuous trails lead east into the **Black Cuillin**, a rough semicircle of peaks rising to about 3000ft, which surround Loch Coruisk. One of the easiest walks is the five-mile round-trip (3hr) from the campsite up **Coire Làgan**, to a crystal-cold lochan squeezed in among the sternest of rockfaces. Above the lochan is Skye's highest peak, **Sgùrr Alasdair** (3258ft), one of the more difficult Munros, while Sgùrr na Banachdich (3166ft) to the northwest is considered the most easily accessible Munro in the Cuillin (for the usual walking safety precautions, see p.49). The Mountain Rescue Service has produced a book of walks for those who are not climbers, widely available locally.

Dunvegan and around

After the Portnalong and Glen Brittle turning, the A863 slips across bare rounded hills to skirt the bony sea cliffs and stacks of the west coast twenty miles or so north to **DUNVEGAN** (Dùn Bheagain). It's an unimpressive place, strung out along the east shore of the sea loch of the same name, though it does make quite a good base for exploring two interesting peninsulas: Duirinish and Waternish.

The main tourist trap in the village is **Dunvegan Castle** (Easter to Oct daily 10am–5pm; £8, gardens only £6; Ⓦ www.dunvegancastle.com), which sprawls on top of a rocky outcrop, sandwiched between the sea and several acres of beautifully maintained gardens. It's been the seat of the Clan MacLeod since the thirteenth century, but the present greying, rectangular fortress, with its uniform battlements and dummy pepper pots, dates from the 1840s. Inside, you don't get a lot of castle for your money and the contents are far from stunning, but there are three famous items, the most intriguing of which is the battered remnants of the **Fairy Flag** which was allegedly carried back to Skye by Norwegian king, Harald Hardrada's Gaelic boatmen after the Battle of Stamford Bridge in 1066. Among the Jacobite mementoes are a lock of hair from the head of Bonnie Prince Charlie (whom the MacLeods, in fact, fought against) and Flora MacDonald's corsets.

Dunvegan has a **tourist office** (April & May Mon–Fri 10am–5pm; June–Oct Mon–Sat 10am–5pm, July & Aug also Sun 10am–4pm; Nov–March Mon–Fri 10am–1.30pm) and some good **accommodation** options in the vicinity. Along the A863 to Bracadale, you'll find the *Old Byre* (Ⓦ www.theoldbyre.net; ❸), a cosy converted farmhouse B&B in Roskill, and *Roskhill House* (Ⓣ 01470/521317, Ⓦ www.roskhillhouse.co.uk; ❸) – confusingly, a further four miles down the road in Ose – once the village post office, now a lovely B&B with a log fire and free wi-fi. The **campsite** on Loch Dunvegan (April–Oct; Ⓣ 01470/521531, Ⓦ www.kinloch-campsite.co.uk) is five minutes' walk from Dunvegan on the road to Colbost. Without doubt, the best place to eat in Dunvegan is *The Old School* (Ⓣ 01470/521421; March–Dec, eves only) whose excellent food belies its appearance from the outside.

Duirinish and Glendale

The hammerhead **Duirinish peninsula** lies to the west of Dunvegan, much of it inaccessible to all except walkers prepared to scale or skirt the area's twin flat-topped basalt peaks: Healabhal Bheag (1600ft) and Healabhal Mhor (1538ft). The mountains are better known as **MacLeod's Tables**, for legend has it that the MacLeod chief held an open-air royal feast on the lower of the two for James V.

The main areas of habitation lie to the north, along the western shores of Loch Dunvegan, and in the broad green sweep of **Glen Dale** (Ⓦ www.glendale-skye.org.uk), attractively dotted with white farmhouses and dubbed "Little England" by the locals, due to its high percentage of incomers searching for a better life. Glen Dale's current predicament is doubly ironic given its history, for it was here in 1882 that local crofters staged a rent strike against their landlords, the MacLeods. Five locals – who became known as the "Glen Dale Martyrs" – were given two-month prison sentences, and eventually, in 1904, the crofters became the first owner-occupiers in the Highlands. All this, and a great deal more about nineteenth-century crofting, is told through fascinating contemporary news cuttings at **Colbost Croft Museum** (Easter–Oct daily 9.30am-6pm; £1), situated in a restored blackhouse, four miles up the road from Dunvegan. A guide is usually on hand to answer questions, the peat fire smokes all day, and there's a restored illegal whisky still round the back.

If you've got kids, you might like to pay a visit to the **Toy Museum** (Mon–Sat 10am–6pm; £3; ⓦwww.toy-museum.co.uk), in **GLENDALE** itself, which has everything from early Meccano sets to a fully equipped mini-crofters' kitchen, plus innumerable Sasha dolls and Star Wars toys.

Beyond Glendale is *Carter's Rest* (ⓣ01470/511272, ⓦwww.cartersrestskye.co.uk; £80), a spotless, high-quality modern **B&B** that serves excellent food. The culinary highlight of the area is the *Three Chimneys* **restaurant** (ⓣ01470/511258, ⓦwww.threechimneys.co.uk; ❾), next door to the Colbost Folk Museum, which serves sublime three-course meals at around £55 a head – the restaurant also has six fabulous rooms at the adjacent *House Over-By* which cost around £300 for dinner, bed and breakfast for two.

Waternish

Waternish is a thin and little-visited peninsula to the north of Dunvegan, whose prettiest village is **STEIN** (pronounced "Steen"), on the west coast looking out over Loch Bay and to the Western Isles. Descending from the heights, you eventually reach a row of whitewashed cottages built in 1787 by the British Fisheries Society. The place never really took off and was more or less abandoned within a couple of generations. Today, however, it's quite a lively place, particularly the sixteenth-century *Stein Inn* (ⓣ01470/592362, ⓦwww.steininn.co.uk; ❸), which has welcoming fires, good **pub food** and is a good place to stay. Next door is the pricier *Lochbay Seafood Restaurant* (ⓣ01470/592235, ⓦwww.lochbay-seafood-restaurant.co.uk; Easter–Oct Tues-Fri only), where you'll need to book ahead.

At the end of the road that runs along the west of the peninsula is **Trumpan Church**, an evocative medieval ruin on a cliff-top looking out to the Western Isles. This peaceful site was the scene of one of the bloodiest episodes in Skye history, when, in a revenge attack in 1578, the MacDonalds of Uist set fire to the church, while numerous MacLeods were attending a service inside. Everyone perished except one young girl who escaped by squeezing through a window, severing one of her breasts in the process. She raised the alarm, and the rest of the MacLeods quickly rallied and, bearing their famous Fairy Flag (see p.529), attacked the MacDonalds as they were launching their galleys. Every MacDonald was slaughtered and their bodies were thrown in a nearby dyke.

Portree

Although referred to by the locals as "the village", **PORTREE** is the only real town on Skye, with a population of around two thousand. It's also one of the most attractive fishing ports in northwest Scotland, its deep, cliff-edged harbour filled with fishing boats and circled by multicoloured restaurants and guesthouses. Originally known as *Kiltaraglen*, it takes its current name – some say – from *Port Rìgh* (Port of the King), after the state visit James V made in 1540 to assert his authority over the chieftains of Skye.

Information and accommodation

Portree's **tourist office** (April–Oct daily; Nov–March Mon–Fri only), just off Bridge Street, will book **accommodation** for you – useful if you haven't booked ahead – and you can go online here. Portree has a couple of centrally located

hostels, but you're better off going to nearby Staffin or Uig. By contrast, Torvaig **campsite** (April–Oct; ⓣ01478/611849, ⓦwww.portreecampsite.co.uk) is well kept, with a friendly owner, and lies a mile and a half north of town off the A855 Staffin road.

Ben Tianavaig 5 Bosville Terrace ⓣ01478/612152, ⓦben-tianavaig.co.uk. The best B&B in the centre of town, with charming hosts, views over the harbour, and free wi-fi. ❸

Cuillin Hills Hotel 10min walk out of town along the northern shore of the bay, ⓣ01478/612003, ⓦcuillinhills-hotel-skye.co.uk. Rooms are spacious and comfortable at this secluded hotel, with splendid views over the harbour and reasonably priced bar snacks. ❾

Gràsmhor Woodend ⓣ01478/611664, ⓦwww.grasmhor.co.uk. Modern B&B sitting in splendid isolation a couple of miles out of Portree along the single-track road to Bracadale. Very welcoming hosts, and bright and cheerful rooms, with great views. ❷

Medina Coolin Hills Gardens ⓣ01478/612821, ⓦmedinaskye.co.uk. Well-run and attractive bungalow B&B, with tasty breakfasts, in a quiet spot near the *Cuillin Hills Hotel*. ❹

Skeabost House five miles northwest of Portree ⓣ01470/532202, ⓦskeabostcountryhouse.com. Late Victorian pile which offers the life of a country gent in the main building, with an original billiard room and, outdoors, fishing, golf and extensive gardens – just don't take a room in the modern annexe. Open March–Oct. ❽

Viewfield House ⓣ01478/612217, ⓦviewfieldhouse.com. For old-school Scots Baronial style, it's hard to beat this hotel on the southern outskirts of town. It's been in the hands of the MacDonalds for over two hundred years, and has a real Victorian air, with stuffed polecats and antiques. Open mid-April to mid-Oct. ❼

The Town

The **harbour** is well worth a stroll, with its attractive pier built by Thomas Telford in the early nineteenth century. Fishing boats still land a modest catch, some of which is sold through *Anchor Seafoods* (Tues–Fri only) at the end of the pier. Up above the harbour is the spick-and-span town centre, spreading out from **Somerled Square**, built in the late eighteenth century as the island's administrative and commercial centre, and now serving as the town's bus station and car park. The **Royal Hotel** on Bank Street occupies the site of *McNab's Inn* where Bonnie Prince Charlie took leave of Flora MacDonald (see box, p.630), and where, 27 years later, Boswell and Johnson had "a very good dinner, porter, port and punch".

A mile or so out of town on the Sligachan road is the **Aros Centre** (daily 9am–5.30pm; ⓣ01478/613750, ⓦwww.aros.co.uk), one of Skye's most successful tourist attractions despite the fact that it's little more than one enormous souvenir shop. If it's wet, you can grab a live RSPB webcam centred on sea eagles' nests and an audiovisual roam around the island (£4). The best bit about Aros is that it hosts gigs and contains a **cinema**, a modern exhibition space, a licensed bar and a popular café, and there's a special play area for small kids. If it's fine, you might consider one of the easy waymarked forest walks from the car park.

Eating, drinking and activities

There's a surfeit of **places to eat** in Portree, all aimed at the tourist trade. The best solution is to head for *Café Arriba*, a truly relaxing place to eat at the top of the road down to the harbour, with an array of imaginative dishes for under £10. For decent seafood, *Sea Breezes* (ⓣ01478/613611; closed Mon), on the harbour, is excellent, but you'll have to book ahead; for good **fish and chips**, pop to the chippy a few doors down. As for **pubs**, the bar of the *Pier Hotel* on the quayside is the fishermen's drinking hole, and the *Tongadale* on Wentworth Street is a lively, convivial place. Currently the most popular evening venue by far, though, is the *Isles Inn* on Somerled Square, which has excellent **bar meals**, a real fire and occasional live music.

For **bike rental**, go to Island Cycles (Ⓣ01478/613121; closed Sun) below The Green. Day or half-day **boat trips** leave the pier for daily excursions to Raasay and Rona (Ⓣ07798/743858, Ⓦwww.skyeboat-trips.co.uk); **diving** can be organized through Dive-and-Sea the Hebrides in Lochbay, towards Dunvegan (Ⓣ01470/592219, Ⓦwww.dive-and-sea-the-hebrides.co.uk).

Trotternish

Protruding twenty miles north from Portree, the **Trotternish peninsula** has some of the island's most bizarre scenery, particularly on the east coast, where volcanic basalt has pressed down on the softer sandstone and limestone underneath, causing massive landslides. These, in turn, have created sheer cliffs, peppered with outcrops of hard, wizened basalt, which run the full length of the peninsula. These pinnacles and pillars are at their most eccentric in the **Quiraing**, above Staffin Bay, on the east coast. Trotternish is easily explored with your own transport, but the Flodigarry Circular bus service #57A and #57C gives access to almost all the coast.

The east coast

The first geological eccentricity on the Trotternish peninsula, six miles north of Portree along the A855, is the **Old Man of Storr**, a distinctive column of rock, shaped like a willow leaf, which, along with its neighbours, is part of a massive landslip. Huge blocks of stone still occasionally break off the cliff face of the Storr (2358ft) above and slide downhill. At 165ft, the Old Man is a real challenge for climbers; less difficult is the half-hour trek up the new footpath to the foot of the column from the woods beside the car park.

Further north, the wonderful amphitheatre of **Staffin Bay** is spread out before you, dotted with whitewashed and "spotty" houses. A single-track road cuts across the peninsula from the north end of the bay, allowing access to the **Quiraing**, a spectacular forest of mighty pinnacles and savage rock formations. There are two car parks: from the first, beside a cemetery, it's a steep half-hour climb to the rocks; from the second, on the saddle, it's a longer but more gentle traverse. Once you're in the midst of the rocks, you should be able to make out "The Prison" to your right, and the 120-foot Needle, to your left; the Table, a great sunken platform where locals used to play shinty, lies above and beyond the Needle, another fifteen-minute scramble up the rocks; legend also maintains that a local warrior named Fraing hid his cattle there from the invading Norsemen.

Most **accommodation** choices on the east coast enjoy fantastic views out over the sea. Just beyond the Lealt Falls there's the very welcoming and comfortable *Glenview Hotel* (Ⓣ01470/562248, Ⓦwww.glenview-skye.co.uk; ❼), with an excellent restaurant. Or for half the price, you can stay at *Hallaig Guest House* (Ⓣ01470/562250, Ⓦwww.hallaig.com; ❸), a comfortable, modern B&B in Marishadder, along the dead-end road to Garros. There's also a **campsite** (Ⓣ01470/562213, Ⓦwww.staffincampsite.co.uk; April–Sept) south of Staffin Bay. In fine weather, you can enjoy good bar snacks on the castellated terrace of the stylish *Flodigarry Country House Hotel*, three miles up the coast from Staffin. Behind the hotel (and now part of it) is the cottage where local heroine Flora MacDonald lived, and had six of her seven children, from 1751 to 1759. You can **camp** or stay at the neat and attractive *Dun Flodigarry* **hostel** (Ⓣ01470/552212, Ⓦwww.hostelflodigarry.co.uk), a couple of minutes' walk away.

Duntulm and Kilmuir

Beyond Flodigarry, four miles further along the A855, lies **DUNTULM** (Duntuilm), whose heyday as a major MacDonald power base is recalled by the shattered remains of a headland fortress abandoned by the clan in 1732 after a clumsy nurse dropped the baby son and heir from a window onto the rocks below; on these same rocks, it is said, can be seen the keel marks of Viking longships. The imposing *Duntulm Castle Hotel* (March–Nov) is close by and provides good pub food as well as wonderful views across the Minch to the Western Isles.

Heading down the west shore of the Trotternish, it's two miles to the **Skye Museum of Island Life** (Easter–Oct Mon–Sat 9.30am–5pm; £2.50; Ⓦwww.skyemuseum.co.uk), an impressive cluster of thatched blackhouses on an exposed hill overlooking Harris. The museum, run by locals, gives a fascinating insight into a way of life that was commonplace on Skye a hundred years ago. Behind the museum in the cemetery up the hill are the graves of **Flora MacDonald** (see box, p.630) and her husband. Thousands turned out for her funeral in 1790, creating a funeral procession a mile long – indeed, so widespread was her fame that the original family mausoleum fell victim to souvenir hunters and had to be replaced. The Celtic cross headstone is inscribed with a simple tribute by Dr Johnson, who visited her in 1773: "Her name will be mentioned in history, if courage and fidelity be virtues, mentioned with honour."

Uig

Skye's chief ferry port for the Western Isles is **UIG** (Uige), which curves its way round a dramatic, horseshoe-shaped bay. Most folk are just passing through, but if you've time to kill, take the a lovely, gentle **walk** up Glen Uig, better known as the **Faerie Glen**, at the east end of the bay. Uig's **campsite** is on a sloping field very close to the pier (Ⓣ01470/542714, Ⓦwww.uig-camping-skye.co.uk) and offers **bike rental**. By contrast, the SYHA **hostel** (April–Sept; Ⓣ0870/004 1155) is a twenty-minute walk away, high up on the south side of the village, with exhilarating views over the bay. If you need to stay near the ferry terminal, *Harris Cottage* (Ⓣ01470/542243, Ⓦwww.harris-cottage.co.uk; April–Oct; ❶), an inexpensive **B&B** a short walk from the pier. If you're staying more than one night, head for *Woodbine House* (Ⓣ01470/542243, Ⓦwww.skyeactivities.co.uk; April–Oct; ❸), a luxurious Victorian house just under a mile from the pier, tastefully furnished by a couple who also run boat trips from Uig. The *Pub at the Pier* offers basic **pub food**, and serves beers from the nearby **brewery**.

The Small Isles

The history of the **Small Isles**, which lie to the south of Skye, is typical of the Hebrides: early Christianization, followed by Norwegian rule, ending in 1266 when the islands fell into Scottish hands. Their support for the Jacobites resulted in hard times after the failed 1745 rebellion, but the biggest problems came with the introduction of the **potato** in the mid-eighteenth century. The consequences were as dramatic as they were unforeseen: the success of the crop and its nutritional value – when grown in conjunction with traditional cereals – eliminated famine at a stroke, prompting a population explosion. In 1750, there were a thousand islanders, but by 1800 their numbers had almost doubled.

Getting to the Small Isles

CalMac (Ⓣ01687/462403, Ⓦwww.calmac.co.uk) runs ferries to the Small Isles every day except Sunday from Mallaig (see p.481). From late April to late September, the **Sheerwater** (Ⓣ01687/450224, Ⓦwww.arisaig.co.uk) operates a daily service from Arisaig (see p.480) to Rùm, Eigg or Muck – advance booking is advisable. This is a much more pleasant way to get there, not least because if any marine mammals are spotted en route, the boat will pause for a bit of whale-watching. With careful studying of both CalMac and Sheerwater timetables, you should be able to organize a day-trip or longer visit to suit you, especially as Arisaig and Mallaig are linked by railway. Be warned, however, that boats to the Small Isles are frequently cancelled in bad weather, so be prepared to holiday for longer than you planned.

At first, the problem of overcrowding was camouflaged by the **kelp** boom, but the economic bubble burst with the end of the Napoleonic Wars and, to maintain their profit margins, the owners resorted to drastic action. The first to sell up was Alexander MacLean, who sold Rùm as grazing land for **sheep**, got quotations for shipping its people to Nova Scotia and gave them a year's notice to quit. He also cleared Muck to graze cattle, as did the MacNeills on Canna. Only on Eigg was some compassion shown: the new owner, a certain Hugh MacPherson, who bought the island from the Clanranalds in 1827, actually gave some of his tenants extended leases.

Since the Clearances, each of the islands has been bought and sold several times, though only **Muck** is now privately owned by the benevolent laird, Lawrence MacEwen. **Eigg** hit the headlines in 1997, when the islanders finally managed to buy the island themselves and put an end to more than 150 years of property speculation. The other islands were bequeathed to national agencies: **Rùm**, by far the largest and most-visited of the group, possessing a cluster of formidable volcanic peaks and the architecturally remarkable Kinloch Castle, passed to the Nature Conservancy Council (now Scottish Natural Heritage) in 1957; and **Canna**, in many ways the prettiest of the isles with its high basalt cliffs, has been in the hands of the National Trust for Scotland since 1981.

Accommodation on the Small Isles is limited and requires **forward planning** at all times of year; formal public transport is nonexistent, but the locals will usually oblige if you have heavy baggage to shift.

Rùm

Like Skye, **Rùm** (Ⓦwww.isleofrum.com) is dominated by its Cuillin, which, though reaching a height of only 2663ft at the summit of Askival, rises with comparable drama straight up from the sea in the south of the island. The majority of the island's twenty or so inhabitants now live in **KINLOCH**, overlooking the large bay on the sheltered east coast, and most are employed by Scottish Natural Heritage (SNH), which runs the island as a National Nature Reserve. SNH have been reintroducing native woodland to the island, overseeing a long-term study of the vast red deer population, and have re-introduced **white-tailed (sea) eagles**, which have since mostly abandoned Rùm in favour of neighbouring islands. You can learn more about the history of the island, and its flora and fauna, in the small **museum** near the old pier.

Rùm's chief attraction is **Kinloch Castle** (March-Oct guided tours coincide with the ferry; £6; Ⓦwww.kinlochcastle.co.uk), a squat, red-sandstone edifice fronted by colonnades and topped by crenellations and turrets, which dominates the village of Kinloch. Completed at enormous expense in 1900 – the red sandstone was shipped in from Dumfriesshire and the soil for the gardens from Ayrshire – and now in need of some serious restoration, its interior is a perfectly preserved example of Edwardian decadence, "a living memorial of the stalking, the fishing and the sailing, the tenantry and plenty of the days before 1914". From the galleried hall, with its tiger rugs, stags' heads and giant Japanese incense burners, to the "Extra Low Fast Cushion" of the Soho snooker table in the Billiard Room, the interior is packed with knick-knacks and technical gizmos accumulated by **Sir George Bullough** (1870–1939), the spendthrift son of self-made millionaire, Sir John Bullough, who bought the island as a sporting estate in 1888. As such, it was only really used for a few weeks each autumn, during the "season", though it employed an island workforce of one hundred year-round. Bullough's guests were woken at eight each morning by a piper; later on, an orchestrion (an electrically driven barrel organ) that was originally destined for Balmoral was crammed in under the stairs and would grind out an eccentric mixture of pre-dinner tunes: *The Ride of the Valkyries* and *Ma Blushin' Rosie* among others (a demo is included in the tour). The ballroom has a sprung floor, the library features a gruesome photographic collection from the Bulloughs' world tours, but the *pièce de résistance* has to be Bullough's **Edwardian bathrooms**, whose baths have hooded walnut shower cabinets, fitted with two taps and four dials, which allow bathers to fire high-pressure water at their bodies from every angle.

There are two gentle waymarked **trails** in the surrounding countryside, both of which start from Kinloch, and take around two hours to complete. For longer walks, you must fill in route cards and pop them into the *White House* (Ⓣ01687/462026), on the road from the ferry, where the reserve manager can give useful advice; they also occasionally offer **guided walks** around the island, including a night-time hike to see the shearwaters on the slopes of Hallival.

The island's best beach is at **KILMORY**, in the north of the island (5hr return from Kinloch) where students frequently get eaten alive by midges while studying red deer. When the island's human head count peaked at 450 in 1791, the hamlet of **HARRIS** on the southwest coast (6hr return from Kinloch) housed a large crofting community. All that remains now are several ruined blackhouses and the extravagant **Bullough Mausoleum** overlooking the sea, which was built by Sir George to house the remains of his father. This is, in fact, the second one to be constructed here: the first was lined with Italian marble mosaics, but when a friend remarked that it looked like a public lavatory Bullough had it dynamited and the current Neoclassical one erected.

Practicalities

Until Rùm passed into the hands of the SNH, it was known as the "Forbidden Isle" because of its exclusive use as a sporting estate for the rich; nowadays, visitors are made very welcome by the SNH staff. Day-trips are possible more or less daily in the summer (see opposite). *Kinloch Castle* was a luxury hotel until the 1990s, and still lets one of its (non-en-suite) four-poster rooms (❷), but it's basically run as an independent **hostel** (Ⓣ01687/462037), with dormitories in the old servants' quarters – advance booking is essential. Wild camping is permitted, and there are two simple mountain **bothies** (three nights maximum stay), in Dibidil, on the southeast coast, and Guirdil, on the northwest coast, plus a basic community **campsite** with hot showers on the foreshore near the old pier.

Wherever you're staying, you can use the hostel kitchen, have a drink in the castle bar, and eat in the hostel's licensed **bistro**, which serves full breakfasts (£7), offers packed lunches (£5) and tasty three-course evening meals (£15) – advance booking essential. There is also a small shop/off-licence/post office on the north side of the bay. Bear in mind that Rùm is the wettest of the Small Isles, and is known for having some of the worst **midges** (see p.47) in Scotland – come prepared for both. Note that overnight visitors cannot bring dogs, but day-trippers can.

Eigg

Eigg (Ⓦwww.isleofeigg.org) – which measures just five miles by three – is made up of a basalt plateau 1000ft above sea level, and a great stump of columnar pitchstone lava, known as An Sgurr, rising out of the plateau another 290ft. It's by far the most vibrant, populous and welcoming of the Small Isles, with a real and strong sense of community. This was given an enormous boost by the 1997 buyout by the 70-odd islanders (along with the local council and the Scottish Wildlife Trust), which ended Eigg's unhappy history of private ownership, most recently by the Olympic bobsleigher and gelatine heir Keith Schellenberg. The anniversary of the buyout is celebrated every year with an all-night ceilidh on the weekend nearest 12 June.

Ferries arrive at the causeway which juts out into **Galmisdale Bay**, in the southeast corner of the island where **An Laimhrig** (The Anchorage), the island's community centre, stands, housing a shop, post office, licensed tearoom and information centre. Davie's minibus meets incoming ferries, and will take you to wherever you need to go on the island (Ⓣ01687/482494; £2). If time is limited, you could simply head through the woods for the nearby **Lodge**, the former laird's house and gardens, which the islanders plan to renovate in the future. With the island's great landmark, **An Sgurr** (1292ft), watching over you wherever you go, many folk feel duty-bound to climb it, and enjoy the wonderful views over to Muck and Rùm. The easiest approach is to take the path that skirts the summit to the north, and ascend from the saddle to the west (3–4hr return). Some visitors prefer to head off to **CLEADALE**, the main crofting settlement in the north of the island, where the beach, known as Camas Sgiotaig, or the **Singing Sands**, is comprised of quartz and squeaks underfoot when dry (hence the name).

If you're just here for the day, make sure you pop into the **tearoom** by the causeway, which has a lovely terrace looking out to sea. A great place **to stay** is ★ *Kildonan House* (Ⓣ01687/482446, Ⓦwww.kildonanhouseeigg.co.uk; dinner, B&B ❻), an eighteenth-century, wood-panelled house beautifully situated on the north side of Galmisdale Bay, with good home-cooking. Alternatively, you can stay in the north of the island at *Lageorna* (Ⓣ01687/482405, Ⓦwww.lageorna.com; dinner, B&B ❼), a beautifully designed modern house in Cleadale, with free wi-fi and a **restaurant** (Easter–Sept) that offers delicious lunches and evening meals to residents and non-residents. *Glebe Barn* (Ⓣ01687/482417) is a very comfortable **bunkhouse** a mile from the pier, and wild **camping** is possible at Galmisdale Bay and at Sue Hollands' organic croft in Cleadale (Ⓣ01687/482480, Ⓔsuehollands@talk21.com), plus there's a **yurt** for hire in the middle of the island (Ⓣ01687/460317). A minibus and **bike rental** are usually available – ask locally for details.

Muck

Smallest and most southerly of the Small Isles, **Muck** (Ⓦwww.isleofmuck.com) is low-lying, mostly treeless and extremely fertile, and as such shares more characteristics with the likes of Coll and Tiree (see p.282) than its nearest neighbours. Its name derives from *muc*, the Gaelic for "pig" – or, as some would have it, *muc mara*, "sea pig" or porpoise, which abound in the surrounding waters – and has long caused much embarrassment to generations of lairds who preferred to call it the "Isle of Monk", because it had briefly belonged to the medieval church.

PORT MÓR, the village on the southeast corner of the island, is where visitors arrive and where most of the thirty or so residents live. A road, just over a mile in length, connects Port Mór with the island's main farm, **GALLANACH**, which overlooks the rocky seal-strewn skerries on the north side of the island. The nicest sandy beach is Camas na Cairidh, to the east of Gallanach. Despite being only 452ft above sea level, it really is worth climbing **Beinn Airein** (2hr return), in the southwest corner of the island, for the 360-degree panoramic view of the surrounding islands.

You can **stay** with one of the MacEwen family, who have owned the island since 1896, at *Port Mór House* (ⓣ01687/462365; full board ❻); the rooms are pine-clad and enjoy great views, and the food is delicious (non-residents welcome). Alternatively, there are a couple of B&Bs, including *Godag House* (ⓣ01687/462371; full board ❺), halfway between Port Mór and Gallanach, or you can try the island's seven-bed **bunkhouse** (ⓣ01687/462042), a characterful, wood-panelled bothy heated by a Raeburn stove. You can also hire the island **yurt** (ⓣ01687/462362; May–Sept), or **camp rough** – ask at the *Green Shed* (ⓣ01687/462990; June–Aug) in Port Mór. The only shop on the island, the *Green Shed* is essentially a craft shop, which springs into life when day-trippers arrive, and also sells seasonal vegetables and serves evening meals on request.

Canna

Measuring a mere four miles by one, and with just a handful of full-time residents, **Canna** is run as a single farm and bird sanctuary by the National Trust for Scotland (NTS). The island enjoys the best harbour in the Small Isles, a horn-shaped haven at its southeastern corner protected by the tidal island of Sanday, linked to Canna by a road bridge. For visitors, the chief pastime is walking: from the dock it's about a mile across a grassy basalt plateau to the bony sea-cliffs of the north shore, which rise to a peak around Compass Hill – so called because its high metal content distorts compasses – in the northeastern corner of the island, from where you get great views across to Rùm and Skye. The cliffs of the buffeted western half of the island are a breeding ground for Manx shearwaters, razorbills and puffins. Some seven miles offshore stands **Hyskeir** (Òigh-sgeir) a curious mass of stone columns sticking up 30ft above the water.

With permission from the NTS, you may **camp rough** on Canna, though you need to bring your own supplies, as there's no real shop to speak of. There's also a traditional bell **tent** for hire, sleeping five (ⓣ01687/460166, ⓦcannafolk.co.uk; April–Oct), tucked away in some woodland. *Tighard*, a substantial, red sandstone, Victorian house half a mile from the jetty, is the island's only **guesthouse** (ⓣ01687/462474, ⓦwww.peaceofcanna.co.uk; ❹); the rooms are spacious, with glorious views, and they'll cook you dinner when the restaurant's not working. The **restaurant**, *Gille Brighde* (ⓣ01687/460164, ⓦwww.cannarestaurant.com; Tues–Sat only), offers lunch and dinner with the emphasis on local produce where possible. Note that Canna is not on the national grid; **electricity** is powered by diesel generators, which are switched off between midnight and 6am.

Travel details

Trains

Fort William to: Mallaig (4–5 daily; 1hr 20min).
Glasgow (Queen St) to: Mallaig (Mon–Sat 3 daily, 1 on Sun; 5hr 10min).
Inverness to: Kyle of Lochalsh (Mon–Sat 3–4 daily, 1–2 on Sun; 2hr 30min).

Buses

From the mainland

Glasgow to: Broadford (3 daily; 5hr 30min); Portree (3 daily; 6hr 15min); Uig (2 daily; 6hr 50min).
Kyle of Lochalsh to: Broadford (Mon–Sat hourly; 25min); Kyleakin (Mon–Sat hourly; 10min); Portree (Mon–Sat 5 daily, 2 on Sun; 1hr).

On Skye

Armadale to: Broadford (Mon–Sat 5 daily, 2 on Sun; 35min); Portree (Mon–Sat 5 daily, 2 on Sun; 1hr 20min); Sligachan (Mon–Sat 5 daily, 2 on Sun; 1hr).
Broadford to: Elgol (Mon–Fri 4 daily, 2 on Sat; 45min); Kyleakin (hourly; 15min); Portree (Mon–Sat 5–10 daily; 40min); Sligachan (Mon–Sat 5 daily, 2 on Sun; 20min).
Dunvegan to: Glendale (school days 2–3 daily; 30min).
Portree to: Duntulm (Mon–Sat 4–5 daily; 55min); Dunvegan (Mon–Sat 3–4 daily; 45min); Glenbrittle (Mon–Fri 2 daily; 50min); Staffin (Mon–Sat 4–5 daily; 35min); Uig (Mon–Sat 7–8 daily, 3 on Sun; 30min).

CalMac ferries

Summer timetable only.

To Canna: Eigg–Canna (Mon & Sat; 2hr 30min); Mallaig–Canna (Mon, Wed, Fri & Sat; 2hr 30min–3hr 50min); Muck–Canna (Sat; 1hr 35min); Rùm–Canna (Mon, Wed, Fri & Sat; 55min).
To Eigg: Canna–Eigg (Mon & Sat; 2hr 15min); Mallaig–Eigg (Mon, Tues & Thurs–Sat; 1hr 15min–2hr 25min); Muck–Eigg (Tues & Thurs–Sat; 35min); Rùm–Eigg (Mon & Sat; 1hr–3hr 30min).
To Muck: Canna–Muck (Sat; 1hr 35min); Eigg–Muck (Tues, Thurs & Sat; 35min); Mallaig–Muck (Tues, Thurs, Fri & Sat; 1hr 40min–4hr 20min); Rùm–Muck (Sat; 2hr 45min).
To Raasay: Sconser–Raasay (Mon–Sat 8–10 daily, 2 on Sun; 15min).
To Rùm: Canna–Rùm (Mon, Wed, Fri & Sat; 55min); Eigg–Rùm (Mon & Sat; 1hr–3hr 30min); Mallaig–Rùm (Mon, Wed, Fri & Sat; 1hr 20min–2hr 30min); Muck–Rùm (Sat; 1hr 10min).
To Skye: Glenelg–Kylerhea (daily frequently; 15min); Mallaig–Armadale (Mon–Sat 8 daily, Sun 4–6 daily; 30min).

15

The Western Isles

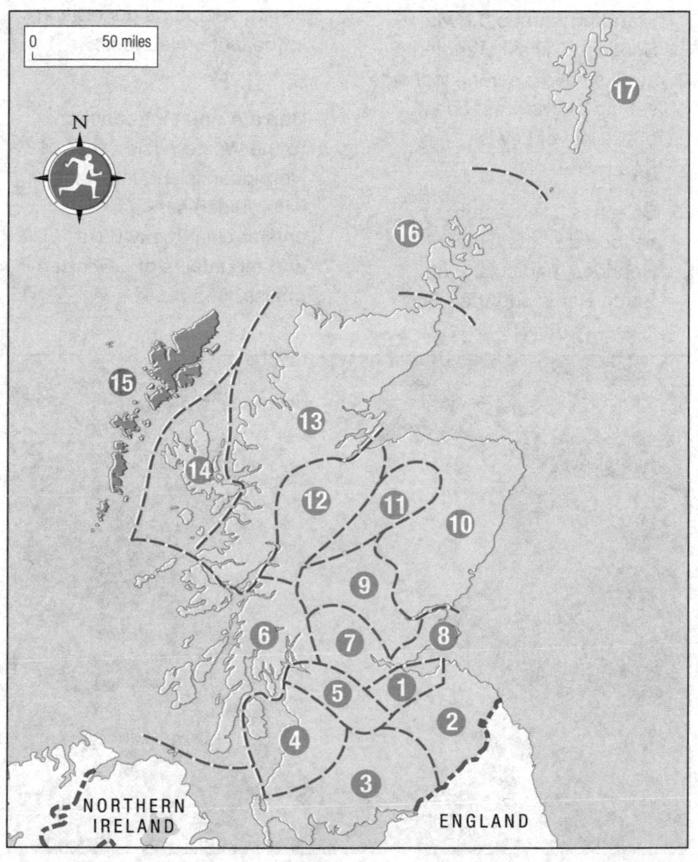

CHAPTER 15 Highlights

* **Gearrannan (Garenin), Lewis** A crofting village of painstakingly restored thatched blackhouses: you can stay in the hostel, or simply have a guided tour round the site. See p.549

* **Calanais (Callanish) standing stones, Lewis** Scotland's finest standing stones have a serene lochside setting on the west coast of the Isle of Lewis. See p.549

* **Beaches** The western seaboard of the Outer Hebrides, particularly on South Harris and the Uists, is strewn with stunning, deserted golden-sand beaches backed by flower-strewn machair. See p.553

* **Roghadal (Rodel) Church, Harris** Roghadal's pre-Reformation St Clement's Church boasts the most ornate sculptural decoration in the Outer Hebrides. See p.554

* **Barra** A great introduction to the Western Isles: a Hebridean island in miniature, with golden sands, crystal-clear rocky bays and mountains of Lewissian gneiss. See p.561

▲ Gearrannan, Lewis

15

The Western Isles

Beyond Skye, across the unpredictable waters of the Minch, lie the wild and windy Outer Hebrides or Outer Isles, now officially known as the **Western Isles** (Ⓦ www.visithebrides.com). A 130-mile-long archipelago stretching from Lewis and Harris in the north to the Uists and Barra in the south, the islands appear as an unbroken chain when viewed from across the Minch, hence their other nickname, the Long Isle. In reality there are more than two hundred islands, although only a handful are actually inhabited, with the islands' total population just under 27,000. This is truly a land on the edge, where the turbulent seas of the Atlantic smash up against a geologically complex terrain whose coastline is interrupted by a thousand sheltered bays and, in the far west, a long line of sweeping sandy beaches. The islands' interiors are equally dramatic, veering between flat, boggy, treeless peat moor and bare mountain tops soaring high above a host of tiny lakes, or lochans.

However, the most significant difference between the Western Isles and the rest of the Hebrides is that the islands' fragile economy is still mainly concentrated around crofting, fishing and weaving, and the percentage of incomers is fairly low. In fact, the Outer Hebrides remain the heartland of **Gaelic** culture, with the language spoken by the majority of islanders, though its everyday usage remains under constant threat from the national dominance of English. Its survival is, in no small part, due to the efforts of the Western Islands Council, the Scottish parliament, and the influence of the Church in the region: the Free Church and its various offshoots in Lewis, Harris and North Uist, and the Roman Catholic Church in South Uist and Barra.

Lewis and Harris form two parts of the same island. The interior of the northernmost island, **Lewis**, is mostly peat moor, a barren and marshy tract that gives way abruptly to the bare peaks of **North Harris**. Across a narrow isthmus lies **South Harris**, with wide beaches of golden sand trimming the Atlantic in full view of the rough boulder-strewn mountains to the east. Across the Sound of Harris, to the south, a string of tiny, flatter isles linked by causeways – **North Uist**, **Benbecula**, **South Uist** – offer breezy beaches, whose fine sands front a narrow band of boggy farmland, which, in turn, is mostly bordered by a lower range of hills to the east. Finally, tiny **Barra** contains all the above landscapes in one small Hebridean package.

In contrast to their wonderful surroundings, villages in the Western Isles are rarely very picturesque in themselves, and are usually made up of scattered, relatively modern crofthouses dotted about the elementary road system. **Stornoway**, the only real town in the Outer Hebrides, rarely impresses. Many visitors, walkers and nature-watchers forsake the main settlements altogether and retreat to secluded cottages, simple hostels and B&Bs.

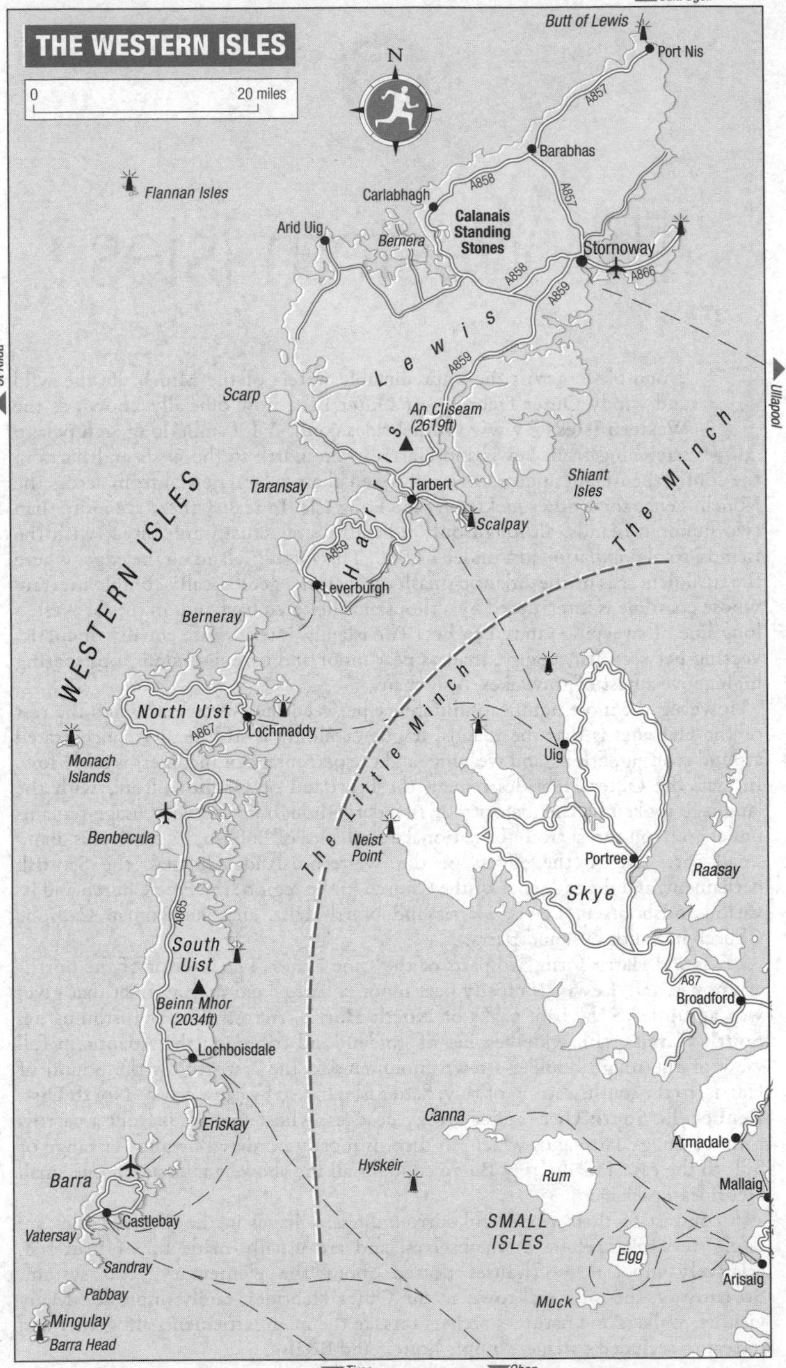
THE WESTERN ISLES
0 20 miles
N
Sula Sgeir
Butt of Lewis
Port Nis
A857
Barabhas
Flannan Isles
Carlabhagh
A858
A857
Calanais Standing Stones
Arid Uig
Bernera
Stornoway
A866
A858
A859
Lewis
A859
St Kilda
Ullapool
Scarp
An Cliseam (2619ft)
The Minch
WESTERN ISLES
Shiant Isles
Taransay
Tarbert
Harris
Scalpay
A859
Leverburgh
Berneray
North Uist
Lochmaddy
A867
Monach Islands
Uig
The Little Minch
Neist Point
Benbecula
Portree
Raasay
Skye
A865
South Uist
Beinn Mhor (2034ft)
A87
Broadford
Lochboisdale
Eriskay
Canna
Armadale
Barra
Hyskeir
Rum
Mallaig
Castlebay
SMALL ISLES
Vatersay
Eigg
Sandray
Arisaig
Pabbay
Muck
Mingulay
Barra Head
Tiree
Oban

Gaelic in the Western Isles

All Ordnance Survey maps and many **road signs** are exclusively in **Gaelic**, a difficult language to the English-speaker's eye, with complex pronunciation (see p.644), though the English names sometimes provide a rough pronunciation guide. If you're driving, it's a good idea to pick up a bilingual Western Isles **map**, available at most tourist offices. We've put the Gaelic first in the text, with the English equivalent in brackets, to try to familiarize readers with their (albeit variable) spellings – the only exceptions are in the names of islands and ferry terminals, where we've stuck to the English names (with the Gaelic in brackets), partly to reflect CalMac's own policy.

Visiting the Western Isles

There are scheduled **flights** from Glasgow, Edinburgh, Inverness and Aberdeen to Stornoway on Lewis, and to Barra and Benbecula. Be warned: weather conditions are notoriously changeable, making flights prone to delay and even cancellation. On Barra, the other complication is that you land on the beach, so the timetable is adjusted with the tides. CalMac **car ferries** run from Ullapool to Stornoway; from Uig, on Skye, to Tarbert (Mon–Sat only) and Lochmaddy (daily); and from Oban to South Uist and Barra, via Coll and Tiree (Thurs only).

A series of causeways makes it possible to drive from one end of the Western Isles to the other with just two interruptions – the **ferry** from Harris to Berneray, and from Eriskay to Barra. The islands have a decent **bus** service, though there are no buses on Sundays. **Bike rental** is also available, but the wind makes cycling something of a challenge – head south to north to catch the prevailing wind. There's a wide choice of **boat trips** offered locally: try Sea Trek (Ⓣ01851/672464, Ⓦwww.seatrek.co.uk), based in Uig, or Kilda Cruises in Leverburgh (Ⓣ01859/502060, Ⓦwww.kildacruises.co.uk) – prices start at around £35 per person for a short RIB wildlife cruise to £180 for a day-trip to St Kilda.

The islands' **hostels** are geared up for the outdoor life, occupying remote locations on or near the coast. Several of them are run by the **Gatliff Hebridean Hostels Trust** or GHHT (Ⓦwww.gatliff.org.uk), and none have phones, so in the height of summer get there early to be sure of a bed; each hostel has hot water, a simple kitchen and space outside for camping. The islands' **B&Bs** and **guesthouses** are often better value than the hotels, and allow you to meet the locals – bed numbers are limited though, so it's always best to **book in advance**.

The Gulf Stream ensures a mild but moist climate, though you can expect the **strong Atlantic winds** to blow in rain on two out of every three days, even in summer – the upside is that means few problems with midges. Lastly, for a lively view on local life, read the **local papers**, in particular the weekly *West Highland Free Press*, published in Broadford on Skye.

Lewis (Leodhas)

Shaped rather like the top of an ice-cream cone, **Lewis** is the largest and by far the most populous of the Western Isles. Nearly half of the island's 18,500 inhabitants – two-thirds of the archipelago's total population – live in the crofting and fishing villages strung out along the northwest coast, between **Calanais** and **Port Nis**, in one of the most densely populated rural areas in the country. On this coast you'll also find the islands' best-preserved **prehistoric remains** – Dùn Charlabhaigh and the Calanais standing stones – as well as a smattering of ancient crofters' houses in various stages of abandonment. The landscape is mostly flat peat bog – hence the island's name, derived from the Gaelic *leogach* (marshy) – but the shoreline is more dramatic especially around Rubha Robhanais (Butt of Lewis), the island's rocky northernmost tip, near Port Nis. The other half of the island's population live in **Stornoway**, on the east coast, the only real town in the Western Isles. To the south, where Lewis is physically joined with Harris, the land rises to over 1800ft, providing an exhilarating backdrop for the excellent beaches that pepper the isolated western coastline around **Uig**.

Some history

After Viking rule ended in 1266, Lewis became a virtually independent state, ruled over by the **MacLeod clan**. King James VI, however, had other ideas and in 1610 granted the lands to their arch-rivals, the MacKenzies of Kintail. The MacKenzie chiefs – the Earls of Seaforth – chose to remain absentee landlords until 1844, when they sold Lewis to **Sir James Matheson**, who'd made a fortune from pushing opium

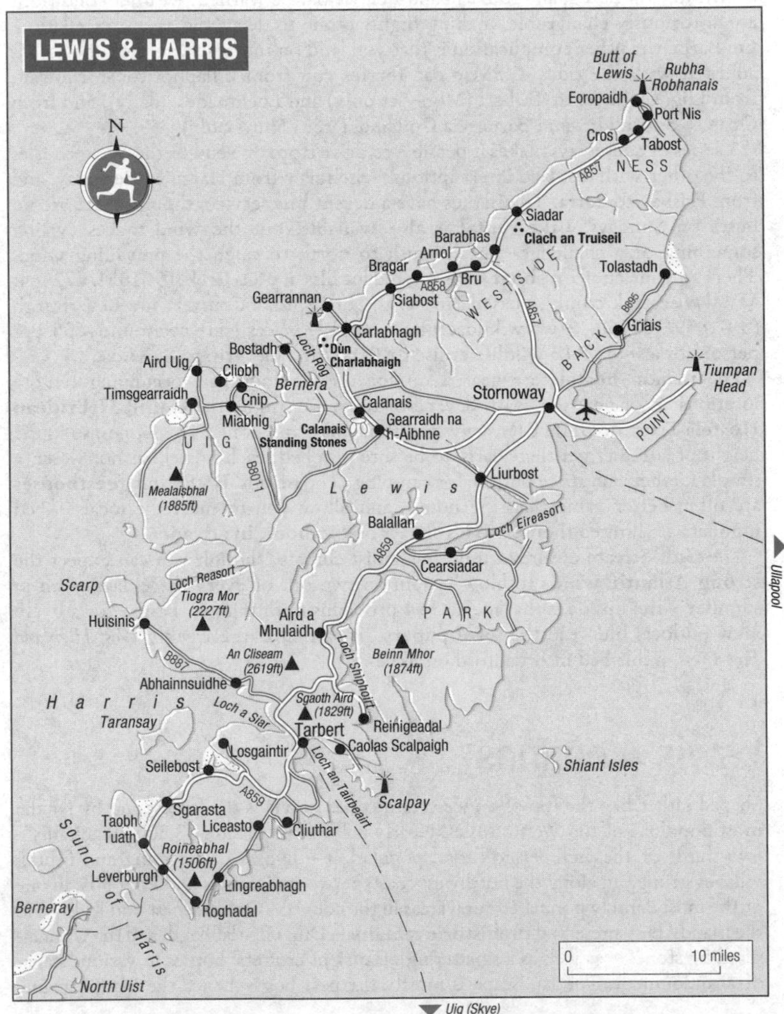

on the Chinese. Matheson was relatively benevolent when the island was hit by potato famine in the mid-1840s, but ultimately opted for eviction and emigration. His chief factor, Donald Munro, was utterly ruthless, and was only removed after the celebrated Bernera Riot of 1874. The 1886 Crofters' Act greatly curtailed the power of the Mathesons; it did not, however, right any of the wrongs of the past.

When **Lord Leverhulme**, founder of the soap empire Unilever, acquired the island (along with Harris) in 1918, he was determined to drag Lewis out of its cycle of poverty by establishing an integrated fishing industry. He founded MacFisheries, a nationwide chain of fishmongers; he built a cannery, an ice factory, roads, bridges and a light railway; he bought boats and planned to use spotter planes to locate the shoals of herring. But the dream never came to fruition. Leverhulme was implacably opposed to the island's centuries-old tradition of crofting, which he regarded as inefficient and "an entirely impossible way of life". In the end, however, it was financial difficulties that prompted Leverhulme to pull out of Lewis in 1923. He generously gifted Lews Castle and Stornoway to its inhabitants, but his departure left a huge gap in the non-crofting economy, and between the wars thousands more emigrated.

Stornoway (Steòrnabhagh)

In these parts, **STORNOWAY** is a buzzing metropolis, with more than six thousand inhabitants and all the trappings of a large town. It's a centre for employment, a social hub for the island and home to the Western Isles Council or **Comhairle nan Eilean Siar**, set up in 1974, which has done so much to promote Gaelic language and culture and to stem the tide of anglicization. For the visitor, however, the town is unlikely to win any great praise – aesthetics are not its strong point, and the urban pleasures on offer are limited.

Arrival, information and accommodation

Stornoway **airport** (Ⓣ01851/707400, Ⓦwww.hial.co.uk) is four miles east of the town centre: the hourly bus takes fifteen minutes, or else it's a £5 taxi ride into town. The octagonal CalMac **ferry terminal** (Ⓣ01851/702361) is on South Beach, close to the **bus station** (Ⓣ01851/704327). You can get bus timetables, a map of the town, a parking disc and other useful information from the **tourist office**, near North Beach at 26 Cromwell St (April to mid-Oct Mon–Sat only; mid-Oct to March Mon–Fri only; Ⓣ01851/703088).

Stornoway's **accommodation** choices have improved dramatically in recent years, but prices are high. The only **hostel** is the *Heb Hostel* (Ⓣ01851/709889, Ⓦwww.hebhostel.co.uk), a clean, centrally located and friendly converted terrace house at 25 Kenneth St. If you're **camping**, it's better to camp away from Stornoway, unless you need to stay near town, in which case use *Laxdale Holiday Park* (Ⓣ01851/703234, Ⓦwww.laxdaleholidaypark.com) which lies a mile or so along the road to Barabhas, on Laxdale Lane; the campsite has a purpose-built **bunkhouse**, as well as a nice sheltered spot for tents.

Cairn Dhu 18a Matheson Rd Ⓣ01851/701611, Ⓦwww.lewisapartments.co.uk. Superbly equipped contemporary apartment, with free wi-fi, in a Victorian villa on the town's nicest leafy street. ❻

Hal O The Wynd 2 Newton St Ⓣ01851/706073, Ⓦwww.halothewynd.com. Reliable, inexpensive town centre B&B in an old townhouse, conveniently situated directly opposite the ferry terminal. ❷

Hebridean Guest House 61 Bayhead St Ⓣ01851/702268, Ⓦwww.hebrideanguesthouse.co.uk. A whole range of smartly refurbished, en-suite rooms on offer here, including a couple of self-catering apartments. ❺

Jannel 5 Stewart Drive Ⓣ0800/634 3270, Ⓦwww.jannel-stornoway.co.uk. A short walk from the town centre, this B&B is run by a delightful landlady, and offers five spacious, immaculate rooms, with free wi-fi. ❹

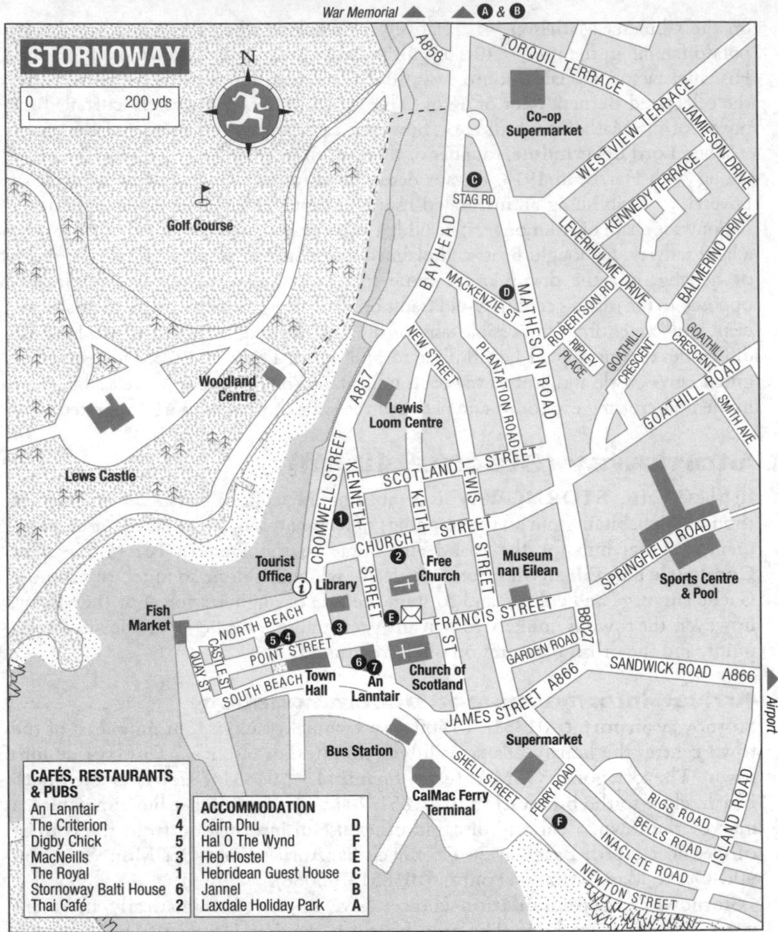

The Town

Stornoway's commercial centre, to the east of the harbour, is little more than a string of unprepossessing shops and bars. The one exception is the old **Town Hall** on South Beach, a splendid Scots Baronial building, its rooftop peppered with conical towers, above which a central clock tower rises. One block east along South Beach, and looking rather like a modern church, you'll find **An Lanntair** (Mon–Sat 10am–late; free; Ⓦ www.lanntair.com) – Gaelic for "lantern" – Stornoway's modern cultural centre, which has an events space, cinema and a gallery, plus a decent café-bar.

Continuing up the pedestrian precinct into Francis Street, you'll eventually reach the **Museum nan Eilean** (April–Sept Mon–Sat 10am–5.30pm; Oct–March Tues–Fri 10am–5pm, Sat 10am–1pm; free; Ⓦ www.cne-siar.gov.uk), housed in the old Victorian Nicolson Institute school. The ground-floor gallery explores the island's history until the MacKenzie takeover and is full of artefacts found during peat-cutting, including a large Viking dish made from alderwood. The first-floor gallery includes lots of information about the herring and weaving industries and houses an old loom shed with one of the semi-automatic looms introduced by Lord Leverhulme in the 1920s.

Northwest of the town centre, across the bay, stands **Lews Castle**, a castellated pomposity built by Sir James Matheson in 1863 after resettling the crofters who used to live here. As the former laird's pad, the castle is seen as a symbol of old oppression by many and it's currently in a state of some disrepair awaiting renovation. For the moment, however, the chief attraction is its mature wooded grounds, a unique sight on the Western Isles, for which Matheson had to import thousands of tons of soil from the mainland. Hidden in amongst the trees is the **Woodland Centre** (Mon–Sat 10am–5pm; free), with an exhibition on the castle, and a decent **café** serving soup, salads and cakes.

Eating, drinking and nightlife

Fish and chips are as popular as ever in Stornoway, but the choice of cafés and restaurants has improved enormously over the last few years. Wherever you decide to eat, be sure to sample the local **black puddings** (or the white and fruit ones) – the best ones are made to a secret family recipe by local butcher, Charles MacLeod, who has his HQ at Ropework Park (ⓣ01851/702445, ⓦwww.charlesmacleod.co.uk). As for **pubs**, *MacNeills* on Cromwell Street (closed Sun) is the liveliest central pub, with a mixed clientele of keen drinkers. *The Criterion*, a tiny wee pub on Point Street (closed Sun), is another option. There's a regular programme of **gigs and films** at An Lanntair, and in mid-July, the annual **Hebridean Celtic Festival** (ⓦwww.hebceltfest.com) hits town, with a festival tent in Lews Castle grounds, and events right across Lewis and Harris.

An Lanntair Kenneth St ⓣ01851/703307, ⓦwww.lanntair.com. Stylish café-restaurant in the An Lanntair arts centre which does decent sandwiches and lighter dishes during the day, as well as more imaginative stuff in the evening. Free wi-fi. Closed Sun.

Digby Chick 5 Bank St ⓣ01851/700026, ⓦwww.digbychick.co.uk. Smart, modern, buzzy little bistro with a real emphasis on using local produce. Sandwiches available at lunchtimes or two courses for around £10; three-course dinners for under £25. Closed Sun.

The Royal Cromwell St ⓣ01851/702109. This hotel has two eating options: the *Boatshed* restaurant, where you can eat traditional fare, and *HS-1*, more of a bar-restaurant with a brasserie-style menu.

Stornoway Balti House 24 South Beach ⓣ01851/706116. Family-run restaurant that's been in Stornoway for over twenty years. The curries are the real thing and the service great, but the real boon is that it serves food until at least 10pm and on Sundays.

Thai Café 27 Church St ⓣ01851/701811. Despite the name, this is actually a restaurant, serving authentic Thai food. No licence so bring your own bottle. Closed Sun.

The road to Ness (Nis)

Northwest of Stornoway, the A857 crosses the vast, barren **peat bog** of the Lewis interior, an empty, undulating wilderness riddled with stretchmarks formed by peat cuttings and pockmarked with freshwater lochans. The whole area was once covered by forests, but these disappeared long ago, leaving a smothering deposit of peat that is, on average, six feet thick, and still being formed in certain places. For the people of Lewis the peat continues to serve as a valuable energy resource; its pungent smoke is one of the most characteristic smells of the Western Isles.

Twelve miles across the peat bog the road approaches the west coast of Lewis and divides, heading southwest towards Calanais (see p.549), or northeast through **BARABHAS** (Barvas), and a whole string of bleak and fervently Presbyterian crofting and weaving villages. These scattered settlements have none of the photogenic qualities of Skye's whitewashed villages: the churches are plain and unadorned; the crofters' houses relatively modern and smothered in grey pebbledash rendering or harling; the stone cottages and enclosures of their forebears often lie half-abandoned in the front garden; a rusting assortment of discarded cars and vans store peat bags and the like.

Eventually, you reach the various densely populated settlements that make up the parish of **NESS** (Nis), at the northern tip of Lewis. Nis has the highest percentage of Gaelic-speakers in the country, at around 75 percent, but the locals are perhaps best known for their annual culling of young gannets on **Sula Sgeir**, a tiny island forty miles north. For an insight into the social history of the area, take a look inside Ness Heritage Centre or **Comunn Eachdraidh Nis** (March–Oct Mon–Fri 10am–4pm; Nov–Feb Mon–Fri noon–4pm; £2; Ⓦ www.c-e-n.org), on the left as you pass through **TABOST** (Habost).

The road terminates at the fishing village of **PORT NIS** (Port of Ness), with a tiny harbour and lovely golden beach. Shortly before you reach Port Nis, a minor road heads two miles northwest to the hamlet of **EOROPAIDH** (Europie) – pronounced "Yor-erpee". Here, by the road junction that leads to the Butt of Lewis, the simple stone structure of **Teampull Mholuaidh** (St Moluag's Church) stands amid the runrig fields, which now act as sheep runs. Thought to date from the twelfth century, when the islands were still under Norse rule, but restored in 1912, the church features a strange south chapel with only a squint window connecting it to the nave. From Europaidh, a narrow road twists to the bleak and blustery northern tip of the island, **Rubha Robhanais** – well known to devotees of the BBC shipping forecast as the **Butt of Lewis** – where a lighthouse sticks up above a series of sheer cliffs and stacks, and is alive with kittiwakes, fulmars and cormorants, with skuas and gannets feeding offshore; its a great place for marine mammal-spotting.

Accommodation is available at *Loch Beag* (Ⓣ 01851/810405, Ⓦ www.lochbeag.co.uk; ❺), a typically dour-looking B&B on the road to Butt of Lewis, run by a very friendly local couple, or at *Galson Farm* (Ⓣ 01851/850492, Ⓦ www.galsonfarm.co.uk; ❹), an attractive converted eighteenth-century farmhouse in Gabhsann Bho Dheas (South Galson), which offers dinner, bed and breakfast, and runs a six-bunk **bunkhouse** close by. The best place to **eat** is *Port Beach House* (Ⓣ 01851/810000; closed Sun), in Port Nis, with great views out to sea, and locally caught fish and seafood on the menu.

Westside

Heading southwest from the crossroads near Barabhas brings you to the **Westside** (An Toabh Siar), an area where several villages meander down towards the sea. In **ARNOL**, the remains of numerous blackhouses lie abandoned by the roadside; at the north end of the village, no. 42 is the **Arnol Blackhouse** (Mon–Sat: April–Sept 9.30am–5.30pm; Oct–March 9.30am–4.30pm; HS; £2.50). The house has been very carefully preserved to show exactly how a true blackhouse, or *taigh-dubh*, would have been. The interior is dimly lit and heated by a small peat fire in the central hearth of bare earth. Smoke drifts up through the thatch, helping to kill any creepy-crawlies, keep out the midges and turn the heathery sods and oat-straw thatch itself into next year's fertilizer. The animals would have slept in the byre, separated only by a low partition, while potatoes and grain were stored in the adjacent barn.

Carlabhagh (Carloway) and Gearrannan (Garenin)

The landscape becomes less monotonous as you approach the parish of **CARLABHAGH** (Carloway), with its crofthouses, boulders and hillocks rising out of the peat moor. A mile-long road leads off north to the beautifully remote coastal settlement of **GEARRANNAN** (Garenin). Here, rather than re-create a single museum-piece blackhouse as at Arnol, a whole cluster of nine thatched crofters' houses – the last of which was abandoned in 1974 – have been restored and put to a variety of uses. As an ensemble, they also give a great impression of what a **Baile Tughaidh**, or blackhouse village (May–Sept Mon–Sat 9.30am–5.30pm; £2.50) must have been like. The first house you come to houses the ticket office and **café**, which serves cheap and cheerful food during the day. Next door, there are toilets and opposite is the GHHT **hostel** (Ⓦ www.gatliff.org.uk); several others have been converted into **self-catering** houses (Ⓦ www.gearrannan.com).

Just beyond Carlabhagh village, **Dùn Charlabhaigh** perches on top of a conspicuous rocky outcrop overlooking the sea. Scotland's west coast is strewn with more than five hundred **brochs**, or fortified towers, but this is one of the best preserved, its dry-stone circular walls reaching a height of more than 30ft on one side. The broch consists of two concentric walls, the inner one perpendicular, the outer one slanting inwards, the two originally fastened together by roughly hewn flagstones, which also served as lookout galleries reached via a narrow stairwell. The only entrance to the roofless inner yard is through a low doorway set beside a crude and cramped guard cell. As at Calanais (see below), there have been all sorts of theories about the purpose of the brochs, which date from between 100 BC and 100 AD; the most likely explanation is that they were built to provide protection from Roman slave-traders.

Calanais (Callanish)

Overlooking the sheltered, islet-studded waters of Loch Ròg, on the west coast, are the islands' most dramatic prehistoric ruins, the **Calanais standing stones**. These monoliths – nearly fifty slabs of gnarled and finely grained gneiss up to 15ft high – were transported here between 3000 and 1500 BC, but their exact function remains a mystery. No one knows for certain why the ground plan resembles a colossal Celtic cross, nor why there's a central burial chamber. It's likely that such a massive endeavour was prompted by the desire to predict the seasonal cycle upon which these early farmers were entirely dependent, and indeed many of the stones are aligned with the positions of the sun and the stars. Whatever the reason for their existence, there's certainly no denying the powerful primeval presence, not to mention sheer beauty, of the stones.

A blackhouse adjacent to the main stone circle serves as a **tearoom** offering limited snacks. On the other side of the stones, the **Calanais Visitor Centre** (April–Sept Mon–Sat 10am–6pm; Oct–March Wed–Sat 10am–4pm; museum £2.50; Ⓦ www.calanaisvisitorcentre.co.uk) has a slightly longer (though no more imaginative) menu and a small museum on the site, but with so much information on the panels beside the stones there's little reason to visit it. If you want to commune with standing stones in solitude, head for the smaller circles in more natural surroundings a mile or two southeast of Calanais, around Gearraidh na h-Aibhne (Garynahine).

The nearest campsite is back beyond Carlabhagh in Siabost; *Eilean Fraoich* **campsite** (Ⓣ 01851/710504, Ⓦ www.eileanfraoich.co.uk; April–Oct) is located behind the old village church. There are several good **accommodation** options near the stones: try *Eshcol* (Ⓣ 01851/621771, Ⓦ www.eshcol.com; ❺), a large, modern and very well-run guesthouse, or *Leumadair* (Ⓣ 01851/612706, Ⓦ www.leumadair.co.uk; ❹), another new-build guesthouse owned by a very friendly Lewis couple, who have a pet hawk. Eating out options are limited, but both guesthouses offer dinner.

Bernera (Bearnaraigh)

Dividing Loch Ròg in two is the island of Great Bernera, usually referred to simply as **Bernera**. Joined to the mainland since 1953 via a narrow bridge that spans a small sea channel, Bernera is a rocky island, dotted with lochans. The chief reason to come here is to see the replica **Iron Age House** (for times contact the tourist office) that has been built above a precious little bay of golden sand beyond the cemetery at **BOSTADH** (Bosta), on the north coast – follow the signs "to the shore". In 1992, gale-force winds revealed an entire late Iron Age or Pictish settlement hidden under the sand; due to its exposed position, the site has been refilled with sand, and a full-scale mock-up built instead, based on the "jelly baby" houses (so called because of their shape) that were excavated. Inside, the house is incredibly spacious, and very dark, illuminated only by a central hearth and a few chinks of sunlight.

Uig (Uuige)

It's a long drive along the B8011 to the remote parish of **Uig**, one of the areas of Lewis that suffered really badly from the Clearances. The landscape here is hillier and more dramatic than elsewhere, a combination of myriad islets, wild cliff scenery and patches of pristine golden sand.

The main road takes you through the narrow canyon of Glèann Bhaltois (Glen Valtos) to **TIMSGEARRAIDH** (Timsgarry), which overlooks **Uig Sands** (Tràigh Uuige), the largest and most prized of all the golden strands on Lewis, where the sea goes out for miles at low tide; the best access point is from the car park near the cemetery in Eadar Dha Fhadhail. It was here in 1831 that a local cow rubbed itself against a sandbank and stumbled across the **Lewis Chessmen**, 78 twelfth-century Viking chess pieces carved from walrus ivory that now reside in Edinburgh's Museum of Scotland and the British Museum in London. You can see replicas of the chessmen in the **Uig Museum** (Mon–Fri noon–5pm; ⓦwww.ceuig.com; £1), housed in Uig School in Timsgearraidh. As well as putting on some excellent temporary exhibitions, the museum has bits and bobs from blackhouses and is

St Kilda

Britain's westernmost island chain is the NTS-owned **St Kilda** (Hiort) archipelago (ⓦwww.kilda.org.uk), roughly forty miles from its nearest landfall, Griminish Point on North Uist. Dominated by the highest cliffs and sea stacks in Britain, Hirta, St Kilda's main island, was occupied on and off for two thousand years, with the last 36 Gaelic-speaking inhabitants evacuated at their own request in 1930. Immediately after evacuation, the island was bought by the Marquess of Bute, to protect the island's millions of puffins, gannets, petrels and other seabirds. In 1957, having agreed to allow the army to build a missile-tracking radar station here linked to South Uist, the marquess bequeathed the island to the NTS. St Kilda is one of only two dozen **UNESCO World Heritage Sites** with a dual status reflecting its natural and cultural significance. Despite its inaccessibility, several thousand visitors make it out here each year; if you get to land, you can see the museum, send a postcard and enjoy a drink at the army's pub, the *Puff Inn*. Several companies offer **boat day-trips** for around £180 per person (see p.543 & opposite). Between mid-May and mid-August, the NTS organizes volunteer **work parties**, which either restore and maintain the old buildings or take part in archeological digs – for more information, contact the NTS (ⓣ0844/493 2100, ⓦwww.nts.org.uk). For the armchair traveller, the best general book on St Kilda is Tom Steel's *The Life and Death of St Kilda*, or else there's the classic 1937 film *The Edge of the World* by Michael Powell (which was actually shot on Foula in Shetland).

staffed by locals, who are happy to answer any queries you have; there's also a **tearoom** in the adjacent nursery that is open during the holidays.

There are several idyllic **places to stay** overlooking the Uig Sands, the most intriguing **being** *Baile na Cille* (Easter–Oct; ⓣ01851/672242, ⓦwww.bailenacille.co.uk; ❺), a chaotic kind of place, run by an eccentric couple, who are very welcoming to families and dogs and dish up wonderful set-menu dinners for £30 a head. The best B&B in the area is *Suainaval* (ⓣ01851/672386, ⓦwww.suainaval.com; ❹), in Cradhlastadh (Crowlista), run by a truly welcoming couple. An entirely different (but equally unusual) experience is to stay at *Gallen Head* (ⓣ01851/672474, ⓦwww.gallanheadhotel.co.uk; ❹), housed in the old RAF station in **AIRD UIG**, three miles north of Timsgearraidh. The concrete buildings themselves are something of an eyesore, but the hotel has been tastefully converted inside and the position, overlooking a rocky inlet, is spectacular.

Sea Trek (ⓣ01851/672464, ⓦwww.seatrek.co.uk), runs from Miabhaig jetty (Cidhe Mhiabhaig) and offers **boat trips** in a RIB to uninhabited islands in Loch Ròg and day-trips to the Flannan Isles, Mingulay and St Kilda. For longer trips around the islands, contact Island Cruising (ⓣ01851/672381, ⓦwww.island-cruising.com), which also sails from Loch Ròg.

Harris (Na Hearadh)

Harris, whose name derives from the old Norse for "high land", is much hillier, more dramatic and much more immediately appealing than Lewis, its boulder-strewn slopes descending to aquamarine bays of dazzling, white sand. The shift from Lewis to Harris is almost imperceptible, as the two are, in fact, one island, the "division" between them embedded in a historical split in the MacLeod clan, lost in the mists of time. For the record, the dividing line comprises Loch Reasort in the west, Loch Shìphoirt (Loch Seaforth) in the east, and the six miles in between (see map on p.544). Harris itself is more clearly divided by a minuscule isthmus into the wild, inhospitable mountains of **North Harris** and the gentler landscape and sandy shores of **South Harris**.

Along with Lewis, Harris was purchased in 1918 by **Lord Leverhulme**. In contrast to Lewis, though, Leverhulme and his ambitious projects were broadly welcomed by the people of Harris. His most grandiose plans were drawn up for Leverburgh (see p.554), but he also purchased an old Norwegian whaling station in Bun Abhain Eadara in 1922, built a spinning mill at Geocrab and began the construction of four roads. Financial difficulties, a slump in the tweed industry and the lack of market for whale products meant that none of the schemes was a wholehearted success, and when he died in 1925 the plug was pulled on all of them by his executors. Since the Leverhulme era, unemployment has been a constant problem in Harris.

Tarbert (An Tairbeart)

Sheltered in a green valley on the narrow isthmus, **TARBERT** is the largest place on Harris and a wonderful place to arrive by boat. The port's mountainous backdrop is impressive, and the town is attractively laid out on steep terraces sloping up from the dock. It boasts Harris's only **tourist office** (April to mid-Oct Mon–Sat only; open to greet the evening ferry), close to the ferry terminal. The office can arrange modest, inexpensive B&B **accommodation** and has a full set of bus timetables, but its real value is as a source of information on local walks.

Harris Tweed

Far from being a picturesque cottage industry, as it's sometimes presented, the production of **Harris Tweed** is vital to the local economy, with a well-organized and unionized workforce. Traditionally the tweed was made by women, from the wool of their own sheep, to provide clothing for their families, using a 2500-year-old process. Each woman was responsible for plucking the wool by hand, washing and scouring it, dyeing it with lichen, heather flowers or ragwort, carding (smoothing and straightening the wool, often adding butter to grease it), spinning and weaving. Finally the cloth was dipped in stale urine and "waulked" by a group of women, who beat the cloth on a table to soften and shrink it whilst singing Gaelic waulking songs. Harris Tweed was originally made all over the islands, and was known simply as *clò mór* (big cloth).

In the mid-nineteenth century, Catherine Murray, **Countess of Dunmore**, who owned a large part of Harris, started to sell surplus cloth to her aristocratic friends; she then sent two sisters from Srannda (Strond) to Paisley to learn the trade. On their return, they formed the genesis of the modern industry, which continues to serve as a vital source of employment, though demand (and therefore employment levels) can fluctuate wildly as fashions change. To earn the official **Harris Tweed Authority (HTA)** trademark of the Orb and the Maltese Cross – taken from Lady Dunmore's coat of arms – the fabric has to be hand-woven on the Outer Hebrides from 100 percent pure new Scottish wool, while the other parts of the manufacturing process must take place only in the local mills. The main centre of production is actually now in Siabost, in Lewis, where the wool is dyed, carded and spun.

If you're looking for **accommodation** close to the ferry terminal, *Rockview Bunkhouse* (Ⓣ01859/502626), on Main Street, is a possibility, but it's best to book ahead as there's no warden on site. There's a very good local **B&B**, *Tigh na Mara* (Ⓣ01859/502270, Ⓦwww.tigh-na-mara.co.uk; ❸), just up the Scalpay road, or the long-established *Harris Hotel* (Ⓣ01859/502154, Ⓦwww.harrishotel.com; ❺), five minutes' walk away. Two miles up the road to Stornoway is the *Ardhasaig Hotel* (Ⓣ01859/502500, Ⓦwww.ardhasaig.co.uk; ❻), idyllically located overlooking West Loch Tarbert and the mountains of North Harris – the food is locally sourced and superbly prepared with dinner around £40 a head.

Other options for **food** include the *Isle of Harris Inn* (closed Sun), next door to the *Harris Hotel*, which has a short seafood specials menu worth perusing. Alternatively, head for the very pleasant *First Fruits* **tearoom** (April–Sept; closed Sun), behind the tourist office, housed in an old stone-built cottage and serving real coffee, home-made cakes, toasties and so forth, plus evening meals (Thurs–Sat; booking essential; Ⓣ01859/502439). **Fish and chips** are dispensed by *Ad's Take-Away* (April–Oct; closed Sun), next to the hostel.

North Harris (Ceann a Tuath na Hearadh)

If you're coming from Stornoway on the A859, mountainous **North Harris** is a spectacular introduction to Harris, its bulging, pyramidal mountains of gneiss looming over the dramatic, fjord-like **Loch Shìphoirt** (Loch Seaforth). From **AIRD A' MHULAIDH** (Ardvourlie), you weave your way over a boulder-strewn saddle between mighty **Sgaoth Aird** (1829ft) and An Cliseam or the **Clisham** (2619ft), the highest peak in the Western Isles. This bitter terrain, littered with debris left behind by retreating glaciers, offers but the barest of vegetation, with an occasional cluster of crofters' houses sitting in the shadow of a host of pointed peaks, anywhere between 1000ft and 2500ft high.

Other than self-catering cottages, the only place to stay in this area is the GHHT **hostel** (Ⓦwww.gatliff.org.uk) in the lonely coastal hamlet of **REINIGEADAL** (Rhenigdale), which until as recently as the 1990s, was only accessible by foot or boat. Nowadays, there's even a bus service, though this must be booked in advance (Ⓣ01859/502871).

The road to Huisinis (Hushinish)

The most attractive road on North Harris is the winding, single-track B887, which clings to the northern shores of Loch a Siar (West Loch Tarbert), and gives easy access to the awesome mountain range of the (treeless) Forest of Harris to the north. Immediately as you turn down the B887, you pass through **Bun Abhàinn Eadarra** (Bunavoneadar), where some Norwegians established a short-lived whaling station – the slipways and distinctive red-brick chimney can still be seen. Seven miles further on, you pass **Abhainnsuidhe Castle** (pronounced "Avan-soo-ee"), built in Scottish Baronial style in 1865 by the Earl of Dunmore. The main road takes you through the gates and right past the front door, much to the annoyance of the castle's succession of owners – as you do, make sure you admire the lovely salmon-leap waterfalls in the castle's pristine grounds.

It's another five miles to the end of the road at the small crofting community of **HUISINIS** (Hushinish), where you are rewarded with a south-facing beach of shell sand that looks across to South Harris. A slipway to the north of the bay serves the nearby island of **Scarp**, a hulking mass of rock rising to over 1000ft, once home to more than two hundred people and abandoned as recently as 1971 (it's now a private holiday hideaway). The most bizarre moment in its history – and the subject of the 2002 film *The Rocket Post* – was undoubtedly in 1934, when the German scientist Gerhardt Zucher conducted an experiment at sending mail by rocket. Zucher made two attempts at launching his rocket from Scarp, but the letter-laden missile exploded before it even got off the ground, and the idea was shelved.

South Harris (Ceann a Deas na Hearadh)

The mountains of **South Harris** are less dramatic than in the north, but the scenery is equally breathtaking. There's a choice of routes from Tarbert to the ferry port of **Leverburgh**, which connects with North Uist: the east coast, known as Na Baigh (The Bays), is rugged and seemingly inhospitable, while the **west coast** is endowed with some of the finest stretches of golden sand in the whole of the archipelago, buffeted by the Atlantic winds. Paradoxically, most people on South Harris live along the harsh eastern coastline of **Bays** rather than the more fertile west side. But not by choice – they were evicted from their original crofts to make way for sheep-grazing.

The west coast

The main road from Tarbert into South Harris snakes its way south and west for ten miles across the boulder-strewn interior to reach the coast. Once there, you get a view of the most stunning **beach**, the vast golden strand of **Tràigh Losgaintir**. The road continues to ride above a chain of sweeping sands, backed by rich **machair** that stretches for nine miles along the Atlantic coast. In good weather, the scenery is particularly impressive, foaming breakers rolling along the golden sands set against the rounded peaks of the mountains to the north and the islet-studded turquoise sea to the west – and even on the dullest day the sand manages to glow beneath the waves. A short distance out to sea is the island of **Taransay** (Tarasaigh), which once held a population of nearly a hundred, but was abandoned as recently as 1974. Day-trips are possible from Horgabost beach (April–Oct Mon–Fri; £20; ⓣ01859/550260, ⓦwww.visit-taransay.com).

Beul-na-Mara (ⓣ01859/550205, ⓦwww.beulnamara.co.uk; ❹) is a very good modern **B&B** in Seilebost, overlooking the sands of Tràigh Losgaintir. A few miles further south, in Na Buirgh (Borve), is a lovely, tastefully converted Victorian crofthouse, *Pairc an t-Srath* (ⓣ01859/550386, ⓦwww.paircant-srath.co.uk; ❻), which also serves up excellent three-course dinners for £35 a head. Beyond lies **SGARASTA** (Scarista), where one of the first of the Hebridean Clearances took place in 1828, when thirty families were evicted and their homes burnt.

There's a particularly magnificent stretch of machair by the golden sands close to the village of **TAOBH TUATH** (Northton), a lovely spot overlooked by the round-topped hill of Chaipabhal at the southwesternmost tip of the island. In the village is the tiny **MacGillivray Centre** (open all year at any time), with a tiny bit of information on the naturalist, William MacGillivray (1796–1852), after whom it's named, and a little on crofting and machair. There's more information on local geology, flora and fauna to be found in **Seallam!** (Mon–Sat 10am–5pm; £2.50; ⓦwww.seallam.com), on the main road, a useful centre for eager ancestor hunters, but also providing interest for kids, literally at their level.

Leverburgh (An t-Ob)

From Taobh Tuath the road veers to the southeast to trim the island's south shore, eventually reaching the sprawling settlement of **LEVERBURGH** (An t-Ob), where a series of brown clapperboard houses strikes an odd Scandinavian note. Named after Lord Leverhulme, who planned to turn the place into the largest fishing port on the west coast of Scotland, it's a place that has languished for quite some time, but has picked up a fair amount since the establishment of the CalMac **car ferry** service to Berneray and the Uists (see below). The hour-long journey across the skerry-strewn Sound of Harris is one of Scotland's most tortuous ferry routes, with the ship taking part in a virtual slalom race to avoid numerous hidden rocks – it's also a great crossing from which to spot seabirds and sea mammals.

For **accommodation**, *Grimisdale* (ⓣ01859/520460, ⓦwww.grimisdale.co.uk; ❻; March–Nov) is the luxury option; a modern guesthouse with loch views from most rooms and free wi-fi. A cheaper option is *Sorrel Cottage* (ⓣ01859/520319, ⓦwww.accommodationisleofharris.co.uk; ❸), a converted crofthouse a mile back towards Taobh Tuath from Leverburgh, that also offers **bike rental**, or the quirky, timber-clad *Am Bothan* (ⓣ01859/520251, ⓦwww.ambothan.com), a luxurious, very welcoming **bunkhouse** close to the ferry. On the north side of the bay is the *An Clachan* co-op store which houses a small **information office**. For some local seafood, home-made cakes and the usual comfort **food**, head for *The Anchorage* (closed Sun), a lively bar and restaurant by the ferry slipway that has great views and the occasional live music night.

Roghadal (Rodel)

A mile or so from Rubha Reanais (Renish Point), the southern tip of Harris, is the old port of **ROGHADAL** (Rodel), where a smattering of ancient stone houses lies among the hillocks. Down by the old harbour where the ferry from Skye used to arrive, you'll find the *Rodel Hotel* (ⓣ01859/520210, ⓦwww.rodelhotel.co.uk; ❻), a solid, stone-built, family-run hotel.

On top of one of the grassy humps, with sheep grazing in the graveyard, is **St Clement's Church** (Tur Chliamainn), burial place of the MacLeods of Harris and Dunvegan in Skye. Dating from the 1520s – in other words pre-Reformation, hence the big castellated tower (which you can climb) – the church was restored in 1873 by the Countess of Dunmore. The bare interior is distinguished by its wall tombs, notably that of the founder, Alasdair Crotach (also known as Alexander MacLeod), whose heavily weathered effigy lies beneath an intriguing backdrop and canopy of sculpted reliefs depicting vernacular and religious scenes – elemental representations of, among others, a stag hunt, the Holy Trinity, St Michael and the devil, and an angel weighing the souls of the dead. Look out, too, for the *sheila-na-gig* halfway up the south side of the church tower; unusually, she has a brother displaying his genitalia, below a carving of St Clement on the west face.

North Uist (Uibhist a Tuath)

Compared to the mountainous scenery of Harris, **North Uist** – seventeen miles long and thirteen miles wide – is much flatter and for some comes as something of an anticlimax. Over half the surface area is covered by water, creating a distinctive peaty-brown lochan-studded "drowned landscape". Most visitors come here for the trout and salmon fishing and the deerstalking, both of which (along with poaching) are critical to the survival of the island's economy. Others come for the smattering of prehistoric sites, the birds, or the sheer peace of this windy isle and the solitude of North Uist's vast sandy beaches, which extend – almost without interruption – along the north and west coast.

There are two **car ferry** services to North Uist: from Leverburgh on Harris to Berneray, from where there are regular **buses** to Lochmaddy, the principal village on the east coast; and from Uig on Skye to Lochmaddy itself.

Lochmaddy (Loch nam Madadh) and around

Despite being situated on the east coast, some distance away from any beach, the ferry port of **LOCHMADDY** – "Loch of the Dogs" – makes a good base for exploring the island. Occupying a narrow, bumpy promontory and overlooked by the brooding mountains of Lì a Tuath (North Lee) and Lì a Deas (South Lee) to the southeast, it's difficult to believe that this sleepy settlement was a large herring port as far back as the seventeenth century.

The only thing to keep you in Lochmaddy is **Taigh Chearsabhagh** (Mon–Sat 10am–5pm; free) a converted eighteenth-century merchant's house that is now home to a vibrant community arts centre that houses a café, post office, shop and an excellent museum, which puts on some seriously innovative exhibitions. Taigh Chearsabhagh was one of the prime movers behind the commissioning of a series of seven sculptures dotted about the Uists – ask at the arts centre for directions to the ones in and around Lochmaddy, the most interesting of which is the **Both nam Faileas** (Hut of the Shadow), 1km north of the town. The hut is an ingenious dry-stone, turf-roofed camera obscura built by sculptor Chris Drury that projects the nearby land, sea and skyscape onto its back wall – take time to allow your eyes to adjust to the light.

Lochmaddy has the island's only **bank** and **tourist office** (April to mid-Oct Mon–Sat only; open to greet the evening ferry; ⓣ01876/500321), near the quayside, which has local bus and ferry timetables and can help with **accommodation**. In Lochmaddy itself, you can stay at the cherry-red, purpose-built *Tigh Dearg* (ⓣ01876/500700, ⓦwww.tighdearghotel.co.uk; ❼), whose stylish modernity are pretty much unique on the Uists; guests get free use of the hotel's

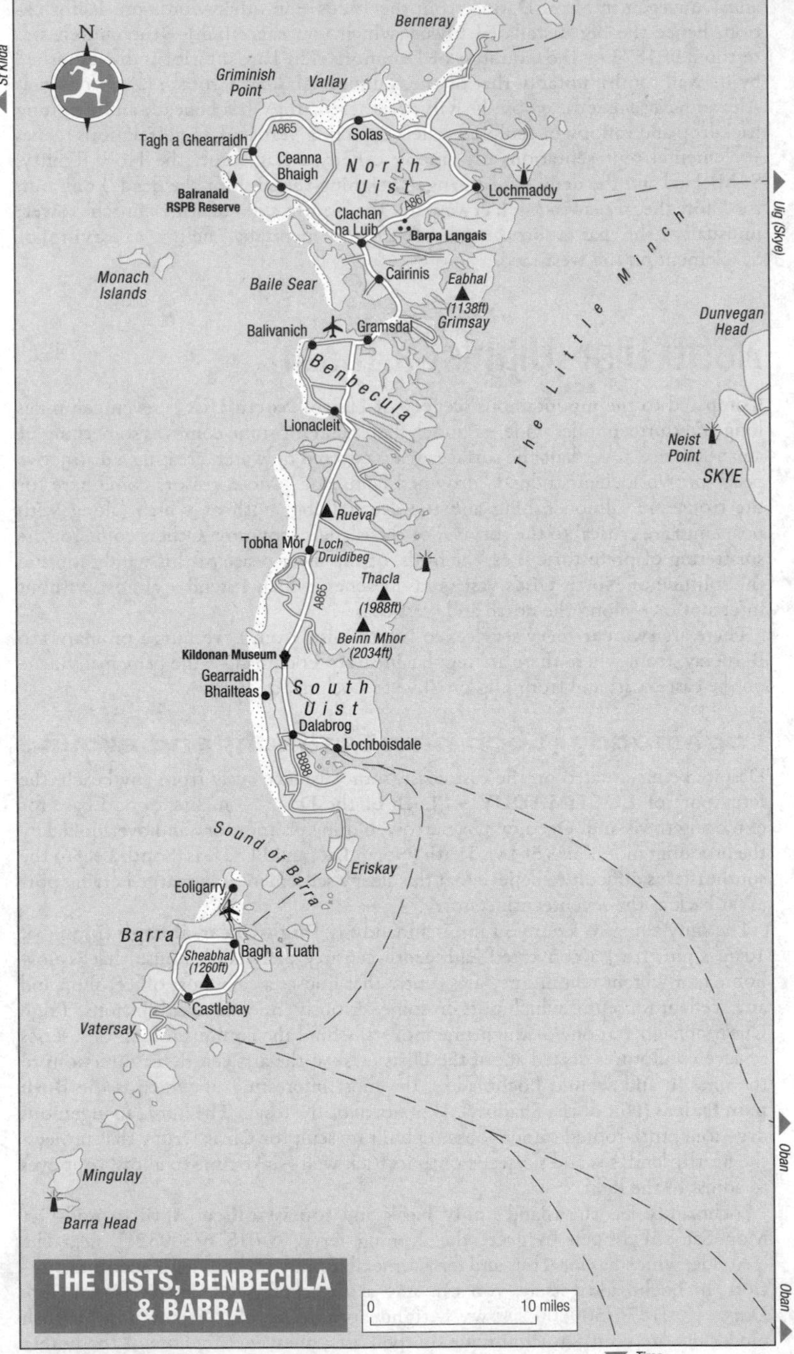
Leverburgh (Harris)
St Kilda
N
Berneray
Griminish Point
Vallay
A865
Solas
Tagh a Ghearraidh
Ceanna Bhaigh
North Uist
Balranald RSPB Reserve
Lochmaddy
Uig (Skye)
A867
Clachan na Luib
Barpa Langais
Monach Islands
Cairinis
Baile Sear
Eabhal (1138ft)
Grimsay
The Little Minch
Dunvegan Head
Balivanich
Gramsdal
Benbecula
Lionacleit
Neist Point
SKYE
Rueval
Tobha Mòr
Loch Druidibeg
Thacla (1988ft)
A865
Beinn Mhor (2034ft)
Kildonan Museum
Gearraidh Bhailteas
South Uist
Dalabrog
Lochboisdale
B888
Sound of Barra
Eriskay
Eoligarry
Barra
Sheabhal (1260ft)
Bagh a Tuath
Castlebay
Vatersay
Oban
Mingulay
Barra Head
0
10 miles
Oban
Tiree

THE UISTS, BENBECULA & BARRA

gym, sauna and steam room and there's free wi-fi. Back towards the main road, there's *Redburn House* (ⓣ01876/500301, ⓦwww.redburnhouse.com; ❸), a nicely renovated Victorian house, and in the opposite direction, the *Uist Outdoor Centre* (ⓣ01876/500480, ⓦwww.uistoutdoorcentre.co.uk; March to mid-Dec), which has **hostel** accommodation and offers activities ranging from sea-kayaking to rock climbing for residents and non-residents alike.

Tigh Dearg serves delicious, quite elaborate **food** in the bar and restaurant, while the *Lochmaddy Hotel*, whose bar is the local **social centre**, serves pretty standard bar meals; if you're looking for something a bit more special, you'll need to head for *Langass Lodge* (see below). There is a small **general store**, but the island's largest supermarket is eight miles away in Solas.

Neolithic sites near Lochmaddy

Several prehistoric sites lie in the vicinity of Lochmaddy. The most remarkable is **Barpa Langais**, a huge, chambered burial cairn a short walk from the A867, seven barren miles southwest. The stones are visible from the road and, unless the weather's good, it's not worth making a closer inspection as the chamber has collapsed and is too dangerous to enter. A mile further down the A867, a side road leads off to *Langass Lodge* (ⓣ01876/580285, ⓦwww.langasslodge.co.uk; ❻), a venerable **hotel** with a stylish modern extension, whose restaurant and bar serves excellent local seafood. Beside the hotel, a rough track leads to the small stone circle of **Pobull Fhinn** (Finn's People), which enjoys a picturesque location overlooking a narrow loch. The circle covers a large area and, although the stones are not that huge, they occupy an intriguing amphitheatre cut into the hillside. Three miles northwest of Lochmaddy along the A865 you'll find **Na Fir Bhreige** (The Three False Men), three standing stones which, depending on the legend, mark the graves of three spies buried alive or three men who deserted their wives and were turned to stone by a witch.

Berneray (Bhearnaraigh)

Berneray (ⓦwww.isleofberneray.com) is a low-lying island immediately to the north of North Uist, and connected to the latter via a causeway that starts some eight miles north of Lochmaddy. Two miles by three, with a population of just over a hundred, the island has a superb three-mile-long sandy beach on the west and north coast, backed by rabbit-free dunes and machair. The island has a wonderful GHHT **hostel** (ⓦwww.gatliff.org.uk), which occupies a pair of thatched blackhouses in a lovely spot by a beach, beyond Loch a Bhàigh and the main village. Alternatively, you can follow in Prince Charles's footsteps and stay (and help out) at "Splash" MacKillop's *Burnside Croft* **B&B** (ⓣ01876/540235; ❸), in Borgh (Borve), overlooking the machair and dunes, and enjoy "storytelling evenings"; bike rental is also available. *The Lobster Pot* **tearoom** (and shop) on the main road, near the ferry terminal, serves toasties and soup and simple early evening meals (closed Sun).

Clachan and Balranald

At **CLACHAN NA LUIB**, by the crossroads with the A867 from Lochmaddy, there's a post office and general store. Offshore, to the southwest, lie two flat, tidal, dune and machair islands, the larger of which is **Baleshare** (Baile Sear), with its fantastic three-mile-long beach, connected by causeway to North Uist. In Gaelic the island's name means "east village", its twin "west village" having disappeared under the sea during a freak storm in the fifteenth or sixteenth century.

Seven miles northwest of Clachan is the **Balranald RSPB Reserve**, best known for its corncrakes, once common throughout the British countryside but now among the country's rarest birds. Unfortunately, the birds are very good at hiding in long grass, so you're unlikely to see one; however, the males' loud "craking" is relatively easy to hear from May to July throughout the Uists and Barra: there are usually one or two making a loud noise right outside the RSPB **visitor centre**, from which you can pick up a leaflet outlining a two-hour walk along the headland, marked by posts. A wonderful carpet of flowers covers the machair in summer, and there are usually corn buntings and arctic terns inland, and gannets, Manx shearwaters and skuas out to sea. On a clear day you can see the unmistakeable shape of St Kilda (see box, p.550), seeming miraculously near.

A couple of miles down the main road from Balranald, the *Claddach Kirkibost Centre* has an excellent **café** (closed Sat & Sun) in a conservatory with sea views, which uses local produce and has internet facilities. **Accommodation** options include *Moorcroft Holidays* (Ⓣ01876/580305, Ⓦmoorcroftholidays.com), an exposed, but very well-equipped **campsite** (and bunkhouse), overlooking the sea just south of Carinis (Carinish), or you can stay on Baleshare at *Bagh Alluin* (Ⓣ01876/580370, Ⓦwww.jacvolbeda.co.uk; ❸), a secluded, modern **B&B** with fantastic views over the island.

Benbecula (Beinn na Faoghla)

Blink and you could miss the pancake-flat island of **Benbecula** (put the stress on the second syllable), sandwiched between Protestant North Uist and Catholic South Uist. Most visitors simply trundle along the main road, which cuts across the middle of the island in less than five miles – not such a bad idea, since the island is scarred from the postwar presence of the Royal Artillery who once made up half the local population. Economically, of course, the area benefited enormously from the military presence, though the impact on the environment and the local Gaelic culture (with so many English-speakers around) was less positive.

The legacy of Benbecula's military past is only too evident in the depressing, barracks-like housing developments of **BALIVANICH** (Baile a Mhanaich), the grim, grey capital of Benbecula in the northwest. The only reason to come here at all is if you happen to be flying into or out of **Benbecula airport** (Ⓦwww.hial.oc.uk), need an ATM, the laundry (behind the bank) or a supermarket. There's no tourist office and no real need **to stay** here, but if you've time to kill, you could head down to *MacGillivray's*, an old-fashioned shop selling everything from tweeds to books, a short distance from the airport on the road to North Uist. For a bite to eat, *Stepping Stone* **café/restaurant** serves up chips with everything during the day, and tries a bit harder (and charges more) in the evenings.

If you're passing along the west side of the island, pop into Baile nan Cailleach, better known as the **Nunton Steadings** (Mon–Sat 10am–5pm; Ⓦwww.nuntonsteadings.co.uk), an unusual three-sided eighteenth-century farm building with a cobbled courtyard, and a small bell tower (used to call the workers in from the fields), that hosts occasional exhibitions and gigs, has free wi-fi and houses a **café.** In **LIONACLEIT** (Liniclate), in the south of the island, there's a small **Museum nan Eilean** (Mon–Sat only; phone for times; Ⓣ01870/602864), located in **Sgoil Lionacleit**, which puts on temporary exhibitions on the history of the islands, as well as occasional live music and other events. For **accommodation**, close to the school, there's *Shell Bay* **campsite** (ⓣ01870/602447; April–Oct) and *Lionacleit Guest House* (ⓣ01870/602176, ⓦwww.lionacleit-guesthouse.com; ❷), a very comfortable modern crofthouse.

South Uist (Uibhist a Deas)

To the south of Benbecula, the island of **South Uist** (ⓦwww.southuist.com) is the largest and most varied of the southern chain of islands. The west coast has some of the region's finest machair and beaches – a necklace of gold and grey sand strung twenty miles from one end to the other – while the east coast features a ridge of high mountains rising to 2034ft at the summit of Beinn Mhor. Whatever you do, don't make the mistake of simply driving down the main A865 road, which runs down the centre of the island like a backbone. To reach the beaches (or even see them), you have to get off the main road and pass through the old crofters' villages that straggle along the west coast; to climb the mountains in the east, you need a detailed 1:25,000 Explorer map in order to negotiate the island's maze of lochans. The only blot on South Uist's landscape is the old Royal Artillery missile range, which dominates the northwest corner of the island.

Rueval to Kildonan

The Reformation never took a strong hold in South Uist (or Barra), and the islands remain Roman Catholic, as is evident from the various roadside shrines and the slender modern Madonna, *Our Lady of the Isles*, which stands by the main road below the small hill of **Rueval**, known to the locals as "Space City" for its forest of aerials and giant "golf balls", which help track missiles launched by the nearby MOD range.

One of the best places to gain access to the sandy shoreline is at **TOBHA MÒR** (Howmore), a pretty little crofting settlement with a fair number of restored houses, many still thatched, including one distinctively roofed in brown heather. A GHHT **hostel** (ⓦwww.gatliff.org.uk) occupies one such house near the village church, from where it's an easy walk across the flower-strewn machair to the gorgeous beach. Close by the hostel are the shattered, lichen-encrusted remains of no fewer than four medieval churches and chapels, and a burial ground that now harbours just a few scattered graves.

Five miles south of Tobha Mòr lies the **Kildonan Museum**, or Taigh-tasgaidh Chill Donnain (April–Oct Mon–Sat 10am–5pm, Sun 2–5pm; £2; ⓦwww.kildonanmuseum.co.uk), with mock-ups of Hebridean kitchens through the ages, two lovely box beds and an impressive selection of old photos, accompanied by a firmly unsentimental yet poetic written text on crofting life in the last two centuries. Pride of place goes to the sixteenth-century **Clanranald Stone**, carved with the arms of the clan who ruled over South Uist from 1370 to 1839. The stone used to lie in the church at Tobha Mòr and was stolen briefly in the 1990s. The museum also runs a café serving sandwiches and home-made cakes, and has a choice of historical videos for those really wet and windy days. A little south of the museum, the road passes a cairn that sits amongst the foundations of **Flora MacDonald**'s childhood home (see box, p.630); she was born nearby, but the house no longer stands.

Apart from the aforementioned hostel, there's the *Orasay Inn* (ⓣ01870/610298, ⓦwww.orasayinn.co.uk; ❺), a modern **hotel** off the road to Loch a Charnain

(Lochcarnan); the rooms are pretty standard, but the location is peaceful and the breakfasts are good – if you're hoping for a bar meal, it's best to book ahead. Just south of Rueval, there's *Kinloch* (ⓣ01870/620316, ⓦwww.kinlochuist.com; ❹), a fine modern **B&B**, run by a keen angler, sheltered by trees and overlooking a freshwater loch. **Bike rental** (and repair) is available from Rothan Cycles (ⓣ01870/620283, ⓦwww.rothan.com), on the main road in Tobha Mòr (Howmore).

Lochboisdale (Loch Baghasdail) and around

LOCHBOISDALE occupies a narrow, bumpy promontory on the east coast, but, despite being South Uist's chief settlement and ferry port, has only very limited facilities. If you're arriving here late at night on the boat from Oban (or from Barra or Tiree), you should try to book accommodation in advance; otherwise, head for the **tourist office** (Easter–Oct Mon–Sat only; open for an hour to meet the ferry; ⓣ01878/700286); next door is a useful coin-operated shower and toilet block (daily 9am–6pm). The town's only **hotel**, the *Lochboisdale*, does decent **bar meals**, occasionally featuring local seafood. For **accommodation**, there are several small, perfectly friendly **B&Bs** within comfortable walking distance of the dock: one of the best (and nearest) being *Brae Lea House* (ⓣ01878/700497, ⓦwww.braelea.co.uk; ❷). There's a bank in Lochboisdale, but the shops are pretty limited; the nearest supermarket is three miles west in **DALABROG** (Daliburgh), where you'll also find the *Uist Bunkhouse* (ⓣ01878/700566, ⓦwww.uistbunkhouse.co.uk; ❶), which offers singles, doubles and family rooms as well as bunks. Another place you could happily hole up in is the *Polochar Inn* (ⓣ01878/700215, ⓦwww.polocharinn.com; ❹), eight miles from Lochboisdale, right on the south coast overlooking the Sound of Barra, and with its own sandy beach close by; the rooms all have sea views, and on the ground floor is a genuine **pub**, serving decent bar meals.

Eriskay (Eiriosgaigh)

Famous for its patterned jerseys and a peculiar breed of pony, originally used for carrying peat and seaweed, the barren, hilly island of **Eriskay** is connected to the south of South Uist by a causeway that was built in 2001. The island, which measures just over two miles by one and shelters a small fishing community of about 150, makes a great day-trip from South Uist. The walk up to the island's highest point, **Ben Scrien** (607ft; 2hr return from the village), is well worth the effort on a clear day, as you can see the whole island, plus Barra, South Uist and across the sea to the Inner Hebrides. On the way up or down, look out for the diminutive Eriskay ponies, who roam free on the hills but tend to graze around Loch Crakavaig, the island's freshwater source.

For a small island, Eriskay has had more than its fair share of historical headlines. The island's main beach on the west coast, Coilleag a Phrionnsa (Prince's Cockle Strand), was where **Bonnie Prince Charlie** landed on Scottish soil on July 23, 1745 – the sea bindweed that grows there to this day is said to have sprung from the seeds Charles brought with him from France. The prince, as yet unaccustomed to hardship, spent his first night in a local blackhouse and ate a couple of flounders, though he apparently couldn't take the peat smoke and chose to sleep sitting up rather than endure the damp bed.

Eriskay's other claim to fame came in 1941 when the 8000-ton **SS Politician** or "*Polly*" as it's fondly known, sank on its way from Liverpool to Jamaica, along with its cargo of bicycle parts, £3 million in Jamaican currency and 264,000 bottles of whisky, inspiring Compton MacKenzie's book, and the Ealing comedy (filmed on Barra in 1948), *Whisky Galore!* (released as *Tight Little Island* in the US). The real story was somewhat less romantic, especially for the 36 islanders who were charged with illegal possession by the Customs and Excise officers, nineteen of whom were found guilty and imprisoned in Inverness. The ship's stern can still be seen at low tide northwest of Calvay Island in the Sound of Eriskay, and one of the original bottles (and lots of other related memorabilia) can be viewed at *Am Politician*, the island's purpose-built pub near the two cemeteries on the west coast, which offers an extensive bar menu and great views out to sea.

Apart from a few self-catering options, the only way to stay on Eriskay is to **camp rough** (with permission). CalMac now runs a **car ferry** to Barra (4–5 daily; 40min) from the southwest coast of Eriskay.

Barra (Barraigh)

Just four miles wide and eight miles long, **Barra** (Ⓦ www.isleofbarra.com) is like the Western Isles in miniature. It has sandy beaches backed by machair, mountains of Lewissian gneiss, prehistoric ruins, Gaelic culture and a laidback, welcoming Catholic population of just over 1300. Like some miniature feudal island state, it was ruled over for centuries, with relative benevolence, by the MacNeils. Unfortunately, however, the family sold the island in 1838 to Colonel Gordon of Cluny, who had also bought Benbecula, South Uist and Eriskay. The colonel deemed the starving crofters "redundant" and offered to turn Barra into a state penal colony. The government declined, so the colonel called in the police and proceeded with some of the most cruel forced Clearances in the Hebrides. In 1937, the 45th chief of the MacNeil clan bought back most of the island, and in 2003 gifted the estate to the Scottish government.

Castlebay (Bàgh a Chaisteil)

The only settlement of any size is **CASTLEBAY** (Bàgh a Chaisteil), which curves around the barren rocky hills of a wide bay on the south side of the island. It's difficult to imagine it now, but Castlebay was a herring port of some significance back in the nineteenth century, with up to four hundred boats in the harbour and curing and packing factories ashore. Barra's religious allegiance is immediately announced by the large Catholic church, Our Lady, Star of the Sea, which overlooks the bay; to underline the point, there's a Madonna and Child on the slopes of **Sheabhal** (1260ft), the largest peak on Barra, and a fairly easy hike from the bay.

As its name suggests, Castlebay has a castle in its bay, the picturesque medieval islet-fortress of Caisteal Chiosmuil, or **Kisimul Castle** (April–Sept daily 9.30am–5.30pm; HS; £4.70), ancestral home of the MacNeil clan. The castle burnt down in the eighteenth century, but when the 45th MacNeil chief – conveniently enough, a wealthy American and trained architect – bought the island back in 1937, he set about restoring the castle. There's nothing much to see inside, but the whole experience is fun – head down to the slipway at the bottom of Main Street, where the HS ferryman will take you over (weather permitting; Ⓣ01871/810313).

To learn more about the history of the island, and about the postal system of the Western Isles, it's worth paying a visit to the Barra Heritage Centre, known as

Dualchas (March, April & Sept Mon, Wed & Fri 10.30am–4.30pm; May–Aug Mon–Sat 10.30am–4.30pm; £2; Ⓦwww.barraheritage.com), on the road that leads west out of town; the museum also has a handy **café** serving soup, toasties and cakes.

The Cockle Strand and Eòlaigearraidh

At the north end of the island, Barra is squeezed between two sandy bays: the dune-backed west side takes the full force of the Atlantic breakers, while the east side has the crunchy shell sands of Tràigh Mhòr, better known as **Cockle Strand**. The beach is also used as the island's **airport**, with planes landing and taking off according to the tides, since at high tide the beach (and therefore the runway) is covered in water. As its name suggests, the strand is also famous for its cockles and cockleshells, the latter being used to make harling (the rendering used on most Scottish houses).

To the north of the airport is the scattered settlement of **EÒLAIGEARRAIDH** (Eoligarry), which has several sheltered sandy bays. Here, too, is **Cille-Bharra** (St Barr's Church), burial ground of the MacNeils (and the author Compton MacKenzie). The ground lies beside the ruins of a medieval church and two chapels, one of which has been re-roofed to provide shelter for several carved medieval gravestones and a replica of an eleventh-century rune-inscribed cross, the original of which is in the National Museum of Scotland in Edinburgh.

Barra practicalities

There are two **ferry terminals** on Barra: from Eriskay, you arrive at an uninhabited spot on the northeast of the island; from Oban, Lochboisdale or Tiree, you arrive at Castlebay itself. Barra Car Hire (Ⓣ01871/890313) will deliver **cars** to either terminal or the airport and Barra Cycle Hire (Ⓣ01871/810284) will do the same with **bikes**. There's also a fairly decent **bus/postbus** service, which does the rounds of the island (Mon–Sat). Barra's **tourist office** (April–Oct Mon–Sat only; open to greet the ferry; Ⓣ01871/810336) is situated on Main Street in Castlebay just round from the pier, and can help book accommodation, though it's as well to book in advance for B&Bs and hotels. Guided **sea-kayaking** is available from the *Dunard Hostel* (see below) and those interested in a **boat trip** to any of the islands around Barra, including **Mingulay**, should phone Donald (Ⓣ01871/890384, Ⓦwww.barrafishingcharters.com) or enquire at the tourist office.

For **accommodation** in Castlebay itself, the *Castlebay Hotel* (Ⓣ01871/810223, Ⓦwww.castlebay-hotel.co.uk; ⑤) is the more welcoming of the town's two options. For a cheaper alternative, try *Tigh-na-Mara* (Ⓣ01871/810304, Ⓦwww.tighnamara-barra.co.uk; April–Oct; ③), a Victorian guesthouse a couple of minutes' walk from the pier, overlooking the sea, or *Dunard Hostel* (Ⓣ01871/810443, Ⓦwww.dunardhostel.co.uk), a relaxed, family-run place just west of the ferry terminal in Castlebay. The best option on Barra is the old church in Bagh a Tuath (Northbay), now home to the *Heathbank Hotel* (Ⓣ01871/890266, Ⓦwww.barrahotel.co.uk; ⑤), a comfortable hotel and local watering hole.

On Main Street, the *Kisimul* **café** (closed Sun) serves breakfast all day and specializes in cheap-and-cheerful Scottish fry-ups and Asian food. For more fancy food, head to the *Castlebay Hotel*'s cosy **bar**, which regularly has cockles, crabs and scallops on its menu, and good views out over the bay. The aforementioned *Heathbank Hotel* serves good bar meals.

Travel details

Buses

Lewis and Harris

For more details, see Ⓦwww.cne-siar.gov.uk/travel

Stornoway to: Arnol (Mon–Sat 6–8 daily; 35min); Barabhas (Mon–Sat 6–9 daily; 25min); Calanais (Mon–Sat 4–6 daily; 40min); Carlabhagh (Mon–Sat 5–6 daily; 45min); Gearrannan (Mon–Sat 3–4 daily; 1hr); Great Bernera (Mon–Sat 4 daily; 1hr); Leverburgh (Mon–Sat 4–5 daily; 2hr); Port Nis (Mon–Sat 6–8 daily; 1hr); Siabost (Mon–Sat 5–6 daily; 45min); Tarbert (Mon–Sat 5 daily; 1hr); Uig (Mon–Sat 4 daily; 1hr–1hr 30min).

Tarbert to: Huisinis (schooldays Mon–Fri 3–4 daily; school holidays Tues & Fri 3 daily; 45min); Leverburgh (Mon–Sat 6–8 daily; 45min–1hr); Leverburgh via the Bays (Mon–Sat 2–4 daily; 1hr); Rhenigdale (Mon–Sat 2 daily; 30min).

Uists and Benbecula

Balivanich to: Eriskay (Mon–Sat 5–7 daily; 1hr 30min); Lochboisdale (Mon–Sat 7–9 daily; 1hr).

Berneray to: Balivanich (Mon–Sat 5–7 daily; 1hr 15min); Eriskay (Mon–Sat 4 daily; 3hr); Lionacleit (Mon–Sat 6–8 daily; 1hr 15min); Lochboisdale (Mon–Sat 6 daily; 2hr 15min); Lochmaddy (Mon–Sat 9 daily; 25min); Solas (4–5 daily; 30min).

Lochboisdale to: Eriskay (Mon–Sat 7 daily; 35min).

Lochmaddy to: Balivanich (Mon–Sat 6 daily; 45min–2hr); Balranald (Mon–Sat 3 daily; 50min); Lochboisdale (Mon–Sat 6 daily; 1hr 30min).

Barra

Castlebay to: airport/ferry for Eriskay (Mon–Sat 4–6 daily; 35–45min).

Ferries

Summer timetable only.

To Barra: Eriskay–Barra (5 daily; 40min); Lochboisdale–Castlebay (Mon, Tues & Thurs; 1hr 30min); Oban–Castlebay (1 daily; 4hr 50min); Tiree–Castlebay (Thurs; 3hr).

To Harris: Berneray–Leverburgh (3–4 daily; 1hr); Uig–Tarbert (Mon–Sat 1–2 daily; 1hr 45min).

To Lewis: Ullapool–Stornoway (Mon–Sat 2–3 daily, 1 on Sun; 2hr 45min).

To North Uist: Leverburgh–Berneray (3–4 daily; 1hr); Uig–Lochmaddy (1–2 daily; 1hr 40min).

To South Uist: Castlebay–Lochboisdale (daily except Sat; 1hr 40min); Oban–Lochboisdale (Tues, Thurs, Sat & Sun; 5hr 20min–6hr 30min).

Flights (British Airways only)

Benbecula to: Barra (Mon–Fri 1 daily; 20min); Stornoway (Mon–Fri 2 daily; 30min).

Edinburgh to: Stornoway (Mon–Fri 2 daily, Sat & Sun 1 daily; 1hr 5min).

Glasgow to: Barra (Mon–Sat 2–3 daily; 1hr 10min); Benbecula (Mon–Fri 2 daily, Sat & Sun 1 daily; 55min); Stornoway (Mon–Fri 3–4 daily, Sat & Sun 1–2 daily; 1hr 10min).

Inverness to: Stornoway (Mon–Fri 3 daily, Sat & Sun 1 daily; 40min).

16

Orkney

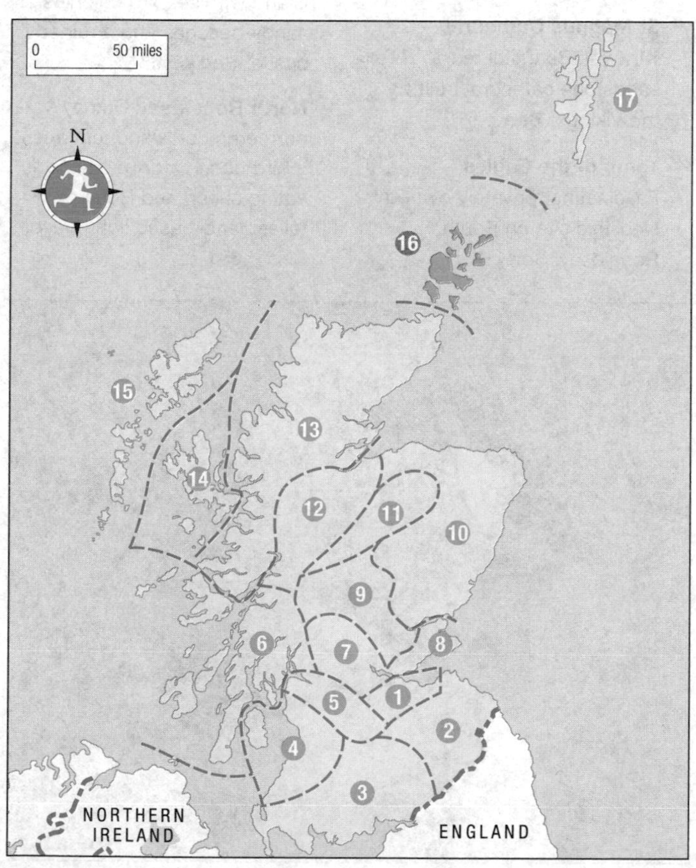
0
50 miles
N
17
16
15
13
14
12
11
10
9
6
7
8
1
5
2
4
3
NORTHERN
IRELAND
ENGLAND

CHAPTER 16 **Highlights**

* **Maes Howe** Orkney's – and Europe's – finest Neolithic chambered tomb. See p.572

* **Skara Brae** Mesmerizing Neolithic homes, crammed with domestic detail. See p.573

* **St Magnus Cathedral, Kirkwall** Beautiful red sandstone cathedral built by the Vikings. See p.576

* **Tomb of the Eagles** Fascinating, privately owned Neolithic site on South Ronaldsay. See p.580

* **Scapa Flow Visitor Centre** Learn about the wartime history of Orkney's great natural harbour and the scuttling of the German Fleet. See p.582

* **Westray** Thriving Orkney island with seabird colonies, sandy beaches and a ruined castle. See p.586

* **North Ronaldsay** Orkney's northernmost island features a bird observatory, seaweed-eating sheep and Britain's tallest land-based lighthouse. See p.591

▲ Puffins and razorbill, Westray

16

Orkney

Orkney is a captivating and fiercely independent archipelago made up of seventy or so mostly low-lying islands, with a population of less than twenty thousand. The locals tend to refer to themselves first as Orcadians, regarding Scotland as a separate entity, and proudly flying their own flag. For an Orcadian, the **Mainland** invariably means the largest island in Orkney rather than the rest of Scotland, and throughout their distinctive history they've been linked to lands much further afield, principally Scandinavia.

Orkney has two chief settlements: **Stromness**, an attractive old fishing town on the far southwestern shore, and the capital, **Kirkwall**, which stands at the dividing point between East and West Mainland. The Mainland is relatively heavily populated and farmed throughout, and is joined by causeways to a string of southern islands, the largest of which is **South Ronaldsay**. The island of **Hoy**, the second largest in the archipelago, south of Mainland, presents a superbly dramatic landscape, with some of the highest sea cliffs in the country. Hoy, however, is atypical: Orkney's smaller, much quieter **northern islands** are low-lying, elemental but fertile outcrops of rock and sand, scattered across the ocean.

For the visitor, the best time to come is in spring and summer when the days are long, the sandy beaches dazzling, the cliffs packed with seabirds and the meadows thick with wild flowers. In autumn and winter, the islands are often battered by gale force winds and daylight is scarce, but the temperature stays remarkably mild thanks to the ameliorating effect of the Gulf Stream. Wind is, of course, a factor, throughout the year, though its almost constant presence does mean that midges are less of a problem, except on Hoy.

Some history

Small communities began to settle in the islands around 4000 BC, and **Skara Brae** on the Mainland is one of the best-preserved Stone Age settlements in Europe. Elsewhere the islands are scattered with chambered tombs and stone circles, a tribute to the well-developed religious and ceremonial practices taking place here from around 2000 BC. More sophisticated **Iron Age** inhabitants built fortified villages incorporating stone towers known as brochs, the finest of which is the **Broch of Gurness**. Later, **Pictish** culture spread to Orkney and the remains of several early Christian settlements can be seen, the best at the **Brough of Birsay**. Around the ninth century, settlers from Scandinavia arrived and the islands became **Norse** earldoms, forming an outpost of a powerful, expansive culture. The last of the Norse earls was killed in 1231, but they had a lasting impact on the islands, leaving behind not only their language but also Kirkwall's great medieval **St Magnus Cathedral**.

After Norse rule, the islands became the preserve of **Scottish earls**, who exploited and abused the islanders, although a steady increase in sea trade did offer some chance

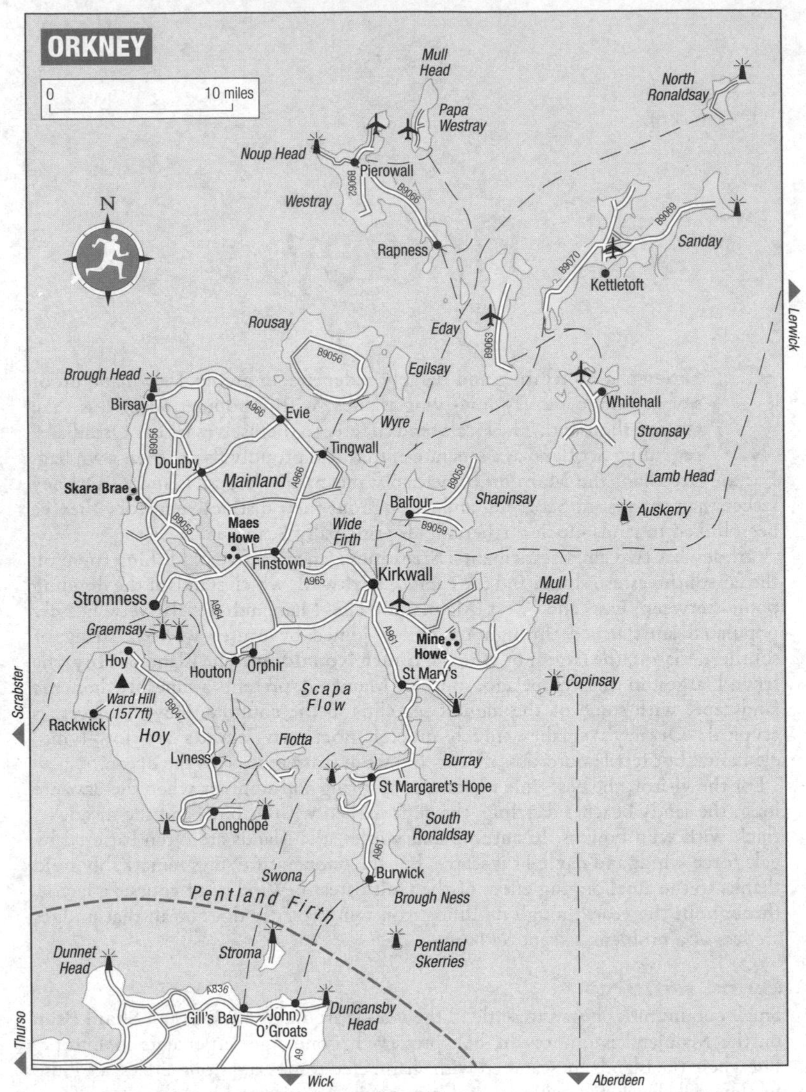

of escape. French and Spanish ships sheltered here in the sixteenth century, and the ships of the **Hudson's Bay Company** recruited hundreds of Orcadians to work in the Canadian fur trade. The islands were also an important staging post in the **whaling industry** and the herring boom, which drew great numbers of small Dutch, French and Scottish boats. The choice of **Scapa Flow**, Orkney's natural harbour, as the Royal Navy's main base brought plenty of money and activity during both world wars, and left the cliff-tops dotted with gun emplacements and the sea bed scattered with wrecks – which these days make for wonderful diving opportunities.

After the war, things quietened down somewhat, although since the mid-1970s the large **oil terminal** on the island of Flotta, the establishment of the

Orkney Islands Council (OIC), combined with EU development grants, have brought surprise windfalls, helping to stem the exodus of young people. Meanwhile, many disenchanted southerners have become "ferryloupers" (incomers), moving to Orkney in search of peace and the apparent simplicity of island life.

Arrival and island transport

Orkney is connected to the Scottish mainland by several **car ferry** routes. Pentland Ferries (Ⓣ01856/831226, Ⓦwww.pentlandferries.co.uk) operates catamarans from **Gills Bay**, near John O'Groats (linked by bus to Wick and Thurso) to **St Margaret's Hope** on South Ronaldsay (3 daily; 1hr). Services to **Stromness** from **Scrabster** (2–3 daily; 1hr 30min), which is connected to nearby Thurso by shuttle bus, are run by Northlink Ferries (Ⓣ0845/600 0449, Ⓦwww.northlinkferries.co.uk), which also operates ferries to **Kirkwall** from **Aberdeen** (4 weekly; 6hr) and from **Lerwick** in Shetland (3 weekly; 5hr 30min). John O'Groats Ferries (Ⓣ01955/611353, Ⓦwww.jogferry.co.uk) runs a **passenger ferry** from **John O'Groats** to **Burwick** on South Ronaldsay (May & Sept 2 daily; June–Aug 4 daily; 40min), its departure timed to connect with the arrival of the Orkney Bus from Inverness; there's also a free shuttle service from Thurso train station for certain sailings. The ferry is small and, except in fine weather, is recommended only for those with strong stomachs. Direct **flights** on Flybe (Ⓦwww.flybe.com) serve Kirkwall airport from Sumburgh in Shetland, Inverness, Aberdeen, Edinburgh and Glasgow.

Bus services (Ⓦwww.stagecoachbus.com) on the Orkney Mainland are infrequent, and skeletal on Sundays – a free timetable is available from the tourist office. On the smaller islands, a minibus usually meets the ferry and will take you to your destination. **Cycling** is not a bad option if the weather holds, since there are few steep hills and distances are modest, though the wind can make it hard going.

Getting to the other islands from the Mainland isn't difficult, though it's expensive: Orkney Ferries (Ⓣ01856/872044, Ⓦwww.orkneyferries.co.uk) operates all the **ferries** and it's essential to book your ticket well in advance, especially if you're taking a car. There are **flights** from Kirkwall to most of the outer isles, operated by Loganair (Ⓣ01856/872494, Ⓦwww.loganair.co.uk), using an eight-seater plane, with discounted fares to North Ronaldsay and Papa Westray and between the islands, if you stay over. Travel between individual islands by sea or air isn't straightforward, but careful study of timetables may reduce the need to travel via Kirkwall. It's worth enquiring from Orkney Ferries about their **additional Sunday sailings** in summer, which often make useful inter-island connections.

Stromness

STROMNESS has to be one of the most enchanting ports at which to arrive by boat, its picturesque waterfront a procession of tiny sandstone jetties and slate roofs nestling below the green hill of Brinkies Brae. As one of Orkney's main points of arrival, Stromness is a great introduction, and one that's well worth spending a day exploring, or using as a base in preference to Kirkwall. Its natural sheltered harbour (known as Hamnavoe) must have been used in Viking times, but the town itself only really took off in the eighteenth century when the Hudson's Bay Company made Stromness its main base from which to make the long journey

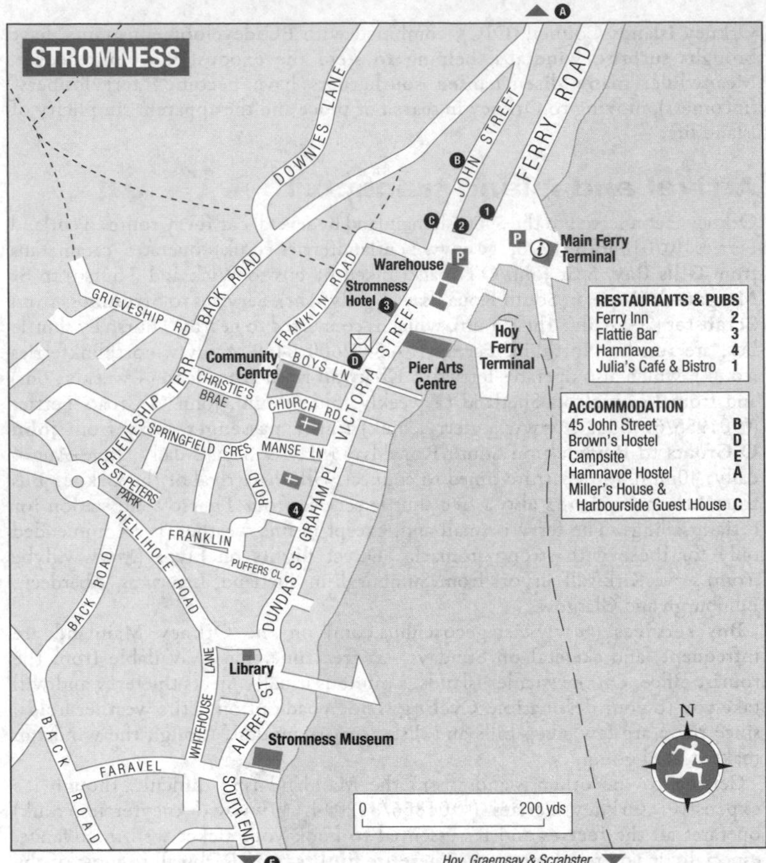

across the North Atlantic, and crews from Stromness were also hired for herring and whaling expeditions – and, of course, press-ganged into the Royal Navy. Today Stromness remains an important fishing port and ferry terminal, and is the focus of the popular four-day **Orkney Folk Festival** (ⓦwww.orkneyfolkfestival.com), held in May.

Information and accommodation

Stromness's modern ferry terminal also houses the **tourist office** (March–Oct daily; ⓣ01856/850716, ⓦwww.visitorkney.com). **Accommodation** is surprisingly thin on the ground. The venerable Victorian *Stromness Hotel* – the town's first – has seen better days, and you're better off heading for the *Miller's House and Harbourside Guest House*, 13 John St (ⓣ01856/851969, ⓦwww.millershouseorkney.com; ③), in the town's oldest property (and a nearby annexe), or the nearby former harbour master's house, *45 John Street* (ⓣ01856/850949, ⓦwww.45johnstreet.co.uk; ③). There's a choice of **hostels**: the *Hamnavoe*, 10a North End Rd (ⓣ01856/851202, ⓦwww.hamnavoehostel.co.uk), is no beauty from the outside, but inside it's all spotlessly clean and well equipped; *Brown's* (ⓣ01856/850661, ⓦwww.brownshostel.co.uk) is a family-run place, right in the centre of town on Victoria Street, with bunk beds in very small, shared rooms. There's also a **campsite** (☎01856/873535; May to mid-Sept) in a superb (though extremely exposed) setting a mile south of the ferry terminal at Point of Ness. **Bike rental** is available from Orkney Cycle Hire, 54 Dundas St (☎01856/850255, ⓦwww.orkneycyclehire.co.uk), near the museum.

The Town

Unlike Kirkwall, Orkney's capital, the old town of Stromness still hugs the shoreline. Its one and only street is a narrow winding affair, paved with great flagstones long before the advent of the motor car, and fed by a tight network of alleyways or closes. The central section, which begins at the *Stromness Hotel* (see above), is known as **Victoria Street**, though in fact it takes on several other names – Graham Place, Dundas Street, Alfred Street and South End – as it threads its way southwards. On the east side of the street the houses are gable-end-on to the waterfront, and originally each one would have had its own pier, from which merchants would trade with passing ships.

The warehouse on the first of the old jetties on Victoria Street now forms half of the **Pier Arts Centre** (Mon–Sat 10.30am–5pm; free; ⓦwww.pierartscentre.com); the other half is a modern glass and steel structure that offers views of the harbour framed like pictures. The gallery has always featured a remarkable collection of twentieth-century British art mostly by members of the Cornish school, such as Barbara Hepworth, Ben Nicholson, Terry Frost, Patrick Heron, and the self-taught Alfred Wallis, but has now also acquired contemporary works, many by northern and Scandinavian artists, which continue the marine themes of the original collection.

Ten minutes' walk from here, at the junction of Alfred Street and South End, is the **Stromness Museum** (May–Sept daily 10am–5pm; Oct–April Mon–Sat 11am–3.30pm; £3.50), built in 1858. Highlights include an early inflatable boat like the one used by John Rae, the Stromness-born Arctic explorer, and some barnacle-encrusted crockery from the German High Seas Fleet that was sunk in Scapa Flow in 1919 (see box, p.579).

Eating and drinking

Stromness has only a few **places to eat**, starting with the daytime-only *Julia's Café and Bistro* situated opposite the ferry terminal, with a sunny conservatory and imaginative meals for under £10. The *Hamnavoe Restaurant*, at 35 Graham Place (April–Sept; ☎01856/850606; Tues–Sun eve only), offers the town's most ambitious cooking, concentrating on local produce, such as grilled sole or peppered monkfish – main courses start at around £15 and booking is essential. The downstairs *Flattie Bar* of the *Stromness Hotel* is a congenial place to warm yourself by a real fire or (depending on the season) sit outside with a **drink**; the most popular pub is, however, the *Ferry Inn*, opposite the terminal.

West Mainland

Stromness sits in the southwesternmost corner of the **West Mainland** – west of Kirkwall, that is – the great bulk of which is fertile, productive farmland, fenced off into a patchwork of fields used either to produce crops or for cattle-grazing. Fringed by spectacular coastline, particularly in the west, West Mainland is littered with some of the island's most impressive prehistoric sites, such as the village of **Skara Brae**, the standing **Stones of Stenness**, the chambered tomb of **Maes Howe** and the **Broch of Gurness**, as well as one of Orkney's best preserved medieval castles at **Birsay**. Despite the intensive farming, there are some areas that are too barren to cultivate, and the high ground and wild coastline include several interesting **wildlife reserves**.

Stenness

The parish of **Stenness**, northeast of Stromness along the main road to Kirkwall, slopes down from Ward Hill (881ft) to the lochs of Stenness and Harray; the first of which is tidal, the second of which is Orkney's most famous freshwater trout loch. The two lochs are separated by a couple of promontories, now joined by a short causeway that may well have been a narrow isthmus around 3000 BC, when it stood at the heart of Orkney's most important Neolithic ceremonial complex, centred on the burial chamber of **Maes Howe**.

The most visible part of the complex between lochs Stenness and Harray is the **Stones of Stenness**, originally a circle of twelve rock slabs, now just four, the tallest of which is a real monster at over 16ft, though it's more remarkable for its incredible thinness. A broken tabletop lies within the circle, which is surrounded by a much-diminished henge (a circular bank of earth and a ditch) with a couple of entrance causeways. Less than a mile to the northwest, past the awesome **Watch Stone** which stands beside the road at over 18ft in height, you reach another stone circle, the **Ring of Brodgar**, a much wider circle dramatically sited on raised ground. Here there were originally sixty stones, 27 of which now stand; of the henge, only the ditch survives.

Maes Howe

There are several quite large burial mounds visible to the south of the Ring of Brodgar, but these are entirely eclipsed by one of the most impressive Neolithic burial chambers in Europe, **Maes Howe** (April–Sept daily 9.30am–5pm; Oct–March Mon–Sat 9.45am–4.30pm; HS; £5.20; ☎01856/761606), which lies less than a mile northeast of the Stones of Stenness. Dating from around 3000 BC, its excellent state of preservation is partly due to the massive slabs of sandstone it was constructed from, the largest of which weighs over thirty tons. To visit the tomb, you must first buy a **timed ticket** for a guided tour, either over the phone or direct from the nineteenth-century meal mill by the main road, which houses the **ticket office**, toilets and interpretive display on the ground floor.

You enter the **central chamber** down a low, long passage, one wall of which is comprised of a single immense stone. Once inside, you can stand upright and admire the superb masonry of the lofty corbelled roof. Remarkably, the tomb is aligned so that the rays of the winter solstice sun hit the top of the Barnhouse Stone, half a mile away, and reach right down the passage of Maes Howe to the ledge of one of the three cells built into the walls of the tomb. When Maes Howe was opened in 1861, it was found to be virtually empty, thanks to the work of generations of grave-robbers, who had left behind only a handful of human bones. The Vikings entered in the twelfth century, probably on their way to the Crusades, leaving large amounts of runic graffiti, some of which are cryptographic twig runes, cut into the walls of the main chamber and still clearly visible today. They include phrases such as "many a beautiful woman has stooped in here, however pompous she might be", and "these runes were carved by the man most skilled in runes in the entire western ocean", to the more prosaic "Thor and I bedded Helga".

Practicalities

Given the density of prehistoric sites around Stenness, and its central position on the Mainland, it's not a bad area in which to base yourself. For **accommodation** look no further than the carefully converted *Mill of Eyrland* (Ⓣ01856/850136, Ⓦwww.millofeyrland.co.uk; ❹), in a delightful setting by a millstream on the A964 to Orphir; it's filled with wonderful antiques and old mill machinery plus all mod cons, and serves enormous breakfasts. Alternatively, you could stay at the excellent *Holland House* (Ⓣ01856/771400, Ⓦwww.hollandhouseorkney.co.uk; ❺), a former manse halfway along the A986 to Dounby, that's tastefully furnished and serves up very good breakfasts.

Skara Brae

North of Stromness, the parish of Sandwick contains the best known of Orkney's prehistoric monuments, **Skara Brae** (April–Sept daily 9.30am–6.30pm; Oct–March Mon–Sat 9.30am–4.30pm, Sun 2–4.30pm; HS; £6.50), beautifully situated beside the white curve of the Bay of Skaill. Here, the extensive remains of a small Neolithic fishing and farming village, dating back to 3000 BC, were discovered in 1850 after a fierce storm ripped off the dunes covering them. The village is amazingly well preserved, its houses huddled together and connected by narrow passages, which would originally have been covered over with turf. The houses themselves consist of a single, spacious living room, filled with domestic detail, including dressers, fireplaces, built-in cupboards, beds and boxes, all ingeniously constructed from slabs of stone.

The **visitor centre** houses an excellent **café/restaurant**, where you can also get takeaway sandwiches to order. If you want to, you can take in the small introductory **exhibition**, with a few replica finds, and some hands-on stuff for kids. You then proceed to a full-scale replica of House 7 (the best-preserved house), complete with a fake wood and skin roof. It's all a tad neat and tidy, with fetching uplighting – rather than dark, smoky and smelly – but it gives you the general idea, and makes up for the fact that, at the site itself, you can only look down on the houses from the outer walls. A short video, in the little building at the far end of the site, helps put the site in context.

In the summer months, your ticket to Skara Brae also covers entry to nearby **Skaill House**, originally built for Bishop George Graham in the 1620s, but much extended since. The last occupant of the house was a Mrs Kathleen Scarth, who died in 1991; her bedroom has been left as it was and is filled with old frocks, an ostrich feather fan and a "twist and slim exerciser".

Birsay and around

Occupying the northwest corner of the Mainland, the parish of **BIRSAY** was the centre of Norse power in Orkney for several centuries before the earls moved to Kirkwall, some time after the construction of its cathedral. Today a tiny cluster of homes is gathered around the imposing sandstone ruins of the **Earl's Palace**, which was built in the second half of the sixteenth century by Robert Stewart, Earl of Orkney, using the forced labour of the islanders, who weren't even given food and drink for their work. By all accounts, it was a "sumptuous and stately dwelling", built in four wings around a central courtyard, its upper rooms decorated with painted ceilings and rich furnishings; surrounding the palace were flower and herb gardens, a bowling green and archery butts. The palace appears to have lasted barely a century before falling into rack and ruin; the crumbling walls and turrets retain much of their grandeur, although inside there is little remaining domestic detail. However, its vast scale makes the Earl's Palace in Kirkwall seem almost humble in comparison.

Just over half a mile northwest of the palace is the **Brough of Birsay**, a substantial Pictish settlement on a small tidal island that is only accessible during the two hours each side of low tide. Stromness and Kirkwall tourist offices have the tide times, which are also broadcast by Radio Orkney (93.7FM; Mon–Fri 7.30–8am). Once you reach the island, there's a small ticket office, where you must pay your **entrance fee** (mid-June to Sept daily; £3), and where you can see a few artefacts gathered from the site, including an antler pin and a game made from whalebone. The focus of the village was – and still is – the sandstone-built twelfth-century **St Peter's Church**, which is thought to have stood at the centre of a monastic complex of some sort – the foundations of a courtyard and outer buildings can be made out to the west. Close by is a large complex of Viking-era buildings, including several houses, a sauna and some sophisticated stone drains.

The best **accommodation** in Birsay is at *Linkshouse* (ⓣ01856/721221, ⓦwww.ewaf.co.uk; ❸), an attractive, stone-built, Edwardian B&B with a bit of character close to Birsay village itself. There's also the large, refurbished *Birsay Outdoor Centre* (April–Sept; ⓣ01856/873535 ext 2415), a **hostel** and **campsite**, half a mile south of the Barony Mills. For **food**, head for the *Birsay Tea Room* just south of the village: it has a superb view of the Brough (binoculars provided) and offers light snacks and home-made cake.

Evie and the Broch of Gurness

The village and parish of **EVIE**, on the north coast, look out across the turbulent waters of Eynhallow Sound towards the island of Rousay. Its chief draw is the **Broch of Gurness** (April–Sept daily 9.30am–5.30pm; HS; £4.70), the best-preserved broch on an archipelago replete with them, still surrounded by a remarkable complex of later buildings. As at Birsay, the sea has eaten away half the site, but the broch itself, dating from around 100 BC, still stands, its walls reaching a height of 12ft in places and its inner cells still intact. The compact group of homes clustered around the broch has also survived amazingly well, with much of their original and ingenious stone shelving and fireplaces still in place. The best view of the site is from the east, where you can clearly make out the "main street" leading towards the broch.

One of the most secluded **accommodation** options on the Mainland is the artfully decorated *Woodwick House* (ⓣ01856/751330, ⓦwww.woodwickhouse.co.uk; ❹), southeast of the main village, which provides an excellent breakfast; some rooms have shared, slightly ancient bathrooms, but the residents' lounge has a real fire and the wooded grounds are delightful (and feature a seventeenth-century doocot). At the other end of the scale, you can stay in the simple *Eviedale* **campsite** (April–Oct; ⓣ01856/751270, ⓦwww.creviedale.orknet.co.uk), situated in a sheltered spot right by the junction of the road to Dounby.

Kirkwall

Initial impressions of **KIRKWALL**, Orkney's capital, are not always favourable. It has nothing to match the picturesque harbour of Stromness, and its residential sprawl is far less appealing. However, it does have one great redeeming feature – its sandstone **cathedral**, without doubt the finest medieval building in the north of Scotland. In any case, if you're staying any length of

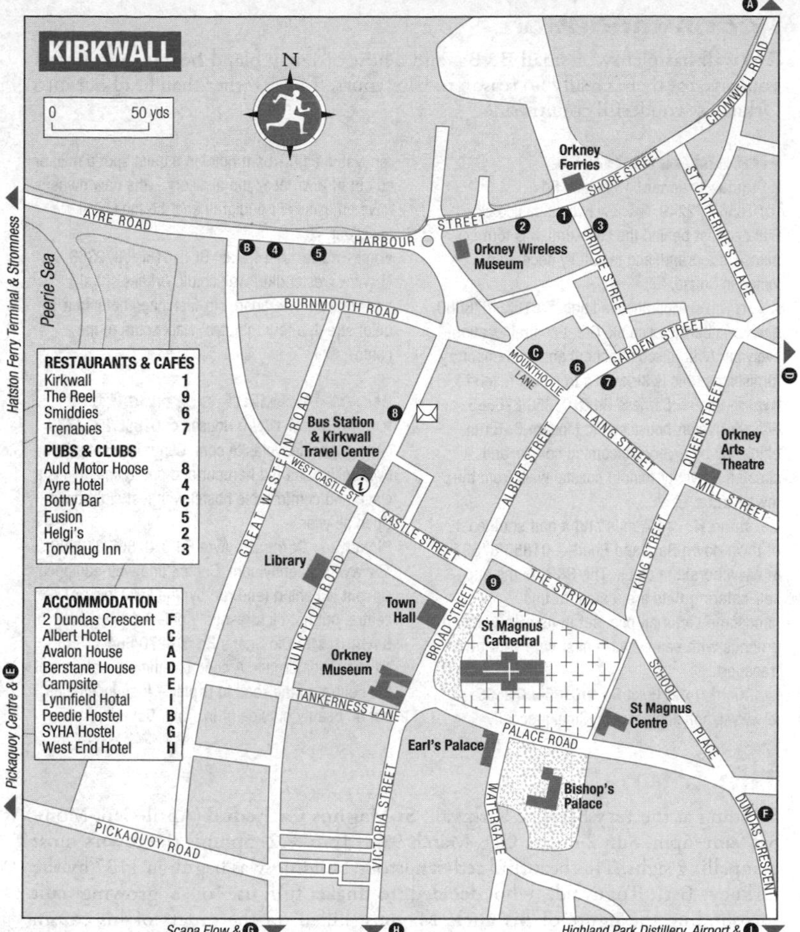

time in Orkney you're more or less bound to find yourself in Kirkwall at some point, as the town is home to the islands' better-stocked shops, including the only large supermarket, and is the departure point for most of the ferries to Orkney's northern isles.

Arrival and information

Northlink **ferries** from Shetland and Aberdeen (and all cruise ships) dock at the Hatston terminal, a mile northwest of town; a shuttle bus will take you into Kirkwall (or to Stromness if you prefer). Kirkwall **airport** is three miles southeast of town on the A960; a bus (Mon–Sat every 30min–hourly, 9 on Sun; 15min) will take you to the **bus station** (aka Kirkwall Travel Centre) on West Castle Street. For **bike rental** head for Cycle Orkney, Tankerness Lane (ⓣ01856/875777, ⓦwww.cycleorkney.com; closed Sun). The helpful **tourist office** (April–Sept daily; Oct–March Mon–Sat only; ⓣ01856/872856, ⓦwww.visitorkney.com) is in Kirkwall Travel Centre, by the bus station.

Accommodation

Kirkwall has plenty of small **B&Bs**, and a host of fairly bland **hotels**, but, unless you have to, there's really no reason to base yourself here rather than head out into Orkney's wonderful countryside.

Hotels and B&Bs

2 Dundas Crescent 13 Palace Rd ⓣ01856/872249, ⓦwww.twodundas.co.uk. Situated just behind the cathedral, this former manse is a grand, and tastefully decorated, Victorian house. ④

Albert Hotel Mounthoolie Lane ⓣ01856/876000, ⓦwww.alberthotel.co.uk. Great central location, lively bar (with disco attached) and contemporary furnishings: this is Kirkwall's trendiest hotel. ⑥

Avalon House Carness Rd ⓣ01856/876665, ⓦwww.avalon-house.co.uk. Modern B&B run efficiently by a very welcoming couple, and situated a twenty-minute coastal walk from the town centre. ③

Berstane House A mile and a half southeast of town down Berstane Road ⓣ01856/876277, ⓦwww.berstane.co.uk. The B&B rooms and self-catering flats are a steal at this handsome Victorian pile, set in its own wooded grounds with sea views – best with your own transport. ①

Lynnfield Hotel Holm Rd ⓣ01856/872505, ⓦwww.lynnfieldhotel.com. Small, recently renovated eight-room hotel in a quiet spot a mile or so out of town near the distillery – the new owners have an excellent pedigree and the food is excellent. ⑥

West End Hotel 14 Main St ⓣ01856/872368, ⓦwww.westendkirkwall.co.uk. Orkney's first hospital is now a good, old-fashioned hotel in a quiet street, a few minutes' walk south of the centre. ⑤

Hostels and campsites

Peedie Hostel 1 Ayre Houses ⓣ01856/875477, ⓦpeediehostel.yolasite.com. Centrally located overlooking the old harbour and out to sea, this is a clean and comfortable hostel with just eight beds. Open all year.

Pickaquoy Campsite Ayre Rd ⓣ01856/879900, ⓦwww.pickaquoy.com. Central and well-equipped, since it is behind (and run by) the local leisure centre, but not picturesque. April–Oct.

SYHA Hostel Old Scapa Rd ⓣ0870/004 1133, ⓦwww.syha.org.uk. A good ten-minute walk out of the centre on the road to Orphir – friendly enough, but no beauty outside or in. April–Oct.

The town

Standing at the very heart of Kirkwall, **St Magnus Cathedral** (April–Sept Mon–Sat 9am–6pm, Sun 2–5pm; Oct–March 9am–1pm & 2–5pm) is the town's most compelling sight. This beautiful red-sandstone building was begun in 1137 by the Orkney Earl Rognvald, who decided to make full use of a growing cult surrounding the figure of his uncle Magnus, killed on the orders of his cousin Haakon in 1117 (see p.585). When Magnus's body was buried in Birsay, a heavenly light was said to have shone overhead, and his grave soon drew pilgrims from far afield. When Rognvald took over the earldom, he built the cathedral in his uncle's honour, moving the centre of religious and secular power from Birsay to Kirkwall.

Today much of the detail in the soft sandstone has worn away – the capitals around the main doors are reduced to artistically gnarled stumps – but it's still an immensely impressive building. Inside, the atmosphere is surprisingly intimate, the bulky sandstone columns drawing your eye up to the exposed brickwork arches, while around the walls is a series of mostly seventeenth-century tombstones, many carved with a skull and crossbones and other emblems of mortality, alongside chilling inscriptions calling on the reader to "remember death waits us all, the hour none knows". In the square pillars on either side of the high altar, the bones of Magnus and Rognvald are buried. In the southeastern corner of the cathedral lies the tomb of the Stromness-born Arctic explorer John Rae, who tried to find Sir John Franklin's expedition; he is depicted asleep, dressed in moleskins and furs, his rifle and bible by his side. Beside Rae's tomb is Orkney's own Poets' Corner, with memorials to, among others, George Mackay Brown, Eric Linklater and Edwin Muir.

The Bishop's Palace, Earl's Palace and Orkney Museum

South of the cathedral are the ruined remains of the **Bishop's Palace** (April–Sept daily 9.30am–5.30pm; HS; £3.70), traditional residence of the Bishop of Orkney from the twelfth century. It was here that the Norwegian king Haakon died in 1263 on his return from defeat at the Battle of Largs. Most of what you see now, however, dates from the time of Bishop Robert Reid, founder of Edinburgh University, in the mid-sixteenth century. The walls still stand, as does the tall round tower in which the bishop had his private chambers; a narrow spiral staircase takes you to the top for a good view of the cathedral and across Kirkwall's rooftops.

The Bishop's Palace also covers entry to the **Earl's Palace**, built by the infamous Earl Patrick Stewart around 1600 using forced labour; which is rather better preserved and a lot more fun to explore. With its grand entrance, fancy oriel windows, dank dungeons, massive fireplaces and magnificent central hall, it is reckoned to be one of the finest examples of Renaissance architecture in Scotland. The roof may be missing, but many domestic details remain, including a set of toilets and the stone shelves used by the clerk to do his filing. Earl Patrick enjoyed his palace for only a few years before he was imprisoned and charged with treason. The earl might have been acquitted, but he foolishly ordered his son, Robert, to organize an insurrection. Robert held out for four days in the palace against the Earl of Caithness, before being captured, sent to Edinburgh and hanged there; his father was beheaded there five weeks later.

Opposite the cathedral stands the sixteenth-century Tankerness House, a former home for the clergy, and now home to the **Orkney Museum** (Mon–Sat 10.30am–5pm; free). A couple of rooms have been restored to how they would have been in 1820, when the building was a private home for the Baikie family. The rest house some of the islands' most treasured finds, among the more unusual of which are a witch's spell box and a lovely whalebone plaque from a Viking boat grave discovered on Sanday.

Eating, drinking and entertainment

Kirkwall has a smattering of decent **food** options. The best **place** in town is *Smiddies*, 21 Albert St (☎01856/875576), which has a great deli and daytime café on the ground floor and a licensed **restaurant** upstairs serving imaginative dishes using Orkney produce, such as spoots (razorfish). Another option is *Helgi's*, 14 Harbour St (☎01856/879293), a popular new **pub** on the harbour front which serves filling bar food. Of the town's **hotels**: the *Kirkwall*, on Harbour Street, is definitely the best option, as it offers **bar meals** at lunch time and very good à la carte menu in the evening. *The Reel*, near the cathedral, is a laidback **café** run by the musical Wrigley Sisters, serving great coffee, sandwiches and cakes, and offering free wi-fi and occasional live music. The alternative is *Trenabies* on Albert Street, a cosy café with booths, that's a classic Kirkwall institution.

Kirkwall has its very own **nightclub**, *Fusion*, on Ayre Road, which caters for all musical tastes and occasionally stages live gigs. The liveliest **pub** is the *Torvhaug Inn* at the harbour end of Bridge Street; another good place to try is the *Bothy Bar* in the *Albert Hotel*, which sometimes has live music, as does *The Auld Motor Hoose*, on Junction Road. The *Ayre Hotel* has regular Orkney Accordion & Fiddle Club nights on Wednesdays – ask at the tourist office or check the *Orcadian* listings for the latest.

Kirkwall's **Pickaquoy Leisure Centre** (Ⓦwww.pickaquoy.com) – known locally as the "Picky" – is a short walk west of the town centre, up Pickaquoy Road past the supermarket. It now serves as one of the town's main large-scale venues and also contains the New Phoenix **cinema** (Ⓣ01856/879900). Kirkwall's chief cultural bash is the week-long **St Magnus Festival** (Ⓦwww.stmagnusfestival.com), a superb arts festival based in Kirkwall and held in the middle of June. For many of the locals, though, the most important event is the agricultural **County Show** held in the middle of August in Kirkwall.

East Mainland and South Ronaldsay

Southeast from Kirkwall, the narrow spur of the **East Mainland** juts out into the North Sea and is joined, thanks to the remarkable Churchill Barriers, to several smaller islands, the largest of which are **Burray** and **South Ronaldsay**. As with the West Mainland, the land here is heavily farmed, but it contains few of Orkney's more famous sights. Nevertheless, there are some good coastal walks to enjoy, an unusual new Iron Age site to explore at **Mine Howe** and, at the **Tomb of the Eagles**, one of the most enjoyable and memorable of Orkney's prehistoric sites.

East Mainland

The northern side of the **East Mainland** consists of three exposed peninsulas that jut out like giant claws. The most intriguing sight is the Iron Age mound of **Mine Howe** (May & Sept Tues & Fri 11am–3pm; June–Aug daily 10am–4pm; £3.50), just off the A960 in the Tankerness peninsula, beyond the airport. Originally Mine Howe would have been a large mound surrounded by a deep ditch, but only a small section has been excavated so far. At the top of the mound a series of steps leads steeply down to a half-landing, and then plunges down even deeper to a small chamber some twenty feet below the surface. Visitors don a hard hat and grab a torch before heading underground. The whole layout is unique and has left archeologists baffled, though, naturally, numerous theories have been put forward, from execution by ritual drowning to a temple to the god of the underworld. Mine Howe's relationship to the nearby mound and broch of Longhowe remains a mystery too.

The Churchill Barriers and Italian Chapel

The southeastern corner of Orkney Mainland is connected to the islands of Lamb Holm, Burray and South Ronaldsay by four causeways known as the **Churchill Barriers**, built during World War II as anti-submarine barriers after the sinking of the battleship HMS *Royal Oak* on October 14, 1939. As you cross the barriers, you can still see the old blockships, which used to form the barrier, rusting away. More than two-thirds of the 1700-strong workforce who built the barriers were Italian POWs, whose legacy is the extraordinary **Italian Chapel** (daily dawn–dusk; free) at the end of the first causeway. This, the so-called "miracle of Camp 60", must be one of the greatest adaptations ever, made from two Nissen huts, concrete, barbed wire and parts of a rusting blockship. It has a great false facade, and colourful *trompe l'oeil* decor, lovingly restored by the chapel's principal architect, Domenico Chiocchetti, in 1960.

Burray

If you're travelling with children, you may like to stop off on the island of **Burray** in order to visit the **Orkney Fossil and Heritage Centre** (April–Sept daily 10am–6pm; £3.50), on the main road across the island. The UV room, where the rocks reveal their iridescent colours, is a particular favourite with

Scapa Flow

Apart from a few oil tankers, there's very little activity in the great natural harbour of **Scapa Flow**, yet for the first half of the twentieth century, the Flow served as the main base of the Royal Navy, with more than a hundred warships anchored here at any one time. The coastal defences required to make Scapa Flow safe to use as the country's chief naval headquarters were considerable and many are still visible all over Orkney, ranging from half-sunk blockships to the Churchill Barriers (see opposite) and the gun batteries that pepper the coastline. Unfortunately, these defences weren't sufficient to save **HMS Royal Oak** from being torpedoed by a German U-boat in October 1939, but they withstood several heavy German air raids during the course of 1940. Ironically, the worst disaster the Flow has ever witnessed was self-inflicted, when **HMS Vanguard** sank on July 9, 1917, after suffering an internal explosion, killing 843 crew and leaving only two survivors.

Scapa Flow's most celebrated moment in naval history, however, was when the entire **German High Seas Fleet** was interned here immediately after World War I. A total of 74 ships, manned by several thousand German sailors, was anchored off the isle of Cava awaiting the outcome of the Versailles Peace Conference. At around noon on Midsummer's Day 1919, believing either that the majority of the German fleet was to be handed over, or that hostilities were about to resume, the commanding officer, Admiral von Reuter, ordered the fleet to be scuttled. By 5pm, every ship was beached or had sunk and nine German sailors had lost their lives, shot by outraged British servicemen. The British government was publicly indignant, but privately relieved since the scuttling avoided the diplomatic nightmare of dividing up the fleet between the Allies.

Between the wars, the largest **salvage operation** in history took place in Scapa Flow, with the firm of Cox & Danks alone raising twenty-six destroyers, one light cruiser, four battlecruisers and two battleships. Despite this, seven large German ships – three battleships and four light cruisers – remain on the sea bed of Scapa Flow, along with four destroyers and a U-boat. Although the remaining vessels can only be salvaged on a piecemeal basis, their pre-atomic-era steel is still extremely valuable as it is radiation-free and is in great demand in the space and nuclear industries. Scapa Flow is also considered one of the world's greatest dive sites. Scapa Scuba (Ⓣ01856/851218, Ⓦwww.scapascuba.co.uk), based in Stromness, offers one-to-one **scuba-diving** tuition for all abilities. If you don't want to get your feet wet, Dawn Star II (Ⓣ01856/876743, Ⓦwww.orkneyboattrips.co.uk) will take you close to the Admiralty buoys and give you a history tour of the harbour; tours begin at St Mary's.

kids. Upstairs, there's a lot of wartime memorabilia, books to read and a rocking horse to play on.

BURRAY VILLAGE, on the south coast of the island, expanded in the nineteenth century during the boom years of the herring industry, but was badly affected by the sinking of the blockships during World War I. The two-storey warehouse, built in 1860 in order to cure and pack the herring, has since been converted into the *Sands Hotel*, where you can sink a pint by the seashore.

South Ronaldsay

At the southern end of the series of four barriers is low-lying **South Ronaldsay**, the largest of the islands linked to the Mainland and, like the latter, rich farming country. It was traditionally the chief crossing point to the Scottish mainland, as it's only six miles across the Pentland Firth from Caithness. Car **ferries** currently arrive at St Margaret's Hope, and there's a small passenger ferry between John O'Groats and Burwick, on the southernmost tip of the island (see p.569 for details).

St Margaret's Hope

The main settlement on South Ronaldsay is **ST MARGARET'S HOPE**, which local tradition says takes its name from Margaret, the Maid of Norway and daughter of the king of Norway, who is thought to have died here at the age of eight in November 1290. As the granddaughter of Alexander III, Margaret had already been proclaimed queen of Scotland and was on her way to marry the English Prince Edward (later Edward II), thereby unifying the two countries. Today, St Margaret's Hope – or "The Hope", as it's known locally – is a pleasing little gathering of stone-built houses overlooking a sheltered bay, and is by far the best base from which to explore the area. As is obvious from the architecture, and the piers, The Hope was once a thriving port. Nowadays, despite the presence of the Pentland Ferries terminal, it remains a very peaceful place.

The village smithy on Cromarty Square has been turned into a **Smiddy Museum** (May & Sept daily 2.30–4.30pm; June–Aug Mon–Fri 11am–1pm & 2–4pm, Sat & Sun noon–4pm; free), which is particularly fun for kids, who enjoy getting hands-on with the old tools, drills and giant bellows. There's also a small exhibition on the annual **Boys' Ploughing Match**, in which local boys compete with miniature hand-held ploughs. The competition, which is taken extremely seriously by all those involved, happens on the third Saturday in August at the beautiful golden beach at the **Sands O' Wright** in Hoxa, a couple of miles west of The Hope. At the same time a **Festival of the Horse** takes place, with the local children, mostly girls, dressing up in spectacular costumes and harnesses.

If you just want a pint, head for the *Murray Arms* **pub** on Back Road. If you want **to stay** in St Margaret's Hope itself you can stay at ★ *The Creel* (Ⓣ01856/831311, Ⓦwww.thecreel.co.uk; ⑥) on the harbour front, with a view over the bay, and one of the best **restaurants** in Scotland – three-course dinners for around £30. There's also a backpackers' **hostel** nearby (Ⓣ01856/831225, Ⓦorkneybackpackers.com; ①), with singles, doubles and family rooms available. More spacious rooms are available from *Roeberry House* (Ⓣ01856/831228, Ⓦwww.roeberryhouse.com; ⑥), a substantial Victorian mansion, boasting spectacular views, in Hoxa. On the eastern side of South Ronaldsay, a mile and a half from the war memorial on the main road, an organic farm called *Wheems* (April–Oct; Ⓣ01856/831556, Ⓦwww.wheemsorganic.co.uk), has a **self-catering bothy** (sleeping 8) for hire, and a field for **camping**, with all the usual facilities, plus a communal yurt.

The Tomb of the Eagles

One of the most enjoyable archeological sights on Orkney is the Ibister chambered cairn at the southeastern corner of South Ronaldsay, known as the **Tomb of the Eagles** (daily: March 10am–noon; April–Oct 9.30am–6pm; Nov–March by appointment; £5.50; Ⓣ01856/831339, Ⓦwww.tomboftheeagles.co.uk). The cairn was discovered and excavated by local farmer, Ronald Simpson of Liddle, who still owns it, so a visit here makes a refreshing change from the usual interpretive centre. First off, you get to look round the family's private museum of prehistoric artefacts; this is the original hands-on museum, so visitors can actually touch and admire the painstaking craftsmanship of Neolithic folk, and also examine a skull. Next you get a brief guided tour of a nearby Bronze Age **burnt mound**, which is basically a Neolithic rubbish dump, beside which there was a large trough, where joints of meat were boiled by throwing in rocks from the fire. Finally you get to walk out to the **chambered cairn** by the cliff's edge, where human remains were found alongside talons and carcasses of sea eagles. To enter the cairn, you must lie on a trolley and pull yourself in using an overhead rope – something that's guaranteed to put a smile on every visitor's face.

If you're looking for **accommodation** in the southern part of South Ronaldsay, try *Eastward Guest House* (Ⓣ01856/831551, Ⓦwww.eastwardhouse.com; ❷), a B&B full of character a couple of miles north of Burwick, housed in a tastefully converted former church.

Hoy

Hoy, Orkney's second-largest island, rises sharply out of the sea to the southwest of the Mainland. The least typical of the islands, but certainly the most dramatic, its north and west sides are made up of great glacial valleys and mountainous moorland rising to over 1500ft, dropping into the sea off the red-sandstone cliffs of St John's Head, and, to the south, forming the landmark sea stack known as the **Old Man of Hoy**. The northern half of Hoy, though a huge expanse, is virtually uninhabited, with just the cluster of houses at **Rackwick** nestling dramatically in a bay between the cliffs. Meanwhile, most of Hoy's four hundred or so residents live on the gentler, more fertile land in the southeast, in and around the villages of **Lyness** and **Longhope**. This part of the island is littered with buildings dating from the two world wars, when Scapa Flow served as the main base for the Royal Navy.

Two **ferry services** run to Hoy: a passenger ferry **from Stromness** to Moaness pier, by Hoy village (Mon–Fri 4–5 daily, Sat & Sun 2 daily; 25min; Ⓣ01856/850624), which also serves the small island of Graemsay; and the roll-on/roll-off car ferry **from Houton** on the Mainland to Lyness (Mon–Fri 6–8 daily, Sat & Sun 2–4 daily; 35min–1hr; Ⓣ01856/811397), which sometimes calls in at the oil terminal island of Flotta, and begins and ends its daily schedule at Longhope. There's a seasonal Hoy Hopper **bus service** (mid-May to mid-Sept Wed–Fri only), which departs from Kirkwall Travel Centre, and is integrated with the ferries.

North Hoy

Walkers arriving at Moaness Pier, near the tiny village of **HOY**, and heading for Rackwick (four miles southwest), should take the well-marked footpath that goes past Sandy Loch and along the large open valley beyond. The single-track road to Rackwick travels along another valley to the south. En route, duckboards head across the heather to the **Dwarfie Stane**, Orkney's most unusual chambered tomb, cut from a solid block of sandstone and dating back to 3000 BC. The sheer effort that must have been involved in carving out this tomb, with its two side-cells, is staggering, and, as you crawl inside, the marks of the tools used by the Neolithic builders on the ceiling are still visible. The tomb is also decorated with copious Victorian graffiti, the most interesting of which is to be found on the northern exterior, where Major Mouncey, a former British spy in Persia and a confirmed eccentric who dressed in Persian garb, carved his name backwards in Latin and also carved in Persian the words "I have sat two nights and so learnt patience."

RACKWICK is an old crofting and fishing village squeezed between towering sandstone cliffs on the west coast. In an area once quite extensively cultivated, these days only a few of Rackwick's houses are inhabited all year round, though the savage isolation of the place has provided inspiration to a number of artists and writers, including Orkney's George Mackay Brown, who wrote "when Rackwick weeps, its grief is long and forlorn and utterly desolate." A small farm building beside the hostel serves as a tiny **museum** (open anytime; free), with a few old photos and a brief rundown of Rackwick's rough history.

Despite its isolation, Rackwick has a steady stream of walkers and climbers passing through it en route to the **Old Man of Hoy**, a great sandstone column some 450ft high, perched on an old lava flow that protects it from the erosive power of the sea. The Old Man is a popular challenge for rock climbers, and a 1966 ascent, led by the mountaineer Chris Bonington, was the first televised climb in Britain. The well-trodden footpath from Rackwick is an easy three-mile walk (3hr round-trip) – the great skuas will dive-bomb you only during the nesting season – and gives the reward of a great view of the stack. The surrounding cliffs provide ideal rocky ledges for the nests of thousands of seabirds, including guillemots, kittiwakes, razorbills, puffins and shags.

Continuing north along the cliff-tops, the path peters out before **St John's Head** which, at 1136ft, is one of the highest sea cliffs in the country and mostly too sheer even for nesting seabirds. Another, safer, option is to hike to the top of **Ward Hill** (1577ft), the highest mountain in Orkney, from which on a fine day you can see the whole archipelago laid out before you.

Practicalities

There are only a few basic places to stay in North Hoy. There are two council-run, SYHA-affiliated **hostels**, housed in converted schools (book via ⓣ01856/873535 ext 2415, ⓦhostelsorkney.co.uk): the *Hoy Centre* (open all year) in Hoy village is large and modern, with all rooms en suite, while *Rackwick Hostel* (April–Sept) has just eight beds but is in Rackwick village itself. You can also **camp** behind *Rackwick Hostel*, or beside the basic heather-thatched *Burnside Bothy* (ⓣ01856/791316) by the beach. Be warned, too that North Hoy is probably the worst place on Orkney for midges. The nearest shop is in Longhope (see opposite), so it's best to take your supplies with you if you're staying overnight. Even if you've just come for a day-trip, you'll want to check out the *Beneth'hill Café* (ⓣ01856/851116; May–Sept only) a short walk from Moaness Pier, a really friendly, simple **café** serving up cullen skink, fresh local crab, home-made puddings and proper coffee – they'll even do you a packed lunch and an evening meal on a Friday.

Lyness and Longhope

Along the sheltered eastern shore of Hoy, high moorland gives way to a gentler environment similar to that on the rest of Orkney. Hoy defines the western boundary of Scapa Flow, and **LYNESS** played a major role for the Royal Navy during both world wars. Many of the old wartime buildings have been cleared away over the last few decades, but the harbour and hills around Lyness are still scarred with the scattered remains of concrete structures that once served as hangars and storehouses during World War II, and are now used as barns and cowsheds. Among these are the remains of what was – incredibly – the biggest cinema in Europe, but perhaps the most unusual remaining building is the monochrome Art Deco facade of the old **Garrison Theatre**, on the main road south of Lyness, now a private home. Lyness also has a large **naval cemetery**, where many of the victims of the various disasters that have occurred in the Flow, such as the sinking of the *Royal Oak*, now lie, alongside a handful of German graves.

The old oil pumphouse, which still stands opposite the Lyness ferry terminal, has been turned into the **Scapa Flow Visitor Centre & Museum** (April–Oct Mon–Sat 9am–4.30pm, Sun 10.30am–4pm, July–Sept Sun until 6.15pm; Nov–March Mon–Fri 9am–4.30pm; free), a fascinating insight into wartime Orkney. As well as the usual old photos, torpedoes, flags, guns and propellers, there's a paratrooper's folding bicycle, and a whole section devoted to the scuttling of the

German High Seas Fleet and the sinking of the *Royal Oak*. The pumphouse itself retains much of its old equipment – you can even ask for a working demo of one of the oil-fired boilers – used to pump oil off tankers moored at Lyness into sixteen tanks, and from there into underground reservoirs cut into the neighbouring hillside. On request, an audiovisual show on the history of Scapa Flow is screened in the sole surviving tank, which has incredible acoustics. Even the **café** has an old NAAFI feel about it.

South Walls

A causeway built during World War II connects Hoy with **South Walls,** a fertile tidal island whose main settlement of **LONGHOPE** was an important safe anchorage during the Napoleonic Wars and World War I. Evidence of Longhope's strategic importance lies to the east of the village at the Point of Hackness, where the **Hackness Martello Tower** (April–Oct daily 9.30am–5.30pm; HS; £4.20) stands guard over the entrance to the bay, with a matching tower on the opposite promontory of Crockness. Built in 1815, these two circular sandstone Martello towers are the northernmost in Britain, and were built to protect merchant ships from American and French privateers. You enter Hackness Tower via a steep ladder connected to the upper floor, where nine men and one officer shared the circular room. Originally, a portable ladder would have been used and retracted, making the place pretty much impregnable: the walls are up to 9ft high on the seaward side, and the tower even had its own water supply.

Practicalities

The most outstanding **accommodation** on Hoy is *Wild Heather* B&B (Ⓣ01856/791098, Ⓦwww.wildheatherbandb.co.uk; ❷), in Lyness, just beyond the naval cemetery. It's a converted mill with just two en-suite rooms, both with sea views and a lovely breakfast conservatory – they'll offer dinners, too, if required. In Longhope itself, there's the small, welcoming *Stromabank Hotel* (Ⓣ01856/701494, Ⓦwww.stromabank.co.uk; ❸), a nicely converted old schoolhouse, which also does good bar **food** in the evening (closed Thurs). There's just one shop by the pier in Longhope.

Shapinsay

Just a few miles northeast of Kirkwall, **Shapinsay** is the most accessible of Orkney's northern isles. A gently undulating grid-plan patchwork of rich farmland, it's a bit like an island suburb of Kirkwall, which is clearly visible across the bay. Its chief landmark is **Balfour Castle**, an imposing baronial pile designed by David Bryce and completed in 1848 by the Balfour family of Westray, who had made a small fortune in India the previous century. The Balfours died out in 1960 and the castle was bought by a Polish cavalry officer, Captain Tadeusz Zawadski, whose family ran the place for many years as a hotel – nowadays, it's an exclusive-use holiday retreat.

The old smiddy, halfway along the village street, houses the **Shapinsay Heritage Centre** (May–Sept Mon–Fri 11am–4.30pm, Sat & Sun 11am–6pm; free), where you can learn everything you ever wanted to know about the island, before availing yourself of its excellent café. The **east coast** from the Bay of Linton to the Foot of Shapinsay has the most interesting cliffs and sea caves and is backed by the only open moorland on the island. On the far northeastern peninsula is Shapinsay's most striking ancient monument, the **Broch of**

Burroughston, a well-preserved strongly fortified Iron Age broch with the substantial remains of living quarters within, a bar hole to make fast the door, and a guard-cell. The finest stretch of sandy beach is at the sweeping curve of **Sandgarth Bay** in the southeast.

Practicalities

Less than thirty minutes from Kirkwall by **ferry** (4–5 daily), Shapinsay is an easy day-trip, but for those wishing to stay, **B&B** is available at the whitewashed *Hilton Farmhouse* (Ⓣ01856/711239, Ⓦwww.hiltonorkneyfarmhouse.co.uk; ❹), which also has a restaurant in the conservatory (booking ahead essential) and offers optional full board. Even if you're just coming for the day, it's worth popping into *The Smithy* (May–Sept; Ⓣ01856/711722), the wonderfully cosy licensed **café** below the heritage centre, which serves delicious food.

Rousay, Egilsay and Wyre

Just over half a mile from the Mainland's northern shore, the hilly island of **Rousay** is one of the more accessible northern isles as well as being home to a number of intriguing prehistoric sites. The group of a dozen or so houses above the ferry terminal is the only settlement of any size, but a single road runs around the edge of the island, connecting a string of small farms that make use of the more cultivable coastal fringes. Many visitors come on a day-trip, as it's easy enough to reach the main points of archeological interest on the south coast by foot from the ferry terminal.

Rousay's diminutive neighbours, **Egilsay** and **Wyre**, contain a few medieval attractions of their own, which can either be visited on a day-trip from Rousay itself, or from the Mainland.

Trumland House to the Knowe of Yarso

Despite its long history of settlement, Rousay is today home to little more than two hundred people (many of them incomers), as this was one of the few parts of Orkney to suffer Highland-style Clearances, initially by George William Traill at Quandale in the northwest. His successor and nephew, Lieutenant General Traill-Burroughs, built a wall to force crofters onto a narrow coastal strip and eventually provoked so much distress and anger that a gunboat had to be sent to restore order. You can learn about the history and wildlife of the island from the well-laid-out display room of the **Rousay Heritage Centre** housed in the back of the ferry waiting room.

It was the aforementioned Burroughs who built **Trumland House**, the forbidding Jacobean-style pile designed by David Bryce in 1873, and hidden in the trees half a mile northwest of the ferry terminal. The house is currently undergoing much-needed restoration, as are the **gardens** (May–Sept Mon–Fri 10am–5pm; £2), though they can still be visited. The road west from Trumland House is bordered over the next couple of miles by a trio of intriguing prehistoric cairns, starting with **Taversoe Tuick**, discovered by workers during the building of a Victorian viewpoint. Dating back to 3500 BC, it's remarkable in that it exploits its sloping site by having two storeys, one entered from the upper side and one from the lower. A little further west is the **Blackhammar Cairn**, which is more promising inside than it looks from the outside. You enter through the roof via a ladder; the long interior is divided into "stalls" by large flagstones, rather like the more famous cairn at Midhowe (see below). Finally, there's the **Knowe of Yarso**, another stalled cairn dating from the same period that's a stiff climb up the hill from the road, but worth it, if only for the magnificent view. The remains of 29 individuals were found inside, with the skulls neatly arranged around the walls; the bones of 36 deer were also buried here.

Midhowe Cairn and Broch

The southwestern side of Rousay is home to the most significant and impressive of the island's archeological remains, strung out along the shores of the tide races of Eynhallow Sound, which runs between the island and the Mainland. Approaching from the east, **Midhowe Cairn** comes as something of a surprise, both for its immense size – it's known as "the great ship of death" and measures nearly 100ft in length – and for the fact that it's now entirely surrounded by a stone-walled barn with a corrugated roof. Unfortunately, you can't actually explore the roofless communal burial chamber, dating back to 3500 BC, but only look down from the overhead walkway. The central corridor, 25yd long, is partitioned with slabs of rock, with twelve compartments on each side, where the remains of 25 people were discovered in a crouched position with their backs to the wall.

A couple of hundred yards beyond Midhowe Cairn is Rousay's finest archeological site, **Midhowe Broch**, whose compact layout suggests that it was originally built as a sort of fortified family house, surrounded by a complex series of ditches and ramparts. These are now partially obscured by later houses, many of which have shelving and stairs still intact. The broch itself looks as though it's about to slip into the sea: it was obviously shored up with flagstone buttresses back in the Iron Age, and has more recently been given extra sea defences by Historic Scotland. The interior of the broch, entered through an impressive doorway, is divided into two separate rooms, each with its own hearth, water tank and quernstone, all of which date from the final phase of occupation around the second century AD.

Egilsay and Wyre

Egilsay, the largest of the low-lying islands sheltering close to the eastern shore of Rousay, makes for an easy day-trip. The island is dominated by the ruins of the twelfth-century **St Magnus Church**, with its distinctive round tower. It is possible that it was built as a shrine to Earl (later St) Magnus, who arranged to meet his cousin Haakon here in 1117, only to be treacherously killed on Haakon's orders by the latter's cook, Lifolf. A cenotaph marks the spot where the murder took place, a quarter of a mile southeast of the church. If the weather's fine, walk due east from the ferry terminal to the coast, where there's a beautiful sandy bay overlooking Eday.

The tiny, neighbouring island of **Wyre**, to the southwest, directly opposite Rousay's ferry terminal, is another possible day-trip, and is best known for **Cubbie Roo's Castle**, the "fine stone fort" and "really solid stronghold" mentioned in the Old Norse *Orkneyinga Saga*, and built around 1150 by local farmer Kolbein Hruga. The outer defences have survived well on three sides of the castle, which has a central keep, with walls to a height of around six feet, its central water tank still intact. Close by the castle stands the roofless twelfth-century **St Mary's Chapel**. To learn more about Cubbie Roo or any other aspect of Wyre's history, pop into the **Wyre Heritage Centre**, near the chapel.

Practicalities

Rousay makes a good day-trip from the Mainland, with regular **car ferry** sailings from Tingwall (30min), linked to Kirkwall by buses. Most ferries also call in at Egilsay and Wyre, but some need to be booked the day before at the Tingwall ferry terminal (Ⓣ01856/751360). A **bus service** runs (on request Ⓣ01856/821360) every Thursday, or there are **minibus tours** available on demand (Ⓣ01856/821234; £16.50), which connect with ferries and last between five and seven hours.

Accommodation on Rousay is limited. If you want to be near the ancient sites, your best bet is the **hostel** at *Trumland Farm* (Ⓣ01856/821252), a working organic farm half a mile or so west of the terminal. As well as a couple of dorms, you can also camp here, and they offer **bike rental**. The *Taversoe*, further along the road, offers unpretentious accommodation (Ⓣ01856/821325, Ⓦtaversoehotel.co.uk; ❸) and does good bar meals (April–Oct daily; Nov–March Wed–Sun only). *The Pier* **pub**, right beside the terminal, serves bar meals at lunchtime and will make up some fresh crab sandwiches if you phone in advance (Ⓣ01856/821359). Don't arrive expecting to be able to buy yourself many provisions, though, as Marion's Shop, the island's main general store, is in the northeastern corner of the island.

Westray

Although exposed to the full force of the Atlantic weather in the far northwest of Orkney, **Westray** (Ⓦwww.westray-orkney.co.uk) shelters one of the most tightly knit, prosperous and independent island communities. It has a fairly stable population of six hundred or so, producing superb beef, scallops, shellfish and a large catch of white fish, with its own small fish-processing factory and an organic salmon farm. Old Orcadian families still dominate every aspect of life, giving the island a strong individual character. The landscape is very varied, with sea cliffs and a trio of hills in the west, and rich low-lying pastureland and sandy bays elsewhere. However, given that distances are fairly large – it's about twelve miles from the ferry terminal in the south to the cliffs of Noup Head in the far northwest – and that the boat from Kirkwall takes nearly an hour and a half, Westray is an island that repays a longer stay, especially as there's lots of good accommodation and the locals are extremely welcoming and genuinely interested in visitors.

The main village and harbour is **PIEROWALL** set around a wide bay in the north of the island, eight miles from the Rapness ferry terminal on the island's southernmost tip. Pierowall is a place of some considerable size, relatively speaking, with a school, several shops and a bakery (Orkney's only one off the Mainland). The village's **Westray Heritage Centre** (May–Sept Mon 11.30am–5pm, Tues–Sat 10am–noon & 2–5pm, Sun 1.30–5.30pm; £2.50) is a very welcoming wet-weather retreat, and a great place to gen up on (and with any luck catch a glimpse of) the Westray Wife or **Orkney Venus**, a remarkable, miniature Neolithic female figurine found in 2009 in the dunes to the northwest of Pierowall.

The island's most impressive ruin, however, is the colossal sandstone hulk of **Noltland Castle**, which stands above the village half a mile west up the road to Noup Head. This Z-plan castle, pockmarked with over seventy gun loops, was begun around 1560 by Gilbert Balfour, a shady character from Fife, who was Master of the Household to Mary, Queen of Scots, and was implicated in the murder of her husband Lord Darnley in 1567. Balfour was eventually forced to flee to Sweden, where he was found guilty of plotting to murder the Swedish king and executed in 1576. To explore the castle, you must first pick up the key, which hangs outside the back door of the nearby farm.

The northwestern tip of Westray rises up sharply, culminating in the dramatic sea cliffs of **Noup Head**, which are particularly spectacular when a good westerly swell is up. During the summer months the guano-covered rock ledges are packed with more than 100,000 nesting guillemots, razorbills, kittiwakes, fulmars and puffins: a truly awesome sight, sound and smell. The four-mile coastal walk along the top of Westray's red-sandstone cliffs from Noup Head south to Inga Ness is thoroughly recommended, as is a quick ascent of **Fitty Hill** (557ft), Westray's highest point. The sea cliffs in the southeast of the island around **Stanger Head** are not quite as spectacular as at Noup Head, but it's here that you'll find **Castle o'Burrian**, a sea stack that was once an early Christian hermitage. It's now the best place on Westray at which to see **puffins** nesting; there's even a signpost to the puffins from the main road.

Practicalities

Westray is served by car **ferry** from Kirkwall (2–3 daily; 1hr 25min; ⓣ01856/872044), or you can **fly** from Kirkwall (Mon–Sat 2 daily, 1 on Sun; 15min). **Guided tours** of the island by minibus can be arranged with Westraak (ⓣ01857/677777, ⓦwww.westraak.co.uk), who will meet you at the ferry, and also offer **bike rental**. A **minibus** (May–Sept; at other times phone ⓣ01857/677758) also meets the ferry and connects with the Papa Westray ferry at Gill Pier in Pierowall; book a seat for the bus on the ferry.

As for **accommodation**, the *Pierowall Hotel* (ⓣ01857/677472, ⓦwww.pierowallhotel.co.uk; ❸), the social hub of Pierowall itself, is unpretentious and very welcoming – the cheaper rooms have shared facilities. Alternatively, you can get top-notch, good-value **B&B** at *No. 1 Broughton* (ⓣ01857/677726, ⓦwww.no1broughton.co.uk; ❸), a renovated mid-nineteenth-century house on the south shore of the bay, with a lovely conservatory and a sauna, or at *The Old Manse* (ⓣ01857/677578, ⓦwww.bandbwestray.co.uk; ❷) in the heart of Pierowall. Westray is positively spoilt for **hostels**. If you want superb sea views and splendid isolation, head for *Bis Geos* (ⓣ01857/677420, ⓦwww.bisgeos.co.uk), a traditional Oracdian croft, on the road to Noup Head, that's been beautifully renovated inside. If you want to be closer to civilization, head for *The Barn* (ⓣ01857/677214, ⓦwww.thebarnwestray.co.uk), an old farm at the southern edge of Pierowall; it's luxurious inside, with family rooms and twins available (❸), has a small **campsite** adjacent to it and a games room and genuinely friendly hosts.

The *Pierowall Hotel* has a popular bar and a well-justified reputation for excellent **fish and chips**, fresh off the boats (much of the catch you're unlikely to have heard of) – you can buy fresh fish from the hotel, too. The island has a couple of **tearooms**, too: *Wheeling Steen* (closed Sun) café-gallery is over by the airfield in the north of the island, while Westraak tour company runs the *Haf Yok* café in Pierowall itself.

Papa Westray

Across the short Papa Sound from Westray is the island of **Papa Westray** (ⓦwww.papawestray.co.uk), known locally as "Papay", with a population of around seventy. Boasting one of Orkney's best-preserved Neolithic settlements, and a large nesting seabird population, it's worthy of a stay in its own right or an easy day-trip from its neighbour.

Papay's visual focus is **Holland House**, occupying the high central point of the island and once seat of the local lairds, the Traill family. Visitors can explore the old farm buildings, including a kiln, a doocot and a horse-powered threshing mill. An old bothy for single male servants has even been restored and made into a small **museum** (open at all times; free), filled with bygone bits and bobs, from a wooden flea trap to a box bed. A road leads down from Holland House to the western shore, where Papay's prime prehistoric site, the **Knap of Howar**, stands overlooking

Westray. Dating from around 3500 BC, this Neolithic farm building makes a fair claim to being the oldest-standing house in Europe. Half a mile north along the coast from the Knap of Howar is **St Boniface Kirk**, a pre-Reformation church that's beautifully simple, with a bare flagstone floor, dry-stone walls, a little wooden gallery and just a couple of surviving box pews. At the northern tip of the island around **North Hill** (157ft), you can see razorbills, guillemots, fulmars, kittiwakes and puffins nesting on the cliffs, particularly around Fowl Craig on the east coast.

Papay is an easy day-trip from Westray, with a **passenger ferry** service from Gill Pier in Pierowall (3–6 daily; 25min), which also takes bicycles. On Tuesdays, the **car ferry** goes from Kirkwall to Papa Westray via North Ronaldsay, which means it takes over four hours; on Fridays, the **car ferry** from Kirkwall to Westray continues on to Papa Westray; at other times, you have to catch a **bus** to connect with the Papa Westray ferry from Pierowall. The bus should be booked ahead, whilst on the Westray ferry (ⓣ01857/677758); it accepts a limited number of bicycles. Papay is also connected to Westray by the **world's shortest scheduled flight** – two minutes in duration, or less with a following wind. You can also fly direct from Kirkwall to Papa Westray (Mon–Sat 2–3 daily, 1 on Sun; 25min) for a special return fare of £20 if you stay overnight.

Papay's Community Co-operative (ⓣ01857/644321) has a **minibus**, which will take you from the pier to wherever you want on the island, and can arrange a "Peedie Package" tour. The Co-op also runs a shop, a two-room, sixteen-bed **hostel** and the *Beltane House* **B&B** (❸), all housed within the old estate-workers' cottages at Beltane, east of Holland House. There's one other B&B, *School Place* (ⓣ01857/644268, ⓔsonofhewitj@aol.com; ❸), in the island's former school, right in the centre of the island. *Beltane House* opens its "bar cupboard" every Saturday night from 8pm, with **bar meals** available – a great way to meet the locals.

Eday

A long, thin island at the centre of Orkney's northern isles, **Eday** shares more characteristics with Rousay and Hoy than with its immediate neighbours, dominated as it is by a great block of heather-covered upland, with farmland confined to a narrow strip of coastal ground. However, Eday's hills have proved useful in their own way, providing huge quantities of peat that has been exported to the other peatless northern isles for fuel, and was even, for a time, exported to various whisky distillers. Eday's yellow sandstone has also been extensively quarried, and was used to build the St Magnus Cathedral in Kirkwall.

The island is sparsely inhabited and has no real village as such. The ferry terminal is at the south end of the island, whereas the chief points of interest (and most of the amenities) are all in the northern half of the island, about four miles away. First off, there's the **Eday Heritage Centre** (daily: April–Oct 9am–6pm; free), housed in the island's former Baptist chapel. As well as historical displays, there's information on the island's new tidal energy testing centre, as well as a café-bar. Less than a mile further north, near the post office, petrol pump and community shop, there's a bird hide by the road, looking south over **Mill Loch**, where several pairs of red-throated divers regularly breed. Clearly visible on the other side of the road is the fifteen-foot **Stone of Setter**, Orkney's most distinctive standing stone, weathered into three thick, lichen-encrusted fingers. The stone clearly held centre stage in the Neolithic landscape, and is visible from the other nearby prehistoric sites. From here, passing the less spectacular Braeside and Huntersquoy chambered cairns en route, you can climb the hill to reach Eday's finest, the **Vinquoy Chambered Cairn**, which has a similar structure to that of Maes Howe. You can crawl into the tomb through the narrow entrance: a skylight inside lets light into the main, beehive chamber, now home to some lovely ferns, but not into the four side-cells. From the cairn, you can continue north to the viewpoint on the summit of **Vinquoy Hill** (248ft), and on to the very northernmost tip of the island, where the dramatic red-sandstone sea cliffs of **Red Head** lie, the summer nesting site of guillemots, razorbills, puffins and other seabirds.

To the west of Vinquoy Hill is the **Red House Croft Restoration Project,** where you can explore the evocative remains of a large nineteenth-century farm (June–Sept Tues–Fri 10am–5pm, Sat & Sun by appointment; free; ⓣ01857/622217); there's a tearoom with a limited menu of food available (ring for evening meal). Perhaps the most unusual attraction is at the former North School, almost opposite the shop, where several internal sections of the Cold War-era **submarine** HMS. *Otter* (call in any time; free; ⓣ01857/622225) have been reassembled in the old school hall – a truly eerie experience.

Visible on the east coast is **Carrick House**, the grandest home on Eday (late June to mid-Sept Sun by appointment; ⓣ01857/622260). First built by the laird of Eday in 1633, it's best known for its associations with the pirate **John Gow** – on whom Sir Walter Scott's novel *The Pirate* is based – whose ship *The Revenge* ran aground on the Calf of Eday in 1725. He asked for help from the local laird but was taken prisoner in Carrick House, before eventually being sent off to London where he was tortured and executed. Highlight of the house is the bloodstain on the floor of the living room, where John Gow was detained and stabbed whilst trying to escape.

Eday is served by regular **car ferry** from Kirkwall (2–3 daily; 1hr 15min–2hr) or you can do a day-trip on the Wednesday **flight** from Kirkwall to Eday. The island's **ferry** terminal is at Backaland pier in the south, not ideal for visiting the more interesting northern section of the island, although if you haven't got your own transport you should find it fairly easy to get a lift with someone off the ferry. Alternatively, **car rental** and **taxis** can be organized through J&J by the pier (ⓣ01857/622206); he also runs **minibus tours** (May–Aug Mon, Wed & Fri; £12).

Eday has an SYHA-affiliated, community-run **hostel** (ⓣ01857/622283, ⓦwww.syha.org.uk), situated in an exposed spot just north of the airport – phone ahead as there's no resident warden. There's also a handful of friendly **B&Bs**, all of which offer full board. Try *Blett* (ⓣ01857/622248; ❹), a crofthouse near Carrick House, which does excellent locally sourced meals. If you fancy a drink, try the *Roadside Public House*, overlooking the ferry terminal, an evening-only **pub** which also offers B&B.

Stronsay

A low-lying, three-legged island to the southeast of Eday, **Stronsay** is strongly agricultural, its interior an almost uninterrupted collage of green pastures. The island features few real sights, but the coastline has enormous appeal: a beguiling combination of sandstone cliffs, home to several seabird colonies, interspersed with wide white sands and (in fine weather) clear turquoise bays. Stronsay has seen two economic booms in the last three hundred years. The first one took place in the eighteenth century, and employed as many as three thousand people; it was built on collecting vast quantities of seaweed and exporting the **kelp** for use in the chemical industry, particularly in making iodine, soap and glass. In the following century, **fishing** on a grand scale came to dominate life here, as Whitehall harbour became one of the main Scottish centres for the curing of herring caught by French, Dutch and Scottish boats. By the 1840s, up to four hundred boats were working out of the port, attracting hundreds of women herring-gutters. By the 1930s, however, the herring stocks had been severely depleted and the industry began a long decline.

WHITEHALL, in the north of the island, is the only real village, made up of rows of stone-built fishermen's cottages set between two large piers. Wandering along the tranquil, rather forlorn harbour front today, you'll find it hard to believe that the village once supported five thousand people in the fishing industry during the summer season, as well as a small army of coopers, coal merchants, butchers, bakers, several Italian ice-cream parlours and a cinema. It was said that, on a Sunday, you could walk across the decks of the boats all the way to **Papa Stronsay**, the tiny island that shelters Whitehall from the north. Papa Stronsay is now home to a new multi million-pound Golgotha Monastery belonging to the Roman Catholic Order of Son of the Most Holy Redeemer – they're happy to take visitors across to (and around) the island by boat, by prior arrangement (ⓣ01857/616389). The old fish market by Whitehall pier houses a small **museum**, with a few photos and artefacts from the herring days; ask at the adjacent café for access.

If the weather's fine, you can choose which of the island's many arching, dazzlingly white beaches to relax on. The most dramatic section of coastline, featuring great layered slices of sandstone, lies in the southeast corner of the island. Signposts show the way to Orkney's biggest and most dramatic natural arch, the **Vat of Kirbuster**. Before you reach the arch there's a seaweedy, shallow pool in a natural sandstone amphitheatre, where the water is warmed by the sun and kids and adults can safely wallow: close by is a rocky inlet for those who prefer colder, more adventurous swimming. You'll find progressively more nesting seabirds, including a few puffins, as you approach **Burgh Head**, further along down the coast.

Stronsay is served by a regular car **ferry** service from Kirkwall to Whitehall (2–3 daily; 1hr 40min–2hr), and **flights**, also from Kirkwall (Mon–Fri 2 daily, 1 on Sat; 25min). There's no bus service, but D.S. Peace (ⓣ01857/616335) operates taxis and offers **car rental**. Of the few **accommodation** options, a good choice is the *Stronsay Fish Mart* **hostel** (ⓣ01857/616386) in the old fish market by the pier, with a well-equipped kitchen, washing machine and comfortable bunk-bedded rooms. The pub opposite is the nicely refurbished *Stronsay Hotel* (ⓣ01857/616213, ⓦwww.stronsayhotelorkney.co.uk; ❹), which once boasted the longest bar in the north of Scotland. The hotel does good pub **food** – try the seafood taster – but otherwise you'll need to bring your own supplies and make use of the island's two shops.

Sanday

Sanday (ⓦwww.sanday.co.uk), though the largest of the northern isles, is also the most insubstantial, a great low-lying, drifting dune strung out between several rocky points. The island's sweeping aquamarine bays and vast stretches of clean white sand are the finest in Orkney, and in dry, clear weather it's a superb place to spend a day or two. The sandy soil is, in fact, very fertile, and the island remains predominantly agricultural even today, holding its very own agricultural show each year at the beginning of August. The island has a long history as a shipping hazard, with many wrecks smashed against its shores, although the construction of the **Start Point Lighthouse** in 1802 on the island's exposed eastern tip reduced the risk for seafarers. Shipwrecks were, in fact, not an unwelcome sight on Sanday, as the island has no peat, and driftwood was the only source of fuel other than cow dung – it's even said that the locals used to pray for shipwrecks in church. The present Stevenson lighthouse, which dates from 1870, now sports very natty vertical black and white stripes. It actually stands on a tidal island, accessible only either side of low tide, so ask locally for the tide times before setting out (it takes an hour to walk there and back). Better still, phone and arrange a tour (ⓣ01857/600341), which allows you to climb to the top of the lighthouse.

Sanday has particularly spectacular sand dunes to the south of the vast, shallow, tidal bay of **Cata Sand**. It's also rich in archeology, with hundreds of mostly unexcavated sites including cairns, brochs and burnt mounds. The most impressive is **Quoyness Chambered Cairn**, on the fertile farmland of Els Ness peninsula. The tomb, which dates from before 2000 BC, has been partially reconstructed, and rises to a height of around 13ft. The imposing, narrow entrance, flanked by high dry-stone walls, would originally have been roofed for the whole of the way into the thirteen-foot-long main chamber, where bones and skulls were discovered in the six small side-cells.

Ferries to Sanday arrive at Loth Pier, at the southern tip of the island, and are met by the **minibus** (Ⓣ01857/600769), which will take you to most points. The airfield is in the centre of the island and there are regular **flights** to Kirkwall (Mon–Fri 2 daily, 1 on Sat; 10min). The fishing port of **Kettletoft** is where ferries used to dock, and where you'll find the island's two **hotels** – the *Belsair* and the *Kettletoft* – both of which do decent pub food and have free wi-fi. There's a good choice of **B&Bs**: *Marygarth Manse* (Ⓣ01857/600467, Ⓦwww.bedandbreakfast-orkney.co.uk; ❷) is a nicely modernized nineteenth-century former manse near the Bay of Brough, while *Ladybank* (Ⓣ01857/600339; ❷), another converted manse, is close to the airfield. If you're on a budget, *Ayre's Rock* (Ⓣ01857/600410, Ⓦwww.ayres-rock-sanday-orkney.co.uk) is a great place to stay: a well-equipped **hostel** and **campsite** overlooking the bay, with washing and laundry facilities, a chip shop (Tues & Sat) and bike rental.

North Ronaldsay

North Ronaldsay – or "North Ron" as it's fondly known – is Orkney's most northerly island. Separated from Sanday by the treacherous waters of the North Ronaldsay Firth, it has a unique outpost atmosphere, brought about by its extreme isolation. Measuring just three miles by one and rising only 66ft above sea level, the island is almost overwhelmed by the enormity of the sky, the strength of wind and the ferocity of the sea – so much so that its very existence seems an act of tenacious defiance. With no natural harbours and precious little farmland, the islanders have been forced to make the most of what they have, and **seaweed** has played an important role in the local economy.

The island's **sheep** are a unique, tough, goat-like breed, who feed mostly on seaweed, giving their flesh a dark tone and a rich, gamey taste, and making their thick wool highly prized. A high **dry-stone dyke**, completed in the mid-nineteenth century and running the thirteen miles around the edge of the island, keeps them off the farmland, except during lambing season, when the ewes are allowed onto the pastureland. North Ronaldsay sheep are also unusual in that they can't be rounded up by sheepdogs like ordinary sheep, but scatter far and wide at some considerable speed. Instead, once a year the islanders herd the sheep communally into a series of **dry-stone punds** near Dennis Head, for clipping and dipping, in what is one of the last acts of communal farming practised in Orkney.

The most frequent visitors to the island are ornithologists, who come in considerable numbers to catch a glimpse of the rare birds who land here briefly on their spring and autumn migrations. As on Fair Isle (see p.607), there's a permanent **Bird Observatory**, which can give advice as to what birds have recently been sighted. **Holland House** – built by the Traill family who bought the island in 1727 – and the two lighthouses at Dennis Head, are the only features to interrupt the flat horizon. The attractive, stone-built **Old Beacon** was first lit in 1789, but the lantern was replaced as long ago as 1809 by the huge bauble of masonry you now see. The **New Lighthouse** (May–Sept Sun noon–5.30pm; at other times by appointment; £4; ⓣ01857/633257), designed by Alan Stevenson in 1854, half a mile to the north, is the tallest land-based lighthouse in Britain, rising to a height of over 100ft. You can climb to the top of the lighthouse, don white gloves (to protect the brass) and admire the view – on a clear day you can see Fair Isle, and even Sumburgh and Fitful Head on Shetland.

The **ferry** from Kirkwall to North Ronaldsay runs just once a week (usually Fri; 2hr 40min), though day-trips are possible on occasional Sundays between late May and early September (phone ⓣ01856/872044 for details). Your best bet is to catch a **flight** from Kirkwall (Mon–Sat 3 daily, 2 on Sun; 15min): if you stay the night on the island, you're eligible for a bargain £20 return fare. A **minibus** usually meets the ferries and planes (phone ⓣ01857/633244) and will take you off to the lighthouse. You can **stay** at the eco-friendly *Bird Observatory* (ⓣ01857/633200, ⓦwww.nrbo.f2s.com), either in an en-suite guest room or in a **hostel** bunkbed; the observatory's *Obscafé* is a sort of pub/restaurant and serves decent meals. Accommodation is also available at *Garso*, a B&B in the northeast of the island (ⓣ01857/633244, ⓔmuir886@btinternet.com; ❸). *The Burrian Inn*, to the southeast of the war memorial, is the island's small **pub**, and does hot food. **Bike rental** can be organized: phone ⓣ01857/633257.

Travel details

Buses

Orkney Mainland

Kirkwall to: Birsay (Mon–Fri 2 daily; 45min); Burwick (5 daily; 40–55min); Evie (Mon–Sat 4–5 daily; 30min); Houton (Mon–Fri 5 daily, 3 on Sat; 20–40min); Kirkwall Airport (Mon–Sat every 30min–hourly, 9 on Sun; 15min); Skara Brae (June–Aug Mon–Fri 2 daily; 1hr 15min); St Margaret's Hope (Mon–Sat hourly; 30min); Stromness (Mon–Sat hourly, 6 on Sun; 30min); Tingwall (Mon–Fri 4 daily, 2 on Sat; 30–40min).

Stromness to: Skara Brae (Mon–Fri & Sun 3–4 daily; 20min); Tingwall (Wed & Fri 2 daily; 1hr).

Ferries

Summer timetable only.

To Orkney

Aberdeen to: Kirkwall (4 weekly; 6hr).

Gill's Bay to: St Margaret's Hope (3 daily; 1hr).

John O'Groats to: Burwick (passengers only; 2–4 daily; 40min).

Lerwick to: Kirkwall (3 weekly; 5hr 30min).

Scrabster to: Stromness (2–3 daily; 1hr 30min).

Inter-island ferries

To Eday: Kirkwall–Eday (2–3 daily; 1hr 15min–2hr).

To Egilsay: Tingwall–Egilsay (3–4 daily; 50min–1hr 45min).

To Flotta: Houton–Flotta (Mon–Fri 4 daily, Sat & Sun 2–3 daily; 45min–1hr).

To Hoy: Mon–Fri 6–8 daily, Sat & Sun 2–4 daily; 35min–1hr); Stromness–Hoy (passengers only; Mon–Fri 4–5 daily, Sat & Sun 2 daily; 25min).

To North Ronaldsay: Kirkwall–North Ronaldsay (Fri; 2hr 40min).

To Papa Westray: Kirkwall–Papa Westray (Tues & Fri; 2hr 15min); Pierowall (Westray)–Papa Westray (passengers only; 3–6 daily; 25min).

To Rousay: Tingwall–Rousay (5–6 daily; 30min).

To Sanday: Kirkwall–Sanday (2 daily; 1hr 25min).

To Shapinsay: Kirkwall–Shapinsay (4–5 daily; 45min).

To Stronsay: Kirkwall–Whitehall (2 daily; 1hr 40min–2hr).

To Westray: Kirkwall–Westray (2–3 daily; 1hr 25min).

To Wyre: Rousay–Wyre (5–7 daily; 10–20min).

Inter-island flights

Kirkwall to: Eday (Wed; 8–26min); North Ronaldsay (2–3 daily; 15min); Papa Westray (Mon–Sat 2–3 daily, 1 on Sun; 12–19min); Sanday (Mon–Sat 2 daily; 10min); Stronsay (Mon–Sat 2 daily; 25min); Westray (Mon–Sat 2 daily, 1 on Sun; 12min).

Shetland

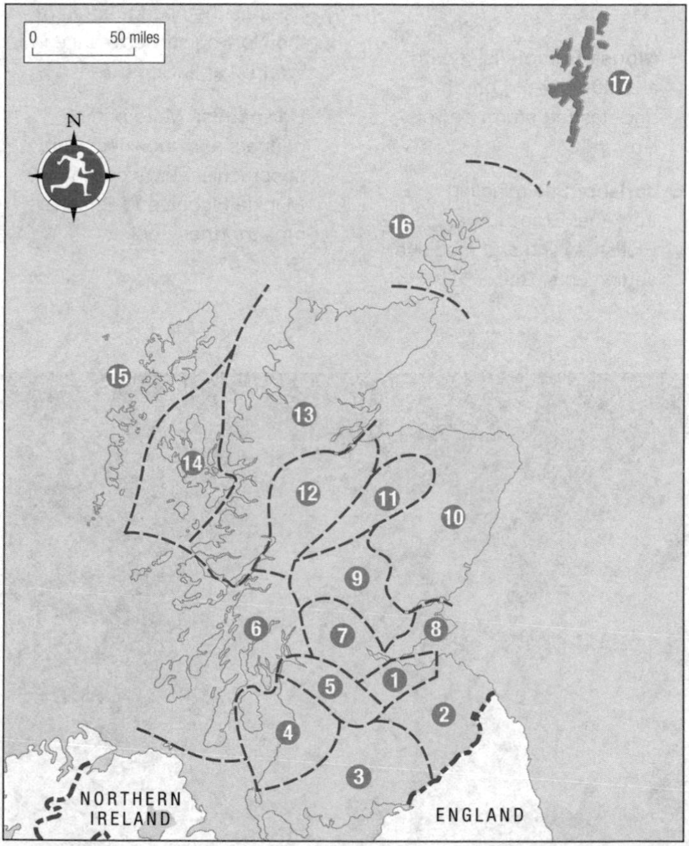

CHAPTER 17

Highlights

* **Traditional music** Catch some local music at the regular informal sessions in Lerwick, or the annual Shetland Folk Festival. See p.602
* **Isle of Noss** Guaranteed seals, puffins and dive-bombing "bonxies". See p.603
* **Mousa** Remote islet with a 2000-year-old broch and nesting storm petrels. See p.604
* **Jarlshof** Site mingling Iron Age, Bronze Age, Pictish, Viking and medieval settlements. See p.606
* **Fair Isle** Magical little island halfway between Shetland and Orkney, with a lighthouse at each end and a world-famous bird observatory in the middle. See p.607
* **Lunna House** Superb B&B in an old laird's house that was used as the headquarters of the Norwegian Resistance in World War II. See p.611
* **Hermaness** More puffins, gannets and "bonxies", and spectacular views out to Muckle Flugga and Britain's most northerly point. See p.617

▲ Folk music in Shetland

Shetland

Shetland is, in nearly all respects, a complete contrast with Orkney. Orkney lies within sight of the Scottish mainland, whereas Shetland lies beyond the horizon. Most maps plonk the islands in a box somewhere off Aberdeen, but in fact they're a lot closer to Bergen in Norway than Edinburgh, and to the Arctic Circle than Manchester. With little fertile ground, Shetlanders have traditionally been crofters rather than farmers, often looking to the sea for an uncertain living in fishing and whaling or the naval and merchant services. The 20,000 or so islanders tend to refer to themselves as Shetlanders first, and, with the Shetland flag proudly and widely displayed, they regard Scotland as a separate and quite distant entity. As in Orkney, the **Mainland** is the one in their own archipelago, not the Scottish mainland.

Most folk come here for the unique **wildlife** and **landscape**. Smoothed by the last glaciation, the coastline's crust of cliffs with caves, blowholes and stacks, testifies to the continuing battle with the weather. Inland (a relative term, since you're never more than three miles from the sea), the treeless terrain is a barren mix of moorland, often studded with peaty lochs.

The islands' capital, **Lerwick**, is a busy little port and the only town of any size; many parts of Mainland can be reached from here on a day-trip. **South Mainland**, a narrow finger of land that runs some 25 miles from Lerwick to **Sumburgh Head**, is an area rich in archeological remains, including the Iron Age **Mousa Broch** and the ancient settlement of **Jarlshof**. A further 25 miles south of Sumburgh Head is the remote but thriving **Fair Isle**, synonymous with knitwear and exceptional birdlife. The **Westside** of Mainland is bleaker and more sparsely inhabited, as is **North Mainland**. A mile off the west coast, **Papa Stour** boasts some spectacular caves and stacks; much further out are the distinctive peaks and precipitous cliffs of the remote island of **Foula**. Shetland's three **North Isles** bring Britain to a dramatic, windswept end: **Yell** has the largest population of otters in Shetland; **Fetlar** is home to the rare red-necked phalarope; north of **Unst**, there's nothing until you reach the North Pole.

It's impossible to underestimate the influence of the **weather** in these parts. In winter, gales are routine and Shetlanders take even the occasional hurricane in their stride, marking a calm fine day as "a day atween weathers". Even in the summer months, more often than not, it will be windy and rainy; though, as they say in the nearby Faroes, you can have all four seasons in one day. Of course, there are some good spells of dry, sunny weather (which often brings in sea mist) from May to September, but it's the **simmer dim**, the twilight which lingers through the small hours at this latitude, which makes Shetland summers so memorable.

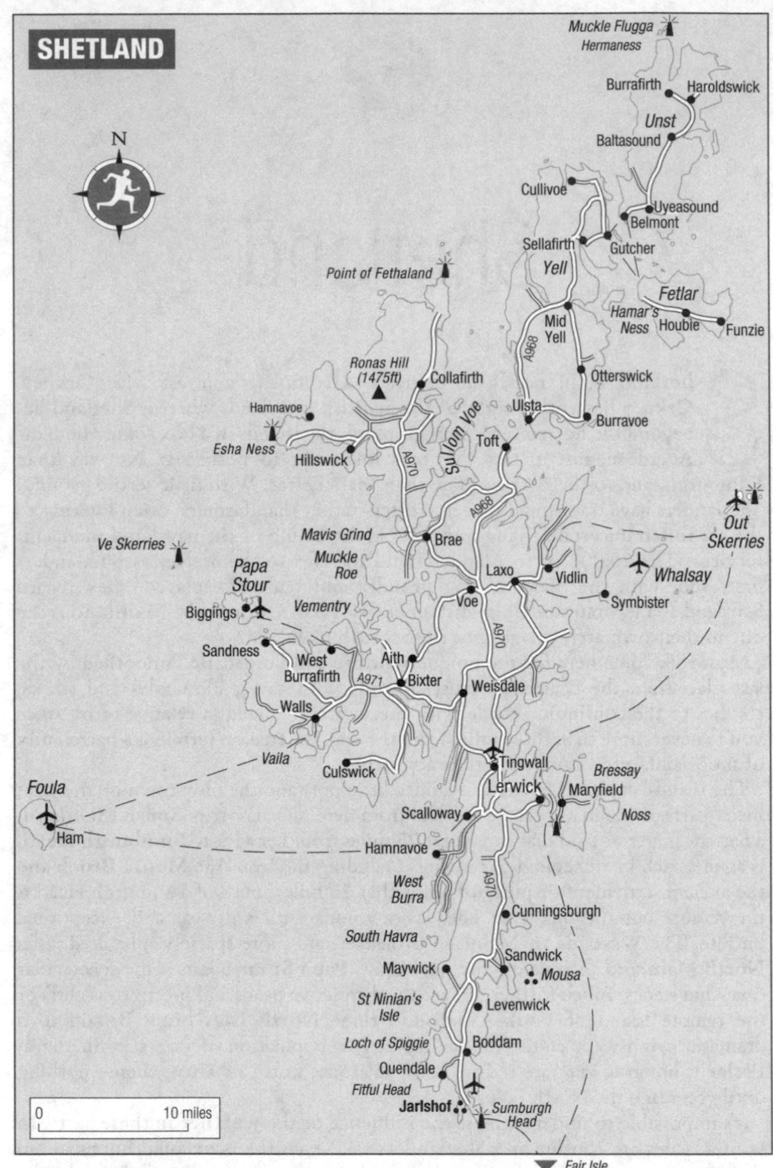

Some history

Since people first began to explore the North Atlantic, Shetland has been a stepping stone on routes between Britain, Ireland and Scandinavia, and people have lived here since **prehistoric times**, certainly from about 3500 BC. The **Norse settlers** began to arrive from about 800 AD, and established Shetland first as part of the Orkney earldom, ruling it directly from Norway after 1195.

Shetland ponies

Shetland is famous for its diminutive **ponies**, but it's still a surprise to find so many of the wee beasts on the islands. Traditionally they were used exclusively as pack animals, though a ninth-century carving on Bressay shows a hooded priest riding a very small pony, and their tails were essential for making fishing nets. During the Industrial Revolution, Shetland ponies were exported to work in the mines in England, since they were the only animals small enough to cope with the low galleries. Shetlands then became the playthings of the English upper classes (the Queen Mother was patron of the Shetland Pony Stud-Book Society) and they still enjoy the limelight at the Horse of the Year show.

The Vikings left the islands with a unique cultural character, most evident today in the place names and in the **dialect** which contains many words from **Norn**, the language spoken here until the nineteenth century (for more on Norn, see p.647).

In 1469, Shetland followed Orkney in being **mortgaged to Scotland**, King Christian I of Norway being unable to raise the dowry for the marriage of his daughter, Margaret, to King James III. The Scottish king annexed Shetland in 1472 and the mortgage was never redeemed. The islands' religious and administrative practice gradually became Scottish, and **mainland lairds** set about grabbing what land and power they could, controlling the fish trade and the tenants who supplied it through a system of truck, or forced barter.

During the two world wars, thousands of naval, army and air force personnel were drafted in and some notable relics, such as huge coastal guns, remain. **World War II** also cemented the old links with Norway, Shetland playing a remarkable role in supporting the Norwegian Resistance (see box, p.604). Since the 1970s, the **oil industry** has provided a substantial income, which the Shetland Islands Council (SIC) have wisely reinvested in the community, building roads, improving housing and keeping the price of ferry tickets down. The oil boom days are over, though, and **tourism** is slowly beginning to play a more important role in the economy. For the moment, however, comparatively few travellers make it out here, and those that do are as likely to be Faroese or Norwegian as British.

Arrival, transport and tours

NorthLink Ferries (ⓣ0845/600 0449, ⓦwww.northlinkferries.co.uk) operates a daily overnight **car ferry** from **Aberdeen** to Lerwick, either direct (12hr) or via Kirkwall (14hr). Flybe (ⓣ0870/850 9850) runs direct **flights** from several airports in Scotland to Sumburgh airport, 25 miles south of Lerwick. There are **inter-island flights** from Tingwall airport, five miles west of Lerwick, to Fair Isle, Out Skerries (via Whalsay on request), Papa Stour and Foula; some Fair Isle flights leave from Sumburgh airport. One-way fares from Tingwall to Foula or Fair Isle are around £35; be sure to book well in advance through Directflight (ⓣ01595/840246) as they're ten-seater planes, and be prepared for the flight to be cancelled due to the weather.

Public transport is pretty good in Shetland, with **buses** fanning out from Lerwick to just about every corner of Mainland, and even via ferries across to Yell and Unst. Various **tours** are also available from specialists such as Shetland Wildlife (ⓣ01950/422483, ⓦwww.shetlandwildlife.co.uk). Given the price of bringing a car on the ferry to Shetland, it's worth considering **car rental** once on the islands: Bolts Car Hire (ⓣ01595/693636, ⓦwww.boltscarhire.co.uk) or Star

Rent-a-Car (Ⓣ01595/692075, Ⓦwww.starrentacar.co.uk) all have vehicles available at Sumburgh airport and Lerwick. **Cycling** is hard going due to the almost constant wind.

The council-run **inter-island ferries** are excellent: journey times are mostly less than half an hour, and fares are kept very low. It's also possible to take **boat trips** for pleasure, to explore the coastline and spot birds, seals, porpoises, dolphins and whales; operators include Shetland Wildlife (see above), Seabirds-and-Seals (Ⓣ07595/540224, Ⓦwww.seabirds-and-seals.com) and Tom Jamieson from Sandwick for the Broch of Mousa (Ⓣ01950/431367, Ⓦwww.mousa.co.uk). The more adventurous should contact Sea Kayak Shetland (Ⓣ01595/840272, Ⓦwww.seakayakshetland.co.uk).

Lerwick

LERWICK is home to just under a third of the islands' total population and is very much the focus of Shetland's commercial life. All year, its sheltered **harbour** is busy with ferries and fishing boats, as well as specialized craft

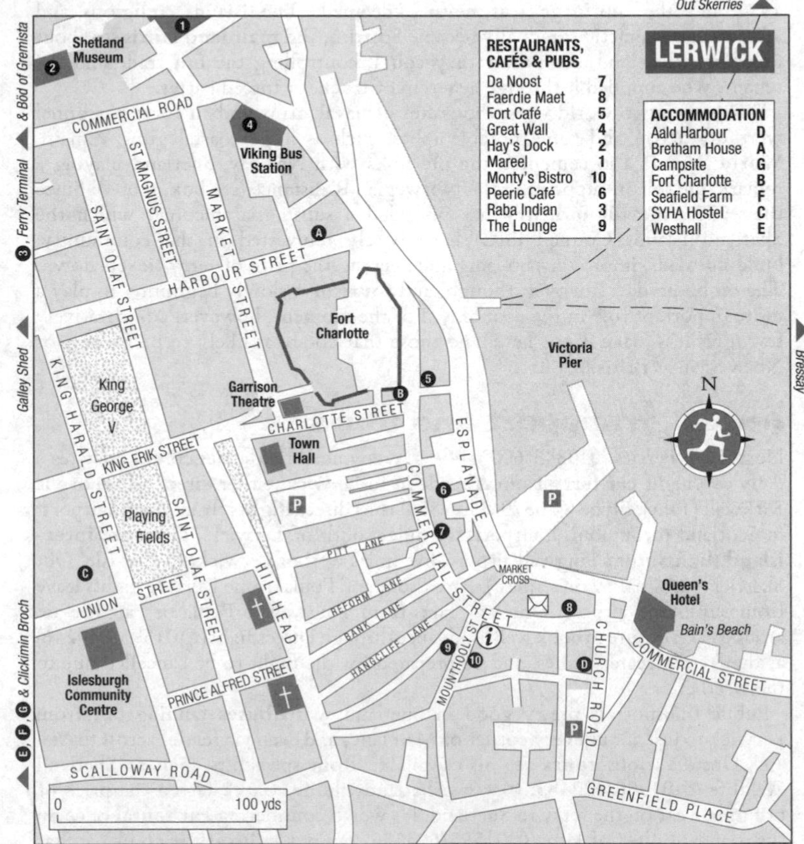

including oil-rig supply, seismic survey and naval vessels from all round the North Sea. In summer, the quayside comes alive with visiting yachts, cruise liners, historic vessels such as the restored *Swan* and the occasional tall sailing ship. Behind the old harbour is the compact town centre, made up of one long main street, Commercial Street; from here, narrow lanes, known as **closes**, rise westwards to the late-Victorian new town.

Leir Vik ("muddy bay") was established to cater for the **Dutch** herring fleet in the seventeenth century, which brought in as many as twenty thousand men during the season. Later, it became a year-round **fishing** centre, and whalers called to pick up crews on their way to the northern hunting grounds. Business was conducted from the jetties of buildings known as **lodberries** (from the Old Norse for "loading rock"), several of which survive beyond the *Queen's Hotel*. Lerwick expanded in the Victorian era, and the large houses and grand public buildings established then still dominate, notably the landmark **Town Hall**. Another period of rapid growth began during the oil boom of the 1970s, with the farmland to the southwest disappearing under a suburban sprawl, the town's northern approaches becoming an industrial estate.

Arrival and information

Lerwick's **ferry terminal** lies in the north harbour, about a mile from the town centre. **Flying** into Sumburgh Airport, you can take one of the regular buses to Lerwick; taxis (around £25) and car rental are also on hand. Buses stop on the Esplanade, very close to the old harbour, or at the Viking Bus Station on Commercial Road, north of the town centre. **Bike rental** is available from Grantfield Garage (Ⓣ01595/692709, Ⓦwww.grantfield-garage.co.uk), on Commercial Road, between the town centre and the ferry terminal.

The **tourist office**, at the Market Cross on Commercial Street (April–Oct Mon–Fri 9am–5pm, Sat & Sun 10am–4pm; Nov–March Mon–Fri 9am–5pm; Ⓣ0595/6693434, Ⓦwww.visitshetland.com), is a good source of information, and will book accommodation for a small fee.

Accommodation

Shetland's best **hotels** are not to be found in Lerwick – the town's **B&Bs** and **guesthouses** are usually better value for money, and will allow you to get closer to Shetland life.

The SYHA **hostel** (Ⓣ01595/692114; April–Sept) at Islesburgh House on King Harald Street, offers unusually comfortable surroundings and has family rooms, a café and laundry facilities. The *Clickimin* **campsite** (Ⓣ01595/741000; May–Sept) enjoys the excellent facilities of the neighbouring Leisure Complex, but its sheltered suburban location, west of the town centre, is far from idyllic.

Hotels, guesthouses and B&Bs

Aald Harbour 7 Church Rd Ⓣ01595/690870. Situated just a minute's stroll from the harbour, this is a well-run B&B with modern furnishings and very welcoming hosts. ❸

Brentham House 7 Harbour St Ⓣ01595/460201, Ⓦwww.brenthamhouse.co.uk. Spacious, newly furnished rooms in a Victorian, bay-fronted terrace; no reception, and no proper breakfast – you pick the keys up from *Baroc*, the bar a couple of doors down. ❹

Fort Charlotte Guest House 1 Charlotte St Ⓣ01595/692140, Ⓦwww.fortcharlotte.co.uk. Small guesthouse with great central location (by the fort), spacious rooms and a friendly proprietor. ❸

Seafield Farm off Sea Rd Ⓣ01595/693853. A very friendly B&B in a huge modern farmhouse overlooking the sea, a mile or so southwest of the

Böds

With only one SYHA hostel in Shetland, it's worth knowing about the islands' unique network of **camping böds** (April–Oct). Traditionally, a böd was a small building beside the shore, where fishermen used to house their gear and occasionally sleep; the word was also applied to trading posts established by Hanseatic merchants. Today, the tourist board uses the term pretty loosely: none of the places they run is strictly speaking a böd, ranging instead from stone-built cottages to weather-boarded sail lofts. To stay at a böd, you must **book in advance** (ⓣ01595/694688, ⓦwww.camping-bods.com), as there are no live-in wardens. All but one of the böds has a solid fuel stove, and all have toilets and a kitchen (though not necessarily hot water, a stove or any cooking utensils), and bunk beds with mattresses. If you're on a camping trip, they're a great way to escape the wind and rain; they're also good value, at around £6–8 per person per night. **Camping rough** is also possible in Shetland, with the landowner's permission, but make sure you're fully equipped for the Shetland wind.

town centre and therefore best for those with their own transport. ❷

Westhall Lower Sound ⓣ01595/694247, ⓦwww.bedandbreakfastlerwick.co.uk. A splendid Vcitorian mansion, known locally as the "Sheriff's Hoose", set in its own grounds a mile or so southwest of town overlooking a bay. Rooms are spacious, the breakfasts are immense and there's free wi-fi. ❺

The Town

Lerwick's attractive main street is the narrow, winding, flagstone-clad **Commercial Street**, set back one block from the Esplanade. The street's northern end is marked by the towering walls of **Fort Charlotte** (daily: June–Sept 9am–10pm; Oct–May 9am–4pm; free), which once stood directly above the beach. Begun for Charles II in 1665 during the wars with the Dutch, the fort was attacked and burnt down by the Dutch fleet in August 1673. In the 1780s it was repaired and given its name in honour of George III's queen. Since then, it's served as a prison and a Royal Navy training centre; it's now open to the public, except on rare occasions when it's used by the Territorial Army.

Although the narrow lanes or **closses** that connect the Street to Hillhead are now a desirable place to live, it was not so long ago that they were regarded as slum-like dens of iniquity, from which the better-off escaped to the Victorian new town laid out on a grid plan to the west. The new town is dominated by the splendid **Town Hall** (Mon–Thurs 9am–5pm, Fri 9am–4pm; free), a Scots Baronial monument to civic pride, built by public subscription.

Lerwick's chief tourist sight is the **Shetland Museum** (Mon–Wed, Fri & Sat 10am–5pm, Thurs 10am–7pm, Sun noon–5pm; free; ⓦwww.shetland-museum.org.uk), housed in a wonderful new purpose-built waterfront building at Hay's Dock, off Commercial Road. The permanent exhibition begins on the ground floor in the Lower Gallery, where you'll find replicas of the hoard of Pictish silver found at St Ninian's Isle (see p.605), the Monks Stone, thought to show the arrival of Christianity in Shetland, and a block of butter, tax payment for the King of Norway, found preserved in a peat bog. Kids can try grinding flour with a quern stone and visit a dark "trowie knowe" where the trows live. Among the boats, artistically suspended in the Boat Hall is a sixareen, amazingly enough, used as a mailboat to Foula. The Upper Gallery concentrates on the last two centuries of the islands' social history from knitting and whaling to the oil industry. The museum also houses Da Gadderie, which puts on temporary art exhibitions, runs the excellent *Hay's Dock* **café**, puts on events and demonstrations, and shows archive films. Meanwhile, out on the waterfront, the wacky Shetland Receivers emit snippets of Shetland conversation, as if blown in on the wind.

Clickimin Broch and the Böd of Gremista

A mile or so southwest of the town centre on the road leading to Sumburgh, the much-restored **Clickimin Broch** stands on what was once a small island in Loch Clickimin. The settlement here began as a small farmstead around 700 BC and was later enclosed by a defensive wall. The main tower served as a castle and probably rose to around 40ft, though the remains are now not much more than 10ft high.

Just beyond Lerwick's main ferry terminal, a mile and a half north of the town centre, stands the **Böd of Gremista** (May–Sept Tues–Sat 10am–1pm & 2–5pm; free), the birthplace of **Arthur Anderson** (1792–1868). The displays explore Anderson's life as beach boy (helping to cure and dry fish), naval seaman, philanthropist, Shetland's first native MP and founder of Shetland's first newspaper, the *Shetland Journal*.

Eating

Shetland produces a huge harvest of fresh fish from the surrounding seas and has its own celebrated local delicacy, *reestit* mutton: steeped in brine, then air-dried, it's the base for a potato soup cooked around New Year. Unfortunately, the **food** on offer in many of Lerwick's hotels and pubs doesn't always live up to its potential.

Cafés

Faerdie-Maet Commercial St (by the post office). Cosy café serving generously filled rolls, as well as cakes, teas, real cappuccino and good ice cream. Closed Sun.

Peerie Café Esplanade. Funky designer shop/gallery/café in an old lodberry, with a good range of cakes, soup and sandwiches, and what is probably Britain's northernmost latte. Closed Sun.

Up Helly-Aa

On the last Tuesday in January, whatever the weather, Lerwick's new town is the setting for the most spectacular part of **Up Helly-Aa**, the largest of several fire festivals held in Shetland from January to March. Around nine hundred torchbearing participants, all male and all in extraordinary costumes, march in procession behind a grand Viking longship. The annually appointed Guizer Jarl and his "squad" appear as Vikings and brandish shields and silver axes; each of the forty or so other squads is dressed for their part in the subsequent entertainment, perhaps as giant insects, space invaders or ballet dancers. Their circuitous route leads to the King George V Playing Field where, after due ceremony, all the torches are thrown into the longship, creating an enormous bonfire. A firework display follows, then the participants, known as "guizers", set off in their squads to do the rounds of more than a dozen "halls" (including the Town Hall) from around 8.30pm in the evening until 8am the next morning, performing some kind of act – usually a comedy routine – at each.

Up Helly-Aa dates from Victorian times, when it was introduced to replace the much older Christmas tradition of rolling burning tar-barrels through the streets, a practice banned in 1874. Seven years later a torchlight procession took place, which eventually developed into a full-blown Viking celebration, known as "Up Helly-Aa". Although this is essentially a community event with entry to halls by invitation only, visitors are welcome at the Town Hall – contact the tourist office well in advance. To catch some of the atmosphere of the event, check out the Up Helly-Aa exhibition in the **Galley Shed** on St Sunniva Street (mid-May to mid-Sept Tues 2–4pm & 7–9pm, Fri 7–9pm, Sat 2–4pm; £3), where you can see a full-sized longship, costumes, shields and photographs.

Restaurants

Fort Café 2 Commercial St. Lerwick's best fish-and-chip shop, situated below Fort Charlotte: takeaway or eat inside in the small café. Closed Sun lunch.

Great Wall Viking Bus Station ⓣ 01595/693988. A Chinese/Thai restaurant located above the bus station. Highly rated by the locals.

Hay's Dock Shetland Museum, Hay's Dock ⓣ01595/741569, ⓦwww.haysdock.co.uk. Bright, modern, licensed café-restaurant in the museum, with a great view over the north bay, and a short but imaginative menu of local dishes, filled bannocks and cakes. Closed Mon & Sun eve.

Monty's Bistro 5 Mounthooly St ⓣ01595/696555. Unpretentious place serving inexpensive, delicious meals and snacks at lunchtimes, and more accomplished cooking in the evening, with friendly service. Closed Sun & Mon.

Raba Indian Restaurant 26 Commercial Rd ⓣ01595/695585. A consistently excellent curry house, with cheerful, efficient service and reasonable prices.

Drinking, nightlife and entertainment

The friendliest **pub** is the upstairs bar in *The Lounge*, up Mounthooly Street, where local musicians often do sessions. The Garrison Theatre (ⓣ01595/692114) by the Town Hall, shows occasional **films** as well as putting on theatre productions, comedy acts and live gigs. There are also **informal sessions** over the summer held regularly in various venues on the islands including *The Lounge* and *Da Noost* on Commercial Street.

For details of **what's on**, listen in to BBC Radio Shetland, 92.7 FM (Mon–Fri 5.30pm), visit ⓦwww.shetland-music.com, or buy the *Shetland Times* on Fridays (ⓦwww.shetlandtoday.co.uk) from any newsagent or the excellent Shetland Times **bookshop**, opposite the post office on Commercial Street. There are numerous music festivals throughout the summer, starting in late April with the excellent four-day **Shetland Folk Festival** (ⓣ01595/694757, ⓦwww.shetlandfolkfestival.com), which embraces a wide range of musical styles, with concerts and dances in every corner of the islands.

Bressay and Noss

Shielding Lerwick from the full force of the North Sea is the island of **Bressay**, dominated at its southern end by the conical Ward Hill (744ft) – "da Wart" – and accessible in five minutes on an hourly car and passenger ferry from Lerwick. Bressay had a population of around 800, thanks to the prosperity brought by the Dutch herring fleet; now, a hundred years or so later, the population is about half that. The chief reason most visitors pass through Bressay is in order to visit **Noss** (see below). If you've time to kill before the ferry back, pop into the **Bressay Heritage Centre** (Tues, Wed, Fri & Sat 10am–4pm, Sun 11am–5pm; free), by the ferry terminal in **MARYFIELD**, where the local history group puts on temporary exhibitions, or go for a pint in the nearby hotel and pub *Maryfield House*. A Bronze Age **burnt mound** – essentially a pile of discarded rocks and charcoal used in fires – has been reconstructed next to the centre. The island's finest walk is out to **Bressay Lighthouse**, three miles south of the ferry terminal at Kirkibuster Ness, built by the Stevensons in the 1850s.

Noss

The tiny but spectacular island of **Noss** – meaning "a point of rock" – lies just off Bressay's eastern shore. Sloping gently into the sea at its western end, and plunging vertically from over 500ft at its eastern end, Noss has the dramatic and distinctive outline of a half-sunk ocean liner. The island is now a nature reserve and sheep farm, partly managed by Scottish Natural Heritage, who operate a RIB as a **ferry** from Bressay (May–Aug Tues, Wed & Fri–Sun 11am–5pm; £3 return; phone Ⓣ0800/107 7818 before setting off). The ferry departs from the landing stage two miles from Maryfield – an easy stroll or short journey on a bike. Another way to see Bressay and Noss is to join one of the **boat trips** that set out from Lerwick: try Seabirds and Seals (mid-April to mid-Sept; £40; Ⓣ07595/540224, Ⓦwww.seabirds-and-seals.com).

On the island, the old farmhouse, or Haa of Gungstie, contains a small **visitor centre**, where the warden will give you a quick briefing and a free map. Nearby is a sandy beach, while behind the haa is a **Pony Pund**, a square stone enclosure built for the breeding of Shetland ponies. As Noss is only one mile wide, it's easy enough to do an entire circumference in one day. If you do, make sure you keep close to the coast, since otherwise you're likely to be dive-bombed by the great skuas (locally known as "bonxies"). The most memorable feature of Noss is its coastline of cliffs, rising to a peak at the massive 500ft **Noup**, from which can be seen vast colonies of cliff-nesting gannets, puffins, guillemots, shags, razorbills and fulmars: a truly wonderful sight and one of the highlights of Shetland.

Central Mainland

The districts of Tingwall and Weisdale, plus the old capital of **Scalloway**, make up the **Central Mainland**, an area of minor interest in the grand scheme of things, but one that is very easy to reach from Lerwick.

Scalloway

Approaching **SCALLOWAY** from the shoulder of the steep hill to the east known as the **Scord**, there's a dramatic view over the town and the islands to the south and west. Once the capital of Shetland, Scalloway's importance waned during the eighteenth century as Lerwick, just six miles to the east, grew in trading success and status. Nowadays, Scalloway is fairly sleepy, though its harbour remains busy enough, with a small fishing fleet and the North Atlantic Fisheries College on the far side.

In spite of modern development nearby, Scalloway is dominated by the imposing shell of **Scalloway Castle**, a classic fortified tower house built with forced labour in 1600 by the infamous Earl Patrick Stewart, and thus seen as a powerful symbol of oppression. Stewart, who'd succeeded his father Robert to the earldom of Orkney and lordship of Shetland in 1592, held court in the castle and became infamous for his cruelty and corruption. He was eventually arrested and imprisoned in 1609, not for his ill-treatment of Shetlanders, but for his aggressive behaviour toward his fellow landowners; he was executed, along with his son, in 1615. The castle itself is well preserved and fun to explore; if the door is locked, the key can be borrowed from the *Scalloway Hotel* (see p.604).

On Main Street, the small **Scalloway Museum** (May–Sept Mon–Sat 10am–noon & 2–4.30pm; free), run by volunteers, holds a few local relics. It explains the importance of fishing and tells the story of the **Shetland Bus** (see box, p.604), a memorial for which stands along the harbour at Mid Shore.

The Shetland Bus

The story of the **Shetland Bus** – the link between Shetland and Norway that helped to sustain the Norwegian Resistance through the years of Nazi occupation – is quite extraordinary. Under threat of attack by enemy aircraft or naval action, small Norwegian fishing boats set out from Shetland to run arms and resistance workers into lonely fjords. The trip took at least 24 hours and on the return journey boats brought back Norwegians in danger of arrest by the Gestapo, or those who wanted to join Norwegian forces fighting with the Allies. For three years, through careful planning, the operation was remarkably successful: instructions to boats were passed in cryptic messages in BBC radio broadcasts. Local people knew what was going on, but the secret was generally well kept. In total, 350 refugees were evacuated, and more than 400 tons of arms, large amounts of explosives and 60 radio transmitters were landed in Norway.

Originally established at **Lunna** in the northeast of the Mainland, the service moved to **Scalloway** in 1942, partly because the village could offer good marine engineering facilities at Moore's Shipyard on Main Street, where a plaque records the morale-boosting visit of the Norwegian Crown Prince Olav. Many buildings in Scalloway were pressed into use to support the work: explosives and weapons were stored in the castle. **Kergord House** in Weisdale was used as a safe house and training centre for intelligence personnel and saboteurs. The hazards, tragedies and elations of the exercise are brilliantly described in David Howarth's book, *The Shetland Bus*; their legacy today is a heartfelt closeness between Shetland and Norway.

Scalloway has very little **accommodation** apart from the *Scalloway Hotel* (ⓣ01595/880444, ⓦwww.scalloway-hotel.com; ❸), on the harbour front, whose bar acts as the local pub, and serves delicious bar **food**. Alternatively, you can stay at the wood-clad *Windward* B&B (ⓣ01595/880769, ⓦwww.accommodation-shetland.co.uk; ❷), at the far western end of the bay, close to the North Atlantic Fisheries College (ⓦwww.nafc.ac.uk). The college also runs *Da Haaf* (ⓣ01595/880747), a daytime coffee bar (Mon–Fri only) serving toasted paninis and pasties, and a restaurant (Wed–Fri lunch, Thurs & Fri eve), which specialises in a wide range of fresh fish, simply prepared, with broad harbour views to enjoy as well.

South Mainland

Shetland's **South Mainland** is a long, thin finger of land, only three or four miles wide but twenty-five miles long, ending in the cliffs of **Sumburgh Head** and **Fitful Head**. It's a beautiful area with wild undulating landscapes, lots of good green farmland, fabulous views out to sea and the mother of all brochs on the island of **Mousa**, just off the east coast. The most concentrated points of interest are at the southern end of the peninsula, with its sea-bird colonies, crofting museum, and **Jarlshof**, Shetland's most impressive archeological treasure.

Mousa

Off the east coast of South Mainland, the island of **Mousa** boasts the most amazingly well-preserved broch in the whole of Scotland. Rising to more than 40ft and looking rather like a Stone Age cooling tower, **Mousa Broch** has a remarkable presence and features in both *Egil's Saga* and the *Orkneyinga Saga*, contemporary chronicles of Norse exploration and settlement. To get to the broch, simply head south from the jetty along the western coastline for about half a mile. The low entrance passage leads through two concentric walls to a central courtyard, divided into separate beehive chambers. Between the walls, a rough (very dark) staircase leads to the top parapet; a torch is provided for visitors.

A small **passenger ferry** runs to Mousa either from Aithsvoe in Cunningsburgh or Leebotten in Sandwick (April to mid-Sept; takes 25min; £13 return; ⓣ01950/431367, ⓦwww.mousaboattrips.co.uk). Thousands of **storm petrels** breed around the broch, fishing out at sea during the day and only returning to the nests after dark. The ferry runs special late-night trips (late May to mid-July Wed & Sat weather permitting), setting off in the "simmer dim" twilight around 11pm. Even if you've no interest in the storm petrels, which appear like bats as they flit about in the half-light, the chance to explore the broch at midnight is worth it alone.

St Ninian's Isle and the Crofthouse Museum

Halfway down South Mainland, a road leads to **BIGTON**, on the west coast. From the village, a signposted track heads down to a spectacular sandy causeway, or **tombolo**, connecting **St Ninian's Isle**. The tombolo – a concave strip of shell sand with Atlantic breakers crashing on either side – is usually exposed so you can walk over to the island, where you'll find the ruins of a medieval church. Excavations in the 1950s revealed **treasure** (28 objects of Pictish silver) hidden in a larch box beneath a slab in the earlier building's floor; the larch probably came from the European mainland, as it didn't grow in Britain at that time. Replicas are in the Shetland Museum in Lerwick and the originals can be seen in the Museum of Scotland in Edinburgh.

Over on the east coast, a back road winds around to the **Crofthouse Museum** (mid-April to Sept daily 10am–1pm & 2–5pm; free) in Southvoe. Housed in a well-to-do thatched croft built around 1870, the museum tries to re-create the feel of crofting life, with a peat fire, traditional box beds and so forth. Adjacent to the living quarters is the byre for the cows and tatties, and the kiln for drying the grain. Crofting was mostly done by women in Shetland, while the men went out haaf fishing for the laird. Down by the nearby burn, there's also a restored thatched horizontal mill.

Sumburgh

Shetland's southernmost parish is known as **Dunrossness** or "The Ness", a rolling agricultural landscape often compared with that of Orkney, dominated from the west by the great brooding mass of Fitful Head (929ft). The main road leads to **SUMBURGH**, whose **airport** is busy with helicopters and aircraft shuttling to and from the North Sea oilfields, as well as passenger services, and **GRUTNESS**, the minuscule ferry terminal for Fair Isle.

Extending the airport revealed a vast Iron Age archeological site known as **Old Scatness Broch & Iron Age Village** (May–Sept Mon–Thurs & Sun 10am–5pm; £4). At the centre of the site are the remains of an Iron Age broch, surrounded by a settlement of interlocking wheelhouses – so called because of their circular ground plan. Visits of the site are led by costumed guides, who will take you around the ongoing dig and inside two of the wheelhouses that have been either partially or wholly reconstructed.

The Mainland comes to a dramatic end at **Sumburgh Head** (262ft), which rises sharply out of the land only to drop vertically into the sea. The Stevenson **lighthouse**, on the top of the cliff, is not open to the public, but the road up to the lighthouse is the perfect site for watching nesting kittiwakes, fulmars, shags, razorbills and guillemots, not to mention gannets diving for fish. This is also the easiest place in Shetland to get close to **puffins**: during the nesting season (May to early Aug), you simply need to look over the western wall, just before you enter the lighthouse complex, and watch them arriving at their burrows a few yards below with beakfuls of sand eels or giving flying lessons to their offspring.

Jarlshof

Of all the archeological sites in Shetland, **Jarlshof** (April–Sept daily 9.30am–5.30pm; HS; £4.70) is the largest and most impressive. What makes Jarlshof so amazing is the fact that you can walk right into a house built 1600 years ago, which is still intact to above head height. The site is big and confusing, scattered with the ruins of buildings dating from the Stone Age to the early seventeenth century. The name, which is misleading as it is not primarily a Viking site, was coined by Sir Walter Scott, who decided to use the ruins of the Old House in his novel *The Pirate*. However, it was only at the end of the nineteenth century that the Bronze Age, Iron Age and Viking settlements you see now were discovered, after a violent storm ripped off the top layer of turf.

The Bronze Age smithy and Iron Age dwellings nearest the entrance, dating from the second and first millennia BC, are nothing compared with the cells that cluster around the **broch**, close to the sea. Only half of the original broch survives, and its courtyard is now an Iron Age aisled roundhouse, with stone piers. However, it's difficult to distinguish the broch from the later Pictish **wheelhouses** that now surround it. Still, it's all great fun to explore, as you're free to roam around the cells, checking out the in-built stone shelving, water tanks, beds and so on. Inland lies the maze of grass-topped foundations marking out the **Viking longhouses**, dating from the ninth century AD and covering a much larger area than the earlier structures. Towering over the whole complex are the ruins of the laird's house, built by Robert Stewart, Earl of Orkney and Lord of Shetland, in the late sixteenth century, and the **Old House of Sumburgh**, built by his son, Earl Patrick.

South Mainland practicalities

There are some excellent **accommodation** choices in the South Mainland, starting with *Mucklehus* (ⓣ01950/422370, ⓦwww.mucklehus.co.uk; ❸), a lovely B&B in a former Master Mariner's house built in 1890 near the beach in Levenwick, eighteen miles south of Lerwick; the rooms are small, but stylish and there's free wi-fi. Further south, there's the *Spiggie Hotel* (ⓣ01950/460409, ⓦwww.thespiggiehotel.co.uk; ❻), which has a lively bar serving real ales and a **restaurant** with great views over the Loch of Spiggie and out to Foula; both serve very reasonably priced and well-presented dishes. And a stone's throw from the *Spiggie* is the comfortable modern B&B, *Setterbrae* (ⓣ01950/460468, ⓦwww.setterbrae.co.uk; ❸). There's also a **camping böd**, *Betty Mouat's Cottage* (book on ⓣ01595/693434; April–Sept), in Scatness, close to the airport. Also at Levenwick is a small, terraced **campsite** run by the local community (May–Sept; ⓣ01950/422207), with hot showers, a tennis court and a superb view over the east coast.

Fair Isle

Fair Isle (Ⓦwww.fairisle.org.uk) measures just three miles by one and a half, marooned in the sea halfway between Shetland and Orkney and very different from both. The weather reflects its isolated position: you can almost guarantee that it'll be windy, though if you're lucky your visit might coincide with fine weather – what the islanders call "a given day". At one time Fair Isle's population was almost 400, but by the 1950s the population had shrunk to just 44, a point at which evacuation and abandonment of the island were seriously considered. **George Waterston**, who'd bought the island and set up a bird observatory in 1948, passed it into the care of the NTS in 1954 and rejuvenation began. Today, Fair Isle supports a vibrant community of around 70.

The north end of the island rises like a wall, while the Sheep Rock, a sculpted stack of rock and grass on the east side, is another dramatic feature. The croft land and the island's scattered houses are concentrated in the south, but the focus for many visitors is the **Bird Observatory**, built just above the sandy bay of North Haven where the ferry from Shetland Mainland arrives. It's one of the major European centres for ornithology, and its work in watching, trapping, recording and ringing birds goes on all year. Fair Isle is a landfall for a huge number and range of migrant birds during the spring and autumn passages. As a result, the island is a haven for twitchers, who descend on the island in planes and boats whenever a major rarity is spotted; for more casual birders, however, there's also plenty of summer resident birdlife to enjoy. The high-pitched screeching that fills the sky above the airstrip comes from hundreds of arctic terns, and arctic skuas can also be seen here. Those in search of puffins should head for the cliffs around Furse, and to find gannets, aim for the spectacular Stacks of Scroo.

Fair Isle is, of course, even better known for its **knitting** patterns, still produced with great skill by the local knitwear cooperative. There are samples on display at the island's **museum** (Mon 2–4pm, Wed 10.30am–noon, Fri 2–3.30pm; free; Ⓣ01595/760244), situated next door to the Methodist Chapel. Particularly memorable are stories of shipwrecks; in 1868 the islanders undertook a heroic rescue of all 465 German emigrants aboard the *Lessing*. More famously, the *El Gran Grifon*, part of the retreating Spanish Armada, was lost here in 1588 and three hundred Spanish seamen were washed up on the island. Food was in such short supply that fifty died of starvation before help could be summoned from Shetland. The idea that the islanders borrowed all their patterns from the shipwrecked Spanish seamen is nowadays regarded as a patronizing myth.

Practicalities

For matters of administration and transport, Fair Isle is linked to Shetland. The passenger **ferry** connects Fair Isle with either Lerwick (alternate Thurs; 4–5hr) or Grutness in Sumburgh (Tues, alternate Thurs & Sat; 3hr); since the boat only takes a limited number of passengers, it's advisable to book in advance (Ⓣ01595/760363). The crossing can be very rough at times, so if you're at all susceptible to seasickness it might be worth considering catching a **flight** from Tingwall (Mon, Wed, Fri & Sat 2 daily) or Sumburgh (Sat).

Camping is not permitted, but full-board **accommodation** is available at the *Fair Isle Lodge & Bird Observatory* (April–Oct; Ⓣ01595/760258, Ⓦwww.fairislebirdobs.co.uk; full board ❻), in en-suite doubles/twins and singles. To guests and visitors alike, the Bird Observatory offers tea, coffee and good home-cooking. There are several other **B&B**s options – all offering full board – including *Upper Leogh* (Ⓣ01595/760248; full board ❺), where you'll be well looked after by spinning and weaving expert, Kathy Coull; the *Auld Haa* (Ⓣ01595/760349; full board ❻), built for the laird in 1700 and now inhabited by an American family; and the *South Light House* (Ⓣ01595/760355, Ⓦwww.southlightfairisle.co.uk; full board ❺), not literally in the lighthouse, but in the adjacent keepers' cottages. There is a shop/post office nearby (closed Tues afternoon, Thurs & Sun).

The Westside

The western Mainland of Shetland – known as the **Westside** – stretches west from Weisdale and Voe to Sandness. Although there are some important archeological remains and wildlife here, the area's greatest appeal lies in its outstanding **coastal scenery** and walks. Cut by several deep voes, the coastline is very varied; aside from dramatic cliffs, there are intimate coves and some fine beaches, as well as, just offshore, the stunning island of **Papa Stour**.

Walls and around

WALLS (pronounced *waas*), once an important fishing port and still the main settlement on the Westside, is now a quiet village that comes alive once a year in the middle of August for the Walls Agricultural Show, the biggest farming bash on the island. It has several good **accommodation** options: the nicely restored *Voe House* (book ahead on Ⓣ01595/694688, Ⓦwww.camping-bods.com; April–Oct), the largest **camping böd** on Shetland, with its own peat fire, and the wonderfully welcoming *Skeoverick* (Ⓣ01595/809349; ❶), a lovely modern crofthouse B&B which lies a mile or so north of Walls. The only **guesthouse** in the area is *Burrastow House* (Ⓣ01595/809307, Ⓦwww.burrastowhouse.co.uk; ❺), beautifully situated about three miles southwest of Walls; parts of the house date back to 1759, and have real character, others are more modern. With fresh Shetland ingredients, and a French chef, the cooking is superb.

Three miles east of Walls lies the finest Neolithic structure in the Westside, dubbed the **Staneydale Temple** by the archeologist who excavated it because it resembled a temple on Malta. Whatever its true function, it was twice as large as the surrounding oval-shaped houses (now in ruins) and was certainly of great importance, perhaps as some kind of community centre. To reach the temple, take the path marked out by black-and-white poles across the moorland for half a mile from the road.

Papa Stour

A mile off the northwest tip of Westside is the rocky island of **Papa Stour**, created out of volcanic lava and ash, which has subsequently been eroded into some of the most impressive coastal scenery in Shetland. In good weather, it makes for a perfect day-trip, but in foul weather or a sea mist it can certainly appear pretty bleak. Its name, which means "big island of the priests", derives from its early Celtic Christian connections. The land is very fertile, and once supported around 300 inhabitants, but in the early 1970s the population crisis was such that the island had to advertise for incomers. Today, the community is down to single figures.

The chief reason to come to Papa Stour is to go **walking**; to reach the best of the coastal scenery, head for the far west of the island. From **Virda Field** (285ft), the highest point, in the far northwest, you can see the treacherous rocks of Ve Skerries, three miles or so northwest off the coast, where a lighthouse was erected as recently as 1979. The couple of miles of coastline from here southeast to Hamna Voe has some of the island's best stacks, blowholes and natural arches. Probably the most spectacular formation of all is **Kirstan's Hole**, a gloup or partly roofed cleft, which extends far inland from the cliff line, and where shags nest on precipitous ledges. Other points of interest include several pairs of red-throated divers that regularly breed on inland lochs such as Gorda Water.

The **ferry** runs from **West Burrafirth**, five miles or so north of Walls on the Westside, to the east coast of Papa Stour (Mon & Sun 1 daily, Wed, Fri & Sat 2 daily; 45min; ⓣ01957/722259) – book in advance, and reconfirm the day before departure. There are **flights** from Tingwall every Tuesday, and a day-trip is feasible; tickets cost around £40 return. The only place to stay is the small, clean, friendly **bunkhouse** (ⓣ01595/873227, ⓦwww.hurdibackhostel.co.uk; April–Sept) at Hurdiback, near the pier, where you can also camp. There's no shop, but the hostel can help with getting supplies. Alternatively, you can stay with the Leasks at *Snarraness House* (ⓣ01595/809375, ⓦwww.shetlandknitwear.com; ❷), a nicely renovated B&B with great sea views, in West Burrafirth.

Foula

Southwest of Walls, at "the edge of the world", **Foula** is without a doubt the most isolated inhabited island in the British Isles, separated from the nearest point on Mainland Shetland by about fourteen miles of often turbulent ocean. Seen from the Mainland, its distinctive mountainous form changes subtly, depending upon the vantage point, but the outline is unforgettable. Its western **cliffs**, the second highest in Britain after those of St Kilda, rise at **The Kame** to some 1220ft above sea level; a clear day at The Kame offers a magnificent panorama stretching from Unst to Fair Isle. On a bad day, the exposure is complete and the cliffs generate turbulent blasts of wind known in Shetland as "flans", which rip through the hills with tremendous force.

Foula has been inhabited since prehistoric times, and the people here take pride in their separateness from Shetland, cherishing local traditions such as the observance of the **Julian calendar**, officially dropped in Britain in 1752, where Old Yule is celebrated on January 6 and the New Year doesn't arrive until January 13. Foula was also the last place that **Norn**, the old Norse language of Orkney and Shetland, was spoken as a first language, in the eighteenth century. Foula's population, which peaked at around two hundred at the end of the nineteenth century, is now around thirty.

Arriving on Foula, you can't help but be amazed by the sheer size of the island's immense, bare mountains, whose summits are often hidden in cloud, known on the Mainland as "Foula's hat". The gentler eastern slopes provide good crofting land and plentiful peat, and it is along this "green belt" that the island's population is scattered. The island, whose name is derived from the Old Norse for "bird island", also provides a home for a quarter of a million **birds**. Arctic terns wheel overhead at the airstrip, red-throated divers can usually be seen on the island's smaller lochs, while fulmars, guillemots, razorbills, puffins and gannets cling to the rock ledges. However, it is Foula's colony of **great skuas** or "bonxies" whom you can't fail to notice. From the edge of extinction a hundred years ago, the bonxies are now thriving, with an estimated three thousand pairs on Foula, making it the largest colony in Britain. During the nesting season, they attack anyone who comes near. Although their dive-bombing antics are primarily meant as a threat, they can make walking across the island's moorland interior fairly stressful: the best advice is to hold a stick above your head or stay on the road and the coast.

Practicalities

Be sure to book and reconfirm your journey by **ferry** (Tues, Thurs & Sat; 2hr; ⓣ07881/823732, ⓦwww.atlanticferries.co.uk), which departs from Walls (or Scalloway) and arrives at Ham, in the middle of Foula's east coast. Day-trips are not possible on the regular ferry, but Cycharters (ⓣ01595/696598, ⓦwww.cycharters.co.uk) do boat trips on Wednesdays. There are also regular **flights** from Tingwall (Mon & Tues 1 daily, Wed & Fri 2 daily); tickets cost around £50 return. From mid-April to October, Foula has its own resident part-time ranger, who usually greets new arrivals and offers local advice; it's also possible to arrange for guided walks (ⓣ01595/753233, ⓦwww.foulaheritage.org.uk). The only **accommodation** on Foula is *Leraback* (ⓣ01595/753226, ⓦwww.originart.com/leraback/leraback.html; ❹), a B&B near Ham, which does full board only; they will collect you from the airstrip or pier. The island's one road runs along the eastern side of the island, and is used by Foula's remarkable fleet of clapped-out vehicles. There's no shop on the island so bring your own supplies.

North Mainland

The **North Mainland**, stretching more than thirty miles north from the central belt around Lerwick, is wilder than much of Shetland, with almost relentlessly bleak moorland and some rugged and dramatic coastal scenery. It is all but split in two by the isthmus of Mavis Grind: to the south are the districts of Delting, home to Shetland's oil terminal (Sullom Voe) and town (Brae), Lunnasting (gateway to the islands of Whalsay and Out Skerries) and Nesting; to the north is the remote region of **Northmavine**, which has some of the most scenic cliffs in Shetland.

Voe and Lunnasting

If you're travelling north, you're bound to pass by **VOE**, as it sits at the main crossroads of the North Mainland. If you stay on the main road, it's easy to miss the picturesque old village, a tight huddle of homes and workshops down below the road around the pier (and signposted Lower Voe). Set at the head of a deep, sheltered sea loch, Voe has a Scandinavian appearance, helped by the presence of the **Sail Loft**, now a large **camping böd** (book ahead on ⓣ01595/694688, ⓦwww.camping-bods.com; April–Oct); it has hot showers and a kitchen, but limited heating. Across the road, the old butcher's is now the *Pierhead Restaurant & Bar* (ⓣ01806/588332); the cosy wood-panelled **pub** has a real fire, occasional live music and offers a good bar menu, a longer version of which is on offer in the upstairs **restaurant**, featuring local scallops and the odd catch from the fishing boats.

LAXO, the ferry terminal for Whalsay (see p.612), lies two miles east of Voe. If you continue along the B9071 past the village, you'll pass **The Cabin** (April–Sept Tues, Thurs, Sat & Sun 1–5pm; free; ⓣ01806/577232), a modern barn packed to the rafters with wartime memorabilia. You can try on some of the uniforms and caps or pour over the many personal accounts of the war written by locals. Three miles or so further north, past **VIDLIN**, the departure point for the Out Skerries, is **Lunna House** (ⓣ01806/577311, ⓦwww.lunnahouse.co.uk; ❹), set above a sheltered harbour nine miles northeast of Voe. Originally built in 1660, the house is best known as the headquarters of the Shetland Bus during World War II (see p.604). It's now a wonderful **place to stay**: the bedrooms, though not en suite, have lovely views and you get a top-class breakfast.

Down the hill from *Lunna House* lies the little whitewashed **Lunna Kirk**, built in 1753, with a beautiful tiny interior that includes a carved hexagonal pulpit. Among its more peculiar features is a "lepers' squint" on the outside wall, through which those believed to have the disease could participate in the service without risk of infecting the congregation; there was, however, no leprosy here, the outcasts in fact suffering from a hereditary, non-infectious skin condition brought on by malnutrition. Several unidentified Norwegian sailors, torpedoed by the Nazis, are buried in the graveyard.

Brae and Sullom Voe

BRAE, a sprawling settlement that still has the feel of a frontier town, was expanded in some haste in the 1970s to accommodate the workforce for the **Sullom Voe Oil Terminal**, just to the northeast. During World War II Sullom Voe was home to the Norwegian Air Force and a base for RAF seaplanes. Although the oil terminal, built between 1975 and 1982, has passed its production peak, it's still the largest of its kind in Europe. Brae may not, at first sight, appear to be somewhere to spend the night, but it does have one of Shetland's better **hotels**, *Busta House* (ⓣ01806/522506, ⓦwww.bustahouse.com; ❻), a lovely laird's house with stepped gables that has been tastefully enlarged over the last four hundred years and which sits across the bay of Busta Voe from the modern sprawl of Brae. Even if you're not staying the night here, it's worth coming for afternoon tea in the Long Room, for a stroll around the lovely wooded grounds, or for a drink and a **bar meal** in the hotel's pub-like bar. A cheaper alternative is the modern crofthouse **B&B** of *Westayre* (ⓣ01806/522368, ⓦwww.westayre.shetland.co.uk; ❸), beyond Busta, overlooking a red sandy bay on the peaceful island of Muckle Roe, which is linked to the mainland by a bridge. Brae's other **food** option is *Frankie's* (ⓣ01806/522700, ⓦwww.frankiesfishandchips.com), a very popular fish and chip café with an attractive interior and views over Busta Voe.

Northmavine

Northmavine, the northwest peninsula of North Mainland, is unquestionably one of the most picturesque areas of Shetland, with its often rugged scenery, magnificent coastline and wide open spaces. The peninsula begins a mile west of Brae at **Mavis Grind**, a narrow isthmus at which it's said you can throw a stone from the Atlantic to the North Sea, or at least to Sullom Voe.

HILLSWICK, the main settlement in the area, was once a centre for deep-sea or haaf fishing, and later a herring station. Down by the harbour, **Da Böd** was founded by a Hanseatic merchant in 1684, later became Shetland's oldest pub, and is now a seal and wildlife sanctuary (ⓣ01806/503348). In 1900, the North of

Scotland, Orkney & Shetland Steam Navigation Company built the **St Magnus Hotel** to house their customers, importing it in the form of a timber kit from Norway. Despite various alterations over the years, it still stands overlooking St Magnus Bay, rather magnificently clad in black timber-framing and white weatherboarding.

If you're looking for a decent **B&B** in the vicinity, head for *Almara* (Ⓣ01806/503261, Ⓦwww.almara.shetland.co.uk; ❸), a mile or two back down the road in Upper Urafirth, which will present you with good food, a family welcome and excellent views. The nicest sandiest **beach** to collapse on is on the west side of the Hillswick isthmus, overlooking Dore Holm, a short walk across the fields from the hotel.

Esha Ness

Just outside Hillswick, a side road leads west to the exposed headland of **Esha Ness** (pronounced "*Ay*sha Ness"), celebrated for its splendid coastline views. Spectacular red-granite **cliffs**, eaten away to form fantastic shapes by the elements, are spread out before you as the road climbs away from Hillswick: in the foreground are the stacks known as **The Drongs**, off the Ness of Hillswick, while in the distance, the Westside and Papa Stour are visible. You can enjoy great views of the Drongs from *Braewick* **café** (Ⓣ01806/503345, Ⓦwww.eshaness.moonfruit.com), five miles along the road to Esha Ness, which serves sandwiches and toasties, plus fancier fare in the evening; the adjacent **campsite** is pretty exposed but you can always book into one of the four wooden wigwams if the wind gets too much.

A mile or so south, off the main road is the **Tangwick Haa Museum** (Easter–Sept daily 11am–5pm; free), housed in a seventeenth-century building, which, through photographs, old documents and fishing gear, tells the often moving story of this remote corner of Shetland and its role in the dangerous trade of deep-sea fishing and whaling. Kids and adults alike will also enjoy the shells and the Shetland wool and sand samples.

The northern branch of the road ends at the **Esha Ness Lighthouse**, a great place to view the red sandstone cliffs, stacks and blowholes of this stretch of coast. A useful information board at the lighthouse details some of the dramatic geological features here, and, if the weather's a bit rough, you should be treated to some spectacular crashing waves. One of the features to beware of at Esha Ness are the blowholes, some of which are hidden far inland. The best example is the **Holes of Scraada**, a partly roofed cleft where the sea suddenly appears 300yd inland from the cliff line. The incredible power of the sea can be seen in the various giant boulder fields above the cliffs: these **storm beaches** are formed by rocks torn from the cliffs in storms and deposited inland.

One of the few places to stay in Esha Ness is *Johnnie Notions* **camping böd** (book ahead on Ⓣ01595/694688, Ⓦwww.camping-bods.com; April–Oct; no electricity), up a turning north off the main road, in the hamlet of **HAMNAVOE**.

Whalsay and Out Skerries

The island of **Whalsay**, known in Shetland as the "Bonnie Isle", is a friendly community of more than a thousand, devoted almost entirely to fishing. The islands' crews operate a very successful pelagic fleet of immense super-trawlers that can fish far afield in all weathers and catch a wide range of species. In addition, the island is extremely fertile, but crofting takes second place to fishing here; there are also plentiful supplies of peat, which can be seen in spring and summer, stacked neatly to dry out above huge peat banks and ready to be bagged for the winter.

Ferries from the Mainland arrive at the island's chief town, **SYMBISTER**, in the southwest, whose harbour is usually dominated by the presence of several of the island's sophisticated, multimillion-pound purse-netters, some over 180ft long. Across the busy harbour from the ferry berth stands the tiny grey-granite **Pier House** (Mon–Sat 9am–1pm & 2–5pm, Sun 2–4pm; free), the key for which resides in the shop opposite. This picturesque little building, with a hoist built into one side, is thought to have been a Hanseatic merchants' store, and contains a good display on how the Germans traded salt, tobacco, spirits and cloth for Whalsay's salted, dried fish from medieval times until the eighteenth century; close by is the Harbour View house that is thought to have been a Hanseatic storehouse or booth. On a hill overlooking the town is the imposing Georgian mansion of **Symbister House**, built in the 1830s in grey granite and featuring a Neoclassical portico. It was built at great expense by Robert Bruce, not because he wanted to live on Whalsay but, so the story goes, because he wanted to deprive his heirs of his fortune. Since the 1940s it has served as the local school and, in the process, has lost some of its grandeur.

Although the majority of folk live in or around Symbister, the rest of Whalsay – which measures roughly two miles by eight – is quite evenly and fairly densely populated. Of the prehistoric remains, the most notable are the two **Bronze Age houses** on the northeastern coast of the island, half a mile south of Skaw, known respectively as the "Benie Hoose" and "Yoxie Biggins". The latter is also known as the "Standing Stones of Yoxie", due to the use of megaliths to form large sections of the walls, many of which still stand.

Car ferries run regularly to Whalsay from Laxo on the Mainland (ⓣ01806/566259; 30min) – book ahead if you have a car. In bad weather, especially southeasterly gales, the service operates from Vidlin instead. There are also request-only **flights** from Tingwall (Mon, Wed & Thurs; ⓣ01595/840246); day-trips are only possible on Thursdays. The only accommodation is at the **camping böd** of *Grieve House* in Sodom (book ahead on ⓣ01595/694688, ⓦwww.camping-bods.com; April–Oct; no electricity). The house has lovely views overlooking Linga Sound, but is hidden from the main road, so ask for directions at the shop on the brow of the hill along the road to the Loch of Huxter. A little further along the road is the *Oot Ower Lounge*, an agreeable **pub** (Fri–Sun only) overlooking the loch, and pretty much the only place to eat and drink on the island (Chinese evening meals Sat only or by arrangement; ⓣ01806/566658), and somewhere you're welcome to **camp**. The island also has an eighteen-hole **golf course**, near the airstrip in Skaw, in the northeast, several shops, and a **leisure centre** with an excellent swimming pool close to the school in Symbister.

Out Skerries

Lying four miles out to sea, off the northeast tip of Whalsay, the **Out Skerries** ("Oot Skerries" or plain "Skerries" as the locals call them), consist of three tiny low-lying rocky islands, with a population of around seventy. That people live here at all is remarkable, and that it is one of Shetland's most dynamic communities is astonishing, its affluence based on fishing from a superb, small natural harbour sheltered by all three islands, and on salmon farming in a nearby inlet. There are good, if short, walks, with a few prehistoric remains, but the majority of visitors are divers exploring the wreck-strewn coastline, and ornithologists who come here when the wind is in the east, in the hope of catching a glimpse of rare migrants.

The Skerries' jetty and airstrip are both on the middle island of **Bruray**, which also boasts their highest point, Bruray Wart (173ft), an easy climb, and one that brings you up close to the islands' ingenious spiral channel collection system for rainwater, which can become scarce in summer. The easternmost island, **Grunay**, is now uninhabited, though you can clearly see the abandoned lighthouse keepers' cottages and the Stevenson-designed lighthouse on the outlying islet of Bound Skerry. The largest of the Skerries' trio, **Housay**, has the most indented and intriguing coastline, to which you should head if the weather's fine. En route, make sure you wander through the Battle Pund stone circle, a wide ring of boulders in the island's southeastern corner.

Ferries to and from Skerries leave from Vidlin on the Mainland (Mon & Fri–Sun; 1hr 30min) and Lerwick (Tues & Thurs; 2hr 30min), but day-trips are only possible from Vidlin (Fri–Sun). Make sure you book your journey by 5pm the previous evening (Ⓣ01806/515226), or the ferry might not run. You can take your car over, but, with less than a mile of road to drive along, it's not worth it. There are also regular **flights** from Tingwall (Mon, Wed & Thurs), with day-trips possible on Thursdays. There is a shop, and a shower/toilet block by the pier, and **camping** is allowed, with permission. Alternatively, you can stay in *Rocklea* (Ⓣ01806/515228, Ⓦwww.rockleaok.co.uk; ❸), a friendly modern **B&B** on Bruray run by Mrs Johnson, who offers optional full board.

The North Isles

Many visitors never make it out to Shetland's trio of remote **North Isles**, which is a shame, as the ferry links are frequent and inexpensive, and the roads fast. Certainly, there is no dramatic shift in scenery: much of what awaits you is the familiar Shetland landscape of undulating peat moorland, dramatic coastal cliffs and silent glacial voes. However, with Lerwick that much further away, the spirit of independence and self-sufficiency in the North Isles is much more keenly felt. **Yell**, the largest of the three, is best known for its vast otter population, but is otherwise often overlooked. **Fetlar**, the smallest, is home to the rare red-necked phalarope, but **Unst** has probably the widest appeal, partly because it is the most northerly land mass in the British Isles, but also for its nesting sea-bird population.

Yell

Historically, **Yell** hasn't had good write-ups. The writer Eric Linklater described it as "dull and dark", while the Scottish historian Buchanan claimed it was "so uncouth a place that no creature can live therein, except such as are born there". Indeed, if you keep to the fast main road, which cuts across the island and links **Yell**'s two ferry terminals, you'll pass a lot of fairly uninspiring peat moorland. Get onto the minor roads, though, and you'll begin to appreciate the island and have much more chance of spotting one of Yell's large population of **otters**; locals can point out the best places to watch for them.

The island's largest village, **MID YELL**, has a couple of shops, a pub and a leisure centre with a good swimming pool, but the only sight as such is at

BURRAVOE, in the island's southeastern corner. Here, there's a lovely whitewashed laird's house dating from 1672, with crow-stepped gables, which now houses the **Old Haa Museum** (April–Sept Tues–Thurs & Sat 10am–4pm, Sun 2–5pm; free). Stuffed with artefacts, the museum has lots of material on the history of the local herring and whaling industry and there's a very pleasant wood-panelled café on the ground floor, too. From May to August, you'll find thousands of **seabirds** (including puffins) nesting in the cliffs above Ladies Hole, less than a mile to the northeast of the village.

Ferries to Yell from Toft on the Mainland are very frequent (20min). Currently, the only place to **stay** is in the *Windhouse Lodge* **camping böd** (book ahead on ⓣ01595/694688, ⓦwww.camping-bods.com; April–Oct), the gatehouse on the main road near Mid Yell; it has a wood- and peat-fired heater and hot showers. **Food** options are limited to two daytime cafés: the aforementioned museum café in Burravoe (closed Mon & Fri) offering soup, snacks and delicious home-baking, and the funky *Wind Dog Café* (ⓣ01957/744321, ⓦwww.winddogcafe.co.uk), at Gutcher, which offers internet access, as well as hosting the odd event throughout the year.

Fetlar

Fetlar is the most fertile of the North Isles, much of it grassy moorland and lush green meadows with masses of summer flowers. It's known as "the garden of Shetland", though that's pushing it a bit, as it's still, relatively speaking, an unforgiving, treeless landscape. Around nine hundred people once lived here and there might well be more than a hundred now were it not for the activities of **Sir Arthur Nicolson**, who cleared many of the people at forty days' notice to make room for sheep. Nicolson's architectural tastes were rather more eccentric than some other local tyrants; his rotting but still astonishing **Brough Lodge**, a rambling castellated composition complete with folly, built in stone and brick in the 1820s, can be seen a mile or so south of the ferry terminal. Today, Fetlar's population lives on the southern and eastern sides of the island. At the main settlement, **HOUBIE**, in the centre of the island on the south coast, there's the **Fetlar Interpretive Centre** (May–Sept Mon–Fri 11am–3pm, Sat & Sun 1–4pm; £2; ⓦwww.fetlar.com), a welcoming museum with information on Fetlar's outstanding birdlife and the archeological excavations that took place near Houbie.

Fetlar is one of very few places in Britain where you can see the graceful **red-necked phalarope** (late May–early Aug): the birds are unusual in that the female does the courting and then leaves the male in charge of incubation. A hide has been provided overlooking the marshes (or mires) to the east of the **Loch of Funzie** (pronounced "Finny"); the loch itself is also a good place at which to spot the phalaropes, and is a regular haunt of red-throated divers.

Ferries to Fetlar (25–40min) depart regularly from both Gutcher on Yell and Belmont on Unst, and dock at **Hamar's Ness**, three miles northwest of Houbie. There's no public transport on Fetlar, so if you don't have a car you should try to negotiate a lift while on the ferry. If you do have a car, bear in mind that there's no petrol station on Fetlar, so fill up before you come across. **Accommodation** is in short supply, so book ahead either at *Gord* (ⓣ01957/733227, ⓔnicboxall@btinternet.com; ❹), the comfortable modern house attached to the island shop in Houbie, which does dinner, bed and breakfast, or at the **camping böd** in Aithbank (book ahead on ⓣ01595/694688, ⓦwww.camping-bods.com; April–Oct), a cosy wood-panelled cottage, a mile east of Houbie. The folk at *Gord* also run the *Garths* **campsite** (ⓣ01957/733227;

May–Sept), a simple field just to the west of Houbie, with toilets, showers and drying facilities. The post office, shop and **café** (closed Thurs & Sun) share one building in Houbie.

Unst

Much of **Unst** (ⓦ www.unst.org) is rolling grassland – a contrast after the peaty moorland of Yell – but the coast is more dramatic: a fringe of cliffs relieved by some beautiful sandy beaches. As Britain's most northerly inhabited island, there is a surfeit of "most northerly" sights, which is fair enough, given that many visitors only come here in order to head straight for Hermaness to see the seabirds and look out over Muckle Flugga and the northernmost tip of Britain, to the North Pole beyond.

Uyeasound and Baltasound

On the south coast of the island, not far from **UYEASOUND**, lie the ruins of **Muness Castle**, a diminutive defensive structure, with matching bulging bastions and corbelled turrets at opposite corners. The castle was built in 1598 by the Scots incomer, Laurence Bruce, stepbrother and chief bullyboy of the infamous Earl Robert Stewart. The inscription above the entrance asks visitors "not to hurt this vark aluayis", but the castle was sacked by Danish pirates in 1627 and never really re-roofed.

Unst's main settlement is **BALTASOUND**, five miles north, whose herring industry used to boost the local population of around 500 to as much as 10,000 during the fishing season. As you leave Baltasound, heading north, be sure to take a look at **Bobby's bus shelter** (ⓦ www.unstbusshelter.shetland.co.uk), an eccentric, fully furnished, award-winning Shetland bus shelter on the edge of the town.

From Baltasound, the main road crosses a giant boulder field of serpentine, a greyish-green, occasionally turquoise rock found widely on Unst, which weathers to a rusty orange. The **Keen of Hamar**, east of Baltasound, and clearly signposted from the main road, is one of the largest expanses of serpentine debris in Europe and is home to an extraordinary array of plantlife. It's worth taking a walk on this barren, exposed, almost lunar landscape that's thought to resemble what most of northern Europe looked like at the end of the last ice age. With the help of one of the SNH leaflets (kept in a box by the stile), you can try to identify some of the area's numerous rare and minuscule plants, including Norwegian sandwort, frog orchid, moonwort and the mouse-eared Edmondston's chickweed, which flowers in June and July and is found nowhere else in the world.

Haroldswick and Hermaness

Beyond the Keen of Hamar, the road drops down into **HAROLDSWICK**, where near the shore you'll find the **Unst Boat Haven** (May–Sept daily 11am–5pm; £2), displaying a beautifully presented collection of historic boats with many tools of the trade and information on fishing. If you want to learn about other aspects of Unst's history, head for the nearby **Unst Heritage Centre** (May–Sept daily 11am–5pm; £2), housed in the old school building by the main crossroads. Less than a mile north of Haroldswick is **SAXA VORD** (also, confusingly, the name of the nearby hill), home to the eyesore former **Saxa Vord RAF base**, now containing a restaurant, bar and hostel, but also a chocolate factory (Mon–Sat 11.30am–5pm, Sun 1–4pm; free), where there's also an exhibition on the history of the RAF on Unst. The former base is also now home to Britain's most northerly brewery, the **Valhalla Brewery**, source of the Shetland Ales you see around the islands, which welcomes visits by appointment (Ⓣ01957/711658, Ⓦwww.valhallabrewery.co.uk).

The road that heads off northwest from Haroldswick leads eventually to the bleak headland of **Hermaness**, home to more than 100,000 nesting seabirds (May–Aug). There's an excellent **visitor centre** in the former lighthouse keepers' shore station, where you can pick up a leaflet showing the marked routes across the heather, which allow you access into the reserve. Whatever you do, stick to the path so as to avoid annoying the vast numbers of nesting great skuas. From Hermaness Hill, you can look down over the jagged rocks of the wonderfully named Vesta Skerry, Rumblings, Tipta Skerry and **Muckle Flugga**. There are few more dramatic settings for a lighthouse than Muckle Flugga, and few sites could ever have presented as great a challenge to the builders, who erected it in 1858. Beyond the lighthouse is **Out Stack**, the most northerly bit of Britain. The views from here are inevitably marvellous, as is the birdlife; there's a huge gannetry on one of the stacks, and puffins burrow all along the cliff-tops.

Practicalities

Ferries shuttle regularly across Bluemull Sound from Gutcher on Yell over to **BELMONT** on Unst (Ⓣ01957/722259; 10min). By far the most unusual **accommodation** is *Buness House* (Ⓣ01957/711315, Ⓦwww.users.zetnet.co.uk/buness-house; ❼), a seventeenth-century Haa in Baltasound still owned and run by the eccentric Edmondstons (of chickweed fame). Another very good bet is *Prestagaard* (Ⓣ01957/755234, Ⓔprestegaard@postmaster.co.uk; ❷), a modest Victorian B&B with just a couple of rooms in Uyeasound, where there's also the very handy *Gardiesfauld* (Ⓣ01957/755279, Ⓦwww.gardiesfauld.shetland.co.uk; April–Sept), a clean and modern **hostel** near the pier which allows **camping**, and offers **bike rental**. *Northern Lights* (closed Mon) is a spacious, bistro-style **café**, with views across the bay, by Unst Boat Haven in Haroldswick, while the *Skibhoul Café & Stores* has the odd chip supper night and will fill your flask. Nevertheless, wherever you stay, you should book yourself in for dinner or self-cater, rather than resort to the bar food at the *Baltasound Hotel*.

Travel details

Buses

Shetland Mainland

Lerwick to: Brae (Mon–Sat 4–6 daily; 45min); Hamnavoe (Mon–Sat 2 daily; 30min); Hillswick (Mon–Sat 1 daily; 1hr 40min); Laxo (Mon–Sat 2 daily; 40min); Scalloway (Mon–Sat hourly; 15min); Sumburgh (Mon–Sat 6–8 daily, 4 on Sun; 45min); Toft (Mon–Sat 3–5 daily; 50min); Vidlin (Mon–Sat 2 daily; 45min); Voe (Mon–Sat 5–6 daily; 35min); Walls (Mon–Sat 1–3 daily; 45min).

Unst

Baltasound to: Haroldswick (Mon–Sat 3–4 daily; 10min).
Belmont to: Baltasound (Mon–Sat 2–3 daily; 20min); Uyeasound (Mon–Sat 1–2 daily; 5min).

Yell

Mid Yell to: Gutcher (Mon–Sat 1–5 daily, 1 on Sun in school term; 20min).
Ulsta to: Burravoe (Mon–Sat 1 daily; 15min); Gutcher (Mon–Sat 1–3 daily, 1 on Sun in school term; 25min).

Ferries to Shetland

Summer timetable only.

Aberdeen to: Lerwick (daily; 12hr).

Kirkwall (Orkney) to: Lerwick (3–4 weekly; 6hr).

Inter-island ferries

Summer timetable only.

To Bressay: Lerwick–Bressay (every 30min–1hr; 7min).

To Fair Isle: Grutness–Fair Isle (Tues & alternate Thurs; 3hr); Lerwick–Fair Isle (Sat & alternate Thurs; 4–5hr).

To Fetlar: Belmont (Unst) and Gutcher (Yell)–Hamar's Ness (Mon–Sat 7–9 daily, 5 on Sun; 25–40min).

To Foula: Scalloway–Foula (Sat & alternate Thurs; 3hr 30min); Walls–Foula (Tues & alternate Thurs; 2hr).

To Out Skerries: Lerwick–Skerries (Tues & Thurs; 2hr 30min); Vidlin–Skerries (1 on Mon, Fri–Sun 3 daily; 1hr 30min).

To Papa Stour: West Burrafirth–Papa Stour (Mon & Sun 1 daily, Wed, Fri & Sat 2 daily; 40min).

To Unst: Gutcher (Yell)–Belmont (every 30–45min; 10min).

To Whalsay: Laxo–Symbister (every 45min; 30min).

To Yell: Toft–Ulsta (every 30–45min; 20min).

Inter-island flights

Summer timetable only.

Sumburgh to: Fair Isle (Sat; 15min).

Tingwall to: Fair Isle (Mon, Wed & Fri 2 daily, 1 on Sat; 25min); Foula (Mon & Tues 1 daily, Wed & Fri 2 daily; 15min); Out Skerries, calling at Whalsay on request (Mon & Wed 1 daily, Thurs 2 daily; 20min); Papa Stour (Tues 2 daily; 10min).

Contexts

Contexts

History

Scotland's colourful and compelling **history** looms large, not just for visitors to the country, but its inhabitants too. Often the nation's history has been defined either by fierce internecine conflict or epic struggles with England, yet from earliest times the influences of Ireland, Scandinavia and Continental Europe have been as important, particularly in aspects of Scotland's creative and cultural development. This has nurtured a sophistication and ambition in Scots that few associate with the land of warring clans and burning castles, peppering the country's story not just with tragic yet romantic heroes, but also notable fighters, innovators and politicians.

Prehistoric Scotland

Scotland, like the rest of prehistoric Britain, was settled by successive waves of peoples arriving from the east. These first inhabitants were **hunter-gatherers**, whose heaps of animal bones and shells have been excavated, amongst other places, in the caves along the coast near East Wemyss in Fife. Around 4500 BC, **Neolithic farming peoples** from the European mainland began moving into Scotland. To provide themselves with land for their cereal crops and grazing for their livestock, they cleared large areas of upland forest, usually by fire, and in the process created the characteristic moorland landscapes of much of modern Scotland. These early farmers established permanent settlements, some of which, like **Skara Brae** on Orkney, were near the sea, enabling them to supplement their diet by fishing and develop their skills as boat-builders. The Neolithic settlements were not as isolated as was once imagined: geological evidence has, for instance, revealed that the stone used to make axe-heads found in the Hebrides was quarried in Northern Ireland.

Settlement spurred the development of more complex forms of religious belief. The Neolithic peoples built large chambered burial mounds or **cairns**, such as **Maes Howe** in Orkney. This reverence for human remains suggests a belief in some form of afterlife, a concept that the next wave of settlers, the **Beaker people**, certainly believed in. They placed pottery beakers filled with drink in the tombs of their dead to assist the passage of the deceased on their journey to, or their stay in, the next world. The Beaker people also built the mysterious **stone circles**, thirty of which have been discovered in Scotland, including that of **Calanais** on the Isle of Lewis. The exact function of the circles is still unknown, but many of the stones are aligned with the position of the sun at certain points in its annual cycle, suggesting that the monuments are related to the changing of the seasons.

The Beaker people also brought the **Bronze Age** to Scotland. Bronze, an alloy of copper and tin, was stronger and more flexible than flint, which had long been used for axe-heads and knives. Agricultural needs plus new weaponry added up to a state of endemic warfare as villagers raided their neighbours to steal livestock and grain. The Bronze Age peoples responded to the danger by developing a range of defences, among them spectacular **hillforts** and **crannogs**, smaller settlements built on artificial islands constructed of logs, earth, stones and brush.

Conflict in Scotland intensified in the first millennium BC as successive waves of **Celtic** settlers, arriving from the south and using iron, increased competition for land. These fractious times witnessed the construction of hundreds of **brochs** or fortified towers. Concentrated along the Atlantic coast and in the northern and western isles, the brochs were dry-stone fortifications (that is, built without mortar or cement) often over 40ft in height; the best-preserved can be found on the Shetland island of **Mousa**.

At the end of the prehistoric period, immediately prior to the arrival of the Romans, Scotland was divided among a number of warring Iron Age tribes, who, apart from raiding, were preoccupied with wresting a living from the land, growing barley and oats, rearing sheep, hunting deer and fishing for salmon. The Romans were to write these people into history under the collective name Picti, or **Picts**, meaning painted people, after their body tattoos.

The Romans

The **Roman conquest** of Britain began in 43 AD. By 80 AD the Roman governor, Agricola, felt secure enough in the south of Britannia (Britain) to begin an invasion of **Caledonia** (Scotland), building a string of forts across the Clyde–Forth line and defeating the Caledonian tribes at the **Battle of Mons Graupius**. The long-term effect of his campaign, however, was slight. Work on a major fort – to be the base for 5000 soldiers – at Inchtuthill, on the Tay, was abandoned before it was finished, and the legions withdrew south. In 123 AD **Emperor Hadrian** sealed the frontier against the northern tribes and built **Hadrian's Wall**, which stretched from the Solway Firth to the Tyne and was the first formal division of the island of Britain. Twenty years later, the Romans again ventured north and built the **Antonine Wall** between the Clyde and the Forth. This was manned for about forty years, but thereafter the Romans, frustrated by the inhospitable terrain of the Highlands, largely gave up their attempt to subjugate the north and instead adopted a policy of containment.

It was the Romans who produced the first **written** accounts of Scotland. These included Greco-Egyptian geographer Ptolemy's map of Scotland, though other descriptions were less scientific, compounding the mixture of fear and contempt with which the Romans regarded their Pictish neighbours. Dio Cassius, a Roman commentator writing in 197 AD, informed his readers:

> **They live in huts, go naked and unshod. They mostly have a democratic government, and are much addicted to robbery. They can bear hunger and cold and all manner of hardship; they will retire into their marshes and hold out for days with only their heads above water, and in the forest they will subsist on barks and roots.**

The Dark Ages

In the years following the departure of the Romans, traditionally put at 410 AD, the population of Scotland changed considerably. By 500 the **Picts** occupied the northern isles, and the north and the east as far south as Fife. Today their settlements can be generally identified by place names with a "Pit" prefix, such as Pitlochry, and by the existence of carved symbol stones, like those found at Aberlemno in Angus. To the west, between Dumbarton and Carlisle, was a population of **Britons**. Many of the Briton leaders had Roman names, which suggests that they were a Romanized Celtic people, possibly a combination of tribes maintained by the Romans as a buffer between Hadrian's Wall and the northern tribes, and peoples pushed west by the Anglo-Saxon invaders landing on the east coast. Both the Britons and the Picts spoke variations of P-Celtic, from which Welsh, Cornish and Breton developed.

On the west coast, to the north and west of the Britons, lived the **Scotti**, Irish-Celtic invaders who would eventually give their name to the whole country. The

The Northern Isles

With their sophisticated ships and navigational skills, the **Vikings**, who began their expansion in the eighth century, soon gained supremacy over the Pictish peoples in Shetland, Orkney, the extreme northeast corner of the mainland and the Western Isles. For the next six centuries the Northern Isles took a path distinct from the rest of what is now called Scotland, becoming a base for raiding and colonization in much of the rest of Britain and Ireland, and a link in the chain that connected the Faroes, Iceland, Greenland and, more tenuously, North America. Norse culture flourished, and buildings such as St Magnus Cathedral in Kirkwall, Orkney, give some idea of its energy. However, there were bouts of unrest, and finally Shetland was brought under direct rule from Norway at the end of the twelfth century.

When Norway united with Sweden under the Danish Crown in the fourteenth century, **Norse power** began to wane and Scottish influence to increase. In 1469, a marriage was arranged between Margaret, daughter of the Danish King Christian I, and the future King James III of Scotland. Short of cash for her dowry, Christian mortgaged Orkney to Scotland in 1468, followed by Shetland in 1469; neither pledge was ever successfully redeemed. The laws, religion and administration of the Northern Isles became Scottish, though their Norse heritage is still very evident in place names, dialect and culture.

first Scotti arrived in the Western Isles from Ireland in the fourth century AD, and about a century later their great king, Fergus Mor, moved his base from Antrim to Dunadd, near Lochgilphead, where he founded the kingdom of Dalriada. The Scotti spoke Q-Celtic, the precursor of modern Gaelic. On the east coast, the Germanic **Anglo-Saxons** had sailed north along the coast to carve out an enclave around Dunbar in East Lothian. The final addition to the ethnic mix was also non-Celtic; from around 800 AD, **Norse** invaders began to arrive, settling mainly in the Northern Isles (see box above) and the northeast of the mainland.

Many of the Britons had been **Christians** since Roman times and it had been a Briton, St Ninian, who conducted the first missionary work among the Picts at the end of the fourth century. Attempts to convert the Picts were resumed in the sixth century by **St Columba**, who, as one of the Gaelic-speaking Scotti, demonstrated that Christianity could provide a bridge between the different tribes. Columba, who established the island of **Iona** as a centre of Christian culture, opened the way for many peaceable contacts between the Picts and Scotti. Intermarriage became commonplace and the Scotti king **Kenneth MacAlpine**, who united Dalriada and Pictland in 843, was the son of a Pictish princess (the Picts traced succession through the female line). Similarly, MacAlpine's creation of the united kingdom of **Alba**, later known as **Scotia**, was part of a process of integration rather than outright conquest. Kenneth and his successors gradually expanded their kingdom by marriage and force of arms until, by 1034, almost all of what we now call Scotland was under their rule.

The Middle Ages

The succession of **Malcolm III**, known as Canmore ("Bighead"), in 1057 marked the beginning of a period of fundamental change in Scottish society. Having spent the previous seventeen years at the English court, Malcolm sought to apply to Scotland a range of ideas he had brought back with him. He and his heirs established a secure dynasty based on succession through the male line and introduced **feudalism** into Scotland, a system that was diametrically opposed to the Gaelic system – the followers of a Gaelic king were his kindred, whereas the followers of a feudal king were vassals bought with land. The Canmores successfully feudalized much of southern and eastern Scotland by making grants to their Norman, Breton and Flemish followers but, beyond that, traditional clan-based forms of social relations persisted.

The Canmores, independent of the local nobility, who remained a military threat, also began to reform the **Church**. This development started with the efforts of **Margaret**, Malcolm III's English wife, who brought Scottish religious practices into line with those of the rest of Europe. **David I** continued the process by importing monks to found a series of monasteries, principally along the border at Kelso, Melrose, Jedburgh and Dryburgh. Similarly, the dynasty founded a series of **royal burghs**, towns such as Edinburgh, Stirling and Berwick, recognized as centres of trade. Their charters usually granted a measure of self-government, vested in the town corporation or guild, and the monarchy hoped this liberality would both encourage loyalty and increase the prosperity of the kingdom. Scotland's Gaelic-speaking clans had little influence within the burghs, and gradually Scots – a northern version of Anglo-Saxon – became the main **language** throughout the Lowlands.

In 1286 Alexander III died, and a hotly disputed succession gave **Edward I**, King of England, an opportunity to subjugate Scotland. In 1291 Edward presided over a conference where the rival claimants to the Scottish throne presented their cases. Edward chose **John Balliol** over **Robert the Bruce**, his main rival; he also obliged Balliol to pay him homage, thus turning Scotland into a vassal kingdom. Bruce refused to accept the decision, thereby continuing the conflict, and in 1295 Balliol renounced his allegiance to Edward and sided with France – the beginning of what is known as the **"Auld Alliance"**. In the conflict that followed, the Bruce family sided with the English, Balliol was defeated and imprisoned, and Edward seized control of almost all of Scotland.

Edward had shown little mercy during his conquest of Scotland – he had most of the population of Berwick massacred – and his cruelty seems to have provoked a truly national resistance. This focused on **William Wallace**, a man of relatively lowly origins who raised an army of peasants, lesser knights and townsmen that was fundamentally different to the armies raised by the nobility. Figures like Balliol, holding lands in England, France and Scotland, were part of an international aristocracy for whom warfare was merely the means by which they struggled for power. Wallace, by contrast, led proto-nationalist forces determined to expel the English from their country. Probably for that very reason Wallace never received the support of the nobility and, after a bitter ten-year campaign during which he notched up a couple of notable victories over English armies, he was betrayed and executed in London in 1305.

With Wallace out of the way, feudal intrigue resumed. In 1306 Robert the Bruce defied Edward and had himself crowned king of Scotland. Edward died the following year, but the unrest dragged on until 1314, when Bruce decisively defeated a huge English army under Edward II at the **Battle of Bannockburn**. At last Bruce was firmly in control of his kingdom, and in 1320 the Scots asserted their right to independence in a successful petition to the pope, now known as the **Declaration of Arbroath**.

In the years following Bruce's death in 1329, the Scottish monarchy gradually declined in influence. The last of the Bruce dynasty died in 1371, to be succeeded by the "Stewards", hence **Stewarts**, but thereafter a succession of Scottish rulers, culminating with James VI in 1567, came to the throne when still children. The power vacuum was filled by the nobility, whose key members exercised control as Scotland's regents. At the close of the fifteenth century, the Douglas family alone controlled Galloway, Lothian, Stirlingshire, Clydesdale

Flodden Field

In 1513, possibly the largest Scots army ever to invade England was decimated by the English at **Flodden Field**, just south of the border. The English king Henry VIII had invaded France and the Scots, under James IV, opted to stand by the Auld Alliance with France and invade England. The Scots army, numbering around 30,000, took the English strongholds of Norham, Eta and Ford before being confronted near Branxton, three miles southeast of Coldstream, by an English force of roughly equal size under the Earl of Surrey.

However, the English artillery was lighter and more manoeuvrable, and forced the Scots to come down off their advantageous position on **Branxton Hill**. Subsequently, the heavily armoured Scottish noblemen got stuck in the mud, and their over-long **pikes** and lances proved no match for the English **bills** (like a hooked halberd). English losses were heavy, but the Scots lost as many as 10,000, including the king himself, his son (an archbishop), nine earls, fourteen lords and numerous Highland clan chiefs, all of whom fought at the head of their troops. After the battle was over, James's blood-stained surcoat was sent to Henry, but his body was denied burial and no one knows what became of it.

If Bannockburn was Scotland's greatest victory over the English, and Bonnie Prince Charlie's last stand at Culloden their most noble defeat, Flodden was simply an unmitigated disaster. It became the subject of numerous songs and ballads and remains a painful memory for Scots even today. The English, meanwhile, have forgotten all about it.

and Annandale. The more vigorous monarchs of the period, notably **James I**, did their best to curb the power of such dynasties, but their efforts were usually nullified at the next regency. **James IV**, the most talented of the early Stewarts, might have restored the authority of the Crown, but his invasion of England ended in a terrible defeat for the Scots – and his own death – at the **Battle of Flodden Field** (see box above).

The reign of **Mary, Queen of Scots** (1542–67), typified the problems of the Scottish monarchy. Mary came to the throne when just one week old, and immediately caught the attention of the English king, Henry VIII, who sought, first by persuasion and then by military might, to secure her hand in marriage for his 5-year-old son, Edward. Beginning in 1544, the English launched a series of devastating attacks on Scotland, an episode Sir Walter Scott later called the "Rough Wooing", until, in the face of another English invasion in 1548, the Scots – or at least those not supporting Henry – turned to the "Auld Alliance". The French king proposed marriage between Mary and the Dauphin Francis, promising in return military assistance against the English. The six-year-old queen sailed for France in 1548, leaving her loyal nobles and their French allies in control. When she returned thirteen years later, following the death of Francis, she had to pick her way through the rival ambitions of her nobility and deal with something entirely new – the religious Reformation.

The Reformation

The **Reformation** in Scotland was a complex social process, whose threads are often hard to unravel. Nevertheless, it is quite clear that, by the end of the sixteenth century, the established Church was held in general contempt. Many members of the higher clergy regarded their relationship with the Church purely in economic terms, and forty percent of known illegitimate births (that is those subsequently legitimized) were the product of the "celibate" clergy's liaisons.

Another spur to the Scottish Reformation was the identification of Protestantism with anti-French feeling. In 1554 **Mary of Guise**, the French mother of the absent Queen Mary, had become regent, and her habit of appointing Frenchmen to high office was seen as part of an attempt to subordinate Scotland's interests to those of France. There was considerable resentment, and in 1560, with English military backing, Protestant nobles succeeded in deposing the French regent. When the Scottish Parliament assembled shortly afterwards it asserted the primacy of Protestantism by forbidding the Mass and abolishing the authority of the pope. The nobility proceeded to confiscate two-thirds of Church lands, a huge prize that did much to bolster their new beliefs.

Even without the economic incentives, Protestantism was a highly charged political doctrine. **Luther** had argued that each individual's conscience was capable of discerning God's will. This meant that a hierarchical priesthood, existing to interpret God's will, was unnecessary and that the people themselves might conclude their rulers were breaking God's laws, in which case the monarch should be opposed or even deposed. This point was made very clearly to Queen Mary by the Protestant reformer **John Knox** at their first meeting in 1561. Subjects, he told her, were not bound to obey an ungodly monarch.

Mary ducked and weaved, trying to avoid an open breach with her Protestant subjects. At the same time, she was engaged in a balancing act between the factions of the Scottish nobility. Her difficulties were exacerbated by her disastrous second marriage to **Lord Darnley**, a cruel and politically inept character, whose jealousy led to his involvement in the murder of Mary's favourite, David Rizzio, who was dragged from the queen's supper room at Holyrood and stabbed 56 times. The incident caused the Scottish Protestants more than a little unease, but they were entirely scandalized in 1567 when Darnley himself was murdered and Mary promptly married the **Earl of Bothwell**, widely believed to be the murderer. This was too much to bear, and the Scots rose in rebellion, driving Mary into exile in England at the age of just 25. The queen's illegitimate half-brother, the Earl of Moray, became regent, and her son, the infant James, was left behind to be raised a Protestant prince. Mary, meanwhile, became perceived as such a threat to the English throne that Queen Elizabeth I had her executed in 1587.

Knox could now concentrate on the organization of the reformed Church, or **Kirk**, which he envisaged as a body empowered to intervene in the daily lives of the people. **Andrew Melville**, another leading reformer, wished to push this theocratic vision further. He proposed the abolition of all traces of episcopacy – the rule of the bishops in the Church – and that the Kirk should adopt a **Presbyterian** structure, administered by a hierarchy of assemblies, part-elected and part-appointed.

The religious wars

James VI disliked Presbyterianism because its quasi-democratic structure – particularly the lack of royally appointed bishops – appeared to threaten his authority. He was, however, unable to resist the reformers until, strengthened by his installation as James I of England after Elizabeth's death in 1603, he restored the Scottish bishops in 1610. Raised in Episcopalian England, James's son **Charles I** had little understanding of Scottish reformism. He believed in the Divine Right of Kings, a concept entirely counter to Protestant thought. In 1637 Charles attempted to impose a new prayer book on the Kirk, laying down forms of worship in line with those favoured by the High Anglican Church. The reformers denounced these changes as "popery" and organized the **National Covenant**, a religious pledge "to recover the purity and liberty of the Gospel as it was established and professed".

Charles declared all the "**Covenanters**" to be rebels, but when he called a General Assembly of the Kirk, the assembly promptly abolished the episcopacy. Charles pronounced the proceedings illegal, but lack of finance stopped him from mounting an effective military campaign – whereas the Covenanters, well financed by the Kirk, assembled a proficient army under Alexander Leslie. In desperation, Charles summoned the English Parliament, the first for eleven years, hoping it would pay for an army. But, like the calling of the General Assembly, the decision was a disaster and Parliament was much keener to criticize his policies than to raise taxes. In response, Charles declared war on Parliament in 1642.

Until 1650, Scotland was ruled by the Covenanters, and the power of the Presbyterian Kirk grew considerably. Laws were passed establishing schools in every parish and, less usefully, banning trade with Catholic countries. The only effective opposition to the theocratic state came from the **Marquis of Montrose**, who had initially supported the Covenant but lined up with the king when war broke out. His army was drawn from the Highlands and Islands, where the Kirk's influence was weakest. Montrose was a gifted campaigner who won several notable victories against the Covenanters, but the reluctance of his troops to stay south of the Highland Line made it impossible for him to capitalize on his successes, and he was eventually captured and executed in 1650.

Largely confined to the peripheries of Scotland, Montrose's campaigns were a side show to the **Civil War** being waged further south. Here, the Covenanters and the English Parliamentarians faced the same royal enemy and in 1643 formed an uneasy alliance. There was, however, friction between the allies. Many Parliamentarians, including Cromwell, favoured a looser form of doctrinal control within the state Church than the Presbyterians did. They also suspected the Scots of hankering for the return of the monarchy, a suspicion confirmed when, at the invitation of the earl of Argyll, the future Charles II came back to Scotland in 1650. To regain his Scottish kingdom, Charles was obliged to renounce his father and sign the Covenant, two bitter pills taken to impress the population. In the event, the "Presbyterian restoration" was short-lived. Cromwell invaded, defeated the Scots at Dunbar and forced Charles into exile. Until the Restoration of 1660, Scotland was united with England and governed by seven commissioners.

Although the restoration of **Charles II** brought bishops back to the Kirk, they were integrated into an essentially Presbyterian structure of Kirk sessions and presbyteries, and the General Assembly, which had been abolished by Cromwell, was not re-established. More than three hundred clergymen, a third of the Scottish ministry, refused to accept the reinstatement of the bishops and were edged out of the Church, forced to hold open-air services, called **Conventicles**, which Charles did his best to suppress.

Charles II was succeeded by his brother **James VII** (James II of England), whose ardent Catholicism caused a Protestant backlash in England. In 1689, he was forced into exile in France and the throne passed to **Mary**, his Protestant daughter, and her Dutch husband, **William of Orange**. In Scotland there was a brief flurry of opposition to William when **Graham of Claverhouse**, known as "Bonnie Dundee", united the Jacobite clans against the government army at the **Battle of Killiekrankie**, just north of Pitlochry. However, the inspirational Claverhouse was killed on the point of claiming a famous victory, the clans dispersed and the threat passed. In Scotland, William and Mary restored the full Presbyterian structure and abolished bishops, though they chose not to restore the political and legal functions of the Kirk, which remained subject to parliamentary control.

The Union

From 1689 to 1697, William was at war with France, a war partly financed by Scottish taxes and partly fought by Scottish soldiers. Yet many Scots, mindful of the Auld Alliance, disapproved of the war and others suffered financially from the disruption to trade with France. There were other economic irritants too, principally the legally sanctioned monopoly that English merchants had over trade with the English colonies. This monopoly inspired the **Darien Scheme**, a plan to establish a Scottish colony in Panama. The colonists set off in 1698, but, thwarted by the opposition of both William and the English merchants, the scheme proved a miserable failure. The colony collapsed with the loss of £200,000 – an amount equal to half the value of the entire coinage in Scotland – and an angry Scottish Parliament threatened to refuse the king taxes as rioting broke out in the cities.

The situation in Scotland was further complicated by the question of the succession. Mary died without leaving an heir and, on William's death in 1702, the crown passed to her sister **Anne**, who was also childless. In response, the English Parliament secured the Protestant succession by passing the Act of Settlement, which named the Electress Sophia of Hanover as the next in line to the throne. The Act did not, however, apply in Scotland, and the English feared that the Scots would invite James Edward Stewart back from France to be their king. Consequently, Parliament appointed commissioners charged with the consideration of "proper methods towards attaining a union with Scotland". The project seemed doomed to failure when the Scottish Parliament passed the **Act of Security** in 1703, stating that Scotland would not accept a Hanoverian monarch unless they had first received guarantees protecting their religion and their trade.

Nevertheless, despite the strength of anti-English feeling, the Scottish Parliament passed the **Act of Union** by 110 votes to 69 in January 1707. Some historians have explained the vote in terms of bribery and corruption. This certainly played a part (the Duke of Hamilton, for example, switched sides at a key moment and was subsequently rewarded with an English dukedom), but there were other factors. Scottish politicians were divided between the Cavaliers – Jacobites (supporters of the Stewarts) and Episcopalians – and the Country party, whose Presbyterian members dreaded the return of the Stewarts more than they disliked the Hanoverians. There were commercial considerations too. In 1705 the English Parliament had passed the Alien Act, which threatened to impose severe penalties on cross-border trade, whereas the Union gave merchants of both countries free access to each other's markets. The Act of Union also guaranteed the Scottish legal system and the Presbyterian Kirk, and offered compensation to those who had lost money in the Darien Scheme.

Under the terms of the Act, both parliaments were to be replaced by a new British Parliament based in London, with the Scots apportioned 45 MPs and 16 peers. There were riots when the terms became known, but no sustained opposition.

The Jacobite risings

When James VII (II) was deposed he had fled to France, where he planned the reconquest of his kingdom with the support of the French king. In 1702, James's successor, William, died, and the hopes of the Stewarts passed to his cousin James, the "Old Pretender" (Pretender in the sense of having pretensions to the throne; Old to distinguish him from his son Charles, the "Young Pretender"). James's followers became known as **Jacobites**, derived from Jacobus, the Latin equivalent of James. The accession to the British throne of the Hanoverian George I, son of

The Highlands

The country that was united with England in 1707 contained three distinct cultures: in south and east Scotland, they spoke **Scots**; the local dialect in Shetland, Orkney and the far northeast, though Scots-based, contained elements of **Norn** (Old Norse); while the language of the rest of north and west Scotland, including the Hebrides, was **Gaelic**. These linguistic differences were paralleled by different forms of social organization and customs. The people of north and west Scotland were mostly **pastoralists**, moving their sheep and cattle to Highland pastures in the summer and returning to the glens in the winter. They lived in single-room dwellings, heated by a central peat fire and sometimes shared with livestock, and in hard times they would subsist on cakes made from the blood of their live cattle mixed with oatmeal. **Highlanders** supplemented their meagre income by raiding their clan neighbours and the prosperous Lowlands, whose inhabitants regarded their northern compatriots with a mixture of fear and contempt.

It would be a mistake, however, to infer from the primitive nature of Highland life that the institutions of this society had existed from time immemorial. This is especially true of the "**clan**", a term that only appears in its modern usage in the sixteenth century. In theory, the clan bound together blood relatives who shared a common ancestor, a concept clearly derived from the ancient Gaelic notion of kinship. But in practice many of the clans were of non-Gaelic origin – such as the Frasers, Sinclairs and Stewarts, all of Anglo-Norman descent – and it was the mythology of a common ancestor, rather than the actuality, that cemented the clans together. Furthermore, clans were often made up of people with a variety of surnames, and there are documented cases of individuals changing their names when they swapped allegiances.

It was not until the late seventeenth century that certain **tartans** became associated with particular clans. Previously, Highlanders wore a simple belted plaid wrapped around the body. The detailed codification of the tartan was produced by the Victorians, whose romantic vision of Highland life originated with George IV's visit to Scotland in 1822, when he appeared in an elaborate version of Highland dress, complete with flesh-coloured tights (for more on tartan, see box, p.460).

Sophia, Electress of Hanover, sparked the **Jacobite uprising of 1715**. Its timing appeared perfect. Scottish opinion was moving against the Union, which had failed to bring Scotland any tangible economic benefits. The English had also been accused of bad faith when, contrary to their pledges, they attempted to impose their legal practices on the Scots. Neither were Jacobite sentiments confined to Scotland. There were many in England who toasted the "king across the water" and showed no enthusiasm for the new German ruler. In September 1715 the fiercely Jacobite John Erskine, Earl of Mar, raised the Stewart standard at Braemar Castle. Just eight days later, he captured Perth, where he gathered an army of more than 10,000 men, drawn mostly from the Episcopalians of northeast Scotland and from the Highlands. Mar's rebellion took the government by surprise. They had only four thousand soldiers in Scotland, under the command of the Duke of Argyll, but Mar dithered until he lost the military advantage. The **Battle of Sheriffmuir** in November was indecisive, but by the time the Old Pretender arrived the following month six thousand veteran Dutch troops had reinforced Argyll. The rebellion disintegrated rapidly and James slunk back to exile in France in February 1716.

Though better known, the **Jacobite uprising of 1745**, led by James's dashing son, Charles Edward Stewart (known as "**Bonnie Prince Charlie**"), had even less chance of success. The Hanoverians had consolidated their hold on the English throne and

Lowland society was uniformly loyalist. Despite a promising start to his campaign, Charles met his match at the **Battle of Culloden**, near Inverness, in April 1746, the last set-piece battle on British soil. Outnumbered and outgunned, the Jacobites were swept from the field, with more than 1500 men killed or wounded compared to the Duke of Cumberland's 300 or so. After the battle, many of the wounded Jacobites were slaughtered, an atrocity that earned Cumberland the nickname "Butcher".

Bonnie Prince Charlie

Prince Charles Edward Stewart – better known as **Bonnie Prince Charlie** or "The Young Pretender" – was born in 1720 in Rome, where his father, "The Old Pretender", claimant to the British throne (as the son of James VII), was living in exile with his Polish wife. At the age of 25, with no knowledge of Gaelic, an imperfect grasp of English and a strong attachment to the Catholic faith, the prince set out for Scotland with two French ships, disguised as a seminarist from the Scots College in Paris. He arrived on the Hebridean island of **Eriskay** (see p.560) on July 23, 1745, with just seven companions, and was immediately implored to return to France by the clan chiefs, who were singularly unimpressed by his lack of army. Charles was unmoved and went on to raise the royal standard at **Glenfinnan** (see p.479), thus signalling the beginning of the **Jacobite uprising**. He only attracted fewer than half of the potential 20,000 clansmen who could have marched with him, and promises of support from the French and English Jacobites failed to materialize. Nevertheless, after a decisive victory over government forces at the **Battle of Prestonpans**, near Edinburgh, Charles made a spectacular advance into England, getting as far as Derby. London was in a state of panic: its shops were closed and the Bank of England, fearing a run on sterling, slowed withdrawals by paying out in sixpences. But Derby was as far as Charles got. On December 6, threatened by superior forces, the Jacobites decided to retreat to Scotland, against Charles's wishes. Pursued back to Scotland by the Duke of Cumberland, he won one last victory, at Falkirk, before the final disaster at **Culloden** (see p.463) in April 1746.

The prince spent the following five months in hiding, with a price of £30,000 on his head, and literally thousands of government troops searching for him. He certainly endured his fair share of cold and hunger whilst on the run, but the real price was paid by the Highlanders themselves, who risked their lives (and often paid for it with them) by aiding and abetting the prince. The most famous of these was, of course, 23-year-old **Flora MacDonald**, whom Charles first met on South Uist in June 1746. Flora was persuaded – either by his looks or her relatives, depending on which account you believe – to convey Charles "over the sea to Skye", disguised as an Irish servant girl by the name of Betty Burke. She was arrested just seven days after parting with the prince in Portree, and held in the Tower of London until July 1747. She went on to marry a local man, had seven children, and in 1774 emigrated to America, where her husband was taken prisoner during the American War of Independence. Flora returned to Scotland and was reunited with her husband on his release; they resettled in Skye and she died at the age of 68.

Charles eventually boarded a ship back to France in September 1746, but, despite his promises – "for all that has happened, Madam, I hope we shall meet in St James's yet" – never returned to Scotland, nor did he ever see Flora again. After mistreating a string of mistresses, he eventually got married at the age of 52 to the 19-year-old **Princess Louise of Stolberg-Gedern** in an effort to produce a Stewart heir. They had no children, and she eventually fled from his violent drunkenness; in 1788, a none-too-"bonnie" Prince Charles died in the arms of his illegitimate daughter in Rome. Bonnie Prince Charlie became a legend in his own lifetime, but it was the Victorians who really milked the myth for all its sentimentality, conveniently overlooking the fact that the real consequence of 1745 was the virtual annihilation of the Highland way of life.

In the aftermath of the uprising, the wearing of tartan, the bearing of arms and the playing of bagpipes were all banned. Rebel chiefs lost their land and the Highlands were placed under military occupation. Most significantly, the government prohibited the private armies of the chiefs, thereby effectively destroying the clan system.

The Highland Clearances

Once the clan chief was forbidden his own army, he had no need of the large tenantry that had previously been a vital military asset. Conversely, the second half of the eighteenth century saw the Highland population increase dramatically after the introduction of the easy-to-grow and nutritious **potato**. Between 1745 and 1811, the population of the Outer Hebrides, for example, rose from 13,000 to 24,500. The clan chiefs adopted different policies to deal with the new situation. Some encouraged emigration, and as many as six thousand Highlanders left for the Americas between 1800 and 1803 alone. Other landowners developed alternative forms of employment for their tenantry, mainly fishing and gathering kelp (seaweed), while others developed **sheep runs** on the Highland pastures, introducing hardy breeds like the black-faced Linton and the Cheviot. But extensive sheep farming proved incompatible with a high peasant population and many landowners decided to clear their estates of tenants, some of whom were forcibly moved to tiny plots of marginal land, where they were to farm as **crofters**.

The pace of these **Highland Clearances** accelerated after the end of the Napoleonic Wars in 1815, when the market price for kelp, fish and cattle declined, leaving sheep as the only profitable Highland product. The most notorious Clearances took place on the estates of the countess of Sutherland, who owned a million acres in northern Scotland. Between 1807 and 1821, around 15,000 people were thrown off her land, often with considerable brutality. As the dispossessed Highlanders scratched a living from the acid soils of tiny crofts, they learnt through bitter experience the limitations of the clan. Famine followed, forcing large-scale emigration to America and Canada and leaving the huge uninhabited areas found in the region today.

By no means all landowners acted cruelly or insensitively, however, and many settlements around Scotland, from Inveraray on the west coast to Portsoy in the northeast, owe their existence to so-called "improving landlords", who invested in infrastructure such as fishing harbours, decent housing and communities of sustainable size. They created a legacy not only in the built environment but also brought economic prosperity to previously disadvantaged areas. Those left crofting, on the other hand, still eked out a precarious existence, often by taking seasonal employment away from home. In 1886, in response to the social unrest, Gladstone's Liberal government passed the **Crofters' Holdings Act**, which conceded three of the crofters' demands: security of tenure, fair rents to be decided independently and the right to pass on crofts by inheritance. But Gladstone did not attempt to increase the amount of land available for crofting and shortage of land remained a major problem until the **Land Settlement Act** of 1919 made provision for the creation of new crofts. Nevertheless, the population of the Highlands has continued to decline since then, with many of the region's young people finding life more appealing, and work opportunities much greater, in the city.

Industrialization

Glasgow was the powerhouse of Scotland's **Industrial Revolution**. The passage from Glasgow to the Americas was much shorter than that from rival English ports and a lucrative transatlantic trade in tobacco had developed as early as the seventeenth century. This in turn stimulated Scottish manufacturing, since, under the terms of the Navigation Acts, Americans were not allowed to trade manufactured goods. Scottish-produced linen, paper and wrought iron were exchanged for Virginia tobacco and, when the American War of Independence disrupted the trade in the 1770s and 1780s, the Scots successfully turned to trade with the West Indies and, most important of all, to the production of cotton. In 1787, Scotland had only 19 textile mills; by 1840 there were nearly 200.

The growth of the textile industry spurred the development of other industries. In the mid-eighteenth century, the **Carron Ironworks** was founded near Falkirk, specializing in the production of military munitions. Here, the capital and expertise were English, but the location was determined by Scottish coal reserves. By 1800 it was the largest ironworks in Europe. The basis of Scotland's **shipbuilding** industry was laid as early as 1802, when the steam vessel *Charlotte Dundas* was launched on the Forth and Clyde Canal. The growth of the iron and shipbuilding industries, plus the extensive use of steam power, created a massive demand for coal, and pit shafts were sunk across the coalfields of southern Scotland.

Industrialization led to a concentration of Scotland's **population** in the central Lowlands. In 1840 one-third of the country's industrial workers lived in Lanarkshire alone, and Glasgow's population grew from 17,000 in the 1740s to more than 200,000 a century later. Such sudden growth created urban overcrowding on a massive scale and, as late as 1861, 64 percent of the entire Scottish population lived in one- or two-room houses. For most Clydesiders, "house" meant a couple of small rooms in a grim tenement building, where many of the poorest families were displaced Highlanders and Irish immigrants, with the Irish arriving in Glasgow at the rate of 1000 a week during the potato famine of the 1840s.

By the late nineteenth century a measure of prosperity had emerged from industrialization, and the well-paid Clydeside engineers went to their forges wearing bowler hats and starched collars. They were confident of the future, but their optimism was misplaced. Scotland's industries were very much geared to the export market, and after **World War I** they found conditions much changed. During the war years, when exports had been curtailed by a combination of U-boat activity and war production, new industries had developed in India and Japan, and the eastern market for Scottish goods never recovered. The postwar world also witnessed a contraction of world trade, which hit the shipbuilding industry very hard and, in turn, damaged the steel and coal industries.

These difficulties were compounded by the financial collapse of the early 1930s, and by 1932 28 percent of the Scottish workforce was unemployed. Some 400,000 Scots emigrated between 1921 and 1931, and those who stayed endured some of the worst social conditions in the British Isles. By the late 1930s, Scotland had the highest infant mortality rate in Europe, while some thirty percent of homes had no toilet or bath. There was a partial economic recovery in the mid-1930s, but high unemployment remained until the start of **World War II**.

The Labour movement

In the late eighteenth century, conditions for the labouring population varied enormously. Handloom weavers, for example, were well paid, whereas the coal miners remained serfs, bought and sold with the pits they worked in. The 1832 **Scottish Reform Act** extended the franchise to include a large proportion of the middle class, and thereafter political radicalism assumed a more distinctive working-class character, though its ideals still harked back to the American and French revolutions. During the next thirty years, as Scotland's economy prospered, skilled workers organized themselves into **craft unions**, such as the Amalgamated Society of Engineers, dedicated to negotiating improvements for their members within the status quo. Politically, the trade unions gave their allegiance to the Liberal Party, but in 1888 **Keir Hardie** left the Liberals to form the Scottish Socialist Party, which was later merged with the Independent Labour Party, founded in Bradford in 1893. Scottish socialism as represented by the ILP was ethical rather than Marxist in orientation, owing a great deal to the Kirk background of many of its members. But electoral progress was slow, partly because the Roman Catholic priesthood consistently preached against socialism.

In the early years of the twentieth century, two small Marxist groups established themselves on what became known as **Red Clydeside**: the **Socialist Labour Party**, which concentrated on workplace militancy, and the party-political **British Socialist Party**, whose most famous member was the Marxist lecturer John MacLean. During World War I (which the BSP opposed) local organizers of the SLP gained considerable influence by playing on the fears of the skilled workers, who felt their status was being undermined by the employment of unskilled workers. After the war, the influence of the shop stewards culminated in a massive campaign for the forty-hour working week. The strikes and demonstrations of the campaign, including one with 100,000 people (and the Red Flag flying) in St George's Square, Glasgow, panicked the government into sending in the troops and tanks. The rank and file had little interest in revolution, however, though many of the activists did go on to become leaders within the newly formed Communist Party of Great Britain.

The ILP, by then an affiliated part of the socialist **Labour Party**, made its electoral breakthrough in 1922, when it sent 29 Scottish MPs to Westminster. They set out with high hopes of social progress and reform, aspirations that were dashed, like trade union militancy, by the 1930s Depression. At the 1945 general election, Labour won 40 seats in Scotland and, in more recent times, the party has dominated Scottish politics. In 1955 the Conservatives had 36 Scottish MPs; by 1997 none at all, though they returned one MP in the 2005 general election and have over a dozen MSPs in the Scottish Parliament.

The ILP MPs of the 1920s combined their socialism with a brand of Scottish nationalism. In 1924, for instance, the MP James Maxton had declared his intentions to "make English-ridden, capitalist-ridden Scotland into the Scottish socialist Commonwealth". The Labour Party maintained an official policy of self-government for Scotland, endorsing home rule in 1945 and 1947, but these endorsements were made with less and less enthusiasm. In 1958 Labour abandoned the commitment altogether and adopted a unionist vision of Scotland, much to the chagrin of many Scottish activists.

Towards devolution

The **National Party of Scotland** was formed in 1928, its membership mostly drawn from the non-industrial parts of the country. Very much a mixture of practical politicians and left-leaning eccentrics, such as the poet Hugh MacDiarmid, in 1934 it merged with the right-wing Scottish Party to create the **Scottish National Party**. The SNP achieved its electoral breakthrough in 1967 when Winnie Ewing won Hamilton from Labour in a by-election. The following year the SNP won 34 percent of the vote in local government elections, and both the Labour and Conservative parties, wishing to head off the Nationalists, began to work on schemes to give Scotland a measure of self-government, the term **devolution** becoming common currency in Scottish politics.

The situation took a dynamic turn in 1974, when Labour were returned to power with a wafer-thin majority. The SNP held seven seats, which gave them considerable political leverage, and devolution was firmly on the agenda. The SNP had also run an excellent election campaign, concentrating on North Sea oil, which was now being piped ashore in significant quantities. Their two most popular slogans, "England expects ... Scotland's oil" and "Rich Scots or Poor Britons?", seemed to have caught the mood of Scotland.

In 1979 the Labour government, struggling to hold onto office, put its devolution proposals before the Scottish people in a **referendum**. The "yes" vote gained 33 percent, the "no" vote 31 percent – but the required forty percent threshold had not been reached. Not for the first time, Scottish opinion had shifted away from home rule; the reluctance to embrace it was based on uncertainty about what might follow, a concern about too many layers of government and, in some areas, a fear that the resulting assembly might be dominated by the Clydeside conurbation.

The incoming Conservative government of **Margaret Thatcher** set its face against any form of devolution. It argued that the majority of Scots had voted for parties committed to the Union – namely Labour, the Liberals and themselves – and that only a minority supported the separation advocated by the SNP. At the same time, the government asserted that any form of devolution would lead inevitably to the break-up of the United Kingdom and, therefore, that the devolution solutions put forward by other parties could not be what the Scottish people wanted, because the inescapable result would be separation.

As the Thatcher years rolled on, growing evidence from opinion polls and central and local government elections suggested that few Scottish voters accepted either this reasoning or the implication that Scots did not know what was good for them. The Conservatives' support in Scotland was further eroded by their introduction of the deeply unpopular **Poll Tax**, a form of local taxation that took little account of income. The fact that it had been imposed in Scotland a year earlier than in England and Wales was the source of further resentment.

Scotland's new political era began with the British general election of 1997, won by Tony Blair's **Labour Party**. Under the stewardship of Scottish Secretary Donald Dewar, the new Labour government moved swiftly to publish its proposals for devolution and a **referendum** was organized for that September. The electorate responded with a clear endorsement: 75 percent voted for a separate Scottish Parliament. The new parliament was given the power to initiate new legislation, and to pass bills without consulting Westminster. Within Scotland it controlled education, health and the environment, while Westminster retained control over foreign affairs, major economic and tax issues and social security.

Scotland's first-ever **general election** took place in 1999 – first ever, given that the last elected Scottish parliament in 1707 had not been under universal suffrage. The form of proportional representation adopted for the election made it unlikely that any one party would achieve an overall majority in the 129-seat assembly, and indeed the final result left Labour needing to enter into a coalition with the Liberal Democrats to achieve a governing majority. The SNP won just under 30 percent of the vote, making them the second largest party.

The coalition enjoyed two parliamentary terms, and made its mark with important decisions such as abolishing tuition fees for Scottish university students and granting state support for the elderly in care – policies to the left of the Labour programme elsewhere in the UK. Under the commanding leadership of **Alex Salmond**, however, the nationalists were able to take advantage of voter disenchantment with Labour in both Holyrood and Westminster, gaining the largest number of seats in the Scottish Parliament in 2007. Salmond formed the new government, albeit as a minority administration requiring the support of one of the other main parties to carry through meaningful legislation. While the SNP remain committed to holding a referendum on independence, Salmond is pragmatic enough to realize that the SNP has yet to gather sufficient support for the issue, hoping to win voters over with a combination of competence and freshness in the way the country is run.

Twenty-first-century Scotland

The Scottish **economy** has benefited from the general prosperity enjoyed in the UK as a whole, but the decline of **heavy industry** has been all but total, and **unemployment** has produced profound social problems in parts of Glasgow, Edinburgh and smaller towns. Meanwhile, in Orkney, Shetland and in northeast Scotland, particularly around Aberdeen, the **oil industry** – although past its boom – continues to underpin an economy which might otherwise have struggled to cope with the uncertainties of agriculture and, especially, fishing.

Though there have been encouraging signs of recent progress, the **Highlands and Islands** remain an economically fragile area that needs special measures, distance from markets being an obvious and fundamental problem. Increasingly, the local environment is seen as a major asset, and the establishment of a system of National Parks has gone some way to creating a firm framework in which tourism can develop alongside local communities and the interests of the natural world.

One aspect of Scottish life which has remained upbeat in the last decade is its **cultural life**. Individuals such as author A.L. Kennedy, classical composer James Macmillan and artist Peter Hewson, along with a plethora of pop and rock acts from Belle & Sebastian to KT Tunstall have given Scotland a substantial presence on the British arts scene. The **Gaelic** language has enjoyed a revival, with old inhibitions about writing in Scots or in Shetland dialect being laid to rest too, and much of the revival of cities such as Glasgow and Dundee is attributed to their focus on the arts. Indeed, contemporary culture is one of the healthiest aspects of Scotland today, and artists have often been able to articulate the richness of Scotland's post-devolution future with more ambition and colour than the country's frequently uninspiring politicians.

Books

Scottish writing is alive and well and so prolific that it can be difficult to keep up with it. This selection covers both classic and modern, and titles marked with ★ are particularly recommended.

Fiction

★ **Iain Banks** *The Bridge*, *The Crow Road*, *Espedair Street*, *A Song of Stone*, *The Wasp Factory*, *Dead Air, The Steep Approach to Garbadale*. Just a few titles by this astonishingly prolific author, who also writes sci-fi as Iain M. Banks. His work can be funny, pacy, thought-provoking, imaginative and downright disgusting, but it is never dull.

Christopher Brookmyre *One Fine Day In the Middle of the Night*, *The Sacred Art of Stealing*, *A Tale Etched in Blood and Hard Black Pencil*. All very funny, inventive novels that refuse to be categorized – you'll probably find them in the crime section, but they're as much politico-satirical.

John Buchan *The Complete Richard Hannay*. This single volume includes *The 39 Steps*, *Greenmantle*, *Mr Standfast*, *The Three Hostages* and *The Island of Sheep*. Good gung-ho stories with a great feel for the Scottish landscape. Less well known, but better, are Buchan's historical romances such as *Midwinter*, a Jacobite thriller, and *Witchwood* (audio only), a tale of religious strife in the seventeenth century.

Anne Donovan *Hieroglyphics,* her first collection of short stories, and *Budda Da*, her first hilarious novel, were both nominated for major prizes, and rightly so. Her latest novel, *Being Emily*, is about growing up in Glasgow.

★ **Lewis Grassic Gibbon** *A Scots Quair.* A landmark trilogy set in northeast Scotland during and after World War I, the events seen through the eyes of Chris Guthrie, torn between her love for the land and her desire to escape a peasant culture.

Alasdair Gray *Lanark: A Life in Four Books*. A postmodern blend of social realism and labyrinthine fantasy. Gray's extraordinary debut as a novelist, featuring his own allegorical illustrations, takes invention and comprehension to their limits.

★ **Neil M. Gunn** *The Silver Darlings*. Probably Gunn's most representative and best-known book, evocatively set on the northeast coast and telling the story of herring fishermen during the great years of the industry.

James Hogg *The Private Memoirs and Confessions of a Justified Sinner*. Complex, dark mid-nineteenth-century novel dealing with possession, myth and folklore, looking at the confession of an Edinburgh murderer from three different points of view.

Jackie Kay *Trumpet*. The protagonist is dead before the novel begins. He was a black Scottish jazz trumpeter, who left a wife in mourning and a son in deep shock, for the posthumous medical report revealed him to be a woman. Kay is also a poet – see p.638.

James Kelman *Busconductor Hines*. The wildly funny story of a young Glasgow bus conductor with an intensely boring job and a limitless imagination. *How Late it Was, How Late* is Kelman's Booker Prize-winning and disturbing look at life as seen through the eyes of a foul-mouthed, blind Glaswegian drunk.

A.L. Kennedy *Looking for the Possible Dance*. This talented writer dissects the difficulties of human relationships on a personal and wider social level. More recent novels *So I Am Glad*, *Original Bliss* and *Paradise* have the same deft touch, as do her collections of short stories, *Indelible Acts* and *What Becomes*.

Alexander McCall Smith *The Sunday Philosophy Club*. Set in middle-class Edinburgh, this is the first of a series of gentle novels with an erudite amateur sleuth.

George Mackay Brown *Beside the Ocean of Time*. A child's journey through the history of an Orkney island, and an adult's effort to make sense of the place's secrets in the late twentieth century. *Magnus* is his retelling of the death of St Magnus with parallels for modern times.

Naomi Mitchison *The Bull Calves* is set in 1747 and comments on the terrible after-effects of Jacobite rebellion. *Lobster on the Agenda*, written in 1952, closely mirrors contemporary life in Kyntyre where Mitchison lived.

Ian Rankin *The Hanging Garden, The Falls* and *Fleshmarket Close*. Superbly plotted dark stories featuring Rebus, the famous maverick police detective who haunts the bars of Edinburgh. Now a TV series and the subject of a guided tour in the city (see p.67).

Dorothy L. Sayers *Five Red Herrings*. A complicated tale involving railway timetables set in Gatehouse of Fleet in Galloway, but solved by Lord Peter Wimsey.

Sir Walter Scott *The Waverley Novels*. The books that did much to create the romanticized version of Scottish life and history.

Muriel Spark *The Prime of Miss Jean Brodie*. Wonderful evocation of middle-class Edinburgh life and aspirations.

Robert Louis Stevenson *Dr Jekyll and Mr Hyde, The Master of Ballantrae, Weir of Hermiston*. Nineteenth-century tales of intrigue and adventure.

Alan Warner *Morvern Callar*. Bleakly humorous story of a supermarket shelf-packer from Oban who finds her boyfriend has committed suicide in her kitchen. It'll grip you. *The Sopranos* tells what happens to five teenage convent choir girls when they go to Edinburgh for a competition, full of an explosive mixture of adolescent sexuality and naivety. Its sequel, *The Stars in the Bright Sky*, sees them off on holiday.

Irvine Welsh *Irvine Welsh Omnibus*. A compendium including *Trainspotting*, *The Acid House* and *Marabou Stork Nightmares*, all of which can also be found as separate titles. Welsh trawls through the horrors of drug addiction, sexual fantasy, urban decay and hopeless youth but, thankfully, his unflinching attention is not without humour.

Poetry

Robert Burns *Selected Poems*. Scotland's most famous bard (see p.192). Immensely popular all over the world, his best-known works are his earlier ones, including *Auld Lang Syne* and *My Love Is Like A Red, Red Rose*.

Douglas Dunn *New Selected Poems 1964–99*. A writer of delicately wrought poetry, ranging from the intensely private to poems involved with Scottish issues.

Kathleen Jamie *The Queen of Sheba, The Donkey's Ears* and *Jizzen*. Although often set in Scotland, her work has a wider significance; its tone is strong, almost angry, and its themes both personal and universal. *Findings* is a prose journal of her travels around her native Scotland.

Jackie Kay *The Adoption Papers, Other Lovers* and *Life Mask*. Her poetry explores being black, Scottish and gay and deals with personal relationships in an accessibly intimate way.

Liz Lochhead *Bagpipe Muzak*. In a strong straightforward style, coupled with shrewd observations, Lochhead speaks with immediacy on personal relationships. Some of her best work is in *Dreaming Frankenstein & Collected Poems*.

Norman MacCaig *Selected Poems*. Justly celebrated for its keen observation of the natural world, MacCaig's work remains intellectually challenging without being arid. His poetry, rooted in the Highlands, uses detail to explore a universal landscape.

Hugh MacDiarmid *Selected Poems*. Immensely influential, not least for his nationalist views and use of Scots, MacDiarmid's poetry is richly challenging. His poem *A Drunk Man Looks at a Thistle* is acknowledged as a masterpiece of Scottish literature.

George Mackay Brown *Collected Poems*. Brown's work is as haunting, beautiful and gritty as the Orkney islands that inspire it. *Travellers*, published posthumously, features work either previously unpublished or which had appeared only in newspapers and periodicals.

Sorley Maclean (Somhairle Macgill-Eain) *From Wood to Ridge: Collected Poems*. Written in Gaelic, his poems have been translated in bilingual editions all over the world, and deal with the sorrows of poverty, war and love.

McMillan and Byrne (eds) *Modern Scottish Women Poets*. The work of more than a hundred women writers of the twentieth century, some of whom have sunk into undeserved oblivion.

Edwin Morgan *New Selected Poems*. A love of words and their sounds is evident in Morgan's poems, which are refreshingly varied and often experimental, commenting on the Scottish scene with shrewdness and humour.

Edwin Muir *Collected Poems*. Muir's idyllic childhood on Orkney at the turn of the century remained with him as a dream of paradise in contrast to his later life in inhospitable Glasgow. His poems are passionately concerned with Scotland.

Don Paterson *God's Gift to Women, Landing Light* and *Nil Nil*. A writer whose work increasingly commands respect for its moving honesty.

Iain Crichton Smith *Collected Poems*. Born on the Isle of Lewis, Crichton Smith wrote with feeling and sometimes bitterness, in both Gaelic and English, of the life of the rural communities, the iniquities of the Free Church, the need to revive Gaelic culture and the glory of the Scottish landscape.

History, politics and culture

Neal Ascherson *Stone Voices*. Intelligent, thought-provoking ponderings on the nature of Scotland and the road to devolution, interspersed with personal anecdotes.

Bella Bathurst *The Lighthouse Stevensons*. Straightforward account of the fascinating lives and amazing achievements of Robert Louis Stevenson's family, who built many of the island lighthouses round Scotland.

Colin Bell *Scotland's Century – An Autobiography of the Nation*. Richly illustrated and readable account of the social history of Scotland, based on radio interviews with people from all walks of life.

Tom Devine *The Scottish Nation 1700–2000*. The best post-Union history, from the last Scottish Parliament to the new one.

David Howarth *The Shetland Bus*. Wonderfully detailed story of the espionage and resistance operations carried out from Shetland by British and Norwegian servicemen, written by someone who was directly involved.

Fitzroy Maclean *Bonnie Prince Charlie*. Very readable and more or less definitive biography of Scotland's most romanticized historical figure, written by the "real" James Bond.

Alistair Moffat *Border Reivers*. A vivid account of nearly 300 years of savage raiding and mayhem which makes us look at the now peaceful area with different eyes.

John Prebble *Glencoe*, *Culloden*, *The Highland Clearances*. Emotive, subjective and accessible accounts of key events in Highland history.

T.C. Smout *A History of the Scottish People 1560–1830* and *A Century of the Scottish People 1830–1950*. Widely acclaimed books, of particular interest to those keen on social history. Smout combines enormous learning with a clear and entertaining style.

Art, architecture and historic sites

Jude Burkhauser *Glasgow Girls: Women in Art and Design 1880–1920*. The lively contribution of women to the development of the Glaswegian Art Nouveau movement is recognized in this authoritative account.

Alan Crawford *Charles Rennie Mackintosh*. Part of the World of Art series, describing the major contribution of Scotland's premier architect and designer.

Philip Long and Elizabeth Cumming *The Scottish Colourists 1900–30*. A recognition of the importance of the work of this group of artists; lavishly illustrated.

Duncan MacMillan *Scottish Art 1460–1990*. Overview of Scottish painting with good sections on landscape, portraiture and the Glasgow Boys. *Scottish Art in the 20th Century 1890–2001* offers a detailed look at modern art.

Steven Parissien *Adam Style*. A well-illustrated account of the birth of the Neoclassical style, named for the two Scottish Adam brothers, Robert and James.

Memoirs and travelogues

Elizabeth Grant of Rothiemurchus *Memoirs of a Highland Lady*. Hugely readable recollections written with wit and perception at the turn of the eighteenth century, charting social changes in Edinburgh, London and Speyside.

Hamish Haswell-Smith *The Scottish Islands*. An exhaustive and impressive gazetteer with maps and absorbing information on all the Scottish islands. Filled with attractive sketches and paintings, the book is breathtaking in its thoroughness and lovingly gathered detail.

Peter Hill *Stargazing*. Engaging account of being a tyro lighthouse keeper on three of Scotland's most famous lighthouses: Pladda, Ailsa Craig and Hyskeir.

Samuel Johnson and James Boswell *A Journey to the Western Isles of Scotland* and *The Journal of a Tour to the Hebrides*. Lively accounts of a famous journey around the islands taken by the great lexicographer Dr Samuel Johnson and his biographer and friend James Boswell.

John Lister-Kaye *Song of the Rolling Earth*. The author tells what led him to become a passionate naturalist and turn a derelict Highland estate into a field study centre where he encourages others to live in harmony with the natural environment. An inspiring story.

George Mackay Brown *Letters from Hamnavoe*. A selection of writings from a weekly column in *The Orcadian*, chronicling everyday life in Orkney during the early 1970s. Gentle and perceptive.

Alasdair MacLean *Night Falls on Ardnamurchan*. A classic story of the life and death of the Highland community in which the author grew up.

Iain Mitchell *Isles of the West, Isles of the North*. In the first book, Mitchell sails round the Inner Hebrides, talking to locals and incomers, siding with the former, caricaturing the latter, and, with a fair bit of justification, laying into the likes of the RSPB and SNH. In *Isles of the North* he gives Orkney and Shetland the same treatment, before sailing off to Norway to find out how it can be done differently.

Robert Louis Stevenson *Edinburgh: Picturesque Notes*. First published in 1879, this is a charming evocation of Stevenson's birthplace – its moods, curiosities and influences on his work.

David Thomson *Nairn in Darkness and Light*. Beautifully written evocation of Nairn in the 1920s.

Betsy Whyte *The Yellow on the Broom*. A fascinating glimpse of childhood in a traveller family, both on the road and in council housing for part of the year to comply with school attendance. Also *Red Rowans and Wild Honey*.

Language

Language

Language

Language is a thorny, complex and often highly political issue in Scotland. If you're not from Scotland yourself, you're most likely to be addressed in a variety of **English**, spoken in a Scottish accent. Even then, you're likely to hear phrases and words that are part of what is known as **Scots**, now officially recognized as a distinct language in its own right. To a lesser extent, **Gaelic**, too, remains a living language, particularly in the *Gàidhealtachd* or Gaelic-speaking areas of the northwest Highlands, Western Isles, parts of Skye and a few scattered Hebridean islands. In Orkney and Shetland, the local dialect of Scots contains many words carried over from **Norn**, the Old Norse language spoken in the Northern Isles from the time of the Vikings until the eighteenth century.

Scots

Scots began life as a northern branch of Anglo-Saxon, emerging as a distinct language in the Middle Ages. From the 1370s until the Union in 1707, it was the country's main literary and documentary language. Since the eighteenth century, however, it has been systematically repressed to give preference to English.

Robbie Burns is the most obvious literary exponent of the Scots language, but there was a revival in the last century led by poets such as Hugh MacDiarmid. Only very recently has Scots enjoyed something of a renaissance, getting itself on the Scottish school curriculum in 1996, and achieving official recognition as a distinct language in 1998. Despite these enormous political achievements, many people (rightly or wrongly) still regard Scots as a dialect of English.

For more on the Scots language, visit Ⓦsco.wikipedia.org.

Gaelic

Scottish **Gaelic** (*Gàidhlig*, pronounced like "garlic") is one of the only four Celtic languages to survive into the modern age (Welsh, Breton and Irish Gaelic are the other three). Manx, the old language of the Isle of Man, died out early last century, while Cornish was finished as a community language in the eighteenth century. Scottish Gaelic is most closely related to Irish Gaelic and Manx – hardly surprising since Gaelic was introduced to Scotland from Ireland around the third century BC. Some folk still argue that Scottish Gaelic is merely a dialect of its parent language, Irish Gaelic, and indeed the two languages remain more or less mutually intelligible. From the fifth to the twelfth centuries, Gaelic enjoyed an expansionist phase, thanks partly to the backing of the Celtic Church in Iona.

Since then Gaelic has been in steady decline. Even before Union with England, power, religious ideology and wealth gradually passed into non-Gaelic hands. The royal court was transferred to Edinburgh and an Anglo-Norman legal system was put in place. The Celtic Church was Romanized by the introduction of foreign clergy, and, most important of all, English and Flemish merchants colonized the new trading towns of the east coast. In addition, the pro-English attitudes held by the Covenanters led to strong anti-Gaelic feeling within the Church of Scotland from its inception.

The two abortive Jacobite rebellions of 1715 and 1745 furthered the language's decline, as did the Clearances that took place in the Gaelic-speaking Highlands from the 1770s to the 1850s, which forced thousands to migrate to central Scotland's new industrial belt or emigrate to North America. Although efforts were made to halt the decline in the first half of the nineteenth century, the 1872 Education Act gave no official recognition to Gaelic, and children were severely punished if they were caught speaking the language in school.

The 2001 census put the number of Gaelic-speakers at under 60,000 (just over one percent of the population), the majority of whom live in the **Gàidhealtachd**, though there is thought to be an extended Gaelic community of perhaps 250,000 who have some understanding of the language. Since the 1980s, great efforts have been made to try and save the language, including the introduction of bilingual primary and nursery schools, and a huge increase in the amount of broadcasting time given to Gaelic-language and Gaelic music programmes, and the establishment of highly successful Gaelic colleges such as Sabhal Mòr Ostaig (Ⓦwww.smo.uhi.ac.uk).

Gaelic grammar and pronunciation

Gaelic is a highly complex tongue, with a fiendish, antiquated **grammar** and, with only eighteen letters, an intimidating system of spelling. **Pronunciation** is easier than it appears at first glance; one general rule to remember is that the stress always falls on the first syllable of a word. The general rule of syntax is that the verb starts the sentence whether it's a question or not, followed by the subject and then the object; adjectives generally follow the word they are describing.

Short and long vowels

Gaelic has both short and long vowels, the latter being denoted by an acute or grave accent.

a as in c**a**t; before nn and ll, as in c**ow**

à as in b**ar**

e as in p**e**t

é like r**ai**n

i as in s**igh**t

í like fr**ee**

o as in p**o**t

ò like enthr**al**

ó like c**ow**

u like sc**oo**t

ù like l**oo**

Vowel combinations

Gaelic is littered with diphthongs, which, rather like in English, can be pronounced in several different ways depending on the individual word.

ai like c**a**t, or p**e**t; before dh or gh, like street

ao like the sound in the middle of colonel

ea like pet, or cat, and sometimes like mate; before ll or nn like cow

èa as in h**ea**r

ei like m**a**te

eu like tr**ai**n, or f**ea**r

ia like f**ea**r

io like f**ea**r, or shorter than street

ua like w**oo**er

Consonants

The consonants listed below are those that differ substantially from the English.

b at the beginning of a word as in big; in the middle or at the end of a word like the p in pair

bh at the beginning of a word like the v in van; elsewhere it is silent

c as in cat; after a vowel it has aspiration before it

ch always as in loch, never as in church

cn like the **cr** in crowd

d like the **d** in dog, but with the tongue pressed against the back of the upper teeth; at the beginning of a word or before e or i, like the j in jam; in the middle or at the end of a word like the t in cat; after i like the ch in church

dh before and after a, o or u is an aspirated g, rather like a gargle; before e or i like the y in yes; elsewhere silent

fh usually silent; sometimes like the **h** in house

g at the beginning of a word as in **g**et; before e like the **y** in yes; in the middle or end of a word like the **ck** in sock; after i like the **ch** in loch

gh at the beginning of a word as in get; before or after a, o or u rather like a gargle; after i sometimes like the y in gay, but often silent

l after i and sometimes before e like the l in lot; elsewhere a peculiarly Gaelic sound produced by flattening the front of the tongue against the palate

mh like the **v** in van

p at the beginning of a word as in pet; elsewhere it has aspiration before it

rt pronounced as **sht**

s before e or i like the **sh** in ship; otherwise as in English

sh before a, o or u like the **h** in house; before e like the **ch** in loch

t before e or i like the **ch** in church; in the middle or at the end of a word it has aspiration before it; otherwise as in English

th at the beginning of a word, like the **h** in house; elsewhere, and in the word thu, silent

Gaelic phrases and vocabulary

The choice is limited when it comes to **teach-yourself Gaelic** courses, but the BBC *Can Seo* cassette and book are perfect for starting you off. Drier and more academic is *Teach Yourself Gaelic*, which is aimed at bringing beginners to working competence. *Everyday Gaelic* by Morag MacNeill is the best phrasebook around. You can do some self-learning on the Gaelic section of the BBC website Ⓦwww.bbc.co.uk, or order learning materials from Ⓦwww.smo.uhi.ac.uk.

Basic words and greetings

yes	tha
no	chan eil
hello	hallo
how are you?	ciamar a tha thu?
fine	tha gu math
thank you	tapadh leat
welcome	fàilte
come in	thig a-staigh
good day	latha math
goodbye	mar sin leat
goodnight	oidhche mhath
cheers	slàinte
yesterday	an-dé
today	an-diugh
tomorrow	maireach
hotel	taigh-òsda
house	taigh
story	sgeul
song	òran
music	ceòl
book	leabhar
bread	aran
water	uisge
whisky	uisge beatha
post office	post oifis
Edinburgh	Dun Eideann
Glasgow	Glaschu
America	Ameireaga
Ireland	Eire
England	Sasainn
London	Lunnain

Geographical and place-name terms

The purpose of this list is to help with place-name derivations from Gaelic and with more detailed map reading.

abhainn	river
ach or auch, from achadh	field
ail, aileach	rock
Alba	Scotland
aonach	ridge
ard, ardan or arden, from àird	a point of land or height
aros	dwelling
ault, from allt	stream
bad	brake or clump of trees
bagh	bay
bal or bally, from baile	town, village
balloch, from bealach	mountain pass
ban	white, fair
bàrr	summit
beg, from beag	small
ben, from beinn	mountain
blair, from blàr	field or battlefield
cairn, from càrn	pile of stones
camas	bay, harbour
cnoc	hill
coll or colly, from coille	wood or forest
corran	a spit or point jutting into the sea
corrie, from coire	round hollow in mountainside, whirlpool
craig, from creag	rock, crag
cruach	bold hill
drum, from druim	ridge
dubh	black
dun or dum, from dùn	fort
eilean	island
ess, from eas	waterfall
fin, from fionn	white
gair or gare, from geàrr	short
garv, from garbh	rough
geodha	cove
glen, from gleann	valley
gower or gour, from gabhar	goat
inch, from innis	meadow or island
inver, from inbhir	river mouth
ken or kin, from ceann	head
knock, from cnoc	hill
kyle, from caolas	narrow strait
lag	hollow
larach	site of an old ruin
liath	grey
loch	lake
meall	round hill
mon, from monadh	hill
more, from mór	large, great
rannoch, from raineach	bracken
ross, from ros	promontory
rubha	promontory
sgeir	sea rock
sgurr	sharp point
sron	nose, prow or promontory
strath, from srath	broad valley
tarbet, from tairbeart	isthmus
tigh	house
tir or tyre, from tìr	land
torr	hill, castle
tràigh	shore
uig	shelter
uisge	water

Norn and Norse terms

Between the tenth and seventeenth centuries, the chief language of Orkney and Shetland was **Norn**, a Scandinavian tongue close to modern Faroese and Icelandic. After the end of Norse rule, and with the transformation of the Church, the law, commerce and education, Norn gradually lost out to Scots and English, eventually petering out completely in the eighteenth century. Today, Orkney and Shetland have their own **dialects**, and individual islands and communities within each group have local variations. The dialects have a Scots base, with some Old Norse words; however, they don't sound strongly Scottish, with the Orkney accent – which has been likened to the Welsh one – especially distinctive. Listed below are some of the words you're most likely to hear, plus some terms that appear in place names, not just in Orkney and Shetland, but also in parts of the Hebrides.

Norn phrases and vocabulary

ayre beach
bister farm
böd fisherman's store
bruck rubbish
burra heath rush
crö sheepfold
eela rod-fishing from small boats
ferrylouper incomer (Orkney)
fourareen four-oared boat
foy party or festival
geo coastal inlet
haa laird's house
hap hand-knitted shawl
howe mound
kame ridge of hills
kishie basket
mool headland
moorit brown
mootie tiny
muckle large
noost hollow place where a boat is drawn up
noup steep headland
peerie /peedie small
plantiecrub (or plantiecrö) small dry-stone enclosure for growing cabbages
quoy enclosed, cultivated common land
roost tide race
scattald common grazing land
scord gap or pass in a ridge of hills
setter farm
shaela dark grey
sixern/sixareen six-oared boat
soothmoother incomer (Shetland)
voe sea inlet

Glossary

Auld Old.

Aye Yes.

Bairn Baby.

Baronial see "Scottish Baronial" opposite.

Ben Hill or mountain.

Blackhouse Thick-walled traditional dwelling.

Bonnie Pretty.

Bothy Primitive cottage or hut; farmworker's or shepherd's mountain shelter.

Brae Slope or hill.

Brig Bridge.

Broch Circular prehistoric stone fort.

Burn Small stream or brook.

Byre Shelter for cattle; cottage.

Cairn Mound of stones.

CalMac Caledonian MacBrayne ferry company.

Carse Riverside area of flat alluvium.

Ceilidh (pronounced "kay-lee") Social gathering involving dancing, drinking, singing and storytelling.

Central belt The densely populated strip of central Scotland between the Forth and Clyde estuaries, incorporating the conurbations of Edinburgh, Glasgow and Stirling.

Clan Extended family.

Clearances Policy adopted by late eighteenth- and early nineteenth-century landowners to evict tenant crofters in order to create space for more profitable sheep-grazing. Families cleared from the Highlands were often put on emigrant ships to North America or the colonies.

Corbett A mountain between 2500ft and 3000ft high.

Corbie-stepped Architectural term; any set of steps on a gable.

Covenanters Supporters of the Presbyterian Church in the seventeenth century.

Crannog Celtic lake or bog dwelling.

Croft Small plot of farmland with house, common in the Highlands.

Crow-stepped Same as corbie-stepped.

Dirk A long dagger.

Dolmen Grave chamber.

Dram Literally, one-sixteenth of a fluid ounce. Usually refers to any small measure of whisky.

Dun Fortified mound.

First-foot The first person to enter a household after midnight on Hogmanay (see p.43).

Firth A wide sea inlet or estuary.

Gàidhealtachd Gaeldom, Highlands or Gaelic-speaking area.

Gillie Personal guide used on hunting or fishing trips.

Glen Deep, narrow mountain valley.

Harling Limestone and gravel mix used to cover buildings.

Hogmanay New Year's Eve.

Howe Valley.

Howff Meeting place; pub.

HS Historic Scotland, a government-funded heritage organization.

Jacobite Supporter of the Stewart claim to the throne, most famously Bonnie Prince Charlie.

Ken Knowledge; understanding.

Kilt Knee-length tartan skirt worn by Highland men.

Kirk Church.

Laird Landowner; aristocrat.

Law Rounded hill.

Links Grassy coastal land; coastal golf course.

Loch Lake.

Lochan Little loch.

Mac/Mc These prefixes in Scottish surnames derive from the Gaelic, meaning "son of". In Scots "Mac" is used for both sexes. In Gaelic "Nic" is used for women: Donnchadh Mac Aoidh is Duncan MacKay, Iseabail Nic Aoidh is Isabel MacKay.

Machair Sandy, grassy, lime-rich coastal land, generally used for grazing.

Manse Official home of a Presbyterian minister.

Mercat Cross lit. Market Cross. The decorative stone or wooden pillar which in medieval towns and cities indicated the central gathering point for the local market; often also the site of proclamations and occasionally other government business such as public executions. Not many remain in situ, though the spot where they sat is often remembered in place names or locals' street knowledge.

Munro A mountain over 3000ft high.

Munro-bagging The sport of trying to climb as many Munros as possible.

NTS The National Trust for Scotland, a heritage organization.

Peel Fortified tower, built to withstand Border raids.

Pend Archway or vaulted passage.

Presbyterian The form of Church government used in the official (Protestant) Church of Scotland, established by John Knox during the Reformation.

RIB Rigid inflatable boat.

RSPB Royal Society for the Protection of Birds.

Runrig A common form of land tenure in which separate ridges are cultivated by different occupiers under joint agreement.

Sassenach Derives from the Gaelic *Sasunnach*, meaning literally "Saxon"; used by Scots to describe the English.

Scottish Baronial Style of architecture favoured by the Scottish land-owning class featuring crow-stepped gables and round turrets.

Sheila na gig Female fertility symbol, usually a naked woman displaying her vulva.

Shinty Stick and ball game played in the Highlands, with similarities to hockey.

Smiddy Smithy.

SNH Scottish Natural Heritage, a government-funded conservation body.

SNP Scottish National Party.

Sporran Leather purse worn in front of, or at the side of, a kilt.

Tartan Check-patterned woollen cloth, particular patterns being associated with particular clans.

Thane A landowner of high rank; the chief of a clan.

Trews Tartan trousers.

Wee Small.

Wee Frees Followers of the Free Presbyterian or Free Church of Scotland.

Wynd Narrow lane.

Yett Gate or door.

Small print and

Index

A Rough Guide to Rough Guides

Published in 1982, the first Rough Guide – to Greece – was a student scheme that became a publishing phenomenon. Mark Ellingham, a recent graduate in English from Bristol University, had been travelling in Greece the previous summer and couldn't find the right guidebook. With a small group of friends he wrote his own guide, combining a highly contemporary, journalistic style with a thoroughly practical approach to travellers' needs.

The immediate success of the book spawned a series that rapidly covered dozens of destinations. And, in addition to impecunious backpackers, Rough Guides soon acquired a much broader and older readership that relished the guides' wit and inquisitiveness as much as their enthusiastic, critical approach and value-for-money ethos.

These days, Rough Guides include recommendations from shoestring to luxury and cover more than 200 destinations around the globe, including almost every country in the Americas and Europe, more than half of Africa and most of Asia and Australasia. Our ever-growing team of authors and photographers is spread all over the world, particularly in Europe, the US and Australia.

In the early 1990s, Rough Guides branched out of travel, with the publication of Rough Guides to World Music, Classical Music and the Internet. All three have become benchmark titles in their fields, spearheading the publication of a wide range of books under the Rough Guide name.

Including the travel series, Rough Guides now number more than 350 titles, covering: phrasebooks, waterproof maps, music guides from Opera to Heavy Metal, reference works as diverse as Conspiracy Theories and Shakespeare, and popular culture books from iPods to Poker. Rough Guides also produce a series of more than 120 World Music CDs in partnership with World Music Network.

Visit www.roughguides.com to see our latest publications.

Rough Guide credits

Text editor: Andy Turner, Annie Shaw
Layout: Ankur Guha
Cartography: Jasbir Sandhu
Picture editor: Sarah Cummins
Production: Louise Daly
Proofreader: Susanne Hillen
Cover design: Nicole Newman, Dan May
Photographer: Helena Smith
Editorial: **London** Keith Drew, Edward Aves, Alice Park, Lucy White, Jo Kirby, James Smart, Natasha Foges, James Rice, Emma Beatson, Emma Gibbs, Kathryn Lane, Monica Woods, Mani Ramaswamy, Harry Wilson, Lucy Cowie, Alison Roberts, Lara Kavanagh, Eleanor Aldridge, Ian Blenkinsop, Joe Staines, Matthew Milton, Tracy Hopkins; **Delhi** Madhavi Singh, Jalpreen Kaur Chhatwal, Jubbi Francis
Design & Pictures: **London** Scott Stickland, Dan May, Diana Jarvis, Mark Thomas, Nicole Newman; **Delhi** Umesh Aggarwal, Ajay Verma, Jessica Subramanian, Pradeep Thapliyal, Sachin Tanwar, Anita Singh, Nikhil Agarwal, Sachin Gupta
Production: Rebecca Short, Liz Cherry, Erika Pepe
Cartography: **London** Ed Wright, Katie Lloyd-Jones; **Delhi** Rajesh Chhibber, Ashutosh Bharti, Rajesh Mishra, Animesh Pathak, Swati Handoo, Deshpal Dabas, Lokamata Sahu
Marketing, Publicity & roughguides.com: Liz Statham
Digital Travel Publisher: Peter Buckley
Reference Director: Andrew Lockett
Operations Coordinator: Becky Doyle
Operations Assistant: Johanna Wurm
Publishing Director (Travel): Clare Currie
Commercial Manager: Gino Magnotta
Managing Director: John Duhigg

Publishing information

This ninth edition published April 2011 by

Rough Guides Ltd,
80 Strand, London WC2R 0RL
11, Community Centre, Panchsheel Park, New Delhi 110017, India

Distributed by the Penguin Group

Penguin Books Ltd,
80 Strand, London WC2R 0RL

Penguin Group (USA)
375 Hudson Street, NY 10014, USA

Penguin Group (Australia)
250 Camberwell Road, Camberwell, Victoria 3124, Australia

Penguin Group (NZ)
67 Apollo Drive, Mairangi Bay, Auckland 1310, New Zealand

Rough Guides is represented in Canada by Tourmaline Editions Inc. 662 King Street West, Suite 304, Toronto, Ontario M5V 1M7

Cover concept by Peter Dyer.

Typeset in Bembo and Helvetica to an original design by Henry Iles.

Printed in Italy by L.E.G.O. S.p.A, Lavis (TN)

672pp includes index

A catalogue record for this book is available from the British Library

ISBN: 978-1-84836-719-7

The publishers and authors have done their best to ensure the accuracy and currency of all the information in **The Rough Guide to Scotland**, however, they can accept no responsibility for any loss, injury, or inconvenience sustained by any traveller as a result of information or advice contained in the guide.

1 3 5 7 9 8 6 4 2

Help us update

We've gone to a lot of effort to ensure that the ninth edition of **The Rough Guide to Scotland** is accurate and up-to-date. However, things change – places get "discovered", opening hours are notoriously fickle, restaurants and rooms raise prices or lower standards. If you feel we've got it wrong or left something out, we'd like to know, and if you can remember the address, the price, the hours, the phone number, so much the better.

Please send your comments with the subject line **"Rough Guide Scotland Update"** to ⓔmail @uk.roughguides.com. We'll credit all contributions and send a copy of the next edition (or any other Rough Guide if you prefer) for the very best emails.

Find more travel information, connect with fellow travellers and book your trip on ⓦwww .roughguides.com

Acknowledgements

The authors would like to thank the National Trust for Scotland, Historic Scotland, VisitScotland, Andrew Deeprose at CalMac and Andy and Annie for their careful and patient editing.

Rob Humphreys would also like to thank: Alasdair Enticknap and Jane Dubrowski for dispatches from Islay and Jura, Val and Gordon for exploring the byways of the Borders and Skye, Val for getting away against the odds to our old stamping grounds, Sara for holding the fort back in Yorkshire, and Kate for hostelling and camping at the wrong time of year.

Donald Reid would also like to thank: Allan Radcliffe, Jo Laidlaw, Anna Millar and Stan Blackley for some capital contributions.

Helena Smith would also like to thank: David at the Lismore Museum for his help, and her parents, Angela and Grahame, for running the best B&B in the whole of Scotland.

Readers' letters

Thanks to all the readers who have taken the time to write in with comments and suggestions (and apologies if we've inadvertently omitted or misspelt anyone's name):

Paul Adderley, Anne Benner, Anthony Bradbury, Jacky Bright, Nancy Brinton, John & Freda Cammack, Margaret Eden, Max Garrone, Shana Goldberg, Emma Harbour, Pat Jeffers, Chris Keeling, Alistair & Solveig McCleery, Sally MacDonald, Jenny MacKay, Karin MacKinnon, Raymond Maxwell, Rachel Pepa, Jane Richards, Jonard Rood, Jane Rooth, Patsy Thompson, Philip Ward, Annie Warwick, Heather White, Sinead Williams, David Wood, Wendy Wood

Photo credits

All photos © Rough Guides except the following:

Title page
Eilean Donan Castle, Loch Duich © Peter Adams/ jonarnoldimages/Corbis

Full page
Forth Rail Bridge © Paul Harris/John Warburton-Lee Photography Ltd

Introduction
Highland dancing © David Moir/Reuters/Corbis
Hiking in the Cairngorms © Cody Duncan/Alamy
Calton Hill, Edinburgh © Bertrand Rieger/Hemis/ Corbis
Loch Lomond © nagelestock.com/Alamy
Puffin with fish © Arthur Morris/Corbis
Mountain bikers, Lairig Ghru © Scottish Viewpoint/Alamy
Glasgow Museum of Modern Art © UK City Images/Alamy
Loch Shiel © Derek Croucher/Alamy

Things not to miss
01 Isle of Eigg © Steve Lewis ARPS/Alamy
02 Ski touring, Cairngorms © Rob Penn/Axiom
03 Hogmanay, Edinburgh © David Moir/Reuters/ Corbis
05 Melrose Abbey © Tim Hurst/Getty
06 Tobermory © Macduff Everton/Getty
08 Aonach Eagach ridge, Glen Coe © Paul Harris/Getty
10 Skye Cuillin © Gavin Hellier/JAI/Corbis
11 Street performers at the Edinburgh Festival © Jeff J. Mitchell/Getty
12 Killer whale © Hugh Harrop/Alamy
13 Glenfinnan viaduct, West Highland Railway © Christophe Boisvieux/Corbis
14 Barnacle geese, Islay © Mike Read/Alamy
15 Jarlshof © Gallo Images/Getty
16 Shetland Folk Festival © Dave Donaldson/ Alamy
19 Rodin sculpture, The Burrell Collection © Neil Setchfield/Alamy
20 Mousa Broch © David Robertson/Alamy
21 Grassmarket, Edinburgh © David Kilpatrick/ Alamy
22 Stirling Castle © Jon Arnold Images Ltd/Alamy
24 Museum of Scotland © Keith Hunter/Arcaid/ Corbis
25 South Harris beach © Patrick Dieudonne/ Robert Harding/Corbis
26 Kinloch Castle © Wild Country/Corbis
28 Red squirrel, Caledonian Forest © Chris Gomersall/Alamy
29 Dunnottar Castle © Jason Hawkes/Corbis

Scottish food and drink colour section
A wee dram © Mar Photographics/Alamy
Venison dish © Brendan MacNeill/Alamy
Haggis ad © TNT Magazine/Alamy
Arborath smokies © Simon Price/Alamy
Mhor Fish © Mhor Fish
The Macallan © Rawdon Wyatt/Alamy
Laphroaig distillery © David Lyons/Alamy
Ardbeg barrels © Andrew McCandlish/alamy

The great outdoors colour section
Stob Ban © Travel Ink/Getty
Buchaille Etive, Glen Coe © Kathy Collins/Getty
Road sign © Duncan Hale-Sutton/Alamy
Mountain biking, Great Glen © John James/ Alamy
Sea-kayaking, Staffa © Alan Payton/Alamy
Ice climbing, Aonach Mhòr © Paul Harris/ Photolibrary
Windsurfers and the Tiree Wave Classic © TNT Magazine/Alamy

Black and whites
p.62 Princes Street Gardens and Edinburgh Castle © Mark A. Johnson/Corbis
p.162 Mountain biker in Galloway Forest Park © South West Images Scotland/Alamy
p.186 Culzean Castle © Patrick Dieudonne/ Robert Harding/Corbis
p.254 Whisky barrels at Laphroaig distillery © Macduff Everton/Corbis
p.422 Stag in the Cairngorms © Roger Antrobus/ Corbis
p.440 The Commando Memorial © Dave Porter/ Alamy
p.470 Loch Lurgainn and Stac Pollaidh, Coigach © Ashley Cooper/Corbis
p.522 The Black Cuillin, Isle of Skye © Patrick Dieudonne/Robert Harding/Corbis
p.566 Puffins and razorbill at Noup Head, Westray © Gareth McCormack/Alamy
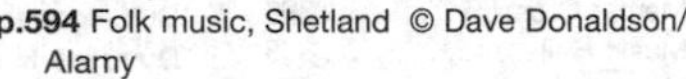
p.594 Folk music, Shetland © Dave Donaldson/ Alamy

ROUGH GUIDES

SMALL PRINT

Index

Map entries are in colour.

INDEX

B

C

E

G

H

I

M

N

O

T

Map symbols

maps are listed in the full index using coloured text

	International boundary		Stately home
	Chapter division boundary		Castle
	Motorway		Museum
	Pedestrianized street		Gardens
	Road		Battlefield
	Track		Campsite
	Steps		Accommodation
	Footpath	P	Parking
	Wall	*i*	Tourist office
	Railway		Post office
	Cable car		Whisky distillery
	Coastline/river		Skiing
	Ferry route		Golf course
	Point of interest		Swimming Pool
	Peak		Bridge
	Viewpoint		Abbey
	Rocks		Monastery
	Lighthouse		Chapel
	International airport		Building
	Waterfall		Church
	Cave		Cemetery
	Ruins/archeological site		Park
	Cairn(s)		Forest
	Hill shading		Beach